African American National Biography

African American National Biography

SECOND EDITION

HENRY LOUIS GATES JR.

EVELYN BROOKS HIGGINBOTHAM

Editors in Chief

VOLUME 12: WHEELER, JOHN HERVEY – ZYDECO, BUCKWHEAT

DIRECTORY OF CONTRIBUTORS

AFRICAN AMERICAN PRIZEWINNERS, MEDALISTS, AND MEMBERS OF CONGRESS

INDEXES

OXFORD
UNIVERSITY PRESS

Oxford University Press is a department of the University of Oxford.
It furthers the University's objective of excellence in research, scholarship,
and education by publishing worldwide.

Oxford   New York
Auckland   Cape Town   Dar es Salaam   Hong Kong   Karachi
Kuala Lumpur   Madrid   Melbourne   Mexico City   Nairobi
New Delhi   Shanghai   Taipei   Toronto

With offices in
Argentina   Austria   Brazil   Chile   Czech Republic   France   Greece
Guatemala   Hungary   Italy   Japan   Poland   Portugal   Singapore
South Korea   Switzerland   Thailand   Turkey   Ukraine   Vietnam

Oxford is a registered trademark of Oxford University Press in the UK and certain other countries.

Published in the United States of America by
Oxford University Press
198 Madison Avenue, New York, NY 10016

Library of Congress Cataloging-in-Publication Data
African American national biography / editors in chief Henry Louis Gates Jr., Evelyn Brooks Higginbotham. – 2nd ed.
p. cm.
Includes bibliographical references and index.
ISBN 978-0-19-999036-8 (volume 1; hdbk.); ISBN 978-0-19-999037-5 (volume 2; hdbk.); ISBN 978-0-19-999038-2 (volume 3; hdbk.);
ISBN 978-0-19-999039-9 (volume 4; hdbk.); ISBN 978-0-19-999040-5 (volume 5; hdbk.); ISBN 978-0-19-999041-2 (volume 6; hdbk.);
ISBN 978-0-19-999042-9 (volume 7; hdbk.); ISBN 978-0-19-999043-6 (volume 8; hdbk.); ISBN 978-0-19-999044-3 (volume 9; hdbk.);
ISBN 978-0-19-999045-0 (volume 10; hdbk.); ISBN 978-0-19-999046-7 (volume 11; hdbk.); ISBN 978-0-19-999047-4 (volume 12;
hdbk.); ISBN 978-0-19-992077-8 (12-volume set; hdbk.)
1. African Americans – Biography – Encyclopedias.   2. African Americans – History – Encyclopedias.
I. Gates, Henry Louis.   II. Higginbotham, Evelyn Brooks, 1945-
E185.96.A4466 2012
920'.009296073 – dc23
[B]
2011043281

1 3 5 7 9 8 6 4 2
Printed in the United States of America
on acid-free paper

African American National Biography

W CONTINUED

Wheeler, John Hervey (1 Jan. 1908–6 Jul. 1978), banker, lawyer, and political activist, was born on the campus of Kittrell College in Vance County, North Carolina. He was the younger of two children born to John Leonidas Wheeler, the president of Kittrell College, and Margaret Hervey. Shortly after John was born, his father left Kittrell to work for the North Carolina Mutual Life Insurance Company in nearby Durham. The family moved again in 1912 to Atlanta, Georgia, where John's father took a position as a regional supervisor for the North Carolina Mutual. The move ensured that John Hervey Wheeler enjoyed a relatively comfortable childhood among Atlanta's black elite. He was a member of the prestigious Big Bethel African Methodist Episcopal church, attended public school in Atlanta up to the seventh grade, earned local fame as an accomplished violinist, and completed his high school education at Morehouse College. Wheeler graduated summa cum laude from Morehouse in 1929 with honors in accounting and finance.

Two Durham businesses expressed an interest in the young graduate: his father's company, the North Carolina Mutual, and the Mechanics and Farmers Bank, which shared office space with the Mutual on Parrish Street, known at that time as the "black Wall Street." The Mechanics and Farmers Bank was the first to offer him a position, and he accepted, in spite of—or perhaps because of—his father's ties to the Mutual. He later discovered, however, that the Mutual had wanted to hire him as an auditor at a monthly salary of $110—nearly double what he received at the Mechanics and Farmers Bank. Wheeler never regretted his choice, however, believing that he had a better chance of rising through the ranks at a smaller company. Indeed, within two years he was promoted from assistant cashier to the vice presidency of the bank. The 1930s were hardly a propitious time to begin a banking career, but Wheeler helped steer the bank through the worst of the Depression. Unlike many other small banks at that time, it never closed its doors, and in 1935 the Mechanics and Farmers became the first financial institution in North Carolina authorized to administer loans from the Federal Housing Administration.

Wheeler's skillful stewardship of the bank marked him as a man to watch among Durham's close-knit black elite. His status was also enhanced by his marriage on Christmas Day 1935 to Selena Warren, the only child of Dr. Stanford Warren, who had helped found the Mechanics and Farmers Bank, the North Carolina Mutual, and Durham's Lincoln Hospital for Negroes. Wheeler shared with his new bride an interest in libraries. He had worked at the Auburn Avenue branch of the Atlanta Public library and had managed Morehouse College Library; she graduated from Howard University and Hampton Institute with degrees in library science and in early 1936 was appointed director of Durham's Stanford L. Warren library. The couple had two children: Julia, born in 1937, would later become president and CEO of the Mechanics and Farmers Bank; Warren Hervey, born six years later, became a pilot and founded his own commuter airline. In 1937, at the age of twenty-nine, Wheeler became the youngest person ever appointed to the Morehouse College Board of Trustees.

Durham prospered during World War II, as its tobacco factories worked around the clock to meet the nation's insatiable desire for cigarettes; one quarter of all the cigarettes produced in the United States were manufactured in the Bull City. African American tobacco workers, many of them Mechanics and Farmers customers, enjoyed steady incomes for the first time in over a decade, and black businesses benefited from the thirty-five thousand soldiers, many of them African American, stationed at nearby Camp Butner. Wheeler recognized, however, that the spoils of the wartime boom were not spread equally among the races. The Mutual's CHARLES CLINTON SPAULDING had worked quietly behind the scenes for decades to improve race relations in North Carolina, but Wheeler believed that the time had come to confront segregation directly. To that end, he enrolled in night classes at the North Carolina College for Negroes Law School in Durham, graduating in 1947. Wheeler was admitted to the North Carolina Bar the same year and later joined the NAACP's Legal Defense Fund.

In 1950, in the case of *Blue v. Durham*, he mounted the first direct challenge to segregated schooling in North Carolina. Wheeler urged a state judge to declare the Durham public schools unconstitutional because spending on white students exceeded spending on blacks by $350 per student. Though the judge refused to declare separate education unconstitutional, he ruled that in Durham such schools were patently unequal, and he enjoined the local school board to equalize spending. Since black North Carolinians had been campaigning for equal school funding for more than two decades, *Blue v. Durham* marked a significant victory and set an important legal precedent for increased funding for other black schools. The ruling also prompted African Americans in Durham to support Wheeler's appointment as the first black member of the city's school board in 1951. The all-white city council narrowly opposed his nomination, however, because they believed that Wheeler would use the post to "snipe," an opinion shared by a local newspaper, which described him as a "belligerent and militant worker for political power" who would only represent the interests of blacks (*Durham Sun*, 4 April 1951). Wheeler's support of an electoral coalition between African Americans and white labor unionists in Durham also frightened white conservatives.

Wheeler assumed the presidency of the Farmers and Mechanics Bank in 1952, upon the death of Spaulding, though to all intents and purposes he had been the bank's chief operating officer for more than a decade. However, after the Supreme Court's landmark 1954 school desegregation ruling in *Brown v. Board of Education*, Wheeler focused increasingly on civil rights. In 1955 he represented the first black undergraduates to integrate the University of North Carolina, and he later worked with FLOYD MCKISSICK in lawsuits that finally integrated the Durham Public Schools.

Wheeler believed passionately in the legal and moral case for integration, but he increasingly turned to economic arguments to persuade white southerners that school desegregation was in their own best interest. Throughout the 1950s he published several articles and gave numerous speeches across the country, attacking the white South's resistance to integration as "economic suicide." In a March 1955 article in the liberal journal *New South*, he argued that the duplication of resources inherent in segregated facilities gave southern states a "disappointingly small return" for their substantial investment in education. North Carolina ranked seventh in the nation in educational spending, he noted, but it was forty-fifth both in median school years completed by its students and in per capita income. Moreover, Wheeler added, the lack of economic opportunities in their home states forced the most talented black high school and college graduates to seek work in the North. Racism and segregation served to retard the economic progress for all North Carolina citizens, he argued, not just blacks.

Wheeler's emphasis on the economic dimensions of racial change brought him to prominence in the Southern Regional Council (SRC), a liberal, interracial organization based in Atlanta, which had roots in the New Deal liberalism of the 1930s. He served as treasurer of North Carolina's SRC affiliate from 1955 to 1961, as chairman of the SRC's Executive Committee from 1961 to 1963, and as the organization's first African American president from 1964 to 1969.

When the student sit-in movement began in North Carolina in 1960, Wheeler again appealed to white leaders in the state to end the economic suicide of segregation, but with little success. In 1961, his arguments eventually struck a chord with newly elected North Carolina governor Terry Sanford, who placed him on a number of state advisory boards on education and employment. Wheeler was also prominent in securing Ford Foundation support for the North Carolina Fund, an innovative antipoverty program launched by Sanford in 1963, which served as a model for President Lyndon Johnson's War on Poverty. President John F. Kennedy had recognized Wheeler's expertise on employment discrimination by appointing him, in 1961, to a four-year term in the U.S. Equal Opportunity Commission, a body that influenced the 1964 Civil Rights Act and that established a permanent Equal Employment Opportunity

Commission. In 1964 Wheeler became North Carolina's first African American delegate to the Democratic National Convention and was appointed as the state party's treasurer four years later.

In his final decade, Wheeler took a less active role in national and state politics, but he remained at the helm of the Mechanics and Farmers Bank, which in 1963 had become the largest black-owned bank in the nation. He also received many awards in appreciation for his lifetime of community service. North Carolina Central University and Duke University in Durham, Johnson C. Smith University in Charlotte, and Morehouse College awarded him honorary degrees. In 1975 Morehouse also dedicated its new business administration and social science building, John H. Wheeler Hall, in honor of his more than five decades of support for his alma mater.

Wheeler died in Durham on 6 July 1978, two weeks after suffering a stroke. Although his contributions as a business leader and as a civil rights lawyer were significant, Wheeler's most important legacy is his long-standing insistence on economic solutions to the deep-rooted racial problems of the South and the rest of the nation.

FURTHER READING
Anderson, Jean Bradley. *Durham County: A History of Durham County, North Carolina* (1990).
Weare, Walter B. *Black Business in the New South: A Social History of the North Carolina Mutual Insurance Company* (1973; repr. 1993).
Wise, Jim. *Durham: A Bull City Story* (2002).
Obituary: *New York Times*, 8 July 1978.

STEVEN J. NIVEN

Whetsol, Artie (1905–5 Jan. 1940), jazz trumpeter, was born Arthur Parker Whetsol in Punta Gorda, Florida. His parents' names are unknown. He became Arthur Parker Schiefe when his widowed mother remarried "Elder" Schiefe, a Seventh-day Adventist minister.

Whetsol's mother ran a boardinghouse in Washington, D.C., where he became a childhood friend of DUKE ELLINGTON and the reed player Otto Hardwick (later known as TOBY HARDWICK). Whetsol and Hardwick attended Garnet Elementary School. Whetsol may have attended Armstrong High School, but he and Hardwick reportedly played in the Dunbar High School orchestra. From 1920 on, he performed with Ellington, the pianist CLAUDE HOPKINS, and the White Brothers, and in June 1923 he traveled to New York City to join Ellington, Hardwick, and others in the Washingtonians, led by the banjoist ELMER SNOWDEN.

Later that year Whetsol returned home, ostensibly to study medicine at Howard University. The writer Mark Tucker reports that no record of Whetsol exists at Howard, and hence nothing is known of his activities before rejoining the then-famous Ellington orchestra in 1928 as its lead trumpeter and a soloist. He is featured on "Black Beauty" (recorded in 1928); "The Dicty Glide" and "Stevedore Stomp" in the film short *Black and Tan* and on "Jungle Jamboree" (all from 1929); "Rocky Mountain Blues" and "Mood Indigo" (both 1930); "Black and Tan Fantasy" (1932); and "A Hymn of Sorrow" in Ellington's film *Symphony in Black* (1934). The victim of a brain tumor, Whetsol began to suffer mental problems in 1935. He returned to Ellington's orchestra until the autumn of 1936, when illness forced his retirement. He died in New York City.

Tucker republished a 1937 press release describing Whetsol as "very loyal … always on the job even when not well … intellectual … tender personality … a bridge fanatic." Ellington summarized Whetsol's stylistic contributions: "We paid quite a lot of attention to our appearance, and if any one of us came in dressed improperly Whetsol would flick his cigarette ash in a certain way, or pull down the lower lid of his right eye with his forefinger and stare at the offending party." He added that Whetsol's "tonal character, fragile and genteel, was an important element in our music."

These sketchy references to Whetsol's life are all that remain. Nonetheless, he is regarded by aficionados as a significant figure in early jazz, both for the unknown specifics of his contributions to the formation of Ellington's big band from childhood to the Washingtonians and for the well documented evidence of his having recorded more than one hundred solos with that band in its prime. In helping to create perhaps the most satisfying integration of sweet dance music and hot jazz, Whetsol's function within the brass section was, as Ellington indicated, to offer the sweet component by playing in a pretty manner. A certain rhythmic stiffness prevented him from being considered among the great jazz soloists, but in the Ellington mix this same quality served as a foil for the raucous and swinging melodies of his colleagues, the trumpeters BUBBER MILEY and COOTIE WILLIAMS and the trombonist JOE NANTON.

FURTHER READING
Ellington, Duke. *Music Is My Mistress* (1973).
Tucker, Mark. *Ellington: The Early Years* (1991).
Tucker, Mark, ed. *The Duke Ellington Reader* (1995).

This entry is taken from the *American National Biography* and is published here with the permission of the American Council of Learned Societies.

BARRY KERNFELD

Whipper, Ionia Rollin (8 Sept. 1872–23 Apr. 1953), physician and public health reformer, was born in Beaufort, South Carolina, the third of five children of WILLIAM J. WHIPPER, a judge and politician, and FRANCES A. ROLLIN, a writer born into Charleston's free black elite. The stage actor Leigh Whipper was her brother. In her very early childhood Ionia grew up in one of the most prominent African American families in South Carolina. But the family suffered in the late 1870s after the end of Reconstruction finished William's political career, and the judge's gambling debts and drinking problem placed a significant financial burden on the family.

After her parents separated in 1880, Ionia, her brother Leigh, her sister Winifred, and her adopted brother Demps moved with their mother to Washington, D.C. Frances Rollin, prominent in Washington's black literary and political circles, found work in the office of her friend, Washington's Recorder of Deeds, FREDERICK DOUGLASS. Along with her siblings, Ionia attended the segregated Washington public schools and was a congregant at ALEXANDER CRUMMELL's Saint Luke's Episcopal Church. Her early exposure to many of Washington's most famed aristocrats of color, as well as the influence of her independent-minded mother, profoundly shaped Whipper's strong sense of well-being. Secure in her own relatively privileged position, she was very much in the vanguard of turn-of-the-century black women reformers who believed in public service for the greater uplift of her race.

Like many of her middle-class black contemporaries, Whipper looked first to a career in education, one of the few avenues open to talented women of color. For a decade, beginning in 1889, she taught in Washington's black public schools, then under the stewardship of GEORGE F. T. COOK and widely recognized as the best black school system in the nation. She then enrolled at Howard University Medical College in 1900, graduating three years later with a specialty in obstetrics. Whipper was one of only four women to graduate.

Although Whipper graduated from Howard in 1903, she did not immediately begin to practice medicine, in part because of her mother's death the year before, which denied her the income that she had expected would pay off her student debts. Instead, she returned to teaching until 1911, when she had earned enough finally to establish her own practice.

For much of her early career, Whipper was one of the very few African American obstetricians in Washington, D.C., and one of the very few female physicians at the maternity ward of the city's Freedmen's Hospital for Negroes. Many of the babies she delivered were born to young, unwed mothers from the city's most impoverished neighborhoods. Shocked by the unsanitary living conditions she found among recent migrants to Washington, Whipper traveled throughout the South during World War I to educate African American mothers and midwives about public health and hygiene.

At the end of the war in 1918, Whipper continued this work under the auspices of the War Work Council for the Young Women's Christian Association. Though she certainly experienced racism in Washington, her work between 1924 and 1929 as a public health lecturer for the Children's Bureau of the U.S. Department of Labor exposed Whipper to the stark racism of the Jim Crow South for the first time. Proud of her professional achievements, she greatly resented having to enter white homes by the back door and being addressed as "auntie" or other, even more demeaning expressions.

In the 1920s she taught obstetrics, hygiene, and pediatrics to nurses and midwives at the Tuskegee Institute in Alabama. Her Tuskegee experience was personally rewarding, and it was invaluable for an entire generation of rural midwives, such as MARGARET C. SMITH, who trained at Tuskegee's rigorous midwifery institute and eventually combined the most recent developments in hygiene with their own black midwife folk knowledge, or "motherwit."

Whipper's main focus remained with the unwed and abandoned young mothers of Washington, D.C. Having opened her own home to several homeless mothers, in 1931 she founded an organization, the Lend-a-Hand Club, to raise funds for a permanent social settlement for black women in Washington. Such a shelter already existed in Washington, but it was open to whites only. The Great Depression was hardly a propitious time to launch such a plan, but by 1941 Whipper had raised enough money to establish the Ionia Rollin Whipper Home for Unwed Mothers, the only such shelter in Washington until desegregation in the 1960s. For much of its existence Whipper was responsible for every aspect of the shelter's functioning, serving as fund-raiser, administrator, teacher, physician, and counselor to hundreds of young women in need, often calling on them in their homes when they were unable to travel to the shelter. Because most of the women she catered for had little money, she asked only that they do housework or other jobs around the shelter.

Whipper, who never married, also served as a mentor to her great-niece, Carol Ione, taking her to services at Washington's predominantly white Bethesda Episcopal Church, as well as at Saint Luke's. Active right up to her death, Whipper spent her final years in semiretirement at the home of her sister-in-law in Saratoga Springs, New York, where she made cakes, crocheted Afghan rugs, and even purchased a loom, at which she worked every day. Following a long illness, Whipper died in New York City.

Although she differed from NANNIE BURROUGHS both in her social background and in her temperament, Whipper shared with her fellow Washington reformer a strong sense of self-reliance, a single-minded focus on the goal of uplifting the less fortunate members of her race, and an adherence to the values of the professional black middle class, described by the historian EVELYN BROOKS HIGGINBOTHAM as the "politics of respectability."

FURTHER READING

Biographical information on Ionia Rollin Whipper can be found in the Leigh R. Whipper Papers at the Moorland-Spingarn Research Center at Howard University in Washington, D.C., and in the file on the Whipper Home at the Martin Luther King Memorial Library in the same city.

Ione, Carol. *Pride of Family: Four Generations of American Women of Color* (1991).

Obituary: *Washington Evening Star*, 24 Apr. 1953.

STEVEN J. NIVEN

Whipper, Leigh (29 October 1876–26 July 1975), actor, director, and writer, was born in Charleston, South Carolina, one of three children born to WILLIAM J. WHIPPER and FRANCES ROLLIN WHIPPER. The former was a lawyer, a Reconstruction Era state legislator, and circuit court judge, and the latter was a writer, educator, and women's rights activist. In 1880, his parents separated, and he moved to Washington D.C. with his mother, his sisters IONIA ROLLIN WHIPPER and Winifred, and their adopted brother Demps. After going through the segregated school system in Washington D.C., he attended Howard University. He graduated cum laude from Howard University in 1985 with an LLB degree; however, he decided to pursue a career in acting instead of establishing a law practice.

Whipper made his acting debut in 1895, performing in a touring show with the Georgia Minstrels. His next recorded performance was in a production of *Uncle Tom's Cabin* in 1898, during which he performed the song, "Old Black Joe." Shortly after *Uncle Tom's Cabin*, he took a break from acting to serve in the Spanish American War. After being released from service, he joined a theatre company in Pennsylvania known as the Philadelphia Stock Company. After leaving the Philadelphia Stock Company, he went on to join the Dudley Theatre of Newport News, Virginia, where he began serving as the manager in the early twentieth century. In 1915, he entered the field of composing, when he served as the lyricist for Irvin C. Miller's "Broadway Raustus."

Whipper's career began to gain rapidly in eminence and prestige in the 1920s. He made his film debut in 1920, playing Tugi in the all black, OSCAR MICHEAUX directed film, *Symbol of the Unconquered*. In addition to his first film role, Whipper's career received another significant boost in 1920 when he became the first African American in history to join the Actors Equity Association. The following year, Whipper became the chairman of the board of directors for the Dressing Room Club, an organization of over 250 African American theatre professionals who worked to raise awareness of the current and historical importance of African Americans in the theatre and funds for members who were struggling financially. In 1923, Whipper portrayed Wallace King in a benefit performance for the foundation entitled *Historic Pageant of the Progress of Negro Theatricals, Past and Present—from 1860–1924*.

He believed strongly in the importance of promoting and producing black cinema, documentaries, theatre, and music, and this belief shaped his career in a variety of ways. In 1922, he began working as a writer for the J. A. Jackson page of *Billboard*, which is described by the magazine as a page dedicated to the "interest of the Colored Actor, Showman and Musician of America." In the same year, he, along with a group of other black film and theatre professionals, formed the Renaissance Film Corporation, which focused on the creation and circulation of short African American documentaries known as "newsreels."

In June of 1925 Whipper made his Broadway directorial debut with his work on the Grainger and Johnson musical, *Lucky Sambo*. It was produced by the Harlem Producing Company, which was formed for the sole purpose of financing the performance. Whipper worked with Grainger again that year, when the latter served as the co-author of Whipper's first play, De Board Meeting. Two years later, in October of 1927, he made his Broadway acting debut as The Crab Man in Dubose and Heyward's *Porgy*. Also that year, Whipper co-wrote another show with Grainger entitled *We's Risin': A Story of the Simple Life in the Souls of Black Folks*, although there is no record it was ever produced.

He continued writing, and in 1930 finished his third play, *Runnin' de Town*, this time collaborating with J.C. Johnson. Also in 1930, he returned to Broadway, playing the role of Evergreen Peppers in the musical *Change Your Luck*. He made yet another Broadway debut in 1932, this time as a playwright when his play *Yeah-Man* (co-authored with Billy Mills) opened in May at the Park Lane Theatre. The next decade held a steady stream of acting work on Broadway for Whipper who appeared as Jim Veal in *Stevedore* (1934), a Negro minister in *White Man* (1936), Aloes in *How Come Lawd?* (1937), Crooks in *Of Mice and Men* (1938), and Eli in *Medicine Show* (1940).

During this period of prosperity, Whipper continued his activism by teaming up with several other prominent theatre professionals to form the Black Actors Guild (of America). Their goals were to portray black theatre professionals in a positive and honorable light, to increase understanding between artists and their communities, to support struggling and/or ailing artists with empathy and financial aid, to promote propriety in performance, and to address issues specific to being an African American artist. He served as the first vice president of the Guild, which grew to include over 600 members, and was active until 1982.

In 1940 Whipper moved from New York to Hollywood. He continued his work on Broadway, performing such roles as the leader of the chorus in an all black production of *Lysistrata* (1946), the judge in *Valpone* (1948), Gullah Jack in *Set My People Free* (1948), Al Giage in *How Long Till Summer* (1949), and Frank Carlisle in *The Shirk* (1952–1953), a role which he reprised in the 1955 film. However, despite his numerous theatrical performances in this period, his primary focus during the 1940s and 1950s was on his film career. He appeared in more than twenty films, the highlights of which include his reprisal of the role of Crooks in the film version of *Of Mice and Men* (1940), his portrayal of Sparks in the Oscar-nominated *The Ox-Bow Incident* (1943), and his depiction of Emperor Haile Selassie in *Mission to Moscow*. He was the first recipient of the Screen Actors Guild Award, was inducted into the Black Filmmakers Hall of Fame in 1974, and was given the prestigious Harold Jackman Memorial Award. He formally retired in 1972, three years prior to his death.

FURTHER READING

Whipper's personal papers can be found in the Manuscripts, Archives, and Rare Books Division of the Schomburg Center for Research in Black Culture at the New York Public Library.

Peterson, Bernard L. *The African American Theatre Directory, 1816–1960: A Comprehensive Guide to Black Theatre Organizations, Companies, Theatres and Performing Groups* (1997).

Peterson, Bernard L. *Profiles of African American Stage Performers and Theatre People, 1816–1960* (2000).

AMBER KARLINS

Whipper, William (1804?–9 Mar. 1876), abolitionist, businessman, and moral reformer, was born in Lancaster, Pennsylvania, the son of a white merchant and his black domestic servant. Very little is known about Whipper's early life or education. In the 1820s he moved to Philadelphia, where he worked as a steam scourer. In March 1834 he opened a free labor and temperance grocery store next door to the Bethel Church in Philadelphia. Whipper supported the temperance movement. He condemned liquor for its destructive effect on Africa and believed that alcohol consumption induced Africans into selling their brothers and sisters to slave traders. As a supporter of the antislavery movement, he also kept a supply of abolitionist books and pamphlets on hand for customers.

In 1835 he moved to nearby Columbia, Pennsylvania, and formed a successful business partnership with the black entrepreneur STEPHEN SMITH. Their eventual holdings included a lumberyard, a merchant ship on Lake Erie, railroad freight cars, and real estate in Pennsylvania and Canada. Smith and Whipper amassed considerable wealth and were classified among the country's wealthiest blacks in the prewar years. Whipper married Harriet L. Smith in 1836.

For more than twenty years Whipper operated a major underground railroad station. Columbia was a major port of entry for fugitive slaves from Virginia and Maryland. Whipper housed as many as seventeen slaves in one night, the next day sending them to Pittsburgh by boat or to Philadelphia by rail in the false end of a boxcar. He estimated that over a thirteen-year period he spent one thousand dollars annually aiding hundreds of fugitive slaves.

In the 1830s Whipper began to participate in the antislavery and black national convention movements. Although he was not considered a great speaker, he gained prominence as an intellectual and moral reformer. In 1832 he helped to lead a petition campaign against a Pennsylvania state measure that restricted immigration of blacks and enforced the 1793

Fugitive Slave Law. Whipper credited the abolitionist movement with giving blacks a heightened sense of self-respect. He felt that the crusade had a more powerful influence on black life than any other influences combined. As a moral reformer, he believed that the movement served as a check on the evil dispositions of blacks and inculcated moral principles.

In his earlier years, Whipper was known as a Garrisonian. As such he felt that political participation and physical resistance by blacks should not be encouraged, and he opposed separatist action until blacks developed strong internal social bonds among themselves. In an 1849 letter to FREDERICK DOUGLASS, Whipper asserted that blacks had no national existence as a people and therefore could have no national institutions. Further, blacks lacked a distinct civil and religious code that generally served as rallying and unifying points for other groups.

As an integrationist, Whipper opposed terms that designated race. Therefore, in 1835 he urged delegates at the annual convention of the Improvement of Free People of Color to adopt a resolution giving up the use of the word *colored*. The convention chose to organize a society with no racial designation, calling it only the American Moral Reform Society (AMRS). At the first annual meeting of the society in 1835, Whipper was elected its secretary and the editor of its journal, the *National Reformer*. His ideology shaped the character of the organization. However, his opposition to racially separate organizations often infuriated those members who wanted the AMRS to address race-specific issues.

Whipper's initial views on the origin and nature of American racism were that prejudice occurred because of the condition in which blacks found themselves, not because of their skin color. If blacks were to overcome their condition, they had to conform to white expectations—that is, blacks had to improve their mental, economic, and moral situations. This, he believed, would ultimately change the attitudes of whites about race.

Although he maintained a lifelong commitment to moral reform, Whipper began to question its antislavery value in the 1840s. He also tempered his opposition to racial separatism in the 1850s. At the 1853 black national convention, he helped draft a plan for the National Council of Colored People and accepted the necessity of separate black schools. Consistent with black abolitionist thought in the 1850s, Whipper abandoned the "condition" argument and increasingly blamed racism on white ignorance.

Although Whipper was for years an opponent of colonization to Africa and a faithful supporter of integration, he became more receptive to the idea of black emigration. He endorsed the African Civilization Society, an organization for which he served as a vice president (c. 1853–1854). He saw emigration as a rational response of people who were dispossessed and persecuted.

In 1853 Whipper visited Canada, where he purchased land on the Sydenham River at Dresden, Ontario. Several of his relatives emigrated, and he had plans to emigrate as well. However, those plans were interrupted by the start of the Civil War. During the war, Whipper promoted black enlistment in the Union army and later served as vice president of the Pennsylvania State Equal Rights League.

After 1865 Whipper conducted his lumber business with his nephew, James Purnell. He had been sole operator of the business since 1842, when his partner had moved to Philadelphia. In 1868 he moved to New Brunswick, New Jersey. Two years later he took a position as a cashier of the Philadelphia branch of the Freedmen's Savings Bank, returning in 1873 to reside in Philadelphia, where he died.

FURTHER READING

McCormick, Richard P. "William Whipper: Moral Reformer," *Pennsylvania History* 43 (Jan. 1976): 23–46.

Quarles, Benjamin. *Black Abolitionists* (1969).

Ripley, C. Peter, ed. *The Black Abolitionist Papers*, vol. 3 (1985).

Sterling Stuckey, comp. *The Ideological Origins of Black Nationalism* (1972).

This entry is taken from the *American National Biography* and is published here with the permission of the American Council of Learned Societies.

MAMIE E. LOCKE

Whipper, William J. (1835–1907), lawyer, politician, and judge, was born William James Whipper, probably in Glenville, Pennsylvania, one of the four children of Benjamin P. Whipper, who later became a minister in Chatham, Canada. There is some uncertainty about the name of William's mother, which in certain sources is given as Mary Ann (maiden name unknown), and in others is recorded as Sophia Patterson. Part of the confusion may have been caused by William J. Whipper himself, who often claimed that his father was the famed Underground Railroad conductor WILLIAM WHIPPER, who was in fact Benjamin's brother. Not long after his family moved from Pennsylvania to Chatham, Canada, William appears to have returned to the United States. By the late 1850s he was working as a law clerk in Detroit, Michigan, and later passed the bar exam in that state, having earlier failed it in Ohio. Around this time Whipper married a woman named Mary Elizabeth.

In the early 1860s he returned to Ohio to practice law, and enlisted in the U.S. Colored Infantry soon after the outbreak of the Civil War. Whipper had a colorful army career, to say the least. Articulate and intelligent but hot-tempered, he was twice court-martialed, once for gambling, which led to his transfer to another company, in which he rose from private to the rank of sergeant. After his second court martial, this time for fighting with an officer, Whipper was reduced to the rank of private. He was involved in active combat in Virginia at the battle of Petersburg, and was present at the surrender of Confederate forces at Appomatox in April 1865. Whipper then moved to South Carolina, where he purchased property on Hilton Head Island, taught in a Freedman's Bureau School in Beaufort, and practiced law. In 1866, his wife joined him in Beaufort, where the couple had a son, Bud, and adopted Demps Powell, a fifteen-year-old boy who had served with Whipper during the Civil War. Mary Elizabeth died, perhaps in childbirth, in 1867, but Whipper did not remain single for long. On 17 September 1868 he married FRANCES ANNE ROLLIN, his law clerk, whom he had met when she was a teacher for the Freedman's Bureau in the South Carolina Sea Islands. Rollin, born into Charleston's antebellum free black elite, published a biography of MARTIN DELANY. The couple had four daughters, two of whom died in infancy, and a son, the actor Leigh Whipper.

1868 proved to be a banner year for William Whipper. In addition to his wedding, he became one of the first three African Americans admitted to the South Carolina bar, represented Beaufort at South Carolina's constitutional convention, and was elected to the state house of representatives. He chaired the house judiciary committee and came to be known by his opponents as the "most rascally of rascally radicals" (cited in Williamson, 331). The "radical" label was in many ways apt. He opposed both corporal and capital punishment and was, like his second wife, a powerful advocate for women's rights. During the constitutional convention he advocated the extension of the vote to women, but found few allies, black or white, among his fellow delegates, who refused even to debate the issue. Although Whipper, like many of his fellow black landowners, opposed the confiscation of former Confederate-owned lands, he recommended in 1869 that plantation workers form labor unions and urged them to demand higher wages from their employers. Whipper's radical rhetoric on the labor question was sometimes undermined by

his actions, however, notably in 1872, when he allegedly refused to pay laborers on his lowcountry rice plantation. He also supported a poll tax on all citizens rather than a property tax to pay for public schools. To opponents who charged that this method disproportionately hurt poor blacks, Whipper replied that the poor should "smoke less segars, or chew less tobacco" (cited in Williamson, 225).

There is also widespread evidence of Whipper's rascality. He spent his money conspicuously, dressed elegantly, rode in the finest carriages, and gambled heavily. He allegedly lost $75,000 in a single night of poker, $30,000 of it on a hand of four aces, defeated by another black legislator's straight flush. The latter anecdote, if true, suggests that Whipper was one of the wealthier black legislators in South Carolina, though his precise fortune is unknown. In 1870 he helped found and served on the boards of the predominantly black-owned Enterprise Railroad Company and the South Carolina Phosphate Mining Company, though both ventures were conspicuous failures. He also founded newspapers in Beaufort and Barnwell County, though his main source of income continued to be his law practice.

Whipper was an ambitious politician, often at odds with his fellow Republicans. He maintained long-running feuds with fellow Beaufort resident and U.S. congressman ROBERT SMALLS, and with the lawyer JONATHAN J. WRIGHT, who defeated him twice for a seat on the state supreme court in 1868 and 1872. After three years out of the House, Whipper was re-elected in 1875, where he again lobbied his fellow Republicans to appoint him to a judgeship on the Charleston circuit. This he finally achieved in December 1875, while the conservative Republican governor, Daniel Chamberlain, was out of town. When the governor returned to Columbia he refused to sign Whipper's commission, an action that precipitated a decisive break between Chamberlain and the state's black Republicans. Chamberlain claimed that Whipper did not have the moral fiber to be a judge, and that his appointment would destroy American civilization, a point echoed by many white newspapers. Whipper responded that he had had a religious awakening and claimed, inaccurately, that he no longer drank or gambled, but to no avail. Although black Republicans rallied to Whipper's defense, white conservatives outmaneuvered them in their successful effort to "redeem" the state from Republican rule in 1876.

After the Compromise of 1877 formally ended Reconstruction in South Carolina, Whipper focused on his Beaufort law firm. His family life was troubled. Frances Rollin, tired of her husband's drinking, gambling, womanizing, and indebtedness, moved to Washington, D.C., in 1880. Whipper followed her there two years later to practice law, returning to Beaufort in 1885, when he was appointed a probate judge. Rollin remained in Washington. Whipper served as judge for three years, but was defeated for re-election in 1888 after a fraudulent vote count. In protest, he refused to pass on his judicial papers to his successor, for which he received a thirteen-month jail sentence. After his release from prison in 1889, Whipper, no longer a heavy drinker and suffering from asthma, was reunited in Beaufort with his wife, who was also ill.

Whipper was one of only six South Carolina Republicans, all black, elected to the state's constitutional convention in 1895. His onetime rival Robert Smalls also attended, though their joint efforts failed to prevent the disenfranchisement of black voters. Whipper died in Beaufort in 1907, thirteen years before the passage of the Nineteenth Amendment gave women the right to vote, as he had demanded in the 1860s. In the 1940s MODJESKA SIMKINS, OSCEOLA MCKAINE, and a new generation of activists in the South Carolina Progressive Democratic Party, would build on Whipper's legacy to ensure that the Nineteenth Amendment also applied to women of color.

FURTHER READING

Holt, Thomas. *Black over White: Negro Political Leadership in South Carolina during Reconstruction* (1977).

Ione, Carol. *Pride of Family: Four Generations of American Women of Color* (1991).

Williamson, Joel. *After Slavery: The Negro in South Carolina during Reconstruction* (1965).

STEVEN J. NIVEN

Whipple, Dinah (c. 1760–13 Feb. 1846), teacher, was born Dinah Chase to an enslaved mother in the household of the Congregationalist minister in the tiny fishing village of New Castle, New Hampshire. Chase was emancipated upon reaching her twenty-first birthday. She moved to the adjacent shipbuilding and mercantile center of Portsmouth, and on 22 February 1781 she married an enslaved man of that city, known as PRINCE WHIPPLE. At the time of Prince's death in 1797, they had seven children. By 1804 the young widow had established a school in her home for the education of Portsmouth's black children.

Dinah Whipple, as the child of an enslaved mother, had been born into slavery. She had later worked as a house servant, and in that capacity she acquired a variety of those skills required to maintain an efficient and gracious household. Her knowledge was useful in later years, when she married Prince Whipple and began to emerge as a leader in the free black community of Portsmouth. Dinah Whipple and her entire family were baptized in and remained faithful to the Congregational Church, although, like other enslaved and free black people, they were restricted to balcony seating. Whipple's high moral standing was noted by white chroniclers of her day.

Her husband, Prince, was a Revolutionary War veteran who had been the servant of William Whipple, a signer of the Declaration of Independence. Prince had come from Guinea, on the west coast of Africa, as a young boy. Like Dinah, he too had grown up enslaved as a household "servant" (the term used in New England for all servants, regardless of legal status). Prince received his freedom papers in 1784, more than four years after he and nineteen other African men had petitioned the New Hampshire legislature for manumission and for an end to the practice of slavery in the state.

During the War of Independence seacoast-area towns of New Hampshire had the largest concentration of black people in the state, a total of more than six hundred, nearly all enslaved. About one-third of that number was located in Portsmouth. By 1800 no slaves were counted in the federal census reports for Portsmouth-area towns and, while the state did not legislate an end to slavery until 1857, no slaves appeared in the New Hampshire census after 1840. Many freemen and free women left Portsmouth in search of employment, a more satisfying social environment, and the security of numbers in larger free-black communities. The Whipples' son Robert was among those. He went to Boston, only fifty miles away, where he died in 1816, at the age of twenty-nine.

Although Dinah Whipple was one of many enslaved people who had been born in the region since the mid-seventeenth century, others had come directly from Africa and the slave-trading markets along the Atlantic coast from Portland, Maine, and Boston, to Baltimore and Charleston and New Orleans, and from the West Indies to South America. Throughout Whipple's lifetime, enslaved and freed laborers often worked alongside European indentured servants in the fields, on the docks and ships, and in the homes of local farmers and merchants.

Whipple's years of servitude had prepared her to be what many of her contemporaries understood as a model for newly freed blacks. In addition to managing her own household, she was literate and informed about the politics of slavery and freedom.

Because of their intimacy with influential white families, albeit as servants, she and her husband were familiar with the radical revolutionary issues and language of the time. Furthermore, as patrons of the church's lending library, they were knowledgeable about classical and contemporary literary thought.

Their home was a small wood-frame house that Prince had provided for his family near the working waterfront and the marketplace, at the edge of William Whipple's townhouse garden. It was here that Dinah Whipple began the Ladies' Charitable African Society School. Such schools at this time provided both children and adults with the kinds of support services needed in the transition from slavery to freedom. The Ladies' Charitable African Society was active in Portsmouth during the same period as the men's African Society. Both benevolent societies had counterparts in communities of free blacks in other northern cities.

In 1832 Dinah Whipple was forced from the house she had shared with her family and students when its deteriorating condition posed a fire hazard. Descendants of William Whipple provided her with another house, along with an annuity. Donations from the church Poor Fund also supplemented her income, allowing her to continue living in a home of her own rather than having to spend her final years in the almshouse.

Together Dinah and Prince Whipple had been among the leaders of the next-largest black community north of Boston. For fifty years after her husband's death, Whipple was a link to the earliest known African American institutions in New England. In a rare tribute to a black person, the editor of the *Portsmouth Journal of Literature and Politics* offered this sentiment on 14 February 1846, acknowledging the passing of Dinah Whipple: "Few, of any color, have lived a more upright, virtuous, and truly Christian life … enjoyed a more calm, tranquil and happy old age, and few have had a more peaceful and happy death" (3).

FURTHER READING

Information regarding the Whipples' marriage date as well as the names of the Whipple children can be found in the *North Church Collection 1640–1970*, MS036, Portsmouth Athenaeum.

Horton, James Oliver, and Lois E. Horton. *Black Bostonians: Family Life and Community Struggle in the Antebellum North* (1979).

Kaplan, Sidney. *The Black Presence in the Era of the American Revolution 1770–1800* (1973).

Sammons, Mark J., and Valerie Cunningham. *Black Portsmouth: Three Centuries of African-American Heritage* (2004).

VALERIE CUNNINGHAM

Whipple, Prince (?–1797), slave, Revolutionary War veteran, abolitionist, and jack-of-all-trades, was born, according to the historical record, in "Amabou, Africa." This location is probably Anomabu in present-day Ghana, which was known as the Gold Coast when Prince Whipple was born. The names of his parents are unknown, but oral tradition published in the mid-nineteenth century implies he was born free and maintains he was sent abroad with a brother (or cousin) Cuff (or Cuffee), but parental plans went awry and the youths were sold into slavery in North America. A collective document Whipple signed with twenty others in 1779 describes their shared experience as being "torn by the cruel hand of violence" from their mothers' "aching bosom," and "seized, imprisoned and transported" to the United States and deprived of "the nurturing care of [their] bereaved parent" (New Hampshire *Gazette*, 15 July 1780).

Prince was acquired by William Whipple, and Cuff by William's brother Joseph Whipple, white merchants in Portsmouth, New Hampshire. William Whipple's household also included Windsor Moffatt and other slaves. There are several possible reasons for the confusion about whether Prince and Cuff were brothers or cousins: linguistic translation difficulties, uncertain community memory after their deaths, and white indifference to such distinctions in a marginalized race.

Likewise, Prince Whipple maintained that his given name reflected his actual status in Africa, although the numerous enslaved black men named Prince suggests the name was frequently given by white owners in sentimentality or mockery. If Prince's name records his African status, it represents an infrequent case of resistance to white renaming, a practice that stripped away African identity and dissociated the enslaved from both the dominant society and their own humanity. However, the persistence of Cuff's African name in a town where only a few other African names persisted lends some credence to this interpretation of Prince's name.

Nineteenth-century tradition spins an elaborate tale of Prince's participation in the American Revolution, fragments of which may be verified, disproved, or called into doubt. No documentation substantiates the claim that Prince accompanied William Whipple, a colonel in the First New Hampshire Regiment, on early revolutionary campaigns or to the Continental Congress in Philadelphia in 1776.

Documentation also argues against a tradition that Prince was with George Washington at the crossing of the Delaware River in December 1776. On that date, William Whipple was attending Congress, first in Philadelphia and then in Baltimore. Were Prince with him, it seems unlikely that William would have sent the enslaved Prince unaccompanied 130 miles to a war zone in which the enemy promised manumission in exchange for defection. The pervasive story about Prince's crossing the Delaware first appears in WILLIAM C. NELL's 1855 *Colored Patriots of the American Revolution*, written at the height of the abolitionist movement. It is unclear whether Nell recorded an undocumented but accurate family tradition circulating among Prince's heirs or a confused family tale, or whether he symbolically attached to one individual the forgotten reality of black participation in both the Revolution and Washington's crossing. Heroic paintings of this event by the nineteenth-century artists Thomas Sully (1819) and Emmanuel Leutze (1851) do indeed include a black man, illustrative of the lingering memory of black participation in the Revolution. New England traditions place other black men in Washington's boat, for example PRINCE ESTABROOK of Lexington (later of Ashby), Massachusetts.

Prince Whipple did, however, participate in the Revolution. He accompanied William Whipple, by then a brigadier general, on military campaigns to Saratoga, New York, in 1777 and Rhode Island in 1778. Prince was attuned to revolutionary philosophy. In 1779 he and Windsor Moffatt were among twenty enslaved men who signed a petition to the New Hampshire legislature for the abolition of slavery in the state. All the signatories were held as slaves in prominent and politically active white patriot families, and thus had ample opportunity to overhear, contemplate, and reinterpret revolutionary rhetoric. However, the petition was tabled, and slavery was not formally abolished in New Hampshire until 1857.

After the Revolution, Prince attained freedom in gradual, if unclear, stages. On Prince's marriage day, 22 February 1781, William Whipple prepared a special document that allowed Prince the rights of a freeman. The actual status conveyed by this document is obscure, as Prince was not formally manumitted until three years later, on 26 February 1784. The document may have been in response to a request from his bride's clergyman owner, who may have wished to legitimize the marriage according to his religious standards. Prince's bride, twenty-one-year-old Dinah Chase of New Castle and Hampton, New Hampshire, was manumitted by her owner on her wedding day.

In freedom, the black Whipples faced the daunting task of making a living in a context of social and economic marginalization. In his widow's obituary, Prince was remembered as "the Caleb Quotem of the old fashioned semi-monthly assemblies, and at all large weddings and dinners, balls and evening parties. Nothing could go on right without Prince." That is, he served as master of ceremonies at the Assembly House balls for white socialites. (Caleb Quotem was an eccentric, voluble character in *The Review, or The Wags of Windsor* [1801], by the English playwright George Colman.) On various occasions, these balls included other black people as caterers and musicians, and it is likely that Prince's role was to bring together this supportive talent. He was "a large, well proportioned, and fine looking man, and of gentlemanly manners and deportment" (*Portsmouth Journal of Literature and Politics*, 22 Feb. 1846). William Whipple died one year after Prince's manumission, and his widow carved a house lot out of the back corner of the pleasure garden behind the Whipple mansion and loaned it to their former slaves. Prince and Dinah, along with Cuff, who had been manumitted in 1784, and his wife Rebecca Daverson (married on 24 August 1786) moved an old house to the lot, where they and their children lived for forty years.

Their home life was crowded. In addition to the adults and first child who occupied the house when the 1790 census was taken, others were soon born, including Prince's daughters, Esther and Elizabeth. In addition, DINAH WHIPPLE operated the Ladies' Charitable African Society School for black children, probably in their house, as well as working for the North Church.

Prince died in Portsmouth in 1797, Cuff in 1816. Dinah's obituary in 1846 described Prince's earlier death as "much regretted both by the white and colored inhabitants of the town; by the latter of whom he was always regarded as their prince." This reminiscence notwithstanding, Prince was not an officer of the Negro Court that held annual coronations in eighteenth-century Portsmouth. However, his signature on the abolition petition alongside those of Portsmouth's black king, viceroy, sheriff, and deputy confirms Prince's active participation in the local black community.

Prince was not buried in Portsmouth's segregated Negro Burial Ground, suggesting that it may have been closed by the 1790s. Following local tradition for black people, his grave in North Burial Ground was marked with two rough stones. Its location was later identified by a grandson, John Smith, and a more impressive stone installed. Today it is marked as that of a Revolutionary War veteran. Prince's age at death is unknown, but he was almost certainly a decade or more older than the age (forty-six) sometimes supposed.

Prince Whipple's life characterizes white Portsmouth's preference for the importation of enslaved children rather than adults, and also exemplifies his generation's participation in and advocacy for a coherent black community. The loaned residence, extended family, and his heirs' continuation in Portsmouth throughout much of the nineteenth century diverge from a local pattern of frequent changes of residence and of filial outmigration. Prince's participation in the Revolution while enslaved may have been elaborated in folk memory. But, along with CRISPUS ATTUCKS and PRINCE HALL, among others, his story reminds us of the significant African American contribution to the American struggle for independence.

FURTHER READING

Kaplan, Sidney. *The Black Presence in the Era of the American Revolution 1770–1800* (1973).

Melish, Joanne Pope. *Disowning Slavery: Gradual Emancipation and "Race" in New England, 1780–1860* (1998).

Nell, William C. *The Colored Patriots of the American Revolution* (1855).

Piersen, William D. *Black Yankees: The Development of an Afro-American Subculture in Eighteenth-Century New England* (1988).

Sammons, Mark J., and Valerie Cunningham. *Black Portsmouth* (2003).

MARK J. SAMMONS

Whitaker, Effie (30 Sept. 1892–11 Mar. 1964), teacher, activist, and advocate for deaf adults in Raleigh, North Carolina, was born Effie C. Pointer, the daughter of Lucinda Pointer and Benjamin Hinton of Raleigh. Nothing is known about her parents. Between 1897 and 1908 Effie attended elementary school at the Joseph K. Brick School in Enfield and attended the First Congregational Church of Raleigh, which also maintained a school funded by the American Missionary Society. Effie was a committed student, and in June 1908 at age sixteen she was sponsored to go to the Hampton Institute. The identity of the sponsor is unclear, but once at Hampton she completed high school and had a smooth transition into college life. She continued her strong religious and benevolence mission by joining, and later becoming president of, the King's Daughter Society, an organization founded in 1886 in New York City as an international

order to encourage the development of an individual's spiritual life and to stimulate Christian activities.

In 1913 Whitaker graduated from Hampton Institute, and by 1914 she had accepted her first teaching position at the Henderson Elementary School in Raleigh. In 1916 she left the Henderson School and accepted a position teaching black deaf and blind children at the Deaf, Dumb, and Blind Institute in Raleigh, which had opened in 1845 but only for white students. The institution began admitting African Americans in 1868, and by 1872 a department within the white school was created for black students. In 1897 a separate school was built for white students in Morganton.

Because Effie was fluent in America Sign Language (ASL) due to learning it from Lovey Mayo from church, she was assigned to teach the youngest children. Although the deaf community remained torn over oral versus signing methods of teaching hearing-impaired students, most schools adopted both approaches. Alexander Graham Bell's theory about teaching deaf students fueled the argument when he opened the Speech School for Teachers of the Deaf in Boston in 1872. Bell was criticized for his strong support of lip reading, yet he refused to waver and even started his own journal, the *Volta Review*, in 1887 to promote his mechanical experiments in hearing and speech. Whitaker was well aware of this debate, but she also understood that deaf students needed to know sign language to communicate with each other. More important, she knew that young, black children needed to know ASL in order to obtain a higher education in settings such as Gallaudet University for the deaf.

In 1919 Effie married Claude E. Whitaker Sr. "Buck," as he was known, graduated from Shaw University in Raleigh, North Carolina, served in the military, and later became the city's first black lithotypist. His work for the *Raleigh Independent* and the *Carolina Tribune*, two local black newspapers, likely opened to Effie the door to publishing.

Effie Whitaker registered for summer school to earn advanced degrees and to attend conferences to learn the latest teaching techniques for special education. During the summer at Hampton University she befriended a white professor from Gallaudet University, Powrie V. Doctor, who was engaged in an evaluation of the school. Doctor also served as assistant editor of the *American Annals of the Deaf*, the oldest journal on deaf education in the world, and published Whitaker's *The Negro Adult Deaf in North Carolina* (1947).

By 1949 Whitaker was spending her summers teaching part time at Shaw, A&T, Johnson C. Smith, and Fayetteville State—all historically black colleges or universities in North Carolina. Her passion for teaching and her ability to comfort the children prompted principal Manuel Crockett to name a dormitory in her honor. In 1952 she received the "mother of the year award," not just for being an exceptional mother to her five children but also for being mother to many children who left home for the first time, to live in a residential school. For thirty-eight years Whitaker took them into her arms, wiped away their tears, and welcomed them to their new home. At a time when deaf children, particularly African Americans, were viewed as unteachable, Whitaker produced students who could go beyond the expected norm of learning to sew, cook, clean, and do manual labor. Her ability to teach blind students and help them to master ASL in the mid-1900s was exceptional.

A high percentage of the children that Whitaker taught had become deaf from high temperatures and meningitis. Thus it was ironic that her son Collins developed meningitis while in the military in Germany and died in 1963. She was a very religious woman, but her son's death placed an insurmountable burden of grief upon her, and she died three months later. Because her husband was a veteran, Whitaker was buried in the National Cemetery for Veterans in Raleigh.

FURTHER READING

A scrapbook compiled by Barbara Crockett Dease and Manuel H. Crockett, titled *Through the Years 1867–1977: Light of Darkness, a History of the North Carolina School for the Negro Blind and Deaf*, is in the North Carolina Collection in the Wilson Library at the University of North Carolina Library at Chapel Hill.

Hairston, Ernest, and Linwood Smith. *Black and Deaf in America* (1983).

Sewell, Joseph L. "The Only Negro Deaf-Mute Lawyer in the United States," *Silent Worker* 39, no. 7 (Mar. 1927).

Valentine, Victory. "Listening to Deaf Blacks," *Emerge* (Dec./Jan. 1996).

Wright, Mary H. *Sounds like Home: Growing Up Black and Deaf in the South* (2002).

MARIETA JOYNER

Whitaker, Forest (15 July 1961–) actor, director, and producer, was born in Longview, Texas, one of four children born to Forest Whitaker Jr., an insurance salesman, and Laura Francis Smith Whitaker, a special education teacher. The Whitakers moved to South Central Los Angeles just prior to the 1965 Watts Riots, when Forest was four years old. Whitaker's parents moved again when he was eleven to Carson, California, on the border of Compton, one of the harshest areas of Los Angeles. With rampant gang violence on the ground and police helicopters flying overhead, Whitaker managed to avoid the area's pitfalls, instead embarking on an academic and artistic path. At his request, Whitaker's dedicated and involved parents allowed him to ride the bus for three or more hours each day to attend the more upscale Palisades High School.

Drawn to academics, football, and music, Whitaker did not consider acting until a speech teacher at Cal Poly Pomona, which he attended on a football scholarship, suggested he try out for the Dylan Thomas play *Under Milk Wood*. Landing the lead role in the play, Whitaker was again awarded a scholarship, this time to study music and acting at a much larger institution, the University of Southern California, and graduated in 1982. Initially headed for a career in opera, Whitaker found greater fulfillment in acting and landed his first legitimate film role in *Fast Times at Ridgemont High* (1982). The small role of hard-hitting football star Charles Jefferson in the teen classic launched his career, along with those of Nicholas Cage and Sean Penn. Small roles in *Vision Quest* (1985) and various television programs followed, but none gave Whitaker the opportunity to flex his acting muscles until his appearance in *The Color of Money* (1986), Martin Scorsese's sequel to *The Hustler*. Working under a renowned director and alongside screen legend Paul Newman and rising star Tom Cruise, Whitaker stole his sole scene as a swindler who outhustles the hustler. In a move that would set a precedent for his serious approach to acting, Whitaker immersed himself in his character both mentally and physically, studying billiards to be believable in the scene. Whitaker also proved his ability to transcend racial lines, landing a role that was originally written for a white yuppie. He would maintain this tradition in many of his roles, later playing characters that had been Jewish or Italian on paper. Whitaker also starred in the war films *Platoon* (1986) and *Good Morning Vietnam* (1987). He took a comic turn in the latter as he starred alongside Robin Williams and turned heads with a subdued performance that accented Williams' flamboyant lead.

In 1988 Whitaker finally landed a lead role, starring as jazz musician CHARLIE PARKER in Clint Eastwood's *Bird* (1988). Again, Whitaker found his bearings as his character through extensive

Forest Whitaker, looking on during a photocall for the presentation of his film *The Last King of Scotland* in Rome, Italy, 15 February 2007. (AP Images.)

research—learning the saxophone, studying music, and even speaking with former acquaintances of the jazz great. Winner of the Best Actor award at Cannes and nominated in the same category for the Golden Globes, Whitaker had earned a name as one of Hollywood's most impressive young actors.

The bulky six foot two inch actor would not take starring roles again for some time. He instead chose supporting roles in smaller films, most notably in *A Rage in Harlem* (1991), which he also co-produced. As a British soldier taken captive by the Irish Republican Army in 1992 surprise hit *The Crying Game*, Whitaker earned critical acclaim as an actor yet again. But it was with *Strapped* (1993), a gritty, hard-core tale of urban street life, that Whitaker earned accolades of a different sort. The realistic and morose tale of Diquan Mitchell (played by unknown actor Bokeem Woodbine), a former Brooklyn drug dealer who goes undercover for the police, was Whitaker's first directorial effort and a huge success for HBO, which financed the film. Directing his first film for a cable station rather than a Hollywood studio granted Whitaker a great deal of leeway, and the actor-turned-director made unconventional choices that resulted in an

authentic and courageous glimpse at inner-city life. From casting unknowns to filming in Harlem and Brooklyn with a local crew and failing to water down the language and themes for a mainstream audience, Whitaker fought hard for the film he envisioned. He subsequently earned a best director nod from the Toronto International Film Festival in 1993. Drawing from the violent environment of his youth, Whitaker brought a legitimate gravity to the film and could have continued making films of a similar strain. Never apt to follow the beaten path, Whitaker moved in the opposite direction in his choices of both directing and acting.

Starring as a gay designer in Robert Altman's *Pret-A-Porter* (1994), an aggressive officer in the mainstream action film *Blown Away* (1994), and an abusive alcoholic father in *Jason's Lyric* (1994), Whitaker once again proved his diversity as an actor. The following year Whitaker landed the unlikely post as director of *Waiting to Exhale*, the tale of four black women in search of love based on the best-selling TERRY MCMILLAN novel. A man whose only directorial effort had been a gang-related film seemed at first an unlikely hire to the film's producers, but Whitaker proved his interest and capability as he emphasized the importance of humanity in the film over gender and race. One of the most successful African American films of all time, *Waiting to Exhale* earned over $80 million worldwide and was one of the first black films to highlight positive images of wealthy African Americans on the screen. Keeping his roles as director and actor mutually exclusive, it would be three years before Whitaker would return to the director's chair. In subsequent years Whitaker balanced his time between mainstream roles in films such as *Species* (1995) and *Phenomenon* (1996), as well as meatier roles in smaller independent films such as Wayne Wang's *Smoke* (1995). Having starred in dozens of films and with his career still on the rise, Whitaker also found personal fulfillment in this period, marrying model Kesiha Nash in 1996. In the coming years the couple had two daughters, Sonnet Noel and True Summer. They became sisters to Ocean Alexander, Whitaker's son from a previous relationship.

Whitaker's return to the director's chair was the romantic drama *Hope Floats* (1998), starring Sandra Bullock and Harry Connick Jr. This time he directed a film that was geared not only primarily toward women but also toward white women. Whitaker's ability to look past pretenses to the heart of a film's universal emotions earned him the position of director, and *Hope Floats* became a moderate summer success.

Switching gears in a return to acting once again, Whitaker's role in Jim Jarmusch's *Ghost Dog: The Way of the Samurai* (1999) was one of his most astounding on-screen performances. Jarmusch and Whitaker talked over their ideas for the script, and in the end Jarmusch's unique and complex title character, Ghost Dog, developed as a soft-spoken and pensive contract killer who follows the ancient code of the Samurai and finds companionship with pigeons. In his typically dedicated fashion, Whitaker spent three months immersing himself in the character prior to filming: reading ancient texts of Eastern mythology, meditating for hours a day, and even living with a pigeon.

Although Whitaker's next mainstream effort, *Battlefield Earth* (2000), was a box-office bomb, his subsequent roles in *Panic Room* (2002) and *Phone Booth* (2003) proved to be much better investments as an actor. Through his production company Spirit Dance Entertainment, Whitaker also produced *Green Dragon* (2001; winner of the Humanitas and Audience awards at the South by Southwest Film Festival), *Door to Door* (2002 TV), *Feast of All Saints* (2002 TV miniseries), and *Chasing Papi* (2003). Spirit Dance Entertainment has a branch in the United Kingdom as well as in the United States, with both focusing on the production of minority films.

As Marcus Clay in *Deacons in Defense* (2003), a historical drama created for the cable channel Showtime, Whitaker's strong performance earned him nominations for the Image Awards, the Screen Actors Guild award, and a win for the Black Reel Awards. Other television roles, including a six-episode arc on NBC's *ER* as well as a thirteen-episode triumph on the FX series *The Shield*, put Whitaker back on the small screen for the first time since the beginning of his career.

Performing in *The Last King of Scotland* (2006) was perhaps Whitaker's most well-known big-screen role, earning him an Academy Award, a BAFTA, and a Golden Globe, among other distinctions. Playing Ugandan dictator Idi Amin, Whitaker once again meticulously researched the role. He interviewed Amin's relatives, ministers, generals, and girlfriends, learned Swahili, and immersed himself in Ugandan culture. In 2009, again forging a distinctive, diversified career path, Whitaker voiced the role of Ira in Spike Jonze's film adaptation of Maurice Sendak's children's book *Where the Wild Things Are*. Whitaker also starred in *Hurricane Season* (2009), a sports drama in which he played the coach of a high school basketball coach who led his team to the state finals the year after Hurricane Katrina; *Our Family Wedding* (2010), a romantic comedy; and *Repo Men* (2010), a science fiction thriller. In 2009 Whitaker was awarded an honorary chieftaincy, the Nwannedinambar of Nkwerre, in Nigeria, after DNA analysis showed he was descended from the Igbo people of Nigeria. His title means, "brother in foreign land."

A respected actor, director, and producer, Forest Whitaker earned his prestigious reputation through unprecedented dedication, unconventional choices, and a knack for molding himself to fit any role that came his way. As Whitaker put it, "That's been my only goal: to do good work and to tell good stories and to be true to the heart of the soul of whatever it was I was doing" (Alexander, p. 478).

FURTHER READING

Alexander, George. *Why We Make Movies: Black Filmmakers Talk About the Magic of Cinema* (2003).

Collier, Aldore. "Forest Whitaker's Big Step: Actor's Portrayal of Dictator Idi Amin in the Last King of Scotland Takes Him to a New Level." *Ebony*, Vol. 62, February 2007.

Donaldson, Melvin. *Black Directors in Hollywood* (2003).

ALEXIS WHITHAM

Whitaker, Mark (7 Sept. 1957–), editor and journalist, was born in Lower Merion, Pennsylvania, to Jeanne Theis Whitaker, a French professor, and Cleophus Sylvester Whitaker Jr., a political science professor. Jeanne Theis was a white native of Madagascar and the daughter of Protestant missionaries. During World War II her parents harbored Jews and other refugees and, to ensure her safety after the 1939 German occupation of France, they sent the fourteen-year-old Jeanne to live with a friend, a biology professor at Swarthmore College in Pennsylvania. She eventually became a French professor at the college.

Whitaker's parents met at Swarthmore, where Cleophus, known as Syl, was an undergraduate and Jeanne was his French professor. The unorthodox courtship between the black student and the white professor resulted in marriage but caused a stir on the small, bucolic campus. The couple left Swarthmore after Cleophus, who graduated with a degree in political science and later earned a doctorate in Political Science from Princeton, secured a teaching job at the University of California, Los Angeles (UCLA). He became a political science professor specializing in political development in Africa, primarily Nigeria.

With two parents employed as professors, the young Whitaker spent the first eight years of his life moving between Swarthmore; Los Angeles; Nigeria; London; Princeton, New Jersey; and Norton, Massachusetts. His father's teaching job at UCLA was followed by teaching stints at the University of Southern California, Princeton, and Rutgers. Whitaker's parents divorced when he was eight, and he and his brother returned to Norton to live with their mother. It was in Norton that Whitaker's passion for journalism began to blossom. While he was still in the seventh grade, he called a local newspaper, the *Attleboro Sun*, in a neighboring town and volunteered to cover sports. He wrote for that paper for two years and then for the newspaper at the George School, a Quaker boarding school he attended. At age fourteen, along with his brother, Paul, he spent a year in a public high school in France during their mother's sabbatical; there the boys learned to speak French.

In 1975, after completing only his junior year of high school, Whitaker enrolled in Swarthmore, the scene of his parents' unconventional courtship. Memories of the relationship lingered on campus, and Whitaker, uneasy with his "celebrity," left Swarthmore after completing a year. He moved to New Brunswick, New Jersey, to live with his father, who by then was a professor at Brooklyn College. During this period Whitaker applied to and was accepted by Harvard on a scholarship. Whitaker excelled in the Ivy League setting. He earned high grades while covering the arts and the admissions office for the prestigious Harvard *Crimson*, whose editorial board he joined. It was while working at the *Crimson* that Whitaker decided to pursue journalism as a career. In 1977, at the age of nineteen, Whitaker was hired as a summer reporting intern at the San Francisco bureau of *Newsweek*, one of the world's most prestigious and largest newsmagazines, with a weekly circulation exceeding 3 million.

Over the next three summers Whitaker, working as either a *Newsweek* stringer or an intern, reported from Boston, Washington, London, and Paris. At Harvard he continued to excel academically: he was elected to Phi Beta Kappa and graduated summa cum laude in 1979. He pursued postgraduate studies in England as a Marshall scholar at Oxford University's Balliol College. In 1981 Whitaker joined *Newsweek* full time, working in the New York bureau. Over the next six years he worked in the international section and wrote cover stories from around the world, including Central America, the Falklands/Malvinas conflict, the Middle East, the Soviet Union, and South Africa.

In 1985, Whitaker married Alexis Gelber, the director of special projects at *Newsweek*, whom he met at the magazine in 1981. The couple have two children, Rachel and Matthew.

From 1987 to 1991 he served as business editor and directed coverage of the Black Monday stock market crash, insider-trading scandals, and the savings-and-loan crisis. In 1991 the shy and congenial Whitaker became assistant managing editor of *Newsweek*, just two positions removed from the top post. Under his leadership, *Newsweek* expanded its technology coverage with the launch of a monthly "Focus on Technology" section and a weekly "Cyberscope" page. The newsweekly also launched an annual newsstand magazine, *Computers & the Family*. Whitaker occasionally wrote essays on race, including a cover story, "The Hidden Race of Successful Blacks," coauthored with ELLIS COSE. The article garnered awards from the Society of Professional Journalists' New York chapter and the National Association of Black Journalists. In the wake of the trial and acquittal of O. J. SIMPSON in 1995, Whitaker wrote a piece called "Whites v. Blacks," which analyzed the different reactions of African Americans and whites to the question of Simpson's guilt or innocence and to the criminal justice system more broadly.

In 1996 Whitaker was promoted to the position of *Newsweek*'s managing editor. In that capacity he directed coverage of the biggest stories of the decade, including the 1996 presidential election, resulting in an eighty-two-page special issue printed the day after the election. He also led the team that produced a special report on the death of Diana, Princess of Wales, in September 1997. That same year he assumed the role of interim editor after the editor, Maynard Parker, became incapacitated with leukemia. Whitaker oversaw the coverage of the scandal that arose concerning President Bill Clinton's relationship with the White House intern Monica Lewinsky, which earned the magazine a coveted National Magazine Award for reporting in 1999. When Parker died in October 1998, Whitaker, at age forty-one, became the first African American at the helm of one of the nation's top newsweeklies. He is also the only African American editor at one of the top one hundred general interest magazines.

Although *Newsweek* still trails its main rival *Time* by more than 1 million in circulation, the magazine has continued to receive national recognition under Whitaker's leadership. Most notably it received a National Magazine Award for general excellence for its coverage of the 11 September 2001, terrorist attacks on the World Trade Center. That same year Whitaker was cited for his editorial leadership by the American Society of Magazine Editors. Whitaker, who in 1999 was awarded an honorary doctorate from Wheaton College in 1999, received the 2003 Trailbrazer Trumpet Award from the Turner Broadcasting Company. The award honored Whitaker for being the first African American to head a major newsweekly, though Whitaker himself has argued that his race is irrelevant to the task. "I'm proud and I'm honored to be in this position," he stated on becoming *Newsweek* editor, "but my goal is to be the very best editor of *Newsweek* that I can be, not just the best black editor" (Kuczynski).

FURTHER READING

Kuczynski, Alex. "Newsweek Names Editor," *New York Times*, 11 Nov. 1998.

MAUREEN M. SMITH

White, Armond (24 Apr. 1953–), film critic, author, and lecturer with often controversial and contrarian views on film, was born and raised in Detroit, Michigan, the youngest of seven children. He and his siblings grew up during the civil rights era in the northwest part of the city at a time when the neighborhood was predominantly Jewish. His father did

Armond White at the New York Film Critics Circle Awards held on 10 January 2011. (AP Images.)

a number of jobs, including working at Ford Motor Factory and playing piano, and attempted to own a gas station and a pool hall. White grew up in a family of movie fans, and classic films like *Cat on a Hot Tin Roof* (1958) and *The Long Hot Summer* (1958) piqued his interest in film, along with international films—from Italian directors like Federico Fellini, Vittorio De Sica, and Luchino Visconti—that White could watch on Canadian television, which was available in his Detroit home.

He has said in interviews with the press that before he even knew what film criticism was he would interpret films through his own perspective, drawing cartoon panels to map out a movie without knowing the lexicon of storyboards, and interpreting films as an untrained novice on an old typewriter. He told a *New York Magazine* reporter in 2009 that his decision to write about film came out of an assignment he received his senior year to write an essay about any book. At a drugstore, he stumbled on the legendary film critic Pauline Kael's second movie review collection, *Kiss Kiss Bang*

Bang (1968) and loved it so much that he has kept a copy of the paperback, along with other reference books about film, around him most of the time for easy reference. With that, he became a "Paulette," or one of the many acolytes of Kael. He associated his love for movies with his Baptist upbringing, telling Marc Jacobson in *New York* magazine, "I'm a believer. I think God is the force for ultimate good in the universe. He made the movies, didn't he? If you cut me open, that's what you'd find: the movies, Bible verses, and Motown lyrics."

He started writing film reviews as an undergraduate at Wayne State University, where he earned a BA, and when he saw Steven Spielberg's *Close Encounters of the Third Kind* (1977) it sparked what became White's lifelong adoration for the director's work. In fact, White would come to be known as a writer who favored several directors, including Brian DePalma, Robert Altman, and Andre Techine.

In 1980 White attended Columbia University to earn a masters' degree in Film History, Theory, and Criticism. Professors Stefan Sharff and Andrew Sarris helped shape his unique perspective on film: Sharff by analyzing films frame-by-frame, and Sarris, one of Kael's greatest rivals, became a great inspiration to White. When he graduated from Columbia, White went to work for the *City Sun*, a radical black Brooklyn newspaper, as an arts editor from 1984 until 1996. He has famously clashed with SPIKE LEE over his less-than-favorable reviews of some of Lee's work (including Lee's three-hour-opus *Malcolm X* (1992), which White said was a movie "with a theme but without a subject") and was informed by Lee's film representatives that he was not welcome at the press screening of Lee's *Get on the Bus* (1996) to which White reportedly replied, "Small mind, big ego," according to Dorothy Giobbe, a reporter for *Editor and Publisher* magazine.

White has become one of America's most polarizing film critics, since he almost always pans popular movies like *Slumdog Millionaire* (2008), *Iron Man* (2008), and *Toy Story 3* (2010), which has led many bloggers and print critics to despise him. However, his criticism is also widely regarded as top-notch. The same year he was banned from Spike Lee's screening, White won the ASCAP-Deems Taylor Award for music criticism.

White's first book, *The Resistance: Ten Years of Pop Culture That Shook the World*, was published in 1995. It includes criticism that discusses hip-hop, popular culture, and film with equal fervor and passion as he examined expression in American culture as a *City Sun* contributor. His unique, acerbic prose at that paper led him to the *New York Press*, an alternative paper, where he began as a contributor in 1997. White has been elected chairman of the New York Film Critics Circle twice: once in 1994 and again in 2009. He has worked as cinema studies lecturer at the Film Society at Lincoln Center. A music video program for the Center's annual video festival that White has been leading since 1993 has attracted international acclaim. He has served on the juries of various film festivals, all while writing and publishing three books of his own and contributing to a variety of publications.

His second book, *Rebel for the Hell of It: The Life of Tupac Shakur*, was published in 2002. Another collection of essays, *Keep Moving: The Michael Jackson Chronicles*, was published in 2009 after Michael Jackson's death.

FURTHER READING
White, Armond. *The Resistance: Ten Years of Pop Culture That Shook the World* (1995).

JOSHUNDA SANDERS

White, Augustus Aaron, III (4 June 1936–), orthopedic surgeon and medical professor, was born in Memphis, Tennessee, the son of Augustus Aaron White, a physician, and Vivian Dandridge, a prominent teacher and librarian in the Memphis public schools. White's father died when the boy was only eight years old. The idealism that motivated White to become involved in civil rights was shaped in his boyhood, when BENJAMIN HOOKS, also a Memphis resident and later the national chairman of the NAACP, was a family friend. As a teenager in the 1950s, White worked to register African Americans to vote at a time when many black activists feared violent reprisals for daring to challenge Jim Crow. Reflecting on his early activism, White later stated: "I reserved some energy to keeping racial issues in the front of my mind and attempting to make a contribution in terms of communication, good will, and influencing people and institutions to be more progressive and egalitarian."

White attended the Mount Herman School in Massachusetts, graduating in 1953. He then entered Brown University, graduating cum laude with a B.A. in 1957. While still an undergraduate at Brown and a member of the football team, White became interested in the orthopedic treatment of injured athletes. Although he was a psychology major, he decided to change course and study orthopedic medicine, and graduated from Stanford University medical school in 1961. From 1960 through 1962 he received a scholarship and a clinical fellowship from the National Medical Fellowships organization, one of the nation's oldest philanthropic bodies dedicated to increasing the number of black and minority medical professionals. White completed his internship at the University of Michigan Hospital in Ann Arbor (1961–1962) and his residency in orthopedic surgery at Yale–New Haven Hospital in Connecticut (1963–1965).

From 1966 to 1968 White served as a captain and military surgeon for the U.S. Army Medical Corps in Vietnam. He recognized that he could have used graduate deferments to avoid participating in a war he did not fully support, but he chose to serve for two reasons: first, as a doctor, he was traveling to Indochina to save lives, not to end them; secondly, White felt obliged to those Americans who had fought and died in World War II to secure his freedom. White kept a diary during his time in Vietnam, and his entries reveal how he often worked around the clock, tending to the wounds of G.I.s and Vietcong sympathizers alike. In September 1966 he watched in horror as:

a young boy was hit in the right hip with God knows what. It completely shattered his femur close to the joint, exploding in him, sending filth and gun powder all through his thigh, lower abdominal wall, scrotum and penis. His sciatic nerve was blown out, as was his femoral artery and 2/3 of the skin of his thigh (White, "Vietnam Memoirs," 19).

Such incidents persuaded White that the war was a "misplaced, misguided effort" (19), but his commanding officer convinced him not to write a letter to President Lyndon Johnson, "respectfully asking him if it's worth it" (19). White did, however, protest the many examples of racism that he experienced during his tour of duty in Vietnam, including the occasion when he passed a U.S. Army compound and demanded, successfully, that a Confederate flag be removed from display on one of the huts. White's anger at being greeted by a symbol of slavery was compounded by the disproportionate casualty rate for black soldiers at that time. Between 1965 and 1967 more than 22 percent of Americans killed in Vietnam were black, even though African Americans were only 11 percent of the U.S. population. For his efforts in commanding a MASH unit in Qui Nhon, Vietnam, White received the Bronze Star in 1967.

White developed a special interest in the biomechanical aspects of orthopedics while under the mentorship of Wayne Southwick, the chairman of Yale's orthopedic surgery department. With Southwick's help he obtained a fellowship to study this subject under a world authority at the Karolinska Institute in Sweden, where he went on to earn a DMSc degree in 1969. White then embarked on what became a lifelong intellectual and clinical crusade to expand the use of biomechanics in orthopedic medicine. He defined biomechanics as utilizing "engineering concepts and technology to scientifically and quantitatively analyze the normal and abnormal functioning of the musculoskeletal system that allows us to move about." It also became evident to White that biomechanics and collaboration with engineers would advance the medical world's understanding of spinal orthopedics.

After completing his clinical training, White became an outstanding professor at Yale and Harvard medical schools. He was associate professor of orthopedic surgery at Yale from 1972 to 1976 and full professor through 1978. He then moved on to Harvard Medical School as professor of orthopedic surgery and has remained there. In addition to his teaching positions at Yale and Harvard, White held visiting professorships at eleven other colleges and universities. He was the main founder of biomechanical laboratories at both Yale and Harvard and also wrote or collaborated on more than two hundred scientific publications. The textbook he coauthored with Manohar M. Panjabi, *The Clinical Biomechanics of the Spine* (1978), was acclaimed widely both in the United States and abroad.

In addition to his teaching positions, White served on the surgical staffs of numerous hospitals in New Haven and Boston. Most notably, he was orthopedic surgeon in chief at Beth Israel Deaconess Medical Center in Boston between 1978 and 1991 and has remained there with emeritus status in orthopedic surgery since 1992. White was also an associate in orthopedic surgery at Brigham & Women's Hospital (1980–1989) and a senior associate in orthopedic surgery at Children's Hospital and Medical Center (1979–1989), both in Boston.

Throughout the late 1970s and 1980s White moved into the leadership ranks of American orthopedic surgeons. He influenced both his peers in the medical profession as well as the broader public to recognize the importance of improving the availability and quality of orthopedic surgery. In many of his writings and presentations, he emphasized that disorders of the spine are one of the most common medical problems in Western nations, affecting an estimated four-fifths of the Western world's population at some point in the life cycle. White's popular book on this subject, *Your Aching Back: A Doctor's Guide to Relief* (1983), sold widely and generated attention throughout the national news media.

Throughout his career, White earned public recognition for his medical achievements and his commitment to racial justice. In 1980 *Ebony* magazine honored him with its award for Black Achievement in the Professions. Two years later the Ciba-Geigy Corporation chose White for its Exceptional Black Scientists Poster Series, a program that distributes posters of prominent black scientists to spur young African Americans to pursue scientific and medical careers. White has also maintained close links with his undergraduate alma mater, Brown University, serving on the university's Board of Fellows from 1981 to 1992. In the spring of 1985, when minority students challenged the administration over discriminatory conditions at Brown, White was selected to chair a committee convened by the university's president to explore the charges of institutional racism and to recommend improvements.

White has also exposed racism within the medical profession and within medical institutions and organizations. "Peer reviewed medical literature," he has noted, "documents that African Americans have higher infant mortality rates, shorter life expectancies, fewer joint replacements, and more amputations than whites" (White, "Justifications," 22). White believes that racially diverse medical schools and hospitals can help to end these disparities and, moreover, that "diversity on clinical teams can enhance rapport between patient and physician" (White, "Justifications," 22). He has also highlighted a wide range of medical studies documenting the inadequate medical treatment received by racial minorities. This evidence, White argued in his 2001 Alfred R. Shands Jr. Lecture, "strongly suggests physician bias and stereotyping, however unconscious, as a cause" (White, "Shands Lecture," 478). In reviewing the many episodes of racial violence and bias that black Americans have endured—from slavery to recent government failures to achieve health-care reform—White found a legacy of bias that "is intimately woven into the fabric of our medical culture"(482). He then provided very specific steps his colleagues in surgery could implement to provide non-biased care. White closed his Shands lecture by remarking that "we, as physicians, can be societal leaders in facing racism clinically, not emotionally but rationally, objectively, and constructively" (482). Throughout his professional career Augustus White has exemplified such leadership.

FURTHER READING

White, Augustus A., III. "Alfred R. Shands, Jr., Lecture: Our Humanitarian Orthopaedic Opportunity," *Journal of Bone and Joint Surgery* 84-A, no. 3 (March 2002): 478–484.

White, Augustus A., III. "Justifications and Needs for Diversity in Orthopaedics," *Clinical Orthopaedics* 362 (May 1999): 22–33.

White, Augustus A., III. "Memoriam," *Brown Alumni Magazine* (May–June 1998).

White, Augustus A., III. "Vietnam Memoirs: River of Blood," *Harvard Medical Alumni Bulletin* (Spring 1993): 17–24.

"Augustus A. White, III, M.D., Dr. Med. Sci.," National Medical Fellowships Web site, http://www.nmf-online.org/Development/scholars/1960s/augustus_white.htm

DAVID MCBRIDE

White, Barry (12 Sept. 1944–4 July 2003), singer, songwriter, musician, and producer, was born in Galveston, Texas, the first of two boys born to Sadie Carter and Melvin White, a machinist. White's father never lived with him because he already had a wife and family on the other side of Los Angeles, the city in which White grew up. His mother had worked briefly as an actor for MGM, appearing in bit parts for three films. Severe arthritis curtailed her film career, and she struggled to raise her two boys with menial jobs and welfare. White grew up on the streets of west Los Angeles, running with gangs, stealing cars, and fighting.

Despite the prominence of street life in his early years, music figured strongly as well. His mother taught him and his brother how to harmonize, and hearing her play Beethoven's "Moonlight" Sonata prompted White to learn the piano at age five. By eight he was singing in the church choir, causing a stir with his natural rhythm and precocious ability to translate deep emotion. When he was fourteen, a change happened that would affect the rest of his life. His voice dropped very low, to the bass level. Its power was immediate; people would turn to look every time he spoke. Young White was uneasy with the newfound attention, but he grew used to the sound of his voice eliciting an excited response from women.

At the age of fifteen he was directing the church choir. This was also the age at which he was arrested for the first time. White was sent to a juvenile facility for stealing tires, and the seven months of confinement convinced him to turn his focus away from the streets. In 1960, shortly after his release, a friend invited him to sing bass in a fledgling rhythm and blues group, the Upfronts. They recorded a few songs, and White played the keyboards during some sessions. His reputation grew with local musicians, and he began to sing with several other local groups, as well as to help with production duties. At seventeen he decided to quit school and head to Hollywood to further his music career.

In 1962 White began doing session work as a singer for Hollywood-based recordings, mostly for the surfer bands that were popular during the time. The work was unsteady, however, and he grappled with how to support Mary Smith, his childhood sweetheart whom he married in 1963, and their two young children. These added responsibilities forced White to seek more traditional employment, and for the next few years he worked construction jobs, at car washes, and he ran a toy store in South Central Los Angeles.

During this time, White still gained a few music industry jobs here and there, even writing two songs for the popular 1960s kids' show *The Banana Splits*. His luck changed when he was offered a position recruiting new talent as the A&R person at Mustang Bronco Records. The Bobby Fuller Four were the label's top act, and White arranged music for the group. He also wrote songs and signed acts. The label closed in 1968, but White came away with valuable lessons about publishing rights and artist independence. After turning down a lucrative record deal with Motown Records, he formed his own publishing company, Savette Publishing, with Aaron and Abby Schroeder the same year. The strain of long years battling poverty took its toll on his marriage, and in 1969 he and Mary divorced, after seven years and four children. That same year, while producing another singer, he met Glodean James, Diane Parson, and Linda James, the three women who would help him successfully launch his career as a songwriter, arranger, and producer. He named the group Love Unlimited, and they earned a Top Ten hit in 1972 with "Walking in the Rain with the One I Love," a song he wrote, arranged, and produced.

After the introduction of his trio of female singers, White continued to cover all bases, releasing his own album, *I've Got So Much to Give*, in 1973 and the debut album of his forty-piece instrumental group, Love Unlimited Orchestra, *Rhapsody in White*, in 1974. Both albums immediately shot up the charts, with Love Unlimited Orchestra's "Love's Theme" becoming the official anthem of the disco age. Once White's signature deep, velvety voice was

Barry White, holding his trophy after receiving the Heritage Award for career achievement at the Soul Train Music Awards in Los Angeles, 15 March 1994. (AP Images.)

unleashed, fans responded immediately. In 1974 alone, White boasted four albums of his own, two for Love Unlimited Orchestra, and another for Love Unlimited, all on the charts at the same time.

At six feet three, over three hundred pounds, and sporting a beard and his trademark processed hairstyle, White captured attention with his looks as well as with his lush productions, expertly crafted grooves, and booming, seductive baritone. Sexy, up-tempo songs, such as "Never Never Gonna Give Ya Up" and "Can't Get Enough of Your Love Baby," quickly established White as an unlikely sex symbol, earning him the monikers "The Maestro" and "Walrus of Love." White had married Love Unlimited's lead singer, Glodean James, in 1973, and together they had a family of seven children, including her two, his four, and the daughter they had together.

The 1970s brought an unprecedented number of hits for White, who earned seven Top Ten singles and eleven gold or platinum albums, which included such songs as the catchy "You're the First, the Last, My Everything" and the steamy "It's Ecstasy When You Lay Down Next to Me." By the 1980s, hip-hop and new wave had taken the place of the disco music that White produced, so the hits stopped, but a loyal following in Europe allowed him to continue to tour and produce records. He and James divorced in 1988, and White geared up for the next decade of music.

White enjoyed a resurgence of popularity when he contributed his unmistakable vocals to "The Secret Garden," along with James Ingram, El DeBarge, and Al B. Sure, for QUINCY JONES's album *Back on the Block* in 1990. He followed up with *Put Me in Your Mix* in 1991, but it wasn't until 1994's *The Icon Is Love*, with his smoldering, mid-tempo single "Practice What You Preach" that White reentered the Top Ten charts for the first time since 1978. His popularity gained an extra boost during the 1990s when his music, and sometimes his presence, were prominently featured on the hit TV show *Ally McBeal*. His recognizable baritone was also heard on another popular show, *The Simpsons*.

In 2000 White was honored with two Grammy Awards for his aptly titled song "Staying Power." He also started doing commercials, lending his voice to ads for McDonald's, Chrysler's Jeep Grand Cherokee, and AT&T. In the midst of his return to the spotlight, his health began failing, and his hypertension forced him to curb his schedule. In 2003 White was on dialysis when he suffered kidney failure and died. He was fifty-eight years old.

Barry White's contributions to music are, like his legendary voice, far-reaching. As a producer, arranger, songwriter, and musician, he gained control of his publishing rights early on, and like RAY CHARLES before him, White would inspire multi-talented African Americans artists such as PRINCE to demand greater independence and control over their music. As one of the architects of disco music, which encompassed soul, rhythm and blues, and dance, he helped create a sound and an attitude that can still be heard in dance clubs today. With a voice that half spoke and half crooned suggestive lyrics, he continued the blues tradition that influenced everybody from rappers to-lounge singers. His legacy lives on in every rhythm and blues, pop, and hip-hop tune that focuses on romance, sumptuous productions, and an irresistible rhythm.

FURTHER READING

White, Barry. *Love Unlimited: Insights on Life and Love* (1999).

Helligar, Jeremy. "Dr. Feelgood," *People* (23 Jan. 1995).

Gregory, Hugh. *Soul Music A–Z* (1995).

Obituary: *Jet* (21 July 2003).

ROSALIND CUMMINGS-YEATES

White, Bukka (12 Nov. 1909?–26 Feb. 1977), blues artist, was born Booker T. Washington White in Houston, Mississippi, the son of John White, a locomotive fireman, and Lula Davisson. He spent his early years on the farm of his mother's father, Punk Davisson, a landowner and fundamentalist church leader. Booker sang in church with his sister and received rudimentary guitar instruction from his father, who played guitar, mandolin, violin, piano, and saxophone.

When Booker was nine, his father bought a guitar for him, and the youngster was soon testing his musical skills at local house parties. In 1920 he hitchhiked about fifty miles west to live with an uncle, Alec Johnson, near Grenada, Mississippi. There and in Clarksdale, White heard a number of accomplished Mississippi Delta blues artists, CHARLIE PATTON among them. "I tried to be a second behind old Charlie Patton," White said in later years.

In his early teens White hopped a northbound freight train and wound up in St. Louis, where he did odd jobs around a roadhouse and took piano lessons. In 1925 he returned to Houston and married Jessie Bea. He combined farming and local performances until his wife died from a ruptured appendix in 1928. Over the next several years, he moved between St. Louis and Mississippi, working briefly with a traveling minstrel show. In 1930, while he was living in Swan Lake, Mississippi, White was contacted by Ralph Lembo, the owner of a furniture store in Itta Bena and a part-time talent scout for RCA Victor Record Company. On 26 May 1930 Lembo took White to Memphis, where he recorded as many as fourteen blues and religious sides. Four titles were issued: "New Frisco Train" and "The Panama Limited," both train blues, and two religious songs, "Promise True and Grand" and "I Am in the Heavenly Way." White returned to Mississippi, where he began performing in roadhouses with the Alabama-born harmonica player George "Bullet" Williams.

In 1934 White married Williams's niece, Susie Simpson, and moved to Aberdeen, Mississippi, about thirty miles east of his birthplace. From 1935 to 1937 he was on the road, working various musical and nonmusical jobs, including stints as a prizefighter and a Negro League baseball pitcher. On one visit to Chicago, White was introduced to Lester Melrose, a music publisher with an ear for blues. Under Melrose's auspices, White recorded two sides for American Record Corporation on 2 September 1937, "Pinebluff Arkansas" and the hit side "Shake 'Em on Down." The record was released on Vocalion and two other labels, Columbia and Conqueror. White's given name was spelled "Bukka" on the record label, a phonetic debasement that stayed with him for the rest of his life. The record sold well enough for Melrose to seek a second session, but by then White was serving a two-year sentence in Parchman Farm, the notorious Mississippi Delta prison, for shooting a man during an altercation in Aberdeen. White said he spent much of his prison time playing music. On 24 May 1939 he was asked to perform for the folklorist Alan Lomax, who had came to Parchman Farm to make field recordings for the Library of Congress. Although unhappy that Lomax would not pay him, White recorded two songs, "Po' Boy" and "Sic 'Em Dogs On."

Released from prison later in 1939, White returned to Chicago for the long-delayed second recording session with Melrose. On 7 and 8 March 1940 White recorded twelve songs, including "Parchman Farm Blues" and "Fixin' to Die Blues," for Vocalion and Okeh, accompanied by a washboard player, probably Washboard Sam. These recordings, for which he received $17.50 per side, were touted for a time as the last great body of "country blues." In the 1940s, though, they were regarded as anachronisms by many blues consumers, whose tastes were becoming increasingly "citified."

Following the 1940 session, White continued to travel back and forth to Mississippi, working briefly with a small band in Chicago. By 1946 he had split up with his second wife and had moved to Memphis, where he occasionally played with Frank Stokes and Memphis Willie Borum. During World War II he spent some time in the navy and recalled entertaining troops in Tokyo. After the war he returned to Memphis, playing less frequently and finally drifting away from music altogether.

In 1959 the blues researcher Samuel Charters mentioned White and White's composition "Fixin' to Die Blues" in his book *The Country Blues*. The song was re-released on the book's companion album, and three years later the folk guitarist Bob Dylan included the song on his debut Columbia album, bringing White to the attention of a growing blues revival audience. Aided by a geographical reference in a song, researchers John Fahey and Ed Denson traced White's whereabouts to Memphis, and in 1963 they took White to California to perform and record for Fahey's Takoma label. Thus began the second stage of White's musical career.

Through the 1960s and the early 1970s White performed for an avid new following, touring with the American Folk Blues Festival in Europe and Dick Waterman's Memphis Blues Caravan in the United States. His performance credits included the Newport Folk Festival in 1966 and a festival coinciding with the Olympics in Mexico City two years later. In the mid-1970s he returned to Memphis, where he later died. Some sources say he had several other significant relationships, probably common-law marriages, and he may have had as many as four children. But the paucity of legal records and the necessity of relying on imperfect recollection when reconstructing the life stories of folk artists makes it difficult to confirm these details.

White brought his blues to life with a percusive slide-guitar style and expressive, hard-edged vocals. He drew on personal experiences and observations to create blues poetry that conjured up images of rural Mississippi. In concert he sometimes improvised new compositions, which he called "sky songs," saying he pulled them out of the sky.

FURTHER READING

Burton, Thomas, ed. *Tom Ashley, Sam McGhee, Bukka White: Tennessee Traditional Singers* (1981).

Charters, Samuel. *The Legacy of the Blues* (1975).

McKee, Margaret, and Fred Chisenhall. *Beale Black and Blue: Life and Music on Black America's Main Street* (1981).

This entry is taken from the *American National Biography* and is published here with the permission of the American Council of Learned Societies.

BILL MCCULLOCH AND
BARRY LEE PEARSON

White, Charles (2 Apr. 1918–3 Oct. 1979), artist, was born Charles Wilbert White in Chicago, to Charles White Sr., a Creek Indian and construction worker, and Ethelene Gary, a domestic worker originally from Mississippi, who had been working since the age of eight. White's parents never married, and after his father died, when Charles was eight, Ethel married Clifton Marsh, a factory worker and alcoholic. The couple divorced when Charles was in his early teens. White's mother encouraged her son's budding artistic voice, and their close relationship underlies his later works, especially images that put the African American woman at the center of black life. The chaos and poverty of his childhood was stabilized by Charles's interest and skill at drawing. He earned good grades until shortly after entering Englewood High School when, having discovered

ALAIN LEROY LOCKE's *The New Negro* and other books by and about African Americans at the local library, he voiced his frustration with the lack of black history and culture in the school's curricula.

At age fourteen Charles undertook a self-guided alternative education at local libraries, art museums, and galleries, and he joined the Arts and Crafts Guild, a circle of local black artists that included ELDZIER CORTOR, WILLIAM BEVERLY CARTER JR., MARGARET TAYLOR GOSS BURROUGHS, and CHARLES SEBREE. He attended art classes at the South Side Settlement House and frequented the John Reed Club, the Artists Union, and other progressive political groups. At ages sixteen and seventeen he won—and was subsequently denied because of his race—two scholarships, from the Chicago Academy of Fine Arts and the Frederick Mizzen Academy of Art, respectively. Chicago's South Side during the 1930s was a vibrant center of African American life and culture, and Charles learned a great deal from his new friends KATHERINE MARY DUNHAM, MARGARET WALKER, GWENDOLYN BROOKS, RICHARD WRIGHT, GORDON PARKS SR., ST. CLAIR DRAKE JR., Marion Perkins, FRANK YERBY, and WILLARD FRANCIS MOTLEY. While poor grades forced him to attend an extra year of high school, his headstrong approach to independent education earned him a scholarship to the Art Institute of Chicago for the 1937 academic year.

During these early years White developed a figurative style that remained at the core of his work for the next four decades. An exceptional draftsman, he would work primarily in black and white and sepia tones. Like the social realists and Mexican muralists Diego Rivera, David Alfaro Siqueiros, and José Clemente Orozco, who greatly influenced his style and subjects, White believed art, through its depiction of the everyday conditions of the working classes and poor, could effect social change. In choosing distinctly American themes, White was influenced by both the murals and history paintings of the American regionalists, especially Thomas Hart Benton, as well as the African American artists CHARLES HENRY ALSTON, AARON DOUGLAS, and HALE ASPACIO WOODRUFF. His drawings, prints, and paintings, steeped in portraiture and biography, view the broad sweep of history, particularly the history and contribution of black Americans, through depictions of the black figure. A celebration of both the major historical figures and everyday heroes of black America, his work began as a corrective to American history and became expressions of fundamental truths about African American life.

White joined the Federal Art Project in 1939, and his first mural, *Five Great American Negroes*, featuring epic portraits of SOJOURNER TRUTH, BOOKER T. WASHINGTON, FREDERICK DOUGLASS, MARIAN ANDERSON, and GEORGE WASHINGTON CARVER, was completed in 1940. While teaching at the South Side Community Art Center, he was commissioned by the Associated Negro Press to produce a mural for the organization's booth at the American Negro Exposition in Chicago. White won first prize for the mural and for *There Were No Crops This Year*, a dark and expressionistic graphite drawing that was used for the cover of the exhibition catalog.

In 1941 White married artist ELIZABETH CATLETT, and after briefly joining his new wife in New Orleans, he moved to New York City in April 1942, having won a Julius Rosenwald Fellowship. Over the next several months White studied with lithographer and graphic artist Harry Sternberg at the Art Students League. Under Sternberg's direction he refocused on drawing and printmaking, and his work became less epic in theme, if not in size. In the fall of 1942 he traveled through the American South, paying close attention to African American folk, cultural, and musical forms. The trip rekindled memories of his regular childhood trips to Mississippi, where three of his uncles were lynched. Sketches made during the trip contributed to his next major work, a twelve-by-seventeen-foot mural for Hampton University in Virginia. *The Contribution of the Negro to Democracy in America*, completed in 1943, was compositionally and iconographically more complex than White's earlier murals.

White won a second Rosenwald Fellowship, and he and Catlett moved to Harlem, where White had already became part of the neighborhood's social and cultural scene. While teaching at the George Washington Carver School, he was drafted into the army, in 1944. Soon after, White's unit was sent to redirect a flood in Missouri, and he contracted tuberculosis and spent nearly two years convalescing at a veteran's hospital in Beacon, New York. He returned to work in 1946, producing Cubist-inflected graphic works, including *Two Heads* (1946) and *Mater Dolorosa* (1946). In an effort to save his flagging marriage, White joined Catlett in Mexico, where she had gone to work on a series of prints at the Taller de Grafica Popular. While the trip was a professional success, introducing White to Rivera, Siqueiros, and other Mexican artists, it proved a personal failure. White and Catlett soon returned to New York to finalize their divorce, after which he found work as a cartoonist for the

Daily Worker and *Congress Vue*. In 1947, despite a relapse that caused a collapsed lung, he received the first of many solo exhibitions at the American Contemporary Art Gallery in New York. White remained committed to progressive political and social change, working with the Workshop for Graphic Art and collaborating with other artists on the portfolio projects *Yes, The People, Mexican Woman, Mexican Boy*, and *Negro USA*. In the late 1940s and early 1950s his images appeared in a number of progressive publications, including the *Daily Worker*, which published his striking 1949 drawing *The Trenton Six*.

In 1950 White married Frances Barrett, a social worker. The same year, the Committee for the Negro Arts, which he helped establish, mounted a show of his work on the theme of the black woman. The following year, the Whites toured Europe, East Germany, and the Soviet Union and were pleased to discover the popularity of the artist's work abroad. Back at home White received several fellowships and exhibitions. By the early 1950s he was focused almost exclusively on graphic work, often using paper as large as five or six feet high. In works like Bessie Smith (1950), *Worker Woman* (1951), and *The Preacher* (1952), White employed greater naturalism, offering rounder, softer figures. In an effort to make his art more affordable and accessible, he produced several portfolios through Masses and Mainstream, the first of which included *The Mother* (1952) and *Ye Shall Inherit the Earth* (1953), portraits of unknown but recognizable contemporary black women.

White's tuberculosis returned in 1956, and he and Frances moved to Altadena, California, a suburb of Los Angeles, in search of milder weather. The couple adopted a girl in 1963 and a boy two years later. White began teaching at the Otis Art Institute in 1965 and became a sought-after public speaker and leader in the Los Angeles art community, serving on several cultural advisory boards. In the 1950s and 1960s his drawings and prints became increasing popular despite the fact that his figurative work—portraits of black men, women, and children, laboring, playing, and at rest—ran counter to the abstract expressionist style currently in vogue in art circles. The 1967 publication of *Images of Dignity: The Drawings of Charles White* (with a forward by Harry Belafonte and an introduction by James Amos Porter) proved a critical and financial success and introduced his work to an even broader audience. Between 1960 and his death in 1979 White took part in 104 exhibitions.

As the 1960s progressed frustration at the increase in racial violence began to inform some of his works, including 1964's *Birmingham Totem* (produced in response to the murderous 1963 church bombing), a dramatic drawing of a naked boy squatting atop a mountain of wooden shards, a defiant Harriet Tubman in *General Moses* (1965), and the series *J'Accuse* (1966) and *Dream Deferred* (1968). His 1968 *I Have a Dream* series, executed after Martin Luther King Jr.'s assassination, gave way to the *Wanted Poster* series the following year. The series's large, sepia-toned paintings appear like flattened-out pieces of crumpled paper printed with several layers of ghosted images. Referencing eighteenth- and nineteenth-century posters and advertisements for slave auctions and monetary rewards for the return of runaway slaves, White depicted black women and children amid fragments of stenciled text suggesting terms of sale and slaves' names and loaded symbols like the confederate and union flags.

In the 1970s White continued experimenting with spatial and background effects. *Black Pope (Sandwich Board Man)* (1973) and *Children's Games #1* (1975) advanced the monochromatic palette and all-over layering of images used in the *Wanted Poster* paintings. In other works, the *Love Letter* lithographs, *Harriet* (1972), and *Mississippi* (1972), for example, White's meticulously rendered figures are sharply defined against negative space, broken only by enigmatic symbols like a bloody handprint or giant seashell. In the last years of his life White returned to color with several large-scale paintings, *Homage to* Langston Hughes (1971), *Homage to* Sterling Brown (1972), and *Mother Courage II* (1974). In 1978 he completed a mural of Mary McLeod Bethune for the opening of the Bethune branch of the Los Angeles Public Library. White's last major work, the mural with its monumental Bethune at its center and a young black boy holding an oversized book at her feet, powerfully evoked his own biography.

In 1979 Charles White died of congestive heart failure at age sixty-one. A few years earlier filmmaker Carlton Moss asked White about his work:

> There is a direct relationship between the content of what I do and this personal history. Actually, I've only painted one picture in my entire life ... each one of these things are segments of a relationship.... I see my totality of 300 years of history of black people through one little fraction ... a family ... my family (*Freedomways*, 137).

FURTHER READING

White's papers are housed at the Archives of American Art, Smithsonian Institution, Washington, D.C.

Barnwell, Andrea D. *Charles White. The David C. Driskell Series of African American Art: Volume 1* (2002).

"Charles White: Art and Soul," *Freedomways* 20.3 (1980).

Studio Museum of Harlem. *Images of Dignity: A Retrospective of the Works of Charles White* (1982).

DAVID MICHEL

White, Charley C. (10 Sept. 1886–16 Nov. 1974), pastor and community leader, was born to Charlie C. White in Shelby County near Center, Texas. His mother worked as a domestic for white families (her name is not known), and his father was a farmer. His parents separated when he was young, but his mother ensured that White received a basic education. At the age of twenty-one he married Lucille Bolton, with whom he would have five children. After his marriage he moved to Richardson, three miles east of Nacogdoches, Texas, where he started a Sunday school. The Sunday school evolved into a small congregation called the Richardson Chapel. This led White to become a licensed Baptist minister. Since his parishioners were poor, White worked on a farm in order to feed his family.

Soon Pentecostalism entered the area and created a stir among Baptist ministers. The Church of God in Christ (COGIC) was doing missionary work in nearby Nacogdoches and attracting Baptists. When some Baptist ministers decided to go and disrupt a COGIC service, they were warned by another that "Them damn niggers got the Bible cold, on everything they say. They are going exactly by it" (White and Holland, 120). White was unable to contain the Pentecostal progress in the area, and his wife was the first in the White family to join the COGIC. She would attend Richardson Chapel on Sunday morning and in the afternoon walked three miles to Nacogdoches. As more of White's members asked for the COGIC to hold a service in Richardson Chapel, White had to oblige. Finally White and his entire congregation joined the COGIC in 1920.

The Richardson congregation was not the first COGIC congregation in Texas; COGIC had planted its first congregation in Houston in 1909. White's wife died in 1926, and he married Martha Allen, a member of his church. Claiming a divine revelation, White moved to Jacksonville, Texas, and planted a new COGIC congregation there in

1928. He would pastor this church until his death. In his new church work, White was much aided by Martha, who sang well and could perform the old gospel songs. The pastor being as poor as his parishioners, White worked odd jobs in order to support himself. He worked in a store, a doughnut factory, and a slaughter pen. At various times his wife picked tomatoes or worked as a domestic.

White's church was Pentecostal, so the services were noisy. Neighbors complained, and the justice of the peace told White to leave town. White told the authorities that he did not understand why he was being told to leave, while the pool halls, domino parlors, and red-light houses were allowed to operate seven days a week. In turn the authorities asked the sheriff to check on White's services. After investigating, the sheriff concluded that the pastor was not doing anything wrong and thereafter left him alone.

White demonstrated concern for the material life of the community. When he was working in the slaughterhouse, he took home scrap meat like pigs' feet, hogs' heads, and livers. He saved some for his family and gave the rest to needy people. This began a tradition that he was to keep for many years. As a new pastor, White held services every night. White's services were well attended, and the crowds extended into the street, which was an intersection. Finally the police had to tell the congregation to move out. White borrowed money and gave a down payment for three lots adjacent to the church. From the same owner he requested the privilege to hold services in nearby lots. Meanwhile he grew tomatoes, cotton, and corn on the lots he had bought and sold them in order to pay off the debt on the land. Later he built a tabernacle where his congregation worshipped for many years.

During the Depression hunger spread throughout rural Texas, and extras from the slaughterhouse were not enough to feed the needy. White started raising vegetables in his yard in order to further assist the hungry. During this time the government bought a large number of cattle from ranchers and decided to waste the meat. This was allegedly done to raise beef prices and because not enough pasture could be found to feed these animals. Aware of this waste, White pleaded with cattle killers and begged to have the meat. He was allowed to pick some good cattle, which he butchered on the spot. He took the meat home and gave it to the hungry. To better serve the poor, White built what he called "God's Storehouse" and put up a sign with the words "Bring ye all the tithes into the storehouse, that there may be meat in mine house" (Malachi 3:10, AV). One side of God's Storehouse was partitioned to hold cured meat, and the other was reserved for dry and canned goods. White extended his generosity to both blacks and whites.

During the Depression, church offerings were no more than thirty or fifty cents, but this did not stop White from going beyond the call of duty. Twice, whole families were housed in his home until they could find a way to help themselves. White's view was, "That is what a preacher's house is for. These people got to have some place to stay" (White and Holland, 166). Another compassionate act was White's provision of Christmas gifts for children of the community, even those who did not belong to the COGIC. On their behalf White went to the town merchants and asked for and received donations and other items such as fruit and candy that he redistributed to the children. He bought toys and set up a big Christmas tree and invited all children to come to church on Christmas Eve. Every year White maintained this tradition and treated the children for Christmas.

In 1939 White built a new sanctuary by himself. The new "White's Temple" was said to be "the nicest colored church in Jacksonville" (White and Holland, 169). During World War II White helped people complete government forms so they could get ration books. He and his church took the crippled and shut-ins on fishing trips, drove the sick to the drugstore, and sometimes managed to have their prescriptions filled for free. As a community leader, he organized a blood bank in 1952 when the local hospital could not treat one of his parishioners' relatives because of the lack of blood supply. His concern even led him to buy pints of blood to keep supplies high when people would not donate blood. Consequently White organized the Citizens' Christian Association, whose purpose was to raise money to pay blood donors. White's prominent role as a minister confirms E. FRANKLIN FRAZIER's conclusion that next to the family the church was the most important institution in the life of rural blacks (Frazier, The Negro in the United States [1957]: 216).

White was the acknowledged leader of the community. Once he was invited by white ministers to rally the other black preachers for an interdenominational revival. Blacks also made him their spokesman, and he petitioned for streetlights, street markers, better roads, and the hiring of blacks on the police force. The need for black police officers arose because white police had been using excessive force when arresting black suspects.

During the civil rights movement White promised the local sheriff that he would check any kind of unrest in the black community. White claimed that he paid no attention to MARTIN LUTHER KING JR. because his priority was finding work for the unemployed and feeding the hungry. He did not encourage opposition to segregation, though he did stand up against the mistreatment of blacks. He campaigned in 1960 for the candidate for sheriff Allen Dotson; four years later White initially refused to work for Dotson's re-election because his deputies were brutalizing black suspects. When Dotson promised to correct his deputies, White again campaigned for him.

White outlived three of his four wives. Martha died in 1955, and he married Geraldine Briscoe in 1956. When Geraldine preceded him in death in 1964, he married Mabel Wade in 1965. Nine years later he died, and his obituary memorialized him as a man who was "happiest when helping others, widows, and orphans."

FURTHER READING
White, C. C., and Ada Morehead Holland. No Quittin' Sense (1969).
Atkins, Rodney L. Let My Work Speak for Me in Northeast Texas: Church of God in Christ (2003).
Mays, Benjamin E. The Negro's Church (1933).

DAVID MICHEL

White, Eartha Mary Magdalene (8 Nov. 1876–18 Jan. 1974), social welfare and community leader and businesswoman, was born in Jacksonville, Florida, the daughter of Mollie Chapman, a former slave, and an unnamed white man of means. She was adopted shortly after birth by freed slaves Lafayette White, a drayman and Civil War veteran, and Clara English, a domestic and cook. Lafayette White died when Eartha was five. Throughout her childhood Clara made Eartha feel as though God had chosen her for a special mission. Listening to stories of hardships that Clara endured as a slave and watching her mother's humanitarian contributions to Jacksonville's "Black Bottom" community convinced Eartha White that she too would someday make a difference in the African American community.

When yellow fever struck Jacksonville in 1893, White went to New York City, where she studied hairdressing and manicuring and attended Madame Thurber's National Conservatory of Music. During the 1895–1896 season, White toured worldwide with the Oriental-American Opera Company, the first black opera company in the United States. On a visit home she met James Lloyd Jordan, a railroad employee; they planned to marry in June 1896, but one month before the wedding Jordan died.

After Jordan's death White quit the tour and returned to Jacksonville, determined to marry "the cause of Christ" and dedicate her life to helping others. Following her graduation from Florida Baptist Academy in 1897, she volunteered as a nurse caring for soldiers wounded in the Spanish-American War. In 1899 she taught blacks in a poor rural school and took a second job as a clerk of the Afro-American Life Insurance Company, becoming its first woman employee. She organized and spoke on behalf of the Colored Citizen's Protective League in 1900. In the same year White attended the first meeting of the National Negro Business League in Boston, where she met BOOKER T. WASHINGTON, who became a lifelong friend.

In 1901 a devastating fire struck Jacksonville, and White transferred to downtown Stanton School while helping the homeless find shelter. Reactivating interest in the Union Benevolent Association founded in 1885, she collected money to build the Colored Old Folks' Home, which was completed in 1902. In 1904 she started the Boys' Improvement Club, received a donation of land for a park, and used her own money to support recreational activities in the new park. She then successfully lobbied for a facility for delinquent girls.

In 1905 White started what she termed a "department store" on $150, and between 1905 and 1930 she owned a taxi service, an employment agency, a janitorial contracting service, and a steam laundry. After a business became profitable, White sold it, using the revenue from the sale to fund a new business. Eventually she received a real estate license, which enabled her to buy and sell property more profitably.

No task was beyond the scope of Eartha White. A respected citizen of Jacksonville, White's reputation grew, and men and women, black or white, counted on her expertise. Called to service during both world wars, White acted as director of War Camp Community Services and coordinator of recreation in Savannah, Georgia, in World War I; she was the only woman delegate at the Southeast War Camp Community Service Conference; and she attended a White House meeting of the Council of National Defense as the only black. An active Republican, White campaigned in her precinct, headed the Negro Republican Women Voters in 1920, and became the only woman member of the Duval County Republican Executive Committee.

The death of her mother in 1920 profoundly affected White. As a tribute to the woman who had been her inspiration, she founded the Clara White Mission in 1928. Modeled after Jane Addams's Hull-House, the mission became a refuge for blacks during the Depression and a center for job training for the unemployed. People of all ages gathered to paint, play music, or join in recreational activities. As a resident herself, White oversaw daily operations. In one month alone more than 2,500 persons were fed. On Sundays she taught the Bible to prison inmates, a practice she continued for fifty years. The police often sent delinquent teenagers to her rather than to jail. As the energetic White saw the need for other services, she expanded into other avenues, founding a maternity home, a child placement center, a community center, and a tuberculosis rest home.

White always maintained that the color of a person's skin did not matter and that all men were made "out of the earth." A follower of the ideals of Booker T. Washington, she thought eliminating prejudice resulted from blacks' improving themselves through education and success in establishing their own businesses. In 1941 continued job discrimination led her to join A. PHILIP RANDOLPH in organizing a protest march on Washington. The march never materialized, but their proposed activities led to President Franklin Roosevelt's Executive Order 8802, which banned employment discrimination in defense industries and in the federal government, and to the establishment of the Fair Employment Practices Committee.

During World War II, White joined the Women's National Defense Program as an honorary colonel, coordinated Red Cross activities, and became the only woman on the Interracial War Camp Community Service Conference. Energized by the people whom she helped, White's service to the community continued as she advanced into her seventies and eighties. In 1967 she took great pride in the completion of the 120-bed Eartha M. White Nursing Home for county and state welfare patients. Underwritten by White and grants from the federal government, the institution had facilities for physical therapy, occupational therapy, and recreational activities.

Honors bestowed upon White included the Good Citizenship Award in 1969 and the Lane Bryant Volunteer Award in 1970, and in 1971 the American Nursing Home Association gave her its Better Life Award. Two years later she received the Booker T. Washington Symbol of Service from the

National Negro Business League. Despite confinement to a wheelchair, White never stopped lending a hand and remained active until her death in Jacksonville.

Known as Jacksonville's Angel of Mercy, Eartha White's remarkable vitality and unending devotion derived from her mother's example as well as her own religious philosophy, and a belief that "service is the price we pay for the space we occupy on this planet." Collecting donations of fruits and vegetables from farmers, trudging down country roads in her tennis shoes when called to an emergency, or simply holding the hand of a person in despair filled White with a renewed purpose of doing "all the good you can … while you can!"

FURTHER READING

White's documents and papers are located in the Eartha White Collection at the University of North Florida library and the Clara White Mission, Jacksonville, Florida.

Duncan, C. Frederick. "Negro Health in Jacksonville," *The Crisis* (Jan. 1942).

Jones, Maxine D., and Kevin M. McCarthy. *African Americans in Florida* (1993).

Taylor, Angela. "She's 94 and Still Busy," *New York Times*, 4 Dec. 1970.

Obituaries: *New York Times*; *Jacksonville Journal*; *Florida Times-Union*, 19 Jan. 1974.

This entry is taken from the *American National Biography* and is published here with the permission of the American Council of Learned Societies.

MARILYN ELIZABETH PERRY

White, George Henry (18 Dec. 1852–28 Dec. 1918), lawyer and member of Congress, was born in Bladen County, North Carolina, the son of Mary (maiden name unknown) and Wiley F. White. With one grandmother Irish and the other half American Indian, White jocularly described himself as no more than "mostly Negro." Like most black boys in the antebellum South, he had little opportunity for education. A biographical sketch in the *New York Tribune* on 2 January 1898 put it in graphic understatement: "His early studies were much interrupted because of the necessity he was under to do manual labor on farms and in the forests, and it was not until he was seventeen years old that his serious education was actually begun." After attending a combination of local schools, public and private, and saving one thousand dollars from farm work and cask making, White enrolled at Howard University.

White graduated in 1877 and returned to North Carolina. He settled in the old coastal town of New Bern, where he quickly became active in local affairs. At various times he was principal of three black schools, including the state normal school, and read enough law with Judge William J. Clark to earn his law license. In 1880 he won a seat in the state house of representatives as a Republican. After an initial defeat in 1882, he was elected to the state senate and served in the legislature of 1885. In 1886, a few weeks before his thirty-fourth birthday, he won a four-year term as district solicitor for the Second Judicial District, defeating the black incumbent and a white Democrat. Reelected to this position in 1890, he was, according to the *New York Freeman*, the only black prosecutor in the country. White prosecuted superior court cases in a six-county area, and his ability was so marked that even his political opponents occasionally praised him. Some whites resented his "presumption" and his demand to be "mistered" like other attorneys, rather than be addressed by an unadorned last name, as was customary with educated African Americans. In 1894 White moved his home from New Bern to Tarboro so he could seek the Republican nomination in the Second Congressional District, a gerrymandered district that had elected three black congressmen since 1874. The district convention "broke up in a row," however, with both White and his brother-in-law, HENRY P. CHEATHAM, claiming to be the regular nominee. After arbitration by the Republican National Committee, White withdrew from the race, but Cheatham was defeated in the general election, thanks partly to Republican disunity. In 1896, after another tumultuous convention, White won the Republican nomination for Congress and defeated the Democratic incumbent and a Populist nominee. Despite a statewide white supremacy campaign in 1898, he was elected to a second term.

As the only black member of Congress, White believed he spoke for all the nation's black people, not just the voters of the Second District, and he was prepared to reply spiritedly to racist pronouncements by southern congressional colleagues. "How long must we keep quiet," he asked, "constantly sitting down and seeing our rights one by one taken away?" He introduced the first federal antilynching bill and denounced disenfranchisement and vote fraud. He also used the patronage power of his office to secure government jobs for his constituents, including some twenty black postmasters.

White supremacy zealots gave Congressman White special prominence during their struggle to defeat the Republican-Populist "fusion" in 1898 and

George Henry White, U.S. Congressman from North Carolina, 1900. (Library of Congress.)

the subsequent movement to disenfranchise North Carolina blacks. Under the editorship of Josephus Daniels, the *Raleigh News and Observer* pilloried White as a belligerent man eager "to invite the issue" of white against black. An incident at a Tarboro circus, in which White refused to surrender his seat to a white man, became an "outrage" to many Democratic journalists anxious to demonstrate the dangers of "Negro domination." In 1900, after White denied from the floor of the House that rape was the primary cause of lynching, noting as well that white men were guilty of abusing black women, Daniels fired off an editorial broadside, describing the "nigger Congressman" as "venomous, forward," and "appealing to the worst passions of his own race."

In fact, the prosperous, middle-aged black lawyer was not a fiery militant. Though some historians have portrayed White as "impetuous" or "vindictive," he was in fact a fairly conventional Republican politician, supportive of tariffs and imperialism and suspicious of civil service reform. On racial matters, he advocated caution and strict respect for the law among both black and white. In the climate of

the turn of the century, however, he was considered radical merely for demanding, as he said in one speech, "all the privileges of an American citizen."

After the passage in 1900 of the state constitutional amendment disenfranchising most black voters, White decided to leave his native state. "I cannot live in North Carolina and be a man and be treated as a man," he told a northern interviewer. In a widely noticed valedictory address during his final session of Congress, he offered the black's "temporary farewell to the American Congress," adding the prediction that "Phoenix-like he will rise up some day and come again."

Unsuccessful in seeking an appointive office, White practiced law, first in the District of Columbia, then in Philadelphia. He continued to support efforts to secure civil rights for African Americans, including lawsuits and organized protests through organizations such as the National Association for the Advancement of Colored People. An investor and visionary, he helped establish an all-black community called Whitesboro in the Cape May region of New Jersey.

White married twice, first to Fannie B. Randolph and, upon Fannie's death, to Cora Lina Cherry, daughter of HENRY C. CHERRY, a former legislator from Edgecombe County. White had one child from his first marriage and three children from his second marriage.

White was an active layman in the Presbyterian Church and a leader among the Colored Masons. He died in Philadelphia.

FURTHER READING

No collection of White's papers exists. A few manuscripts in his handwriting are preserved in the legislative papers and court documents of the Second Judicial District, available at the North Carolina Department of Archives and History in Raleigh, and scattered letters. White's personality is revealed in his congressional speeches and in his testimony before the Industrial Commission, *Report of the Industrial Commission*, vol. 10, 1901.

Anderson, Eric. *Race and Politics in North Carolina, 1872–1901: The Black Second* (1981).

Christopher, Maurine. *America's Black Congressmen* (1971).

Justesen, Benjamin R. *George Henry White: An Even Chance in the Race of Life* (2001).

This entry is taken from the *American National Biography* and is published here with the permission of the American Council of Learned Societies.

ERIC ANDERSON

White, Jacob C., Jr. (1837–11 Nov. 1902), educator, reformer, abolitionist, and businessman, was born in Philadelphia, Pennsylvania, one of ten children of Elizabeth Miller White, a seamstress, and Jacob Clement White Sr. (1806–1872). His father, a prominent abolitionist, barber, dentist, free produce storekeeper, and successful businessman, became one of the city's wealthiest African Americans. He invested in real estate in Pennsylvania and New Jersey and became president of the Benezet Joint Stock Association and owner of Mount Lebanon Cemetery, the foundation of the family's wealth. White's father was greatly respected by the city's black community and became active in the Moral Reform Society and executive secretary of the Philadelphia Vigilance Committee—his wife founded a female auxiliary to help raise funds for the committee. Jacob Jr. regularly saw his parents assist fugitive slaves, many passing through his Philadelphia home.

White grew up a prominent member of the city's black elite, groomed by his father for leadership. He attended the Lombard Street School for African Americans and later graduated from the famed Institute for Colored Youth (ICY), a Quaker-run school—later becoming Cheyney University—which trained generations of black teachers. White studied under CHARLES L. REASON, perhaps the mid-nineteenth century's most important black teacher. Early on, White showed remarkable ability, particularly in his speeches and essays. As a fifteen-year-old, he penned a brief defense of the free produce movement, urging his brethren to boycott slave-made goods such as cotton, sugar, rice, and tobacco and assist the "down-trodden and oppressed slave" (Ripley, 4:138). He was a founding member of Philadelphia's Banneker Institute (1854), a collection of about forty of the city's young black men who regularly met to debate antislavery strategy, sponsor speakers and literary events, commemorate black history, and maintain a library. The Banneker Institute became a leadership training ground for White and his associates who bonded in the fight against slavery and for full civil rights.

Following graduation from the ICY in 1857, White taught mathematics and other subjects there and increasingly took on administrative duties—while also forming the Pythians, an early all-black baseball team, of which he served as secretary and manager. In 1864 he became principal of the Roberts Vaux Consolidated School, founded in 1836, a position he held until 1876. The school began humbly with forty-nine students in the basement of the Zoar Methodist Church, but developed under his care. In recognition of his achievements as an administrator, the city hired White to take over the new Robert Vaux School, Philadelphia's first black public grammar school, in February 1876, and he remained the school's principal until 1896.

In addition to his teaching career and antislavery activism, White helped lead black Philadelphia's temperance movement. First emerging in 1788 in the city's Free African Society, temperance principles quickly suffused all the major northern black communities by the early 1830s. White took the lead in promoting temperance in Philadelphia among the rising black generation of the 1850s. Unlike previous temperance advocates, however, White did not focus on morality but on black issues and black concerns. The future of black Americans, he asserted, depended upon "sobriety, industry, and a willingness to aggressively assert their rights." He warned that drink would destroy black social and economic success and endanger their freedom. Even "respectable groggries" should be avoided, White warned, because "our liberties, and our rights" depend upon black leaders to "fight their battles and contend with our enemies for our rights ..." (Yacovone, 297).

During the Civil War, White served as a correspondent and agent for New York's *Weekly Anglo-African*, the most important black paper of the war years. Every week he ordered five hundred copies of the paper for city residents, a level of sales that helped keep this important paper afloat during one of the most important periods of American history. He also was the city's agent for the *Pine and Palm*, the organ of the Haitian Emigration Bureau, although White never strongly supported emigration and advocated black recruitment for the Union Army. After the war White assumed leadership roles in the Pennsylvania State Equal Rights League and in the Social, Civil, and Statistical Association, and for the rest of his life retained membership in the Pennsylvania Society for Promoting the Abolition of Slavery and the Relief of Free Negroes, an organization that provided assistance to black schools such as Hampton and Tuskegee, and to other relief associations. He served as recording secretary of the Pennsylvania branch of the Equal Rights League, working closely with other former, well-known black abolitionists like GEORGE B. VASHON and Joseph C. Bustill, all of whom sought to reestablish "Justice and Enfranchisement without regard to race or color" (*Christian Recorder*, 17 Feb. 1866). Philadelphia's

Social, Civil, and Statistical Association sought the same goals, but also provided relief to the freedmen after the war, especially at Port Royal, South Carolina, and brought many prominent speakers to the city's black audiences. FREDERICK DOUGLASS, William Lloyd Garrison, FRANCES ELLEN WATKINS HARPER, William D. Kelley, Henry Ward Beecher, and General Benjamin F. Butler, all spoke under the auspices of White's association.

His wife, Caroline E. White, of whom little is known, died in 1895. Her illness likely prompted White to help found Philadelphia's Frederick Douglass Memorial Hospital, a medical and nurse's training facility—he served as president of the hospital's board. White also was an elder in the city's First (Colored) Presbyterian Church and superintendent of the church's Sabbath school. A successful businessman, educator, and reformer, White, like his father, came to symbolize the economic, social, and intellectual achievements of the city's important African American community.

FURTHER READING

Martin, Tony. "The Banneker Literary Institute of Philadelphia: African American Intellectual Activism before the War of the Slaveholders' Rebellion," *Journal of African American History* (Summer 2002).

Richings, G. F. *Evidences of Progress Among Colored People* (1896).

Ripley, C. Peter. *Black Abolitionist Papers,* vols. 3–4 (1991).

Winch, Julie, ed. *The Elite of Our People: Joseph Wilson's Sketches of Black Upper-Class Life in Antebellum Philadelphia* (2000).

Yacovone, Donald. "The Transformation of the Black Temperance Movement, 1827–1854: An Interpretation," *Journal of the Early American Republic* 8 (Autumn 1988).

DONALD YACOVONE

White, Jesse Clark, Jr. (23 June 1934–) educator, athlete, and politician, was born in Alton, Illinois, the fourth of seven children raised by Jesse White, the owner of a janitorial service, and Julia Mae White, a homemaker. In 1943 White's family moved to Chicago, where he attended Schiller Elementary School and Waller High School (later Lincoln Park Academy). A star athlete in high school, White earned all-city honors in both basketball and baseball. He attended Alabama State College (now Alabama State University) on a scholarship and earned all-conference honors in both sports.

After graduating from Alabama State with a degree in Physical Education, White signed a contract to play baseball for the Chicago Cubs organization. Shortly after the contract was signed, the U.S. Army drafted him. White spent two years in the army (1957–1959), serving as a paratrooper in the 101st Airborne Division.

In 1959 he received an honorable discharge from the army. He returned to Chicago and served in both the U.S. Army Reserve and the Illinois National Guard. He also resumed playing professional baseball and played for the Chicago Cubs organization from 1959 to 1966, rising to Triple-A ball as a centerfielder. Also in 1959 he began teaching during the off-season as a physical education instructor for the Chicago Park District and at Schiller School, which he had attended as a child.

In the winter of 1959 White organized a gymnastics show at the Rockwell Gardens Public Housing Project. That led him to create the Jesse White Tumbling Team, an organization designed to provide a positive alternative for inner-city, at-risk youth. Members of the team abided by strict rules, which included staying away from gangs, drugs, and alcohol and staying in school and maintaining at least a C average. In the 2000s the team consisted of 150 members, male and female, with ages ranging from six to sixteen. The tumblers performed more than one thousand shows a year. They performed throughout the United States and Canada and in Japan, Hong Kong, and Bermuda. The team was featured on commercials, national television shows, and movies. More than 8,500 children went through the program.

White served as a teacher and school administrator for the Chicago Public Schools for thirty-three years. In 1974 he successfully ran for the Illinois House of Representatives as a Democrat. Two years later, he lost a primary for renomination, the only election he ever lost. In 1978 he again ran for the Illinois House and this time was successful. He was reelected to the House six times. His diverse near–North Side district included wealthy lakefront areas and Cabrini-Green, one of the poorest housing projects in the nation. In the House, White served as chairman of the Committee on Human Services and also served on the Education Committee and the House Select Committee on Children and Aging.

In 1992 White was elected Cook County Recorder of Deeds. He was reelected in 1996. As recorder, White modernized the office and brought in state-of-the-art technology to facilitate new services, allow easier access to records, and speed the recording process.

In 1998 he was elected Illinois secretary of state, winning election by more than 400,000 votes. He was reelected in 2002, receiving 68 percent of the vote and winning by more than 1.3 million votes. He won all 102 Illinois counties and received the largest vote total for any candidate for Illinois statewide office in more than a quarter century. In 2006 he was elected to a third term as secretary of state, winning by more than 1 million votes.

As secretary of state, White managed 21 departments, 136 driver services facilities, and more than 3,500 employees. He also served as state librarian and archivist. During his time as secretary of state, White led the fight to clean up corruption in an office that had been plagued with scandal. He managed the largest distribution of new license plates in Illinois history, fought for tougher DUI laws, and made many services available online. His office operated the largest organ donor registry in the nation, with more than 5.5 million Illinois residents registered as potential organ donors. White's many honors and awards included his election to the Southwestern Athletic Conference Hall of Fame, the Alabama State University Hall of Fame, and the Chicago Public League Basketball Coaches Association Hall of Fame.

FURTHER READING
Davis, Rick. *They Call Heroes Mister: The Jesse White Story* (2006).

DAVID A. JOENS

White, John H. (18 Mar. 1945–), photographer and Pulitzer Prize–winning photojournalist, was born in Lexington, North Carolina, one of six children of an African Methodist Episcopal Zion minister, whose name is now unknown, and Ruby Mae Leverett White. White proved a slow student and was once told by a teacher that he would grow up to be nothing more than a garbageman. His father reportedly answered that remark by telling his son that what he did mattered less than wanting to be the best at whatever goal he had set for himself. White purchased his first camera at age thirteen for fifty cents and ten bubblegum wrappers. When he began studying commercial art at Central Piedmont Community College in Charlotte, North Carolina, he decided to become a professional photographer.

A turn in the U.S. Marine Corps gave White his first professional photography experience. When

he returned to civilian life he had a difficult time finding work; little demand existed for African Americans in any profession during the late 1960s. He finally found a job at the *Chicago Daily News* in 1969 and decided to settle in Chicago. After the *Daily News* stopped publishing, White became a photographer for the city's major daily, the *Chicago Sun-Times*, in 1978.

Great photojournalism is the product of skill, circumstance, and strength of character. White's instincts as a photographer pushed him to follow the action, no matter how dangerous the situation or how frightened he was. While in South Africa with the Reverend JESSE JACKSON, a gun was held in his face by a police officer who had just shot several people. The officer was enforcing a local law against documenting police activity.

White has more than 300 awards to his name, including three first-place National Headliner Awards. In 1982 he earned the prestigious Pulitzer Prize for feature photography. He was the first photographer inducted in to the Chicago Journalism Hall of Fame and is unique in having been the Chicago Press Photographer Association's Photographer of the Year five times. In 1999 he received the city's Chicago Medal of Spirit.

While making his name shooting breaking news and historical events in Chicago and beyond, White also developed a reputation as an inventive and inspiring teacher. In addition to his duties as a full-time photojournalist for the *Sun-Times*, White taught and was head of Columbia College Chicago's photojournalism department. He became known for the tactics and tools he used to prepare students for the realities of photojournalism.

White always managed to be where the action was, and to capture it. On Halloween morning in 1998, White was investigating a report that senior citizens were being evacuated from a building because of a ruptured gas main. After making his way around a police roadblock, he jumped out of his car with two cameras loaded and set to the proper shutter speed and exposure. Moments later, when an explosion rocked the side of the building, he captured it on film. White called the shot a crisis demanding "everything you know," with no time to think about it. "You see everything in an instant. Our lives, our work, our profession is about capturing an instant that's forever. So we see more than just a fireball, more than just a building, more than just a person—you see all those things" (*News Photographer*, Apr. 1999).

One of White's most important assignments was seemingly less exciting at the outset than an explosion. He first photographed Joseph Cardinal Bernardin in 1979, while both were at an airport awaiting the arrival of Pope John Paul II. White was struck by the Catholic cardinal's presence and felt an immediate connection with him, despite their obvious differences. "There I was, a black photojournalist, the Protestant son of a Protestant minister, the brother of three Protestant ministers, and I felt Cardinal Bernardin's luminous spirit when we met" (*New Catholic Explorer*, 6 Sept. 1996).

White followed Bernardin more closely after he was named archbishop of Chicago in 1982, and the two became friends. He photographed Bernardin often for the *Chicago Sun-Times* over the next fourteen years, documenting his initial Mass in Chicago's Grant Park, his acquittal from charges of sexual misconduct, and his struggle with cancer. White's first book documenting the cardinal, titled *This Man Bernardin*, was published in 1996. The book was a critical success for White and a record-breaking bestseller for its publisher, Loyola Press. White called the photographic memoir "an assignment from God" (*New Catholic Explorer*, 6 Sept. 1996). The follow-up, *The Final Journey of Joseph Cardinal Bernardin*, presented White's candid photographs of the cardinal in his last days as he struggled with cancer. White considered his time with the cardinal "a privilege—a front-row seat to his life, and an opportunity to be exposed to his life and to the people he shepherds" (*New Catholic Explorer*, 6 Sept. 1996).

White used his camera as his passport to the world. He toured Russia, South Africa, Europe, the Middle East, and Asia on assignment. He was one of the few Vatican-approved photographers to cover Pope John Paul II's 1979 visit to Mexico. He also was one of 200 photographers to participate in the "Day in the Life of America" campaign in 1986, the largest photographic project in American history. White's photos of Nelson Mandela, who was released after twenty-seven years in a South African prison, garnered him numerous awards in 1996. On a trip to the former Yugoslavia with the Reverend Jesse Jackson in 1999, White documented the momentous release of three captured United States soldiers.

"A photographer can be the eyes for the world," White said in an interview with the *New Catholic Explorer*; "it's a privilege and a tremendous responsibility" (6 Sept. 1996). White's achievements may be notable, but his standards for his work were as lofty as they were simple. In an October 2004 interview with *Christianity Today*, White stated plainly, "I want to see through the eyes of God."

FURTHER READING

McGill, Denise. "John H. White: Mercy Over Justice," *Christianity Today* (Oct. 2004).

Miner, Michael. "Instinct, Readiness Capture Moment after Severed 24-inch Gas Line Blows," *News Photographer* (Apr. 1999).

"NikonNet Fetes Chicago Photographer John H. White," *PHOTOgraphic* (May 2002).

"NikonNet's April 2002 'Legends Behind the Lens' Presents the Photos of Pulitzer Prize–Winning Photojournalist John H. White," *PR Newswire*, 5 Apr. 2002.

BRENNA SANCHEZ

White, Josh (11 Feb. 1915–5 Sept. 1969), folk and blues vocalist and guitarist, was born Joshua Daniel White in Greenville, South Carolina, the son of Dennis White, a teamster and preacher, and Daisy Elizabeth Humphrey. The fifth of eight children born into a poor African American family, White received little formal education. He later completed the sixth grade and may have attended high school for a time. As a child he was exposed to music through his mother, a leading singer in the church choir. At age seven he began to serve as "lead boy" (guide) for blind guitarists. His masters included John Henry Arnold, Blind Joe Taggart, and (possibly) BLIND LEMON JEFFERSON. Watching these itinerant street musicians as he traveled throughout the South and to Chicago, White taught himself to play the guitar. In 1928 he accompanied Taggart at a recording session.

Discovered by a scout for ARC records (predecessor to Columbia Recording Company) at age fourteen, White released a series of "race" records, including "Low Cotton" and "Jesus Gonna Make Up My Dying Bed," in the early 1930s under the name Pinewood Tom (for blues) and Josh White, the Singing Christian (for spirituals). He moved to New York City and played at clubs, where his appeal to urban white audiences allowed him to survive the decline of "race" records. He broadcast regularly from 1932 to 1935 with the Southernaires on NBC radio. During the 1930s he performed solo, with the Josh White Singers, and with jazz and blues musicians such as SIDNEY BECHET and BESSIE SMITH. White married Carol Carr in 1934; they had four children.

By the early 1940s White was an established part of the folk music scene. He performed regularly with LEADBELLY at New York City's Village Vanguard. He also played with SONNY TERRY, BROWNIE McGHEE, Woody Guthrie, and, occasionally, the Almanac Singers. He sang at Leadbelly's funeral in 1949.

White achieved a unique sound. Contemporaries reported being impressed by his clear diction and sonorous baritone. Though he sometimes sang a cappella, he usually accompanied himself, fingerpicking a small-bodied rosewood guitar strung with heavy steel strings. He punctuated rhythmic chord patterns with virtuoso single-line riffs that employed bent notes, slides, and other blues techniques. Pete Seeger claimed that "guitar players all over the country imitated Josh's guitar styles," according to Dorothy Schainman Siegel in *The Glory Road*. White was so popular among players that a guitar company marketed an instrument under his name.

White's repertoire ranged from spirituals to bawdy blues and topical protest songs. In later years it expanded to include English, Irish, and Australian ballads. His best-selling single, "One Meat Ball," sold more than one million records. Many of his songs expressed his strong commitment to social reform. In the early 1940s he released two albums that featured antiracist blues and ballads.

Strikingly good-looking and able to project a warm personality onstage, White performed in a number of shows and revues. In 1939–1940 he played Blind Lemon Jefferson in the musical *John Henry*, starring PAUL ROBESON. He appeared again with Robeson in 1942 in the LANGSTON HUGHES operetta *The Man Who Went to War*. In the late 1940s he appeared in *Blue Holiday* (starring ETHEL WATERS), *A Long Way from Home*, and *How Long Till Summer*. He also appeared in two musical film shorts, *Tall Tales* (1940), with Burl Ives, and *To Hear Your Banjo Play* (1947), with Terry and McGhee. White had small parts in the films *Crimson Canary* (1945) and *Dreams That Money Can Buy* (1948) and a major role in *The Walking Hills* (1949). White's career broke musical and social barriers. His tour with Libby Holman in the 1940s is identified as the "first mixed race duo" by *The Oxford Companion to Popular Music* (1991). He fused African American and international folk genres in his own performances, and in the 1940s he toured with the Haitian dancer JOSEPHINE PRÉMICE. He also privately helped other musicians; he cared for BIG BILL BROONZY during that blues master's last illness.

President Franklin D. Roosevelt and his wife admired and befriended White; Eleanor Roosevelt became godmother to White's son. White performed at the inaugural balls in 1941 and 1945 and was the first African American folk artist to give a command performance at the White House. During the war he went on a goodwill tour of

Josh White, photographed by Albert A. Freeman, with his guitar in 1945. (Library of Congress.)

Mexico (1942) and broadcast weekly for the Office of War Information.

In 1950 White accompanied Eleanor Roosevelt on a goodwill tour of Europe, during which he performed before capacity audiences. He interrupted the tour to return home to confront accusations that he was a communist. Although he appeared without subpoena before the House Un-American Activities Committee and denied supporting communism, his career suffered in the United States. He remained popular, however, in England, where he recorded in the 1950s, and in Scandinavia. During his 1951 tour of England, he broadcast on the British Broadcasting Corporation, and in 1961 he appeared on a series of British television shows.

With the folk revival of the 1960s, White enjoyed something of a comeback, with occasional television appearances and bookings at major clubs and folk festivals. In the summer of 1961 he suffered the first of four heart attacks. Despite declining health and injuries, he continued to perform, touring Canada, Australia, and England as late as 1966–1967. He died during heart surgery in Manhasset, New York.

According to the writer Studs Terkel, "During the early 1940s Josh was one of the first voices … that brought folk music to big cities on records and radio stations." White's fusion of ethnically diverse vocal traditions helped legitimate the broad cosmopolitan interests of folk musicians in the 1960s. He influenced many performers, including Pete Seeger, and is said to have served as a model for HARRY BELAFONTE. His acoustic guitar technique has rarely been equaled. White received an honorary doctorate of folk anthology from Fisk University in 1949. He is the subject of a play by Peter Link, *Josh the Man and His Music*, which was produced in 1983 with his son Josh Jr. playing his father.

FURTHER READING

A few items pertaining to White are included in the People's Song Library Collection at Wayne State University Archives of Labor and Urban Affairs in Detroit.

Siegel, Dorothy Schainman. *The Glory Road: The Story of Josh White* (1982, repr. 1991).

Obituary: *New York Times*, 6 Sept. 1969.

DISCOGRAPHY

The Josh White Song Book (1963).

This entry is taken from the *American National Biography* and is published here with the permission of the American Council of Learned Societies.

MICHAEL H. HOFFHEIMER

White, Lulu Belle (Aug. 1900–6 July 1957), civil rights activist, was born Lulu Belle Madison in Elmo, Texas, to Henry Madison, a farmer, and Easter Norwood, a domestic worker. Lulu, who had five brothers and six sisters, received her early education in the public schools of Elmo and Terrell, Texas. Following her high school graduation she attended Butler College, an African American school in Tyler, Texas, for one year before transferring to Prairie View College (later Prairie View A&M University), an African American land-grant institution, from which she received a B.A. in English in 1928.

On 28 June 1928 Lulu married Julius White, a businessman, nightclub owner, and promoter of public entertainment. After teaching school for nine years Lulu White resigned her post to devote herself fully to the NAACP. In 1939 she became acting president of the Houston branch of the NAACP, and just a few years later, in 1943, she was elevated to the post of full-time executive secretary of the Houston branch, making her the first woman in the South to hold that position.

In her role as executive secretary White traveled to towns throughout most of the state to garner contributions, organize new branches, and reactivate old ones. Her job entailed managing the office, conducting branch activities, and helping to organize other branches, but most especially she directed membership and fund-raising drives. Members' dues were essential in keeping the NAACP viable, providing the basic revenue not only for local branches but also for state and national operations, the salaries for all the organization's workers, publicity, cost of publications, travel expense, and other miscellaneous expenditures. In Texas, White seemed the right person for the job. Under her guidance the Houston branch grew from 5,674 members in 1943 to 12,700 in 1948, an increase that reflected White's aggressive fieldwork in recruiting new members as well as the extent of her appeal to black Texans and black Houstonians. This work would earn her the title of director of state branches in 1946.

By taking the helm of Texas's NAACP in 1943 White placed herself squarely in the forefront of the black movement for political equality, beginning with the elimination of the state statute that held only whites were eligible to vote in the Democratic primary. Sharp-tongued and unafraid of speaking her mind to both whites and blacks, White boldly created a movement for the elimination of the all-white primary. The success of the movement would require courage, passion, spontaneity, and a leader who had the time, resources, and energy to encourage people to join the NAACP and to fight for civil rights. The movement found these qualities in White.

Since White was already familiar with black Texans' struggle to retrieve the ballot, she needed no briefing on this issue. Not only did she become directly involved in *Smith v. Allwright* (1944), last of the U.S. Supreme Court's so-called White Primary cases and the one that at last brought an end to the state's all-white primary, but she also was in daily contact with NAACP national headquarters and served as liaison between the national office, the local chapter, and the black press. In anticipation of a favorable court decision White mounted a "pay your poll tax" campaign two months prior to the Court's decision. When in April of 1944 the U.S. Supreme Court declared the all-white Democratic primary statute unconstitutional, White hailed the decision a "second emancipation" (*Houston Informer*, 10 Apr. 1944).

The success of the NAACP in overturning the primary law launched a new era in both black politics and Democratic Party elections. Throughout the 1940s and 1950s White argued that a strong black voice was needed to shape governmental policies at both the local and state levels. She urged African Americans to assume greater roles in the political lives of their communities, to learn about political organizations, and to prepare for future leadership positions. She argued convincingly that those who understood the movement for social change must identify with it fully and must interpret it to others. Not only did White urge blacks to vote and seek office but she also conducted voter registration seminars, helped select candidates, aided in drafting platforms, and used black churches to address public issues—all without actually campaigning for specific candidates. In part as a result of her efforts black voter registration increased and several blacks became candidates for office in the 1940s.

Just as White viewed the vote as a necessary ingredient to full citizenship, she believed that if blacks were to enter the mainstream of American life, it was necessary to expand equality through economics. To this end she encouraged her allies to seek employment at white establishments, a task she was willing to personally undertake. Her energetic pursuit of equal opportunities often took her on a stormy path; some white managers refused to see her, while others slammed doors in her face or were simply evasive. Ever persistent, she staged solo as well as group demonstrations, one of which resulted in having "colored" and "white" signs removed from the soda fountain at one of Houston's department stores in 1946.

As a tactic for achieving economic justice White advocated that blacks work with organized labor, without whom, she argued, black workers possessed little bargaining power in disputes with employers. Though White's advocacy for a coalition with labor caused many to label her a communist, she did nothing to discourage the label, and indeed in 1948 she worked to get Henry Wallace's Progressive Party on the presidential ballot in Texas.

When in June 1945 the NAACP announced that it would challenge segregated public professional education in Texas, White was at the forefront of the movement to integrate the University of Texas Law School. It was White who found the plaintiff, HEMAN SWEATT, who, represented by the NAACP legal team, pursued the case *Sweatt v. Painter* to the U.S. Supreme Court. Sweatt won the case and later credited White's leadership for maintaining his own resolve.

White stepped down as executive secretary of the Houston chapter of the NAACP on 19 June 1949,

after a long-standing feud with Carter Wesley, editor of the *Houston Informer*, over the issue of integration. But White's resignation did not signal the end of her political activism. In her work as director of state branches for the Texas NAACP she continued to fight for political and economic opportunities—demanding that the Houston city council pass an ordinance to allow city hospitals to employ black doctors, staging demonstrations against the prohibition of black women from trying on clothing in department stores, and working towards the integration of yellow cab companies. White's friendship with WALTER WHITE, DAISY LAMPKIN, THURGOOD MARSHALL, and ROY WILKINS enabled her to exert influence in the NAACP nationally. As such she went on to become a field-worker for the national office of the NAACP. A mobilizer, organizer, and foot soldier, White dedicated her life to fighting to dismantle the apartheid system in the United States. The week before her death, the national NAACP established the Lulu White Freedom Fund in her honor. She is buried in Paradise South in Houston, Texas.

FURTHER READING
Beeth, Howard, and Cary D. Wintz, eds. *Black Dixie: Afro Texans History and Culture in Houston* (1992).
Hine, Darlene C. *Black Victory: The Rise and Fall of the White Primary in Texas* (2003).
Pitre, Merline. *In Struggle against Jim Crow: Lulu B. White and the NAACP, 1900–1957* (1999).
Shabazz, Amicar. *The Opening of the Southern Mend: Desegregation of Higher Education in Texas, 1865–1965* (2003).
Taylor, Quintard, and Shirley Ann Wilson Moore, eds. *African Women Confront the West 1600–2000* (2003).

MERLINE PITRE

White, Reginald Howard (Reggie) (19 Dec. 1961–26 Dec. 2004), professional football player and minister, was born in Chattanooga, Tennessee, to unmarried parents, nineteen-year-old Thelma Dodd, and Charles White, a semiprofessional baseball player. As a child growing up within the close-knit extended family the Dodds provided, White was mostly influenced by his aunts and cousins, but especially by his maternal grandmother. Mildred Dodd was called "Mother" by all, and she was the first to introduce the young White to the Christian faith. At the age of thirteen, White declared his faith in Jesus Christ and began his quest for truth, living his life by the lessons he learned in the Bible. The future "Minister of Defense" would grow physically and mentally in his convictions and in his dedication to his new identity. In 1979, White, now seventeen, was ordained as a minister at St. John's Baptist Church, where he testified openly and unapologetically to both his peers and adults to the power of God's love. Through his dedication and adherence to the tenets of his faith, White became an example of servitude in his community. White would establish the cornerstone of the excellence he would experience both on the football field and in the pulpit as an ordained minister. At Chattanooga's Howard High School, White stood out from his peer group because of his size. As a fourteen-year-old, he was six-foot-three and weighed more than 200 pounds. Understandably, this did not go unnoticed by the football coaches. The future two-sport athlete would come under the influence of Robert Pullman, a former college defensive lineman for the University of Tennessee Volunteers Football team and the head football coach of the Howard High School Hustling Tigers. With Pullman's guidance and commitment, White was able to achieve the kind of mental toughness and durability needed to be successful in any endeavor. Pullman constantly challenged. By his senior year, White had met every challenge placed before him on the athletic field and began to reap the benefits incrementally. In 1979, he was named to both the All-State football and basketball teams, to the All-American Football Team, to the All-Chattanooga basketball and football teams, and he was recognized by the Associated Press as the nation's top two-sport athlete (future National Basketball Association Hall-of-Famer Patrick Ewing was the runner-up).

As a highly touted athlete, White was recruited by a number of prestigious universities, including UCLA, the University of Michigan, the University of Alabama, and the University of Tennessee. Although he enjoyed and was attracted to the multiracial, multiethnic environment and overwhelming sense of acceptance on the UCLA campus, White chose to stay close to home and attend the University of Tennessee. It was in Knoxville, under the guidance of head football coach Johnny Majors, that White's endurance, instilled in him by coach Pullman and his Christian faith—and initiated by his grandmother—would propel the adolescent boy of uncertain promise into becoming one of the most dominant defensive lineman in all of college football. While at the University of Tennessee, White set school records for the most sacks in a career (32), in a season (15), and in a game (4). After

Reggie White of the Green Bay Packers reacting after sacking San Francicso 49ers quaterback Steve Young in Green Bay, Wisconsin, 1 November 1998. (AP Images.)

four years of college, the six-foot-five, 280-pound White realized his dream of becoming a professional football player when he was selected in the first round of the 1984 U.S. Football League (USFL) draft by the Memphis Showboats. In two seasons with the Showboats, White piled up 192 tackles, seven fumbles, and 23.5 sacks in just 34 starts.

As a venerable student of the game, White used the opportunity to play in the now-defunct league as a catalyst to come into his own. It was while a member of the Showboats that White practiced, developed, and honed his ability to completely change the outcome of football games. Using speed that was uncommon for a big man, as well as strength and leverage, White would literally pick up offensive linemen, a majority of them weighing more than three hundred pounds, and throw them aside in an effort to make a defensive play in the opposing team's backfield. White possessed the ability to make big plays, and quite often he alone changed the momentum of a game.

In 1985 White married Sara Copeland; they would have two children, son Jeremy and daughter

Jacolia. Also in 1985 White was drafted in the first round by the NFL's Philadelphia Eagles. Although he lived and played in Philadelphia, White maintained a church in Memphis, Tennessee, of which he was the pastor. In 1993, after eight seasons with the Eagles, playing in more than 121 games, producing an astounding 124 sacks, and more than 1,000 tackles, White became the most heavily recruited defensive free agent in the league. He chose to play with the Green Bay Packers, adopting the city of Green Bay, Wisconsin, and its citizens as members of his extended family.

In 1996 the Inner City Church of Knoxville, the church where White had been an associate minister, burned down. White's church was one of a number of black churches that had been the target of arson. Through the support of White's teammates and adoring fans, more than $250,000 was raised to rebuild the church. Unfortunately, the church was never rebuilt and the funds never recovered.

Playing six more seasons with the Packers, White helped lead the organization to two Super Bowl appearances, Superbowl XXX in 1995, and Super Bowl XXXI in 1996, where the Packers beat the New England Patriots.

In 1997 White was diagnosed with a systemic lung disorder called sarcoidosis, but he received treatments for the condition and was cleared by his doctors to return to the Packers organization. Upon his return, White achieved his finest honor yet—being named, for the second time in his career, the NFL's Defensive Player of the Year, following the 1998 season. In that same year, during what was thought to be a celebrity visit to the Wisconsin Legislature, White shocked lawmakers when he made negative comments concerning homosexuality, racism, and the gifts of different races. White's remarks are believed to have cost him a lucrative job as a sports analyst with CBS Sports. After a short retirement, White returned to football, playing the 1999 season with the Carolina Panthers. He officially retired in 2000 as the NFL's all-time sacks leader, with 198. In December 2004 White died of a heart attack, believed to be related to his previous diagnosis of sarcoidosis.

FURTHER READING

White, Reggie. *Fighting the Good Fight* (1999).
White, Reggie. *Reggie White in the Trenches: The Autobiography* (1996).
Kopay, David. "Dear Reggie White: You Just Don't Get It," *New York Times*, 2 Aug. 1998.
Shapiro, Leonard. "Minster of Defense, Man of Conviction; Character, His Integrity Was Everything Any NFL Player Should Aspire to Be," *Washington Post*, 27 Dec. 2004.
Sports Publishing. *Reggie White: A Celebration of Life* (2005).
Wiggins, David, ed. *African Americans in Sport* (2004).
Obituary: *New York Times*, 27 Dec. 2004.

PELLOM MCDANIELS III

White, Sarah (27 Sept. 1958–), union organizer and human rights activist, was born Sarah Claree White in Inverness, Mississippi, the daughter of Willie White, a farm laborer, and Annie Bell White, a worker at a dry-cleaning store. She was the fifth child in an impoverished family with eleven children. When Sarah was two years old, her mother was severely injured in an automobile accident. Her father left the family shortly after the accident, and Clara Grayson, her maternal grandmother, raised the children through much of White's childhood in a three-room shotgun house at the edge of a cotton field. In 1971, when she was twelve years old, a tornado struck Inverness, killing dozens and destroying much of the town, including their home. They were forced to move to Moorhead, another small town in Sunflower County, in the Mississippi Delta.

During the 1960s Sunflower County became a special focus of the civil rights movement. It was the home of Senator James Eastland, one of the most powerful and intransigent Dixiecrats in Congress, and FANNIE LOU HAMER, an impoverished sharecropper whose courageous struggle for voting rights made her a nationally recognized leader in the civil rights movement. By the 1970s, when White entered Gentry High School in Indianola, Mississippi, the school had already been officially desegregated, but racial integration was largely in name only since only a few whites too poor to pay tuition at the private school attended Gentry. After graduation White received a scholarship to nearby Mississippi Valley State University, earning a B.A. in Elementary Education in 1981.

White briefly worked as a substitute teacher, but after her son Antoine was born she decided to take a job on the night shift at Con Agra, one of the many catfish processing plants then opening up in Mississippi. In 1983, seeking better hours and a more secure income, she found a job at the new Delta Pride plant in Indianola, working as a catfish skinner. Delta Pride was launched in 1981 by 178 white farmers who wanted to experiment with producing something other than cotton. The venture was an unexpected success. Sales of Delta Pride catfish soared, and in six years the plant grew from fifty workers to more than a thousand. More than 90 percent of the workers were black women, many of them former welfare recipients working as sole providers for their families.

White told the 1996 North American Labor History Conference that she remembered starting out at Delta Pride on the "kill line." "We worked sun-up to sun-down, 12 and 13 hour shifts. We couldn't even take our children to the doctor or we would be fired. We stood on those lines all day and we could only wash the fish blood out of our faces during the 10-minute break when we would go to the bathroom. And the bathrooms didn't have any doors. The supervisor would come right into the bathroom, rushing us to return to the lines."

One of White's co-workers, Mary Young, was feisty and talkative. In the fall of 1985 White and Young were contacted by organizers from the United Food and Commercial Workers Union. With three other workers ("four skinners and a long gunner"), they secretly met union representatives at a motel in Greenville, Mississippi. White had been very shy since childhood, but as the union sign-up campaign intensified, the union staffer Bobby Moses convinced her that she had to speak up. "He wanted us to tell the community the truth about the conditions at Delta Pride, so that they would get involved.... I had to come out of that shyness to do it. So in the end, I had to change myself to change Delta" (White, 46).

All catfish plants in the Delta were nonunion in 1986. In March of that year students and parents in Indianola conducted a successful school boycott, demanding the hiring of a black school superintendent. The energy of the boycott spilled over to the union organizing drive at Delta Pride. White and Young led a union committee inside the plant, while many community activists helped on the outside. On 10 October 1986, workers at Mississippi's largest catfish producer, Delta Pride, voted for UFCW Local 1529 as their union, 489 to 349.

By 1987 the union won its first contract, but many problems remained. White, now chief union steward at the sprawling plant, had to cope with numerous loopholes (she called them "gapholes") in the contract. Workers were "crippled by the fast and furious pace of the assembly line, which forces them to perform the same motions, over and over, thousands of times an hour" (Bates, 24). More than a hundred workers reported accidents that severed fingers and limbs, or reported carpal tunnel syndrome injuries that left them permanently disabled.

As negotiations on a new contract began in 1990, Delta Pride refused to settle health and safety grievances. White reported that "a little thing," the company's bathroom policy, was the issue that finally forced workers out on strike. The company had enforced a policy allowing every worker to use the bathroom only six times a week for five minutes each time. In negotiations, company managers infuriated workers by demanding an even more stringent rule—that workers now use the bathroom only on their lunch break.

More than a thousand Delta Pride workers walked out on strike on 12 September 1990. The strike, which was not settled until 12 December, became the largest labor dispute by any group of workers, black or white, in Mississippi history. Hundreds of workers picketed the plant daily, joined by many supporters. White and other strike leaders went on national tour to secure support for their struggle. The strike escaped the usual labor confines and became a civil rights crusade. Pickets walked in front of supermarkets, urging shoppers to boycott Delta Pride catfish. A huge crowd in Saint Louis cheered White when she said that the "plantation mentality, it still exists. We're going down in history as black women in Mississippi who tried to do something" (*Saint Louis Post Dispatch*, 8 Oct. 1990).

White was among the strikers who testified before Congress, telling legislators about the crippling injuries, sexual harassment, and plantation discipline that the workers endured. By the time the three-month strike ended, she was profoundly changed. Moved by the truck caravans sent by strike supporters bringing clothes, food, and toys for Christmas, White said, "I'll never be the same person again. Till the day I die I'll be dedicated to help any people who want to change their lives."

In the years following the strike, White served first as a volunteer union organizer and later as a staff representative of UFCW Local 1529. She organized unions at catfish and poultry processing plants, nursing homes, and warehouses in Mississippi, Alabama, Arkansas, and North Carolina. By the mid-1990s, however, catfish processing companies began to set up new plants, and they fended off most unionization efforts. The plants also began bringing in Spanish-speaking workers from Mexico and Central America, often housing them on company property. The percentage of nonunion catfish plants began to rise, and management at unionized plants demanded givebacks on union overtime protections to compete with the nonunion plants.

In this more difficult antilabor climate, White was determined to learn more about what she called the "struggle of the mind." She began reading African American, labor, and women's history. She studied Fannie Lou Hamer's life, MARTIN LUTHER KING JR's legacy, and the writings of the Marxist-Humanist philosopher Raya Dunayevskaya. And she became active with a new organization, the Mississippi Workers Center for Human Rights (MWCHR), based in Greenville, Mississippi. The MWCHR, founded in 1996 by the attorney Jaribu Hill, provides education, advocacy, and organizing support for low-wage workers who are abused in the workplace. White was elected president of MWCHR's board of directors, and she played a major role in bringing black women together in the Fannie Lou Hamer Sister Roundtable and in the Southern Human Rights Organizers' Conference.

White had become an accomplished orator and was a widely requested speaker at conferences of both activists and scholars. Her 1998 appearance at the Black Radical Congress "electrified and moved the Congress." As she recounted the story of the catfish workers' struggle, "people were moved to tears. Ms. White provided the perfect context for the congress" (*Jackson Advocate*, 2 July 1998).

In 2000 and again in 2001 White traveled to South Africa, meeting with union activists and women's groups. She considered these trips to be highlights of her life. White was a featured speaker at the United Nations Conference on Racism, held in Durban, South Africa, in 2001, where her testimony on "the legacy of slavery" in Mississippi energized the crowd (*BBC News Online*, 10 Sept. 2001).

As controversy over federal policies on immigration intensified in 2006, Sarah White spoke and wrote about the way catfish-processing plant owners imported workers from Latin America and kept them isolated on company property, working in nonunion plants. White expressed her concern that these non-union plants were driving down wages and benefits for everyone. She appealed to union leaders for additional resources to organize immigrant workers (Trice). White's comments were repeatedly quoted during debates over immigration reform in Congress.

FURTHER READING

Sarah White's papers are housed in the Vivian G. Harsh Research Collection of Afro-American History and Literature at the Chicago Public Library.

White, Sarah. "Change in a Closed Little Town." *Southern Exposure* (Fall/Winter 1997).

Bates, Eric. "The Kill Line," *Southern Exposure* (Fall 1991).

"Fishy Business," *Southern Exposure* (Fall 1991).

Trice, Dawn Turner. "Immigration Issues Real in Delta," *Chicago Tribune*, 11 June, 2006.

Turner, Lou. "Struggles in the Delta," *News and Letters* (22 May 1987).

Zook, Kristal. "Catfish and Courage," *Essence* (April 2003).

MICHAEL FLUG

White, Slappy (20 Sept. 1921–7 Nov. 1995), comedian and actor, was born Melvin White in Baltimore, Maryland. Little is known of his early childhood except that he grew up in impoverished circumstances and often danced on the streets for small change. At age fourteen White briefly performed with a circus touring through Baltimore. Although he did not have any formal performance training, his strong dancing and physical abilities attracted many of his first comedic collaborators.

In the late 1930s White began to frequent and occasionally perform in nightclubs. Although he later was known for his verbal comedy, he began his career as a physical comedian. In the late 1940s he toured and performed as a comedic partner with the pantomimist Willie Washington. Washington and White performed as the Two Zephyrs and were known for their baggy clothing, clowning, and slapstick routines. Their trademark props included a pair of dice and two menacing razors, what Darryl Littleton referred to as "ill-informed images of the slick city Negro brandishing a razor in one hand and a pistol in the other" (86–87). Later White was known for his ability to play to and be accepted by white audiences, but the Two Zephyrs were often considered too brash and caustic.

After White split with Washington, between 1952 and 1958 he teamed with two other partners. In 1956 he moved to Los Angeles, where he met the comedian Willie Lewis. The format of the Lewis and White partnership varied significantly from that of the Two Zephyrs. Lewis deliberately spoke few words in their act, and White began to develop his own verbal humor abilities. White began to write his own material as opposed to purely improvising around a comedic scenario.

Although White never considered himself a political comedian, throughout his early career he utilized material that referenced racial segregation. He often ended his shows with a section called the "Brotherhood Creed." In this scenario he pulled two gloves out of his pockets and placed a white glove on one hand and a black glove on the other. After a recitation concerning the desire to create racial harmony, he brought his hands together to symbolize that idea. Throughout the remainder of his career, White's performances involved similar expressions of racial commentary and humor.

In 1945 White married the actress and singer PEARL BAILEY. They had no children. In 1946 Bailey made her Broadway debut in *St. Louis Woman*. At roughly the same time White formed a duo with the comedian REDD FOXX. Foxx and White were an influential comedic team who represented a shift in African American comedy from early "old school black stage comics" to a "younger, more articulate" style of comics that also included NIPSEY RUSSELL (Watkins, 258). The old-school comics, such as MOMS MABLEY and PIGMEAT MARKHAM, continued to play on the chitlin circuit, a string of theaters and nightclubs that played to all-black audiences, whereas the younger comics began to play to white and mixed audiences, reflecting perhaps the growing desegregationist climate of post–World War II America. White and Foxx began by performing in chitlin circuit venues, but by the early 1950s they also performed to white audiences throughout the United States.

White's marriage to Bailey ended in 1953. At that time Foxx and White were hired to perform as part of DINAH WASHINGTON's show in Los Angeles. The high-profile jazz and blues singer, nicknamed the "Queen of Rock 'n' Roll," was integral in setting a standard to pay black comedians a decent wage. White and Foxx earned one thousand dollars per week for playing in Washington's show.

In 1957 Foxx and White split and moved on to separate solo careers. They occasionally worked together throughout the remainder of their lives, although White primarily focused on stand-up comedy. His first significant solo performance was in 1957, when he played the Cotton Club in Miami Beach. His first evening was awkward and uncomfortable, as the producers requested he insert humor that would play well to a largely Jewish audience. White was asked to include a series of jokes that involved Yiddish punch lines—which he did not quite understand. While White struggled with this new experience, he quickly adapted by avoiding humor that was considered racially derogatory. In addition he avoided vulgar or "blue" jokes during his routine. This was one of the major differences between his material and that of Foxx.

In 1959 White was invited to perform at the Concord Hotel in Monticello, New York, becoming the first black comic to appear in the Catskills. He then appeared in Larry Steele's *Smart Affairs Revue* in Atlantic City, New Jersey. During his eight seasons in Atlantic City, White perfected his stand-up act. The revue provided him with steady employment as well as many touring opportunities. In 1959 he met the rock and roll singer LAVERN BAKER during a joint appearance in Kansas City, Missouri. They married in 1960 and soon purchased a home in White Plains, New York.

In 1967 White formed his fourth career duo with the comic Steve Rossi. Rossi was also a successful comedian at the time and had formerly partnered with the comedian Marty Allen. Although White and Rossi were not officially the first black and white comic team, they performed in high-profile clubs in New York, Los Angeles, and Las Vegas.

White always identified himself as a live stand-up comic; however, he occasionally appeared in television and film. On 27 December 1970 White and Rossi appeared on the *Ed Sullivan Show*. In 1971 White made his feature film debut with Rossi in *The Man from O.R.G.Y.*, a low-budget sexploitation film. In 1972 White made a guest appearance on Redd Foxx's immensely successful television sitcom *Sanford and Son*, reuniting with his former comedy partner. White played the character of Melvin (his actual name) and appeared in five episodes during the first season.

White also acted with the veteran comedian Mabley in the 1974 film *Amazing Grace*, directed by Stan Lathan. Although Mabley and White did not perform together in their earlier years, the film served as an opportunity to join two contemporaries who had traveled in different comedic directions. White's final film appearance was in 1992 with Billy Crystal in *Mr. Saturday Night*. The film tells the story of an aging comedian who is relegated to touring nursing homes. His inclusion in the film demonstrated White's comfort at poking fun at his own career.

FURTHER READING

Foxx, Redd, and Norma Miller. *The Redd Foxx Encyclopedia of Black Humor* (1977).

Littleton, Darryl. *Black Comedians on Black Comedy: How African-Americans Taught Us to Laugh* (2006).

Vanderzee, James. *Harlem Heyday* (1982).

Watkins, Mel. *On the Real Side* (1994).

Watkins, Mel. *Stepin Fetchit: The Life and Times of Lincoln Perry* (2005).

DONNY LEVIT

White, Solomon (12 June 1868–Aug. 1955), baseball player and manager and chronicler of early "blackball" years, also known as "Sol," was born in Bellaire, Ohio, an industrial town across the Ohio river from Wheeling, West Virginia. Nothing is known of his parentage or early life. In 1883 White began his baseball career with a three-year stint with his hometown Bellaire Globes, an amateur team barnstorming the Ohio Valley. In 1886 White moved to the Wheeling Green Stockings of the Ohio State League and, after an abortive seven-game 1887 season with the Pittsburgh Keystones of the National Colored League, he returned to the integrated Wheeling club, reportedly batting .370 for the remaining fifty-two games, including 84 hits and 54 runs. Meanwhile, segregationist practices solidified in major league baseball, represented by Chicago star Adrian "Cap" Anson's July 1881 refusal to play against a team with a black player. To play, African American players filled the rosters of integrated minor league teams and organized their own circuits and ball clubs.

In 1889 White began the year with Trenton in the integrated Middle States League. After thirty-one games and a .333 batting average, he joined the black New York Gorhams earning ten dollars per week. In 1890 White's Cuban Giants became the York (Pennsylvania) Monarchs, moving the team into the Eastern Interstate League, an integrated circuit. As the Monarchs' second baseman, his signature position, the right-handed White—at five foot nine and 170 pounds—batted .356, fifth best in the league, with eighty-four hits and seventy-eight runs. White's 1891 season was split between the Cuban Giants, soon bankrupt, and the New York Big Gorhams, representing Ansonia in the Connecticut State League, which folded by mid-summer. The Big Gorhams became a touring team, recording one hundred wins and four defeats versus weak amateur and semiprofessional teams. At some point in the year White left to join the Harrisburg Giants, apparently taking other teammates with him and leading sportswriters to dub Harrisburg the "Polka-Dots." From 1892 to 1894 White labored for J. B. Bright's Cuban Giants, the Pittsburgh Keystones, the Black Boston Monarchs, and a Hotel Champlain team in upstate New York, where he also waited tables. In 1895 White played 10 games for Fort Wayne, Indiana, in the integrated Western Tri-State League, being paid $80 while batting .385 with 20 hits and 15 runs. When the league disbanded in June, White joined the Adrian (Michigan) Page Fence Giants, owned by a barbed-wire company, hitting .404 with 21 safeties and 15 runs in just 12 games. At the end of the season White entered Ohio's Wilberforce University as a theological student and began a four-year pattern of summer ball and winter school. In 1897 White moved to the Cuban X-Giants for three years. White returned in 1900 to the Page Fence team, which had now become the Columbia Giants of Chicago. In 1901 the Cuban X-Giants welcomed White back as second baseman and captain.

In 1902 White began his longest and most successful tenure in baseball as player-manager of the Philadelphia Giants. Recruited by owner H. Walter Schlicter, sports editor of the *Philadelphia Item*, White played shortstop and second base while guiding the Giants to a record of 81 wins and 43 losses. After claiming the "blackball" championship, White's Giants lost two postseason exhibition games to the American League Champion Philadelphia Athletics. In 1903, with salaries ranging from sixty dollars to ninety dollars per month, the Philadelphia Giants and the Cuban X-Giants joined the white Independent League. Before the 1904 season White's squad acquired the pitching stars RUBE FOSTER and Danny McClellan, the left fielder Preston "Pete" Hill, and the catcher GEORGE "CHAPPIE" JOHNSON, becoming one of the great "blackball" teams of all time, even moving south to win Cuba's winter league title. The Philadelphia squad reached its peak in 1905, with a record of 134 wins and 21 losses, and in 1906 at 108-31, both times claiming the "blackball" championship.

White's greatest contribution to Negro League baseball and the sport in general was as author of *Sol White's Official Base Ball Guide*, published in 1907. Providing information about the origins and evolution of Negro League baseball, White's unique chronicle profiles special contests, star players, managers, the Cubans, and the "Colored" game. While noting the difficulties faced by the "Colored player," White was optimistic that one day black players would walk "hand in hand with the opposite race in the greatest of all American games—baseball."

In 1910 White organized his own Brooklyn Royal Giants in the International League of Colored Baseball Clubs. The circuit did not last more than a few weeks, and manager White moved in 1911 to the New York Lincoln Giants, which folded by 4 July. Following one more ill-fated season in 1912 as manager of the Boston Giants, White's baseball career ended except for a few isolated responsibilities: secretary, Columbus, Ohio, club in the National Negro

League (1920); manager, Fear's Giants of Cleveland, a black minor league squad (1922); manager, Cleveland Browns, Negro National League (1924); and manager, Newark Browns, Eastern Colored League (1926). White's remaining years are not well known. Apparently he lived in Harlem, where he died, and wrote a column of observation for the *Amsterdam News* and the *New York Age*.

FURTHER READING

Sol White's Official Base Ball Guide (1907) has been reprinted by Camden House (1984).

Holway, John B. *Blackball Stars, Negro League Pioneers* (1988).

Petersen, Robert. *Only the Ball Was White* (1970).

This entry is taken from the *American National Biography* and is published here with the permission of the American Council of Learned Societies.

DAVID BERNSTEIN

White, Walter Francis (1 July 1893–21 Mar. 1955), civil rights leader, was born in Atlanta, Georgia, to George White, a mail carrier, and Madeline Harrison, a former schoolteacher. The fourth of seven children, White, whose parents had been born in slavery, grew up entrenched in black Atlanta's leading and most respected institutions: his family attended the prestigious First Congregational Church, and he received his secondary and collegiate education at Atlanta University, from which he graduated in 1916. (His siblings enjoyed similar religious training and educational opportunities.) With blond hair, blue eyes, and a light complexion, White was a "voluntary Negro," a person who could "pass" for white yet chose not to do so. His black racial identity was annealed by the Atlanta riot of September 1906. For three days white mobs rampaged through African American neighborhoods, destroying property and assaulting people; the thirteen-year-old White realized, as he put it in his autobiography, that he could never join a race that was infected with such toxic hatred.

Upon graduation from college, White became an executive with the Standard Life Insurance Company, one of the largest black-owned businesses of its day. Part of Atlanta's "New Negro" business elite, White was a founder of a real estate and investment company and looked forward to a successful business career. He also participated in civic affairs: in 1916 he was a founding member and secretary of the Atlanta branch of the NAACP. The branch experienced rapid growth, largely because, in 1917, it stopped the school board from eliminating seventh grade in the black public schools.

White was an energetic organizer and enthusiastic speaker, qualities that attracted the attention of NAACP field secretary JAMES WELDON JOHNSON. The association's board of directors, at Johnson's behest, invited White to join the national staff as assistant secretary. White accepted, and in January 1918 he moved to New York City.

During White's first eight years with the NAACP, his primary responsibility was to conduct undercover investigations of lynchings and racial violence, primarily in the South. Putting his complexion in service of the cause, he adopted a series of white male incognitos—among the cleverer ones were itinerant patent-medicine salesman, land speculator, and newspaper reporter intent on exposing the libelous tales being spread in the North about white southerners—and fooled mob members and lynching spectators into providing detailed accounts of the recent violence. Upon White returning to New York from his investigative trips, the NAACP would publicize his findings, and White eventually wrote several articles on the racial carnage of the post–World War I era that appeared in the *Nation*, the *New Republic*, the *New York Herald-Tribune*, and other prestigious journals of liberal opinion. By 1924 White had investigated forty-one lynchings and eight race riots. Among the most notorious of these was the 1918 lynching in Valdosta, Georgia, of MARY TURNER, who was set ablaze. Turner was nine months pregnant, her womb was slashed open, and her fetus was crushed to death. White also investigated the bloody race riots that left hundreds of African Americans dead in Chicago and in Elaine, Arkansas, during the "red summer" of 1919, and the 1921 riot in Tulsa, Oklahoma, that resulted in the leveling of the black business district and entire residential neighborhoods. White's investigations also revealed that prominent and respected whites participated in racial violence; the mob that perpetrated a triple lynching in Aiken, South Carolina, in 1926, for example, included local officials and relatives of the governor.

White wrote of his undercover investigations in the July 1928 *American Mercury* and in *Rope and Faggot* (1929), a detailed study of the history of lynching and its place in American culture and politics that remains indispensable. His derring-do in narrowly escaping detection and avoiding vigilante punishment was also rendered in verse in LANGSTON HUGHES's "Ballad of Walter White" (1941).

At the same time that he was exposing lynching, White also emerged as a leading light in the Harlem Renaissance. He authored two novels. *The Fire in the*

Walter Francis White, civil rights activist and NAACP leader, c. 1935. (Library of Congress.)

Flint (1924) was the second novel to be published by a New Negro, appearing just after JESSIE FAUSET's *There Is Confusion*. Set in Georgia after World War I and based on White's acquaintance with his native state, *The Fire in the Flint* tells the story of the racial awakening of Kenneth Harper, who pays for his new consciousness when a white mob murders him. The novel was greeted with critical acclaim and was translated into French, German, Japanese, and Russian. His second work of fiction, *Flight* (1926), set in New Orleans, Atlanta, and New York, is both a work about the Great Migration of blacks to the North and story about "passing." *Flight*'s reviews were mixed. White's response to one of the negative reviews—by the African American poet FRANK HORNE, in *Opportunity* magazine—is instructive. He complained to the editor about being blindsided and parlayed his dissatisfaction into a debate over his book's merits that stretched over three issues. To White there was no such thing as bad publicity—in art or in politics. The salient point was to keep a topic—a book or a political cause—firmly in public view, which would eventually create interest and sympathy.

White's dynamism and energy was central to the New Negro movement. He was a prominent figure in Harlem's nightlife, chaperoning well-connected and sympathetic whites to clubs and dances. He helped to place the works of Langston Hughes, COUNTÉE CULLEN, and CLAUDE MCKAY with major publishers, and promoted the careers of the singer and actor PAUL ROBESON, the tenor ROLAND HAYES, and the contralto MARIAN ANDERSON.

When James Weldon Johnson retired from the NAACP in 1929, White, who had been looking to assume more responsibility, succeeded him. As the association's chief executive, White had a striking influence on the civil rights movement's agenda and methods. In 1930 he originated and orchestrated the victorious lobbying campaign to defeat President Hoover's nomination to the Supreme Court of John J. Parker, a North Carolina politician and jurist who had publicly stated his opposition to black suffrage and his hostility to organized labor. During the next two election cycles, the NAACP worked with substantial success to defeat senators with significant black constituencies who had voted to confirm Parker. The NAACP became a recognized force in national politics.

During Franklin Roosevelt's New Deal and Harry Truman's Fair Deal, White raised both the NAACP's public profile and its influence on national politics. White's success owed much to his special knack for organizing the more enlightened of America's white elites to back the NAACP's programs. Over the decade of the 1930s, he won the support of the majority of the Senate and House of Representatives for a federal antilynching law; only southern senators' filibusters prevented its passage. His friendship with Eleanor Roosevelt likewise gave him unparalleled access to the White House. This proved invaluable when he conceived and organized Marian Anderson's Easter Sunday 1939 concert at the Lincoln Memorial, which was blessed by the president and had as honorary sponsors cabinet members, other New Deal officials, and Supreme Court justices. As NAACP secretary and head of the National Committee against Mob Violence, White convinced President Truman in 1946 to form a presidential civil rights commission, which the following year issued its groundbreaking antisegregationist report, *To Secure These Rights*. In 1947 he persuaded Truman to address the closing rally of the NAACP's annual meeting, held at the Washington Monument; it was the first time that a president had spoken at an association event.

As secretary, White oversaw the NAACP's legal work, which after 1934 included lawsuits seeking equal educational opportunities for African

Americans. He was also instrumental in convincing the liberal philanthropists of the American Fund for Public Service to commit $100,000 to fund the endeavor, though only a portion was delivered before the fund became insolvent. After 1939 the day-to-day running of the legal campaign against desegregation rested with CHARLES HAMILTON HOUSTON and THURGOOD MARSHALL's NAACP Legal Defense Fund, but White remained intimately involved in the details of the campaign, which culminated with the Supreme Court's 1954 *Brown v. Board of Education* ruling that declared the doctrine of "separate but equal" unconstitutional.

White had married Gladys Powell, a clerical worker in the NAACP national office, in 1922. They had two children, Jane and Walter Carl Darrow, and divorced in 1948. In 1949 he married Poppy Cannon, a white woman. This interracial union provoked a major controversy within both the NAACP and black America at large, and there was widespread sentiment that White should resign. In response, White, who was always an integrationist, claimed the right to marry whomever he wanted. He weathered the storm with the help of NAACP board member Eleanor Roosevelt, who threatened to resign should White be forced from office. Though White maintained the title of secretary, his powers were reduced, with ROY WILKINS taking over administrative duties. White continued to be the association's public spokesperson until his death on 21 March 1955. In declining health for several years, he suffered a fatal heart attack in his New York apartment. Unlike other NAACP leaders such as W. E. B. DuBois and Charles Houston, Walter White was neither a great theoretician nor a master of legal theory. His lasting accomplishment lay in his ability to organize support for the NAACP agenda among persons of influence in and out of government and to persuade Americans of all races to support the cause of equal rights for African Americans.

FURTHER READING

The bulk of Walter White's papers are in the Papers of the National Association for the Advancement of Colored People, deposited at the Library of Congress in Washington, D.C., and the Walter Francis White/Poppy Cannon Papers, deposited at the Beinecke Rare Books and Manuscript Library, Yale University, New Haven, Connecticut.

White, Walter. *A Man Called White* (1948).

Cannon, Poppy. *A Gentle Knight: My Husband Walter White* (1956).

Janken, Kenneth Robert. *WHITE: The Biography of Walter White, Mr. NAACP* (2003).

Obituaries: *New York Times*, 22 Mar. 1955; *Washington Afro-American*, 26 Mar. 1955.

KENNETH R. JANKEN

White, William Jefferson (25 Dec. 1832–17 Apr. 1913), minister, educator, editor, and Reconstruction office holder, was born near Ruckersville in Elbert County, Georgia. Although much about White's early life remains shrouded in mystery, oral accounts and surviving records suggest that his father, William, was a white planter, and that his mother, Chaney, was a Native American woman who "probably had Negro admixture" (Donaldson, 136). During the 1850s White settled in Augusta, Georgia, a bustling cotton trade center on the Savannah River. After working for a lumber company, he earned a living as a carpenter and coffin maker for a local funeral home. During one of his job assignments, he met Josephine Elizabeth Thomas, a mulatto seamstress who worked for a prominent, white Augusta family. On 7 October 1855 White joined Josephine's church, Springfield Baptist—the oldest African American congregation in Augusta. A year later the two married and lived as a free man and an enslaved woman until he purchased her freedom. They had ten children. One son, Lucien Hayden White, served as music editor of the *New York Age* newspaper. A daughter, Claudia White Harreld—one of the first college graduates of Spelman in Atlanta—later served on the faculty of her alma mater.

Although White lacked formal schooling, his mother's tutorials in rudimentary reading and writing sparked his lifelong passion for education. Defying Georgia law, he conducted clandestine schools for enslaved Augusta families and then established a "Sabbath school" at Springfield Baptist in 1859. In the spring of 1867 he was appointed an agent of the Freedmen's Bureau and supervised the development of schools for newly emancipated slaves throughout the state. While traveling, White endured threats from vigilantes who opposed his educational mission and his political campaigning on behalf of the Republican Party. When the Bureau disbanded in 1869, White secured an assignment as an assistant assessor in Augusta's Internal Revenue office, "the first black to hold that federal position" (Foner, *Freedom's Lawmakers*, 229).

In April 1866, White pursued the ministry and was ordained to preach by his pastor at Springfield Church in Augusta. In February 1867 Richard C.

Coulter, a former slave from Augusta and a representative of the National Theological Institute in Washington, D.C., returned to his hometown and solicited White's help in developing a training school for ministers in the city. With the financial support of Springfield Baptist, the contributions of African American citizens, and subsequent funding from the American Baptist Home Missionary Society, White pursued Coulter's proposition and established the Augusta Baptist Institute. Although constrained financially and constantly threatened by white critics, the school attracted strong students. For a time the Institute was housed at Harmony Baptist Church, which was founded by Reverend White and some members of Springfield Baptist in the spring of 1868. But when resources proved scarce and conditions became increasingly dangerous, White endorsed relocating the Institute to Atlanta in 1879. He continued his association with the school (later renamed Morehouse College), serving on its board of trustees for several years. He also served on the boards of neighboring Spelman Seminary and Atlanta University.

In January 1873 White joined Colored Methodist minister LUCIUS H. HOLSEY and others in persuading Augusta's local school board to acquire and fund the black schools once supported by the Freedmen's Bureau and the American Missionary Association. A few years later White and his colleagues initiated a petition drive that ultimately led to the establishment of "The Colored High School"—the first publicly funded high school for African American students in Georgia. During the summer of 1880 White personally recruited RICHARD R. WRIGHT, an Atlanta University graduate, to lead the school, which was later named in honor of Atlanta University President Edmund Asa Ware.

A founding member of the Georgia Equal Rights and Education Association, White actively supported the Republican Party and served as a delegate to state and national conventions. At an October 1875 Colored Convention held in Augusta, White joined African Methodist Episcopal minister HENRY MCNEAL TURNER and other black Republicans in deploring racial violence and appealing for improved educational resources and land reform. Five years later White invited three hundred citizens to Macon for a meeting of the Georgia Consultation Convention to debate similar issues.

A successful career in journalism and publishing bolstered White's work in education, politics, and religion. On 28 October 1880 he began publishing the *Georgia Baptist* newspaper, a weekly periodical endorsed by members of the Missionary Baptist Convention of Georgia, early issues of the paper. The pages of the *Georgia Baptist*, which carried the masthead "Great Elevator, Educator, and Defender of the People," provided White and other African American leaders a visible platform to address a number of critical issues. When a group of black Baptists, led by Savannah pastor E. K. LOVE, called for increased self-determination and attempted to wrestle control of Atlanta Baptist College away from the American Baptist Home Mission Society, White launched a series of editorials criticizing the "separatist" move as detrimental to the longevity of the school. When the Augusta school board decided to close Ware High School in the summer of 1897, White penned lengthy objections in his newspaper. Drawing from the recent 1896 *Plessy v. Ferguson* Supreme Court decision, he and his colleagues demanded separate but equal educational facilities and charged that white high schools should be closed if Ware was dissolved. The school's eventual closing prompting a celebrated lawsuit by parents. The case, *Cumming v. Richmond County*, made its way to the U.S. Supreme Court. In December 1899 the court ruled in favor of the local school board.

As much as White used the *Georgia Baptist* to support educational opportunities and to convey messages of morality, respectability, and race pride to readers, he also railed against segregation, disfranchisement, debt peonage, and violent assaults upon black men and women. Although White championed interracial cooperation, his public criticisms of racial bigotry and discrimination nearly cost him his life on several occasions. In May 1900, when a white mob lynched an African American laborer for allegedly murdering the son of a wealthy, white cotton merchant, White's *Georgia Baptist* republished a caustic editorial from the *Washington Bee* that hailed the black man as a hero. Within days, an indignant band of nearly three hundred white men stormed the minister's neighborhood in a thwarted attempt to destroy the newspaper office. Taking refuge in the local jail, White subsequently repudiated the *Washington Bee* insert and issued a lengthy apology.

Despite the enormous challenges White encountered, he remained active on a number of fronts. He attended sessions of the American Negro Academy, organized by Episcopal minister ALEXANDER CRUMMELL. He frequently participated in discussions at W. E. B. DuBOIS's Atlanta University Conferences, and he championed the founding of the Niagara movement in 1905. In February 1906 and again the following year, White organized the Georgia Equal Rights Convention and worked in collaboration with DuBois and Turner in demanding civil and political rights for African Americans in direct opposition to BOOKER T. WASHINGTON's Tuskegee Institute. Washington supporters, such as Atlanta editor BENJAMIN J. DAVIS and prominent evangelist CHARLES T. WALKER, publicly criticized the gathering, but White's convention drew support from Boston publisher WILLIAM MONROE TROTTER, J. MAX BARBER, editor of the *Voice of the Negro* magazine, and Augusta educator LUCY CRAFT LANEY.

Seven months after the celebrated gathering in Macon, White and his associates watched as their political prospects dwindled with the Atlanta Race Riot. As violence paralyzed Atlanta, newspapers reported rumors that a vigilante group in Augusta—purported to be the Ku Klux Klan—intended to target White for his outspoken statements against segregation. Concerned for his family's safety and hoping to avert similar danger in Augusta, White secretly left the city and went into exile for a number of weeks, only to resume preaching and publishing. Although White had every incentive to leave his home permanently, he remained in Augusta and continued his political and social activism. When he died at sunset on 17 April 1913, his fame and influence extended well beyond the borders of Georgia. In an ironic twist, Washington telegraphed a letter of sympathy to the family and informed them that he honored the minister for his "great unselfishness; for his pride in his race and for his unflinching devotion to its best interests." In a poignant eulogy published in a local white newspaper, Augusta minister SILAS X. FLOYD concluded: "In more respects than one, Dr. White was our most remarkable colored citizen. The story of his life, when told, sounds like romance" (Donaldson, 168).

FURTHER READING
Donaldson, Bobby J. "Standing on a Volcano: The Leadership of William Jefferson White," *Paternalism in a Southern City: Race, Religion, and Gender in Augusta, Georgia*, Edward Cashin and Glenn T. Eskew, eds. (2001).

BOBBY J. DONALDSON

White, William Sylvester, Jr. (27 July 1914–16 Feb. 2004), pioneer black naval officer, was born in Chicago, Illinois, the only child of William S. White Sr. and Marie Houston White. His father was a chemist and pharmacist and his mother was a public school teacher. They were graduates of Fisk University in Nashville, a traditionally black school. Both had postgraduate degrees and emphasized to their son the importance of education. In an oral history interview, White recalled, "I knew that the opportunity to go to school was a precious opportunity which should not be wasted…. My father used to tell me that his mother told him that almost anything you get, the white folks can take away from you—except learning" (Stillwell, 243). White attended public schools, including Hyde Park High School in Chicago. Small in physical stature, he ran track and played soccer in high school. He earned a bachelor's degree from the University of Chicago in 1935 and a law degree from the same university in 1937. White chose the law because it was among the few professions available to African Americans in the 1930s and because, as he put it, "it depended more on the powers of reasoning rather than memorization" (Stillwell, 243).

As White embarked on his legal career in the late 1930s, there were no lucrative job offers. He had a small neighborhood practice of his own and initially worked in the offices of two other black attorneys in the city. In 1939 White was incredulous when offered the opportunity to become an assistant U.S. attorney for the Northern District of Illinois. When assured that the offer was legitimate, he accepted the job despite the fact that he was obviously the token black in the office. He worked mostly on the civil side, handling contracts and regulatory cases for the government. He was given little courtroom experience, perhaps because of a concern by superiors that he might not be able to persuade white juries to convict white defendants. He enjoyed the work nonetheless, explaining, "I didn't concentrate on the hole; I concentrated on the doughnut" (Stillwell, 244). The same year he married George Vivian Bridgeforth; they were divorced in the 1980s. The couple had twin daughters, Carolyn Craven and Sala Marilyn Steinbach, born in December 1944. Carolyn died in 2001.

White enlisted in the navy in October 1943 and went through recruit training in segregated Camp Robert Smalls at the Great Lakes Naval Training station north of Chicago. By that time the navy had some one hundred thousand black sailors but no black officers. White was one of sixteen enlisted men who in January 1944 comprised the first class of black officer candidates. His postgraduate degree was among the few in the group. Between January and mid-March, the men went through a cram course that included training in such areas as navigation, communications, gunnery, propulsion machinery, seamanship, naval history, and the navy disciplinary system. Of the sixteen, twelve, including White, were commissioned as naval reserve ensigns, and a thirteenth became a warrant officer. The other three men remained in the enlisted ranks. Years later the pioneer officers collectively became known as the Golden Thirteen.

Although the navy had gone through a rigorous selection process, including FBI checks, to pick the officer candidates, it was not ready to give them full-fledged opportunities in the fleet—despite their training. The service was still reluctant to have white personnel working for black officers, thus White's service as a commissioned officer was entirely ashore. He was initially stationed at Great Lakes, though he and his cohorts were not allowed to use the officers' club there. He served as a training station public relations officer, assigned to create news releases and radio programs that highlighted the achievements of black personnel. The releases were geared mostly toward black publications. His other role was as information officer on the staff of the white admiral in command of the Ninth Naval District. In 1945 he was reassigned to Washington, D.C., in general public relations activities. He also joined LESTER GRANGER, an official of the National Urban League, on a wide-ranging tour of naval facilities to ascertain the extent to which the navy's then-limited integration policies were being implemented.

White left active service as a lieutenant (junior grade) in 1946. He then resumed his earlier civilian position as an assistant U.S. attorney. He remained in that job until 1954 when he became assistant state's attorney for Cook County, Illinois, based in Chicago. From 1955 to 1961 he was deputy commissioner of Chicago's Department of Investigation. White's professional career took another turn in 1961 when he joined the cabinet of Illinois' newly elected Governor Otto Kerner Jr., a Democrat, serving from 1961 to 1964 as director of the Department of Registration and Education. During that time he was also chairman of the state's Board of Vocational Education and Rehabilitation and Board of Natural Resources. In 1964 White became judge of the Circuit Court of Cook County and in 1968 was appointed presiding judge of juvenile court. Donald P. O'Connell, former chief judge of the circuit court, said of White: "Syl was a pioneer in establishing programs for juveniles that would divert non-violent offenders from custodial care into programs that didn't require the children

be kept in detention" (*Chicago Tribune*). During his term on the court Judge White recognized the sincere interest that many individuals had in helping young offenders find constructive paths, and he himself sought ways to use the law to help those in need. In 1980 White became a justice of the Illinois appellate court, one step below the state supreme court. One of his notable opinions came in a case that ruled that the forces of HAROLD WASHINGTON, Chicago's first black mayor, were in control of the city council. Justice White held that post until his retirement in 1990.

In addition to his activities on the bench, White had a variety of teaching experiences in the legal field, often as an adjunct professor, and he wrote articles on the subject of juvenile justice. In 1972 the Cook County Bar Association honored him as Judge of the Year. Also in 1972 the John Howard Association selected him for the Outstanding Service in the Juvenile Delinquency Field Award. Justice White died in 2004.

FURTHER READING

Stillwell, Paul, ed. *The Golden Thirteen: Recollections of the First Black Naval Officers* (1993).
Reminiscences of William Sylvester White, Member of the Golden Thirteen (1990).
Obituary: *Chicago Tribune*, 20 Feb. 2004.

PAUL STILLWELL

Whitehead, Colson (1969–), novelist and essayist, was born in New York City and lived in various Manhattan neighborhoods over the course of his childhood with his parents Arch and Mary Ann, both businesspeople working in the city. Whitehead graduated from Harvard College in 1991 and lived in San Francisco for less than a year before returning to New York to take an editorial assistant post at the *Village Voice*, where he established himself as a television and popular culture critic. After leaving the staff of the *Village Voice*, Whitehead began writing for numerous periodical publications, including *New York Magazine*, *Vibe*, and *Spin*, in addition to his novelistic output.

Published in 1999, Whitehead's first novel, *The Intuitionist*, announced his emergence as a major contemporary American author with its markedly positive popular and critical reception. A finalist for the Ernest Hemingway/PEN Award for First Fiction and winner of the Quality Paperback Book Club's New Voices Award, *The Intuitionist* brought Whitehead's writing into the purview of critics and scholars, owing in large part to its nuanced and delicate dissection of race, class, and gender within the frame of its highly inventive, allegorical plot.

In the novel, Lila Mae Watson, the first black female elevator inspector appointed to the Department of Elevator Inspectors, finds her status and professional abilities under fire after the free fall crash of an elevator she had previously inspected and certified. A devotee of the Intuitionist camp of inspection technique and procedure, Lila Mae must defend not only her perfect inspection record but also the entire Intuitionist methodology and practice against the impending investigation and rival Empiricist faction. She must prove herself innocent of the charges of negligence brought about by the Empiricists, who wish to undermine and discredit Intuitionist practice, which relies mainly on touch, feel, and sensations, not only upon the visible and verifiable world.

Concerned heavily with race, *The Intuitionist*, though set in an unnamed time and place, allegorizes pre–civil rights urban America, with its recumbent xenophobia and stringent social divisions. Writing within the detective fiction genre (though arguably in a postmodern manifestation of the form), Whitehead directed Lila Mae's quest with a light touch, affording his protagonist a diffident agency that sets her apart from the surrounding cast of characters and positions her keenly for uncovering the conspiratorial plot running deep within the Guild of Elevator Inspectors. At the same time, Lila Mae also brings to the narrative's forefront the more insidious cultural logic of racism, perhaps most cleverly rendered in the departmental response to the fact that the inventor of elevator safety brakes and the author of the founding Intuitionist text, James Fulton, was a black man, though one who passed as white. The uncovering of Fulton's racial background throws the impasse between the Intuitionists and the Empiricists into greater relief, since whichever faction dominates the guild possesses formidable social and political power.

Following the success of *The Intuitionist*, Whitehead's second novel, *John Henry Days* (2001), further bolstered his literary reputation. A work of fiction that played with the distinction between myth and history, agency and determinism, *John Henry Days* was nominated for both the Pulitzer Prize and the National Book Critics Award for fiction and helped earn Whitehead the New York Public Library Young Lions Fiction Award. Likewise selected as a *New York Times* Book Review Editors' Choice and a *Los Angeles Times, Washington Post*, and Salon.com Book of the Year, *John Henry Days*

brought Whitehead's writing to an even larger reading public.

In this novel, Whitehead took as his subject an actual historical event—the 1996 John Henry Days Festival in Talcott, West Virginia—and mused upon both the folk history of JOHN HENRY's fabled competition against a steam drill at Big Bend Tunnel in 1872 and the myth of John Henry that has since proliferated and permeated the American national imagination. In the novel's frame narrative, the junketeer and glossy journalist J. Sutter, challenging the record for attending the most consecutive press junkets, travels to Talcott to cover the festival and the unveiling of the John Henry stamp, which stands as its main event. Mixing genres and narrative forms, the novel confidently moves among different forms of writing and presentation, casting the technological, historical, and sentimental with a striking evenness of tone—a feature of Whitehead's writing that has invited comparisons with Don DeLillo, Thomas Pynchon, William Gaddis, and other accomplished postwar American novelists.

Around J. Sutter and the goings-on of the festival, Whitehead introduces a cast of at least twelve major characters with their own connection to John Henry—both the myth and the man—in a complex narrative that shifts abruptly not only among the perspectives of its characters but also across time and geographical space. John Henry, both the fictional character rendered in certain sections within the novel and the American folk legend, provides an epic myth that Whitehead weaves and reworks in both parodic and reverent guises: man versus machine or, perhaps, the teleological narrative of historical progress. As in *The Intuitionist*, Whitehead's work proves especially attentive to issues of race and class, making a clear case for the historical provenance of American racism that pervades society not only in the post–Civil War era but also at the contemporary moment.

With two successful novels behind him, in 2002 Whitehead was awarded a MacArthur Fellowship (popularly referred to as the "Genius Award"), which carried with it a five-hundred-thousand-dollar grant. Soon after receiving the fellowship, Whitehead published his first book-length work of nonfiction, a paean to New York City written largely in response to the 11 September 2001 terrorist attacks, titled *The Colossus of New York: A City in Thirteen Parts* (2003). Though the attacks themselves are not directly mentioned, the book remains expressly and obsessively concerned with both memory and the constant morphing and revamping of city space that provides its foundational condition. Impressionistic and imagistic, *The Colossus of New York* does not attempt to masquerade as a work of popular history; rather, it serves as a work of memory that demonstrates Whitehead's insistence on the simultaneity of recording and reconstructing that goes into any act of writing.

Colson Whitehead's virtuoso prose and adept handling of multiple genres and styles distinguished him as one of America's most aggressive and ambitious contemporary novelists. When asked by Salon.com editor Laura Miller about the pressures of treating race within the American novel, Whitehead responded:

> There were two rigid camps in the '60s: the Black Arts movement, denouncing James Baldwin and Ralph Ellison for being too white, and Ralph Ellison calling the Black Arts writers too militant and narrow, not universal enough. Now I think there are a lot more of us writing and a lot more different areas we're exploring.... I'm dealing with serious race issues, but I'm not handling them in a way that people expect.

Melding the serious with the comical, the true with the fantastical, Whitehead's writing challenged conventional literary treatment of race and gender, while at the same time doing so without recourse to a flat and unmoving didacticism. Whitehead's work in the 2000s has reflected this commitment to expanding the horizons of fiction. His introspective novel *Sag Harbor* (2009), a finalist for the PEN/Faulkner Award, depicts affluent African American teens in the summer of 1985. Two years later, Whitehead published *Zone One*, a literary take on the zombie genre that employs familiar tropes from apocalyptic science fiction films in order to critique topics as diverse as popular culture, gentrification, consumerism, and nostalgia.

FURTHER READING

Larimer, Kevin. "Industrial Strength in the Information Age: A Profile of Colson Whitehead," *Poets and Writers Magazine* 29.4 (July/Aug. 2001).
Miller, Laura. "The *Salon* Interview: Going Up," Salon.com. Available at http://www.salon.com/books/int/1999/cov_si_12int.html.
Zalewski, Daniel. "An Interview with Colson Whitehead: Tunnel Vision," *New York Times Book Review*, 13 May 2001.

ZACH WEIR

Whiteside, Larry (19 Sept. 1937–15 June 2007), pioneering black sports journalist best known for his work as a baseball beat writer and national baseball reporter for the *Boston Globe*, was born Lawrence W. Whiteside in Chicago to Myrtis Wells Whiteside and her husband Alonzo Whiteside. From 1955 to 1957 he attended Wilson Junior College and in 1957 entered Drake University in Des Moines, Iowa. While attending Drake, Whiteside began working for the *Des Moines Register* and from 1958 to 1959 was a researcher for the Johnson Publishing Company. In 1959 he graduated with a B.A. in Journalism and was hired as a sports reporter by the *Kansas City Kansan*, eventually serving as assistant sports editor. In 1960 his reporting on the Kansas City Athletics baseball team earned him membership in the Writers Association of America. In 1963 he joined the *Milwaukee Journal*. Although primarily a sports reporter for the *Journal*, on occasion Whiteside was assigned to cover contemporary civil rights issues.

While at the *Journal* Whiteside covered the Milwaukee Braves baseball team, whose roster included several players who would eventually enter the National Baseball Hall of Fame, including HANK AARON, third baseman Eddie Mathews, and pitcher Warren Spahn. When the Braves franchise was transferred to Atlanta after the 1966 season, Whiteside remained at the *Journal* covering other sports. When the Seattle Pilots franchise moved to Milwaukee in 1970 and became the Brewers, baseball once again became Whiteside's primary beat. The 1970 season also marked Whiteside's tenth year as a member of the Baseball Writers Association of America, making him eligible to vote for the induction of players in the National Baseball Hall of Fame, a prestigious honor among baseball writers. He became only the fourth black reporter to qualify as a voter, following WENDELL SMITH of the *Pittsburgh Courier*, SAM LACY of the *Baltimore African American*, and Bob Teague of the *New York Times*.

While covering the Brewers, Whiteside became acquainted with the team's majority owner Allen "Bud" Selig. Selig, who later became commissioner of baseball, offered Whiteside a position with the Brewers in the public relations department, but he turned Selig down. In 1971, taking notice of the lack of black representation in the sports departments of major American newspapers, Whiteside began accumulating what he referred to as "The Black List," to aid sports editors who wished to hire qualified, black reporters. Whiteside's original list included only nine names, but in little more than a decade it had expanded to more than ninety. Young, black journalists soon came to know Whiteside as both a mentor and an important ally in the advancement of their careers.

In 1973 *Boston Globe* sports editor Ernie Roberts offered Whiteside the opportunity to become the first black reporter in the paper's sports department. Whiteside was well aware of his pioneering position, later telling author Howard Bryant in *Shutout: A Story of Race and Baseball in Boston*, that he was offered the position because "[the *Globe*] desperately needed a black" (Bryant, 111). Despite some trepidation over Boston's reputation as a city that made life difficult for blacks, he accepted the job. Whiteside and his wife, Elaine (Fain), a public school guidance counselor, boarded at a black rooming house before purchasing a house in Newtonville, a nearby Boston suburb. They later had one son, Anthony L. Whiteside. Whiteside had joined the *Globe* during a time in which the newspaper's sports department was earning a reputation as perhaps the most dynamic and talented in the nation, and he worked with such notable young reporters as Peter Gammons, Bob Ryan, and Leigh Montville. Although he covered a variety of sports for the *Globe*, including boxing and Boston Celtics basketball games, Whiteside became best known as a beat reporter covering the Boston Red Sox; he became the first black reporter for a major American daily newspaper to cover Major League Baseball on a full-time basis and even traveled with the team.

The beginning of Whiteside's tenure at the *Globe* also coincided with a period of racial unrest in Boston, sparked by the issue of busing to counteract racial segregation in the city's school system. In 1974 U.S. District Court Judge W. Arthur Garrity ruled that the schools were unconstitutionally segregated and implemented a busing plan developed by the Massachusetts State Board of Education. Although Whiteside did not avoid addressing racial issues in his reporting, he was not in a position that allowed him the latitude to report on race or other issues unless they directly affected the Boston Red Sox. The last Major League Baseball team to integrate, the Red Sox had a problematic history in regard to race. Whiteside was acutely aware of his role as a pioneer in the press box and sought to avoid being stereotyped as a writer known only for his writing on race. As Dave Smith, who succeeded Roberts as the *Globe* sports editor, later told the newspaper, Whiteside was "Low-key when it came to racial issues. He obviously realized his position at the time. It was groundbreaking, so to speak, and he knew what responsibilities he had and handled them well" (*Boston Globe*, 16 June 2007).

In 1985, for instance, black Red Sox coach Tommy Harper went public with a complaint that for many years during spring training white members of the Red Sox had received passes to a nearby segregated Elks Club, an act that revealed a shocking level of racial insensitivity in the Red Sox front office. When the story became public, the team severed ties with the Elks Club; but at the end of the season the team fired Harper, causing him to file a complaint with the Federal Equal Opportunity Commission. As Whiteside later told Bryant, he had become aware of the issue twelve years before in 1973. Whiteside had discussed the Elks incident with Harper, who had been an outfielder with the team and whom Whiteside knew from Harper's days playing for the Milwaukee Brewers. Harper was offended, as was Whiteside. He wanted to write the story at the time, but Harper talked him out of it because, as Bryant noted, "They were both new in town … Whiteside was the only black in the press box…. Neither needed the heat of a racial scandal" (Bryant, 125). Yet Whiteside did not ignore the issue. On several occasions he even asked for a pass to the Elks Club just to see if he would be turned down, and he was. After Harper's 1985 complaint, Whiteside backed the player publicly, telling *New York Times* reporter David Margolick that he found the practice personally "appalling," but that he had not written about it because "I always felt I was there to cover the news, not to make it" (*Boston Globe*, 23 Mar. 1986).

Among the most notable events Whiteside covered while at the *Globe* were the 1978 American League Eastern Division playoff games between the Red Sox and the New York Yankees, the 1986 World Series, and pitcher Roger Clemens's record-setting twenty-strikeout performances in 1986 and 1996. In addition to his newspaper writing, Whiteside occasionally contributed magazine pieces to *Baseball Digest* and the *Sporting News*. In 1973 the Milwaukee Press Club gave him the Sports Writer of the Year Award. In 1987 he became the first sportswriter to receive a John S. Knight Professional Journalism Fellowship at Stanford University, where he studied law and labor issues from 1987 to 1988. In 1999 Whiteside received a career achievement award from the National Association of Black Journalists. His final byline in the *Globe* appeared on 24 August 2000, and in 2002 he received a legacy award from Boston's Sports Museum. Whiteside retired from the *Globe* in 2004, and in the spring of 2007 he was nominated by the Boston Chapter of the Baseball Writers Association of America for the J. G. Taylor Spink Award, the association's highest honor. In his final years, Whiteside suffered a stroke and was afflicted with Parkinson's disease. He died at Kindred Hospital-Boston in Brighton, Massachusetts, at age sixty-nine.

FURTHER READING

Bryant, Howard. *Shutout: A Story of Race and Baseball in Boston* (2002).

Gaspar, Christopher L. "Larry Whiteside; *Globe* Writer Aided Other Black Journalists," *Boston Globe* (June 2007).

Who's Who Among Black Americans, 1994–1995 (1994).

GLENN STOUT

Whitfield, James Monroe (10 Apr. 1822–23 Apr. 1871), poet, abolitionist, and emigrationist, was born in Exeter, New Hampshire, the son of parents whose names are unknown. Little else is known of his family except that he had a sister, a wife, two sons, and a daughter.

A celebrated poet, Whitfield published two volumes of poetry, *Poems* in 1846 and *America, and Other Poems* in 1853, the latter launching his career as an abolitionist and emigrationist. The authors Richard Barksdale and Keneth Kinnamon point out Lord Byron's influence on his poetry's "brooding melancholy and latent anger" but see his strong abolitionist protest as more important. His poem "America" voiced the paradox of America as he saw it: "a boasted land of liberty" and "a land of blood and crime." One of the most forceful writers and speakers for the abolitionist cause, Whitfield was seen by FREDERICK DOUGLASS as unjustly "buried in the precincts of a barber's shop" by the "malignant arrangements of society," and MARTIN ROBINSON DELANY appraised his potential to be the equal of John Greenleaf Whittier and Edgar Allan Poe. Jane R. Sherman praises Whitfield as "outstanding [among nineteenth-century black poets] for his metrical smoothness and breadth of classical imagery" and his poetry as "among the most robust and convincing of the time ... describ[ing] the crippling of a creative soul by race prejudice" (176).

Whitfield's life exemplifies the ambivalence of African Americans toward the emigration, abolitionist, and civil rights movements of the nineteenth century as well as the frustrations of talented African Americans barred from the pursuits of higher education. On one hand he signed the 1853 Rochester Colored National Convention's "Address to the People of the United States" that called for whites to allow blacks full access to what Whitfield accepted as his "native land" in his poem "America"

and that simultaneously accepted segregation. On the other hand, a few months later he signed Delany's 1853 call for the National Emigration Convention and, in letters to the *Frederick Douglass Paper*, advocated emigration and the establishment of a black nation. As late as 1862 he, along with almost 240 blacks, petitioned Congress for funds to "promote the emigration of free colored resident natives of the United States to Africa or to the tropical regions of America" (Miller, 265).

Whitfield, along with JAMES THEODORE HOLLY and Martin Delany, became one of the most prominent supporters of nationalist emigration during the 1850s. Whitfield's letter to the *Frederick Douglass Paper* began the extended debate over the Rochester convention proposals and Delany's call for emigration. His exchanges with William J. Watkins, Douglass's associate editor, and subsequent letters from the public anticipated the death knell for a viable emigration movement. Whitfield argued the connection between blacks' acceptance of their separate position in American society, from which they would advocate their right to full participation, and emigration, from which they could form a separate black nationality to both elevate the race and free the slaves. He saw his embracing of emigration as a logical extension of the Rochester convention and the National Council it had established, and he advocated the emigration of a few blacks to form a nationality where they "can help strike an effective blow against the common foe" (Sherman, 174) should efforts for equality in the United States fail. By raising the nationality issue, Whitfield and Delany drew negative responses from Canadian and American blacks, who saw themselves as part of a nation already, and Douglass saw to it that his paper used its unprecedented influence to discredit the emigration movement. Nonetheless, Whitfield served as one of the five notable delegates to Delany's 1854 National Emigration Convention in Cleveland. That convention's constitution of the National Board of Commissioners was ridiculed by anti-emigrationists (who were by far the majority) as an impracticable and foolish plan of political neophytes. The national black community met the plan with either indifference or ambivalence, except in Cincinnati, where leaders sought unsuccessfully to rally black support for emigration in opposition to white supporters of slavery and colonization. White colonizationists advocated removal of all blacks from the United States. Black emigrationists, on the other hand, advocated voluntary emigration and sought to maintain family and political ties with those remaining in the United States to advance the uplift of the race.

Although Whitfield and significant other nationalist-emigrationists did not attend the 1858 Chatham (Canada) convention, with its broadened platform and more inclusive title, the Association for the Promotion of the Interests of the Colored People of Canada and the United States, that followed the Cleveland convention, he remained active in the emigration movement until 1858. He signed a prospectus (published in the *Provincial Freeman*, 6 Dec. 1856) for a quarterly to publicize the nationalist-emigrationist cause, the *African American Repository*. Whitfield edited the *Repository* for a year, publishing the first issue in July 1858.

Whitfield then moved to San Francisco and may have traveled to "tropical regions." Settling in California in 1862, he worked as a barber, briefly moving to Portland, Oregon, then to the towns of Placerville and Centerville in Idaho, before returning to establish a "hairdressing shop" in San Francisco. On New Year's Day on the fourth anniversary of the Emancipation Proclamation, Whitfield published *A Poem*, a history of the founding of America and of slavery and its effects. Whitfield dedicated this poem to PHILIP ALEXANDER BELL, the editor of the *Elevator*, a San Francisco publication in which Whitfield published poems and letters from 1867 to 1870.

Whitfield, a Masonic grand master of California, died in San Francisco of heart disease. He ranks among the leading articulate and prescient nationalist-emigrationists who, sadly foreseeing the intractability of American racism, embraced America's highest ideals and argued vociferously against racism while simultaneously struggling to realize the dream of establishing a black nation to free the slave and uplift the race worldwide.

FURTHER READING

Miller, Floyd J. *The Search for a Black Nationality: Black Emigration and Colonization, 1787–1863* (1975).

Robinson, William H. *Early Black American Poets* (1969).

Sherman, Jane R. "James Monroe Whitfield, Poet and Emigrationist: A Voice of Protest and Despair," *Journal of Negro History*, Apr. 1972.

This entry is taken from the *American National Biography* and is published here with the permission of the American Council of Learned Societies.

JOHNNELLA E. BUTLER

Whitfield, Norman Jesse (12 May 1943–16 Sept. 2008), songwriter, arranger, and record producer, was born in Harlem, New York. When Whitfield was a teenager, his family moved to Detroit, Michigan, where he graduated from Northwestern High School. Whitfield, who was initially known for his skill with a pool cue, displayed musical talent as a songwriter and record producer at Thelma Records as he worked with the Sonnettes and as a tambourinist for Richard "Popcorn" Wylie's group, Popcorn and the Mohawks.

Whitfield, desiring to work as a songwriter at Motown Records, was a frequent visitor to the company's headquarters at 2648 West Grand Boulevard, although Motown's founder, BERRY GORDY JR., ordered Whitfield to leave the premises on more than one occasion. Gordy was eventually impressed with Whitfield's determination to be affiliated with Motown, and he allowed Whitfield to assist Billie Jean Brown, who was in charge of quality control for the company. Whitfield's salary was fifteen dollars a week.

Whitfield's first success at Motown was "Pride and Joy" (1963), recorded by MARVIN GAYE and written by Whitfield, Gaye, and William "Mickey" Stevenson. The song ranked tenth on *Billboard*'s Pop Chart and second on *Billboard*'s R & B Chart. Over the years, Whitfield continued to team up with other songwriters including EDWARD HOLLAND, Cornelius Grant, and Barrett Strong, and their collaborations number among Motown's most memorable hit records. Whitfield's best-selling song, "I Heard It Through the Grapevine," was recorded by GLADYS KNIGHT and the Pips in 1967, reaching number two on the Pop Chart. One year later, Gaye's version of the song remained at the top of *Billboard*'s Pop Chart for seven weeks. Whitfield is especially known for his work with the Temptations. While SMOKEY ROBINSON wrote and produced the Temptations' earliest hits, Whitfield provided subsequent hits for the group including "Ain't Too Proud to Beg" (1966); "Beauty's Only Skin Deep" (1966); "(I Know) I'm Losing You" (1966); You're My Everything" (1967); "(Loneliness Made Me Realize) It's You That I Need" (1967); "I Wish It Would Rain" (1967); "I Could Never Love Another (After Loving You)" (1967); "Cloud Nine" (1968); "I Can't Get Next to You" (1969); "Runaway Child, Running Wild" (1968); "Don't Let the Joneses Get You Down" (1969); "Ball of Confusion (That's What the World Is Today)" (1970); "Psychedelic Shack" (1970); "Just My Imagination (Running Away with Me)" (1971); "Superstar (Remember How You Got Where You

Norman Whitfield arrives at the 35th annual induction ceremony for the National Academy of Popular Music's Songwriters Hall of Fame in New York on 10 June 2004. (AP images.)

Are)" (1971); and "Papa Was a Rollin' Stone" (1972). Whitfield received his first Grammy Award in 1972, when "Papa Was a Rollin' Stone" was named the "Best R&B Vocal Performance by a Group." With the exception of "Pride and Joy," all of the afore-mentioned songs were produced by Whitfield, who began producing records at Motown as early as 1964 with the Velvelettes' "Needle in a Haystack" and "He Was Really Saying Something." Whitfield shared writing credits on both songs. His additional hit records include EDWIN STARR's "War (What Is It Good For?)" (1970) and the Undisputed Truth's "Smiling Faces Sometimes" (1971).

Whitfield left Motown in the mid-1970s. In 1976 he wrote and produced the music for the film *Car Wash,* which featured the comedian RICHARD PRYOR in the starring role. The soundtrack album, recorded by the group Rose Royce on the MCA label, includes three hit singles: "Car Wash," "I Wanna Get Next to You," and "I'm Going Down." The title song, "Car Wash," was Number One on *Billboard*'s Pop and R&B

Charts. Also in 1976, Whitfield won the Grammy Award for "Album of Best Original Score Written for a Motion Picture or Television Special." Whitfield established his own record label and produced two additional Rose Royce albums; among the group's most successful songs from this period are "Wishing on a Star" (1977), "Ooh Boy" (1977), and "Love Don't Live Here Anymore" (1978). Whitfield Records' label was "W," which was the Motown logo, "M," inverted. In 1984 Whitfield returned to Motown Records to produce the Temptations' hit single, "Sail Away," a song cowritten by Whitfield. He was inducted into the Songwriters Hall of Fame in 2004.

Whitfield, who resided in Toluca Lake, California, died on 16 September 2008 in Los Angeles. His survivors include one daughter and four sons.

FURTHER READING

Dahl, Bill. *Motown: The Golden Years* (2001).

George, Nelson. *Where Did Our Love Go? The Rise and Fall of the Motown Sound* (1986).

Gordy, Berry. *To Be Loved: The Music, the Magic, the Memories of Motown: An Autobiography*. (1994).

Obituaries: *The New York Times*, 18 Sept. 2008; *USA Today*, 18 Sept. 2008; *New York Amsterdam News*, 25 Sept. 2006.

LINDA M. CARTER

Whitfield, Owen (14 Oct. 1892–11 Aug. 1965), labor organizer, community activist, preacher, and farmer, was born Owen Hones Whitfield into a sharecropping family near Jonestown, Mississippi, in the heart of the Delta. His father's name was Thomas Whitfield; his mother's name is unknown. Like most children in the cotton South, Whitfield attended school sporadically. The Whitfield family moved frequently in search of better farm-ing opportunities and often supplemented their income with wage work. During moves through Tennessee, Arkansas, and Mississippi, Whitfield was able to save enough money from odd jobs to enroll at Okolona College, a small Baptist college in Mississippi, in 1912. He studied theology for two years, during which time he met and married Zella Glass, a thirteen-year-old cotton picker.

Newly married and with the first of seven chil-dren on the way, Whitfield continued his search for profitable farming. In 1922 the Whitfields moved to southeast Missouri, a burgeoning new cotton frontier. There Whitfield joined a nascent commu-nity of migrants, many of whom were prosperous tenant farmers and landowners. These patriarchs nurtured their communities and kin groups with MARCUS GARVEY's black nationalist ideology. As young sharecroppers the Whitfields would have found themselves at the bottom of this hardening, hierarchical system based on land tenure, relative wealth, and the prerogatives of age. Yet Whitfield slowly rose in the community hierarchy. He made use of his education to assume leadership in four local churches by 1930. Preaching lent Whitfield newfound prestige and authority. It also placed him in close touch with the aspirations and hardships of the mass of poor farmers in his congregations.

The onset of the Great Depression of the 1930s and the effects of inequitable agricultural policies during the early New Deal decimated what rough prosperity these farmers had achieved. Cotton prices plummeted, and government efforts to raise them further reduced available farmland and provided incentives for plantation owners to evict their sharecroppers entirely. Community elders failed to confront the crisis. As a rising young leader, Whitfield was uniquely poised to address the concerns of his followers.

Whitfield came to see his preaching as a means of empowering the rural poor. After flirting with a radical variant of black nationalism in 1934 he became attracted to the efforts of the Socialist-led Southern Tenant Farmers' Union (STFU), a labor organization of white and black tenant farmers combating unfair government policies. In the summer of 1936 Claude Williams, a white radical preacher and union official, convinced Whitfield that the STFU was the right vehicle for mobilizing Christian radicalism for political purposes. Whitfield's successful promulgation of a working-class gospel catapulted him into the union leadership.

Beginning in 1937 Whitfield mobilized his fellow tenant farmers to demand that the New Deal ensure their basic social and economic rights. By 1938, however, he increasingly became convinced that the STFU had to multiply its power to cause change. He was central to the STFU decision to join the Communist-led United Canning, Agricultural, and Packing and Allied Workers of America (UCAPAWA), an affiliate of the Congress of Industrial Unions (CIO), that year. Whitfield argued that the CIO would unite his followers with a national movement and that the CIO "culture of unity" would help build trust between black and white farmers in the South.

Looking to apply the power of this new alliance to alleviate the suffering of landless farmers, Whitfield organized a roadside protest of more than 1,500 destitute sharecroppers along major highways in southeast Missouri in January 1939. Their display of poverty caused by unfair agricultural policy, Whitfield reasoned, would force the federal government to intervene. It worked. The protest startled the nation and President Franklin D. Roosevelt. In February 1939 Whitfield aired the demands of rural workers to Roosevelt himself in the Oval Office. He was able to secure an expansion of federal efforts to aid poor farmers, including an ambitious public housing scheme and a public health program. He also helped acquire land in Missouri where evicted sharecroppers founded a cooperative settlement known as Cropperville.

Almost overnight Whitfield emerged as a national labor leader and activist. The recipient of an award from the Schomburg Library in Harlem, New York, Whitfield was feted by New York mayor Fiorello LaGuardia and President Roosevelt again in early 1940. That same year he electrified the National Negro Congress (NNC) meeting with his calls to use religion to mobilize civil rights and labor activism. Through groups such as the NNC, which was dedicated to using labor unions to push for civil rights, Whitfield provided a key link between agricultural and industrial workers, especially in the South.

Whitfield's new role led him into industrial campaigns in urban areas. In 1942 UCAPAWA reassigned him to Memphis, Tennessee, to organize workers in the cotton-processing industry. There he used his radical gospel to appeal to black and white workers, many of them recently from the fields. Whitfield worked in conjunction with the People's Institute of Applied Religion, a group created by Claude Williams. Whitfield later joined UCAPAWA's tobacco workers' strike in Winston-Salem, North Carolina. In addition to this union work he organized a citizens' committee to register black voters and helped direct a local electoral campaign.

These years exhausted Whitfield. While remaining a UCAPAWA officer, Whitfield returned to Cropperville in late 1943. There he used the exigencies of World War II to embolden his demands for federal aid to the rural poor. In 1944, however, his wife, Zella, fell ill, and Whitfield retreated from public view. He continued to speak for the People's Institute, for the most part locally, but increasingly he focused on raising food to support the war effort. He briefly worked for the St. Louis Council of the National Negro Congress in 1946. Whitfield's previous relations with Communists dogged him. In the early stages of the postwar Red Scare, his institutional allies either disbanded or cut back their activities because of political pressure. In addition, conservatives in Congress gutted many of the New Deal programs that Whitfield had helped bring to the aid of the rural poor. Though his public career was over, he did write occasionally for the *National Guardian*, a progressive weekly published by Cedric Belfrage, after 1948. Claiming the need for better schooling for their children, the Whitfields left Cropperville in 1950. Whitfield continued to preach at a series of area churches, finally settling in Mounds, Illinois. He died in Cape Girardeau, Missouri, in 1965.

In his lifetime, Whitfield worked to transform the aspirations and struggles of black southerners, first in the cotton fields of southeast Missouri and later in southern cities, into concerted collective action in pursuit of social and economic justice. He did this by refashioning their core beliefs in the power of religion, the dignity of hard work, and the life-giving bonds of family and civic responsibility into a vibrant indigenous protest movement tooled for the political realities of the New Deal. Whitfield's career illustrates the rich network of interchange between urban and rural working-class movements, locating the roots of the civil rights unionism of the 1940s in lives and labors of rural southerners.

FURTHER READING

The papers of the Southern Tenant Farmers' Union, located at the University of North Carolina at Chapel Hill, contain a number Whitfield's writings.

Cantor, Louis. *Prologue to the Protest Movement: The Missouri Sharecropper Roadside Demonstration of 1939* (1969).

Roll, Jarod H., and Erik S. Gellman. "Owen Whitfield and the Gospel of the Working Class in New Deal America, 1936–1946," *Journal of Southern History* 72 (May 2006).

Obituary: *New York Times*, 13 Aug. 1965.

JAROD H. ROLL

Whitman, Albery Allson (30 May 1851–29 June 1901), epic poet and clergyman, was born in Hart County, Kentucky. His father, Caswell Whitman, was enslaved, and the status of his mother, born Caroline Bronner (sometimes Brawner), is uncertain. Albery was one of five children born to the pair. He had two older siblings, Richard Gillem and David Whitfield, and two younger siblings, Julia Catherine and Robert Taylor.

Albery Whitman is an enigma in the realm of African American history, both literary and social. Unlike many figures who achieved relative prominence, Whitman left no autobiography or memoirs to offer clues to his eventful life. From the time of his birth until 1 January 1863 he was a slave, working on the plantation of his birth. At the age of twelve Albery became an orphan. After the death of his father he began a brief career as an itinerant worker, working in many different towns throughout Kentucky and Ohio, developing an affinity for travel that stayed with him the rest of his years. Between 1864 and 1870 Whitman worked in a plough shop and with a railroad construction crew. During this time he also attended school, though his formal education remained sparse by any standards. Whitman was, however, able to obtain enough education to become a primary teacher. He went on to teach in both Kentucky and Ohio.

The year 1870 found Whitman enrolled as a student at Wilberforce University. At Wilberforce, a recently founded institution of higher learning with strong ties to the African Methodist Episcopal (AME) Church, he met the Reverend DANIEL ALEXANDER PAYNE, the first president and founder of Wilberforce University and an AME minister, who became an influential force in Whitman's life. Though no records of Whitman's graduation have been found, at least one source, JAMES CORROTHERS, asserts in his 1916 autobiography, *In Spite of the Handicap*, that Whitman had indeed graduated from Wilberforce (64). In any event, he continued his association with Wilberforce and its president for several years to come. Around this time Whitman began his work with the AME Church. He was no stranger to the profession; at least one brother, Richard, preceded him in the ministerial work, and his younger brother, Robert, was also ordained as a minister.

In 1871 Whitman published his first work of poetry. However, no extant copies of *Essays on the Ten Plagues and Miscellaneous Poems* have been found. *Leelah Misled* followed quickly in 1873. His second work of epic poetry tells the story of a young white woman seduced by a philandering plantation owner.

In 1874 Whitman worked in Springfield, Ohio, continuing his ministry within the AME Church. In the *Christian Recorder* Whitman described the process of building a church there and the subsequent visit and compliments from the Reverend Payne. From there, Whitman traveled throughout Ohio, helping to build churches and delivering sermons as an AME minister. He was noted for his eloquence in sermonizing and his enthusiasm in helping to build, literally and figuratively, the AME

Church. Letters litter the archives of the *Christian Recorder*, singing Whitman's praises and characterizing him as noble, talented, and successful. For his part, Whitman seemed sincere about his work and gratified about the praise that he received from his mentor, Bishop Daniel Payne.

Not a Man and Yet a Man, Whitman's third work, was published in 1877. The hero of this work, Rodney, is mixed race and endures many of the harrowing dangers of slavery, including sale into a harsher slavery in the Deep South. This poem received much notice from the literary world. Payne noted, in his 1888 memoir *Recollections of Seventy Years*, that both William Cullen Bryant and Henry Wadsworth Longfellow, two of Whitman's literary idols, had given favorable reviews of the work.

Whitman's lasting esteem for Wilberforce and for Payne is evident in the preface to the poem as well. It includes a dedication to the university for its role in producing educated black leaders. Also in the preface, Whitman described himself as a general financial agent of the school. He did not offer any further explanation of the attachment; however, a portion of the proceeds from sales of the book went toward the maintenance of the school. In addition, Whitman composed an original sacred lyric, which was performed at the dedication of Wilberforce on 20 June 1878, and he took part in these proceedings.

During this time, Whitman met and married Kate, affectionately "Caddie," White. No records have been found to indicate an exact date of marriage, but their first child, Caswell, was born in 1875. Altogether the couple had four children, and they may have adopted a fifth. The Whitmans' four daughters went on to enjoy a bit of fame themselves, as a vaudeville act.

Records of the Whitmans, in 1880, locate the family in Kentucky. At this time Albery Whitman was quite active in the Richmond Conference of the church. The early part of this decade saw the Whitman family's steady progression westward. They moved first to Arkansas, then Kansas, and finally Texas, where Whitman's efforts to build churches and deliver sermons continued. In 1884 he published perhaps his most controversial work, *The Rape of Florida*, which was republished as *Twasinta's Seminoles* in 1885. By this time the tone of his preface had changed. It challenged more strongly the placid acceptance of racism by African Americans, urging an emancipation of both body and mind.

The Reverend W. J. SIMMONS, in *Men of Mark* (1887), placed Whitman in Kansas and in poor health in 1887. There are suggestions that he struggled throughout his career with alcoholism, and his deteriorating physical condition could have been related to that. Despite the fact that there is no evidence that his careers as a clergyman and author suffered as a result, Payne does refer, in his memoirs, to Whitman's consumption of alcohol, blaming it for Whitman's failure to rise to prominence as an American author.

Meanwhile, having returned to Kansas, Whitman by 1890 was ministering at the St. James Church in Lawrence. A few years later, in 1893, he published *The World's Fair Poem*, which represented a departure from his normally epic style. The collection of two poems, "The World's Fair Poem" and "The Freedman's Triumphant Song," protested against white stereotypes about African Americans and endorsed African Americans as meaningful contributors to American life. The publication of *The World's Fair Poem* came on the heels of the Chicago World's Fair, from which African Americans were almost summarily excluded. The title poem was presented at the Memorial Art Palace in Chicago on 22 September 1893. Among those gathered for the occasion were other elders of the AME Church, all for the purpose of protesting the discrimination evident in the planning and implementation of the exposition.

Whitman ended his careers in both the church and as an author in Atlanta, Georgia. In 1899 he ministered at St. Phillip's Church in Savannah, Georgia. Early in 1901 he published his final work, *An Idyl of the South*; like "The World's Fair Poem," *Idyl* was a collection of two shorter poems, "The Octoroon" and "The Southland's Charms and Freedom's Magnitude." Again, as many scholars note, the tone of his preface in this work is significantly changed from that of earlier works; it is almost conciliatory. While on a lecture circuit in Anniston, Alabama, in 1901, Whitman contracted pneumonia. He returned to Atlanta, dying from the illness one week later.

Of Whitman, REVERDY C. RANSOM wrote, "This man, I think, was lonely. There were few among us with whom he could have communion of mind and spirit" (*The Pilgrimage of Harriet Ransom's Son* [1949]: 64). Given the scarcity of information about his life, this pronouncement becomes all the more poignant. Most of the texts contain only short paragraphs that mention the man, his works, and his writings. Though there are records praising his eloquence, no extant sermons have been found. Similarly, though he was a noted poet in the nineteenth century and one of the earliest known

African American epic poets, his work has been the subject of only a few substantial critical inquiries. In the early twenty-first century, however, his poetry began to receive long overdue attention. Perhaps the resurging scholarly interest will enable a younger generation to establish a new communion with a man who, in many ways, was representative of his time.

FURTHER READING

Whitman, Albery A. *Leelah Misled* (1873).

Whitman, Albery A. *Not a Man and Yet a Man* (1877).

Brawley, Benjamin. *The Negro Genius: A New Appraisal of the Achievement of the American Negro in Literature and the Fine Arts* (1937).

Payne, Daniel A. *Recollections of Seventy Years* (1888).

Simmons, William J. *Men of Mark* (1887).

LAROSE M. DAVIS

Whitman, Alice, Alberta, Essie, and Mabel, vaudeville musical group known as the Whitman Sisters. Mabel (1880–1942), Essie (1882–1963), and Alberta (1888–1964) were the daughters of ALBERY ALLSON WHITMAN, a minister in the African Methodist Episcopal church (and a notable poet), and his wife Caddie Whitman. A fourth member of the group was Alice (1900–1969). There were rumors about Alice's parentage, but no definitive information has yet been found. She may have been a fourth daughter of Albery and Caddie, or she may have been adopted after Albery's death (for more see George-Graves, p. 25 and n. 53). Whatever the circumstances of her birth or membership in the Whitman family, Alice was in any case considered one of the four Whitman Sisters in the singing group. The Whitmans also had a brother, Caswell. They began performing by singing and dancing in their father's church and on evangelical tours. Then in 1899 Will Accooe, a musical director who worked on many black musical comedy productions, such as *A Trip to Coontown*, *The Cannibal King*, and *The Sons of Ham*, created a short singing and dancing skit for Essie and Mabel, who rented a hall and started performing professionally. They then began touring Missouri and Florida managed by their mother under the name the Danzette Sisters. Their first big break came as a filler act at the Orpheum Theater in Kansas City. In a *Chicago Defender* article, Mabel claimed that they were an instantaneous hit. They then signed to tour the predominately white Orpheum and Kohl & Castle circuits. They toured several white circuits including the Greenwald circuit, the Keith & Proctor circuit, the Percy C.

Williams circuit, and the Poli & Fox circuit. Alberta joined her sisters on a European tour, where according to the Whitman relative Ernestine Lucas, the sisters gave a command performance before British royalty. Eventually they changed the name of the act to The Whitman Sisters' New Orleans Troubadours and began signing other performers.

In 1905 they moved their base of operations from Atlanta to Chicago as part of the Great Migration. Although based in the Midwest, they often performed in New York, Washington, D.C., and the South. Even though they played for both white and black audiences, many accounts praised the Whitmans for staying "loyal" to their black constituency. At a time when any successful black person became a symbol for the possibilities of the entire race, the Whitmans served their community well. In return, black audiences stayed loyal to the Whitman Sisters.

The act was always considered a class act with no "blue" (bawdy) material. The sisters also ensured their respectable reputation by insisting on a strict moral code for themselves and the other performers. In a new town, they always visited the church, gave generously as the collection plate was passed and even performed in churches.

Working with the Whitman Sisters was the nonpareil of arts educations. Company members learned to sing, dance, act, and tell jokes. They also learned how to behave themselves. Boys and girls could not travel together unless married. All children were required to take school lessons with Dave Payton (Mabel's husband). And if anyone was caught breaking the rules, he or she was immediately fired. Parents knew that their children were safer touring with the Whitman Sisters than with other companies. Mabel and her sisters served as surrogate mothers.

Alice Whitman, the youngest sister, who had been caring for Caddie in her final days, joined the group in 1909 after their mother's passing. Baby Alice, as she was known, was famous for her cutesy, girly singing and dancing. She also switched images and became the sex symbol of the company. She did the shimmy, the shake, and snake-hips. She performed in a duet act with sister Alberta who dressed as a man. Alberta became the dapper beau brummel to Alice's ingénue. She did one of the first "flash" acts, which consisted of crowd-pleasing acrobatics along with dance. Essie was known for her record-breaking low contralto singing voice that reportedly made Sophie Tucker sound like a soprano.

Mabel also sang and danced. She created a "pick" (or pickaninny) act called *Mabel Whitman and the*

Dixie Boys in which she surrounded herself with very talented children. However, her most important role was as the company manager. Because of her hard work the company enjoyed atypical success and longevity. In the early years, she insisted on keeping all production responsibilities in the family. Mabel handled bookings and business, Essie designed and built costumes, and Alberta was the accountant and composer. During these years, Mabel Whitman was said to have been the only black woman managing her own company and booking them at the best southern venues. Mabel's status as female entrepreneur and independent manager-owner of the Whitman Sisters was an exception to the rule, and she offered a rare opportunity for black performers to work for a black manager in a black show. According to Bill Reed, "no finer actor-manager ever existed than the act's unquestioned leader, Mabel Whitman."

For over forty years, the Whitman Sisters persevered in the face of wars, the Great Depression, and the decline of vaudeville. The show offered something for everyone: jubilee songs and coon shouts, cakewalks and breakdowns, comedians, midgets, cross-dressers, beautiful dancing girls, pickaninnies, a jazz band, and, after their invention in the 1920s, talkies. One of the favorite acts that went on to further fame was the comedy duo of Butterbeans and Susie (JODIE "BUTTERBEANS" EDWARDS and his wife, Susie Edwards). They performed a husband-and-wife act in which the henpecked husband had to negotiate issues with his domineering, nagging wife. Butterbeans was a particularly small man which added to the comedy as he tried to stand up to his much-larger wife. Susie sang the blues and cakewalked, and Butterbeans performed the Itch, also known as the Heebie Jeebies, in which he scratched himself in syncopation.

In another act the sisters performed in black-haired wigs and blackface. At one point they left the stage, took off the make-up and wigs, let their dyed blonde hair down, and came back onstage. Essie claimed, "The audience was always puzzled and someone was sure to ask, 'What are those white women doing up there?' Then they would recognize us as the performers and laugh in amazement" (Sterns, p. 86).

In a third act Mabel performed a plantation act similar to typical minstrel shows. However, in addition to having the stereotypical Mammy figure happily cooking while children sang and danced, Mabel also sang religious songs to elevate this complicated and highly problematic racialized image.

Part of the Whitman Sisters' significance is due to the ways in which they negotiated race, class, and gender on and off stage: They passed for white; Mabel complicated the images and symbolism of minstrelsy; Alberta was a skilled cross-dresser; and they insisted on integrated audiences. No matter what buttons they were pushing, however, they always maintained a very high-class, respectable reputation. By doing this they were allowed to challenge other norms.

Whatever the weather, crowds packed into the standing-room-only local theater house, or perhaps a black church set up to accommodate theatrics, to see the Whitman Sisters revue. If they could not get inside they waited outside to catch a glimpse of the show or to hear some of the songs. The reviews in the paper were usually raves. All of the most distinguished members of the African American community, including professionals and the clergy, went to see the Whitman Sisters, who for a few weeks at a time would take a city by storm.

In 1928, the Whitman Sisters bought a new house in Chicago, which became a home base for many traveling African American performers. During the Depression, Essie founded the Theatrical Cheer Club to aid performers down on their luck.

In the later years of the company the Whitman Sisters joined the black vaudeville traveling circuit TOBA, which alternately stood for Theater Owners' Booking Association, Tough on Black Actors, and Tough on Black Asses. The circuit earned its reputation due to the difficult conditions and poor salaries. The Whitman Sisters had top billing, however, and were therefore spared many of the hardships of the lesser acts.

From 1930 to 1943 the company produced at least six shows that toured on TOBA and in independent black houses. The known shows are *Faststeppers* (1930), *Spirit of 1930* (1930), *Wake up Chillun'* (1930), *January Jubilee* (1931), *Step Lively Girls* (1931), and *Swing Revue* (1936). After *Swing Revue* closed, Alice went on to perform in other New York revues and was a soloist in nightclubs and theaters. That same year Essie survived a serious car accident and claimed that God had called her to do religious work. She left the stage for the pulpit and became an evangelist.

The Whitman Sisters company struggled to stay active after *Swing Revue* but finally folded after Mabel's death in 1942 from pneumonia.

In May 1963, a fire destroyed the sisters' home on Chicago's Southside. Alberta, then age seventy-four, escaped the flames by herself, and Alice, sixty-three, was carried down a ladder by firefighters. But

Essie, who was eighty-one and had been suffering from a heart ailment, was rushed to Provident Hospital after firefighters carried her from the second floor of the house. She died in the hospital of a combination of shock, burns, and smoke inhalation.

The next year Alberta passed away in Chicago after a "prolonged illness." In 1969 Alice died of a cerebral hemorrhage in Chicago.

Mabel, Essie, Alberta, and Alice left behind them an important legacy. The helped launch the careers of many entertainment stars including COUNT BASIE, Bunny Briggs, Jeni Legon, Willie Robinson, Butterbeans and Susie, BILLY KERSANDS, JACKIE "MOMS" MABLEY, MA RAINEY, and ETHEL WATERS. They helped move the industry away from racist practices. They provided entertainment for countless black and white audiences. And they challenged assumptions about race and gender identity. They well deserved the title the Royalty of Negro Vaudeville.

FURTHER READING

George-Graves, Nadine. *The Royalty of Negro Vaudeville: The Whitman Sisters and the Negotiation of Race, Gender and Class in African American Theatre, 1900–1940* (2000).

Stearns, Jean, and Marshall. *Jazz Dance: The Story of American Vernacular Dance* (1994).

NADINE GEORGE-GRAVES

Whittaker, Johnson Chesnut (23 Aug. 1858–14 Jan. 1931), military cadet and educator, was born one of a set of twins, on the plantation of James Chesnut Sr. near Camden, South Carolina, the son of James Whitaker, a freedman, and Maria J. (maiden name unknown), a slave. His twin brother died in an accident at the age of thirteen.

Johnson Whittaker (he added the second *t* sometime later in life) spent his early years in slavery, his mother at times serving as personal slave to Maria Boykin Chesnut, the author of *A Diary from Dixie* (1905). His father had purchased his own freedom, but at the birth of the twins he refused responsibility for them and an older son because he insisted that never before had twins been born in his family.

With the coming of emancipation, Whittaker and his mother, both light-skinned, took up residence in Camden, where she worked as a domestic and Johnson attended a freedman's school. After five years he began receiving special tutoring from a local black minister while he worked as a bricklayer's assistant. In 1874 he entered the University of South Carolina, briefly integrated during Reconstruction, in Columbia. He did so well during his two years there that one of his teachers, RICHARD GREENER, Harvard's first black graduate, recommended him as a candidate for appointment to West Point. He entered the military academy in 1876 on the nomination of a local white Republican congressman, S. L. Hoze.

The man destined to become the military academy's first black graduate, HENRY O. FLIPPER, was in his final year when Whittaker arrived. The two men shared a room because no white cadet would room with either of them. Flipper passed along his nonviolence philosophy, which Whittaker, who was deeply religious, accepted enthusiastically. Throughout his time at West Point, he responded to insults and total social ostracism with patience. He refused to allow any provocation to take his mind off his ultimate goal—graduation. When a white cadet struck him, for example, Whittaker did not fight back but reported the offender to academy authorities. As a result, West Point cadets labeled him a coward.

On 6 April 1880, as Whittaker slept alone in a two-man room, three masked men entered, dragged him out of his bed, lashed his legs to the bed's side, and tied his arms in front of him. They slashed his ear lobes, gouged his hair, and made him look into a mirror that they then smashed against his forehead. He later recalled hearing one say, "Let us mark him as we mark hogs down South." After they had completed their vicious work, the attackers warned Whittaker not to make any noise. "Cry out, or speak of this affair, and you are a dead man," they said, and also told him he should leave the academy.

The next morning, when Whittaker was absent from reveille, another cadet was sent to his room and discovered him unconscious, surrounded by pools of blood. West Point authorities quickly decided that he had mutilated himself to avoid final examinations two months later.

General John M. Schofield, the military academy superintendent, established a court of inquiry to begin meeting on 9 April. The board took more than three thousand pages of testimony, some of it casting grave doubts on the West Point position. Nonetheless, it found Whittaker guilty of mutilating himself. Hoping to clear his name, Whittaker demanded a court-martial. A panel that began hearings on 3 February 1881 recorded nine thousand pages of testimony. After taking his June 1880 oral examinations, Whittaker was placed on leave.

Meanwhile, O. O. Howard, the onetime head of the Freedmen's Bureau, replaced Schofield as West Point superintendent.

Like the court of inquiry, the court-martial was a national cause célèbre. Three presidents (Rutherford B. Hayes, James A. Garfield, and Chester A. Arthur), army commanding general William T. Sherman, and the nation's major newspapers all followed these judicial proceedings closely. Former South Carolina Governor Daniel Chamberlain and leading army lawyer Asa Bird Gardiner were on opposite sides in the four-month trial. Once again Whittaker was found guilty; his race continued to be the major determinant in the military court decision.

On 1 December 1881 the army's judge advocate general, D. G. Swaim, found irregularities and prejudice in the proceedings and overturned the decision. Benjamin Brewster, the attorney general, agreed on 17 March 1882, and five days later President Arthur officially threw out the guilty verdict. Whittaker was exonerated. That same day, however, Secretary of War Robert T. Lincoln, the Great Emancipator's son, issued an army special order discharging Whittaker from the military academy for failing an oral examination in June 1880. Whittaker was innocent of wrongdoing, but he was separated from the academy anyway.

Whittaker tried for several years to fight the dismissal, even going on a brief national speaking tour to drum up support. "With God as my guide," he said in his first speech, "duty as my watchword, I can, I must, I will win a place in life!" Unsuccessful in his efforts to reverse the dismissal, he moved back to South Carolina, where he became a teacher in Charleston and Sumter, a member of the South Carolina bar in 1885, and a lawyer and school principal in Sumter. In 1890 he married Page Harrison, the daughter of a white Sumter city employee and his black wife. They had two sons, one of whom became a college president.

In 1900 Whittaker became secretary of the college and principal of the academy at the Colored Normal, Industrial, Agricultural, and Mechanical College of South Carolina (later South Carolina State University) in Orangeburg. In 1908, because of a son's asthma, the family moved from Orangeburg to Oklahoma City, where they had to contend with nightly gunfire when they moved into a white neighborhood. Whittaker became a teacher at all-black Douglass High School and in the early 1920s became the school's principal. One of his students was the future novelist RALPH ELLISON.

In 1925, at the age of sixty-seven, Whittaker returned to the black college in Orangeburg, South Carolina, again as principal of the academy. He maintained his post until his death there, a revered teacher but unknown outside of his community. It was not until the publication of a book about him and a made-for-television motion picture (*Assault at West Point*, 1994) that Whittaker received the lieutenant's bars denied him in the 1880s. On 24 July 1995 in a White House ceremony, President Bill Clinton presented to Whittaker's descendants a posthumous commission.

FURTHER READING

The records of his court of inquiry and his court-martial are preserved in the Records of the Judge Advocate General (Army), RG 153, National Archives.

Marszalek, John F. *Assault at West Point: The Court Martial of Johnson Whittaker* (1994).

Marszalek, John F. *Court-Martial: A Black Man in America* (1972).

This entry is taken from the *American National Biography* and is published here with the permission of the American Council of Learned Societies.

JOHN F. MARSZALEK

Whittaker, Miller F. (30 Dec. 1892–14 Nov. 1949), professor, architect, and college president, was born Miller Fulton Whittaker in Sumter, South Carolina, to JOHNSON CHESNUT WHITTAKER and Page Harrison Whittaker on 30 December 1892. His father, a former cadet at the United States Military Academy at West Point, was at the center of a violent racial incident in early April 1880 in which he was found unconscious and bound to his bed with slashed earlobes and his hair cut in several places. Having been court-martialed and found guilty of fabricating a story (self-inflicted wounds), Whittaker was expelled from the academy. Two years later, U.S. President Chester A. Arthur overturned his court-martial; nevertheless, the expulsion was upheld. Johnson Whittaker served as a teacher at the Avery Institute in Charleston, South Carolina, and would later be admitted to the South Carolina bar where he practiced law in Sumter in 1885. Johnson Whittaker later served as a professor at the historically black South Carolina State College (State College) in Orangeburg from 1900 to 1908 and 1925 to 1931.

Miller Whittaker was educated during his early years at Sumter City Schools, attended the Normal Department at State College, and later graduated from Oklahoma City High School. He received a

B.S. degree in 1913 and a M.S. degree in 1928, both from Kansas State College. He also studied at Harvard and Cornell.

Whittaker, a registered architect in the state of South Carolina and Georgia, served as a professor of physics at State College from 1913 until 1932. During his tenure, he headed the Division of Mechanic Arts and designed and supervised the construction of several buildings on campus. During World War I, Whittaker was commissioned as a second lieutenant and spent a year in France serving with the 371st and 368th Infantry regiments.

On 30 May 1932, Whittaker was officially named the third president of South Carolina State College after the death of then current president Robert Shaw Wilkinson sixteen days earlier. During his seventeen-year tenure as president of State College, Whittaker made sweeping reforms to the institution. He raised the academic standards by seeking to recruit faculty who held doctoral degrees (this would not be a reality until the end of his tenure and during the next administration), implemented a faculty ranking and tenure system, and required faculty members to engage in professional activity and join professional organizations in their respective fields.

The reorganization of the instructional program during Whittaker's administration was vital. The institution was placed on the approved lists of colleges of the Southern Association of Colleges and Secondary Schools (SACSS) in 1932 and would be categorized as a *Class A* college by 1941. Recognized by SACSS, State College moved away from the industrial-agricultural educational model (which was the common educational curriculum for black schools) to a college that offered a both a liberal arts and industrial-agricultural curriculum along with a graduate and professional schools (law) during Whittaker's tenure. The institution also phased out its high school department, which had long provided an invaluable service to many African American high school students who attended segregated, inferior schools or had no high school to attend in the state of South Carolina (the former Morehouse college president Dr. BENJAMIN MAYS benefited from State College's high school). The War Department also approved a ROTC unit, and the institution experienced physical growth both from a surge of returning servicemen (World War II) and a series of academic, administrative, and residence halls.

Despite the many improvements of State College during his tenure, as the president of a state-supported black institution in the segregated South, Whittaker faced many problems. State College was disproportionately allocated the least amount of money in comparison to the four other state-supported institutions (which were all white). Moreover, then-governor J. Strom Thurmond often used President Whittaker's office to secretly visit his daughter (ESSIE MAE WASHINGTON-WILLIAMS), who was a student at State College during the 1950s. Whittaker understood the political implications if he did not comply with the racial status quo. Like his successor BENNER C. TURNER, dean from 1950–1967, Whittaker chose not to challenge the status quo and was subsequently rewarded by the state with funding—albeit modestly—allowing him to improve the conditions at his institution.

Like college presidents throughout the United States he also presided over a time of significant social change. There were significant challenges to the traditional relations between the races, the sexes, and young and old. Prior to the 1954 *Brown* decision, there were several Supreme Court and federal court decisions that challenged racial segregation in graduate in professional schools. In 1947, John Wrighten, an African American World War II veteran, successfully sued to be admitted into the University of South Carolina School of Law. The federal judge ruled that the Wrighten had to be admitted or the State of South Carolina had to create a separate but equal law school for African Americans. The South Carolina General Assembly immediately created a law school on the campus of State College appointing BENNER C. TURNER (a Harvard Law graduate and then law professor at North Carolina Central College in Durham) as its dean.

Like other racial diplomats in the segregated south, Whittaker had to walk a tightrope to please both the white power structure in South Carolina and African American students and their families. He faced a major test of his loyalties when he was asked to testify by THURGOOD MARSHALL in June of 1947 during John Wrighten's suit to desegregate the University of South Carolina's law school. Maceo Nance, who would later serve as the fifth president of State College and who was a student at the time, noted that Whittaker "was in a very uncomfortable and untenable position" ("Maceo Nance"). While he had the legal obligation to comply with the racial status quo of South Carolina and support a separate black law school, Whittaker testified that a law school with no library, no classroom, and no faculty would not be feasible to begin operation that September. His testimony helped Marshall and the NAACP Legal Defense Fund to successfully win the suit that forced the state of South Carolina to desegregate the University of South Carolina's law school, create a truly separate but equal law school for African Americans, or abolish legal education in the state of South Carolina.

Whittaker suffered a series of heart attacks in 1949 and eventually succumbed to one on 14 November 1949. Benner C. Turner, the dean of the law school, would later be officially named as the fourth president of State College on 1 August 1950 and would carry on Whittaker's agenda of advancing the institution. Whittaker never married or had children. He was a member of Williams Chapel AME Church (in Orangeburg) and Omega Psi Phi Fraternity. Miller Whittaker faced many challenges that reflected the travails of the black college president during the early and mid-twentieth century. He was willing, to a degree, to remain silent on social issues with the understanding that the governor and state legislature would award appropriations and improve the conditions of the institution; nevertheless, it should be acknowledged that he successfully administered and improved academic standards at State College through the Great Depression, World War II, and the early NAACP efforts to integrate education.

FURTHER READING

Burke, William L., and William C. Hine. "The South Carolina State College Law School: Its Roots, Creation, and Legacy," in W. Lewis Burke and Belinda F. Gergel, eds., *Matthew J. Perry: The Man, His Times, and His Legacy* (2004).

Cho, Nancy. "Johnson C. Whittaker." BlackPast.org, accessed 2 November 2010, http://www.blackpast. org/?q=aah/whittaker-johnson-c-1858-1931

"Maceo Nance." William C. Hine Oral History Interviews, 14 March 1989. South Carolina State University Historical Collections, Miller F. Whittaker Library.

Potts, John F. *A History of South Carolina State College* (1978).

Reid, Richard. "The S.C. State Presidency; Miller F. Whittaker," *The (Orangeburg) Times and Democrat,* 27 May 2008.

Obituary: "Dr. Whittaker, State College, Dies." *Times and Democrat,* 15 November 1949.

TRAVIS D. BOYCE AND
WINSOME CHUNNU

Whitten, Jack (5 Dec. 1939–), painter, was born in Bessemer, Alabama, one of seven children of Mose Whitten, a coal miner, and Annie Bell Whitten, a seamstress. Jack took art classes and studied the saxophone while attending Carver Junior High School and Dunbar High School, from which he graduated in 1957. Whitten was a premedical student at Tuskegee Institute in Alabama from 1957 to 1959 before shifting to a concentration in art at Southern University in Baton Rouge, Louisiana, between 1959 and 1960. In 1959 he participated in his first art exhibition, a group show at Xavier University in New Orleans. He moved to New York in 1960 to complete his formal art education at the Cooper Union for the Advancement of Science and Art. His next exhibition opportunities were in 1962 and 1963 when his paintings were included in shows in New York at the Westerly Gallery and Edios Group.

Whitten married Florence Squires in 1962, and they had one child, Keita. Already closely associated with artists JOE OVERSTREET, William White, Lawrence Compton, and Haywood (Bill) Rivers, he soon met BOB THOMPSON, Emilio Cruz, and ED CLARK. Like most experimental painters in the city, Whitten frequented the popular Cedar Bar, a trendy gathering spot for abstract Expressionists in Greenwich Village where he was introduced to painters Willem de Kooning and Mark Rothko. By the time he graduated from Cooper Union in 1964, he was also personally acquainted with ROMARE BEARDEN, Norman Lewis, JACOB LAWRENCE, and CHARLES WHITE. He was awarded the John Hay Whitney Opportunity Fellowship.

Whitten's first marriage having ended, he and Mary Whitten exchanged vows in 1968 and had one daughter, Mirsini. In the fall he took a yearlong appointment at Queens College teaching art survey, painting, and drawing. For two years beginning in 1967 he pursued a new direction in his work, focusing on creating his first series of black, white, and gray paintings, presenting them in his first one-person gallery exhibition at Allan Stone Gallery in New York in 1969. He spent the summer of 1969 on the island of Crete, which became his summer residence for many years. He returned to a yearlong adjunct position, teaching figure drawing at Pratt Institute in Brooklyn in 1970. He also took a job as a part-time lecturer in drawing and painting at Manhattan Community College the same year, a position he held for five years. In 1971 he added another part-time job to his workload teaching painting at Cooper Union.

Adopting a large-scale painting style in the early 1970s that essentially established his personal drip pour method (a predetermined general format similar to yet distinct from that of Jackson

Pollock) requiring a considerable amount of paint, Whitten worked out a trade with the Aquatec acrylic paint manufacturer Leonard Bocour. Whitten also received a National Endowment for the Arts Individual Artist Fellowship in painting in 1973 and a Xerox Corporation grant in xerography (a copier-based form of image manipulation) in 1974; he had his first solo exhibition at the Whitney Museum of American Art in New York in the fall of the same year. In 1975 he received a New York State Council on the Arts Creative Artists Public Service Grant, followed by the Solomon R. Guggenheim Fellowship in 1976.

From 1975 to 1979 Whitten made a number of paintings for his *Greek Alphabet* series. In this body of work he eliminated color for the second time in his career; his aim was to explore the spatial implications of two-dimensional formats where surface texture and process are emphasized in the interaction of black, white, and gray hues. The *Greek Alphabet* series was exhibited at Montclair State College in New Jersey in February 1977 and at the Robert Miller Gallery in New York in 1978. Whitten became an adjunct professor of painting at the School of Visual Arts in New York in 1979. In his artwork he continued to experiment with smaller tools and innovative application techniques. He forced thick paints—oils and acrylics—through screening materials, achieving his base image when excess paint was removed. He next used afro picks, combs, brooms, handmade rakes, and saw blades to incise unexpected markings into added bands of color, emphasizing the optical and plastic presence of his surfaces.

A devastating fire destroyed Whitten's home and studio in 1980, and he discontinued the experimentation with unusual tools for three years and began using acrylics as his primary paint type. After rebuilding his home and studio, he began to aggressively explore paint applications and tools in 1983, pouring acrylics into molds, cutting the color sections into tile-like formats, and assembling the pieces on canvas along with such common items as hair, coffee, and foil to create mosaic, mixed-media canvases. In November 1983 the Studio Museum in Harlem mounted a retrospective of his work, Jack Whitten: Ten Years, 1970–1980. This latest work was presented in shows at the Onyx Gallery in New York (1983), the Cure Gallery in Los Angeles (1990), and the Newark Museum in New Jersey (1990). He also received the Sambuca Romana Contemporary Fellowship (1983).

Whitten continued teaching at various New York schools as his reputation advanced in the field of reductive painting. He received a Joan Mitchell Foundation Grant in 1995, and during the 1990s exhibited at galleries in New York, Michigan, and Illinois.

Whitten later participated in more than one hundred group exhibitions that presented the most recent examples of his reductive, mixed-media paintings at such major venues as the Pennsylvania Academy of the Fine Arts, the Museum of Contemporary Art in Los Angeles, the Galerie de l'Ecole des Beaux-Arts (France), the Kunstmuseum Bonn in Germany, and the Museu d'Art Contemporani in Spain.

His work is represented in the permanent collections of such prominent institutions as the Metropolitan Museum of Art, the Museum of Modern Art, the Whitney Museum, the Studio Museum in Harlem, the Newark Museum, Wadsworth Athenaeum, and the University of Delaware's Paul R. Jones Collection.

FURTHER READING

Onyx Museum of Art. *Jack Whitten—New Works* (1984).

Wright, Beryl J. *Jack Whitten* (1990).

AMALIA K. AMAKI

Wickham, DeWayne (22 July 1946–), journalist, was born in Baltimore, Maryland. He was the third of John Trevillian and DeSylvia (Chase) Wickham's five children. John and DeSylvia Wickham were a cab driver and store clerk, respectively.

In his autobiography *Woodholme: A Black Man's Story of Growing Up Alone* (1995) Wickham recounted how in the early hours of 17 December 1954, his father, apparently distraught that he could not afford to buy Christmas gifts for his family, shot and killed his wife and then turned the .32-caliber revolver on himself. Wickham's parents were found inside his father's powder-blue 1950 Plymouth station wagon. Besides John Wickham's suicide note to his mother, a twenty-dollar money order, and the couple's wedding rings, police also recovered twenty-one photographs of a black boy—his school pictures, Wickham wrote.

The Wickham children were parceled out among relatives. Eight-year-old DeWayne and his brother John Rodney were taken in by their mother's sister, Annette McClain, who along with her husband, their six children, and neighbors in Baltimore's Cherry Hill public housing project, "all helped to insulate me from the people and things that were too painful a reminder of all that

I wanted to forget," he wrote. Nevertheless, growing up parentless took a toll on the sensitive boy. Those early years were colored by anger, fear, confusion, and Wickham's failure to conform. He was kicked out of three high schools in his junior year, and finally dropped out of a fourth school in 1964. That same year, on 14 October, as the Vietnam War raged, Wickham enlisted in the U.S. Air Force. He served in areas of the Southeast Asia war zone and earned a Vietnam Service Medal and the Republic of Vietnam Campaign Medal. By the time Wickham was honorably discharged on 16 September 1968, he had attained the rank of sergeant.

By then Wickham had been married for three years to Ruth Ann Frederick. They had two daughters, Vanessa Denise and Zenita Ann. The couple divorced in 1984, and in 1987 Wickham married Wanda Nadine Persons. His third daughter, Mikella Nicole, was born in 1994.

Wickham made up for the early interruptions in his education. He received a high school equivalency diploma while in the military in 1965, a B.S. in Journalism in 1974 from the University of Maryland and a master's degree in Public Administration from the University of Baltimore.

Wickham's 1968 discharge from the air force coincided with momentous events that would help shape the hard-charging journalist that he would become. MARTIN LUTHER KING JR. and Robert F. Kennedy were assassinated that spring; SHIRLEY CHISHOLM, the first black woman to seek the presidency, was elected to Congress; black students, alleging discrimination, took over the administration building at Boston University; and the Kerner Commission warned the nation of the hell there would be to pay if America continued its drift toward two societies—one black and one white—separate and unequal.

It can be argued that Wickham entered journalism at the right time for someone of his temperament and talents. A natural-born organizer, Wickham thoroughly understood that if the mainstream U.S. media hoped to avoid the looming disaster the Kerner commissioners foresaw as the dramas unfolded in America's black urban ghettoes, and as the civil rights battlegrounds increasingly shifted from South to North, it had to empower more people of color to call the shots. Wickham realized that white-majority newsrooms had to do more than merely hire blacks who could write well. Those newsrooms also had to hire black reporters and editors who had the willingness, the knowledge, and the courage to report on and from communities that were wary of the "white" press because of its history in directly and indirectly aiding and abetting racism and segregation.

So it is no wonder that Wickham was among the forty-four African American media professionals who boldly formed the National Association of Black Journalists on 12 December 1975 in Washington, D.C. Their agenda was clear: it was to press for the hiring of more blacks in the media and for more to be promoted into top editing and newsroom management positions. Wickham was elected NABJ president in 1987. Under his leadership NABJ's membership and treasury both swelled. In Sheila Brooks's essay commissioned by NABJ to salute its past presidents, she wrote that Wickham "strongly challenged the industry's notion of workplace opportunities." In later years, Wickham would go on to cofound The Trotter Group, an organization of black columnists, and to found the Institute for Advanced Journalism Studies at North Carolina A&T State University in Greensboro, North Carolina.

Wickham was a reporter and columnist for many of the nation's most prestigious news organizations. They included: *USA Today*; the Gannett News Service, which syndicated his columns to more than 130 newspapers; *U.S. News & World Report*; *Black Enterprise* magazine; and *The Sun* and *The Evening Sun*, of Baltimore. Wickham, who served on many industry boards, also worked for a time as a news analyst for CBS News and as executive editor of news for BlackAmericaWeb.com. USA Today Books published a collection of Wickham's columns, *Fire at Will*, in 1989. He also edited *Thinking Black: Some of the Nation's Best Black Columnists Speak Their Mind* (1996) and wrote *Bill Clinton and Black America* (2002).

A multiple award-winner, Wickham and his wife donated significant amounts of their personal funds to scholarships and internships for aspiring journalists, and in 1995 Wickham established The Woodholme Foundation, which awards college scholarships annually to youths who, as did Wickham, struggle to carve a normal life out of families riven by strife. Wickham devoted his life to creating opportunities for aspiring and seasoned black journalists to travel nationally and internationally to report stories of major importance to people of color.

FURTHER READING
Wickham, Dewayne. *Woodholme: A Black Man's Story of Growing Up Alone* (1995).

Coleman, Trevor W. "Black America's White Knight," *New Crisis* (March/April 2002)

Powell, Tracie. "Engineering a Grand Plan: A Man on a Mission," *Black Issues in Higher Education* (July 2005).

Valentine, Victoria L. "Black on Black Silence," *New Crisis* (July 2005).

Wayne, Dawkins. *Black Journalists: The NABJ Story* (1997).

Williams, Roland T. "Woodholme: A Black Man's Story of Growing Up Alone," *African American Review* (Spring 1999).

BETTY WINSTON BAYÉ

Wideman, John Edgar (14 June 1941–), writer and educator, was born in Washington, D.C., to Edgar Wideman, a laborer, and Betty (French) Wideman. Shortly before his first birthday, he moved with his family to the predominantly African American Homewood section of Pittsburgh, Pennsylvania, which was originally founded by, among others, Wideman's maternal great-great-great-grandmother, Sybela Owens, a runaway slave. A fine student, Wideman excelled at Pittsburgh's Peabody High School before accepting a Benjamin Franklin Scholarship to attend the University of Pennsylvania, where he became captain of the basketball team. He graduated Phi Beta Kappa in 1963 from the University of Pennsylvania with a B.A. in English, and in 1965 married Judith Ann Goldman, with whom he had three children: Daniel, Jacob, and Jamila. As the second-ever African American Rhodes Scholar, Wideman studied philosophy at Oxford University's New College, from which he graduated in 1966.

Literary success came quickly to Wideman. After returning to the United States from Oxford, he served as a Kent Fellow in the University of Iowa's Writers' Workshop for the 1966–1967 academic year. At Iowa he completed his first novel, *A Glance Away*, which was published in 1967—the peak of the civil rights era—when Wideman was just twenty-six years old. Unlike other African American writers of his generation, such as Black Arts Movement activists LEROI JONES (AMIRI BARAKA), LARRY NEAL, and ADDISON GAYLE JR., Wideman did not seek to make race the most important aspect of his work. *A Glance Away* told the story of Eddie Lawson, an African American struggling to get his life together after overcoming drug addiction, and Robert Thurley, a white professor of English, who were both haunted by a sense of incompleteness and failed promise. Wideman soon followed that novel with two others, *Hurry Home* (1970) and *The Lynchers* (1973), in which he examined the lives of white as well as black characters and consequently offered his art to readers on a broader canvas than his contemporaries of the Black Arts Movement did. By the time Wideman reached his mid-thirties, he was generally accepted as one of the best and most important African American male writers of his generation, earning him a position as a literary descendant of the giants of African American literature—including RICHARD WRIGHT, JAMES BALDWIN, and RALPH ELLISON— as well as comparisons to T. S. Eliot, William Faulkner, Virginia Woolf, and even William Shakespeare.

After the release of *The Lynchers*, Wideman made a conscious effort to find a new language and vision to use in his storytelling. Beginning with *Damballah* in 1981 and continuing in *Hiding Place* (1981) and *Sent for You Yesterday* (1983)—in what would be released as *The Homewood Trilogy* in 1985— Wideman set out on a personal journey to recreate the world in which his maternal great-great-great grandmother had lived and to capture the essence of what she and others like her had experienced when they established themselves in Pittsburgh, at the intersection of the Allegheny, Monongahela, and Ohio Rivers. Also during this time Wideman wrote a memoir entitled *Brothers and Keepers*, in which he examined the circumstances by which two brothers (himself, a writer and college professor, and his brother Robbie, a convicted murderer currently serving a life sentence) ended up with such different lives. The book also looked closely at the responsibilities of love and brotherhood, at society's values, and at attitudes toward crime and punishment. A growing sense of his personal past and present led Wideman to examine the ways in which history resided within the cultural memory of race and community. Eventually, it led him to write *Fatheralong*, a memoir detailing his journey with his father to Promised Land, South Carolina, the town that his paternal grandparents fled in search of freedom—a town that was not present on most maps, just as, Wideman pointed out, there was no presence of slavery's history in the *Chronological History of South Carolina (1662–1825)*. Since *Damballah*, Wideman used his writing as a means of bringing to life voices that had been silenced by white America and of capturing the essence of urban African American life. He presented readers with characters struggling to break through walls and cages and to make places for themselves in the world. In doing so, Wideman celebrated African

American vernacular speech and music and offered invaluable insights into the conflicts pushing against the hearts and minds of his protagonists. Perhaps most importantly Wideman—through his work and his teaching—helped move African American literature from the margins of American letters to its rightful place in the center.

In addition to the aforementioned books Wideman authored the novels *Reuben* (1987), *Philadelphia Fire* (1990), *The Cattle Killing* (1996), *Two Cities* (1998), and *Fanon* (2007), as well as the short story collections *All Stories Are True* (1992), *The Stories of John Edgar Wideman* (1993), *Fever* (1998), *God's Gym* (2005), and another memoir, *Hoop Roots* (2001). He also published articles on a range of African American figures, including MALCOLM X, SPIKE LEE, MICHAEL JORDAN, EMMETT TILL, and THELONIUS MONK in *The New Yorker*, *Vogue*, *Esquire*, and the *New York Times Magazine*. The only person to do so, he won the PEN/Faulkner Award for Fiction twice: for *Sent for You Yesterday* in 1984 and for *Philadelphia Fire* in 1990. He received many other awards, including the DuSable Museum Prize for Nonfiction (1985), the National Magazine Editors' Prize for Short Fiction (1987), the American Book Award for Fiction (1990), the Lannan Literary Fellowship for Fiction (1991), and a MacArthur Award (1993).

In addition to his brother's incarceration, Wideman also had to deal with the 1988 sentencing of his son Jacob to incarceration for twenty-five years to life after being convicted of a 1986 murder in Flagstaff, Arizona. Wideman's son was tried as an adult even though he was under the age of eighteen at the time. Wideman's other son, Daniel, became a published writer. His daughter, Jamila, played professional basketball in the Women's National Basketball Association (WNBA) from 1997 to 2000 and in the Israeli Women's Basketball League from 1999 to 2000.

Throughout his writing career, Wideman taught at various universities. His first teaching job was in the University of Pennsylvania's English department, where he also created and served as the first chair of Penn's African American Studies program. From Penn, he moved on to the University of Wyoming, where he spent more than ten years, then to the University of Massachusetts at Amherst, where he was a professor of creative writing and American studies. In 2004 he moved to New York City with his second wife, journalist Catherine Nedonchelle, and her son. In the same year he became the Asa Messer Professor and professor of Africana studies and English in the Department of Africana Studies of Brown University in Providence, Rhode Island.

FURTHER READING
Wideman, John Edgar. *Brothers and Keepers* (1984).
Wideman, John Edgar. *Fatheralong: A Meditation on Fathers and Sons, Race and Society* (1994).
Wideman, John Edgar. *Hoop Roots* (2001).
Coleman, James W. *Blackness and Modernism: The Literary Career of John Edgar Wideman* (1989).
Tusmith, Bonnie, ed. *Conversations with John Edgar Wideman* (1998).

DANIEL DONAGHY

Wiggins, Thomas Bethune. *See* Blind Tom.

Wilberforce, Daniel Flickinger (24 Feb. 1857–1927), missionary, educator, and tribal chieftain, was born in Bonthe, Sherbro Island, Sierra Leone, and named for Daniel Flickinger, an American missionary visiting a nearby mission station. Little is known about his parents, both members of the Sherbro tribe who worked at the mission station. Wilberforce sailed to America in 1871 while working as a nurse for an American missionary couple suffering from an African fever.

In a remarkable turn of events the young Wilberforce met Daniel Flickinger, the man for whom he had been named years earlier, in New York City. After hearing that Wilberforce had already acquired a basic education and wished to continue his schooling, Flickinger arranged for him to travel to Dayton, Ohio, and begin studies in December 1871 at the expense of the Church of the United Brethren in Christ, an American denomination begun in 1767. Wilberforce thus became one of at least seventy Africans who studied in the United States during the late nineteenth century, most with the aim of returning to their country of origin as missionaries. Wilberforce lived with an African American family, attended a black church, and studied at Dayton High School and Union Biblical Seminary, becoming the first black student ever admitted to the former institution.

While in Dayton Wilberforce converted to Christianity, joined the United Brethren Church, and received his preaching license in September 1878. In that same year he graduated at the top of his class from Dayton High School, married an African American woman named Elizabeth Harris, and sailed for Africa as a missionary.

Soon after returning to Sierra Leone, Wilberforce was made superintendent of the United Brethren mission schools there. In 1887 he became principal of the Clark Training and Theological School, and served there for several years.

Wilberforce's relationship with United Brethren supporters in America was greatly complicated by the denomination's schism in 1889, although he managed to sidestep most public controversy for the next decade. In 1895 Wilberforce was appointed superintendent of the Imperri mission, run by the more conservative wing of the church, a position he held on and off until he resigned in the fall of 1903.

Wilberforce enjoyed fame and popularity within the mostly white United Brethren Church as his work in Sierra Leone prospered during the 1880s and 1890s. He and his wife, Elizabeth, visited America with their children (Lucy, Joseph, Christopher, and Lillie) three times between 1878 and 1901. Wilberforce was an entertaining lecturer capable of drawing large crowds. The family also maintained connections with their supporters through letters published in denominational journals. These measures helped make Wilberforce something of a United Brethren hero, a notable achievement in light of the racial prejudice that infected nearly every aspect of American society during these years and that even marred Wilberforce's relationships with some of his white missionary colleagues. One minister urged every Sunday school to display a picture of Wilberforce, and a church magazine ran a photo of Wilberforce clad in African garb on its front cover during the summer of 1901.

Perhaps the most harrowing period of Wilberforce's adventure-filled life occurred during the Hut Tax Rebellion of 1898, when a violent uprising sparked by British colonial taxation in Sierra Leone nearly cost him his life. Rebel forces massacred seven American missionaries, several African missionaries, and several hundred African converts. Hearing that war parties were executing all English speakers, Wilberforce and his young family fled into the bush and remained in hiding while a relative bargained for their lives. The Wilberforces escaped, but rebels burned their home, possessions, and mission buildings to the ground. Mistaken reports that the Wilberforces had been murdered circulated in the United States, and word that they had survived evoked relieved praise for Wilberforce and his family from ministers and denominational leaders.

In the aftermath of the rebellion, colonial administrators recruited Wilberforce to serve as paramount chief of the Imperri district. His duties included accepting the surrender of rebels, holding peace talks, and directing reconstruction efforts in his district. In early 1899 Wilberforce returned to Danville, the village from which he and his family had fled nine months earlier, and resumed religious services in a makeshift building. He wrote in a letter to American supporters that "although the warriors had sought to take our lives, I had come to shake hands with them."

Elizabeth Wilberforce, suffering from the traumatic events she and her family had endured, traveled with her children to Dayton, Ohio, arriving in June 1899, while Daniel remained in Sierra Leone to participate in the reconstruction effort. He joined his family in May 1901 and lectured to large crowds before returning to Sierra Leone in the fall. All four Wilberforce children studied in American schools, Lucy and Lillie until they returned to Africa with their parents, Joseph and Christopher at Central College and Otterbein College until they married African American women and sailed for Sierra Leone as missionaries in 1906.

Wilberforce's relationship with the conservative United Brethren began to sour as early as 1900, when his responsibilities as paramount chief prevented him from devoting himself to missionary work and garnered criticism from denominational superiors impatient to rebuild their war-torn mission. Unwilling to abdicate the chieftaincy, Wilberforce resigned the superintendency of the Imperri mission in 1903. Wilberforce and his sons also angered conservative leaders by moving back and forth between the two factions of the United Brethren Church as they sought institutional support for their work in Africa. Additionally Wilberforce believed that some of the white United Brethren missionaries were not culturally sensitive enough, and he pressed for the increased use of African missionaries. Charges about his own moral shortcomings curtailed his efforts. In 1905, in a decision reported by the *New York Times* and *Washington Post*, conservatives severed all ties with Wilberforce, claiming that he had failed to answer charges of polygamy and had refused to accept the correction and discipline of church leaders. Wilberforce's silence on the matter makes it difficult to assess the truth of the charges.

Little is known about Wilberforce after 1905, although he and his family continued their missionary work with support from the rival faction of the United Brethren Church. Wilberforce was tried on charges of cannibalism in 1906 and acquitted, escaping a death sentence. Again, whether the charge was based on fact, rumor, or malice is unknown. He died in 1927 in Sierra Leone.

Throughout his life Wilberforce was seen by supporters and critics as a symbol of the abilities or shortcomings of Africans and African Americans. A biography by the early African American historian GEORGE WASHINGTON WILLIAMS praised him as "a striking illustration of the capabilities of the Negro" and the white missionary leader Daniel Flickinger cited his academic success and exemplary spiritual life as proof that some Africans could be educated and used as missionaries, while newspaper reports about his ejection from the conservative mission echoed a denominational official who described Wilberforce as a "dark back-slider for Africa."

FURTHER READING

Daniel Flickinger Wilberforce's letters are in the Huntington University Archives in Huntington, Indiana.

Fleming, George D. *Trail Blazers in Sierra Leone* (1971)

Flickinger, Daniel K. *Fifty-Five Years of Active Ministerial Life* (1907).

Flickinger, Daniel K. "Rev. D. F. Wilberforce," *Missionary Monthly* (November 1901).

Mills, J. S. *Mission Work in Sierra Leone, West Africa* (1898).

Williams, George W. *History of the Negro Race in America* (1882).

ANDREW WITMER

Wilder, Douglas (17 Jan. 1931–), governor of Virginia, was born Lawrence Douglas Wilder in Richmond, Virginia, the son of Robert J. Wilder Sr., a door-to-door insurance salesman, church deacon, and a strict disciplinarian, and Beulah Richards, an occasional domestic and mother of ten children, including two who died in infancy. Wilder's paternal grandparents, James and Agnes Wilder, were born in slavery and married on 25 April 1856 in Henrico County, Virginia, north of Richmond. They were later sold separately, and on Sundays, James would travel unsupervised to neighboring Hanover County to visit his wife and children. According to family lore, he was so highly regarded that if he returned late, the overseer would feign punishment by beating on a saddle. Agnes Wilder, a house servant, learned to read while overhearing the lessons of a handicapped child for whom she cared. Less is known of the origins of Wilder's mother. She was raised by a grandmother and aunt in Richmond after her mother and stepfather died. Her father's identity is unknown.

Douglas (later called Doug by non-family members) was the next to youngest of the Wilder children and one of only two boys who survived. He was named for FREDERICK DOUGLASS, the fiery abolitionist, and PAUL LAURENCE DUNBAR, the contemplative poet. He grew up in what the family describes as "gentle poverty," surrounded by sisters and as the apple of his mother's eye. Clever and high-spirited, the young Douglas shined shoes, hawked newspapers, and teased the family that "some rich people left me here, didn't they?" "They're coming back for me, aren't they?" he would ask (Baker, 8). As a youth in segregated Richmond, Douglas had few associations with whites, other than as an elevator boy in a downtown office building and, while in college, as a waiter at private country clubs and downtown hotels.

Shortly after graduating in 1951 from Virginia Union University with a degree in chemistry, Wilder was drafted into the U.S. Army. While serving in the Seventeenth Infantry Regiment's first battalion during the Korean War, he and a comrade captured twenty North Koreans holed up in a bunker, an action that won Corporal Wilder a Bronze Star. Back in the United States, Wilder began work as a technician in the state medical examiner's office. In 1956 he enrolled in the Howard University law school, taking advantage of a state stipend encouraging African Americans to pursue advanced degrees out of state. Wilder married Eunice Montgomery in 1958, and after his graduation in 1959 they returned to Richmond, where his focus was less on dismantling segregation than on establishing a successful law practice. Over time he became known as one of the city's leading criminal trial attorneys. That record was blemished somewhat by a 1975 reprimand from the Virginia Supreme Court for "inexcusable procrastination" in a car-accident case. Wilder apologized for and did not repeat the mistake.

In 1969 Wilder entered politics by winning a special election to a state senate seat against two white opponents in a majority-white district. Arriving as the first black member since Reconstruction of a body still dominated by rural white conservatives, Wilder made waves with his maiden floor speech denouncing the state song, "Carry Me Back to Ol' Virginny." Over the next several years he pursued a legislative agenda that was liberal by Virginia standards. He fought for fair-housing laws, pushed for a national holiday honoring MARTIN LUTHER KING JR., and opposed the reinstatement of the death penalty. Although he later claimed to have done

Douglas Wilder, as Governor-elect of Virginia, photographed in his Richmond office in January 1990. (AP Images.)

so primarily as a courtesy, he introduced legislation calling for statehood and voting rights for the District of Columbia, whose residents are largely African American. In 1978 Wilder's marriage, which produced three children, ended in divorce.

A pivotal moment in Wilder's rise came in 1982, when a moderate Democratic legislator, Owen B. Pickett, launched his campaign for a U.S. Senate seat by invoking the name and record of Harry Flood Byrd Jr., the retiring senator and the epitome of segregationist Old Virginia. Already angry at the treatment of black lawmakers in the 1982 assembly, Wilder threatened to run as an independent if Pickett did not withdraw. Governor Charles S. "Chuck" Robb and other Democratic kingpins calculated the odds of winning without the black vote and advised Pickett to exit. He did. Wilder had demonstrated the power of black voters in Virginia. When he announced his candidacy for lieutenant

governor in 1985, the white establishment fretted, but no Democrat was willing to challenge his nomination. Benefiting from lackluster Republican opposition, Wilder ran a lively, shoestring campaign, hoarding his dollars for a final television blitz. He captured almost 52 percent of the vote, including support from an estimated 44 percent of white Democrats who voted.

In the four years leading up to his 1989 race for governor, Wilder honed his trademark blend of contentiousness and charm. He quarreled over politics with former governor Robb and his successor, Gerald Baliles. As the election approached and Wilder's chief rival for the Democratic nomination dropped out of the race, friction gave way to civility. Slight in stature, immaculately dressed, his mustache shaved, and his once bold Afro trimmed to a sedate silver cap, Wilder wooed audiences with an easy, engaging laugh and an increasingly centrist, nonthreatening message. He declined offers from JESSE JACKSON and other nationally prominent black politicians to travel to Virginia to campaign, and he deliberately avoided references to race and the historic nature of his campaign. Wilder drew support from a broad network of social acquaintances, but as in past campaigns, he kept few confidantes, relying on a small circle of advisers whose members fell in and out of grace.

Perhaps the determining event of the governor's campaign occurred on 5 July 1989, when the U.S. Supreme Court ruled in *Webster v. Reproductive Services* that states could restrict abortions beyond the limits set in 1973. Wilder deftly framed the issue as a matter of personal freedom. He trusted the women of Virginia to make the proper individual choice, he said. Wilder's opponent, former Republican attorney general J. Marshall Coleman, attempted to soften his hard-line, antiabortion message adopted in order to win a three-way contest for the Republican nomination. But in public opinion polls, both campaigns saw women in the vote-rich Washington, D.C., suburbs swing to Wilder.

Entering the final weekend of the campaign, opinion polls showed Wilder leading Coleman by as much as eleven percentage points. As soon as the voting ended on election night, an exit survey taken by Mason-Dixon Opinion Research appeared to confirm that margin. The celebration began. But as the evening wore on, the "landslide" turned into a cliffhanger. Wilder won by 6,741 votes of a record 1,787,131 cast. As in previous American elections involving black candidates, it appeared that many voters simply lied when asked about their vote.

In office Wilder encountered an unexpected $1.4 billion budget shortfall. By his second year, revenues lagged further. Rather than raise taxes, the option adopted by almost every other state during the recession of the early 1990s, Wilder instituted across-the-board spending cuts, laid off state workers, canceled salary increases, and insisted on holding the line on taxes. He pushed also for creation of a "rainy-day fund" to help tide the state over in future economic crises. His managing of the economic crisis was widely applauded, particularly after Virginia was cited twice in a row by *Financial World* magazine as the nation's best managed state. Wilder also won acclaim for the passage of legislation limiting guns sales in Virginia to one per month, thereby halting extensive gun running from Virginia to the northeast, and for extensive appointments of African Americans to prominent government posts. Less lauded was his 1991 bid for the Democratic presidential nomination, a campaign that alienated many Virginia voters before his voluntary withdrawal and during which he engaged in public spats with Robb and other prominent Democrats, including some members of the legislative black caucus. An article in *U.S. News & World Report* stated that "Virginia's governor is capable of transcendent, triumphal moments and of astonishing pettiness" (13 May 1991).

Prohibited by the Virginia constitution from seeking more than one consecutive gubernatorial term, Wilder left office in January 1994. That spring he mounted a brief, independent run for Robb's U.S. Senate seat. Both money and support lagged, and Wilder withdrew. Out of office, Wilder hosted a radio call-in show and was appointed to a distinguished professorship at Virginia Commonwealth University, which subsequently named its school of government and public affairs after him. Wilder was also the driving force behind the creation of the National Slavery Museum in Fredericksburg, Virginia. Although his later political career never reached the heights suggested by his 1989 election, he returned to elected office in 2004 as mayor of his hometown, Richmond.

FURTHER READING

Wilder's papers are housed at the L. Douglas Wilder Library at Virginia Union University and at the Library of Virginia, both in Richmond, Virginia.

Baker, Don. *Wilder: Hold Fast to Dreams* (1989).

Edds, Margaret. *Claiming the Dream: The Victorious Campaign of Douglas Wilder of Virginia* (1990).

Jeffries, Judson L. *Virginia's Native Son: The Election and Administration of Governor L. Douglas Wilder* (2002).

Yancey, Dwayne. *When Hell Froze Over: The Story of Doug Wilder: A Black Politician's Rise to Power in the South* (1990).

MARGARET E. EDDS

Wilkens, Lenny (28 Oct. 1937–), basketball player, coach, and general manager, was born Leonard Randolph Wilkens Jr. in Brooklyn, New York, the second oldest of the five children of Leonard Wilkens, an African American chauffeur, and Henrietta Cross, an Irish American candy shop worker. While in many parts of the country such an interracial marriage would have been the cause of discrimination or worse, in the impoverished immigrant melting pot of Bedford-Stuyvesant it went largely unnoticed. Life in Bedford-Stuyvesant, one of the toughest parts of Brooklyn, became more difficult when Wilkens Sr. died in 1942. Henrietta Wilkens, sustained by love for her family and the Irish Catholic Church, worked tirelessly to provide for her children. Young Lenny was expected to contribute and began work as a house cleaner, work that gave the nine-year-old Wilkens a sense of pride at being able to fulfill his duty as man of the house, helping to support the family.

When he was in the eighth grade Wilkens had his first exposure to basketball, playing pickup games in the Police Athletic League. He was usually the last one to be picked, something that inspired him to improve his game and to work to shed his unflattering nickname "Heaver." Wilkens joined the Catholic Youth Organization Basketball League, where a priest, Father Thomas Mannion, put him on the path to basketball success, suggesting that the young player improve his ball handling and passing. Wilkens later attributed his success to the fact that in the 1950s street ball was primarily about passing, moving without the ball, and the pick and roll. Wilkens's early basketball experience taught him the value of the team over the individual, lessons which would be central to his subsequent success as a professional player, coach, and general manager. Wilkens's only experience as a member of his high school basketball team came as a senior, when he played on the varsity team for half of the year before graduating early.

Perceiving Wilkens's tremendous potential both as a scholar and an athlete, Father Mannion encouraged him to attend college. Mannion wrote to Father Bagley, the athletic director at Providence

College, and lobbied for Wilkens to be given a basketball scholarship, which came to pass after a scout saw him play in a summer league game. At Providence College, Wilkens excelled. He played point guard for the freshman team and led them to a perfect 23-0 record. In addition, he continued to perform well academically, maintaining a B average and turning down the special treatment usually offered to athletes. As a sophomore, now the starting varsity point guard, Wilkens led Providence in scoring and was the youngest player named to the Eastern Conference Athletic League All-Conference team. During his junior year the team made the National Invitational Tournament (NIT), and Wilkens was praised in the media for his outstanding play. When he was a senior his team again made the NIT, and even though Providence lost in the finals, Wilkens was named the tournament's most valuable player. By the time Wilkens finished his college career he had become the second highest scorer in school history, but was known more for his defense, rebounding, and ball handling. Academically, he had earned a degree in economics and planned to attend graduate school.

Wilkens's final collegiate game was the annual East/West All-Star game, one of the forums most favored by NBA scouts. Wilkens performed exceptionally and was named co-MVP. In spite of all his achievements, the idea of playing basketball professionally never crossed his mind. His last basketball ambition was to be named to the 1960 Olympic team, for which the East-West All-Star game was supposed to have been a tryout. Ultimately, however, Wilkens was not chosen, something he attributed to the selection committee's desire to maintain an "appropriate" black-white ratio for the team. For the first time, Wilkens would later write in his autobiography, he felt as if racism had prevented him from receiving the credit that was his due.

It was not until Wilkens realized that he could make more money playing basketball than as an accountant that he committed to playing professionally. In 1960 he signed with the St. Louis Hawks for $9,500, and after breaking into the starting lineup late in the season he excelled. The next year, because Wilkens had belonged to ROTC in college, he began serving active duty at Fort Lee, Virginia. He only played for the Hawks on weekends, when games did not conflict with his naval obligations. He retired as First Lieutenant Wilkens.

In 1962 Wilkens married Marilyn Reed. The couple eventually had three children, two girls and a boy. When the new couple bought their

Lenny Wilkens (no. 14), of the St. Louis Hawks, during a playoff game against the San Francisco Warriors at the Oakland Coliseum, 30 March 1968. (AP Images.)

first house, their white neighbors would not talk to them, began trying to sell their houses, and poisoned the Wilkens's dog. In spite of the racist atmosphere, Wilkens continued to shine on the court with the Hawks. The 1967–1968 season was Wilkens's last with the Hawks, after which a contract dispute led to his being traded to the Seattle Supersonics, an expansion team in its second year. Over his seven years with the Hawks, Wilkens had been an All-Star four times.

After just one year in Seattle Wilkens was asked to both coach and play the next season. In a total of three years as player/coach Wilkens lead the Supersonics to thirty-six, thirty-eight, and then forty-seven wins in the eighty-two-game season. In his final year he set the franchise record for wins. When Seattle's management changed, it brought in a new coach, Tom Nissalke, and Wilkens was traded to the Cleveland Cavaliers, an expansion team that had only been in existence for two years. Now thirty-five, Wilkens saw his hopes of winning an NBA championship slipping away.

After the 1973–1974 season Wilkens was offered a coaching position with the Portland Trailblazers, which had entered the league in 1970. He accepted the job on a three-year contract. In the 1974–1975 season he once again played a dual role as player/coach but decided to retire as a player after that season to concentrate on coaching. Unfortunately, because of injuries to the team's star player, Bill Walton, Coach Wilkens won only thirty-seven games in 1975–1976, down from thirty-eight in 1974–1975, and was fired.

After one year as a CBS broadcaster, Wilkens was approached by the Sonics, then in the market for a general manager, and Wilkens accepted. He quickly made several roster moves and assembled a team for the coming season. When the rookie coach Tom Hopkins proved ineffective, Wilkens replaced him, and the Sonics finished the season with a 47-35 record, losing to the Washington Bullets in the NBA finals. The next season Wilkens and the Sonics finished with a franchise best 52-30 record and beat the Washington Bullets to become NBA champions. The 1984–1985 season was his last as the Sonics' coach, and 1985–1986 was his last as the team's general manager. For the 1986–1987 season he returned to coaching with the Cleveland Cavaliers. During the MICHAEL JORDAN era, Wilkens's team was never able to win an NBA title. Wilkens felt that his team was fated to lose after its star defender Ron Harper was traded to the Los Angeles Clippers, leaving the Cavaliers with no single player capable of defending Jordan.

Wilkens finally got to represent his country in the 1992 Barcelona Olympics as an assistant coach to the Dream Team, the first group of professional basketball players to represent the United States. Wilkens tore his Achilles tendon while in Barcelona but put off surgery to see the team win the gold medal. As a result blood clots formed in his lungs and Wilkens almost died. Despite this he returned to coach the Cavaliers in the 1992–1993 season. After a winning but subpar season he resigned and took a job with the Atlanta Hawks. While with the Hawks Wilkens passed Red Auerbach to become the coach with the most wins in NBA history. In addition to this he was named head coach of the U.S. Olympic basketball team in 1996 and won a second gold medal. Wilkens coached the Hawks until the 1999–2000 season, and then coached the Toronto Raptors the next three seasons. In the 2003–2004 season Wilkens became coach of the New York Knicks; he resigned in January 2005 after a tumultuous losing season to become Isiah Thomas's assistant general manager for the New York Knicks. Wilkens is one of only two men enshrined in the Basketball Hall of Fame as both player and coach. Over his forty-year NBA career Wilkens won more games than anyone else, and saw the league change from one of cramped buses, coach flights, and players with summer jobs and no pensions to a big-money game with private jets and salary caps. Throughout this career the basketball lessons he learned playing Brooklyn street ball remained the cornerstones of a coaching philosophy emphasizing teamwork and self-sacrifice.

FURTHER READING
Wilkens, Lenny. *The Lenny Wilkens Story* (1974).
Wilkens, Lenny. *Unguarded: My Forty Years Surviving in the NBA* (2000).

JACOB ANDREW FREEDMAN

Wilkerson, Doxey (24 Apr. 1905–17 June 1993), educator, community and civil rights activist, was born Doxey Alphonse Wilkerson in Excelsior Springs, Missouri, the son of a Methodist minister and a civic-minded mother. As was the case with many Jim Crow–era black families looking for avenues to further their children's education, Wilkerson's father moved his family from Excelsior Springs thirty miles west to Kansas City, so his son could benefit from a larger public educational system. Ironically, the year of Wilkerson's birth, the Kansas legislature enacted statutes that created segregated schools in Kansas City. After graduating from Sumner High School, Wilkerson attended the University of Kansas where he received a bachelor's degree in English in 1926 and his master's in Education in 1927. That same year he was hired as an assistant professor of English and secondary education at Virginia State College in Petersburg, Virginia. He quickly became known as a quiet but forceful advocate for social change. He worked closely with Edna Colson, professor of elementary education, and other black Virginia educators to promote a more progressive curriculum for African American schools.

In 1935 Wilkerson joined the faculty at Howard University in Washington, D.C., as associate professor of education and director of the summer school. One year later he was appointed to President Franklin Roosevelt's Advisory Committee on Education. Initially Wilkerson's committee research focused on vocational education, but he also worked on a range of issues affecting southern African Americans that resulted in the publication of his *Special Problems of Negro Education* (1939), a volume of data and analysis. In the final chapter titled "Democracy in Negro Education," Wilkerson called for a more equitable distribution of wealth and fundamental improvement of African American education to help guarantee fulfillment of American ideals and national stability—recurring themes for Wilkerson. One of his students at Howard, EDMUND W. GORDON, who would go on to a distinguished career as a psychologist and professor at Yale, would later refer to Wilkerson as "a scholar's scholar."

With the worsening Depression and the growing international crises that would soon plunge the world into war, Wilkerson increasingly saw his work defined by radical politics. His teaching, public speaking, and writing focused on addressing structural issues of racial inequality, arguing that the neglect of educational opportunities for African Americans was a drag on the entire society. An active member of the American Federation of Teachers (AFT), where he served as national vice president from 1937 to 1940, Wilkerson argued that the calls for renewed national defense and "Americanism" were eroding the nation's commitment to democratic education. In the AFT "Program of Action" (1941), which he coauthored just before the war, he warned that the very substance of the nation's liberty was at risk if teachers and other progressive-minded citizens failed to see the need for "courageous" action.

His commitment to equality was demonstrated repeatedly. The famous black concert singer MARIAN ANDERSON was denied access to Constitution Hall based on race. Many, including Wilkerson, his lifelong friend PAUL ROBESON, and Eleanor Roosevelt, spearheaded an effort to move the concert to the Lincoln Memorial, where on 9 April 1939 Anderson sang before 75,000 people. The Lincoln Memorial concert marked one of the defining moments in civil rights history. Late in the 1930s Wilkerson's reputation as a scholar of African American education grew and he was appointed a senior researcher on the Carnegie Foundation investigation of the "Negro problem." The principal investigator was the respected Swedish economist, Gunnar Myrdal. The massive 1,500-page study, published in 1944 as *The American Dilemma: The Negro Problem and Modern Democracy*, carefully documented the social, political, and economic issues related to race in America. Myrdal's study validated what Wilkerson and countless other African Americans had been saying for generations: there

was no "Negro problem," rather the "problem" was with white America.

Wilkerson broke with conventional political ideology and on 15 June 1943 he resigned from Howard University and joined the Communist Party. He was first appointed education director of the Maryland state organization, which included the Washington, D.C., area. That same year he was elected vice president of the International Labor Defense (ILD), which had provided legal services in such high-profile cases as the Sacco and Vanzetti trial in the late 1920s and the SCOTTSBORO BOYS during the 1930s. After the war, the ILD merged with the National Federation of Liberties to form the Civil Rights Congress (CRC), which would petition the United Nations in 1951 to argue that by its inaction the U.S. government was complicit in the lynching of thousands of African Americans. Working with Wilkerson on the CRC's petition, *We Charge Genocide: The Crime of Government Against the Negro People* (1951), were his good friends WILLIAM L. PATTERSON of the Communist Party and Paul Robeson. He wrote a weekly column for the *Daily Worker* and in 1946 joined the staff of the Jefferson School of Social Science in New York. It was at "Jeff," the party's flagship school for adult education with an enrollment over ten thousand, that Wilkerson entered his most ideologically productive period.

During the first half of the 1940s and into the 1950s Wilkerson authored numerous essays on black freedom and the book *The Negro People and the Communists* (1944), but he understood Communist ideology all too well to limit his critique of American capitalism to race. He worked with other notable left-leaning writers including the radical feminist Eleanor Flexner in "Marxism and the Woman's Question," a mimeographed pamphlet published by the Jefferson School in 1953, and the labor and Marxist writer James S. Allen in *The Economic Crisis and the Cold War* (1949). But Wilkerson's discontent with internal party struggles, the revelations about Stalinist Russia, and the mounting pressure on Communists during the 1950s, led him to resign from the party in 1957. That same year the Jefferson School closed. One year later he joined the faculty at Bishop College in Dallas, Texas, but that was short lived as the administration dismissed him the next year when he participated in lunch-counter sit-in demonstrations. He had begun his dissertation on the education of Virginia's African Americans before the war at the University of Michigan, but his party affiliation led the university to reject his student status, so after he left Bishop College, he completed his Ph.D. at New York University in 1959.

His former student and good friend Edmund W. Gordon, by then the chair of the department of social sciences at Yeshiva University in New York City, urged him to come to that institution. He joined the Yeshiva faculty in 1962 and was soon appointed chairman of the department of curriculum and instruction. He retired from Yeshiva in 1973 and joined the Westport, Connecticut–based consulting firm of Mediax, which had been contracted to evaluate Head Start. He continued to argue, as he had throughout his career, that the problems associated with schooling were not located in the individual child but rather in structural problems related to social and economic inequalities. For the next twenty years Wilkerson traveled widely, wrote, and spoke about the "American Dream" for all children. He died in Norwalk, Connecticut.

FURTHER READING

Katz, William A. "The Poor: A Problem of Priority. An Interview with Dr. Doxey Wilkerson," *Equal Opportunity Review* (March 1973).

Jackson, John P., Jr. *Social Scientists for Social Justice: Making the Case Against Segregation.*

Obituaries: *New York Times* and *The Hour* (Norwalk, Conn.), 18 June 1993.

MICHAEL JAMES

Wilkerson, Isabel (March 1961–), journalist and the first African American woman to win the Pulitzer Prize in journalism, was born in Washington, DC., to Alexander Wilkerson, a civil engineer and Tuskegee airman, and Rubye Wilkerson, a school teacher. Her mother, from Georgia, and her father, from southern Virginia, migrated to Washington, DC, where they met at Howard University. Wilkerson would later write in her epic first book, *The Warmth of Other Suns* (2010), that their story piqued her interest in southern migrants moving to the urban North in what she would later call an "internal immigration."

Wilkerson's interest in journalism began early. She edited her high school newspaper before she went on to attend her parents' alma mater. As a student at Howard, she rose through the ranks at the college newspaper, *The Hilltop,* to become editor-in-chief. Her flair for narrative reporting was noticed in the early 1980s, when she won a national Sigma Delta Chi Mark of Excellence Award for best feature reporting by a college student.

Her newspaper career began at the *Detroit Free Press* in 1983. She stayed there until she went to work on the metro desk at the *New York Times* in 1984. She worked in various positions at the *Times,* working her way up from being a metro reporter to a national correspondent. In 1991, when she was just thirty years old, she was promoted to Chicago bureau chief. It was a rare move that allowed the freedom to spend a lot of time reporting stories of significance that would lead to her growing renown.

One of her best-known stories is about a ten-year-old boy named Nicholas that included these lines: "He is all boy—squirming in line, sliding down banisters, shirt-tail out, shoes untied, dreaming of becoming a fireman so he can save people—but his walk is the stiff slog of a worried father behind on the rent." Distinctive reporting like that led to her gaining growing recognition in journalism when she became the first African American woman to win the Pulitzer Prize (and the first black person in history to win for individual reporting) in 1994. The Pulitzer committee praised her for the "high literary quality and originality of her work," and she was also awarded a George Polk Award by Long Island University. Bill Keller wrote in the introduction for *Class Matters* (2005), a collection of pieces written by correspondents, that Wilkerson was a "tenacious reporter and mellifluous writer," for returning to a source she wrote about for the powerful 1993 "Children of the Shadows" series, to which she had contributed before she left the *Times* in 1995 to pursue a number of other projects. These projects included the book that took her fifteen years to write—*The Warmth of Other Suns: The Epic Story of America's Great Migration* (2010), the most comprehensive and detailed account of African Americans' migration from the Deep South to the urban North during the twentieth century. Support for the project began with a publisher's advance in 1997, and a fellowship from the Guggenheim Foundation followed in 1998.

The New Yorker and the *New York Times Book Review,* among many others, had nothing but praise for the exhaustive, sometimes harrowing, but always moving accounts so lovingly chronicled in the book. Among the reviews Wilkerson favored most was the *Wall Street Journal*'s review, which asserted "that *Warmth* 'does for the Great Migration what John Steinbeck did for the Okies in his fiction masterpiece, *The Grapes of Wrath.*' Steinbeck's book was a touchstone for Wilkerson as she crafted *Warmth*…which tells the story of the Great Migration through three migrants, Ida Mae Gladney (Mississippi to Chicago), Dr. Robert Pershing Foster (Louisiana to Los Angeles), and George Starling (Florida to Harlem). Wilkerson settled on these central characters after interviewing more than 1,200 people" (Burns).

Wilkerson said the book had been researched in the North but was written by necessity in the South. "I needed to be in the land of my forebears," she said. In her conversations with her sources, she learned ultimately that "they had left the South, but the South had never left them" (Burns).

In 2006 Wilkerson stated, "It was something in my history that I had taken for granted, but if my parents had not been participants in this movement, I wouldn't be here today" (Urquhart).

She taught journalism at a number of universities after leaving the *Times*, including Harvard University's Nieman Foundation, Princeton University, Emory, and Boston University. *The Warmth of Other Suns* won the 2010 National Book Critics Circle Award for Nonfiction, among many other awards. By 2011 she was working as Director of Narrative Nonfiction and a professor at Boston University. She married Roderick Watts, a psychology professor, in 1989. The couple later divorced. Wilkerson also served as an advisor to the Migration Survey of the National Geographic Society and as a board member of the Center for the Public Integrity, a journalistic research organization in Washington, DC.

FURTHER READING

Burns, Rebecca. "Isabel Wilkerson." *Atlanta Magazine*, 50, no. 8 (Dec. 2010).

Correspondents of the *New York Times. Class Matters* (2005).

Urquhart, Kim. "Write from the Heart." *Emory Report*, 25 Sept. 2006.

JOSHUNDA SANDERS

Wilkerson, Vernon Alexander (21 Aug. 1901–24 May 1968), biochemist, educator, and physician, was born in Fort Scott, Kansas, and grew up in Kansas City, Missouri. His parents' names and occupations are unknown. After attending Sumner High School in Kansas City from 1913 to 1917, he entered the University of Kansas, where he majored in chemistry and graduated with an AB in 1921. He stayed an additional year at Kansas before attending the medical school of the University of Iowa, Iowa City, where he earned an MD in 1925. During his medical studies he listed his place of residence as Council Bluffs, Iowa. Next came a year of internship at Kansas City General Hospital No. 2, followed by a one-year appointment as house surgeon at Wheatley-Provident Hospital, also in Kansas City. These hospitals, located in a racially segregated city, served the African American community exclusively and provided one of the few means available anywhere in the country for black medical graduates to acquire postgraduate training.

In 1927 Wilkerson returned to General Hospital No. 2 as assistant surgeon and simultaneously established himself in private practice, working in the local black community. In 1928 he married Vivian Cheatham, with whom he had three children. That marriage ended, and he later married a woman named Helen (her maiden name and the date of marriage are unknown); they had no children.

Wilkerson was so highly regarded that in 1929 he became one of a select few invited by NUMA P. G. ADAMS, the newly appointed and first black dean of the Howard University School of Medicine, to accept a fellowship to pursue doctoral studies with the expectation of returning to Howard to teach. This program, supported by the Rockefeller-funded General Education Board (GEB), was part of a larger campaign at Howard to upgrade the medical curriculum, train full-time teachers in the preclinical sciences, and provide better educational and research opportunities for promising black scholars.

Wilkerson was among the first five GEB Fellows. He registered at the University of Minnesota, while others variously attended the University of Chicago, the University of Michigan, and Columbia University. His major was agricultural biochemistry; his minor, physiology. Working under the supervision of Ross Aiken Gortner, chief of the Division of Agricultural Biochemistry, Wilkerson carried out a study of the forms of nitrogen in pig embryos at various stages of development. One of Wilkerson's conclusions was that mammalian embryos appeared to be governed more by their inherent chemical nature than by variations in maternal nutrition. The project became his doctoral thesis and was published in condensed form (with Gortner as coauthor), first as part of the journal series of the Minnesota Agricultural Experiment Station and then in the *American Journal of Physiology*. Awarded a Ph.D. in 1932, Wilkerson was said to have been the first African American to earn a doctorate at the University of Minnesota. The dean of the graduate school called him "one of the most brilliant students to ever attend the University, [earning] one of the highest grades ever recorded in a Ph.D. examination."

Wilkerson arrived at Howard University in spring or summer 1932 to help build a biochemistry department to replace the old physiological chemistry program. He served as acting head until 1935, when his appointment became permanent. According to the foundation officer Robert A. Lambert, the Howard administration was pleased with the way Wilkerson and other GEB fellows—Roscoe L. McKinney (anatomy), Arnold H. Maloney (pharmacology), Joseph L. Johnson (physiology), HILDRUS A. POINDEXTER (bacteriology), and Robert S. Jason (pathology)—seemed "equal to their new responsibilities, though none of them was really adequately prepared to take over the headship of a department." In addition to administrative responsibilities, their teaching loads were heavy. Wilkerson, assisted by two or three others, delivered lectures and organized laboratory sessions in general biochemistry for all medical and dental students, provided a basic course for students in the dental hygiene program, taught an upper-level course on blood chemistry, led a seminar, and supervised students doing advanced research.

Although this left little time for his own research, Wilkerson remained productive by working long hours into the night. He continued his work on embryonic growth and developed a new interest, the chemistry of human epidermis. He published eight papers during this time, all but two related to his skin research, which sought to define and analyze the distinctive chemical properties of the skin's outer layer. Later he investigated the viscosity of whole blood and blood plasma as well as the possible relationship between certain lymphatic and plasma proteins. Highly regarded, especially in Europe, Wilkerson's research was often cited in the scientific and medical literature. He was elected to membership in the American Society of Biological Chemists in 1936 and served in 1944 as president of the International Society of Biological Chemists. He served on the Nobel Prize selection committee for medicine in 1952, the year Selman A. Waksman won the award for the development of streptomycin.

Wilkerson carried on his research against growing odds. His teaching load, already heavy, almost doubled during World War II, when, for example, two medical classes graduated at Howard in 1944. Furthermore, financial support was minimal. Lambert noted that the GEB fellows had felt "discouragement in not finding on their return [to Howard] the facilities for research which they had during their fellowship study." Although the Howard administration attempted to garner small grants for apparatus and supplies, Wilkerson spent much time and energy improvising equipment essential to his work. Such pressures, in addition to growing family responsibilities, likely played a part in his departure from full-time academics and return to private practice. In 1948 he resigned as Howard's biochemistry department head and opened the Medical Arts Building at 61 K Street, Washington, D.C., a practice catering primarily to the inner-city poor. He remained as part-time lecturer in biochemistry at Howard until 1966. He also served as consulting biochemist for Freedmen's Hospital from 1948 until his death in Washington, D.C.

FURTHER READING
Crisis 39 (May 1932): 163.
Obituaries: *Journal of the National Medical Association* 60 (July 1968): 344–345; *Washington Post*, 27 May 1968.
This entry is taken from the *American National Biography* and is published here with the permission of the American Council of Learned Societies.

KENNETH R. MANNING

Wilkins, Ernie (20 July 1919–5 June 1999), jazz composer, arranger, and saxophonist, was born Ernest Brooks Wilkins in St. Louis, Missouri, the eldest son of Ora Webster, a hospital nurse originally from Mississippi. The name of his father is unknown. Ora's brother Berry, who worked as a cook, apparently took some role in the household. Ernest's brother Jimmy, two years his junior, became a successful jazz trombonist. As a child, Ernest—known at the time as "Pudd" or "Pudding"—had been exposed to jazz on his uncle's Victrola phonograph, but when he was perhaps ten years old his mother gave him a violin for Christmas, "so I could have some 'culture,'" Wilkins later recounted (Rusch, 3).

One of Wilkins's earliest jazz influences was a neighborhood friend, the saxophonist JIMMY FORREST. It was Forrest who encouraged Wilkins to take up the saxophone in high school and gave him his first lessons on the instrument. Wilkins's interest in arranging also began at this time, in part inspired by his listening to recordings by the big bands of JIMMIE LUNCEFORD, DUKE ELLINGTON, CHICK WEBB, and EARL HINES. He created his first arrangements by teaching different combinations of riffs orally, humming lines to his high school bandmates. At the saxophone Wilkins worked to learn the recorded solos of LESTER YOUNG and CHU BERRY; he was especially impressed by ANDY KIRK's saxophonist Dick Wilson.

After a period of freelance gigs in the St. Louis area, the nineteen-year-old Wilkins joined Eddie Randle's Blue Devils, one of the top local jazz bands. Supported by leader Randle, Wilkins wrote his first arrangements for this group. Although these early efforts were later described by Wilkins as "kind of sad," Randle's continuing encouragement won out (Rusch, 4). From 1940 to 1942 Wilkins attended Wilberforce University in Ohio, on scholarship, studying harmony and composition, and performing with the school jazz band. Wilkins then joined the navy and served as a musician. He was stationed at the Great Lakes Boot Camp and performed with the (then and future) jazz stars WILLIE "THE LION" SMITH, GERALD WILSON, Al Grey, Jerome Richardson, and CLARK TERRY, among others. After World War II Wilkins returned to St. Louis before joining the orchestra of Earl Hines as a saxophonist and arranger. He found similar work in the late 1940s with the Jeter-Pillars and George Hudson orchestras, and began taking interest in the modern arranging styles of the bebop music writers Gil Fuller and TADD DAMERON.

In 1951, on the recommendation of the trumpeter Clark Terry, Wilkins was brought into the COUNT BASIE Orchestra. Although Wilkins later recalled some dissatisfaction at having to simplify his Ellington-, BILLY STRAYHORN- and Dameron-influenced writing to fit Basie's style, it was with this group that Wilkins made his reputation. In fact, it was Wilkins who—along with the arrangers Neal Hefti, Frank Foster, and Frank Wess—defined the new Basie sound of the 1950s, one of the most influential styles in the history of the genre: a direct, hard-swinging, section-based orchestration style, incorporating the phrasing of contemporary bebop into the blues riff format Basie had pioneered with his earlier groups. Highlights of Wilkins's Basie period—he performed with the band from 1951 through 1954 and continued to write for Basie throughout his career—include such recordings as "The Blues Done Come Back," "Sixteen Men Swinging," "Peace Pipe," and "Every Day I Have the Blues," which featured the vocalist JOE WILLIAMS. In 1956 Basie recorded Wilkins's extended composition "From Coast to Coast," which displayed his Ellington and Dameron influences.

After leaving Basie, Wilkins entered his busiest period of writing and recording. The late 1950s found him arranging numerous small group sessions for Basie sidemen Joe Newman and Frank Wess; vocal sessions for SARAH VAUGHAN, Patti Page, DINAH WASHINGTON, and Mary Ann McCall; big band arrangements for the DIZZY GILLESPIE and Harry James orchestras; and a series of albums for RCA, where he served as house arranger for the producer Jack Lewis. There were also memorable albums supporting jazz stars like SONNY ROLLINS, Jimmy Cleveland, and KENNY CLARKE, as well as

two big band albums under Wilkins's own name, in 1959 and 1960. In 1953 Wilkins had married Vallie McCain; the couple divorced and had no children.

The 1960s, however, were not as fruitful. Having moved to Detroit for work in the pop music field, by mid-decade Wilkins was in the midst of a heroin addiction that effectively took him off the professional scene. He entered rehabilitation at the end of 1966 and joined the Hart's Island Phoenix House therapeutic community in 1967. One of the Phoenix organization's great success stories, Wilkins recalled in an interview with Ira Gitler, "Drugs are not the problem … but the symptoms of the person's problem" (15). After graduating from the program Wilkins continued to be active with Phoenix House as a counselor and community volunteer.

Wilkins's friend Clark Terry gave him his first comeback gig, hiring the saxophonist to write and play for Terry's big band in 1969, a group that toured the international jazz festival circuit and recorded through the 1970s. By 1971 Wilkins was performing in a New York-based quintet with the saxophonist Chris Woods and had recorded his own album of contemporary "electric" big band arrangements. In March of 1977 New York's Jazzmobile, Inc., recorded Wilkins conducting a twenty-piece big band and a forty-piece orchestra in a performance of his own composition "Four Black Immortals," a tribute to PAUL ROBESON, JACKIE ROBINSON, MALCOLM X, and MARTIN LUTHER KING JR.

The final chapter of Wilkins's career was a happy one. Not only was he "back on the scene" but his dream of leading his own big band also came to life. After moving to Denmark in 1979 he established the Almost Big Band, a thirteen-piece ensemble featuring the American expatriates Tim Hagans, Richard Boone, Sahib Shihab, Kenny Drew, and Ed Thigpen. In 1981 Wilkins's career achievements were recognized when he was awarded the Queen of Denmark's Ben Webster Jazz Award, presented at an all-star tribute concert including performances by THAD JONES, Idrees Sulieman, and Duke Jordan.

Wilkins continued leading the Almost Big Band—recording four albums with the group—until suffering a stroke in 1991. He lived in Copenhagen with his second wife, Jenny Mikkelsen, whom he had married in 1975, until his death from complications related to his stroke. The success of Wilkins's comeback career remains one of jazz's most inspirational stories.

FURTHER READING
Gitler, Ira. "Ernie Wilkins Returns," *Downbeat* (3 Apr. 1969).

Rusch, Bob. "Ernie Wilkins: Oral History," *Cadence* (Mar. 1977).

Obituary: *New York Times*, 8 June 1999.

JOHN WRIGGLE

Wilkins, J. Ernest, Jr. (27 Nov. 1923–1 May 2011), mathematician and engineer, was born in Chicago, the son of J. Ernest Wilkins, a prominent lawyer, and Lucile Beatrice Robinson, a schoolteacher with a master's degree. Wilkins developed an intense interest in mathematics at an early age, and with the encouragement and support of his parents and a teacher at Parker High School in Chicago, he was able to accelerate his education and finish high school at the age of thirteen. After graduation, he was immediately accepted by the University of Chicago, where he was the youngest student ever admitted by that institution. Within five years, Wilkins received three degrees in Mathematics, a B.A. in 1940, an M.S. in 1941, and a Ph.D. in 1942. He was also inducted into Phi Beta Kappa in 1940 and Sigma Xi, the Scientific Research Society, in 1942. While at the university, he was university table tennis champion for three years and won the boys' state championship in 1938.

After earning his Ph.D. from the University of Chicago, Wilkins received a Rosenwald Fellowship to carry out postdoctoral research at the Institute for Advanced Study in Princeton, New Jersey. During his stay, from October 1942 to December 1942, he worked on four papers. All were published within one year, with three appearing in the *Duke Mathematical Journal* and one in *Annals of Mathematics*.

In January 1943 Wilkins began teaching at Tuskegee Institute in Alabama, where he had accepted a position as instructor of freshmen mathematics. However, in March 1944 he was recruited to work in the Metallurgical Laboratory at the University of Chicago as part of the Manhattan Project, the United States' program to develop an atomic bomb. At the laboratory, he was given the title of "Associate Physicist" rather than "Mathematician," a designation that allowed him to receive a higher salary. Wilkins worked under Eugene Wigner, who directed the Theoretical Physics Group, which provided the theoretical basis for the design of the Hanford, Washington, fission reactor. Wilkins's duties consisted of applying his expertise in mathematics to help resolve various issues related to the understanding and design of reactors. During his stay at the Metallurgical Laboratory, Wilkins made several major contributions to the field of nuclear-reactor physics. It was in his Manhattan District reports that the concepts now referred to as the Wilkins effect, and the Wigner-Wilkins and Wilkins spectra for thermal neutrons, were developed and made quantitative.

At the completion of his duties at the Metallurgical Laboratory, Wilkins accepted a position as mathematician in the Scientific Instrument Division of the American Optical Company in Buffalo, New York. There he worked on the design of lenses for microscopes and ophthalmologic instruments. His research on "the resolving power of a coated objective" was published in the *Journal of the Optical Society of America* (1949, 1950), and was the first of a long series of publications, extending over four decades, on various problems related to apodization—methods that can be used to improve the resolving power of an optical system. In addition to the solution of several specific problems, Wilkins brought to the field of apodization a certain mathematical rigor, whose absence left many earlier results suspect.

On 22 June 1947 Wilkins married Gloria Louise Stewart; they had two children. Gloria Wilkins died in 1980. In May 1950 Wilkins moved to White Plains, New York, to accept the position of senior mathematician at the United Nuclear Corporation. After accepting a series of increasing managerial responsibilities, he became manager of the Research and Development Division, a group of about thirty individuals in mathematics, physics, chemistry, and metallurgy doing contract work for the Atomic Energy Commission in the areas of theoretical reactor physics and shielding. Wilkins developed and applied a variety of mathematical tools to problems in these fields, and some of his methods are now presented in the standard textbooks. In addition, his work with H. Goldstein on the transport of gamma rays through various materials was the standard reference for many years and is still cited in the current literature.

Although Wilkins's work required him to provide mathematical support to the engineering staff, he discovered that many of them did not approach him for aid until their projects were substantially complete, often resulting in cost overruns. Wilkins concluded that his colleagues might respond better if he were a fellow engineer, and in 1953 he entered the Department of Mechanical Engineering at New York University. He graduated in 1957 with a BME magna cum laude and in 1960 received an MME degree. As he had hoped, his engineering colleagues at United Nuclear Corporation greatly increased their early consultations with him.

In September 1960 Wilkins accepted a position at the General Atomic Company in San Diego, California, as assistant chair of the Theoretical Physics Department. Shortly thereafter, he was promoted to assistant director of the John Jay Hopkins Laboratory, followed by further promotions to director of the Defense Science and Engineering Center and director of Computational Research. His managerial responsibilities included making sure that safety concerns were being treated seriously, ensuring the progress of various technical projects, and providing both technical and policy advice to his administrative superiors. Particular programs included work on thermoelectricity, the design of high-temperature gas-cooled nuclear reactors, plasma physics as it relates to fusion reactors, and Project ORION, a program exploring the use of nuclear power to propel rockets.

In March 1970 Wilkins accepted a position at Howard University in Washington, D.C., as Distinguished Professor of Applied Mathematics and Physics. During his stay at Howard he supervised seven M.S. theses and four Ph.D. dissertations. Wilkins had become a member of the American Nuclear Society in 1955; his increasing participation in the activities of the organization and his international prominence in several areas of mathematics and engineering led to his selection as national president in 1974–1975. In 1976 he was inducted into the National Academy of Engineering. The citation for this honor reads, "Peaceful application of atomic energy through contributions to the design and development of nuclear reactions."

In September 1976 Wilkins took a sabbatical leave from Howard University to go to the Argonne National Laboratory in Argonne, Illinois. As a visiting scientist, he provided mathematics consultation in reactor physics and engineering. He also continued his own research interests in apodization and "a variational problem in Hilbert space." Before Wilkins could return to Howard, he received an offer to return to industry as vice president and associate general manager for Science and Engineering at EG and G Idaho, Inc., in Idaho Falls, Idaho. He accepted this responsibility and began work in March 1977, officially resigning from the faculty at Howard in 1978. In 1978 he was promoted to deputy general manager for Science and Engineering, but he continued his position as vice president, with the responsibility of ensuring the high quality of work and of representing the company in its dealings with the U.S. Department of Energy and the Nuclear Regulatory Commission.

In 1984 Wilkins retired from EG and G Idaho and returned to Argonne National Laboratory as a Distinguished Argonne Fellow. That summer he married Maxine G. Malone, who died in 1997; they had no children. At the completion of his stay at Argonne in May 1985, Wilkins went into full retirement. However, he continued to work as a consultant and adviser to a number of technical companies, professional organizations, and universities. It was during this period that Wilkins initiated a new area of research concerned with the real zeros of random polynomials, published in the *Proceedings of the American Mathematical Society* (1988, 1991).

Wilkins's retirement ended in 1990 when he accepted the position of Distinguished Professor of Mathematics and Mathematical Physics at Clark Atlanta University in Atlanta. A major factor influencing this decision was the opportunity to collaborate with ALBERT TURNER BHARUCHA-REID, an internationally recognized mathematician, on random polynomials. Unfortunately, Bharucha-Reid died before Wilkins arrived at the university, but Wilkins continued his research, publishing over the next decade five fundamental papers on the mean number of real zeros for random hyperbolic, with the French mathematician Adrien-Marie Legendre, and trigonometric polynomials. During this period he also supervised eleven M.S. theses in the Department of Mathematical Sciences. Wilkins retired from Clark Atlanta University in August 2003, and in September he married Vera Wood Anderson in Chicago.

J. Ernest Wilkins Jr.'s distinguished career as a research mathematician and engineer, and his contributions to research and management, have been recognized by a large number of honors and awards received throughout his life.

Wilkins died in Foutain Hills, Arizona, at the age of 87.

FURTHER READING

A complete copy of J. Ernest Wilkins Jr.'s *curriculum vita*, along with other bibliographic materials, is in the Special Collections of the Atlanta University Center of the Woodruff Library in Atlanta.

Donaldson, James. "Black Americans in Mathematics," in *A Century of Mathematics in America, Part III* (1989): 449–469.

Newell, V. K., ed. *Black Mathematicians and Their Works* (1980).

"Phi Beta Kappa at 16." *The Crisis*, Sept. 1940, 288.

Tubbs, Vincent. "Adjustment of a Genius." *Ebony*, Feb. 1958: 60–67.

Obituary: *Chicago Tribune*, 4 May 2011.

RONALD E. MICKENS

Wilkins, Joe Willie (7 Jan. 1921–28 Mar. 1979), bluesman, guitarist, and vocalist, was born in Bobo, Coahoma County, Mississippi, the only surviving child of Parlee Johnson and Frank Wilkins, sharecroppers. His father was known widely in the Mississippi Delta for his guitar playing and singing, and his friends included the guitarists Willie Brown and Richard "Hacksaw" Harney, the violinist Fiddlin' Sam Harris, and the accordion player Walter "Pat" Rhodes—all were Wilkins's earliest teachers. As a child Wilkins first learned to play the harmonica, but his mother made him give it up because playing it caused his nose to bleed. He soon learned to play other instruments, including the fiddle, before settling on the guitar.

Wilkins's musical influences were many and varied. He absorbed ideas from other musicians and from listening to recordings by CHARLIE PATTON and BLIND LEMON JEFFERSON. Although he immersed himself in his father's guitar sound and in the blues of the northern Mississippi Delta, he also heard other musical styles on the jukebox at a local tavern. Wilkins studied the records on the jukebox until he could replicate them exactly; locals called him the "Walking Seeburg" (Seeburg was the brand name of the jukebox) for his ability to play any song from the jukebox upon request. His precocious absorption and mastery of the entire spectrum of black popular music of the 1920s and 1930s contributed greatly to his becoming the primary blues guitar stylist of the post–World War II era.

In 1941, several months after the inaugural broadcast of the *King Biscuit Time* show over Helena, Arkansas, radio station KFFA, SONNY BOY WILLIAMSON, the harmonica virtuoso, recruited Wilkins to join the guitarist ROBERT LOCKWOOD JR. and himself on the influential show. *King Biscuit Time* (sponsored by the Interstate Grocery Company to promote its King Biscuit Flour and later its Sonny Boy Corn Meal) was the first African American radio programming regularly heard in the mid-South. The show broadcasted every day at noon—when agricultural workers and other laborers broke for lunch—for fifteen minutes and featured Williamson with his distinctive and expressive singing and original compositions. *King Biscuit Time* was heard everywhere across the Delta, and soon other radio stations throughout the region were also broadcasting midday blues shows. In 2004 *King Biscuit Time* was still broadcasting daily from station KFFA, though it no longer featured live music.

It was in Helena and at KFFA that Williamson and Wilkins, who had by this time adopted the electric guitar, developed a true blues ensemble sound (including at various times Joe Willie "Pinetop" Perkins, Willie Love, Robert "Dudlow" Taylor, Houston Stackhouse, ELMORE JAMES, and James "Peck" Curtis). They became the prototype for the next decade's Chicago blues bands of MUDDY WATERS, HOWLIN' WOLF, and others. It was at KFFA and in jukes scattered throughout the Delta that his innovative synthesis of the Delta style of his father and the Texas single-string picking popularized by T-BONE WALKER matured into a definitive and influential sound.

Wilkins and Williamson were ramblers and frequently did stints at other radio stations in Arkansas, Mississippi, Louisiana, and Tennessee. Often they performed and broadcast with other musicians, including ROBERT NIGHTHAWK, Willie Nix, Little Milton Campbell, Elmore James, Charlie Booker, Big Amos Patton, James Cotton, Willie Love, ROOSEVELT SYKES, Floyd Jones, WALTER HORTON, LITTLE WALTER JACOBS, Jimmy DeBerry, Forest City Joe Pugh, Henry "Little Wolf" Palmer, Woodrow Adams, MEMPHIS SLIM, and Robert Lockwood Jr., among many others. This included stints on Nighthawk's competing KFFA blues shows, *Mother's Best Flour* and *Bright Star Flour*. Of special importance in the history of the blues were Williamson and Wilkins's, and later Wilkins's with his own bands, broadcasts over West Memphis, Arkansas, station KWEM. In the late 1940s and 1950s a whole generation of blues guitarists were mentored by Wilkins from his base in West Memphis, including Pat Hare, L. D. McGee, HUBERT SUMLIN, B. B. KING, Willie Lee Johnson, and ALBERT KING. These guitarists also laid the foundation for the development of Memphis rock and roll in the 1950s. Though Wilkins spent some time in Detroit and Chicago, he always soon returned to the South to be close to his parents, thus forsaking greater recognition and more income so that he could stay at home. It was this renowned stubbornness which earned Wilkins the nickname "Mule."

A sought-after sideman, Wilkins first recorded with Sonny Boy Williamson for Jackson, Mississippi's, Trumpet label in 1951. Subsequently Wilkins played guitar on recordings by Willie Love, Floyd Jones, ARTHUR CRUDUP, Elmore

James, Willie Nix, Roosevelt Sykes, Little Walter Jacobs, Walter Horton, Mose Vinson, Memphis Al Williams, Joe Hill Louis, and Jimmy Deberry for Sun, Chess, Trumpet and other labels. A 45-rpm single was released by Joe Willie Wilkins and His King Biscuit Boys (including Roland "Boy Blue" Hayes and Houston Stackhouse) by the Mimosa label in 1973. In 1977 Adamo released an LP of mostly live recordings of Wilkins, and following his death from a heart attack in Memphis, additional live recordings were released. There was an aborted attempt by Sun Records to record Wilkins's deep, rich Delta voice in the 1950s, but it was Wilkins's 1973 Mimosa single that first preserved his exceptional singing.

Best known for his single-string lead and sophisticated rhythm guitar playing (often played simultaneously) Wilkins was also an outstanding slide guitarist. Wilkins's first slide guitar recording was a remake of his and Williamson's composition "Mr. Downchild," originally recorded for Trumpet in 1951; Wilkins's slide version appeared in 1973 on Mimosa. Wilkins's Adamo LP includes several live recordings of his slide technique: a version of ROBERT JOHNSON's "Me and the Devil Blues" and a remake of Muddy Waters's "I Feel Like Going Back Home" (which was based on a song recorded by Frank Wilkins's friend Willie Brown). Indeed Waters recalled that while touring the South soon after the 1948 release of his song by Aristocrat, he heard someone performing the song on the car's radio. He was startled that the radio performance was better than his own hit record; the performer was Wilkins.

A heavy drinker since early in life, Wilkins suffered from related health problems as early as the 1950s. He lived with several women for extended periods of time, including Alice (Helena) and Margaret (Nighthawk's adopted sister with whom he had at least one child), but it was his wife, the dancer and singer Louise "Carrie" Etheridge, with whom he spent most of his adult life. It was with Carrie that Wilkins spent his last years living in the house that his parents had built in industrial north Memphis. In the 1970s Wilkins still played the small Delta jukes he had played for decades, but he also performed on the college/festival circuit, bringing his music to new audiences, including at the American Folklife Festival, Ann Arbor Jazz and Blues Festival, Monterey Jazz Festival, River City Blues Festival, and as the star act of the traveling Memphis Blues Caravan. Wilkins also appeared in the BBC production *The Devil's Music: A History of the Blues* (1976).

Wilkins influenced almost every significant blues guitarist of the 1950s. Little Milton Campbell said "Joe Willie taught me a heck of a lot … he is very artistic; sounds like two guitarists at once—he plays rhythm and lead at the same time. He influenced me tremendously. Me personally, I think he's the greatest of the blues guitarists" (Hay, 199). According to Jimmy Rogers, "Joe Willie Wilkins was my favorite. He had a tone. He carried a good bottom … Joe Willie … I got a lotta licks from" (Brisbin, "Jimmy Rogers," 17), and to Willie Johnson, Wilkins "could play the blues the way he developed it … he could play bass on his guitar and lead all at the same time. He'd stretch them fingers, man. Joe Willie, he was a terrific guitar player" (Brisbin, "Howlin' Wolf's," 45). Muddy Waters said of Wilkins, "The man is great, the man is stone great. For blues, like I say, he's the best" (Hay, 224). The Trumpet label discographer Marc Ryan wrote, "His ultimate contribution to the development of a modern blues guitar style is immense; his precociously early refinement and dissemination of his music place him alongside T-Bone Walker and LONNIE JOHNSON as a progenitor of the genre" (Ryan, 43). In 1993 the African country of Gambia—from that area of the continent that ethnomusicologists have identified as the ancestral source of the blues—paid tribute to Wilkins by issuing a postage stamp in his honor.

FURTHER READING

Brisbin, John Anthony. "Howlin' Wolf's Early Guitarists: Willie Johnson," *Living Blues* (1995).
Brisbin, John Anthony. "Jimmy Rogers: I'm Havin' Fun Right Today," *Living Blues* (1997).
Hay, Fred J. "Goin' Back to Sweet Memphis": *Conversations with the Blues* (2001).
O'Neal, Jim. "Joe Willie Wilkins," *Living Blues* (1973).
Obituary: *Living Blues* (1979).

DISCOGRAPHY

Ryan, Marc. *Trumpet Records: An Illustrated History with Discography* (1992).

FRED J. HAY

Wilkins, Roger Wood (24 Mar. 1932–), journalist, educator, and attorney, was born in Kansas City, Missouri, the only child of Earl William Wilkins, a business manager for the *Kansas City Call* newspaper, and Helen Natalie Jackson, a YWCA organizer. At age eight, shortly after the death of his father, Wilkins and his mother moved to Harlem, New York, and shared a seventh-floor apartment with his grandmother and an aunt. An exceptionally bright student, he was envied and bullied in middle school. Fortunately his mother's second marriage to a Michigan doctor in 1944 landed him in a less hazardous albeit unwelcoming neighborhood in Grand Rapids in the only home occupied by a black family. Self-assured and athletic, he soon adapted to his new environment and in his senior year at Crestin High School was elected president of the student council. Wilkins majored in political science at the University of Michigan at Ann Arbor where he was president of the graduating class of 1953, which also included the actor JAMES EARL JONES.

When Wilkins enrolled in the university's law school he quit his part-time factory job, and thanks to his uncle ROY WILKINS, the soon-to-be executive secretary of the NAACP, he found work as a summer intern with the NAACP Legal Defense and Education Fund then headed by the future U.S. Supreme Court justice THURGOOD MARSHALL. Upon receiving his law degree in 1956 he married his college sweetheart, Eve Estelle Tyler. Wilkins had just been hired by the Brooklyn, New York, law firm of Delson, Levin & Gordon to practice international law when he ran out of military draft exemptions and was forced to alter his career plans. Reclassified 4A, he wound up working as a welfare caseworker for ten months in Cleveland, Ohio, and witnessed firsthand the misery of persons in poverty-stricken, dysfunctional families and the ineptness of government intervention. He resumed his law practice in Brooklyn but became disillusioned with his profession and in 1962 took a post as special assistant to the administrator of the Agency for International Development (AID) in the U.S. State Department. His time in government service in Washington, D.C., was extended when he accepted positions as community relations director at the U.S. Department of Commerce in 1964 and assistant attorney general in the U.S. Department of Justice in 1966. Leaving behind the heady world of capital power politics and exclusive cocktail parties, in 1969 he was employed by the Ford Foundation as a program director for experimental human services and assistant to the president until 1972.

Possessed by a strong desire to live a more meaningful life in the service of those less fortunate, and still troubled by his own privileged status and upbringing in contrast to that of so many underprivileged African Americans, he again changed careers. Choosing journalism as the vehicle to press for social and political reforms, in 1972 Wilkins found a degree of personal satisfaction and accomplishment working as a member of the editorial board of the *Washington Post*, and in 1973

shared with Bob Woodward and Carl Bernstein the Pulitzer Prize for Public Service for the newspaper's coverage of the Watergate scandal. From 1974 to 1979 he was both on the editorial board and a columnist writing on urban issues for the *New York Times*. A few months after his divorce from his first wife he married the artist Mary Meyer in 1977, but they were divorced just nine months later. By 1980 Wilkins was the associate editor of the *Washington Star*. In February 1981 he married Patricia King, a law professor, with whom he had his third child.

In yet another career switch, in 1982 he began more than two decades of teaching as a professor of history and American culture at George Mason University in Fairfax, Virginia. Tall, handsome, urbane, and with sterling credentials as a former federal government insider and prestigious newspaper editor and columnist, Wilkins, from his vantage point in the ivory tower, was in demand to appear on major television news–interview shows such as PBS's *McNeil/Lehrer News Hour* (the *NewsHour with Jim Lehrer* since 1995), *NBC Nightly News*, and ABC's *Nightline*, among others; on radio his opinions as a commentator were heard on National Public Radio (NPR), CBS Radio Network, and the Mutual Broadcasting System. The same attributes that made him attractive to television and radio audiences also kept him busy on the lecture circuit. Since the mid-1980s he has regularly published articles on society and politics, book reviews, interviews, and speech transcripts in the liberal news magazine the *Nation* (he has been a member of its editorial board since 1979), the *New York Times*, the *Washington Post*, the *Boston Globe*, the *Los Angeles Times*, the *San Francisco Chronicle*, the NAACP's the *Crisis*, *Newsday*, and *Mother Jones*, and he contributed writings to numerous other newspapers, magazines, and journals, including the *Chronicle of Higher Education*, *Emerge*, *Social Education*, *USA Today*, *Media Studies Journal*, the *Baltimore Sun*, *Education Digest*, and the *Virginia Quarterly Review*. Wilkins also wrote and narrated two documentaries for the PBS show *Frontline*: "Keeping the Faith" (1987) on the black church, and "Throwaway People" (1990) on destitute black males.

Prominent national organizations for which Wilkins has served as a board member include the NAACP Legal Defense Fund, the Pulitzer Prize Board (chairman, 1987–1988), the PEN/Faulkner Foundation, the African American Institute, and the University of the District of Columbia. Long active in the fight against South African apartheid, in 1990 he coordinated the visit of the South

African freedom fighter Nelson Mandela to the United States. Among his awards and recognitions are several honorary degrees from universities and the Roger Baldwin Civil Liberties Award from the New York Civil Liberties Union. In 1982 Wilkins published his critically acclaimed autobiography, *A Man's Life*. His other books are the award-winning *Jefferson's Pillow: The Founding Fathers and the Dilemma of Black Patriotism* (2001) and a coedited book, *Quiet Riots: Race and Poverty in the United States* (1988).

FURTHER READING

Gwinn, Mary Ann. "Patriotic Dilemma," *Seattle Times*, 13 Jan. 2003.

Miller, Roger. "Pulitzer Winner to Speak at IWU Annual King Festival," *Pantagraph*, 27 Dec. 2000.

ROBERT FIKES JR.

Wilkins, Roy (30 Aug. 1901–8 Sept. 1981), reporter and civil rights leader, was born Roy Ottaway Wilkins in St. Louis, Missouri, the son of William DeWitte Wilkins, a brick kiln worker, and Mayfield Edmundson. Upon his mother's death in 1905, Wilkins was sent with his brother and sister to St. Paul, Minnesota, to live with their aunt and uncle, Elizabeth and Sam Williams, because his mother worried that her husband could not handle raising their three children and would send them back to Mississippi. The family had fled Mississippi after an incident in which William had beaten a white man over a racial insult.

Wilkins grew up in a middle-class household in a relatively integrated neighborhood. A porter who oversaw operations in the personal car of the chief of the Northern Pacific Railroad, Sam Williams taught Wilkins the virtue of education. Stressing the importance of faith, Sam and Elizabeth also regularly took Wilkins to the local African Methodist Episcopal Church. He developed an interest in writing in high school and then went on to the University of Minnesota, where he became the first black reporter for the school's newspaper. Wilkins also served as editor of the *Saint Paul Appeal*, a weekly African American paper, and was an active member of the city's NAACP branch.

After graduating from college with honors in 1923, Wilkins became a reporter with the *Kansas City Call*. He covered the NAACP's Midwestern Race Relations Conference and was deeply inspired by JAMES WELDON JOHNSON's message stressing the need for African Americans to fight for constitutional rights. Wilkins was outraged over the widespread racism in Kansas City in housing, public accommodations, education, law enforcement, and employment, but his middle-class values of thrift and hard work also led him to look disdainfully at blacks who behaved in ways that affirmed negative white stereotypes. "A lot of the things we suffered came as wrapped, perfumed presents from ourselves," he later wrote (Wilkins, 73). Wilkins soon became secretary of the Kansas City branch of the NAACP, and in 1929 he married Aminda Badeau, a social worker who came from a prominent St. Louis family. The couple had no children.

Wilkins's writing and NAACP work soon caught the attention of WALTER WHITE, the executive secretary of the national organization, and in 1931 White persuaded Wilkins to move to New York to become his chief aide. His duties included writing, lecturing, raising money, and speaking out against racial injustice. When Will Rogers used a racial epithet four times in a radio broadcast, for example, Wilkins organized a nationwide effort to bombard the National Broadcasting Company with telegrams of protest. In 1932 he traveled to Mississippi to do an undercover investigation of the low pay and horrible working conditions suffered by African Americans working for the U.S. Army Corps of Engineers. Wilkins's findings encouraged Senator Robert Wagner of New York to hold hearings on the conditions, and as a result the workers received modest pay increases. In 1934 Wilkins became editor of *The Crisis*, the NAACP's magazine, and brought changes to the periodical that boosted its financial position and broadened its coverage. W. E. B. DuBois, the magazine's former editor, looked upon Wilkins and his changes with disdain, and the two would later clash over DuBois's growing radicalism. Throughout the 1930s and 1940s Wilkins also battled Communists within the NAACP. Holding a strong faith in America's democratic promise, he disagreed profoundly with their philosophy and viewed them as politically harmful to the struggle for racial equality.

Upon Walter White's death in 1955, Wilkins was unanimously selected as the new executive secretary of the NAACP, a post he would hold for twenty-two years. Wilkins strongly believed that working through the courts for legal changes and lobbying presidents and lawmakers in Congress for civil rights legislation offered the best way to effect lasting, significant improvements for African Americans. He regularly testified before Congress on behalf of legislation, met with every president from Harry Truman through Jimmy Carter, rallied NAACP branches

Roy Wilkins, Assistant Secretary of the NAACP, dressed as a workman during his investigation of workers' conditions on the Federal Flood Control Project in Memphis, Tennessee, 1932. (Library of Congress.)

and other progressive organizations to support various civil rights initiatives, and appeared before Democratic and Republican conventions to urge both parties to take strong stands for racial equality. Wilkins's efforts helped produce such landmark federal laws as the 1964 Civil Rights Act, which outlawed segregation in public accommodations and employment discrimination; the Voting Rights Act of 1965; and the Fair Housing Act of 1968. Like many other civil rights leaders, Wilkins found President Lyndon Johnson to be a valuable ally. Conversely, he regularly criticized Dwight Eisenhower and John F. Kennedy for doing too little.

As direct-action protests became more prominent in the 1950s and early 1960s, Wilkins steadfastly held to his legalistic approach. He was initially skeptical about seminal protests, such as the Montgomery bus boycott and the 1963 March on Washington, though he ultimately supported them. Similarly, Wilkins and BAYARD RUSTIN urged the Mississippi Freedom Democratic Party (MFDP) to accept President Johnson's compromise offer of two at-large seats at the 1964 Democratic

convention if they would moderate their demands for broader representation. The MFDP's FANNIE LOU HAMER and ROBERT P. MOSES refused to compromise, however.

Fearing that civil rights protests might turn to violence and play into the hands of the Republican presidential candidate Barry Goldwater, a staunch conservative who had opposed the 1964 Civil Rights Act, Wilkins also organized an effort among several black leaders that summer to call for a moratorium on civil rights demonstrations until after the presidential election. Wilkins often criticized MARTIN LUTHER KING JR. and groups such as CORE and SNCC, because he doubted that direct action would lead to meaningful change. "When the headlines are gone, the issues still have to be settled in court," he observed (Branch, 557). Wilkins's views also reflected his personal jealousy over the growing popularity of such groups and King. "The other organizations," he angrily commented, "furnish the noise and get the publicity while the NAACP furnishes the manpower and pays the bills" (Branch, 831). Wilkins especially feared that King and the Southern Christian Leadership Conference would erode the NAACP's financial and political strength in the South. Thus, though the two leaders often worked together, they maintained an uneasy relationship throughout the 1960s. King believed the NAACP was often too timid, while Wilkins saw King as a self-promoter. Wilkins distanced himself and the NAACP from King as the SCLC leader grew more critical of the Vietnam War.

Wilkins came under sharp attack from more radical African Americans in the mid- to late 1960s for his unwavering faith in integration, willingness to work with white allies, and confidence in American institutions. Critics also alleged that the NAACP was too timid and had no program to help African Americans economically. Wilkins bristled at these charges and fired back that Black Power was "the father of hatred and the mother of violence" (Fairclough, 320). Younger African Americans sympathetic to Black Power, Wilkins insisted, were "unfair, ungrateful, and forgetful" regarding NAACP accomplishments (*New York Times*, 9 Sept. 1981). One radical group, the Revolutionary Action Movement, even hatched plans to assassinate Wilkins in 1967, though no attempt on his life was carried out, because police raided the group's headquarters and broke up the plot.

At the same time he faced these conflicts with external rivals, Wilkins battled critics within the NAACP. A group of junior NAACP board members known as the Young Turks challenged Wilkins's positions on economic issues, race riots, and the NAACP's endorsement of Johnson in the 1964 presidential election. Supporting Johnson contradicted the organization's longstanding policy of nonpartisanship, but Wilkins saw the right-wing Republican Goldwater as a threat to recent civil rights advances. Critics also believed that Wilkins wielded too much power within the organization. The Young Turks endorsed structural changes that would give more power to local branches and would strip some authority from the national leadership. They first made their case at the NAACP's annual convention in 1965, when they came within one vote of removing Wilkins from the leadership post. The feud lasted for three years. By 1968, however, Wilkins had firmly consolidated his power and put down the rebellion. His means included co-opting some of the Turks' agenda and, at the 1968 NAACP convention in Atlantic City, calling in law enforcement officials to keep order, turning off microphones and lights when some of the Turks attempted to speak, and tabling the dissenters' proposals quickly, with little or no debate. Wilkins continued to advocate for laws and programs to improve black life in education, housing, employment, health care, and other areas throughout the 1970s. He sharply criticized Republican presidents Richard Nixon and Gerald Ford over school desegregation, busing, and voting rights, but failing health slowed his activities somewhat. In 1969 he had suffered a second bout with cancer. Ill health forced him to retire from the NAACP in 1977, when he was replaced by BENJAMIN HOOKS. Four years later, Wilkins died from kidney failure at New York University Medical Center. Upon hearing of Wilkins's death, JESSE JACKSON observed that he was "a man of integrity, intelligence, and courage who, with his broad shoulders, bore more than his share of responsibility for our and the nation's advancement" (*New York Times*, 9 Sept. 1981).

FURTHER READING

Roy Wilkins's papers are housed at the Library of Congress, Washington, D.C.

Wilkins, Roy, with Tom Mathews. *Standing Fast: The Autobiography of Roy Wilkins* (1982).

Branch, Taylor. *Parting the Waters: America in the King Years, 1954–1963* (1988).

Eick, Gretchen Cassel. *Dissent in Wichita: The Civil Rights Movement in the Midwest, 1954–72* (2001).

Fairclough, Adam. *To Redeem the Soul of America: The Southern Christian Leadership Conference and Martin Luther King, Jr.* (1987).

Obituary: *New York Times*, 9 Sept. 1981.

TIMOTHY N. THURBER

Wilkinson, Henry B. (14 Oct. 1889–29 Mar. 1961), poet and U.S. Army veteran, was born Henry Bertram Wilkinson in Philadelphia, Pennsylvania, the second of five surviving children of the Barbadians Mary Elizabeth Clarke, a seamstress, and William Lawrence Wilkinson, a carpenter, himself the son of a "colored" slave manumitted in the parish of St. Philip, Barbados, in 1834.

When Henry was four, the family departed Philadelphia's black ghetto, a district hostile to the social and economic advancement of its black citizenry (as W. E. B. DuBois documented in 1899 in *The Philadelphia Negro*), and returned to Barbados. There Wilkinson received his elementary and only formal education, leaving school at age twelve to become a pupil-teacher (trainee).

In 1909 Panama beckoned Wilkinson, as it did thousands of other West Indians in search of economic opportunity. Two years later, on 24 August 1911, he left the canal zone, with its deadly and debilitating tropical diseases and a Jim Crow system based on "race" and nationality, and returned to the United States, where he enlisted in the U.S. Army at Fort Slocum, New York, in April 1912. In the highly segregated armed forces, he was automatically assigned to the Colored Twenty-fourth Infantry and was stationed in Southeast Asia before being transferred to France during World War I. In keeping with the army's policies, Wilkinson, like most African American soldiers, was compelled to serve in a support unit rather than in a combat division.

After an honorable discharge from the army in 1920 with the rank of battalion sergeant major, Wilkinson settled down to family life in New York. The 1930 federal census showed him living in Kings County, Brooklyn, with his wife Rita Stoute, also of Barbadian ancestry, and their two daughters, and employed as a clerk at the U.S. post office.

Wilkinson's apprentice verse had appeared in the *Service*, the *Honolulu Star-Bulletin*, and the *Stars and Stripes*, the organ of the American Expeditionary Force during World War I. It was only after the war that he turned his attention seriously to poetry with the publication of his three collections *Idle Hours* (1927), *Shady-Rest* (1928), and *Desert Sands* (1933). In 1933 Wilkinson, for some unknown reason, rejected a proposal from a Boston publishing house for a 120-page collection of poems titled *Wanderlust*. This was also the period when some of his poems appeared in literary journals in Barbados and Trinidad and in *Negro World*, which also serialized his fictional work *All*

Men Are Liars. In 1941 he brought out the long poem *Transitory: A Poem for a Peaceful World*, by all evidence his last published work. Wilkinson's notes mention other texts that, like *Wanderlust*, have apparently not survived. A few unpublished poems are among the papers of Arthur Schomburg in New York City and Arthur Spingarn at Howard University.

Wilkinson shares with COUNTÉE CULLEN, the black poet he most revered ("Lines to Cullen"), a breadth of vision and a penchant for older poetic conventions, as illustrated by the rhetorical excesses in his verse. His poetry is also distinguished by its multiplicity of themes: death, friendship, love, war, natural landscapes (especially those of his Caribbean upbringing), and patriotism, as exemplified in his odes to George Washington, Cullen, Charles Lindbergh, the statue of liberty ("Miss Liberty"), and Theodore Roosevelt ("The Square Deal"). Additionally, several poems ("Miriam's Rebellion," "Judas," and "Ishmael") thoughtfully use religious figures to explore personal and universal dilemmas.

In the tradition of his more famous and radical contemporaries, such as CLAUDE MCKAY, Wilkinson also critically addressed the conflicts and contradictions of American society, especially in the area of race relations, from the perspective of one whose patriotism and service to the United States are beyond question. In "Somewhere," "My Brother's Keeper," and "Black Boy" he confronts his ambivalent status as an African American, protesting social injustice and interrogating attitudes toward race, particularly the failure of whites to acknowledge the humanity of blacks and their contribution to modern civilizations. "What record do I bear? / In all the arts and sciences / I nobly did my share," the poet asserts plaintively in "Somewhere," one of his most poignant and best-known poems, published in *The Beacon* in April 1932.

"Black Dancers," "My Ambition," and "Belated Message" also celebrate the African cultural heritage, bemoaning its loss and vilification in the New World setting. But Wilkinson's verse is equally critical of black militancy and those facets of black culture he considered inimical to the well-being of the African American community itself and the wider society in general. "Harlem" provides a painful if uncompromising glimpse of a vibrant yet decaying world and illustrates Wilkinson's ambivalent relationship to black folklife. Some poems about blackness, such as "El Mundo Negro" and "Race Pride," also disturb the modern reader with their tones of self-flagellation, passivity, and appeasement.

Wilkinson's affinity for traditional poetic conventions that may be attributable to his West Indian socialization, and the influence of Cullen proved a barrier to the effectiveness and appeal of his verse and left him further out of step with his contemporaries. Repeatedly he protested the marginalization of his poetry by black editors and critics. Poems such as "Retrospection" and "To the Critics" and his letters to the influential bibliophiles Schomburg and Spingarn reveal this quest for recognition and validation by a sophisticated African American audience. He donated copies of his poetry collections to Schomburg's fledgling institution out of this desire and determination to be memorialized in what he anticipated would become an important record of black cultural achievement.

Henry B. Wilkinson was probably the most prolific and significant of a number of minor Caribbean American voices that lent diversity to the Harlem canon. The rhetorical excesses and idiosyncrasies of his verse notwithstanding, he deserves recognition for his contribution through his art to the debate about self and community that challenged entrenched racial ideologies and indicted social inequity. In addition to articulating alternative and sometimes controversial perspectives, Wilkinson's work expanded the possibilities of African American writing through its broader vision of the poet as a person singing to all people about their common humanity. His work demonstrates as well a considerable grasp of Western ideas and poetic conventions despite his limited formal education. Those tensions and conflicts that surface throughout his verse are the expected consequences of his socialization in both a British colony and a black metropolis.

Wilkinson died in New York City and is buried at the Long Island National Cemetery in Farmingdale, New York.

FURTHER READING

Wilkinson's work and correspondence are in the Schomburg Center for Research on Black Culture in New York City and the Moorland Spingarn Research Center at Howard University in Washington, D.C.

"Henry B. Wilkinson," in *The New Writer's Who's Who* (1934?).

Wade, Carl A. "Lost Voices in a Minor Key: Three Caribbean American Poets and the Harlem Renaissance," in *Journal of Caribbean Studies* vol. 18, nos. 1 and 2 (Fall 2003/Spring 2004).

CARL A. WADE

Wilkinson, Marion Birnie (23 June 1870–19 Sept. 1956), clubwoman and civil rights activist, was born Marion Raven Birnie, in Charleston, South Carolina, to Richard Birnie, a cotton shipping agent, and Anna (Frost) Birnie. Both the Birnies and the Frosts, descendants of antebellum free black families, were members of the black social and economic elite in post–Civil War Charleston. Birnie's family taught her that her relative privilege obliged her to serve those less fortunate in her community. Richard Birnie was a trustee of the Avery Normal Institute, an American Missionary Association school established in Charleston in 1865. In 1888 Marion Birnie graduated from Avery with high honors. She went on to teach at her alma mater until her marriage nine years later.

Her father was a lay leader at St. Mark's Episcopal Church in Charleston, and her future husband, Robert Wilkinson, was a choirboy there. As a young woman Birnie represented the woman's auxiliary from her church at the annual Conference of Church Workers Among Colored People, held in Charleston in 1896, where she read a paper on woman's work. In 1896 she was also president of the African American branch of the Women's Christian Temperance Union (WCTU), a Christian-oriented temperance association that emphasized social reform and endorsed woman suffrage.

On 29 June 1897 Marion Birnie married Robert Shaw Wilkinson. In 1911 he was named president of South Carolina State College in Orangeburg, South Carolina, one of the most important centers of education for blacks in the state. He also became a director of two local banks and president of the South Carolina Negro Business League. The Wilkinsons, who had four children (Helen, Robert, Frost, and Lula), enjoyed considerable financial stability. The family had a chauffeur and two servants, sent out their laundry, and hired State College students to help around the house.

Known as "Mother Wilkinson" Marion Wilkinson was loved by South Carolina State College students. She was in charge of the dining hall and the boarding department and was an unofficial adviser to many students. In 1908 she founded a branch of the YWCA at State College, chaired its advisory board for over twenty-seven years, and in 1925 oversaw the building of the "Y-Hut," the first YWCA building on an African American college campus. Wilkinson was also involved in the national YWCA as a member of the committee convened by LUGENIA BURNS HOPE to appeal for greater control over black branches in the South.

Wilkinson's most significant role, however, was as the president of the South Carolina Federation of Colored Women's Clubs, which she helped found in 1909. The federation sought to improve living conditions for African American families through campaigns for better health and education, and it also protested against discrimination and lynching, and worked to increase black economic prosperity and pride through knowledge of black history. The federation also emphasized improving rural education through sewing and cooking classes and campaigned to extend the school term. In 1910 Wilkinson began a local women's club, the Sunlight Club of Orangeburg, and presided over it for forty years. The club was founded to help the poor in Orangeburg, initially by donating goods to the poorhouse. The Sunlight Club later built a community center for use by various youth organizations and others in Orangeburg.

Wilkinson was instrumental in the decision of the Federation of Colored Women's Clubs to build a home for troubled black girls in 1917, originally known as the Fairwold Home for Delinquent Girls and later renamed the Marion Birnie Wilkinson Home for Girls. Members of the federation raised over $30,000 to build the home, while Wilkinson helped organize a committee of black and white community members to lobby the state legislature for aid. Although it already provided funds for homes for white boys, white girls, and black boys, the legislature appropriated only $4,000 from 1924 to 1926 and refused to sanction Fairwold as the official state home for black girls. Funding for such an official home did not come until 1949. The original home was destroyed by fire in December 1925, and largely because of Wilkinson's good relationships with white Episcopalians, the church donated land for a new home in Cayce. Despite major fund-raising efforts, in 1932 the federation, strapped for money, changed the mission of the home from the care of delinquents to the care of orphans in order to secure funding from the Duke Foundation. Wilkinson stressed the teaching of practical skills, such as housekeeping and farming, along with culture and the arts.

Wilkinson's campaign for white support for Fairwold dovetailed with her leadership in the state branch of the Commission on Interracial Cooperation (CIC), which was founded in 1919 by the Tuskegee Institute principal ROBERT RUSSA MOTON, the New York investment banker George F. Peabody, and Harry F. Byrd, later governor of Virginia and U.S. senator, among others. In early 1920 Wilkinson and Lugenia Burns Hope were among ten

African American women who met with two white Methodist women. This in turn led to a meeting of black and white women, including MARGARET MURRAY WASHINGTON and CHARLOTTE EUGENIA HAWKINS BROWN, in October 1920, during which the participants organized the women's division of the CIC. When South Carolina participants in that meeting subsequently organized a women's division for their own state CIC in 1922, Wilkinson drew together a committee of black women to parallel the white women's group. She served as vice chair of the committee for many years, exercising considerable leadership in the CIC's efforts to improve race relations, gain better accommodations on railroad cars, prevent lynchings, improve justice and education for African Americans, and increase knowledge of black literature and history. In recognition of her work Wilkinson was appointed to the national CIC's board of directors. She maintained friendly relations with many whites in South Carolina, using her position as a women's club leader and college president's wife to demand justice for African Americans.

Wilkinson was a member of an important network of black women educators and clubwomen in the early twentieth century and was involved in several national organizations in addition to the YWCA and the CIC. She was vice president at large of the National Association of Colored Women (NACW) from 1920 to 1922, held several other offices in the NACW, and was vice president and honorary president of the regional Southeastern Federation. Wilkinson also served as vice president of the International Council of Women of the Darker Races and took great interest in its black history program. She believed that it was crucial to expose clubwomen in South Carolina to national leaders, and she invited prominent women such as MARY McLEOD BETHUNE and Charlotte Brown to speak in Orangeburg and elsewhere.

Wilkinson remained active in her church as well. When she moved to Orangeburg in 1911 there was no black Episcopal church there, so in 1912 she and her husband founded the St. Paul Episcopal Mission. They held services at their home and Wilkinson served as treasurer for over forty years, while her husband was senior warden and lay reader until his death, at which time their son-in-law, Fredrick M. Sheffield, succeeded him.

Wilkinson was on the county executive committee of the Red Cross and a member of the board of trustees of Voorhees College in Denmark, South Carolina. She also had a love for gardening, and was instrumental in creating the Rose Garden at State College and in convincing the white Orangeburg Horticultural Society to donate azaleas to black churches.

The most influential clubwoman in South Carolina and a crucial leader in the state interracial movement, Marion Birnie Wilkinson demonstrated throughout her life the many ways in which educated African Americans attempted to uplift the race within the confines of segregation. Known as a "lady," she was well-respected by both blacks and whites and was often praised for her unselfish generosity.

FURTHER READING

The Book of Gold: Fiftieth Anniversary, South Carolina Federation of Colored Women's Clubs, 1909–1959 (1959).

Drago, Edmund L. *Initiative, Paternalism, and Race Relations: Charleston's Avery Normal Institute* (1990).

Fortieth Anniversary Booklet of the South Carolina Federation of Colored Women's Clubs, 1909–1949 (1949).

Gordon, Asa H. *Sketches of Negro Life and History in South Carolina* (1929; repr. 1971).

Johnson, Joan Marie. *Southern Ladies, New Women: Race, Region, and Clubwomen in South Carolina, 1890–1930* (2004).

JOAN MARIE JOHNSON

Willet, Chappie (6 Sept. 1907–30 Mar. 1976), jazz composer, arranger, and pianist, was born Francis Robert Willet in Philadelphia, Pennsylvania, the son of Chester Willet, originally from New Jersey, and Elizabeth "Lizzie" Hill of Virginia. The Willet family, which included Francis and his older sister, Elizabeth, lived in the row house neighborhood of South Philadelphia, often taking in boarders to supplement their income. Like the majority of African Americans and Italian immigrants in their neighborhood, both of Willet's parents worked in catering or domestic service.

Willet's early education has not been documented, but by 1930 he was attending West Virginia State College, a land-grant school in Institute, West Virginia, where he was involved in music both in and out of school. He studied composition with an instructor, Joseph William Grider, composed the school "Cheering Song," and performed on piano in various recitals and concerts sponsored by the school. Willet—already performing under the name "Chappie"—also led, arranged, and composed for the Campus Revelers, an eleven-piece dance band that performed and broadcast from various hotels and country clubs in the nearby Charleston area. (The future Benny Carter and CLAUDE HOPKINS drummer Keg Purnell claimed membership in Willet's Revelers.) After graduation in the spring of 1933 Willet again found work as a musical director, this time with Edwards's Collegians, a popular territory band out of Bluefield, West Virginia, led by the pianist Phillip H. Edwards and featuring alumni of West Virginia State, Bluefield Institute, and Wilberforce University. Willet was brought in as a front man and arranger, updating the Collegians' repertoire with more jazz-influenced swing arrangements. Although the band continued under Willet through the summer of 1934 as Chappie Willet's Greystone Ballroom Orchestra, the Depression finally took its toll: the group, having never recorded, disbanded in Philadelphia. After working jobs in Philadelphia and Chicago, Willet eventually found regular employment in New York City, writing for nightclub floor shows and dance acts. By September of 1937 Willet was working at the Cotton Club, where he wrote the dance specialty number for FAYARD NICHOLAS of the Nicholas Brothers dance act. He also procured his own office space in midtown Manhattan, where he worked with songwriters and arrangers including Porter Grainger, Donald Heywood, and Russell Wooding. Willet is reported to have provided scores for floor shows at numerous New York nightclubs throughout the late 1930s and 1940s, including Connie's Inn, the Ubangi, and the Zanzibar, as well as theaters like the Apollo and the Lafayette. His collaborators included the dance acts HONI COLES and Cholly Atkins, Charles "Cookie" Cook and Ernest "Brownie" Brown, Ford Lee "Buck" Washington and JOHN BUBBLES, and the choreographer Clarence Robinson, among others.

Willet also found work with the various swing bands that played these shows, providing material for their recording sessions or film appearances. His arrangements were recorded by the bands of Teddy Hill ("Uptown Rhapsody" and "Blue Rhythm Fantasy"), LUCKY MILLINDER ("Prelude to a Stomp" and "Rhythm Jam"), CAB CALLOWAY ("I Ain't Gettin' Nowhere Fast"), and Red Norvo ("Jump Jump's Here" and "A-Tisket, A-Tasket"). With LOUIS ARMSTRONG, Willet developed a long-term relationship that included writing "Jubilee" for Armstrong's film feature *Every Day's a Holiday* (1938) and such classic recordings as "I've Got My Fingers Crossed," "Struttin' with Some Barbecue," and "Satchel Mouth Swing."

At the Cotton Club Willet collaborated with the composer DUKE ELLINGTON on Ellington's score for the spring 1938 *Cotton Club Parade* show, including dance numbers like "I'm Slappin' Seventh Avenue (With the Sole of My Shoe)" and "Swingtime in Honolulu." When the drummer Gene Krupa left Benny Goodman to start his own big band in April of 1938, Krupa hired Willet to help create his book and to write Krupa's radio theme song, "Apurksody." Krupa remembered: "Chappie Willet was my first arranger and we got some great things from him.... I'll never forget how much he did for bands that had to play shows" (Klauber, 46).

Krupa went on to record Willet's arrangements, including "Grandfather's Clock," "I Know That You Know," an extended performance of "Blue Rhythm Fantasy" (Parts 1 & 2), and "Jungle Madness," performed in a 1940 Krupa orchestra film short. Willet's big band instrumental pieces were typically up-tempo, tour de force numbers showcasing the particular band's ensemble or soloist virtuosity. His arrangements had a reputation among players as harmonically advanced (whole-tone and chromatic harmonies were a favorite device) and challenging to play. "Blue Rhythm Fantasy" in particular gained notice as possessing a modern sound.

The 1940s saw more assignments from Armstrong and, increasingly, the JIMMIE LUNCEFORD Orchestra. One of Lunceford's recordings, Beethoven's Sonata "Pathétique," op. 13, exemplified another of Willet's specialties: rearranging well-known classical material into the big band swing idiom and ensemble showpiece. Other examples of Willet's "jazzing the classics" include Christian Sinding's "Rustle of Spring," performed by Lucky Millinder, and Sergei Rachmaninoff's Prelude in C# Minor, performed by Duke Ellington. In 1944 Willet wrote a campaign song for ADAM CLAYTON POWELL JR., titled "Let My People Go Now!" The tune's lyrics were provided by LANGSTON HUGHES.

Willet eventually expanded his business to include studio recording, talent management, and a school for aspiring stage performers. But with the demise of the swing era following World War II, Willet appears to have quickly faded from the New York scene. By the early 1950s most of the venues he had worked at were closed, and most of the big bands had disintegrated. Returning to Philadelphia, Willet lived his final years in obscurity. He died a few weeks after suffering a heart attack, at age sixty-eight, virtually unnoticed by the music and entertainment community.

FURTHER READING

Klauber, Bruce. *World of Gene Krupa: That Legendary Drummin' Man* (1990).

Panassié, Hugues, and Madeleine Gautier. *Guide to Jazz* (1956).

DISCOGRAPHY

Mills Blue Rhythm Band 1936–1937 (Classics CD 731).

JOHN WRIGGLE

Williams, Aaron (22 Aug. 1932–), ventriloquist, was born in Atlanta, Georgia, the only child of Alonzo Williams and Laura Powell, a live-in maid. As a small boy, Williams moved to Dayton, Ohio, with his grandmother, whom he thought of as his mother. Williams's mother eventually joined her family in Dayton.

Williams's mother died when he was eight, and he went to live with his Aunt Ola Mae and his Uncle James Jackson in Dayton. He attended Dunbar High School, where he was a high jumper and ran the half mile as a member of Dunbar's 1948 Ohio state track championship team. After he graduated in 1951 he worked at a local bowling alley, as he had done throughout his high school years. Later he took a job at Chevrolet parking cars. In 1952, at the age of twenty, Williams met Ernestine Hatcher. The couple married the same year; they had two children, Romana and Monique. While still twenty years old, Williams obtained a job at the Wright Air Force Base as a messenger. After he was laid off from this job, he began to drive a taxi to make a living. At other times he worked for Goodwill Industries.

In 1957 Williams left Dayton and moved to Los Angeles, California, to pursue better employment opportunities. His first job in the city was as a dishwasher. At this point Williams was frustrated, hated Los Angeles, and wanted to return to Dayton. He eventually found work in a printing company, where he remained until 1962.

During this time Williams made his first attempt at a show business career when he put together a short-lived roller-skating act with a friend. In 1956 he was offered a job as a ventriloquist, backing up a singing group. Williams quit his job and was paid only one time. But the interest in ventriloquism stuck. He returned to work at the printing company and began doing ventriloquist shows on the weekend. During one of these shows, Williams met the comedian Mantan Moreland, who became a close friend. Moreland encouraged him to get out and perform, and he helped Williams find a ventriloquist job in a small club. What started as a short-term gig turned into a two-year booking.

Williams and his wooden friend Freddie found work in larger clubs, and his ventriloquist act became popular. While working at a club called the Persian Room, Williams got his big break when a publicist at American International Pictures saw the act and was impressed with his performance. Through this connection Williams met the Smothers Brothers, who invited him to audition for their CBS show. In 1968 Williams made his television debut on *The Smothers Brothers Show*. Soon afterward he appeared on Johnny Carson's *The Tonight Show*, which was hosted by HARRY BELAFONTE and included appearances by MARTIN LUTHER KING JR., Bobby Kennedy, NIPSEY RUSSELL, Paul Newman, and LENA HORNE. That same year he appeared on *The Pat Boone Show*, which was cohosted by the comedian RICHARD PRYOR.

In 1970 Williams performed with RAY CHARLES in Huntsville, Alabama. In 1971 Williams joined the Los Angeles County Sheriff's Department, where he acted as the department's safety education field deputy. In this role he made over three thousand public appearances with four of his ventriloquist dummies, Freddie, Grandpa Ike, Aunt Ida, and McTuff the Dog. He continued to perform in the 1970s and 1980s, appearing on *The Merv Griffin Show*, *The Mike Douglas Show*, *The Diana Shore Show*, Dick Clark's *American Bandstand*, and *The Joey Bishop Show*. In 1999 he retired from the Los Angeles County Sheriff's Department after thirty-two years of service. After a long and often varied career, Williams is remembered for his skill at ventriloquism, his integration of *The Smothers Brothers Show*, and his commitment to public safety.

FURTHER READING

"Black Ventriloquist to Integrate Smothers Show with White Dummy," *Variety* (6 Sept. 1968).

Jenkins, Walter. "Aaron and Freddie Take a Bow," *Black Stars* (Dec. 1975).

CHARLIE T. TOMLINSON

Williams, Anthony (c.1795–c. 1834), was a sailor who fought in the Battle of Lake Erie during the War of 1812. He was a native of Salem, Massachusetts. If born in Massachusetts in the mid 1790s, it is most likely that he was born free. Slavery had been abolished by 1783 in Massachusetts as a result of the QUOK WALKER case. The 1790 Federal Census lists no slaves in the state. It is possible that Anthony Williams made a living as a merchant sailor, given his residence in one of New England's most active seaports and his subsequent naval service.

Anthony Williams joined the navy by early 1813, likely in New England; his listed rating was that of

WILLIAMS, AUSTIN "HEAVY" 93

ship's boy, an indicator of both his youth, probably a teenager, and slight experience. During this time, the rating of ship's boy was held by white and black youths alike, their job being to serve a ship's officers as both messenger and servant and during times of battle as an ammunition handler, called a "powder monkey", carrying powder to the ship's gun positions as supplies needed replenishing, an important and dangerous task.

The term "powder monkey" is not a racist one because it was applied to both whites and blacks alike. It is instead a descriptive term; the young men performing this work were required to scurry at great speed from the magazine to one or more gun positions carrying powder, often bowed or bent over while doing so to avoid, as far they could, being hit by enemy shot and shell fire. This position was usually held by boys under the age of eighteen (roughly fourteen to eighteen years old).

Upon Williams's transfer to the Great Lakes theater of operations he was assigned to serve aboard a small gunboat, the two-gun schooner *Somers*, one of five merchant schooners purchased by the navy and outfitted as men of war in 1812. When the American naval commander assigned to Lake Erie, Oliver Hazard Perry, arrived on the scene in March 1813, he found that he had not enough men to man the vessels. An appeal to the man in charge of the overall Great Lakes command, Commodore Isaac Chauncey, netted Perry but 55 men to man the five schooners and it may be that Anthony Williams was among them. The *Somers* subsequently sailed to Presque Isle Bay in June 1813 and remained undermanned, as did the rest of Perry's fleet, until another 150 soldiers and sailors from the Lake Ontario fleet were sent as reinforcements. Despite their small numbers, African American sailors such as Williams, JOHN DAVIS, and NEWPORT HAZARD composed as much as 20 percent of the navy's crew strength during the war and, although largely unheralded even to this day, played an important part in naval battles waged both on the high seas and in the inland waters.

The only military action in which Anthony Williams was a known participant during his naval service was the Battle of Lake Erie. Fought on 10 September 1813, the battle resulted in a decisive victory for Perry's Lake Erie squadron over an experienced British fleet and subsequent American control of the lake and surrounding territory. William's vessel, the schooner *Somers* commanded by Thomas Almy and manned with a crew of twenty-four and six soldiers, played a secondary role in the action, but was noted for its long-distance gunnery and a

shot that damaged an enemy ship's rudder. Anthony Williams, as ship's boy, was almost certainly active in the traditional battle role of "powder monkey" during the several hours of fighting and afterward received a share of the prize money resulting from the capture and sale of the enemy ships. Following the War of 1812, Anthony Williams moved to Meadville, Pennsylvania, at an unknown date and was a resident there at the time of his death in 1833 or 1834.

FURTHER READING

Altoff, Gerard T. *Amongst My Best Men: African-Americans and the War of 1812* (1996).

GLENN ALLEN KNOBLOCK

Williams, Austin "Heavy" (?–?), anti–labor union activist in the Chicago meatpacking industry during the time of the Stockyards Labor Council (SLC), particularly 1916–1919, was one of the few men known by name for his leading role in anti-union agitation among African American employees, and those seeking work from the large and smaller packing companies.

Williams's birth, previous experience, and later life are unknown, although there are faint clues for speculation. Even his motives and loyalties are unclear, and probably more complex than any partisan for or against organized labor may have credited. He may have been born around 1874 in Texas, the son of Lizar Williams, who had been born, like Williams's father, in Georgia. If so, he was living in 1910 in a rooming house in Fort Worth, working at odd jobs.

According to two African American SLC floor committeemen, Williams was the leader of a group of men who came from Texas around 1916, joined the union, then quit three or four months later, beginning to agitate for others not to join. Union leaders believed that the entire group was recruited by the packinghouse owners for that specific purpose. One of the committeemen, FRANK CUSTER, told a Federal Mediation and Conciliation Service hearing "It seems as though the Wilson Company is taking my race up from Texas, using that as a big stick, using them as something to cut their own throats, to run themselves down lower than they are today. Out in that Wilson plant, there is as much as 15 men out of Texas working upon that floor that is not in the union" (Records of the Federal Mediation and Conciliation Service [FMCS], p. 290).

The other committeeman, ROBERT BEDFORD, said Williams was not a butcher by skill or experience. However, Bedford also testified that when he first came to work at the Wilson plant, Williams was sawing rumps. Williams himself testified that his job in June 1919 was "seeing after the truckers," a gang of twelve to fourteen men, who "catches the guts from the cattle" (FMCS, p. 426). Bedford observed that Williams walked the floor doing nothing, his principle job being "to buttonhole new men, tell them to keep out of the union." Williams had told Bedford, newly returned from a period of layoff, "Let me tell you, when they get after you about this union, don't you join it. If you join the union you are against the company. You are not with the company, and you won't last long" (FMCS, p. 153).

Williams's record justifies some skepticism about his statement that "the union is all right" but that "some of the men when they put a button on … it makes them think they are all of it." But like many of his contemporaries, he may have been genuinely conflicted at times as to where his best interests lay. He maintained that "if they had worked along steady they would have gotten me, worked along easy they would have gotten me" (FMCS, p. 429). He also admitted he had joined the union three years earlier, and then quit. Williams was, by all contemporary accounts, a popular man and a persuasive speaker. He observed that he came to oppose the union "Because I seen it was going down…. I wanted to see which way my money was going" (Barrett, pp. 215–216).

While SLC leaders worked hard to recruit African Americans into the union, many union workers who thought of themselves as "white" associated dark skin color with strikebreaking, putting the words "nigger scabs" together. In turn, newly arrived African Americans, accustomed to southern customs, interpreted any hostility against them for not being in the union as racial hostility, especially since European immigrants who spoke limited English had few words to explain that they only refused to work with "the colored fellows" who were not wearing union buttons (Trotter, p. 96).

Williams became a leader of the Wilson Efficiency Club, at the (colored) Wabash Avenue YMCA, which included, in its efforts to socialize newly arrived migrants from the South, warning them to stay away from the "white man's union." On the shop floor, he was known for verbal bullying, and in particular, according to Custer, for harassing a man so persistently that "he couldn't go to the toilet to make a passage without he would be there to take him off the seat" (FMCS, p. 265). Bedford recounted similar incidents. Williams generally did not initiate a fistfight, but if he could provoke a man to hit him first, would take the opportunity to punch back.

It wasn't always just about the union. Williams was known to take care of the time card, at quitting time, of a worker who wanted to go home early, expecting to be tipped half the pay for the remaining hours of the day. He got sore at workers who didn't pay him. The fact that Williams was never suspended or fired for "stealing an afternoon's pay" was one point raised by the union to show he was being protected by the company. Williams and his work gang, according to Bedford, routinely sauntered in to work half an hour late, but union members were sent home for the day on the rare occasion that one came in five or eight minutes late.

Williams's followers threw bricks at union members, and one was defended by a Wilson company attorney after attacking a black union member with a pritching iron (used to turn cattle carcasses). Williams was especially resistant to the SLC's campaign to make all plants "100 percent union," which produced spontaneous work stoppages demanding that anyone who would not join the union be fired. In some departments, such as the cattle-killing floor at Wilson's, this might be twelve to fourteen nonunion holdouts among 140 union members; while the nonunion men were a mix of black and white, tension was sharp and often physical.

How long Williams worked for Wilson, and where he went afterward, has never been established. If he is the Austin Williams born in Texas in 1874, he seems to have left the plant before the strike of 1921–1922 that broke the SLC and drove the Amalgamated Meatcutters Union out of organizing the major industrial plants. The man who told Wilson Co. employees not to join the union testified in 1919 that he was married, his children grown, living with his wife and a married daughter (FMCS, pp. 446–447). In 1920, a man named Austin Williams, classified by the census as black, was living in Chicago with his wife Amanda, daughter Bama, and her husband Isaiah Lott. But he wasn't working in the stockyards: he and Lott were wage employees managing a grocery store.

It appears that sometime after 1900, this Williams had married Mandy Watson, the widowed landlady of a boarding house he was living at, in Palestine, Texas. Bama Watson was Williams's step-daughter by this marriage. There is insufficient information to know if this is the same Austin Williams, nor is there better information as to where the man who plagued Bedford and Custer's efforts to organize the Wilson Company came from. In any event, there is no record of how long Austin Williams lived, or where or how he died. What is known of his life illuminates one of the many contradictions of one wave of the great northward migrations.

FURTHER READING
Records of the Federal Mediation and Conciliation Service (FMCS), "Violation of Agreement by Employers," Honorable Samuel Alschuler, Arbitrator, 20 June 1919. National Archives, College Park, MD, RG 280, Case 33/864, Box 42.

Barrett, James R. *Work and Community in the Jungle: Chicago's Packinghouse Workers, 1894–1922* (1987).

Halpern, Rick, and Roger Horowitz. *Meatpackers: An Oral History of Black Packinghouse Workers and Their Struggle for Racial and Economic Equality* (1996).

Trotter, Joe William. *The Great Migration in Historical Perspective: New Dimensions of Race, Class, and Gender* (2001).

CHARLES ROSENBERG

Williams, Bert and George Walker (12 Nov. 1874– 4 Mar. 1922) and (1873–6 Jan. 1911), stage entertainers, were born, respectively, Egbert Austin Williams in Nassau, the Bahamas, and George Williams Walker in Lawrence, Kansas. Williams was the son of Frederick Williams Jr., a waiter, and Julia Monceur. Walker was the son of "Nash" Walker, a policeman; his mother's name is unknown. Williams moved with his family to Riverside, California, in 1885 and attended Riverside High School. Walker began performing "darkey" material for traveling medicine shows during his boyhood and left Kansas with Dr. Waite's medicine show. In 1893 Williams and Walker met in San Francisco, where they first worked together in Martin and Selig's Minstrels.

To compete in the crowded field of mostly white blackface performers, "Walker and Williams," as they were originally known, subtitled their act "The Two Real Coons." Walker developed a fast-talking, city hustler persona, straight man to Williams's slow-witted, woeful bumbler. Williams, who was light-skinned, used blackface makeup on stage, noting that "it was not until I was able to see myself as another person that my sense of humor developed." An unlikely engagement in the unsuccessful Victor Herbert operetta *The Gold Bug* brought Williams and Walker to New York in 1896, but the duo won critical acclaim and rose quickly through the ranks of vaudeville, eventually playing

Koster and Bial's famed New York theater. During this run they added a sensational cakewalk dance finale to the act, cinching popular success. Walker performed exceptionally graceful and complex dance variations, while Williams clowned through an inept parody of Walker's steps. AIDA OVERTON WALKER, who later become a noteworthy dancer and choreographer in her own right, was hired as Walker's cakewalk partner in 1897 and became his wife in 1899. They had no children. The act brought the cakewalk to the height of its popularity, and Williams and Walker subsequently toured the eastern seaboard and performed a week at the Empire Theatre in London in April 1897.

Vaudeville typically used stereotyped ethnic characterizations as humor, and Williams and Walker developed a "coon" act without peer in the industry. For the 1898 season, the African American composer WILL MARION COOK and the noted poet PAUL LAURENCE DUNBAR created *Senegambian Carnival* for the duo, the first in a series of entertainments featuring African Americans that eventually played New York. *A Lucky Coon* (1898), *The Policy Players* (1899), and *Sons of Ham* (1900) were basically vaudeville acts connected by Williams and Walker's patter. In 1901 they began recording their ragtime stage hits for the Victor label. Their popularity spread, and the 18 February 1903 Broadway premiere of *In Dahomey* was considered the first fully realized musical comedy performed by an all-black company. In 1900 Williams had married Charlotte Louise Johnson; they had no children.

Williams and Walker led the *In Dahomey* cast of fifty as Shylock Homestead and Rareback Pinkerton, two confidence men out to defraud a party of would-be African colonizers. Its three acts included a number of dances, vocal choruses, specialty acts, and a grand cakewalk sequence. Critics cited Williams's performance of "I'm a Jonah Man," a hard-luck song by Alex Rogers, as a high point of the hit show. *In Dahomey* toured England and Scotland, with a command performance at Buckingham Palace arranged for the ninth birthday of King Edward VII's grandson David. The cakewalk became the rage of fashionable English society, and company members worked as private dance instructors both abroad and when they returned home.

Williams composed more than seventy songs in his lifetime. "Nobody," the most famous of these, was introduced to the popular stage in 1905:

When life seems full of clouds and rain, And I am filled with naught but pain, Who soothes my thumping, bumping brain? Nobody!

The sense of pathos lurking behind Williams's plaintive delivery was not lost on his audience. Walker gained fame performing boastful, danceable struts, such as the 1906 "It's Hard to Find a King Like Me" and his signature song, "Bon Bon Buddie, the Chocolate Drop," introduced in 1907. During this period Williams and Walker signed their substantial music publishing rights with the black-owned Attucks Music Publishing Company.

Walker, who was more business-minded than Williams, controlled production details of the 1906 *Abyssinia* and the 1907 *Bandanna Land*. Walker demanded that these "all-Negro" productions play only in first-class theaters. His hard business tactics worked, and Williams and Walker played several theaters that had previously barred black performers. In 1908, at the height of their success, the duo were founding members of The Frogs, a charitable and social organization of black theatrical celebrities. Other members included composers BOB COLE and JOHN ROSAMOND JOHNSON, bandleader JAMES REESE EUROPE, and writer/directors Alex Rogers and Jesse Shipp.

During the tour of *Bandanna Land*, Walker succumbed to general paresis, an advanced stage of syphilis. He retired from the stage in February 1909. Aida Walker took over his songs and dances, and the book scenes were rewritten for Williams to play alone. Walker died in Islip, New York.

Williams continued doing blackface and attempted to produce the 1909 *Mr. Lode of Koal* without Walker. His attention to business details languished, and the show failed. Williams's performances, however, received significant critical praise, and he gained stature as "an artist of pantomime" and "a comic genius." In 1910 he joined Florenz Ziegfeld's *Follies*. He told the *New York Age* (1 Dec. 1910) that "the colored show business— that is colored musical shows—is at the low ebb just now. I reached the conclusion last spring that I could best represent my race by doing pioneer work. It was far better to have joined a large white show than to have starred in a colored show, considering conditions."

Williams was aware of the potential for racial backlash from his white audience and insisted on a contract clause stating that he would at no time appear on stage with any of the scantily clad women in the *Follies* chorus. His celebrity advanced, and he became the star attraction of the *Follies* for some eight seasons, leaving the show twice, in 1913 and 1918, to spend time with his family and to headline in vaudeville. His overwhelming success prompted educator BOOKER T. WASHINGTON to quip, "Bert Williams has done more for the race than I have. He has smiled his way into people's hearts. I have been obliged to fight my way." An Actor's Equity strike troubled Ziegfeld's 1919 edition of the *Follies*, and Williams, who had never been asked or allowed to join the union because of his African ancestry, left the show. In 1920 he and Eddie Cantor headlined Rufus and George Lemaire's short-lived *Broadway Brevities*. In 1921 the Shuberts financed a musical, *Under the Bamboo Tree*, to star Williams with an otherwise all-white cast. The show opened in Cincinnati, Ohio, but in February 1922 Williams succumbed to pneumonia, complicated by heart problems, and died the next month in New York City.

Although Williams's stage career solidified the stereotype of the "shiftless darkey," his unique talent at pantomime and the hard work he put into it was indisputable. In his famous poker game sketch, filmed in the 1916 short *A Natural Born Gambler*, Williams enacted a four-handed imaginary game without benefit of props or partners. His cache of comic stories, popularized in his solo vaudeville and Ziegfeld *Follies* appearances, were drawn largely from African American folk humor, which Williams and Alex Rogers duly noted and collected for their shows. Williams collected an extensive library and wrote frequently for the black press and theatrical publications.

The commercial success of Williams and Walker proved that large audiences would pay to see black performers. Tall and light-skinned Williams, in blackface and ill-fitting tatters, contrasted perfectly with short, dark-skinned, dandyish Walker. Their cakewalks revived widespread interest in African American dance styles. Their successful business operations, responsible for a "$2,300 a week" payroll in 1908, encouraged black participation in mainstream show business. The *Chicago Defender* (11 Mar. 1922) called them "the greatest Negro team of actors who ever lived and the most popular pair of comedy stars America has produced."

FURTHER READING

Charters, Ann. *Nobody: The Story of Bert Williams* (1970).

Johnson, James Weldon. *Black Manhattan* (1930).

Rowland, Mabel. *Bert Williams: Son of Laughter* (1923).

Sampson, Henry T. *Blacks in Blackface: A Source Book on Early Black Musical Shows* (1980).

Smith, Eric Ledell. *Bert Williams: A Biography of the Pioneer Black Comedian* (1992).

Woll, Allen. *Black Musical Theatre—From Coontown to Dreamgirls* (1989).

Obituaries: *New York Times*, 8 Jan. 1911 (Walker) and 5 Mar. 1922 (Williams).

This entry is taken from the *American National Biography* and is published here with the permission of the American Council of Learned Societies.

THOMAS F. DEFRANTZ

Williams, Big Joe (16 Oct. 1903–17 Dec. 1982), blues musician, was born Joe Lee Williams in Crawford, Mississippi, the son of John Williams, a tenant farmer and sawmill hand, and Cora Lee Logan. Joe's mother, who was in her early teens, placed the youngster in the care of her father, Bert Logan, a musician who played accordion and guitar. Inspired by his grandfather and by a cousin, Jesse Logan, who also played guitar, Joe showed an early aptitude for the local vernacular music. He won a dance contest at age nine, crafted a one-string guitar called a "diddley bow," carved a cane fife or "fice," as it was known locally, and often beat rhythm on a bucket for musicians at his grandfather's Saturday night suppers.

After an argument with his stepfather, an incident he later sang about in "Stepfather Blues," Williams decided to strike out on his own. Although it is not clear when this happened, Williams recalled decades later that he became "a walking musician, all down through that Delta and all through the hills." Williams continued to lead an itinerant existence for the rest of his life.

His early travels, during the 1920s, took him throughout the South. Around 1930 he settled briefly in St. Louis, but by 1932 or 1933 he was traveling the South again, this time with a protégé, DAVID "HONEYBOY" EDWARDS. Throughout the Depression Williams relied on his rural audiences to meet his meager needs, traveling as a hobo and performing as "Poor Joe" or "Big Joe."

Williams made his first documented recordings after landing in St. Louis in the mid-1930s. At the time he was playing at clubs, rent parties, and on the city's streetcars, working with well-known bluesmen such as St. Louis Jimmy Oden, PEETIE WHEATSTRAW, J. D. Short (his cousin), and Charley Jordan. Through these contacts, Williams met the Chicago-based music publisher Lester Melrose, who signed him to RCA Victor Record Company's subsidiary label Bluebird. On 25 February 1935 Williams went to Chicago for his first session. Six songs were issued, including "49 Highway Blues," "Stepfather Blues," and "Somebody's Been Borrowing That Stuff," with the St. Louis guitarist Henry Townsend sitting in on the latter two.

That same year Williams returned to Chicago and, on Halloween, did a second session for Bluebird, accompanied by Townsend, the one-string fiddle player Chasey Collins, and a washboard player called Kokomo. One of the four issued sides, "Baby, Please Don't Go," eventually became a blues standard.

On 5 May 1937 in Aurora, Illinois, Williams recorded with Robert Lee McCoy, better known as ROBERT NIGHTHAWK, and the harmonica virtuoso SONNY BOY WILLIAMSON, a trio often cited as the forerunner of the Chicago blues band sound of the late 1940s and 1950s. In Chicago on 27 March 1941 Williams had another Bluebird session, working with William Mitchell, who did a vocal imitation of a string bass. The session yielded another popular recording, "Crawling King Snake." After a final 1945 session Williams ended his successful ten-year relationship with Bluebird.

Beginning in 1957 Williams was launched on a second career during which he was promoted as a folk blues artist. He recorded on Robert G. Koester's Delmar (now Delmark) label, collaborated with the pianist Erwin Helfer on several singles released on Collector Jen, and in 1958 recorded for Delmar again. In 1959 and 1960, now married to Mary (maiden name and date of marriage unknown) and staying at what the recording executive Chris Strachwitz described as a "dreadful flea-bag hotel" in Oakland, California, Williams made his LP debut on the World-Pacific album *Down South Summit Meeting*, recorded with the harmonica player SONNY TERRY and the guitarists BROWNIE McGHEE and LIGHTNIN' HOPKINS. He also recorded for the Arhoolie label, owned by Strachwitz. Williams's wife died in 1961; the number of their children, if any, is unknown.

Williams was among the first artists to reach out to new audiences during the so-called "blues revival." Harmonica player Charlie Musselwhite, a one-time Williams roommate, said Williams helped spark the revival that occurred in Chicago's North Wells Street nightclub district in the early 1960s: "There was a little bar down the street called Big John's. They asked Joe to come down and play. They thought Joe was kind of like a folk singer. They didn't know what they were getting into.... Joe asked me to play with him and the place was packed. The crowd loved it. So they started booking other blues bands and then other clubs started having blues" (personal interview, 9 June 1990).

In New York, Williams added to his folk blues credentials by playing with young Bob Dylan, jamming as Big and Little Joe. Through the 1960s and 1970s Williams recorded for various small independent labels and toured extensively in the United States and Europe. In 1976 he performed at the Bicentennial Festival of American Folklife in Washington, D.C.

As failing health curtailed his travels, Williams returned home to Crawford, Mississippi. He died in Macon, Georgia, and ten years later was inducted into the Blues Foundation's Hall of Fame in Memphis, Tennessee.

Williams's music was distinctive partly because he played in open G, or Spanish, tuning, and partly because he played a guitar that he had customized by adding three strings, doubling the first, second, and fourth strings. He developed the most percussive guitar sound of any recording artist of his time, comparable to CHARLIE PATTON, whom he claimed to have bested in a music contest. With his gruff voice and intense, declamatory vocal style, Williams epitomized the country bluesman. Moreover, he made his mark on every major phase of blues history—in the rural South in the early years of country blues, in St. Louis when it was a blues center, in Chicago at the beginning of the golden years of Chicago blues, and in the blues revival. Despite a talent for fantastic invention—he claimed that he was invisible on certain days—Williams became a valued oral historian of the blues during the last twenty years of his life.

FURTHER READING

Bloomfield, Michael. *Me and Big Joe* (1980).

Charters, Samuel. *The Legacy of the Blues* (1977).

McKee, Margaret, and Fred Chisenhall. *Beale Black and Blue: Life and Music on Black America's Main Street* (1981).

Obituary: *Living Blues* 57 (Autumn 1983).

DISCOGRAPHY

Dixon, Robert M. W., and John Godrich. *Blues and Gospel Records: 1902–1943* (1982).

Leadbitter, Mike, and Neil Slaven. *Blues Records 1943–1970*, vol. 2 (1994).

This entry is taken from the *American National Biography* and is published here with the permission of the American Council of Learned Societies.

BILL MCCULLOCH AND
BARRY LEE PEARSON

Williams, Billy Leo (15 June 1938–), baseball player, was born in Whistler, Alabama, to Frank Williams, a laborer and former semipro baseball player, and Jessie Mae Williams, a homemaker. Emerging from the same Alabama hotbed that bred stars like HANK AARON, WILLIE MAYS, and WILLIE MCCOVEY, Williams became a standout athlete at a young age, and he was a highly coveted prospect at Whistler High School. After graduating from high school in 1956 he worked part-time as a busboy and bricklayer (David Porter, ed., *African-American Sports Greats* [1995], 375). The Chicago Cubs signed him for a pittance in 1956, offering him, in Williams's words, "a cigar and a bus ticket" (Derek Gentile, *The Complete Chicago Cubs* [2002], 407). Williams was sent to the rookie league in Ponca City, Oklahoma.

While in the minor leagues, Williams befriended future longtime teammate Ron Santo, in spite of their very different experiences. Unlike Santo, who was Caucasian, and Williams's future teammate ERNIE BANKS, who bypassed the minors and jumped straight to the major league, Williams was subject to the inherent racism of smaller minor-league towns in the Midwest and South. He was forced to stay in a different hotel from the rest of the team and was exposed to vitriolic abuse on the field.

To some it was clear from the start that Williams was on his way to stardom; in February 1959 Rogers Hornsby, a Hall-of-Fame second baseman, visited the Cubs' prospect camp and predicted that Williams and his smooth swing would be a fixture in the majors. Williams did not immediately live up to Hornsby's adulation in 1959, hitting just .152 during a brief call-up. While spending much of 1960 in the minors for more seasoning, Williams married Shirley Ann, whose maiden name was Williams as well; the couple had four daughters. By 1961 he was the starting outfielder in Chicago. With 25 home runs and 86 RBIs that season, he won the National League Rookie of the Year Award. His efforts, however, were overshadowed by Roger Maris's and Mickey Mantle's season-long chase of Babe Ruth's single-season home run record.

Throughout the 1960s and early 1970s "Sweet-Swinging" Billy Williams was an indispensable player on the team. He set a then-record in the National League by playing in 1,117 consecutive games between September 1963 and September 1970. When, on 29 June 1969, he broke the National League record for consecutive games played set by the St. Louis Cardinals great Stan Musial, the Cubs held "Billy Williams Day" at Wrigley Field. Although he enjoyed great popularity in Chicago, Williams garnered little press outside of the Midwest, as he was overshadowed first by Santo and Banks and later by Canadian pitcher Fergie Jenkins.

Though Williams never won the most valuable player award, he finished second twice: once in 1970, when he led the league in runs and hits and set personal highs in home runs (42) and RBIs (129), and again in 1972, when he led the league in batting and slugging percentage and was named the *Sporting News* Player of the Year. By the end of his career he had totaled 426 home runs, 1,475 RBIs, a .290 batting average, and six All-Star game selections. Williams spent all but two of his playing seasons with Chicago; he was traded to the Oakland Athletics after 1974. He tallied 23 home runs as the designated hitter in helping the A's reach the World Series in 1975, but he retired the following season after hitting just .211. Williams served as a coach and batting instructor for the Cubs from 1978 through 1982, and then for Oakland from 1983 through 1985.

Williams was elected to the National Baseball Hall of Fame in January 1987 after falling four votes short the previous year. In his inauguration speech six months later Williams called on the audience and Major League Baseball to demand equal treatment in hiring policies for coaching, managerial, and executive positions. He concluded his speech by saying: "Baseball has been considered America's favorite pastime. Now let's make it the sport that reflects the true spirit of our great country" (Cooperstown, N.Y., 26 July 1987). Four months after his Hall of Fame speech Williams turned down a Triple-A managing position, asserting that he ought to have been a candidate for the Cubs' manager, a job that was vacant as well. Williams enjoyed two more stints with the Cubs as first-base coach, bench coach, and hitting instructor, and he saw Chicago hire its first black manager, Don Baylor, prior to the 2000 season. Williams himself finally made it to the front office in November 2001, as an assistant to the Cubs' president Andy MacPhail.

Though soft-spoken during his playing career, even in the face of racist threats, Williams remained a vocal critic of the lack of minorities in administrative jobs in baseball. His speech at the Hall of Fame came just three months after the Los Angeles Dodgers executive Al Campanis asserted in a *Nightline* interview on 6 April 1987, nine days shy of the fortieth anniversary of JACKIE ROBINSON's debut in the majors, that blacks "may not have some of the necessities to be, let's say, a field manager or perhaps a general manager" (*New York Times*, 22 June 1998). Though Campanis was promptly fired, his comments put the spotlight on a sport that filled only 2 percent of its front-office positions

with minorities. A minority committee was formed to discuss action, and the commissioner began to tackle the issue. By the time Williams became a top-level executive with the Cubs, the number of minorities in baseball administrative positions had risen to more than 15 percent.

FURTHER READING
Williams, Billy, and Irv Haag. *Billy: The Classic Hitter* (1974).
Berkow, Ira. "Billy Williams Says No," *New York Times*, 7 Nov. 1987.
Santo, Ron, with Phil Pepe. *Few and Chosen: Defining Cubs Greatness across the Eras* (2005).

ADAM W. GREEN

Williams, Camilla Ella (18 Oct. 1922–29 Jan. 2012), opera singer and college professor, was born in Danville, Virginia, to Cornelius Booker Williams, a butler and chauffeur, and Fannie (Carey) Williams, a homemaker. Camilla's parents, both firm believers in education and church involvement, insisted that all four of their children (Camilla was the youngest) go to college and sing in the church choir. Alexander Carey, her maternal grandfather, was a singer and choir leader.

Preparing to be a teacher, Williams graduated with honors from Virginia State College, now Virginia State University, in 1941. One of Williams's professors at Virginia State College was the distinguished composer and pedagogue UNDINE SMITH MOORE. Moore's poignant composition "Watch and Pray" is dedicated to Williams. One of her schoolmates at Virginia State College, who graduated in 1942, was the renowned jazz musician Billy Taylor. Taylor-Williams Hall, a student residence on the campus, is named in their honor.

Williams's career as a teacher in the Danville schools (she taught music and third grade) was short-lived, only one year. In 1942 her performance at the University of Philadelphia as guest soloist with the Virginia State College a cappella choir so impressed the university's alumni association that it offered her a scholarship in voice at the university. She accepted the offer, enrolled there, and began serious voice studies with Marion Szekely-Freschl. Williams supported herself during this period by working in the evenings as an usher at a Philadelphia theater, receiving assistance from a former employer of her mother, and benefiting from a fund that had been established for her at Virginia State College. While Szekely-Freschl remained her principal vocal mentor, she also worked, in

Camilla Ella Williams on 31 May 1946. (Library of Congress.)

Philadelphia and in New York, with Rose Dirman, Sergius Kagan, Ralf Berkowitz, Borislava Bazala, and Cesare Sodero.

Williams's journey to international prominence began when she won the MARIAN ANDERSON Scholarship Award in 1943 (and again in 1944), and first place in the Philadelphia Orchestra Youth Auditions in 1944. The latter award carried with it a performance with the orchestra; for her concert with the orchestra, Williams sang the "Alleluja" from Wolfgang Amadeus Mozart's motet *Exultate Jubilate*, "Dove Sono" from Mozart's *Le nozze di Figaro*, and "Casta Diva" from Vincenzo Bellini's *Norma*. In 1946 Williams signed with the New York City Opera, becoming the first African American singer to receive a contract with a major American opera company for a full season (ROBERT TODD DUNCAN preceded her at New York City Opera, but his contract was not for a full season). Her debut on 15 May 1946 was as Cio-Cio-San in Giacomo Puccini's *Madama Butterfly*. Her performance was an unqualified success, receiving rave reviews from the New York press. The renowned soprano Geraldine Farrar, who had sung Butterfly in the

Metropolitan Opera's first production of the opera in 1906, was at the performance and told *Newsweek* that of all sopranos currently doing the role, Williams was already one of the greatest.

Despite her success, Williams was still subject to the racial insults of the time. In 1947 the New York City Opera was scheduled to perform *Madama Butterfly* in a segregated theatre in Washington, D.C. Echoing the notorious banning of Marian Anderson from performance at the city's Constitution Hall in 1939, the contract stated that Camilla Williams could not be involved in the production. Laszlo Halasz, the company's director, cancelled the production rather than submit to the insult.

As a regular member of the New York City Opera for several seasons, Williams sang several other major roles in addition to Butterfly: Nedda in Ruggiero Leoncavallo's *I Pagliacci*, Mimi in Puccini's *La Bohème*, and on 28 October 1948 she created the title role in the company's first production of Giuseppe Verdi's *Aida*.

She repeated her Butterfly role in 1955 with the Vienna State Opera, the first black artist to appear there. She also sang in the first Viennese performance of Gian Carlo Menotti's *The Saint of Bleecker Street* (1955). In New York she was Princess Ilia in the Little Orchestra Society's first performance of Mozart's *Idomeneo* (1950), and with the National Negro Opera Company, Marguerite in Charles Gounod's *Faust* (1952). She also sang in the first New York performance of George Frideric Handel's *Orlando* (1971).

The New York press was divided on Williams's effectiveness as a recitalist but united in praising her ability in lyric Theater. In other places around the world she was critically acclaimed in both settings. Truly an international personality and a musical ambassador, Williams performed in all of the world's major music centers, as well as in Alaska, in fourteen countries in Africa, in Taiwan, Korea, Philippines, Laos, South Vietnam, Poland, and Israel.

Before becoming the first black professor of voice at Indiana University in 1973, she was on the faculties of Brooklyn College, Bronx Community College (a community college of the city of New York), and Queens College. In 1983 Camilla became the first black professor of voice at Central Conservatory of Music, Beijing, People's Republic of China.

In 2012, Williams died of cancer at her home in Bloomington, Indiana. She was 92.

FURTHER READING

Cheatham, Wallace McClain. *Dialogues on Opera and the African American Experience* (1997).

Gray, John. *Blacks in Classical Music* (1988).

Sokel, Martin L. *The New York City Opera* (1981).

Story, Rosalyn. *And So I Sing* (1990).

Obituary: *Los Angeles Times*, 31 January 2012.

WALLACE MCCLAIN CHEATHAM

Williams, Carla (1965–), photographer, writer, and curator, was born in Los Angeles, California, the third of four daughters born to Evelyn Williams, a homemaker, and Wendell Williams, an aerospace industry employee. Carla showed no signs of interest in becoming an artist during her childhood, even though she already had an affinity and talent for taking photographs. As a high school senior she indicated that she could not imagine going off to college "to major in something utterly useless like art" (Williams, e-mail interview, May 2005).

Williams first became seriously interested in art during her sophomore year at Princeton University after she enrolled in a photography course. The university darkrooms were located in the basement of the visual arts building; it was there also that the mandatory interviews conducted prior to registration for an art class were held. She later described that first journey to the basement as a "conversion experience" about art and photography (Williams, e-mail interview, May 2005). She described it as being "like Dorothy entering Oz." The venture opened up a magical world for her that she "wanted to inhabit." From that point on she never looked back and made the decision that photography would be her career.

Williams earned her bachelor's degree in Art and Archaeology in 1986 and continued her studies at the University of New Mexico, receiving her M.A. and MFA in Photography in 1988 and 1996. Before her matriculation at New Mexico, she interned in the department of photographs at the J. Paul Getty Museum in Malibu, California, from 1991 to 1992, where she cataloged and researched the work of the renowned photographers Aaron Siskind (1903–1991), Charles Fletcher Lummis (1859–1928), Edward S. Curtis (1868–1952), Karl Moon (active from the late 1890s to the 1910s), and Adam Clark Vroman (1856–1916).

In 1997 Williams became the artist-in-residence at Light Work, a Syracuse University–based center providing direct support to artists working in photography and digital imaging. In 1999 she developed and launched the Internet site http://www.carlagirl.net to publish her photographs and writings, a bibliography on artists of the African diaspora, images of women of African descent, and links to other sites on photography, black artists, women artists, queer artists, and other subjects relevant to the visual arts, including an extensive international arts events calendar. She received a Rockefeller Foundation Fellowship at Stanford University for 2002–2003, and won an artist residency from the Helene Wurlitzer Foundation in Taos, New Mexico, in 2005.

Williams became editor of the journal *exposure: The Society for Photographic Education* in 2004, was an art reviewer for the *Santa Fe Reporter* in 2000, and was a writer for the J. Paul Getty Museum from 1997 to 1999. Among her books are THURGOOD MARSHALL: *Journey to Freedom* (2002), *The Black Female Body: A Photographic History* (coedited with DEBORAH WILLIS; 2002) and *They Called Her Hottentot: The Art, Science, and Fiction of Sarah Baartman* (also coedited with Deborah Willis; 2006). Williams also contributed essays to a number of other publications, including *Photography from 1839 to Today, George Eastman House, Rochester, New York* (1999), *Picturing Women* (2006), and *A Century of African American Art: The Paul R. Jones Collection* (2004).

Williams also worked as a curator in the prints and photographs division of the Schomburg Center for Research in Black Culture in New York from 1992 to 1993, as visual resource curator for the Thaw Art History Center of the College of Santa Fe between 1999 and 2002, as guest curator for Allegiances: Flags, Banners, Photographs, Books at Glendale Community College in Arizona in 1993, as curator at the Wilson Centre for Photography in Topanga, California, from 1993 until 1997, as co-curator of Patriot Acts for the California Lawyers for the Arts 30th Anniversary Celebration in Fort Mason in October 2004, as co-curator of Who Am I: Beacon Youth Photography @ BUILD in San Francisco in 2004, and as guest curator of the companion exhibition to Recovered Views at de Saisset Museum of Santa Clara University in 2005. As a teacher, Williams was instructor of photography at Pomona College in Claremont, California, in 1994 and was adjunct professor at the Marion Center for Photographic Arts at the College of Santa Fe in New Mexico from 2001 to 2002.

Williams's work was shown at the Sawtooth Building Galleries, Winston-Salem, North Carolina, in 1988, where she won the Canon Excellence Award and was also exhibited there in 1990; at the Teaching Gallery at the University of New Mexico and at the University Museum in Albuquerque in 1991; at the Lindhurst Gallery at the University of Southern California in Los Angeles in 1992; at the Light Factory in Charlotte, North Carolina, in 1992; at the Salena Gallery at Long Island University in Brooklyn, New York, in 1993; at the Bathhouse Exhibition at the Arts Festival of Atlanta in 1995; at Ohio University in Athens, Ohio, in 1998; at Washington State University in Richland in 1998; at Dixie College in Saint George, Utah, in 1998; at the Dinnerware Gallery in Tucson, Arizona, in 1999; at the College of Santa Fe Fine Arts Gallery in New Mexico in 2000; at the Anacostia Museum of the Smithsonian Institution in Washington, D.C., in 2000; at Alfred University in Alfred, New York, in 2000; at Calvin College in Grand Rapids, Michigan, in 2001; at the Center for Contemporary Arts in Santa Fe, New Mexico, in 2004; and at California College of the Arts in San Francisco in 2004. Her work is in the collections of the Art Museum at Princeton University, of the University Art Museum at the University of New Mexico, and of Light Work in Syracuse, New York.

FURTHER READING

Arnold, Brian. *Precedence: Emmet Gowin and His Students* (2000)

Collins, Lisa Gail. *The Art of History: African American Women Artists Engage the Past* (2002)

Light Work. "Carla Williams" in *Contact Sheet 94* (1998).

AMALIA K. AMAKI

Williams, Cathay (Sept. 1844–?), cook, laundress, and Buffalo Soldier, was born into slavery in Independence, Missouri. Nothing is known of her parents, except that her father was reported to be a free black man. At some point in her early childhood, she went with her master's family to a farm near Jefferson City, where she toiled as a house servant until the start of the Civil War.

Probably in the summer of 1861, when she was nearly seventeen years old, Williams fled the plantation and joined the large group of escaped and newly freed slaves seeking the protection of Union troops occupying Jefferson City. Within months she was pressed into service as a laundress and cook for a Union regiment, possibly the Eighth Indiana Infantry. She maintained that position for nearly two years, accompanying the troops on campaigns in Missouri and Arkansas. In the summer of 1863 Williams found employment as a government cook in federal-controlled Little Rock. Within a year she was a regimental laundress and cook again, purportedly working throughout the Red River campaign in Louisiana before being sent east, where she said she obtained employment as "cook and washer woman" for the staff of General Philip Sheridan during the second Shenandoah Valley Campaign in Virginia. By January 1865 Williams was back with her old regiment, traveling with them to Savannah, Georgia, until the end of the war.

After the cessation of hostilities, Williams managed to return to Missouri to reunite with her family. In November 1866, in the company of a male cousin and a "particular friend," she disguised herself as a man and enlisted in the U.S. Army in St. Louis under the alias of William Cathey. Her reasons for doing so have never been clearly delineated. She may have viewed the military as an opportunity for a decent livelihood and a semblance of respect, since as a black woman in postwar Missouri her economic prospects were dim. Her years with the Union army undoubtedly made the military seem a familiar place in which to stake her future. Or perhaps her motivation was a strong desire to accompany her cousin and her friend.

Army regulations of the time forbade the enlistment or commissioning of women as soldiers, but since recruiters did not seek proof of identity and because army surgeons often failed to fully examine enlistees, it was not very difficult for women to infiltrate the military. During the Civil War, for example, hundreds of women pretended to be men and served in both the Union and Confederate armies. Williams, however, holds the distinction of being the only known female Buffalo Soldier, and the only documented African American woman to serve in the U.S. Regulars in the nineteenth century. At least three black women served as soldiers in the Civil War: Lizzie Hoffman and another unidentified woman in the U.S. Colored Troops, and Maria Lewis, passing as a white man, in a New York cavalry regiment.

Williams, using the name William Cathey, informed the recruiting officer that she was twenty-two years old and a cook by occupation. Her enlistment papers reveal that she was illiterate at the time of her induction. The recruiting officer described Private William Cathey as five feet, nine inches tall, with black eyes, black hair, and black complexion. She was one of the tallest soldiers in her company. An army surgeon reportedly examined her upon enlistment and determined that she was fit for duty. The exam was obviously a farce or incomplete, as neither the surgeon nor the recruiter realized that she was a woman. Assigned to Company A of the segregated Thirty-eighth U.S. Infantry, Private Cathey did not have an illustrious or exciting army career. She was an average soldier, never singled out for praise or punishment, and, apparently, neither distinguished nor disgraced herself. Opinions held of Private Cathey by her fellow soldiers and officers are unknown.

From her enlistment until February 1867, Williams was stationed at Jefferson Barracks, except for one visit to a St. Louis hospital for treatment of an undocumented illness. By April 1867 Private Cathey and her company had marched to Fort Riley, Kansas, where she and fifteen others were described as "ill in quarters" for two weeks. In June 1867 her company arrived at Fort Harker, Kansas, and the following month they arrived at Fort Union, New Mexico, after a march of 536 miles. By October the company was encamped at Fort Cummings, New Mexico. It appears that Private Cathey withstood the marches as well as any man in her unit, and although she participated in her share of soldierly obligations, the company never engaged the enemy or saw any direct combat while she was a member. In January 1868 her health began to deteriorate, and she was hospitalized for rheumatism that month and again in March. In June the company marched for Fort Bayard, New Mexico, where she was admitted into the hospital in July and diagnosed with neuralgia, a catch-all term for any acute pain of the nervous system. She did not report back to duty for a month.

On 14 October 1868 Private Cathey and two others in Company A were discharged from the Thirty-eighth Infantry on a surgeon's certificate of medical disability. She had served her country for just less than two years. Although Cathey's discharge papers do not indicate that the surgeon was aware of her true sex, Williams later related that she grew tired of being a soldier and eventually confessed her true identity to obtain release from the military. Indeed, none of the records of the Thirty-eighth Infantry—including carded medical records, enlistment papers, and the muster rolls and returns of Company A, Thirty-eighth U.S. Infantry—reveal any awareness of a woman in the ranks.

Upon resuming civilian life, she traveled to Fort Union and worked as a cook until some time in 1870, when she moved to Pueblo, Colorado, and worked as a laundress for two years. She next moved to Las Animas County, Colorado, staying for a year, again working as a laundress. She finally settled, more or less permanently, in Trinidad, Colorado, making

her living as a laundress, seamstress, and nurse. In 1875 Williams told her life story to a St. Louis journalist traveling in Colorado, who described her as "tall and powerfully built, black as night, muscular looking." The full newspaper article published the following year remains the only written story of her life told in her own voice. In the mid-1880s Williams moved to Raton, New Mexico, where she may have operated a boarding house. By 1889 she was back in Trinidad, hospitalized for nearly a year and a half with an undisclosed illness.

Williams was probably indigent when she left the hospital, so in June 1891 she petitioned for an "invalid pension" based upon her military service. Her sworn application gave her age as forty-one, and she declared that she was the same William Cathey who served as a private in the Thirty-eighth Infantry. She produced her original discharge certificate as proof. She claimed she was suffering from deafness, contracted in the army, she referred to her rheumatism, and she declared she was eligible for the government pension because she could no longer sustain herself by manual labor. A supplemental declaration, filed the following month, contended that she had contracted smallpox at St. Louis in 1868, and, while still recovering, swam the Rio Grande on the way to New Mexico. She believed that the combined effects of smallpox and exposure led to her deafness. All of her pension papers were signed by her, as she had learned to read and to write since her time in the army more than two decades earlier.

On 8 September 1891 a medical doctor in Trinidad, commissioned by the Pension Bureau, examined Williams. Charged with providing a thorough examination of the patient and a complete description of her physical condition, the doctor described her as five feet, seven inches tall, 160 pounds, and "stout." He reported that she was not deaf and he could find no evidence of rheumatism. Most horrifying, the doctor reported that all her toes on both feet had been amputated, and she could walk only with the aid of a crutch, but he provided no explanation of the cause of amputation. Other than the loss of her toes, the doctor stated she was in good general health and gave his opinion as "nil" on a disability rating. In February 1892 the Pension Bureau rejected her claim for an invalid pension, and Williams never received any government assistance. The bureau rejected her claim on medical grounds, but it never questioned her identity. No one appeared to doubt that William Cathey of the Thirty-eight Infantry and Cathay Williams of Trinidad were the same person.

Nothing definite is known of Williams after her pension case closed, although it is believed that she died before 1900. Where and how she lived, the date and place of her death, and her final resting place are undetermined.

FURTHER READING

Records pertaining to Cathay Williams's military service as Private William Cathey can be found at the National Archives in Washington, D.C., in Record Group 94; and her pension application file (SO 1032593), in Record Group 15.

Tucker, Phillip Thomas. *Cathy Williams: From Slave to Female Buffalo Soldier* (2002).

"Cathay Williams Story." *St. Louis Daily Times*, 2 Jan. 1876.

DE ANNE BLANTON

Williams, Clara Belle (29 Oct. 1885–3 July 1994), educator and philanthropist, was born in Plum, Texas, as Clara Belle Drisdale. Her parents, Isaac and Malinda Drisdale, were former slaves and had six children, of whom Clara was the eldest. The family name, Drisdale, was the surname of the family that had owned her parents when they were slaves. Her grandfather, Stephen Drisdale, had been brought to America from the coast of Africa.

Determined to better himself, Clara's father taught himself how to read in order to take advantage of a chance to go to school, making him an early role model for his daughter's aspirations. In 1901 Clara won a full four-year scholarship to Prairie View Normal and Independent College (now Prairie View A&M University) in Prairie View, Texas, graduating in 1905 as the valedictorian of her class. Founded in 1876, Prairie View was the first state college in Texas exclusively for black students. Clara briefly taught school in Austin, Texas, but from 1907 to 1914 she was a professor of domestic arts and assistant dean of women at Prairie View. She also attended the University of Chicago in the summer of 1910.

Around 1907, she also began teaching in the segregated schools of Cameron, Texas, for thirty dollars a month. It was there that she met Jasper Buchanan Williams, whom she would marry on 21 January 1917 after a ten-year engagement, which had allowed Jasper to provide for his family, allowing his ten brothers and sisters to attend school. The couple later had three sons.

The Williamses soon moved to El Paso, Texas, where they opened a drugstore that was later destroyed in a fire. As a result of the fire the couple moved to Las Cruces, New Mexico, where Clara

Williams began teaching again. She taught for twenty-seven more years, while Jasper became a barber until a stroke paralyzed him. Williams was employed as a primary school teacher at the segregated BOOKER T. WASHINGTON School. Washington only had one high school teacher, and the school still used outhouses. While they were living in Las Cruces the family also homesteaded 640 acres.

In 1937 Clara Williams became the first African American to graduate from New Mexico College of Agriculture and Mechanic Arts (now New Mexico State University), receiving a bachelor's degree in English. At the time of her graduation some members of her summer graduating class objected to her marching in the ceremonies. In order to avoid any confrontation she chose to receive her diploma in the office of the registrar. She was fifty-one at the time. In 1939 she was accepted by and permitted to enroll in the graduate school.

Williams's three sons, Jasper, Charles, and James, all attended New Mexico State in later years. In 1943 Charles became the second African American to graduate from the school. Each of the sons went on to a medical career: James as an internist, Jasper as an obstetrician/gynecologist, and Charles as a surgeon. James, who served in the Army Air Corps in World War II, belonged to a unit assigned to the famed Tuskegee Airmen and was part of a group that was once refused entrance to a club at Freeman Field near Seymour, Indiana.

Clara Belle Williams retired from teaching in 1951 and moved to Chicago to be with her sons. In 1963 she used her life savings to purchase and refurbish a medical center on Chicago's South Side. She also went to work at a health center, the Williams Clinic, so named because it was built and operated by her sons from 1961 to 1995. The clinic at one point employed more than twenty-five doctors and had its own pharmacy and lab.

The state of New Mexico became aware of Clara Belle Williams's achievements. In 1961 a street on the New Mexico State University campus was named in honor of the family, and in 1980 she was given an honorary doctorate of laws degree. At the age of ninety-four she claimed that she was still not done with learning and registered for a Spanish class to "brush up on her skills" (*Panorama-NMSU Alumni Magazine*, Summer 2005). In 1991 New Mexico State established the Clara Belle Williams Endowed Scholarship Fund and in February 2005 renamed a hall as the Clara Belle Williams Hall.

Other achievements throughout her life included winning the Outstanding Mother and

Businesswoman award from the Fine Arts Guild of Chicago in 1966 and the 1977 Scroll of Merit from the National Medical Association. She was also named to the National Education Association Teaching Hall of Fame and even appeared as a guest on the *Today* show in April 1981. Clara Belle Williams died in Chicago in 1994 aged 108.

FURTHER READING

Materials relating to Williams are in the Rio Grande Historical Collection of the Branson Library of New Mexico State University.

JEFF BERG

Williams, Clarence (8 Oct. 1898 or 1893–6 Nov. 1965), blues and jazz musician, publisher, and music producer, was born in Plaquemine, Louisiana. The names and occupations of his parents are unknown. In 1906 his family moved to New Orleans. Williams's first instrument was the guitar, which he abandoned before he reached his teens to concentrate on the piano. Most of his learning was done by ear or by watching others, although he did receive eight lessons in the early 1910s, at the end of which he believed he knew all he needed to know about piano playing. At the age of twelve he left home to join BILLY KERSANDS's traveling minstrel show as a pianist, master of ceremonies, dancer, and comedian. Williams spent most of his teenage years in the clubs of New Orleans's legendary Storyville district as a pianist and songwriter. During this time he met the pianist and composer JELLY ROLL MORTON, who played an important role in transforming ragtime music into jazz and represented the main musical influence on Williams.

Williams's entrepreneurial skill and multifaceted musical talents exhibited themselves early in his life. About the year 1915 he founded his first publishing company, which lasted for two years, with the bandleader and songwriter ARMAND JOHN PIRON. Among the copyrights they handled were "Brownskin, Who You For" and Piron's oft-covered jazz classic "I Wish I Could Shimmy Like My Sister Kate." Williams formed his own jazz group that featured the jazz soloists BUNK JOHNSON, KING OLIVER, and SIDNEY BECHET, and they toured the South in the mid-1910s. At nineteen he served as a musical director for Salem Tutt Whitney's The Smart Set, a black touring company that produced musicals. He also toured briefly in 1917 with blues songwriter-entrepreneur W. C. HANDY.

At the end of World War I, Williams moved to Chicago and attempted to take advantage of the local activity surrounding jazz music by opening a music store and publishing company on State Street. Williams peddled his compositions door-to-door and on street corners from Texas to New York. He was one of the first African Americans to demonstrate his songs in five-and-dime stores, which were usually segregated. Despite extensive effort, the business failed. Not easily deterred, Williams relocated to New York City in 1919 and launched a publishing company that initiated his meteoric rise in the music business. That year Piron's "Sister Kate" marked its first significant commercial success. For the next two decades, dozens of hit songs in the blues, jazz, and vaudeville genres emanated from the company, and most of them were credited to Williams.

Being in New York City, home of the major record companies, represented a boon for Williams. Spurred on by the unprecedented sales of MAMIE SMITH's "Crazy Blues" (1920), the first popular vocal recording by an African American, these companies were starting to realize the previously untapped financial potential of a popular music market aimed at African Americans. Williams, with his combination of songwriting, publishing, band leading, and piano skills, proved invaluable in their efforts to exploit this market. By 1923 Williams became manager of the Race Artists' Section of Okeh Records and remained in that position for eight years. He directed sessions for his own groups and for others, sometimes playing piano or singing. He often selected the material to be performed, much of which was published under his company's banner. Perhaps Williams's most valuable skill to these companies was his ability to spot emerging and important artists. Many jazz legends made early recorded appearances on Williams's sessions long before they were famous, including Bechet, LOUIS ARMSTRONG, BUBBER MILEY, COLEMAN HAWKINS, and DON REDMAN.

Williams proved instrumental in the first recordings of BESSIE SMITH, the best-selling blues artist of the 1920s. Frank Walker, the head of Columbia Records' "race" music division, recalled seeing Smith perform in Alabama in 1917 and six years later had Williams find her so she could record for the company. Williams played piano and contributed two original songs to her first eight sides. One of them, "Baby Won't You Please Come Home" (1919), became a blues standard and one of Williams's most covered compositions. A bitter disagreement over a one-sided personal representation contract that Williams had Smith sign with him led to a divisive impasse between them, though they would be reunited in the recording studio in the late 1920s and early 1930s. In 1923 Smith's debut recording, "Down Hearted Blues," featured her joined only by Williams. His piano playing was not virtuosic, but he provided a bittersweet ambience that complemented the song and attractively lined the edges of Smith's vocal performance. It is no accident that a disproportionate amount of Smith's best sides are the relatively few times Williams was paired with her, including "Black Mountain Blues" (1930) and "Long Old Road" (1931).

Williams's talents as a simple but effective accompanist were regularly heard alongside the rich array of 1920s female vocal blues talent, including ETHEL WATERS, ALBERTA HUNTER, VICTORIA SPIVEY, and SIPPIE WALLACE. However, the female vocalist most identified with Williams was EVA TAYLOR, whom he met as a result of his work as an accompanist. They married in 1921. Taylor's successful career endured longer than most black female vocalists of the period; she appeared on recordings and radio well into the 1930s. The biggest hits by the Williams bands of the 1920s (such as the Blue Five, Morocco Five, and Blue Seven) usually showcased Taylor's vocals on Williams's songs. Some examples are "Everybody Loves My Baby (But My Baby Don't Love Nobody but Me)," "Cake Walking Babies from Home" (both from 1925 and featuring Armstrong), and the suggestive "Shake That Thing" (1926). Many of the mid-1920s Blue Five recordings are now considered early jazz classics, especially "Texas Moaner Blues" and "Mandy, Make Up Your Mind," two tracks from 1924 that document Armstrong and Bechet's definition of the jazz solo. Williams's skill at maintaining a relaxed and friendly atmosphere in the studio encouraged artists to perform at their highest level. "He could somehow manage to get the best out of them, and to this day hasn't received the credit he really deserves," marveled Walker in a 1950s interview (Shapiro and Hentoff, 239).

Throughout the late 1910s and the 1920s Williams contributed additional jazz and blues standards: "Royal Garden Blues" (1919), cowritten with the non-related Spencer Williams; "Tain't Nobody's Business if I Do" (1922); "Gulf Coast Blues" (1923); "West End Blues" (1928); and what may have been his most financially successful composition, "Squeeze Me," written with FATS WALLER in 1925. Some latter-day authors have accused Williams of claiming popular "unwritten" tunes of the day rather than composing his own and of taking credit for songs that he only helped promote. No conclusive evidence has been found on these charges, but

such situations were not uncommon in the music business of Williams's era.

Williams was also part of an exclusive group of black artists (others included JAMES P. JOHNSON, WILLIE "THE LION" SMITH, and Waller) contracted to record piano rolls for the QRS Company in 1923. Beginning in 1926 Williams embarked on a moderately successful series of recordings that utilized novelty "washboard" instrumentation that musically and humorously straddled the line between the hillbilly and vaudeville genres. In 1927 Williams wrote the music for an unsuccessful Broadway production titled *Bottomland*.

After his position at Okeh ended, Williams concentrated on administering his publishing and continuing his songwriting. His appearances on recordings and his string of hit songs subsided during the 1930s. Throughout the 1930s and 1940s Williams acted as an agent for black recording artists, arranging recording sessions with major record labels. By 1941 he had ceased to record, and two years later he sold his publishing interests to the Decca Recording Company for a large sum. Afterward Williams enjoyed a wealthy and private semiretirement as the proprietor of a hobby shop in Harlem. He died in New York City.

Williams played a significant role in enlarging the scope of the commercial possibilities for black music, which led to the rise of the African American music market and the dominance of blues- and jazz-influenced music on American radio airwaves in the 1920s and 1930s. He was one of the first African Americans to wield real power in the music business as an entrepreneur, executive, and artist. Williams was one of the main progenitors of the recording and songwriting legacy of the opening decade of recorded jazz and blues—writing, cowriting, and recording many of the standards identified with the music for decades to come. Despite his many achievements, Williams told an interviewer in the 1960s that there was a significant amount of struggle involved as well. He called the blues a "mood" that represented a "carry-over from slavery—nothing but trouble in sight for everyone. There was no need to hitch your wagon to a star, because there weren't any stars. You got only what you fought for" (Patterson, 56).

FURTHER READING
Lord, Tom. *Clarence Williams* (1976)
Patterson, Lindsay, ed. *The Negro in Music and Art* (1967).

Shapiro, Nat, and Nat Hentoff, eds. *Hear Me Talkin' to Ya* (1955).

Obituary: *New York Times*, 9 Nov. 1965.

DISCOGRAPHY

Rust, Byron. *Jazz Records, 1897–1942*, 4th rev. ed. (1978).

This entry is taken from the *American National Biography* and is published here with the permission of the American Council of Learned Societies.

HARVEY COHEN

Williams, Claude "Fiddler" (22 Feb. 1908–25 Apr. 2004), violinist and guitarist, was born Claude Gaberial Williams in Muskogee, Oklahoma, the son of Lee J. Williams, a blacksmith, and Laura Williams, a homemaker. The youngest of six children, Williams learned to play piano, guitar, and four-string mandolin from his brother-in-law Ben Johnson. He taught himself the violin in his youth after hearing Joe Venuti play. After becoming proficient on violin, Williams joined his brother-in-law's string band. The band traveled by train on a circuit between Muskogee, Tulsa, and Oklahoma City. The band performed ragtime, popular standards, and blues for tips in barbershops, hotels, and on the street.

In 1927 Williams joined T. Holder's Dark Clouds of Joy at the Louvre Ballroom in Tulsa. The band alternated between Tulsa and Oklahoma City playing "jitney dances," so called because the management would give away a car, commonly referred to as a jitney, as a door prize on Saturday nights. Williams modeled his big tone after the reed and brass sections. A strong soloist, he improvised off song chord changes.

In December 1928 ANDY KIRK took over the band after an irregularity with the payroll and shortened the name to Clouds of Joy. In July 1929 the band opened at the Pla-Mor Ballroom in Kansas City, a wide-open entertainment mecca for the Midwest. Kirk moved the band's headquarters to Kansas City and established a regional circuit. In January 1930 the band replaced the FLETCHER HENDERSON band at the Roseland Ballroom in New York. Williams resisted Kirk's repeated requests to set aside his violin and concentrate on playing guitar with the rhythm section. When Williams fell ill while on the road, the band left him behind.

Back in Kansas City Williams worked for a year with a small ensemble at a "taxi dance" hall, where men paid to dance with the women who were employed there. After a short stint with the Chick Stevens band in Peoria, Illinois, Williams joined the Eddie Cole band in Chicago, featuring NAT "KING" COLE. A top local pianist with a stutter, Cole had yet to discover he could sing. Williams left the band when work became scarce during a southern tour and returned to Chicago.

In early fall 1936 COUNT BASIE sent for Williams to join his Barons of Rhythm at the Reno Club in Kansas City. With the support of John Hammond and the Willard Alexander Agency, Basie expanded the band to fourteen pieces for a tour to New York. Lacking suitable arrangements, the band got off to a rough start. The band arrived in New York to mixed reviews. George Simon in his "Dance Band Reviews" column in *Metronome* in February 1937 tempered his criticism of the band's debut in New York by praising Williams's "good hot fiddle passages." Nevertheless, at the urging of Hammond, Basie let Williams go for guitarist Freddie Green, a steady rhythm player, during an engagement at the Hotel William Penn in Pittsburgh, Pennsylvania.

Williams returned again to Kansas City and formed the Three Swing Men of Swing, a string trio that opened at Lucille's Paradise, a popular club on 18th Street. In 1938 Williams moved to Flint, Michigan, and joined a WPA band (the WPA, for Works Projects Administration, was a New Deal government agency that provided economic assistance to artists and others during the 1930s Depression). During World War II Williams worked a day job welding tanks before being inducted into the service in 1944. Discharged after nine months of service, he returned to Chicago where he worked with the Four Shades of Rhythm as well as with guitarist Austin Powell, the former leader of the Cats and the Fiddle.

Williams traveled briefly with Powell, but the band ran out of work, leaving Williams stranded in New York. As a result, Williams traveled to the West Coast, where he replaced the guitarist in ROY MILTON's Solid Senders. Williams changed to the electric guitar and adapted to the band's orchestral style of rhythm and blues. The Milton band toured widely up the West Coast and across the Midwest. Williams left the group in Wichita and returned yet again to Kansas City.

During the 1950s and 1960s Williams worked mainly in Kansas City, playing the Blue Room, Orchid Room, Fandango, and other small nightclubs. Williams, doubling on guitar and violin, employed organist Charles Kynard, alto saxophonist Eddie "Cleanhead" Vinson, and other top players. In the late 1960s, when work became scarce in Kansas City, Williams freelanced in Los Angeles.

In the early 1970s Williams teamed up with pianist JAY MCSHANN and toured the Midwest. Although they both hailed from Muskogee and had come of age musically in local bands, they had previously had little opportunity to work together. Williams's fluid phrasing complemented McShann's boogie-woogie and barrelhouse piano style. In 1972 McShann recorded the *Man From Muskogee* for the Sackville label. The recording prominently featured Williams, giving his career a boost. The next year McShann and Williams appeared at the JVC Jazz Festival (an extension of the Newport, Rhode Island, Jazz Festival) at New York's Lincoln Center. They worked regularly together throughout the 1970s, touring Europe and recording prolifically. Williams and McShann went their separate ways in 1979.

In 1984 Williams joined the cast of the revue *Black and Blue* in Paris. Originally booked for a six-week run, the revue, celebrating the legendary Cotton Club, ran for eight months. Williams left the revue before it opened on Broadway and returned to Kansas City to care for his ailing wife, Mabel, to whom he was married for over fifty years.

Williams enjoyed critical acclaim during the last two decades of his career. In 1985 he was the subject of the documentary *Fiddler's Dream*. In 1989 he became one of the first inductees into the Oklahoma Jazz Hall of Fame. In 1990 he was featured with Billy Taylor on *CBS News Sunday Morning*. Williams played for President Bill Clinton's first inaugural, then returned in 1998 for an encore performance in the East Room of the White House. He played a regular circuit of jazz festivals, conducted clinics, recorded numerous CDs, and toured internationally well into his nineties.

Throughout his career, which virtually spanned the history of jazz, Williams refused to compromise and refused to replace his violin with a rhythm section guitar. By virtue of his perseverance in the face of adversity, longevity, and devotion to his instrument, Williams enjoyed a great deal of well-deserved acclaim in the twilight of his career.

FURTHER READING

Driggs, Frank, and Chuck Haddix. *Kansas City Jazz: From Ragtime to Bebop—A History* (2005).
Haddix, Chuck. "Fiddler's Triumph," *Down Beat* (March 1999).

DISCOGRAPHY

Count Basie. *Swingin' at the Chatterbox: 1937* (Stardust Records 139-2).

King of Kansas City (Progressive 7100).
Swingtime in New York (Progressive Records 7093).

CHUCK HADDIX

Williams, Cootie (24 July 1910–15 Sept. 1985), jazz trumpeter, was born Charles Melvin Williams in Mobile, Alabama. His parents' names are unknown. When Williams was a small child, his father, the owner of a gambling house, took him to hear a brass band, which the boy described as sounding like "cootie, cootie, cootie," thus giving rise to his lifelong nickname. His mother, who played piano and organ, died when Williams was eight, and he and his three brothers were raised by a live-in aunt. After two years studying piano and violin, at age seven he entered the school band, where he played drums, trombone, and tuba before ultimately settling on the trumpet, which he then studied with Charles Lipskin. At fourteen he worked for a summer with Billy Young's Family Band, a traveling act whose youthful members included the later renowned LESTER YOUNG. That same year Williams met the clarinetist and saxophonist EDMOND HALL, who was then playing in Pensacola, Florida. In 1924, when Hall was asked to join "Eagle Eye" Shields's orchestra in Jacksonville, he accepted on the condition that the teenaged Williams also would be hired.

In late 1926 or early 1927 Hall and Williams left Shields and moved to Miami to work with the Alonzo Ross De Luxe Syncopators, a band that also traveled all over Florida and Georgia. While in Savannah in August 1927, the band was recorded, but for some reason Williams was not present at the session. When the records were released, though, they so impressed the manager of New York City's Roseland Ballroom that he hired the band to play at his Rosemont Ballroom in Brooklyn starting on 18 March 1928. However, the Syncopators apparently were not up to New York standards, and they were fired after only two weeks. By this time Ross had been replaced as pianist by Arthur "Happy" Ford, who, after termination of the Rosemont job, quickly found work for Williams and Hall in his quartet at a taxi dance hall (a dime-a-dance ballroom so named for the time-metered practice by which women collected tickets from their "suitors") called the Happyland. After hours Williams and Hall often went to jam sessions at Harlem's Band Box, where the trumpeter was heard by the drummer CHICK WEBB, who in turn hired him for a job at the famous Savoy Ballroom. Williams worked with Webb for three weeks at the end of 1928 and then in January 1929 joined the FLETCHER HENDERSON Orchestra as a temporary replacement for the lead trumpeter Russell Smith. To Williams's understanding, he had been hired only for a brief tour, but immediately after the band returned to New York in mid-February to resume its regular stand at the Roseland Ballroom, Williams was invited to stay on as first trumpeter.

However, Williams had already been approached by DUKE ELLINGTON to replace BUBBER MILEY as featured soloist in his band. Albeit with mixed feelings over his obligation to Henderson, Williams accepted the offer and made his debut recordings with Ellington on 18 February 1929. Until this time Williams had been noted as a powerful, LOUIS ARMSTRONG–inspired open-horn trumpeter who rarely if ever played with a mute. He had a large, full tone that projected itself easily whether playing lead or solo, but Ellington had something else in mind for his new acquisition. Miley, a virtuoso in his own right, was a specialist in the so-called "wa-wa" style of trumpet playing, a technique of plunger-muted guttural growling that he had mastered in his own unique fashion after having first been impressed by Johnny Dunn and KING OLIVER. Although Ellington never actually told the young, fat-toned trumpeter to imitate Miley, Williams nevertheless started experimenting with this new technique on his own, using his bandstand mate, the trombonist JOE "TRICKY SAM" NANTON, as his nightly exemplar. It was not until the recording of "Doin' the Voom Voom" on 10 September 1929, seven months after he had joined the band, that he can be heard growling, tentatively, on record. But only a few days later, on "Jazz Convulsions" and "Mississippi," he emerges as a convincing, full-fledged Miley disciple.

Williams stayed with Ellington for almost twelve years, appearing on hundreds of recordings and broadcasts with such outstanding fellow sidemen as JOHNNY HODGES, BARNEY BIGARD, HARRY CARNEY, REX STEWART, Nanton, and LAWRENCE BROWN. But the time came, in November 1940, when Benny Goodman, with Ellington's consent, asked Williams to join his band for a year. Realizing that his star trumpeter would receive even greater exposure by playing in the most successful white swing band of the time, Ellington not only gave his blessings but also helped negotiate a substantial raise in pay. Williams's first assignment was the now-historic sextet date of 7 November that produced "Wholly Cats," "Royal Garden Blues," "As Long as I Live," and "Benny's Bugle" with the nonpareil combination of Goodman's inventive clarinet, Georgie Auld's robust tenor sax, COUNT BASIE's prodding piano, CHARLIE CHRISTIAN's pacesetting guitar, and his own incendiary growl trumpet.

Williams was also featured on several of Goodman's big-band recordings, such as "Superman" and "Pound Ridge," but it is undeniably the sextet titles that offer the best evidence of his flawless skill in an improvising context. Goodman's work schedule was easily the equal of Ellington's during this busy prewar period, and Williams's reputation was at its peak. Earlier, on 16 January 1938, he had appeared along with Hodges and Carney as a featured Ellingtonian at Goodman's historic Carnegie Hall concert, and in both 1939 and 1940 he was voted in as a member of *Metronome*'s All-Star Band. He also won similar awards from *Esquire* in 1944, 1945, and 1946.

After his contract with Goodman expired in October 1941, Williams told Ellington that he was ready to come back, but his former leader encouraged him to take advantage of his new popularity and go out on his own. After a few months of preparation, on 1 April 1942 he recorded his first session as a big-band leader. Successful from the start, his orchestra enjoyed long residencies at the Savoy Ballroom throughout the forties, and at various times his personnel included future modern jazz and rhythm and blues stars such as BUD POWELL, EDDIE "LOCKJAW" DAVIS, CHARLIE PARKER, PEARL BAILEY, Sam "The Man" TAYLOR, Eddie "Cleanhead" Vinson, and Willis "Gator" Jackson. But because of changing popular tastes, in 1948 Williams had to reduce his personnel at the Savoy to a sextet. When the thirty-two-year-old ballroom was torn down in 1958, Williams disbanded and spent some time touring as a single. He then formed a quartet and worked at the Embers, the Round Table, and other venues. After a long hiatus from the studios, he started recording again in 1957 and in July 1958 appeared at the Newport Jazz Festival as a member of the Ellington Alumni All Stars. He toured Europe with a small band in early 1959 and recorded his last album as leader in April 1962. In July 1962 Williams rejoined Goodman for a short time and, in a striking reversal of historical sequence, then went back to the Duke Ellington Orchestra in September, where he remained, except for a 1973 illness, through Ellington's death in May 1974. He continued to play under the son Mercer Ellington's leadership into the next year. Williams spent his final years of activity touring Europe, during which time he recorded in Holland in 1976.

Although open-minded in his acceptance and encouragement of younger jazzmen such as Bud Powell, Charlie Parker, and THELONIOUS MONK, whose "'Round Midnight" he chose for his band's theme, as a trumpet stylist Williams was considered passé by the generation that had produced DIZZY GILLESPIE, FATS NAVARRO, and MILES DAVIS. But he was still capable of great playing, as is evidenced by his latter-day appearances with Ellington, where, unburdened by the responsibilities of leading a band, he was required only to exhibit his most unique attributes—his majestic, Armstrong-like open-horn tone, his inimitable mastery of the plunger mute, and those adroitly placed, dramatically shaded, massive blocks of sound that had always lent so much authority to his presence within the Ellington fold. A chronic sufferer of high blood pressure, Williams played only sporadically from 1976 on. He died in Jamaica, New York, and was survived by his wife, Catherine.

FURTHER READING

Allen, Walter C. *Hendersonia: The Music of Fletcher Henderson and His Musicians* (1973).
Dance, Stanley. *The World of Duke Ellington* (1970).
Dance, Stanley. *The World of Swing* (1974).
McCarthy, Albert. *Big Band Jazz* (1974).
Schuller, Gunther. *The Swing Era* (1989).

This entry is taken from the *American National Biography* and is published here with the permission of the American Council of Learned Societies.

JACK SOHMER

Williams, Daniel Barclay (22 Nov. 1861–1895), educator and first black university classicist in the state of Virginia, was born in Richmond, Virginia, apparently to a single mother. In April 1865, when Williams was three years old, Richmond fell to Union troops under Ulysses S. Grant, mere days before the South's ultimate surrender at Appomattox. Retreating Confederates set fire to their capital, but the two-day blaze presented Richmond's black population with some unprecedented prospects. Williams was among the first generation of Southern blacks to gain legal access to public schools, and his mother put enough trust in his talent to enroll him early on. Upon his graduation from Richmond Normal School in 1877, Williams was awarded a gold medal for his superior scholarship and conduct, as well as a silver medal for excellence in orthography. These early successes prefigured the steep rise to prominence of a life cut short in its prime.

The end of Federal Reconstruction efforts in 1877 left the freedmen once more at the mercy of their former owners, but this did not deter Williams from continuing his pursuit of an education. In the fall, the sixteen-year-old ventured beyond the Mason-Dixon Line and into Massachusetts, where he matriculated at Worcester Academy. Williams completed his studies there at the top of his class in 1880 and gained admission to prestigious Brown University. During his freshman year at college, Williams's academic ascent came to a sudden halt. For reasons glossed over by his contemporary biographers (though most likely due to financial difficulties), Williams was forced to leave Rhode Island and resettle in his native city, Richmond. Yet even this humbling episode had its positive aspects. Upon his return to the South, Williams found his true calling in the education of his race. And according to nineteenth-century accounts of his life, he did not abandon his college studies altogether. Williams was apparently able to complete Brown's requirements for a B.A. through independent readings in Richmond, and accordingly, many of his later writings express his respect for the self-educated.

While pursuing his off-campus studies, Williams lived on a teacher's salary. For the next five years, he managed a private school in segregated Richmond, teaching higher mathematics, science, and philosophy, as well as various languages he had acquired. Williams is known to have been proficient in German and French, as well as Hebrew, Latin, and Greek. During the academic year of 1884–85, Williams was also an instructor in the public schools of Henrico County, and he was in charge of Richmond's Moore Street Industrial School for three months, starting in March 1885. Williams's immediate circle of students was not the sole beneficiary of this burst of didactic productivity.

Williams completed his B.A. program later that summer, at age twenty-four, and went on to teach at the all-black Virginia Normal and Collegiate Institute (VN&CI) in Petersburg, Virginia (today Virginia State University), where in 1887 he accepted the chair of ancient languages and held the position of instructor in methods of teaching and school management. By then, Williams had already published his debut features for a wider reading public. *The Negro Race: The Pioneers in Civilization* (1883) is a multilayered attack on common perceptions of black cultural inferiority and constitutes a true pièce de résistance. In the Jim Crow era, many white Americans rationalized the nation's unashamed discriminations by pointing to blacks' alleged failure to attain to a degree of "civilization" equal to that of Europeans. In *The*

Negro Race Williams argued that the two aboriginal white cultures, ancient Greece and Rome, had in fact received their civilizing impulses from black Africa via Egypt. Moreover, Williams refuted the frequent claim that blacks had since been reduced to unproductive paupers by pointing to the race's intellectual, professional, and material successes since Emancipation.

In his speeches and various published essays of successive years, he extolled the achievements of impressive individuals, praised their patriotism, and delineated many events in which black men had proved valiant soldiers, brilliant educators, and moral exemplars. He hoped that his sketches would inspire his young readers in the same way that the ancient historian Thucydides came to outshine his renowned forerunner, Herodotus. Reports of Williams's own achievements played no trivial role in this approach. His literary successes at a young age allowed for comparisons to the ancient Athenian playwright Aristophanes and American poets like William Cullen Bryant. As he drew such parallels, as he peppered his publications with quotes from Virgil in Latin, St. Paul in Greek, and Goethe in German, and as he made a career as a professor of ancient languages, Williams demonstrated a familiarity with the highest spheres of learning that many had thought unattainable for an African American.

This variety of interests and agendas is reflected in the titles of Williams's works. Aside from various other journalistic engagements, he contributed a series of articles on "The Latin Language" and "The Education of the Negro" to *The Industrial Herald* and the *Richmond Planet* between 1883 and 1884. He published *Why We Are Baptists?* in 1884 and again in 1885, when he also printed *The Life and Times of Captain R. A. Paul*. The next in a line of nine books was *Science, Art, and Methods of Teaching* (1887), which was the first publication by a faculty member of the VN&CI and was adopted as a textbook. *Freedom and Progress* was published in 1890, followed by *Science and Art of Elocution* in 1894. His works on education and oratory were particularly influential; *Freedom and Progress*, for example, went through as many as four revisions.

Williams's oeuvre evidences a lifelong effort to harmonize his academic training with his zealous religiosity. If the two collided, the latter took precedence. Daniel B. Williams was a stalwart believer in the literal truth of the Bible; he ranted against the "death-breeding infidelity" of the likes of Rousseau and Voltaire and considered Jesus Christ the only

"original" teacher with no debts to intellectual forerunners. He was a stern advocate for temperance, rejected the Darwinian theory of evolution, and in a gloomy tale of Enlightenment thought winning out over church doctrine, he labeled reason a "naked harlot."

During his decade at the VN&CI, Williams proved a congenial instructor. Hundreds of college students and prospective teachers watched a slender young man with chinstrap beard, mustache, and receding hairline lecture on a variety of subjects, ranging from Tacitus, Horace, and Homer to Demosthenes. One of his textbooks of choice was fellow black classicist WILLIAM SAUNDERS SCARBOROUGH's *First Lessons in Greek*. Williams rose quickly through the ranks. He laid the foundations for the institution's classics library, became head of the Ancient Languages department, and also served as dean of the Collegiate department. Livingstone College in Salisbury, North Carolina, awarded him an honorary A.M. degree in 1889, and Shaw University in Raleigh, North Carolina, followed up with an honorary Ph.D. in 1891.

Sketches of Williams's life appeared in the notable newspapers of the period, and he traveled his beloved home state as a public speaker. On the side, he made time to care for his aging mother, to publish his own poetry (see Thomas Herringshaw's *Local and National Poets of America* [1890]), and to write for the *Progressive Educator*. Yet in many respects, Williams stood against the currents of his time. Though he recognized the importance of manual training to wider swaths of the black population, he did urge the more gifted to pursue a college education, which along with tireless diligence and Christian morality he considered most beneficial to the advancement of his race. Some black leaders of national influence, such as BOOKER T. WASHINGTON, did not share his appreciation for university instruction, and prominent white Virginians like Paul Cabell (who served on the university's board of supervisors) bluntly rejected providing blacks with a classical education. It is a testimony to Williams's role in fighting these adverse trends that in 1902, seven years after his premature death at age thirty-four, the VN&CI closed its collegiate branch for what would be twenty years.

FURTHER READING
Johnston Memorial Library at Virginia State University holds the Personal Library and Papers of Daniel Barclay Williams.

Becker, Trudy Harrington. "Daniel B. Williams, 1861–1895," *Classical Outlook* 76.3 (1999).

Mitchel, John, Jr. "A Sketch of the Life of Professor D. B. Williams, A.M." in Daniel B. Williams, *Freedom and Progress and Other Choice Addresses on Practical, Scientific, Educational, Philosophic, Historic, and Religious Subjects*, 4th ed. (1890).

Penn, I. Garland. *The Afro-American Press, and Its Editors* (1891).

MATHIAS HANSES

Williams, Daniel Hale (18 Jan. 1856–4 Aug. 1931), surgeon and hospital administrator, was born in Hollidaysburg, south central Pennsylvania, the son of Daniel Williams Jr. and Sarah Price. His parents were black, but Daniel himself, in adult life, could easily be mistaken for being white, with his light complexion, red hair, and blue eyes.

Williams's father did well in real estate but died when Daniel was eleven, and the family's financial situation became difficult. When Williams was seventeen, he and a sister, Sally, moved to Janesville, Wisconsin. Here Williams found work at Harry Anderson's Tonsorial Parlor and Bathing Rooms. Anderson took the two of them into his home as family and continued to aid Williams financially until Williams obtained his MD.

Medicine had not been Williams's first choice of a career; he had worked in a law office after high school but had found it too quarrelsome. In 1878 Janesville's most prominent physician, Henry Palmer, took Williams on as an apprentice. Williams entered the Chicago Medical College in the fall of 1880 and graduated in 1883. He opened an office on Chicago's South Side and treated both black and white patients.

Late in 1890 the Reverend Louis Reynolds, a pastor on the West Side, asked Williams for advice about his sister, Emma, who had been turned down at several nursing schools because of her color. As a result Williams decided to start an interracial hospital and a nursing school for black women. He drew on black and white individuals and groups for financial support. Several wealthy businessmen, such as meat-packer Philip D. Armour and publisher Herman H. Kohlsaat, made major contributions to the purchase of a three-story building at Dearborn and Twenty-ninth Street and its remodeling into a hospital with twelve beds. Provident Hospital and Training School Association was officially incorporated on 23 January 1891 and opened for service on 4 May of that year. The Training School received 175 applicants for its first class, and Williams selected 7 for the eighteen-month course.

Provident had both white and black patients and staff members, although the lack of suitably qualified black physicians led to some problems. Williams appointed black physicians and surgeons who had obtained their medical degrees from schools such as the Rush Medical College and his own alma mater and who, in addition, had suitable experience. However, he had to deal diplomatically with some leaders of the black community who were pushing the appointment of young George Cleveland Hall, who had a degree from an eclectic school and only two years of experience (mostly in Chicago's red light district). Hall (and his equally aggressive wife) never forgave Williams for this early judgment to oppose Hall's appointment.

The hospital soon became overcrowded, but many donations—again including major contributions from Armour and Kohlsaat—resulted in the construction of a new sixty-five-bed hospital at Dearborn and Thirty-sixth streets. The new Provident opened in late 1896.

In 1893 a longtime Chicago friend of Williams, Judge Walter Q. Gresham, recently named secretary of state by President Grover Cleveland, urged Williams to seek the position of surgeon in chief at Freedmen's Hospital in Washington, D.C. This, Gresham pointed out, would bring Williams onto the national scene. Williams, believing that Provident was in good hands, finally agreed to Gresham's suggestion and in 1894 was appointed to Freedmen's where his predecessor, CHARLES B. PURVIS, unhappy at being replaced and often with the aid of Hall, made life as difficult as possible for Williams.

Williams, nevertheless, accomplished much at Freedmen's. He reorganized the staff interracially, created an advisory board of prominent physicians for both professional and political help, and founded a successful nursing school. Williams also began an internship program, improved relationships with the Howard University Medical School, and helped establish an interracial local medical society.

Williams also worked hard on the national scene and became one of the founders of the National Medical Association in 1895. Because at the time the American Medical Association did not accept black physicians, such a national organization was a necessary part of the educational and professional growth for black health-care givers. In 1895 Williams turned down the presidency but did become vice president of the organization.

With the election in 1896 of a new U.S. president, the control of Freedmen's became involved

AMERICAN NEGRO EMANCIPATION CENTENNIAL

BIOGRAPHIES OF NOTABLE NEGROES

WILLIAMS, Daniel Hale, 1858 - 1931
Negro surgeon--Daniel Hale Williams "performed the first recorded successful heart operation in 1893" was born in Hollidaysburg, Pa., but at an early age his family moved to Janesville, Wis., where he was educated through high school. He worked in the office of the surgeon general of the state for two years, and then entered Northwestern University Medical School. He taught anatomy at Northwestern after receiving an M. D. in 1833, and in 1891 founded Provident Hospital in Chicago, where he started a nursing school for Negro girls. He gained worldwide recognition for the heart operation. President Grover Cleveland invited him to Washington to head Freedmen's Hospital, where he started another nursing school. Dr. Williams was a member of the surgical staffs of many hospitals, and was made a Fellow of the American College of Surgeons. He wrote many articles on surgery.

COPYRIGHT 1964 CRAWFORD STUDIO

Daniel Hale Williams performed the first successful recorded operation on the membrane surrounding the heart in 1893. (Library of Congress.)

in partisan congressional hearings. These were sufficiently upsetting for Williams, but then William A. Warfield, one of Williams's first interns at Freedmen's, accused his chief, before the hospital's board of visitors, of stealing hospital supplies. Although the congressional hearings came to no conclusion and the board of visitors exonerated Williams, he had become soured on Washington and resigned early in 1898.

In April 1898 Williams married Alice Johnson in Washington, D.C. The couple moved to Chicago, and Williams returned to his old office. There the Halls continued to undermine the Williamses' professional and social lives. Hall finally forced Williams to resign from Provident in 1912 because the latter had become an associate attending surgeon at St. Luke's Hospital and was, therefore, "disloyal" to Provident. That this was a trumped-up charge was apparent from the fact that, since 1900,

Williams had regularly had patients in up to five other hospitals at the same time.

National recognition, however, counterbalanced such sniping; in 1913 Williams was nominated to be a charter member of the American College of Surgeons, the first black surgeon to be honored in this manner. At the board of regents meeting to act on this, a surgeon from Tennessee objected because of the social implications in the South. After vigorous discussion, during which it was pointed out that "if you met him [Williams] on the street you would hardly realize that he is a Negro," Williams was accepted.

As a surgeon, Williams is best known for his stitching of a stab wound to the pericardium of Jim Cornish, an expressman, on 9 July 1893. After Williams had realized that conservative care would not be sufficient for Cornish, he searched the medical literature for reports of surgery in this area. Finding none, he nevertheless decided to perform surgery. Cornish lived for fifty years after the operation. While strictly speaking not an operation on the heart itself, this was the first successful suturing of the pericardium on record.

Perhaps more important surgically was Williams's successful suturing of a heavily bleeding spleen in July 1902, one of the earliest such operations in the United States. Williams also operated on many ovarian cysts, a condition that had not been believed to occur in black women. In 1901 he reported on his 357 such operations, almost equally divided between black and white patients. Well aware of the lack of training opportunities available to black surgeons in the South, Williams readily accepted an invitation near the end of the century to be a visiting professor of clinical surgery at the Meharry Medical College in Nashville, Tennessee. He spent five or ten days there without pay each year for over a decade. He began operating in a crowded basement room, but by 1910 growing financial support for the college programs resulted in a separate hospital building with forty beds. Williams also operated and lectured at other schools and hospitals in the South.

In 1920 Williams built a summer home near Idlewild, Michigan, to which he and his wife moved. There Alice died of Parkinson's disease a few years later, and Williams then succumbed to diabetes and a stroke.

Williams became known for his long and successful efforts for medical care and professional training for blacks, although much of his work was multiracial. His logically developed and pioneering surgery, especially on the pericardium and the spleen, increased the possibilities and scope of surgical action.

FURTHER READING

Beatty, William K. "Daniel Hale Williams: Innovative Surgeon, Educator, and Hospital Administrator," *Chest* 60 (1971): 175–82.

Buckler, Helen. *Daniel Hale Williams: Negro Surgeon* (1954; repr. 1966).

This entry is taken from the *American National Biography* and is published here with the permission of the American Council of Learned Societies.

WILLIAM K. BEATTY

Williams, Doug (9 Aug. 1955–), football player, coach, and executive, was born Douglass Lee Williams in Zachary, Louisiana, the sixth of eight children to Robert Williams, a construction worker and disabled World War II veteran, and Laura (maiden name unknown), a school cook. He grew up in Zachary sharing a room with three brothers and idolizing his older brother Robert, who served as a mentor and coach and steered Doug toward football, which he started playing in the eighth grade. Like most boys, he wanted to play quarterback and got the chance his junior year of high school.

In 1973 Williams attended Grambling University in Louisiana, where he had a football scholarship. Redshirted his freshman year, he did not play and almost quit the team, but his coach, EDDIE ROBINSON, convinced him to stay. Early in his second season he replaced starter Joe Comaux and held the starting position for the next four years, from 1974 to 1977. During his career at Grambling Williams had a 36-7 record and won or shared the Southwestern Athletic Conference (SWAC) championship every year. He had only one game his entire college career without a touchdown pass and threw for more than eight thousand yards and a school-record ninety-three touchdown passes. His senior year he finished fourth in Heisman Trophy voting and was named All-American and Louisiana College Athlete of the Year. He graduated with a B.S. in Health and Physical Education.

In 1978 the Tampa Bay Buccaneers drafted Williams as the seventeenth pick in the first round of the National Football League's (NFL) college draft. Williams was just the second black quarterback to be drafted in the first round, but he was the first to become a regular starter (the first drafted was Eldridge Dickey in 1968 by the Oakland Raiders, but he was converted to wide receiver). Hoping to revive a moribund franchise, the Buccaneers named the rookie Williams their starting quarterback. In 1979, Williams's second season, he led the team to its first winning record (10-6) and won the franchise's first playoff game, against Philadelphia. Williams's and the Buccaneers' success continued. He led the team to the playoffs in 1981 and 1982. In that latter year he also married Janice Goss, whom he'd met in college; the couple had one child.

Following the 1982 season Williams entered contact negotiations with the Buccaneers. His salary of $120,000 a year was far less than that earned even by most backup quarterbacks and ranked Williams fifty-fourth in the league for quarterbacks. Negotiations with Tampa Bay were acrimonious. Williams believed that his salary and subsequent offers from Tampa Bay were low because he was black. Though he had little respect for the Buccaneers' owner Hugh Culverhouse—Williams called him a redneck—he did respect the team's head coach John McKay and wanted to continue playing for Tampa Bay. After his wife died from a brain tumor in 1983, however, Williams broke off negotiations with the franchise.

Williams played two seasons in the United States Football League (USFL) for the Oklahoma (later Arizona) Outlaws until the USFL folded in 1986. No NFL team approached him until the Washington Redskins' head coach Joe Gibbs signed Williams as a backup, a development Williams felt was the result of blacklisting on the part of the Buccaneers. He spent two seasons, 1986 and 1987, playing behind Jay Schroeder and saw little game action. Williams married again in 1987, to Lisa Robinson, but they divorced a year later.

During the 1987 season Williams played in only three games, twice replacing Schroeder after the starter was benched for poor performance. When the Redskins made the playoffs Coach Gibbs named Williams as the starting quarterback. Williams led the Redskins on an improbable playoff run, beating the Minnesota Vikings in the National Football Conference championship to propel the Redskins to the Super Bowl. When reporters tried to make a big deal of the fact that he was the first black quarterback to lead a team to the NFL's championship game, Williams responded, "I'm not a black quarterback. I'm the Washington Redskins quarterback" (Williams, 149).

The Redskins faced the Denver Broncos in Super Bowl XXII on 31 January 1988 in San Diego, California. After a slow start that saw the Redskins go down 10-0 and Williams injure his knee,

Doug Williams, photographed on 31 January 1988. As quarterback for the Washington Redskins, he was voted most valuable player of Super Bowl XXII. (AP Images.)

Williams put on an offensive display for perhaps the most impressive quarter in Super Bowl history. He led five straight touchdown drives, including throwing four touchdown passes, to lead the Redskins to a 35-10 first half lead. The Redskins went on to win 42-10, and Williams was named the game's Most Valuable Player. He set or tied several Super Bowl records: passing yards (340), touchdown passes (four), longest completion (eighty yards), and longest touchdown pass (eighty yards). Williams's first act after the victory was to hug his old coach, Eddie Robinson.

Williams would play two more seasons with the Redskins before the team released him in 1990. His release and a subsequent lack of interest from other NFL teams proved to Williams what he long believed—that the NFL did not want black quarterbacks. Following his historic Super Bowl victory, Robinson called Williams the JACKIE ROBINSON of quarterbacks, but Williams felt that this could be true only if black quarterbacks became commonplace.

From 1990 to 1993 Williams ran the Doug Williams Foundation. Established shortly after Williams's Super Bowl victory, the foundation offered a variety of programs in the Washington, D.C., area relating to school, life skills, and sports. Williams spent the next few years at a variety of coaching stops, including head coach at Chanceyville High School in Zachary, assistant coach at the Naval Academy in 1994, assistant coach of the Scottish Claymores of the World Football League from 1995 to 1996, and head coach of Morehouse College in 1997, before replacing Robinson as the head coach at Grambling in 1998. He coached there for seven years, compiling a 52-18 record, and won three consecutive SWAC championships and SWAC Coach of the Year in 2000, 2001, and 2002. He married his third wife, LaTaunya (maiden name unknown), in 2002, and they had four children. In 2001 he was inducted into the College Football Hall of Fame.

Williams's football career came full circle when he returned to the Tampa Bay Buccaneers as a personnel executive in 2004. Upon his return to the NFL Williams remarked that he was amazed at the strides made by black athletes, particularly quarterbacks, of whom more than a dozen were on team rosters as starters or backups.

FURTHER READING

Williams, Doug, with Bruce Hunter. *Quarterblack: Shattering the NFL Myth* (1990).
Current Biography (1999).
Dyer, Scott. "Louisiana Officials Mounted Fierce Effort to Keep Williams at Grambling," *Black Issues in Higher Education* 21.2 (Mar. 2004).

MICHAEL C. MILLER

Williams, Dudley Eugene (18 Aug. 1938–), dancer, was born in New York City, son of the carpenter Ivan Williams and the housewife Austa Beckles Williams, both from St. Croix, Virgin Islands. With his older brother Ivan Leroy and mentally disabled younger sister Patricia, Williams spent his childhood in the culturally mixed East River Projects, often swirling around on his roller skates and ice skates in imitation of stars like Sonja Henie. At ten, Williams insisted on piano lessons. At twelve, he began a once-a-week, one-dollar-a-session class in "interpretive dance," learning ballet-based movement from Sheldon B. Hoskins. Earlier tap lessons, however, had been a disaster: "I wanted to *dance*," Williams said, "and they were going toe, ball, heel" (Oral History Project, 2002). Drum lessons were likewise unsuccessful—telling lapses in a performer later famed for lyricism.

Having missed piano auditions at High School of Performing Arts, Williams successfully auditioned for its dance department—the first in what he saw as a series of happy accidents shaping his career—where he studied ballet and modern dance. Graduating in 1958, he went to Juilliard on scholarship for one year, studying ballet with Antony Tudor and Margaret Craske and modern dance with José Limon, Bertram Ross, and Yuriko, then attended classes the following year without formally enrolling. Living with his parents, who had moved to Bay Chester Avenue in the Bronx, Williams studied on scholarship with May O'Donnell, performing with her company, and also with the Hava Kohav Dance Company, the Corybantes (founded by his friend Eleo Pomare), and in musical Theater at Jones Beach and the New York World's Fair. He also studied on scholarship with Martha Graham, teaching after he had been at her school only a year, and performing in small roles until he was formally accepted into the company in 1961. Later he would become a soloist, featured in *Secular Games, Witch of Endor*, and *Diversion of Angels*, and debuting *Plain of Prayer* in 1968.

Dissatisfied with his prospects at Graham, which he considered to be a woman's company, Williams bought a freighter ticket for Europe in late 1963. But the day before he was due to depart, ALVIN AILEY called, in urgent need of a dancer who could step into Talley Beatty's *Road of the Phoebe Snow* and *Congo Tango Palace*. Williams accepted with the proviso that he be exempted from partnering, and in 1964, starred in those pieces as well as Ailey's self-choreographed solo, *Reflections in D*. Soon after, he also took over "I Want to Be Ready," a solo that James Truitte had choreographed based on a Lester Horton floor exercise called a coccyx balance, which Ailey had edited and included in *Revelations*; it would become a Williams signature, performed hundreds of times over the next decades. Although he danced and taught for both Graham and Ailey until 1968, Williams finally resigned from Graham "because Alvin was more human to me, more about what was going on in the world" (Interview with the author, 2010).

Barely five feet, eight inches tall, Williams weighed just over 120 pounds during most of his career, but, like the equally slight Graham, had a larger-than-life stage presence. Musically sophisticated, Williams breathed just before or after the beat, furthering the illusion of elongation given by his body's naturally balletic line. And, at a time when male dancers were often accessories or afterthoughts, his nonpartnering status made him sui generis: Not merely a cavalier or an athlete but a dancer with immense dignity and exemplary technique, sufficient unto himself. Williams would star in Ailey's *Gymnopedies* (1970), *Love Songs* (1972), *Night Creature* (1974), and *Three Black Kings* (1976), becoming known as Ailey's male muse.

By the 1980s, he was also famous for career longevity. In 1984, Williams not only originated major roles in Ailey's *For Bird with Love* and Donald McKayle's *Collage*, he also celebrated his twentieth anniversary with the company at an 11 December City Center gala, dancing *Reflections in D* and an excerpt from *Love Songs*, debuting Loris Anthony Beckles's *Anjour*, then leading the finale of *Revelations*. In 1986, Ailey created major roles for him in *Survivors* and *Opus McShann*; when Ailey died in 1989, the fifty-one-year-old Williams performed "I Want to Be Ready" at the memorial. In 1994, Williams celebrated his thirtieth anniversary with the company, then his fortieth in 2004. Finally, Williams gave his last performance with the Ailey company at the New Jersey Performing Arts Center in Newark on 8 May 2005, aged sixty-six.

But he did not stop dancing. Cofounding Paradigm as a performing outlet for older dancers with Gus Solomons Jr. and Carmen deLavallade in 1998, he danced with that company for a decade. Remaining on the Ailey School faculty, he also conducted master classes throughout the United States in a demonstration-dependent style that turned teaching into a kind of performance.

FURTHER READING

Tapes and transcripts of Oral History Project interviews conducted with Williams in 2002 by Robert Tracy are housed in the New York Public Library for the Performing Arts.

Dunning, Jennifer. *Alvin Ailey: A Life in Dance* (1996).

Horosko, Marian. *Martha Graham: The Evolution of Her Dance*, rev. ed. (2002).

Pogrebin, Robin. "Can't Stop Dancing to the Music of Life," *New York Times*, 22 Dec. 2003.

MARY LISA GAVENAS

Williams, Edward Christopher (11 Feb. 1871–24 Dec. 1929), librarian, educator, and writer, was born in Cleveland, Ohio, the only child of Daniel P. Williams, from a prominent African American family in Ohio, and Mary Kilkary, a white woman born in Tipperary, County Cork, Ireland. Williams attended public schools, graduated from the Cleveland Central High School, and enrolled at Adelbert College of Western

Reserve University (later Case Western Reserve University). Though fair enough to pass for white, Williams never hid his racial heritage, and despite the prevailing racism of the era he flourished in college. Acknowledged by his instructors and peers as an outstanding student and athlete, Williams was elected to Phi Beta Kappa in his junior year and participated in a number of team sports, varsity baseball among them. He received his bachelor's degree in 1892 and was class valedictorian.

After graduation Williams was appointed first assistant librarian of Adelbert College, and in 1894 he became head librarian of Western Reserve's Hatch Library, where he remained until 1909. Williams achieved distinction during his tenure at Western Reserve in a number of ways. Beginning in 1896 he oversaw the library's move from its cramped location to a new structure, and he worked aggressively for a larger staff, increased holdings, and improved physical equipment. In 1899 Williams went on leave in order to attend the New York State Library School in Albany, finishing the bulk of the two-year course in one year. Williams is widely considered the first professionally trained African American librarian. Upon his return to Ohio, Williams resumed working as a librarian and educator. In addition to his library duties he taught various courses on library science and tutored students in foreign languages.

In 1902 Williams married Ethel Chesnutt, daughter of CHARLES WADDELL CHESNUTT, the writer, and a graduate of Smith College. They had one son, Charles, who went on to become a lawyer in Washington, D.C. Williams became a charter member of the Ohio Library Association, acting as its secretary in 1904, and he chaired the association's constitution committee and college section. Williams also served as second vice president of the New York State Library Association in 1904.

A new chapter of Williams's life began in 1909, when he resigned from the library, moved his family to Washington, D.C., and became principal of M Street High School (later the Paul Laurence Dunbar High School), an institution renowned for academic excellence. In that same year he joined the Mu-So-Lit Club, a cultural men's group, and in 1916 he helped organize a drama committee for the local chapter of the NAACP.

Williams served as principal until 1916, at which time he resumed his role as a librarian by accepting a position at Howard University. Tireless as ever, Williams assumed multiple roles, becoming librarian, director of the library training class, professor of bibliography, and an instructor of foreign languages and literature. As head librarian Williams worked for years to improve every aspect of the library, which he felt lacked adequate space, equipment, books, and staff for an institution of Howard's stature. As an instructor and administrator he provided sound, firm leadership in the development and teaching of library science courses at the university. He also offered a wide variety of courses in French, German, and Italian language and literature, and his course on Dante was the first of its kind to be offered at a historically black college. Williams also served as director of both student organizations and the library committee, edited the Howard University *Record*, and during a number of his summer vacations he worked in Harlem at the 135th Street branch of the New York Public Library.

Already an accomplished educator and librarian, Williams began to blossom as a writer, becoming an integral figure of Washington's cultural life. He was instrumental in founding a locally influential literary society, helped nurture the talents of poets such as GEORGIA DOUGLAS JOHNSON and CARRIE CLIFFORD, and was in contact with a number of emergent literary figures, including JEAN TOOMER, ZORA NEALE HURSTON, MARY BURRILL, and ANGELINA GRIMKÉ. His book club, which often discussed African American literature, met on Wednesday nights at the Carnegie Library. An important mentor and organizer during an era of intense creativity, Williams also wrote three plays that were performed at Howard: *The Exile* (1924), a two-act drama set in fifteenth-century Florence during the power struggle between the Salviati and Medici families; *The Chasm* (1926), cowritten with WILLIS RICHARDSON; and *The Sheriff's Children* (n.d.), an adaptation of Chesnutt's short story of the same name. In addition Williams wrote at least two unpublished short stories, "The Colonel" and "The Incomparable Dolly," both of which feature socially conservative men who fall in love with younger modern women. Williams was, moreover, known by his contemporaries as the author of a number of unsigned essays and poems, and he perhaps published in A. PHILIP RANDOLPH and CHANDLER OWEN's little magazine, the *Messenger*, under the pseudonym "Bertuccio Dantino."

Williams's most important literary work, however, is his novel, *When Washington Was in Vogue*, which is most likely the first African American epistolary novel. Published serially and anonymously in the *Messenger* in 1925–1926 under the title *The Letters of Davy Carr: A True Story of Colored Vanity Fair*, the novel did not appear in book form and under Williams's name until 2004. *When Washington Was in Vogue* consists of a series of letters written by the fictional Captain Davy Carr, a World War I veteran on a visit to Washington to research the slave trade, to his friend and former comrade-in-arms, Bob Fletcher, who is living in Harlem. Davy describes the mores and foibles of Washington's black social elite and, as the novel progresses, he falls in love with his landlady's daughter, Caroline, a vivacious, younger flapper.

Awarded a Julius Rosenwald Fellowship, Williams left Howard in 1929 in order to pursue further education in library science at Columbia University. He traveled to New York but soon fell ill and returned to Washington, where he died at age fifty-eight.

FURTHER READING
Some archival material concerning Edward
    Christopher Williams can be found in the Founders
    Library, Howard University.
Josey, E. J. "Edward Christopher Williams: Librarian's
    Librarian," *Negro History Bulletin* 33 (Mar. 1970).
Porter, Dorothy. "Edward Christopher Williams," In
    Dictionary of American Biography, eds. Rayford W.
    Logan and Michael R. Winston (1994).

ADAM MCKIBLE

Williams, Ella V. Chase (1852 or 1854–?), educator and founder of African American schools in the post-Reconstruction South, was born in Washington, D.C., the eldest of six children of William H. Chase, a blacksmith from Maryland, and Lucinda (Seton) Chase, who was freeborn in Virginia. Her parents were prominent members of a Washington black community of business owners and professionals. The family belonged to the prestigious Fifteenth Street Presbyterian Church where black abolitionist FRANCIS GRIMKÉ was minister. When William Chase died as the result of an accident in 1844, Lucinda Seton Chase raised her six children to value education and encouraged her daughters to pursue careers in that field.

Williams first attended school in the basement of the Fifteenth Street Presbyterian Church, which was one of the earliest schools for African Americans in Washington. After her father died, she attended the Washington, D.C., public schools. At the age of sixteen, Williams entered the Howard Normal and Preparatory school, attending from 1870 through 1873. There is no record that Williams received a teaching certificate from Howard, but she must have, as she is known to have taught in the Washington, D.C., public schools from 1879 to 1882, and without a certificate it would have been nearly impossible for her to teach there.

On 1 December 1882 Ella Chase married Emory Williams, a Presbyterian minister. The large wedding was officiated by Grimké at the Fifteenth Street Presbyterian Church. Shortly after their marriage, the Williamses embarked on what was to be their life's work: building schools. Toward that end, the Presbyterian Board of Missions for Freedmen sent them in 1883 to South Carolina to build a school and a church, but the couple encountered significant prejudice and racism from white Presbyterians (In 1839 the Presbyterian Church had split over slavery along regional lines into a Southern branch and a Northern branch; the church did not reunite until 1983).

Because of the hostility from southern white Presbyterians, in 1893 the Williamses launched a movement to organize African American churches into a separate synod. Four years later, in 1897, Reverend Williams petitioned the Presbyterian General Assembly to pass a resolution allowing African Americans to form their own church. The resolution passed and the Colored Presbyterian Church was formed in 1898.

In 1885 the Williamses founded Ferguson College in Abbeville, South Carolina, which promoted the "industrial, literary, musical, and religious advancement" of African Americans (Parker, 167). It was named after the Reverend James A. Ferguson of New Jersey, one of the earliest contributors to the founding of the school.

Reverend Williams was president of the college, and Ella Williams was its principal. Together they taught all elementary grades (the basics were taught out of necessity, but the school curriculum went well beyond elementary education) to the more than fifty students in daily attendance. The Presbyterian Board of Missions for Freedmen gave a small amount of money to the school. The plans the Williamses had for expanding the school, however, met with objections from the white southern church. Undeterred, Williams helped her husband raise money from northern Presbyterians for the expansion, and in 1889 they started to build a four-story brick building that would house classrooms and teachers and serve as a boarding hall for students. Their success was greatly resented by whites in the area, however, and before the building was completed, it was completely destroyed by a fire in 1890. In 1891 ownership of Ferguson College was transferred to the Board of Missions for Freedmen, which had made a small contribution toward its rebuilding.

Williams continued her work as principal of the college, and her husband remained president, though the Presbyterian Board of Missions for Freedmen owned the school. In 1893 Emory Williams published an editorial in Ferguson College's weekly newspaper about the control of the school by the Board of Missions for Freedmen, an editorial that offended board members. When he refused to retract his comments, he and Williams were removed from their positions. The church appointed Baltimore minister Thomas Amos the new president of Ferguson College.

Also in 1893 the Colored Presbyterian Church synod that Emory and Ella Williams had worked hard to establish, in a close vote, removed Reverend Williams from the African American conference for reasons that are now unknown. Undaunted and resilient, in 1894 the Williamses started another college in Abbeville, the Ferguson and Williams College. At the same time Emory Williams was accepted as pastor of a Presbyterian church, whose name is unknown. By 1897 Ella Williams was running Ferguson and Williams College while her husband traveled throughout the South to gain support for the separate Colored Presbyterian Church. In November 1904 the African American Synod of the Presbyterian Church held a conference at Ferguson and Williams College. The synod did not last, however, and Emory Williams died in 1910.

Throughout Williams's work for African American education in the South after Reconstruction, she led various church boards and contributed articles for the *Atlantic Beacon*, the Ferguson College weekly, and her brother William Chase's newspaper in Washington, D.C., the *Washington Bee*.

The date of Ella V. Chase Williams's death is unknown. In 1919 Ferguson and Williams College closed and the buildings became the Abbeville Memorial Hospital.

FURTHER READING

Copies of catalogs of Howard University Normal and Preparatory Schools in the late 1800s can be found in the Moorland-Spingarn Research Center in the Howard University Libraries. Information about Ella V. Chase's attendance at Howard University is available at Howard University, Office of Records, Washington, D.C.

Murray, Andrew E. *Presbyterians and the Negro—A History* (1966).

Parker, Inez Moore. *The Rise and Decline of the Program of Education for Black Presbyterians of the United Presbyterian Church U.S.A. 1865–1970* (1977).

Wilmore, Gayraud S. *Black Religion and Black Radicalism: An Examination of the Black Experience in Religion* (1972).

LINDA SPENCER

Williams, Emily Augustine Harper (1 Dec. 1873–2 Sept. 1933), educator, was born in Detroit, Michigan, to a prosperous family that was part of Detroit's growing affluent black intelligentsia. Her parents' names and occupations are not known, but she was the elder of two sisters who enrolled in the College of Literature, Arts and Sciences at the University of Michigan in Ann Arbor, approximately forty miles west of Detroit. Harper entered the university in October 1892. During her first two years in Ann Arbor, she roomed in the home of a white socialite and faculty wife, Mrs. Gayley-Browne, to whom Harper later attributed her devotion to teaching and public service activities that specifically benefited African Americans in the South. Harper studied literature and philosophy and—although she was the only African American woman in her class—experienced social acceptance and inclusion in campus social events. Writing in 1924 about her undergraduate days in Ann Arbor, Harper even recalled the cold winters and strict university rooming codes with fondness:

I think most often of the hour between supper and study when we used to go coasting down Corkscrew Hill and I cherish today a chip from the fence that I gathered in my glove the night our sled overturned right at the bottom of the hill. Then there was the oyster roast Hallow E'en night away across the [Huron] river on the Heights. We were a jolly party of girls and all went well until the supper was over and we started home. It seemed so late that we were afraid to go home. Our various landladies gave us no trouble, however. They didn't even wait up for us… most of our pranks were innocent, I am sure. Youth is our period of superlatives and I find my letters home of those days full of "the very best time" as a characterization of each event (Response to University of Michigan Alumnae Council questionnaire).

As an undergraduate student at the University of Michigan, Harper's sense of politicized race consciousness was just emerging.

Harper graduated from the University of Michigan in 1896. That autumn she obtained a position as a teacher of English, French, and Latin at the academically prestigious M Street High School for black students in Washington, D.C. The school attracted a superlative teaching faculty led by the principal Robert H. Terrell, a Harvard graduate, and including his wife, MARY CHURCH TERRELL. Many of M Street's students came from beyond the District of Columbia, including from New England and the South, to study there. Harper's salary in 1896 was $650 per year, but by the time she left the school in 1901 it had risen to $800. The M Street faculty was largely devoted to inculcating in black students the belief that they must excel academically in the classical fields of philosophy, Latin, Greek, French, mathematics, and literature in order to compete professionally with white elites on their own terms. Harper was uncertain about this educational strategy and about the confrontational race politics behind it.

When in 1901 an opportunity arose for her to move to the Armstrong Manual Training School, a rival of the M Street School, Harper accepted a teaching position there. The Armstrong School curriculum emphasized gender-specific vocational training: metalworking, athletics, and military drills for the boys, who were called "cadets," and music and manual arts courses, including sewing, dressmaking, and "domestic science," for the girls. Harper taught some of the courses open to both sexes, including English literature and history. She quickly also became "lady" principal at the school, responsible for overseeing girls' vocational studies and discipline among the female students. During the academic years of 1901 through 1904 Harper taught at the Armstrong School, but during the summer sessions she made extra money teaching English at the renowned Hampton Institute, a postsecondary college for blacks in Hampton, Virginia. Its summer sessions offered teacher training courses for aspiring black elementary and secondary teachers. There she met the 1897 Harvard graduate and Hampton Institute faculty member William Taylor Burwell Williams, whom she married at St. Matthew's Church in Detroit on 29 June 1904.

As a newly married woman now living on the grounds of the Hampton Institute, Emily Williams resigned from the faculty of the Armstrong School and briefly stopped teaching altogether. However, in the autumn of 1906 she became a member of the Hampton Institute's Night School faculty, and she continued in that capacity until the end of the 1910 academic year. For two years, 1910–1912, she returned

to the institute's regular staff as an English teacher, and she served as the institute's assistant librarian from 1912 to 1919. Her social activities during this period supported her husband's increasing administrative responsibilities at Hampton Institute and his broad activities in progressive black politics. W. T. B. Williams was a close associate of BOOKER T. WASHINGTON, founder of Tuskegee Institute, and in 1911 he became president of the National Negro Educational Association, making him one of the country's most prominent black educators. Emily Williams maintained her own interests, organizing the Treble Clef Club of Hampton, a musical society for affluent and educated black women, and serving as its president from 1907 to 1917. It was Williams's first foray into the growing club movement for middle-class black women. In 1912 the national convention of the National Association of Colored Women (NACW) was held in Hampton, and Williams was instrumental in coordinating local arrangements for the meeting. With MARGARET MURRAY WASHINGTON, "lady" principal of the Tuskegee Institute and wife of Booker T. Washington, installed as president, several new NACW officers and department heads were named, including Mary Fitzbutler Waring as chair of the health and hygiene department and Williams as chair of the music department, a post she held until 1920.

In 1919 Williams and her husband moved to Tuskegee, Alabama, where W. T. B. Williams succeeded Washington as dean of Tuskegee Institute. Emily Williams was an English instructor at Tuskegee Institute from 1919 until her death in 1933. She wrote several articles and reviews in the *Southern Workman*, wrote the pamphlet *American Authors' Birthdays*, and served as president of a women's literary society at Tuskegee Institute from 1920 to 1924. Her club work also continued on a national scale. In 1920 she was the secretary and in 1922 the recording secretary of the NACW. In 1920 some NACW leaders, including Mary Church Terrell, MAGGIE LENA WALKER, and MARY MCLEOD BETHUNE, founded a new organization that focused on international linkages between black women in the United States and those in the Caribbean, Africa, and Europe. Williams took an active role in the new group, which was called the International Council of Women of the Darker Races. It endorsed the cross-cultural cooperative ideals that had informed W. E. B. DuBois's Pan-African Congress, convened in Paris in 1919. Williams was a central activist in the new organization, chairing its department of education from 1922 to 1924. In 1922 she was dispatched to Haiti as the head of a small delegation to investigate the status of black women and children in that country. Her report was delivered at the council's August 1923 national conference, which was held at the National Training School for Women and Girls in Washington, D.C. Williams died in Tuskegee, Alabama.

FURTHER READING
An alumni questionnaire completed by Williams in 1911, the University of Michigan Alumnae Council questionnaire she completed in 1924, and a 1926 letter written by her are in the University of Michigan's Bentley Historical Library in the Alumni Association Necrology File. Her employment with the black schools in Washington, D.C., is documented in the Minutes of the Board of Trustees of Public Schools in and for the District of Columbia in the Charles Sumner School Museum and Archives, Washington, D.C.

Neverdon-Morton, Cynthia. *Afro-American Women of the South and the Advancement of the Race, 1895–1925* (1989)

LAURA M. CALKINS

Williams, Eugene (1902–27 July 1919), was the first victim of the Chicago Race Riot of 1919. Little is known of his parents or his early life, but his death spurred an important legal precedent when the city paid compensation to his mother, Luella Williams, for her loss.

In a 1968 interview, Eugene's friend John Turner Harris recalled the tragic events of almost fifty years earlier that led to the death of Eugene Williams and rocked the city of Chicago. As Harris recounted, it was approaching 90 degrees on Sunday, 27 July 1919, when the fourteen-year-old Harris and four other teenage African American boys, including seventeen-year-old Eugene Williams, decided to skip church and go swimming in Lake Michigan. The boys were not headed for the black-patronized Twenty-fifth Street beach, nor did they intend to swim at the white beach at Twenty-ninth Street. Instead they were going to their own private spot located in between. Tied up at this spot was a raft built by the boys during the hot summer days of that year. The boys were not expert swimmers, but they could hang onto the raft and propel it forward by kicking. Meanwhile, at Twenty-ninth Street, angry white swimmers were hurling both curses and rocks to frighten away a group of African Americans who earlier had tried to enter the water there. Minutes later, however, the blacks returned, this time armed with rocks. Soon, an interracial battle erupted.

Innocently unaware of this rioting, the five boys continued to "swim, kick, dive, and play around" (Tuttle, 6). But passing by the breakwater near Twenty-sixth Street, they noticed a white man standing on the end of the breakwater and throwing rocks at them. Eugene Williams had just bobbed out of the water, Harris recalled, when the white man threw a rock that struck Williams on the forehead. Harris could tell that Williams was injured because he slid back into the water, "and you could see the blood coming up" (Tuttle, 6–7). Harris shouted for a lifeguard, but it was too late; Williams drowned. Next, the boys paddled to shore and alerted the black police officer at Twenty-fifth Street as to what had happened. Together they marched to Twenty-ninth Street and pointed out the man they believed to be the rock thrower to the white police officer on duty, Daniel Callahan. But Callahan refused to permit the black police officer to arrest the white man. By then hundreds of blacks and whites had swarmed to the beach; volleys of rocks were exchanged, gunshots erupted, and a black man fell dead. Rumors of atrocities on both sides quickly swept through Chicago, which had been on the verge of a racial conflagration for several weeks.

Eugene Williams's death was the spark that ignited five days of interracial violence in the city. In one of the bloodiest race riots in American history, thirty-eight people were killed (twenty-three blacks and fifteen whites), and more than five hundred people were injured. But Williams's story did not end there.

After the riot, Eugene Williams's mother, Luella Williams, filed a lawsuit against the City of Chicago, charging the city with failure to fulfill its duty to "control" its public streets and beaches "in a safe and proper manner so that pedestrians going along and up same would not be … killed" (Bukowski, 3). Mrs. Williams's suit was filed under a 1905 statute passed by the Illinois General Assembly in the wake of a series of bloody labor conflicts; the law held that cities or counties were liable for wrongful deaths due to rioting. Chicago's corporation counsel moved to have the suit dismissed, but his motion was denied. The suit resulted in a finding for the plaintiff, with the jury awarding her "damages at the sum of $4,500" (Bukowski, 3). On 11 January 1923 both sides agreed to set aside the judgment, because nine days earlier the Chicago city council had voted to award Mrs. Williams the same amount of money. The council also moved that day to make the same offer in seventeen other suits. In July 1923 the council agreed to offer compensation in four additional suits.

The City of Chicago did not label its payments as "reparations," but they functioned in that way. In the latter half of the twentieth century the notion of reparations became hotly debated. This was true whether the historical issue was American slavery, the Japanese American internment camps during World War II, or race riots, such as those in Rosewood, Florida, in 1923 (where reparations were eventually paid in 1994) or Tulsa, Oklahoma, in 1921 (where they were not). In the early twenty-first century critics continued to argue that there was insufficient precedent for the payment of reparations, but the story of the life and tragic death of Eugene Williams is proof that such a precedent does exist. Indeed, according to University of Alabama law professor Alfred L. Brophy, the Chicago compensation cases constitute one of the "absolutely essential pieces of the reparations case" (Bukowski, 8).

FURTHER READING

Brophy, Alfred L. *Reconstructing the Dreamland: The Tulsa Riot of 1921: Race, Reparations, and Reconciliation* (2002).

Brophy, Alfred L. *Reparations Pro & Con* (2006).

Bukowski, Doug. "Paying Up and Moving On" (unpublished essay, 2000).

Chicago Commission on Race Relations. *The Negro in Chicago* (1922).

Spear, Allan H. *Black Chicago: The Making of a Negro Ghetto, 1890–1920* (1967).

Tuttle, William M., Jr. *Race Riot: Chicago in the Red Summer of 1919*, 2d ed. (1996).

WILLIAM M. TUTTLE JR.

Williams, Fannie Barrier (12 Feb. 1855–4 Mar. 1944), lecturer and clubwoman, was born in Brockport, New York, the daughter of Anthony J. Barrier and Harriet Prince, free persons of color. She graduated from the State Normal School at Brockport in 1870 and attended the New England Conservatory of Music in Boston and the School of Fine Arts in Washington, D.C. She then taught in southern schools and in Washington, D.C., for a short time. In 1887 Barrier retired from teaching to marry S. Laing Williams, a prominent attorney in Chicago.

Williams became known for her club work and lecturing. Though many of her early lectures and written works supported the militant, egalitarian protest ideology of FREDERICK DOUGLASS, she later became a staunch supporter of BOOKER T. WASHINGTON's accommodationist views, including his emphasis on industrial education and practical training. She encouraged employers to hire qualified black women for clerical positions and sought other job opportunities for blacks. She did not, however, reject the value of education beyond that of industrial training.

Williams's prominence arose from her efforts to have blacks officially represented on the Board of Control of the Columbian Exposition in 1893. She was able to persuade the board to include black affairs in the exhibits planned for the celebration. At the exposition, Williams delivered an address, "The Intellectual Progress of Colored Women in the U.S. since the Emancipation Proclamation," to an enthusiastic, integrated audience of the World's Congress of Representative Women. In this address, Williams dismissed the charges of sexual immorality so commonly aimed at black women with the claim that continued harassment by white men was the source of the problem. She stated that after Emancipation black women were quick and eager to "taste the blessedness of intelligent womanhood," and she urged white women who were concerned about morality to find ways to help black women.

In 1895 Williams was a state representative at the National Colored Women's Congress, which was convened by the Negro Department of the Cotton States and International Exposition in Atlanta, Georgia. In the same year, following an initial rejection, she became the first black woman admitted to the Woman's Club of Chicago. She was also the first black woman to be appointed to the Chicago Library Board, on which she served from 1924 to 1926. Active in many community and civic organizations, she was a director of the Frederick Douglass Center, Chicago's first interracial organization, and a member of the Abraham Lincoln Center. She also worked with the PHILLIS WHEATLEY Home Association. She was a founding member of the National League of Colored Women in 1893 and served as president of the Woman's Council, which hosted the 1899 meeting of its successor, the National Association of Colored Women. She wrote a column about women's activities for T. THOMAS FORTUNE's *New York Age* and the *Chicago Record-Herald*.

Williams's political activism, which began with the 1893 Columbian Exposition in Chicago, continued with the black women's club movement. She often spoke about the need for black women to emancipate their minds and spirits. In the speech "Club Movement among Colored Women of America," she stated that "the struggle of an enlightened conscience against the whole brood of

Fannie Barrier Williams worked tirelessly in the social reform and women's club movements. (Austin/Thompson Collection.)

miseries [is] born out of the stress and pain of a hated past." Williams advocated feminist thinking through her efforts in the club movement. She noted that black women had reached an age in which they were moving beyond the patriarchal notion of women doing what men felt they ought to do. "In our day and in this country, a woman's sphere is just as large as she can make it." Williams's activism focused on the social condition of the entire race, which distinguished the black women's club movement from that of white women. She strongly supported education of black women in order to move them out of domestic work, where sexual harassment was so prevalent. She also advocated voting rights and equal employment opportunities.

Williams sought to combat and defy Jim Crow laws in whatever manner she could. She once used her light complexion and knowledge of French to ride in the white-only section of a southern train. She wrote in "A Northern Negro's Autobiography" (1904) that "[I] quieted my conscience by recalling that there was a strain of French blood in my ancestry, and too that their barbarous laws did not allow a lady to be both comfortable and honest."

Williams worked closely with Dr. DANIEL HALE WILLIAMS in establishing the Provident Hospital in 1891. It housed the first training school for black nurses in Chicago, which she helped organize, and which was distinctive for its biracial staff of doctors. After her husband's death in 1921, Williams withdrew from many of her activities. She died in Brockport.

FURTHER READING

Williams, Fannie Barrier. "A Northern Negro's Autobiography." *Independent*, 14 July 1904.

Williams, Fannie Barrier, and Mary Jo Deegan. *The New Woman of Color: The Collected Writings of Fannie Barrier Williams, 1893–1918* (2002).

Lerner, Gerda. *The Black Woman in White America: A Documentary History* (1972).

Meier, August. *Negro Thought in America, 1880–1915: Racial Ideologies in the Age of Booker T. Washington* (1963).

This entry is taken from the *American National Biography* and is published here with the permission of the American Council of Learned Societies.

MAMIE E. LOCKE

Williams, Frances E. (17 Sept. 1905–2 Jan. 1995) actress, activist, and organizer, was born Frances Elizabeth Jones in East Orange, New Jersey, the youngest of three children of William Henry Jones, who drove a delivery wagon for a grocery store, and Elizabeth (Nelson) Jones, a laundress. In 1907 the Jones family moved from New Jersey to Pittsburgh, Pennsylvania. Shortly after arriving there, her father died. A year later Elizabeth Jones remarried Ben Williams, and the family moved to Cleveland, Ohio, where Williams worked as footman for a department store.

When she was only five years old, Williams got her first job babysitting. In junior high, she worked weekends with her mother catering. While in high school, she was employed at Sherbundy's, an exclusive restaurant on Euclid Avenue, making enough money to help out the family. At Saint Andrews, the family church, Williams was a member of the choir, Sunday school superintendent, president of the altar guild, and a member of the Elks. Her introduction to the theater began at the Saint Andrews theater workshop.

Knowing Williams's athletic abilities as well as her organizing skills, Thomas Fleming, one of the first black city councilmen in the country, recommended her for the position of activities director at the Central Avenue Bath House in the "Roaring

Third," a poor section in Cleveland. The neighborhood's population was a mixture of Italian and German immigrants, and newly arrived African American migrants from the South. At the Bath House, Williams organized a swimming program and trained the drill teams who performed in the Sunday parades.

Down the street from the Central Avenue Bath House was the Playhouse Settlement, founded in 1915 by Russell and Rowena Jelliffe. It was the only settlement house in the city that welcomed African Americans. Williams and her friend E. Warren, Thomas Fleming's niece, organized games and craft projects at the settlement playground. When the Jelliffes asked her to work for them at the Playhouse Settlement, she eagerly accepted. Her job was to interview incoming students, assign them to an activity group, and oversee two clubs. Eventually she became the settlement's first resident worker and lived there for fourteen years until she left to study theater in the Soviet Union. Williams's experiences at the settlement house resonated with her throughout her life. It stimulated her budding curiosity and satisfied her abundant energy. At the settlement house, not only was she a social worker, but in their theater she became a writer, director, and organizer.

Though she began with the children's theater, writing and directing some of the plays, she also performed in the settlement's adult theater with performers such as Hazel Mountain Walker and John Marriott. The sixty-seat theater was always packed. Sustaining tickets sold out the house for a year during which they presented plays such as *Scarlet Sister Mary*, *Cinderella*, and *Stevedore* (*The Plain Dealer* magazine, Sept. 1990, 18–26). In 1921 CHARLES GILPIN, who played Emperor Jones and was one of the first African American actors on Broadway, came to see their performance of *Scarlet Sister Mary*. After the show he went backstage, encouraged the actors to make their "little theater" into a "real Negro theater," and gave them fifty dollars toward their cause. To honor him they renamed their group the Gilpin Players. In 1925 they performed Ridgeley Torrence's *Granny Maumee*, their first play about black life. Among those who visited the theater were W. E. B. DuBois, ALAIN LOCKE, and ETHEL WATERS.

With the Jelliffes' consent the volunteers formed an African Art Club and raised $1,500 for Paul Bow Travis to purchase African artifacts from Africa. The collection has since been given to the Cleveland Museum of Art and the Cleveland Historical Society. In 1927, after the theater was remodeled and decorated with African masks and hangings, the name was changed to Karamu House, from a Swahili word meaning "central meeting place."

At Karamu, Williams developed lifelong friendships with artist Zell Ingram and writer LANGSTON HUGHES. Ingram worked in the arts and crafts department in the late afternoons after he finished his own classes at the Cleveland School of Arts. Hughes, who wrote for the Central High School publication, needed a place to express himself creatively. Karamu House gave him that outlet. He wrote poetry and children's plays, many of which were performed in the theater. The three friends were like sister and brothers going on hikes and having picnics and cookouts together. When Hughes decided to go to Cuba and Haiti, he asked Williams and Ingram to accompany him; however, Williams's family succeeded in dissuading her from going.

Despite all she had learned at Karamu House, Williams was dissatisfied, feeling that the Jelliffes shared little with her. "What I learned about theater was almost accidental," she said in her biography. During her fourteen years at Playhouse Settlement and Karamu House, Williams had been in eighty-five productions, written and directed some of the plays, made costumes, and designed sets—in short, she was responsible for whole productions, yet she felt she needed to learn more about the technique of theater.

Hughes, who had left Karamu and become involved in the Harlem Renaissance, urged Williams to come to New York to attend the Writer's Congress, where she would meet writers, directors, and artists from the Soviet Union. There she met Friedrich Wolf, author of *Sailors of Cattarro*, which was being produced by the Theatre Union in New York. Wolf had lived in the Soviet Union for years. By the time she left his hotel, she had made up her mind to study theater there. In the spring of 1934, Williams set out for the USSR. Williams studied at the Meyerhold theatre and at the Natalie Satz Children's Theatre. After two years there and in Helsinki, Finland, Williams returned home in 1936.

Instead of returning to Cleveland, she went to New York and auditioned for a part in *You Can't Take it With You*, a comedy written by George S. Kaufman and Moss Hart. Shortly after Williams joined the cast, the play went on a lengthy road tour. While in Chicago, Williams met her soon-to-be second husband, William Anthony Hill, a social worker. (In 1932 she had married George

Ferguson, a businessman, but they divorced after one year.)

When the tour ended, Williams went back to New York where she and Hill were married. While in New York, Williams became an active member of Actors' Equity Association, the labor union representing American actors and stage managers, and the newly formed Negro Actors Guild.

At this time, Williams made two films for African American director OSCAR MICHEAUX, *Lying Lips* (1939) and *The Notorious Elinor Lee* (1940), for which she is uncredited.

In 1941 Williams and Hill moved to Los Angeles. Ethel Waters, who was preparing to go on tour with *Mamba's Daughters*, hired Williams as her assistant and understudy. Upon their return, Williams joined the Actors' Lab. The only African American on the staff, Williams took a full schedule of classes, worked in every area of production from stage management to lights and wardrobe, and was a member of the executive board. Williams was embarrassed by the roles available for African American performers, and she initially refused to accept a part that called for her to speak in heavy dialect; but in order to get work she had to relent. She made her Hollywood debut in 1946 with *Magnificent Doll*. After this she appeared in a number of films, including *Her Sister's Secret* (1946), *The Reckless Moment* (1949), and *Show Boat* (1951). In the latter films, Williams refused to wear the bandanna the wardrobe woman presented her. In fact, she was presented with seventeen kerchiefs, all of which she refused. By the late 1950s Williams had gained a reputation as a fighter. Many times she was called upon to intervene on behalf of the actors, dancers, and other workers who were being treated unfairly by the studios.

As a teenager Williams worked with the Democratic Party and the Future Outlook League in Cleveland. While in the Soviet Union in 1934, her knowledge of political machinations grew. However, her awareness broadened considerably in the late 1940s when she became involved with progressive groups such as those at the Actors' Lab and Actors' Equity. In 1948, at the urging of her friends, Williams ran for the California State Assembly on the Progressive Party ticket. After nine years of marriage, Williams and Hill, who had become a noted ceramist, divorced. Despite their separation, however, Hill supported her campaign. Though Williams didn't win the election, she made a strong showing.

In 1951, as a trade unionist and a member of the board of the National Negro Labor Council (NNLC), Williams attended the first NNLC convention. Attacked by the House Committee on Un-American Activities (HUAC) and labeled "subversive," "Communist dominated," and "a tool of the Soviet Union," the NNLC was soon disbanded. However, before its demise, the NNLC was able to win jobs for blacks in several industries including the department-store chain Sears Roebuck (Foner, 301).

During the 1950s Williams was hired as assistant director for *The Salt of the Earth*, a film about the striking members of Mine Mill Local 890 against the Delaware Zinc Company in Silver City, New Mexico. A groundbreaking film, *Salt of the Earth* portrayed the struggles of the mineworkers fighting for equality in all areas. Of particular significance, it highlighted equality for women. The film shoot was not without conflict. According to Lorenzo Torrez, one of the mineworkers who appeared in the film, had Williams not been there, the role of the miners would have been minute. Finally the film helped garner public support for the trade union movement throughout the South and Southwest.

In 1961 Williams replaced CLAUDIA MCNEIL in the Broadway run of *A Raisin in the Sun*. In the 1960s Williams and her brother Bill, who had retired from the post office in Cincinnati, Ohio, traveled throughout Mexico and finally settled in Mazatlán where they stayed for nine years until his death. Upon her return to the United States, Williams began teaching drama at Dorsey High School in Los Angeles, which led to her involvement in the formation of nine theaters in the area, including the Inner City Cultural Center, the Native American Theater, and the East-West Players.

In the mid 1970s, though still active in film, Williams became even more involved in local and national, as well as international, issues. In 1975 she attended the Women's Conference in East Berlin, Germany. In 1976 she co-chaired the United Front for Justice in South Africa. In 1978 she helped form the local chapter of the National Anti-Imperialist Movement in Solidarity with African Liberation (NAIMSAL). The Los Angeles Chapter of NAIMSAL became one of the first groups to picket the South African Embassy. Also in 1978 Williams traveled to Chicago to help form Women for Racial and Economic Equality (WREE). In addition, as a representative of the World Peace Council, and though suffering from severe arthritis, Williams traveled to Moscow, Greece, Cuba, Suriname, and Lisbon, Portugal, as well as to Angola for that nation's first independence day celebration. In 1979 she represented the Coalition for Black Trade

Unions on the Police Crimes Tribunal Grand Jury. In 1986 she helped organize Art Against Apartheid, a group of committed artists who performed in schools around Los Angeles to inform students about apartheid in South Africa.

In 1987 after appearing in over forty films and a host of television shows and commercials, Williams auditioned for and won a role in *Frank's Place*, which ran for only one year. After *Frank's Place*, Williams continued to appear in films and commercials, to present adult and children's plays, poetry readings, and jazz at her Frances Williams Corner Theater, and to raise funds for various projects such as the Paul Robeson Cultural Center and the Aquarius Bookstore that had been burned down following the Rodney King verdict.

Two weeks after celebrating her eighty-ninth birthday, Williams suffered a stroke, and after a short stay in Centinela Hospital she was placed in a convalescent hospital, where her health steadily declined. She died in 1995.

FURTHER READING

Frances E. Williams's papers are housed at the Southern California Library for Social Studies and Research, Los Angeles, Calfornia.

Christian, Anna. *Meet It, Greet It, and Defeat It, the Biography of Frances E. Williams, Actress/Activist* (1999).

Foner, Philip Sheldon. *Organized Labor and the Black Worker, 1619–1980* (1974).

UCLA Oral History Program, Dept. of Special Collections, Interview with Frances E. Williams.

ANNA CHRISTIAN

Williams, George Washington (16 Oct. 1849– 2 Aug. 1891), soldier, clergyman, legislator, and historian, was born in Bedford Springs, Pennsylvania, the son of Thomas Williams, a free black laborer, and Ellen Rouse. His father became a boatman and, eventually, a minister and barber, and the younger Williams drifted with his family from town to town in western Pennsylvania until the beginning of the Civil War. With no formal education, he lied about his age, adopted the name of an uncle, and enlisted in the United States Colored Troops in 1864. He served in operations against Petersburg and Richmond, sustaining multiple wounds during several battles. After the war's end Williams was stationed in Texas, but crossed the border to fight with the Mexican republican forces that overthrew the emperor Maximilian. He returned to the U.S. Army in 1867, serving with the Tenth Cavalry, an all-black unit, at Fort Arbuckle, Indian Territory. Williams was discharged for disability the following year after being shot through the left lung under circumstances that were never fully explained.

For a few months in 1869 Williams was enrolled at Howard University in Washington, D.C. But with an urgent desire to become a Baptist minister, he sought admission to the Newton Theological Institution in Massachusetts. Semiliterate and placed in the English "remedial" course at the outset, Williams underwent a remarkable transformation. He became a prize student as well as a polished writer and public speaker and completed the three-year theological curriculum in two years. In 1874, following graduation and marriage to Sarah Sterret of Chicago, Williams was installed as pastor of one of the leading African American churches of Boston, the Twelfth Baptist. A year later he went with his wife and young son (their only child) to Washington, D.C. There he edited the *Commoner*, a weekly newspaper supported by FREDERICK DOUGLASS and other leading citizens and intended to be, in Williams's words, "to the colored people of the country a guide, teacher, defender, and mirror." It folded after about six months of publication.

The West beckoned, and Williams moved in 1876 to Cincinnati, where he served as pastor of the Union Baptist Church through the end of the next year. Also engaged as a columnist for a leading daily newspaper, the Cincinnati *Commercial*, he contributed sometimes autobiographical pieces on cultural, racial, religious, and military themes. He spent what spare time he had studying law in the office of Judge Alphonso Taft, father of William Howard Taft. Even before passing the bar in 1881, Williams had become deeply immersed in Republican politics—as a captivating orator, holder of patronage positions, and, in 1877, an unsuccessful legislative candidate. In 1879 the voters of Cincinnati elected him to the Ohio House of Representatives, making Williams the first African American to sit in the state legislature. He served one term, during which he was the center of several controversies, ranging from the refusal of a Columbus restaurant catering to legislators to serve him to a furor in the African American community over his support for the proposed closing of a black cemetery as a health hazard. Williams's effort to repeal a law against interracial marriage failed; he also supported a bill restricting liquor sales.

By this time Williams had developed an interest in history. In 1876 he delivered an Independence Day Centennial oration titled "The American Negro from 1776 to 1876." While in the legislature, Williams made regular use of the Ohio State Library to collect historical information. After completing his stint as a lawmaker in 1881, he devoted his full attention to writing *History of the Negro Race in America from 1619 to 1880: Negroes as Slaves, as Soldiers, and as Citizens*. Based on extensive archival research, interviews, and Williams's pioneering use of newspapers, and published in two volumes by G. P. Putnam's Sons in 1882–1883, the work was the earliest extended, scholarly history of African Americans. Comprehensive in scope, it touched on biblical ethnology and African civilization and government but gave particular attention to blacks who served in America's wars. Widely noticed in the press, Williams's *History of the Negro Race in America* was, for the most part, well received as the first serious work of historical scholarship by an African American. Williams followed it in 1887 with another major historical work, *A History of the Negro Troops in the War of the Rebellion, 1861–1865*. Drawing on his own experiences (but also on the wartime records then being published for the first time), Williams wrote bitterly of the treatment of black soldiers by white northerners as well as by Confederates. Despite disadvantages, their conduct, in his opinion, was heroic, and he concluded that no troops "could be more determined or daring." Though not as widely heralded as his earlier volumes, *A History of the Negro Troops in the War of the Rebellion* was generally well reviewed by the white and black press. Williams also planned a two-volume history of Reconstruction in the former Confederacy, but he never went beyond incorporating some of the materials he had collected for the project into his lectures in the United States and Europe. In his writings and lectures, Williams expressed an optimism based on faith in a divine power that preordained events and enlisted adherents to assist in evangelizing the rest of the world's peoples.

Williams had begun to lecture extensively early in the 1880s, and by the end of 1883 had returned to Boston, where he practiced law. He later resided in Worcester and continued his research at the American Antiquarian Society. In March 1885, lame-duck president Chester Arthur appointed Williams minister to Haiti. He was confirmed by the U.S. Senate and sworn in during the final hours of the outgoing Republican administration, but before Williams could assume the post, Democrat Grover Cleveland appointed someone else to it.

Ever restless and aggressively ambitious, Williams turned his sights toward Africa, already an occasional subject of his writing and public speaking. He attended an antislavery conference in Brussels in 1889 as a reporter for S. S. McClure's syndicate and there met Leopold II, king of the Belgians. In the following year, without the blessing of the king but with the patronage of Collis P. Huntington, an American railroad magnate who had invested in several African projects, he visited the Congo. After an extensive tour of the country, which took him from Boma on the Atlantic coast to the headwaters of the Congo River at Stanley Falls, he had a clear impression of what the country was like and why. Having witnessed the brutal conduct and inhumane policies of the Belgians, Williams decided to speak out. He published for circulation throughout Europe and the United States *An Open Letter to His Serene Majesty, Leopold II, King of the Belgians*, thus becoming a pioneering opponent of Leopold's policies and anticipating later criticisms of Europe's colonial ventures in Africa. Among the barrage of charges against the king was that his title to the Congo was, at best, "badly clouded" because his treaties with the local chiefs were "tainted by frauds of the grossest character." He held the king responsible for "deceit, fraud, robberies, arson, murder, slave-raiding, and general policy of cruelty" in the Congo. "All the crimes perpetrated in the Congo have been done in *your* name," he concluded, "and *you* must answer at the bar of Public Sentiment for the misgovernment of a people, whose lives and fortunes were entrusted to you by the august Conference of Berlin, 1884–1885." While the attack inspired denunciations of Williams in Belgium, it was little noted in the United States, though Williams had already written a report on the Congo for President Benjamin Harrison at the latter's request. A closer scrutiny of conditions in the Congo would come only after such "credible" persons as Roger Casement of the British foreign office and Mark Twain made charges against Leopold that echoed those of Williams and WILLIAM H. SHEPPARD.

Following his exploration of the Congo and southern Africa, Williams fell ill in Cairo, Egypt, after giving a lecture before the local geographical society (he had not been in robust health since being wounded in the army). Separated but not divorced from his wife, he subsequently went to London with his English "fiancée," Alice Fryer, intending to write a lengthy work on colonialism in Africa. There, tuberculosis and pleurisy overtook him, and he died in Blackpool. In the United States, his death was noted in the national media as well as in the black press.

To the end, George Washington Williams remained a difficult person to understand fully. To many on both sides of the racial divide he possessed a curious combination of rare genius, remarkable resourcefulness, and an incomparable talent for self-aggrandizement. Although Williams was justifiably chided during his lifetime for making inflated claims about his background, W. E. B. DuBois did not hesitate to pronounce him, long after his death, "the greatest historian of the race."

FURTHER READING

There are numerous Williams letters in collections of other people's correspondence, including the George F. Hoar Papers at the Massachusetts Historical Society in Boston and the Collis P. Huntington Papers at the George Arents Library at Syracuse University.

Franklin, John Hope. *George Washington Williams: A Biography* (1985).

This entry is taken from the *American National Biography* and is published here with the permission of the American Council of Learned Societies.

JOHN HOPE FRANKLIN

Williams, Henry Sylvester (19 Feb. 1869–26 Mar. 1911), convened the first Pan-African Conference in July 1900 in London, England, in the midst of a legal career that included admission to the bar in England, South Africa (Cape Colony), and Trinidad and election as probably the first African-descended borough councillor in Britain.

Williams was born on Arouca, Trinidad, the son of Henry Bishop Williams, a wheelwright, and Elizabeth Williams, immigrants from Barbados. Barbados was strongly influenced by British culture, while Trinidad had a majority French–Creole African population, with Indian indentured laborers imported starting in 1845. Williams attended a village government school, closely associated to the Church of England, to which he belonged his entire life.

At age fifteen, he passed an examination for admission to the Men's Normal School in Port-of-Spain, and in 1886 he passed a teaching exam (Mathurin, p. 21). His first teaching assignment, in 1887, was La Fortunee–Bien Venue Government School, named for the two large sugar estates from which his students came, owned by the Glasgow firm of Charles Tennant, Sons & Co. In July 1888 he was transferred to the Canaan School, also being appointed local registrar of births and deaths (Mathurin, p. 24). In 1889 he moved to the San Juan

Government School, where he became a founding member of the Trinidad Elementary Teachers Union.

In 1891 he sailed for New York. There is no evidence for where he traveled or how he supported himself in the United States. By 1893 he had moved to Nova Scotia, where he enrolled as a general student in the faculty of law at Dalhousie University. Nova Scotia, at the time, had the largest African-descended population in Canada; descended from transported Jamaican maroons, men enlisted to fight in the British Army during the American Revolution, enslaved property of exiled American loyalists, and later refugees from enslavement in the United States (Mathurin, p. 30).

He went to London in 1896, supporting himself as a lecturer for the Church of England Temperance Society, and the National Thrift Society, enrolling in a Latin course at King's College. Williams founded the African Association 24 September 1897 to encourage unity, promote the interests of all British subjects of African descent, and present direct appeals to imperial and local governments. In December of the same year, he was admitted to Gray's Inn, one of four Inns of Court where aspiring lawyers studied in London. He passed an exam in Roman law within three months and two months later an exam in constitutional law and legal history. Williams also contributed to the South Place Ethical Society's Sunday afternoon lecture series on "Empire," a critique of British administration in Trinidad. Denouncing crown rule as "heartless" and a "synonym for racial contempt" (Mathurin, p. 36), Williams called for representative government, free universal education, and an increase in the wage scale. His text was printed and circulated to members of Parliament, without immediate effect.

In 1898 Williams married Agnes Powell, who worked in a book depot of the Church of England Temperance Society (Mathurin, p. 36). Agnes's mother and her sister Amy were supportive, but her father, Captain Francis Powell of Gillingham, Kent, refused his consent and never received Williams at his home. Powell shared the infatuation of imperial institutions with skin color as a measure of character. The Williams's first son, Henry Francis Sylvester, was born in 1899.

Williams convened the world's first Pan-African Conference at Westminster Town Hall in London, 23–25 July 1900, with the curious endorsement of BOOKER T. WASHINGTON, who had attended a meeting and corresponded with Williams the previous year (Marable, p. 79). He may have expected that the more African Americans learned about European treatment of Africans, the more tolerable conditions in the South would seem. Americans attending included the educator ANNA JULIA COOPER, women's club leader Ada Harris, a young college professor named W. E. B. DuBois, and African Methodist Episcopal Zion Church Bishop ALEXANDER WALTERS, president of the Afro-American Council, who was elected to preside at the conference. Among the thirty-three participants were the intellectual Benito Sylvain of Haiti (also representing Emperor Menelik of Ethiopia), composer Samuel Coleridge-Taylor of London, Edinburgh-trained physician John Alcindor of Trinidad and London, and Underground Railroad veteran HENRY "BOX" BROWN. The conference opened with a welcoming speech from the bishop of London, Mandell Creighton, who on the second day invited all to what Walters described as a "magnificent repast" (Lewis, pp. 249–250).

The conference, meeting under the motto "Light and Liberty," agreed to found a Pan-African Association, resolved to ameliorate the condition of people of African descent throughout the world, including Africa, to encourage friendly relations between the Caucasian and African races, to secure civil and political rights for Africans and their descendants in all parts of the world, and to encourage African peoples everywhere in educational, industrial, and commercial enterprises (Juguo, p. 95). A closing speech by DuBois offered his first public declaration that "The problem of the twentieth century is the problem of the colour line," asking how far differences of race would be used as "the basis of denying to over half the world the right of sharing to their utmost ability the opportunities and privileges of modern civilization" (Lewis, pp. 250–251).

Elected general secretary, Williams submitted a memorial from the new association to Queen Victoria, forwarded an address to Emperor Menelik and the presidents of Liberia and Haiti, representing the three nations with African leadership in the world, and delivered an address to the nations to French, German, and other diplomatic channels. He passed his bar exam in October 1900, but was not immediately admitted to practice law, due to a rule requiring eating at least three times per term in the dining hall at Gray's Inn. He had been too busy organizing the conference. He set out on a tour of Jamaica, Trinidad, and the United States to develop Pan-African Association chapters. He drew large crowds in Jamaica, but got a mixed reception on building chapters. He was enthusiastically welcomed in Trinidad, where many chapters were formed, but they faded soon after he left. The conference had provided for branch vice presidents in the United States (DuBois), Haiti, Abyssinia, Liberia, southern Africa, western Africa, and the British West Indies, but none took up the work of building sustained, effective chapters. Williams was warmly welcomed by Bishop Walters in the United States, where the National Afro-American Council was meeting 7–9 August 1901 in Philadelphia, and delivered an address on "The Union of the Negro Races."

Even before his return to London, Williams had heard that officers in Britain had dissolved the association and then changed the name to Anglo-African Association. Even Dr. Joseph Robert Love, editor of the *Jamaica Advocate*, who had been supportive of Williams's visit, emphasized "British birth" and the rights of British Negroes, opining that "only through British authority can the Pan-African Association achieve its high aims." Although Williams worked to reconstitute a new executive board and revive the Pan-African Association, it had ceased to exist by 1902.

Admitted as a barrister of the English bar in May 1902, Williams left for South Africa, where he was admitted to the bar by Henry de Villiers, Cape Chief Justice. The rest of the bar, self-conscious of their pale skin color, boycotted him as much as possible, but he was able to practice in the courts, serve on the board of managers of Wooding's Private Preparatory School (for Cape colored children), and present to Cape Attorney General T. L. Graham grievances of the nonwhite populations regarding trial by juries that were limited to people designated as white. After spending two weeks with Chief Lerothodi in Basutoland (now Lesotho), Williams returned to England early in 1905.

In London, Williams established a law practice, sought to present grievances to the colonial office from south and west Africa and from the Caribbean, and was elected on a Progressive liberal and Labor fusion ticket to the borough council for Marylbone. In 1907 he went to Liberia to aid the government in resisting an attempt by the British consul to make the nation a virtual British colony, and in August of the same year he moved with his family back to Trinidad.

He developed a thriving law practice in Port-of-Spain, where most barristers were black and colored Trinidad natives, while the judges were entirely English. He was the main speaker in October to the Workingmen's Association—he may have been the connection for endorsement of the association by Scottish labor leader Keir Hardie. Williams was stricken with a kidney ailment in late 1910 and died in March 1911. His fifth child, a boy, was born five days after Williams's death.

FURTHER READING

Juguo, Zhang. *W. E. B. DuBois: The Quest for the Abolition of the Color Line* (2001).

Lewis, David Levering. *W. E. B. DuBois: Biography of a Race, 1868–1919* (1994).

Marable, Manning. *Black Leadership* (1998).

Mathurin, Charles Owen. *Henry Sylvester Williams and the Origins of the Pan-African Movement, 1869–1911* (1976).

CHARLES ROSENBERG

Williams, Hosea (5 Jan. 1926–16 Nov. 2000), civil rights activist, was born in Attapulgus, Georgia, to an unwed teenage mother who died while Williams was still a child. Raised in poverty by his grandparents, Williams left home at age fourteen and wandered for a period of time before joining the army to serve during World War II. Returning as a wounded veteran, he endured further physical assault at the hands of Georgia whites who severely beat him for drinking from a water fountain.

Using his veteran's benefits, Williams gained a master's degree in Chemistry from Atlanta University and worked until 1963 for the Department of Agriculture in Savannah, Georgia. Williams married Juanita Terry and settled into a middle-class lifestyle. Anguish at not being able to purchase sodas for his sons in a drugstore provided the emotional trigger that launched Williams into civil rights activism in the 1950s.

Williams maintained his job with the Department of Agriculture while also working under W. W. Law in the local NAACP. Williams led sit-ins and marches in Savannah to break segregation, and he also led voter registration drives. In 1961 Williams devised the night march as a tactic. He was arrested time and again, noting later in his life that he had been in jail over one hundred times. His ability to inspire people to march and to organize marches became his hallmark trait in the movement.

Because Williams was considered too aggressive and uncouth by state NAACP leaders, he was turned down for advancement. Stung by this rejection, especially in light of his successful work in desegregating Savannah stores and businesses, in 1962 Williams offered his services to MARTIN LUTHER KING JR. and the Southern Christian Leadership Conference (SCLC). Williams remained loyal to King throughout King's life and also remained active in the SCLC, serving in positions of leadership until 1979.

While respecting King's nonviolent philosophy, Williams's style was tenaciously aggressive, and he occasionally clashed with other leaders in the SCLC. ANDREW YOUNG, another King confidant, was the opposite of Williams, more cultured and intellectual and more willing to employ negotiation as a tactic in civil rights battles. Williams also fought with the SCLC organizer JAMES BEVEL over strategies, particularly after the 1965 march in Selma, Alabama. Yet King appreciated the diverse talents of his top staff and recognized that he could not do without Williams when direct action was needed.

Following his work in Savannah, Williams worked with the SCLC in St. Augustine, Florida, as well as in Selma, Alabama. In Selma, Williams joined JOHN LEWIS in the front row of marchers who crossed the Edmund Pettus Bridge on Sunday, 7 March 1965, to be met with a vicious attack from police and state troops. "Bloody Sunday" was filmed and played on televisions throughout America, engendering outrage that enabled President Lyndon Johnson to push for the passage of the Voting Rights Act.

After Selma, the SCLC split over two proposed plans. Bevel called for statewide boycott in Alabama and a strong effort to unseat white power in the state. Williams countered with a proposal for a program called the Summer Community Organization and Political Education, SCOPE, which would extend voting rights campaigns to 120 southern counties using methods developed by the Student Nonviolent Coordinating Committee in the 1964 Mississippi Freedom Summer campaign. King decided to attempt both. The economic boycott fared poorly, while Williams's program, SCOPE, received more SCLC funding and attention. Williams claimed that SCOPE was successful during the summer of 1965 in registering thousands of new voters. However, critics of the program doubted the numbers and said that SCOPE was hampered by poor field administration and financial irresponsibility of SCLC staffers as well as by white resistance in southern communities.

When SCOPE ended in the fall of 1965 Williams remained in Alabama working on voter registration drives while King turned his attention to Chicago. Williams joined King in Chicago in December 1966, where Williams again worked on voter registration, though with little success. Williams assisted King in the 1967 Poor People's Campaign, an attempt to draw national attention to poverty by encouraging thousands of impoverished people to dwell in a tent city in Washington, D.C. While working on this campaign in the spring of 1968, Williams joined King in Memphis to assist black sanitation workers in their strike. Williams was waiting for King in the Lorraine Hotel parking lot on 4 April 1968 when King was assassinated by James Earl Ray.

Hosea Williams remained in the SCLC in positions of leadership until 1979. He also served in Georgia politics, serving at various times as Georgia state senator, Atlanta city council member, and DeKalb County commissioner. His interest in civil rights continued, and he led two well-publicized marches in Forsyth County, Georgia, in 1987 to highlight Ku Klux Klan activity in that county. In 1971 Williams also began the Hosea Feed the Hungry and Homeless organization, which grew to serve thousands of people Thanksgiving and Christmas dinners. After Williams's death in 2000, under his daughter Elizabeth Omilami's direction, the nonprofit organization increased its scope to offer a wide range of social services to the poor in Atlanta and other locations.

FURTHER READING

More information may be found in the SCLC collection and in the audio visual and oral history collections at the King Library and Archives, Martin Luther King Center for Nonviolent Social Change, Atlanta, Ga.

Branch, Taylor. *Pillar of Fire: America in the King Years, 1963–1965* (1999).

Fairclough, Adam. *To Redeem the Soul of America: The Southern Christian Leadership Conference and Martin Luther King, Jr.* (1987).

Garrow, David J. *Bearing the Cross: Martin Luther King, Jr., and the Southern Christian Leadership Conference* (1988).

Raines, Howell. *My Soul Is Rested: Movement Days in the Deep South Remembered* (1977).

Obituary: *The Independent* (London), 27 Nov. 2000.

MARY A. WAALKES

Williams, Isaac D. (1821–1898), slave-narrative author, businessman, and entrepreneur, was born in King George, Virginia, one of five children. Little is known about Isaac's parents except that his father was a free man. His mother's status is unknown. It is believed, although not certain, that as a boy Isaac served not as a slave but as an indentured servant. However, when Isaac's father was presented with the choice of either being enslaved or leaving for Liberia, he smuggled himself to England, parting ways with his family forever. Isaac was placed under the guardianship of John O. Washington, owner of a plantation with over 700 slaves. Williams had been meant to apprentice as a carpenter until the age of twenty-one, when he would have been responsible for deciding his own fate. But Washington died when Williams was seventeen, and although no new guardian was appointed, he continued to live and work on the plantation. Williams's stewardship officially changed hands when Washington's widow married again and John Braxton became the executor of the estate. When Braxton was arrested as a debtor, Williams, his brother, and his three sisters were all sent to the auction block. Williams was leased for $180 to Drewey B. Fitzhugh, who, knowing Williams had no protector, later arranged to purchase him formally from the Washington estate for $500. When this occurred, Williams felt for the first time that he was a slave. At some point during his five years (1849–1854) at the Fitzhugh farm, which was about five miles from the Washington estate, Williams married Eliza Wheeler.

While on the Fitzhugh farm, Williams met two Massachusetts men who were opposed to slavery. They often held clandestine meetings in the woods, where Williams was enraptured by their descriptions of life, enterprise, and business in the North. As he retold these stories of freedom and prosperity to the slave populations of the Fitzhugh and surrounding farms, Williams was targeted by area farmers, who learned of Williams's stories and demanded that Williams be sold to discourage their own slaves from attempting an escape. Fitzhugh complied, and Williams was bought first by George Ayler and then by a Dr. (first name unknown) James. While Williams was being transported to Georgia, he and a friend, Henry Banks, escaped and evaded slave hunters for three weeks by digging a cave into the bank of Williams Creek, approximately forty-five miles from Fredericksburg, Virginia. The pair were found, shot during their capture, and then jailed to await the return of James, who had proceeded south to Georgia. In prison Williams persisted in his attempts to escape by trying to pry the bars off his cell window. On the morning that James was due to arrive, Williams was on the verge of despair. In this fragile mental state he decided to kneel before God and swear that he would never attempt to escape again unless it was God's will that he do so. Williams's autobiography (as told in 1884 to "Tege") reported that he then heard a voice in his head that he took to be God telling him to return to the window. Williams then was able to remove the window's bars and glass. Williams and Banks escaped a second time and made their way back to the Fitzhugh farm, where they met up with a third escaped slave, Christopher Nicholas. At the farm Williams said goodbye to his wife and his mother, and on 1 December 1854 the three escaped slaves began their journey to Pennsylvania, where Banks had free cousins.

Along their journey Williams, Banks, and Nicholas avoided virtually all human contact, white or black, and drew near Pennsylvania by mid-December. The weather became colder, and snow set in. Around Christmas, they were all desperate enough to approach a man in the woods for help. This man gave the runaways food and put them in contact with Stephen Whipper, an agent of the Underground Railroad who was paid by abolitionists to help slaves escape. Whipper told the three men that their destination was St. Catharines, Canada, just twelve miles north of Niagara Falls. Progress toward freedom became easier for Williams, both mentally and physically, when he began to recognize parts of their passage from his dreams. He believed that this was the second time that God gave him a sign that his escape would be successful. Once in Philadelphia, the three were hidden in trains for the last leg of their journey to St. Catharines, where Hiram Wilson, an agent for the American Anti-Slavery Society, educator, and operator of a fugitive relief station, provided each with a set of clothes, boots, and an axe so they could begin to make their own livings as free men. As Williams recalled, "It was a curious coincidence that the day we entered Canada as free men was Christmas, and what a glorious Christmas present we had ..." (Williams, 49).

Williams worked chopping wood until the lead that remained in his hand from when he was shot in Virginia began to inflame his arm and shoulder, preventing him from working. As he was nearing the end of his means, he met one of the Underground Railroad agents who had helped him cross into Canada, the Reverend J.-W. LOGUEN. Loguen gave Williams money for train fare to his own hometown, Syracuse, New York, where he paid for a physician to operate on Williams's hand. While recovering, Williams gave talks to local teachers about the experience of slavery. These talks were well received, and he was asked to speak at a Presbyterian church in People Grove, New York. He gave two speeches, each so popular that Williams left with over one hundred dollars in donations in his pocket. This was more than enough money to support himself until his hand healed.

Williams worked for the Great Western Railway of Canada from 1855 to 1867, and his companion Banks worked with Williams until Banks enlisted in the Union army. In 1868 Williams moved back to the United States, taking up residence in East Saginaw, Michigan, where he bought a house and several rental properties that generated enough income for him to live comfortably. After establishing himself in the North, Williams returned South in search of his mother and his wife, whom he had left behind when he fled north in 1854. He stopped in Washington for an audience with President Ulysses S. Grant. Having heard stories about the Ku Klux Klan, Williams asked Grant if he thought it would be safe for him to travel to the South. Grant told him that he believed there would be no danger in his returning. Ultimately Williams escaped the shadow of slavery to become a successful businessman and entrepreneur who lived comfortably in Michigan until his death.

FURTHER READING

Williams, Isaac D. *Sunshine and Shadow of Slave Life: Reminiscences as Told by Isaac D. Williams to "Tege"* (W. F. Goldie) (1975 [1885]). Accessible online at http://docsouth.unc.edu/neh/iwilliams/menu.html.

JACOB ANDREW FREEDMAN

Williams, J. Mayo "Ink" (25 Sept. 1894–2 Jan. 1980), professional athlete, blues producer, and record company executive, was born in Pine Bluff, Arkansas, the son of Daniel and Millie McFall Williams. When Williams was seven his father was murdered while waiting to catch a train. Subsequently Williams's mother relocated the family to her hometown of Monmouth, Illinois. In high school Williams demonstrated great athletic ability, winning the 50-yard dash in the Illinois High School State Championship in 1912. He was found to be even more capable on the football field, earning a scholarship to Brown University where he played football in 1916, 1917, 1919, and 1920. Williams served in the army in 1918 as World War I drew to a close, and did not receive his degree until 1921.

After he graduated from college Williams played professional football until 1926, joining the rosters of such teams as the Canton Bulldogs, Hammond (Indiana) Pros, Dayton Triangles, and Cleveland Tigers. Williams was one of three

African Americans to play during the first year of the American Professional Football Association (now known as the National Football League). In retrospect, however, it might appear that football was merely a passing fancy for Williams, whose business acumen and passion for music would catapult him to the forefront as a pioneering blues producer and industry trendsetter in the field of "race records," 78 rpm recordings made by and marketed primarily to African Americans.

Evidence indicates that Williams's nickname "Ink" dates back to his college days, but others have argued that the moniker had just as much to do with his ability to sign black entertainers to recording contracts. In any event Williams proved to be an ambitious businessman and aggressive promoter when Paramount Records hired him to head its Chicago-based race records division in 1924. Among the artists Williams first recorded were the vaudeville singer GERTRUDE "MA" RAINEY and the self-accompanied Papa Charlie Jackson. Other notable blues performers, including BLIND LEMON JEFFERSON, BLIND BLAKE, and IDA COX, would soon be discovered. Williams's race records kept Paramount in business at a time when its other record sales were lackluster at best.

Early on, Williams employed the same exploitative practices to which unethical white record company executives subjected black artists. Williams took advantage of entertainers' unfamiliarity with copyright laws, even supplying liquor to some performers in order to get them to sign away their rights. Flat fees were often paid for a recording session with the promise of royalties, but even those who sold well seldom saw any royalty income. Additionally Williams registered copyrights through his own Chicago Music Publishing Company on the race recordings he supervised, and would later be accused of taking credit for songs he did not compose. Interestingly THOMAS A. DORSEY, who would become known as the "Father of Gospel Music," was one of the writers who composed and arranged songs for Williams's company to earn extra money.

By the time Williams left Paramount in 1927 to start the Chicago Record Company, releasing blues, jazz, and gospel music on his own Black Patti label, it appeared that he was destined for success. In spite of having Chicago's finest vocalists and musicians at his beck and call, however, Williams's venture failed within the first year due to inefficient distribution, particularly outside of Chicago.

Williams soon found himself working for Brunswick Records and its subsidiary Vocalion, for whom he recorded performers such as CLARENCE "PINE TOP" SMITH, LEROY CARR, and "TAMPA RED" WHITTAKER. With the stock market crash of 1929 and the onset of the Great Depression, Williams soon became unemployed.

Returning to football, he became the coach at Atlanta's Morehouse College in the early 1930s, but resumed working in the music business when Decca Records offered him a job. Between 1934 and 1945 Williams recorded ALBERTA HUNTER, MAHALIA JACKSON, BLIND BOY FULLER, SISTER ROSETTA THARPE, Marie Knight, SLEEPY JOHN ESTES, and others before leaving Decca to work as a freelance producer and once again establish his own record company ventures. His Southern and Harlem labels, initially based in New York, folded in 1949, leaving behind his Chicago-based Ebony Records, which he operated until 1972.

The Archives Committee of the Jazz Institute of Chicago had planned to interview Williams at length, but he passed away at a Chicago nursing home before an interview could be arranged. Williams's wife, Aleta, of whom few details are known, had predeceased him in death in 1968. Posthumously Williams was inducted into the Blues Foundation's Hall of Fame in 2004.

FURTHER READING
Barlow, William. *"Looking Up at Down": The Emergence of Blues Culture* (1989).
Charlters, Samuel. *The Bluesmen: The Story and the Music of the Men Who Made the Blues* (1967).
Weissman, Dick. *Blues: The Basics* (2005).
Obituary: *Come For to Sing* (Chicago folk magazine), Autumn 1980.

GREG FREEMAN

Williams, James (1 Apr. 1825–after 1873), entrepreneur and author of a slave narrative, was born John Thomas Evans in Elkton, Cecil County, Maryland. According to his narrative, which is the source of most of the biographical information available about his life, he was born the slave of Thomas Moore, who owned his mother Abigail. When he was a child, he and his mother were sold to William Hollingsworth; soon after, Abigail ran away. One of her daughters, left with Moore, also attempted to escape from slavery but failed. James Williams lived with Hollingsworth until he was thirteen. One day, after being punished especially severely and threatened with sale to Georgia, he took one of Hollingsworth's horses and gradually made his way north to the area around Somerset, Pennsylvania.

There he was reunited with his mother, who had married William Jourdan.

Taking the name "James Williams," he worked several jobs—mostly tied to agriculture—across Pennsylvania in the late 1830s and 1840s and began a peripatetic existence, some of which is described (and some perhaps fabricated) in his narrative. His narrative describes his work with the Underground Railroad during this period and details his claim that he fired the first shot in the September 1849 Philadelphia riot centering on the attacks of the "Moyamensing Killers" on Philadelphia's black population. These events led him to flee briefly to New York. Returning to Philadelphia in 1850, Williams briefly ran an ice cream and fruit business, but continued problems with the law led him to move back and forth between Philadelphia and New York—and even as far as Boston, where he reportedly met fugitive slave and activist WILLIAM CRAFT.

In March of 1851 Williams decided to move to California. After a stay in Panama, he arrived in Sacramento in May. He mined with little success, first in Negro Hills and then in Kelsey's Diggings, before working as a hod carrier (a laborer who carried materials to masons) and restaurateur in Sacramento. He there ran into trouble with a slaveholder visiting California—after one of the slaveholder's female slaves left with Williams, the slaveholder confronted Williams at pistol-point—and was forced to leave his business and escape first to San Francisco and then to Mexico. Back in California within a year, he again worked a variety of jobs as a watchman, miner, junk-store owner, and wagon driver. Williams claimed to have been active in the 1857 Archy case, the key fugitive slave case in California during the period, in which ARCHY LEE asserted his right to freedom arguing that his owner Charles Stovall was a resident of—rather than a visitor to—California. Specifically, Williams's narrative asserts that he helped lead the rescue of Lee when Stovall attempted to move him out of state. Williams then relocated briefly to Vancouver and then to Nevada.

In the late 1850s and early 1860s, Williams continued to work as a miner, driver, and merchant. He accumulated property in both Carson City and Sacramento. In 1865 he sold his Carson City property for a significant profit and returned to Sacramento, where, after an extended illness, he worked between 1867 and 1869 as an agent of the Sacramento African Methodist Episcopal Church. During this period he also worked as a caterer. Williams provided a large luncheon for Sacramento's 1869 Emancipation Day celebration that was praised by the black press. He moved briefly to San Francisco in late 1869 and then back East. But he soon returned to California and, from 1870 to 1871, he worked as a whitewasher and agent for Siloam Baptist Church in Sacramento, finally leaving this church, too, claiming in his narrative that "as a general thing, amongst the people of color in their churches, you can never do enough" (Williams, 51).

The events of the following year remain cloudy and may represent one of the key reasons Williams composed a narrative. A friend from the East named Elizabeth ("Lizzie") Thompson supposedly asked Williams to aid her in moving to California. According to his narrative, Williams loaned her money, paid her rent, and "remained her security" (Williams, 52). Thompson seems to have then befriended an Alfred Linchcomb. Soon after, in February of 1872, the house she was renting burned down, and she died in the blaze. Williams accused Linchcomb of both arson (and so murder) and the theft of Thompson's jewelry, but the San Francisco police arrested Williams. Though he was discharged after two weeks in jail, in the words of his narrative, he was "wounded and injured for life in my reputation" (Williams, 55). The black press was especially critical of Williams—referring to him as "Gassy" Williams, sarcastically saying that he had been Thompson's "gallant," and intimating that he was an accomplice in Thompson's murder after swindling Thompson and her mother. In a letter published in the 30 March 1872 *Christian Recorder, Pacific Appeal* editor Peter Anderson asserted that, prior to the fire, Thompson's throat "had been cut from ear to ear."

Williams soon sold his whitewashing business and took a job whitewashing for the Central Pacific Railroad, but only a few months later, in August of 1872, he was again arrested, charged in Thompson's murder. Though he was again released, he wanted both to clear his name and to replace his income: "all I can receive for damages" for being arrested, he claimed in his narrative, "is for the people to buy my book" (Williams, 55). That narrative, first published in 1873, was composed of both an autobiography and various stories of other escaped slaves such as HENRY "BOX" BROWN that borrow from WILLIAM STILL's *The Underground Rail Road*. Williams seems to have consciously pitched the narrative toward white readers, making fairly snide remarks about California black churches and asserting that "be it known, that the Anglo-Saxon race were my best friends through it all" (Williams, 60).

The details of the end of his life remain uncertain, though his narrative went through at least three more editions in California in the 1870s and one in Philadelphia in the 1890s. James Williams provided an important voice among black participants in the Gold Rush and its aftermath.

FURTHER READING

Williams, James. *Fugitive Slave in the Gold Rush* (2003), which includes his 1873 narrative.

Beasley, Delilah. *Negro Trail Blazers of California* (1919).

ERIC GARDNER

Williams, Jesse (fl. 1812), a sailor during the War of 1812, was a crewman on the *Constitution* and on the *Lawrence* during the Battle of Lake Erie. Nothing is known about Jesse William's personal life except for the fact that he was a free man and a Pennsylvania native. Williams joined the navy in 1812 and was designated an "ordinary seaman," a second-tier position among enlisted sailors. That Jesse Williams had at least some experience as a sailor under his belt by the time he joined the navy is indicated by his rating; further down in the hierarchy of sailors was the position of ship's boy, one usually held by younger men, black or white, without experience, whose job it was to serve as officer's servants and cabin attendants. Williams's service came at a time before segregation among the enlisted ranks became the norm in the navy, and white and black seamen served side by side with relatively few problems, even if black sailors were not always appreciated by their white officers. Further proof of Williams's skill was his assignment to the crew of the *Constitution*'s number three long gun as "first sponger." Here, his role was to sponge down the gun tube after every firing so as to eliminate any sparks or fire prior to reloading. It was a wet and dirty job, but a vital one to keep the gun operating. We may also be sure that Williams would also have the skill, based on repetitive drilling and observation, to serve in other gunnery positions should the need arise due to battle casualties. Williams received his baptism of fire during the *Constitution*'s battle with the British frigate *Java* on 29 December 1812, one of the great naval battles of the War of 1812. The *Constitution* and its gunners battered their equally matched British opponent into submission after an action that lasted nearly two hours.

In early 1813, several months after the *Constitution*'s victory, a number of its men, Jesse Williams included, were sent to join the Great Lakes fleet. These skilled and battle-tested men would be an important addition to a fleet, as yet untested in battle. They were first sent to Sackets Harbor, New York, on Lake Ontario, where the Great Lakes fleet was commanded by Commodore Isaac Chauncey. When Oliver Hazard Perry was subsequently transferred to Chauncey's command in March 1813, tasked with finalizing the construction of the Lake Erie fleet, one of the things he needed most was sailors to man his ships. Perry made repeated requests for men to Chauncey, subsequently going directly to the secretary of the navy to get the men he needed. With pressure from above, Chauncey finally acted, sending 150 men to Perry from his Lake Ontario fleet. However, Perry had mixed feelings about the men he received; though "pleased to see anything in the shape of a man," he also commented that they were "a motley set, blacks, Soldiers, and boys" (Altoff, p. 36). Displeased by his junior officer's complaints, Chauncey vigorously responded that "I regret that you are not pleased with the men sent you … for to my knowledge a part of them are not surpassed by any seaman we have on the fleet, and I have yet to learn that the Colour of the skin, or cut and trimmings of the coat, can effect a man's usefulness. I have nearly 50 Blacks on board this ship [the *General Pike*], and many of them are amongst my best men" (Altoff, p. 37). Perry had to settle for the men that Chauncey sent him, men such as Jesse Williams, ISAAC HARDY, JESSE WALLS, JAMES BROWN, and ROBERT BROWN, and he would not be disappointed in the end, for it was this "motley" set of sailors that helped him win the decisive Battle of Lake Erie.

Sent to Lake Erie at an unknown date, perhaps as late as August 1813, Jesse Williams was assigned to Perry's newly built flagship, the twenty-gun brig *Lawrence*. Whether Perry personally conversed with Williams is unknown, but his experience in a gun crew aboard the *Constitution* was almost certainly a deciding factor in his posting to the vessel that, in the near future, would lead the American fleet into action. That battle developed in the early hours of 10 September 1813 in the waters of western Lake Erie off Put-In-Bay when the squadron of nine American ships, led by Perry in the *Lawrence*, faced a British fleet of six ships. Despite Perry's well-formulated battle order, most of the other ships in his fleet lagged behind, leaving the *Lawrence* to battle alone against the combined firepower of the British fleet. The battle was hard fought, but the men of the *Lawrence* held their own and returned broadside for broadside in a contest that lasted two hours. Perry's flagship suffered 80 percent casualties among its crew; among the many wounded was Jesse Williams. With his flagship still afloat, but crippled, Perry boldly transferred his command to the brig *Niagara*, which had not yet joined the fight, and subsequently sailed to meet the British fleet once again, soon turning the tide toward victory. When the Battle of Lake had ended, the British were effectively swept from Lake Erie and the area of Ohio, the Michigan Territory, and western Upper Canada was under American control.

After his vigorous service in the War of 1812, little is known of Jesse Williams. He likely resided in Philadelphia, perhaps sailing out of that port as a merchant seaman. On 4 July 1820 he was a resident of that city when his attorney, Peter Sprout, applied on his behalf "for to obtain the prize medal designed and ready kept to be presented as one of the brave victors of Lake Erie by the generous and patriotic State of Pennsylvania" (Montgomery, p. 289). This prize medal was approved by the state in January 1814 and was a silver medal of two dollars weight inscribed with the name of those "who nobly and gallantly volunteered on board the American Squadron" (Montgomery, p. 247). Jesse Williams and his fellow black sailors were, indeed, among those noble and gallant men.

FURTHER READING

Altoff, Gerard T. *Amongst My Best Men: African-Americans and the War of 1812* (1996).
Montgomery, Thomas L., ed. *Pennsylvania Archives, Sixth Series* (vol. 9, 1907).

GLENN ALLEN KNOBLOCK

Williams, Joe (12 Dec. 1918–29 Mar. 1999), blues and popular singer, was born Joseph Goreed in Cordele, Georgia, the son of Willie Goreed and Anne Beatrice Gilbert, whose occupations are unknown. At the age of "about three" Joe, his mother, and grandmother moved to Chicago, where he was educated at Austin Otis Sexton Elementary School. From age ten Joe funded his own education, which concluded at Englewood High School, by singing locally. At age twelve he founded the Jubilee Boys, who sang in Chicago churches, while earning between twenty and thirty dollars singing at late-night clubs. At age sixteen, family members decided he would be professionally known as Williams. That year he dropped out of school and was soon singing four nights a week with the Johnny Long band. His repertoire was primarily the mainstream popular songs of the day, usually written by whites for those with a "white" point of view. "Moonlight and Shadows," a tune from *The Jungle Princess* (1936), a Dorothy Lamour film introducing the sarong, is an example. But by 1938 Williams had also been "opened up to the blues," a genre singularly African American in origin and appeal.

During the next twelve years Williams sang mostly mainstream ballads in many cities and with many groups. He also worked as a janitor, a door-to-door salesman, and a doorman. His personal life was chaotic. In 1943 he married Wilma Cole but was divorced in 1946. Williams suffered a nervous breakdown, which lasted most of 1947. That year he married Ann Kirksey but they too were divorced in 1950. By the end of the decade his singing career had virtually ended.

Things began to change in 1950. Williams was in a nightclub audience listening to the COUNT BASIE band when someone recognized him and called on him to sing a few numbers. He responded with several standards, including DUKE ELLINGTON's "Solitude" and FATS WALLER's "Honeysuckle Rose" and "Ain't Misbehavin'." He received fifty dollars for his efforts and decided to pursue a singing career again. In 1951 he married Lemma Reid; they had two children and were divorced in 1964.

In 1955, after receiving what he later called a "vague offer" the year before from the Basie band, Williams got a clear one and accepted. By then Basie was already a phenomenon. Although most of America's memorable bands—excepting Ellington's—had collapsed after World War II, when the public seemed more interested in new sounds and television, Basie's ensemble had become one of the most innovative.

The first Basie recording session, in 1955, featuring Williams proved historic. It included "Every Day (I Have the Blues)," previously identified with its creator, Peter Chatman. Williams's eight-minute tour de force showed his uncanny flexibility, vocal range, and control. That same year Williams created major hits with "In the Evening," "The Comeback," and "All Right, Okay (You Win)." The 1955 *Down Beat* magazine poll named Williams America's top male vocalist.

Williams stayed with Basie, touring and recording more blues classics, until 1960. Then he struck out on his own with a wider repertoire, though in subsequent years there were frequent reunions with the legendary bandleader. Williams often gave Basie credit for his own renascence, but it is demonstrable that the Basie band achieved wider popularity after Williams joined it. Both were national treasures.

In 1965 Williams married Jillean Hughes d'Eath, an Englishwoman whom he had met in New York. They remained married until Williams's death. In 1967 they moved to Las Vegas, where Williams's particular mixture of mainstream and blues singing to a big band accompaniment commanded a year-round audience. There he remained for the rest of his life, though he regularly undertook national and international tours and made recordings. He appeared as a soloist with the Boston Pops and the symphony orchestras of Cincinnati and Detroit. Williams appeared in two films, *Jamboree* (1957) and *Cinderfella* (1960). During the 1980s he appeared regularly on television as BILL COSBY's father-in-law, Grandpa Al. In 1988 Williams founded a scholarship fund for music students at the Community College of Southern Nevada in Las Vegas.

Referring to his straightforward versions of mainstream music, Williams once said, "There's nothing wrong with singing a song the way it was written, with making a song say 'Please like me'" (*New York Times*, 31 Mar. 1999). He died in Las Vegas a day after collapsing on the sidewalk, having left (without permission) a hospital where he had been confined for a week with respiratory problems related to chronic emphysema.

Williams was the most popular blues singer of his era, rivaled only by RAY CHARLES, enveloping multiethnic audiences with the richness and flexibility of his baritone voice. Mixing the sound and phrasing of jazz with the blues, Williams began the creation of "urban blues." "Joe definitely dressed the blues up," the singer Kevin Mahogany recalled. "He made it okay to listen to the blues for those who misperceived what they were all about. You didn't have to be downtrodden, sitting out in a field, and moaning about your life" (liner notes to *The Ultimate Joe Williams*, Verve 559 700 2).

The awards and honors Williams accumulated during the last half of his life included selection as best male vocalist by the International Critics Poll in 1955, 1974–1978, 1980, 1981, 1983, 1984, and 1989–1991; best male vocalist, *Billboard* disc jockey poll 1959; and best male vocalist, Grammys, 1985 and 1992. Popularizing mainstream music to an essentially blues audience, Williams was one of the most honored entertainers of the late twentieth century.

FURTHER READING

Gourse, Leslie. *Every Day: The Story of Joe Williams* (1985).

Gourse, Leslie. *Louis' Children: American Jazz Singers* (1984).

Leblanc, Ondine. *Contemporary Musicians: Profiles of the People in Music*, vol. 11 (1994).

Obituaries: *Las Vegas Review-Journal*, 30 Mar. 1999; *New York Times*, 31 Mar. 1999.

This entry is taken from the *American National Biography* and is published here with the permission of the American Council of Learned Societies.

JAMES ROSS MOORE

Williams, John Alfred (5 Dec. 1925–), novelist, journalist, and teacher, was born in Jackson, Mississippi, to John Henry Williams and Ola Mae, whose maiden name is unknown. Soon after his birth, the family returned to Syracuse, New York, where his father was a laborer and his mother a domestic. Williams attended Central High School in Syracuse, leaving in 1943 to enter the U.S. Navy. After service in the Pacific theater during World War II, he returned to Syracuse, completed high school, and, in 1947, married Carolyn Clopton; the couple had two sons, Gregory and Dennis. Williams entered Syracuse University and graduated in 1950 with a bachelor's degree in Journalism and English. He did graduate work in 1951–1952 before financial circumstances forced him to withdraw; he and Clopton also divorced in 1952.

Williams held several paid writing positions in the 1950s: he was a public relations writer in Syracuse, publicity director for Comet Press Books, editor of *Negro Market Newsletter*, a publisher's assistant, and European correspondent for both *Ebony* and *Jet* magazines. He incorporated these experiences into his first novel, *The Angry Ones* (1960), which draws mainly on his employment at Comet Press.

Williams's second novel, *Night Song* (1962), marks the start of his deep exploration of African American music, especially jazz. An account of the life of Richie "Eagle" Stokes, a fictitious saxophonist who closely resembles CHARLIE PARKER, the novel describes the opportunities and limitations that an artistically talented black man must confront in his attempt to forge meaningful art in racist America. On the strength of it, Williams was informed that he would be selected to receive the *Prix de Rome* from the American Academy of Arts and Letters.

After receiving the informal letter of congratulations that promised him the prize, the author had an interview with the director of the academy, supposedly a mere formality. Instead, after the interview, the director informed Williams that the award had been rescinded. (Williams fictionalized the events in *The Man Who Cried I Am* [1967] and recounted them in "We Regret to Inform You That," an essay reprinted in his collection *Flashbacks* [1973].) The director offered no explanation, though Williams speculated that his impending marriage to Lorrain Isaac, a white Jewish woman, was the cause. At this writing, Williams remains the only candidate to ever have had the prize retracted. Williams later married Isaac in 1965, and the couple had a son, Adam.

Williams produced another fine novel, *Sissie*, in 1963 and a compelling travelog about his exploration of America, *This Is My Country, Too*, in 1964. It was the publication of *The Man Who Cried I Am*, however, that won him international acclaim and secured his literary reputation. The novel recounts the experiences of Max Reddick, a terminally ill expatriate African American writer. As his marriage and his health deteriorate, Max pursues information left to him by a writer friend, Harry Ames. Ames, who is clearly modeled on RICHARD WRIGHT, has discovered an international plot for the subjugation of black peoples; a subset of this plot, the King Alfred Plan, is a blueprint for the annihilation of African Americans. Knowledge of King Alfred proves fatal for Max, as it has for all other blacks who have discovered it.

This novel appeared when the struggle for American racial equality was swinging away from the nonviolent resistance of the Southern Christian Leadership Conference to the more aggressive stance of the Black Power movement. Williams reflects that shift through his negative portrayal of Paul Durrell, a MARTIN LUTHER KING JR. figure whom the novelist portrays as little more than a government puppet. He intensifies that critique in his stinging biography of King, *The King God Didn't Save* (1970).

Williams's work portrays the activist as a failure whose outmoded integrationist views necessarily gave way to the militancy of the black power movement. In his introduction he argues, "So now the man is dead, and time is already proving that his philosophy began to die before he did" (23). He builds on that idea, claiming that strife is the natural outcome of white America's racist past. In telling the story of King's being hit by a brick during the Marquette Park march, for instance, Williams remarks that the minister had won the Nobel Peace Prize, an award that elsewhere in the world would have afforded him some protection. Not so in America; indeed, in Williams's view white Americans' inability to recognize and revere King "damned them to a restless racial future—which

they well deserve and, in fact, have long deserved" (97). One finds a similar tone in the novel that he wrote while working on the King biography, *Sons of Darkness, Sons of Light* (1969).

At almost exactly the same time that Williams was writing these two books, he began his teaching career. Subsequent to his initial appointment as teacher and lecturer in writing at City College of the City University of New York, he has held positions at more than a dozen colleges and universities. His commencement of teaching coincided with a shift in his fiction toward a fascination with history. This did not translate into a de-emphasis on contemporary social commentary, however; rather, it provided him a means of extending his commentary through his contextualization of the present era within a larger continuum. One sees a masterly example of this in *Captain Blackman* (1972).

Grievously wounded in a Vietnam firefight, the novel's eponymous hero moves backward in time, hallucinating the entire history of African Americans' military activity up until World War II. When he emerges from his coma, he reflects on his own career, which includes World War II, the Korean War, and the Vietnam War. Although the novel ends with a somewhat fanciful call for infiltration and subversion of the American military, it provides a solidly researched, powerful commentary on the neglected contributions that African American soldiers have made to a nation that has perpetually, systematically denied them their humanity.

Captain Blackman also exhibits Williams's most striking formal achievement: a flexible chronology that embroiders a linear plot with facts, dates, and experiences that thoroughly complicate the reader's understanding of what history is and how it is constructed. This pattern demonstrates Williams's rejection of history as a monolithic, fundamentally accurate, and basically just entity. Much of his fiction identifies a plethora of intellectual-economic-racial tensions that infiltrate the telling of American history and distort the reader's perception of past (and present) events. A subsequent generation of African American writers who concern themselves with historical questions, including JOHN EDGAR WIDEMAN, Charles Johnson, and TONI MORRISON, cite Williams as an important influence on their work.

In some of his later works, Williams applies the historical lens to more personal subjects. As Gilbert Muller notes, *!Click Song* (1982) provides a sequel to *The Man Who Cried I Am*. *!Click Song*'s narrator, Cato Caldwell Douglass, is Max Reddick's emotional and spiritual heir; nevertheless, his interest in aesthetics saves him from the destruction that political activity visits on Reddick. In *The Berhama Account* (1985), Williams effectively mixes the personal and the political, setting a love story against the backdrop of effective political action. *The Berhama Account* shows a small Caribbean nation addressing its racially inspired internal strife in the wake of a specious assassination attempt. In the midst of all this social upheaval, a cancer survivor and journalist reignites an old affair and finds personal salvation in the relationship. On many levels this plot represents a rewriting of *The Man Who Cried I Am*, with a shift in emphasis away from the annihilation plot and toward the possibility of enduring human connection.

The same is true in Williams's compelling *Clifford's Blues* (1999), which recounts the story of the gay black jazz musician Clifford Pepperidge's confinement in the Dachau Nazi concentration camp near Munich, from 1933 until 1945. (The plot of the novel is not entirely fictional; several African Americans, including the jazz singer VALAIDA SNOW, were interned in concentration camps by the Nazis). Saved from the general camp population by his musical abilities and by a gay SS officer's sexual desire for him, Pepperidge spends his years in Dachau never fully suffering what most prisoners do and yet always remembering that he is not, cannot be, free. In the face of this, Pepperidge struggles to retain some sense of self. The emphasis on his experiences with jazz as a salvific force lends an air of hopefulness to the work. Williams tempers that hope, however, with a constant reminder that racism in America is little better than the discrimination that lands Pepperidge in Dachau initially; furthermore, by leaving the question of Pepperidge's survival unresolved, he complicates the notion that black identity and selfhood are sustainable, no matter what resources one brings to the struggle.

The appearance of this powerful novel, almost four decades after the publication of Williams's first book, indicates that in the early twenty-first century his is a vital and viable career. Furthermore, it demonstrates how his evolving approach to literature and his views about racial questions mirror shifts in the larger national populace. From an early hopeful emphasis on the chance for racial amelioration, through his strong hand in the articulation of a revolutionary black arts ethos, to a rich, subtle engagement with the issue of what black life means in America, Williams spans a range of attitudes and literary techniques that make his one of the most important American literary voices of his age.

FURTHER READING
Cash, Earl A. *John A. Williams: The Evolution of a Black Writer* (1975).
Muller, Gilbert H. *John A. Williams* (1984).

WILLIAM R. NASH

Williams, John Taylor (1 May 1859–8 June 1924), physician and diplomat, was born in Cumberland County, North Carolina, one of seven children of free black parents Peter Williams, a successful lumberman, and Flora Ann McKay, who taught her son to read at an early age. After the family moved to nearby Harnett County in 1867, his father engaged an educated white widow to tutor his children, in exchange for working on her farm. According to one account, within two years John Williams had "mastered Webster's blue back speller and other books"; by age sixteen, the avid reader was well versed in memoirs, history, and biographies (Powell, p. 210).

As a teenager, John entered the state normal training school at Fayetteville (now Fayetteville State University), where he graduated at the top of his class in 1880. Williams then became a schoolteacher, holding teaching positions near his home in Lillington and in a number of common schools across the state, from Southport to Charlotte, where he was then hired as assistant principal of the public graded schools for black students.

In 1883 Williams resigned his post as assistant principal to enter the first class at the new Leonard Medical College of Shaw University in Raleigh, where he studied for the next three years. After graduating with an M.D. degree in 1886, he became one of the first physicians of his race to be licensed by the state board of medical examiners, and soon established his practice in Charlotte, one of the state's largest cities. As a surgeon there, he assumed charge of Union Hospital and was a visiting surgeon at Samaritan Hospital; he also served on the Mecklenburg County Board of Health.

Williams was married in 1887 to his first wife, May E. Killian of Raleigh, who died soon afterward. In 1890 he married the schoolteacher Jennie E. Harris, a graduate of Scotia Seminary and Livingstone College, and the niece of the wealthy black industrialist WARREN CLAY COLEMAN. They had one daughter, Aurelia.

In 1888 Williams was appointed by Governor Alfred Scales as a captain in the North Carolina State Guard, after serving as surgeon for the Guard's First Battalion. He also became a successful businessman, operating the Queen City Drug Company in partnership with his Shaw classmate, Dr. MANASSA

T. Pope, and acquiring substantial investments in real estate, from farmland acreage to a small hotel in Charlotte. Politically active as a Republican, Williams won election in 1889 as a Charlotte city alderman and was reelected alderman in 1891.

Williams also became a founding member of Charlotte's Grace African Methodist Zion (AME) Church and a trustee of the AME Zion Publishing Company. Active in the denomination since his youth, Williams held a number of church offices, serving as a regular lay representative at church meetings and representing the state's Western Conference in 1892 at the denomination's General Conference in Pittsburgh, Pennsylvania.

In 1897 Williams was among those African Americans recommended by Governor Daniel Russell and other state Republican leaders for appointment to federal office by President William McKinley. McKinley selected Williams as the U.S. consul to Sierra Leone, then a British colony in West Africa. He joined a select group of black professionals appointed as consuls by McKinley, including the attorneys MIFFLIN W. GIBBS of Arkansas and CAMPBELL L. MAXWELL of Ohio, and the physicians LEMUEL W. LIVINGSTON of Florida and HENRY W. FURNISS of Indiana.

Williams sailed for Sierra Leone shortly after his confirmation by the U.S. Senate in February 1898. He served as U.S. consul in Freetown for the next eight years, sending widely read dispatches about colonial Africa and gaining reappointment by President Theodore Roosevelt in 1902. He resigned in April 1906, returning home to Charlotte to resume his surgical practice.

Active to his last day at Grace Church, Dr. Williams was serving as the preacher's steward at Sunday services in June 1924 when he suffered a stroke and died an hour later, after being taken to his nearby home. Three days later, he was brought back to the church for his funeral. He was sixty-five years old.

A lengthy obituary in the *Charlotte Observer* hailed Williams as "one of the oldest Negro physicians in the state," recalled his local service and consular posting overseas, and noted that he was "held in high esteem by the people of both races" (*Charlotte Observer*, 10 June 1924). The John Taylor Williams Middle School, a public magnet facility located near his home, is named in his honor.

FURTHER READING
Powell, William S. "John Taylor Williams," in *Dictionary of North Carolina Biography*, Vol. 6 (1986).

Obituary: *Charlotte Observer*, 10 June 1924.

BENJAMIN R. JUSTESEN

Williams, Kenny J. (4 Sept. 1927–19 Dec. 2003), university professor, was born Kenny Jackson in Omaha, Nebraska, the only child of the Reverend JOSEPH HARRISON JACKSON and Maude Thelma (Alexander) Jackson. Kenny's father was a distinguished pulpit orator and well-regarded writer who traveled widely, especially after he became head of the National Baptist Convention USA, Inc., in 1953, and had responsibility for its eight million members. Although Maude Jackson often accompanied her husband on his trips, he had to be in Kentucky while she stayed in Nebraska for the birth of their baby, a fact commemorated in their daughter's unusual first name. The family moved to Chicago in 1941, when Kenny's father became pastor of the Olivet Baptist Church there. In Chicago, her father's well-stocked library and her mother's work with amateur dramatic groups helped prepare Kenny for the intellectual life she would pursue. Although she was not born there, Chicago became her hometown emotionally and remained a focus for her own writing wherever she lived.

After her graduation from the Hyde Park High School, Kenny followed her mother's interest in the YWCA/YMCA movement by spending the first three of her undergraduate years at George Williams College, named for the YMCA's founder and then located, like her high school, in Hyde Park on Chicago's South Side. The practice teaching required there for teacher certification inspired her to pursue a career in education. In her senior year Jackson transferred to Benedict College in Columbia, South Carolina, a historically black college with Baptist ties. At Benedict she majored in English and earned her baccalaureate degree in 1949. Returning to Chicago, she completed in a single year (1950) at DePaul University the first of her two master's degrees. At DePaul she began her study of literary Chicago by compiling for her thesis a critical bibliography of Chicago novels.

After teaching English for two years (1951–1953) at Alabama State College in Montgomery and for four years (1953–1957) at the Hampton Institute in Virginia, Jackson left for further graduate study at the University of Pennsylvania. During summers she studied history at the National University of Mexico and library administration at the University of Chicago. She also traveled through Europe and parts of the Middle East, often accompanying her father during his trips on behalf of the church.

At the University of Pennsylvania, Jackson's studies were centered in the American Civilization Department. She earned her second M.A. there in 1959, followed by her Ph.D. in 1961 with a dissertation on Henry Blake Fuller's Chicago novels. Even before the completion of her doctorate, Jackson was hired as an associate professor by Tennessee Agricultural and Industrial State College in Nashville, and she left there as a full professor in 1964 to return to Chicago. While in Tennessee, in 1962, she married Emory Wardell Williams, a high school counselor; they had no children. She began to publish professionally under her married name, and she continued to be known as Kenny J. Williams after the marriage broke up a decade later.

In Chicago, Kenny Williams helped build the English Department of the new Northeastern Illinois State University and remained there as associate, later full, professor of English from 1964 until 1977. During those years she also served the fledgling university in many other capacities ranging from secretary of the graduate faculty to chairperson of the faculty senate. By self-directed study, she became an authority on African American authors, particularly those earlier writers whose works had never appeared in the curriculum during her student days. She also began taking on significant duties in national professional organizations, among them the American Association of University Professors, the Modern Language Association, the American Studies Association, and the Society for the Study of Midwestern Literature, which conferred on her its MidAmerica Award in 1986. Such experience helped bring Williams to the attention of the Department of English at Duke University, in Durham, North Carolina, which she joined in 1977 as a tenured full professor. In keeping with her training, at Duke she taught the received canon of nineteenth-century American literature, which she insisted was her academic specialty, not African American literature, but she did help to broaden it by including more black writers. She was a continuing member of the university's Afro-American Studies Advisory Committee and its President's Council on Black Affairs. She was considered something of a maverick among her peers at Duke University because of her conservative academic, social, and political views. While remaining a member of the Modern Language Association, she joined the traditionalist American Literature Association when it was founded in 1989 and served on its executive board. She also was an active participant in the Association of Literary Scholars and Critics and helped organize at Duke a chapter of the conservative National Association of Scholars. Williams's growing national reputation was recognized by colleagues through visiting professorships that took her back to the University of Pennsylvania in 1969 and to the University of California at Irvine in 1971. Her acknowledged academic status along with her lifelong enthusiasm for the Republican Party led to her appointment in 1991 by President George H. W. Bush as one of the twenty-six members of the National Council on the Humanities, the body that reviews grant applications and advises the National Endowment for the Humanities.

Among Williams's several dozen articles in professional journals, her long 1987 *Callaloo* essay, "An Invisible Partnership and an Unlikely Relationship: WILLIAM STANLEY BRAITHWAITE and Harriet Monroe," restored Braithwaite, a black literary critic, to a prominent place in literary history. The thesis of her first book, *They Also Spoke: An Essay on Negro Literature in America* (1970), was that "Negro literature is really American literature—nothing more nor nothing less" (xi), and this thesis was further elaborated in most of her subsequent articles and books. Those publications continued to be centered on Chicago while having broader implications for American culture. They included such wide-ranging books as *In the City of Men: Another Story of Chicago* (1974) and *Prairie Voices: A Literary History of Chicago from the Frontier to 1893* (1980) as well as the more narrowly focused *A Storyteller and a City: Sherwood Anderson's Chicago* (1988). Rounding out the Chicago theme, she and Bernard Duffey edited *Chicago's Public Wits: A Chapter in the American Comic Spirit* (1983). Williams died of cancer at her Durham, North Carolina, home.

FURTHER READING
The bulk of Williams's professional papers, which include her correspondence with a number of important literary figures, have joined those of her father at the Chicago History Museum while smaller collections are at Duke University and the University of North Carolina, Chapel Hill.
Greasley, Philip A., ed. *Dictionary of Midwestern Literature* (2001).
Velazquez, Rita C., ed. *Directory of American Scholars*, 9th ed. (1999).

CHARLES BOEWE

Williams, Lacey Kirk (11 Jul. 1871–29 Oct. 1940), pastor of Mt. Olivet Baptist Church in Chicago (1915–1940), president of the National Baptist

Convention from 1922 until his death in 1940, and president of Victory Mutual Life Insurance Co., was born in Eufala, Barbour County, Alabama, to Levi Shorter and Elizabeth Hill. His parents had previously been enslaved on opposite sides of the Alabama–Georgia state line. Williams, whose father adopted that surname as a new family name after marrying Hill, moved in 1877 with his family to Brazos Bottom, Texas, where his father saw better economic opportunity.

Converted and baptized in 1884 at Thankful Baptist Church, which numbered his parents among its founders, he was awarded a second-grade certificate in 1890, authorizing him to teach in public schools of Burleson County. He taught at River Lane School, eventually becoming the principal; on 16 August 1894 he married Georgia Lewis, one of his former pupils. They had one son, L. K. Williams Jr., who followed his father into the ministry. Ordained as a minister by the Baptist church in 1894, Williams served as pastor of several rural Texas churches, including Thankful Baptist. He continued his education at Hearne Academy and in 1902 at Bishop College, Marshall, Texas, where he also became pastor of Bethesda Church. Called to Macedonian Baptist Church in Dallas in 1907, he moved to Mount Gilead Baptist Church in nearby Fort Worth in 1909. Williams earned a B.A. from Arkansas Baptist College in 1913, and an honorary Doctor of Divinity degree from Selma University, Alabama, in 1914.

He served as president of the Baptist Missionary and Educational Convention in Texas until 1915, when he was called as pastor to Olivet Baptist Church, Chicago, established in 1850. According to the church's history, he was expected to "sustain relations between the Olivet Church and the white Baptists of Chicago" and also "unite the Negro Baptists of Chicago" (Fulop, Timothy Earl, *African American Religion: Interpretive Essays in History and Culture*, 1997, p. 335, fn. 26). From this post, he worked with the *Chicago Defender*, which had a greater southern circulation than any northern black newspaper, to recruit southern citizens of African descent to migrate to the city—probably the most organized of the many northward migrations from southern plantations and towns to northern cities. Olivet housed the Bethlehem Baptist Association, offering services to help "the race coming from the south" adjust to their new urban home.

The foundation for this work was laid by his predecessor, Elijah John Fisher, who expanded church membership from six hundred when he arrived from Georgia in 1902 to four thousand, with substantial resources to sustain a program of social services. Newly arrived migrants found food, clothing, assistance in finding housing and jobs, and eventually a health clinic, as well as social, educational, and recreational activities. By 1920 these programs employed sixteen people full-time. Shortly after World War I, Williams wrote in the *Chicago Whip* that black churches had a special responsibility to "make efficient and assimilate a rural element into modern city life." He saw helping northbound migrants as a moral duty, a golden opportunity, and the obligation of "humanity-loving and God-fearing men" (Best, p. 14).

In Williams's first two years, Olivet expanded to over seven thousand members; he relocated his congregation to a building newly purchased from First Baptist Church, the oldest Baptist congregation with a predominantly "white" membership—which was anxious to move out of a neighborhood rapidly changing in complexion. He pioneered a "mixed type" preaching style, intended to satisfy the intellectual elite who predominated in the pre-migration membership and the more emotional and demonstrative style that new arrivals from the south expected.

Williams and Olivet offered some limited support to efforts by the Chicago Federation of Labor and the Stockyards Labor Council to organize the meat packing industry in 1917–1919. Although lukewarm at best, accompanied by warnings against radicalism, this was far more than the unions obtained from most black churches, which received substantial grants from the packing companies. AME Bishop Archibald Carey typified majority opinion among ministers when he said "the interests of my people lies with the wealth of the nation and the class of white people who control it" (Halpern, p. 53).

Williams was one of six members "representing the Negro people" appointed by Illinois Governor Frank Lowden to the Commission on Race Relations, which published a study entitled *The Negro in Chicago* after the race riot of 1919; he was the only minister among the six. The same year, he was elected president of the Illinois General Baptist State Convention.

When the National Baptist Convention—the fifth-largest denomination in the United States ("Religion: Negro Baptists," *Time*, 25 Aug. 1930)—met in 1922 to elect a successor to its first president, ELIAS CAMP MORRIS, a two-month campaign resulted in "bitter feelings" and "the ugliest things ever said by one preacher about another" (*The*

Papers of Martin Luther King, Jr., 2007, Vol. 6, p. 18, citing three contemporary sources). Williams, who had already served as vice president, prevailed over Peter James Bryant, of Atlanta's Wheat Street Baptist Church. In 1928 he was also elected vice president of the Baptist World Alliance.

In 1927 Bishop College awarded Williams an honorary LL.D. He contributed an article to the *Chicago Tribune* in 1929 entitled "The Urbanization of Negroes: Effect on Their Religious Life," criticizing the "palpable excusable neglect" by northern black churches of migrants arriving from the south (Best, p. 13). By the 1930s, Olivet's membership passed twelve thousand, up to that time the largest Protestant congregation in America. By 1931 the "Progressive" movement within the NBC opposed William's leadership, which, like that of his next two successors, was seen by many as autocratic.

In 1936 Williams was chosen by Republican National Chairman John Hamilton to head the party's drive for black votes in the west; *Time* magazine observed that "Unlike most of the other important Negroes in the 1936 campaign, who have more white blood in them than black, Republican Williams is an old-fashioned chocolate color" ("RACES: Black Game," 17 Aug. 1936). Both parties, *Time* also noted, "were aware that local machines in the North can give Negroes a semblance of political equality without running into social difficulties." Williams died in an airplane crash on his way to Flint, Michigan, to speak at a Republican rally for Wendell Willkie, running for president against incumbent Franklin D. Roosevelt.

FURTHER READING

Best, Wallace D. *Passionately Human, No Less Divine: Religion and Culture in Black Chicago, 1916–1952* (2005).

Halpern, Rick. *Down on the Killing Floor: Black and White Workers in Chicago's Packinghouses, 1904–54* (1997).

Hayne, Coe. "Negro Education That Paid." *Missionary Review of the World* 45 (1922): 464.

Horace, Lillian B., and L. Venchael Booth. *"Crowned with Glory and Honor": The Life of Rev. Lacey Kirk Williams* (1978).

Sernett, Milton C. *Bound for the Promised Land: African American Religion and the Great Migration* (1997).

CHARLES ROSENBERG

Williams, Lavinia (2 July 1916–19 July 1989), dancer and choreographer, was born in Philadelphia, Pennsylvania. Little is known of her early life, although she claimed that one of her first memories as a dancer was her playful gyrations on top of a box at her Portsmouth, Virginia, home. A self-proclaimed "born performer" Williams regularly entertained her family, particularly her grandmother, a janitor for a local dance school (Williams Collection). Faced with the realities of a segregated southern community during the 1920s Williams entered through the back door of a dance school to take private ballet lessons at the end of the day from a Russian instructor.

As a young African American ballet dancer in the white ballet world of the 1930s, Williams quickly learned that she would be denied access to the premier dance companies in the U.S. "Being brought up in America," Williams recalled, "you were told you were not supposed to be a ballet dancer because you're black and your behind is too big, and your feet are flat … I could never get a job in America as black ballet dancer because they took away that part of me, [they] took away my ballet technique and made it modern or acrobatic" (Williams Collection). Williams's candid statement highlights the institutional and systematic discrimination that black dancers encountered with respect to the black female body and African Americans' approach to modern dance and ballet. During the emergence and popularity of modern dance in the United States, African American dancers were subject to the primitive and inferior trope in the dance world.

By 1937 Williams, who also possessed a strong interest in drawing, was awarded a scholarship by the Art Students League in New York City. While sketching ballet dancers at Eugene Von Grona's American Negro Ballet she was invited to audition; her acceptance served as one of the driving forces to a noteworthy dance career that spanned the United States, Europe, and the Caribbean. Von Grona's Negro Ballet provided her with steady work for a couple of years, and in 1938 she married Lev Sergeivitch Termen (Leon Theremin), the Russian inventor of an electronic instrument that would ultimately be incorporated into the soundtracks of many Hollywood science fiction films. The marriage lasted less than a year due to a mysterious disappearance by Termen.

In August 1940 Williams joined the cast of Agnes de Mille's *Obeah.* Her performance in de Mille's theatrical production helped to cultivate Williams's interests in the culture and art of the Caribbean. The Caribbean, Williams asserted, symbolized a "missing link to Africa" and allowed for a more complex understanding of the African experience in the Americas (Williams Collection). KATHERINE DUNHAM, the noted African American dancer, choreographer, and anthropologist, sought out Williams in 1941 and within a few months Dunham had assigned her as a student instructor in her budding dance company.

Dunham's dance philosophy influenced Williams's understanding of African-influenced dance and ethnology profoundly. Central to the Dunham dance technique was the importance of research and comprehension of an ethnic group's culture as a way to better understand, participate in, and choreograph a people's dance styles. Participation in a culture and obtaining a so-called "authentic" knowledge of why people danced and for what purpose remained essential to Dunham's and Williams's dance pedagogy.

From 1941 to 1945 Williams trained dancers in Dunham's company. She also enjoyed considerable success touring with Dunham throughout the United States and Canada and also performing in such films as *Cabin in the Sky* and *Stormy Weather* (both 1943), which were both choreographed by Dunham and featured her dance company. After 1945 Williams toured Europe in NOBLE SISSLE's United Service Organizations' (USO) revival of *Shuffle Along*, and while in Italy and Austria Williams studied with renowned dancer Kyra Nijinsky.

After a grueling tour of Europe, Williams returned to Brooklyn, New York, where she opened a dance studio in her basement apartment. During this time she balanced a career, a marriage to Shannon Yarborough, and motherhood, raising two daughters, Sara and Sharron. The spring of 1951 signaled a turning point for Williams when the Haitian government and local officials sponsored the Haiti Week festival in New York City. The events showcased the best in Haitian culture and introduced Americans to the tourist attractions of the country. During the week's festivities, Papa Augustin, a prominent Haitian drummer, invited several members from the festival committee to watch Williams teach at her studio. Jean Brierre, a celebrated Haitian poet, remarked that with Williams's extensive dance pedigree and ballet experience she would be a tremendous asset to the training of Haitian performers. In 1952 the Haitian government invited her as a national dance instructor for a period of six months to improve the technical skill of Haitian dancers.

On 23 April 1953 Williams arrived in Haiti with her daughters. Some of her early responsibilities included dance instruction at the Lycée des Jeunes Filles, training teachers at the Bureau of Sports, offering physical culture and body conditioning classes to La Troupe Folklorique Nationale, and also directing the troupe. Additionally, she served as Mistress of Ceremony at the open-air Théâtre de Verdure, narrating traditional dances to tourists. Williams also broadcast *Glimpses of Haiti*, a weekly radio program that educated foreigners about the cultural and historical richness of the nation.

By the 1950s Haiti was a center for Caribbean cultural tourism. The Haitian government and African American leaders such as WALTER WHITE, executive secretary of the NAACP, launched several public relation campaigns to develop Haiti's economic infrastructure and promising tourist industry. Haitian dance, painting, and music became "natural resources" or cultural commodities to attract middle-class and elite tourists from the United States and Europe who wished to avoid the precariousness of post–World War II Europe. Williams's technical training of Haitian dancers complemented the nation's postwar program to promote the cultural arts, in conjunction with structural investment, to strengthen the failing Haitian economy.

After a year in Haiti, Williams came to believe that it could be a potential center of black cultural production, where "people could come from all over the world for study, and for rhythmical inspiration" (*Dance Magazine*, Oct. 1956). In 1954, she organized the Haitian Academy of Folklore and Classic Dance, which represented a microcosm of her dream to create "an establishment which may someday incorporate not only dancing, but music, painting, drama, opera, and all of the other related subjects to help found a University of 'Beaux Arts of Haiti'" (*Haiti Sun*, 25 July 1954). Her Pan-African ideals resulted in institution-building, social and economic development through cultural exchange and tourism, and an effective promotion of racial and cultural identity.

Williams lived in Haiti until 1972, when she was invited by Prime Minister Forbes S. Burnham of Guyana to aid in that country's plan to establish a National Dance School and to promote musical and dance training among Guyanese youth. From 1973 to 1976 she directed the national school, and from 1976 to 1980 the Bahamian administration also called upon her to "create dances unique to the nation." Williams's post-Haiti career involved a Pan-Caribbean vision where the development of dance and choreography served as a tool to enable relatively new independent Caribbean nations, which, in many ways, still suffered under the remnants of colonialism, to create identities and cultural traditions distinctive to their multifaceted cultural heritage and post-colonial experience.

Long considered one of the forerunners of Caribbean dance, along with Beryl McBurnie and Ivy Baxter, Williams maintained a deep connection to the history and movement of African-descended peoples. Williams believed in the power of dance to entertain, to educate, and to move audiences. "We [African-descended peoples] are rhythm … it's a subconscious effort," she stated in 1983 (Williams Collection). And with that rhythm she influenced a generation of Caribbean dancers, in addition to dancers in the United States, where she taught at New York University, the ALVIN AILEY School, and the City College of New York during the early 1980s. In 1984, Williams returned to Haiti; she died of a heart attack on the island in July 1989.

FURTHER READING

The Lavinia Williams Collection can be found at the Schomburg Research Center for Black Culture, New York Public Library, New York, New York.

Yarborough, Lavinia Williams. "Haiti Where I Dance and Teach" *Dance Magazine* (October 1956).

Polyné, Millery. "'To Carry the Dance of the People Beyond': Jean Léon Destiné, Lavinia Williams and *Danse Folklorique Haïtienne*," *Journal of Haitian Studies* 10:2 (Fall 2004).

Obituary: *New York Times*, 10 August 1989.

MILLERY POLYNÉ

Williams, Leon Lawson (21 July 1922–), politician and public administrator, was born in Weeletka, Oklahoma, the eldest son of the twelve children of Lloyd Williams, a laborer, and Elvira Lott. Williams moved with his impoverished family to Bakersfield, California, during the Great Depression in 1934. Soon after his graduation from Kern County Union High School in 1941, Williams settled in San Diego, California, where he found work as a mechanic's helper at the North Island Naval Air Station. In 1946 he married Dorothy Nisley. Williams enrolled in courses at San Diego City College in 1947 and, after completing military duty in the army air corps, became a full-time student at San Diego State College, where he graduated with a bachelor's degree in psychology in 1950. As a college student, in 1947 and 1948, Williams, along with some fellow black and white students under the direction and training of the local NAACP president JACK KIMBROUGH,

participated in an effective desegregation plan, wherein white students were positioned in dozens of white-owned restaurants to observe and later act as legally competent court witnesses to the denial of service to their black classmates as customers.

Williams's first job out of college was as a social worker, and he rose to the rank of supervisor in the county welfare department. By 1957 he was working as an administrative officer for the San Diego County Sheriff's Department, and by the early 1960s he was on the county's Democratic Party Central Committee. In 1966 Williams was hired as director of the Neighborhood Youth Corps, an inner-city employment agency, and in 1968 he was interim executive director of the San Diego Urban League. Such prominence in the community of southeast San Diego made him a viable candidate to fill a vacancy on the city council. He was strongly supported by Mayor Fred Curran, his friend since their college days. Favored over a prominent Mexican American candidate, Williams was appointed by the majority on the council to fill its Fourth District seat in January 1969, thus becoming the council's first African American member. The following year he married Martha Jones.

Announcing that he wanted to transform the city into "a gem of human habitation" and emphasizing measures to relieve social unrest and juvenile delinquency in his largely black and Latino district, Williams won the November election. He was reelected on three occasions and served on the city council until 1982, when his protégé William Jones, another African American, succeeded him. In 1983 Williams won election to the San Diego County Board of Supervisors, another first for an African American, and in 1985 and 1990 he was elected by its members to serve as chairman.

Williams began his long involvement with the Metropolitan Transit Development Board (MTDB) in 1976, when he was appointed a member of the new agency that became one of the nation's leaders in the rebirth of light rail transportation. He became chairman of the MTDB in 1994 and oversaw initiatives to reduce traffic congestion and increase usage of publicly financed transportation primarily in the form of buses, commuter trains, and a steadily expanding trolley system. He worked to make such transportation an affordable, convenient, and safe alternative to automobiles.

Other career milestones for Williams included serving as consultant to the Federal Mart Corporation, director of the San Diego College of Retailing, president of the California State

Association of Counties, director of the San Diego Region Water Reclamation Board, life membership in the NAACP, and chairman of the Service Authority for Freeway Emergencies. He also served as a member of the powerful California Coastal Commission, the League of California Cities, the National League of Cities, the California Constitution Commission, the San Diego Black Leadership Council, and the Los Angeles–San Diego Rail Corridor Agency.

Williams maintained a reputation as a soft-spoken, mild-mannered but effective liberal Democrat who preferred working behind the scenes and away from the glare of cameras and reporters. He was especially noted for his efforts at reconciliation and consensus-building to solve problems. A political colleague once described Williams's method for getting things done as "political judo" because he seemed to have the ability to take the momentum of an issue and turn it back on itself, and he could persuade people to reexamine issues they opposed and eventually adopt them as though they were their own original ideas. Williams told one reporter, "My mission is to include people, to include everybody if possible, to include the homeless, to include the blacks, to include the Asians, to include everybody, include the right-winger, the left-winger, because we are all human beings" (Weintraub, 1).

Williams worked to improve the physical condition and economy of his district, and in 1981 he launched the Southeast Economic Development Corporation. He helped create the county's Human Relations Commission, was one of the earliest city politicians to call for funding for AIDS research and education, and championed environmental protections. He also pushed for much-needed downtown redevelopment and occasionally fought with the San Diego Police Department, whose treatment of minority-race suspects was a recurring source of tension, particularly in his district. Williams took law courses at the University of San Diego and worked toward a doctorate in public administration at the U.S. International University (later Alliant International University), though he did not take the degree. In 1993 Williams married Margaret Jackson. His three marriages produced four natural children, and he parented two stepchildren. In recognition of his service to the people of San Diego, Williams received numerous awards and commendations, including the Black Achievement and Freedom Award in 1981 from Action Enterprises, the Distinguished Service to the Community Award from the Black Federation

of San Diego, the San Diego NAACP's Outstanding Contributions Award in 1978 and its Distinguished Service Award in 1985, and the Percy Benbough Award for Distinction in Government Leadership from the San Diego Historical Society in 2002.

FURTHER READING
Josey, E. J., ed. *Who's Who among African Americans* (2004).
"Leon Williams Announces for 4th Council District," *San Diego Union*, 21 June 1969.
Pasqua, Sandra. "The Towering Leon Williams," *San Diego Metropolitan*, Feb. 2001.
Weintraub, Daniel M. "Williams' Quiet, Political Artistry Builds Solid, Satisfied Constituency," *Los Angeles Times*, 30 Nov. 1986.

ROBERT FIKES JR.

Williams, Marie Smith. *See* Selika (Marie Smith Williams).

Williams, Marion (29 Aug. 1927–2 July 1994), gospel singer, was born in Miami, Florida, the tenth of eleven children of Robert and Ethel Williams. Her West Indian father, who worked as a butcher and taught music on the weekends, died when she was nine, and a few years later her mother had both legs amputated due to diabetes. To help support her family, Williams left school after the ninth grade to work all day at various low-level jobs. On Sundays she attended two Pentecostal churches, where she developed her voice and musicianship. Recognized for her exceptional talent from early on, she first soloed at the age of three and later performed sacred music on street corners and in revivals.

In 1943 Williams started performing in churches around Florida with a gospel group, the Melrose Singers. Several years passed before she started traveling nationally, which was sparked by an impromptu solo. At the request of Reverend Leola Cosby, the Ward Singers, a well-known female gospel quartet, allowed Williams to perform during one of their Philadelphia concerts. According to group member Willa Ward-Royster, "When the time came, a short, plump girl took the stage, opened her mouth—and brought the house down. She sang with unbelievable versatility, command, and spirit" (Ward-Royster, 72). After joining the Ward Singers, Williams became a star (along with CLARA WARD) of the most powerful and successful gospel group of the period. The Ward Singers recorded "Surely God Is Able," Clara Ward's arrangement of a WILLIAM HERBERT BREWSTER song. Williams led the song's final verse, helping to make it the first million-selling record by a gospel group. In 1950 the Ward Singers, along with MAHALIA JACKSON and others, brought gospel music to Carnegie Hall for the first time, which led to a series of annual gospel concerts. The group, again along with Jackson, also became the first gospel singers at the Newport (Rhode Island) Jazz Festival in 1957. During this period the Ward Singers regularly attracted capacity crowds in large venues, although their success did not shield them from segregation and racial hostility on their travels. Williams appeared with the group on television on the *Today* show and Steve Allen's *Tonight* show.

Williams's experience with the Ward Singers brought her considerable exposure and enabled her to sing gospel as a full-time occupation, yet she eventually found it necessary to move on. GERTRUDE WARD, who managed the group and its finances, and her daughter, Clara, purportedly reaped a disproportionate amount of the group's earnings and made efforts to distinguish themselves from the other group members. This prompted Williams, along with Kitty Parham, Frances Steadman, and Henrietta Waddy, who were on salary, to leave the group on the verge of another *Today* show appearance. Since Williams was pregnant at the time with her son, Robin, her departure satisfied the wishes of the Wards, who did not want the stigma of an unwed mother attached to their group.

The four women who left formed a new group in 1958 named the Stars of Faith, which Esther Ford later joined. According to gospel historian and producer Anthony Heilbut, the group struggled because they lacked the caliber of compositions sung by the Ward Singers, the managerial abilities of Gertrude Ward, and, in particular, the previously no-holds-barred vocal approach of Williams, the group's star. Instead, Williams pulled back and allowed other members of the group to lead, which failed to satisfy audiences' expectations. The Stars of Faith got their big break after three difficult years. Motivated by Williams's musical talent and inspired by her group's Christmas music, musical producer Gary Kramer commissioned a gospel musical with a script written by LANGSTON HUGHES. The resulting work, *Black Nativity*, opened off-Broadway to packed houses in 1961, and traveled for four years in America and then Europe. Williams and ALEX BRADFORD starred in the production, which brought them international acclaim. She sang lead on several songs, including the popular "When Was Jesus Born."

Williams left the Stars of Faith in 1965 for a solo career. Over the following years she toured Africa, performing under the auspices of the U.S. State Department, and later she performed at various European jazz festivals. In the United States, she toured college campuses, shifting her repertoire to include some folk songs in order to satisfy the tastes of her predominantly white audiences. Like a few other great gospel performers, such as Mahalia Jackson and Dorothy Love Coates, Williams resisted the temptation to fully "cross over" into a secular market by performing nonsacred music. She did, however, perform in venues not traditionally affiliated with gospel music, such as nightclubs. A *Village Voice* review suggested that rather than compromising her Christian values, Williams transformed one nightclub into a virtual church through the power of her performance (Crouch, 57). In spite of her worldwide travels, Williams never achieved the popularity of Jackson. Late in life, Williams's reputation spread and she started to receive long-deserved recognition. Critics responded favorably to several of her albums, including *Strong Again* (1991) and *Can't Keep It to Myself* (1993). Her songs offered testimony to the expressive power of her booming soprano voice, noted for its wide range and timbral variety and her singular ability to phrase lyrics. The music critic Dave Magee proclaimed that "she was nothing less than the greatest singer ever" (Henke, 771). In addition to being a featured performer in a Bill Moyers documentary entitled *Amazing Grace*, she sang background tracks for the movies *Mississippi Masala* and *Fried Green Tomatoes*.

In June 1993 Williams received a John D. and Catherine T. MacArthur Foundation "genius" award, which included a grant of $374,000. She recalled that upon hearing the news, "I thought I was in heaven and the angels were talking to me … When I got off the phone, I went into the room where [the church mothers and daughters] were all sitting and waiting. I said, 'The Lord has opened up not a window, but doors in heaven and poured me out a blessing like I have never had before'" (Fitzgerald, 48). Following this good news, she was honored by President Bill Clinton for her lifetime achievements at the Kennedy Center in Washington, D.C., and her name was added to the Philadelphia, Pennsylvania, Music Alliance's Walk of Fame. Sadly, Williams never fully benefited from her MacArthur grant because of her untimely death of vascular disease at Philadelphia's Albert Einstein Medical Center in 1994.

Williams will be remembered as a vocalist of the highest order who channeled her explosive power into richly nuanced evocations of religious faith.

Through dramatic shifts in timbre and dynamics, interpolated words of praise, spontaneous hums and hollers, and other expressive devices, her vocal ingenuity inspired many singers, including SHIRLEY CAESAR, ARETHA FRANKLIN, and LITTLE RICHARD, who took his signature whoop from Williams. Her voice represents the gold standard of twentieth-century gospel music artistry.

FURTHER READING

Crouch, Stanley. "Marion Williams Transforms the Cookery," *The Village Voice* (6 August 1980).

Fitzgerald, Sharon. "The Glorious Walk of Marion Williams," *American Visions* 8 (December 1993/January 1994).

Heilbut, Anthony. *The Gospel Sound: Good News and Bad Times* (1971)

Henke, James, et al., eds. *Rolling Stone Album Guide: Completely New Reviews: Every Essential Album, Every Essential Artist*, 3rd ed. (1992).

Santelli, Robert. "Marion Williams: The Genius of Gospel," *Gadfly* (Nov./Dec. 1999).

Ward-Royster, Willa, as told by Toni Rose. *How I Got Over: Clara Ward and the World-Famous Ward Singers* (2000).

Obituary: *Philadelphia Inquirer*, 6 July 1994.

BRIAN HALLSTOOS

Williams, Mary Lou (8 May 1910–28 May 1981), pianist, composer, and arranger, was born Mary Elfrieda Scruggs in Atlanta, Georgia, the daughter of Mose Scruggs and Virginia Winn. Her father left home about the time she was born. Her mother remarried, to Fletcher Burley, and the family moved to Pittsburgh, Pennsylvania, when Mary Lou was four. She began to play the piano at about the same time, learning first from her mother and then from the many pianists who frequented the family's home. She learned to play ragtime, boogie-woogie, and blues, and her uncle and grandfather paid her to play their favorite popular and classical tunes. Her stepfather took her to play in local gambling halls and similar venues and to Pittsburgh theaters to see musicians like the pianist LOVIE AUSTIN. Neighbors invited her to play at parties, and she even performed for wealthy white families like the Mellons, thus earning the rubric "the little piano girl of East Liberty." At the age of twelve she sat in with McKinney's Cotton Pickers when the group passed through Pittsburgh. Though she studied music at Westinghouse Junior High School, it was these other experiences and the hours she spent listening to the recordings of JELLY ROLL MORTON, EARL HINES, and FATS WALLER that provided her true music education.

By the age of fifteen Mary Lou was on the road full time, playing with a small band that backed a vaudeville act known as Seymour & Jeanette. The baritone saxophonist John Williams also was in the band and befriended her, defending her right to play against managers and performers who objected to working with a woman. While on a gig in New York City, Mary Lou also played for a week with DUKE ELLINGTON's Washingtonians. John formed his own group, the Synco Jazzers, in 1925, and the couple married in 1926. The following year they moved to Oklahoma City, where John joined Terrence T. Holder's Dark Clouds of Joy Orchestra. Mary Lou continued to manage the Jazzers for a time.

In 1928 the Clouds of Joy settled in Kansas City, where Mary Lou played with Jack Teagarden, ART TATUM, TADD DAMERON, and even a teenage THELONIOUS MONK, firmly establishing her reputation. In 1929 ANDY KIRK assumed leadership of the renamed Clouds of Joy Orchestra. Mary Lou first played with the group in 1930, as a last-minute substitute for regular pianist Marion Jackson during an audition for a record executive. The executive liked the group, but he was even more impressed with Williams and insisted that she play on the subsequent recording date. She recorded six titles, four written wholly or partly by her. Though she was only nineteen and still an eclectic stylist, her solo on "Somethin' Slow and Low" showed that she had learned well the lessons of two of her chief models, Earl Hines and JAMES P. JOHNSON. Her strong left hand could play a ragtime bass, boogie-woogie, or swing while her right hand added lovely melodies, sophisticated harmonies, or counterrhythms.

Williams traveled with the band to New York City in 1930 and made occasional special appearances with them; at times, she waited in the car outside, only coming in to play a popular boogie-woogie piece or two if the audience seemed receptive to a woman musician. She joined the band full time in 1931, soon supplying Kirk with a half-dozen arrangements a week, which were characterized by a unique "light, bouncy swing." Following Henderson and Ellington, she divided the orchestra into sections, contrasting brass with reeds and producing creative harmonies by combining instruments in various forms—placing a trumpet, for instance, among four saxes. Scores like "Mary's Idea," "Walkin' and Swingin'," and especially "Froggy Bottom" (1936) made the Kirk band one of the most popular of its era. Williams was also the group's star soloist, playing in a variety of styles: a Gershwinlike solo on "Gettin' Off a Mess;" modernistic, in-and-out-of-key playing on "You Rascal You" and "Mess-a-Stomp;" and old-fashioned, barrelhouse piano on "Little Joe from Chicago." She provided excellent support for other soloists and filled in creatively during ensemble passages. She was, in short, one of the great swing-band pianists. Her powerful rhythmic skills led her to be billed as "The Lady Who Swings the Band." While with Kirk she also did arrangements for LOUIS ARMSTRONG, Benny Goodman, Earl Hines, and Tommy Dorsey. Two of her 1937 arrangements for Goodman, "Roll 'Em" and "Camel Hop," are particularly noteworthy.

In 1942 Williams left the band and formed her own small group in New York City with her second husband, the trumpeter Shorty Baker, whom she had married by May of that year after a divorce from her first husband. She led an all-women group in 1945 and 1946 that included the talented guitarist Mary Osborne, and she worked as a staff arranger for Duke Ellington for a short time, writing the well-known "Trumpets No End" in 1946 and providing the Ellington band with fifteen arrangements. She made a series of recordings from 1944 to 1947 under a variety of names: "Mary Lou Williams and Her Chosen Five," with FRANKIE NEWTON on trumpet, VIC DICKENSON on trombone, and Edmund Hall on clarinet; "Mary Lou Williams and Her Orchestra"; and a trio that included the trumpeter Bill Coleman. In 1945 she wrote the *Zodiac Suite*, each section written in honor of a particular musician, and each evoking a different sound—the first, for instance, brings to mind Debussy, the second Ellington. Three movements from the suite were performed that year at Carnegie Hall by the New York Philharmonic Orchestra.

While much of her playing during this period was an adaptation of the boogie-woogie style for which she was best known, she also added dissonances, sophisticated rhythms, and tone clusters that reflected the more modern approach of the bop revolution. Indeed, she became an important figure in the bop movement, serving as mentor and friend to Thelonious Monk, BUD POWELL, and DIZZY GILLESPIE. Compositions like "Froggy Bottom," "Roll 'Em," "What's Your Story, Morning Glory?" and "In the Land of Oo-Bla-Dee" successfully integrated bop innovations into the swing style, and Williams contributed several scores to Gillespie's big band.

Frustrated by the commercialism of the music business, Williams moved to Europe in 1952, but there she also found her talents constrained by market demands. She retired from music in 1954 to pursue religious and charitable activities. Moving first to the French countryside and then back to New York City, she began a "street ministry" to musicians hurt by alcoholism, drugs, and illness. She converted to Catholicism in 1957. Her apartment became almost a rest home, complete with cots and a soup kitchen. She established the Bel Canto Foundation to help needy musicians, ran a thrift shop to raise money, and used the profits from her own record company, Mary Records, to support her work.

Encouraged by Gillespie, Williams resumed her career in 1957, appearing at the Newport Jazz Festival. By the early 1960s she was again composing prolifically, focusing in particular on religious themes. She wrote a choral hymn, "St. Martin de Porres," which won the Grand Prix—Academie du Disque Francais; a cantata, "Black Christ of the Andes" (1963); and three masses. The last of these, the "Music for Peace" mass (1970), was commissioned by an American priest in the Vatican, choreographed as "Mary Lou's Mass" by ALVIN AILEY in 1971, and performed at St. Patrick's Cathedral in New York City and in many other churches worldwide. She conducted musical workshops in storefronts and on college campuses and appeared throughout the sixties and seventies in concert and on numerous radio and television shows, including *The Today Show*, *Sesame Street*, and *Mr. Rogers' Neighborhood*. Concerned that young blacks seemed unaware of their own rich musical heritage, she became a proselytizer for jazz itself. In 1970 she recorded *The History of Jazz*, a commentary with musical examples, and repeated similar programs many times in concert. As her close friend the Reverend Peter F. O'Brien later noted, "The American Black man, in the Spirituals, the Blues, and in Jazz, had created something new and unique. And the music was powerful, beautiful, full of love and healing to the soul" (O'Brien liner notes, *From the Heart* [1971]).

Throughout these years, Williams's playing remained based on a rock-steady rhythmic pulse and a driving sense of swing, decorated with lovely melodic ideas. She recorded a number of critically acclaimed albums, including *Zoning* (1974); *Live at the Cookery* (1976); *Free Spirits* (1976), a trio album that is perhaps the best of her later recorded work; *My Mama Pinned a Rose on Me* (1977), an album of mostly blues; and a solo recital in 1978 that covered the entire stylistic range of her playing. The title tune on *Free Spirits* contains some of her most powerful, modernist playing. Indeed, Williams remained drawn to adventurous, modern ideas; in 1977 she performed in concert with the avant-garde pianist CECIL TAYLOR. During the last decade of her life she was honored with a Guggenheim Fellowship (1972–1973) and from 1977 until shortly before her death was an artist-in-residence at Duke University, where she taught jazz history and led the jazz orchestra. She died at home in Durham, North Carolina. A month after her death, pianists and a big band performed several of her compositions in a tribute at town hall in New York City.

Williams was an important swing pianist who sought constantly to broaden her style, and she was open to all kinds of modernist musical expressions. Influenced by such musicians as Fats Waller, Art Tatum, TEDDY WILSON, and MILT BUCKNER, she never abandoned the basic blues feeling that was at the core of her playing. Duke Ellington, in his book *Music Is My Mistress* (1973), wrote that "Mary Lou Williams is perpetually contemporary.... Her music retains a standard of quality that is timeless. She is like soul on soul" (169).

FURTHER READING

Dahl, Linda. *Morning Glory: A Biography of Mary Lou Williams* (2001).

Kernodle, Tammy L. *Soul on Soul: The Life and Music of Mary Lou Williams* (2004).

Schuller, Gunther. *The Swing Era: The Development of Jazz, 1930–1945* (1989).

Obituary: *New York Times*, 30 May 1981.

This entry is taken from the *American National Biography* and is published here with the permission of the American Council of Learned Societies.

RONALD P. DUFOUR

Williams, Melvin, Jr. (3 Nov. 1955–), United States naval officer, was born in San Diego, California, the son of MELVIN G. WILLIAMS SR. and Dora (Ruth) Williams. Williams's father served in the navy as an enlisted man and had an outstanding career, retiring as a master chief petty officer in 1978. Because he was "exposed to the navy," Williams also contemplated a navy career. "The thing that got my attention was my father's sea stories, mostly positive. I recall hearing my father and his friends laugh and I thought that this was something that sounds fun. As I got older I knew that I wanted to serve our country, and the navy became my first choice" (Telephone interview, 14 March 2007). His decision to join the navy was strengthened by the family's

move to Suitland, Maryland, in 1968, where he worked as a newsboy for the *Washington Post* and "received an education" by reading the headlines and discussing the events of that historic year with his parents. The importance of service and the understanding of national issues were thereby reinforced. His exposure to the navy was heightened when he got a job as a busboy at the Officers' Club at the Washington Navy Yard. Williams subsequently applied to the Naval Academy, but was not at first accepted. He then enlisted into the Navy Reserves in June 1973 and attended the U.S. Naval Academy Preparatory School for a year before going on to the Naval Academy in 1974.

At the Naval Academy, things went well for Williams. As he recalled, "everyone was challenged, and with the increase in minority enrollment I had only positive race-related experiences." Williams gained further confidence and exposure to the navy way of life by attending the traditional Army-Navy football game and occasionally visiting the Pentagon where his father worked in the Flag Mess. Working toward a B.S. in Mathematics, Williams also had to decide on his career specialty, a decision influenced by his Naval Academy company officer, Lieutenant Commander Jim Brown, "a surface nuclear qualified officer who saw something in me and gave me an opportunity to consider a career in nuclear power." Because he had "experience watching his father serve in the challenging submarine community," Williams decided to choose nuclear-powered submarines because he felt that it presented him with the most challenging career opportunity.

Upon graduation with the class of 1978, which also included future notable CECIL HANEY, Williams attended nuclear power school and prototype training before attending submarine school in Connecticut. He married Donna Freeland, his high school sweetheart, following graduation from the Academy; the couple would have one son, Melvin III, in 1979. Williams saw his first submarine duty when he served on the fast-attack submarine USS *Jack* as a division officer from 1980 to 1982, making two deployments and performing damage control and main propulsion systems duties. In this tour he "learned a lot about what was required of a submarine officer." From 1982 to 1984 Williams served as a joint service cruise missile (Tomahawk) project officer at the Defense Mapping Agency in Washington, D.C., and earned a master's degree at Catholic University in Engineering in 1984. His service as project officer proved valuable in his future submarine duties.

Williams next served on the missile submarine USS *Woodrow Wilson* (Gold crew; all missile submarines have two crews and two captains, each referred to as the Blue or the Gold, so that the boat may remain constantly deployed—while one crew is at sea, the other is ashore for rest and training) from 1984 to 1987 as engineer officer. As he recalled, this "was a very large increase in responsibility because about 60 percent of the crew were under the engineers' watch…. It was exciting, challenging, and I made mistakes, but it helped me in my leadership development." Missile submarines are assigned set patrol routes, so that the missiles they carry remain within range of certain enemy targets. Because the enemy (at this point in time, the Soviets) knew that these subs were out there (but not precisely where they were), the submarines were viewed as a deterrent threat, the idea being that enemies would not launch arms against the United States because they knew that American boats were out there and could quickly retaliate. Even today missile boats perform similar deterrent patrols. The Soviets of course made these same patrols, and both sides had their fast-attack submarines out in the Atlantic tracking boats belonging to the other side. During Williams's four deterrent patrols in the Atlantic on the *Woodrow Wilson*, the ship earned the Meritorious Unit Commendation.

Following a stint of duty on the Atlantic Fleet Nuclear Examining Board from 1987 to 1989, Williams's next submarine assignment was on the fast-attack submarine USS *Louisville* as executive officer. From September 1989 to January 1992 Williams and the crew earned the Navy Unit Commendation and played a historic part in combat operations against Iraq in Operation Desert Storm. Indeed, the *Louisville* executed the first Tomahawk cruise missile strike by a nuclear submarine in history. This duty gave Williams valuable experience and insight that would become hallmarks in his career—he later stated that "it was my first exposure to combat operations (with the associated uncertainty) and reinforced in my mind the need for advance preparedness and training for all contingencies possible. This was an appreciation for the value of readiness." Williams's subsequent shore duty at the Bureau of Naval Personnel was followed by his appointment to command of the Trident missile submarine USS *Nebraska*, nicknamed "Big Red," as skipper of the Gold crew in August 1994.

Williams's rise to command was historic in two ways—not only was he just the fourth African American ever named to command a submarine (joining C. A. "PETE" TZOMES, TONY WATSON, and WILLIAM BUNDY) in a group that would later become known as the Centennial 7, but he was also the first African American officer to command a U.S. Navy ballistic missile submarine. However, while Williams's achievement as an African American gaining this command was highlighted by the press, he downplayed this achievement. Williams would acknowledge these matters when asked, but as a naval officer he did not dwell on the navy's past record of diversity or lack thereof. Interestingly, he was also one of the first officers at the rank of commander to command a Trident submarine. Such a command previously required the higher rank of captain and Williams knew that he had to succeed. Indeed, he did just that; his crew, in close cooperation with the Blue crew, earned the *Nebraska* not only a Meritorious Unit Commendation, but also the navy and air force's Top Strategic Missile Unit Omaha Trophy Award for excellence, a first for a Trident submarine.

Williams's subsequent career as a naval officer was equally accomplished, as well as varied. In addition to furthering his education as a joint service officer to the highest levels, he steadily increased his major command responsibilities. He commanded Submarine Squadron 4 in Groton, Connecticut, from 1999 to 2000 and subsequently served as chief of staff for Carrier Strike Group 5 in Yokosuka, Japan, as second in command of the navy's only forward-deployed carrier strike group. During Operation Enduring Freedom, after the terrorist attacks of September 2001, his service during deployments "opened my aperture and broadened my navy experience… I learned quickly that leadership is leadership regardless of your background." For this service, Williams received the Legion of Merit (this being his fourth time, it was presented with Gold Star in lieu of a fourth award) for his group's combat effectiveness and "highly effective warfighting deliberate planning process" and "focus on planning and readiness" that "contributed to the short notice response and superior performance … and his exceptional professional ability, personal initiative, and total dedication to duty" (Clark, Legion of Merit Citation). Subsequent to this duty, Williams was elevated to flag rank as rear admiral and served as commander of Submarine Group 9 in Bangor, Washington, followed by duty as director of Global Operations at Strategic Command headquarters at Offutt Air Force Base in Nebraska. This job involving joint operations with all branches of the military provided Williams with valuable insights into a wide variety of military operations.

Williams was promoted to vice admiral, just the sixth African American naval officer to attain this rank after SAMUEL GRAVELY, Walt Davis, J. PAUL REASON, Ed Moore, and Dave Brewer. In 2005 Williams became deputy commander of U.S. Fleet Forces Command. Through all of his years of service, Williams found that "the common thread has been the privilege serving and defending our country … My passion is serving others through leadership and helping others to grow and learn."

FURTHER READING

The quotations in this entry are from the author's telephone interview with Vice Admiral Melvin Williams Jr. on 14 March 2007 and follow-up e-mail exchanges.

Clark, Admiral Vernon E. *Legion of Merit—Captain Melvin G. Williams, Jr.* (Citation dated 19 March 2002).

United States Navy Biographies. "Vice Admiral Melvin G. "Mel" Williams, Jr." Available online at http://www.navy.mil/navydata/bios/navybio. asp?bioid=299.

GLENN ALLEN KNOBLOCK

Williams, Melvin, Sr. (27 May 1933–), master chief petty officer, United States Navy, was born in East St. Louis, Illinois, the oldest of eight children of Robert and Dimple Williams. His parents migrated to the area from Mississippi after the devastating floods of 1927. Williams's mother worked as a domestic and his father worked as a longshoreman and truck driver. Although Williams graduated from a segregated high school in St. Louis in 1951, he lived with his aunt in 1949 in Tacoma, Washington, attending an integrated school there. He described that year as "life changing"—in Tacoma, Williams "learned how to get along and study and became a better student" (Telephone interview, 10 March 2007). In his first job after high school graduation, Williams "earned a man's wages" working as a "gandy dancer"—laying railroad tracks on an all-black section gang on the Wabash Line Railroad before joining the navy in late 1951.

The navy that Williams had joined was, like the rest of the American military, in a state of flux when it came to African American service. Although President Harry S. Truman had officially desegregated the military in 1947, all the service branches were slow to implement change. Williams went to navy boot camp in San Diego and "loved it because it wasn't segregated," but he soon learned that he would be assigned to the rating of steward, a role traditionally assigned to blacks and other minorities in the navy since the 1890s. Though Williams was assured that he could later change his rating, this proved untrue and "the entire experience was quite a shock" (Knoblock, 180). In fact, many young black recruits joining the navy with a high school diploma, "a big deal back then," resented their assignment to the Steward's Branch and subsequent duty serving white officers. How, then, did such men survive their navy experience? The answer, at least for Williams, lay in those stewards that came before them: "We had to be calmed down and the stewards that came in during the years from 1932–1945 helped us … they were there for us, taught us to endure, and how to survive. They set the stage for those of us who stayed in [the navy]…. I liked their style and wanted to emulate them." Williams proceeded to do just that and, although he did not know it then, he became a primary force in moving the navy toward true racial equality years later.

Williams married Ruth Pettes in 1953. The Williamses had four children: Melvin Jr., Sharon, Veronica, and Kenneth.

Williams's first sea duty came aboard the carrier USS *Hancock* where he served from 1953 to 1955, followed by assignments on other surface craft until 1959. By the time he left the destroyer USS *Hollister*, however, Williams had been a third-class petty officer for eight years and was "worried and nervous" about the lack of promotion for himself and other stewards. He seriously considered leaving the navy, but reenlisted at the ten-year mark instead and volunteered for submarine duty. Starting out on USS *Carp* in 1961, Williams earned his silver dolphins (dolphins are the distinctive uniform insignia of a submariner, indicating that the wearer has "qualified" as a submariner by learning all aspects of submarine operations) and subsequently served on three more submarines and made nine Polaris patrols combined on the USS *Thomas Jefferson* and USS *James K. Polk* from 1961 to 1968. During this time Williams rose to chief steward and became recognized for his distinguished leadership, a fact firmly evidenced with his subsequent assignment to the presidential yacht *Sequoia*. Though a prestigious appointment, Williams later recalled that "I didn't want it [duty on *Sequoia*] … When I asked why I was being sent there, they told me they only took the best" (Knoblock, 225). This position became the springboard for Williams's later opportunities, for it was on *Sequoia* from 1968 to 1970 that Williams became experienced in dealing with foreign dignitaries, government officials from the president on down, and high-ranking naval officers and U.S. Navy Department officials. From the *Sequoia*, Williams was assigned to the Pentagon as lead chief in the Flag Mess of the chief of naval operations (CNO), Admiral Elmo Zumwalt.

In Zumwalt, Williams found a kindred spirit, one who was committed to the ideal of equality for all who served in the navy. With the knowledge that he had a ready audience, Williams offered his ideas on the racial situation to Zumwalt and others on an ever-increasing basis. His letter and suggestions in May 1970 to Colonel Theus, chairman of the Inter-Service Task Force on Education in Race Relations, referencing racial incidents occurring on Okinawa between black and white servicemen, were incorporated into the group's findings. When racial conflicts flared up on several navy ships, including the carrier USS *Kitty Hawk*, in 1972, Zumwalt asked Williams for his opinions about the overall causes of the disturbances. In 1974 he was part of a three-man group assigned to investigate the complaints of stewards at the Naval Academy. But Williams's greatest contribution to the navy came when he prepared a position paper in June 1974, submitted to Admiral Zumwalt, regarding a proposed rating change for stewards. The early 1970s were a difficult time for race relations in the navy and the treatment and highly publicized misuse of its Steward's Branch. While at the Pentagon, Williams learned that the navy was considering abolishing the steward's rating and merging it with that of commissaryman. With years of service in a wide variety of naval branches, he was determined to offer his insights about how this merger might be managed successfully and proceeded to draft his ideas. Ironically, his work in helping the navy, which "didn't know how to change … but was worth saving," most benefited not African Americans but men from the Philippines and other Pacific islanders who constituted over 80 percent of Steward's Branch personnel. Indeed by 1974 blacks constituted less than 5 percent of navy stewards, whereas whites (first admitted to serve as stewards in 1967) constituted 12 percent. Williams's efforts were truly an exercise in promoting diversity and fairness. Following the submission of his position paper to Zumwalt, Williams was appointed as senior member to an eleven-man Steward Rating Study Group. In September 1974 he received a Letter of Appreciation for his "thoroughness and professionalism" and "very successful results" (from Williams's personal service records). When the Steward's Branch of the navy was effectively eliminated on 1 January 1975 and the new rating of mess management specialist (renamed culinary specialist in 2004) was created, Williams's original ideas were adopted almost in their entirety. Putting his own ideas to the test, Williams returned to sea duty from 1976 to 1978 as a master chief mess management specialist on the destroyer tender *Piedmont*. While on this tour Williams was promoted to command master chief with responsibilities for the well-being and morale of the entire crew. Not only did his ratings change result in a newfound pride among those in the navy's food service division, but they also generated real opportunities for promotion and future career possibilities. He retired in 1978.

Williams's son, MELVIN WILLIAMS JR. became just the fourth African American ever to command a submarine in December 1993 when he became skipper of the USS *Nebraska*. While visiting his son's ship, Williams recalled the powerful emotion of the day, stating that "I had lunch in the wardroom…. I looked up at the mess management specialist who was serving my food and saw he was a white American. I looked up to the head of the table and in the commanding officer's seat, I looked into the face of my son…. I get choked up thinking about it now" (Knoblock, 256).

In addition to his son, a vice admiral and fleet force deputy commander, his grandson, Marine Major Ahmed Williamson, graduated from the Naval Academy and earned a Bronze Star for his service in Iraq in 2005, and his granddaughter, Dallis Rawls, became an air force captain. After retirement, Williams worked on a number of initiatives to gain official recognition for the stewards that served in World War II.

FURTHER READING

Many of the quotations in this entry came from the author's interview with Mel Williams on 10 March 2007, as well as personal correspondence dating from 2004 through 2007.

Knoblock, Glenn A. *Black Submariners in the United States Navy, 1940–1975* (2005).

GLENN ALLEN KNOBLOCK

Williams, Milton Alexander, Sr. (28 June 1938–3 Dec. 2005), elder, pastor, and bishop of the African Methodist Episcopal Zion Church, was born in Mocksville, in Davie County, North Carolina, the son of Booker T. and Lillian Gaither Williams. He had two brothers and two sisters.

After graduating from Central Davie High School, Williams enrolled at Livingstone College in Salisbury, North Carolina, a school founded and supported by the AME Zion Church. His early ministry was intertwined with his education, as he delivered his first sermon in 1958 at his family's home church, St. John AME Zion in Mocksville, then served as pastor of Steward Chapel and Hayden Grove Circuit, North Carolina, 1958–1963. During this time, he earned a bachelor's degree from Livingstone in 1960, also being ordained that year as a deacon in the AME Zion church. Entering Hood Theological Seminary (also in Salisbury and linked with Livingstone), he was ordained as an elder in 1962 at Charlotte, North Carolina, by Bishop WILLIAM J. WALLS, and completed a master's degree in Divinity (M.Div.) at Hood in 1963. He was a member of the Alpha Phi Alpha fraternity.

Williams married Lula Mae Goolsby, a teacher in the Charlotte-Mecklenburg school system, and herself a future minister of the AME Zion Church, 8 June 1963 at Cedar Grove Baptist Church at Mocksville. Reverend Williams held two more, early ministerial assignments in his native North Carolina, Snow Hill in Newton, 1963–1964, and Wardell Chapel in Shelby, 1964–1965. In keeping with original Methodist tradition and practice, the AME Zion church has an itinerant ministry; pastors are subject to reassignment at any time, and are generally renewed in their current church assignment, or transferred by their bishops, at meetings of the Annual Conference.

Williams moved to Buffalo, New York, in 1965, initially assigned to Durham Memorial AME Zion Church, where he served as pastor until 1970. That year, he was chosen as presiding elder of the Rochester-Syracuse-Buffalo District. He served three terms as chair of the Buffalo branch of the National Association for the Advancement of Colored People (NAACP). When race riots broke out in 1967, Williams received threatening phone calls, then suffered a broken arm and burned hand fleeing an arson attack on his home. He served as president of the Community Action Organization of Erie County, and director of the local Girl Scout Council, the Black Business Development Corporation, and the National Council of Christians and Jews.

In 1971 Williams established Shaw Memorial AME Zion Church in Buffalo, in the building of the historic Plymouth Methodist Episcopal Church, which had lost most of its membership in an exodus to the Buffalo suburbs. The Western New York Conference of the United Methodist Church donated the property to the Western New York Conference of the AME Zion Church. Williams carried both responsibilities until 1981, also serving as executive secretary of the AME Zion Minister's and Laymen's Association, 1974–1982. Shaw Memorial remained relatively small in numbers and, after Williams's transfer to Big Zion AME Zion, Mobile, Alabama, in 1981, eventually closed. The building later housed an art museum.

Reverend Williams was elected to the board of bishops in 1988, the 82nd bishop in the history of the church, at the 43rd Quadrennial General Conference. The General Conference, in conformance with traditional practice in most Methodist denominations, is the highest governing body, meeting every four years, with both ministerial and lay delegates. Bishops fill an administrative function, rather than making authoritative pronouncements on matters of faith and doctrine.

Williams was initially assigned as presiding prelate of the 12th Episcopal District, 1988–1992, traveling from his home in Charlotte, North Carolina, to West Africa and Britain. During this time he organized three new conferences, Mid-Ghana and Côte d'Ivoire in Africa and Manchester-Midland in England. Opening six churches in the French-speaking West African nation fulfilled a long-held goal for AME Zion, of moving beyond the English-speaking nations of West Africa. Moving to the 5th Episcopal District in 1992, renamed in 1996 the Mid-Atlantic II district, Williams began twelve years of service overseeing the Virginia, Philadelphia-Baltimore, East Tennessee–Virginia, India, London-Birmingham, and Manchester-Midland conferences.

In 1995 Williams participated in a ministerial protest against "gangsta rap" lyrics found to be sacrilegious, demeaning toward women, and sexually explicit, organized by C. DELORES TUCKER, president of the National Political Congress of Black Women. Williams was host bishop for the AME Zion bicentennial 1996 General Conference, with Full Gospel AME Zion Church in Temple Hills, Maryland, as host church. He also observed the 200th anniversary by initiating and supervising formation of Judah Temple AME Zion Church, in Prince George's County, Maryland. Reverend Scot C. Moore was called as Judah Temple's first pastor, located in the first suburban county surrounding the District of Columbia to have an African American majority population.

Bishop Williams's tenure in the Mid-Atlantic II Episcopal District was unavoidably marked by the high-profile dispute over the property of Full Gospel AME Zion Church, which grew from twenty-four members in 1981 to twenty thousand in 1996, when it hosted the General Conference. Three years later, Reverend John A. Cherry, who led the church during its substantial growth, announced that God had told him to "get out of Zion" (*Christianity Today,* 12 June 2000; *Baltimore Sun,* 8 Sept. 2000). AME Zion, like most Christian denominations that have not adopted a strictly congregational form of government, vests ownership of church property in the denomination, not the local church, so it was Williams's duty to insist that Cherry couldn't take the property with him.

Litigation lasted several years, and was not fully resolved until 2009, after Williams's death. Courts are barred by the First Amendment from making any judgment on matters of faith and doctrine, and often defer on church property disputes to the internal governance of the church, although litigation was prolonged by Maryland statute and case law, which, according to the state court of appeals, "contemplates a congregational form of government." The real property in dispute, but not the personal property, ultimately returned to the new Full Gospel AME Zion, established after Cherry's departure.

A lifetime member of the NAACP, Williams served on the Board of Trustees of Livingstone College, and served as chair or vice-chair of several boards, including Christian Education, International Evangelism, and Statistics and Records. In August 2004, reassignment among the board of bishops again moved Bishop Williams to his final responsibility overseeing the Midwest District. After little more than a year, Bishop Williams died at his home in Belleville, Illinois, at the age of sixty-seven; services were held in Varick Auditorium at Livingstone College, in Salisbury, North Carolina. He was survived by his wife, Reverend Lula G. Williams, an ordained elder of the church; a brother, Barry Williams; daughters Angela, Cynthia, and Milicent; one son, Reverend Milton A. Williams Jr.; and seven grandchildren.

FURTHER READING

Hoggard, Bishop James Clinton. *African Methodist Episcopal Zion Church, 1972–1996* (1998).
Obituaries: *Greensboro News and Record* (NC), 10 Dec. 2005, B9; *Buffalo News* (NY), 9 Dec. 2005, D5; *Salisbury Post* (NC), 8 Dec. 2005; *Charlotte Observer* (NC), 9 Dec. 2005

CHARLES ROSENBERG

Williams, Moses (1849–23 Aug. 1899), Civil War and Indian Wars soldier and Medal of Honor recipient, was born in Carroll, Orleans Parish, Louisiana. While nothing certain is known about his early life, his place of birth suggests that Williams was likely born enslaved and working on one of the many cotton plantations in Orleans Parish until the arrival of the Union Army during the Civil War in early 1862. When the army of General Ulysses Grant set up a supply depot in the area during the campaign against the key Confederate stronghold of Vicksburg, Mississippi, the depot quickly grew into a large settlement with the arrival of large numbers of black refugees. Among them was Moses Williams, who arrived to the Union lines without his parents, according to army records, and subsequently gained employment as a laborer.

Moses Williams began his career as a cavalryman on 11 October 1864, when he enlisted in the Union Army at Vicksburg, Mississippi, joining Company I of the 3rd Regiment of U.S. Colored Cavalry. Recruited by and credited to the state of Massachusetts, Williams was paid a $200 enlistment bounty. Standing but five feet, four inches tall, he nonetheless stood out among his fellow soldiers, and in less than a month, on 10 November, was promoted to corporal. During his year and a half of Civil War service, Williams performed scouting duties, took part in the unit's raids in Mississippi to destroy Confederate rail lines, and battled Confederate forces at Franklin, Mississippi, from December 1864 to January 1865. The experience Williams gained as a cavalryman in the Civil War would serve him well in the future. At the war's end, Williams was mustered out of the Union Army on 26 January 1866 and returned to Orleans Parish, living in Lake Providence and earning a living as a farmer. His time as a civilian would not last long.

After the end of the Civil War, the substantial contribution made by the black soldiers serving in the Union Army had made an impression on army officials in Washington, DC, and by 1866 Congress had authorized the establishment of six regiments (later reduced to four) to be manned entirely by black enlisted men and noncommissioned officers, to be led by white senior officers. Many of the recruits for these regiments, including the 9th and 10th Cavalry regiments, were found among those men who had fought in the Civil War. While the recruiting efforts for the 9th Cavalry Regiment began in the area of New Orleans, they soon were expanded, and the area of Lake Providence, Louisiana, proved to be profitable; among the fifty or so men recruited here was the Civil War veteran Moses Williams. He joined the 9th Cavalry on 1 October 1866, enlisting for a period of five years, and by doing so became one of the first professional black soldiers in the U.S. Army. Employed on the frontier fighting a variety of Native American tribes in a long-running conflict known as the Indian Wars, these soldiers, men like Williams, EMANUEL STANCE, THOMAS BOYNE, and HENRY JOHNSON, played a key role in facilitating America's great westward expansion and soon gained the nickname "Buffalo Soldiers."

By the end of his first term of service in 1871, Moses Williams had achieved the rank of first sergeant and was one of the 9th Cavalry's most experienced soldiers. To recount Moses Williams entire army career, which lasted over thirty years, would be to also tell the storied history of the 9th Cavalry; they are one and the same. However, Moses Williams's finest moment as a soldier, one that would eventually result in the award of the Medal of Honor, occurred in 1881 in the Cuchillo Negro Mountains in New Mexico during the Apache Campaign. On 16 August, Company I of the 9th Cavalry received word that a group of about fifty warriors under the command of Nana, one of the greatest of the Apache chiefs, had attacked the Chavez ranch and brutally murdered its owner and his family, as well as several ranch hands. Elements of Company I, along with a group of angry citizens, took off in pursuit of the Apache warriors and soon caught up with them. Thus began a series of running battles that lasted for hours; Lieutenant George Burnett commanded the front group, while Sergeant Moses Williams was placed in command of the right flank, with citizen soldiers manning the left. Despite fierce Apache fire, the black troopers gradually forced the Apaches to retreat from one ridge line to another until they reached the foothills of the Cuchillo Negro Mountains and were forced to make a final stand. The men under Burnett's command, including Moses Williams, tried to circle to the rear of the Apache position, but were nearly caught in a trap, saved from possible destruction by William's keen eye in spying a warrior lying in wait. A gun battle then ensued, which resulted in Burnett losing his horse, and nearly all of his black troopers, except Williams and AUGUSTUS WALLEY, beating a hasty retreat. While Burnett and Walley stayed in position and returned fire against the Apaches, Williams was sent down to gather the command and bring them back, which he succeeded in doing. The battle continued on, with the Apache warriors more than holding their own,

until the commander of Company I, Lieutenant Gustavus Valois, ordered Burnett and his men to retreat. Williams and Walley, along with Burnett, covered the retreat with gunfire while the remainder of the men made it to safety below. Just as the rearguard was ready to withdraw, three wounded soldiers called for help; the men were pinned down several hundred yards away in the open, but Burnett and Williams provided cover fire. Two of the men made it to safety on their own, while Private Walley dashed to the third, too badly wounded to move, and carried him back on horseback. As Burnett, Williams, and Walley were about to leave again, a fourth wounded man was located; he, too, was rescued, this time by Burnett, with Williams providing the cover fire. Soon thereafter, the battle was ended; while Nana and his Apache warriors had eluded capture, the actions of First Sergeant Moses Williams, Private Walley, and Lieutenant Burnett had helped save the day for the cavalry. All three of these men would eventually receive the Medal of Honor, but, for reasons unknown, recognition would not come for over a decade. Moses Williams received the award on 12 November 1896; though recognition was late in coming, there is no doubt that Williams's actions during the fight were the most notable. Burnett would later comment about Williams' "coolness, bravery, and unflinching devotion to duty in standing by me in an open exposed position under a heavy fire" (Schubert, p. 83).

Just a few years after receiving the Medal of Honor, Ordnance Sergeant Moses Williams retired from the army in 1898 and settled in Vancouver, Washington. Sadly, he would die of a heart attack the following year, leaving behind his wife and child. He is buried in the Vancouver Barracks Cemetery in Vancouver, where a Medal of Honor headstone marks his final resting place.

FURTHER READING

Hanna, Charles W. *African American Recipients of the Medal of Honor* (2002).
Schubert, Frank N. *Black Valor: Buffalo Soldiers and the Medal of Honor, 1870–1898* (1997).

GLENN ALLEN KNOBLOCK

Williams, Paul Revere (18 Feb. 1894–23 Jan. 1980), architect, was born in Los Angeles, California, to Chester Stanley Williams and Lila Wright Churchill. Orphaned by the age of four, he was raised by foster parents. His foster father, Charles Clarkson, was a bank janitor. Paul was one of only a few African American students at Sentous

Elementary School on Pico Street. While at Los Angeles Polytechnic High School, Paul decided to become an architect after reading about the African American architect WILLIAM SIDNEY PITTMAN, BOOKER T. WASHINGTON's son-in-law and a graduate of Tuskegee Institute and Drexel Institute in Philadelphia.

Paul graduated high school in 1912, and the following year he went to work for Wilbur Cook Jr., a landscape architect. Two years later he took a job as a draftsman for noted Pasadena residential architect Reginald Johnson, and in 1919 Hollywood architect Arthur Kelly hired him as a junior architect. Williams's art training had begun with evening classes from 1915 to 1920 at the Los Angeles *atelier* of the Beaux Arts Institute of Design, where he learned rendering techniques and the use of color. From 1916 to 1919 he attended the School of Architecture at the University of California at Los Angeles, although he left before earning a degree. In 1922 Williams took a position in the office of John Austin, an architect specializing in schools and government buildings.

Williams married Los Angeles native and socialite Della Mae Givens in June 1917. They had two children, Marilyn Francis and Norma Lucille, the latter of whom became an interior designer. In 1923 Williams opened his own office at the 1400 Stock Exchange Building in downtown Los Angeles. He secured his first major construction project by promising auto industrialist Everett Lobban Cord a complete set of sketches for a house, fifteen-car garage, swimming pool, and stables within twenty-four hours. Williams won the commission for the $250,000 country house. From the 1930s to the 1950s—his most productive period—Williams's office was located on the top floor of the swank Wilshire Building in downtown Beverly Hills. Williams was the most successful African American architect of his era in a business that necessitates a delicate balance of art and commerce. In 1948 his practice grossed $140,000. His drafting room, which at the firm's height included twenty full-time people, was an interracial mix of Chinese, German, and African American architects. Unlike James Garrott, another Los Angeles African American architect, Williams did not go out of his way to apprentice "junior" architects. With as many as thirty projects on the boards simultaneously, he needed experienced architects in order to meet production deadlines.

A competitive tennis player, Williams was lithe and muscular. His matinee-idol good looks and

Paul Revere Williams, architect, photographed c. 1950s. (Schomburg Center for Research in Black Culture, New York Public Library.)

chic Southern California "cool" style of attire helped Williams get his foot in the door of potential white clients. Once inside, he marketed himself assiduously. Williams was a medal-winning freehand artist who rendered all the buildings he designed. He taught himself to sketch upside down (right side up to the client). An eye-catching attention-getter, the technique also positioned him on the opposite side of the table from clients, avoiding a hovering stance that made some white clients uncomfortable. Swiftly and with flair, Williams sketched design ideas before awestruck potential clients. By 1935 Williams had received commissions for close to forty houses.

During the 1930s and 1940s Williams became known as the "architect to the stars of Hollywood," and over the years his celebrity clients included Tyrone Power, Robert Holden, ZaSu Pitts, Julie London, Lon Chaney, William Paley, Charles Cottrell, Will Hays, Desi Arnaz and Lucille Ball, Anthony Quinn, and Otto Preminger. In 1956 Williams teamed up with his daughter Norma in designing the interior of Frank Sinatra's swinging bachelor's pad, creating custom-designed chandeliers, lamps, and furniture. Williams also designed several Hollywood restaurants and lounges famous for celebrity watching: Chasen's (1936), Perino's (1949), and the Beverly Hills Hotel Polo Lounge (1959).

Williams's architectural style captured the casual, informal, Mediterranean "look" characteristic of hot, sunny climates such as Southern California's. Williams was neither an innovator nor trendsetter like Frank Lloyd Wright, whom he knew personally and admired professionally. For nonresidential buildings he generally chose a "historic" Tudor or Georgian style, applying exterior details to a functional façade. For palatial homes he used a more modernist approach. Williams described his design philosophy in *Architecture Magazine* in 1940 as "the pleasing assembly of parts and not the assembly of pleasing parts." Williams was a master of interior color coordination and was meticulous about interior architectural detailing, whether it was the joinery of a spiral grand stair or cabinetry trim. Williams was a versatile residential architect capable of designing $100,000 country houses as well as small, practical houses for World War II veterans. A collection of his floor plans for houses costing less than $5,000 were compiled in two books Williams wrote in 1946: *Small Homes of Tomorrow* and *New Homes for Today*. With the publication of these books, Williams became the first African American architect to have his books distributed nationwide. Flattering profiles on Williams in *Life*, and later *Ebony*, further heightened his name recognition and attracted clients.

Over his career Williams made a profound impression on the architecture of Los Angeles. While most of his business came from wealthy white clients building homes in upscale Los Angeles neighborhoods like Beverly Hills, Pacific Palisades, and Bel Air, his firm also designed commercial real estate, schools, and public buildings. Williams's designs include the Shrine Auditorium, the Hollywood YMCA, the Los Angeles County Court House, and the MCA Building in Beverly Hills, for which he won an American Institute of Architects (AIA) award in 1939. In the 1960s Williams served as an associate architect in the design of the Los Angeles International Airport, whose futuristic look became a visual icon of its era.

In 1936, acting on a referral from a friend in the industry who was a former client of Williams's, Adam Gimbel commissioned Williams to renovate the Beverly Hills annex of the Saks Fifth Avenue department store. Williams's use of motifs more typical of residential architecture—oval recessed ceilings, bowed counters, and curvilinear display cases—was credited with increasing retail sales. Other commercial projects followed over the years, including designs for the Arrowhead Springs Hotel, the W. & J. Sloan department store, the Palm Springs Tennis Club, the Golden State

Mutual Life Insurance building, and the renovation of the Ambassador Hotel. Ecumenical in pursuit of church commissions, Williams designed the First Church of Christ, Scientist, in Reno, Nevada (1939), and St. Nicholas Orthodox Church (1948) and Founders Church of Religious Science (1960), both in Los Angeles. In 1962, at the behest of television comedian and benefactor Danny Thomas, Williams volunteered to design St. Jude's Children's Hospital in Memphis, Tennessee.

Williams was well aware, however, that as an African American, he could not live in many of the neighborhoods in which he designed houses. In the July 1937 *American* magazine article "I Am a Negro," Williams conceded, "Sometimes I have dreamed of living there," referring to a client's home. "I could afford such a home. But this evening, leaving my office, I returned to my small, inexpensive home in an unrestricted, comparatively undesirable section of Los Angeles … because … I am a Negro." Williams did, however, make several contributions to the architecture of Los Angeles's African American community, including the Second Baptist Church (1924) and the 28th Street Colored YMCA.

Williams was the first African American architect with enough government buildings in his portfolio to qualify as having a government practice. As early as 1925 Williams was commissioned to design a U.S. Post Office in Ontario, California. President Herbert H. Hoover appointed him to direct the designing of a Negro Memorial to be erected in Washington, D.C. (which was never built). In 1937, in association with Washington, D.C., African American architect Hilyard Robert Robinson, Williams designed the 274-unit Langston Terrace Public Housing, the first federally financed public housing project. Back in Los Angeles, he worked as chief architect of the Pueblo Del Rio, a housing project built in 1941. After World War II Williams and six engineers formed Allied Engineers, Inc., which was contracted in 1947 by the Defense Department to design U.S. Navy bases in Los Alamitos, Long Beach, and San Diego, California. He was also the architect for the Grave of the Unknown Sailor (1953) at Pearl Harbor.

Williams gathered an impressive list of "firsts." He was the first African American appointed to serve on the Los Angeles Planning Commission, which he did beginning in 1920. In 1923 he became the first black American architect licensed in the state of California; in 1935, the first admitted to the AIA; and in 1957, the first elevated to the distinguished rank of AIA Fellow. In 1943 he was the first African American chosen to serve on a Los Angeles County grand jury, and in 1953 he became the first architect to win the NAACP's prestigious Spingarn Medal.

Paul Williams closed his office in the mid-1970s, having designed more than three thousand buildings, and gracefully transitioned into retirement. Suffering from diabetes, he died at age eighty-six in 1980. His funeral was held at the First African Methodist Episcopal Church in Los Angeles, which he had designed seventeen years earlier.

FURTHER READING

Hudson, Karen E. *Paul Revere Williams: A Legacy of Style* (1993).

DRECK WILSON

Williams, Peter, Jr. (1780?–17 Oct. 1840), clergyman and abolitionist, was born in New Brunswick, New Jersey, the son of PETER WILLIAMS SR., a slave, and Mary Durham, a black indentured servant from St. Kitts. A patriot soldier during the American Revolution, his father was sexton and undertaker for John Street Methodist Church in New York City. In an unusual arrangement, the church in 1783 purchased him from his departing Loyalist master and allowed him to purchase himself over time, completing his freedom in 1796. A founder of the African Methodist Episcopal Zion Church and a tobacconist and funeral home owner, he was a leader of the small black middle class in New York City.

Williams Jr. was educated first at the African Free School and tutored privately by a white minister, Reverend Thomas Lyell, of John Street Methodist Church. He became involved in Sunday afternoon black congregations at Trinity Episcopal Church, and in 1798 he was confirmed by John Henry Hobart. Williams was licensed by the Episcopal bishop in 1812 when the fledgling black Episcopalian group elected him lay reader. In the next six years Williams organized the congregation as a separate institution, acquired land, and constructed a church costing over eight thousand dollars, much of it contributed by wealthy white Episcopalians. In 1819 the new edifice was consecrated as St. Philip's African Church. The following year the wooden church burned down. It was fully insured, however, and a new brick church was quickly constructed. Baptismal rolls indicate that the church's membership included primarily black middle-class tradesmen and female domestics. Among the young candidates for baptism were future abolitionists JAMES MCCUNE SMITH, GEORGE THOMAS DOWNING, ALEXANDER CRUMMELL, and CHARLES L. REASON.

Williams was a significant figure in black New York politics. He published a speech he had delivered celebrating the close of the slave trade in 1808, *An Oration on the Abolition of the Slave Trade: Delivered in the African Church, in the City of New York*. He was a prominent member of the African Society for Mutual Relief, a benefit and burial organization. In 1817 he preached the funeral sermon after the death of his close friend, colonizationist PAUL CUFFE SR.

Despite deep reservations about the white American Colonization Society, Williams remained open to the possibility of voluntary black migration out of the United States. He favored colonization to the black republic of Haiti and visited there in 1824. In 1830 he delivered a speech at St. Philip's for the benefit of the Wilberforce colony in Canada. He also helped JOHN BROWN RUSSWURM emigrate to Liberia in 1829 under the aegis of the American Colonization Society. Williams increasingly believed, however, that blacks should remain in the United States to work for full citizenship. He eventually denounced the efforts of the American Colonization Society as racist.

Although Williams enjoyed equality in reform organizations, he was forced to accept an inferior status within the Episcopal Church, where he finally advanced to priesthood in 1826. His mentor, Bishop Henry Hobart, counseled him not to seek representation for himself or St. Philip's at the diocesan convention, even though all white clerics and churches assumed this privilege. Williams nevertheless accepted these limitations.

Williams was ubiquitous in black reform efforts in the late 1820s and 1830s. He was cofounder in 1827 of *Freedom's Journal*, the first black newspaper. A staunch believer in black education, in 1833 he helped found the Phoenix Society in New York, which enabled poor blacks to attend school, encouraged church attendance, and established a library. Williams personally assisted several young blacks, including Alexander Crummell, and frequently wrote letters of recommendation to potential white employers. Very active in the early black national convention movement, Williams was inspired by the 1831 convention to attempt to establish a manual training college in New Haven, Connecticut (the attempt was unsuccessful).

In 1833 Williams became deeply involved in the American Anti-Slavery Society as one of six black managers. In 1834 he suffered terribly for his beliefs.

During early July, white mobs, angered by abolitionist efforts and competition with blacks for jobs, and inflamed by rumors of interracial marriages, terrorized New York Citsy blacks for three days. After hearing rumors that Williams performed an interracial marriage, a mob sacked and burned St. Philip's and its rectory. Rather than support and defend Williams, Bishop Benjamin T. Onderdonk demanded that Williams refrain from public abolitionist activity. Reluctantly, Williams acceded to Onderdonk's commands. In a moving statement, published in New York newspapers, he described childhood conversations with his father about his Revolutionary War service. His father's words, he said, "filled my soul with an ardent love for the American government." Williams longed for the day when his brethren "would all have abundant reason to rejoice in the glorious Declaration of American Independence." He also expressed his lifelong love for New York City. Although his congregation supported him, acquiescence cost him much respect among younger, more militant black abolitionists. Williams continued to work for social reform and led St. Philip's until his death in New York City.

FURTHER READING

Williams, Peter, Jr. "Response to Bishop Benjamin T. Onderdonk," *Journal of Negro History* 11 (1926): 181–85.

DeCosta, B. F. *Three Score and Ten: The Story of St. Philip's Church* (1889).

Porter, Dorothy, ed. *Early Negro Writing, 1760–1834* (1971).

Ripley, C. Peter, et al., eds. *The Black Abolitionist Papers* (5 vols., 1985–1992), especially vol. 3.

This entry is taken from the *American National Biography* and is published here with the permission of the American Council of Learned Societies.

GRAHAM HODGES

Williams, Peter, Sr. (1749–21 Feb. 1824), tobacconist, sexton of John Street Methodist Church, and founding trustee of the African or Zion Chapel (later named "Mother Zion," the first African Methodist Episcopal Zion, or AMEZ, church in the United States), was born on Beekman Street in New York City, the son of the African slaves George and Diana. At the time of his birth as many as one in five New York City residents were slaves, a percentage greater than any other British colonial area north of the Chesapeake. Two events in Peter Williams's early adulthood dramatically shaped his future. At some undetermined time, his owners sold him to James Aymar in New York

City. From Aymar, Williams learned the tobacconist trade, providing him skills that would one day make him one of the wealthiest blacks in the city. Also as a young man Williams attended Methodist meetings, and he converted to Methodism in the mid-1760s. Soon thereafter he married a fellow Methodist convert, Mary Durham, also called Molly. Peter and Mary had one son, PETER WILLIAMS JR., who was born sometime around 1780.

In the wake of a series of revivals known as the Great Awakening, blacks in North America heard Christian messages with greater frequency. Itinerant ministers preached to lower-class audiences, who had formerly avoided services in established churches. Many blacks found the Methodists particularly attractive, for the group's ministers condemned slavery as a sin and encouraged new converts to free their slaves. Methodists also allowed gifted blacks to exhort others as lay ministers. During the Revolutionary War, Williams briefly lived in New Jersey, where he earned distinction for protecting a Patriot Methodist minister from detection by British troops. According to tradition Williams did not reveal the minister's location despite the threat of death and promise of financial reward. Williams's master was a Loyalist; when he left the country at war's end he sold Williams to New York City's John Street Methodist chapel for forty pounds. Williams must have preferred sale to his home church, for he knew the members and their opposition to slavery. He offered the chapel his own watch as a down payment.

Although Methodists condemned slavery as a sin, the church's trustees did not immediately free Williams, who worked as a sexton and undertaker at the John Street chapel to purchase his freedom. By 1785, just two years after the church had bought him, he had repaid the forty pounds in full, though he was not officially freed until 1796, perhaps working additional time as a condition of his manumission. He and his wife lived in the parsonage, where Mary cooked and cleaned for the Methodist ministers who resided there. Williams left the parsonage to open his own business, but he and his wife remained close to the ministers and entertained them at their new home. Early Methodists regularly met in class meetings, intense emotional gatherings where believers shared prayers and testimony in mutual support of the faith. Peter and Mary attended segregated meetings with other blacks; meetings were also usually divided by sex. Class meetings created camaraderie among blacks, especially black men, who had largely avoided organized Christianity before the Revolution. In the early 1790s Philadelphia's black Methodists had begun to worship separately from whites, under the leadership of RICHARD ALLEN, who would later become the first African Methodist Bishop in America. In 1796 black men in New York's Methodist classes, led by JAMES VARICK, who would later become the AMEZ Church's first bishop, and William Hamilton, who actively promoted abolition and moral reforms, petitioned and won from Methodist leaders the same right. Williams did not attend the same class as most of the prominent African Methodist leaders such as Varick and Hamilton, but worshiped with a group whose members mostly remained with the white-run church.

As the Methodist Church increased its membership in the southern states, its early opposition to slavery gave way to greater accommodation. Some Methodist leaders began to promote the colonization of free blacks as a solution to race relations in America. Consequently black Methodists in the northern states pushed for greater independence from the white church. In 1801 New York's African Methodists erected a church building and incorporated it independently of the white body. In 1822 they established a new black-run denomination, which would eventually take the title of the African Methodist Episcopal Zion Church. Peter Williams hosted class meetings for black members in his home, served as a trustee for the black church, and raised money for subscriptions so the African Methodists could erect their own building. But despite this support of fellow black Methodists, he kept close ties to the John Street chapel. Within a few years after the subscription effort Williams stepped down as the church's trustee, perhaps because some blacks disapproved of his close relationships with the white leadership.

In the years after 1800 Williams concentrated on his tobacconist business and set up shop in his Liberty Street home. New York property tax assessments list him among the wealthiest blacks in the city. One source names him as one of the first individuals to use machines in tobacco processing. Despite this mechanical prowess Williams never learned to read or write; his wife helped with figures in his shop, and his son kept his books. Mary died in 1821; Williams followed her in 1824. Their funerals at John Street were heavily attended. Williams was a beloved figure among white Methodists, and an important liaison between white and black Methodists. In the late 1810s, when white and African Methodist leaders gathered to discuss the institutional separation of the black church, they did so in Williams's house. He probably never advocated separation from the white church, nor did he take public stances on issues of social reform and abolition, such as those his son advocated.

Because he was illiterate and left no writings of his own, individuals have often evaluated Williams' legacy not on its own terms but according to their own agendas. Thus white Methodists such as the nineteenth-century church historian J. B. Wakeley praised Williams as a model of industry and piety to which all blacks should aspire. Some black leaders such as the AMEZ bishop William Walls conversely implied that Williams was a patsy for white church leaders because he did not promote independence for the black church and even supported white oversight of that church. Williams Sr. was a transitional figure in African American religious history. Unlike JUPITER HAMMON a generation earlier, he did not preach submission, and indeed his own life stood as an example of striving after liberty and prosperity. But unlike his son (who after 1800 left Methodism to become a reformer in the Episcopal Church) or other African Methodist leaders he did not forcefully promote social reforms or a wholly independent black-run church. Rather, Williams reflected the ethos of early Methodism and was committed to the short-lived vision of an interracial church.

FURTHER READING

Williams, Peter, Jr. "To the Citizens of New York" (14 July 1834), in *The Mind of the Negro as Reflected in Letters Written During the Crisis*, ed. Carter G. Woodson (1926; rpt. 1969).

Bradley, David Henry, Sr. *A History of the African Methodist Episcopal Zion Church*, vol. 1 (1956).

Nell, William C. *The Colored Patriots of the American Revolution* (1855).

Rush, Christopher. *A Short Account of the Rise and Progress of the African Methodist Episcopal Church in America* (1843).

Wakeley, J. B. *Lost Chapters Recovered from the Early History of American Methodism* (1858).

Walls, William J. *The African Methodist Episcopal Zion Church: The Reality of the Black Church* (1974).

Obituaries: New York *Commercial Advertiser* and *Evening Post*, both 21 Feb. 1824.

KYLE T. BULTHUIS

Williams, Preston Noah (23 May 1926–), Presbyterian theologian and ethicist, was born in Alcolu, South Carolina, the son of Anderson

James Williams and Bertha Bell McRae. He spent his early years on the farm his family had purchased soon after emancipation, where nearby the Westminster Presbyterian Church stood on a corner of the family property. But he spent most of his youth growing up in racially mixed Homestead, in metropolitan Pittsburgh, where he attended Grace Memorial Presbyterian Church.

Williams graduated Phi Beta Kappa with an AB from Washington and Jefferson College in 1947, and he earned his master's degree from the same institution in 1948. He enrolled in Johnson C. Smith Theological Seminary in Charlotte, North Carolina, where he earned his bachelor of divinity in 1950. Later that same year the Pittsburgh Presbytery of the Presbyterian Church (USA) ordained Williams as a minister.

In 1954 Williams received his master of sacred theology from Yale Divinity School, where he took classes with Robert L. Calhoun and H. Richard Niebuhr. Williams then served as a college chaplain and taught religion at the historically black colleges of Knoxville College, Tennessee; North Carolina College at Durham (later North Carolina Central University); and Lincoln University, Pennsylvania.

Williams married Constance Marie Willard on 4 June 1956, and they had two children, Mark Gordon and David Bruce. From 1956 to 1961 Williams served as assistant chaplain at Pennsylvania State University. In 1961 he began a Ph.D. program at Harvard University; while he pursued his doctorate, he served as Protestant chaplain at nearby Brandeis University. Beginning in 1966 Williams taught at the Boston University School of Theology, where he was later named the Martin Luther King Jr. Professor of Social Ethics. In 1967, at the end of his first year of teaching, Williams earned his Ph.D. from Harvard University; his dissertation was "Religious Responses to the New Deal: The Reaction of William Henry Cardinal O'Connell, Monsignor John A. Ryan, Clarence E. Macartney, and Reinhold Niebuhr to the Economic Policies of the New Deal."

In the following years Williams became active in the National Committee of Negro Churchmen, subsequently renamed the National Convention of Black Churchmen and later the National Convention of Black Christians (NCBC). Led by the Reverend Dr. Benjamin F. Payton, then director of the National Council of Churches' Commission on Religion and Race, an ad hoc gathering of staff from New York City's Interchurch Center together with pastors from Harlem drafted a response to the rising Black Power movement. Called upon to denounce STOKELY CARMICHAEL's Black Power movement as un-Christian, they sought instead to affirm their appreciation for the goals of the militant movement and at the same time express their loyalty for the nonviolent tradition of MARTIN LUTHER KING JR. They circulated their Black Power statement nationally for signatures and published it as a full-page ad in the *New York Times* on Sunday, 31 July 1966. The following year the group convened a formal meeting in Dallas, Texas, and appointed the Committee on Theological Prospectus to report to the next annual convention in St. Louis, Missouri. The Reverend Dr. Gayraud S. Wilmore Jr. became the first chair of the Committee on Theological Prospectus, and when Wilmore stepped down, Williams became cochair of the committee with Bishop Joseph Johnson Jr. of the Christian Methodist Episcopal Church.

Williams participated in several conferences to explore the new black theology movement. He and a growing cohort of African American theologians participated in a 1969 conference at Howard University, "The Black Revolution: Is There a Black Theology?" The conference papers were published in a special issue of the *Journal of Religious Thought*. A few months later Williams and several other members of the new movement participated in a May 1969 conference at Georgetown University, "Black Church/Black Theology." Just a few weeks earlier JAMES FORMAN had delivered his "Black Manifesto" at the April 1969 meeting of the Black Economic Development Conference held at Wayne State University, demanding that the Interreligious Foundation of Community Organization (IFCO) collect half a billion dollars from American churches and synagogues for reparations to African Americans. Within the next few weeks Foreman and his supporters disrupted worship services (most notably at New York City's Riverside Church) and staged sit-ins at several national denominational headquarters. In response the NCBC affirmed its support of Foreman, and its Committee on Theological Prospectus drafted a statement titled "Black Theology," published with a commentary by Williams in the 15 October 1969 issue of the *Christian Century*.

In 1971 Williams joined the faculty of Harvard University Divinity School as the Houghton Professor of Theology and Contemporary Change. Throughout his career, he served Harvard in several other capacities, as acting dean of the Divinity School from 1974 to 1975; as chair of the Ethics

Department; as adviser to Harambee, the black student organization at Harvard Divinity School; and as cochair of the Harvard University Black Faculty and Administrators Association.

At Harvard, Williams became involved in an effort, first proposed in 1969, to establish a research center for African American studies. When Harvard founded the W. E. B. DuBois Institute for African American Research, named in honor of the first African American to earn a Ph.D. at Harvard, Williams served as its acting director from 1975 to 1977. Under Williams's guidance, the institute awarded four doctoral fellowships in its first year; CORNEL WEST was a member of that first doctoral fellowship class. The institute subsequently expanded its offerings to include conferences, lectures, research, and publishing at Harvard as well as community after-school programs and high school enrichment projects in metropolitan Boston.

Williams continued his active career of writing and service at Harvard. In 1972 he became an editor at large for the *Christian Century*. From 1974 to 1975 he served as president of the American Society of Christian Ethics, and from 1975 to 1976 he served as president of the American Academy of Religion. An expert on King, Williams served on the advisory board of the Martin Luther King Jr. Papers Project. He taught and lectured in India, Korea, England, Japan, Canada, and the Caribbean.

In 1998 Williams became the founding director of the Summer Leadership Institute (SLI), an annual program of Harvard's Center for the Study of Values in Public Life, a two-week program to educate and empower urban ministry practitioners in neighborhood community and economic development. During its first decade the SLI enabled nearly five hundred lay and clergy graduates to establish or strengthen housing developments, shopping malls, charter schools, and job programs.

Williams received numerous honors. Tuskegee University awarded him an honorary doctor of humane letters in 1993, and Harvard honored him with the Harvard Foundation Medal for Interracial and Race Relations in 1994 and the W. E. B. DuBois Medal in 2000. When Williams retired from Harvard in 2002, he became the first recipient of the Harvard-Divinity School Preston N. Williams Black Alumni/Alumnae Award, named in his honor. He was named the Houghton Professor of Theology and Contemporary Change Emeritus. In October 2006 Yale Divinity School awarded him its Alumni Award for Distinction in Theological Education. Through his teaching, his writing, and his work with the W. E. B. DuBois Institute and the Summer Leadership Institute, Williams left his mark on countless scholars, students, and community organizers.

FURTHER READING
The Andover Harvard Library at Harvard Divinity School contains archival material on Williams.

Williams, Preston N. "Christian Realism and the Ephesian Suggestion: Influences That Have Shaped My Work," *Journal of Religious Ethics* (1997).

Finnin, William M., Jr. "Ethics of Universal Wholeness: An Assessment of the Work of Preston N. Williams," *Iliff Review* (1977).

DAVID BRUCE MCCARTHY

Williams, Robert Franklin (26 Feb. 1925–15 Oct. 1996), civil rights radical, broadcaster, and writer, was born in Monroe, Union County, North Carolina, the fourth of five children of John Williams, a railroad boiler washer, and Emma (Carter) Williams. In school Robert excelled at history, an interest encouraged by his grandmother, Ellen Williams, who passed on to the young boy tales of slavery and of the violent white supremacy campaigns of the 1890s. Ellen also passed on to Robert the rifle owned by his grandfather, Sikes Williams, who had been a prominent Republican Party activist and newspaper editor.

Even at an early age Robert understood the powerful sexual dynamics that shaped Southern race relations. One incident in particular from Robert's childhood haunted him. As an eleven-year-old he looked on in horror as Monroe's burly police chief, Jesse Helms Sr. (the father of the U.S. senator), dragged a black woman to the city jail, "her dress up over her head, the same way that a cave man would club and drag his sexual prey" (Tyson, 1). Williams was mortified by the woman's screams and by the laughter of white bystanders, but it was the silence and inaction of the black male witnesses to the attack that troubled him most. Much of Williams's later militancy grew from this incident, which convinced him that black men had a duty to protect their families, and encouraged him to embrace the necessity of armed self-defense.

After leaving school in 1942 the seventeen-year-old Williams apprenticed as a machinist in a National Youth Administration labor camp and studied at Elizabeth City State Teachers College, before leaving North Carolina for Detroit, Michigan, in 1943 to work as a mill operator with the Ford Motor Company. Following Detroit's bloody race riot in June 1943 Williams left the city for a job in the California shipyards, where he also witnessed racial violence, before returning to Monroe in 1944. Frustrated by the lack of job opportunities Williams moved north again, to Harlem, New York, where he worked on the docks before being drafted into the army in July 1945. He served first at Fort Bragg, North Carolina, before being transferred to Camp Crowder, Missouri, where he joined a Signal Corps battalion. Despite his high scores on a radio aptitude test Williams did not receive his desired posting as a radio operator, but was instead assigned as a clerical typist. Williams's outspoken views soon earned him a reputation as a troublemaker, at least among white officers, and he spent much of his military service in the brig for insubordination and for being absent without leave (AWOL) on several occasions.

Discharged from the army in November 1946 Williams returned again to Monroe, where he found a cadre of around 150 like-minded black veterans, all skilled in the use of weaponry and determined to defeat segregation. In March 1947 forty of these veterans, including Williams, thwarted a plan by the Ku Klux Klan to parade through the streets of Monroe the body of a black man executed for killing his white employer. Around that time Williams met Mabel Ola Robinson, then still in high school, and married her in June 1947, shortly after her sixteenth birthday. The couple moved to Detroit the following year, following the birth of their first son, Robert Jr., and later had two more sons, Franklin and John.

While working as a laborer in Detroit's Cadillac plant in 1949 Williams submitted a largely autobiographical article to the Detroit *Daily Worker* about a Southern-born black veteran who vowed to someday return to the South "more efficient in the fight for the liberation of [his] people" (Tyson, 63). After he was sacked by Cadillac for threatening a supervisor Williams did indeed return South, in 1950, where he took classes at West Virginia State, the North Carolina College for Negroes, and Johnson C. Smith College. With the encouragement of LANGSTON HUGHES, among others, he published a number of his poems and other writings in journals such as PAUL ROBESON's *Freedom*, where his 1952 essay urging greater black student militancy appeared next to a short story by LORRAINE HANSBERRY. Williams enrolled in the U.S. Marine Corps in 1954 but was dishonorably discharged the following year after protesting his assignment to a position in supply; Williams insisted that the Marine Corps recruiters had promised him an assignment with information services, where he was to train as a journalist.

Although the Supreme Court had issued its historic *Brown v. Board of Education* decision in 1954 Williams returned to Monroe to find the local NAACP branch ill-equipped to respond to the desegregation ruling. Aided by fellow veterans and a largely working-class membership recruited in Union County's pool halls, barber shops, and beauty salons, Williams transformed the Monroe NAACP into one of the most vibrant branches in the South. Within a year he had increased NAACP membership from six to two hundred by focusing on issues such as equal access to public recreational facilities. Following the death of a black child in a dangerous swimming hole in 1957 Williams rallied the NAACP—and some white Quaker and Unitarian allies—to demand that African American children receive the same access to swimming lessons and to the publicly funded swimming pool that white children enjoyed.

It was, however, Monroe's remarkable 1958 "Kissing Case" that propelled Williams to national, and even international, prominence. The case had its roots that October in a kissing game played by several Monroe children, in which a ten-year-old black boy, Hanover Thompson, and an eight-year-old white girl, Sissy Sutton, kissed each other. When Sutton innocently told her parents about the game her mother vowed to kill Thompson; her father went searching for him and his eight-year-old friend David Simpson with a shotgun. Allegedly to "protect" them the Monroe police arrested Simpson and Thompson at gunpoint, took the two young boys to jail, where they were beaten, terrorized by guards wearing Klan regalia—in what the police claimed was a Halloween joke—and kept in custody without access to parents or lawyers for six days. In November 1958 the children, who had received no legal representation, were sentenced to an unspecified number of years—perhaps until they were twenty-one—in a youth detention center.

In addition to providing an armed NAACP guard at the Thompson and Simpson homes, Williams worked closely with the *New York Post* reporter TED POSTON to publicize the young boys' plight. However, they soon found that, as with the SCOTTSBORO BOYS a quarter of a century earlier, state and national NAACP officials were reluctant to take on a case involving interracial relationships, albeit one in which the alleged "offense" was a far cry from the charge of rape in Scottsboro. Williams turned, therefore, to the Committee to Combat

Racial Injustice (CCRI), a New York–based Trotskyite organization, which helped to spread publicity about the case in the global left-wing press. Several reports in the mainstream European press also criticized the white authorities in Monroe for their hysterical reaction to the case, and prompted tens of thousands of letters of protest to the United States Information Agency and to North Carolina's governor Luther Hodges. Hodges initially tried to deflect criticism by attacking Williams's links to the CCRI and by questioning the morality of the Thompson and Simpson families. By February 1959, however, Hodges, then engaged in an ambitious campaign to secure foreign investment in North Carolina, bowed to international pressure and released the two boys.

The "Kissing Case" resulted in increased media coverage of Williams, whose down-home militancy provided a sharp contrast to inspirational southern preachers such as MARTIN LUTHER KING JR. and bureaucrats such as the NAACP's ROY WILKINS. In spring 1959 Wilkins removed Williams from the presidency of the Monroe NAACP following Williams's remark that it was time for African Americans to "meet violence with violence," given the failure of Southern courts to protect their rights (Tyson, 149). At that year's NAACP Convention Wilkins and DAISY BATES persuaded delegates to uphold Williams's suspension, but the Monroe activist remained unrepentant. He befriended MALCOLM X and debated the issue of violent and nonviolent civil rights strategies in public with BAYARD RUSTIN and in print with King. The differences between Williams and King were relatively small in theory—both accepted the principle of armed self-defense as a matter of last resort—but were radically different in tone and style. Williams's bravado and willingness to pose with all kinds of weaponry gave some credence to King's depiction of him as a loose cannon.

In August of 1961, following armed clashes between whites and civil rights demonstrators, Williams escaped to Canada. Pursued by the North Carolina authorities and the FBI on flimsy kidnapping charges, Williams settled in Cuba, under the protection of Fidel Castro, who provided him with a weekly show on Radio Havana. "Radio Free Dixie" found an audience among young blacks in the Northern inner cities and in the Southern civil rights movement, but Williams chafed at the dogmatism of the Castro regime and its own unwillingness to tackle racism. In 1964 Williams moved to Vietnam, where he advised Vietcong leader Ho Chi Minh, a fellow former Harlemite, and encouraged black Americans to oppose U.S. military intervention in Indochina. In exile he became a powerful icon and inspiration to young black militants like HUEY NEWTON and ELDRIDGE CLEAVER, who acknowledged the influence of Williams's *Negroes with Guns* (1962) on the Black Panther Party.

Williams moved to China in 1965, where he remained with his family until 1969, at which time he negotiated their safe return to the United States. Although Williams was still wanted by the FBI, President Richard Nixon's State Department was then engaged in renewing diplomatic relations with China and hoped to learn much from the North Carolina activist, who was close to Chairman Mao and other Communist Party officials. After a year as a Ford Foundation Fellow at the University of Michigan's Center for Chinese Studies Williams settled in Baldwin, a small town in Western Michigan where he taught and lectured occasionally and was active in the local NAACP.

Williams did not, however, return to national prominence. He rebuffed the entreaties of a new generation of black militants seeking an inspirational leader, and rejected what he saw as their militant posturing and tactical naivety. Shortly after his return Williams reminded reporters that he had always considered himself "an American patriot" who "believed in the Constitution of the United States." The only problem with "the greatest document in the world" (Tyson, 304), he noted, was that federal, state, and local governments had often ignored it when it came to African Americans. In 1976, after North Carolina ended efforts to prosecute him on kidnapping charges, Williams traveled to the state for the first time in twenty-five years. He returned to Monroe every summer after that, and he was buried in his hometown on 22 October 1996, five weeks after dying of Hodgkin's disease in Grand Rapids, Michigan. At his funeral service, ROSA PARKS acknowledged the ideological and tactical differences that she and Martin Luther King had with Williams. Nonetheless, Parks noted, she and King had "always admired Robert Williams for his courage and commitment to freedom." Such work, her eulogy concluded, "should go down in history and never be forgotten" (Tyson, 307).

FURTHER READING
Williams, Robert. *Negroes With Guns* (1962; 1998).
Tyson, Timothy B. *Robert F. Williams and the Roots of Black Power* (1999).
Obituary: *New York Times*, 19 Oct. 1996.

STEVEN J. NIVEN

Williams, Sally Isaac (Aunt Sally) (1796?–after 1860), slave, mother, and subject of an early slave narrative, was born to parents who were slaves on a plantation in Fayetteville, North Carolina. Her exact birth date and the names of her parents remain unknown. As a field hand first and later a handmaiden to her mistress, Williams's mother could not spend much time with her daughter. This meant that Williams, like many other slave children, was mostly left to her own devices as a child.

When Williams was ten years old she had her first encounter with tragedy when her closest playmate was struck with an illness and died suddenly. Saddened deeply by her friend's death, she spoke to her master, who rented Williams and one hundred other slaves from his sister. Williams asked him about the afterlife and her friend's fate, having been exposed to organized religion for the first time at her friend's funeral. Her master told her that there was no life after death and squashed temporarily the glimmer of hope that these thoughts had provided her.

It was around this age that Williams began to be given various jobs to perform, including carrying dinner to the field hands. This duty resulted in her first whipping, when the overseer discovered that she had dropped food on her way to the field. Williams was kept busy at night helping her mother prepare cotton to be spun. The only recreation available was an occasional Saturday night dance, which would draw slaves from several surrounding plantations.

Although spared some of the harshest mistreatment that slaves often underwent, Williams did not have a youth of contentment. Her mother was often away, and Williams's master, whom she admired, had temporarily crushed her hope of a better life through religion. This hope was reawakened when a revivalist meeting was held near her master's plantation. This type of revival was commonly referred to as a "camp meeting" because participants would camp out in a field for an extended religious gathering. Originally a prominent feature of Presbyterian practice in Scotland, these meetings produced such emotionally charged religious expression that the Presbyterians abandoned them in the United States. However, their immense popularity caused the practice of camp meetings to be adopted by the Methodist Church, leading to their rapid expansion during the period before the Civil War.

Although the specific affiliation of the meeting that Williams attended is unclear, its effect upon her spiritual life was not. She left the camp meeting and returned home anxious about how to answer the call of the Lord. According to her biography, when she returned she was overcome with worry about how to serve the Lord and passed into a trancelike state for two days, during which she "thought the Lord Jesus came to her with the most loving words … and told her to be his child" (Williams, 45).

Armed with youthful optimism and a new sense of spiritual direction, Sally was given yet another reason to be hopeful for happiness when by order of her mistress she was married at the age of thirteen. She wed Abram Williams, a fellow slave from the plantation. Abram's age at marriage is unknown; however, he was kind, and Sally quickly came to love him. The ceremony was held at the main house, and Sally Williams's mistress had arranged for a Methodist preacher to preside over the ceremony, exposing Sally to organized religion for a third time. Her mother was away when the marriage took place, and when she returned she was saddened, telling her daughter, "Sally, gettin' married's de beginnin' o' sorrow; my heart aches to think what ye've got to bar!" (Williams, 59)

The couple remained together for an unclear period of time before Abram was sold. During this time they had three children. The first was Isaac, and the second was unnamed, dying shortly after birth. The third and final child was Daniel, who was only months old when his father was sold. Abram was to be sold to a neighboring plantation, where despite their close proximity the couple would not be allowed to see each other. This impossibility made Sally Williams contemplate escape, knowing that she could stay with a friend in Fayetteville.

She plotted an escape but remained unsure whether it would be considered a sin. She dismissed these uncertainties when she overheard her master talking to a man about the need to get more out of his slaves because of his shaky financial situation. She knew that this would have meant bigger tasks and harsher taskmasters. She decided to leave that night and traveled four miles with her children to the center of Fayetteville. They arrived undetected and were welcomed with open arms by her friend, identified in the biography only as "Aunt Marthy." Williams and her sons arrived in October, and around New Year's received news that her master was going to hire out all his slaves after the New Year. She boldly proceeded to the field where this was taking place and agreed with her master that for six dollars a month, paid directly to him, she could hire her own time out as she saw fit. Having always loved cooking, she rented a small house and began to sell beer and cakes out of it.

Abram was now able to make regular visits to see his wife and their children. Sally Williams's business selling beer, cakes, and coffee was successful and afforded her the power to buy material comforts for her family. When her master agreed to renew their contract at the end of its first year, she was overjoyed. Just as it appeared that stability was entering her life, happiness was disrupted when Abram was caught gambling by his master. Abram's punishment was to be sold south to New Orleans. The morning of his departure Sally Williams closed her shop and took Abram a farewell breakfast. She neither saw nor heard from Abram again.

Williams and her sons continued to prosper in Fayetteville, living well enough to generate talk of Sally exceeding her proper place in society. When her oldest son, Isaac, turned twelve, Williams was able to convince her master to allow her to hire his labor out at a rate of two dollars a month. Her master even agreed to have Isaac taught to read during this period. Isaac's ability to read gave Williams's life a new feeling of depth and purpose because it allowed her free access to the Bible.

After four years, under pressure from her master to find a new husband, Williams selected Lewis Beggs, an African American freeman who worked as a carpenter. They had one child, Lewis. When Lewis was three years old Williams's mistress died and left her slaves to her nephew. Looking for quick cash, he immediately sold all three of Williams's children. A year later Williams herself was sold to a slave trader from Alabama. Before leaving Fayetteville, Williams attempted one escape, which she aborted after making noise while trying to climb a fence. She never again attempted to escape. The next morning her mother and oldest son said goodbye to her inside a slave pen.

On the march to Alabama all of the slaves were shackled, except for Williams, a young girl she was taking care of, and an old woman. According to her biography it was the woman's age, the girl's youth, and Williams's dignity that made their owner dislike putting them in irons. As with many similar pieces of period writing, *Aunt Sally* transmitted a message of the hope of redemption for the players involved in the slave trade. For example, George Leland, the slave trader who bought Williams, was reported to have sworn to a preacher, while transporting Williams and her group back to Alabama, that he would find these slaves good homes and then leave the trade forever. Leland also swore to Williams that he would not sell her. However, because of the selectiveness of Leland in selling his slaves he was unable to do so in either a timely fashion or

to the highest bidder. Because of these factors he was unable to pay his debts, meaning that the slaves would be sold at sheriff's auction. However, before the auction Leland managed to secure private sales of several more slaves, including Williams.

Williams was sent to Dallas County, Alabama, as property of the Cones, to be used as a seamstress and cook. She settled into life on the new plantation and lived in relative stability for approximately twenty years. Her greatest disappointment with her new owners was that she was allowed to attend church only on sacrament Sundays. Taking one of the few holidays she was ever granted to attend a wedding at a neighboring plantation, she encountered a free man, Daniel, whose boat was in port for repairs. Daniel was from North Carolina and was friends with Williams's cousin Mary Ann Williams. Daniel agreed to take a letter and a shawl back to North Carolina for Mary Ann. The shawl, one of Sally's prized possessions, would be recognized and thus prove their relationship. Williams soon received letters from both her cousin and her oldest son, Isaac. Isaac also wrote to the Cones saying that he wished to buy his mother's freedom. Isaac Williams, having escaped from slavery, taken up residence in Detroit, and become a Methodist preacher, was economically secure enough to purchase his mother. Unfortunately, Sally Williams's mistress refused for an entire year to let her son buy her.

Williams made her first voyage as a free woman to meet her son in New York City. When her son arrived they traveled to Detroit, where Williams lived with her son and his family until she died. Because Williams's biography was written shortly after she arrived in Detroit, at the approximate age of sixty-four, information about the concluding years of her life is unknown. However, the most historically compelling years of her life are well documented.

Constantly guided and sustained by her Christian (probably Methodist) faith, Sally Isaac Williams's journey through life was one of hope and perseverance. Through boldly escaping, negotiating an agreement with her master to hire out her own time, and giving her oldest son the opportunity to learn to read, she was able both to maintain a sense of self-respect and to escape the South as a free woman.

FURTHER READING
Aunt Sally: or, The Cross the Way of Freedom.
  A Narrative of the Slave-life and Purchase of the

Mother of Rev. Isaac Williams of Detroit, Michigan (1858). Available online at http://docsouth.unc.edu/neh/sally/sally.html.

JACOB ANDREW FREEDMAN

Williams, Serena and Venus Williams (26 Sept. 1981–) and (17 June 1980–), respectively, professional tennis players, are the fourth and fifth daughters, respectively, born to Richard Williams, a security agency owner, and Oracene Price, a nurse. Venus Ebone Starr Williams was born in Lynwood, California, and Serena Williams in Saginaw, Michigan. Both girls were homeschooled. By age ten Venus had won the under-twelve division tennis title in Southern California and was on the front page of the *New York Times* and in *Sports Illustrated*. In 1991 the family moved from Compton, California, so that Venus could accept a scholarship at Rick Macci's tennis academy in Haines City, Florida.

At the age of fourteen, in October 1994, Venus turned professional at the Bank of the West Classic in Oakland, California, where she nearly upset second-ranked Arantxa Sanchez Vicario. She also put in limited appearances on the circuit before making her major debut at the 1997 French Open. At the start of the 1997 season she was ranked 211th in the world. By the end of the year she had climbed to 64th. Serena, meanwhile, attended a private high school in Miami, and she, too, turned pro at age fourteen, in 1995. Although she was ranked only 304th in 1997, Serena defeated fourth-ranked Monica Seles and seventh-ranked Mary Pierce at a tournament in Chicago, in only her fifth professional tournament.

During the 1998 season Venus reached the semifinals of the U.S. Open, advanced to the quarterfinals at the Australian Open, the French Open, and Wimbledon, and won her first career singles title, the IGA Tennis Classic in Oklahoma City. Her serve was clocked that year at an unprecedented 127 miles per hour. Serena started the year ranked number 96, but climbed to number 40 after besting several higher-ranked players and losing narrowly to the world's top-ranked player, Martina Hingis. In 1999 Venus defended her Lipton title by beating Serena in the first WTA Tour final between siblings and won her first singles title on clay, in Hamburg, Germany. That year the Williamses became the first sisters to be ranked simultaneously in the top ten and the first sisters in the twentieth century to win a Grand Slam doubles crown at the French Open. Serena continued to improve her game, winning her first singles title at an indoor tournament in Paris.

Serena's dramatic breakthrough came at the 1999 U.S. Open, when, seeded seventh, she upset Martina Hingis, Lindsay Davenport, and Monica Seles, the number one, two, and four seeds, respectively, to win her first career Grand Slam singles title. Serena was the first African American woman to win the singles title since ALTHEA GIBSON won the last of her five U.S. championships in 1958. She and Venus also joined forces to win the U.S. Open doubles title that year. The year 2000 proved to be even more successful for the Williamses. Venus won her first two Grand Slam singles titles, at Wimbledon and the U.S. Open, and she and Serena won the Wimbledon doubles title. At the Olympic Games in Sydney, Australia, Venus won the singles gold medal, and when the two sisters then took the gold medal in the doubles, she became the first tennis player to win both Olympic titles since 1924.

At the 2001 U.S. Open, Venus faced her sister Serena for the title in the finals. The match was an exciting event that drew a crowd of celebrities and high television ratings, in part, at least, because the two sisters had become superstars in a sport traditionally dominated by white athletes. It was the first time since 1884 that two sisters had played each other in a Grand Slam final, and the first time that two African Americans had competed against each other in the final. Their father, Richard, had a difficult time watching the match and left before its conclusion, when Venus beat Serena, 6-2, 6-4. To cap off her banner year, Venus received the ESPY award for Outstanding Women's Tennis Performance.

Serena's first title in 2001 generated controversy when she was scheduled to face Venus in the semifinal of the State Farm Evert Cup in Indian Wells, California. When Venus withdrew from the match, rumors circulated that their father had ordered her to not play against Serena. He charged the crowd with racism, saying, "I really just think a lot of people in tennis and the business world are jealous of me. They'd rather see me sweeping the floor at the U.S. Open or picking cotton somewhere. But I'm not" (*Newsweek*, 2 July 2001). The sisters continued their winning ways and their emerging rivalry into 2002, with Serena dominating her older sister. She beat Venus for the first time since 1999 in Miami and again in the finals of the French Open, after which they became the first siblings to be ranked first and second in the world. Serena won three Grand Slam titles in 2002, Wimbledon, the French Open, and the U.S. Open, putting her in the select company of only seven women who have won three consecutive major titles. Venus won four WTA tour

Serena Williams, left, walks past her sister Venus during their center court match at the Australian Open Tennis Championships in Melbourne, Australia, Wednesday, 21 January 1998. (AP Images.)

titles and was runner-up to Serena at Wimbledon and the U.S. Open.

Serena continued to dominate Venus in the 2003 season, besting her for the Australian title, the one Grand Slam title Serena had not been able to win. She also defeated Venus in the ladies' singles at Wimbledon, in a match that many observers viewed as a complex psychological battle. Serena appeared initially unwilling to punish her sister's weaknesses—Venus was suffering from leg, hip, and stomach injuries—but she eventually recaptured the form that had led her to the final with some ease. Venus later revealed that she had played through great pain and would have retired from the match had her opponent been anyone other than her sister.

The two years following Serena's second Wimbledon title were difficult for the sisters. On 14 September 2003 their elder sister, Yetunde Price, was shot and murdered in Compton, a suburb of Los Angeles. This tragedy stunned the Williams sisters and though it would later inspire them to further success, in the immediate aftermath it

encouraged a step back from the professional tennis circuit. Serena and Venus returned in 2004 but knee and wrist injuries, respectively, compounded their difficulties. During this relative slump, Serena pursued acting opportunities while Venus established a successful interior design company. Success in the Australian Open for Serena, and at Wimbledon by Venus in 2005 suggested their woes were behind them. However, injury and motivational problems continued in 2006. In 2007, Serena once again won the Australian Open, this time against all expectations. Entering the tournament unseeded, Serena defeated the top seed, Maria Sharapova, in the final. Speaking to her critics after the victory she asserted that "the thing that makes me happiest is playing tennis" (Clarey). Even more surprising to many commentators was Venus's victory at Wimbledon the same year. Ranked 48th in the world at the start of 2007 and seeded only 23rd at Wimbledon, Venus defeated Marion Bartoli of France in the final, marking her fourth victory at the All England Club, and her sixth Grand Slam. Of particular significance, the 2007 final was the first at Wimbledon where women's prize money equaled that of men's, a cause long championed by Billie Jean King and Martina Navratilova, among others, and which Venus Williams had lobbied for in an op-ed piece in the London *Times* in 2006.

The role of Richard Williams, their father and coach, remains controversial. Williams has been outspoken in defending his daughters from criticism, claiming that their critics are motivated by a combination of racism and jealousy. When his daughters sign endorsement deals, Williams requests that the companies donate goods to the black community. He has also criticized the WTA for being "a close-knit community that tends to embrace its own. We've never been a part of it. But then, we never planned to be a part of them either. We're a part of ourselves. People can criticize me and complain about me, but no one wants to see a tournament that Venus and Serena aren't in. We breathed life into this game, and people dislike us for it" (*Newsweek*, 2 July 2001). Richard Williams's criticisms can hardly be leveled at advertisers and the media, however, who have ensured that the Williams sisters have become the most prominent women in professional sports. In 2000 Venus signed a five-year, $40 million contract with Reebok International, the highest amount ever paid to a female athlete. She and Serena together signed a deal with Avon, making them the first athletes since JACKIE JOYNER-KERSEE to represent the world's largest direct seller of beauty products. Avon, then in the process of aggressively marketing its products to the growing global teenage market, could hardly have chosen better examples of attractive, successful young womanhood. As one Avon representative stated, "These were two very young women who were all about empowerment and caring and sharing. Their appeal goes very far and wide" (*Advertising Age*, 22 Jan. 2001). In 2005, the ABC Family Network commissioned the sisters to star in their own reality television show, *Venus and Serena: For Real*.

From 2007 to 2011 the Williams sisters remained the most recognized tennis players on the planet, and, along with TIGER WOODS, enjoyed greater global fame than any other African American athletes. Both, however, suffered from injuries and faced some criticism in the tennis world for avoiding many events on the tennis tour in favor of appearing mainly at grand slam tournaments, in addition to their many business and charitable ventures. As a result, their position in the rankings—determined by participation in all tour events—declined significantly. Venus, who repeated at Wimbledon in 2008—defeating her sister—won no other grand slam events between 2008 and 2011, although she did appear in the 2009 Wimbledon Final, losing to Serena. Venus and Serena also won Ladies Doubles titles at Wimbledon (2008 and 2009); the Australian Open (2009 and 2010); the U.S. Open (2009) and the French Open (2010). Venus also won the 2008 Olympic Gold Medal in Beijing, defeating her sister in the final. Injuries and illness—she was diagnosed with Sjögren's syndrome, an autoimmune disease—plagued Venus throughout 2011. She would end that year ranked outside of the top 100 for the first time since 1997. Nonetheless she continued to lead the WTA tour among active players in terms of career singles titles—43—four more than Serena, and a figure that placed her 10th in the all-time rankings.

In 2008 Serena Williams won her first US Open in six years, and followed up by winning back-to back Australian Open and Wimbledon titles in 2009 and 2010, for a total of 13 grand slams, six more than Venus. Serena struggled with foot injuries in 2011, and also suffered a pulmonary embolism, but still managed to win two tournaments and reach the final of that year's U.S. Open, where she lost to Australian Samantha Stosur in straight sets. Both in that final and in the 2009 semi-final at the U.S. Open, Williams was fined for "unsportsmanlike" conduct. She ended 2011 ranked 12th in the world. In 2009 both sisters became part-

owners of the Miami Dolphins National Football League franchise. Serena Williams's autobiography, *On the Line*, was published in that same year. In 2012, Serena retained her Wimbledon Singles title, regained the US Open crown, and won Gold at the London Summer Olympics. Both sisters also won the Ladies' Doubles at Wimbledon and the Women's Doubles Gold in London.

Despite the earlier successes of LUCY DIGGS SLOWE, ORA WASHINGTON, Althea Gibson, and ARTHUR ASHE, most Americans have tended to view tennis as a white upper-class sport. Like TIGER WOODS in golf, the Williams sisters have taken it as their mission to persuade African Americans that it is their game too.

FURTHER READING

Clarey, Christopher. "After Times of Grief and Doubt, a Tennis Ace Is Hungry Again." *New York Times*, 28 Jan. 2001.

Jenkins, Sally, and David Bailey. "Double Trouble," *Women's Sports and Fitness*, Nov./Dec. 1998.

Noel, Peter, and Amanda Ward. "Fear of the Williams Sisters," *Village Voice*, 14 Nov. 2000.

Samuels, Allison. "Life with Father," *Newsweek*, 2 July 2001.

Stein, Joel. "The Power Game." *Time*, 3 Sept. 2001.

MAUREEN M. SMITH

Williams, Sherley Anne (25 Aug. 1944–9 July 1999), fiction writer, poet, literary critic, and children's author, was born in Bakersfield, California, to Jesse Winson and Lena Silver Williams, laborers. Sherley and her sisters (Ruby, Jesmarie, and Lois) grew up poor, with their parents working as crop pickers in Fresno, California, and needing welfare assistance to live in Bakersfield's low-income housing projects. Despite its poverty, exacerbated by Winson's death from tuberculosis before Williams's eighth birthday, the family was very close, with each child growing up optimistic about what the future might hold.

Williams began her writing career while still a student at Edison Junior/Senior High School in Fresno. There, she was inspired by the autobiographies of black female entertainers such as EARTHA KITT, KATHERINE DUNHAM, and ETHEL WATERS, who overcame difficult childhoods to enjoy fruitful adult lives. Her mother tried to discourage Williams's interest in reading, believing that books would fill her daughter's head with dreams that could never be fulfilled. Lena Silver Williams died when Sherley Anne was sixteen, and Sherley Anne was placed into the custody of her eldest sister, Ruby, who was divorced and struggling to support a daughter of her own. That year before leaving for college, Williams and her sister managed to live on public assistance and whatever odd jobs—picking cotton, cutting grapes, stocking department store shelves during holiday seasons—the two of them could secure. In addition, they benefited from a small cash payment that Williams received for having a story published in *Scholastic Magazine*.

After graduating from Edison in 1962, Williams enrolled at Fresno State College (now called California State University at Fresno). As a freshman, she fell in love with the imagery, characters, and variations of black speech captured in the poems of LANGSTON HUGHES and STERLING ALLEN BROWN. Williams earned a B.A. in History in 1966 and in 1967 enrolled in courses at Howard University in Washington, D.C. That same year, she published a short story, "Tell Martha Not to Moan," in the *Massachusetts Review*. (The story would later be anthologized in, among other highly regarded collections, *The Black Woman*, edited by TONI CADE BAMBARA.) Also at Howard, Williams became a proponent of the "Black Aesthetic," which she defined in part as "those elements in our lives on which constructive political changes, those that do more than blackwash or femalize [sic] the same old power structure, can be built" (*Callaloo* 22.4: 769–770). Williams studied at Howard for a year before working from 1970 to 1972 as a consultant in curriculum development and a community educator at Federal City College. From there, she moved on to Brown University in Providence, Rhode Island, where she joined the faculty of the black studies department and, in late 1972, completed her master's degree. Though she understood that earning a Ph.D. would make it easier to advance in academia, she did not continue in Brown's doctoral program because

> I didn't want to spend the rest of my life poring over other people's work and trying to explain the world thru [sic] their eyes. Rather, what I gain from books, and it is often a great deal—no book affected my life so much as reading Langston Hughes' *Montage on a Dream Deferred*, for here was my life and my language coming at me—must be melded with, refracted through my experiences and what I know of my contemporaries, my ancestors, my hopes for my descendants (and the "my" is used in the collective sense, implying *we*, implying *our*) (*Callaloo* 22.4: 770).

Williams left Brown in 1972 to teach at California State University at Fresno before leaving in 1975 to become the first African American female faculty member of the English Department at the University of California, San Diego, where she worked until her death in 1999. Williams's first book publication, *Give Birth to Brightness: A Thematic Study in Neo-Black Literature* (1972), examined the work of JAMES BALDWIN, LeRoi Jones (AMIRI BARAKA), and ERNEST J. GAINES. Her first book of creative work was *The Peacock Poems* (1975), which, in the tradition of Hughes and Brown, uses variations of black dialect and musical forms such as the blues and spirituals to explore the hardships of Williams's early years, especially those when both of her parents were alive. The book was nominated for the National Book Award and the Pulitzer Prize and was followed in 1982 by *Someone Sweet Angel Chile*, which offers further reflections on Williams's childhood and, by invoking historical figures ranging from FREDERICK DOUGLASS to BESSIE SMITH, attempts to locate her individual story within the larger scope of African American history. *Someone Sweet Angel Chile*, which, like *The Peacock Poems*, was nominated for a National Book Award, secured Williams's place among major contemporary African American poets, particularly those influenced by the blues, spirituals, and black dialect. Williams earned an Emmy Award for a television performance of poems from the book, which helped to create a receptive audience for her next work, a historical novel entitled *Dessa Rose* (1986), which received widespread critical acclaim and was named a 1986 Notable Book by the *New York Times*. Constructed as a neo-slave narrative, *Dessa Rose* tells the story of a pregnant black slave, Dessa, who teams with Rufel, a white plantation mistress, to forge an ingenious and dangerous money-making enterprise. The two arranged for Rufel, whose profligate husband had vanished, to sell Dessa and others into slavery, only to help them escape soon afterward, before selling and helping them escape again.

Williams wrote three other celebrated works: *Letters from a New England Negro* (1992), a full-length play that premiered in Chicago, and two children's books: *Working Cotton* (1992), which received a CORETTA SCOTT KING Book Award and was named a Caldecott Honor Book by the American Library Association in 1993, and *Girls Together* (1999). In addition, she wrote *Ours to Make* (1973) and *The Sherley Williams Special* (1977) for television, *Traveling Sunshine Good Time Show and Celebration* (1973) for the stage, and an introduction to ZORA NEALE HURSTON's *Their Eyes Are Watching God* published by the University of Illinois Press (1991). Leaving behind one child, a son named John Malcolm, Williams died of cancer on 9 July 1999 in San Diego. At the time of her death, Williams was working on the sequel to *Dessa*

Rose. A musical adaptation of *Dessa Rose*, by Lynn Ahrens and Stephen Flaherty, opened at Lincoln Center in New York City on 21 March 2005.

FURTHER READING

Fisher, Dexter, ed. *The Third Woman: Minority Women Writers of the United States* (1980).
Stetson, Erlene, ed., *Black Sister: Poetry by Black American Women*, 1746–1980 (1981).
Washington, Mary Helen, ed. *Midnight Birds: Stories By Contemporary Black Women Writers* (1980).

DANIEL DONAGHY

Williams, Smokey Joe (6 Apr. 1886–25 Feb. 1951), baseball player and manager, was born Joseph Williams in Seguin, Texas, the son of an unknown African American father and Lettie Williams, a Native American. He attended school in San Antonio, but it is not known how many years he completed. As a young boy Joe was given a baseball, which he carried with him everywhere and which he even slept with under his pillow. He pitched in the sandlots around Seguin until 1905, when he began playing professionally with the San Antonio Black Broncos. Williams quickly became the ace of the pitching staff and in the following seasons posted records of 28–4, 15–9, 20–8, 20–2, and 32–8, all with San Antonio except 1906, when he played with Austin. In the autumn of 1909 he signed to play with the Trilbys of Los Angeles, California, which marked the first of many years that he played baseball in both summer and winter. In 1910 Joe was recruited by Chicago Giants' owner FRANK LELAND, who wrote, "If you have ever witnessed the speed of a pebble in a storm you have not even seen the speed possessed by this wonderful Texan Giant" (Riley, 856). The Giants were the only black team in the semiprofessional Chicago League that season. Williams then played during the 1910–1911 winter in California, where he compiled a 4–1 record with seventy-eight strikeouts in sixty innings. After another season with the Giants, Williams made his first visit to Cuba, where he tied for the most wins, with a 10–7 record for the 1911–1912 Cuban Winter League champion Havana Reds. In the spring of 1912 he toured with the Chicago American Giants on the West Coast and defeated every Pacific Coast League team except Portland, finishing the tour with a 9–1 record.

After the 1912 tour Williams joined the New York Lincoln Giants for $105 a month; he remained with the franchise through 1923. At this point of his career he was called "Cyclone," but later in his career he would become better known as "Smokey Joe." With the Lincoln Giants, Joe joined another hard-throwing right-hander, "Cannonball" DICK REDDING, and the duo pitched the Lincolns to the Eastern Championship in 1912. After the close of the 1912 regular season, Williams shut out John McGraw's National League champion New York Giants 6–0 on four hits while fanning nine. A week later he tossed another four-hit shutout, defeating Hal Chase's All-Stars, a team composed mostly of New York Yankees. Joe was at his best against white major leaguers and compiled a lifetime 20–7 record against them. When the weather turned cold, the Lincoln Giants toured Cuba, where Joe split a pair of games with Cuban ace José Mendez. After the tour ended, Williams stayed on the island and had a 9–5 record to lead the Fe team to the 1913 Cuban Winter League championship.

After returning to the United States for the 1913 summer season, Williams jumped to the Mohawk Giants of Schenectady, New York; but the Lincoln Giants quickly paid him five hundred dollars to return, and he pitched the team to their finest season, capping the year with six victories in the championship series against Rube Foster's Chicago American Giants. When the triumphant Lincoln Giants returned to New York, a large crowd was on hand at Olympic Park to welcome them home. In the fall Williams resumed his postseason performances against major leaguers. He struck out sixteen in a two-hit 9–1 win over Mike Donlin's All-Stars, fanned nine in defeating Hall-of-Famer Grover Cleveland Alexander and the Philadelphia Phillies 9–2, whiffed twelve in a 1–0 loss to Earl Mack's All-Stars, avenged that loss when he fanned fourteen to take a 7–3 win over the same team, and hurled a three-hit 2–1 victory over a white all-star team that featured Chief Bender, the Philadelphia Athletics ace pitcher.

In 1914 Williams joined the Chicago American Giants during their preseason spring barnstorming tour through the Northwest and pitched a no-hitter against Portland. Back with the Lincoln Giants for the regular season, he compiled a record of 41–3 against all levels of opposition. In the fall Williams again faced major league opposition, defeating the Philadelphia Phillies 10–4, and then fanning a dozen as he battled Hall-of-Famer Rube Marquard and the New York Giants to a 1–1 draw that was ended by darkness.

Williams suffered two injuries in 1915, a broken arm and a broken wrist, and missed much of the season, but was back in action by the fall exhibition games against major leaguers. He struck out nine in a 3–0 shutout over a combination of players from the Federal League's Buffalo and Brooklyn franchises, and fanned ten in pitching a three-hit 1–0 shutout over the National League champion Philadelphia Phillies. In the winter of 1915–1916 Williams pitched for the Chicago American Giants in California, making his last appearance on the West Coast. Later that winter he also made his final appearance in Cuba, when he joined the struggling San Francisco franchise for the second half of the season. He finished with a lifetime 22–15 record in the Cuban Winter League.

In 1917 Hilldale, a team based in the Philadelphia suburb of that name, scheduled a postseason series against major leaguers and recruited Williams to pitch. Williams rose to the occasion and defeated Connie Mack's Philadelphia Athletics 6–2, beating Athletics' ace Joe Bush, and then whiffed ten in a ten-inning 5–4 win over Rube Marquard and Chief Meyers's All-Leaguers. Joe also fanned twenty and tossed a no-hitter against John McGraw's National League champion New York Giants but lost the game 1–0 on an error. According to oral accounts, in this game Giants' star Ross Youngs gave him the nickname "Smokey Joe."

As manager of the Lincoln Giants, Williams took his team to Palm Beach, Florida, in the winter of 1917–1918 to represent the Breakers Hotel in the Florida Hotel League, where they opposed Rube Foster's Royal Poinciana team. In one memorable match-up, Williams struck out nine and tossed a two-hitter to out-duel his old rival Dick Redding 1–0. Williams continued playing and managing in the winter Florida Hotel League for several years, including a stint as manager of the Royal Poinciana team in 1926.

There was no dominant team in the East in 1918, but when Williams pitched, the Lincoln Giants were the best team. He defeated rival Brooklyn Royal Giants' ace lefthander John Donaldson 1–0 and 3–2 on successive weekends, and in the fall he continued his pitching prowess against major leaguers and fashioned an 8–0 shutout over Marquard and his All-Nationals team. On opening day 1919 the largest crowd to ever attend a game in Harlem watched Williams hurl a no-hit 1–0 masterpiece over Redding and the Brooklyn Royal Giants.

In 1922 Williams married Beatrice Johnson, a Broadway showgirl, and they had one daughter. In the spring of 1924 he became a victim of the Lincoln Giants' preference for young players and was released. He joined the Brooklyn Royal Giants and, although he was their top pitcher, was released after the season. Williams then joined the Homestead Grays in 1925 and remained with the franchise through 1932. During his years with the Grays, the nickname "Smokey Joe" was used almost exclusively, and he developed a mystique about his age, encouraging people to think that he was older than he was, that the press kept alive.

In 1929 owner CUM POSEY entered the Grays in the American Negro League, and Williams, appointed captain, compiled a 12–7 record. The league folded after its only year of existence, and in the absence of an eastern league, the Grays returned to independent play. In 1930 Williams and Chet Brewer hooked up in a historic pitching duel under the Kansas City Monarchs' portable lighting system, with Joe fanning twenty-seven batters in the twelve-inning game while allowing only one hit in a 1–0 victory. At the end of the season the Grays defeated Williams's old team, the New York Lincoln Giants, in a playoff for the Eastern championship. In 1931 the Grays fielded one of the greatest teams in the history of the Negro Leagues. As an aging veteran, Williams paired with the youthful JOSH GIBSON to form an exceptional battery.

Following his retirement from baseball, Williams worked as a bartender in Harlem. In 1950 he was honored with a special day at the Polo Grounds in ceremonies before a game between the New York Cubans and Indianapolis Clowns. Less than a year later, in 1951, he died of a brain hemorrhage in New York City. In a 1952 poll conducted by the *Pittsburgh Courier*, Smokey Joe was chosen the greatest pitcher in the history of black baseball, winning over SATCHEL PAIGE by one vote. In 1999 he was elected to the National Baseball Hall of Fame in Cooperstown, New York.

FURTHER READING
Holway, John. *Black Ball Stars: Negro League Pioneers* (1988).
Peterson, Robert. *Only the Ball Was White* (1970).
Riley, James A. *The Biographical Encyclopedia of the Negro Baseball Leagues* (1994).

JAMES A. RILEY

Williams, Spencer, Jr. (14 July 1893–13 Dec. 1969), film writer, director, and actor, was born in Vidalia, Louisiana, to Spencer Williams Sr. and Pauline Williams Tatum, the president of the local Woman's Relief Corps. At the age of seventeen, he moved to New York City and found work backstage in the Theater for the producer Oscar Hammerstein. As a "call boy," the stagehand who is responsible for giving the performers a five-minute warning before their entrances, Williams met several celebrities, including Bert Williams, the African American star of the *Ziegfeld Follies*, who served as something of a mentor to the young man.

After serving in the army during World War I and attaining the rank of sergeant, Williams returned to find employment in the newly burgeoning film industry, both as a performer (notably in Buster Keaton's silent classic *Steamboat Bill, Jr.*) and behind the camera. He was hired by Paramount's Christie Comedies production company as a writer, adapting comic short stories about African American life for film. Although this material relied heavily on the caricatures and comic tropes of the minstrel show, Williams is credited with trying to "squeeze honest black roles into the crevices of white movies" (Cripps, p. 222) and was the screenwriter of the first all-black "talkie," 1928's *Melancholy Dame*. In the same year he directed his first movie, the all-black silent western *Tenderfeet*, and he continued working as a performer, technician, and writer of "race pictures" (films with black casts designed for African American movie houses).

Impressed by his work, in 1940 the producer Alfred Sack offered Williams the opportunity to create his own films, and Williams moved to Texas to make race pictures for Sack Amusement Enterprises. The first film he created for Sack was 1941's *The Blood of Jesus*, the story of a woman who is accidentally shot by her husband and, finding her spirit at the crossroads between Heaven and Hell, must resist the temptations of drinking and dancing in order to find redemption. Shot around Dallas for a budget of $5,000 (miniscule even by 1940 standards), this Baptist allegory was commercially successful and is generally considered to be Williams's best work, praised in recent years as "magnificent" by the *New York Times* and appearing on *Time* magazine's list of "The 25 Most Important Films on Race." His ability to make a commercially successful film on a shoestring budget made Williams popular with both his crew, who praised his speed and professionalism, and with Alfred Sack, who gave Williams free reign to continue making movies both religious (such as *Brother Martin: Servant of Jesus*) and secular (*Dirty Gertie from Harlem, U.S.A.*; *Juke Joint*) for the rest of the 1940s.

In 1950, Williams seized on an opportunity that was both entrepreneurial and a way to help his fellow veterans, and he moved to Tulsa, Oklahoma, to cofound the American Business and Industrial College, a technical school for returning African American servicemen going to college on the G.I. Bill. He was in Tulsa for only a year when he accepted the role of Andy in the new television version of the popular, problematic *Amos & Andy* radio show. Created by Freeman Gosden and Charles Correll, two white minstrel show performers who voiced their characters in an exaggerated black dialect, *Amos & Andy* was a comedy about two ignorant friends—Amos, the childlike innocent and Andy, the blustering dimwit—who were constantly thwarted in their attempts to get rich quick. Gosden and Correll had originally planned to play the parts on the television show themselves, wearing blackface, but they eventually hired an all-black cast who brought their talents and experience to these decades-old stereotypes. Although the show was successful with viewers and sponsors, in the face of sustained condemnation from the NAACP over what the president Walter White saw as the program's offensive caricatures of African Americans, CBS cancelled the series in 1954 after seventy-nine episodes.

Williams worked very little after the cancellation of *Amos & Andy*, living off his pension and veteran's benefits, and he passed away from kidney failure at the Sawtelle Veterans Administration Hospital in Los Angeles at the age of seventy-nine. He was survived by his widow, Eula, and his films were largely forgotten until the discovery of several canisters of his movies in a warehouse in Tyler, Texas, in 1983. The consequent reevaluation of his work has rightfully placed Spencer Williams beside Oscar Micheaux as the only African American auteurs in midcentury American film.

FURTHER READING

Cripps, Thomas. *Slow Fade to Black: The Negro in American Film, 1902–1942* (1977).

Ely, Melvin Patrick. *The Adventures of Amos 'n' Andy: A Social History of an American Phenomenon* (1991).

Weisenfeld, Judith. *Hollywood Be Thy Name: African American Religion in American Film, 1929–1949* (2007).

MALCOLM WOMACK

Williams, Stanley "Tookie" (29 Dec. 1953–13 Dec. 2005), cofounder of Los Angeles's Crips gang, author, Nobel Prize nominee, and antigang activist, was born in New Orleans, Louisiana, and moved to South Central Los Angeles in 1959, after his parents (names unknown) divorced. Gang rivalry was prevalent in the area, and Williams was intrigued by the thrilling stories he heard from older neighborhood boys who had served time in prison. As a teenager, he spent time in a variety of juvenile detention centers in California and Utah for drug use, fighting, and suspected burglary.

Back in South Central, Williams earned a reputation as an expert street fighter and, along with high school friend Raymond Lee Washington, founded the Crips in 1971. Although the Crips—a derivative of "crib"—was originally founded to protect and defend the members and their families from gang aggression, it rapidly increased in membership and violent activity to rival the area's other notorious gang, the Bloods. Spin-off Crip gangs formed across the United States and in countries as far away as Germany and South Africa.

In 1981, at age twenty-six, Williams was convicted of multiple homicides for the shooting of four people during two separate 1979 robberies. The conviction landed him on San Quentin's death row, though Williams consistently maintained his innocence. After several years in prison, including over six years in "the hole" (solitary confinement) for fighting with other inmates, Williams embarked on a period of intense study and self-improvement. He began to memorize scores of words and definitions from a dictionary given to him by a prison chaplain, and he read books about black history and culture, law, psychology, politics, math, and religion. Williams reached a critical realization during this period of reeducation: his gang activity had been rooted in intense self-hatred. His new regimen of self-examination, study, and discussion became focused on making amends, in whatever way possible, for the wrongs of his past.

In January 1993 journalist Barbara Becnel visited San Quentin to interview Williams for a book she was writing about the history of the Crips and Bloods. The two forged a friendship that would result in many years of collaborative antigang activism. Later that year Williams videotaped a speech to be shown at a gang summit in Los Angeles. The speech, rooted in Williams's new understanding of gangs as brothers acting out their self-hatred on one another, called for an end to the rivalry between the Crips and the Bloods. Becnel facilitated the effort and hired a crew to film the speech.

In another visit with Becnel, Williams expressed his desire to write a book dissuading children from following in his footsteps. He dictated text to Becnel over the prison phone, and she transcribed and edited what later became a series of children's books. Subtitled "Tookie Speaks Out against Gang Violence," the 1996 series is intended for children in

grades one through five. In straightforward, easy-to-read language, the books explain the perils of gang culture: mobbing, gangbanging, and drug abuse are all candidly defined and discussed. Titles include *Gangs and Weapons*, *Gangs and Your Neighborhood*, *Gangs and Self-Esteem*, and *Gangs and the Abuse of Power*. The eight small volumes explain the source of gang violence as fear. Each book emphasizes positive choices and ends with a sincere call to avoid gangs. Although sometimes considered controversial, even inappropriate, the series soon met with international success. Royalties are donated to activist groups such as Mothers against Gang Wars and the Institute for the Prevention of Youth Violence.

In 1998, again with Becnel's assistance, Williams published a lengthier book for young adult readers, *Life in Prison*. It provided a blunt account of daily prison life through photographs and chapters focusing, for example, on strip searches, prison health care, "the hole," and homesickness. One of Williams's goals in writing the book was to strip the glamour from conventional conceptions of gang life. *Life in Prison* garnered praise from many arenas and was named one of the American Library Association's "Quick Picks for Reluctant Readers."

The books' success led to other projects. "Tookie's Corner," an educational Internet Web site begun in 1997, provided a forum for children to post questions and receive Williams's answers (www.tookie.com). It also contained Williams's public apology for creating the Crips and a multipage document called "The Tookie Protocol for Peace," a prototype for countering urban street violence. Working with Becnel and other activists, Williams established the Internet Project for Street Peace, which taught computer skills, literacy, leadership, and violence-prevention strategies to ten- to fourteen-year-olds at the nonprofit Neighborhood House for North Richmond, not far from San Quentin. These children then communicated by means of the Internet with at-risk children in South Africa, another country with escalating gang violence. The project impressed Winnie Mandela, who visited Williams at San Quentin in October 1999 to discuss strategies for combating South Africa's gang problems.

Perhaps Williams's most controversial experience was his nomination for multiple Nobel Prizes. Lauding Williams's children's books and antigang activism, a member of Switzerland's parliament nominated him for the Nobel Peace Prize in 2000. In subsequent years, Williams received several nominations for both the Peace and Literature prizes, but he never received either award.

Although a 2002 decision by the Ninth Circuit Court rejected the appeal against Williams's death sentence, it recommended clemency and suggested that California's governor, Gray Davis, commute his sentence in light of Williams's antigang efforts while incarcerated. Still, in February 2005, another appeal was denied, and his execution was scheduled for December. As the date approached, activists held rallies, vigils, and peaceful protests across the United States. A campaign to raise awareness of the situation was centralized through an Internet site. It included information on contacting Governor Arnold Schwarzenegger, signing petitions promoting Williams's pardon, and donating to the campaign. News coverage included a variety of views on Williams and the death penalty and sometimes even featured interviews with Williams himself. While supporters of the death penalty generally remained focused on the violent murders of which Williams was convicted, death penalty opponents tended to emphasize the ongoing stream of constructive projects and programs springing from Williams's prison cell.

Williams continued his work from death row. Always active in antigang projects, Williams published a sizable volume of memoirs in 2004 and was working on a collection of essays, *Thoughts of Thunder: A Manifesto for the Mind*, when his execution date arrived. His authorship and activism from death row bear witness to the possibility of rehabilitation in the face of impending execution. Williams meditated on his uncertain future in his memoirs and concluded that perhaps "merely demonstrating that this awakening was possible was my mission" (*Blue Rage, Black Redemption*, 293).

FURTHER READING
Williams, Stanley "Tookie." *Blue Rage, Black Redemption: A Memoir* (2004).
Sevcik, Kimberley. "Has Stanley Williams Left the Gang?" *New York Times* (10 Aug. 2003).
Van Slambrouck, Paul. "On Death Row, an Author and Nobel Nominee," *Christian Science Monitor* (28 Nov. 2000).
Wagner, Venise. "An Inspiration from Death Row," *San Francisco Chronicle* (11 Dec. 2000).
Willwerth, James. "Lessons Learned from Death Row: A Repentant Founder of the Crips Writes Books to Warn Kids off Gangs," *Time* 148, 15 (23 Sept. 1996).
Obituary: *New York Times*; 13 Dec. 2005.

GINNY CROSTHWAIT

Williams, Tony (12 Dec. 1945–23 Feb. 1997), drummer, was born Tillmon Anthony Williams in Chicago, the son of Tillmon Williams, a saxophonist. Nothing is known about his mother. His family moved to the Boston area when he was two. The younger Williams started playing drums before he was ten, and his father allowed him to sit in at jazz clubs as soon as he was able. By the time Tony was eleven, he was playing on his own. He studied with Boston educator and drummer Alan Dawson and as a young teenager he played with both ART BLAKEY and MAX ROACH. He was also influenced by PHILLY JOE JONES, Jimmy Cobb, and Louis Hayes. Williams took his craft seriously even at that young age, practicing eight hours a day in the late fifties and early sixties. By the age of fifteen he enjoyed an active freelance career in the greater Boston area. He often played with organ trios and experimental musicians, presaging his later career in jazz fusion.

In 1959 and 1960 Williams played with the saxophonist SAM RIVERS, who became his first important mentor. Williams worked with Rivers in a band led by pianist Leroy Fallana. The two played in a variety of settings, including some of the period's so-called "third stream" experiments in jazz and classical fusion, notably with a chamber group called the Boston Improvisational Ensemble. In late 1962 the saxophonist JACKIE MCLEAN came to a Boston club called Connelly's, where Williams was part of the house rhythm section. McLean was so impressed by the young drummer's virtuosity and imagination he talked Williams's family into allowing Tony to accompany him to New York City. Williams lived in McLean's house for two months and he appeared on his classic album, *One Step Beyond*.

In 1963 MILES DAVIS heard Williams and invited him to join the new quintet Davis was forming. Williams remained with this group until 1969, the drummer on the brilliant string of recordings Davis made with WAYNE SHORTER, Ron Carter, and HERBIE HANCOCK. His clean, spare sound on the ride cymbal and his unprecedented, flexible approach to tempos were central to the rhythmically elastic sound of the group's performances. Williams further disconnected the drums from a strict timekeeping function, playing meterless percussive sounds over a steady beat. His blinding speed and use of polyrhythms and displaced accents created a more supple, less definable pulse. During this time Williams also played with a range of the most important improvisers in jazz, including Rivers and ERIC DOLPHY (on Dolphy's album *Out to Lunch*), and he made two studio recordings with his own groups. On *Life Time* (1964) he was accompanied by Rivers, Hancock, Bobby Hutcherson on vibes, and

Richard Davis and Gary Peacock on bass. Williams himself wrote four of the compositions on the album, each with different instrumental combinations; the trio piece "Memory," with Hutcherson and Hancock, was particularly impressive. The second recording, *Spring*, included Rivers, Hancock, Peacock, and Wayne Shorter on tenor sax, and it highlighted Williams's fondness for enigmatic lyricism.

During Williams's last years with Davis, the jazz great had become increasingly interested in electric instruments and rock rhythms. Williams took this trend one step further in founding Lifetime, the first jazz-rock fusion group, with Larry Young on organ and John McLaughlin on electric guitar. In truth, the move should not have been surprising at all. His early interest in organ trios, his fanatical love of the Beatles (he had a Beatles poster on his wall while he was playing with Davis in 1965), and his fondness for JIMI HENDRIX and the group Cream were all clear indications of his broader rhythmic and aural interests. He certainly had no objection to "free" music, having been impressed by ORNETTE COLEMAN as early as 1959 or 1960. And unlike many jazz purists, Williams embraced electric instruments. They were, he believed, simply another sound to be exploited. Lifetime's first album, *Emergency* (1969), was recorded in only two days and suffered from horribly distorted studio sound and Williams's own rather anemic vocals. But it also successfully combined the improvisational excitement of jazz with the raw energy of rock and was filled with spectacular instrumental performances. Williams used heavy, parade band sticks for a bigger sound—the cymbal crashes and bass drum bombs were louder than ever. Jazz fans and critics were simply not ready for a stripped-down ensemble playing amplified guitar and rock rhythms, punctuated by dissonant sound effects and a piercing jazz organ, but rock audiences loved it all. The second album, *Turn It Over* (1970), added Cream's Jack Bruce on electric bass. The recording was cleaner and the tunes had a bluesier feel, but more importantly, it abandoned any connection with the sophistication of jazz and projected a darker, far more aggressive sound.

But the group's music began to drift. McLaughlin left in 1971 to join Miles Davis's own electric group, and Williams brought in several new players, notably bassist Ron Carter and two additional percussionists, for 1971's *Ego.* Larry Young left before the rhythm and blues–influenced 1972 album, *Bum's Rush*, and

Williams himself increasingly dominated the stage. Lifetime recorded three more albums with constantly shifting personnel before it finally disbanded.

Williams subsequently returned to more traditional jazz formats. From 1976 to 1978 he toured and recorded several albums with "The Great Jazz Trio" (Hank Jones on piano and Carter on bass). He also played with the Davis tribute group, VSOP, in 1976, 1977, 1979, and 1983, touring extensively and making several recordings. In 1977 he settled in the San Francisco area and studied composition at the University of California, Berkeley. Over the next several years he played with SONNY ROLLINS and toured with the Herbie Hancock Quartet.

In 1985 Williams released an album under his own name for the first time since 1978. *Foreign Intrigue* was a sextet with trumpeter Wallace Roney, saxophonist Billy Pierce, pianist Mulgrew Miller, vibraphonist Hutcherson, and bassist Carter; the mix of young lions and modernist veterans provided the perfect context for the drummer's return to straight-ahead jazz. Williams recorded six albums for Blue Note with this group (with shifting bass players) over the next seven years, culminating in 1992's *Tokyo Live*, a two-CD set that served as a summation of the group's passionate hard-bop style.

After disbanding this group, Williams toured with a Miles Davis tribute group in 1992 with Hancock, Shorter, and Carter; a recording by the group won a Grammy in 1995. He also made several television appearances, notably on the *Miles Ahead* documentary of the PBS "Great Performances" series. His last jazz recording came in 1996, with *Young At Heart*, on Columbia Records, a trio session with pianist Miller and bassist Ira Coleman; Williams was more restrained than he had been in years, providing sophisticated, swinging support on standards such as "Green Dolphin Street" and "Body and Soul." Perhaps appropriately, however, Williams's very last recording was "Wilderness," his first orchestrated composition, written for a twenty-piece string orchestra. Evoking the Americana of composers such as Aaron Copland, the piece reflected Williams's ongoing study of extended compositional forms. He died suddenly, suffering a heart attack after routine gallbladder surgery. He was survived by his wife, Colleen, whom he had married in 1994.

Tony Williams became one of jazz's most influential post-bop drummers at an astonishingly early age. He was intuitive in accompanying soloists, excelled in delicate and light playing filled with dramatic contrasts, and his own solos were colorful essays in flexible rhythm. His musical interests seemed to parallel those of his broader artistic generation, moving from the aggressive hard bop championed by McLean and others, to the more supple experimental music of Davis, then to Williams's own unique and pioneering jazz-rock fusion. His return to more traditional jazz forms in the 1980s and 1990s mirrored the contemporary direction of the jazz community. In the end, stereotyped definitions of jazz proved too constraining for his imagination. His untimely death cut short an original, creative musical path.

FURTHER READING

De Barros, P. "Tony Williams: Two Decades of Drum Innovation," *Down Beat* (Nov. 1983).

Gibbs, V. "Tony Williams: Report on a Musical Lifetime," *Down Beat* 43 (Feb. 1976).

Point, Michael. "Tony Williams: The Final Interview," *Down Beat* 64 (April 1997).

Taylor, Arthur. *Notes and Tones: Musician to Musician Interviews*, 3d ed. (1993).

Underwood, Lee. "Tony Williams: Aspiring to a Lifetime of Leadership," *Down Beat* 46 (Dec. 1979).

Woodson, C. D. "Solo Jazz Drumming: An Analytical Study of the Improvisational Techniques of Anthony Williams," thesis, UCLA, 1973.

Obituaries: *The New York Times*, 26 Feb. 1997; *Jazz Times*, 27 May 1997.

RONALD P. DUFOUR

Williams, Walter E. (31 Mar. 1936–), author, educator, and economist, was born Walter Edward Williams in Philadelphia, Pennsylvania. His father and namesake was a latherer, someone who prepared foundations for the plasterer during the construction of plaster houses; he divorced Williams's mother, Catherine (Morgan) Williams, when Williams was a young child. Williams's mother was left to raise him and his younger sister alone in the Richard Allen housing projects, a predominantly low-income black neighborhood in North Philadelphia, until her marriage later to Thomas Burchett.

In his teens Williams held a number of low-wage jobs to help support his family while attending Benjamin Franklin High School from 1950 to 1954. Despite being economically one of the lowest-ranking schools in Pennsylvania, Benjamin Franklin provided Williams with a solid learning experience including no-nonsense teachers and a first-class curriculum. Being black was not an excuse to do poorly in school; Williams had the ambition to get out of poverty and succeed.

On 6 August 1959 Williams was drafted into the U.S. Army in what the economist would later call a "government confiscation of labor services," since he was forced to leave his job with the Yellow Cab Company. He trained at Fort Jackson, South Carolina, and Fort Stewart, Georgia, before being sent to Korea for one year. During this time Williams married Conchetta "Connie" Taylor on 31 May 1960. They later had one child, a daughter.

Prior to serving in the army Williams had visited his birth father and grandmother in Los Angeles, California. There he had learned of the opportunities available for subsidized higher education and briefly attended Los Angeles City College. Following his release from the army on 3 July 1961, Williams and his wife made plans to move to Los Angeles. They both worked until they had saved $800 to move in December 1961. In February 1962 Williams enrolled at California State University, Los Angeles, from which he received his B.A. in Economics in 1965 before continuing on to the doctoral program at the University of California, Los Angeles (UCLA).

While attending university, from 1963 to 1967 Williams worked as a probation supervisor for the juvenile division of the Los Angeles County Probation Department. After receiving his M.A. in Economics from UCLA in 1967, he returned to his alma mater as an assistant professor from 1967 to 1971, as he continued to work toward his doctoral degree. At this point, Williams faced an educational disaster: along with the majority of his doctoral class, he failed the comprehensive examination in microeconomic theory. Although crestfallen, he was also pleased. His professors' willingness to fail him convinced Williams that they were more concerned with producing competent economists than with meeting a racial quota. With his professors' support and additional study, Williams was able to retake and pass the exam, and he began writing his dissertation. During these last years of schooling Williams met and exchanged ideas with THOMAS SOWELL, a like-minded black economist who taught briefly at UCLA. Williams also served on the research staff at the Urban Institute in Washington, D.C., from 1971 to 1973, researching poverty and racial discrimination.

Earlier, David Caplovitz's *Poor Pay More: Consumer Practices of Low-Income Families* (1963, 1967) had excited concern for low-income consumers who were forced to pay higher prices than higher-income consumers for lower-quality food and other goods. This study was heavily cited, and it influenced subsequent legislation passed to prevent the exploitation of America's poor. Williams's further investigation into this phenomenon would eventually become his dissertation, "The Low-Income Market Place." He found that high prices and low quality were directly associated with the increased risks, especially crime, that every business serving low-income neighborhoods encountered. He concluded that merchants were responding rationally to market conditions and predicted that policy failing to recognize this would only worsen the situation. Williams completed his dissertation in 1972 and received his Ph.D. in Economics.

The following year Williams took a position in his hometown at Temple University. When Temple's Department of Economics proposed a new course in "black economics," Williams was appalled and asked his colleagues if the laws of supply and demand were different for blacks than they were for other racial groups. He criticized the practice of heaping guilt upon whites for events long past. This idea later evolved into his famous "Proclamation of Amnesty and Pardon Granted to All Persons of European Descent" completed in the 1990s. This proclamation "pardoned" whites for their historical crimes against blacks—Williams's effort to improve race relations in America.

In 1976 the Joint Economic Committee of the Congress of the United States commissioned Williams's *Youth and Minority Unemployment* (1977) while he was a National Fellow at the Hoover Institute at Stanford University in California. Williams cited minimum wage laws and labor union monopolies as the root causes of black unemployment. Minimum wage laws, he argued, prevented youths from holding jobs because employers could not hire at a market-determined wage but were instead required to pay a (higher) legislated wage. Labor unions sought state regulation to prevent employers from making contracts with individual workers so that they could charge monopoly prices for their labor. Williams, in direct opposition to popular opinion, recommended the elimination of these controls as the best way to improve youth unemployment conditions. In 1977 Williams began working as a columnist, first writing for the *Philadelphia Tribune*, the oldest black-owned daily newspaper in America, founded by Christopher J. Perry in 1884. By 1981 Williams had a nationally syndicated column with Heritage Features Syndicate, acquired by Creators Syndicate in 1991. Williams critiqued policies such as affirmative action, gun control, and socialized health care

while voicing support for capitalism, immigration, and even succession, soon gaining popularity among American libertarians and conservatives of all races.

In June 1981 Williams left Temple University as a full professor of economics to take a position as the John M. Olin Distinguished Professor of Economics at George Mason University in Fairfax, Virginia. There he wrote *The State Against Blacks* (1982) on how state legislation aggravated economic conditions for low-income blacks. Beginning in 1986 he worked in South Africa, collecting information for his book *South Africa's War Against Capitalism* (1989), in which he criticized the state-granted monopolist power given to white labor unions. In 1992 Williams began appearing as a substitute host on radio for the *Rush Limbaugh Show*. He also served as chairman of the Department of Economics at George Mason from 1995 to 2001 and wrote commentaries for the Public Broadcasting Service (PBS) from 2001 to 2002. His ability to make basic economic principles understandable to the general public earned him the honorary title of "The People's Economist" from his admirers. Refusing to ally himself with a political party, Walter E. Williams claimed a mission to preserve liberty in America. "If liberty dies in America," he argued, "it'll die everywhere."

FURTHER READING
Williams's publications and an online archive of selected syndicated columns are available through his faculty website at George Mason University, accessible at http://www.gmu.edu/departments/economics/wew/.

JENNIFER VAUGHN

Williams, Wayne (27 May 1958–), convicted murderer and alleged serial killer, was born in Atlanta, Georgia, to Homer and Faye Williams, both schoolteachers. Williams attended Frederick Douglass High School, where he was an honors student, and matriculated to Georgia State University but soon dropped out.

Williams was known around his neighborhood as a bit of an oddball and a teller of tales, but his only run-in with law enforcement came as a teenager in a 1976 incident in which he was arrested for impersonating a police officer. The charges were later dropped. His employment history is spotty. Apparently, he fancied himself a kind of radio personality, though his broadcast booth was a room in his parents' Atlanta residence. He also did a bit of freelance photography

Wayne Williams, center, is led from the Fulton County Jail in Atlanta during his trial, 18 January 1982. (AP Images.)

and videography, using a police scanner to tip him to area accidents, which he then rushed to film.

In 1979 what are thought to be the first killings in the Atlanta child murder case took place. Two young boys, Edward Smith, who was fourteen years old, and Alfred Evans, who was either twelve or thirteen, had gone missing for several days. On 28 July, a woman stumbled upon their bodies clumsily hidden in the bushes along a thoroughfare. In September a fourteen-year-old, Milton Harvey, vanished while running an errand for his mother. A month later, nine-year-old Yusef Bell disappeared during a trip to the grocery store for a neighbor. His body was found sometime later in

the derelict E. P. Johnson Elementary school building, strangled. The recovery of Bell's body touched off an outcry in the city and a promise by city officials to crack down on the rash of violence against Atlanta's African American children.

The investigation was a long one, however, and the police were slow to conclude that a serial killer was the culprit. Over the course of the following two years, police identified as many as thirty-one victims, some strangled, some bludgeoned, some stabbed. Some investigators and observers have argued that as many as sixty other potential victims were arbitrarily excluded from the police department's tally of "official" victims.

Near the end of the series of killings, adults joined the list of victims. On 30 March 1981, Larry Rogers, a twenty-year-old, was found strangled. Police theorized that his killer was in fact the Atlanta Child Killer. Just a day later, another adult, twenty-one-year-old Eddie Duncan, was added to the list. More adult victims followed.

Atlanta, and much of the country, was in a state of shock and panic. Theories as to the nature of the killer ranged from claims that a cult of Satanists were responsible—a possibility advanced by the civil rights activist ROY INNIS—to a gang of Ku Klux Klansmen bent on targeting young blacks and terrorizing the city's African American community.

The break in the case came on 22 May 1981. Because several of the victims had been found in the Chattahoochee River, police had taken to staking out areas near bridges in hopes of catching the killer as he (or they) moved to dispose of evidence. It was on that Friday night that a pair of Atlanta policemen staked out near the James Jackson Parkway Bridge heard a loud splash in the water and saw a car driving away with its headlights switched off. The officers radioed ahead to a waiting FBI agent, who stopped the car. Inside was Wayne Williams. Questioned, Williams claimed to be a music promoter looking for the house of a singer he wished to audition, but the address and phone number he gave to police turned out to be made up. When two days later the body of Nathaniel Carter was pulled from the Chattahoochee, Williams was treated as the primary suspect in the case. He subsequently failed a number of polygraph tests and much of his alibi turned out to be false. Fiber evidence found on the victim was linked to various sources in Williams' home, including a family pet. On 21 June 1981, Williams was arrested and charged with the murder of Carter and that of Jimmy Payne, a twenty-one-year-old missing since April. Williams's connection to the Payne killing has long been a source of controversy surrounding the case.

The trial began in January of the following year. Much of the evidence against Williams appears to have been circumstantial. The fiber evidence used by prosecutors, though incriminatory, was hardly conclusive. The fibers themselves were of an extremely common variety, such as might be found in countless other homes. Other potentially exculpatory evidence was never presented to the jury (several witnesses who had seen Carter alive *after* the famous Chattahoochee splash incident were never called to testify). Nevertheless, Williams himself proved a less-than-perfect witness, and his on-stand outbursts seem to have convinced the jury of his probable culpability. On 27 February, the jury returned a verdict of guilty on two counts of first-degree murder. Williams was sentenced to two consecutive life sentences.

Questions remained, however, as to both the nature and the number of victims, as well as regards Williams's guilt. In 2005 some of the murder cases were reopened by police in DeKalb County, where several of the crimes had taken place, but no new evidence was found. In 2007 DNA testing of the fibers that had sealed Williams's fate likewise proved inconclusive. Some authorities have claimed that the greatest proof of Williams's guilt is that the series of murders stopped after he was arrested, while others counter that numerous victims who appear to fit the Atlanta Child Killer's pattern appeared thereafter. Whatever the case, Williams remained in prison as of 2012 and has never stopped asserting his innocence.

FURTHER READING

Baldwin, James. *The Evidence of Things Not Seen* (1985).
CNN.com. *Cold-Case Squad to Probe Decades-Old Atlanta Murders.* Television broadcast (7 May 2005).
Headley, Bernard. *The Atlanta Youth Murders and the Politics of Race* (1998).

JASON PHILIP MILLER

Williams, Wesley (26 Aug. 1897–3 July 1984), battalion chief in the New York City Fire Department, was born in New York City, the eldest son of James H. Williams, chief red cap (porter) of the New York Central Railroad station (now Grand Central Terminal), and Lucy (Metrash) Williams. Williams spent some of his early childhood years with his mother's family in Norwalk, Connecticut, where he attended the Marvin Elementary School. In 1903 the Williamses moved to the Bronx after Williams's father started working as a porter and they later moved to Harlem. When Williams was twelve years old he won a roller-skating contest thanks to the training advice of Charles Ramsay, his aunt's neighbor. Ramsay taught Williams the principles of Benarr Macfadden's "Physical Culture" philosophy: to breathe fresh air, eat fresh foods rich in vitamins, and exercise through progressive resistance training. It was believed that by following these principles one could maximize physical and mental strength.

Williams dropped out of school at the age of sixteen to work for the Flynn and O'Rouke Company, which helped excavate tunnels for the new subway system. Williams's father insisted that he stop this risky job after he heard about tunnels caving in. He then began to work part-time as a red cap in New York's Pennsylvania Station and as a parcel-post truck driver. Williams was emerging as a gifted athlete in swimming, baseball, basketball, handball, and weightlifting, and he wanted a more exciting career than working as a red cap or a driver. In 1918 he planned to take the civil service exam for the police department, but instead he took the fire department exam. Out of a field of 1,700 candidates, Williams was the only one to score 100 percent on the physical exam, and he ranked thirteenth overall. The department nonetheless balked at hiring Williams because of his race, and it required the intervention of former New York police commissioner, mayor, governor, and U.S. President Theodore Roosevelt on Williams's behalf before the Fire Department of New York (FDNY) would hire Williams.

The FDNY predominantly comprised men of Irish descent. When Williams's friends at the Harlem YMCA found out about his appointment, they suggested that he take up boxing. Some of the prizefighters who worked out at the Harlem Y, such as Joe Gennet, Panama Al Brown, and SAM LANGFORD instructed him in the art of boxing. After completing probationary training Williams was appointed on 10 January 1919 to Engine Company 55 at 363 Broome Street in Manhattan. The captain of the station, refusing to work with a black man, retired on Williams's first day of duty. The rest of the men in the company put in for transfers. Headquarters decided to place a one-year moratorium on transfers out of the company. The men refused to talk to Williams, but a representative for the men advised him that they would talk to him if he agreed to sleep in a bed of his own in the basement. Williams refused. His coworkers were further angered when Williams qualified to be an engine driver, a coveted position for a fireman.

Besides enduring cruel acts, such as having chicken entrails placed in his boots, his fire coat slashed with a razor, and his helmet crushed under the wheels of the fire engine, Williams had to give up competing in public sporting contests to become a fireman. He could not defend his Amateur Athletic Union (AAU) weight-lifting championship in the one-arm dead lift at 625 pounds. The clean-and-jerk heavyweight record was a mere 250 pounds—Williams was lifting 345 pounds. In 1924 Williams became the FDNY's heavyweight boxing champion.

If Williams was not busy doing his probationary service duty chores, which sometimes meant cleaning urine or feces out of the spittoons, then he was working out in his own private gym in the hose tower. He was often alone studying the rules and regulations of the FDNY, and despite the difficulties, successfully endured his probationary period, becoming New York City's first black lieutenant in 1927. It was unusual to promote a man to be an officer in the same company he had worked as a fireman. He was promoted to captain in 1934 at 55 Engine, and battalion chief in 1938.

It was not until the late 1930s that more blacks were allowed to join the FDNY. Those who entered the fire department in 1938 and 1939 encountered the same Jim Crow policy that Williams had endured. Many times these men would call on Williams to intervene on their behalf. Williams advised the black firefighters to form an organization that would take their concerns to headquarters. Twelve other men joined with Williams in 1940 to form the Vulcan Society, which became instrumental in leading the fight against racism and the Jim Crow rules in the FDNY. Through the next several decades the Vulcan Society continued to act in the interest of African American firefighters. In the early 2000s it took additional steps to increase the number of African Americans hired by the FDNY.

Williams retired from the fire department in 1952. Living in the Bronx, New Jersey, and then Harlem, he gave speeches at churches and schools describing his experiences in the fire department, and the lifelong benefits of practicing Physical Culture.

FURTHER READING

Wesley Williams's papers, dated 1909–1984 and 1919–1984, are housed in the Schomburg Center for Research in Black Culture's Manuscripts, Archive and Rare Books Division in New York City, New York.

Leuthner, Stuart. *The Railroaders* (1983).

Marshal, David. *Grand Central* (1946).

CHARLES FORD WILLIAMS

Williams, William Taylor Burwell (3 June 1866–26 March 1941), educator, was born in Clarke County, Virginia. His parents, Edmund and Louisa Johnson Williams, formerly enslaved, were illiterate and worked as farm laborers. Williams's first teachers were minimally trained rural blacks. He was subsequently taught by educated northerners of both races, who came South as missionaries to the black community. In spite of this inauspicious beginning, he graduated, cum laude, from Harvard University.

By 1883, having absorbed all that local schools could offer, Williams, like many others of the era, began teaching. He was seventeen years old and earned thirty dollars monthly, three times his father's salary. Williams taught at Peace and Plenty School in Clarke County and supervised the other teacher assigned there. In 1886, he enrolled at Hampton Institute in Hampton, Virginia.

Williams worked as a janitor and waiter at Hampton to finance his education. He also taught eighty students at Hampton's elementary school and Sunday school classes for children and adults. He graduated as valedictorian of the class of 1888, completing the three year course in two years.

Williams was influenced by Samuel Armstrong, Hampton's founder, and by Hollis Frissell, the Institute's vice-principal. Both believed industrial education was most appropriate for blacks. This model, designed to prepare students to be effective laborers, deemphasized literature, languages, and the arts. Williams, perceived as different from other blacks, was encouraged to pursue academic education. Frissell arranged for Williams's admission to his alma mater, the elite Phillips Academy in Andover, Massachusetts. With a scholarship funded by the Congregational Church, Williams studied modern and ancient languages, geometry, physics, and history. He won prizes for oratory, was editor of the school newspaper, and graduated in 1893.

Although he passed Yale's entrance exam, Williams enrolled at Harvard with a scholarship arranged by Armstrong. In addition to courses similar to those at Phillips, he studied economics, government, geology, philosophy and fine arts. He graduated in 1897.

Following graduation, Williams was principal of an Indiana primary school serving southern migrant children and adults. He believed both industrial and academic education would benefit his students. Since financial resources were limited, Williams sought donations from local businesses and convinced skilled community members to volunteer as instructors. He thought community involvement and support were essential to a successful school.

The early twentieth century brought expanded contributions by northern philanthropic groups to the education of southern blacks. John D. Rockefeller funded the General Education Board (GEB) in support of industrial education, Quaker heiress Anna T. Jeanes established an endowment for the benefit of rural schools for blacks and the fund established by industrialist John F. Slater financed teacher training. In view of his education and teaching experience, Williams was an ideal person to implement the goals of these philanthropists.

In 1902 he was appointed Field Agent for the GEB, in 1906 for the Slater Fund and in 1910 for the Jeanes Fund. As Field Agent, he traveled throughout the South, observing conditions in black schools and making recommendations for financing improvements. Usually blacks attended schools for three months annually while whites attended between six and nine. There were race based disparities in teacher salaries, books and other supplies were inadequate and most black teachers were educationally deficient.

Adopting Williams's recommendations, the trustees of the funds lengthened the school year for blacks and supplemented teacher salaries. They funded construction and staffing of teacher training schools and financed and expanded college libraries. Among the trustees were William Howard Taft and Andrew Carnegie. Realizing that many trustees favored industrial education, Williams, sometimes surreptitiously, encouraged more emphasis on academic subjects. Before Negro History Week was established, he encouraged teachers to include black history and biographies in their lessons. Believing the entire community was responsible for the education of its children, he castigated parents of truant children, encouraged teachers to make their lessons relevant to students' lives and lobbied churches and fraternal groups for donations to supplement inadequate government funding of black schools. Deeply interested in enhancing the role of ministers in the educational process, Williams taught an annual summer course for clergymen.

While serving as Field Agent, Williams was editor of *The Southern Workman*, Hampton's journal which circulated internationally. He wrote prolifically, his articles reaching African American scholars as well as less educated subscribers. This broadened his sphere of influence. In 1909 and 1910 Williams accompanied BOOKER T. WASHINGTON on tours of southern schools. He was president of the American Teachers Association whose members included JOHN HOPE, president of Atlanta Baptist College, forerunner of Morehouse. He was president of the Sumner Literary Society and held office in the Virginia Tennis Association and the Negro Organization Society, an umbrella group established by Booker T. Washington. Williams was also a member of the Odd Fellows, Prince Hall Masons, Alpha Phi Alpha Fraternity and the exclusive black organization, Sigma Pi Phi Boulé. He considered these groups vehicles for the uplift of African Americans.

Commissioned by the United States Department of Labor, Williams authored a 1917 study of black migration from the South. In 1919 he became vice-principal of Tuskegee and was charged with upgrading the academic department. He traveled to Haiti to review their educational system and returned recommending that blacks invest money and skills in that nation's development. Four years after Morehouse College awarded him an honorary doctorate, he became Tuskegee's first Dean.

In June 1904, Williams married Emily Harper, a musician who also taught at Tuskegee. In 1933, Emily died and in 1937 Williams married the widowed Kate Greene. Although childless, he reared as his own a niece and nephew and financially supported the education of countless other relatives and friends.

During Williams' lifetime, racism in America restricted African American opportunities for advancement. He challenged that situation by promoting the interdependence of all people of color and by arguing that African Americans should be exposed to all forms of education. In 1934, he received the NAACP's highest honor, the Spingarn Medal for his contributions to the education of African Americans. At the age of seventy-five, while still actively engaged in his life's work, he suffered a heart attack and died at his Tuskegee home.

FURTHER READING

The majority of W. T. B. Williams's professional papers are located at Tuskegee University. Some of his personal papers are included in the Blackwell Chapman Tyler Washington Papers, portions of which have been donated to the Library of Virginia in Richmond. Phillips Academy and Hampton and Harvard Universities maintain vertical files with clippings about his activities and accomplishments. Many of the reports prepared by Williams for the General Education Board are housed at the Rockefeller Archives in Pocantico Hills, New York.

Anderson, James D. *The Education of Blacks in the South, 1860–1935* (1988).

Gatewood, Willard B. *Aristocrats of Color: The Black Elite 1880–1920* (1990).

Hammond, L. H. "An Educational Leader," *The Southern Workman* pp. 478–481 (October 1922).

DONNA TYLER HOLLIE

Williamson, Fred (5 Mar. 1938–), football player, sportscaster, actor, director, screenwriter, and producer, was born in Gary, Indiana, where his father was a steelworker and his mother a homemaker. Williamson earned a track scholarship to Northwestern University, where he studied architecture, but football coach Ara Parseghian recruited him for an additional spot. After college Williamson played for the San Francisco 49ers in 1960 before jumping to the National Football League's new rival, the American Football League. In four seasons with the Oakland Raiders and three with the Kansas City Chiefs, he was an outstanding defensive back, earning the nickname "The Hammer" for his practice of hitting opposing players in the head with his forearm while tackling them.

Williamson's "unsportsmanlike" play earned him great notoriety. Before the first Super Bowl, played in January 1967, he boasted that he would knock Green Bay Packer receivers Boyd Dowler and Carroll Dale out of the game. Instead Williamson's head collided with the knee of running back Donny Anderson, leading to his exit from the game in the fourth quarter. Williamson reportedly never took off his Super Bowl ring in the years afterward. His playing days ended following the 1967 season with thirty-five interceptions in 104 games, and he scored two touchdowns on interception returns.

According to Williamson he deliberately created "The Hammer" as a marketable personality, wearing white shoes to stand out on the field and constantly bantering in the style of MUHAMMAD ALI. He knew that because coaches and the media would not care about him once his playing days were over, he had to establish a new identity to prosper and would have to combat the view that football players are not intelligent.

Following in the footsteps of his contemporary, Cleveland Browns running back JIM BROWN, Williamson moved from football to acting. After appearing on television in episodes of *Ironside*, *The Outsider*, and *Star Trek*, Williamson received a significant boost with a part in Robert Altman's immensely popular Korean War satire *M*A*S*H* (1970). As football star–turned–army captain "Spearchucker" Jones, his role poked fun at the racial attitudes of the 1950s and, more importantly, the 1970s.

Following twelve appearances in the groundbreaking situation comedy *Julia* as star DIAHANN CARROLL's boyfriend, Williamson moved on to concentrate on film work. Starting with *The Legend of Nigger Charley* in 1972, he starred in a series of films in the genre that came to be known as "blaxploitation." Unlike the often-didactic films of the previous two decades that presented African Americans generally as noble and self-sacrificing, the genre movies of the 1970s, usually Westerns or crime dramas, presented a more aggressive, militant stance. This new attitude was summarized by the advertising slogan for *The Legend of Nigger Charley:* "Somebody warn the West. Nigger Charley ain't running no more."

Following leading roles in such films as *Hammer* (1972), *Black Caesar* (1973), *The Soul of Nigger Charley* (1973), *That Man Bolt* (1973), *Hell up in Harlem* (1973), *Black Eye* (1974), and *Three the Hard Way* (1974), Williamson and his wife, Linda, the mother of his five sons, formed Po' Boy Productions to gain more control over his films. Because of the demand for Williamson's services, *That Man Bolt* was filming in Los Angeles while *Hell up in Harlem* was shooting in New York, necessitating a body double for some scenes in the latter film.

In addition to producing many of his films, Williamson also wrote and directed *Adios Amigo* (1976), *No Way Back* (1976), *The Last Fight* (1983), *Steele's Law* (1991), and *Vegas Vampires* (2003), and directed more films written by others. All of Williamson's films feature shooting, fighting, and explosions. The emphasis on action over dialogue made them popular around the world.

Though best known for his work in low-budget action films, Williamson also appeared in more mainstream movies such as *From Dusk Till Dawn* (1996) and *Starsky and Hutch* (2004). When Quentin Tarantino, his costar in *From Dusk Till Dawn*, claimed to be a huge fan, Williamson was skeptical until Tarantino started quoting dialogue from several of the actor's blaxploitation films.

Williamson produced *Original Gangstas* in 1996 as a response to the "gangsta" posing of the world of hip hop. Along with Jim Brown, PAM GRIER, Ron O'Neal, RICHARD ROUNDTREE, and PAUL WINFIELD, all veterans of the blaxpoitation era, Williamson starred as a football coach who returns home to Gary, Indiana, and reunites with old friends to combat the violence of local gangs and restore a sense of respect to the community. Williamson cast more than forty local gang members in the film directed by Larry Cohen, who had made *Black Caesar* and *Hell up in Harlem*.

Williamson's varied career also included being a nude centerfold in *Playgirl* in 1973. He was the first African American analyst on ABC's *Monday Night Football* in 1974, teaming with Howard Cosell, Frank Gifford, and Alex Karras. He appeared in print and television advertisements for Reebok athletic shoes, Miller Lite beer, and King Cobra malt liquor. A cigar smoker, he owned a twelve-acre tobacco plantation in Jamaica.

In 2000 Williamson was named spokesman for the Illinois organ donor program. Spurred by the death of legendary Chicago Bears running back WALTER PAYTON, Illinois Secretary of State JESSE WHITE said he appointed Williamson to increase awareness of the program among African Americans.

In *Black Directors in Hollywood*, Melvin Donaldson observed that Williamson contributed to the international recognition of the African American presence in films through his entrepreneurship and indestructible ego. Though Williamson was more concerned with filmmaking as a business than as art, he dealt with Hollywood, as he did with all his endeavors, on his own terms.

FURTHER READING

Alexander, George. *Why We Make Movies: Black Filmmakers Talk about the Magic of Cinema* (2003).

Donaldson, Melvin. *Black Directors in Hollywood* (2003).

Malone, Janice. "'Original Gangsta': A Conversation with Fred Williamson," *New Pittsburgh Courier*, 26 June 1996.

MICHAEL ADAMS

Williamson, John Hendrick (3 Oct. 1844–9 Jan. 1911), barber, newspaper editor, public official, and six-term state legislator, was born in Covington, Georgia, the son of James Williamson, a slave, and an unknown mother. Little is known of his childhood, although he reportedly taught himself to read against the wishes of his owner, who hired him out to reduce his free time. The determined youth responded by borrowing his white playmates' schoolbooks at night, then tutoring them each morning.

His parents were owned by General John N. Williamson, a wealthy white attorney. In 1858 John Hendrick Williamson moved to Louisburg, North Carolina, with his widowed mistress Temperance Perry Williamson. By the end of the Civil War, he had become a skilled and popular barber, and in 1865 he became a delegate to the first statewide Freedmen's Convention. Two years later he was appointed a Franklin County voter registrar by the controversial general Daniel E. Sickles, military commander of the Reconstruction-era Second District.

Despite his youth, Williamson was elected as a Franklin County delegate to North Carolina's 1868 constitutional convention, and immediately ran as a Republican for the state legislature from the predominantly black Franklin County. One of twenty

African Americans elected that year, he was also among the fourteen legislators who later signed a glowing public endorsement of the newly elected U.S. president, Ulysses S. Grant. "Our cause has triumphed," the men wrote to the *North Carolina Standard* on 2 December 1868. "By his election our status is settled. We are men!"

This was the beginning of a durable political career for Williamson, whose six legislative terms were the most served by any nineteenth-century African American in the state. After serving in separate 1868–1869 and 1869–1870 sessions of the North Carolina General Assembly, he was reelected four times, in 1870, 1872, 1876, and 1886. Besides serving on the House committees on Agriculture, Mechanics, and Mining (1869–1870) and Propositions and Grievances (1870–1872), he was not afraid to take unpopular stands on principle, such as proposing an unsuccessful bill to prohibit sale of liquor in part of his home county during his first term, or opposing reorganization of the state militia. He and other African American legislators also opposed, albeit unsuccessfully, the 1871 impeachment and removal of Republican Governor William W. Holden, a stalwart ally of freedmen.

Williamson's electoral record was not unblemished, including reelection losses in 1874 and 1878. But his final reelection defeat, in 1888, was perhaps his most painful, coinciding with that year's statewide white supremacist Democratic campaign. Yet Williamson remained popular in Louisburg and in statewide politics, serving as a justice of the peace, for a decade on the Franklin County board of education, and on the Republican state executive committee in 1886. In 1881 he became vice president of the statewide convention of African Americans. He also attended four Republican National Conventions (1872, 1884, 1888, and 1892) as a delegate from his congressional district.

Outside the political arena, Williamson excelled as a journalist. From 1881 until 1888, as secretary of the North Carolina Industrial Association, which sponsored the state's annual fair for African American citizens, he helped found the association's newspaper, the *Banner*. After its 1883 merger with the *Goldsboro Enterprise*, Williamson worked briefly on the new *Banner-Enterprise* with the co-editors George Allen Mebane and Ezekiel E. Smith. The chronicler I. Garland Penn described the original *Banner* as well-subscribed and devoted more to educational and industrial interests of the race than to political issues (Penn, 182). The *Banner-Enterprise*

shifted its focus to more controversial topics, and Williamson soon tired of philosophical differences with Smith and Mebane. Williamson sold his interests to Mebane and in 1885 founded his own Raleigh weekly, the *North Carolina Gazette*, which soon became the state's largest African American newspaper, with substantial advertising revenues from white businesses.

In the early 1890s Williamson retired from active journalism, and the *Gazette* came under the ownership of James Hunter Young, a controversial lawyer, federal official, and outspoken party activist. Unlike Young, but like many black Republicans, Williamson had lost enthusiasm for the national party during the Benjamin Harrison administration, despite having served as a state delegate to the president's 1889 inauguration. Yet Williamson had even less enthusiasm for the Populists, with whom his party was now considering "fusion." Out of frustration with the situation, he undertook a quixotic bid for the Fourth District's congressional seat in 1892, running as an independent Republican in a four-way race against the incumbent Democrat Benjamin H. Bunn, the regular Republican nominee John Sanders, and the Populist candidate William F. Strowd. Williamson proposed federal payments to former slaves—to be split with former owners—and endorsed the dredging of the Tar River inland to Louisburg, but these issues gained him little traction in the campaign. The Democrat Bunn was narrowly reelected, and Williamson finished a distant third, after Sanders withdrew.

Williamson served in 1896 as an alternate delegate from his district to the party's St. Louis convention, which nominated William McKinley and inaugurated a brief era of high-level appointments for black Republicans. By 1899, as the southern Republican Party grappled with its new "lily-white" faction, Williamson gradually drifted toward the Democrats. His letter that year to Georgia's Governor Allen D. Candler, a proponent of whites-only Democratic primaries, was a despairing commentary on his disappointment with the party he had served for so long. Williamson's letter was printed in the *Atlanta Constitution* in September 1899 and was reprinted shortly thereafter in the *Franklin (NC) Times*.

Even during his time as an active Republican, Williamson had maintained cordial relationships with white Democrats, including the influential publisher Josephus Daniels. Daniels became a leading proponent of white supremacist politics in 1898, but continued to speak deferentially, even fondly, of Williamson, recalling their longtime friendship in his memoirs. Williamson had helped him gain admission to the 1892 Republican National Convention, Daniels wrote, after he arrived without notice in Minneapolis to cover the event.

Williamson married Clara A. Barnes on 11 August 1865. They had at least six children. Due in part to his large family, he retained a strong interest in the education of African American children, and with the principal Ephraim Dent helped found Louisburg's Episcopal School in 1894. The school operated well into the twentieth century, offering elementary classes under the supervision of the town's Episcopal parish.

After a lengthy illness, Williamson died in a Goldsboro, North Carolina, hospital. In 2006 a state highway historical marker in his memory was approved to stand near his Louisburg grave.

FURTHER READING

No collection exists of John H. Williamson's personal papers. Scattered copies of issues of his two best-known newspapers, the *Banner* and the *North Carolina Gazette*, are on microfilm in the North Carolina State Archives in Raleigh, and in the North Carolina Collection at Wilson Library, University of North Carolina at Chapel Hill.

Crow, Jeffrey J., Paul D. Escott, and Flora J. Hatley. *A History of African Americans in North Carolina* (1992).

Foner, Eric. *Freedom's Lawmakers: A Directory of Black Officeholders during Reconstruction* (1993).

Kenzer, Robert C. *Enterprising Southerners: Black Economic Success in North Carolina, 1865–1915* (1997).

Penn, I. Garland. *The Afro-American Press and Its Editors* (1891).

Obituary: *Franklin* (North Carolina) *Times*, 13 Jan. 1911.

BENJAMIN R. JUSTESEN

Williamson, Sonny Boy (5 Dec. 1899?–25 May 1965), blues artist, was born Aleck Miller in Glendora, Mississippi, the son of Millie Ford, a sharecropper; his father's name is unknown. He grew up on a farm near Yazoo City, where his mother and stepfather, Jim Miller, moved when he was young. He began learning to play the harmonica, or mouth harp, around the age of five, supposedly performing religious music before switching to blues, and was playing at local parties as a teenager.

By his own account, Miller's career as a wandering musician began in 1928. Using the name Little Boy Blue, he ranged as far afield as New Orleans and became a familiar figure in Mississippi, Arkansas, and Tennessee, always recognizable by the heavy belt of harmonicas he wore around his waist. Throughout the 1930s he worked with many of the emerging blues artists of the day, among them ROBERT JOHNSON, ROBERT JUNIOR LOCKWOOD, Sunnyland Slim, and HOWLIN' WOLF. In 1937 Miller courted and married Howlin' Wolf's half-sister, Mary, who was then living in Parkin, Arkansas.

In late 1941 in Helena, Arkansas, Miller began a career in radio. Ever the hustler, he talked his way into a regular time slot on a new radio station, KFFA. With Lockwood as his guitarist and Interstate Grocery as his sponsor, he broadcast blues on weekdays at lunchtime to promote his local club dates. One of the sponsor's products, King Biscuit Flour, provided the show's name, *King Biscuit Time*, and the artists their name, King Biscuit Entertainers. With the addition of sidemen like Peck Curtis, Robert "Dudlow" Taylor, Pinetop Perkins, and Joe Willie Wilkins, the Entertainers soon became a full-fledged band. Featuring electronically amplified instruments, a first for radio listeners in the Mississippi Delta region, the show became so popular that the sponsor later marketed corn meal with Miller's picture on the label.

Although he was using the name Miller when he came to KFFA, he soon adopted the name Sonny Boy Williamson. It is possible he took the name to capitalize on the reputation of then-popular harmonica player and blues recording star JOHN LEE "SONNY BOY" WILLIAMSON. Nevertheless, most blues artists agreed that Miller was the superior musician. Miller, according to Lockwood, "could play rings around little Sonny Boy—and every damn body else that was playing harp at that time." Miller went to his grave claiming to be the "original" and "only" Sonny Boy—although the name was just one of nearly a dozen he adopted during his career, including Alex Miller, Willie Miller, Sonny Boy Williams, Willie Williamson, Biscuit Miller, Footsie, and Goat.

Miller left KFFA in 1944 and resumed the life of a traveling musician and occasional radio artist. By the late 1940s he had married again, this time to Mattie Lee Gordon (or Jones) and had settled in West Memphis, Arkansas.

Although Miller claimed to have recorded earlier, his first documented session took place in 1951 for the Trumpet label in Jackson, Mississippi. Starting with the hit "Eyesight to the Blind," he recorded for Trumpet until 1954 as both a featured artist and sideman—most notably on ELMORE JAMES's "Dust My Broom."

With the murder of John Lee Williamson in Chicago in 1948, Miller became the foremost Sonny Boy Williamson (although older musicians generally referred to him as Sonny Boy No. 2). Through his Trumpet recordings his name spread, and by 1953 he was beginning to work the Midwest, where he came to the attention of Chicago-based Chess Records. Chess, the major blues label of the time, bought his contract, and his first record on the subsidiary Checker label, "Don't Start Me Talking," rose to number 3 on the rhythm and blues charts. Despite several other hits in the late 1950s, he remained third in the Chess blues hierarchy behind MUDDY WATERS and Howling Wolf.

In his sixties, losing the support of his traditional audience, Miller turned his attention overseas, where he once again achieved stardom. Traveling on a passport issued to one "Sonny Boy Williams," he went to Europe in 1963 with the American Folk Blues Festival, staying on once the tour ended. In Europe he indulged his eccentricity, dressing as a banker in bowler hat and tails. Despite his temper and steady drinking, audiences from France to Poland embraced him warmly, particularly the British. Beginning in 1963 he did a number of European sessions, working with touring Chicago artists and with newcomers such as Britain's Eric Clapton. He also played with Brian Jones, Jimmy Page, and John Mayall, influencing a generation of young blues rockers who, in turn, brought their versions of the blues back to the United States during the so-called British Invasion of the 1960s.

Following his European successes in 1963 and 1964, Miller returned home to Helena in deteriorating health. He told KFFA he wanted his old job back, explaining that he had come home to die. After several *King Biscuit Time* broadcasts, he died in Helena and was buried in Tutwiler, Mississippi.

Much of what is known about Sonny Boy Williamson No. 2 seems contradictory. Fellow musicians described him as a con man and a hard taskmaster. The blues artist Eddie Burns said Miller had a temper so volatile that he once fired his whole band when it showed up late and provided a full evening's music and entertainment by himself. On the other hand, the songwriter WILLIE DIXON, who traveled with Miller in Europe, said he was a "beautiful guy."

By any of his names, Sonny Boy Williamson No. 2 was one of the blues tradition's most influential and historically important artists. He participated in all major blues eras, right up to the blues/rock transition of the 1960s, and was the single most important blues radio personality ever, his programs inspiring countless other artists. The list of artists who played with him in the South, the North, and over the airwaves reads like a Who's Who of the blues, among them B. B. KING, EARL HOOKER, Willie Nix, Fred Below, Willie Love, and Baby Boy Warren. And even though many older artists disapproved of the name he appropriated, they all acknowledged that Sonny Boy No. 2 was a great musician—a true original.

A commemorative marker was erected at his grave as a tribute in 1980, and that same year he was inducted into the Blues Foundation's Hall of Fame.

FURTHER READING
Leadbitter, Mike, and Neil Slaven. *Blues Records 1943–1966* (1968).
Oliver, Paul, ed. *The Blackwell Guide to Blues Records* (1989).

DISCOGRAPHY
Down and Out Blues (Checker, CHD-9257).
King Biscuit Time (Arhoolie, 2020).
Sonny Boy Williamson II: The Harp from the Deep South (Blues Encore, CD52018).

This entry is taken from the *American National Biography* and is published here with the permission of the American Council of Learned Societies.

BILL MCCULLOCH AND
BARRY LEE PEARSON

Williamson, Sonny Boy (30 Mar. 1914–1 June 1948), blues harmonica player, was born John Lee Curtis Williamson in Jackson, Tennessee, the son of Rafe Williamson and Nancy Utley, occupations unknown. His father died shortly before he was born, and he was raised by his mother, who later remarried. As a boy, Williamson sang with a gospel quartet at Blair's Chapel CME Church on the outskirts of Jackson. When he was nine or ten, his mother gave him a harmonica, or mouth harp, as a Christmas gift, and he began teaching himself to play, starting with the gospel tunes he sang in church. At least two other Tennessee musicians later claimed to have known him then: John "Homesick James" Williamson, a guitarist from Somerville, said he and Williamson were boyhood friends, and JAMES "YANK" RACHELL, a mandolinist from Brownsville, claimed Williamson was a youngster riding a bicycle in Jackson when they met.

Though still in his teens, Williamson was anxious to work with Rachell at country dances. Reluctant at first, Rachell finally gave in, and the two became partners. Around this time, Williamson also met two other musicians from Brownsville: SLEEPY JOHN ESTES, a country blues guitarist who often played with Rachell, and harmonica player Hammie Nixon, six years Williamson's senior and a major influence on his style. In various configurations, Williamson worked with these bluesmen, playing local suppers and juke joints, and by 1929 they were playing throughout Arkansas and Tennessee.

By 1930 Williamson was visiting Memphis, home to several noted mouth-harp players, including jug-band artists Will Shade and Noah Lewis, who had been an early influence on Nixon. In Memphis, Williamson, known by now as Sonny Boy Williamson, picked up repertoire and techniques from an informal group of jug-band and street musicians who played in Church Park and on the city's streetcars. He also began an association with Mississippi piano player Albert Luandrew, better known as Sunnyland Slim.

Through most of the 1930s Williamson commuted between the burgeoning blues centers in the North and his home in Jackson, where in November 1937 he married Lacey Belle Davidson, the coauthor of many of his compositions. It was Williamson's second marriage, though little is known about his first wife, Sally Mae Hunt. The number of his children, if any, is unknown.

A 1934 commute took Williamson to Chicago, where he met BIG BILL BROONZY and other transplanted southern artists. In 1936 he was in St. Louis, forming harmonica-guitar trios with Robert Lee McCoy (better known as ROBERT NIGHTHAWK), BIG JOE WILLIAMS, and Henry Townsend, among others. A year later, pianist Walter Davis, who doubled as a scout for RCA Victor Record Company's Bluebird label, arranged a meeting with Chicago-based music publisher Lester Melrose. That led to a recording session on 5 May 1937 in Aurora, Illinois, featuring Williamson with guitarists Williams and Nighthawk. The session yielded a half-dozen sides, including the classics "Good Morning, Little School Girl," "Bluebird Blues," and "Sugar Mama Blues." Six months later, a second Aurora session, which included Walter Davis and Henry Townsend, produced another blues standard, "Early in the Morning." While staying with Townsend in St. Louis in 1937, Williamson began working again with Yank Rachell, his first partner. That laid the groundwork for a third recording session in Aurora on 13 March 1938, on which Big Joe Williams rounded out the group.

In 1939 Williamson sent for his wife and moved to Chicago permanently. Starting that year and continuing through 1947, Williamson had at least one recording session each year, except for a two-year break during World War II. He cut 120 sides, including classics such as "Sloppy Drunk Blues," "Checkin' Up on My Baby," "Hoo-doo Hoo-doo," and "You Better Cut That Out." The recordings from that period document a change in Williamson's music. He generally worked with a piano player—Walter Davis, Joshua Altheimer, BLIND JOHN DAVIS, Eddie Boyd, or Big Maceo. Guitarists included BIG BILL BROONZY, TAMPA RED, and, in a final session on 12 November 1947 for RCA Victor, Willie Lacey on electric guitar, an innovation Williamson had resisted, at least on recordings, up to that point. He used drummers Charles Sanders, Fred Williams, Armand "Jump" Jackson, and Judge Riley, and bass players such as Ransom Knowling and WILLIE DIXON. These sessions helped spur the evolving postwar ensemble sound that would be brought to fruition after Williamson's death by artists such as MUDDY WATERS, who supposedly played guitar in Williamson's band from time to time after he first hit Chicago in 1943.

In 1946 Williamson and fellow southern blues artists Broonzy and MEMPHIS SLIM participated in a New York recording session set up by folklorist Alan Lomax. The session, now available as *Blues in the Mississippi Night*, yielded a combination of commentary and music describing blues in relation to the oppressive conditions faced by African Americans in Mississippi, content then considered so controversial that Lomax concealed the identities of the three artists with pseudonyms—"Sib" in Williamson's case.

During the 1940s Williamson also made his mark outside the recording studio. He was a regular in Chicago's open-air Maxwell Street Market. He worked top blues clubs such as Sylvio's and the Plantation Club and was considered by fellow musicians to be the most popular blues-band leader in Chicago. Sidemen included the cream of the city's blues talent.

Returning from a late-night engagement at the Plantation Club on 1 June 1948, Williamson was assaulted and robbed. According to legend, he managed to stagger home, where he awakened his wife, said, "Lord, have mercy," and died in her arms. His body was shipped to his home in Jackson for burial in the Blair's Chapel cemetery.

It should be noted that late in his career Williamson was known professionally as Sonny

Boy Williamson No. 1, to distinguish him from Aleck Miller (SONNY BOY WILLIAMSON), an older, Mississippi-born harmonica player who assumed Williamson's name and was often referred to as Sonny Boy Williamson No. 2. Although No. 2 went to his grave claiming to be the original Sonny Boy, other artists of that era generally condemned him for trying to cash in on Williamson's name.

A highly influential artist, Williamson changed the way the harmonica was played by those who followed him, including his most famous protégé, LITTLE WALTER JACOBS. He exemplified a traditional black folk style in which the harmonica acted as a second voice, responding to the vocal phrasing, as opposed to the more melodic phrasing common to the string-band or jug-band tradition, and thus he brought the harmonica to the forefront as a lead instrument. As fellow bluesman OTIS SPANN told author Rick Milne in a 1960s interview, "The first Sonny Boy put the harp in the union…. Then the price of harps went up."

An accomplished vocalist with a distinctive, personable delivery, Williamson turned a supposed speech impediment into an attractive, even imitated, vocal style. As songwriters, he and his wife composed a remarkable number of blues songs that have become part of the traditional repertoire of Chicago artists. From country string band to jug band to acoustic piano-guitar-harmonica trios to the full amplified Chicago blues sound, Sonny Boy Williamson participated in the changing blues tradition as a shaping force, taking it from its rural roots to its urban flowering as the immediate forerunner of rock and roll.

FURTHER READING

For general information see the collected records and recollections on file at the Jackson-Madison County Public Library, Jackson, Tennessee.

Broonzy, Big Bill. and Yannick Bruynoghe. *Big Bill Blues: William Broonzy's Story* (1992).

Evans, David. "Goin' Up the Country," in *Nothing But the Blues*, ed. Lawrence Cohn (1993).

Harris, Sheldon. *Blues Who's Who: A Biographical Dictionary of Blues Singers* (1979).

Leadbitter, Michael, ed. *Nothing But the Blues* (1971).

Rowe, Mike. *Chicago Breakdown* (1973).

DISCOGRAPHY

Dixon, Robert M. W., and John Godrich. *Blues and Gospel Records: 1902–1943* (1982).

Leadbitter, Mike, and Neil Slaven. *Blues Records 1943–1970*, vol. 2 (1994).

Oliver, Paul, ed. *The Blackwell Guide to Blues Records* (1989).

This entry is taken from the *American National Biography* and is published here with the permission of the American Council of Learned Societies.

BILL MCCULLOCH AND
BARRY LEE PEARSON

Willis, Deborah (1948–), artist, educator, and art historian specializing in African American photographic history, was born in North Philadelphia, Pennsylvania. Her father, Thomas, was a police officer, and her mother, Ruth, was a hairdresser. Willis grew up with four sisters in a tight-knit and loving family. Her father, the family photographer, and his cousin (who name is not known) who owned a photographic studio, constantly took pictures of daily family life, including her mother's visual transformation of the neighborhood women as a hairdresser. Willis was mesmerized by images in the media and noted how blacks were portrayed as criminals or outsiders to the normal, suburban white family. Willis also noted that African Americans were omitted completely from history books except for references to slavery in the antebellum South. In LANGSTON HUGHES and Roy DeCarava's lyrical photo essay *The Sweet Flypaper of Life* (1955), Willis discovered tender images of black Americans that resembled those in her family's photographs and her own visual memories.

Even as a young person Willis realized that images were powerful and could change how people see the world. She began teaching photography in her Philadelphia neighborhood in her late teens, and after moving to New York in 1969, she taught photography in Brooklyn at the Neighborhood Youth Corps photography program in Ocean Hill-Brownsville. As a college student she traveled to Huntington, West Virginia, with the Center for Community Studies to help Appalachian families through employment training in 1968.

In 1975 Willis earned a BFA in Photography at the Philadelphia College of Art (later the University of the Arts). She continued her education at Pratt Institute in Brooklyn, where she earned a master of fine arts degree in Photography in 1980. Early in her career she participated in several group shows in New York, including Women Photographers: Reflections of Self at Fordham University in 1986, Prisoners of War: In My Native Land and On Foreign Soil at the New School for Social Research Gallery in 1992, and Occupations and Resistance at the Alternative Museum in 1992. Word of her work spread, and notable national exhibits included Words and Pictures (Light Factory, Charlotte, North Carolina, 1992) and Encounter 6: Deborah Willis (Center for Creative Photography, Tucson, Arizona, 1994). Personal narrative and visual history were two important themes for her, and she drew on family stories and symbolic heirlooms, from her father's aspiration to become a tailor to her aunt Cora's quilts. Her images are of common moments in her own life, and include mementoes from family stories and scenes such as pictures of the ladies in her mother's beauty shop or decaying houses in the old South. Weaving and textiles were central to the installation work she exhibited in *Conceptual Textiles* (1995–1996), *Deborah Willis: Photo/Quilt Stories* (1996), and *Fabricated Memories* (2000). Willis told personal histories through her photographs and assembled textiles, presenting their content and form as narratives generally absent from American history and its canonical art history. Willis saw her personal photographic history intertwined with the history of other African Americans, and placed narratives of the everyday African American experience back into the mainstream media and historical consciousness of the twentieth century. These narratives focus on family and relationships, home life, and a positive black urban experience. In 2001 she presented the autobiographical *Family History Memory*, which included her experiences with breast cancer.

From 1980 to 1992 Willis worked at the New York Public Library's Schomburg Center for Research in Black Culture, first as its curator of photographs and later as prints and exhibitions coordinator. At the Schomburg she began researching African American photographic history, tracing its role in shaping the visual memory of American culture. Her M.A. in Art History and Museum Studies, which she received from the City College of New York in 1986, also focused her study on the photograph as an art object and visual artifact that reframed cultural perspectives. After her tenure at the Schomburg Center, Willis became the associate director for research and collections, exhibition curator, and museum specialist at the Center for African American Research and Culture at the Smithsonian Institution in Washington, D.C. Her contributions included the monumental text for the traveling exhibition, Reflections in Black: A History of Black Photographers, 1840 to the Present (2000), the first comprehensive anthology of African American photography. Among the awards and honors accorded to her were the

Golden Light Photographic Book of the Year Award (1993), a grant from the Anonymous Was a Women Foundation (1996), and a MacArthur Foundation Fellowship (2001). Having earned a Ph.D. in Cultural Studies from George Mason University in 2003, Willis focused upon the identity and interpretation of the "New Negro" in photographic images for her dissertation topic.

Willis's professional career subsequently expanded from research and curatorial work to pedagogical pursuits. She taught photographic history at the Brooklyn Museum, New York University, and the City University of New York. In 2000 she was appointed the Lehman Brady Chair in Documentary Studies and American Studies at Duke University in Durham, North Carolina. She went on become professor of photography and imaging at New York University's Tisch School of the Arts in 2001. Willis had one son, Hank Willis Thomas, who was also a photographer and cultural critic.

FURTHER READING

Ferris, Alison. "Deborah Willis: Fabricated Histories," *Fiberarts* (Mar./Apr. 1999).

Kennedy, Winston. "Deborah Willis, Artist and Scholar," *International Review of African American Art* 7.2 (2000).

Royster-Hemby, Christina. "Reflected in the Lens," *Baltimore City Paper*, 3 Mar. 2005.

Sligh, Clarissa T. "Picturing Us: Together—Deborah Willis and Hank Willis Thomas," *International Review of African American Art* 20.3 (2005).

JENNIFER LYNN HEADLEY

Willis, William Shedrick, Jr. (11 July 1921–6 Aug. 1983), anthropologist, was born into a prosperous, college-educated family, in Waco, Texas. Willis's father, William Willis Sr., the high school principal of an all-black school, resigned that position in protest of what he considered unfair and racially motivated restrictions regarding appropriate behavior for a person in that job. He went on to put his abilities to work as owner of a construction company, building homes for poor African Americans. The Ku Klux Klan drove the family out of Waco in 1923, and they relocated to Dallas.

In 1942 Willis received a B.A. in History from Howard University in Washington, D.C., and, after serving in World War II, earned his Ph.D. in Anthropology from Columbia University in 1955. His dissertation, "Colonial Conflict and the Cherokee Indians, 1710–1760," was in that branch of anthropology called ethnohistory. Willis continued to pursue the study of relations among Native Americans, blacks, and whites, but much of his work centered on the dilemma of race and racism in anthropology, especially as represented by the career of Franz Boas, one of the major founders and shapers of the field of anthropology. Exposing this dilemma was one of Willis's key contributions to anthropology. Willis knew that racism in anthropology hid behind a mask of "objectivity," which conveniently ignored colonial domination of the peoples whom anthropologists study. Sometime in the early 1950s, Willis married Gene Willis (maiden name unknown). Information about his personal life, however, is limited.

Willis's understanding of anthropology's racism came from firsthand experience. In spite of his brilliant academic career in graduate school, the groundbreaking nature of his dissertation, and recommendations from major figures in the profession, Willis found it difficult to get an academic job. He worked as a lecturer at Columbia University from 1958 to 1959, then at City College of New York during the 1959–1960 academic year, before returning to Columbia in 1965. When he did finally get an academic job at Southern Methodist University in Dallas in 1965, he again ran into racism, eventually resigning from SMU in 1972 after attaining the position of associate professor. That same year Willis published "Skeletons in the Anthropological Closet," an essay condemning the field's combination of racism at home and colonialism abroad. However, he continued working in the field, embarking on a major study of Boas's works and life.

Willis sought to establish the significance of Boas not only in promoting a nonracist understanding of race, especially by examining the scholar's famous commencement speech at Atlanta University in 1906, but also calling attention to Boas's efforts to establish an area of studies within anthropology in particular and in academic studies generally that would advance the cause of racial justice and understanding. At the time of his death Willis was working on a manuscript titled "Boas Goes to Atlanta," which detailed Boas's role in the future of African American studies. Willis left copious material detailing Boas's efforts at recruiting African Americans and other minorities, including women, into anthropology, as well as his role in promoting Melville Herskovits's work in African American studies.

Willis's work built upon Boas's understanding that the perspectives of indigenous peoples were, by their very definition, unavailable to even the most perceptive outsider; in this way Willis anticipated a strain of humanistic anthropology that came after him. Willis argued that Boas's 1906 speech had an immediate effect in the black community. The Eleventh Atlanta Conference on Negro Health and Physique, for example, quoted Boas's address at length and with great approval. Willis noted that Boas was deeply committed to black equality and that his writings influenced both BOOKER T. WASHINGTON and W. E. B. DuBois, even as white racists within the field prevented Boas from implementing policies that would have enabled anthropology to take a greater role in the anticolonial and antiracist movements.

Willis died before he could complete the project, but it is clear from his papers that he came to respect Boas and his work.

FURTHER READING
Willis's papers are at the American Philosophical Society in Philadelphia, Pennsylvania.
Sanday, Peggy Reeves. "Skeletons in the Anthropological Closet: The Life Work of William S. Willis Jr.," in *Pioneers in African-American Anthropology*, eds. Ira E. Harrison and Faye V. Harrison (1998).

FRANK A. SALAMONE

Willmott, Kevin (31 Aug. 1958–), independent filmmaker, playwright, director, actor, professor, and community activist, was born in Junction City, Kansas, the son of Lee Douglas Willmott, a hodcarrier and plastic tender, and Ruth Lee Willmott, a homemaker. Junction City, located in the central part of the state, in many ways owes its existence and takes its character from its proximity to Fort Riley, an army post dating from the 1850s that was home to the Tenth Cavalry, the Buffalo Soldiers, one of two all-black cavalry units created essentially to guard settlers from Indian attack following the Civil War.

Junction City's unusual history helped form Willmott's viewpoint from the beginning. Contributing to the early presence of the Buffalo Soldiers in the nineteenth century was a substantial population of African American settlers originally attracted to Kansas as a free-state haven for escaped and manumitted slaves. As a result Junction City, unlike most of the rest of the state, had a substantial black population when Willmott was growing up. In addition, social segregation was a fact of life in Kansas, and even if the city was too small to support the separate schools that existed in nearby Topeka,

Kevin Willmott, an assistant professor in the film department at the University of Kansas, speaks during a news conference on 9 January 2004. (AP Images.)

for instance, an all-black business and entertainment district known throughout the Midwest as East Ninth Street was established. This area, home to beauty shops, cab stands, jazz clubs, and brothels alike, supplied many of the available jobs for African American residents, including Willmott's mother, who ran a restaurant there. The area also formed the subject of his first play, later to be his first film, *Ninth Street*.

Another major influence in Willmott's life was a Catholic priest named Frank Coady. In 1974, at the age of sixteen, partly in response to the times but because of the deteriorating racial situation in the Junction City schools, Willmott participated in a series of protests that culminated in his being expelled from public school. Essentially without skills or education, he took a job helping to maintain the local Catholic cemetery. There he met then-Deacon Coady, who became his mentor. Coady, according to Willmott, introduced him to a level of spirituality and social concern he had never known, and he enrolled as a junior at St. Xavier High School,

converting to Catholicism soon after. His association with Coady, along with the fact that Junction City was the poorest community in an economically disadvantaged state, instilled in Willmott a sensitivity to social injustice, and he became a lifelong champion of homeless and poor people.

Following his graduation from St. Xavier in 1976 Willmott attended nearby Marymount College, a Catholic institution in Salina, Kansas, where in 1982 he earned a B.A. in Theater. In 1981, during his senior year, he wrote, produced, and acted in his first play, *Ninth Street*, which focused on two alcoholics (one of whom he played) who spend their time sitting outdoors on a couch, making *Waiting for Godot*–like observations of passing people and events. Drawing in part on his memories of his parents, the play humanized the district often known to outsiders only as home to the vice trade. In addition, the work was essentially an antiwar statement. Willmott attributed much of the altruistic sentiment embodied by the play to the influence of the community and antiwar activist Daniel Berrigan, whom he met while at Marymount (in fact, he later named one of his sons Berrigan).

Willmott's social concerns extended from his plays and screenplays to his work as an activist. In 1982, following his graduation from Marymount, he organized a sit-in at the Junction City Chamber of Commerce office to protest the lack of minority contractors in a local public housing project. This action, along with another protest over the all-white makeup of the local fire department, led to his meeting activist and comedian DICK GREGORY, who offered him advice about how best to utilize his social energies by cultivating his artistic talents. That same year he met and married Becky Reedy; over the next several years the couple would have five children.

After earning an MFA in Dramatic Writing in 1988 from New York University's Tisch School of the Arts, Willmott, encouraged by the success of his fellow NYU alumnus and noted filmmaker SPIKE LEE, decided to make *Ninth Street* into a film, moving to Lawrence, Kansas, to do so. Because he had little outside backing, adapting his stage play to screen took seven years. The play's connections between spiritual transcendence and the well-being of the community attracted the attention of the noted actors Martin Sheen and ISAAC HAYES, both of whom agreed to appear in the film for no pay. Sheen's part, in fact, was written especially for him and was based on Willmott's old mentor, Father Frank Coady. Hayes played the owner of the local black cab company.

In 1975 Willmott joined the faculty in the school of film at the University of Kansas. Following this, he cowrote and directed one play, *T-Money and Wolf* (1995), cowrote one teleplay produced by NBC, *The 70's* (2000), and adapted and directed another play, *The Watsons Go to Birmingham–1963* (2005).

During this same period, his newfound sense of financial security allowed him to write and direct his second film, a fake documentary, or "mockumentary," titled *C.S.A.* (2004), which Spike Lee supported with advice and by lending his name as a "Spike Lee Presentation." *C.S.A.*, at once a satirical comedy and a critique of the intransigence of racism in America, was based on the hypothetical premise that the South had won the Civil War and slavery continued nearly 150 years later. At base the film concerned the ways in which racial stereotypes going back to Zeb Coon and STEPIN FETCHIT, plus codes for racism like the Confederate flag, persist as hidden symbols in our culture, despite the ostensible eradication of the realities that underlie them. *C.S.A.*, like his earlier films and plays, revealed Kevin Willmott's continuing interest in exposing social injustices through the popular forms of the screen and the stage.

FURTHER READING

Kaufman, Will. *The Civil War in American Culture* (2006).

Loeb, Jeff. "A Conversation with Kevin Willmott," *African American Review* (Summer 2001).

JEFF LOEB

Wills, Harry (20 Jan. 1889–21 Dec. 1958), professional boxer, was born Harrison Coleman Wills in New Orleans, Louisiana, the son of Strother G. Wills and Georgie B. Kenner. He grew up in New Orleans in an impoverished waterfront neighborhood and received little formal education. While in his teens he worked as a stevedore and frequented horse racing tracks. He hoped to become a jockey but soon became too big. Eventually he found work on freighters, and it is believed that he was introduced to boxing during a long voyage abroad.

Wills returned to New Orleans, where he had his earliest recorded fight in 1910. By 1913 he was fighting such competent black heavyweights as Joe Jeannette and Jeff Clark. In May and June 1914 Wills gained attention by boxing Jeannette on even terms and beating the great SAM LANGFORD in fights in which official decisions were not given. At six feet two and 220 pounds, Wills towered over Langford by six inches and outweighed him by 30 pounds.

In August 1914 Wills went to the West Coast, where he gained a series of wins, mostly over white fighters. He suffered the first major setback of his career in Los Angeles on 26 November 1914, when he was knocked out by Langford in fourteen rounds after earlier scoring eleven knockdowns. He returned to New Orleans in December but was beaten on points by Sam McVea.

Over the next several years Wills fought Langford fifteen more times. In 1916 Langford again knocked out Wills, but Wills generally had the best of the series, and by 1918 Langford had ceased to be able to compete seriously with him. Wills also fought other good black heavyweights, including Sam McVea six times and Jack Thompson ten times. Indeed, all of Wills's opponents during the years 1915 to 1918 were black, and the overwhelming majority of all of his fights were with other black men. During these years, in reaction to the controversial black heavyweight champion JACK JOHNSON, promoters seldom matched black fighters with white fighters, and whites often "drew the color line," refusing to box black fighters. Wills's earnings from his boxing career were so small that he continued to work as a stevedore between fights, first in New Orleans and later in West Hoboken, New Jersey.

In 1917 Wills was stopped in two rounds by Battling Jim Johnson when he suffered a broken arm, but he easily won a rematch. Wills thereafter won all of his fights (either officially or, in the case of no-decision fights, unofficially by "newspaper decisions") until 1926, except for a 1922 loss to Bill Tate on a foul and a draw with Tate in a rematch. In 1920 he gained an important victory when he knocked out white heavyweight Fred Fulton, and in 1922 he knocked out a major black rival, Kid Norfolk, in two rounds.

In 1922 some of the influential New York sportswriters, especially George Underwood, boxing writer for the *New York Telegram*, and Nat Fleischer, editor of *The Ring* (a boxing magazine), called for the white heavyweight champion, Jack Dempsey, to defend his title against Wills. Although Dempsey and his manager, Jack Kearns, were willing to have the heavyweight title defended against Wills, Tex Rickard, the great fight promoter of the period, opposed it. Rickard had promoted the Jack Johnson–Jim Jeffries fight in 1910 and was blamed for the "humiliation" of the white race after Johnson defeated Jeffries. He feared race riots if another black became heavyweight champion and claimed that unnamed political forces did not want the fight. Even so, a contract was signed for a fight between Dempsey and Wills in July 1922 in New York, contingent upon a reliable promoter's being found to stage the fight within sixty days. Neither Rickard nor any other promoter came forward. In February 1923 William Muldoon, the chairman of the New York State Boxing Commission, stated that he would not permit a heavyweight title fight in New York because Americans were opposed to any person earning more for a few minutes' work than the president of the United States made for a full term. New Jersey was also mentioned as a possible site for a Dempsey-Wills fight, but the authorities would not allow it.

In 1924 Wills's reputation suffered somewhat when he was unable to knock out the much smaller Bartley Madden in a fifteen-round fight. Although hampered by an injured thumb, Wills decisively beat Argentine heavyweight Luis Angel Firpo in twelve rounds at Jersey City (newspaper decision) on 11 September 1924. After two impressive knockouts by Wills over white heavyweights Charley Weinert and Floyd Johnson in 1925, there was renewed pressure from sportswriters for a Dempsey-Wills fight.

This led to an ultimatum to Dempsey by the New York State Boxing Commission that he would be barred from fighting in the state unless he fought Wills. Kearns refused to accept the Wills fight and Rickard refused to promote it, and instead a fight between Dempsey and Gene Tunney was arranged. The License Committee of the New York Boxing Board refused to allow a Dempsey-Tunney fight, but Rickard simply moved the fight to Philadelphia, where it occurred on 23 September 1926.

Paddy Mullins, Wills's manager, had turned down possible fights for Wills with Tommy Gibbons and Tunney, insisting that Wills would meet only Dempsey. Tunney, by defeating Gibbons, secured the match with Dempsey and won the heavyweight title. On 12 October 1926 Wills fought Jack Sharkey in Brooklyn, New York, and suffered a bad beating, losing every round until being disqualified in the thirteenth, thus ending his heavyweight title chances.

On 13 July 1927 Wills made an attempt to put himself back into contention for the heavyweight title by fighting a young Spanish heavyweight, Paulino Uzcudun, in Brooklyn. Wills's cleverer boxing held his opponent at bay for a couple of rounds, but the aggressive Uzcudun scored a four-round knockout. Afterward Wills had only three minor fights, the last in 1932.

In 1916 Wills had married a former model and schoolteacher, Sarah (maiden name unknown), who proved to be a good manager of money and handled the family finances well. Eventually the couple bought six apartment houses in New York City, made their own home in one of them, and managed them for many years. Wills lived quietly with his wife in New York City until his death there.

Wills was both a hard puncher and a good orthodox boxer. He was more agile than most of his opponents and, unlike many tall heavyweights, was a good fighter at close quarters. He had the ability to tie up his opponents with one arm and flail away with the other, to good effect.

The probable outcome of the Dempsey-Wills fight that never occurred has continued to be a matter of debate. Although the consensus is that Dempsey would have won, there is no doubt that Wills was prevented from getting his well-merited opportunity by the prevailing racist fears. Always gentlemanly and affable, Wills was almost the opposite in personality from the controversial Jack Johnson and would have been a well-liked champion. It is probable that the unjust denial of a heavyweight title fight to Wills worked to the benefit of the next African American heavyweight challenger to appear, JOE LOUIS.

Wills had approximately one hundred professional fights, winning almost half of them by knockout and most of the rest by decision (either official or in the opinion of newspaper reporters). He lost fewer than ten fights. He was elected to the International Boxing Hall of Fame in 1992.

FURTHER READING

Dempsey, Jack, and Barbara Piattelli Dempsey. *Dempsey* (1977).

Fleischer, Nat. *Black Dynamite*, vol. 5: *Sockers in Sepia* (1947).

Fleischer, Nat. *Jack Dempsey: Idol of Fistiana* (1929, 1972).

Jones, Jersey. "The Legend That Was Harry Wills," *The Ring*, Mar. 1959.

Kennedy, John B. "If Dempsey's Afraid Let Him Say So," *Collier's*, 20 Mar. 1926.

Roberts, Randy. *Jack Dempsey: The Manassa Mauler* (1979).

Obituary: *New York Times*, 22 Dec. 1958.

LUCKETT V. DAVIS

Wills, Maury (2 Oct. 1932–), baseball player, was born Maurice Morning Wills in Washington, D.C., the seventh of thirteen children of the Reverend Guy O. Wills, a machinist at the Washington navy yard and Baptist minister, and Mabel (maiden name unknown), an elevator operator. Though small, Maury excelled in sports, playing football, basketball, and baseball. His life changed when he met the Washington Senators' second baseman Jerry Priddy, who encouraged Maury to work hard at baseball. He started playing semipro baseball at age fourteen, and his father even held special Sunday services so Maury and his brothers could play baseball in the afternoon. When Wills graduated from Cordoza High School in 1950 he signed a contract with the Brooklyn Dodgers. He married Gertrude Elliot in 1949, while still in high school. They had six children before divorcing in 1965.

Wills attended his first spring training in 1951 at "Dodgertown" in Vero Beach, California. Vero Beach was segregated, so Wills had to travel to nearby Gifford for food and entertainment. The Dodgers assigned him to their Class D affiliate in Hornell, New York, where he led the league in steals in 1951 and 1952. Wills's fielding skills as a shortstop and his speed in the base paths led him on a steady but slow climb through the minor leagues, including

stops in Pueblo, Colorado, in 1953–1954 and 1956; Fort Worth, Texas, where he was the first black player on the team, in 1955; Seattle, Washington, in 1957; and Spokane, Washington, in 1958. Bobby Bragan, Wills's manager in Spokane, taught Wills to be a switch hitter, a move that would finally propel Wills to the major leagues.

During the 1959 season the Dodgers (who had moved to Los Angeles in 1958) promoted Wills to the major leagues to replace the injured shortstop Don Zimmer. Wills started slowly but ended up becoming the team's starting shortstop, helping the Dodgers win the 1959 World Series, four games to two, over the Chicago White Sox. Over the next three seasons the Dodgers remained unsure of Wills and auditioned numerous shortstops, but Wills beat out the competition every time. In 1960 he set a team record with fifty steals, leading the major leagues, a feat he repeated in 1961 while also claiming his first Gold Glove award. Wills's speed, uncanny ability to get on base, and skill as a base runner transformed the Dodgers from a power hitting team to one built on speed and defense. The Dodgers rewarded Wills by naming him team captain in 1962.

The 1962 season was a defining moment for Wills's career as he finished with 104 steals, breaking the major league record of ninety-six steals held by Ty Cobb since 1915. The Dodgers moved into a new, pitcher-friendly stadium for the season, and manager Walter Alston built the team's offense around Wills's base stealing, turning him loose to steal at will. As Wills approached Cobb's record, league commissioner Ford Frick ruled that Wills had to beat the record in 156 games, the same number Cobb played in 1915. Wills stole his ninety-seventh base in game 156, getting his record. Wills was named the National League Most Valuable Player, won a second Gold Glove, and broke another record by playing in all 165 Dodger games (162 regular games and a three-game playoff against the San Francisco Giants).

The Dodgers and Wills continued to have success, winning the World Series again in 1963 and 1965. Wills led the major leagues in stolen bases for six consecutive seasons, 1960 to 1965. During off-seasons Wills was a regular in Las Vegas. An accomplished banjo player, Wills started playing with Milton Berle in 1962 before starting his own act at the Sahara casino in 1963. He often included teammates in his act and never realized that the celebrities he met were just as much in awe of him as he was of them.

Maury Wills, infielder for the Los Angeles Dodgers, on 8 March 1972. (AP Images.)

In 1966 the Dodgers traded Wills to the Pittsburgh Pirates, where he played for two seasons before the Montreal Expos selected him in the expansion draft. He almost retired because of a poor start to the season, but he was traded back to the Dodgers. He was named a Dodger Centennial Celebrity during the 1969 season, an honor he called the highlight of his life. Wills remained the Dodger shortstop through the 1971 season, when he won Major League Baseball's Shortstop of the Year award. The Dodgers released Wills after the 1972 season as the team looked to younger players. He finished his playing career with 2,134 hits, a career .281 batting average, and 586 stolen bases. Never known for power, he had only twenty career home runs, and only one of those on purpose. After his release Wills went into broadcasting, taking over for his former teammate Sandy Koufax on NBC's *Game of the Week*. He managed in the Mexican Leagues during the winter and coached base-running skills to a number of teams. In 1979 NBC dropped Wills, and he moved to HBO to work on its show *Race for the Pennant*. He spent a year at HBO before becoming manager of the Seattle Mariners in August 1980, fulfilling his wish to manage a major league team. His tenure at Seattle was short. Wills managed only eighty-two games over two seasons, finishing with a record of 26-56.

Wills's life took a bad turn after he was fired in Seattle. He became addicted to cocaine, and for three years never left his house; however, he beat his drug habit in 1988 and began to rebuild relationships with his family and former teammates. During his recovery he worked with many organizations dedicated to helping children stay away from drugs. He also returned to baseball, working as a roving base-running instructor for fifteen major league teams. Wills was a Dodger at heart, and was ecstatic to return to Los Angeles in 2000 as the team's base-running and bunting instructor. In 2002 Dodger fans voted him Dodger Stadium's most exciting player.

FURTHER READING

Wills, Maury, and Mike Celizic. *On the Run: The Never Dull and Often Shocking Life of Maury Wills* (1990).
Wills, Maury, and Steve Gardner. *It Pays to Steal* (1963).
Delsohn, Steve. *True Blue: The Dramatic History of the Los Angeles Dodgers, Told By the Men Who Lived It* (2001).

MICHAEL C. MILLER

Willson, Joseph (22 Feb. 1817–21 Aug. 1895), author, printer, and dentist, was born in Augusta, Georgia, the fourth of five children of John Willson, a Scots-Irish banker, and Elizabeth Keating, a free woman of color. Although they never married, Elizabeth eventually took Willson's last name. Shortly before his death in 1822, John Willson wrote a will leaving his "housekeeper" (the term he used to describe Elizabeth's role in his household) and her children two hundred shares of stock in the Bank of Augusta and appointed his friend, the prominent attorney John P. King, as their guardian (by the time Willson wrote his will, Georgia law required free people of color to have a white guardian to administer their property). King sent young Joseph to school in Alabama, but he and Elizabeth agonized about the family's prospects, given that the Georgia legislature seemed intent on restricting virtually every aspect of the lives of the state's free people of color. Eventually Elizabeth decided to move with her children to what she hoped would be the more congenial setting of Philadelphia, Pennsylvania. King used John Willson's bequest to buy the family a home on Morgan Street in that city's Spring Garden section. A friend the Willsons made soon after their arrival in Philadelphia did much to ease their transition. Frederick Augustus Hinton, an influential lay member of the church they joined, St. Thomas's African Episcopal, was also a zealous abolitionist. In 1833, when Joseph Willson graduated from the Pennsylvania Abolition Society's Clarkson School, he tried without success to secure an apprenticeship as a printer. Hinton intervened on his behalf, writing Boston's abolitionist leader William Lloyd Garrison and challenging him to live up to his egalitarian principles by hiring Willson. Garrison agreed to do so, and Willson spent the next few years in the Boston office of the *Liberator* mastering the printer's trade before setting up on his own shop in Philadelphia.

After Willson's return to Philadelphia sometime prior to 1838, Hinton again took him under his wing (in 1837 the two became brothers-in-law when Hinton married one of Joseph's sisters). Hinton's influence opened doors for Willson, literally and figuratively. Willson joined the Young Men's Antislavery Society, which Hinton had helped found. He made the rounds of the various African American literary and mutual improvement societies and attended meetings on everything from abolition to voting rights. He was invited into the homes of the black elite but also witnessed the poverty endured by many of the city's black residents. It was the sheer diversity of black life in Philadelphia—a diversity he was convinced eluded most whites—that prompted Willson in 1841 to write *Sketches of the Higher Classes of Colored Society in Philadelphia, by a Southerner.*

Although he used a pen name, his authorship was an open secret. In many respects *Sketches* prefigured W. E. B. DuBois's *The Philadelphia Negro* (1899). *Sketches* explored class differences in one of the largest free communities of color in the United States and eloquently challenged whites to judge black people as individuals, not as "one consolidated mass" (82). It was also a heartfelt appeal for black unity. Willson begged those in the "higher classes" to abandon counterproductive feuding and work for the greater good of all African Americans. Witty and insightful, *Sketches* attracted considerable attention in the African American and antislavery press, although it likely did not reach many white readers outside the ranks of abolitionists.

At some point in the mid-1840s Willson returned to Georgia, where he married Elizabeth Harnett, whose background was strikingly similar to his own: her mother was a free woman of color and her father a well-to-do Scottish immigrant. The couple made their home in Philadelphia with Willson's mother. They had five children.

When Willson's mother died in 1847, she left an estate worth well over twenty thousand dollars. Willson used his share to purchase a house in Moyamensing, on the southern fringe of Philadelphia. Moving from Spring Garden, a largely white section of the city, into the heart of Philadelphia's most vibrant African American neighborhood represented an unmistakable declaration of racial identity. The years immediately following his mother's death saw many changes in Willson's life, some tragic. Hinton succumbed to cholera in 1849, robbing Willson of his mentor, while the decision of Willson's younger brother John to remain in Spring Garden and "pass" into the white community estranged the siblings. On the positive side, Joseph Willson found solace in his role as husband and father. He also branched out professionally, abandoning the printer's trade in favor of dentistry.

Several factors prompted Joseph and Elizabeth Willson to leave Philadelphia for Cleveland, Ohio, in the mid-1850s. The eldest of their children was approaching school age, and they disdained Philadelphia's rigidly segregated public schools. The schools in Cleveland were open to all. Joseph Willson had also been advised that Cleveland had far fewer medical professionals than Philadelphia. He would have no trouble attracting both black and white patients. Their expectations of a better life in Cleveland proved well founded, and Willson soon enjoyed a thriving practice. He and Elizabeth were accepted into the city's African American upper class, and they also made many white friends. The Willson children graduated from the public schools. Leonidas Willson became one of the first African Americans admitted to the Ohio bar, while the Willson daughters all became teachers in the school system. The Willsons valued their privacy, but in the summer of 1878 they were thrust into the limelight when their daughter JOSEPHINE BEALL WILLSON BRUCE wed U.S. Senator BLANCHE K. BRUCE from Mississippi. Eager to give their readers a glimpse into the lives of the "higher classes of colored society," newspaper editors across the nation dispatched reporters to Cleveland to cover every aspect of the Willson-Bruce wedding, much to the family's consternation.

In the mid-1880s Joseph and Elizabeth Willson moved to Indianapolis, where two of their daughters had teaching posts. Willson spent his remaining years there. His death, the result of complications from diabetes, attracted little attention outside his immediate circle. His obituary in the *Washington Bee* (7 Sept. 1895), for instance, dwelled less on his achievements than on the fact that he was Senator Bruce's father-in-law.

FURTHER READING
Gatewood, Willard B.. *Aristocrats of Color: The Black Elite, 1880–1920* (1990).
Winch, Julie, ed. "The Elite of Our People": *Joseph Willson's Sketches of Black Upper-Class Life in Antebellum Philadelphia* (2000).
Obituary: *Washington Bee*, 7 Sept. 1895.

JULIE WINCH

Wilson, Alyce McCarroll (1907?–26 Sept. 1987), social worker and settlement house director, was born in Birmingham, Alabama, to parents whose names and occupations are now unknown. Wilson graduated from Fisk University in Nashville, Tennessee, in the late 1920s, earning a certificate of music. Shortly after graduation she arrived in Omaha, Nebraska, where she worked as a social worker. Wilson was a diligent member of the Alpha Beta Chapter of the Delta sorority and served as a founding member of Delta sorority chapters in her hometown, as well as a chapter at Fisk University and the Gamma Xi Alumnae Chapter of Omaha. While still in her thirties, Wilson was appointed director of Woodson Center, an African American settlement house in South Omaha.

The idea of settlement houses originated in London in the nineteenth century to help immigrants adjust to their new surroundings and to help eradicate social inequalities by providing educational opportunities for the working class. In 1908 Omahans supported the opening of a social settlement house in South Omaha (a separate municipality until it was annexed by the city of Omaha in 1915) to help the families of white immigrants. Hundreds of immigrants had settled near the South Omaha stockyards, where they could find work on the railroads or in meat processing. Settlement house workers in Omaha were charged with providing recreational and educational opportunities for people from diverse countries and cultural backgrounds. The Woodson Center maintained this tradition, in effect functioning as a combined facility for the meetings of voluntary associations, a mutual aid society, and a community recreation center.

Wilson's Woodson Center had a unique beginning: it developed as a result of segregation in the white South Omaha Social Settlement House. With the number of African Americans in South Omaha rapidly increasing, the white directors of the Social Settlement House grudgingly allowed African American children to use the center's facilities from 1908–1926, but only when they were not being utilized by white children. African Americans and whites were instructed to use the facility at alternate times. As the population of South Omaha grew, this arrangement became increasingly strained.

In 1926 a second house, called the Culture Center, was established for African Americans. Located at 2915 R Street, two blocks from the segregated social settlement facility, the Culture Center served South Omaha's African American population for decades. In 1930 Social Settlement moved to the west side of Omaha and the Culture Center began serving a diverse population in South Omaha from its new and expanded location at 30th and R Street. In 1937 it was renamed Woodson Center, after the historian CARTER GODWIN WOODSON. Woodson Center staff members soon voted to become financially independent of the Social Settlement House, reporting thereafter directly to the Omaha Community Chest. Included in Woodson Center's bylaws was a requirement that the organization be supervised by an interracial board that was not less than 51 percent African American. This requirement created an opportunity for the hiring of qualified African American staff. Wilson took the directorship and institutionalized her vision of community service at Woodson Center for the better part of four decades.

Under Wilson the Woodson Center became the site of a nursery school during the day, a recreational facility for children after school, and a night school for adults. It provided a clinic operated by visiting nurses, a tutoring location for primary and secondary school students, and a counseling and food distribution center. On weekends and during the summer the facility was used for dances, bowling, and sports. Plays and musicals were attended at the center by African Americans from all over the city. Woodson Center also served as a meeting place for scores of self-improvement associations featuring etiquette, sewing, cooking, and woodworking clubs. It provided a meeting place for African American fraternal organizations and sponsored Boy Scout troops.

In the tradition of the women's club movement, much of the work carried out at the center was conducted by women. Wilson worked closely with other community women such as Katherine Fletcher and with Woodson Center employees Beatrice Mosley and Claudell Thomas, who became Wilson's lifelong friends. Woodson Center was one of six original African American social service agencies in Omaha whose program goals provided for improvement in the quality of life for African Americans. Wilson took this mission to heart working daily to reallocate resources to those most in need of support.

Wilson had no children of her own and dedicated her life to the Woodson Center, working most nights until 10 p.m. She also served as a member of professional and social service organizations including the National Association of Social Workers, Planned Parenthood, the Omaha Occupation and Industrialization Center, and the National Federation of Settlements. Wilson was a civil rights advocate and served as a charter member of the Nebraska Equal Employment Opportunity Commission. She was highly respected for her contributions to the lives of South Omaha youth and received numerous awards, including two from the Urban League (1967 and 1985), and recognition from the South Omaha Optimists Club, the South Omaha Neighborhood Association, the South Omaha Women's Club, the Omaha Housing Authority, Bethel Baptist Church, and the Black Heritage Series.

After Wilson's retirement from the center in the mid-1970s she received a number of moving tributes from generations of community members who had attended Woodson Center as children and teenagers. At one of the tributes Wilson was described first as "a mother, father, counselor, and teacher" who gave young people the "motivation and enthusiasm to look beyond where we are" ("Alyce Wilson Tribute" video, Woodson Center, Omaha, Nebraska, 1985), while another attendee remembered Wilson as "a lady who has given her all to this community." Wilson believed that there was something good about each young person and was seeking to find that out. Bumpy Curtis recalled, "We used to play ball at the white settlement. We had to be more than good to play up there, we had to be better. A lot of times we would win the title and the white team would say we forfeited the game because not all of our players had uniforms. We'd cry, and Mrs. Wilson would say, 'Don't worry about it. Where there's a will there's a way.' Eventually we did win a title." Wilson and her staff taught girls to make aprons and biscuits, and was "like a second mother." One adult of Hispanic heritage recalled that Wilson had let him into the center for the first time when he was barefoot. In truth Wilson had hundreds of "children," some of whom later returned to the center to work for her or to offer various kinds of support. Ann Sails said that "though it was preferred for women to stay home with their children in those days, our mothers worked," so "Mrs. Wilson became a mother to all of us."

FURTHER READING

"Alyce Wilson Tribute." Video, Woodson Center, Omaha, Nebraska (1985).

Nebraska Writers' Project. *The Negroes of Nebraska* (1935), accessible online at http://www.memoriallibrary.com/NE/Ethnic/Negro.

"Social Settlement, Omaha Nebraska." Nebraska State Historical Society Archives Collection Record RG 5337, Lincoln, Nebraska.

Obituary: *Omaha World Herald*, 28 Sept. 1987.

TEKLA ALI JOHNSON

Wilson, August (27 Apr. 1945–2 Oct. 2005), playwright, was born Frederick August Kittel in Pittsburgh, Pennsylvania, the fourth of six children of Frederick Kittel, a German baker who immigrated to the United States at age ten, and Daisy Wilson, a cleaning woman. Frederick Kittel was an infrequent visitor to the family's two-room apartment in the city's racially mixed Hill District. As an adult, August symbolically severed ties to his father by taking his mother's maiden name, Wilson.

In 1959 David Bedford, Wilson's stepfather, moved the family to the white suburb of Hazelwood, Pennsylvania, where Wilson attended Central Catholic High School. He suffered racial taunts from other students and transferred the following year to Gladstone High School, where the greatest assault on his intelligence came from a black teacher who accused him of plagiarizing a twenty-page paper, believing that Wilson was not capable of writing such lucid prose. Confused and frustrated, Wilson dropped out of school in the ninth grade. He worked at a series of odd jobs, wandered the streets, and found solace in the public library, where he took responsibility for completing his own education, devouring the works of LANGSTON HUGHES, JAMES BALDWIN, RICHARD WRIGHT, and the Welsh poet Dylan Thomas. With no career goal in mind, he joined the army just shy of his eighteenth birthday and was discharged a year later, unable to conform to the strict rules of the military.

Wilson's life started to come into focus on 1 April 1965, when he purchased a twenty-dollar typewriter and began to explore the written word as a critical means of self-expression and as a viable occupation. His first efforts were highly charged poems that might be appreciated for their passion, though their precise meanings could be a mystery even to their author. Wilson's aesthetic sensibilities were forged by the emerging Black Arts Movement, which identified culture as an important battleground and enlisted black artists in every medium as soldiers in the struggle for racial liberation. Just as W. E. B. DuBois influenced artists of his generation with the publication of "Criteria of Negro Art" during the Harlem Renaissance, Wilson and his cohorts were influenced by AMIRI BARAKA, who, in his poem "Black Art," called for "poems like fists" and urged his generation to use their creative talents to achieve collective ends. Imbued with this philosophy, Wilson drew inspiration from blues musicians such as BESSIE SMITH and visual artists such as ROMARE BEARDEN for both their cultural relevance and their aesthetic excellence.

Wilson began to establish his credentials and reputation as both an artist and an advocate for black Theater by becoming a founding member of the Center Avenue Poet's Theater Workshop and, with Rob Penney in 1967, an organizer of the Black Horizon Theater Company. "Youngblood," as Wilson was called by his friends, published his first poems, "MUHAMMAD ALI" and "For MALCOLM X and Others," in *Black World* and the *Negro Digest* in 1969. In 1972 his three-year marriage to Brenda Burton, a member of the Nation of Islam, with whom he had one child, ended in divorce. The following year Wilson wrote his first play, *Recycle*, exploring the painful disintegration of a marriage. *The Homecoming*, a play based on the mysterious death of the legendary blues guitarist BLIND LEMON JEFFERSON, was performed at the University of Pittsburgh's Kuntu Theater in 1976. Yet Wilson still considered himself to be primarily a poet until 1978, when he accepted an assignment in St. Paul to write children's plays for the Science Museum of Minnesota.

Writing convincing dialogue was difficult for Wilson until he was encouraged by his friend Claude Purdy at the Playwrights Center in Minneapolis to listen to the authentic voices of his characters and allow them to tell the story. In 1977, drawing on this advice, Wilson completed *Black Bart and the Sacred Hills*, a musical satire based on the infamous white outlaw. In 1978 Wilson moved to St. Paul, where he met Judy Oliver, a social worker whom he married in 1981. Wilson then wrote *Jitney* (1979), a two-act play centered on the lives of men in a gypsy cab station who confront the problems of urban renewal, the Vietnam War, and a developing generation gap. The local acclaim that *Jitney* received allowed Wilson to begin thinking of himself as a serious playwright. Later, in describing his development, Wilson said with pride, "I consider it a blessing that when I started writing plays in earnest, in 1979, I

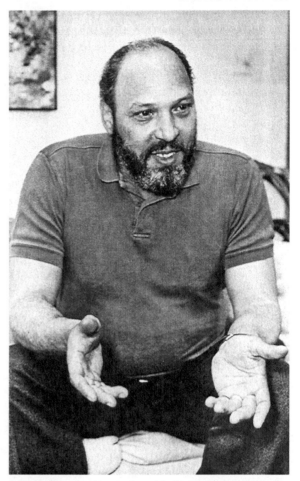

August Wilson, in his apartment in St. Paul, Minnesota, discusses winning the Pulitzer Prize for Drama, 16 April 1987. (AP Images.)

had not read Chekov. I hadn't read Ibsen. I hadn't read Tennessee Williams, Arthur Miller, or O'Neill. … It took me eight years to find my own voice as a poet. I didn't want to take eight years to find my voice as a playwright" (Lahr, 53).

Critics have not missed the irony that America's most celebrated black playwright, whose plays make millions on Broadway, are financed by white producers, and win the acclaim of New York socialites, was, in fact, an "unrepentant black nationalist" (*New York Times*, 2 Feb. 2003) who publicly championed independent black theater and supported race-specific casting. Taking note of this apparent contradiction, HENRY LOUIS GATES JR. opined, "The Revolution will not be subsidized" (Gates, 138). However, Wilson's entrée into the elite circles in which he traveled was made possible by the support of a black network, particularly Lloyd

Richards, an influential black insider who had directed LORRAINE HANSBERRY's *A Raisin in the Sun* in 1959. By 1982, when Wilson met him, Richards was dean of the Yale Drama School and director of the National Playwrights Conference of the Eugene O'Neill Center in Waterford, Connecticut, which invited Wilson to be one of fifteen playwrights that summer to have their work critiqued and staged. Wilson's play was M.A. *Rainey's Black Bottom*, set in a recording studio in Chicago during the 1920s. The depth and complexity he wove into a single day in the life of the audacious blues singer and her musicians elevated Wilson's exposition of racism beyond mere agitprop to a nuanced tale of exploitation, the struggle for dignity, and the dangers of uncontrolled and misdirected rage. Richards brought Wilson and the actor CHARLES DUTTON, who would play the male lead in M.A. *Rainey's Black Bottom*, to the Yale Repertory Theater, where Richards was the artistic director and their future producer, Ben Mordecai, was the managing director. Together with Wilson they further refined the play before taking it to the Cort Theater on Broadway in 1984. It won both the New York Drama Critics' Circle Award and a Tony nomination in 1985. Richards would direct Wilson's next six plays, usually opening at the O'Neill, continuing at Yale, and traveling a circuit of local theaters on the way to Broadway, where each play in turn also won the Drama Critic's Circle Award.

Wilson and Richards next produced *Fences* (1987). Set in the 1950s and partly based on Wilson's stepfather, the play uses a sports plot to explore the physical and emotional barriers that fragment the lives of black men. *Fences* garnered a Pulitzer Prize and a Tony Award and grossed $11 million. Wilson's favorite play, *Joe Turner's Come and Gone* (1988), set in 1911, explores themes of cultural dislocation and the search for identity as the main characters struggle to make the transition from slavery to freedom and have difficulty embracing an African heritage infused with occult mystery. *The Piano Lesson* (1990) turns on the dilemma of a family in the 1930s confronted with a decision to keep or sell the piano that links them with their past. This play earned Wilson a second Pulitzer and brought him together with his third wife, Constanza Romero, who designed costumes for the Yale production; they had one child. *Two Trains Running* (1992) takes place in a 1960s diner that becomes a window into the hearts and minds of its patrons, each of whom presents a slice of black life. *Seven Guitars* (1996) is ostensibly about a group of musicians in the 1940s who gather to remember the life of a blues guitarist tragically cut down on the verge of fame. Ultimately, however, their soliloquies combine to bespeak the blues of an entire people.

With the Broadway production of *Jitney* (2000), Richards was replaced by Marion McClinton, who directed Wilson's plays until his death in New York after a brief battle with liver cancer at the age of sixty. Wilson's break with Richards divided his career into two eras that were, nevertheless, united by an overarching objective: capturing the African American experience by devoting one play to each decade of the twentieth century. With *King Hedley II* (1999), a look at the desperate conditions and pandemic ills of the 1980s, and *Gem of the Ocean* (2002), a play set in 1904 about a man on the run who passes through a labyrinth of challenges leading to self-discovery, Wilson was poised to achieve his goal. He did so just months before his death with the publication of *Radio Golf* in 2005. Wilson placed race at center stage in the American theater and advanced a philosophical discussion about the roles of history and art. In fact, no playwright in history had explored so much of the African American odyssey in drama. Shortly after his death, the Virginia Theater in New York City was renamed the August Wilson Theater in his honor; it was the first Broadway theater to bear the name of an African American.

FURTHER READING

Bogumil, Mary L. *Understanding August Wilson* (1999).

Gates, Henry Louis, Jr. "The Chitlin Circuit," in *African American Performance and Theater History*, ed. Harry J. Elam Jr. and David Krasner (2001).

Lahr, John. "Been Here and Gone," *New Yorker*, 16 Apr. 2001.

Shannon, Sandra G. *The Dramatic Vision of August Wilson* (1995).

SHOLOMO B. LEVY

Wilson, Butler (22 July 1860–1 Nov. 1939), civil rights attorney and political activist, was born in Atlanta, Georgia. Little is known of his parents, except that his father was a black physician. Wilson graduated from Atlanta University and then attended Boston University Law School, where he received a degree of Juris Doctor in 1883. He became one of the social and political black elite of Boston, who enjoyed economic privilege but who were also dedicated to improving the quality of life for all African Americans. An interesting note is that Butler Wilson was among the first Negro golfers in post–Civil War America. He played with Dr. George Grant, the inventor of the first patented golf tee (and one of the country's first Negro dentists), and with other civil rights activists and socially prominent blacks such as ARCHIBALD GRIMKÉ (later president of the Washington, D.C., branch of the NAACP) and the noted restaurateur Howard Lee.

Butler Wilson began his legal career in 1883 as an office apprentice for Judge GEORGE L. RUFFIN. Justice Ruffin had been the first black graduate of Harvard Law School and Boston's first black judge (it took seventy-five years for Boston to appoint a second one).

Wilson married Mary Evans, a physical education teacher who dedicated her life to the cause of civil rights for black Americans. She wrote articles for black community newspapers, organized a Women's Service Club to aid black men in uniform, and helped organize a New England–area membership drive for the NAACP that coincided with the migration of many African Americans from the South in the years 1915 to 1929.

Wilson gradually made a name for himself as a prominent Boston attorney, representing white as well as black clients, at a time and place where segregation and discrimination were commonplace. Wilson also edited a community newspaper called *The Hub*, with his friend and colleague Archibald H. Grimké, as a vehicle for spreading their civil rights philosophies. In 1899 Wilson addressed an audience of Boston blacks at a gathering to commemorate the forty-eighth anniversary of Charles Sumner's election to the United States Senate. "We can no longer, with safety, allow men, however honest and earnest they may be, to lead us along dangerous paths. We seek to obtain rights, not to surrender them." Wilson spoke in support of an alternative to the established position, represented by BOOKER T. WASHINGTON, that Wilson believed failed in not condemning Jim Crow and in discouraging the pursuit of higher education for average African Americans.

In 1905 Wilson continued to lend his support to the cause of civil rights when he signed a petition in support of the Niagara Movement. W. E. B. DuBois had sent out a call to the Negro community's "educated tenth" for "organized determination and aggressive action on the part of men who believe in Negro freedom and growth." Fifty-nine men from seventeen states signed, and twenty-nine attended the conference held in a hotel on the Canadian side of the Erie River near Buffalo, New York. The Niagara Movement's causes included freedom of speech, freedom of the press, and the right to vote, and its principles included the abolition of caste distinctions based on race and color and a belief in brotherhood and the right to higher education, dignity of employment, and self-determination.

Wilson was a cofounder of the Boston branch of the NAACP. The NAACP, which evolved in part from the Niagara Movement, was founded in 1909 by a group of multiracial activists. It was originally called the National Negro Committee. White descendants of abolitionists made up the majority of the Boston branch's early leadership. The first president was Francis Jackson Garrison, the youngest son of William Lloyd Garrison, who served from 1912 to 1916. In 1911 Boston hosted the NAACP's first national gathering outside New York. In the decade that followed, the Boston branch was the association's largest and strongest. It also remained the most integrated— almost every other branch had become, by 1920, almost entirely African American. One of the most notable endeavors for the Boston branch was the attempt by Wilson and his colleagues to pass U.S. Congressman Leonidas Dyer's antilynching legislation (initiated in 1918). Dyer was a Republican representative from St. Louis, Missouri. The Dyer Bill was passed by the House of Representatives on 26 January 1922, and was given a favorable report by the Senate committee assigned to report on it in July 1922. The bill would have made lynching a federal crime, and would have provided compensation for victims' families from county funds up to $10,000. Despite Wilson's efforts to find support for the bill, its passage was ultimately halted by a filibuster in the Senate.

Wilson was also leader in the Boston NAACP's most successful civil rights case in the higher education arena. In the fall of 1921 a handful of African American students, including Wilson's own son Edward, along with the grandson of Mississippi senator BLANCHE K. BRUCE, were admitted to Harvard University but were barred from living in the freshman dormitory because an integrated living situation might be offensive to students from the southern states. A petition and an editorial campaign led in the spring of 1923 to the overturn of the discriminatory edict.

In the 1920s and 1930s Wilson made a name for himself representing black defendants in extradition proceedings against southern states. Southern courts and penitentiaries of that era were notorious for their inhumane treatment of African American convicts. Wilson did what he could to protect the prisoners' constitutional rights.

Wilson died in 1939, eleven years after the passing of his wife, Mary.

FURTHER READING

DuBois, W. E. B. *The Autobiography of W. E. B. DuBois:-A Soliloquy on Viewing My Life from the Last Decade of Its First Century* (1968).

Schneider, Mark. "The Boston NAACP and the Decline of Abolitionist Impulse." *Massachusetts Historical Review*. 1999. Accessible online at: http://historycooperative.org/journals/l?schneider.html.

Smock, Raymond W. "Washington, Booker T." *World Book Online Reference Center*, 2007. http://www.worldbookonline.com/wb/Article?id=ar592920

JOLIE A. JACKSON-WILLETT

Wilson, Cassandra (4 Dec. 1955–), jazz singer and songwriter, was born Cassandra Fowlkes in Jackson, Mississippi, the third and youngest child of Hermann Fowlkes, an electric bassist and high school music teacher, and Mary, an elementary school teacher who eventually earned her Ph.D. in Education. Wilson's parents sparked her early interest in music: her mother loved Motown, and her father was dedicated to jazz. The first album she recalled ever hearing came from her father's collection, MILES DAVIS's *Sketches of Spain*. The musicians who passed through her home and the performances she attended increased her interest in music. Perhaps more importantly, her father encouraged Cassandra to develop eclectic listening habits, which later led her into a nontraditional jazz repertoire.

Like many jazz musicians, Wilson's formal musical education consisted of classical lessons; she studied piano from around the age of six to thirteen and played clarinet in the middle school concert and marching bands. When she tired of this training, she asked her father to teach her the guitar. Instead, he gave her a lesson in self-reliance—some Mel Bay method books. She explored the instrument on her own, developing what she described as an "intuitive" approach. During this time she began writing her own songs, adopting a folk style. She sang and played guitar in a folk trio during high school and also appeared in musical Theater productions, crossing racial lines in a recently desegregated school system; the other members of her trio were white males. Perhaps even more startling, she starred as Dorothy in *The Wizard of Oz* during her junior year. Wilson attended Jackson State University and graduated with a degree in mass communications, a career path that met with her mother's approval because of its potential to provide financial security. Outside of the classroom, the busy student spent her nights working with R&B, funk, and pop cover bands, and also singing in local coffeehouses. The Black Arts Music Society provided her with her first opportunities to perform bebop. In 1981 she moved to New Orleans for a job in the public affairs department of a local television station. She did not stay long. Working with mentors who included elder statesmen Ellis Marsalis and Alvin Batiste, Wilson found encouragement to pursue jazz performance seriously and moved to the New York City area the following year.

Her focus turned toward improvisation. Heavily influenced by the singer BETTY CARTER, she learned to scat and studied ear training with the trombonist Grachan Moncur III. Frequenting jam sessions, she met the alto saxophonist Steve Coleman, who encouraged her to abandon the standard jazz repertoire in favor of developing original material. She would become the vocalist associated with the M-Base Collective, in which Coleman was the leading figure. The M-Base Collective was a stylistic outgrowth of the Association for the Advancement of Creative Musicians (AACM) and Black Artists Group (BAG) that reimagined the grooves of funk and soul within the context of avant-garde jazz. Although the voice—typically treated as the focal point of any arrangement in which it is included—was not an obvious choice for M-Base's complex textures or dissonant free melodies, Wilson wove herself into the fabric of these settings with wordless scatting and lyrics. She can be heard on Coleman's *Motherland Pulse* (1985); *On the Edge of Tomorrow* and *World Expansion* (1986); and *Sine Die* (1987). Wilson recorded and toured with the alto saxophonist Henry Threadgill in the avant-garde trio New Air. A decade her senior and an AACM member, Threadgill was lauded as a composer for his ability to transcend stylistic boundaries, a trait he and Wilson shared. The two were married briefly, and their son, Jeris, was born in 1989.

Like fellow M-Base artists, Wilson signed to the Munich-based, independent label JMT. She released her first recording as a leader in *Point of View* in 1986. The majority of her JMT albums that followed—including *Days Aweigh* (1987), *Jumpworld* (1989), *She Who Weeps* (1990), *Live* and *After the Beginning Again* (1991)—were dominated by originals by Wilson that kept close to the M-Base style. She recorded material by Coleman, Jean-Paul Bourelly, and James Weidman, as well as material that she cowrote with them. She also recorded a

Cassandra Wilson performs during the JVC Jazz Festival in Newport, Rhode Island, on 10 August 2003. (AP Images.)

few standard tunes. Her throaty contralto gradually emerged over the course of these recordings, making its way to the foreground. Although Wilson was neither the fleetest nor most agile vocalist, preferring to linger in the bottom of her range, she developed a remarkable ability to stretch and bend pitches, elongate syllables, and manipulate tone and timbre from dusky to hollow.

Whereas these recordings established her as a serious musician (jazz singers as a group are not acknowledged as composers), Wilson received her first broad critical acclaim for the album of standards recorded in the middle of this period, *Blue Skies* (1988). With it, she stepped into a void of younger, mainstream vocal talent. DEE DEE BRIDGEWATER and Patti Austin had left jazz for pop. With the exception of ELLA FITZGERALD and SARAH VAUGHAN, veteran singers such as Betty Carter, CARMEN MCRAE, ABBEY LINCOLN, and SHIRLEY HORN were still working in relative obscurity following jazz's lean years in the 1960s and 1970s. With Wilson cast as the savior of an embattled tradition, critical reception for the far less conventional projects to which she immediately returned after *Blue Skies* ranged from lukewarm to downright hostile.

Her signing with Blue Note records in 1993 marked a crucial turning point in her career and a major breakthrough to audiences beyond jazz, with albums selling in the hundreds of thousands of copies. Beginning with *Blue Light 'Til Dawn* (1993), her repertoire moved toward a broad synthesis of blues, pop, jazz, world music, and country. Although she continued to perform originals and standards, she adopted songs as diverse as ROBERT JOHNSON's "Come On in My Kitchen," Joni Mitchell's "Black Crow," The Monkees' "Last Train to Clarksville," and Hank Williams's "I'm So Lonesome I Could Cry."

Not only did Wilson effectively reconnect vocal jazz with its blues roots; she was arguably the first to fashion post–British Invasion pop convincingly into jazz, trailblazing a path that many since have followed. Furthermore, producer Craig Street drew from pop production techniques to create a rich ambient environment around her voice, magnifying it and giving sonic depth to Brandon Ross's sparse but incredibly vivid arrangements, which used steel guitar, violin, accordion, and percussion.

Wilson's 1996 album, *New Moon Daughter*, won the Grammy for Best Jazz Vocal Performance. In 1997 she recorded and toured as a featured vocalist with WYNTON MARSALIS's Pulitzer Prize–winning composition, *Blood on the Fields*. Her projects after that time included the Miles Davis tribute *Traveling Miles* (1999); the heavily blues-based *Belly of the Sun* (2002), recorded in the Clarksdale train station; *Glamoured* (2003), with sumptuous covers of Bob Dylan's "Lay Lady Lay" and Willie Nelson's "Crazy"; and *Thunderbird* (2006), which used sampling techniques drawn from hip hop. In 2000 Wilson married actor Isaach de Bankolé, who directed the concert film *Traveling Miles: Cassandra Wilson* (2000). Arguably the most important vocalist who had emerged since the 1980s, *Time* magazine named her "America's best singer" in 1996.

FURTHER READING

Wilson, Cassandra. "What Betty Taught Me," *Jazziz* (January 1999).

Giddins, Gary. "Cassandra Wilson," in *Visions of Jazz: The First Century* (1998).

Watrous, Peter. "Jazz through the Voice of Cassandra Wilson," *The New York Times* (21 March 1994).

LARA PELLEGRINELLI

Wilson, Ed (28 Mar. 1925–26 Nov. 1996), sculptor, was born Edward N. Wilson Jr. in Baltimore, Maryland, to Edward Wilson, a registrar for a historically black college, and his wife, a homemaker. Wilson and his sister grew up in an industrious family whose roots began in Freetown, a freedmen's township in modern-day Somerset County on the Eastern Shore of Maryland. His grandfather had been a businessman, a superintendent of black schools in their area, and a lay preacher.

Wilson began informal art studies while he was still in elementary school. At age seven he was bedridden for more than a year with rheumatic fever. During his confinement his mother encouraged him to draw, paint, and weave. Upon recuperating Wilson returned to school and finished as the salutatorian of his elementary school class. In junior and senior high school he abandoned his art studies and became involved in sports. He proved exceptional in football, basketball, wrestling, and track. Immediately after graduating from high school in 1943, Wilson planned to attend the University of Iowa as a civil engineering student; however, he was drafted into the military for World War II. He spent three years in the armed forces, during which time he traveled throughout Asia, where he experienced a measure of freedom from the discrimination that he had known in the United States.

After his discharge from the military in 1946 Wilson enrolled at the University of Iowa, the first integrated school he had ever attended. He initially studied painting in the country's first university-level studio-based fine arts program; but during the course of his studies he became interested in sculpture. He entered a master's degree program immediately after completing his bachelor of fine arts degree. In 1953, after earning a master of arts degree from Iowa, Wilson accepted a teaching position at the historically black North Carolina College (now North Carolina Central University) in Durham. While at North Carolina College he sculpted primarily in stone and wood, but by 1960 he had begun welding and working with metals. He won two awards for his sculpture: the portrait award from Baltimore Museum of Art in 1956 and the Purchase Prize from Howard University in 1961.

Although Wilson's work was always informed by his experiences with racism, he did not become involved in the civil rights movement until the late 1950s. He joined the Congress of Racial Equality's (CORE) civil rights protests. His CORE activities inspired many of his works of that period including his *Minority Man* sculptures, which were elongated wooden statues of black men with clasped hands and upturned heads. Wilson wanted to depict the begging stereotype he believed was associated with minorities. His other influences included jazz music, writers of color such as RALPH ELLISON and JAMES BALDWIN, and the West African cultural movement known as Negritude.

In 1964 Wilson accepted a teaching position at the Harpur College of Arts and Sciences at the State University of New York (SUNY) in Binghamton. Binghamton did not have a studio art department, and Wilson was hired to develop a standardized curriculum for an undergraduate degree program in fine arts and to find faculty for the program. As such, Wilson became the first chairman of the department of art and art history. He also discovered the major disparities between the resources available to black schools and those available to predominantly white schools. At North Carolina College his annual budget had been $437; at Binghamton it was $46,000.

Wilson's time in New York was arguably his most productive and defined him as a public artist. After a successful solo exhibition at SUNY-Binghamton, the city of Binghamton commissioned him to design the John F. Kennedy Memorial Park. The project featured a central monument, *The Seven*

Seals of Silence, which represented human apathy in the wake of social problems. The park was completed in 1969 to critical acclaim.

Wilson was commissioned for many other public sculptures throughout the 1970s and 1980s. Begun in 1969 and completed in 1971, he created *Second Genesis*. Later displayed at the Lake Clifton High School in Baltimore, the sculpture served as a response to the era's increased reliance on technology and mechanized labor. In 1973 he created *Falling Man* for SUNY-Binghamton. In 1977 the Boys and Girls High School—formerly New Boys High School—in Brooklyn, New York, commissioned the piece entitled *Middle Passage*. This work was inspired in part by ROBERT HAYDEN's poem of the same title and was informed by Wilson's trips to historical slave sites in South Carolina and Nigeria. The work included panels of bas-relief sculptures depicting the kidnapping of Africans, slave ships, and the transportation of slaves across the Atlantic Ocean. The following year he suffered a heart attack and decided to dedicate his time to public art and teaching. In 1984 the city of Baltimore commissioned a piece that he called *Jazz Musicians*. In addition to the public works, Wilson created bronze portraits of renowned African Americans such as the composer and bandleader DUKE ELLINGTON.

Wilson's health continued to fail into the 1990s, and in 1994 he had quadruple bypass surgery. He never fully recovered from the surgery and stopped making artwork as a result of his weakened condition. Although he no longer sculpted, he continued to mentor his students. Since his students were mostly young women, his political and social concerns developed a feminist interest. As Wilson stated in an interview, he did not want them to succumb to the societal pressure of having to choose to have a family over a career in the arts. In the same interview, he proclaimed his belief that artists were the only group that could elevate society from its overly racialized environment. His work as a public artist and mentor to emerging artists of color continued in the community until his death on 26 November 1996. Wilson died at his home in Vestal, New York.

FURTHER READING

Much of the material for this essay comes from personal interviews by the author with Ed Wilson.

Mshana, Fadhili. *A Conversation with Ed Wilson* (2000).

Riggs, Thomas. *The St. James Guide to Black Artists* (1997).

CRYSTAL AM NELSON

Wilson, Edith Goodall (6 Sept. 1896–30 Mar. 1981), blues and popular singer, was born Edith Goodall in Louisville, Kentucky, the daughter of Hundley Goodall, a schoolteacher, and Susan Jones, a housekeeper. She grew up in a mixed middle-class and working-class black neighborhood of small, neat cottages. Like many African Americans, she began singing in the church and at community social clubs. She completed her elementary education but by the time she was fourteen had dropped out of school. Her first taste of performing in an adult venue came in the White City Park talent shows in Louisville.

Eventually, Edith teamed with the pianist Danny Wilson and his sister, Lena Wilson, a blues singer. The trio performed in Kentucky and Ohio and later Chicago, where jazz was making inroads. Edith married the pianist around 1919. Danny Wilson had had some musical training, which enabled him to teach his wife how to use her voice. He also encouraged her to sing a variety of ballads, light classics, and blues. After performing in small clubs around Chicago for two years, the trio moved to Washington, D.C., in 1921. Their musical exposure in the nation's capital and in clubs around Atlantic City, New Jersey, helped prepare them for the much tougher competition of New York City.

Wilson was appearing in the musical revue at Town Hall, *Put and Take*, when Columbia Records signed her in September 1921 as the label's first blues singer. Johnny Dunn's Original Jazz Hounds, with Danny Wilson on piano, backed her on the first release, "Nervous Blues," by PERRY BRADFORD. From 1921 until 1925 Wilson recorded thirty-one vocals, most of them blues, but a few of them humorous novelties such as "He May Be Your Man (But He Comes to See Me Sometime)." This song was among the most popular with Wilson's audiences during blues festivals in the 1970s. Wilson's voice, a light, plaintive soprano, was more refined—some jazz critics termed it "citified"—than those of most blues singers. This was partly the result of the training she received from her husband, who advised her to continue expanding her repertoire. In all, she made about forty recordings during the 1920s.

Wilson's stage career received a boost when she toured briefly on the TOBA (Theater Owners' Booking Association) circuit to promote her recordings. A fine comedian, she was offered roles in shows that featured both comedy and singing. She appeared in Lew Leslie's first major venture in producing black shows at Manhattan's Plantation Room in 1922. Noted for her blues and for songs featuring double entendres, she also sang at the Cotton Club in Harlem.

Wilson's first trip abroad was with Leslie's *Dover Street to Dixie*, which starred FLORENCE MILLS and played London's Pavilion in 1923. A theatrical version of the revue, *Dixie to Broadway*, opened at New York's Broadhurst Theater in 1924, then toured until early 1925. Wilson and Doc Straine were partners from 1924 until 1926, with Wilson singing the blues as part of their comedy routine. They traveled on the Keith theatrical circuit and, according to press reports, were highly popular. They also recorded two comedy songs about a bossy woman. That personality often became a Wilson feature in her later Broadway shows. Subsequent revues in which she traveled abroad included *Chocolate Kiddies* and two more Leslie shows, *Blackbirds, 1926* and *Blackbirds of 1934*. Wilson was a quick study with languages. Her fluency enabled her to perform blues and popular songs in French and German as well as the languages of other countries where she appeared.

Wilson's versatility kept her in demand in revues in the United States and overseas throughout the 1920s and 1930s. Her vocal style easily adjusted to the changing tastes and big-band arrangements of the swing years. During the 1930s she was featured on occasion with orchestras led by CAB CALLOWAY, JIMMIE LUNCEFORD, LUCKY MILLINDER, NOBLE SISSLE, and SAM WOODING. Later, in 1945, she worked with LOUIS ARMSTRONG in *Memphis Bound*, but the Broadway show, excepting her own performance, received poor notices.

At the end of the 1930s Wilson moved to Los Angeles and began a new phase of her career with a nonsinging role in the film *I'm Still Alive* (1940). She appeared in other movies, her most important part coming in the classic *To Have and Have Not* (1944) that starred Humphrey Bogart and Lauren Bacall. During the mid-1940s Wilson toured on the major Burt Levy and Orpheum circuits and served with the USO.

Wilson, who had been widowed in 1928, married her second husband, Millard Wilson, in 1949. Eventually, they moved to Chicago and remained together until her death.

Wilson's career took a social and political twist when she was signed by the Quaker Oats Company to be the radio voice of its Aunt Jemima character for pancake mix commercials. The opportunity resulted from her portrayal of the Kingfish's wife on the "Amos 'n' Andy" radio show. In her Aunt Jemima role she toured on behalf of many charitable projects. Notwithstanding her charitable activities, however, black civil rights leaders and influential activists criticized her for what they saw

as the exploitation of her talents to promote minstrel show stereotypes. She refused to give in to the pressure, insisting that her work was for good causes for which she was not being given proper credit. Wilson was dropped from the role in 1965, and eventually Quaker Oats bowed to criticism and retired the Aunt Jemima character.

Nearly seventy, Wilson resumed her singing career, performing regularly at clubs in the Chicago area. She appeared on local television shows and recorded an exemplary album for the Delmark label in 1976. At eighty, she was singing with the verve and sophistication that were hallmarks of her younger years. She performed in local and national blues and jazz festivals, including the 1980 Newport Jazz Festival, and made her final appearance on Broadway in a 1980 show, *Blacks on Broadway*, produced by Bobby Short. She died in Chicago, having remained a highly regarded performer to the end.

FURTHER READING
Harrison, Daphne. *Black Pearls: Blues Queens of the 1920s* (1988).

DISCOGRAPHY
Godrich, John, and Robert M. W. Dixon, comp. *Blues and Gospel Records, 1902–1942* (1969).

This entry is taken from the *American National Biography* and is published here with the permission of the American Council of Learned Societies.

DAPHNE DUVAL HARRISON

Wilson, Ellis (30 Apr. 1899–7 Jan. 1977), painter, was born in Mayfield, Kentucky, one of seven children of Frank Wilson, a second-generation barber, and Minnie Wilson, a founding member of the local Second Christian Church. Frank Wilson was an amateur artist, and two of his paintings proudly hung in the Wilson home. Ellis later credited his parents with encouraging his educational and artistic pursuits. The Wilsons lived in The Bottom, the largest of several African American sections of Mayfield, a small town in the heart of western Kentucky's tobacco-growing region. After graduation from the Mayfield Colored Grade School, Ellis studied for two years at the Kentucky Normal and Industrial Institute (later Kentucky State University), an all-black school in Frankfort. In 1919 he transferred to the School of the Art Institute of Chicago, where he won several student prizes and studied with the school's first African American instructor, WILLIAM MCKNIGHT FARROW, among others. Following graduation in 1923 Wilson remained in Chicago, working as a commercial artist and in several service jobs, including at the YMCA cafeteria.

In 1928 Wilson moved from Chicago to Harlem, New York. Although he sold a few illustrations, including one that graced the cover of *Crisis* magazine in March 1929, he was primarily a painter of still lifes and urban street scenes. Throughout his life Wilson did not support himself through sales of his art; rather he worked as a handyman and at other jobs. After three years in Harlem Wilson moved to West 18th Street in Greenwich Village, where he produced work that depicted black life. His reserved temperament, however, kept him from direct participation in black politics. Wilson was not the only African American artist to move downtown; PALMER HAYDEN, BEAUFORD DELANEY and JOSEPH DELANEY, and RICHMOND BARTHE lived nearby. In 1931 Wilson began several years of weekend study with the painter Xavier J. Barile and took free evening classes at the Mechanics' Institute. Throughout the 1930s his paintings were included in exhibitions of work by African American artists, including the Harmon Foundation shows in 1930 and 1933, AUGUSTA SAVAGE's Salon of Contemporary Negro Art in 1934, and the American Negro Exposition in Chicago in 1939. Wilson joined the newly established Harlem Artists Guild in 1935, and along with many other African American artists, including AARON DOUGLAS, DOX THRASH, CHARLES ALSTON, JACOB LAWRENCE, and ERNEST CRICHLOW, Wilson worked for the Works Progress Administration (WPA) Federal Arts Program. From 1935 through 1939 he was assigned to a mapping division that produced detailed maps and dioramas of New York City's five boroughs. During World War II, from 1940 to 1944, he worked in a New Jersey aircraft engine factory. While not at work on the floor of the plant he produced sketches and paintings of black factory workers.

In 1939 Wilson began applying annually to the Simon Guggenheim Memorial Foundation for a fellowship award. "Practically all of my life I have been painting under difficult conditions," he wrote in his first application, echoing the experience of many African American artists of the period; "Lack of money and time, especially time, have prevented me from painting as much and as often as I have wanted to. ... I am most interested in painting the Negro. Unfortunately, this type of painting hasn't a large following at present." Wilson argued in his 1940 application, "I want to continue to paint the Negro! There is such a wide, rich field of unexplored material to work from. Although I have been

painting the Negro for a number of years, I feel I have only begun to go beneath the surface." When he finally won a fellowship in 1944 (renewed the following year), he used the award money to travel through the American South, where he sketched black fishermen, lumberjacks, fieldworkers, mothers with children, the open markets in Charleston, South Carolina, and African Americans from the Sea Islands. The resulting paintings, influenced in part by the social realism movement, offer little in the way of specific locales or identifiable portraits; rather they evoke African American life in the rural South through emotion, color, and texture.

Kentucky welcomed Wilson home with a 1947 exhibition at the Mayfield public library and a solo exhibition the following year at the Speed Museum in Louisville. Wilson found champions in Justus and Senta Bier, art critics for Louisville's *Courier Journal*, who published several complimentary articles about him, including a 1950 Sunday magazine story with color reproductions of his work. In 1952 a painting, later lost, depicting an African American fisherwoman won Wilson a $3,000 prize from the Terry Art Institute in Miami. He used this prize to finance the first of several trips to Haiti, after which his painting style, while still representational, employed bolder colors—pinks, purples, sea blues—and more geometric and elongated figures. These Haitian-inspired paintings earned reviews in both *Art News* and *Art Digest* in 1954 and an exhibition in 1960 at the New York Contemporary Arts Gallery. The next exhibition of Wilson's work came eleven years later in a joint retrospective curated by DAVID DRISKELL entitled *Paintings by Ellis Wilson, Ceramics and Sculpture by* WILLIAM E. ARTIS.

Wilson was by all accounts a shy and private man. He preferred sketching on site and painting alone in his studio. His intimate, often small paintings of African American and Haitian subjects engaged in the details of daily life were generally painted in oil on wood or board. Because he was a lesser-known artist and had no heirs, historians have been challenged in documenting his oeuvre. Though he rarely dated or titled his work it appears that Wilson produced nearly three hundred paintings in his lifetime. Upon his death in New York, Wilson was buried in an unmarked pauper's grave.

Interest in Wilson was rekindled in the 1980s after one of the artist's best paintings, "Funeral Procession" (c. 1950s), was featured as a key story element on the *Cosby Show* (SEE BILL COSBY). In a 1985 episode from the television show's second season, Claire Huxtable learns that a painting by her "great uncle Ellis" is up for auction at Sotheby's. After buying the painting for $11,000 (in real life Wilson never sold a painting for more than $300), the painting hung above the fictional Huxtable family's fireplace, appearing in the background of every episode. The original "Funeral Procession" is located in the Aaron Douglas Collection at the Amistad Research Center. Wilson's paintings are held by several important collections, including the Howard University Gallery of Art, the Studio Museum in Harlem, and the National Museum of American Art.

FURTHER READING

Murray State University. *The Art of Ellis Wilson* (2000).

LISA E. RIVO

Wilson, Ernest Judson (28 Feb. 1899–26 June 1963), Negro League baseball player, was born in Remington, Virginia, of parents whose names and occupations are unknown. As a teenager he played baseball on sandlots in the Foggy Bottom neighborhood of Washington, D.C. As he matured, Wilson grew into a squat five feet eight inches, weighing 185 pounds. He had wide shoulders that shrank to a small waist—reminiscent of a smaller but similarly proportioned Babe Ruth. Although Wilson was pigeon-toed and had bowed legs, he possessed great speed. But before he could sign professionally with a Negro League team, he was drafted into the U.S. military near the end of World War I. He served as a corporal in Company D, 417th Service Battalion, Quartermaster Corps.

Upon discharge, Wilson signed with the Baltimore Black Sox in 1922. As Wilson laced line drives off the fence during his Black Sox tryout, Negro League great SATCHEL PAIGE gave him the nickname "Boojum" because of the sound his balls made when they hit the fence. "Boojum" would stick with him throughout his career. With the Black Sox, Wilson established himself as one of the finest hitters in the Negro Leagues. In his second year with the team, Wilson had a .373 batting average, which led the league in hitting. Although Wilson was never an outstanding defensive third baseman, he played the position effectively, often knocking down ground balls with his body instead of catching them with his glove.

Wilson was a lock to hit over .300 each year and even over .400 on occasion. He played with the Baltimore Black Sox from 1922–1930. Wilson then moved over to the Homestead Grays of Homestead, Pennsylvania, during the 1931 season and part of the 1932 campaign. Wilson finished the 1932 season with the Pittsburgh Crawfords. In 1933 he signed with the Philadelphia Stars where he played until 1939, when he returned to the Grays until 1945. On each of these teams Wilson dominated at the plate.

In 1923 Wilson batted a league-leading .373. In 1945, when he retired from the Negro Leagues, he held a lifetime average of .345. In the winter Wilson played baseball in Cuba and during the winters of 1925 and 1926, he hit .403 and .441, respectively. Against white major leaguers in exhibition games, Wilson had a .442 career lifetime average.

Wilson also played on some of the best teams in Negro League baseball history. He was on teams that won four championships in six years between 1931 and 1934. The 1931 Grays team is thought to be one of the greatest Negro League teams in history; Wilson was its captain.

Wilson had a reputation for hitting in the clutch during his twenty-three year career. In the East-West Negro League All-Star game in 1934, a game that is regarded as one of the greatest games in Negro League history, Wilson singled home COOL PAPA BELL for the first and only run of the game in the eighth inning. Wilson was selected as a starter in the first three East-West All-Star games, which began in 1933. He batted .455 during the contests.

Besides his clutch hitting, Wilson was also known for his temper. Along with Chippy Britt, OSCAR CHARLESTON, and E. VICTOR HARRIS, Wilson was named one of the "Big Four of the Big Badmen" by sportswriters. On the field Wilson was so confident of his abilities that he actually dared pitchers to throw the ball. He often got in fights with umpires. During his most brutal fight, however, Wilson was (initially) innocent: Wilson interceded between Jake Stephens, his roommate and second baseman, as he argued with an umpire. Stephens managed to punch the umpire who thought that Wilson delivered the blow. The umpire kicked Wilson out of the game. Wilson then turned his rage at the umpire and three policeman had to intercede, beating Wilson with patrol sticks until they were able to cart him off to jail.

In 1934, during the championship series between the Chicago American Giants and Wilson's Philadelphia Stars, Wilson struck the home plate umpire after a controversial call. The umpire ejected him from the game but then, minutes later, rescinded the objection, claiming that he did not know that Wilson struck him. Philadelphia won the game 4-1 and the umpire later claimed that he reversed his original ejection because Wilson threatened him.

Off the field Wilson was just as intense. Although Wilson and Jake Stephens were best friends, they sometimes argued. Stephens, after a night of drinking, woke up Wilson one night after the East-West All-Star game. Wilson picked Stephens up and supposedly dangled him out the sixteenth story window of the hotel, holding his leg with one hand. Eventually Wilson pulled Stephens back into the hotel room and the two continued their friendship.

Wilson's toughness off the field was matched only by his toughness on the field. Wilson played through a myriad of injuries during his career. He often crowded the plate, and in 1926 a pitch cracked his elbow. Doctors told him he was done for the season, but two weeks later he returned to the lineup. The only major injury that put him out for considerable time was when the Philadelphia Stars team bus was in an accident in 1938.

Wilson became a player-manager with the Stars in 1937. He continued in that role with the Homestead Grays in 1940. Under his reign the Grays won the Negro National League pennant in each of his seasons until he retired in 1945.

Wilson suffered from epilepsy during the end of his career. After he left the game, Wilson worked in construction in Washington, D.C., building the Whitehurst Freeway. In the last days of his life, the only man Wilson recognized was Stephens, the same man he supposedly dangled out of a hotel window during his playing days. Wilson died in Washington, D.C.

Along with Oliver Marcelle and JUDY JOHNSON, Wilson is regarded as one of the greatest third basemen in Negro League history. Satchel Paige considered Wilson one of the best hitters to ever play the game.

FURTHER READING

Holway, John B. *The Complete Book of Baseball's Negro Leagues* (2001).

Lanctot, Neil. *Negro League Baseball—The Rise and Ruin of a Black Institution* (2004).

Riley, James A. *The Biographical Encyclopedia of the Negro Baseball Leagues* (1994).

LOU MANZO

Wilson, Flip (8 Dec. 1933–25 Nov. 1998), comedian, actor, and writer, was born Clerow Wilson Jr. in Jersey City, New Jersey, the son of Clerow Wilson and Cornelia Wilson, whose maiden name was also Wilson. His father, a handyman, was unable to support the large family of twelve children, and the boy

was given up to foster care at an early age. Although his schooling was sporadic, he managed to appear in a number of school plays, including one in which he played the part of Clara Barton. Drag comedy would later become central to his success. He gained the nickname "Flip" as a teenager because of his inclination to break into sudden impromptu comic performances. Friends said he appeared to be "flippin' out." At age sixteen he left school and enlisted in the U.S. Air Force, serving from 1950 to 1954. It was there that he began to find his vocation as a comedian, delivering comic monologues and putting on skits for his fellow servicemen.

Following his discharge, Wilson settled in San Francisco, hoping to begin a show business career in the city's nightclub scene, which was gaining a reputation as a hotbed of stand-up comedy. It was also one of the few places in the United States where black comedians could find work. While supporting himself as a bellhop at the Manor Plaza Hotel, he insinuated his way into the house nightclub by putting on an act, gratis, as a drunken bellhop during the breaks taken by featured acts.

Gaining notice this way, Wilson was offered several gigs at local nightclubs and eventually made it onto the national circuit. Most of the clubs were cheap bars, known in the business as "toilets," and he often was forced to hitchhike from city to city during the late 1950s as he continued to write new material and develop a repertoire of original characters. By the end of the decade he was playing better venues, including the Fontainebleau Hotel in Miami Beach and the Apollo Theater in New York.

A turning point came in 1965, when Johnny Carson invited Wilson to appear on *The Tonight Show* after hearing the veteran comedian REDD FOXX's favorable comment about Wilson's nightclub act. This led to a string of guest appearances for Wilson on some of television's most popular programs, including *The Ed Sullivan Show* and *Rowan and Martin's Laugh-In*. In 1969 he starred in his own prime-time comedy special on NBC. Its critical and commercial success led to the premiere of his weekly series, *The Flip Wilson Show*, in 1970.

Following the classic comedy-variety format developed by such early television stars as Milton Berle and Jackie Gleason, Wilson typically began the hour with a monologue in front of a stage curtain and then presented himself and his guest stars in a series of short comic sketches and musical numbers. It was in these sketches that Wilson developed his signature characters. They included Geraldine, a sassy, outspoken woman who reveled in testing

Flip Wilson, dressed in his famous character "Geraldine," with comic Tim Conway, during the taping of *The Flip Wilson Show* in 1973. (AP Images.)

the limits of female propriety; the ultraspirited, if somewhat shifty, Reverend LeRoy of the Church of What's Happening Now; and Freddie the Playboy, a silver-tongued ladies' man. Geraldine was by far the most popular. Drag humor was nothing new to prime-time television; Berle had made liberal use of it in the medium's earliest days. Wilson, however, reinvigorated the art by creating an enduring persona in Geraldine. He used the character's unabashed sexuality to push television content into areas that tested the limits of the still-vigilant network censorship codes of the 1970s. Geraldine was especially frank on the subject of her boyfriend, Killer, whom Wilson also played on occasion. "The devil made me do it!"—her all-purpose excuse for misbehavior—achieved the status of a national catchphrase.

Wilson became a television star of the first magnitude, winning two Emmy Awards and a Golden Globe for the show. This was all the more remarkable in light of the commercial failure of earlier attempts to have such well-established African American stars as NAT KING COLE and SAMMY DAVIS JR. serve as hosts of prime-time variety hours. During the peak of his stardom Wilson continued his live performances, becoming a frequent

headliner in Las Vegas. He won a Grammy Award in 1970 for "Best Comedy Recording" with his album of stand-up monologues, *The Devil Made Me Buy This Dress*, which he produced for his own record company, Little David.

After the 1974 cancellation of *The Flip Wilson Show*, the comedian's career took an unexpected—though not really unusual—turn for a television star. Professing a desire for the stable family life he had never known, he retreated from the national spotlight, only occasionally emerging from his Malibu home to perform. "I accomplished what I set out to do," he explained to an interviewer. "I wanted the whole cookie and I got it. Now I want to spend more time with my children—make sure they don't go through what I did" (Mel Watson, *New York Times*, 27 November 1998).

Over the next six years, his work was limited to minor roles in just three films: *Uptown Saturday Night* (1974), directed by SIDNEY POITIER and starring Poitier, BILL COSBY, and HARRY BELAFONTE; *Skatetown, U.S.A.* (1979); and *The Fish That Saved Pittsburgh* (1979). In 1980 he became corporate spokesperson for the soft drink maker 7-Up, but his contract was voided following his arrest on misdemeanor cocaine charges within a year's time. Two attempts at new television series during the 1980s both ended in early cancellations. In 1990 he surprised some critics with his dramatic performance as God in "Zora Is My Name," a play concerning the life of writer ZORA NEALE HURSTON, on PBS's *American Playhouse*. Though he would remain financially secure, Wilson never again would achieve anything like the fame he had known in the early 1970s.

Flip Wilson's personal life was complex. His 1957 marriage to the dancer Peaches Wilson (her maiden name) ended in divorce that same year. Soon after, he entered into a long-term relationship with Blonell Pitman, eventually adopting Pitman's daughter, Michelle. Between 1960 and 1970 the couple had four children of their own; they never married, however. In 1979 Wilson wed Cookie Mackenzie, but this second marriage ended in a 1985 divorce.

Wilson told *Jet* magazine in a 1997 interview that he did not miss his acting career and that he had spent a good deal of the last two decades reading Eastern philosophy, especially the works of Kahlil Gibran. The comedian died of liver cancer at home in Malibu.

The first African American to host a successful prime-time variety show on television, Flip Wilson created several signature comic characters whose appeal transcended race. As Paul Brownfield of the *Los Angeles Times* wrote, "If RICHARD PRYOR and DICK GREGORY represented a school of black comics who translated their backgrounds into crackling, confrontational comedy routines, Wilson was from a different school—not as angry or political, and thus not as much of a threat to white audiences" (28 Nov. 1998).

FURTHER READING

Current Biography Yearbook (1969).

Obituaries: *New York Times*, 27 Nov. 1998; *Jet*, 14 Dec. 1998.

This entry is taken from the *American National Biography* and is published here with the permission of the American Council of Learned Societies.

DAVID MARC

Wilson, Frank H. (4 May 1886–16 Feb. 1956), actor and playwright, was born Frank Henry Wilson in New York City. Little is known about his family and early life, although it is known that he attended the American Academy of Dramatic Arts. Wilson supported himself with a job as a postman while also pursuing his acting and writing career.

Wilson began his career in vaudeville, spending twelve years as a baritone singer, but his true calling was the stage, where he worked as a playwright and as an actor. Wilson's career as a playwright began in 1914, when he wrote one-act plays for the Lincoln and Lafayette theaters in Harlem. During these early years of the century, African American leaders organized a push for recognition of African American arts as a road to civil rights. Wilson's career as playwright and actor was set in the midst of early debates over the form and definition of African American theater. That debate proceeded on two very different levels. The first concerned what might be called the cultural question: what kind of theater constituted art? Clearly, the successful musical comedies and variety shows that filled Broadway stages were not high art. A second level of debate concerned the social role of art: what were the proper aims of art? In this, African American leadership was divided. W. E. B. DuBois argued that art must always be propaganda, while ALAIN LOCKE argued that aesthetics must be the guide to African American arts and letters. Wilson's work followed DuBois's challenge for playwrights to deal honestly with African American life.

Beginning in 1925 the two major African American periodicals of the time, the NAACP's *Crisis* and the National Urban League's *Opportunity*, sponsored competitions among writers and artists. Wilson's one-act play *Sugar Cain* won the 1925 *Opportunity* prize. On 6 February 1928 Wilson's play *Meek Mose*, about an African American preacher who believes that "the meek shall inherit the earth," opened on Broadway, while Wilson was acting the title role in Dubose Heyward's play *Porgy*. Although *Meek Mose* would be produced again in 1934 by the Federal Theatre's Negro Drama Unit of New York under the title *Brother Mose*, Wilson's play was considered a failure. His *The Wall Between* (1929) was scheduled for Broadway but was cancelled when the Depression hit.

Wilson found greater success in his acting career. He had had his first triumph in 1926 in Paul Green's Pulitzer Prize–winning play, *In Abraham's Bosom*. When the play's lead, Jules Bledsoe, failed to appear, Wilson exchanged his small part for the leading role. His performance, which *New York Times* critic Brooks Atkinson called "almost letter perfect" and "swift, direct and extraordinarily moving" (20 Feb. 1926, sec. 7), earned him the role permanently. His performance as Porgy in 1927 earned him recognition as one of the best African American actors of the time, among the ranks of CHARLES GILPIN and PAUL ROBESON. His subsequent successes included *Sweet Chariot* (1930), *We the People* (1931), the musical play *Singin' the Blues* (1931), Frederick Schlick's prison drama *Bloodstream* (1932), and *They Shall Not Die* (1934), a play by John Wexley based on the SCOTTSBORO BOYS case.

While the majority of Wilson's success came on the stage, he acted in films as well, and he appeared in a variety of Hollywood productions and "race" films, films made by either African American or mixed-race production companies for black audiences. Wilson's debut was in the film version of *The Emperor Jones* (1933), with Paul Robeson in the title role. Next he portrayed Moses in the film adaptation of the popular Broadway play *The Green Pastures* (1936), co-starring with Rex Ingram, EDDIE "ROCHESTER" ANDERSON, and Edna Mae Harris. Wilson also performed in sound-era race films, including *Paradise in Harlem* (1939), which he co-scripted. Other screenwriting credits included *Murder on Lenox Avenue* (1941), one of the last "black gangster" movies. Wilson also performed for radio, and played the role of Jackson Papaloi on *Young Dr. Malone*, a soap opera that ran from 1939 to 1960.

Shortly before his death, Wilson appeared on television in the role of Henry in *Floodtide*, the first episode of *The Elgin Hour*, a series of live dramas sponsored by the Elgin Watch Company. Frank Wilson died in Queens, New York, at the age of sixty-nine. Although his plays are not included in anthologies of African American drama such as Alain Locke's 1927 *Plays of Negro Life* or James V. Hatch's 1974 *Black Theater*, Wilson's plays remain important examples of African American theater during a time when African American aesthetics were being defined.

FURTHER READING

Bogle, Donald. *Toms, Coons, Mulattoes, Mammies, & Bucks: An Interpretive History of Blacks in American Films* (2001).

Cripps, Thomas. *Slow Fade to Black: The Negro in American Film, 1900–1942* (1993).

Wilson, Sondra Kathryn, ed. *The Opportunity Reader* (1999).

MARY ANNE BOELCSKEVY

Wilson, Fred (1954–), curator and artist, was born in the Bronx, New York. His mother and father, both native New Yorkers, were of Caribbean and African American descent respectively. While Wilson identified with the analytical and critical capacities of his civil engineer father, he credited his mother, an art teacher, with nurturing his creativity from a young age. Growing up in Brooklyn, the Bronx, and suburban Westchester County, Wilson attended New York's High School of Music and Art, and frequented the New York City museums throughout his youth. He received a bachelor of fine arts from the State University of New York (SUNY) at Purchase in 1976, though even as an art student he seemed to have been more interested in spatial relationships and performance than in a traditional medium such as painting. In his senior year of college he traveled to West Africa, spending time in Ghana, Nigeria, Togo, and Benin, in an experience that he claimed, in a 1994 interview with Lisa Corrin, changed his life and profoundly affected his relationship to his African heritage.

After graduation Wilson organized art programs for East Harlem schools and freelanced as an educator at New York's Metropolitan Museum of Art, the American Crafts Museum, and the Museum of Natural History. In 1981 Wilson began working in arts administration at the Just Above Midtown Gallery before being hired by the Bronx Art Council as the curator for their Longwood Arts Gallery. For his first exhibition there in 1987 Wilson transformed three rooms into a nineteenth-century salon, an ethnographic gallery, and a modernist white cube, so that the contemporary artists' works that he installed in these fabricated spaces shifted dramatically with each different context.

This first installation, technically a curatorial project rather than an artistic commission, was instrumental in establishing Wilson's signature *modus operandi*—that of creating installations that mimic the form of museum exhibitions rather than constructing physical objects from traditional materials. For the next five years Wilson continued to transform gallery spaces into museum-like installations that engaged and critiqued normative museum practices of classification and display. "Mining the Museum" (1992) was the artist's first opportunity to work from within the institutional structure of the museum itself, in this case the Maryland Historical Society, and turned out to be both Wilson's watershed project and the one with which he attained national acclaim. After extensive scholarly research on the Society's holdings, numerous interviews and collaborations with over one hundred people, Wilson reinstalled the entire third floor of the Baltimore museum. He literally "mined" the dusty basement storage of the Society, combing its lost and "forgotten" areas to excavate artifacts that represented the region's repressed histories of slavery and social injustice, such as the slave shackles that he exhibited alongside fine silver in a display he wryly entitled "Metalwork: 1700–1870."

Throughout the 1990s Wilson created site-specific installations for numerous museums, engaging each institution's specific histories on issues ranging from anti-Semitism to colonialism and primitivism. In these varied and diverse projects, Wilson continued to use the museum itself as his medium, often creating installations that mimicked the form of museum exhibitions. Indeed because so much of Wilson's work was rooted in ideas, critics often thought of him as a conceptual artist, although in fact Wilson worked with the language of the visual and made his arguments visually rather than (or in addition to) textually. Composing his own labels and wall text, painting the walls, and reconfiguring the architectural space of the museum, as well as rearranging the museum's objects, Wilson examined the means by which historical narratives are created in the museum context. He hoped to incite the viewer to question why museums presented certain histories and excluded others—usually those of minorities and the exploited. Wilson therefore employed the museum as both a site of institutional power and as a microcosm of American society to raise provocative questions about power and the representation of cultures.

The recipient of several prestigious awards including a John D. and Catherine T. MacArthur Foundation Achievement Award (1999) and a Larry Aldrich Foundation Award (2002), Wilson represented the United States at the 2003 Venice Biennale. For that installation, Wilson examined local histories of Renaissance blacks in Venice, using the Shakespearean drama *Othello* as a means to address the larger issue of the representation of black peoples in Western art. He also employed distinctive local materials and traditions—such as black glass from the Venetian glassworking community of Murano—to evoke broader concepts such as transparency, race, and the culturally freighted meanings of color. In this and other recent work Wilson shifted away from his traditional habitus of the museum, opening up his practice to new materials and techniques. Yet despite the eclecticism of Wilson's work, he retained his longtime interest in the construction and representation of race.

Wilson's 2005 exhibition at the Aldrich Contemporary Art Museum in Ridgefield, Connecticut, *Black Like Me* comprised sculpture and installations mostly fabricated from black glass. In his subsequent 2006 show at PaceWildenstein Gallery in New York, *Fred Wilson: My Echo, My Shadow, and Me*, the artist continued to explore the expressive medium of glass in works that slithered down walls and seeped suggestively across the floor. These works exploited not only the fluid beauty of liquid glass and the powerful literary motif of doubling, but suggested Wilson's new, more personal engagement with African American history through the lens of his own identity.

FURTHER READINGS

Berger, Maurice. *Fred Wilson: Objects and Installations 1979–2000* (2001).

Corrin, Lisa G. *Mining the Museum: An Installation by Fred Wilson* (1994).

Hassan, Salah. *Fred Wilson: Speak of Me As I Am: 50th Venice Biennale* (2003).

LEORA MALTZ LECA

Wilson, Gerald (4 Sept. 1918–), trumpeter, bandleader, arranger, composer, and educator, was born in Shelby, Mississippi, to Shelby J. Wilson, a blacksmith, and Lillian (Nelson) Wilson, a schoolteacher who also taught music. The second of four children, Wilson began taking piano lessons from his mother, an accomplished pianist, at the age of five. His love of music expanded through the spiritual songs heard in church, and by the music he

listened to on the radio. Wilson began playing the trumpet while attending Manassa High School in Memphis, Tennessee, where his parents had sent him to live with friends of the family. In 1934 he moved to Detroit, Michigan, where he once again lived with friends of the family. He attended Cass Technical High School, a school that has produced a remarkable number of performing artists, where he played trumpet in the band and studied composition and orchestration.

Between 1934 and 1939 Wilson played with many of the top bands in Detroit, led by such bandleaders as Stutz Anderson, GLOSTER CURRENT, and Chic Carter. In 1939, while playing an out-of-town engagement with Carter in Dayton, Ohio, Wilson received a message from bandleader JIMMIE LUNCEFORD inviting him to replace trumpet player SY OLIVER. Lunceford, while visiting Cass Technical High School several years earlier, had heard Wilson play in the school band. Wilson eagerly accepted Lunceford's offer. In addition to performing with Lunceford's band, the twenty-one-year-old Wilson was given the opportunity and responsibility to compose and arrange tunes for the touring ensemble. In this role he wrote such classic compositions as "Hi Spook" and "Yard Dog Mazurka."

While fulfilling an engagement with the band in Los Angeles in February 1940, Wilson fell in love with the beauty and climate of Los Angeles and decided that he would one day settle there. That move came two years later, after he left Lunceford in 1942. He was immediately drafted by the U.S. Navy, but did not report until 1943. In the meantime he played briefly with high-profile Los Angeles–based bands led by LES HITE and Benny Carter, respectively.

When Wilson finally reported to the military he was chosen to play trumpet in the navy band. The band also included trumpeter CLARK TERRY, who would become one of the great jazz trumpet players. Wilson and Clark were among the first African Americans to serve in the navy. On his honorable discharge in 1944, Wilson returned to Los Angeles. He immediately formed his first band, the Gerald Wilson Jazz Orchestra. The band played all the major jazz venues around Los Angeles and performed at the hot spots in San Francisco, St. Louis, New York, Chicago, and Salt Lake City. Though in great demand, the ensemble broke up after two years of touring. Wilson, however, continued to perform with some of greatest musicians of the era and to perfect his composing and arranging skills. From the late 1940s through the 1960s Wilson was one of the most sought-after composers in jazz and popular music. Many of his compositions and/or arrangements were recorded by such artists as RAY CHARLES, Bobby Darin, CARMEN McRAE, SARAH VAUGHAN, Nancy Wilson, and DUKE ELLINGTON. He arranged or orchestrated more than fourteen compositions for Ellington, including "If I Give My Heart to You," "Smile," "You Gotta Crawl Before You Walk," and the incomparable "You're Just an Old Antidisestablishmentarianismist."

Wilson also continued to record and play trumpet with numerous jazz icons of the era, including DIZZY GILLESPIE, ILLINOIS JACQUET, COUNT BASIE, and to serve as bandleader for BILLIE HOLIDAY. With Gillespie's band in 1949 Wilson's progressive arrangements stood out, as on "Out of this World" and his own "Couldn't Love, Couldn't Cry."

Wilson became one of the first African Americans to score music for major motion pictures and television. His film-scoring résumé included scenes in *Anatomy of a Murder* (1959, starring James Stewart and Lee Remick), *Where the Boys Are* (1960, starring George Hamilton and Yvette Mimieux), and *Love Has Many Faces* (1964, starring Lana Turner). He also appeared in 1951 with the bandleader Benny Carter in *An American in Paris*, starring Gene Kelly. For television, Wilson scored several scenes for NBC's *Hollywood My Home Town* and was the musical director for *The Redd Foxx Show* on ABC. In addition, Wilson made his television acting debut in CBS's *The Line Up*, with Jack Lloyd, for which he also wrote the music.

During the early 1960s Wilson signed with Pacific Jazz Records, with which he released ten albums, including *You Better Believe It, Moment of Truth, Portraits, On Stage, The Golden Sword, Live and Swinging, California Soul,* and *Eternal Equinox.*

Dedicated to education, Wilson accepted numerous teaching assignments in California. He taught jazz courses at California State University, Northridge; at California State University, Los Angeles; and at UCLA.

Wilson's numerous awards and honors included six Grammy nominations, Best Big Band and Best Composer/Arranger in the Downbeat International Critics Poll, a Paul Robeson Award, an NEA American Jazz Masters Fellowship, and two American Jazz Awards for Best Arranger and Best Big Band.

FURTHER READING
Carr, Ian, Digby Fairweather, and Brian Priestley. *The Rough Guide to Jazz* (2004).

Shipton, Alyn. *A New History of Jazz* (2001).
Yanow, Scott. *Jazz on Film* (2004).

DISCOGRAPHY
The Complete Pacific Jazz Recordings of Gerald Wilson & His Orchestra (1961–1969) (Mosaic 198).
Theme from Monterey (MamaJazz, MMF1021).
State Street Sweet (MamaJazz, MMF1010).

DONALD JAMES

Wilson, Harriet E. (c. 1828–?), servant and writer, was born Harriet Adams to parents whose names and occupations remain unidentified. Very little is known about the woman who, in 1859, published *Our Nig*, the first novel published by an African American in the United States and one of the first novels published by a black woman in any country. Harriet was probably born in 1827 or 1828 in Milford, New Hampshire, according to her marriage record and federal census records. Although there is no record of Harriet's education, the quality of writing in *Our Nig* and the skillful use of epigraphs, including excerpts from Shelley, Byron, and Thomas Moore, indicate that she received some schooling. Evidence suggests that Harriet spent her childhood and adolescence living with and in service to the Nehemiah Hayward family. Following nineteenth-century trends in poor relief, Harriet would have been "bound out" to the Haywards as an indentured servant. After the Haywards moved to Baltimore in 1847, it appears that Harriet remained behind and supported herself until 1850, when her name appears on Milford's charity roll.

Records show that in 1851 Harriet married Thomas Wilson in Milford and that in the spring of 1852 a son, George Mason Wilson, was born in nearby Goffstown. There is no further trace of Thomas Wilson, who seems to have abandoned his wife before the birth of their son. Because Milford's charity reports for 1851–1854 are missing, there is no evidence as to whether Wilson needed financial assistance during these years. She is, however, listed on Milford's charity rolls in 1855 and 1856, and documents indicate that her son, then three years old, spent a month on the county poor farm in 1855. Charity reports for 1857–1859 list only "Harriet E. Wilson's child," suggesting that Wilson left her son behind in New Hampshire. City directories show that Wilson was most probably living in Boston during these years.

On 18 August 1859 a "Mrs. H. E. Wilson" copyrighted *Our Nig*, and the book was published several weeks later, on 5 September. Wilson states in the preface to *Our Nig* that she was motivated to write the book by financial reasons: "Deserted by kindred, disabled by failing health, I am forced to some experiment which shall aid me in maintaining myself and child.... I sincerely appeal to my colored brethren universally for patronage." Sadly, only five months after the publication of *Our Nig*, Wilson's seven-year-old son, George Mason, died of "bilious fever." Wilson reappears on Milford's 1863 charity roll, after which there is no trace of her in either Milford or Boston records. The date of her death is unknown.

Our Nig; or, Sketches from the Life of a Free Black, in a Two-Story White House, North. Showing That Slavery's Shadows Fall Even There, By "Our Nig" was printed by G. C. Rand and Avery in Boston, Massachusetts, in 1859. *Our Nig*'s protagonist is Alfrado, nicknamed Frado, the daughter of Mag, a white servant, and Jim, a free black artisan. After her father's death, Frado, then five or six years old, is abandoned by her mother and left with the Bellmonts, a white family for whom she works as an indentured servant until she is eighteen. Most of the novel describes the brutal treatment and severe deprivation Frado receives at the hands of Mrs. Bellmont and her daughter. Despite occasional attempts by the male members of the Bellmont family to protect her, Frado is treated so harshly that her health is permanently ruined. In the last pages of the book, Frado marries Samuel, a fugitive slave "lecturer" who, before deserting her, discloses "that he had never seen the South, and that his illiterate harangues were humbugs for hungry abolitionists" (128). Their son is born on the county poor farm, and Frado is forced to give him over to the county's care shortly after he is weaned. Looking for work, she travels through New England, facing contempt by racists unwilling to help, until a kind woman gives her a recipe for a home remedy, which Frado begins to sell. *Our Nig* ends with an appeal to the reader for financial assistance.

When the scholar HENRY LOUIS GATES JR. bought *Our Nig* at a used bookshop in 1981, he could not foresee that his fifty-dollar investment would alter African American literary scholarship, causing a literary sensation. Gates and his research team found only a handful of nineteenth- and twentieth-century references to the novel, most of which listed the author as white or male or both. But after a copyright search at the Library of Congress yielded the name "Mrs. H. E. Wilson," Gates set out to identify the novel's author and establish her race. Research confirmed, through city directories, that a "Harriet Wilson" lived in Boston during the time of *Our Nig*'s publication. They then found an 1850 census document listing Wilson's race as black. (The questionnaire's choices were "white," "black," or "mulatto.") Further historical detective work produced Wilson's 1851 marriage record and the 1860 death certificate of her son, George Mason. "Ironically," Gates explained, "George's death certificate helped to rescue his mother from literary oblivion.... The *record* of his death, *alone*, proved sufficient to demonstrate his mother's racial identity and authorship of *Our Nig*" (xiii).

Gates's reconstruction of Wilson's life, augmented by other scholars, shows the novel to be a semiautobiographical work written by Harriet E. Wilson. While the novel's fictional form allows Wilson greater narrative and creative possibilities than traditional autobiography, *Our Nig* is grounded in the economic deprivation and racism Wilson herself had experienced. Wilson borrows heavily from her own life in fashioning Frado's life, although some events, including the mixed marriage of Frado's parents, are probably fictional creations.

The complexity of *Our Nig* begins with its title. Gates was immediately drawn to Wilson's daring and ironic use of the racist epithet *"Our Nig"*: "Harriet E. Wilson allows these racist characters to name her heroine, only to *invert* such racism by employing the name, in inverted commas, as her pseudonym of authorship" (li). The descriptive phrasing of Wilson's subtitle, *in a Two-Story White House, North. Showing That Slavery's Shadows Fall Even There*, highlights the book's explicit indictment of northern racism and the hypocrisy of many northern abolitionists. "My mistress was wholly imbued with *southern* principles," Wilson offers in *Our Nig*'s preface. Anticipating a hostile reaction from abolitionists, she continues, "I have purposely omitted what would most provoke shame in our good anti-slavery friends at home." By the novel's end, however, Wilson has dropped her accommodating tone: "Strange were some of her adventures. Watched by kidnappers, maltreated by professed abolitionists, who didn't want slaves at the South, nor niggers in their own houses, North. Faugh! to lodge one; to eat with one; to admit one through the front door; to sit next to one; awful!" (129). While Wilson's candor underlies the novel's daring, it also doomed sales of her book. "All the abolitionists chose to ignore *Our Nig*," Gates explains. "There were two things you couldn't do if you were a foe of slavery. One was to write about racism in the North—and this book is all about racism in the North. Second, the man Alfrado marries is a black man pretending to be an escaped slave" (*New York Times*, 8 Nov. 1982).

Our Nig is the first representation in American fiction of an interracial marriage in which the wife is white and the husband is black. Furthermore, this unusual literary union is brought about by a black man's pity for a destitute white woman and is presented in a positive light: "He loved Mag to the last. So long as life continued, he stifled his sensibility to pain, and toiled for her sustenance long after he was able to do so" (15). Along with Wilson's fundamental reconfiguration of the theme and character of the "tragic mulatto," the novel's other characters—the brutal Bellmont women, ineffectual Bellmont men, the "fugitive slave" con artist, Samuel—are equally complex, refusing to adhere to strict literary racial or gender stereotypes.

"Wilson's achievement," Gates argues, "is that she combines the received conventions of the sentimental novel with certain key conventions of the slave narrative, then combines the two into *one new form*" (lii). *Our Nig* conforms to many of the conventions of the sentimental novel but deviates from the formula in its ambiguous ending, in which the heroine neither triumphs nor lives happily ever after. Instead, Wilson appeals directly to the reader for financial support. In the tradition of slave narratives, which often include testimonial letters from whites to help get works published, *Our Nig* appends three supporting letters attesting to the truthfulness of the narrative and pleading for the "friends of our dark-skinned brethren and sisters" to help the author by buying the book. Scholars continue to debate whether the letters are, in fact, authentic recommendations or were created by Wilson to mimic the slave narrative model.

When ALICE WALKER first encountered *Our Nig*, she "sat up most of the night reading and pondering the enormous significance of Harriet Wilson's novel *Our Nig*. It is as if we'd just discovered PHILLIS WHEATLEY—or LANGSTON HUGHES" (quoted in Wilson, vii). Since its rediscovery, *Our Nig* has been canonized by its inclusion in major anthologies and classroom curricula worldwide. Written during a critical period for African Americans marked by the DRED SCOTT decision (1857), the Fugitive Slave Act of 1850, and the Kansas-Nebraska Act (1854), *Our Nig* offers unique insights into the circumstances of a quarter-million free blacks in the North and especially into the lives of black women living in small-town New England. Before the rediscovery

and verification of *Our Nig*, it was believed that the first African American–authored novel published in the United States was written after the Civil War by a man. "Harriet Wilson's novel," Gates concludes, "inaugurates the Afro-American literary tradition in a manner more fundamentally *formal* than did either WILLIAM WELLS BROWN or FRANK J. WEBB" (xlvi–xlvii).

FURTHER READING

Wilson, Harriet E. *Our Nig; or, Sketches from the Life of a Free Black, in a Two-Story White House, North. Showing That Slavery's Shadows Fall Even There*, ed. Henry Louis Gates Jr., with an afterword by Barbara A. White (1859; repr. 2002).

LISA E. RIVO

Wilson, J. Finley (28 Aug. 1881–18 Feb. 1952), journalist and civic leader, was born James Finley Wilson in Dickson, Tennessee, the son of James L. Wilson, a preacher, and Nancy Wiley. He attended Fisk University in Nashville, Tennessee, although he did not graduate; afterward he traveled the United States, living in Missouri, Wyoming, Utah, Colorado, Arizona, and Alaska, and worked in various jobs including as a miner, a porter, a waiter, and a cowboy.

In 1903 in Denver and Boulder, Colorado, Wilson joined a lodge of the Improved Benevolent and Protective Order of Elks of the World, an organization that had been started by a black porter, Arthur J. Riggs, in Cincinnati, Ohio, in 1897 to provide charitable relief and social outlets for people of color.

Wilson began his career in journalism in 1905 as a reporter for the *Baltimore Times*. During his career, he edited the *Salt Lake City Plaindealer* and wrote for the *New York Age* as well as the *Harrisburg (Pennsylvania) Advocate-Verdict*. He was instrumental in the founding of the *Norfolk Journal and Guide*. In 1920 he was elected vice president of the National Negro Press Association, and he became president the following year, subsequently serving in that office for three years.

While working as a journalist, Wilson also advanced through the ranks of the Elks fraternity. On 28 August 1922 he was elected Grand Exalted Ruler of the Improved Benevolent and Protective Order of Elks of the World, which he developed into one of the largest and most important African American organizations in the country, expanding from 30,000 to 500,000 members in nine hundred lodges throughout the United States and other countries including England, Canada, Cuba, and Bermuda. Wilson married Leah Belle Farrar of Richmond, Virginia, in 1924. They had no children.

This new Elks organization stood in distinction to the older, exclusively white fraternity known as the Benevolent and Protective Order of Elks. During the 1920s and 1930s, Wilson's so-called "Negro Elks," the Improved Benevolent and Protective Order of Elks of the World (IBPOEW), attracted many members from the ranks of blue-collar workers as well as educated professional black men who came together in the fraternity to offer assistance to needy members and their families and to work toward improving living conditions for blacks.

Although white men were not admitted to Wilson's fraternity, he insisted that it welcome members of other ethnicities, including Japanese and Chinese men, into its ranks. He said, "It behooved the black man to make friends with all the sons of men—and still further in view of the fact that our organization is based upon the Christian religion, it should be our slogan, 'whosoever will, let him come.'" During his nearly thirty-year tenure as Grand Exalted Ruler of the Elks, Wilson traveled the nation setting up new lodges; he was immensely popular and became known simply as "the Grand."

Under Wilson's leadership, the Elks worked for the cause of civil liberties and strove to improve health and education among minorities through concrete measures such as college scholarships and youth programs such as the Daughter Elks and the Junior Herd. The Elks fraternity gained a position of national political influence and provided social advancement as well as improved business contacts for individual members within their own communities. Because of Wilson's direction, Elks' parades in major U.S. cities came to be regarded as important social events, and those attending were edified by speakers such as W. E. B. DuBois and Ralph Bunche.

Wilson personally visited public officials such as Tennessee Governor Austin Peay in 1923 to establish open communication and secure fair legal treatment for his fellow "black Elks" when their efforts to expand their organization were being impeded by lawsuits from the "white Elks." Personally, Wilson was fearless. He once defended himself with a gun, refusing to be forced off a Pullman train because he was black.

In 1925 the Elks' Grand Lodge established as its official publication the *Washington Eagle*, of which Wilson was founder, editor, and publisher. Wilson also edited the *John Brown Reader* with his long-time friend and colleague, William C. Hueston, and established John Brown's Farm near Harpers Ferry, West Virginia, as a memorial to the great abolitionist.

At the Grand Lodge meeting of 1927 Wilson established the Elks' Commission on Civil Liberties and issued a call to seventy-five black fraternities throughout the country to gather in Washington, D.C., to discuss the problem of racism. In 1933 Wilson was elected president of the Colored Voters League of America.

At the Elks' Grand Lodge meeting in Indianapolis, Indiana, in 1933, Wilson reported on his activities, including raising money to help with the legal defense of several black youths who had been falsely accused of raping a white girl in Scottsboro, Alabama. In his speech he said that he looked forward to economic recovery after the Great Depression, and he encouraged members to support black banking institutions and insurance companies. He also encouraged black Americans to participate in politics and to vote; he praised the policies of the New Deal and said that there must be a "comprehensive policy of financial rehabilitation of the colored race in America which is a part of the trunk-line program of the National Recovery Administration of Franklin D. Roosevelt."

In 1936 Wilson reported on the expansion of the fraternity into the southern states of South Carolina, Georgia, Louisiana, Texas, and Florida. He also emphasized the importance of physical exercise and athletics, introducing Elks member Jesse Owens as an example. He was often in the forefront of national debate over racial issues, speaking out against all forms of discrimination, including poll taxes, hate crimes by the Ku Klux Klan, lynching, and police brutality against African Americans.

One of Wilson's most famous speeches, delivered at the National Baptist Convention in Cleveland, Ohio, in 1941, was also published as a pamphlet, *The Colored Elks and National Defense*. In that speech, which typified the way he spent his life dealing with such issues, Wilson stressed the need for higher living standards and better nutrition and housing for blacks, as well as equal employment opportunities and wages. He emphasized the need for better insurance and health care in addition to Social Security coverage for agricultural and domestic workers.

Wilson praised President Franklin D. Roosevelt's 1941 actions ordering an end to discrimination in defense related industries and federal government employment. Wilson advocated the integration of the armed forces during World War II, and he urged blacks to get involved in civic and church groups as agents for social change and to contribute to the national defense effort by supporting the USO and by purchasing defense savings bonds. Denouncing prejudice and espousing patriotism, Wilson encouraged all Americans to work together to fight against the evils represented by both Nazism and racism; in the "National Defense" speech he said, "I have tried to show how these handicaps to equal citizenship rights affect not only the ability of our people to serve their country's cause, but as well holds back the real national unity which must exist if democracy is to triumph."

Wilson assumed leadership of the International Association of Colored People of the World in 1945, the year it was established. That same year, Wilson helped found the Federated Organization of Colored People, which took part in State Department meetings when the United Nations was formed. He served as a delegate to the World Conference on Human Rights in 1947.

Wilson traveled around the country for many years, often at his own expense, recruiting members for the Elks and rallying people to work for better living conditions in the inner cities and an end to discrimination. He was a powerful orator, but he also related well to individuals. He urged blacks to act within the law but strive to change and improve the legal system, to work diligently to improve their own physical and financial well-being, and to build bridges of understanding with other ethnic, religious, and political groups.

Because of his prominence as one of the most beloved and influential leaders in the black community, Wilson was respected by many national political figures who sought his counsel and endorsement, including President Roosevelt. He died in Washington, D.C.

Wilson was one of the most charismatic leaders of the black community in America during the first half of the twentieth century. Though he worked as a professional journalist for some years, he is best remembered for bringing the "Colored Elks" fraternity to national prominence as a respected voice for the disadvantaged. An early proponent of civil rights, he spread a message of peaceful, constructive engagement in society as the means of improving the quality of life among black people.

FURTHER READING

Elks (IBPOEW) records are at their Grand Lodge Headquarters in Winton, North Carolina.

Wesley, Charles H. *History of the Improved Benevolent Protective Order of Elks of the World, 1898–1954* (1955).

Obituaries: *Washington Post*, 20 Feb. 1952; *Negro History Bulletin*, May 1952; *Chicago Defender*, 1 Mar. 1952; *Journal of Negro History*, July 1952.

This entry is taken from the *American National Biography* and is published here with the permission of the American Council of Learned Societies.

BRUCE GUY CHABOT

Wilson, Jackie (9 June 1934–21 Jan. 1984), singer, was born Jack Leroy Wilson, in Detroit, Michigan, the son of Eliza Lee. Nothing is known about his father. Known as Sonny and described as "a tough street kid," he began singing, at his mother's urging, at the Russell Street Baptist Church, becoming a member of the Ever Ready Gospel Singers in his early teens.

The often-repeated tale that Wilson won the Detroit Golden Gloves is erroneous, but he did box briefly as a professional, posting a 2-8 record. While finishing Highland Park High School he sang with several spiritual-oriented groups and won several amateur contests at the Paradise Theater. Before he turned to the popular idiom, he wanted to be "the world's best known gospel singer," remembered his wife Freda. He never studied music but listened to a wide range of acts, including the Dixie Hummingbirds, the Mills Brothers (HARRY MILLS and HERBERT MILLS), the Ink Spots, JAMES CLEVELAND, LOUIS JORDAN, and Al Jolson. Still billing himself as Sonny, Wilson recorded two singles in 1951; he garnered interest from several people in the music industry that December at a talent show staged by the bandleader Johnny Otis.

Wilson's break finally came in early 1953, when an audition earned him a place in the group Billy Ward and the Dominoes. CLYDE McPHATTER, lead singer, "was my man," remembered Wilson. "I fell in love with the man's voice." He "learned a lot from Clyde," including the "high-pitched choke" that became one of Wilson's trademarks (Shaw, 442–443). The internship with his idol was brief, as McPhatter left after a few weeks to join the Drifters, and Wilson, at age eighteen, became the featured vocalist. The group released its most successful record of his four-year tenure in April 1956, "St. Therese of the Roses," which rose to number thirteen on the pop charts.

By then Ward—"a strict disciplinarian," according to Wilson, but "a nice man"—had molded his lead singer into a polished showman. In 1957

Detroit-based agent Al Green convinced Wilson to pursue a solo career. Green had recently met the young songwriters BERRY GORDY (who later founded Motown Records) and Roquel "Billy" Davis (whose pen name was Tyran Carlo), and that July, Wilson recorded their composition "Reet Petite." Green died while this minor hit was climbing the charts, and Nat Tarnopol, one of his assistants, took over as Wilson's manager.

"Reet Petite" launched Wilson as a solo artist, and over the next two years other Gordy-Carlo songs made him a star. "To Be Loved" (1958), "That's Why" (1959), and "I'll Be Satisfied" (1959) were all hits, and "Lonely Teardrops" (1958) reached number seven on the pop charts. It would become Wilson's signature number. Only in his early twenties, Wilson was already an amazing talent, "the epitome of natural greatness," according to Gordy. Producer Dick Jacobs remembered that at the first recording session, Wilson's near-operatic range left veteran musicians "slack-jawed and goggle-eyed in disbelief." "Jackie ... opened his month," said Jacobs, "and out poured that sound like honey on moonbeams" (Pruter).

But it was as a live performer that Wilson was becoming a legend. Splits, spins, and knee drops were an integral part of his incredibly athletic act, and Wilson was soon being billed as "Mr. Excitement." Handsome, confident, and flashy, he worked audiences into a frenzy, with women screaming and men agreeing that Wilson "was just as pretty as he thought he was."

Fan zealousness proved dangerous in 1961. A woman who claimed that Wilson would not speak to her in the lobby of his New York apartment building went to his room and shot him twice as he attempted to disarm her. He was hospitalized for a month, and one bullet, lodged one-sixteenth of an inch from his spine, had to be left in his body. By this time Wilson's career had leveled off. He was still producing hits, but Gordy and Davis were no longer writing for him, and Tarnopol was encouraging him to record songs that would be popular with patrons of nightclubs such as New York's Copacabana and the Las Vegas casinos. Tarnopol, Wilson, Jacobs, and Brunswick Records have all been criticized for the choice of material, but at the time most of the major record companies were unsure of how to market their black acts to appeal to white audiences. SAM COOKE and ARETHA FRANKLIN experienced similar problems. Instead of broadening Wilson's following, Brunswick lost contact with his fan base, and in the mid-1960s he

Jackie Wilson waves as he leaves New York's Roosevelt Hospital with his mother Elizabeth Lee, left, and his wife Freda Wilson on 18 March 1961. (AP Images.)

went three years without placing a song in the top forty of the pop charts.

"Yeah, it's true I've recorded some things you don't expect from an R&B singer," Wilson admitted. "But I don't know that I am an R&B singer." He was proud to "have been accepted by the white world" and saw merit in classically based arrangements such as "Alone at Last" and "Night." "Now they knew I wasn't just a screamer," he believed. "Some people say I'm a soul singer," Wilson continued, "but I've [also] got the gospel in me" (Shaw).

A brief career resurrection began in late 1966 when Tarnopol paired Wilson with Chicago producer Carl Davis. "Whispers (Gettin' Louder)" put Wilson back on the charts, and 1967's driving "(Your Love Keeps Lifting Me) Higher and Higher" became the biggest hit of his career, topping the rhythm-and-blues charts and going to number six on the pop charts.

It would, however, be his last substantial hit. Wilson remained a popular live performer, but by the 1970s he was considered an oldies act. On 29 September 1975, while headlining a Dick Clark revue at the Latin Casino in Cherry Hill, New Jersey, Wilson suffered a massive coronary in the middle of "Lonely Teardrops." He was rushed to a local hospital, but oxygen deprivation during the twenty-five minutes that it took to get him stabilized left him brain-damaged and in a coma. After four months he regained consciousness but never the ability to speak or take care of himself. A series of New Jersey and Pennsylvania hospitals and nursing homes cared for him during his last eight years before he died of pneumonia in Mount Holly, New Jersey.

Wilson was married three times, although during court battles over guardianship his second wife claimed that they had never divorced. He wed Freda Hood in 1951 and had four children with her, fathered another child with his 1967 bride Harlean Harris, and had two more children with Lennie "Lynn" Bell, whom he married in 1971. The murder of his eldest son in 1969 caused him great distress. This incident, a chaotic personal life, and his fading career intensified drug and alcohol use that ultimately led to his collapse.

Wilson's legacy, however, is not that of a fallen star living out his final days in nursing homes, beset with financial problems so great that money had to be raised for a gravestone. It is of the athletic and vocally gifted performer who influenced an entire generation of singers, beginning with early fan Elvis Presley and continuing on through MICHAEL JACKSON. According to Gordy, Wilson "set the standard I would be looking for in artists forever." When asked who stands out from his decades in the music business, Dick Clark replied that Wilson, who was elected to the Rock and Roll Hall of Fame in 1987, "heads the list.... In person or on record, there was only one Mr. Excitement" (Pruter).

FURTHER READING

Gordy, Berry. *To Be Loved: The Music, the Magic, the Memories of Motown* (1994).

Lee, Cooper, B. "Jackie Wilson—Mr. Excitement? Mr. Musical Diversity? Mr. Song Stylist? or Mr. Stage Show?" *Popular Music and Society* 17 (Summer 1993).

Pruter, Robert. *Jackie Wilson—Mr. Excitement* (1992).

Shaw, Arnold. *Honkers and Shouters: The Golden Years of Rhythm and Blues* (1978).

This entry is taken from the *American National Biography* and is published here with the permission of the American Council of Learned Societies.

KENNETH H. WILLIAMS

Wilson, John Woodrow (14 Apr. 1922–), artist and educator, was born in Roxbury, Massachusetts, one of four children of Reginald and Violet Wilson, immigrants from British Guiana. Wilson's parents held working-class positions in the Boston area but were forced onto public relief at the onset of the Great Depression. In 1938 Wilson attended the Roxbury Boys Club, where he took art classes taught by graduate students from the School of the Museum of Fine Arts, Boston. These students passed on the techniques of their teacher, the Russian émigré painter Alexandre Iacovleff, whose lessons stressed the meticulous rendering of the human form. Wilson's student drawings, often emulative of Iacovleff's conté crayon technique, were so impressive that his instructors brought a portfolio of his work to the attention of the School of the Museum of Fine Arts, which led to a full scholarship in 1939.

At the School of the Museum of Fine Arts Wilson's instructor was Karl Zerbe, who emphasized the rudiments of life drawing in his curriculum and encouraged Wilson to pursue his interest in social issues, particularly those that affected African Americans. Zerbe's personal experiences of fleeing Nazi Germany had an influence on Wilson, who saw similarities between Nazi oppression and racial discrimination in the United States. While in art school Wilson also became familiar with the writings of ALAIN LOCKE, JAMES BALDWIN, JAMES PORTER, and RICHARD WRIGHT. Speaking of this time the artist later recalled, "I wanted to create images that would be as powerful as what Richard Wright and James Baldwin wrote about, but I wanted to do it visually" (Hills, 29).

After graduating in 1945 with the highest honors from the School of the Museum of Fine Arts, Wilson began working toward a B.S. in Education from Tufts University (completed in 1947) and had his first one-man exhibition at the Boris Mirski Gallery, Boston, in 1946. One year later the School of the Museum of Fine Arts awarded the artist with the prestigious James William Paige Fellowship, which stipulated study in Europe. Wilson traveled to Paris, where he found various races peacefully coexisting, again highlighting for him the harsh segregation still prevalent in the United States. During his two-year sojourn Wilson also worked in the studio of the avant-garde painter Fernand Léger. Utilizing a realist manner up until this point, Wilson strove to depict his subjects in accurate detail. Under Léger's wing, however, the artist would concentrate on the formal elements of the composition rather than the details of the chosen subject. Works from this time, such as *Boulevard de Strasbourg* (1949), executed in casein (a water-based paint), reflect Léger's teachings with their simplified forms and bold colors.

After returning to the United States in 1950 Wilson married Julia Kowitch, a fellow social-ist, and shortly thereafter received the John Hay Whitney Fellowship (1951–1952) and additional funding which allowed him to pursue additional training in Mexico. Wilson was inspired by the work of the Mexican modernists (for example, José Clemente Orozco, David Alfaro Siqueiros, and Diego Rivera) after seeing a 1942 group exhibition at Harvard University's Fogg Art Museum; he identified with the Mexican artists' ambition to create a style unique to their culture. During his five-year stay Wilson studied in Mexico City at the Instituto Politecnico (1952), the Escuela de las Artes del Libro (1952–1955), and the Esmeralda School of Art (1952), where he created a powerful mural depicting Ku Klux Klansmen lynching an African American man (*The Incident*, 1952). With his friend and fellow artist ELIZABETH CATLETT, he also worked at the famous Taller de Gráfica Popular, a printmaking collective with the aim of bettering social conditions for the working classes and the dispossessed.

Wilson returned to the United States in 1956 with his wife and daughter Rebecca (born 1953), and further expanded his family with the birth of a son, Roy (born 1956), and another daughter, Erica (born 1966). Wilson spent two years working as a graphic designer in Chicago, but the commercial aspect of this position did not suit him, so he moved his family to New York City in 1958, where he would teach art at the New York City Board of Education (1959–1964) and the Pratt Institute Evening School (1958). In 1964 Boston University hired Wilson to help shape its art department, and it was there that he would stay until his retirement in 1986. During this significant tenure as a professor Wilson, in 1969, assisted Elma Lewis in the establishment of Boston's Museum of the National Center of Afro-American Artists (NCAAA) and served as a consultant to the Museum of Fine Arts in the selection of a new director. Besides continuing to show his prints, drawings, and paintings in exhibitions throughout the United States and abroad, Wilson also expanded his artistic repertoire to include sculpture. *Eternal Presence*, the seven-foot-high African American bronze head that the artist is perhaps best known for, was commissioned by the Museum of the NCAAA in 1982 and installed in 1987. Making use of a variety of artistic sources—Pre-Columbian Olmec Heads, the stylized forms of the Mexican muralists, and the tranquil nature of contemplative Buddha statues—this monument to African American strength was created to honor the history of black people in Massachusetts. Additional commissions included a monument to Dr. MARTIN LUTHER KING JR. for the Buffalo Arts Commission, Buffalo, New York, unveiled in 1985, and a sculpture for the Roxbury Community College, *Father and Son Reading*, unveiled in 1990. Most notably, the National Endowment for the Arts selected Wilson from a group of 180 artists to create a memorial bust of Dr. Martin Luther King Jr. for the U.S. Capitol building, unveiled in 1986, which was the first representation of an African American within this famous structure.

Following his retirement from teaching, Wilson had more time to devote to art, and was the recipient of a Painters and Sculptors Grant Award (The Joan Mitchell Foundation, New York, 2000) and the subject of a 2004 retrospective exhibition organized by Faulconer Gallery (Grinnell College, Grinnell, Iowa). The Museum of Modern Art in New York, the Philadelphia Museum of Art, the Smithsonian American Art Museum in Washington, D.C., and numerous other major museums hold the artist's work in their permanent collections, signifying his achievement as a great painter, printmaker, and sculptor.

FURTHER READING
Gaither, Edmund Barry, and Shelley R. Langdale. "John Wilson/Joseph Norman: An Introduction," in *Dialogue: John Wilson/Joseph Norman* (1995).
Hills, Patricia. "A Portrait of the Artist as an African-American: A Conversation with John Wilson," in *Dialogue: John Wilson/Joseph Norman* (1995).
Jenkins, Kay Wilson, curator. *John Wilson: A Retrospective* (2004).
Tarlow, Lois. "Profile: John Wilson," *Art New England* 19.5 (Aug./Sept. 1998).

MELISSA A. KERR

Wilson, Lionel (4 Mar. 1915–23 Jan. 1998), the first mayor of Oakland, California (and the first Alameda Superior Court judge) of African descent, and an active member of the East Bay Democratic Club, was born in New Orleans, Louisiana, the son of Jules and Louise Wilson. His father was a carpenter and plasterer.

The family moved to Oakland in 1918 when Wilson was three years old, at the urging of a maternal uncle, Ponce Barrios, who had found work in the shipyards. Living first with Barrios, the family settled in the northern end of West Oakland between 28th and 32nd streets, near Myrtle, Chestnut, and Linden.

The Wilsons had five more children in Oakland. Wilson later recalled that schools in the neighborhood were predominantly attended by children of Portuguese, Italian, and Irish ethnic families, with 10 to 15 percent African Americans.

In 1932 Wilson graduated from McClymonds High School and entered the University of California, eventually settling on a major in economics and a minor in political science. Three credits short of qualifying for a degree, he dropped out for a year and a half, returning to graduate with a bachelor's degree in 1939. From 1940 to 1942 he was a maintenance worker at the Alameda Naval Air Station, while also working on the recreational staff at the North Oakland YMCA. He married his wife, Dorothy, several months before being drafted into the army in 1943. He served in Europe and attained the rank of first sergeant.

In 1946, Wilson entered Hastings College of Law. While his wife stayed at home with three children, Wilson continued to work part-time at the Oakland YMCA, also taking up janitorial work in his younger brother's dental office. After graduating in 1949 he passed the bar exam on his first attempt. For about fifteen months Wilson worked in the law office of George Vaughns, the senior black lawyer in the East Bay, before opening his own practice. In 1950 he was elected president of the Berkeley, California, NAACP.

In 1959 Wilson was elected president of the East Bay Democratic Club, which he had helped to revive, and secretary of the Berkeley-Albany Bar Association. He was appointed to the Municipal Court in Oakland in 1960 by Governor Edmund G. "Pat" Brown Sr. Though he had lived in Berkeley after returning from military service, he had to move across the city line to 62nd and Market Streets in Oakland to accept the appointment. He was appointed by Governor Brown to an opening on the Alameda County Superior Court in 1964.

In 1965 Wilson was appointed chair of the Oakland Economic Development Commission, recalling years later that he had declined to serve until Oakland Mayor John Houlihan committed not to interfere with the commission's deliberations. The city was divided into seven districts, each with its own community organization and district council. The Commission administered both federal and private antipoverty grants.

Formed in Oakland at the time of Wilson's ascendance to public service, the Black Panther Party (BPP) would inevitably cross paths with him. One of Wilson's earliest encounters with the party may

Lionel Wilson, mayor of Oakland, stands to the right of U.S. President George H. Bush, who came to the city on 20 October 1989 to view the damage caused by the massive Loma Prieta earthquake days earlier. (AP Images.)

have been the appearance of the Panther cofounder Bobby Seale in his courtroom, an event mentioned briefly in Seale's autobiographical *Seize the Time*. Seale's strong but unsuccessful campaign for mayor in 1973 blazed a trail for Wilson's more traditional campaign four years later. In 1972, Wilson was one of four black representatives appointed by Mayor John Reading to serve on the New Oakland Committee, which by Wilson's own description "was formed out of fear when the Panthers announced that they were going to move on the white business community" (Pearson, p. 246).

After Huey P. Newton fled to Cuba to avoid criminal charges in Oakland, Wilson was invited by the Black Panther chair Elaine Brown to serve on the board of the Educational Opportunities Corporation, an initiative of one-time Panther supporter David Horowitz to sustain the Oakland Community Learning Center. In turn, Wilson supported Brown for membership on the OEDC. When Wilson ran for mayor of Oakland in 1977, Brown mobilized Panther support to register thousands of new voters, and provided most of Wilson's get-out-the-vote workers. Wilson wryly noted that he was the first person to win the office of mayor without the endorsement of the *Oakland Tribune*. The *Tribune*, and the Knowland family that had long owned the paper, had been virtual kingmakers in local politics for decades.

Although some BPP members served in Wilson's staff, his first years were disappointing to all the constituencies who voted for him, and to Wilson himself, because the mayor's office simply didn't have much authority. Oakland's charter assigned most administrative authority to the appointed city manager, not to the elected mayor—a part-time position presiding over city council meetings, but not responsible for preparing the city budget or day-to-day administration of city departments. In 1977 Wilson resigned from the board governing the BPP learning center, a result of the scandals—among them the attempted murder of Crystal Grey, a key witness in Newton's trial for the murder of Kathleen Smith in the early 1970s—that followed Newton's return that same year, After Newton's death in 1989, Wilson spoke of how promising Newton's life had been, and what a pity it was that he couldn't get it all together (Pearson, p. 319).

In 1981, Wilson was reelected with over seventy percent of the vote in a four-way race. By the mid-1980s Oakland had a new city manager and a new director of economic development, both of them African American. In 1985, he was challenged for reelection by Wilson Riles Jr., the son of California's first school superintendent of African descent. Wilson won sixty percent of the vote, and a third term, extended by eighteen months due to a charter amendment altering the election cycle. Although the race raised fears that Riles's aggressive campaign would "split the Black community" (*Jet*, 6 May 1985, p. 4), Wilson's decisive win—and his even more decisive loss to yet another African American five years later—showed that simple racial blocs no longer defined city politics.

In 1990 Wilson had the honor of welcoming Nelson Mandela to Oakland. Recently freed from prison in South Africa, he appeared before 78,000 people at the Oakland Coliseum as part of his first world tour. That same year, Wilson lost a bid for a fourth term, winning just 17 percent of the vote in a seven-person primary. He was succeeded in January 1991 by the state assemblyman Elihu Harris. Aged seventy-five, Wilson observed: "This is the first time that the people have turned me down. All they're saying really is that they felt it was time for a change. And I accept that" (*Jet*, 25 June 1990, p. 8).

Less than eight years later, at the age of eighty-two, Wilson died of cancer at his Montclair district home. He was survived by his wife; three sons—Lionel B. Wilson Jr., Steven, and Robin Wilson; four brothers; and a sister.

FURTHER READING

Morris, Gabriel. "Attorney, Judge, and Oakland Mayor: Lionel Wilson," *Online Archive of California* (2007).

Pearson, Hugh. *The Shadow of the Panther: Huey Newton and the Price of Black Power in America* (1995).

Self, Robert O. *American Babylon: Race and the Struggle for Postwar Oakland* (2003).

Thompson, J. Phillip. *Double Trouble: Black Mayors, Black Communities, and the Call for a Deep Democracy* (2006).

CHARLES ROSENBERG

Wilson, Margaret Bush (30 Jan. 1919–11 Aug. 2009), civil rights activist and attorney, was born Margaret Berenice Bush in St. Louis, Missouri—as she has been known to point out, before the passage of the Nineteenth Amendment giving women the right to vote. Her father, James T. Bush, a real estate broker, and her mother, Margaret Berenice (Casey) Bush, a committee executive of the St. Louis NAACP in 1920, were both instrumental in shaping young Margaret's views on racism. She attended public schools and graduated from Sumner High School in St. Louis with honors in 1935. She received a B.A. in Economics and Mathematics, cum laude, from Talladega College in Alabama in 1940. During her senior year she received a JULIETTE DERRICOTTE fellowship, named after the writer and educator.

In the late 1930s when Margaret Bush was still an undergraduate, Missouri did not allow blacks to attend its state-supported law schools. The state paid tuition stipends for residents of color to attend out-of-state schools, although black lawyers were allowed to practice law in Missouri once they had graduated and passed the bar. The state's discrimination against blacks seeking a legal education was challenged by the NAACP. In that case, *Gaines v. Canada* (305 U.S. 337), the Supreme Court ruled that Missouri must either allow black students to attend the University of Missouri Law School or provide "separate but equal" law school facilities. Rather than integrate, Missouri created the all-black

Lincoln University School of Law, and Margaret Bush enrolled. In 1943 she received her LLB degree from Lincoln (now merged with the University of Missouri School of Law). She passed the bar and was only the second black woman admitted to practice in Missouri. In 1944 she married Robert E. Wilson Jr.; the couple would divorce in 1968.

In 1946 Margaret Wilson's father, James T. Bush, was involved in helping the J. D. Shelley family buy a home in a previously all-white neighborhood. The family was later forced to move out of the home when the Missouri Supreme Court ruled that the racial laws governing the property were enforceable. Bush was the founding president of the Real Estate Brokers Association of St. Louis, the organization that spearheaded the *Shelley v. Kraemer* case. The young Wilson was counsel for the organization and obtained its corporate charter. Two years later, in 1948, the U.S. Supreme Court held that such covenants were unenforceable in the courts, and the Shelley family moved back into their home.

In 1954 Wilson was elated when the *Brown v. Board of Education* decision was handed down, and she celebrated with colleagues and friends. The next year, her five-year-old son, Robert E. Wilson III, started kindergarten at one of St. Louis's first integrated schools. He went on to graduate from Harvard Law School and to launch a career as a New York attorney as well as a principal with a private investment group.

After devoting time to private law practice during the 1950s, Wilson served as assistant attorney general for Missouri in 1961–1962. In 1965 she joined the Missouri Office of Urban Affairs and two years later became an administrator for Community Services and Continuing Education programs in the Missouri Department of Community Affairs. Her commitment to housing and community issues continued as deputy director and acting director of the St. Louis Model City Agency and then as director of St. Louis Lawyers for Housing from 1969 to 1972.

In 1975 Wilson was elected as chair of the NAACP national board of directors, a position she held for nine years. She then became chair of the board of trustees of Mutual Real Estate Investment of New York in 1984. As senior partner in the firm Wilson and Associates, she practiced law in St. Louis and also was admitted to practice before the U.S. Supreme Court. She was chair of the American Bar Association (ABA) Special Committee on Youth Education for Citizenship for three years, 1991 to 1994. Other activities include serving on the American Bar Association's Gavel Awards Committee from 1995 to 1997, as a member of the ABA Standing Committee on Public Education, and as the 1998 national chair of the ABA's Law Day.

Wilson also served as chair of the boards of trustees of St. Augustine's College and Talladega College. Other boards benefiting from her expertise included the Land Reutilization Authority of the City of St. Louis and the Intergroup Corporation. Her service was honored with many civic and professional awards, including honorary degrees from St. Paul's College, Smith College, Washington University, Kenyon College, Talladega College, Boston University, Morgan State University, Alabama State University, and the University of Missouri–St. Louis. She also received the 1996–1997 Distinguished Lawyer Award from the Bar Association of Metropolitan St. Louis. Fueled by her lifelong commitment to racial justice and equal opportunity, Wilson's work in civil rights was monumental in helping the movement. She died in St. Louis at the age of 90.

FURTHER READING
"Baugh to Head African and Afro-American Studies," *The Record* (21 January 2005).
"Legal Eagle," *The Crisis* (March/April 2007).
"Margaret Bush Wilson Is Honored by United Negro College Fund," *St. Louis Post-Dispatch* (2 Dec 2001).
                                                CHESYA BURKE

Wilson, Mary (6 March 1944–), singer and original member of the Supremes, was born in Greenville, Mississippi, to Sam Wilson, a butcher, and Johnnie Mae Wilson. She was the great-grandchild of slaves. At three her parents sent her to live in Detroit, Michigan, with her aunt, I. V. Pippin, an employee of Hudson's Dry Cleaners, and her uncle, John L. Pippin, an employee of the Chrysler auto company. Briefly, she thought of the Pippins as her biological parents.

When Mary Wilson was six years old, however, her mother settled in Detroit. After a period of living with relatives and some employment, Wilson's mother became welfare dependent. She moved twelve-year-old Mary and her two younger siblings to Detroit's Brewster Projects, a government-owned housing complex. Wilson was bused from the projects to Algers Elementary School in 1956 when integration of public schools began. Graduating in 1962 from Northeastern High School in Detroit, she credited a largely Polish faculty for a positive experience with integration and helping her to realize her future goals.

In 1959, at age fourteen, Wilson became part of a singing group, the Primettes. Other original members were FLORENCE BALLARD, DIANA ROSS, Betty McGlown, and Marvin Tarplin on guitar. Under the direction of Milton Jenkins, and later Jesse Greer, they played small venues such as sock hops. In 1960 the Primettes performed for an audience of several thousand at the Detroit-Windsor Freedom Festival amateur talent contest and won first place.

Later that year the Primettes approached Motown Records, then known as Hitsville, U.S.A., and auditioned for BERRY GORDY JR. Not immediately offered a recording contract, they were allowed to observe other artists record. Richard Morris, a recording engineer and musician at Hitsville, helped the Primettes rehearse and worked to promote the group; they played larger venues and began recording at Flick and Contour Studios. Meanwhile, McGlown left the group. Tarplin also left to work with SMOKEY ROBINSON and the Miracles. Gordy assigned the remaining Primettes to record with Robinson, who was affiliated with Hitsville-Motown. In 1961 the group, which now included Barbara Martin, signed a contract and started recording for Motown. The Primettes changed their name to the Supremes.

The quartet did live shows and went on tour, starting in Cincinnati and Pittsburgh, sharing the bill with other acts such as GLADYS KNIGHT and the Pips. When in 1962 Martin left the group, the Supremes permanently became a trio: Wilson, Ross, and Ballard. Out of high school but still underage, the chaperoned trio traveled in the fall of 1962 with "The Motortown Revue," which included other Motown artists such as the Temptations, STEVIE WONDER, and MARVIN GAYE. They went on tour to Chicago, Washington, D.C., and New York, where they played the famed Apollo Theater.

The group found itself in the midst of a civil rights movement that was unfolding. The Revue's performance in a ballpark in Birmingham, Alabama, was the first in the community with an integrated audience, but after a racial incident there, bullet holes were found in the windows of their tour bus.

Wilson studied music while learning vocalization, choreography, and staging along with other artists under Motown's direction. The Supremes' image was one of sophistication, doing complex three-part harmonies but singing in a variety of styles from jazz to show tunes. Teaming up with writer-producers Brian Holland, LAMONT DOZIER, and Eddie Holland (HDH) in 1963, a few Supremes records received regional and some national airplay.

Having recorded the Supremes, who had shared the lead singing for three years without a hit record, Gordy rearranged the group with Wilson and Ballard as background singers. Wilson returned to singing leads in the group after Ross eventually left the Supremes.

The tours gradually expanded to include better venues. In 1964 the Supremes—Wilson, Ross, and Ballard—became one of the first Motown acts to perform outside the United States when they played the Clay House Inn, a black supper club in Bermuda. Afterward the trio did a three-month Caravan of Stars tour with promoter Dick Clark, host of the television show *American Bandstand*. The Supremes also began European tours starting with Great Britain in 1964 and later toured elsewhere, including the Far East.

Meanwhile Motown released the Supremes' "Where Did Our Love Go," and in August 1964 the record became the number-one song in the country. Later that year their next two number-one singles, "Baby Love" and "Come See About Me," were released. Number-one hits continued (eventually totaling twelve), and American and foreign television performances and commercials followed, including many appearances on *The Ed Sullivan Show*. They performed for fund-raisers, such as one for President Lyndon B. Johnson in the 1960s. The *New Musical Express* named the Supremes the number-three group in the world; *Music Biz* labeled the group the top female trio in 1965.

The Supremes were the first black pop group of the sixties, and one of the youngest, to play New York City's Copacabana in 1965, one of the most prestigious nightclubs in the country. That same year they were featured on the cover of *Time* and *Ebony* magazines and were the first pop group to play New York's Philharmonic Hall in Lincoln Center. They gave a Royal Command Performance at the London Palladium in 1968. They received the NAACP Image Award for Best Female Group in 1972, and they were inducted into the Rock and Roll Hall of Fame in 1988.

During the seventies Mary Wilson began a solo career after the Supremes' last farewell concert in 1976; the group officially disbanded in 1977. Wilson was an original member who remained with the Supremes throughout most of its history. As a solo performer, Wilson toured the world, recorded, acted on stage and television, and participated in celebrity charity events.

Wilson married Pedro Ferrer on 11 May 1974 and gave birth to three children; she also took in her cousin's eldest child. Wilson sought a divorce in 1981; she wrote openly about her professional and personal experiences in two books: *Dreamgirl: My Life as a Supreme* (1986) and *Supreme Faith* (1990).

She was honored in 1973 with a Mary Wilson Day in Detroit when she was praised as an example of the power of black women everywhere.

FURTHER READING

Wilson, Mary, Patricia Romanowski, and Ahrgus Juilliard. *Dreamgirl: My Life as a Supreme* (1986).
Wilson, Mary, and Patricia Romanowski. *Supreme Faith* (1990).

ROSE PELONE SISSON

Wilson, Milton James (20 July 1915–2 Sept. 2003), founder of business schools at Texas Southern and Howard Universities, was born in Paducah, Kentucky, to Jess Wilson, a Pullman porter, and Rhea (Day) Wilson, a teacher. He graduated from Lincoln High School in Paducah.

After high school, Wilson attended the University of Illinois, where he majored in mathematics. His maternal grandparents lived there, and in order to pay in-state tuition, he registered under their address. His father had been laid off by the railroad during the Depression, and Wilson needed to cut his costs. Early in one of his calculus classes, the professor asked to speak with him. She told him that although he was one of the top three students in the class, he would never have the opportunity to work for the large corporations that would recruit his white classmates. She suggested that he switch his major to commerce, where perhaps his opportunities would be broader.

Wilson discussed the idea with his mother, who encouraged him to make the switch. One of the first requirements for commerce majors was an accounting course. One of his classmates in this course was the son of the business-school dean. Both students excelled in the class, and they had a friendly competition to get the highest scores on the examinations. Soon the dean called him in and told him, "My son says you should major in accounting" (Personal interview, Silver Spring, Maryland, 16 Nov. 1991). Unfortunately, school administrators soon discovered that Wilson was not a resident of Illinois. The university gave him the choice of leaving or paying the incremental tuition he owed as a Kentuckian. Because of his financial situation, he had no choice but to leave, and he chose West Virginia State, a black university where a friend of his was enrolled. His friend found him a local address, which enabled him to pay only $25 per semester in tuition. He worked for his room and board, taking two jobs in order to stay solvent in the middle of the Depression. Wilson was almost certain that the administration of West Virginia State was aware that he was not from West Virginia, but his presence and tuition payments were never challenged.

While a student, Wilson was very impressed with accounting professor Dallas Brown, who inspired him to become a certified public accountant (CPA). To earn accreditation as a CPA, candidates had to meet an educational requirement, pass a difficult examination, and work for an accounting firm. While the first two requirements were challenging for most African Americans, in the 1930s the final requirement was almost impossible to achieve. White-owned accounting firms would not hire African Americans, and the first black-owned firm was not opened until later. Wilson sought other employment, and found a job in Indiana with the National Youth Administration grading high school math papers.

Wilson married Zelda Summers on 29 May 1941; they had three children: Milton Jr., Rhea Ann, and Zelda Catherine. Subsequently, Wilson moved several times, heading the business department at a junior college in Texas before moving to Kentucky to become chief accountant for Samuel Plato, a pioneering black architect and contractor. Wilson developed an accounting system for Plato's federal contract to build $3.5 million in defense housing that led to a job as a cost accountant for the federal government's Office for Emergency Management in Washington, D.C. While he was in D.C., one of his professors at West Virginia State recommended him for a position teaching accounting at Hampton University. Wilson went to visit his supervisor at the Office for Emergency Management and asked about his career prospects there. The supervisor said that he could get a small promotion, but beyond that, because of his race, he had no opportunity to advance higher in the ranks. Wilson talked it over with his wife, and decided to take the job offer at Hampton.

While working for Hampton, in 1945 he finished his master's of commercial science in business administration at Indiana University, one of the top accounting programs in the country. He was soon offered a position at Dillard University in New Orleans, where he became head of the business department. He asked the vice president for academic affairs for a raise, and was told that he was already one of the best-paid professors in the school and would need a Ph.D. to get a raise. He wrote to his alma mater, Indiana University, to apply for a doctoral fellowship, which he was granted. He wrote his dissertation on differences in tax liability under federal law versus state law. When he earned his doctorate in September 1951, he became only the second African American (and only by a matter of months) to earn a doctorate in accounting in the United States.

While he was in graduate school, he decided to take the CPA examination. Indiana was one of the few states in which a CPA candidate could count teaching experience toward the experience requirement, so, because of his years of teaching at Hampton and Dillard, when he passed the test he immediately became a CPA. He was the twenty-fifth African American CPA in the United States and the first in Indiana. He knew that he was fortunate to be able to earn this credential and reported that he helped other African Americans to gain CPA experience once he had "sneaked in" (Personal interview, Silver Spring, 16 Nov. 1991).

During this period the state of Texas was sued for not admitting HEMAN SWEATT to the University of Texas Law School in Austin, because the state provided no "separate but equal" law school for African American Texans (Tushnet). In response, the state created the Texas State University for Negroes, and Wilson was invited to start a business school at what would soon be renamed Texas Southern University. The president of the new university had worked with Wilson at Hampton University. While the state lost its case to keep the University of Texas Law School segregated, Wilson reported that the "whole idea [of creating Texas Southern] was to keep large numbers of blacks from attending the University of Texas" (Personal interview, Silver Spring, 16 Nov. 1991).

Through its reciprocity agreement with the state of Indiana, when Wilson moved in 1952 he became a CPA in Texas, the first African American to do so. Nevertheless, the State Society of Certified Public Accountants, the professional organization for CPAs, would not admit Wilson as a member. Wilson needed the signatures of two CPAs to sponsor his membership application, and one of his employees, a Jewish accounting professor, happily signed the sponsorship and found a friend to co-sponsor, partly because he was angry with the State Society's poor treatment of Jews. Despite the fact that Wilson had the required signatures, the society rejected his application. Wilson was told that the rejection resulted from Society members' worries that he might attend the dances it sponsored.

In the 1950s it was not uncommon for southern states' professional associations to exclude African Americans or to hold conferences at segregated hotels (Hammond, 69). But by the late 1960s, civil rights pressure had changed the demographics of the firms, and Wilson, along with two of his colleagues at Texas Southern, became a member of the Texas State Society of CPAs in 1969.

Wilson served as dean at Texas Southern for twenty years. While there he maintained a part-time CPA firm in Houston with one of his TSU colleagues, and the two of them provided experience to African Americans who had no other opportunities in the field. In 1957 he joined the faculty at the Harvard Business School for one year, during which time he developed several useful contacts. He later applied to the Ford Foundation for a grant to expand the faculty and the library at TSU to help earn accreditation from the American Assembly of Collegiate Schools of Business (AACSB), and one of the assistant deans he had met at Harvard helped facilitate the application. Wilson landed the first Ford Foundation grant to a black business school, and Texas Southern became the first historically black college to earn AACSB accreditation.

Through the Ford Foundation and Indiana University, Wilson helped establish a school of business in Dacca, Pakistan, in 1966. In 1970 Indiana University tried to lure Wilson away from Texas Southern, but Wilson accepted a position with Howard University instead. He chose the job at Howard after he and his wife talked about it. His mother had been an educator and they both thought that she would have been happier with his dedicating his life to the education of other African Americans. Wilson became the first dean of the Howard University Business School, which he also led to AACSB accreditation; its undergraduate program was accredited in 1976 and its graduate program in 1980. When Wilson joined Howard in 1970, there were fifteen faculty members and a $500,000 annual budget; in 1988 he had seventy faculty and a $6 million budget. He was particularly successful in raising money for Howard University from the major public accounting firms—the same firms with which he had been unable to find employment early in his career (Hammond, 111).

Wilson served on several boards of directors, including boards for Great Western Savings and Loan Association, United National Bank, and the American Assembly of Collegiate Schools of Business.

He served on numerous committees designed to advance minority participation in the accounting profession including those for the academic association, the American Accounting Association, and the association for professional CPAs, the American Institute of Certified Public Accountants.

After 59 years of marriage, Zelda Summers Wilson died in January 2001. Wilson married Imelda Pradia on 6 November 2002. Wilson died at the age of 88 on 2 September 2003.

FURTHER READING

Much of the material for this entry derives from personal interviews with Milton Wilson.

Hammond, Theresa. *A White-Collar Profession: African American Certified Public Accountants since 1921* (2002).

Tushnet, Mark. *The NAACP's Legal Strategy against Segregated Education, 1925–1950* (1987).

Obituary: *Houston Chronicle*, 6 September 2003.

THERESA A. HAMMOND

Wilson, Nancy Sue (20 Feb. 1937–), jazz singer and performer, was the oldest of six children born in the southern Ohio town of Chillicothe. Her father, Olden, worked in an iron mill. Her mother, Lillian Ryan, was a domestic worker. She discovered her love of music early on. Her father bought albums for the family, and Nancy soon began to entertain her parents and siblings with her singing. She was a member of her church choir. When she was a teenager, her family relocated to Columbus (she had grandparents nearby), and there Wilson attended West High School. While there, she entered and won a school contest that led to her hosting a radio request program during which she also sang. She graduated from West High School in 1955.

That year, Wilson matriculated to Central State College in Ohio (later Central State University), where she enrolled in the normal school, but she wanted badly to pursue a musical career and dropped out after only a year. In 1956 she joined Rusty Bryant's band and worked her way up to lead vocalist. The group toured widely for the next several years and even cut an album under the Dot label. Around the same time, Wilson met and fell under the influence of the jazz great CANNONBALL ADDERLEY. Under his advice, she relocated to New York, where she began to perform in clubs at night and work as a secretary during the day. She did not hold this latter position for long. Almost immediately, Wilson made enough of a splash that she was hired to sing in one of the city's premiere nightclubs every night. A recording of one of her first performances made its way to the offices of Capitol Records, and in short order Wilson was offered a recording contract. In 1960 she married the drummer in her club band, Kenneth Dennis. The couple went on to have a son. They divorced in 1970.

Her musical career now underway, Wilson saw her first album, *Like in Love*, pressed in 1959. Her first single, "Guess Who I Saw Today?" became a small hit and convinced Capitol that the label had a star on its hands. In 1962 she cut an album with her mentor Adderley, *Nancy Wilson/Cannonball Adderley*, an effort that secured her a national audience as well as a reputation as a jazz singer of the first order. The following year, her smash single "Tell Me the Truth" appeared, and with it Wilson's success was secure. For the next several years, her albums would fly to the top of the charts. In 1964 she won a Grammy Award for her album *How Glad I Am*. She also began to appear on television programs, and in 1967 NBC offered her her own show. *The Nancy Wilson Show* ran only between 1967 and 1968, but the show won an Emmy in 1975. Over the course of her long career, Wilson appeared in numerous television programs— both entertainment and variety shows and fictional dramas—among them *The Dean Martin Show* (1969), *The Carol Burnett Show* (1969–1970), *Hawaii Five-O* (1970), and *Police Story* (1974). Meanwhile, she made herself a presence at the era's high-profile civil rights events and became an outspoken advocate for equality and justice. In 1965 she marched in Selma, Alabama. In 1970, following her divorce from her first husband Kenneth, she married Wiley Burton, a minister, with whom she would go on to have two daughters, Samantha and Sheryl. They remained married until 2008, when Burton died.

Wilson's career continued to flourish. She had long established herself as one of her generation's all-time jazz vocal greats. During her long career, she recorded some seventy albums. She became quite popular all over the world, especially in Japan, where in 1983 she won the Tokyo Song Festival. Her awards and honors are numerous and include the Global Entertainer of the Year Award from the World Conference of Mayors (1986), an NAACP Image Award (1986), and an Essence Award (1992), among many others. Wilson won three Grammy Awards, her latter two for *R.S.V.P (Rare Songs, Very Personal)* (2005) and *Turned to Blue* (2007). She was nominated for a Grammy twenty times. In 2003 the National Endowment for the Arts named her an American Jazz Master.

In the first decade of the twenty-first century, frail health sometimes kept Wilson from performing or appearing in public. In 2010, however, she was performing live shows again. A cherished musical icon, Wilson's body of work will last as long as people listen to jazz.

FURTHER READING

Dahl, Linda. *Stormy Weather: The Music and Lives of a Century of Jazzwomen* (1984).

Warren, Nagueyalti. "Nancy Wilson." In *Notable Black American Women* (1992).

JASON PHILIP MILLER

Wilson, Olly (7 Sept. 1937–), composer, was born Oliver Woodrow Wilson in St. Louis, Missouri, the third of four children born to Oliver Wilson, Sr., an insurance salesman and butler, and Alma Grace (Peoples) Wilson, a seamstress. Wilson grew up in a musical household; not only did the family sing at home and in church, but his father was a gifted tenor who sang at social functions around town and in amateur choirs. Wilson began studying the piano around age seven and within a few years was playing at church and accompanying his father. At age ten he also began lessons on the clarinet, which he would later play in the band at Sumner High School. There he came under the influence of the bandmaster Clarence Hayden Wilson, a former president of the National Association of Negro Musicians who helped further inflame the young Wilson's passion for music. Becoming increasingly interested in jazz and popular music during his early high school years, Wilson began playing the piano at local clubs and even started his own jazz band, for which he wrote and arranged music. Growing up in such a musically rich city, Wilson was exposed to a wide range of black music genres that included not only jazz and R&B, but also spirituals, gospel, and the blues, all of which would leave a distinctive mark on his own compositional style.

Upon graduation in 1955 Wilson attended Washington University in St. Louis on a clarinet scholarship, becoming one of a small handful of blacks enrolled at an institution that had only recently been integrated in the wake of the Supreme Court's landmark decision in *Brown v. Board of Education* (1954). There he undertook a serious study of works by composers across the history of Western classical music and began to compose in this tradition, drawing inspiration both from acknowledged twentieth-century classical masters such as Béla Bartók and Igor Stravinsky and from

jazz greats including MILES DAVIS and CHARLIE PARKER. He continued to play the piano and clarinet with jazz groups at school and around town, but his performing interests gradually shifted toward the double bass, which he had begun to learn in his later high school years. Wilson progressed rapidly on the bass and before long was playing with professional ensembles such as the St. Louis Philharmonic and the St. Louis Summer Chamber Players.

Receiving his bachelor of music degree in 1959, Wilson went on to earn a master's in Composition at the University of Illinois in 1960, after which he taught at Florida A&M University for two years. In 1962 he enrolled in the doctoral program at the University of Iowa and was awarded a Ph.D. in composition two years later, thereafter returning to teach at Florida A&M for an additional year. From 1965 to 1970 he was a professor at the Oberlin Conservatory of Music in Ohio, during which time his compositions met with considerable success. Wilson's music had already been performed by the Dallas Symphony Orchestra at a Composer's Symposium of 1964, and in 1967 it was featured as part of the Black Composer's Concert Series in Atlanta. While many of his compositions from this period were influenced by the German composer Arnold Schoenberg's groundbreaking twelve-tone method—using all twelve notes of the chromatic scale in serial fashion—Wilson nonetheless integrated elements of the African American musical tradition into his works. He also took an interest in the burgeoning field of electronic music, which he studied in 1967 at the University of Illinois's Studio for Experimental Music. In 1968 his work *Cetus* for electronic tape won first prize at the International Electronic Music Competition sponsored by the Dartmouth Arts Council. This piece was chosen by a panel of blind judges that included the celebrated modern composer Milton Babbitt, and thus this victory represented an important milestone for black composers, who had been deemed by some as incapable of writing music that could stand on an equal footing with that of their white colleagues.

Two years later, in 1970, Wilson joined the composition faculty at the University of California, Berkeley. Shortly thereafter he was awarded a Guggenheim fellowship, which allowed him to study West African music in Ghana from 1971 to 1972. He received a second Guggenheim fellowship in 1977 and served the following year as an artist-in-residence at the American Academy in Rome. Over the next several years, Wilson received many more such honors, including a grant from the Rockefeller Foundation in 1991 and election to the American

Academy of Arts and Letters in 1995. Meanwhile, his music was increasingly performed throughout the United States and in Europe. Beginning in the 1970s Wilson received several prestigious commissions to compose new works, including ones from such venerated organizations as the Boston Symphony Orchestra, the New York Philharmonic, and the Chicago Symphony Orchestra. Also during this time, Wilson conducted various chamber ensembles in performances of both his own works and those of other contemporary composers. In 1993 he was appointed chair of the music department at Berkeley, a post he occupied for four years, and from 1995 to 1998 he held an endowed professorship at the university. In addition to his composing and his teaching duties, Wilson published a number of articles throughout his academic career. Most of these were concerned with the relationship between African and African American music, as well as with an overall attempt to identify the defining characteristics of such music. One of these traits Wilson termed the "heterogeneous sound ideal," which he defined as the aim of achieving highly contrasting sound qualities, or timbre, in black vocal and instrumental music.

Wilson retired from Berkeley in 2002, although he continued to compose and to conduct performances of new music. Despite certain changes in compositional style over the course of his life, Wilson consistently sought to reconcile elements of African and African American music with those of the European classical tradition, an approach exemplified by his well-known work *Sometimes* (1973), scored for tenor and electronic tape and based on the spiritual "Sometimes I Feel Like a Motherless Child." As a successful composer and teacher as well as an eloquent spokesman on behalf of the black perspective in American music, Wilson exerted a powerful influence on a generation of younger composers who themselves searched for ways of expressing their unique cultural voice in an increasingly pluralistic musical world.

FURTHER READING

Baker, David M., Lida M. Belt, and Herman C. Hudson, eds. *The Black Composer Speaks* (1978).

Banfield, William C. *Musical Landscapes in Color: Conversations with Black American Composers* (2003).

Southern, Eileen. "Conversation with Olly Wilson: The Education of a Composer," *The Black Perspective in Music* 5 (1977) and 6 (1978).

JASON GEARY

Wilson, Orlandus (1917–30 Dec. 1998), gospel singer, was born in a rural area that is now Chesapeake, Virginia, to Maurice Wilson, a farmer, and Annie Cole Wilson, a teacher. Raised on a small farm along the James River, Wilson was one of seven children. His father initially operated a small farm and later sharecropped. His mother, a graduate of Hampton Institute, taught school for three years before turning her full-time attention to their burgeoning family. Growing up poor in Tidewater, Virginia, Wilson and all of his siblings attended public school. They walked more than two miles daily to the nearest school open to African American children. Their neighbors and the other members of the Union Bethel Baptist Church provided their most important social network. Wilson's father had no musical talents but his mother sang in the ladies quartet and led their weekly practice sessions. In addition to his early exposure to music at church, Wilson received a harmonica for Christmas on which he performed imitations of barnyard animals, trains, and the sounds of a fox hunt.

Around 1930 Orlandus Wilson, along with his brother James, formed a quartet—the Jollet Four—to sing at local churches. One of its members was William Langford, who would eventually sing with Wilson in the Golden Gate Quartet. The Jollet Four performed in local churches and participated in quartet contests, singing a repertoire of mostly older spirituals such as "Go Down, Moses," "I Wouldn't Take Nothing for My Journey Now," and "Sometimes I Feel Like a Motherless Child." A few years later Langford moved to Portsmouth, Virginia, where he joined the Golden Crowns Quartette, while Wilson remained in the country attending school and working at a nearby Planters Peanuts processing plant. Needing talent for his new group, the Golden Gate Quartet, and recalling his old friend's skills, Langford asked Wilson's parents' permission for Wilson to try out for the group and come into the city twice a week for rehearsals after work. The Golden Gate Quartet's members included Willie Johnson and William Langford (alto and lead), "Peg" Ford (an older man who sang bass), and Henry Owens (baritone).

Within several years the group had gained local fame singing nearly every weekend at churches, some of them many hours away. By 1936 their fame had grown to the point that they were on the road for several weeks at a stretch. Because of the travel Wilson could only "sub" into the group for local appearances but could not join them for extended engagements. When Ford was no longer able to travel with the group, the members, led by Langford, went to Wilson's parents asking if the nineteen-year-old might join the group on a full-time basis. Maurice and Annie Wilson reluctantly agreed, and Orlandus Wilson took his place in the Golden Gate Quartet, where he stayed for the next sixty-two years.

Buoyed by success on local radio and regular touring in Virginia and the Carolinas, the group easily supported itself for nearly a year before a recording deal with RCA's Bluebird division and several appearances on NBC's *Magic Key* radio program placed the group in the national spotlight. Langford had tremendous range and an emotional voice, Owens filled in the middle, and Wilson provided the group with a solid anchor. But it was Willie Johnson's innovative lead singing, in a narrative style that emphasized texts from the New Testament of the Bible, that distinguished the group from others.

From 1937 into the early 1950s, the Golden Gate Quartet was one of the most popular African American gospel quartets in the United States, participating in John Hammond's groundbreaking 1938 Carnegie Hall Spirituals-to-Swing concert, landing a weekly radio program on CBS, and enjoying a long run at New York City's chic Café Society. President Franklin Delano Roosevelt invited them to entertain at his January 1941 inaugural gala. In the early 1940s the Golden Gate Quartet appeared in such Hollywood films as *Star-Spangled Rhythm* and *Hollywood Canteen*. During this period they continued to record for RCA and Columbia before switching to Mercury in 1948. But the group began to change in the late 1940s. First William Langford left, followed by Johnson and Owens. By 1950 Orlandus Wilson was the only "original" member left in the Golden Gate Quartet, and he became its de facto leader.

The world of gospel quartet singing was changing, too: in the early 1950s rhythm and blues and rock and roll began to replace the a cappella sound. In 1955 the Golden Gate Quartet toured Europe with immense success. This initial tour was quickly followed by two equally triumphant trips. Spurred by their success abroad and faced with an uncertain racial climate and a changing musical landscape at home, the group soon decided to relocate. Following a 1958 twenty-eight-country tour arranged by the U.S. State Department, Wilson and his group members decided to take up permanent residence in Paris. During this time they recorded several dozen albums and toured Europe regularly,

but they did not perform in the United States until 1994. They returned to New York City in order to be inducted into the Hall of Fame of the United in Group Harmony, an organization devoted to preserving the history of vocal harmony. Wilson remained at the helm of the Golden Gate Quartet, managing, handling musical arrangements, and composing new material until two months before his death in Paris.

FURTHER READING
Obituary: *New York Times*, 31 Dec. 1998.
This entry is taken from the *American National Biography* and is published here with the permission of the American Council of Learned Societies.

KIP LORNELL

Wilson, Shadow (25 Sept. 1919–11 July 1959), jazz drummer, was born Rossiere Wilson in Yonkers, New York. Virtually nothing is known of Wilson's parents, early background, or personal life. The singer and bandleader Billy Eckstine said that Wilson's given name was Rossier Van Donnel, adding, "We called him Shad." Starting in 1935 he worked with the bands of Frankie Fairfax and Jimmy Gorham in Philadelphia. When the Gorham band moved to New York in 1938, leadership transferred first to the pianist Bill Doggett and then to LUCKY MILLINDER from May 1938 to early 1939, when Millinder declared bankruptcy.

Wilson played with the orchestras of JIMMY MUNDY in 1939, Benny Carter and TINY BRADSHAW in 1940, and LIONEL HAMPTON from 1940 to 1941. According to the pianist Sir Charles Thompson, Hampton "wanted the drummers to play a back beat [strong accents on the second and fourth beats] all the time, and that was bad for a pianist. Shadow Wilson joined and he wouldn't be influenced. He had a lot of will power. One time there was a move to fire him, but all the fellows liked Shadow so well and their sentiment was so strong that Lionel had to keep him. After Shadow left, there were never any great drummers with Lionel" (Dance, 338–339).

Wilson joined EARL HINES's orchestra in 1941 and is remembered as one of Hines's finest drummers. Late in 1943 he was among nine of Hines's sidemen—including BILLY ECKSTINE, CHARLIE PARKER, and DIZZY GILLESPIE—who simultaneously gave notice, in part because they wanted to explore their own developing bebop style and in part because they were discouraged by Hines's undertaking yet another grueling tour of the South. Eckstine had scarcely begun organizing a new big band when Wilson was drafted in the spring of 1944. Somehow extricating himself from army duty, Wilson was a member of the big band of saxophonist Georgie Auld by September, when Jo Jones was drafted out of COUNT BASIE's orchestra. Basie wanted to hire Wilson to replace Jones immediately; Wilson joined two months later, after fulfilling his commitment to Auld. Recordings with Basie demonstrate his ability to drive a big band; on "Queer Street" (1945) he is heard as a soloist.

Jones returned from the army in early 1946, and Wilson left Basie to play with the tenor saxophonist ILLINOIS JACQUET's group through 1947. During that year Wilson also took part in celebrated recording sessions with TADD DAMERON's sextet and with THELONIOUS MONK's quartet; the faster of two versions of Dameron's "Our Delight" demonstrates how well Wilson transferred his forthright, well-rehearsed big band style to a combo setting.

Wilson briefly returned to Basie's orchestra in 1948, and he played with Woody Herman's big band during 1949. He rejoined Jacquet from 1949 to 1950 before touring in ERROLL GARNER's trio from 1950 to 1952. A recording such as Garner's "Lover" (1950) demonstrates the subtle side of Wilson's musical personality: quiet but briskly energetic swing rhythms, meticulous accents coordinated with Garner's piano arrangement of the tune, and a brief flurry of snare drum soloing to end the piece. The drummer Kelly Martin reports that Wilson was an avid baseball fan, and whenever Garner's trio was in New York at the same time as the Yankees, Wilson would fake a hand injury and—without asking Garner—hire Martin as a substitute.

In 1951, during the course of Wilson's association with Garner, the drummer participated as a freelance player in a session with the tenor saxophonist EDDIE "LOCKJAW" DAVIS, the organist Bill Doggett, and the bassist OSCAR PETTIFORD. According to Davis, these were the first tenor and organ recordings, although the archetypal tenor-organ groups (with organ foot pedals replacing string bass and, optionally, with electric guitar added as well) had not yet evolved. Wilson again played with Jacquet's band from 1952 to 1954, worked with Hines again in a seven-piece group in 1954, and was part of the trio accompanying the singer ELLA FITZGERALD from 1954 to 1955. From 1957 to 1958 he was a member of Monk's quartet with JOHN COLTRANE at the Five Spot in New York. Intermittently through the decade Wilson also worked with the saxophonist SONNY STITT, with whom he recorded. During this same period he also recorded with the pianist

HERBIE NICHOLS, the trumpeter Joe Newman, and the saxophonist Lee Konitz.

According to the trombonist DICKY WELLS, "Before he died, Shadow Wilson told me that before he went with Basie he had one way of playing in mind—the latest thing, that was it! Then he got hungry and found out, and began playing with a beat to satisfy the band. He was very versatile and a good drummer, and he played for the musicians on the order of BIG SID [CATLETT]" (Dance, 93). After stopping all work for several months because of illness, Wilson died of bronchial pneumonia in New York.

FURTHER READING
Dance, Stanley. *The World of Count Basie* (1980).
Gitler, Ira. *Jazz Masters of the '40s* (1966).
McCarthy, Albert. *Big Band Jazz* (1974).
Obituary: *Jazz Magazine*, no. 52, 1959.
This entry is taken from the *American National Biography* and is published here with the permission of the American Council of Learned Societies.

BARRY KERNFELD

Wilson, Sunnie (7 Oct. 1908–14 Mar. 1999), hotelier and entertainment entrepreneur, was born William Nathaniel Wilson in Columbia, South Carolina. His mother, Rebecca (Butler) Wilson, worked as a cook and maid, and his father, William Wilson, whom Sunnie barely knew, worked as a Pullman porter and hotel waiter. As a young child, Rebecca moved Sunnie and his older sister Irene to live with his maternal grandparents. His grandfather's status as a doctor allowed him entrée into Columbia's elite black society. While in high school, he worked several odd jobs. One summer he went with his uncle to New York. His outgoing personality and a bit of good fortune landed him a job as a bellboy at the exclusive Lotus Club, a private millionaires' club. When he returned to South Carolina, he completed high school with the help of a private tutor and went on to study drama at Allen University in Columbia.

Wilson struggled to earn enough money to pay for his tuition and expenses. While a student, he opened a soda fountain and ice cream parlor called The Pals Shop. He did very well the first year but competition from other stores soon forced him to close. With few opportunities in his hometown, he set his sights on the North. In 1927 he interrupted his studies and moved to Detroit, Michigan, lured by Henry Ford's promise of jobs paying five dollars a day at the automotive plant. Unable to get on at the plant, he worked odd jobs and took up organizing parties to make ends meet. His side job soon became his lifelong passion. During the Great Depression, Wilson distinguished himself in the entertainment and hospitality industry. He managed nightclubs, led show bands, and booked acts and musicians for local clubs and engagements. Wilson often managed black-and-tan establishments, or clubs that catered to interracial crowds. He socialized with some of the biggest names in music, including LOUIS ARMSTRONG and DUKE ELLINGTON. He was also reportedly well liked among the local gangsters and bootleggers.

His self-confidence and friendly manner helped him forge social and economic connections with politicians, entertainers, and businesspeople in Paradise Valley, the business center of black Detroit's east side. In the early 1930s, many considered him the unofficial "mayor" of Paradise Valley. His civic and community activities included helping the poor, registering voters, and establishing an amateur boxing training center at a local church. In 1936 he managed the Brown Bomber Chicken Shack, a restaurant and club co-owned by the boxer JOE LOUIS, one of Wilson's closest friends. The "Shack" offered valet parking and an upscale ballroom that featured entertainers such as Duke Ellington, the Marx Brothers, Louis Armstrong, and CAB CALLOWAY.

In 1941 Wilson bought his own club, the Forest Club, which was larger than New York's Madison Square Garden. The Forest Club included a roller-skating rink, bowling alley, and a 107-foot bar, the longest bar in the city. He featured top-ranked entertainers at his club, but he also used it to demonstrate his commitment to the community. The club hosted a night school for adults, etiquette classes run by local black sororities, and black auto workers' union organizing meetings. He persuaded other black businesses in the area to donate toys, clothes, and food, and he distributed them from the club at Christmas. In the mid-1940s, with Joe Louis as an investor, he opened the 62-room Mark Twain Hotel to cater to blacks. Though Detroit had two other larger hotels owned by blacks, the Mark Twain was more affordable for Wilson's key market: black entertainers. Wilson would put up entertainers even if they did not have any money, but he still provided luxury accommodations and services. In 1949 he hosted PAUL ROBESON when no other venue would book him because of Robeson's connection to the Communist Party.

When the Forest Club's lease ended in 1951, Wilson poured his energy into helping legalize alcohol in Idlewild, an exclusive resort village for blacks in Michigan. The same year he opened a lounge in the Mark Twain Hotel called the Swamp Room. During the 1950s and early 1960s the Mark Twain hosted a diverse group of musical guests that highlighted the diverse and growing entertainment choices for the black community. Established and up-and-coming gospel, blues, and jazz musicians such as LESTER YOUNG, DIZZY GILLESPIE, and B. B. KING as well as young rhythm-and-blues stars such as JACKIE WILSON and Sam Cooke came through his hotel's doors. In 1959 the city targeted Paradise Valley for "slum clearance" and tore down many black business landmarks, symbolizing the end of an era in the black business district. After a brief stint owning two hamburger stands in the early 1960s, Wilson opened Sunnies Celebrity Room, one of the few black-owned bars left in the city. The bar closed in 1987. From the early 1970s to the late 1980s, Wilson turned to public life, working as a fund-raiser and goodwill ambassador for the mayoral campaigns of COLEMAN A. YOUNG.

Wilson kept his personal life very private. Although little is known of his wife, he had been married, and had a daughter, Sharon Wilson Cardwell. The city awarded him the Spirit of Detroit Award in 1987, and the Urban League awarded Wilson its Distinguished Warrior Award in 1993 for his assistance to African American victims and businesses decades earlier during the 1967 riot and for his testimony against corrupt and abusive police afterwards. Wilson had been one of the very earliest and most vocal critics of police brutality in Paradise Valley. Wilson helped Paradise Valley blossom into a vibrant cultural and social center of African American community in Detroit. In the postwar years, however, he especially lamented the decline of African American businesses in Paradise Valley and other previously segregated communities in the North and Midwest. He criticized African Americans for abandoning communities such as Paradise Valley and Idlewild by the 1970s, even though he also strongly believed that African Americans should be part of the American mainstream. He believed that African Americans could not achieve political and social equality without a strong business foundation. After his death, the Detroit African American business and civic community established the Sunnie Wilson Spirit of the Champ Award, which honors both Wilson and Joe Louis. It recognizes citizens who have overcome challenges to achieve personal and/or professional success. He died of cancer at a Detroit hospital.

FURTHER READING

Wilson, Sunnie, with John Cohassey. *Toast of the Town: The Life and Times of Sunnie Wilson* (1998).

Bak, Richard. *Joe Louis: The Great Black Hope* (1998).

Moon, Elaine Latzman. *Untold Tales, Unsung Heroes: An Oral History of Detroit's African American Community, 1918–1967* (1994).

Obituary: *Detroit Free Press*, 16 March 1999.

SHENNETTE GARRETT

Wilson, Teddy (24 Nov. 1912–31 July 1986), musician, was born Theodore Shaw Wilson in Austin, Texas, the son of James Augustus Wilson, an English professor at Tuskegee Institute, and Pearl Shaw, the chief librarian at Tuskegee. Wilson grew up in Tuskegee, and as a teenager he heard early recordings by LOUIS ARMSTRONG, Bix Beiderbecke, KING OLIVER, and other jazz pioneers. He also spent summer vacations with one of his mother's sisters in Detroit, where he heard groups like the FLETCHER HENDERSON Orchestra. Wilson studied music at Tuskegee and at Talladega College, focusing on the piano but also studying the violin. After a year in college he spent his summer vacation in 1928 in Chicago, where his exposure to many jazz greats profoundly influenced him. His parents convinced him to stay in college another year, but the following summer he moved to Detroit to pursue his musical career. He worked with various territorial bands, and in Toledo, Ohio, he heard the great pianist ART TATUM for the first time and frequently played with him.

Tatum's complex harmonic improvisation had a strong impact on the young Wilson, whose own increasingly melodic playing also influenced Tatum. Wilson himself always focused on melody and rhythm above all. Tatum generally stayed close to the original melody of a tune while exploring its harmonic implications. Wilson, on the other hand, constantly invented his own melodies and rarely played anything the same way twice. He also played with more restricted dynamics, and his touch emphasized clarity and clear articulation. Above all, his playing was tasteful. He had no interest in calling attention to himself, a quality that made him the perfect ensemble player.

In 1931 Wilson moved to Chicago, where he came under the influence of EARL HINES. When Hines left his permanent position at the Grand Terrace ballroom to go on the road, Wilson filled in with Clarence Moore's band. He also played with Armstrong and Jimmie Noone. In 1933 the producer John Hammond heard Wilson on a radio broadcast with Moore's band and arranged for him to travel to New York to play and record with Benny Carter's group, the Chocolate Dandies. Hammond introduced him to Benny Goodman, who hired Wilson to join him and drummer Gene Krupa in the influential Benny Goodman Trio in 1936. The pianist became the first black musician to be publicly featured with a white group in the United States.

In one memorable year, 1935, Wilson played and recorded with a variety of artists, made his debut as a leader of his own instrumental groups and of recordings with BILLIE HOLIDAY, and began to play with the Goodman trio. The recordings he made with Holiday are among his greatest achievements, his rhythmically steady Mozartian clarity serving as the perfect foil for Holiday's emotive, rhythmically free style in songs like "These Foolish Things." Wilson left Goodman in 1939 and led his own big band for a short time in 1939 and 1940, but he lacked the personal charisma and showmanship that was essential to success in such a venture. He thereafter concentrated on his work with small groups and as a soloist, occasionally rejoining Goodman to tour or record.

A series of recordings Wilson made in April 1941 are typical of his creative output during this period, particularly an extraordinary rendition of "I Know That You Know." In this up-tempo piece and in others, Wilson smoothes out the powerful left hand of the stride style while playing lyrical single-note lines with his right hand and adding subtle dynamic shadings throughout. While he could provide a powerful sense of swing when the piece demanded (as in "Sailin'" with a Goodman septet), his playing was most notable for its beautiful delicacy and symmetry. Wilson later commented that the introduction of microphones liberated him, allowing him to introduce a much softer style than that favored by FATS WALLER or Hines. Similarly, the "muscle" supplied by Goodman drummers like Krupa and the emotionality of singers like Holiday allowed Wilson to pursue a less visceral approach. And like many other jazz players of his era, Wilson was profoundly influenced by classical musicians, particularly Mozart. He often played classical music for his own pleasure, had a substantial record collection, and kept abreast of classical pianists' careers.

By 1942 only Tatum surpassed Wilson in influence among jazz pianists. And though Wilson made few creative advances for the remainder of his career, essentially ignoring the newer styles that

Teddy Wilson performs during a tribute to Erroll Garner at the Newport Jazz Concert at Carnegie Hall, New York City, on 29 June 1977. (AP Images.)

appeared, he continued to play widely. He taught regularly at the Juilliard School of Music in New York City from 1945 to 1952 and there and at other colleges periodically thereafter. During the 1960s he played in Europe, Japan, South America, and Australia, and in the 1970s he appeared regularly at Michael's Pub in New York City and annually at the Newport Jazz Festival. His playing in these later decades was often routine, and his repertoire rarely varied, but even at this "ordinary" level his style retained its remarkable, well-crafted sense of beauty. Teddy Wilson epitomized urbane sophistication in both his playing and personal life. Performing with grace and subtlety, he refined Hines's complex cross-rhythms, Waller's powerful stride style, and Tatum's harmonic sophistication into a personal, instantly recognizable style. Though he rarely moved beyond the achievements of his early career, he remained one of the most subtly satisfying of jazz pianists, influencing Hank Jones, Jimmy Rowles, Tommy Flanagan, Dick Katz, and many other modern players.

Wilson was married four times and had five children. His first marriage was in 1931 to Irene Armstrong, a songwriter and pianist better known by her name from a later marriage, Irene Kitchings. Wilson then married Janice Carati, with whom he had his first child, a son. After their divorce he married Blanche Louth. They had two sons before their divorce. He married for a final time to Joanne Roberts, with whom he had a son and a daughter. Wilson died in New Britain, Connecticut.

FURTHER READING

Lyons, Len. *The Great Jazz Pianists, Speaking of Their Lives and Music* (1983).
Schuller, Gunther. *The Swing Era: The Development of Jazz, 1930–1945* (1989).
Tirro, Frank. *Jazz: A History*, 2d ed. (1993).
Obituaries: *New York Times* and *Washington Post*, 1 Aug. 1986.

This entry is taken from the *American National Biography* and is published here with the permission of the American Council of Learned Societies.

RONALD P. DUFOUR

Wilson, William Joseph (1818–? Dec. 1878), abolitionist leader, educator, boot maker, and freedman's bank administrator, was born near Shrewsbury on the New Jersey coast where his family operated an oyster boat. In the late 1830s Shrewsbury, located near the Revolutionary War battlefield at Red Bank, had a total population of 5,166, with 441 free blacks and twenty-five slaves. Wilson had attended a small common school that had white and black students, but nothing else is known about his life until he moved to New York City, probably in 1837, and opened a boot-making shop. The same year that he began advertising his shop, he married Mary Ann Garret Marshall, a black New Yorker.

Shortly after moving to New York, Wilson became involved in the fight for black suffrage and remained at the head of the effort until the 1860s. In 1837 he began serving on a black suffrage ward committee and lectured, organized petition drives, mobilized other African Americans, and formed local organizations in an attempt to remove the property restrictions that had effectively disenfranchised the majority of black males. He also became a member of the board of managers of the New York State Suffrage Association. Although by 1850 he had accumulated enough property to qualify for the vote, his own status did not diminish his commitment to securing such rights for all, regardless of race or class. As a boot maker, Wilson emerged as a labor leader, participating in the American League of Colored Laborers. Led by SAMUEL RINGGOLD WARD, HENRY BIBB, FREDERICK DOUGLASS, and Lewis Woodson, the League declared that through "Union and CONCERT OF ACTION," it would improve black life. In particular, the organization attempted to create a fund that would loan money to black businessmen who could not get credit from white-owned banks (*North Star*, 13 June 1850).

In the early 1840s Wilson became a teacher in the black schools in Brooklyn, New York, and later a principal of Colored Public School No.1, where he shared teaching duties with a Miss J. E. Brown. The school's student population fluctuated between 120 and 400 students, and Wilson earned a well-deserved reputation as an effective educator. He saw in the black poet PHILLIS WHEATLEY a model for all African American youth. By the age of twenty-two, Wilson maintained, Wheatley had accomplished more than "America's paler daughters" at any age (Brown, 231). Undoubtedly, he used Wheatley, a former slave, as a model for his students to show what ambition and drive could accomplish—a theme he would later develop further. In 1851 even the *New York Times* took note of his school's public examinations and declared that the students' performances reflected the effectiveness of the school's staff.

Beginning in December 1851 Wilson became the regular Brooklyn correspondent for *Frederick Douglass' Paper*, and during the Civil War he wrote a similar series for the *New York Weekly Anglo-African*. Writing under the pseudonym "Ethiop" for the two most important black papers of the mid-nineteenth century, Wilson commented on a wide range of subjects of interest to free blacks across the North. His opinionated essays often sparked heated—sometimes sarcastic—debate, usually with his abolitionist colleague JAMES MCCUNE SMITH who wrote under the pseudonym "Communipaw." Indeed, the two often jousted on fundamental questions regarding black life. Wilson could provoke controversy and anger, but he always retained the respect of his audience, which clearly savored his epistles. A missed publication deadline meant that Wilson's letter would be delayed for a week or more, raising a hue and cry from Douglass's subscribers. In appreciation of Wilson's contributions, and that of other correspondents such as Communipaw, Douglass remarked that they were the "equal in ability to those of any other paper in the country" (*Frederick Douglass' Paper*, 17 Dec. 1852). One correspondent who had met Wilson for the first time in 1854 after reading his many essays, came away feeling that Ethiop was a "modest, discreet, warmhearted and sensible man, able ready and willing to work for the cause of his people" (*Frederick Douglass' Paper*, 17 March 1854).

During the 1850s Wilson wrote passionately to increase black racial pride: "through my veins flow, freely flow, dark Afric's proudest blood," he proclaimed in *Frederick Douglass' Paper* (8 Jan. 1852). While other black leaders continued to attack the institution of slavery and American racial attitudes, Wilson increasingly focused his attention upon what he believed blacks should do to combat the effects of racial prejudice. He insisted that African Americans needed a "monied class," a "black aristocracy," that would serve as a catalyst for black economic and social development. Such a class, to his mind, would "give fixity and stability to our people" and put an end to all plans for black colonization or emigration. Black wealth would inspire other blacks to climb up to success and put down white accusations of black inferiority. Pushing aside claims from his brethren that blacks "can't" acquire wealth so long as whites oppress them, Wilson asserted that it "is said that so deeply do we feel degraded, so depressed are we by weight of the wrongs heaped upon us, that we can scarcely look up, much less rise up…. As a man acquires, the greater is his desire for greater acquisitions; and the nearer he approaches the goal of his ambition…." For Wilson, blacks had been depressed and dejected for so long that they lacked faith and pride in their own abilities. "We have not got steam up enough yet; this is all…. Let us then knock in the head, forever, the *Dogma* 'that, because we feel depressed we cannot rise'" (*Frederick Douglass' Paper*, 15, 22 Jan. 1852).

In arguing for creation of a black aristocracy—a concept reincarnated by W. E. B. DuBois as the "Talented Tenth" at the century's end—Wilson was asking others to follow his own example. Not only had he created his own business at age nineteen, but by 1860 he had accumulated five thousand dollars of real estate and another one thousand dollars of personal estate. The assertion he heard over and over again that blacks cannot acquire wealth was wrong. "'CANNOT,' the bug-bear 'CANNOT,'" to Wilson was "a *hideous monster*, pursuing us everywhere" (*Frederick Douglass' Paper*, 5 Feb. 1852). All they lacked, Wilson contended, was confidence and the right education. Education with a purpose, aiming to establish black businesses, black stores, and black workshops, which would in turn hire black workers and, thus, stimulate black enterprise, black ambition, and black elevation. In spite of white racism and through determination, Wilson had risen, and he believed that with inspiration and a sound education the mass of African Americans could succeed as well.

In 1862 and 1863 Wilson gave a series of anti-slavery speeches at the New York's Cooper Institute in response to the Emancipation Proclamation that caused an uproar among members of Brooklyn's board of education. Forced to resign his teaching position, he moved to Washington, D.C., and offered his services to the American Missionary Association (AMA). With his wife and daughters, Annie and Mary Marshall, working as assistants, Wilson took over as head of the AMA's Camp Baker School for freedmen. Firm in his principles, he refused to hire white teachers, informing the AMA that he wanted only "good competent earnest devoted *colored persons.*" Blacks must lead in these kinds of efforts, he asserted. Taking a back seat to the "dominant class" would, Wilson contended, teach the wrong lesson and keep blacks subordinate. The AMA refused his request for more teachers of any race, regardless of the growing number of his students, so he hired his own (Richardson, 23–24). Despite conflicts with his employer, the Camp Baker School became one of the best in the District.

At the close of the Civil War, Wilson became corresponding secretary of the committee for the "Colored People's National Monument to the Memory of Abraham Lincoln," an effort led by HENRY HIGHLAND GARNET (*Christian Recorder,* 3 June 1865). As he had attended various black state and national conventions in the mid-1850s, Wilson helped organize the 1869 black national convention in Washington, D.C. He served as chairman of the finance committee and won approval of his resolution urging Congress to pay bounties to those blacks who had served in the Civil War regardless of previous condition or servitude.

Perhaps needing a larger salary than the AMA could provide, Wilson eventually quit his teaching position and became a cashier for the new Freedman's Savings Bank. True to his insistence that blacks must learn to accumulate wealth, Wilson argued that the bank represented a great opportunity for blacks in the District and in Richmond, Virginia, to create capital and advance free of white domination. He actively recruited investors, assuring them that even small deposits in a Freedman's bank account would, over time, prove a godsend.

While Ethiop had shown himself to be an effective teacher and essayist, he lacked accounting skills and soon faced a forty-thousand-dollar deficit—an enormous sum. He left the bank in 1874 under a cloud of suspicion shortly before it failed, losing its depositors' funds. Wilson unsuccessfully sought another teaching position with the AMA and slipped into poverty and obscurity until his death four years later in Washington, D.C. One of the North's leading black intellectuals before the Civil War, Wilson was recognized by his peers as a man of destiny and influence. According to WILLIAM WELLS BROWN, the former slave, abolitionist leader, and novelist, Wilson was someone who "wakes us from our torpidity and coldness to a sense of our capabilities" (Brown, 235).

FURTHER READING

Brown, William Wells. *The Black Man: His Genius and His Achievements* (1863).

Richardson, Joe M. *Christian Reconstruction: The American Missionary Association and Southern Blacks, 1861–1890* (1986).

Ripley, C. Peter, et al., eds., *Black Abolitionist Papers*, vol. 4 (1991).

Stauffer, John, ed. *The Works of James McCune Smith, Black Intellectual and Abolitionist* (2006).

DONALD YACOVONE

Wilson, William Julius (20 Dec. 1935–), sociologist, was born in Derry Township, Pennsylvania, one of six children of Esco Wilson, a coal miner and steelworker, and Pauline Bracy. Wilson grew up in Blairsville, a small mining town outside of blue-collar Pittsburgh, and his family struggled alongside neighboring black families, all of whom experienced firsthand the slow decline of American manufacturing in the postwar era. Blairsville, Wilson later suggested, helped him realize the importance of work in organizing personal and family life, a theme that would echo in all of his writings. On graduating from high school, Wilson left for Ohio, where he attended Wilberforce University, receiving a B.A. in 1958. After earning an M.A. at Bowling Green State University in 1961, he headed west to study at Washington State University. He earned his doctorate there in 1966, a year after he received his first full-time teaching position, as an assistant professor of sociology at the University of Massachusetts at Amherst.

Although Wilson is best known for his work on urban poverty in the United States, he began his career as a comparativist, focusing in particular on race relations in South Africa under apartheid and America during the civil rights era. In the late 1960s and early 1970s he began work on *Power, Racism and Privilege* (1973), a set of essays in which he examines the relationship of race and social inequality in South Africa and the United States. Wilson married Beverly Huebner in 1971; they had two children. Wilson also had two children from a previous marriage to Mildred Hood.

In 1972 Wilson began teaching in the Department of Sociology at the University of Chicago. In doing so, he continued a long-standing tradition at the university, one that could be traced to the writings of Robert Park and E. FRANKLIN FRAZIER, of addressing American race relations. Wilson credited his arrival in Chicago for helping him to see the variegated class structure in America's black community. While the city's class-segregated black neighborhoods motivated his thinking, Chicago itself did not appear prominently in either of his first two books. This changed in the late 1970s as Wilson initiated several major research initiatives in the city.

As a young scholar, Wilson was committed to the spirit of the American left—he would play a guiding role in the Democratic Socialists of America in the 1970s. However, he bucked the trend of his liberal colleagues by questioning what he felt to be the overtly polemical character of civil rights–era political discourse. Looking concretely at the changing place of black Americans in U.S. society, he noticed the growing cleavages, mostly along class lines, and wondered whether this signaled a need for a new political platform. As he would remark years later in a *New Yorker* profile, "You had to live in Chicago to appreciate the changes that were taking place. I felt we had to start thinking about the black class structure…. One segment seemed to be improving, with higher incomes, better life styles, while the rest were falling further and further behind" (Remnick). Liberal-democratic policies did not take this bifurcation into account; neither did social scientists adequately capture the import of this phenomenon for American race relations.

During the late 1970s and 1980s, Wilson focused intently on the social and political implications of the changing class dynamics within the black community, questioning whether different strata of black Americans experienced daily life uniquely and thus needed different kinds of social support. He wrote *The Declining Significance of Race* (1978) as a means of specifying the unique configuration of race relations in post–civil rights era America.

Numerous critics and observers have interpreted this work in terms of the growing distance it seemed to create between Wilson and segments of the black intellectual and political leadership. Many black public figures interpreted Wilson as being skeptical of government intervention in providing redress for black Americans; more extreme critics suggested that Wilson was championing the end of racism. Wilson took great pains to state that racism continued to oppress America's black community and that his argument about the diminishing impact of race was in terms of *economic* advancement, not quality of life in general. He insisted that affirmative action and government subsidies were reaching mostly middle-class blacks, not the poor who lived in depressed inner cities. In noneconomic areas, discrimination, segregation, and outright antipathy to black Americans continued to be pressing problems that the nation needed to contend with. With this argument, Wilson had charted his own ground and faced the criticism of conservatives and liberals alike.

The Declining Significance of Race was also a significant academic achievement in terms of its mode of argumentation. Wilson had presented a historical argument about the relative weight of race and class as factors inhibiting the social advancement struggles of black Americans. Skillfully using a mix of statistical data and secondary sources, Wilson analyzed the intersection of race and class in distinct historical periods: the preindustrial, antebellum South; early-nineteenth- century industrialization; the period between the World Wars; and the modern era. It would no longer be sufficient to speak of "racism" as a continuous social process. Wilson took what historians often argued—that American race relations were continuously evolving—gave it an empirically rigorous treatment, and then presented it to social scientists in such a way that they were forced to reconceptualize and analyze anew the black experience. The public reception of the work missed this important contribution, focusing instead on the title of the book and the possible fallout for black political practice.

As Wilson prepared for the writing of *The Truly Disadvantaged*, perhaps his most influential and widely praised book, Chicago assumed a prominent role. His presence at the university drew a cadre of like-minded graduate students and young faculty, many of whom would move on to prominent academic careers in urban studies. Wilson supervised several empirical projects in the city's African American inner-city neighborhoods. Some were

William Julius Wilson's book *The Truly Disadvantaged* is an unflinching assessment of the causes of urban poverty. (Library of Congress.)

large-scale survey studies under his direct supervision, and others were solitary, often rich ethnographic investigations by his graduate students in fields as diverse as boxing, gangs, religious behavior, and domestic life. His focus on U.S. inner cities eventually helped to sponsor a rejuvenated interest in urban poverty in America's leading research institutions.

As he marshaled empirical data on the city, Wilson found himself in a new political battle. On the one hand, with their writings on the supposed dysfunctionality within black inner-city communities, Reagan-era intellectuals such as Charles Murray and Lawrence Mead provided fodder for an increasingly conservative public attitude towards welfare and urban inequity. Liberals challenged them—as they did in the 1960s—by suggesting that these communities were not rife with social pathology, but that black social structure was different because of the impact of racism, discrimination, and slavery. Once again, Wilson found himself challenging both views: in *The Truly Disadvantaged*

(1987), he acknowledged that black Americans were growing farther from the social mainstream, but unlike conservatives, he suggested that a compromised economic opportunity structure was at the root of high crime, low marriage rates, and other indicators of nonnormative behavior.

Wilson's unflinching assessment of the conditions of inner-city communities may not have won him immediate political support, but a growing number of scholars and policy makers noted the significance of his argument. *The Truly Disadvantaged* received scholarly and popular awards and was listed as one of the fifteen notable books of 1987 by the *New York Times*. Perhaps the greatest sign of the book's reach was President Bill Clinton's admission that *The Truly Disadvantaged* had the strongest impact on his own thinking on race and urban America. In 1990 Wilson was elected as president of the American Sociological Association, the first time that an African American had held that post since E. FRANKLIN FRAZIER had forty-two years earlier. In 1996 Wilson took up a post in the Kennedy School of Government at Harvard University, where he eventually became the Lewis P. and Linda L. Geyser University Professor. He continued to write prolifically on U.S. urban poverty, but his research also returned to his comparative roots. He incorporated experiences of white and Latino urban communities into his writings and worked actively to shape a research agenda on European and American urbanism, notably in *When Work Disappears: The World of the New Urban Poor* (1996). In *There Goes the Neighborhood* (2006), Wilson combined the themes of urban poverty and ethnicity by using four Chicago communities as microcosms of wider problems concerning deprivation.

Since the civil rights era, no author has been more influential in shaping our understanding of poverty in American society than William Julius Wilson. This description has been given to Wilson not only by scholars and policy makers but also by a U.S. president. In his academic career, Wilson has accumulated numerous honorary doctorate degrees and awards, two of the most prestigious being a MacArthur Foundation Fellowship in 1987 and the National Medal of Science, the highest scientific honor in the United States. When he received the latter award from President Clinton in 1998, the citation praised William Julius Wilson for having "revitalized the field of urban sociology, pioneering methods of interdisciplinary social science research, advancing understanding of the interaction between the macroeconomic, social structural, cultural and behavioral forces that cause and reproduce inner city poverty."

FURTHER READING

Biographical information on Wilson can be found on the Harvard University Web site: http://ksgfaculty. harvard.edu/william_wilson.

Remnick, David. "Dr. Wilson's Neighborhood." *The New Yorker*, 29 April & 6 May 1996, 96–107.

SUDHIR ALLADI VENKATESH

Wilson, William Othello (September 1867–18 January 1928), U.S. Army soldier and Medal of Honor recipient, was a native of Hagerstown, Maryland. Nothing is known about his life prior to joining the army as a young man, but his activities later in life suggest that he had likely attended school and was well educated.

As a young man, William Wilson would later move to Minnesota at an unknown date. He was residing in the area of St. Paul and working as an upholsterer when he enlisted in the army there on 21 August 1889. At this time, there were only four segregated units, two cavalry and two infantry regiments, in which African Americans could serve. These units were employed on the frontier and would soon gain the collective nickname "Buffalo Soldiers" for their skill and valor fighting native peoples on the western plains. The regiment in which Wilson enlisted, serving in Company I, was the 9th Cavalry, which, along with the 10th Cavalry, was the oldest and most storied of the army's black regiments. Wilson excelled at army life and within a year had risen to the rank of corporal, was an excellent marksman, and served as his company's acting quartermaster sergeant. He was serving with his regiment at Fort Robinson, Nebraska, in the winter of 1890 when the Ghost Dance religion took hold among the plains Indians, prophesying the return of the great buffalo herds and the destruction of the white man. In anticipation of problems with the Sioux Nation on the Pine Ridge Reservation in the Dakota Territory due to the rapid rise of the Ghost Dance religion, nearly half of the army's cavalry regiments were dispatched to the reservation to quell a possible revolt. On 29 December 1890 the one-sided Battle of Wounded Knee took place, during which many Sioux women and children were massacred by the white 7th Cavalry. In response to this battle the 9th Cavalry was sent to the scene to the aid of the 7th Cavalry on 30 December. In an effort to make quick time the regimental wagon train was left behind under the guard of several companies, including Corporal William Wilson and Company I, while the rest of the men rode on to Pine Ridge. Within hours of the arrival there of the main body of the 9th Cavalry, Corporal Wilson came dashing into the reservation on horseback with the report that the wagon train had been attacked by a group of fifty Sioux warriors. With one black trooper killed and the wagon train in danger of being captured, Captain John Loud had quickly decided to send a messenger ahead to seek help. When no one else would volunteer for the dangerous mission, Wilson stepped forward to volunteer; saddling up his horse, he galloped out of the encircled wagon train and soon had ten warriors pursuing him. Despite the danger, Wilson was able to elude the warriors and make it to Pine Ridge for help. Because of Wilson's daring ride, reinforcements were soon on the way and the wagon train was saved without further loss. Later that busy day the black cavalrymen were sent to the rescue of the 7th Cavalry Regiment when it was attacked at nearby Drexel Mission.

On 1 January 1891, the first regimental order of the year issued by Major Guy Henry commended Corporal William Wilson, stating that his "soldierlike [sic] conduct is worthy of emulation and reflects great credit not only upon Corpl. Wilson but also upon the 9th Cavalry" (Schubert, p. 126). While Wilson was a hero among the men of the 9th Cavalry, it is interesting to note that it was not his officers that directly recommended him for the Medal of Honor. During this time, the medal could still be awarded based on an application by the man himself, as long as he had endorsements to support his claim, and Wilson, indeed, had plenty of support. Not only did Wilson send to army headquarters in August 1891 the regimental order that praised his deed, but also letters of support from two of his officers, including Captain Loud. Within a month, Corporal Wilson was awarded the Medal of Honor at Fort Robinson, Nebraska.

The service of the Buffalo Soldiers in the U.S. Army, men like William Wilson, WILLIAM MCBRYAR, and MOSES WILLIAMS, is not just important for the many valorous deeds they performed in combat; these skilled fighters were also instrumental in the development and acceptance in the army of blacks as professional soldiers. Their high standard of service and the honors they achieved served as proof to white army leaders then and in the future that African American soldiers could and should be an integral part of our nation's military command.

While full recognition of this fact would take years to achieve, the well-earned reputation of the Buffalo Soldiers is a legacy that has lasted to this day.

Following his service in the Pine Ridge Campaign in 1890–1891, William Wilson would continue in the army for but a short time. For reasons unknown, the previously acclaimed soldier deserted his unit for a brief time, stole a rifle, and cashed several forged checks. Though he was court-martialed for these offenses and originally sentenced to several years in prison, Wilson's sentence was overturned by a sympathetic officer and he was instead merely reduced to the rank of private. Wilson left the army for good on 5 September 1893, when he deserted after attending an army marksmanship competition in Nebraska. Instead of returning to Fort Duchesne, Utah, he only made it to Denver, Colorado, before turning around and heading back to his hometown of Hagerstown, Maryland. The army never did find William Wilson, and he thus holds the distinction of not only being the last black soldier to earn the Medal of Honor on American soil, but also the only recipient to desert from the army.

William Wilson would later marry Margaret Jackson in Hagerstown in 1898 and for a time resided with Margaret's parents, Percy and Hannah Jackson. The Wilsons had seven children, including their oldest, Percy, and a daughter named Anna. William Wilson generally supported his family by working a variety of common jobs, but was also known for his penmanship around town and the "elegant calling cards" (Schubert, p. 130) he created. Wilson died at the Washington County Hospital in Hagerstown and was buried in the Jewish Cemetery in nearby Halfway, Maryland.

FURTHER READING

Hanna, Charles W. *African American Recipients of the Medal of Honor* (2002).

Schubert, Frank N. *Black Valor: Buffalo Soldiers and the Medal of Honor, 1870–1898* (1997).

GLENN ALLEN KNOBLOCK

Wimberly, Dred (15 March 1849–16 June 1937), carpenter, public official, and legislator, was born on a cotton plantation near Tarboro in Edgecombe County, North Carolina, the son of slave parents whose names are not known. Little is known of his education before the Civil War, although he briefly attended the common schools of Tarboro after the war ended.

Wimberly was raised as a field hand, working for planter James S. Battle at the Walnut Creek plantation. After the war ended, Wimberly initially chose to remain as a wageworker on the Battle plantation, and he established a strong relationship with new overseer Kemp Plummer Battle, a future president of the University of North Carolina at Chapel Hill. Wimberly was given new responsibilities and was trusted enough to be allowed to drive delivery wagons of poultry and other produce to Raleigh, a two-day trip, alone.

A farmer and skilled carpenter, he gradually became an active member of the Republican Party, first serving on the Edgecombe County school committee during the late 1870s. In 1878 local party leaders approached him to become a candidate for one of the county's two seats in the North Carolina House of Representatives. Wimberly recalled, years later, that he felt inadequate for such a position, but finally consented under persistent pressure. "I didn't think I was qualified to hold the job," Wimberly said. "They nominated me anyhow, and I was elected" (Raleigh *News and Observer*, 17 Feb. 1935). He easily won that election, amassing a majority of just under 2,000 votes over his Democratic opponent, Archer Braswell, in the predominantly black county. One of three African Americans to represent Edgecombe County in the General Assembly of 1879–1880, he joined Clinton W. Battle in the House and Franklin Dancey in the state senate. While in the legislature, Wimberly supported public works improvements and served on two committees, those on immigration and on salaries and fees. Having resigned from his county school committee, Wimberly used his new office to continue to promote public education, later claiming to have provided the tie-breaking vote in favor of renewing state appropriations for the state university after its closure during Reconstruction, as a personal favor to Kemp Battle (Raleigh *News and Observer*, 17 Feb. 1935); there is, however, no conclusive record of Wimberly's role in such a vote. Wimberly did not seek reelection in 1880, choosing instead to return to his Tarboro farm.

In 1886 party leaders called him back to public service, renominating him for his old seat in the house of representatives. Again he won a convincing victory, serving on Edgecombe County's all-black delegation, joined by R. C. Crenshaw in the house and by Robert S. Taylor in the senate. In the 1887 North Carolina General Assembly he served on the house committees on education and finance, and he actively supported the establishment of the North Carolina College of Agriculture and Mechanical Arts at Raleigh, the state's first land-grant institution of higher education (later known as North Carolina State University).

In 1888 Wimberly was selected as the Republican Party's nominee to represent the Fifth District (Edgecombe County) in the state senate. He won the seat with little difficulty, joining house members Edward Bridgers and Daniel Justice in the 1889 General Assembly. The session was uneventful, but the increasingly racist tone of statewide elections made Wimberly the last African American senator from Edgecombe for nearly a decade. When the 1889 session ended, Wimberly chose never again to seek public office.

He did remain active in Republican politics, serving in 1900 as an alternate delegate from the "Black Second" congressional district to the Republican national convention in Philadelphia, which renominated President William McKinley and selected Theodore Roosevelt as his running mate. In early 1901 Wimberly moved to Washington, D.C., where he was given a custodial position in the U.S. House of Representatives. He lived and worked there for several years before returning to live in Rocky Mount, North Carolina, some thirty miles from his previous Tarboro farm, where he spent the remaining years of his life working as a carpenter. A devout Baptist, Wimberly was a deacon and active member of the Primitive Baptist Church of Edgecombe County.

Wimberly was married twice. On 7 October 1869, he was married to Kisiah Wimberly, by whom he had four children, including one daughter, Mary Ann, and three sons (Andrew, Frank, and James). Following her death, he married Ella Jenkins on 11 February 1891, by whom he fathered seven more children, including four sons (Allen, Jim, John, and Luther) and three daughters (Annie, Della, and Lucy).

Dred Wimberly died in Rocky Mount, nearly five decades after leaving the legislature. That same year Democratic leader Josephus Daniels, publisher of the Raleigh *News and Observer*, paid tribute to Wimberly and his nineteenth-century General Assembly colleagues, declaring that "they upheld education when no one else did. They laid the foundations for the common schools, where the schools had few or no friends" (Raleigh *News and Observer*, 19 June 1937).

In 1965 a state highway historical marker in Wimberly's honor was erected in front of the Rocky Mount house where he spent his final years.

FURTHER READING

Anderson, Eric. *Race and Politics in North Carolina, 1872–1901: The Black Second* (1981).

Obituary: Raleigh *News and Observer*, 19 June 1937.

BENJAMIN R. JUSTESEN

Winfield, Dave (3 Oct. 1951–), baseball player, was born David Mark Winfield in St. Paul, Minnesota, to Frank Winfield, an airline skycap, and Arline Winfield, an audiovisual operator. Born on the day New York Giant Bobby Thomson hit his "shot heard 'round the world" against the Brooklyn Dodgers, Winfield blossomed into a natural athlete. Developing a close bond with his mother when his father left the family, Winfield also became a fan of Minnesota's new baseball team, the Twins, and their minority stars Zoilo Versalles and Tony Oliva. He played in a number of amateur leagues with his older brother, Steve, including the American Legion.

Drafted by the Baltimore Orioles out of St. Paul's Central High School, where he graduated in 1969, Winfield opted instead to attend the University of Minnesota. As a walk-on starter for the Gophers' basketball team, he was an imposing six feet six inch power forward, helping them win the 1972 Big Ten championship. Winfield also became a star pitcher on Minnesota's baseball team and spent two summers with the semipro Alaska Goldpanners. After an injured elbow forced him to the sidelines his junior year, he split time on the mound and in the outfield his senior year. Winfield led Minnesota to the semifinals of the 1973 College World Series, where he was named most valuable player after two stellar pitching performances. He was selected by the San Diego Padres as the fourth pick of the 1973 draft, but he was also drafted in two other sports by three teams: in basketball by the NBA's Atlanta Hawks and the ABA's Utah Stars, and in football by the NFL's Minnesota Vikings, despite not playing a single game in college.

Winfield was promoted to the majors after the draft, skipping the minor leagues. He batted .277 his first year with San Diego and cracked the 20-home-run barrier in 1974. He steadily improved over his eight seasons with the Padres, making the All-Star Game for the first time in 1977. In that same year Winfield started the David M. Winfield Foundation in San Diego, which provided health services, scholarships, drug awareness programs, and free tickets to underprivileged children.

Winfield became a bona fide star in 1979, when he hit thirty-four home runs, led the league in runs batted in (RBIs), and won his first of seven Gold Gloves. After free agency negotiations with a number of teams following the 1980 season, he landed with the New York Yankees. His agent and close

Dave Winfield, the New York Yankees left fielder, bats against the Cleveland Indians in New York City on 23 September 1982. (AP Images.)

friend, Al Frohman, drew up the deal with George Steinbrenner, tricking the Yankee owner into signing a contract with complicated cost-of-living increases. Steinbrenner, thinking he was signing Winfield to a $16 million deal, ended up paying the slugger $23 million over ten years.

Though Winfield led the Yankees in most batting categories in the strike-shortened 1981 season, he was publicly chastised by Steinbrenner for his sub-par postseason play. Getting just one hit in the World Series loss to the Los Angeles Dodgers, Winfield was dubbed "Mr. May" by Steinbrenner early the next year, an overt comparison to "Mr. October," the clutch-hitting Reggie Jackson.

During the off-season Jackson left the Yankees to join the California Angels, and Winfield responded to Steinbrenner's challenge during the 1982 season by hitting 37 home runs, driving in 106 RBIs, winning his first American League Gold Glove, and being named to his sixth All-Star team. Staying with the Yankees, Winfield remained one of the best players in the league, tallying at least 97 RBIs each season after 1981 and intimidating base runners with his powerful arm in right field. Nevertheless, the stigma Steinbrenner attached stayed with him; the New York fans and media eventually turned on Winfield for not winning a championship. Despite Winfield's success, "the Boss" sought to rid himself of the pricey slugger, even violating their contract by stopping prearranged $300,000 payments to Winfield's charity organization. Following the 1983 season, when Winfield hit 32 home runs and posted 116 RBIs, Steinbrenner noted that he did not hit for a high average. In 1984 Winfield adjusted his swing and stayed in the batting race all season—against teammate and fan favorite Don Mattingly, who eventually won by three points.

Winfield endured personal trouble in New York as well. Sandra Renfro, a flight attendant with whom he had had a daughter (Shanel), filed a common-law marriage suit against him in 1985; meanwhile gambling accusations and his foundation's financial problems severely hurt his reputation; and, perhaps most importantly, his mother's health was failing. Winfield arranged to marry his longtime girlfriend, Tonya Turner, in February 1988, just eight months before he lost his mother to breast cancer. Winfield would have twins with Tonya in 1994, Davie Mark II and Arielle Arline. Winfield's feud with the Yankee owner exploded when Steinbrenner agreed to pay a gambler, Howard Spira, $40,000 for information about him. After the story broke in 1990, Spira was indicted on extortion charges and Steinbrenner was suspended for two years from the Yankees' day-to-day operations by Commissioner Fay Vincent. That same year, after sitting out 1989 with a herniated disk, Winfield was traded to the California Angels. The outfielder returned to form, earning the *Sporting News*'s Comeback Player of the Year Award and hitting 47 home runs over two seasons with the Angels.

Winfield signed with the Toronto Blue Jays for the 1992 season and became their cleanup hitter. Once vilified in Canada for accidentally hitting and killing a seagull during warm-up throws against the Blue Jays in 1983, Winfield became a fan favorite. In the World Series, his two-run double in the eleventh inning of Game Six secured Toronto (and Canada) its first championship. Two years later, as the designated hitter for his hometown Minnesota Twins, Winfield received the Roberto Clemente Award for his community service. He finished his career with the Cleveland Indians, retiring after an off-season shoulder surgery in February 1996.

Winfield stayed busy in retirement, continuing his ownership of numerous Burger King franchises, starting a lighting company for commercial buildings, serving on various boards, and working as a senior adviser for the Padres. He was elected to the Hall of Fame in 2001, gaining entry on his first attempt.

One of the finer all-around athletes to play the game, Winfield was also a successful businessman, community representative, and advocate for equal hiring within the sport. Following prejudiced comments by Dodgers executive Al Campanis in a 1987 *Nightline* interview, Winfield joined a coalition determined to see more minority representation in the sport's front offices. A year and a half later Bill White was named the National League president, becoming the highest-ranking black executive in American sports.

FURTHER READING

Winfield, Dave, with Tom Parker. *Winfield: A Player's Life* (1988).

Doctor, Ken, ed. *Dave Winfield: 3,000 and Counting* (1993).

Durso, Joseph. "Dave Winfield Finds Baseball and Business the Perfect Mix," *New York Times* (9 Feb. 1981).

Reilly, Rick. "I Feel a Whole Lot Better Now," *Sports Illustrated* (29 June 1992).

ADAM W. GREEN

Winfield, Hemsley (20 Apr. 1907–15 Jan. 1934), actor and dancer, was born in Yonkers, New York, the son of Osbourne Winfield, a civil engineer, and Jeraldine (maiden name unknown but perhaps Hemsley), an actress and playwright. Educated at public schools, Winfield showed an early interest in theater, perhaps prompted by his mother's involvement. In 1924 he received his first role in a major production, Eugene O'Neill's *All God's Chillun Got Wings*, performed by the Provincetown Players and starring a rising PAUL ROBESON. Winfield acted in other productions in the 1920s but soon turned to producing and directing. In April 1927 he put on his own play, *On*. The play was not critically received, but its production is indicative of the growing little theater movement of the early twentieth century, during which community and small theaters attracted larger audiences and offered greater and more varied opportunities to aspiring actors, writers, and directors. Winfield continued in this arena in 1928 and 1929, directing different versions of the popular *Salome*—once even playing the role of Salome when his female lead failed to show up—and collaborating with his mother in a production called *Wade in de Water* in 1929.

Around this same time he began taking dance lessons, and this led him to shift his attention from theater to dance.

On 6 March 1931 Winfield's newly formed dance company, the Bronze Ballet Plastique, performed at the Saunders Trade School in Yonkers in a benefit for the Colored Citizens Unemployment and Relief Committee. This was Winfield's first collaboration with African American dancer Edna Guy, who had received much of her training from Ruth St. Denis, one of the founders of concert dance in America. Guy and Winfield went on to create the New Negro Art Theatre Dance Group, which placed itself by name and mission in the artistic resurgence now known as the Harlem Renaissance.

It was within this highly creative and receptive environment that, on 29 April 1931, Winfield and Guy performed what they called the "First Negro Dance Recital in America." Playing to an overflowing audience in the Theater at the top of the Chanin Building on Forty-second Street, the innovative duo hoped to initiate a new tradition in African American dance separate from the swing and jitterbugging that characterized Harlem's dance halls. Concert dance provided a new means of expression, one that was more profound than the entertaining theatrics of social dancing for which African Americans were thought to be naturally talented. Winfield and Guy sought to place African Americans within the emerging artistic movement of modern dance, which was then dominated by the austere and serious works of Martha Graham and Doris Humphrey. The influential *New York Times* dance critic John Martin, recognizing the value of their purpose, described the performance as the "outstanding novelty of the dance season." In a further exploration of Winfield's group, Martin called Winfield's choreography "crude" but supported his effort to establish an African American tradition in concert dance that neither mimicked European traditions nor restricted itself to what short-sighted whites delimited as "Negro art" (*New York Times*, 14 Feb. 1932).

Throughout 1931 and 1932 Winfield and Guy performed this program of the New Negro Art Theatre Dance Group in settings around New York City. In December 1932 they were included in a large benefit for the Dancers Club, a newly founded organization to aid struggling dancers, at the Mecca Temple, where they performed alongside the famous dancers Ruth St. Denis, Charles Weidman, and Fred Astaire. Soon after, Winfield received the opportunity to choreograph the opera *The Emperor Jones* at the Metropolitan Opera in New York. Dancing the role of the Witch Doctor, Winfield became the first African American to perform at the Metropolitan. His choreography and performance received praise for depicting authentic sounds and movement of the African jungle. He was thus fast accomplishing the establishment of a concert dance tradition for African Americans.

In October 1933 Winfield and noted African American sculptor AUGUSTA SAVAGE led a discussion on the topic "What Shall the Negro Dance About?" at a forum sponsored by the Workers Dance League, an organization associated with the Communist Party, held at the YWCA in Harlem on 138th Street. Fittingly, the forum recognized the social as well as artistic implications of African Americans' producing their own art and also considered the political relevance of such actions. There is no evidence that Winfield was a member of the Communist Party, but he was keenly aware of the injustices facing African Americans, and he used modern dance to promote new and broader perspectives of African Americans and their capabilities. Unfortunately for the movement he initiated, Winfield's artistic responses to the question "What Shall the Negro Dance About?" were cut short; soon after the forum, he died of pneumonia in New York City, at the tragically young age of twenty-six.

Despite his premature death, Winfield had made startling progress. Others who had been inspired by him, in particular Edna Guy, took up his mission of creating an African American concert dance tradition, and by the late 1930s African Americans, led by the dancer-choreographers KATHERINE DUNHAM and PEARL PRIMUS, were making significant contributions to concert dance.

FURTHER READING
Emery, Lynne Fauley. *Black Dance from 1619 to Today*, rev. ed. (1988).
Long, Richard. *The Black Tradition in American Dance* (1989).
Thorpe, Edward. *Black Dance* (1990).
Obituaries: *New York Amsterdam News*, 17 Jan. 1934; *New York Times*, 16 Jan. 1934.
This entry is taken from the *American National Biography* and is published here with the permission of the American Council of Learned Societies.

JULIA L. FOULKES

Winfield, Paul (22 May 1941–7 Mar. 2004), stage and screen actor, was born in Los Angeles, California, to Lois Beatrice Edwards, a garment worker. His mother married Clarence Winfield when Paul was

eight, at which time he adopted the name Paul Edward Winfield. The family moved to Oregon for a brief period, and while there Winfield saw *Home of the Brave* (1949), a film that portrayed African Americans in a different light than did most movies of the late 1940s and early 1950s. JAMES EDWARDS's leading part as an African American soldier in a mixed-race outfit revolutionized Winfield's thinking and prompted him to consider acting as a career. The family returned to Los Angeles, where Winfield enrolled in Manual Arts High School and became proficient in acting and music. He performed in the Speech and Drama Teachers Association Drama Festival and won the top prize for three consecutive years. As a result he received a scholarship to Yale University.

The scholarship was a great honor; however, Winfield was not sure of how he would be accepted in a predominantly white Ivy League environment and instead chose a two-year scholarship at the University of Portland. He continued his studies by enrolling in classes at various universities over the years, including Stanford and UCLA. Winfield left his studies in 1964 to pursue his acting career, just a few credits short of completing his degree.

In 1964 Winfield received his first break when he was cast in LeRoi Jones's (AMIRI BARAKA) play *The Dutchman and the Toilet*. Soon after, he signed a contract with Columbia Pictures and appeared in small parts in films like *Who's Minding the Mint?* (1967). It was following such roles in film and television that Winfield was cast as DIAHANN CARROLL's boyfriend in the television show, *Julia* (1968). The show, which focused on the life of a widowed nurse (played by Carroll) and her young son (Marc Copage), was the catalyst that created a new trend in broadcast television and opened doors for African American performers on the small screen. Around this time Winfield also appeared in *The Lost Man* (1969), opposite SIDNEY POITIER. This was Winfield's first major film role.

Throughout these early years Winfield remained actively involved in the stage, first with the Stanford Repertory Theatre and then, after 1969, with the Inner City Cultural Center Theater in Los Angeles. Winfield's acclaim was bolstered in 1972 when he starred in the film *Sounder*, opposite CICELY TYSON. His performance earned him an Academy Award nomination for Best Actor—at that time he was only the third African American to receive that honor. The film, set in southern Louisiana during the Depression, is the story of a sharecropper who is jailed for stealing food to feed his family.

In 1975 Winfield relocated to San Francisco, where he began a committed relationship with Charles Gillan Jr., a television set designer. They remained together until Gillan's death in 2002.

After returning to Los Angeles, Winfield was offered many film and television roles. One of the most notable was that of civil rights activist Dr. MARTIN LUTHER KING JR. in the television miniseries *King*. The series also featured performances by Cicely Tyson, Roscoe Lee Brown, OSSIE DAVIS, AL FREEMAN JR., and Dr. King's daughter, Yolanda King. Winfield was nominated for an Emmy. Next, he appeared in *Roots: The Next Generations*, Georg Stanford Brown and John Erman's 1979 sequel to ALEX HALEY's *Roots*. His Emmy hopes became a reality in 1995 when his guest appearance on the series *Picket Fences* was honored. Alex Haley's *Queen* and *Scarlett* were television productions in which Winfield was featured, as well as HBO's *Tyson* (1995), in which he portrayed the boxing promoter DON KING.

In his later years Winfield performed in a variety of films and television series. He appeared in such films as *Star Trek II: The Wrath of Khan* (1982), *The Terminator* (1984), *Dennis the Menace* (1993), *Mars Attacks!* (1996), and *Second to Die* (2002). Winfield's television performances included *Star Trek: The Next Generation*, *Babylon 5*, and *Touched By an Angel*. Additionally, he provided voice for a number of animated series, including *The Simpsons*, *Spider-Man*, *Batman Beyond*, *The Charmings*, and *The Magic School Bus*. He continued his involvement with the stage, appearing in a number of productions of Shakespeare's plays, including *Richard III* and *Othello*, and on Broadway in the comedy *Checkmates* (1988), in which he had the starring role.

Aside from acting, Winfield played cello and fostered several hobbies that included breeding champion dogs and renovating homes. After suffering a prolonged hospitalization following a diabetic coma, he became an advocate for nutrition and health education in the African American community. While openly devoting time and efforts to promoting cultural diversity and acceptance in the entertainment arena, and though he lived in a committed relationship, Winfield did not publicly spend time campaigning for gay rights.

Besides his numerous performance nominations and awards, including a NAACP Image Award, Winfield was honored for his civic work by the Congress of Racial Equality (CORE) and the California Federation of Black Leadership, among others. Winfield died in Los Angeles of a heart attack.

FURTHER READING
Dictionary of Blacks in the Performing Arts (1990).
Who's Who among African Americans (1998–1999).
SIBYL COLLINS WILSON

Winfrey, Oprah (29 Jan. 1954–), talk show host, actor, and entrepreneur, was born Oprah Gail Winfrey in Kosciusko, Mississippi, to eighteen-year-old Vernita Lee, and Vernon Winfrey, a twenty-year-old soldier. Vernita intended to call the baby "Orpah," after the biblical figure, but accepted "Oprah" when the name was misspelled by a clerk. Shortly after her daughter's birth, Vernita left Mississippi for Milwaukee, Wisconsin, leaving her newborn under the watchful eye of Oprah's paternal grandparents, Hattie Mae Bullock and Earless Lee, who were pig farmers. In 1960 Oprah went to Milwaukee to join her mother, who was working as a maid and who had given birth to a second daughter, Patricia. Another child, Jeffrey, followed a few years later, and Vernita struggled to support herself and her three young children. Bright and precocious, Oprah skipped several grades in elementary school but, despite her siblings and her early academic achievements, she felt the same loneliness and isolation she had experienced in Mississippi. Her outlet became performing and public speaking. Oprah spent fourth grade with her father and his wife, Zelma, in Nashville, Tennessee, but returned to Milwaukee after the school year ended.

The traumatic events of the next several years had lifelong consequences. Vernita's Milwaukee apartment was increasingly crowded with visitors and, at one point, Oprah shared her bed with a fourteen-year-old cousin who sexually molested her. Shortly after, she was sexually abused by her father's brother. Behavioral problems soon surfaced, and while she was performing well academically— she won a scholarship to an all-white high school in suburban Milwaukee—Oprah's behavior became increasingly rebellious. By age fourteen, she was running away and stealing from her mother, and she had become sexually promiscuous. Failing to get her daughter admitted to a home for wayward teens, Vernita sent Oprah to live with Vernon and Zelma Winfrey in Nashville. A few months after her arrival, Oprah gave birth to a son, who died several weeks after delivery. She has never revealed the name of the father.

Vernon and Zelma, who had no children of their own, insisted on Oprah's obedience. Oprah, or Gail as she was known in high school, thrived under her father's strict discipline and high expectations.

Oprah Winfrey relaxes in her studio office following a morning broadcast in Chicago, Illinois, on 18 December 1985. (AP Images.)

She excelled in school, made friends, was elected senior class president, and got a part-time job reading the news at WVOL, a predominantly black local radio station. In 1971 Oprah graduated from Nashville High School and won a local beauty pageant, Miss Fire Prevention, after which she enrolled at Tennessee State University. While in college she worked evenings at WTVF-TV in Nashville.

In 1976, several credits shy of graduation, Winfrey left Tennessee State for a job anchoring the evening news at WJZ-TV, Baltimore's ABC affiliate. Promoting their new hire, the station peppered billboards with the question, "What's an Oprah?" WJZ management itself wasn't quite sure, and attempted a makeover, sending Winfrey to a voice coach and to a salon, where she lost her hair to a botched permanent. Having arrived with little technical training and virtually no journalistic background or education, Winfrey was ill prepared for the constraints of objective news reporting. Within a year, she was moved off the news desk to *People Are Talking*, a morning talk show where she could practice her more emotional and subjective journalistic style. In this format, Winfrey found her niche. She remained as co-host of the show until

1983, when she was hired as host of *A. M. Chicago* at WLS-TV, Chicago's ABC affiliate. Within months *A. M. Chicago*'s ratings surpassed those of the popular *The Phil Donahue Show*. Winfrey had turned a faltering show into a hit.

In 1985 *A. M. Chicago* was expanded from a half-hour to a one-hour format and re-launched as *The Oprah Winfrey Show*. That same year Winfrey starred with DANNY GLOVER and WHOOPI GOLDBERG in Steven Spielberg's adaptation of ALICE WALKER's novel *The Color Purple*, earning both Oscar and Golden Globe nominations. Winfrey's meteoric rise began in 1986 when *The Oprah Winfrey Show* went into national syndication. Within six months the show was the highest-rated talk show and the third-highest-rated program in syndication. Within a decade, twenty-four talk shows had followed *The Oprah Winfrey Show* into national syndication.

Winfrey's syndication deal placed her in charge of her own public relations, an indication of her savvy approach. Indeed, news stories from the mid-1980s set the tone for much of Winfrey's future press coverage, highlighting her ease on camera and her open, hands-on approach with guests and audiences. Reports also focused on the biographical details of her life, including revelations of sexual abuse, issues with regard to her weight, and the influence of such role models as SOJOURNER TRUTH and MADAME C. J. WALKER. Proof that Winfrey's celebrity was solidifying came in December 1986 when she was interviewed by Mike Wallace on *60 Minutes*. Her cameo appearance in *Throw Momma from the Train* in 1987 was the first of several films in which she played herself.

Winfrey formed Harpo Productions (Oprah spelled backwards) in 1986 and acquired ownership of *The Oprah Winfrey Show* in 1988, the same year she was named broadcaster of the year by the International Television and Radio Society. Harpo Entertainment Group, chaired by Winfrey and headquartered in an 88,000-square-foot production facility, now includes production, film, video, and print divisions. In 1989 Winfrey combined her talents by producing and starring in *The Women of Brewster Place*, a television movie based on the book by GLORIA NAYLOR, and about which the *New York Times* commented, "There hadn't been this kind of assembly of black actors for any TV productions since *Roots*" (12 Mar. 1989). Under the umbrella "Oprah Winfrey Presents," Winfrey has produced, and occasionally starred in, the television movies *There Are No Children Here* (1993); *Before Women Had Wings* (1997); *David and Lisa* (1998), starring SIDNEY POITIER; *The Wedding* (1998), based on the novel by DOROTHY WEST; *Tuesdays with Morrie* (1999); and *Amy and Isabelle* (2001).

In 1998 Winfrey returned to the silver screen in Jonathan Demme's film adaptation of TONI MORRISON's Pulitzer Prize–winning 1987 book *Beloved*. Winfrey, who produced the film, starred as Sethe, opposite Beah Richards and DANNY GLOVER. "What I love about the story of *Beloved*," Winfrey wrote in her 1998 book *Journey to Beloved*, "is that it allows you to *feel* what slavery was like; it doesn't just intellectually *show* you the picture" (19).

Despite her various projects, *The Oprah Winfrey Show* remains the heart of Winfrey's empire. The highest-rated talk show for eighteen consecutive seasons, it has earned thirty-five Emmy Awards. Each week 21 million American viewers watch the show, which is broadcast in 109 countries. Twenty-five thousand letters arrive at the Harpo offices each week, and the show earns $260 million a year in advertising sales.

Statistics only hint at the range and depth of Winfrey's influence on American culture. Through programs showcasing "real people" discussing heretofore "private" issues before a live audience, Winfrey and her many imitators changed both popular debates and private attitudes by introducing such new or previously ignored topics as women's empowerment, talk therapy, and new age self-help into the mainstream. Because of Winfrey, these revolutions *were* televised and, certainly, altered as a result. It seemed that the personal stories and voices of everyday Americans, especially women, were being heard for the first time. The show also engendered a revolution in television itself, changing syndication and advertising patterns, expanding the role of women in the medium, and bringing about the explosion of talk-television, which paved the way for "women's programming," celebrity brand-naming, and reality, home, and how-to TV. From the beginning, Winfrey's unique approach to broadcasting, drawing on forerunners such as Donahue and Barbara Walters, rested on her success with on-air guests and audience members. Winfrey's wit and easy, conversational style, along with her empathetic manner, endeared her to audiences. "She's like the one friend you trust," explained a woman waiting in line at *The Oprah Winfrey Show*, "the one you know has good taste" (*Los Angeles Times*, 9 Mar. 1997). Winfrey has both fomented and served Americans' growing interest in celebrity and good taste, consistently booking top musicians, Hollywood stars, politicians, television personalities, and cultural figures on her show. Notable black figures, such as MICHAEL JORDAN, MICHAEL JACKSON, QUINCY JONES, BILL COSBY, and MAYA ANGELOU were celebrated and placed on equal footing with white stars. Such was the power of Winfrey's show that an on-air appearance often catapulted ordinary guests into the realm of minor celebrity.

Over the years, Winfrey transformed herself from a poor, female, and overweight outsider to the ultimate insider—rich, powerful, popular, and connected. Worldwide audiences are kept abreast of her lavish lifestyle (she owns several homes, including a $50 million estate in Montecito, California) and the machinations of her private life, especially her long-time romantic relationship with businessman Stedman Graham Jr. Tabloid reports also chronicled her often tumultuous family relationships, stemming in part from her sister's revelations of Oprah's past, and Oprah's rift with her brother, who died of AIDS in 1989.

Winfrey features two Oprah personas on her show. "Celebrity Oprah" gives audiences behind-the-scenes access to her life and celebrity friends, albeit in a carefully selected way. In 2002 she began airing a daily half-hour show, *Oprah after the Show*. "Everyday Oprah," however, struggles with the same problems as her audience. Issues of importance to Winfrey off-air, chiefly topics relating to weight, body image, and self-esteem, are consistent themes on-air. Winfrey's 15 November 1988 show, during which she revealed how she lost sixty-seven pounds on a liquid diet, won a 16.4 rating. Winfrey soon regained weight, and she shared that fact with audiences. In the early 1990s she hired a chef and a trainer and lost seventy pounds. Winfrey parlayed her weight-loss success into a minor industry, beginning with the 1996 publication of *Make the Connection: Ten Steps to a Better Body and a Better Life*.

Most pointedly with her popular—and legally trademarked—segments "Get with the Program," "Remembering Your Spirit," and "Change Your Life TV," Winfrey uses her show as a forum for group therapy, but also as a bully pulpit. Most significantly, she took on the issues of child and sexual abuse, revealing on-air in 1990 that she had been molested as a child. The following year, she testified before Congress in support of the National Child Protection Act, which established a national database of convicted child abusers. "Oprah's Bill," as the legislation came to be known, was signed into law by President Bill Clinton in 1993.

Winfrey, who chairs the Oprah Winfrey Foundation and the Oprah Winfrey Scholars Program, brought her philanthropic endeavors to the air with the establishment of Oprah's Angel Network in 1997. When she asked viewers to send in their spare change, the show raised $3.5 million. The Angel Network went on to raise a total of $12 million and established the "Use Your Life Award," which provides $100,000 to individuals whose work benefits the broader community. Recently, Winfrey has shown a new interest in Africa, establishing Christmas Kindness South Africa 2002, and donating $10 million to build the Oprah Winfrey Leadership Academy for Girls South Africa, about which she told *TV Guide*, "I'm going to teach classes in leadership and life lessons from Chicago via satellite. I am all about girl power!" (4 Oct. 2003).

One measure of her influence was seen in 1996 when Winfrey remarked off-the-cuff during a show on mad cow disease, "It has just stopped me cold from eating another hamburger." After what the plaintiffs dubbed the "Oprah crash of 1996," which saw cattle prices plummet, a group of Texas cattle ranchers sued her. In 1998, following a jury's ruling in her favor, *Time* magazine wrote, "The winner's

Oprah. She's the most powerful woman in the United States. Laws be damned" (12 Jan. 1998).

If her criticism could send a market into decline, Winfrey's recommendation could also send a stock soaring. Such was the case with Oprah's Book Club, launched in 1996. Each of the book selections became instant best sellers. In recognition of her unprecedented influence on the publishing industry, Winfrey was presented with the National Book Foundation's Fiftieth Anniversary Gold Medal.

Winfey has evolved from television personality to celebrity to media mogul to synergistic pioneer. In addition to the relationship between Oprah's Book Club and Harpo Productions, which owns the rights to many of the books selected, Winfrey has introduced a host of projects with the "Oprah" brand name. In 1995 "Oprah Online," a collaboration with AOL, debuted. Three years later she cofounded Oxygen Media Inc., a cable network offering shows inspired by *The Oprah Winfrey Show* material. Another outgrowth of the show, the syndicated series *The Dr. Phil Show*, was launched in 2002. In 2000 Winfrey expanded into a new medium with the wildly successful *O, The Oprah Magazine*, copublished with Hearst Magazines. Winfrey owns a stake in Granite Broadcasting, a media company that owns eleven television stations. In 1999 Winfrey brought her entrepreneurial lessons into the classroom, coteaching "Dynamics of Leadership" with Stedman Graham at the J. L. Kellogg Graduate School of Management at Northwestern University.

Winfrey's major honors include a George Foster Peabody Individual Achievement Award, Lifetime Achievement and Bob Hope Humanitarian Award Emmys from the National Academy of Television Arts and Sciences, and an International Radio and Television Society Foundation Gold Medal award. In 2003 *Forbes* magazine disclosed that Winfrey, the world's richest entertainer after Steven Spielberg, had become the first African American woman billionaire. Winfrey constantly tops lists of the most influential, popular, or powerful people in America. As Fran Lebowitz told *Time* magazine in 1996, "Oprah is probably the greatest media influence on the adult population. She is almost a religion" (17 June 1996).

For years on her talk show Winfrey had given audience members generous gifts, often distributed in gift bags and hidden under their seats. An extravagant September 2004 giveaway turned into a public relations disaster when Winfrey gave each of the 276 members of her studio audience a new car. Because the cars were technically prizes and not gifts, the audience members, who had all been selected for that episode because of difficult circumstances in their lives, were responsible for paying as much as $7,000 in taxes on the cars.

In 2004, 2005, and 2006 *Time* magazine included Winfrey on its 100 Most Influential People in the World list. She was also named to the NAACP Hall of Fame in 2005.

Oprah's Book Club, having focused solely on fiction since it began in 1996, introduced its first work of contemporary nonfiction in 2005: *A Million Little Pieces* by James Frey. After a Web site called *The Smoking Gun* revealed parts of the memoir about the author's struggle with drug addiction to be fabricated, Winfrey publicly chastised Frey in a face-to-face interview on her show, telling him that he had "duped" her and millions of readers. As a result of the controversy, the book's publishers, including Random House, which had initially rejected Frey's book when he had shopped it as a work of fiction, publicly stated that future editions of the book would be issued with a disclaimer acknowledging that portions of the book were not factual.

Winfrey was profiled on PBS's February 2006 special *African American Lives*, Professor HENRY LOUIS GATES JR.'s exploration of the ancestry of nine prominent African Americans, including musician QUINCY JONES, comedian WHOOPI GOLDBERG, and Gates himself. The interest generated in Winfrey's background by *African American Lives* led to the follow-up special *Oprah's Roots* in January 2007, in which genealogical and scientific research turned up Winfrey's descent from the Kpelle people of Liberia.

That same month the Oprah Winfrey Leadership Academy for Girls opened in Henley-on-Klip, South Africa. Over five years, Winfrey used $40 million of her own fortune to fund the school, located near Johannesburg. The 152 seventh- and eighth-grade girls of the inaugural class, all from impoverished backgrounds across South Africa, were personally selected by Winfrey to attend the school based on what she determined was their future leadership potential.

In May 2007, during an appearance on CNN's *Larry King Live*, Winfrey endorsed Democratic senator BARACK OBAMA in his run for president. Winfrey, who for many years had denied any political aspirations of her own, had never before publicly endorsed a candidate in any election.

More than a household name, or even a brand name, Oprah has become part of American language itself, as critics write about the "Oprahization" or "Oprahfication" of American culture. Although she will continue to appear each day on television, at least through the 2007–2008 season, she can rarely be found in front of a small screen; Winfrey rarely watches television, complaining, "It promotes false values" (*Life*, Sept. 1997).

In May 2011, after 25 years, the final episode of *The Oprah Winfrey Show* aired.

FURTHER READING

Lowe, Janet. *Oprah Winfrey Speaks: Insight from the World's Most Influential Voice* (1998)

Mair, George. *Oprah Winfrey: The Real Story* (1994)

LISA E. RIVO

JULIE WOLF

Winkfield, Jimmy (1882–1974), jockey and trainer, was born in Chilesburg, Kentucky, the youngest of seventeen children in a family of sharecroppers. He first worked at the racetrack shining shoes and made his way to stable hand, then exercise rider, and finally jockey. At the age of sixteen he was riding in races. Nicknamed "Wink," he secured a place in racing history by age twenty-two for winning the Kentucky Derby back-to-back: in 1901 on His Eminence and in 1902 on Alan-A-Dale. During his career he won an amazing twenty-six hundred races. He also was a talented horse trainer in his later years.

In 1904 Winkfield fled the United States (rumor had it that he had a falling out with a racehorse owner) and raced in Russia. There he continued his winning career, taking the Russian and Moscow derbies more than once. He scored victories in other races in Germany, Russia, and Poland. Winkfield's success in Russia was curtailed when the Bolshevik Revolution broke out in 1917. He fled to France, continued to race, and eventually retired in 1930.

Winkfield next turned to raising and training horses on his farm in France. He briefly returned to the United States during World War II, when the Nazis took his farm. Following the war he returned to France, where he died. In 2004 he was inducted into the Hall of Fame at the National Museum of Racing.

FURTHER READING

Hotaling, Edward. *The Great Black Jockeys* (1999)

Renau, Lynn S. *Jockeys, Belles, and Bluegrass Kings: The Official Guide to Kentucky Racing* (1995)

Saunders, James Robert, and Monica Renae Saunders. *Black Winning Jockeys in the Kentucky Derby* (2003).

KELLY M. JORDAN

Winn, Mississippi (31 Mar. 1897–14 Jan. 2011), super-centenarian, was born in Benton, Louisiana, the tiny parish seat of Bossier Parish in the northwest corner of the state. Her parents were Mack and Ellen Winn, who are believed to have been born into slavery and after Emancipation were probably subsistence farmers. Winn was the thirteenth of fifteen children.

Not much is known of Winn's quiet life. It is likely that she did not attend school, or at least not for very long. She never married, but she did have a child out of wedlock. The child died while still young, however, and apparently Winn never had another. Throughout her long life, she worked as a domestic and cook in and around Benton. Her sunny demeanor won her the nickname "Sweetie."

What makes Winn so remarkable was her advanced age. At the time of her death, she is believed to have been the oldest African American and the seventh-oldest person then living anywhere in the world. She was—as far as records can show, at least—the one-hundredth-oldest known human being. As of the early twenty-first century, statistics suggest that only one in five million people live to reach the age of 110. The majority of them are women.

Winn spent much of her life in Benton. Sometime around the late 1950s she relocated to Seattle, Washington, to live with a younger sister. However, upon that sister's death in 1975, she returned to Louisiana and took up residence in Shreveport, which is where she lived for the rest of her life. On her 110th birthday, the mayor of Shreveport declared a day (31 March) in her honor, and she became something of a cause célèbre for state and national politicians, attracting the notice and praise of President BARACK OBAMA and Louisiana governor Bobby Jindal, among many others. Winn lived on her own until the age of 103, only then moving into an assisted-living facility. There she lived another ten years. At the time of her death, she was thought to be one of only two Americans whose parents had been slaves, the second being Mamie Reardon of South Carolina. Reportedly, however, the history of slavery in Winn's family is a subject she notably refused to discuss.

FURTHER READING

Pollard, Leslie J. *Complaint to the Lord: Historical Perspectives on the African American Elderly* (1996).
Obituary: *Los Angeles Times*, 15 Jan. 2011.

JASON PHILIP MILLER

Mississippi Winn poses for a photo for a gerontology studies group on 19 July 2010 in Shreveport, Louisiana. (AP Images.)

Winston, Isabella (3 Feb. 1888–13 Sept. 1971), huckster, vendor, and entrepreneur, was born Isabella Wallace in Louisa County, Virginia, south of the town of Gordonsville, the daughter of McKaylor Wallace and Maria (Coleman) Wallace. Little information about her background is available. She credits her mother with having used business profits to build their first house, which burned in the 1920s. Following this tragedy, Winston's mother built another home farther from the road and spent much of her life caring for her livestock and attending church. Isabella married Douglas Winston—the exact date of her marriage is not known—and was widowed by age thirty-seven with ten children.

As head of household, Isabella Winston bore the responsibility for feeding her large family. Following a generational tradition, she made her living as a "waiter carrier" (as they called themselves), meeting local trains and serving the passengers fried chicken and other foods. In later years, sharing her memories with the local newspaper, the *Orange County (VA) Review*, Winston described groups of African American women who walked to town with baskets of fried chicken and other cooked food stacked on trays that they skillfully carried on their heads. In those days, she recalled, "wings and a gizzard brought five cents" (*Orange County Review*, 9 July 1970). Unlike the customers, however, Winston's children had fewer choices. She indicated that it was not until her children were much older that they knew other parts of the chicken existed besides wings, backs, and feet. Clearly the best pieces were reserved for her commercial enterprise so her children could have life's necessities.

Little is known about the sum of her economic activities, but Winston was far from anomalous. In Gordonsville sources suggest that black women contributed significantly to the town's commercial economy and social welfare. The waiter carriers entered the center of commercial activity as early as 1870, prior to the town's incorporation. It was a time when the small town marked the junction of the Orange and Alexandria Railroad and the Chesapeake and Ohio Railroad. Amid the bustle of emerging hotels, shops, and businesses, this group of women catered to hungry passengers, who purchased meals through the open windows of their coaches. The census records of 1910 provide a basis for identifying the other women who served as "chicken" or "snack" vendors. Among them were Laura Swift, Adeline Daniel, Penny Daniel, Frances Taylor, Laura Washington, Eliza Vest, Henrietta Broadus, and Mary Bowles. Many of these women used their business profits to purchase homes and to start new enterprises. Hattie Edwards recalled that when she eventually left her trade at the train platform, she transferred these street vending skills to Hattie's Inn, a small eatery in the African American section of Gordonsville.

These kinds of market activities were not limited to Gordonsville, Virginia. Countless locales in North Carolina, South Carolina, Georgia, Louisiana, and Mississippi attest to a similar presence of black women selling chicken, rolls, and other foods at train stations and on roadsides. During the Civil War, artists, writers, and soldiers mentioned the presence of "mulatto" or "Negro" women surrounding their cars with sweet potato pie and other foods for sale. Travel guides are another source for uncovering the lives of ordinary women who made their living in the invisible economy. In Corinth, Mississippi, Julia Brown and her daughter Lizzie built their trade on the passenger train traffic by selling fried chicken and fruit pie lunches.

The waiter carriers employed similar aggressive techniques to combat municipal ordinances and health regulations that sought to suppress their limited prosperity. At the railroad crossing, passengers were the source of much competition and the ultimate demise of the waiter carriers. In order to compete, the waiter carriers resorted to selling their wares outside the legal selling area at the train stops. This system of sale continued unabated despite the advent of the dining car and the invention of the train vestibule. Eventually the waiter carriers were driven out of business by licensing regulations and the modernization of trains, including air-conditioned railroad cars with windows that would not open. The legacy of these women was so legendary among many regular travelers that one writer dubbed Gordonsville "the chicken capital of the universe" (*The Free-Lance State of Fredericksburg*, "Area News," 13 Sept. 1976).

Although clearly an exaggeration, this culinary title reflects a history of African American female entrepreneurs that had its origins in early American slavery, when Africans became involved in selling and trading foodstuffs in local markets. The foundation for these economic ventures can be traced back to western African women, who were experts in trading and bartering. In addition to the other areas in which African women claimed proficiency, they also excelled in food production, preparation, and presentation. In the South, where farming and planting were the order of the day, some enslaved black women carved out time amid the arduous plantation labor demands to participate in the marketplace economy. In many of the largest southern cities—such as Richmond, Nashville, Charleston, and New Orleans—as well as in whistle-stop towns, black women could be seen working the public markets with their baked goods, produce, and other foodstuffs. So adept were they at negotiating and bartering that their skills often drew the attention and ire of local whites because they dominated this sector of the economy. According to the *South Carolina Gazette*, one antebellum writer complained that almost on a daily basis black country women could be found huckstering goods such as poultry, fruit, and eggs "from morn till night, *buy[ing]* and *sell[ing]* on *their own accounts*" (Olwell, 101). Their incorrigible behavior of exorbitantly pricing goods to "get so much more for themselves" (Olwell, 102) was seldom thwarted by the local laws that sought to prevent these enterprises from succeeding.

In the broader context of entrepreneurship, these mostly small-scale transactions have not been given much recognition. This is but one of the many reasons it is difficult to find much information on Winston and other waiter carriers. Little is known about their participation in the economic growth of their communities. In small towns and locales where the local economy is dependent on barter and exchange transactions, the contributions of these women would not have gone unnoticed. Their purchases of large amounts of chicken, bread, coffee, and other food items undoubtedly expanded the profitability of other local businesses. Moreover many of these women were credited with establishing the foundations for African American businesses.

The town of Gordonsville, however, has not forgotten the waiter carriers. Since 2000 the town has held a heritage celebration where, among other events, these women are recognized. In 2002 a plaque was dedicated to the vendors for their "memorable contribution to Gordonsville's economy and history."

FURTHER READING

The Free-Lance State of Fredericksburg, "Area News," 13 September 1976.

Leving, Boyce. "Fried Chicken, Ham Once Made Gordonsville Station Famous," Charlottesville (VA) Daily Progress, 18 Nov. 1955.

Olwell, Rovert. "'Loose, Idle, and Disorderly': Slave Women in the Eighteenth-Century Charleston Marketplace," in More Than Chattel: Black Women and Slavery in the Americas, ed. David Barry Gaspar and Darlene Clark Hine (1996).

Thomas, William H. B. Gordonsville, Virginia: Historic Crossroads Town (1971).

"Waiter Carrier Recalls the 'Fried Chicken' Days," Orange County (VA) Review, 9 July 1970.

Walker, Juliet E. K. "Racism, Slavery, and Free Enterprise: Black Entrepreneurship in the United States before the Civil War," Business History Review 60 (Autumn 1986).

PSYCHE WILLIAMS-FORSON

Withers, Ernest C. (7 Aug. 1922–15 Oct. 2007), photojournalist and commercial photographer, was born Ernest Columbus Withers to working-class parents, Earl and Pearl Withers, in strictly segregated Memphis, Tennessee. When Withers was nine his mother died, and his father, a truck driver and driver for the postal service, married Minnie Clay. Withers credits Minnie, who was a seamstress, with helping him to develop the keen sense of detail that is evident in his photographs. Withers's first foray into photography occurred when, as a freshman at Manassas High School, he

borrowed his sister's camera to photograph a visit to his school by Marva Trotter Louis, wife of the boxer JOE LOUIS. Withers began photographing other school and community events. He began to think seriously about photography as a profession after marrying his high school sweetheart, Dorothy Curry, in February 1942 and starting their family of eight children in 1943.

In 1943 Withers joined the army. Assigned to the 1319 Engineering Regiment, he requested photography training. The Army School of Photography at Camp Sutton, North Carolina, provided Withers with darkroom experience and large-format camera skills. Stationed on the island of Saipan in 1945, Withers found his first opportunity to work as a commercial photographer by providing troops with photos of themselves to send home.

Upon returning to Memphis in 1946, Withers continued his career as a commercial photographer. An early subject of his photography was Negro League baseball. Withers was a fan of the league and had friendships with its players. However, Withers's attendance at the games was for a practical purpose, to make saleable photographs to support his growing family.

In 1948, following racial strife over a police shooting of an unarmed black veteran, Memphis mayor Edward Hall Crump, known as "Boss" Crump, strayed from his strict segregationist policies and allowed the hiring of a small detail of black police officers to be assigned to the black community. Attracted by the steady pay, Withers became one of the first black police officers in Memphis. In addition to photographing Negro League baseball, funerals, weddings, and assorted community events, Withers documented the musical crossroads of Beale Street in Memphis. At various times Withers ran a studio on Beale Street, and his position as a police officer gave him greater access to its music clubs, where he photographed everyone from COUNT BASIE to Elvis Presley, RILEY "B. B." KING, ARETHA FRANKLIN, RUTH BROWN, RUFUS THOMAS, LIONEL HAMPTON, and HOWLIN' WOLF. As was usually the case, Withers's first priority was to make saleable prints, but his images document Memphis's importance in the history of American music. Early in Withers's career, Nat D. Williams, known as "Nat Dee," became an important associate. Williams, a public school teacher, radio personality, promoter, and journalist in Memphis, commissioned Withers's photographs to promote his various community events. One of the more notable events Withers documented for Williams

Ernest C. Withers, photojournalist of the Civil Rights era, speaks during a presentation of images from his 70-year career at a special award ceremony at Parsons School of Design in New York, Monday, 14 February 2005. (AP Images.)

was the rise of WDIA AM, the first radio station in the nation to have entirely black programming. Nat Dee himself was a disc jockey on WDIA, as was a young B. B. King, who Withers photographed throughout his long career.

Withers is most well known, however, for the images he produced during the critical years of the civil rights movement. After being forced out of the police department in the early 1950s by hostile white officers, he began selling photographs to the local black newspapers, the *Memphis World* and the *Tri-State Defender*. Under the tutelage of Nat Williams and L.-Alex Wilson, a reporter, editor, and general manager for the Memphis *Tri-State Defender* and later editor of the parent *Chicago Defender*, Withers became an accomplished photojournalist and extensively documented the emerging movement in the South. He first gained national exposure in 1955 during the infamous murder trial in which Roy Bryant and J. W. Milam were acquitted by an all-white jury of the brutal slaying of the fourteen-year-old Chicagoan EMMETT TILL in Money, Mississippi. Bryant and Milam later admitted to *Look* magazine that they had indeed killed Till, who had angered them by whistling at a white woman during his visit with Mississippi relatives. Withers photographed the trial during the day and then helped his friend, Mississippi NAACP field secretary MEDGAR EVERS, search out potential witnesses at night. After the trial Withers produced and distributed a photo pamphlet of the murder and trial titled *Complete Photo Story of Till Murder Case*. The pamphlet included text by the black writer Raymond Tisby and was sold throughout the country. Unfortunately, economic necessity and the fact that national newspapers often did not utilize black journalists forced Withers to sell undeveloped rolls of his images to white journalists. As a result, Withers was not credited for many of his published photographs, including the famous shot of Emmett Till's uncle pointing out the accused in the courtroom. Withers was satisfied to have the story told, regardless.

In addition to the Till case, Withers photographed the Montgomery bus boycott in 1955–1956 and the integration of Central High School in Little Rock, Arkansas, in 1957–1958. Withers's mentor L. Alex Wilson was severely beaten while covering the Little Rock story and eventually died from Parkinson's-like symptoms resulting from his injuries. Withers himself endured several beatings and attacks during his coverage of civil rights events, including during the funeral of the martyred civil rights leader Medgar Evers in 1963. This attack was precipitated by his photographing a white man attempting to stab a black man.

Though Withers made no claims to having been anything other than a photographer, the back stories behind many of his photographs speak of a man engaged in the struggle. Not only did Withers photograph the violence surrounding JAMES MEREDITH's 1962 admission to the University of Mississippi, known as Ole Miss, but he also assisted in transporting Meredith to and from the campus. Withers covered the Memphis sanitation workers' strike in 1968 and helped make famous their *I Am A Man* picket signs—signs that he helped cut the pickets for. Withers also captured MARTIN LUTHER KING JR.'s visits to Memphis, the only image of King and RALPH ABERNATHY seated at the front of a Montgomery city bus after the successful bus boycott there, King in his room at the Lorraine Hotel before his assassination, his autopsy, and his

Atlanta funeral. While male leaders were often the focus of news stories, Withers did not neglect to photograph women and the masses of people crucial to the movement.

Despite Withers's insistence that his work was motivated by economic necessity, his images display a familiarity and intimacy with his subjects that reflect his position as an insider. Indeed, the culture of segregated Memphis dictated that the majority of Withers's photos were of the African American community, and his work is a virtual museum of African American life in the South. The fact that Withers himself was a black man in the midst of these events gave him different access—and a different perspective—than was usually possible in the mainstream media. In fact, he was often the first or only photographer to photograph events in their early stages.

During his career Withers received recognition from his peers as a photojournalist, and he was inducted into the Black Press Hall of Fame in 1998. In 1984 Withers published a book of his photographs titled *Reflections in History: Pictures Tell the Story, Vol.-1*. In 1987 an exhibition of his civil rights photographs was organized at the University of Mississippi. However, he did not receive significant recognition for the artistry and historical significance of his work until a traveling exhibition titled Let Us March On! Selected Civil Rights Photographs of Ernest C. Withers: 1955–1968 was developed at the Massachusetts College of Art and the accompanying, same-titled book was published in 1992. In 2000 the Chrysler Museum of Art organized an exhibition and published an overview of his work titled *Pictures Tell the Story*. Withers's portfolio contains an estimated 5 million images, and many of these have been presented in exhibitions across the country. In addition to numerous local and national newspapers, Withers's work has appeared in such publications as *Time*, *Life*, *Newsweek*, *Ebony*, and *Jet*. In the twenty-first century he remained a practicing photographer and maintained a Beale Street studio. He shared his knowledge and experience with communities and college campuses, where he received several honorary doctoral degrees. Withers died at the age of 85 in Memphis, his longtime home.

In September 2010, a major investigation by the *Memphis Commercial Appeal* revealed that Withers was an informant for the FBI between 1968 and 1970. Records reviewed by that newspaper indicate that Withers's close links to King and other civil rights leaders made him the perfect source for the FBI's COINTELPRO program of surveillance of alleged domestic radicals. As a photographer, "he could go everywhere with a perfect, obvious professional purpose," historian David Garrow told the *Appeal*. Following King's assassination Withers also played a major role in the FBI surveillance and arrest of more than 30 members of a Memphis black nationalist group, the Invaders. Despite the revelations of Withers's FBI links, former King lieutenants ANDREW YOUNG and JAMES LAWSON, as well as former Invaders, remained sanguine about the photographer's legacy. In Young's view the publicity generated by Withers's photographs was more important to the movement than any information he might have given to the FBI. "I don't think Dr. King would have minded him making a little money on the side," Young told the *Appeal*.

FURTHER READING

Furst, Michelle. *Let Us March On! Selected Civil Rights Photographs of Ernest C. Withers: 1955–1968* (1992).

Perrusquia, Marc. "Photographer Ernest Withers doubled as FBI informant to spy on civil rights movement." *Memphis Commercial Appeal*, 12 Sept. 2010.

Withers's photographs can be viewed at the Panopticon Gallery online at http://www.panopticongallery.com/artist/ernest_withers/#Withers_01.jpg.

Withers, Ernest C. *The Memphis Blues Again: Six Decades of Memphis Music Photographs* (2000).

Withers, Ernest C. *Pictures Tell the Story* (2000).

Wolff, Daniel J. *Negro League Baseball* (2004).

Obituary: *Los Angeles Times*, 18 Oct. 2007.

JARED T. STORY

Withers, William (Bill) (4 July 1938–), singer, guitarist, and songwriter, was born William H. Withers Jr. in Slab Fork, West Virginia, the youngest of six children of William H. Withers Sr., a coal miner, and Mattie Galloway. After his father's death in 1951, Withers was reared by his mother and his grandmother. His mother worked as a maid. Withers served in the U.S. Navy from 1956 to 1965. While he was on duty in the Far East, he made his first attempts at songwriting.

After his discharge from the navy, Withers moved to Los Angeles in 1967 and began pursuing a musical career. While promoting his compositions, he worked at a factory. Clarence Avant of Sussex Records gave Withers his first break. The result was the classic album *Just as I Am* (1970), which included the hits "Ain't No Sunshine" and "Grandma's Hands." "Ain't No Sunshine," which

William "Bill" Withers in his office in Beverly Hills, Calif., on 21 June 2006. (AP Images.)

was covered by many performers, was awarded a Grammy. Withers toured on the strength of his debut, even appearing at New York's Apollo Theater, the epicenter of African American musical performance. In 1973 he married Denise Nicholas, an actress who starred in *Room 222*, a television show of the late 1960s and early 1970s. (She later had other roles in film and television and published fiction). Their marriage ended in divorce in 1974. In 1976 Withers married Marcia Johnson, a businesswoman; the couple had two children. Marcia managed her husband's publishing concerns.

Soul, folk, and religious music provided Withers's melodies, while romance, broken hearts, and hard times informed his lyrics. He said the neighborliness of the West Virginia coal-mining families in the rough times of his childhood inspired his lyrics. Such themes appeared in his second album, *Still Bill* (1972), which included two huge hits, "Lean on Me" and "Use Me." The first is about the faithful support one person offers another, while the second is about a love affair gone bad but still feeling so good that the singer will not walk out on his or her selfish lover. "Lean on Me" held the number one spot for both pop and rhythm and blues singles on the Billboard chart. The song was also incorporated into church music. These early hits joined the most popular and most covered songs of American soul music. A concert album, *Bill Withers Live at Carnegie Hall* (1973), completed the trilogy of his great early work. In an essay by Clayton Riley, "For the Love of the Nation," which is included in a 1997 reissue of this concert

album, Withers is quoted describing the women in his family as people who "did housework outside their homes, took jobs as maids and maintained themselves as good, solid people, folks who lived as examples of what words like character really mean…. Plain folks, you see. With an awful lot going for them that others don't always see. I did. My good fortune" (Riley). Conflict with Sussex Records disrupted Withers's career in the mid-1970s and precipitated his switch to Columbia Records, but he continued to write and sing a series of hits that he recorded, including "The Same Love That Made Me Laugh," "Make Love to Your Mind," and "Lovely Day." In 1974 he performed in Zaire (now the Democratic Republic of the Congo) with ETTA JAMES, JAMES BROWN, and B. B. KING at a show accompanying the landmark fight the "Rumble in the Jungle" between MUHAMMAD ALI and GEORGE FOREMAN. One more giant hit, "Just the Two of Us" (1981), awaited Withers as he moved into the second decade of his musical career. This modern classic love song, recorded with GROVER WASHINGTON JR., earned Withers several Grammy nominations and won him the award for Best Rhythm and Blues Song of 1981.

Withers's last label recording was *Watching You, Watching Me* in 1985, but he continued to write and perform at a light pace, a state probably best described as semiretirement. The documentary film *When We Were Kings* (1996) features Withers's jazzy, African-inflected performance of "Ain't No Sunshine." Like many black musicians of the second half of the twentieth century, he was sampled by modern rap and hip hop performers, including WILL SMITH, TUPAC SHAKUR, Kanye West, and LL COOL J. In 2001 Withers asserted his right in court to use BillWithers.com as a domain name on the Internet, and he prevailed against parties who attempted to use that domain name for commercial purposes. In 2005 he was inducted into the Songwriters Hall of Fame.

FURTHER READING
"On the Scene: Bill Withers, Now There's Sunshine," *Playboy* (Feb. 1973).
Riley, Clayton. "For the Love of the Nation," on *Bill Withers Live at Carnegie Hall* (1997).

JOHN DANIEL SAILLANT

Witherspoon, Jimmy (8 Aug. 1920?–18 Sept. 1997), blues musician, was born in Gurdon, Arkansas. The exact year of his birth has been the subject of much speculation and may have been confused by subsequent recounts by relatives. His parents were

Leonard Witherspoon, a railway brakeman, and Eva Tatum, who played piano in a nearby church. The family was musical but strictly religious. Witherspoon sang in his church choir but was discouraged from his true love, the blues. He won his first singing contest when he was five years old. His father died when he was still just a boy.

In his teens, Witherspoon decided to make a go of it as a professional musician. He ran away from Arkansas and headed west to Los Angeles, where he arrived sometime in the mid-1930s. While looking for work in the music scene, he took on various jobs to make ends meet. He saw a performance by BIG JOE TURNER and thereafter was more determined than ever to make it as a blues performer. This was easier said than done, however, and in 1941 Witherspoon joined the Merchant Marine. One night on leave in Calcutta, India, he happened upon a show featuring the pianist Teddy Weatherford. While the band was playing "Why Don't You Do Right?" Witherspoon was seized with inspiration. He went up to the bandstand and began to sing along with the music. The performance—which was broadcast on U.S. Armed Forces Radio—was a hit, and Witherspoon's musical career was under way.

In 1944 his stint with the Merchant Marines came to a close. He relocated to San Francisco and rejoined his mother, who had moved there several years earlier. He took work at a steel mill and performed in local clubs on his days off. As luck would have it, he was seen and discovered by JAY McSHANN, one of the predominant band leaders of the day. McShann made Witherspoon his lead singer, and he remained with the band until 1948. A year later, however, he cut a recording of "Ain't Nobody's Business" with McShann and some of his former mates that turned into a major hit, staying on the R&B charts for thirty-four weeks, something that had never been done before. In 1951 Witherspoon married Rachel (maiden name unknown). The couple divorced just two years later having had no children together.

The next several years were difficult ones. Following the success of "Ain't Nobody's Business," Witherspoon cut several records with a number of different labels, but to little notice. The emergence of rock-and-roll and a lack of public interest in blues music took their toll. Witherspoon began to play smaller and smaller clubs, and he experienced financial hardships. In 1953 he and Rachel divorced; he was also forced to declare bankruptcy.

Success came again in 1959, when Witherspoon was invited to play at the Monterey Jazz Festival.

There he appeared with such greats as COLEMAN HAWKINS, SARAH VAUGHAN, and EARL "FATHA" HINES. The resulting live album, *Jimmy Witherspoon at the Monterey Jazz Festival*, was a major hit and is considered a blues classic. It reignited Witherspoon's popularity and ensured his place in the pantheon of great blues performers, and in the ensuing years Witherspoon toured both the United States and Europe. As had long been the case, jazz and blues performers who fell on hard times in the States found warmer audiences and greater success (to say nothing of more hospitable race relations) abroad.

The success of Monterey spurred Witherspoon into an extremely prolific period of recording, and he cut dozens of albums between 1962's *A Spoonful of Blues* to 2010's *Live 59*. In the meantime, he worked with all the greats of the day, BUCK CLAYTON, T-BONE WALKER, KENNY BURRELL, Robben Ford, and JIMMY WOODE, to name but a very few. In 1962 he married Diana Williams, but they would divorce in just a few months. In 1978 he was apparently engaged to Sharon Rivera, but it is not clear that they ever married. He had three children, but with whom is also not entirely clear.

In the late 1970s Witherspoon was diagnosed with throat cancer. He endured treatment and, after time away for rehabilitation and learning how to use his now-changed voice, continued singing and touring. Albums from this time include *Spoon Concerts* (1989), *Live at Condon's* (1990), *Spoon's Blues*, and *Taste of Swing Time* (both 1995). By the mid-1990s Witherspoon's cancer had returned. His last album, *Live at the Mint* (1996), recorded with the guitarist Robben Ford, was nominated for a Grammy Award for Best Traditional Blues album. Witherspoon died a year later of throat cancer. He is remembered today as one of the blues greats of his generation.

FURTHER READING

Cohn, Lawrence. *Nothing but the Blues: The Music and the Musicians* (1993).

Obituary: *New York Times,* 22 Sept. 1977.

JASON PHILIP MILLER

Witten, Juan Bautista "Big Prince" (c. 1756–1830s), sergeant in the free black militia who helped defend Spanish Florida from Indians, pirates, and the United States Marines, was born in Guinea on the west coast of Africa in about 1756, according to his own estimates. He spent perhaps the first twenty years of his life in Guinea, the next ten in South

Carolina, another thirty-five in Spanish Florida, and he ended his days in Matanzas, Cuba.

Witten's African name and the circumstances of his enslavement are unknown, but in the 1770s the man that English records later called Big Prince was carried across the Atlantic by slave traders to be unloaded at Sullivan's Island, South Carolina, the largest slave port of its time. The Charleston planter Peter Witten purchased Witten and named him Big Prince, perhaps in reference to his great size, for the African was described as "6' and brawny" (Landers, 77). Big Prince became a carpenter on Witten's plantation, and by 1777 he had formed what would be a lifetime bond with an enslaved "county-born" woman named Judy on the neighboring plantation of William Canty. Within a year Judy and Prince had a son named Glasgow, and the following year their daughter, Polly, was born.

Before long the chaos of the American Revolution engulfed the Witten family. The Canty plantation where Judy and the children lived changed hands several times during the confusion of 1781–1782. In this tumultuous period the Witten family, like many others, was plundered as the spoils of war and came into the hands of Colonel William Young, the commander of a Loyalist cavalry troop. When the Loyalists finally evacuated Charleston, South Carolina, in 1782 Young took Big Prince Witten and his family to Georgia with him, and two years later, when the American Patriots aided by free black militiamen from Saint Domingue (modern Haiti) liberated Savannah, Young moved the Wittens even further southward to the frontier post of Point Petre, Georgia, just across the St. Marys River from British Florida.

At the end of the American Revolution, Florida was returned to Spain, and this change of governments gave the Wittens a new hope. In June or July of 1785 the Wittens escaped from Colonel Young, but he commissioned the Georgia Patriot Lieutenant Colonel Jacob Weed to recapture them. After several failed attempts the Wittens also escaped from Weed and crossed the St. Marys River into what had become Spanish Florida.

Taking advantage of a religious sanctuary policy first established in Spanish Florida in 1693, the Wittens and almost 250 other escaped slaves stated that they fled to Florida to become Catholics. On this basis they were accepted into the colony as free subjects of the Spanish Crown. After learning the Catholic catechism all the Wittens were baptized. Prince Witten became Juan Bautista, Judy took the name María, and the children became Domingo and María Francisca.

The Wittens quickly learned to take full advantage of their new free status and their rights as Spanish subjects. They registered Domingo in the free Catholic school in St. Augustine, and his subsequent literacy greatly helped the family. Prince Witten's talents as a skilled carpenter were sought after, and he signed work contracts with various employers on his own terms. When one employer tried to make Judy do field work rather than the laundry and cooking that the couple had agreed to, Witten went to court stating he "could not permit it" (Landers, 88). Before long Witten secured government contracts to quarry coquina rock and cut timber, hiring other free blacks to work for him. Judy helped the family economy by raising pigs for sale and training young girls to be domestics. She also went to court when she felt her rights were violated, and she once filed suit against the richest planters in Spanish Florida. Francisco opened a shoemaking shop and trained young black apprentices, as his mother did. Within a decade the Wittens were living next door to two of St. Augustine's most prominent figures, and they had acquired a slave of their own.

After twenty-one years living as man and wife, in 1798 Prince and Judy further elevated their social status by marrying in the Catholic church in St. Augustine. Their elite neighbor and patron served as their marriage sponsor, and in turn the Wittens became favored godparents for many other free black families. In 1796 daughter María Francisca married Jorge Jacobo, one of the slave rebels from Saint Domingue who had taken up residence in St. Augustine only three months earlier. This wedding united some of the most important free black families in the colony.

As all able-bodied Spanish subjects were required to do, Witten joined the militia and saw frequent service. Although it is difficult to determine if Witten had already acquired military experience during the southern campaigns of the American Revolution, his military service for the Spaniards is well documented. In the summer of 1795 he helped defend the colony from the Revolutionary Legion of the Floridas, a mercenary force sponsored by the French Republic's first minister to the United States, Edmond Charles Genet, to "liberate" Florida from the Spanish monarchy. The grateful Spanish governor noted the significant service of his "excellent company of free blacks" (Landers, 208). Witten also fought against Mikasuki Indians in the Indian Wars of 1800–1803, and on that occasion his son and his new son-in-law fought with him. Witten received a land grant from the Spanish government as reward and soon built a prosperous homestead, but it was burned by Georgian invaders in the so-called Patriot rebellion of 1812. Witten became a hero in that invasion, leading the black and Indian troops who defeated a unit of the United States Marines who were covertly aiding the Georgians. Claimants who later filed damage suits against the United States government usually refer to the black militia as "Prince's Black Company." In the next decade Witten and his French-speaking in-laws and their black companies fought Latin American filibusters of assorted new "republics" before the United States finally acquired Florida.

Spanish sovereignty in Florida ended on 10 July 1821, and free black families like the Wittens had to make some hard choices. Some free blacks trusted cession treaties and remained in Florida, but the white supremacist planters who immigrated into the new territory soon acquired most of their land and installed new laws to restrict them. Anticipating that certain shift in racial politics, Prince Witten led most of Florida's polyglot free black community into exile in Cuba, where once again they remade their lives.

FURTHER READING

Cusick, James. *The Other War of 1812: The Patriot War and the American Invasion of Spanish East Florida* (2003)

Landers, Jane. *Black Society in Spanish Florida* (1999)

JANE G. LANDERS

Wolfe, George C. (23 Sept. 1954–), playwright, theater director and producer, and arts administrator, was born in Frankfort, Kentucky, the third of four children of Costello Wolfe, a clerk at the state department of corrections, and Anna (Lindsey) Wolfe, a teacher who became principal of a private black elementary school, which the Wolfe children attended. George spent the summer before high school in New York City with his mother while she was doing research toward her doctorate in education. There he saw his first professional theater productions, *Hello Dolly* with PEARL BAILEY and a revival of *West Side Story*. The next summer he went with his mother to Miami University in Oxford, Ohio, where he attended a youth theater program, returning to Frankfort with new ambitions and confidence. "If I joined a club and didn't become president, I'd quit the club," he later boasted (*New York Times Magazine*, 8 Nov. 1988).

After high school Wolfe spent a year at his parents' alma mater, Kentucky State University, before transferring to Pomona College in Claremont, California. After graduating with a B.A. in Theater in 1976 he spent three years in Los Angeles pursuing an acting career while teaching theatre at the Inner City Cultural Center. In 1979 he moved to New York City and enrolled at New York University's Graduate Musical Theatre Writing Program, earning an M.A. in 1983. By 1985 Wolfe's musical *Paradise* was mounted off-Broadway.

It was his next production, however, which began at the Crossroads Theatre in New Brunswick, New Jersey, before moving to the Public Theater in New York, that jump-started his career and began a string of theatrical successes. *The Colored Museum* (1986), which the theater critic Frank Rich called "a most liberating revolt," consisted of eleven exhibits, or satiric sketches, that Wolfe described as "where the myths and madnesses of black/Negro/colored Americans are stored" (*New York Times*, 15 Aug. 1986). Confronting, debunking, and even reclaiming a gallery of historical and contemporary images of African Americans, the skits take on subjects as diverse as JOSEPHINE BAKER, a feisty drag queen, "buppies" (or black urban professionals), and LORRAINE HANSBERRY's seminal play *Raisin in the Sun*. "I can't live inside of a museum," Wolfe explained, "and I don't think a culture that's as vibrant as black culture can live inside of a museum. So I just found a way to tear down walls" (*American Visions*, Apr. 1991). The play's tackling of taboo material began with an African American flight attendant clad in a pink miniskirted uniform announcing, "Welcome aboard Celebrity Slaveship … to put on your shackle, take the right hand and close the metal ring around your left hand like so … Also, we ask that you please refrain from call-and-response singing between cabins, as that sort of thing can lead to rebellion … if there's anything I can do to make this middle passage more pleasant, press the little button over-head and I'll be with you faster than you can say 'Go Down, Moses.'" *The Colored Museum* ran for nine months in New York, followed by major productions in London and Los Angeles. A television version aired on PBS in 1991.

The play introduced themes and forms that continued to occupy Wolfe as both a director and writer, including a fondness for ritualized stylizations and spare aesthetics drawn in part from Bertolt Brecht and Japanese Kabuki and Noh Theater, and the use of humor and music in disarming audiences, providing an opening for bold and challenging material. The play illustrated an attention to spoken language indicative of an extraordinarily articulate

George C. Wolfe, left, and Savion Glover, director and choreographer, respectively, of *Bring in 'Da Noise, Bring in 'Da Funk*, pose with their awards after both won honors at the 50th Annual Tony Awards in New York City on 2 June 1996. (AP Images.)

and verbal man enamored with the theatrical use of speech by southerners and African Americans and appropriate to a childhood stutterer intensely aware of the rhythms of speech. *The Colored Museum* revealed Wolfe's deep and passionate interest in African American history, particularly the fragmented nature of African American identity. "We are these bizarre mutt creatures who are African-American at their base but have all these other kinds of incredibly violent contradictions coursing through our veins," Wolfe expounded in 1993. "And it is those violent contradictions that generally have sprung forth the most extraordinarily brilliant things you'd ever want to find: jazz, blues, the writings of ZORA [NEALE HURSTON], the rhythms of TONI MORRISON, BILLIE HOLIDAY. It's MILES DAVIS, JOHN COLTRANE, the brightest who explore those extraordinary contradictions, who celebrate them" (Rowell, 620).

In 1990, having written the libretto for *Queenie Pie* (1986) based on a story by DUKE ELLINGTON, and contributed to the multi-author play *Urban Blight* (1988), Wolfe was made one of four artistic directors

at New York's Public Theater. In that capacity he directed a well-received version of Bertolt Brecht's *The Caucasian Chalk Circle* adapted by THULANI DAVIS and curated "Moving beyond the Madness: A Festival for New Voices," a program of performance artists that included Danitra Vance, John Leguizamo, and ANNA DEAVERE SMITH. In 1990 he wrote and directed the Obie Award–winning *Spunk* (1990), an adaptation of three short stories by Zora Neale Hurston, about whose writing Wolfe said, "That language is just like taking a shower in something luxurious, it's so extraordinary." During this time Wolfe was also writing a musical about the pioneering jazz musician JELLY ROLL MORTON. *Jelly's Last Jam*, with GREGORY HINES in the lead role and Wolfe directing, arrived on Broadway in 1992 after premiering in Los Angeles in 1991. The show, which the critic John Lahr praised in *The New Yorker* as "a watershed … [it] opens the musical up to new mythologies, new aesthetics, and a new historical sophistication," ran for 569 performances and garnered eleven Tony Award nominations, winning three. With *Jelly's Last Jam* Wolfe proved his contention that musicals are "pieces that are very specifically about America, and America is about the collision of rhythms and about who owns history" (Savran, 346). "Where are the stories of black people stored?" Wolfe asked rhetorically in 1993. "They're not stored in the history books; they're just beginning to be. In my theory, they're stored in the music" (Rowell 620). The critical and financial success of *Jelly's Last Jam* prepared the way for Wolfe's selection as the director for the Broadway production of Tony Kushner's groundbreaking play *Angels in America*. An astonishingly powerful and complex theatrical enterprise, part one of *Angels*, *Millennium Approaches*, opened in May 1993, while part two, *Perestroika*, opened the following November. Together, the play ran seven hours. In addition to a Pulitzer Prize for Kushner, the play won seven Tony awards, including best play of 1993 and 1994, and best direction for 1993.

In 1993—while directing rehearsals of *Angels* and completing the film version of *Fires in the Mirror*, Anna Deavere Smith's play about racial unrest between blacks and Hasidic Jews in Crown Heights, Brooklyn—Wolfe was named producer of the Public Theater/New York Shakespeare Festival with authority over all artistic and managerial decisions for the Public's six stages. Wolfe, who at the time had writing and directing successes but no substantial producing or managerial experience, assumed the position after the controversial dismissal of JoAnne Akalatis. Wolfe, a charismatic, supremely confident visionary talent with a skill for talent scouting and promotion, much like the Public's founder Joseph Papp, was the trustees' unanimous choice.

During his tenure at the Public, Wolfe spearheaded a change in tone, stressing the friendly treatment of patrons and press and hiring a director of community affairs tasked with bringing in black, Asian, and Hispanic audiences. Wolfe, a gay man, prioritized productions, as well as ancillary programming, by and about racial, ethnic, and sexual minorities and emphasized the nurturing of writers and artists. Under his reign the Public inaugurated programs like the *New Work Now Series*, opened Joe's Pub, a cabaret and performance space, and transferred nine productions to Broadway. As a result, donations and grants increased substantially, box office revenues doubled, and the endowment grew from ten million dollars to forty million. While running the Public, Wolfe continued to direct, and his version of Shakespeare's *The Tempest* moved from Central Park to Broadway in 1995. A second directorial effort, Anna Deavere Smith's award-winning play *Twilight: Los Angeles, 1992*, opened on Broadway a few months later.

A collaboration with the dancer SAVION GLOVER born out of a workshop session at the Public yielded Wolfe's next Broadway hit. *Bring in 'Da Noise, Bring in 'Da Funk*, which Wolfe wrote and directed and Glover choreographed, opened on Broadway in 1996. It ran for 1,135 performances and netted four Tony awards, including Wolfe's second for direction. Simultaneously chronicling the history of tap dancing and black America, *Bring in 'Da Noise* captured dance's essential communicative power, which for Wolfe also characterized folk art and the early blues, two of his other passions.

While *Bring in 'Da Noise* was the hottest ticket on Broadway, Wolfe was experiencing a series of personal trials. His mother, with whom he was especially close, died in 1996. Shortly thereafter a fire destroyed his Greenwich Village home. The following spring he was diagnosed with kidney failure and spent a year on dialysis before receiving a kidney transplant in 1998 from his brother William. The personal characteristics—tenacity, combativeness, drive, boldness—that made Wolfe a professional success and, according to some collaborators, "difficult," served him well in surmounting these challenges. "In the same way that Charles Brown's friend Pig Pen moves through life in a whirl of grime," Alex Witchel wrote of the director's boundless energy, "Wolfe moves through it practically vibrating. He's like the cork from a Champagne bottle, still going, propelled by a blast of bubbles" (*New York Times Magazine*, 8 Nov. 1988). Wolfe continued directing during his illness, mounting *On the Town* in Central Park, *Macbeth* at the Public, and the opera *Amistad* at the Lyric Opera of Chicago.

By the late 1990s Wolfe's health had improved, but he was about to encounter his first professional setbacks. Wolfe and the Public lost heavily on two lavish Broadway musicals, a revival of *On the Town* in 1998, which Wolfe directed, and *The Wild Party*, which he directed and co-wrote in 2000. Between the two, the Public lost an estimated eleven to fourteen million dollars. These losses combined with New York's struggling economy following the terrorist attacks of 2001 forced the Public to lay off 15 percent of its staff and to limit productions. Critics held that the fiscal damage was due in part to Wolfe's arrogance, particularly his insistence on opening *The Wild Party* directly on Broadway, bypassing the Public's stage.

Wolfe weathered the storm, however, and in 2002 he returned to Broadway, directing two plays, both of which were originally mounted at the Public: *Elaine Stritch at Liberty*, the salty one-woman show that won the 2002 Tony Award for best special theatrical event, and SUZAN-LORI PARKS's Pulitzer Prize–winning play *Topdog/Underdog*. That same year he wrote and directed the musical revue *Harlem Song* for the Apollo Theater and in 2003 he directed *Radiant Baby*, a new musical about the 1980s graffiti artist Keith Haring, at the Public. In 2004 Wolfe reunited with Tony Kushner, directing *Caroline, or Change*, a family drama/musical about race in the 1960s. As the play was opening on Broadway Wolfe announced that he would leave his post as producer of the Public Theater in the 2004–2005 season. Wolfe continued his association with the organization as a trustee and occasional director and directed *A Midsummer Night's Dream* in summer 2005. In 2006, Wolfe directed an outdoor run of Berthold Brecht's *Mother Courage*, at the Delacorte Theater in New York's Central Park, with Meryl Streep and Kevin Kline, and returned to Broadway in 2011 as the supervising director of the revival of *The Normal Heart*, Larry Kramer's path-breaking play about the emergence and impact of HIV/AIDS in New York City in the early 1980s. *The Normal Heart* won the 2011 Tony Award for Best Revival of a Play. Wolfe branched out to film in 2008, directing the romantic drama, *Nights in Rodanthe*, starring Richard Gere and set on the Outer Banks of North Carolina.

FURTHER READING

Rowell, Charles H. "'I Just Want to Keep Telling Stories': An Interview with George C. Wolfe," *Callaloo* (Summer 1993).

Savran, David. *The Playwright's Voice* (1999).

Witchel, Alex. "The Man Who Would Be Papp," *New York Times Magazine* (8 Nov. 1998).

LISA E. RIVO

Womack, Bobby (4 Mar. 1944–), soul singer and songwriter, was born Robert Dwayne Womack in Cleveland, Ohio, one of five sons of a steelworker, Friendly Womack Sr., and Naomi (Reed) Womack. Friendly, who sang and played guitar in the Voices of Love gospel quartet, ended up rearing a quintet's worth of talented musicians; by the early 1950s Bobby and his brothers Cecil, Curtis, Friendly Jr., and Harry were touring the country as the Womack Brothers, sharing stages with revered performers such as the Five Blind Boys of Alabama and the Pilgrim Travelers. Bobby excelled as both a vocalist and a guitarist, already displaying the versatility that would be the hallmark of his solo career.

In 1953 the Womack Brothers opened for the Soul Stirrers, then fronted by the charismatic, ambitious Sam Cooke. Cooke was in the midst of making the transition to secular pop, which he did at the peril of alienating his religious fans, and over the next nine years he attempted to persuade the Womacks to do the same. He took a special interest in Bobby, whom he attempted to hire for his band, but Womack, still a teenager, remained wary of choosing the path of sin—or at least the wrath of his observant father. Finally in 1962 the Womack brothers signed with Cooke's SAR Records as the Valentinos. They cut their first single in less than two hours, converting a pair of traditional spirituals into impassioned proto-soul. "Lookin' for a Love" became an instant hit (later covered by the J. Geils Band), and the Valentinos went on the road with JAMES BROWN. In 1964 the Valentinos released the Womack composition "It's All Over Now," which almost immediately became the first number-one single for the Rolling Stones. In a year that saw the Valentinos' future brighten and Womack reap a significant amount of money from the rights to "It's All Over Now," he also finally joined on as a regular member of Cooke's band.

Cooke's murder that same year marked the end of the first phase of Womack's career. Following SAR's demise, the Valentinos stayed together just long enough to record some undervalued sides for Checker Records. For Bobby it marked the loss of his mentor and set into motion a series of events that placed his career in peril. Then twenty years old, he married Cooke's widow, Barbara Campbell; at best, this association overshadowed his own reputation, while at worst, it led some to ostracize him. As a result Womack retreated behind the scenes for the remainder of the decade, playing guitar on key southern soul sessions and contributing songs to records by RAY CHARLES, ARETHA FRANKLIN, JOE TEX, and KING CURTIS. His association with WILSON PICKETT proved especially fruitful, with Pickett scoring hits with the Womack-penned gems "I'm in Love," "Ninety-Nine and a Half," and "I'm a Midnight Mover." In 1968 Womack's own recording career showed some life, as he charted with the rough-hewn plaint "What Is This?"

The 1970s saw Womack emerge as a star in his own right, even as he made high-profile contributions to albums by Janis Joplin and SLY (and the Family) STONE. In 1970 Minit Records, for which Womack had recorded "What Is This" and the subsequent singles "More Than I Can Stand" and "How I Miss You Baby," folded and sent its roster over to United Artists. Rather than asking Womack to continue working in the southern soul vein, the label granted Womack full creative freedom. He responded with 1971's classic album *Communication* and its no less successful follow-up, 1972's *Understanding*. Despite having been recorded at American Sound Studio, a hub for funky soul, *Communication* and *Understanding* drew from a variety of influences. Womack's remarkably successful covers of James Taylor's "Fire and Rain" and the Carpenters' "(They Long to Be) Close to You" showed him putting his own distinct stamp on others' material while respecting their original intent. But it was Womack originals such as "That's the Way I Feel About 'Cha" and "Woman's Gotta Have It" that announced his arrival as a chart force. Ironically it was the B-side of his 1973 version of Neil Diamond's "Sweet Caroline"—the wistfully cautionary "Harry Hippie"—that ended up as Womack's first gold-certified release. That same year, Womack wrote the score for the blaxploitation film *Across 110th Street*, with the title cut providing him yet another hit. He continued his run for the next few years, with a remake of "Lookin' for a Love" matching the sales of "Harry Hippie." But by 1975 his marriage had fallen apart, he was living dissolutely, and United Artists cut ties with

Bobby Womack, left, gets a hug from Chubby Checker at the Hard Rock Café in New York City on 17 January 1990. (AP Images.)

him after a dispute over Womack's desire to record a collection of country songs, released that year as *BW Goes C&W*. Womack moved to Columbia Records, smoothing out his sound somewhat for *Home Is Where the Heart Is* (1976) and *Pieces* (1977). However, Womack grew impatient with the label's treatment of him and ended the decade mired in obscurity.

Yet once again, Womack surprised the world by returning with the thoughtful masterpiece *The Poet* (1981), and its sequel *The Poet II* (1984). He immediately found himself embroiled in legal disagreements with Beverly Glen, the small operation that Womack had considered his only option at the time. His highly restrictive contract kept him from recording elsewhere, but it did not keep Womack from achieving unprecedented acclaim abroad, most notably in Great Britain. The year 1985 saw Womack emerge from his legal woes and enjoy yet another boom period; *So Many Rivers* produced the hit single "I Wish He Didn't Trust Me So Much," and in 1986 longtime fans the Rolling Stones featured Womack on "The Harlem Shuffle," a duet with Mick Jagger. Rolling Stones guitarist Ron Wood also helped revive Womack's career after an early 1990s lull, releasing the aptly titled *Resurrection* on his Slide imprint in 1994. In

1999 Womack fulfilled a promise to his late father by recording the all-gospel set *Back to my Roots*, and that same year released a Christmas album, *Traditions*. He toured regularly and raised money for the fight against diabetes, from which Womack himself suffered. In 2006, he published his autobiography, *Midnight Mover: The True Story of the Greatest Soul Singer in the World*, which recounted his colorful, often tumultuous journey through over fifty years of pop music.

FURTHER READING

Womack, Bobby. *Midnight Mover: The True Story of the Greatest Soul Singer in the World* (2006)

DISCOGRAPHY

Anthology (EMI 90299).

NATHANIEL FRIEDMAN

Wonder, Stevie (13 May 1950–), songwriter, singer, multi-instrumentalist, producer, and political activist, was born Steveland Judkins in Saginaw, Michigan, to Calvin Judkins and Lula Mae Hardaway, who separated early in his life. Steveland came into the world with the odds stacked firmly against him; he was poor, black, and born two months premature with a birth weight barely reaching four pounds. He spent his first fifty-two days in an incubator, resulting in the permanent loss of his eyesight. Stevie was raised largely by his mother under difficult economic and social circumstances. Calvin, a street hustler, forced his wife to work as a prostitute for a short period before the family moved from Saginaw to Detroit's Brewster Housing Projects in 1953. The couple separated shortly thereafter.

Despite his hardscrabble upbringing, Stevie never thought himself disadvantaged. With unwavering optimism, he compensated for his impairment by developing his other senses. By age five Stevie showed an aptitude for music, taking up percussion and imitating the day's top R&B artists, including LITTLE WALTER JACOBS, JIMMY REED, and the Coasters, heard on WCHB's *Sundown* show. At eight, without formal training, Stevie played piano and harmonica, sang in the Whitestone Baptist Church's gospel choir, and busked on street corners.

In 1960 one of Stevie's best friends, Gerald White, convinced his brother Ronnie White of SMOKEY ROBINSON and the Miracles to give his friend an audition. The confident ten year old, who bragged he could "sing badder than Smokey," backed up his audacious claim with a show-stopping performance.

White brought Stevie to BERRY GORDY JR., owner of Detroit's fledgling Motown label, where Stevie played every instrument in the studio. Lula signed her son's recording contract, which stipulated his earnings be held in a trust until he turned twenty-one.

Motown producer and songwriter Clarence Paul became Wonder's producer and mentor. His first two recordings, *The Jazz Soul of Little Stevie*, an all-instrumental album showcasing Wonder's instrumental virtuosity, and *A Tribute to Uncle Ray*, a homage to his idol RAY CHARLES, were held back until 1963. His first release, the 1962 single "I Call It Pretty Music (But the Old People Call It the Blues)," written by Paul, was released under the Gordy-coined moniker Little Stevie Wonder; it failed to chart.

Despite his early recordings' lack of commercial success, Wonder gave electrifying live performances. And Gordy captured Wonder's dynamism on a 1963 live recording of "Fingertips Pt 2," a seven-minute, two-sided single, complete with Wonder's inspired harmonica improvisations and an uproarious audience call and response. It became Wonder's first number 1 single and the first live recording to top the charts. That track and the single "Workout Stevie Workout" propelled Wonder's album *The 12 Year Old Genius* to number 1.

With a Song in My Heart, an album of treacly ballads, and *Stevie at the Beach*, an improbable surf album, predictably failed to chart. In 1965 Wonder embodied Motown's infectious pop and soul fusion with "Uptight (Everything's Alright)," a number 1 single and title cut that he cowrote. The album also contained a countrified, gospel-inflected version of Bob Dylan's "Blowin' in the Wind," showcasing the sixteen-year-old's burgeoning political consciousness.

Down to Earth, released in 1967 with the un-Motown-like album cover of Wonder in a ghetto landscape, featured the number 1 R&B song "I Was Made to Love Her." The summer following the album's release saw racial confrontations turn into full-scale urban riots in Newark, New York City, Cleveland, Washington, Chicago, Atlanta, and Detroit, and in April 1968 MARTIN LUTHER KING JR. was assassinated. Wonder became more politicized, performing at benefits for the Southern Christian Leadership Conference (SCLC) in Chicago and for SCLC's Poor People's March on Washington in 1968.

From 1968 to 1970 Wonder's fame grew precipitously on the strength of four top 10 hits: "For Once in My Life," "My Cherie Amour," "Yester-Me, Yester-You, Yesterday," and "Signed, Sealed, Delivered, I'm Yours." After graduating from Michigan School for the Blind in 1969, Wonder was able to devote himself full-time to music, and he began moving beyond Motown's rigid hit-factory system, coproducing and playing most of the instruments on 1969's *Signed, Sealed, Delivered*. The record included a broader repertoire, including his inspired rendition of the Beatles' "We Can Work It Out," the socially conscious ballad "Heaven Help Us," and, especially, the title track, written with his paramour Syreeta Wright, a Motown secretary and backup singer, whom he married in 1970. The couple divorced two years later.

That same year, with his Motown contract about to expire, Wonder was granted full artistic control of *Where I'm Coming From*, the first album he produced and cowrote himself. The album contained a more cohesive political message with songs like "Think of Me as Your Soldier," expressing his opposition to the Vietnam War, and "I Wanna Talk to You," commenting on the widening generation gap.

In May 1971 Wonder turned twenty-one and received a million dollars from his Motown trust. He remained unsigned while holing up in the late JIMI HENDRIX's state-of-the-art Electric Ladyland Studio in New York. With his groundbreaking album *Music of My Mind* in hand, Wonder successfully renegotiated his Motown contract, winning complete artistic control, increased royalty rates, and his own publishing company, Black Bull.

Wonder's new artistic freedom resulted in an extraordinary burst of creativity that cemented his place as one of the twentieth century's most important musicians. The five successive albums he released in the early to mid-1970s, *Music of My Mind* (1972), *Talking Book* (1972), *Innervisions* (1973), *Fulfillingness' First Finale* (1974), and *Songs in the Key of Life* (1976), represent a body of work and a creative zenith few artists ever reach. At Electric Ladyland, Wonder delved into sound and instrument experimentation with synthesizers, Moogs, and clavinets, creating category-defying hybrids—parts jazz, R&B, rock, soul, and pop. At a session with RICHIE HAVENS, Wonder met engineers and electronic musicians Robert Margouleff and Malcolm Cecil, who became his collaborators and teachers. While *Music of My Mind* had only one single, the breezy, jazz-inflected "Superwoman (Where Were You When I Needed You)," the album's progressive music experimentation represented an enormous paradigm shift.

Stevie Wonder performing a duet with Roberta Flack at the United Nations on 13 May 1985. (AP Images.)

Following a 1972 summer tour opening for the Rolling Stones, Wonder began work, with the help of Margouleff and Cecil, on one of his most seminal recordings, *Talking Book*. The album yielded two consecutive number 1 hits, the romantic, melodious "You Are the Sunshine of My Life," and the classic funk jam "Superstition," featuring Wonder's jaunty clavinet backed by bawdy horns.

Innervisions, another Wonder masterpiece, was filled with spirituality and introspection ("Visions," "Jesus Children of America," "Higher Ground"), ballads ("All in Love Is Fair," "Golden Lady"), jazz influences and psychedelia ("Too High"), political statements ("Living for the City," "He's Misstra Know It All,"), and Latin grooves ("Don't You Worry about a Thing"). Thirty years later tracks like "Higher Ground," "Living for the City," "Don't You Worry about a Thing," and "Golden Lady" remained in heavy rotation at radio stations across the globe.

On 6 August 1973, while Wonder was driving with his brother on a South Carolina highway, a log from a truck slammed into Wonder's forehead and fractured his skull. He lay in a coma for a week before regaining consciousness and was forced to stop performing until the following January. While convalescing, he met Yolanda Simmons, who became his partner and the mother of two of his children, Aisha and Keita, although they never married. In 1974 Wonder won five Grammy Awards for *Innervisions*, including Album of the Year.

Wonder's new zeal for life on 1974's *Fulfillingness' First Finale* was evident on songs like "Smile Please," the metaphysical "Heaven Is 10 Zillion Light Years Away," the syncopated and stomping "Boogie On Reggae Woman," and the politically charged "You Haven't Done Nothin.'" The album went on to win four Grammy Awards.

Wonder's *Songs in the Key of Life* remains his veritable magnum opus, a double album featuring some of his finest work, including "Sir Duke" (a tribute to DUKE ELLINGTON), "I Wish," "Isn't She Lovely" (about his daughter Aisha), "Pastime Paradise," and "As." While detractors called the work sprawling and excessive, most saw the ambitious recording as the musical culmination of his career.

While most critics would agree that Wonder's creativity dropped off after 1980, his commercial success continued to grow. *Hotter than July*

(1980) included the hit "(Master Blaster) Jammin'," a tribute to Bob Marley, and "Happy Birthday," an anthem to the battle Wonder had spearheaded to make Martin Luther King's birthday a national holiday. In 1982 he had a number 1 single with his duet with Paul McCartney, "Ebony and Ivory." That same year he released *Musicquarium*, a greatest hits album that produced two new hits, "That Girl" and "Do I Do." Wonder's 1984 Oscar-winning soundtrack for *The Woman in Red* featured "I Just Called to Say I Love You," his biggest-selling single. In 1989, at age thirty-nine, Wonder was inducted into the Rock and Roll Hall of Fame. Although he scored the soundtrack for SPIKE LEE's 1991 film *Jungle Fever* and released the 1995 Grammy-winning album "Conversation Peace," his output flagged in the 1990s. His next studio album did not arrive until ten years later, but "A Time to Love" was widely viewed as a return to form. During this interregnum, Wonder married Kai Millard Morris, with whom he has two children.

Throughout the 1990s and into the 2000s, Wonder's legacy was enriched by the neo-soul movement, the members of which rightfully deified him, and by hip-hop, with many artists, including TUPAC SHAKUR, Wu-Tang Clan, and A Tribe Called Quest, sampling his music and introducing him to a new generation.

FURTHER READING

Horn, Martin E. *Innervisions: The Music of Stevie Wonder* (2000).

Love, Dennis, and Stacy Brown. *Blind Faith: The Miraculous Journey of Lula Hardaway, Stevie Wonder's Mother* (2002).

Swenson, John. *Stevie Wonder* (1986).

Werner, Craig. *Higher Ground: Stevie Wonder, Aretha Franklin, Curtis Mayfield, and the Rise and Fall of American Soul* (2004).

ANDY GENSLER

Wood, William Vernell (23 Dec. 1936–), football player, was born in Washington, D.C.; little is known of his parents or early childhood. He starred in both high school football and basketball in the city's Cardozo High School. As a quarterback, he played in the District's first integrated high school championship football game between a Catholic and a public school in 1955. The game was played between Cardozo, which was all-black, and Gonzaga High School, an all-male and (then) all-white school run by the Roman Catholic order, the Society of Jesus (Jesuits). Wood also played in the

first integrated public school basketball game in the District, when his team faced all-white McKinley Tech in 1954, the year of the Supreme Court's *Brown v. Board of Education* school desegregation decision.

In 1955 after Wood graduated high school, his former Boys Club coach, Bill Butler, wrote to several colleges touting Wood's athletic potential. He was finally invited to the University of Southern California (USC). At USC the somewhat undersized (five feet, ten inches) Wood continued to play quarterback, which was unusual for a major college in the late 1950s—few African Americans were chosen for that position. Wood was the first African American quarterback in Pac-10 conference history.

After graduation from USC, Wood went undrafted by any pro football team at that position (despite another spirited letter-writing campaign on his behalf by Butler), but he was invited to try out for the Green Bay Packers as a free safety in 1960. Other teams ignored the letters, but the Packers were entering their second season under a new young coach, Vince Lombardi. Though smallish for an NFL safety, the speedy Wood, who proved to be a jarring tackler and valuable punt returner, helped to build one of the great Green Bay sides. After a year on the bench Wood earned a starting position in 1961, which he kept until his retirement in 1971. With Wood at safety, the Packers won world championships in 1961 and 1962, after losing the 1960 title game to the Philadelphia Eagles. From 1962 through 1971 Wood was named All-NFL nine times and was considered the premier safety in the game. During this time, he also appeared in eight Pro Bowls and six NFL Championship Games, and he helped the Packers win five NFL titles. Wood led the NFL in both interceptions and punt return average in 1962, helping the Packers to a World Championship season in which they defeated the New York football Giants by a score of 26-7 in the title game.

He was a vocal leader, both on the field and off, of the Packer dynasty, more so than unassuming quarterback Bart Starr or playboy halfback Paul Hornung. By 1967 the Packers, who won the first Super Bowl that year, had eight African American players on their roster. Wood's exceptional pass coverage and hard tackling in the first two Super Bowl games (1967 and 1968) helped bring him national fame. In "NFL Films," it was the chipper Wood who was shown on the sidelines telling his giddy Packer mates, "Guess who got it? The 'Hammer,'" when talkative Kansas City Chiefs cornerback (and future blaxploitation actor) FRED WILLIAMSON was accidentally knocked out cold by the knee of Packer guard Gale Gillingham during a play. Williamson had boasted that he would fell a Green Bay receiver during the game with his forearm shiver that he had labeled "The Hammer."

Wood intercepted forty-eight passes in his twelve NFL campaigns returning two for touchdowns. He also scored twice on punt returns. So exceptional was his leaping ability that the Packers would post him at the goal line on an opponent's field goal attempts so that he could attempt to block the kick (the goal posts were stationed at the goal line when he played).

In 1973 Wood was named head coach of the Philadelphia Bells in the upstart World Football League, the first black head coach in major professional football since FRITZ POLLARD guided the Akron Pros in the early 1920s. Wood, who was also the first black head coach in the Canadian Football League when he was hired by Herb Trawick to lead the Toronto Argonauts in 1980, was inducted into the Pro Football Hall of Fame in 1989.

In November 2006 Wood moved to an assisted care facility, with one of his two sons, having endured many surgeries as a result of his career as one of the smallest safeties in the pro game. Knee replacements, a hip replacement, and a degree of dementia beset the former hero, whose NFL pension paid out only $1,100 a month. In 2007 Wood's friends and supporters hosted benefits to assist him in paying for his five-figure medical bills. His plight resembled that of many former players, even much younger than Wood, who challenged the NFL and its union regarding better medical benefits for its former players. In 1992–93 Wood's son, Willie Jr., coached in the Arena Football League for the Indianapolis Firebirds.

FURTHER READING

Harrington, Denis J. *The Pro Football Hall of Fame: Players, Coaches, Team Owners, and League Officials, 1963–1991* (1991).

Hollander, Zander. "Great Moments in Pro Football," (1969).

Maske, Mark. "He's in Need, But Too Proud to Beg," *Washington Post*, 15 March 2007.

BIJAN C. BAYNE

Woodard, Beulah Ecton (11 Nov. 1895–13 July 1955), artist and sculptor, was born on a farm near Frankfort, Ohio. Woodard was the youngest of three children of William P. Ecton. A former slave, he had

fought in the Civil War and later became a successful businessman in Ohio and California. Little is known of his wife, Woodard's mother. Several of Woodard's relatives were artists; one of her grandmothers was an expert weaver and a male relation (either her grandfather or uncle) was a sculptor. While Woodard was still an infant, her family moved to Vernon, California. Her passion for studying Africa's history and cultures began at the age of twelve when her family was introduced to a visitor from Africa.

As a student at Polytechnic High School, Woodard studied architectural drawing. After graduation she found a job in a café and began to experiment with clay in her free time. She went on to study sculpture at the Los Angeles School of Art, the Otis Art Institute (now known as the Otis College of Art and Design), and the University of Southern California.

Woodard lived briefly in Chicago, Illinois, where she met and married Brady E. Woodard in 1928. Upon returning to Los Angeles, Woodard initially focused solely on being a wife and homemaker. However, she eventually returned to her art and set up a small sculpture studio in the rear of her home. The Harlem Renaissance, also known as the New Negro Movement, was an exhilarating time for African American writers, visual artists, and performers during the mid-1920s, but the artists' ability to sustain themselves financially was most often based on the largesse of wealthy white patrons. Although a cultural philosophy based on an African aesthetic was promoted during this period, patrons of African American artists were known to favor those artists of mixed heritage, possibly because they were viewed as being more exotic. Woodard withstood these temptations. On one occasion, a female patron would have paid for Woodard to study abroad had Woodard been willing to pretend she was a Native American. One historical account of this episode states that Woodard declined the offer (LeFalle-Collins, 39), while according to another, she remained home at her parents' request (Benjamin, 65).

Woodard's first exhibition was in the office of a California newspaper in 1935. The editor and publisher of the *California News*, James Rodney Smith, placed her sculptures in the office's windows and also allowed her to advertise in the paper. The subsequent exposure prompted Miriam Matthews, the first African American librarian in Los Angeles, to exhibit Woodard's sculptures in the Vernon branch of the Los Angeles Public Library and later at the Los Angeles Central Library that same year.

The interest generated by the library exhibitions led to several commissions for Woodard by way of the city's Urban League, culminating with Woodard holding a one-woman show at the Los Angeles County Museum of Art in the fall of 1935. She was the first African American artist to do so. The two-month exhibition featured nineteen African masks made of clay and papier-mâché, some adorned with beads and feathers. Because they were based on Woodard's cultural anthropological research, her sculptures were not considered stereotypical interpretations; instead, California art critics thought her masks sensitively rendered and strikingly detailed

Thousands of people both black and white came to view Woodward's work. The widespread press coverage of the show was monumental in establishing her career not only as a sculptor but also as an academic lecturer. Woodard's passion was two-fold: to instill ethnocultural self-esteem in African Americans and to develop in others a love and appreciation for all things African.

The next phase of her creative expression revealed her skill as a realist sculptor. In addition to using clay, Woodard carved and molded bronze, stone, and wood into the likenesses of everyday African Americans. Her preference for realism—to portray people and objects as they appeared in real life without sentimentality—converged with her desire to portray African Americans' dignity. Woodard created sculptures of the famous and non-famous. Among her best-known works are *Bad Boy*, *Sharecropper*, and *Maudelle*, all executed around 1936–1937. A 2002 Internet article by the artist CARLA WILLIAMS named the performer MAUDELLE BASS WESTON as the inspiration for *Maudelle*. Weston, professionally known by her maiden name, was a dancer and model who had also posed for the Mexican painter and muralist Diego Rivera. In a departure from her character studies, Woodard also created the sculpture *She*, which symbolized the quiet strength of all black womanhood.

Striving to nurture other African American artists, Woodard founded the Los Angeles Negro Art Association in 1937. Throughout her career she continued to exhibit, produce commissions, and win awards. In 1950, also for the purpose of cultivating talented young black artists, Woodard helped establish the Eleven Associated Artists Gallery in Los Angeles.

Woodard's sculptures and commissioned busts of Los Angeles's upper class eventually led to her international renown. Unfortunately, her death in the summer of 1955 preceded a major exhibition of her work that had been slated to tour several museums in Germany.

FURTHER READING

African American Registry. "Beulah Woodard Was an Early California Artist." http://www.aaregistry.com (2005).

Benjamin, Tritobia Hayes. "Triumphant Determination: The Legacy of African American Women Artists," in *Bearing Witness: Contemporary Works by African American Women Artists*, curated by Jontyle Theresa Robinson (1996).

Farrington, Lisa E. *Creating Their Own Image: The History of African-American Women Artists* (2005).

LeFalle-Collins, Lizzetta. "Working from the Pacific Rim: Beulah Woodard & Elizabeth Catlett," in *Three Generations of African American Women Sculptors: A Study in Paradox*, curated by Leslie King-Hammond and Tritobia Hayes Benjamin (1996).

JONETTE O'KELLEY MILLER

Woodard, Lynette (12 Aug. 1959–), basketball player born in Wichita, Kansas, the youngest child of Dorothy Woodard (maiden name unknown), a homemaker, and Lugene Woodard, a fireman. Woodard developed a love of basketball from her older brother, who taught her how to shoot using a sock. Growing up in Wichita, Woodard attended Marshall Junior High School. In her last year there that she was recruited to play varsity basketball for the high school. However, Woodard choose to develop her skills and played for the junior high. A year later, when she did attend Wichita North High School and joined the basketball team at five foot eleven she helped the team to a state championship in 1975 and then again in 1977. In 1977, she became an All American. In 1977, when Woodard graduated from high school, she chose to stay close to home and went to the University of Kansas (KU) in Lawrence. Woodard graduated in 1981 with a Bachelor of Arts in Speech Communication and Human Relations.

During her four years at KU, Woodard received the Kodak All-American honor four times and scored 3,649 points, the most points in NCAA women's basketball history, averaging 26 points a game. She also received the GTE Academic All American award in 1980 and 1981. Her total scored points during those four years led to her being named the all-time collegiate career-scoring leader and the most prolific scorer in women's college basketball history. In 1978 Woodard led the nation in rebounding and in 1979 led the nation in scoring. In 1981 she won the Wade Trophy, given annually to the best women's basketball player in National Collegiate Athletic Association (NCAA) Division I Competition. In 1982 she received the Broderick Award and the NCAA Top Five Award. She also had the most field goals and attempted field goals in NCAA women's basketball history. She set KU records in the areas of most rebounds (1,714), free throws made (505), steals (522), and games played (139) in KU's women's basketball history. For the 1980s, Woodard was the Big 8 player of the decade.

After graduation, Woodard joined an Italian Women's League team and led the league in the most points scored. In 1983 Woodard played for the USA National Team. In 1984 she was captain of the U.S. women's basketball team for the Los Angeles Olympic Games and won the gold medal. After the Olympics, Woodard stopped playing basketball, taking a position at her alma mater University of Kansas. However, in 1985 Woodard became the first female Harlem Globetrotter. Woodard traveled around the world with the Globetrotters for two years making a name for women in basketball. After her tenure with the Globetrotters, Woodard went back overseas to play for the Italian Women's League team again, this time taking them to the Italian League Championship in 1989. That same year, Woodard was inducted into the National High School Hall of Fame. In 1991 Woodard went to play for a Japanese League team. Woodard returned to the United States in 1992 to take a position as the athletic director for the Kansas City, Missouri, school district. She spent two years in that position before she relocated to New York City to become a registered stockbroker for Magna Securities Corp.

In 1997 Woodard was drafted in an elite selection for the newly formed WNBA (Women's National Basketball Association) Cleveland Rockers. Woodard would continue to work as a stockbroker in the off-season. In 1998, she went to play for the Detroit Shock, though she retired a year later. A guard, Woodard averaged 5.7 points, 3.3 rebounds, and 1.6 assist per game throughout her career. Upon retiring, Woodard became an assistant basketball coach at the University of Kansas. She would remained assistant coach until 2004, when she became interim head coach after the head coach stepped down for medical reasons. In 2004 Woodard became a financial consultant for AG Edwards Brokerage Services. In 2005 Woodard became a Registered Investment Advisor for Cornerstone Securities.

Throughout her life, Woodard has been honored on many different occasions. She has been inducted into ten different halls of fame including the Walk of Stars Hall of Fame–Kansas City (2001), Naismith Hall of Fame as a Team Induction for the Harlem Globetrotters in 2002 and then again as a player in 2004, Black Legend's Professional Basketball Hall of Fame (2003), Women's Basketball Hall of Fame (2005), and the African-American Sports Hall of Fame (2006). Woodward received the Flo Hyman Award presented by President Bill Clinton (and named for volleyball great, FLO HYMAN), among many other prestigious awards. Woodard has made a name for herself and paved the way for girls who want to play basketball.

FURTHER READING

Johnson, Roy. "Far above the Crowd." *Sports Illustrated*, 26 Jan. 1981, 43.

Lidz, Franz. "Move Over, Georgia Brown." *Sports Illustrated*, 6 Jan. 1986, 44.

"Lynette Woodward," The Lynette Woodward Group, LLC, http://www.lynettewoodward.com/bio.htm

ELIZABETH OKIGBO

Woodbey, George Washington (5 Oct. 1854–1937), minister, author, pamphleteer, and Socialist Party activist, was born a slave in Johnson County, Tennessee, the son of Charles Woodbey and Rachel Wagner Woodbey. While little is known about Woodbey's parents and early life, it is clear that he worked as a manual laborer in his youth. Woodbey was largely self-educated, attending only two terms of common school, yet he learned to read after gaining freedom during the Civil War. His experience of servitude spurred his gradual allegiance to socialism. As Woodbey wrote, he was "one who was once a chattel slave freed by the proclamation of Lincoln and now wishes to be free from the slavery of capitalism" (Foner, 10).

By 1874 Woodbey had been ordained a Baptist minister in Emporia, Kansas. Like many blacks confronted with the failure of Reconstruction, Woodbey migrated westward. It is estimated that some seven thousand black families fled Tennessee and Kentucky, and like Woodbey, many of these migrants settled in Kansas. Woodbey established himself as a political reformer in both the Republican and Prohibition parties in Kansas before moving to Nebraska. His political ascendancy in progressive circles was marked by his run for lieutenant governor in Nebraska on the Prohibition Party ticket in 1896.

Shortly thereafter Woodbey abandoned the Prohibition Party for William Jennings Bryan and the Populist Party, which introduced Woodbey to the various radical political ideologies on the midwestern political scene. Many Populists had grown disillusioned with what they perceived as Bryan's subservience to big business and had gravitated to Eugene V. Debs's Social Party of America. Woodbey was no exception. His exposure to Edward Bellamy's *Looking Backward* awakened his socialist convictions. The main character in Bellamy's novel awakes in the year 2000, after falling asleep more than one hundred years earlier, to find that the capitalist exploitation in place before his slumber had gradually evolved into a state of brotherhood and equality. But it was Debs's persuasive speeches that inspired Woodbey to leave the Populist Party and embrace socialism. As a Christian minister Woodbey was predisposed to Debs's gradual and reformist brand of socialism.

After traveling to San Diego, California, in 1902 to reunite with his mother, Woodbey's socialist views flourished. Now a member of the Socialist Party, Woodbey delivered a number of persuasive speeches that impressed the local Socialists. He was soon elected to the California executive board of the Socialist Party. His passion, faith, and oratorical ability also led to a post as a minister at the Mount Zion Baptist Church on Thirtieth and Greely streets in San Diego, an important cultural center for San Diego's black community, as well as a refuge from the racism alive throughout the city.

Woodbey's project to combine Christianity with socialism faced many obstacles, one of which was the Mount Zion Church itself, which grew impatient with his socialist politics. Although he was a popular minister at the church for more than a decade, the congregation was increasingly critical about their revered preacher's socialist agitation. Woodbey was briefly jailed in 1902 and 1908 for acts of civil disobedience and arrested during the famous 1912 free speech fights. Despite his church's distaste for radical politics, Woodbey did not hesitate to criticize even the most influential black leaders of his day. In a 1903 speech before a packed audience in Los Angeles, Woodbey described BOOKER T. WASHINGTON as a "good servant of capitalism." Though Woodbey risked professional ruin by criticizing such a powerful figure, he nonetheless remained loyal to the more radical currents in American culture. He firmly established himself as the leading black Socialist of the first two decades of the twentieth century and was internationally recognized among Socialists. His pamphlets—most notable among them *What to Do and How to Do It, or Socialism vs. Capitalism* (1903), *The Bible and Socialism* (1904), and *The Distribution of Wealth* (1910)—were translated into several languages. The aim of these writings was to foster a socialist society through electoral politics and to emphasize the link between Christianity and socialism, and Woodbey's ability to describe socialist theory in plain language added much to their appeal.

Woodbey's reputation as a radical reformer quickly spread, something which undoubtedly raised eyebrows at the Mount Zion Church. In 1908 Woodbey was the sole black delegate at the national Socialist Party convention. He was selected as Debs's vice presidential running mate on the Socialist Party ticket that same year. After the convention Woodbey launched a speaking tour in northern areas with significant black populations to promote the Socialist Party line. At least one important black preacher, George Slater Jr., was inspired by Woodbey's oratory. Slater, who was a pastor at the Zion Tabernacle in Chicago, Illinois, credited Woodbey's speeches for his "conversion" to socialism. Like Woodbey he also attempted to recruit blacks into the Socialist Party, writing political articles in the *Chicago Daily Socialist*.

With Woodbey's stature firmly established in socialist circles, the Mount Zion Church voted to discharge him in 1915 because, as one member explained, he mixed "too much socialism with his bible, and this the members of the church resented" (Foner, 35). Although little is known about Woodbey's life after 1915, it is believed that he abandoned preaching for socialist politics during the 1920s. Woodbey's influence reached into the twenty-first century. Well-known scholars such as JAMES HAL CONE and CORNEL WEST cited Woodbey's example as having in part inspired their own attempts at conjoining socialism and Christianity.

FURTHER READING

Craig, Robert H. *Religion and Radical Politics: An Alternative Christian Tradition in the United States* (1992).

Foner, Philip S., ed. *Black Socialist Preacher: The Teachings and Writings of Reverend George Washington Woodbey and His Disciple Reverend George W. Slater, Jr.* (1983).

Madyun, Gail, and Larry Malone. "Black Pioneers in San Diego, 1880–1920," *Journal of San Diego History* (Spring, 1983).

CARL MIRRA

Woodby-McKane, Alice. *See* McKane, Alice Woodby.

Wooding, Sam (17 June 1895–1 Aug. 1985), band leader and pianist, was born Samuel David Wooding in Philadelphia, Pennsylvania, the son of a butler and a laundress whose names are unknown. Wooding claimed that a performance by the vaudeville comedy team BERT WILLIAMS and GEORGE WALKER inspired his interest in music as a career. Although he sang, played piano, and even composed from an early age, Sam did not receive formal musical training, in the form of private lessons, until after he graduated from South Philadelphia High School for Boys. Following a career as a band leader in Europe and the United States, he enrolled in the University of Pennsylvania for further musical study, earning a B.A. in 1942 and an M.Ed. in 1945.

During World War I Wooding played tenor horn from 1917 to 1919 in the 807th Pioneer Infantry Band, one of a number of all-volunteer black military bands that played in France as part of the morale effort. The Pioneer Band was led by the Ziegfeld Follies arranger William Vodery, who would have been well acquainted with popular theatrical and syncopated dance music; however, Wooding stated that the band performed only military music and marches. After the war, in 1919, Wooding returned to Atlantic City and organized his first band, the Society Syncopators. By 1920 he was playing and leading ensembles in clubs in Detroit and New York City, playing first in Barron's Club and then at the Nest Club in 1923. In July 1924 he and his group replaced FLETCHER HENDERSON's band at the Club Alabam.

In 1925 the Russian impresario Leoni Leonidof signed Wooding and his band to accompany a black theatrical revue, *The Chocolate Kiddies*, destined for Berlin. Wooding and his ensemble were to supply all the music for the revue as well as perform. The ten-member group Wooding took with him included Tommy Ladnier, who had played trumpet with KING OLIVER, the trombonist Herb Flemming, and Garvin Bushell on reeds. All of these performers have written memoirs of their time in Europe.

With a cast of forty singers and dancers, the revue provided German audiences with supposedly authentic depictions of African American life in Harlem and on a southern plantation. The music consisted of four numbers by DUKE ELLINGTON and Joe Trent, other popular songs, works by Stephen Foster, traditional African American spirituals, and even "jazzed-up" arrangements of concert music. Wooding's ensemble performed alone as the second act.

Although American jazz and dance music were quite popular in Germany, no band consisting entirely of American performers had appeared in Germany prior to the arrival of Wooding and his orchestra. The band proved to be the most successful part of the revue, receiving thunderous and enthusiastic response. Within six weeks of the revue's opening, Wooding had signed a recording contract with the German Vox label and recorded four tunes from the revue, becoming the first jazz ensemble to record in Europe. These recordings, available on a Biograph reissue, provide a good idea of the exuberant, though unpolished, quality of the young band. Wooding's arrangements are generally in the style of the "symphonic jazz" popularized by Paul Whiteman, whom Wooding admired, and they feature some notable solos by his sidemen.

Program listings from subsequent performances indicate that the group's repertory consisted of works ranging from early jazz standards like "St. Louis Blues" and "Memphis Blues" to *Rhapsody in Blue* and jazzy arrangements of Tchaikovsky's *1812 Overture*, John Philip Sousa's "Stars and Stripes" march, and even operatic selections from Verdi, Wagner, and Gounod. Wooding's revue orchestra recorded again in Berlin in 1926 and gave several live broadcasts over the Berlin radio.

After the revue closed in Berlin, it toured for another year, playing dates throughout Germany, eastern Europe, Scandinavia, Russia, Turkey, England, and Italy. Wooding left the revue in 1926, and he and his ensemble continued touring throughout Europe, Russia, and South America. Often the first African Americans their audiences had ever seen, the band experienced some racist press coverage. More often they met with initial curiosity followed by genuine enthusiasm and admiration. After returning to the United States in 1927 Wooding turned down a job at the then unknown Cotton Club, and instead chose to resume touring Europe. The band recorded both in Paris and in Barcelona in 1929, and finally disbanded in Belgium in 1931 as the worsening economic climate and political changes, especially in Germany, made it difficult to book performances.

After returning to the United States in 1932, Wooding resumed his career as a band leader, but given his unknown standing in his native country, he had difficulty finding a steady position. He returned to school at the University of Pennsylvania and founded the Southland Spiritual Choir and other vocal ensembles that toured the United States with some success throughout the 1930s and 1940s. He also worked for a time as a public school music educator and ran his own recording studio.

In 1953 he began performing with singer Rae Harrison, whom he married (date unknown) and for whom he composed songs. They toured extensively throughout the world during the late 1950s and 1960s, resided in Germany for a time, and made recordings. By 1975 Wooding had returned to New York and organized another big band with the intention of performing his old arrangements along with new material that featured Harrison as lead singer. The ensemble performed until two years before Wooding's death in New York City. An earlier marriage, before 1925, to Ethel (maiden name unknown) produced one child who predeceased Wooding in 1980.

Although still little-known in the United States, Sam Wooding achieved a remarkable number of firsts: he led the first American jazz band to play in Germany, to record in Europe, and to tour extensively. The band was notable as well for providing audiences throughout Europe, Scandinavia, and Russia with their first exposure to true American jazz.

FURTHER READING

Wooding's papers are at the Schomburg Center for Research in Black Culture, New York City.

Bushell, Garvin. *Jazz from the Beginning* (1988).

Cook, Susan C. "Jazz as Deliverance: The Reception and Institution of American Jazz during the Weimar Republic," *American Music* 7 (Spring 1989).

Deffaa, Chip. "Sam Wooding: Jazz Pioneer," *Mississippi Rag*, June 1986; July 1986.

Flemming, Herb. "Old Sam: The Man Who Brought Jazz to Europe," *Jazz Journal* 21 (1968).

Obituary: *Variety*, 7 Aug. 1985.

This entry is taken from the *American National Biography* and is published here with the permission of the American Council of Learned Societies.

SUSAN C. COOK

Woodruff, Hale Aspacio (26 Aug. 1900–26 Sept. 1980), artist and teacher, was born in Cairo, Illinois, the only child of Augusta (Bell) Woodruff, a domestic worker, and George Woodruff, who died when his son was quite young. After his father's death, Woodruff and his mother moved to east Nashville, Tennessee. Art instruction was not available in his segregated public school, so Woodruff drew on his own, mostly copying from books, and later as a cartoonist for his high school newspaper.

After graduating from high school in 1918, Woodruff moved to Indianapolis, Illinois, where he held several menial jobs while living at the YMCA. From 1920 to 1922 he studied landscape painting with William Forsyth at the Herron School of Art, while drawing weekly cartoons for the local African American newspaper, *The Indianapolis Ledger*. After a short stint in Chicago, where he studied briefly at the School of the Art Institute of Chicago, he returned to Indianapolis. By the mid-1920s he had experienced some success as a working artist, exhibiting at a few local galleries, the Herron Art Museum, and the YMCA's annual Indiana artists' exhibition. In 1924 he won third prize in *Crisis* magazine's Amy Spingarn Prize contest, bringing him to the attention of NAACP leaders W. E. B. DuBois and WALTER WHITE. The following year he became the membership director of the Senate Avenue YMCA, the country's largest African American YMCA branch, through which he met and was inspired by the many African American political and cultural leaders who came to speak.

When his painting *The Old Women* won a bronze award from the Harmon Foundation in 1926, Woodruff's dream of studying painting abroad took shape. In September 1927 he left for Paris, funded by one hundred dollars in prize money and financial support from local patrons. PALMER HAYDEN, a fellow African American painter, helped situate Woodruff in Paris, where he enrolled in two small art schools, the Académies Scandinave and Moderne. Over the next year and a half he wrote tourist features, essentially dispatches to his hometown paper, often accompanied by his own drawings, for *The Indianapolis Star*. In the winter of 1928, Woodruff made a pilgrimage to see HENRY OSSAWA TANNER in Normandy, a visit that had a lasting and profound effect on the young artist. In 1929 Woodruff moved to Cagnes-sur-Mer, a village in the south of France where African American painter WILLIAM H. JOHNSON had lived several years earlier.

Through his visits to Parisian galleries and shops Woodruff had been introduced to African art, then in vogue with collectors and modern artists. While this exposure proved pivotal to his later work, the watercolors and paintings Woodruff produced in France were primarily influenced by the Postimpressionists and early modernists, especially Picasso, Braque, and Cézanne. In 1930 he had a few small exhibitions in Paris. More importantly, however, his works, including the paintings *Old Farmhouse in Beauce Valley* (c. 1927), *Old Woman Peeling Apples* (1929), and *The Card Players* (1930), were being exhibited in the United States in the Harmon Foundation annual shows and had piqued the interest of American collectors.

Having run out of money, Woodruff left France in the fall of 1931, accepting JOHN HOPE's offer of a teaching post at Atlanta University. As the school's first and only art instructor, Woodruff taught students from its affiliate colleges, Spelman and Morehouse, the university's Laboratory High School, Oglethorpe elementary school, summer school workshops, and People's College. Over the next fifteen years Woodruff built an art curriculum that included innovative interdisciplinary arts courses, and he recruited sculptor NANCY ELIZABETH PROPHET and other art faculty. He also secured crucial financial and material gifts to the art department. He launched an annual student exhibition and brought traveling exhibitions to the campus, offering students—and faculty—opportunities to view historical and contemporary art unavailable to them in Atlanta's segregated facilities.

Within a few years Atlanta University had become a center for young black artists. Woodruff endowed students with self-confidence, encouraging them to exhibit and take risks with their work, especially by working from their own experience and backgrounds. He organized his students into a "Painter's Guild," explaining to *Time* magazine in 1942, "We are interested in the South as a field, as a territory: its particular rundown landscapes, its social and economic problems, and [its] Negro people." Woodruff's students, including Wilmer Jennings, Frederick Flemister, Eugene Grigsby, Hayward Oubre, and Lawrence A. Jones, many of whom depicted African American figures, became known as the Atlanta School.

Woodruff's influence on black artists was felt beyond his own classroom. In 1942 he initiated, and continued to jury, an annual exhibition of African American artists at Atlanta University. Within three years the Atlanta Annuals had become the chief national outlet for black artists to exhibit, sell, and win prize money for their work. By 1970, the last year of the Annuals, more than nine hundred black artists had been exhibited and the university had amassed one of the nation's largest collections of African American art.

Influenced by social realism, American regionalism, and the Mexican muralists, Woodruff's own work began to shift in style and subject within several years of his return from France. From the early 1930s until after World War II, Woodruff depicted the distinctly American landscape of the segregated American South in paintings like *Big Wind in Georgia* (c. 1933), *Picking Cotton* (c.1936), and *Cigarette Smoker* (n.d). He joined African American artists CHARLES ALSTON, CHARLES WHITE, DOX THRASH, ROBERT BLACKBURN, and ELIZABETH CATLETT in adopting the democratizing medium of printmaking, producing linoleum and woodblock prints, such as *Returning Home, Old Church and Sunday Promenade*, and *Relics*, that offered an unsentimental view of life and poverty in black southern communities. In 1935 he contributed two haunting linocuts, *Giddap* and *By Parties Unknown*, to an art exhibition on lynching sponsored by NAACP.

In the summer of 1934 Woodruff apprenticed himself to Mexican artist Diego Rivera in Mexico City, an experience that deeply affected both his teaching and painting. Woodruff's first murals, *The Negro in Modern American Life, Literature, Music, Agriculture, Rural Life, and Art* (1934), and two panels for the Atlanta School of Social Work in 1935, were sponsored by the Works Progress Administration (WPA). Woodruff's next major mural, commissioned by Talladega College, was a series of three six-by-ten-foot panels depicting the 1839 slave mutiny led by CINQUE aboard the *Amistad*, the 1840 trial of the slaves who participated, and their triumphant return to Sierra Leone in 1842. Completed in 1939 but begun more than a year earlier, the work was the result of nine months of painting preceded by months of intensive historical research, including trips to New Haven, Connecticut, the site of the trial, to view the letters, documents, and drawings of *Amistad* participants. The paintings' bright colors, sculptural figures, and focus on dramatic gesture show Woodruff's debt to the Mexican muralists. The commission also included a second set of four murals celebrating the founding of Talladega College and the newly completed Slavery Library on campus. After the success of the *Amistad* murals, Woodruff received other mural commissions, including the recently rediscovered panels *Effects of Bad Housing* and *Effects of Good Housing*, completed in 1942.

Woodruff had married Theresa Ada Baker, a teacher from Topeka, Kansas, in 1934, and the couple had a son, Roy, the following year. When Woodruff received a Rosenwald Fund Fellowship in 1943 (renewed in 1944), the family moved to New York, where for the first time in twelve years

Woodruff devoted himself solely to painting. He returned briefly to Atlanta for the fall term of 1945, before joining the faculty of the Department of Art Education at New York University the following semester, a position he held until retiring in 1968. In 1948 Woodruff and Charles Alston collaborated on a two-part mural celebrating the contributions of African Americans to California, commissioned for the lobby of a new one-million-dollar Los Angeles headquarters of Golden State Mutual Life Insurance Company, one of the West's largest black-owned businesses.

Woodruff's move to New York in the early 1940s coincided with seismic shifts in the history of painting brought about by artists like Jackson Pollock, Willem de Kooning, Franz Kline, and Helen Frankenthaler, who were forging a new, purely abstract, non-representational style. Just when Woodruff began experimenting with abstraction is difficult to pinpoint because he often left his works undated. His works from the late 1940s, however, show an increased interest in abstraction and patterning and illustrate a more hearty, gestural use of paint. By the 1950s, in works like *Carnival* (1950) and *Europa and the Bull* (1958), he was producing abstracted landscapes in muted tones of blues, greens, burgundy, and mustard yellow.

Just as he had amended the vocabulary of the social realists and American regionalists, Woodruff offered a unique brand of abstraction, steeped in an African American context. Like the abstract expressionists' preoccupation with mythology and psychology, Woodruff also turned to signs and symbols drawn from the waking and subconscious mind. In Woodruff's case, however, the subject was the African American collective experience. Years before the Black Arts Movement and Africobra, he was investigating themes of black pride and Afrocentrism, folding African elements into paintings like *Afro Emblems* (1950), *Ancestral Memory* (1966), and especially the *Celestial Gates* (1953) series. His project, however, was more complex than introducing African motifs and forms; he was questioning the slippery boundary between celebrating—and appropriating—African art, and by extension, Africa.

In 1950 Woodruff returned to Atlanta University to work on a mural project he had proposed more than a decade before. Woodruff came to view the resulting *Art of the Negro* cycle as the most significant work of his career. While representational and highly narrative, the six eleven-foot murals employed the themes and style he would explore further in his abstract works. The mural begins with a panel called *Native Forms*, which is a survey of the traditional arts of Africa, including cave painting, sculpture, and masks. The second panel, *Interchange*, shows the exchange of ideas between ancient Africa and the West, and was followed, in panel three (*Dissipation*), by the destruction and looting of African artifacts during colonialization, exemplified by the British burning of Benin in 1897. The fourth panel illustrates *Parallels* in the arts of Africa, Oceana, and the native peoples of the Americas, while panel five, called *Influences*, references the sculpture of Henry Moore and the paintings of Amadeo Modigliani, along with other examples of modern art's debt to African art. The final panel, *Muses*, features seventeen black artists from ancient Africa to contemporary America.

In 1963, hoping to further the goals of the civil rights movement, Woodruff and ROMARE BEARDEN established Spiral, a weekly discussion group of ten to sixteen African American artists that included Alston, Norman Lewis, RICHARD MAYHEW, ERNEST CRICHLOW, and EMMA AMOS. While the group disbanded in 1966, it laid the groundwork for the Black Arts Movement groups of the late 1960s and 1970s. In the mid-1960s he served as chair of visual arts committee for the United States exhibition at the First World Festival of Negro Arts in Dakar, Senegal, and as the U.S. representative on two State Department–sponsored trips to Africa. In 1967 Woodruff received solo exhibitions at New York University, the Museum of Fine Arts in Boston, the San Diego Art Museum, and the Los Angeles County Museum of Art. A year before his death in 1980, a major retrospective of his work was held at the Studio Museum in Harlem.

FURTHER READING

Reynolds, Gary A., and Beryl J. Wright. *Against the Odds: African-American Artists and the Harmon Foundation* (1989).

Studio Museum in Harlem. *Hale Woodruff: 50 Years of His Art* (1979).

LISA E. RIVO

Woods, Brent (c.1850–31 Mar. 1906), U.S. Army soldier, Indian Wars veteran, and Medal of Honor recipient, was born enslaved in Somerset, Pulaski County, Kentucky. Nothing is known of his early life, but he gained his freedom by the end of the Civil War in 1865. Woods subsequently made a living as a farmer before he signed up for the military service that would remain his occupation for most of the remainder of his life.

On 10 October 1873, Woods journeyed to Louisville, Kentucky, where he joined the army. Described as a mulatto and measuring in at five feet, six inches in height, Woods was assigned to Troop B of the 9th Cavalry Regiment. This unit was one of six all-black army regiments (soon after consolidated into four) authorized by Congress in 1866, which included the 9th and 10th Cavalry Regiments and the 24th and 25th Infantry regiments. These newly formed regiments would soon be assigned duty on the western frontier and quickly made a name for themselves, gaining the collective nickname "Buffalo Soldiers," and were famed for their prowess in helping to open the West for the flood of settlers that arrived in the years after the end of the Civil War.

The duties performed by African American soldiers such as Woods, MOSES WILLIAMS, and ADAM PAINE, included scouting and protecting wagon trains and new settlements, mining camps, and outposts from raids by the Native American peoples that did not willingly accept the invasion of their tribal homelands. The duty these black soldiers performed, often in extreme weather conditions, was arduous at best, and often deadly; the Native American warriors they battled knew their land well and often made quick-strike raids on frontier settlements, and then faded into the landscape, sometimes waiting in ambush for the soldiers that pursued them. Indeed, because of their outstanding service, the Buffalo Soldiers were integral in helping to facilitate the westward expansion of America.

On 19 August 1881, with nearly eight years of cavalry experience behind him, Sergeant Brent Woods was among a group of seventeen troopers led by Second Lieutenant George Smith, along with twenty miners led by George Daly, who were in pursuit of the famed Apache chief Nana and his warriors in the northern part of New Mexico Territory. At Gavalin Canyon, near modern day Taos, New Mexico, the troopers and miners were ambushed by an outnumbered Nana and took heavy fire. Daly was killed in the initial fire, while Smith was killed soon after he ordered his troopers to dismount. With Lieutenant Smith dead, command of the troopers fell to Sergeant Woods, who quickly rallied both his troopers and the miners and organized their positions. Woods then led his men in an assault on the Apache position; when they were pinned down by heavy fire from Nana's warriors, Woods continued the assault on his own. During

Brent Woods, Medal of Honor recipient (c. 1900). (Library of Congress/Daniel Murray Collection.)

his advance he was lightly wounded, but continued on and kept up a continuous fire that soon forced the Apache warriors to abandon their position and leave the canyon. Had it not been for Sergeant Brent Woods's leadership, the troopers and miners might have been overwhelmed, and one of the miners later commented that "That Sergeant Woods is an S.O.B. in a fight. If it hadn't been for him, none of us would have come out of that canyon" (Hanna, p. 97).

It was not until 12 July 1894, nearly thirteen years after performing his heroic deeds, that Woods was awarded the Medal of Honor. It is uncertain whether the award was initiated at Woods's own request, as was allowable at this time, or by an officer in the 9th Cavalry who had knowledge of his heroics. Brent Woods would continue his army career until his retirement after nearly thirty years of service on 22 November 1902 at the Presidio in California. Woods would subsequently return to his native Kentucky, living with his wife Pearl near Somerset. He would enjoy his retirement until his death at the early age of fifty-five, perhaps worn out by his years of western service. He was subsequently buried in a lonely grave, his service to his country all but forgotten. However, this changed in 1984 when Brent Woods was reburied in the Mill Springs National Cemetery in Nancy, Kentucky, grave 930 in section A, with full military honors and a Medal of Honor headstone as a result of the efforts of a friend of his widow.

FURTHER READING

Hanna, Charles W. *African American Recipients of the Medal of Honor* (2002).

Neal, Tricia. "Civil War Hero from Pulaski to Be Honored." *Commonwealth Journal,* Feb. 12, 2008. http://somerset-kentucky.com/local/x681542730/ Civil-War-hero-from-Pulaski-to-be-honored,

GLENN ALLEN KNOBLOCK

Woods, Geraldine Pittman (29 Jan. 1921–27 Dec. 1999), biologist, civic leader, and minority education and career consultant, was born in West Palm Beach, Florida, to Oscar Pittman and Susie King Pittman. Throughout her life she was often called "Jerry." Despite both Pittman's parents leaving school after eighth grade, they became prosperous through their lumber business, farms, restaurants, and rental properties. However, they urged Pittman to obtain as much formal education as she possibly could. Through the end of third grade, she attended a private school run by the Episcopal church, then transferred to Industrial High School (apparently taking a grade-level curriculum) because no other public school in her hometown permitted black students.

Although she enjoyed science, she had some learning difficulties at school and, for her family and teachers, a science career for a young black woman was not on the radar. However, she was an avid reader and an active participant in church and musical activities. Although her father died when she was in high school, Jerry was able to continue her education as he and her mother had wished. She graduated from high school in 1938 and went on to Alabama's historically black Talladega College.

In 1940 Pittman's mother became gravely ill and sought treatment from Johns Hopkins University Hospital in Baltimore, Maryland. To be close to her mother, Pittman transferred to nearby Howard University in Washington, D.C. She began to blossom in her science studies, impressing her professors so much that they helped her get into the graduate biology program at Harvard-Radcliffe. Meanwhile her mother recuperated. Pittman received her B.S. in zoology from Howard in 1942.

Although intimidated at first by the majority-white environment and the state-of-the-art laboratory equipment at Harvard-Radcliffe, Pittman quickly applied herself and excelled in her graduate studies. She earned her master's degree in neuroembryology in 1943 and her doctorate in the same life science in 1945. She not only earned her graduate degrees within a two-year span, but was inducted into the honorary society Phi Beta Kappa.

From 1945 to 1946 Pittman taught biology at Howard University. On 30 January 1945, Jerry Pittman wed Robert Woods, a dental student at historically black Meharry Medical College in Nashville, Tennessee. They had a commuter marriage until he graduated in 1947 and the couple moved to Los Angeles. There he launched a dentistry practice near Inglewood with the assistance of friends, and she became a full-time homemaker. The couple had three children: Jerri, Jan (married surname Rocks), and Robert Jr.

When the children entered their teens, Jerry Pittman Woods dedicated herself to volunteer community service. Initially she was active at the local level, but word spread about her leadership abilities. Soon she was making a difference at the state and national levels, too. She served on the boards of the Young Women's Christian Association and Family Services of LA, as well as that of Claremont College's Center for Educational Opportunity. Pittman Woods had two stints on the interviewing panel of the personnel board, California Department of Education. From 1963 to 1967 she was national president of the historically African American Delta Sigma Theta sorority. In this role she advocated for the establishment of the federal Head Start preschool program, and attended its official launch ceremony at the White House in 1965. In 1967 she helped to start the sorority's Delta Research and Educational Foundation. From 1966 to 1970 she was appointed to President Lyndon Johnson's Defense Advisory Committee on Women in the Armed Services, chairing it from 1967 to 1970.

From 1969 to 1987 Jerry Pittman Woods was employed as a special consultant on minority education and career development to the National Institute of General Medical Sciences (NIGMS), part of the federal government's National Institutes of Health (NIH). She was determined to improve recruitment and support, especially financial assistance, of minority students interested in biomedical sciences. She was just as concerned about boosting the ability of scientists at minority institutions to compete for research grants and enjoy other opportunities for professional advancement. Pittman Woods was instrumental in creating and gathering vital professional and political backing for two enduring and critical programs within NIGMS: Minority Biomedical Research Support (MBRS) and Minority Access to Research Careers (MARC). Because of her dedicated efforts, NIGMS began to offer support for minority biomedical scientists at every stage of career development, from high school student to university faculty member.

Even as she worked diligently at NIH, Pittman Woods found time and energy for many other public service roles, including vice chair, Community Relations Foundation of Southern California (1968–1972); trustee, California Museum of Science and Industry (1971–1979); graduate studies advocacy board member, Meharry Medical College (1972–1975); advisory committee member, Air Pollution Manpower Development, Environmental Protection Agency (1973–1975); and national board member, Girl Scouts USA (1975–1978). In her most notable capacity other than her work at NIH, Pittman Woods became the first woman ever to head Howard University's board of trustees, from 1975 to 1988. She was awarded honorary doctorates from Howard, Talladega, Meharry, Benedict College, Bennett College, and Fisk University.

Even after her retirement from public life in 1991, Pittman Woods stayed in touch with her colleagues at NIH. She enjoyed hearing about the continued successes of the MBRS and MARC programs and the scientists who participated in them. When she was seventy-eight years old, Geraldine Pittman Woods died of cancer complications at her home in Aliso Viejo, California. Her husband of fifty-four years, their three children, and three grandchildren were among the survivors. Dr. Ruth Kirschstein, NIGMS director from 1974 to 1993, called Pittman Woods "a person ahead of her time" who never forgot what it was like to be an African American trailblazer in the sciences and who "worked tirelessly" to create opportunities for other scientists of color (quoted in *NIGMS Minority Programs Update* obituary). In 2000 Howard University Medical School established its Geraldine P. Woods Endowment Fund. In 2003 the Annual Biomedical Research Conference for Minority Students (ABRCMS) created the Geraldine Woods Award to honor advocates for underrepresented minority groups in the biomedical sciences.

FURTHER READING

"Geraldine Pittman Woods," in *Distinguished African American Scientists of the 20th Century*, ed. James

H. Kessler, Katherine A. Morin, Jerry S. Kidd, and Renee A. Kidd (1996).

Mitchell, Jilliene, "ABRCMS Commemorates NIGMS Anniversaries," *NIGMS Minority Programs Update* (Winter 2003).

Smith, Jessie Carney, "Geraldine Pittman Woods," in *Notable Black American Women*, ed. Jessie Carney Smith (1992–1996).

Obituaries: *NIGMS Minority Programs Update*, Winter 2000;

Washington Post, 12 Jan. 2000.

MARY KRANE DERR

Woods, Granville T. (23 Apr. 1856–30 Jan. 1910), mechanical and electrical engineer and inventor, was born in Columbus, Ohio. Nothing is known of Woods's parents except that they may have been named Tailer and Martha Woods. The effects of racism in Columbus, shortly before and during the Civil War, were somewhat blunted by the economic influence of a sizable African American population, which included artisans and property holders, and by growing sympathy among whites for abolitionism. Only a few years before Woods's birth, the city established a system of segregated schools for black children, which provided him an education until he was ten years old.

Like almost all American engineers during the nineteenth century, Woods obtained his technical training largely through self-study and on-the-job experience, rather than from formal schooling. Sometime after 1866 he began apprenticing as a blacksmith and machinist, probably in Cincinnati, where several decades earlier German immigrants had established a flourishing machine tool industry. Machinists considered themselves members of an elite profession, and by and large they selected only the most promising and ambitious candidates for apprenticeships. Success depended on a vivid spatial imagination, mathematical adroitness, and draftsmanship. Indeed, Woods's letters patent displayed abundant evidence of all these talents, most apparently the latter. His drawings were consistently rendered with the flair of a first-rate draftsman—presumably Woods himself.

Most of Woods's inventions were electromechanical devices and systems related to railroad technology. His interest in these fields grew out of an eclectic early experience with railroads and from dogged self-study. In November 1872 Woods moved east and was soon hired as an engineer on the St. Louis and Iron Mountain Railroad in Missouri. Given his training and youth, he likely operated lathes and drill presses in a machine shop. During his employment with Iron Mountain, he began studying electricity—at least three years before Thomas Edison patented his revolutionary lighting system. Since almost no American university provided such training, Woods had to learn about electricity from technical books and periodicals. Woods left the Iron Mountain Railroad in early 1876, and then spent two years studying at Stern's Institute of Technology. In February 1878 he signed on to the British steamer *Ironsides* as chief engineer. Two years later he returned east, where he handled locomotives for the Southern Railway, whose line ran near Danville, Kentucky.

Sometime after 1880 Woods began his career as an inventor in Cincinnati, probably only to sell one or two ideas. He chose a propitious historical moment and region. Cincinnati was home to a larger and more cohesive and prosperous African American community than that which resided in Columbus, and southwestern Ohio boasted some of the best machine shops in America. With few corporations willing to invest in their own research laboratories, independent inventors like Woods filled a niche by feeding the burgeoning appetite of those corporations for technological innovation. From the outset he made money. His first patent, filed on 18 June 1883, was a replacement for Alexander Graham Bell's crude telephone transmitter (that is, mouthpiece). His second invention followed almost immediately, an improved steam-boiler furnace. Significantly, he sold the transmitter to two local investors for a modest fee. This success sharply contrasted with the typical experience of a patentee during the period, when ownership of almost all inventions remained forever in the hands of their profitless inventors.

Woods resided in Cincinnati for most of the 1880s, applying for some seventeen patents while he lived there. Around 1886 he founded the Woods Electric Company. One newspaper reported Woods's intention to capitalize his new firm at $1 million and to sell shares for $50, which suggests that he planned a large-scale factory, but if so the proposal fell through and the firm functioned only as a temporary assignee—that is, the legal owner—for ten of his patents. The company last appears in the historical record in April 1890, as assignee on Woods's last Ohio patent.

By August 1891 Woods had relocated to the New York City area. Earlier, he had traveled extensively among large northeastern cities, probably as an engineering consultant, so he likely moved to be

Granville T. Woods patented over thirty-five inventions in his lifetime. (AP Images.)

nearer to his work. He lived out the remaining seventeen years of his life in New York, maintaining the vigorous pace he had established in Ohio. The U.S. Patent Office issued him twenty-eight letters patent for his New York inventions, seven of which listed a brother, Lyates, as co-inventor. Incredibly, he found assignees for all but five. As an engineer, Woods was no revolutionary, and his inventions characteristically tackled problems associated with established technological systems. He focused primarily on inventing communications, power distribution, and control devices for electric trains, a cutting-edge technology that large cities such as New York, Boston, Philadelphia, and Washington, D.C., were increasingly adopting. In 1884 he filed a patent application for "Telegraphony," a combination telegraph and telephone system that he sold to American Bell Telephone. His "Induction Telegraph System" enabled moving railroad cars to exchange telegraph messages, which proved crucial for preventing collisions. Today his most recognizably famous idea is the "third rail," a high-current electrical conductor laid inside the two ordinary rails that guide the wheels of an electric-powered train. The Woods invention with the widest-ranging importance, though, was a method of regulating the rotational velocity of electric motors. Formerly, motors were slowed by diverting part of their electrical current to resistive elements that transformed the excess power to dangerous waste heat. Woods devised a dramatically safer tapped-inductive system that wasted far less energy. The speed of virtually almost every alternating-current electric motor today is controlled by a similar method.

Regrettably, no historian has thoroughly assessed the true technological and commercial significance of all Woods's inventions. For that matter, no one has accurately determined their number, although one reliable authority on black inventors in 1917 credited him with "upwards of 50 different inventions" (Baker, 1917). The fact that Woods sold the rights to well over half of his patents to corporations, many of which included future electrical giants like Westinghouse, General Electric, and American Bell, and one for a reported ten thousand dollars, however, indicates that he was not only a prolific inventor but also a commercially successful entrepreneur and respected engineer.

Woods died in New York City of a cerebral hemorrhage, some five years after applying for his last known patent in October 1904, and perhaps in poverty. He left a distinguished but ambiguous legacy. On one hand, he merits a place in the top tier of independent electrical inventors of the late nineteenth and early twentieth centuries. On the other hand, his position with respect to African American history must remain unfixed. Americans have admired the "Black Edison" for well over a century, but even contemporary African American writers rarely mentioned public statements on his part, except for matters of patent litigation, or when he lectured to Cincinnati audiences "on the various laws and theories that pertain to electricity and magnetism" (*Cleveland Gazette*, 7 Aug. 1886). Doubtless, white journalists, who almost entirely ignored him, deserved blame for much of the mystery surrounding Woods. But to the extent that he chose his reticence, he resembled engineers in general, who, thanks to the increasing influence of capitalism during the nineteenth century, began to adopt a hands-off approach to political and social questions, rather than risk their clients and employers. In any case, his exceptional success as an independent inventor depended on an ability to negotiate a career in an increasingly discriminatory society, and it is difficult to see how a more outspoken individual could have survived professionally in such an environment.

FURTHER READING

Baker, Henry E. "The Negro in the Field of Invention." *Journal of Negro History* II, January 1917.

Brodie, James Michael. *Created Equal: The Lives and Ideas of Black American Innovators* (1993).

Haber, Louis. *Black Pioneers of Science and Invention* (1970).

James, Portia P. *The Real McCoy: African American Invention and Innovation, 1619–1930* (1989).

Jenkins, Edward S. *To Fathom More: African American Scientists and Inventors* (1996).

GARY L. FROST

Woods, Lois Lee Prestage (18 May 1923–12 Jan. 2007), educator and lawyer, was one of three children born to Mattie Bendy Prestage and James Prestage, a World War I veteran, in Woodville, Texas. When Lois was four her family moved to Houston where she grew up in Fourth Ward. At a very young age, Prestage worked in the city's public libraries where she honed her reading and writing skills. She married Herman B. Woods on 8 July 1949. No children were born of their marriage. She was a member of the historic Antioch Missionary Baptist Church for over fifty years.

In the 1940s, Woods graduated from BOOKER T. WASHINGTON High School and entered Houston College for Negroes located at Jack Yates High School. While she was in college, HEMAN MARION SWEATT applied for law school at the University of Texas (UT) but was denied admission because he was black and thereafter he sued the school. On 4 March 1947 in the midst of the court battle, the state established the Texas State University for Negroes (later Texas Southern University) in order to deny Sweatt access to UT while complying with the doctrine of "separate but equal" treatment of blacks and whites. This new university took over the existing Houston College for Negroes where Woods was attending. In 1948 she completed her bachelor of arts degree at the Texas State University for Negroes with majors in history and government and a minor in sociology.

Undeterred by the lack of blacks or women in the field of law, Woods decided to apply to law school. She first applied to the private South Texas College of Law in Houston but was refused admission because of her skin color. She then sought admission to the law school at the Texas State University for Negroes. In 1948 three female students, Lois Woods, Leona Dorsey, and Earline Ross enrolled with twenty male students in the second class of the new law school.

Woods was a dedicated and active law student. She was an executive board member of the Law School Students' Association, a member of the Barristers' Club, and a recipient of the fellowship aid for the 1950–1951 academic school year.

Although three women entered with the second class of the law school only one, Lois Woods, would graduate. Woods became the first female law graduate of the Texas State Negro University when she received her LLB on 29 May 1951. After her law school graduation, she took the Texas Bar examination in Austin. Her score was three points below the required passing score. Despite her love for the law, Woods decided against retaking the bar examination and opted not to practice law but instead to pursue a teaching career.

Understanding the importance of education, Woods did not stop pursing her education after law school. Her quest for knowledge continued through many phases. After law school Woods entered the Maxwell School of Citizenship at Syracuse University (later Maxwell School of Syracuse) where she received her master of arts in Social Science on 2 August 1968. She also received her Certification of Supervision & Administration from Texas A&M University and Special Education Certification from University of Houston in 1974. She later took graduate classes at Western Michigan and University of Colorado.

Woods began her career educating others at Houston Independent School District (HISD) in 1955; her career there spanned thirty-two years. She worked as a community relations specialist, teacher, curriculum writer, and supervisor during her tenure at HISD. In 1968 Woods was also employed as an instructor in the sociology and economics departments at Texas Southern University. She also tutored in the history department as late as the 1980s.

In January 1988, Woods started her employment at the University of Houston, University Park, as an Instructor of Special Programs (GED) in the University of Houston's High School Equivalency Program. In her classroom, Woods taught many students from outside the United States who were learning English as a second language.

Woods received many honors for her dedication to the field of education. In 1989 she was honored as the Achiever of National Women of Achievement Award, an award she would receive a second time years later. For her generous contributions her alma mater, THURGOOD MARSHALL School of Law, the Lois Lee Prestage Woods Scholarship, and the Prestage Woods Women's Legal Society were established in her honor.

In a speech Woods gave in 2003 she reminisced about her life as a law student: study groups, civil rights protests, library duty and working as a teaching assistant, contending with segregation, discrimination, and the scrutiny of cynics who hoped the school would fail. Woods was very proud of this time in her life, a time when she traveled a road not normally traveled by women, especially black women. She voluntarily retired from the University of Houston in January 2005.

Woods died at Park Plaza Hospital in Houston, Texas. On 17 February 2007, the Texas Senate adopted Senate Resolution No. 205 "In memory of Lois L. Woods of Houston," extending its sincere condolences to the bereaved family as an expression of deepest sympathy from the Texas Senate.

FURTHER READING

Harris, LaKeisha. "TMSL's First Female Graduate Prestage Woods Recounts Triumphs and Struggles," in *The Gavel*, 10–23 Nov. 2003.

Lum, Lydia. "TSU feeds appetite for learning," in *Houston Chronicle*, 22 Feb. 1998.

Texas Senate Resolution No. 205 "In memory of Lois L. Woods of Houston," 17 Feb. 2007.

DECARLOUS SPEARMAN

Woods, Mattiebelle (31 Oct. 1902–17 Feb. 2005), journalist and activist, was born in Louisville, Kentucky, the daughter of Ira and Anniebelle Woods. Her mother's family trained horses for the Hansberg family in Milwaukee, Wisconsin, which provided them with connections to other elite families in the area. It is not known when the Woods family made the move to Milwaukee, but Anniebelle Woods found work at the Astor Hotel and was able to introduce Mattiebelle to the exclusive world of this wealthy German American community, allowing her to learn German. Mattiebelle established connections that she used later in her community activism. At West Division High School, she became immersed in Milwaukee's black community.

In 1921, when Woods was nineteen, she married George Beard; they had one daughter. Shortly after their daughter's birth, George Beard died in a car crash. Woods married again, but her second marriage was short-lived. Raising her daughter alone, Woods became a social and political activist who defied the social mores of the time and the prejudice around her. She was known for saying that she looked away from racism and that she would not allow her race to hinder her life. She instead quietly engaged in the fight for civil rights by opening doors for others through her position in Milwaukee's high society.

A known figure in the community, Woods became a reporter for the African American press in the 1940s, reporting on Milwaukee's growing black political and social groups. She had the honor of attending a news conference given by Eleanor Roosevelt and interviewing her.

Woods's lifelong political activism centered on voting rights, stemming from her realization that black people in the United States had to learn the significance of voting. She remained an election supervisor until her death. Woods became a Democrat in 1940, beginning more than sixty years of political work. In 1947 she helped elect Leroy Simmons, the first African American Democrat in the Wisconsin Assembly. Following this victory, she was influential in the African American assemblyman Isaac Coggs's election to the Wisconsin Assembly in 1953. Her acquaintance with the politically powerful reached an apex when MARTIN LUTHER KING JR. was a guest at her home. As a reporter for the *Chicago Defender's* Milwaukee edition, Woods met other celebrated African Americans, such as W. E. B. DUBOIS and RAY CHARLES.

Woods's work in the community extended to fund-raising as well as working the election polling stations. One of her first of awards was from the Community Chest, which later on became the United Way. In the 1950s the Community Chest did not fund African American charities, but Woods's influence was instrumental in creating funding for the National Urban League in Milwaukee; for this assistance she was presented with an Urban League award. Woods later became one of the YMCA's biggest fund-raisers in Milwaukee. Numerous successful fund-raising ventures opened doors for her, allowing her to travel into areas of the city where African Americans were often not welcome.

In 1954 Woods became a co-chair of the United Negro College Fund while continuing to write. In 1964 she reported in the *Milwaukee Courier's* first edition, then over the years she freelanced for the magazines *Ebony* and *Jet* and for the *Milwaukee Defender*, *Star*, and *Globe*.

At a time when black women were not acknowledged in mainstream beauty contests, Woods organized various African American beauty pageants. She helped bring the Ebony Fashion Fair to Milwaukee and was the founder and director of Miss Bronze Milwaukee in 1955, the Ten Best-Dressed Black Women in Wisconsin 1970, and Miss Black Teen Wisconsin.

Throughout her life, Woods was acknowledged for her role in the Milwaukee community.

In 1994 President Bill Clinton and First Lady Hilary Rodham Clinton invited Woods to the White House, and President George W. Bush sent her birthday greetings. Milwaukee mayor John Norquist created Mattiebelle Woods Day in 2000. She was recognized for her civic contributions as well, receiving awards from the National Association of Black Journalists in Milwaukee in 2002, the NAACP, the Milwaukee Press Club, and the Top Ladies of Distinction.

Woods died at the age of 102 in Milwaukee. Before her death she was the oldest African American journalist alive and was still publishing her weekly "Partyline" column in the *Milwaukee Courier*, producing her work on a typewriter in her bedroom. She was the oldest poll worker in Milwaukee and worked at the polling booth as an election supervisor the day before she died. On 3 March 2005, just weeks after her death, the U.S. Senate passed a resolution honoring Woods, "the First Lady of the Milwaukee Black Press," and her contributions to her family, journalism, and her city. After her death Marquette University in Milwaukee created a four-year $1,000-per-year scholarship in Woods's honor for freshmen attending the Diederich College of Communications. Upon her death, Governor Jim Doyle of Wisconsin issued a statement that Woods was "one of Wisconsin's finest citizens. She was a trailblazer for women, for journalists, and for the African American Community as a whole."

ZISCA ISABEL BURTON

Woods, Sylvia (2 Feb. 1926–19 July 2012), chef, restaurateur, and executive, was born Sylvia Pressley in Hemingway, South Carolina, the only child of midwife Julia Pressley and Van Pressley, a World War I veteran who died three days after his daughter's birth. After Sylvia's third birthday her mother placed her in the care of her grandmother while she migrated to Brooklyn, New York, in search of higher-paying work as a laundress. By Sylvia's eighth birthday her mother returned to Hemingway, having saved enough money to purchase a sizable farm and build a small home. Hardworking and determined, her mother and grandmother earned the community's respect, owning over sixty acres and serving as the town's only midwives. Their inspirational examples imbued Woods with "strength, faith and self-sufficiency" (Woods, 36).

In 1937 Sylvia met Herbert Woods, and despite their youth (he was twelve; she was eleven), they fell in love and vowed to marry upon adulthood. After completing high school Sylvia entered La Robert

Sylvia Woods outside her restaurant, Sylvia's, in the Harlem neighborhood of New York City, during the restaurant's 40th anniversary celebration, Thursday, 1 August 2002. (AP Images.)

Cosmetology School in Brooklyn while Herbert enlisted in the navy and was stationed in San Francisco. Following graduation from cosmetology school in 1942, Sylvia returned to Hemingway and operated a beauty shop. Despite the distance they remained committed and on 18 January 1944, Sylvia Pressley married Herbert Woods. Their union produced four children: Van, Bedelia, Kenneth, and Crizette.

Between 1945 and 1950 the Woods family moved between New York, California, and South Carolina, before settling permanently in Harlem, New York. Initially, Herbert worked as both a taxi and truck driver while Sylvia stayed at home as a full-time mother. After the birth of their second child, financial needs grew and Sylvia styled hair in her home and worked in a hat factory. In 1954 she began working as a waitress at Johnson's Luncheonette, a small Harlem establishment with six booths and fifteen counter seats. Having never waited tables before she recalled, "I was scared to death. I told him that I had worked in a restaurant.... [he] knew I was lying, since the only restaurant in Hemingway was segregated. But he gave me the job anyway"

(Woods, 36). The job changed the course of her life.

Cooking and serving soul food within her family had always provided a means of maintaining heritage and strengthening community bonds for Woods. She enjoyed serving food and soon learned to manage the restaurant. Determined and hardworking, she became owner Andrew Johnson's most trusted and valued employee. As her hours increased, and hoping to expose her children to country life, she sent them to live temporarily in Hemingway.

In 1962 Johnson offered to sell his restaurant to Woods. Although blacks in the North faced less overt hostility than those in the South, equal opportunity did not exist. The majority of financial institutions were owned and operated by white men, and Woods feared that she would be denied a business loan based on her race and gender. Thus her mother mortgaged her farm and provided Woods with the necessary capital to purchase the property. On 1 August 1962 Sylvia's Restaurant welcomed customers for the first time. Serving authentic Southern fare, including fried chicken, candied yams, barbecue, corn bread, and collard greens, the restaurant's popularity steadily expanded. The NAACP rewarded Woods's business initiative with its Woman of the Year award in 1978, and the following year food critic Gael Greene from *New York Magazine* favored her with a rave review. Shortly thereafter Sylvia's became a regular destination for foreign tourists and celebrities. To accommodate the growing crowds, Woods gradually expanded the restaurant until it held 250 seats and a banquet hall, spanning almost an entire city block in Harlem.

Over thirty years Sylvia's Restaurant grew to a multimillion-dollar enterprise and Woods, dubbed the "Queen of Soul Food," published her first cookbook, *Sylvia's Soul Food: Recipes from Harlem's World-Famous Restaurant* in 1992. The entire family contributed to the restaurant's success. As Sylvia prepared recipes and oversaw cooking, Herbert purchased real estate overseeing corporate growth, and each of their children worked full time at the restaurant and helped expand Sylvia's name into other venues. Her daughter Bedelia developed the successful Sylvia's Catering Corp., while Van, her eldest son, launched a line of prepared Sylvia's soul food specialties, including marinades, sauces, canned goods, and mixes, sold at supermarket chains nationwide. The potential for expansion attracted the attention of the J. P. Morgan Community Development Corporation, which helped promote the distribution of Sylvia's prepared foods and helped finance a satellite restaurant in Atlanta in 1997. Based on the success of her prepared food products, Woods developed a line of beauty products for African Americans, also marketed under the Sylvia's trademark.

While creating quality brand name products, Woods published a second cookbook, *Sylvia's Family Soul Food Cookbook: From Hemingway, South Carolina, to Harlem* (1999). This work featured favorite recipes compiled from a cooking contest held in Hemingway and also served as a memoir. Woods peppered the pages with family photographs and detailed histories, including short narratives to complement each recipe. The book provides a rich source of information about Woods's heritage. In June 2001 Herbert died of prostate cancer in Manhattan. Though deeply affected by the loss of her lifelong partner, Woods, buoyed by her children and grandchildren, continued to build her legacy, establishing the Sylvia and Herbert Woods Scholarship Endowment Foundation to support education in the local community.

When she first opened the restaurant's doors, blacks across America were fighting for basic civil rights. Few suspected that Woods, a thirty-six-year-old African American woman when the restaurant opened, would become the president of a multimillion-dollar company. She remained modest, attributing her success to her family, her faith, and the strong sense of a loving community: "You got to make people feel like you appreciate them. That love and affection and caring will carry you where money can never carry" (*New York Times*, 3 Sept. 1997).

Sylvia Woods died at her Mount Vernon, New York, home in July 2012. She was 86.

FURTHER READING

Woods, Sylvia, and family. *Sylvia's Family Soul Food Cookbook: From Hemingway, South Carolina, to Harlem* (1999).

Haber, Barbara. *From Hardtack to Home Fries: An Uncommon History of American Cooks and Meals* (2002).

Obituary: *New York Times*, 19 July 2012.

MARILYN MORGAN

Woods, Tiger (30 Dec. 1975–), golfer, was born Eldrick Woods to Earl Woods, a retired army lieutenant colonel who had been the first black baseball player at Kansas State University, and Kultida Punsawad, a native of Thailand and army secretary who met Earl when he was stationed in Thailand during the Vietnam War. Kultida chose the name Eldrick because it begins with the first initial of Earl's name and ends with the first initial of her name. The fusion of identities thus symbolized by his name would have far-reaching influences on the boy's life. The sobriquet Tiger was chosen by Earl in honor of his army buddy Colonel Nguyen Phong, whom Earl nicknamed Tiger because of his courage. Earl, who had three children from a previous marriage, married Kultida in 1969 while he was based at Fort Hamilton in Brooklyn, New York. He was forty-two years old and three months shy of retiring from the army when a fellow black officer invited Earl to play golf for the first time. Thus, Earl began cultivating a love for the greens that would propel his son into the world of golf.

African American golfers had played in mostly segregated venues since Reconstruction. In 1896 JOHN SHIPPEN became the first black golf professional when he was invited to play in the second U.S. Open Championship at the Shinnecock Hills Golf Club, but when some white golfers refused to play with an African American, Shippen was forced to pretend that he was half Shinnecock Indian in order to participate. In 1899 Dr. George

Grant, a black Boston dentist, patented the first golf tee—and though he did not make any money from his invention, variations on his design revolutionized the game. CHARLES SIFFORD was the first African American to finally break the "Caucasian only" barrier when he entered the Professional Golfers Association (PGA) in 1962. The following year ALTHEA GIBSON did the same in the Ladies Professional Golfers Association (LPGA) when she put down her tennis racket and began swinging a golf club.

As an infant, Tiger was often placed in a high chair in the garage so that his father could hit golf balls into a net while at the same time watching the child. When Earl put an improvised club into Tiger's hands, the eleven-month-old prodigy swung from his left side—as it had appeared from his perspective in the high chair. When Earl placed Tiger in the correct position, Tiger intuitively switched the club to his right, and the astonished father began to sense that his son was a natural. At the age of two Tiger made his first television appearance, on *The Mike Douglas Show*, where he demonstrated his putting (and charm) with comedian Bob Hope. Tiger was featured in *Golf Digest* magazine at the age of five and appeared on the ABC program *That's Incredible*.

Despite the early recognition of Tiger's talent, golf did not entirely consume his childhood to the exclusion of all other interests and activities. Earl was not the overbearing father of Little League infamy, trying to live vicariously through his son's playing. Kultida was an exacting disciplinarian who did not exempt the boy wonder from household chores, excuse poor academic performance, or tolerate arrogance. Nor did Tiger have to be prodded to practice; on the contrary, he enjoyed listening to subliminal tapes that told him, "You have the power to move mountains." Tiger and his family were the first black residents to move into their neighborhood in Cypress, California. Growing up in what became a diverse community, Tiger experienced a world filled with video games, rap music, and shopping malls—and though he liked *The Simpsons* more than the *Cosby Show*, he was inescapably a product of the black middle class of the 1980s. In high school he played basketball, football, and baseball and showed aptitude in each. At six feet, two inches in height, he could have pursued these more popular sports, but golf was his first love, only passion, and undeniable forte.

Kultida worked hard to make sure that his Asian identity was not overshadowed by his brown skin.

She took him to Thailand when he was nine and instructed him in Buddhist traditions, which Tiger came to cherish. She taught him to be proud of his Thai ancestry even though most people were not aware of it. Exasperated by a media that referred to her son as black exclusively, she once scolded a reporter that to do so was to "deny his grandmother and grandfather. To deny me!" (*Sports Illustrated*, 27 Mar. 1995, 62). Tiger would one day tell an audience on *The Oprah Winfrey Show* that he was a mixture of Caucasian, black, Indian, and Asian, which made him a "Cablinasian." This racial construction displeased some African Americans who suspected that Woods was uncomfortable being black, but it encouraged others who resented racial categories that blotted out parts of their identities, and it prompted some members of Congress to introduce a "Tiger Woods Bill" to make "mixed race" an option on the 2000 census forms. Earl was confident that Tiger could handle the social challenges that awaited him and focused instead on building Tiger's mental toughness for the pressure he would encounter in high stakes tournaments. For example, he would try to break Tiger's concentration before his son took a shot by jingling coins in his pocket, coughing, or dropping his golf bag. Tiger developed the ability to remain focused in tight situations and became a relentless competitor.

As a teenager Woods amassed a room full of trophies, including an unprecedented three consecutive U.S. Junior Amateur Championships; when he won the first one at fifteen, he became the youngest player to ever do so. In 1994 he became the youngest player to win a U.S. Amateur Championship, which he did by staging the largest comeback in tournament history. Later that year Woods enrolled at Stanford University on a golf scholarship and decided to major in economics. By the end of his freshman year he had successfully defended his U.S. Amateur title, played in his first professional major—the Masters, where he was the only amateur in the field to make the cut—and was named NCAA First Team All-America. By his sophomore year Woods had garnered a record-setting three U.S. Amateur Championships and was winning other tournaments all over the country, all while maintaining a B average. The decision to drop out of Stanford in August 1996 and become a professional golfer was a difficult one, but the $40 million endorsement deal from Nike and $20 million deal with Titleist helped to ease the pain.

Success as a professional was not guaranteed for Woods. Like other sports, golf has seen many

Tiger Woods won the Bay Hill Invitational in Orlando, Florida, on Sunday, 18 March 2001. (AP Images.)

amateur stars fail to meet expectations when put up against seasoned veterans; others prove unable to handle the pressures and distractions that come with celebrity status. Winning even one major tournament over the course of a long professional career is quite an achievement. Woods, in comparison, became the number 1 player in the world in just forty-two weeks as a pro, smashing records as he went. His first major victory was the Masters in 1997 at the Augusta National Golf Club. This exclusive all-male club in Georgia did not admit its first black member until 1990. On the final day of competition, Woods wore a red shirt, as he always does on the last day of play because his mother said that red is his lucky color of power. As he approached the final hole on that day, his ailing father was waiting to greet him, along with LEE ELDER, who had been the first black golfer to play in the Masters at Augusta, doing so the year Woods was born. With this win, Woods became the first African American to win a major, and he did so by twelve strokes, the widest margin of victory in the history of that vaunted tournament. By tradition, the winner of the

Masters chooses the menu for the following year's dinner. Realizing this honor would fall to Woods, a previous Masters champion, Fuzzy Zoeller, told reporters, "Tell him not to serve fried chicken, or collard greens, or whatever the hell *they* serve" (Callahan, 61). Despite the firestorm of controversy that ensued, Woods took such comments in stride and proceeded to become golf's greatest ambassador, bringing millions of minority players to the game and attracting television viewers to the sport in numbers that rivaled baseball and basketball.

Woods went on to play on the United States teams for the Ryder Cup and the Presidents Cup. He won the PGA Championship in 1999 and from 2000 through 2001 built up a phenomenal string of victories that demonstrated his growing prowess. He opened the 2000 season by winning the Mercedes Championship and then captured the U.S. Open Championship by fifteen strokes, breaking a record that had stood since 1899. He then won the British Open at St. Andrews, Scotland, by eight strokes on the course where the modern game of golf was born, and registered the best score (19 under 269) in the history of the British Open. With this victory Woods became the youngest player, at age twenty-four, to complete the Career Gland Slam—winning the four top tournaments over the course of one's career. Only four other players have achieved this feat. However, Woods was not finished; he won the PGA Championship again in 2000 to become the first player to win the U.S. Open, British Open, and PGA Championship in the same year. And when he won the Masters again early in 2001, Woods became the first person in history to own all the major crowns of modern golf at the same time. In 2002, he retained the Masters and added a second U.S. Open title.

When Jack Nicklaus began to establish his dominance over golf a generation earlier, Bobby Jones, a leading competitor, said of Nicklaus, "He plays a game with which I am not familiar" (Callahan, 55). Similarly, Woods unveiled a game never before seen: long off the tees, skillful on the fairways, and accurate on the putting greens. He stated that his professional goal was to surpass Nicklaus's record of eighteen major PGA titles. He delayed marriage and child rearing to pursue this quest. For a short period after his U.S. Open victory in 2002, Woods's march to further success stumbled. He failed to win a major in 2003 and 2004, and lost his world number 1 ranking. Some critics identified problems with his swing; others cited his marriage to Elin Nordegren, a Swedish model, on 5 October 2004. However, in 2005 Woods's form returned with victories in the Masters and the British Open. At the latter tournament a year later, Woods gave arguably his greatest performance. His beloved father had died less than three months previously. At Hoylake, Woods offered a wonderfully controlled display, combining mental toughness with shot accuracy to win by two shots. When Woods finished his last round, the hitherto contained emotion poured out, and he told the watching gallery: "I just miss my dad so much. I wish he could have been here to witness this," he told the BBC. Woods won the British Open again in 2006, and captured his third USPGA title (his twelfth major) the same year.

When Woods met Nelson Mandela in South Africa, Mandela urged him to do something with his fame to help others. Woods subsequently established the Tiger Woods Foundation, whose goal was to help American youth through scholarships, charitable gifts, and educational programs. Woods, like his good friend MICHAEL JORDAN, chose to avoid most political issues—particularly those pertaining to race. His reticence about admitting women into the PGA or rescinding the male-only membership rules at Augusta, two controversies that erupted in 2003, disappointed those who believed that Woods had a special obligation to be outspoken on such matters. However, Woods did not relish becoming a role model, nor did he see himself becoming a champion of causes like MUHAMMAD ALI or JACKIE ROBINSON.

Woods's dominance of the golf world continued throughout the first decade of the 21st century. He won the USPGA Championship in 2007 and the US Open in 2008, a season shortened by injury— leaving him second all time in terms of victories in the majors, four behind Jack Nicklaus. Woods was also PGA Player of the Year and PGA leading money winner in 2007 and 2009, but his form hit a slump in the two years that followed, a result of injuries and the media circus that followed the publication in the tabloids and on the Internet of lurid details about his private life. The scandal led to Woods briefly checking in to a rehabilitation clinic for a sex addiction, and making a public apology to his fans for his marital indiscretions. In the wake of that admission and Woods' subsequent decline in form, a number of Woods's major sponsors ended their relationship with him, including Gillette, Accenture, Tag Heuer, AT&T, *Golf Digest*, and Gatorade. While the sportswear company Nike continued to sponsor Woods, sales of Woods-related Nike products declined significantly between 2010 and 2011. Woods's divorce from Elin Nordegren further cut into his wealth, although he remained one of the richest people on the planet. Shortly before the scandal, Woods's became the first athlete to have career earnings above $1 billion. In 2008 Woods had pocketed more than $200,000 per round of tournament golf he played. By 2011 his failure to make the cut in several majors, or win any tournaments at all in 2010-2011 resulted in a decline to $25,000 per round, approximately what he had earned in his rookie season of 1996.

FURTHER READING

Callahan, Tom. *In Search of Tiger* (2003).
McDaniel, Pete. *Uneven Lies: The Heroic Story of African Americans in Golf* (2000).
Reilly, Rick. "Goodness Gracious, He's a Great Ball of Fire," *Sports Illustrated*, 27 Mar. 1995.
Strege, John. *Tiger: A Biography of Tiger Woods* (1998).

SHOLOMO B. LEVY

Woodson, Carter Godwin (19 Dec. 1875–3 Apr. 1950), historian, was born in New Canton, Virginia, the son of James Henry Woodson, a sharecropper, and

Anne Eliza Riddle. Woodson, the "Father of Negro History," was the first and only American born of former slaves to earn a Ph.D. in History. His grandfather and father, who were skilled carpenters, were forced into sharecropping after the Civil War. The family eventually purchased land and eked out a meager living in the late 1870s and 1880s.

Woodson's parents instilled in him high morality and strong character through religious teachings and a thirst for education. One of nine children, Woodson purportedly was his mother's favorite, and was sheltered. As a small child he worked on the family farm, and as a teenager he worked as an agricultural day laborer. In the late 1880s the Woodsons moved to Fayette County, West Virginia, where his father worked in railroad construction, and where he himself found work as a coal miner. In 1895, at the age of twenty, he enrolled in FREDERICK DOUGLASS High School where, possibly because he was an older student and felt the need to catch up, Woodson completed four years of course work in two years and graduated in 1897. Desiring additional education, Woodson enrolled in Berea College in Kentucky, which had been founded by abolitionists in the 1850s for the education of ex-slaves. Although he briefly attended Lincoln University in Pennsylvania, Woodson graduated from Berea in 1903, just a year before Kentucky passed the "Day Law," prohibiting interracial education. After college Woodson taught at Frederick Douglass High School in West Virginia. Believing in the uplifting power of education, and desiring the opportunity to travel to another country to observe and experience the culture firsthand, he decided to accept a teaching post in the Philippines, teaching at all grade levels, and remained there from 1903 to 1907.

Woodson's worldview and ideas about how education could transform society, improve race relations, and benefit the lower classes were shaped by his experiences as a college student and as a teacher. Woodson took correspondence courses through the University of Chicago because he was determined to obtain additional education. He was enrolled at the University of Chicago in 1907 as a full-time student and earned a bachelor's degree and a master's degree in European History, submitting a thesis on French diplomatic policy toward Germany in the eighteenth century. Woodson then attended Harvard University on scholarships, matriculating in 1909 and studying with Edward Channing, Albert Bushnell Hart, and Frederick Jackson Turner. In 1912 Woodson earned his Ph.D.

in History, completing a dissertation on the events leading to the creation of the state of West Virginia after the Civil War broke out. Unfortunately, he never published the dissertation. He taught at the Armstrong and Dunbar/M Street high schools in Washington from 1909 to 1919, and then moved on to Howard University, where he served as dean of arts and sciences, professor of history, and head of the graduate program in history in 1919–1920. From 1920 to 1922 he taught at the West Virginia Collegiate Institute. In 1922 he returned to Washington to direct the Association for the Study of Negro Life and History full time.

Woodson began the work that sustained him for the rest of his career, and for which he is best known, when he founded the association in Chicago in the summer of 1915. Woodson had always been interested in African American history and believed that education in the subject at all levels of the curriculum could inculcate racial pride and foster better race relations. Under the auspices of the association, Woodson founded the *Journal of Negro History*, which began publication in 1915, and established Associated Publishers in 1921, to publish works in black history. He launched the annual celebration of Negro History Week in February 1926 and had achieved a distinguished publishing career as a scholar of African American history by 1937, when he began publishing the *Negro History Bulletin*.

The *Journal of Negro History*, which Woodson edited until his death, served as the centerpiece of his research program, not only providing black scholars with a medium in which to publish their research but also serving as an outlet for the publication of articles written by white scholars when their interpretations of such subjects as slavery and black culture differed from those of mainstream historians. Woodson formulated an editorial policy that was inclusive. Topically, the *Journal* provided coverage in various aspects of the black experience: slavery, the slave trade, black culture, the family, religion, and antislavery and abolitionism, and included biographical articles on prominent African Americans. Chronologically, articles covered the sixteenth through the twentieth centuries. Scholars, as well as interested amateurs, published important historical articles in the *Journal*, and Woodson kept a balance between professional and nonspecialist contributors.

Woodson began celebration of Negro History Week to increase awareness of and interest in black history among both blacks and whites. He chose the second week of February to commemorate the birthdays of Frederick Douglass and Abraham Lincoln. Each year he sent promotional brochures and pamphlets to state boards of education, elementary and secondary schools, colleges, women's clubs, black newspapers and periodicals, and white scholarly journals suggesting ways to celebrate. The association also produced bibliographies, photographs, books, pamphlets, and other promotional literature to assist the black community in the commemoration. Negro History Week celebrations often included parades of costumed characters depicting the lives of famous blacks, breakfasts, banquets, lectures, poetry readings, speeches, exhibits, and other special presentations. During Woodson's lifetime the celebration reached every state and several foreign countries.

Among the major objectives of Woodson's research and the programs he sponsored through the Association for the Study of Afro-American Life and History (the name was changed in the 1970s to reflect the changing times) was to counteract the racism promoted in works published by white scholars. With several young black assistants—RAYFORD W. LOGAN, CHARLES HARRIS WESLEY, LORENZO J. GREENE, and A. A. TAYLOR—Woodson pioneered in writing the social history of black Americans, using new sources and methods, such as census data, slave testimony, and oral history. These scholars moved away from interpreting blacks solely as victims of white oppression and racism toward a view of them as major actors in American history. Recognizing Woodson's major achievements, the NAACP presented him its highest honor, the Spingarn Medal, in June 1926. At the award ceremony, John Haynes Holmes, the minister and interracial activist, cited Woodson's tireless labors to promote the truth about Negro history.

During the 1920s Woodson funded the research and outreach programs of the association with substantial grants from white foundations such as the Carnegie Foundation, the General Education Board, and the Laura Spellman Rockefeller Foundation. Wealthy whites, such as Julius Rosenwald, also made contributions. White philanthropists cut Woodson's funding in the early 1930s, however, after he refused to affiliate the association with a black college. During and after the Depression, Woodson depended on the black community as his sole source of support.

Woodson began his career as a publishing scholar in the field of African American history in 1915 with the publication of *The Education of the Negro Prior to 1861*. By 1947, when the ninth edition of his textbook *The Negro in Our History* (1922) appeared, Woodson had published four monographs, five textbooks, five edited collections of source materials, and thirteen articles, as well as five collaborative sociological studies. Among Woodson's major works are *A Century of Negro Migration* (1918), *A History of the Negro Church* (1921), *The Mis-Education of the Negro* (1933), and *The African Background Outlined* (1936). Covering a wide range of topics, he relied on an interdisciplinary method, combining anthropology, archaeology, sociology, and history.

Among the first scholars to investigate slavery from the slaves' point of view, Woodson studied it comparatively at institutions in the United States and Latin America. His work prefigured the concerns of later scholars of slavery by several decades, as he examined slaves' resistance to bondage, the internal slave trade and the breakup of slave families, miscegenation, and blacks' achievements despite the adversity of slavery.

Woodson focused mainly on slavery in the antebellum period, examining the relationships between owners and slaves and the impact of slavery upon the organization of land, labor, agriculture, industry, education, religion, politics, and culture. Woodson also noted the African cultural influences on African American culture. In *The Negro Wage Earner* (1930) and *The Negro Professional Man and the Community* (1934) Woodson described class and occupational stratification within the black community. Using a sample of twenty-five thousand doctors, dentists, nurses, lawyers, writers, and journalists, he examined income, education, family background, marital status, religious affiliation, club and professional memberships, and the literary tastes of black professionals. He hoped that his work on Africa would "invite attention to the vastness of Africa and the complex problems of conflicting cultures."

Woodson also pioneered in the study of black religious history. A Baptist who attended church regularly, he was drawn to an examination of black religion because the church functioned as an educational, political, and social institution in the black community and served as the foundation for the rise of an independent black culture. Black churches, he noted, established kindergartens, women's clubs, training schools, and burial and fraternal societies, from which independent black businesses developed. As meeting places for kin and neighbors, black churches strengthened the political and economic base of the black community and promoted racial solidarity. Woodson believed that the "impetus for the uplift of the race must come from its ministry," and he predicted that black ministers would have a central role in the modern civil rights movement.

Woodson never married or had children, and he died at his Washington home; he had directed the association until his death. For thirty-five years he had dedicated his life to the exploration and study of the African American past. Woodson made an immeasurable and enduring contribution to the advancement of the study of black history through his own scholarship and the programs he launched through the Association for the Study of Negro Life and History.

FURTHER READING

Two small collections of Woodson's papers exist at the Library of Congress Manuscript Division and the Moorland-Spingarn Research Center at Howard University.

Goggin, Jacqueline. *Carter G. Woodson: A Life in Black History* (1993).

Meier, August, and Elliott Rudwick. *Black History and the Historical Profession, 1915–1980* (1986).

This entry is taken from the *American National Biography* and is published here with the permission of the American Council of Learned Societies.

JACQUELINE GOGGIN

Woodson, Waverly B., Jr. (3 Aug. 1923–12 Aug. 2005), World War II soldier and Bronze Star medalist, was born in Philadelphia, the son of Waverly and Louise Woodson. His father, a laborer in the lumber industry and later a post office worker, was a native of Virginia, while his mother was from Pennsylvania. He had at least one sibling, Lloyd, who was several years younger. While little is known about young Woodson's early life in Philadelphia, he would later comment that he never experienced racism before joining the army.

Woodson joined the army in 1942 and after completing basic training was eventually assigned to the 320th Anti-Aircraft Balloon Battalion (AABB). This was an all-black unit, one of hundreds of segregated service units, including transportation, port, supply, and field artillery groups, organized by the army in the aftermath of the attack on Pearl Harbor in December 1941. Early in World War II, in keeping with its segregationist policies already in existence, the army had decided that African American volunteers and draftees would serve in

these support units and would not be sent directly into combat. It would not be until 1943 that these policies would begin to change, when pressure from the public gained strength; when African American soldiers were finally utilized as combat troops, men like Woodson, ROBERT J. PEAGLER, WILLY JAMES, and RUBEN RIVERS would soon prove that they were the fighting equal of any white soldier.

Private Woodson joined the 320th AABB at Camp Tyson in Routon, Tennessee. This facility, completed in early 1942, was the site of the army's barrage balloon training operations. While many of these units were white, some were manned by black soldiers. Having grown up in a northern urban environment, it was here in the South that Woodson first experienced racism firsthand. He would later recall that "the atmosphere was terrible. Everything was totally segregated. The feeling was that blacks were inferior to whites. Most of the officers were white. There were not many black officers, and they only made it to 1st or 2nd lieutenant" (Galloway, p. 6). Woodson's specialist duties in the 320th included supply procurement and training as a company medic. While the army's use of barrage balloons during the war was largely considered ineffectual, utilizing a technology that was past its prime, Woodson's training as a combat medic would later prove most valuable.

When the army's barrage balloon program was reduced, Camp Tyson was subsequently utilized as a base for training units scheduled to be shipped for overseas service. Among these units was Waverly Woodson's 320th AABB. Little did the men of this unit know that when they were sent to England in early 1944, they would soon take part in one of the most important actions of the war, the D-Day landings in France at Normandy. The African American presence as part of this historic battle on 6 June 1944 has largely been forgotten, though nearly two thousand black soldiers landed at the beaches of Normandy while serving in support units, and others served aboard the naval ships that supported the landings. Woodson would later state that "when you talk to white people, they will swear up and down that there were no black people in the first wave, but I went in without my unit. I was put on another LST. I'm very light-skinned and a lot of the men thought I was white" (Latty, p. 51). How Woodson became separated from his unit prior to boarding an LST (landing ship, tank) in England is unknown, but perhaps the ship and its crew were in need of a medic and Woodson was the closest one available. In any event, Waverly Woodson, now a sergeant, went in with the first wave in the early hours of 6 June 1944 at Omaha Beach, the most hotly contested of all the D-Day landing sites. On the way in, his ship was damaged by a mine and subsequently hit by German artillery fire, killing most of the men aboard. As Woodson later vividly related:

> I was hit in the back and groin....I swam to the shore and crawled on the beach to a cliff out of range of the machine guns and snipers.... there wasn't any other medic around here on Omaha Beach...and so I set up a first aid station....Bullets and shells were flying everywhere. It seemed like everybody was either dead or screaming, "Doc, Doc help me." I took a bullet from the shoulder of one, and dressed the gaping hole in the shoulder of another. I even amputated a right foot. At one point I heard all this shouting coming from the sea. There were thirty Tommies [the nickname for British soldiers] drowning, so I waded in and dragged out four of them and gave them artificial respiration and revived them (Latty, p. 30).

Indeed, though wounded, Woodson worked for over thirty hours straight and attended to as many as three hundred men before collapsing from severe blood loss and fatigue. After being hospitalized for several days, Sergeant Woodson returned to the beaches at Normandy, working for another twelve hours straight on D-Day plus four until too exhausted to continue.

Despite the swirl of events surrounding D-Day, including numerous acts of individual heroism, Woodson's actions did not go unnoticed, and he was soon recommended by his white commanding officer for an award for valor, as were four other black soldiers of the 320th AABB. While many of the records regarding Woodson's award case file are no longer extant, there is strong evidence to suggest that he was recommended for the Medal of Honor, our nation's highest award for military valor (Converse et al., p. 80). If this was the case, Waverly Woodson was among a select group of men, being only one of perhaps two African American soldiers (and possibly the only one) to be recommended for such an award. However, in the end, the Medal of Honor was not forthcoming, and Woodson was instead awarded the Bronze Star. To this day, many people, including historians and former soldiers alike, believe that Waverly Woodson Jr. was deserving of the Medal of Honor, and would have received it were it not for the color of his skin. Whatever

the debate about which medal Woodson deserved to receive, one thing is clear; not only is Woodson worthy of recognition for his individual acts of heroism, but also as an important example of the overall important contributions made by black soldiers during World War II.

After World War II, Woodson married his sweetheart, Joann, and continued in the army, staying stateside rather than going to Korea. He ended his military service in 1952 after serving ten years. He and his wife subsequently moved to Clarksburg, Maryland, where they lived the rest of their lives, raising their three children, one son and two daughters. In later years, Waverly Woodson became better known for his heroics on D-Day and was often interviewed about his actions that day. In 1994 he was invited by the French government to attend festivities honoring the fiftieth anniversary of the event, and was presented with a medal during a ceremony on Omaha Beach.

FURTHER READING

Converse, Elliott V., III, Daniel K. Gibran, John A. Cash, Robert K. Griffith Jr., and Richard H. Kohn. *The Exclusion of Black Soldiers from the Medal of Honor in World War II* (1997).

Galloway, Joseph L. "Debt of Honor." *U.S. News Online.* http://www.wiz-worx.com/366th/usnews/medal. htm.

Latty, Yvonne. *We Were There: Voices of African American Veterans, from World War II to the War in Iraq* (2004).

GLENN ALLEN KNOBLOCK

Woodyard, Sam (7 Jan. 1925–20 Sept. 1988), jazz drummer, was born Samuel Woodyard in Elizabeth, New Jersey. His parents' names are unknown. His father played drums on weekends. Sam quit school on his sixteenth birthday and began working nonmusical jobs while playing drums on Saturday nights. He married in 1942, and evidently he married again later in life, but details are unknown.

Woodyard toured in the rhythm and blues groups of Paul Gayten in 1950 and Joe Holiday in 1951, and he worked with the jazz trumpeter ROY ELDRIDGE in 1952. In 1953, while with Holiday again in Philadelphia, he transferred into the organist MILT BUCKNER's trio, with which he remained into 1955. He then joined DUKE ELLINGTON's big band from July 1955 to November 1966, leaving only for brief periods in 1959 and 1965. Among his notable recordings are *Ellington at Newport* (1956), *Such Sweet Thunder* (1956–1957), "Mr. Gentle and Mr. Cool" on the album BILLY STRAYHORN: *Live!* (1958), and "La plus belle Africaine" on *Soul Call*

(1966). He may be seen and heard drumming in two film shorts, both titled *Duke Ellington and His Orchestra*, produced in 1962 and 1965.

After working in a trio accompanying the singer ELLA FITZGERALD, Woodyard settled in Los Angeles. During the early 1970s he suffered from ill health, presumably a result of his alcoholism. He worked occasionally with the trumpeter Bill Berry's band, and he played conga with the Ellington (1973) and Buddy Rich bands (1974). In 1975 he toured Europe and worked with the pianist Claude Bolling's band. He was based in New York City in the late 1970s, and he performed at numerous jazz festivals. He recorded an album with a group of all-star jazz musicians, *Swingin' the Forties with the Great Eight* (1983). He died of cancer in Paris, France.

Woodyard is remembered especially for his contribution to Ellington's "Diminuendo and Crescendo in Blue" in a lengthy, cathartic, rhythm and blues oriented performance that was the sensation of the 1956 Newport Jazz Festival. He was a spongy drummer whose approach fit well into the loose-jointed rhythmic conception that governed Ellington's band during his membership. He also brought to the band an irrepressible enthusiasm that manifested itself not only in his swinging drumming but also in episodes of uninhibited accompanimental shouting, grunting, and scat singing.

FURTHER READING

Carriére, Claude. "Jam with Sam," *Jazz Hot*, no. 318 (July–Aug. 1975).

Dance, Stanley. *The World of Duke Ellington* (1970, 1981).

Obituaries: *New York Times*, 23 Sept. 1988; *Jazz Journal International* 41, Nov. 1988.

This entry is taken from the *American National Biography* and is published here with the permission of the American Council of Learned Societies.

BARRY KERNFELD

Work, John Wesley, III (15 June 1901–17 May 1967), composer and educator, was born in Tullahoma, Tennessee, the son of JOHN WESLEY WORK JR., an educator who became president of Roger Williams College, and Agnes Haynes, a contralto and soloist who assisted her husband in training and leading the Fisk Singers. Work was born into a musical family. His grandfather John Wesley Work Sr., a former Kentucky slave, directed a Nashville church choir whose members included some of the original Fisk Jubilee Singers. His uncle Frederick Jerome Work

collected and arranged folk songs, and his brother Julian Work became a well-known composer. In 1898 Work's father accepted a teaching position at Fisk University and moved the family to Nashville. The younger Work, who began composing while in high school, matriculated at Fisk, where he earned an AB in History in 1923 but pursued formal music study in theory and voice.

After graduating from Fisk, Work studied voice at New York's Institute of Musical Art (now Juilliard) from 1923 to 1924 and afterward studied at Columbia University. When his father died in 1925, Work brought his mother and three younger siblings to live with him in New York while he completed his studies. On 19 September 1928 he married Edith Carr McFall, who had been his classmate at Fisk. They had two sons.

Fisk's new president, Thomas E. Jones, sought to revive the spirituals tradition, and Work's mother returned to Nashville to train new singers. In February 1927, during Work's final semester at Columbia, his mother suffered a fatal stroke while on tour in St. Louis. Work returned to Fisk with his wife and assumed his mother's duties. Working toward his Columbia degree during the summers, he completed his master's thesis in 1930, later published as *American Negro Songs and Spirituals* (1940). This landmark collection became a valuable source for researchers and musicians. Work was awarded a Rosenwald Fellowship in both 1931 and 1932, which allowed him to take a leave of absence from Fisk and study composition at Yale University, where he earned a BMus, a conservatory degree, in 1933. Returning to Fisk, Work taught theory and composition. In 1946 he became director of the Jubilee Singers, and in 1950 he was named chairman of Fisk's Music Department. He conducted the Jubilee Singers until 1957.

Work's Yale mentor George Herzog encouraged him to continue his research. Work's students served as important sources of information as he collected and transcribed songs he learned from them. He also taught them that folk music could be valuable in their work as schoolteachers. He was one of the first African American scholars to apply ethnomusicology in his research and to use a portable recorder in the field. He not only collected songs but also studied the music's cultural context. He moved beyond earlier collectors' single-minded focus on spirituals and other sacred songs by studying blues, work songs, and instrumental music. Work used a portable phonograph disc recorder during fieldwork in rural Alabama in 1938, and in 1939 and 1940 he recorded local singers in the Nashville area. He presented his findings in Fisk's annual Robinson Music Lecture Series in a lecture titled "Negro Folk Music." He published his previous fieldwork on Alabama African American folk music collected during the summer of 1938 as a part of the 1941 *Musical Quarterly* article "Plantation Meistersinger."

A tragic fire on 23 April 1940 in Natchez precipitated Work's most important study. Reading of the event in the newspaper, he realized that the tragedy should be commemorated in song. When Work and the sociologist CHARLES S. JOHNSON first suggested the project idea, the university president was hesitant to endorse it, suggesting that Work and his team of African Americans partner with white researchers from the Library of Congress. To win the president's approval, Work partnered with the Library of Congress's Alan Lomax, who undertook fieldwork with the sociologist Lewis Wade Jones, assisted by Johnson.

Work and Lomax disagreed on many issues, including the research site and the project's focus, as Lomax took control of the project and its content. Nonetheless, Work successfully concentrated their efforts on the Delta region in what became known as the Fisk University–Library of Congress Coahoma County Study, focusing on Clarksdale, Mississippi, as an important blues center. Although relegated mostly to transcribing recordings made by Lomax and his assistants during two field trips in 1941 and in 1942, Work made the first field recordings of the bluesmen MUDDY WATERS and SON HOUSE. The interracial team finally concluded its research in mid-1942, and Work prepared his manuscript for publication in 1943. Lost for many years, it was finally located and published in 2005 as *Lost Delta Found: Rediscovering the Fisk University–Library of Congress Coahoma County Study, 1941–1942.*

As a formally trained musician, Work composed vocal music and arrangements of spirituals for most of his life. During his most prolific period, from 1946 to 1956, he composed more than fifty works for orchestra, chamber music, solo instruments, chorus, voice, and keyboard instruments. He completed his organ suite *From the Deep South* in 1936. In 1941 he composed the cantata *The Singers* (based on a poem by Henry W. Longfellow), which won first prize in the Fellowship of American Composers competition in 1946, when it premiered at the organization's convention in Detroit. His instrumental works seldom employ the folk song form. Among his best known are the orchestral

suite *Yenvalou* (1946) and the piano piece *Sassafras* (1946). *Yenvalou*, inspired by a three-month trip to Haiti, is based on Haitian musical themes. His *Golgotha Is a Mountain* (1949) is based on ARNA BONTEMPS's poem of the same name.

Work's piano pieces *Scuppernong* (1951) and *Appalachia* (1954) date from this period. His *My Lord, What a Morning* was performed by choirs from Germany, Sweden, Great Britain, South America, France, Yugoslavia, Japan, Canada, and the United States as part of the 1956 Festival of Music and Art. It was also performed at the United Nations and in New York's Philharmonic Hall. In 1957, after a twelve-week European tour, Work's health weakened, and he stepped down as chair and director at Fisk to concentrate on composing, teaching, and research. Work remained at Fisk and became professor emeritus in 1966, although he continued to teach part-time. During his long career he received several honors, including an award from the National Association of Negro Musicians in 1947 and an honorary doctorate from Fisk in 1963. A member of the American Society of Composers, Authors, and Publishers (ASCAP) and other organizations, he composed more than one hundred works before his death in Nashville at age sixty-six.

FURTHER READING

Work, John W., Lewis Wade Jones, and Samuel C. Adams Jr. *Lost Delta Found: Rediscovering the Fisk University–Library of Congress Coahoma County Study, 1941–1942* (2005).

GAYLE MURCHISON

Work, John Wesley, Jr. (6 Aug. 1873–7 Sept. 1925), composer, conductor, singer, scholar, and folk song collector, was born in Nashville, Tennessee, the son of John Wesley Work Sr., a Nashville church choir director, and Samuella Boyd. The senior Work composed and arranged music for his choirs, which included members of the original Fisk Jubilee Singers, and that work instilled in the younger Work a love of African American folk music, especially spirituals. Work attended public schools in Nashville and graduated from Meigs High School in about 1891. After studying music, Latin, and history at Fisk University, he studied classics at Harvard for two years, beginning in 1896. He sang in the Mozart Society, which awakened further interest in spirituals. He returned to Fisk, where he spent a year as a library assistant while completing a master's degree before assuming teaching duties in 1898. He taught Latin and history at Fisk until 1923. In 1897 he married Agnes Haynes; they had five children.

While teaching, Work continued to pursue his interest in music. Part of a larger movement to preserve, study, and perform African American spirituals, he first began organizing student singing groups around 1898. With the help of his wife, an accomplished contralto, he trained and performed with Fisk student groups that toured to raise money for the college, emulating the original Fisk Jubilee Singers. Becoming a leading authority on African American music, Work lectured and wrote scholarly articles about the spirituals. Defending the spirituals as the only true American folk music, his prominence made Fisk University one of the leading centers for its study. He compiled several important collections of African American folk song, becoming the first major African American scholar and collector of those songs. In 1901 he and his brother Frederick Jerome Work published *New Jubilee Songs as Sung by the Fisk Jubilee Singers*, a collection of harmonized slave songs and spirituals. They published their second collection, *Folk Songs of the American Negro*, in 1907. In the preface Work's remarks critiqued the then prevalent attitude of African American resentment and ambivalent feelings toward the spirituals; he went on to argue that the spirituals expressed "the Negro's inmost life, both intellectually and spiritually, they are the only true course of our history. If any man would read the Negro's life, let him study his songs" (Work and Work, *Folk Songs of the American Negro*). His words resonated with those of W.E.B. DuBois, but Work went further by offering the spirituals as works of musical art and cultural expressions that not only reflected emotion but also chronicled African American history.

From 1909 to 1916 Work toured as a member of the Fisk Jubilee Singers quartet, singing tenor (others included Alfred King, Noah Ryder, and James Meyers). The group recorded for the Victor Talking Machine Company. These recordings represent some of the earliest recordings of African American spirituals and are among the first recordings made by the Fisk singers. In 1915 Work revised and reissued the groundbreaking study *Folk Songs of the American Negro*. He continued to lead Fisk groups until 1917.

Due to backlash and controversy surrounding the study and performance of African American music at Fisk, whose curriculum emphasized the European classical music tradition (as did music study at many other historically black colleges and universities at the time), Work was forced to resign his post in 1923. He then became president of Roger Williams University in Nashville, a position he held until his death. His wife continued to conduct the Fisk singers after his death. Two of their sons were professional musicians: Julian Work became a composer, and JOHN WESLEY WORK III continued his father's work collecting spirituals and composing using the African American idiom.

FURTHER READING

Brooks, Tim. "'Might Take One Disc of This Trash as a Novelty': Early Recordings by the Fisk Jubilee Singers and the Popularization of 'Negro Folk Music,'" *American Music* 18 (Autumn 2000): 278–316.

Lovell, John, Jr. *Black Song: The Forge and the Flame* (1972).

Southern, Eileen. *The Music of Black Americans*, 3d ed. (1997).

Southern, Eileen, ed. *Biographical Dictionary of Afro-American and African Musicians* (1982).

Work, Frederick Jerome, with introduction by John Wesley Work. *Folk Songs of the American Negro* (1907).

Work, Frederick Jerome, and John Wesley Work. *New Jubilee Songs as Sung by the Fisk Jubilee Singers of Fisk University* (1902).

GAYLE MURCHISON

Work, Monroe Nathan (15 Aug. 1866–2 May 1945), sociologist, was born in rural Iredell County, North Carolina, the son of Alexander Work and Eliza Hobbs, former slaves and farmers. His family migrated to Cairo, Illinois, in 1866 and in 1876 to Kansas, where they homesteaded, and Work remained to help on the farm until he was twenty-three. He then started secondary school and by 1903 had received his M.A. in Sociology from the University of Chicago. That year he accepted a teaching job at Georgia State Industrial College in Savannah.

Living in the deep South for the first time, Work became concerned about the plight of African Americans, who constituted a majority of Savannah's population. In 1905 he answered a call from W. E. B. DuBois to attend the conference that established the Niagara Movement, a militant black rights group that opposed BOOKER T. WASHINGTON's accommodationist approach to black advancement. While continuing to participate in the Niagara Movement, Work founded the Savannah Men's Sunday Club. It combined the functions of a lyceum, lobbying group, and civic club, engaging in such activities as petitioning the city government, opening a reading room, organizing youth activities, and conducting a health education campaign among lower-class African Americans. Quickly accepted into the city's black elite, he married Florence E. Henderson in 1904. Their marriage lasted until his death, but no children survived infancy.

In 1908 Work was offered a position at Washington's Tuskegee Institute in Macon County, Alabama. As an ally of DuBois, Work found it difficult to accept the position, but he did. By 1908 he had begun to doubt the efficacy of protest. A streetcar boycott had not halted legalized segregation in Savannah, and the Niagara Movement had failed to expand. Work had begun to see another way to use his talents on behalf of black advancement. He was not a dynamic speaker or a natural leader, but a quiet scholar and researcher. He believed that prejudice was rooted in ignorance, and this suggested reliance on education rather than protest. In a 1932 interview Work declared that while still a student, "I dedicated my life to the gathering of information, the compiling of exact knowledge concerning the Negro." Disillusioned about the power of protest, Work believed that the resources and audience available at Tuskegee would allow him to make his skills useful: "It was the center of things relating to the Negro," he noted.

Although Washington had hired Work primarily as a record keeper and researcher for his own articles and speeches, Work used every opportunity to expand the functions of his Department of Records and Research. In 1908 he began compiling a day-to-day record of the African American experience. His sources included newspaper clippings, pamphlets, reports, and replies to his own letters of inquiry. All were organized by category and date, providing the data for the *Negro Yearbook* and the Tuskegee Lynching Report, both of which began in 1912. Each year he distributed the Tuskegee Lynching Report to southern newspapers and leaders to publicize the extent and injustice of lynch law. Under his editorship, nine editions of the *Negro Yearbook* provided information on discrimination and black progress to educators, researchers, and newspaper editorialists. In 1928 Work supplied another valuable research tool with the publication of *A Bibliography of the Negro in Africa and America*. It was the first extensive, classified bibliography of its kind.

Work did not spend all his time compiling data for others; he was also a teacher, department head, crusader, and researcher. He published over seventy articles and pamphlets. His research usually highlighted either the achievements of Africans and African Americans or the obstacles to black progress. Earlier than most black scholars, Work wrote in a positive manner about African history and culture. In a 1916 article for the *Journal of Negro History*, he declared that "Negroes should not despise the rock from which they were hewn." Work also investigated African American folktales and their African roots. Even before the Harlem Renaissance, Work celebrated the distinctiveness of African American culture. His meticulous scholarship was widely recognized in the academic community. In 1900 he became the first African American to publish an article in the *American Journal of Sociology*; the article dealt with black crime in Chicago and pointed to the lack of social services for African Americans. In 1929 he presented a paper at the American Historical Association annual meeting.

Although Work eschewed protest when he left the Niagara Movement and went to Tuskegee, he remained a quiet crusader for change. Early in his career Work developed a special interest in black health issues. In Savannah he started health education programs through the churches. He encouraged Booker T. Washington to establish National Negro Health Week in 1914. Work organized the week for seventeen years before it was taken over by the United States Public Health Service. He was also deeply concerned with the problem of lynching, and he became active in a southern-based movement to eradicate the evil. Work's estrangement from DuBois made cooperation with the National Association for the Advancement of Colored People's antilynching campaign difficult, but Work found allies in the Atlanta-based Commission on Interracial Cooperation and the Association of Southern Women for the Prevention of Lynching. The latter groups sought to change the South through education, while the NAACP sought change through legislation. Through his contacts in the antilynching campaign, Work became actively involved in numerous interracial groups in the South.

Monroe Work overestimated the power of education to eliminate prejudice, but his numerous articles and his quiet, dignified presence in biracial professional organizations and reform groups undoubtedly helped to dispel some of the southern white stereotypes of African Americans. He accepted the constraints required to work in the deep South in order to use his abilities to change it. After his death, in Tuskegee, two of his protégés established the Tuskegee Civic Association, which brought majority rule and desegregation to Macon County. Monroe Work was one of the lesser-known figures who tilled the soil from which the civil rights movement sprouted in the 1950s and 1960s.

FURTHER READING

A small collection of Work's personal papers is kept in the Tuskegee University Archives in Alabama, and a 1932 interview by Lewis A. Jones and other biographical materials can be found among the Jessie P. Guzman papers also at Tuskegee.

McMurry, Linda O. *Recorder of the Black Experience: A Biography of Monroe Nathan Work* (1985)

This entry is taken from the *American National Biography* and is published here with the permission of the American Council of Learned Societies.

LINDA O. MCMURRY

Wormley, James (16 Jan. 1819–18 Oct. 1884), restaurateur and hotelkeeper, was born in Washington, D.C., the son of Pere Leigh Wormley and Mary (maiden name unknown). Both his parents were free people of color before their 1814 arrival in Washington, where his father became proprietor of a livery stable on Pennsylvania Avenue between Fourteenth and Fifteenth streets, near the famous Willard Hotel. Wormley's early life is obscure, but it is certain that he went to work at a young age as a hack driver for his father, whose business was thriving by the 1820s. Eventually Wormley bought a horse and carriage of his own and began to work independently. Wormley's exposure to the city's fine hotels and high society through his clientele, which inevitably included many prominent public figures, might have influenced his later vocation.

In 1841 Wormley married Anna Thompson; they had four children. In 1849 he left his home to join the multitude of prospectors who traveled to California during the gold rush. Shortly before or after this, he was engaged as a steward aboard the elegant riverboats that plied the Mississippi. Eventually Wormley returned to Washington, where he worked as a steward at the fashionable Metropolitan Club. On the eve of the Civil War he opened a catering business at 314 I Street near Fifteenth Street, next door to a candy store run by his wife. By the mid-1860s he had expanded his business to include a restaurant at the same address. Wormley's restaurant attracted members of Washington's political elite, particularly the Radical Republicans. The patronage of such men as Senator Charles Sumner, after whom Wormley named one of his sons, and Henry Wilson, later vice president under Ulysses S. Grant, ensured the establishment's success.

The next step in Wormley's career entailed a brief absence from Washington and his family. In 1868 Reverdy Johnson, recently appointed ambassador to Great Britain, persuaded Wormley to accompany him to London as his personal steward. One of Wormley's tasks was the preparation of such exotic American dishes as diamondback terrapin (a turtle caught in Chesapeake Bay and the Potomac River), which Johnson was persuaded would do much to "warm up" the reserved British worthies he was required to entertain at embassy functions.

When Wormley returned to Washington, he lost no time in capitalizing on the reputation he had gained as a connoisseur of fine dining. United States representative Samuel Hooper of Massachusetts agreed to buy a five-story building on the southwest corner of H and Fifteenth streets and rent it to Wormley when Wormley was unable to finance the purchase himself. In 1871 Wormley opened the hotel that soon made him famous.

Wormley's Hotel, which included as an annex the building that housed his old restaurant on the other side of the block, could accommodate 150 guests in the sleeping apartments of its upper four stories. The halls and corridors were wide, and the rooms were spacious and elegantly furnished. The dining rooms on the ground floor acquired a reputation for attentive service and an elaborate menu, and the bar in the basement, where patrons also found a first-class barbershop, was known for its outstanding selection of wines and liquors. The hotel boasted the latest innovations of the day, including elevators, telephones, and electric bells for room service. The parlors on the upper floors were also beautifully appointed. One of them, known as the Sumner Parlor, was decorated with furnishings from the house of Wormley's old friend Sumner, which Wormley purchased from the estate after Sumner's death. In 1876 the room rate at Wormley's was a competitive five dollars a day.

With Lafayette Square, the White House, and the Departments of the Navy and the Treasury all near at hand, Wormley's Hotel was ideally located to serve the congressmen, diplomats, and other politicians who already knew Wormley as a restaurateur. Among his long-term residents were Vice President

Schuyler Colfax, Assistant Secretary of State John Hay, and Senator Roscoe Conkling of New York. The hotel was equally popular with foreign dignitaries. The German legation resided there during the 1880s, as did at various times members of the French and Chilean diplomatic corps. Wormley's Hotel also housed delegates to the Pan-American Congress in 1889–1890.

Wormley's Hotel acquired a small but significant place in American history in the aftermath of the disputed presidential election of 1876. A conference held at the hotel in February 1877 among representatives of the Republican candidate Rutherford B. Hayes and a group of southerners led by Major E. A. Burke yielded the "Wormley Agreement," which became in turn the basis for the "Compromise of 1877." In effect the southerners acquiesced to Hayes's accession to the presidency in return for the withdrawal of the northern states' military support for the remaining Reconstruction governments in the South. Wormley played no part in and likely had no awareness of these negotiations, whose outcome signaled the North's final abandonment of southern blacks to the ravages of southern reaction. It is no small irony, nonetheless, that the hotel in which these dealings took place was owned by one of the capital's most prominent African American citizens at a time when the city was noted for the enterprise and brilliance of its black citizenry.

Wormley's hotel and restaurant business continued to prosper until his death in Boston. In an obituary, the *Washington Star* called him "one of the most remarkable colored men in the country" (18 Oct. 1884). The well-known black minister FRANCIS GRIMKÉ remarked that Wormley "demanded respect from others and respected himself." A public school on Prospect Avenue between Thirty-third and Thirty-fourth streets, built in the year of Wormley's death and named in his honor, remained in service until the 1950s.

FURTHER READING

Proctor, John Clagatt. "Figures of a Vanished Past Linked with 15th Street," *Washington Star*, 27 Dec. 1936.

Waynes, Charles E. "James E. Wormley of the Wormley Hotel Agreement," *Centennial Review* 19 (Winter 1975).

Woodson, Carter G. "The Wormley Family," *Negro History Bulletin* 11, no. 4 (Jan. 1948).

Obituaries: (Washington, D.C.) *Evening Star*, 18 Oct. 1884; *Washington Post*, 18 Oct. 1884.

This entry is taken from the *American National Biography* and is published here with the permission of the American Council of Learned Societies.

JOHN INGHAM

Wright, Binkley T. (23 Sept. 1909–10 Oct. 2001), Tulsa Race Riot participant and survivor, was born in Tulsa, Oklahoma. His parents' names are now unknown, although it is known that his father worked as a bank janitor.

In the late evening of 30 May 1921 eleven-year-old Binkley Wright was attending the 10:00 p.m. showing of a play held at the Dixie Theater in downtown Tulsa with some friends. The theater, which was restricted to use by blacks only, was nonetheless located in the white section of the town. Ten minutes or so into the show Wright and the other audience members were dismissed because of disturbances outside of the theater. On his way home to Greenwood, in the northern part of Tulsa, Wright witnessed blacks running in the streets and talking about an impending race riot. When he arrived home, he told his parents what had happened and asked what a race riot was. While corroborating his son's account with what neighbors had heard, Binkley's father learned about the events that had transpired earlier in the day and that had led to the evening's rumors of a race riot. Binkley's father gave his wife his gun, left her and their son at a neighbor's house, and headed for downtown Tulsa to join the growing group of black men assembling at the courthouse.

Nearly twelve hours prior to this, the following events had transpired: nineteen-year-old Dick Rowland, an African American, took a department store elevator to a floor where the "colored only" restrooms were located. The only other person in the elevator car was Sarah Page, a seventeen-year-old white woman, who operated the elevator. At some point during their return to the first floor, Page screamed. Rowland was seen running away by a clerk. By 4:00 P.M. of the same day, the *Tribune*, a white newspaper, reported that Rowland had attempted to rape Page. The paper reported that Rowland had been apprehended and placed in jail shortly after the incident occurred.

Word of Roland's arrest began to spread quickly in Tulsa (and was still spreading by 10:00 P.M. when Binkley Wright was attending the play). This made already tense race relations much worse: black Tulsans had been politically engaging whites to overturn Jim Crow laws and struggling to get equal funding for black public schools. Although blacks had won a victory in the U.S. Supreme Court decision *Guinn v. United States* (which declared Oklahoma's grandfather clause unconstitutional), white Tulsans were able to circumvent the ruling by having the legislature limit black voter registration to a two-week period and, thus, disfranchise a significant number of eligible voters. Moreover, although Oklahoma law prohibited lynching, the actual practice of lynching blacks (as well as whites) in Oklahoma was not only widely accepted but was often facilitated by local policemen, who turned over those they had arrested to local mobs instead of waiting for a trial. Such a series of events had transpired eight months earlier in a town only ninety miles from Tulsa when a jailed black man was released to a mob and hanged.

Kindled by the ongoing tensions and encouraged by the widespread yet implicit social backing of lynching, whites believed it was in their right to lynch the rapist Rowland and thus "defend" Page's honor. On the other hand, blacks believed it was their duty to protect Rowland from mob violence by keeping him safely in jail until his trial. These are the reasons why on the night of 30 May the Dixie Theater closed early, why Binkley's father headed to downtown Tulsa, and why a multitude of whites and blacks descended upon the courthouse where Rowland was held.

Although the sheriff gave assurances that Rowland would not be moved from the jail, that did little to prevent a scuffle that ensued between the two groups and a shot being fired. Meanwhile, elsewhere throughout the city, whites were arming themselves and blacks in Greenwood were preparing to defend themselves against any mob with whatever they weapons they had at their disposal—guns, bricks, and even sticks. Black cab drivers transported ammunition from an unknown location to supply the black rioters. The fighting continued into the next day, 31 May, when Binkley Wright (along with his friends, Douglas Jackson and Virgil Whiteside) were asked to load and reload the shotguns and rifles with the supplied ammunition on behalf of the black men who were busy fending off whites. Wright and his "pass-the-ammunition" team continued to help the next day, 1 June, as well.

In the end the efforts of the "pass-the-ammunition" team and the blacks they supported proved no match for the mob of whites, 250 of whom had actually been deputized (one of the deputized "whites" was WALTER WHITE, a blond-haired, blue-eyed African American and future executive secretary of the NAACP, who had just mingled into the crowd to ascertain the situation). The "pass-the-ammunition" team and the blacks they supported were also no match for the two machine guns supplied by the National Guard nor for the airplanes, which some black Tulsans said had fired upon them from above. The Wright family, like many other black Tulsans, lost everything they owned in the fire that burned Greenwood to the ground.

After the riot Wright's parents were divorced, and Wright moved with his mother to California. As an adult, Wright married Clotie Lewis, also a Tulsa Race Riot survivor. Lewis was one of the performers at the play Wright was attending the night of 30 May. It is not known whether or not they had children. During his lifetime Wright's name was included among those race riot survivors who sought reparations for the role that city and state played in the massacre. He died of natural causes in Los Angeles on 10 October 2001. His wife died two years later.

Rowland was never tried for attacking Page because she refused to press charges as early as a few hours after the assault allegations. A few days after the riot, the *Tribune* admitted to fabricating some aspects of the very allegations that Page refused to pursue. After being released from jail the morning of 31 May, Rowland left Tulsa, and Page is said to have followed him. Although some accounts of the riot reported that Rowland may have had a relationship with Page and the alleged assault might have been a part of a lover's quarrel, Wright said in an interview that his father, a bank janitor, had told him that Rowland, a bank porter, was without a doubt courting Page at the time.

FURTHER READING
Wright, Binkley. Interview by Eddie Faye Gates, chair, Oklahoma Commission to Study the Tulsa Race Riot of 1921. Tape recorded February 2000. Available online at http://www.tulsareparations.org/BWright.htm.
Brophy, Alfred L. *Reconstructing the Dreamland: The Tulsa Riot of 1921 Race, Reparation, and Reconciliation* (2002)
Hirsch, James S. *Riot and Remembrance: The Tulsa Race War and the Legacy* (2002)

TERESA A. BOOKER

Wright, Charles S. (4 June 1932–), novelist and journalist, was born Charles Stevenson Wright in New Franklin, Missouri, the only child of Stevenson Wright, a laborer, and Dorothy Hughes, a homemaker. By the time he was four years old his parents had separated and his mother had died. After her death Wright's maternal grandparents raised him. Influenced by his grandfather's great passion for reading, Wright became a voracious reader of books and what he later called a "newspaper fanatic" (O'Brien). He attended public schools in New Franklin and Sedalia, Missouri, but dropped out of high school in his junior year, in part because of the segregated school's poor facilities and the general unavailability of books for the black students. Among Wright's most vivid teenage memories was reading an issue of *Life* magazine and being startled to see a feature on *Black Boy*, the novelist RICHARD WRIGHT's autobiography. The coincidence of sharing a last name (they were unrelated), coupled with the idea that a black author could receive national recognition, had a major impact on Wright.

After leaving school Wright hitchhiked to California but soon returned to Missouri. He attended the Lowney Handy Writers Colony in Marshall, Illinois, for a few summers before being drafted into the army in 1952. He became an army cook and traveled to Korea and Japan. Upon his discharge in 1954 Wright settled for several years in St. Louis, making ends meet with a twenty-six-week armed services stipend and a job as a stock boy. He also returned to the Handy Writers Colony, where he wrote what he later regarded as a "very bad" first novel about the Korean War (O'Brien).

In the late 1950s Wright moved to New York, a city he had always dreamed of living in. There he held a variety of jobs, all the while continuing to write. His second novel, *No Regrets*, a first-person narrative of an affair between an East Village black beatnik and an upper-class white girl whom he impregnated, was rejected by several New York publishers. Wright's copy of the manuscript was later lost. Wright submitted his plan for his next novel, "The Messenger," a story loosely based on his own experiences as a New York City messenger. Within a week he had a contract with the publisher Farrar, Straus and Giroux. Published in 1963, *The Messenger* garnered praise from both critics and other writers, including JAMES BALDWIN, Norman Mailer, and Kay Boyle. The novel cemented Wright's reputation as a rising young writer of great promise and firmly established his signature literary style—a highly idiosyncratic and dynamic synthesis of naturalistic, surreal, and fantasy-based forms that often alluded to vaguely autobiographical experiences.

One of the first African American authors of the 1960s to consciously use postmodern methods and techniques in both his fiction and nonfiction writing, Wright sought to blur and even erase the imposed literary boundaries between realistic and fictional forms. This conscious blending of both vernacular and avant-garde literary techniques was prominent in Wright's next and most famous novel *The Wig* (1966), a scathing satire of the destructive impact of the pretensions and delusions of the Great Society–American Dream myth during the mid-1960s, and its effect on African Americans' human identity and sanity. Wright's novel, which both he and his publisher felt would be a great success, instead opened to mixed reviews and poor sales. Nevertheless the *New York Times* literary critic Conrad Knickerbocker wrote in his rave review that *The Wig* was "a brutal, exciting, and necessary book." The novelist ISHMAEL REED called it "one of the most underrated novels written by a black person in this century" and credited the book with influencing his own prose technique (O'Brien). Many critics later acknowledged *The Wig* as Wright's most important literary achievement and as one of the 1960's most innovative novels.

Deeply discouraged by *The Wig*'s reception, Wright left the United States to live in Paris, Morocco, and Veracruz, Mexico, before finally returning to New York City in 1971. During the next seven years Wright traveled extensively and wrote a regular column, "Wright's World," for the *Village Voice* newspaper. These essays—collected, amended, and supplemented by other work including journalistic reportage and lyrical musings, and combining both fiction and social commentary—became a new book. Wright wanted to use the title "Black Studies: A Journal" but the publicity department at Farrar, Straus and Giroux felt the book would, as Wright wrote in his work, "get put on the wrong bookshelves." Wright's editor suggested its eventual title, *Absolutely Nothing to Get Alarmed About*. Published in 1973, the book vividly records the shattered dreams, hopes, and illusions of the 1960s, and the subsequent social despair that began gripping the country in the early 1970s following the assassinations of political leaders, the horror of the Vietnam War, and the failure of the War on Poverty and other Great Society programs. Rooted in fact yet galvanized by a restless imagination, *Absolutely Nothing to Get Alarmed About* extended the tradition of mixing fiction with social reality that characterized Wright's earlier work.

After 1973 Wright kept a low public profile. While continuing to travel extensively he completed *Erotic Landslide*, a short-story collection, and an unpublished play, "Madam Is on the Veranda." After twenty years of virtual obscurity Wright made a triumphant return to mainstream publishing in 1993 with the publication of his three novels in one volume, titled *Absolutely Nothing to Get Alarmed About: The Complete Novels of Charles Wright*. Wright found a whole new generation of readers and critics for his trilogy. Beside the new critical praise that greeted the re-publication, Wright won the Ruth Lilly Poetry Prize, a $75,000 cash award, in 1994.

FURTHER READING
Wright, Charles. *Absolutely Nothing to Get Alarmed About* (1973).
Klinkowitz, Jerome. *Literary Disruptions: The Making of a Post-Contemporary American Fiction* (1975).
O'Brien, John. *Interviews with Black Writers* (1973).

KOFI NATAMBU

Wright, Cleo (16 June 1916–25 Jan. 1942), lynching victim, was born Ricedor Cleodas Watson near Gethsemane in Jefferson County, Arkansas, the first child of Albert Leak Watson, a logger, and Alonzo (Woolfolk) Watson, a farmer. Both parents had children from previous marriages. Wright believed, probably incorrectly, that his natural father was named Henry Wright and adopted that surname as an alias around 1937 after robbing a grocery store. Cleo Wright's early life was fairly typical of rural blacks in the Jim Crow South in the years between World War I and World War II: he attended the local segregated grade school, but only after the vital work of bringing in his mother's cotton crop, among other tasks, had been completed.

A talented pianist, tap dancer, and baseball pitcher, Wright made friends easily. Like many adolescent young men he got into fights occasionally, though only if provoked, and he did not have a violent reputation. In 1932, however, he left school to work as a logger with his father. He also began dating women, usually older than himself, and he became increasingly uncomfortable living under his parents' strict, and strictly religious, supervision. Two years later he left home for the first time to work at a New Deal Civilian Conservation Corps (CCC) camp, returning to Gethsemane briefly before enlisting in the U.S. Navy in September 1935.

Wright's service in the navy was brief and troubled. He chafed at the constant discipline, frequently disobeyed orders, was often ill or feigned illness, and was given an "undesirable discharge for reason of unfitness" after only seven months (Capeci, 83). Though his dismissal was technically

less serious than a "dishonorable" discharge, Wright returned to Arkansas angered and depressed by the termination of his military career. He found work for a while as a truck driver in Pine Bluff, but was unemployed in May 1937 when, accompanied by his half-brother Wiley Humphrey and two other men, he stole $80 from a Chinese grocer in Wabbaseka, Arkansas. The robbers did not use force during this daytime robbery, but neither did they wear masks; and within just a few days Humphrey had been arrested and the stolen money recovered from the Watson home.

Although Wiley Humphrey refused to name his accomplices, Cleo fled across the Arkansas state line to Sikeston, Missouri, to escape the authorities, adopting the surname Wright in the process. He found work no easier to find or hold onto in the Depression-era Missouri "boot heel" than it had been in Arkansas, and within six months of arriving in Sikeston he was imprisoned for sixty days in the county jail for tampering with a state police commander's automobile. Released from prison in late 1937 Wright found work as a laborer, avoided trouble with the law, and married Ardella Gay in February 1940. A child was born after Wright's death. Although they knew about his criminal past Wright's employers and new relatives viewed him as a hardworking family man. In May 1940, however, Wright was again imprisoned, this time for burglary, but was released on parole seven months later in February 1941. Wright appears to have fulfilled all of his parole obligations in the eleven months that followed, and found work as a laborer in an oil mill. Early on 25 January 1942, however, two white policemen arrested Wright while he was walking down a street in Sikeston's black neighborhood. Seeking a black man who had assaulted and stabbed Grace Sturgeon, a white woman, a mile and a half across town thirty minutes earlier and finding Wright's clothes spattered with blood, the policemen searched him and found him in possession of a bloodstained knife. As soon as they confiscated it Wright took out another knife and stabbed Hess Perrigan, one of the officers who was pistol-whipping him, in the face. Perrigan responded by shooting Wright four times at point-blank range. The policemen then arrested Wright, who confessed to having attacked Sturgeon and then was given minimal treatment for his head injuries and bullet wounds.

Although the circumstantial evidence of Wright's guilt was compelling, a white Sikeston mob determined that there would be no trial. Shortly before

The charred body of Cleo Wright, who was burned by a mob after being taken from the custody of officers, is observed by a crowd in Sikeston, Missouri on 27 January 1942. (AP Images.)

noon on Sunday, 25 January 1942, the mob, numbering around 700, stormed the cell near city hall where Wright was being held. They tied Wright's legs to the rear bumper of a Ford automobile and drove to a black Baptist church in Sikeston, where they stopped, doused him with five gallons of gasoline, and set their victim ablaze as the astonished black parishioners looked on in horror. Wright mercifully died within minutes of being set on fire. In March 1942 a grand jury established to investigate the lynching handed down no indictments.

The lynching of Cleo Wright was in many respects typical. It happened in response to an alleged attack on a white female by a young, black male drifter with a criminal past in a small rural town, this one on the northern edge of the Mississippi Delta. That Wright did not sexually assault Mrs. Sturgeon was of little consequence to the broad cross-section of local whites who joined the mob as a warning to other black men not to challenge white supremacy. The

timing of Wright's murder, however, just six weeks after the United States' entry into World War II, had profound implications for the national campaign against lynching. The NAACP, among other groups, had long campaigned to force the federal government to investigate the national disgrace of more than 3,800 lynchings since 1890. Southern white resistance, especially in the U.S. Senate, had twice thwarted efforts to secure passage of federal anti-lynching legislation. Yet after the Japanese attack on Pearl Harbor the Roosevelt administration finally took a more aggressive stance against racial hate crimes such as lynching, as part of its campaign to achieve national unity and to counter Japanese propaganda that, correctly, charged the U.S. government with racism.

At a time of growing civil rights consciousness, notably with A. PHILIP RANDOLPH's March on Washington Movement and the NAACP's "Double V" campaign against fascism abroad and racism at home, African Americans and their liberal allies expressed outrage about the Wright lynching. In February 1942 their protests persuaded Attorney General Francis Biddle to investigate the case, the first federal investigation of racial hate crimes since Reconstruction. While the efforts of FBI agents and the attorneys of the civil rights section of the Justice Department failed to secure any indictments of those responsible for the brutal slaying of Cleo Wright, the NAACP's executive secretary, WALTER WHITE, believed that the federal investigation of this case produced a precedent for the future prosecutions of lynchings.

FURTHER READING

Capeci, Dominic. *The Lynching of Cleo Wright* (1998).
Zangrando, Robert L. *The NAACP's Campaign against Lynching* (1980).

STEVEN J. NIVEN

Wright, Elizabeth Evelyn (3 April 1872–14 Dec. 1906), educator and college founder, was born in Talbotton, Georgia, the seventh child of impoverished and illiterate parents. Her father, John Wesley Wright, a former slave, was a carpenter; her mother, Virginia Rolfe, a Cherokee Indian who maintained her tribal affiliation, earned money, from time to time, as a fortune teller, and had twenty-one children.

Wright acquired basic literacy and numeracy at a school for blacks operated in the St. Philip's African Methodist Episcopal Church in Talbotton. Her opportunity to leave her home environment came, when, by chance, she picked up a discarded newspaper page which introduced her to the Tuskegee Institute in Alabama. Here she enrolled in September 1888 in a special work-study preparatory program intended for students who could not pay full fees. She was assigned to kitchen duty.

Wright's chronic poor health, coupled with her intelligence and her iron determination to become a teacher, brought her to the attention of OLIVIA DAVIDSON WASHINGTON, BOOKER T. WASHINGTON's second wife, herself very frail. She obtained for Wright a sponsorship from Judge George W. Kelley of Massachusetts, a Tuskegee trustee. The two became lifelong friends. He would sponsor Wright's first efforts to found a school in South Carolina and later serve as the President of the Board of Trustees of the institution that she founded.

Following Davidson's death in 1889, Wright came under the wing of Margaret James Murray,

the so-called Lady Principal of Tuskegee, who would become Booker T. Washington's third wife (MARGARET MURRAY WASHINGTON). When illness forced Wright to withdraw temporarily from Tuskegee in 1892, Murray sent her to recuperate and to work in Hampton County, South Carolina, with another Tuskegee trustee, Almira S. Steele. She, the widow of a Massachusetts businessman, had founded an orphanage in 1884 in Chattanooga, Tennessee, mainly for African American children, and, several years later, a school for African American children in Hampton County, South Carolina. Steele would become another lifelong friend, supporter, and school trustee.

Their work was cut short in April 1893 when arsonists burned down the school. Wright, her health temporarily restored, accompanied Steele to Chattanooga where the latter resumed work with her orphanage, the Steele Home for Needy Children, and the former returned to Tuskegee in September 1893, graduating in May 1894, and determined to resume teaching in South Carolina.

Wright made several attempts, two of them sponsored by Judge Kelley, to found schools in Hampton, Colleton, and Bamberg Counties in South Carolina. In June 1896, she was joined by a young nurse from Ohio, Jessie Dorsey, sent to her by Almira Steele from the Battle Creek Sanitarium in Michigan where one had trained and the other had been a patient and probably, at this point, a convert to the Seventh Day Adventist faith. Dorsey and Wright became lifelong friends and colleagues. Two of their efforts to found a school failed owing to arson. Two additional efforts failed, one of them because the owner of the land attempted to cut down the timber on it before the sale had been completed, and another because of the objections of an influential African American preacher.

In addition to white opposition to Wright's projects, there seems also to have been an element of prejudice against Seventh Day Adventists on the part of the local African American clergy, mostly Baptists. Although Wright had been raised in the African Methodist Episcopal Church, she had become a non-denominational Christian. Almira Steele and Jessie Dorsey, however, had become committed Seventh Day Adventists probably owing to the influence of Dr. James Harvey Kellogg, the founder and Medical Superintendent of the Battle Creek Sanitarium where Wright would be hospitalized three times.

It is clear that Kellogg, an exponent of holistic medicine and the co-inventor of corn flakes, also influenced Wright. Early on, for instance, she established a regimen at the school, lasting for several years, of two meals a day, an Adventist practice possibly recommended by Kellogg as a means of reducing the sexual urge. When Wright set up her first Board of Trustees in 1898, she invited Kellogg to serve on it.

What permitted Elizabeth Wright to found a school that would endure was a recommendation that she seek to purchase land for it in Denmark, South Carolina, a small village in Bamberg County with a reputation for being relatively friendly to blacks. She was directed to a twenty-acre plot with several useable structures on it owned by State Senator Stanwyx G. Mayfield. When Wright approached Mayfield in March 1897, he agreed to assist her if she could present a letter of recommendation from Booker T. Washington. She obtained the letter and while accumulating the purchase price of $2,000 for Mayfield's land, she opened her school in temporary quarters on the top floor of a store in the Sato section of Denmark.

Voorhees College dates its start-up, as the Denmark Industrial School for Colored Youth, to 14 April 1897. Mayfield's property proved to be too small for her to realize her ambition to create an industrial and agricultural institution on the model of Tuskegee. She needed considerably more land for a model farm, stock raising, buildings for carpentry and mechanical training, residence halls for students, not to mention classrooms for traditional courses and housing for teachers and staff.

In 1900, a 280 acre tract, about a mile east of the Mayfield purchase, owned by a Dr. S. D. M. Guess, became available for $3,000. Determined to raise money to purchase this land, Wright was somehow referred to Ralph Voorhees of New Jersey, a blind philanthropist and former businessman whose ancestors had made a fortune in the Atlantic slave trade.

Wright managed to obtain an invitation to visit Ralph and Elizabeth Voorhees at their Clinton, New Jersey, home in April 1901. Although she understood that the interview must not exceed ten minutes, the Voorhees's were so captivated by her that they kept her overnight. She returned to Denmark the next day with a pledge for $3,000. Voorhees increased his gift to $4,500 plus $500 towards the construction of a building when Guess, who first stalled on his commitment to sell the land, raised his price to $4,500. A condition for the grant was that the school bear Ralph Voorhees's name. Thus, the institution was renamed The Voorhees Industrial School for Colored Youth.

The school took off. Voorhees and other northern donors were relatively generous, and the school gained much local support from the white and the black communities. But the effort involved in founding and managing the school took its toll. Wright continued to suffer from periodic bouts of "fever," probably malaria, and "gastritis." Nevertheless in 1906 she married Martin Menafee, a Tuskegee graduate who, in 1900, had become the business manager of the school. The wedding took place on 2 June 1906, officiated by two ministers who were members of the Board of Trustees.

Wright's health then took a turn for the worse. She was hospitalized at the Battle Creek Sanitarium in October 1906 and underwent a lengthy operation in November, conducted by Dr. Kellogg, to heal stomach ulcers. She died at the Sanitarium on 14 December 1906. Her body was inhumed on the Voorhees College campus.

Elizabeth Wright owed her success to luck, persistence in pursuing her ambition, and a talent for winning the support of wealthy northern patrons like Ralph and Elizabeth Voorhees, Olivia Stokes, and George Foster Peabody, politically and socially influential local figures like Senator Mayfield and his mother-in-law, Ellen Kennerly, the grassroots African American community, and, of course, Booker T. Washington, at that time a major arbiter of African American fortunes. She also adhered carefully to the parameters of African American higher education as they had been laid down by Samuel Chapman Armstrong and Booker T. Washington, parameters that nevertheless included subtle but deliberate academic drift towards the ideals and the practices of traditional American liberal arts higher education. A junior college branch was added to the school in 1929. In 1964, the institution became a four-year liberal arts college.

Clearly Booker T. Washington supported Wright's efforts. He regularly offered her advice, sent Tuskegee graduates to work with her, and invited her to attend important functions at Tuskegee. In Volume 2 of *The Story of the Negro* (1909), Washington lavished praise on Wright as an example of what a black woman graduate of Tuskegee could do. Elizabeth Evelyn Wright was a remarkable educational leader whose vision lives on at Voorhees College.

FURTHER READING
Blanton, Robert J. *The Story of Voorhees College, from 1897 to 1982* (1983).
Coleman, J. F. B. *Tuskegee to Voorhees: Elizabeth Evelyn Wright* (1922, 1966).

Morris, J. Kenneth. *Elizabeth Evelyn Wright (1872–1906): Founder of Voorhees College* (1983).

Washington, Booker T. *The Story of the Negro, Vol. 2* (1909).

LELAND CONLEY BARROWS

Wright, Jane (30 Nov. 1919–), physician, chemotherapist, and educator, was born Jane Cooke Wright in New York City to LOUIS TOMPKINS WRIGHT, a cancer researcher, surgeon, and civil rights leader, and Corrine Cooke, a teacher in the New York City school system. She attended Ethical Culture and Fieldston Schools before entering Smith College in 1938, where she initially contemplated a career in art rather than the sciences. She loved to paint, was a member of Smith's honorary art society, and had served as the art editor of her high school yearbook. Her father, however, feared that life as an artist would be an uncertain one, and at the end of her sophomore year, she chose a premed major. Ultimately Jane Wright was drawn to the field because of a "desire to serve with both the heart and mind" (Wright, 7) She won a scholarship to New York Medical College, where she was graduated with honors, third in her class, in 1945.

Although Jane Cooke Wright would go on to become one of the first chemotherapists to demonstrate regression of solid tumors in humans, she did not start off her medical career fighting cancer. Wright worked at Bellevue Hospital first as an intern and then as an assistant resident in internal medicine, a specialty she chose because it offered her a more regular schedule to be with her family. She began a residency in internal medicine at Harlem Hospital in 1947, married the lawyer David Dallas Jones, and took some time off to give birth to the first of their two girls, Jane. (She gave birth to daughter Allison two years later.) In 1948 she became chief resident in internal medicine at Harlem Hospital. Wright briefly pursued a career as a school and private physician, but she was not satisfied with the work. She joined her father at the Cancer Research Foundation in 1949 where she tested triethylene melamine and antimetabolites on patients with leukemia and other lymphatic types of cancer. When her father died in 1952 she succeeded him as director.

In 1955 Wright became the director of cancer chemotherapy and adjunct professor of research surgery at New York University Bellevue Medical Center, where she pioneered a method involving *in vivo* (in human patient) and *in vitro* (in cell culture) assessment of the effectiveness of cancer drugs. Testing each chemical on the patient's own tissue culture enabled her to determine the most effective course of treatment. In her thirty-five-year career of cancer research Wright researched nearly all types of cancer. She proved especially successful in treating advanced malignant melanoma using triethylene thiophosphoramide. She utilized single drug therapy to treat leukemia, Hodgkin's disease, and ovarian and breast cancers. Wright also advanced the technique of perfusion as a means of directing drugs to the cancer site. She was named professor of surgery and associate dean of her alma mater in 1967, the highest post attained by a black woman in medical administration at that time. The deanship ended in 1975, but Wright continued teaching chemotherapy to physicians. She published hundreds of scientific articles and wrote chapters in nine textbooks on cancer or cancer research.

Wright worked as a leader in cancer research at the local, state, and national levels of cancer research. She was a lifetime member of the board of directors for the New York City division of the American Cancer Society. In 1971 she served as the first female president of the New York Cancer Society. As a member of the 1964–1965 President's Commission on Heart Disease, Cancer and Stroke Wright helped to create regional centers for diagnosis and treatment of these diseases. One of the founding members of the American Society of Clinical Oncology, she was its secretary-treasurer from 1964 to 1967. Wright also served on the twelve-member panel of the National Advisory Cancer Council of the Department of Health, Education, and Welfare from 1966 to 1970 and the editorial board of the *Journal of the National Medical Association* from 1962 to 1980.

Wright shared her expertise with people outside of the United States. The State Department sent her to survey cancer in Ghana shortly after the creation of its new government in 1957. In 1961 she went on a medical safari sponsored by the African Medical and Research Foundation to remote areas of Kenya in a medical mobile unit. In the 1980s Wright led Cancer Update Citizen Ambassador Delegations to China, Eastern Europe and the Soviet Union, and South Africa. The Cancer Update delegations allowed physicians from different countries to exchange knowledge about advances in cancer research.

In addition to being a pioneer in cancer research, Wright served on the Manhattan Council New York State Commission Against Discrimination (1949–1962) and the Manhattan Council New York

State Commission of Human Rights (1962–1968). She was elected to the board of trustees for Smith College from 1970 to 1980. Her work earned her numerous awards and honors. She received honorary doctorates from Woman's Medical College of Pennsylvania and Denison University. In 1975 Clarke College honored her with the Finer Womanhood Award, and the American Association for Cancer Research paid homage to Wright for her contributions to cancer chemotherapy. Smith College presented her with the Smith Medal in 1968 and the Otelia Cromwell Award in 1981, awards bestowed on distinguished alumnae. Although a cure for cancer had not been found by the time Wright retired in 1987, she remained hopeful that one would be discovered. As she told a group of high school students in Stamford, Connecticut, on 3 February 1981, "There is deep satisfaction in knowing you are part of a continuing process … that you have picked up where others have left off and that others will pick up where you leave off" (Wright, 6–7). If her dream is to be realized, it will take more men and women as dedicated to cancer research as Jane Cooke Wright.

FURTHER READING

The Jane C. Wright Papers are housed in the Sophia Smith Collection, Smith College, in Northampton, Massachusetts.

Wright, Jane C. Speech delivered at Stamford High School, Stamford, Connecticut, 3 Feb. 1981. Jane C. Wright Papers, Sophia Smith Collection, Smith College, Northampton, Massachusetts.

Jenkins, Edward Sidney. "Jane Cooke Wright—Mother of Chemotherapy (1919–)," in *To Fathom More: African American Scientists and Inventors* (1996).

KARA M. MCCLURKEN

Wright, Jeffrey (7 Dec. 1965–), actor and producer, was born in Washington, D.C. His father died when he was a year old; his mother, an attorney employed by the United States Customs Department, raised him with the assistance of her sister, a nurse. Wright attended the elite St. Alban's School for Boys, a respected private, college preparatory institution, located on the grounds of the world-renowned Washington National Cathedral. With early aspirations of becoming an attorney, in 1983 he enrolled at the prestigious and highly selective Amherst College in Massachusetts. Unsuspectingly, Wright developed an interest in acting during his senior year; and, when in 1987 he earned a Bachelor of Arts in Political Science from Amherst, instead of attending law school, he accepted an acting scholarship from New York University (NYU). After two months with the Theater Department at NYU, Wright was presented the opportunity to act in a LORRAINE HANSBERRY play and decided to pursue a professional career as an actor on his own terms.

Wright was instantly successful, securing roles in off-Broadway productions; and in 1990 he achieved his first role in a major film, *Presumed Innocent*, starring Harrison Ford, in which he portrayed an attorney. Subsequently, while continuing in the theater, he began appearing in television roles, among them *Separate but Equal* (a dramatization of the NAACP Legal Defense Fund's victory in *Brown v. Board of Education*, starring SIDNEY POITIER as THURGOOD MARSHALL). In 1994 Wright was cast as Norman "Belize" Arriaga, in the award-winning Broadway production of *Angels in America: Perestroika*; for his portrayal of a gay nurse forced to care for a homophobic patient dying of AIDS he won a Tony Award for Best Featured Actor in a Play. In 1996 he played the lead role in the critically acclaimed biopic/drama film *Basquiat*, opposite the actors Davis Bowie and Benecio del Toro, as the acclaimed painter JEAN-MICHEL BASQUIAT, who died of a drug overdose just as he began to receive international recognition. The movie also portrayed racial disparities in the 1980s art scene in New York City, which Wright knew quite well. He had moved to New York City to attend NYU only one month before Basquiat died, and had lived in a building where the artist had spent much time; they thus knew many of the same people.

Subsequently, his film career accelerated with notable supporting roles in films such as *Celebrity* directed by Woody Allen (1998) and lead roles such as his performance in the director JOHN SINGLETON's remake of the 1970s Blaxploitation classic *Shaft* (2000), opposite actor SAMUEL L. JACKSON; for his portrayal he won the Toronto Film Critics Association Award for Best Supporting Performance, Male. In 2001 Wright won the American Film Institute Actor of the Year Award for male in a movie or miniseries for his characterization of the Reverend Dr. MARTIN LUTHER KING JR. in the cable movie *Boycott*. The same year he appeared as Howard Bingham, the MUHAMMAD ALI biographer, in *Ali*, starring Wil Smith as Ali.

Wright has an affinity for the stage and remained a presence in Theater, winning an Obie Award in 2002 for his performance in the SUZAN LORI PARKS play *Topdog/Underdog* opposite Don Cheadle. Already he had achieved recognition as a versatile and multifaceted actor, and his opportunities continued to flourish. In 2003 *Angels in America* was produced for HBO cable-television, with the actors Al Pacino and Meryl Streep; for his portrayal of "Belize," again Wright won commendations including the 2003 Hollywood Foreign Press Association award for Best Actor in a Supporting Role Television Series, and the Black Reel Award for Television: Best Actor (2004), Emmy Award for Outstanding Supporting Actor in a Miniseries or a Movie (2004), and a Golden Globe Award for best Performance by an Actor in a Supporting Role in a Series, Mini-Series, or Motion Picture Made for Television (2004). The San Diego Film Critics Society Awards named Wright Best Supporting actor for his role in *Broken Flowers* (2005). He won Best Supporting Actor from Black Reel Awards in 2006 for his performance in *Lackawanna Blues*. Black Reel Awards recognized Wright again in 2008 for his portrayal of the Blues Hall of Fame artist MUDDY WATERS in *Cadillac Records*. Wright also portrayed General and Secretary of State COLIN POWELL in Oliver Stone's movie about the former United States President, *W* (2008). Wright has also had a recurring role as CIA agent Felix Leiter, in the James Bond series in *Casino Royale* (2006) and *Quantum of Solace* (2008). Wright also produced *Blackout* (2007) and *One Blood* (2009).

Wright is vocal on social and political issues, particularly as they concern racial disparities. In 2008 he endorsed U.S. Senator BARACK OBAMA for president of the United States and hosted numerous fundraisers for his campaign. A highly publicized brawl in a Louisiana bar during the filming of *W.* necessitated his absence from a visible seat at the inauguration of President Obama. Toward the end of the first decade in the twenty-first century he spent valuable time launching his Taia Peace Foundation, an economic-development company in Sierra Leone to help rural communities manage their natural resources.

Wright met his wife, the Scottish-Nigerian actress Carmen Ejogo, on the set of *Boycott* (2001), where they portrayed the couple Martin Luther King Jr. and CORETTA SCOTT-KING. They were married in August 2000 and together have two children, Elijah and Juno.

Wright starred on Broadway in 2010, in the lead role of Jacques Cornet in *A Free Man of Color*, a swashbuckling drama about the wealthiest person of color in New Orleans in 1801, prior to the Louisiana Purchase. In 2011 he appeared in two major movies, the techno-thriller *Source Code*, and the George Clooney directed political thriller, *The Ides of March*.

FURTHER READING

Artz, Andrea. "The Wright Stuff." *The New Yorker*, 14 Aug. 2000.

Cagle, Jess, and David E. Thigpen. "Cinema: Mr. Wrong Is Mr. Wright." *Time*, 26 June 2000.

Healy, Mark. "A Deep Blue State: Actor Jeffrey Wright Hits Chicago in Sharp Navy Suits." *GQ*, January 2009.

Ordona, Michael. "More Than a Riff." *Los Angeles Times*, 4 Dec. 2008.

SAFIYA DALILAH HOSKINS

Wright, Jeremiah A., Jr. (22 Sept. 1941–), pastor, community activist, and author, was born in the racially mixed Germantown section of Philadelphia to Jeremiah Alvesta Wright Sr. and Dr. Mary Elizabeth Henderson Wright.

Wright Sr. served as pastor of Grace Baptist Church of Germantown from 1938 until his retirement in 1980. Dr. Mary Wright was a schoolteacher and the first vice principal at Germantown High and Girls Schools. Both parents profoundly influenced their son, instilling in him values that shaped his intellectual pursuits, spiritual life, and political activism.

Wright attended historic Central High School in Philadelphia, graduating in 1959. Central was an all-boys school and 90 percent white at the time of his attendance. Founded in 1838, the school had established a tradition of excellence in education, and fellow classmates considered Wright a model student among the 211th graduating class. Following in his father's footsteps, Wright enrolled in Virginia Union University, a historically black university in Richmond established in 1865. He stayed for only two years, however. Inspired by President John F. Kennedy's call to service, Wright left Virginia Union to join the Marine Corps in 1961, becoming Private First Class in the Second Marine Division. In 1963 he left the Marine Corps for the U.S. Navy, where he remained until 1967. Wright's military career was marked with distinction. He graduated valedictorian from the Corpsman school at the Great Lakes Naval Training Center and, having trained as a cardiopulmonary technician at the National Naval Medical Center in Bethesda, Maryland, he graduated second in his class. For his skill and accomplishment, Wright was chosen to serve on the medical team that cared for President Lyndon Baines Johnson after surgery to remove his gall bladder and a kidney stone in 1966. He received three White House letters of commendation for his service.

Jeremiah Wright, President Barack Obama's former pastor, speaks with reporters before giving an address to the Veterans of the Mississippi Civil Rights Movement Conference at Jackson State University in Jackson, Mississippi, on 25 March 2010. (AP Images.)

Having decided against making the military his life's career, Wright enrolled in Howard University, another historically black institution. He received a B.A. in 1968 and an M.A. in English the next year. At the University of Chicago Divinity School, where he enrolled as a doctoral student, Wright studied the history of religion, learned Greek and Hebrew, and read such theologians as Paul Tillich, H. Richard Niebuhr, and JAMES CONE, the latter of whom made an indelible mark on his thinking and ministry. He was awarded an M.A. in 1975. After the University of Chicago Wright earned a Doctor of Ministry degree from United Theological Seminary in Dayton, Ohio, where he studied with the eminent theologian and pastor SAMUEL DEWITT PROCTOR. The degree was awarded in 1990, long after Wright had accepted the pastorate at Trinity United Church of Christ (TUCC) on Chicago's South Side.

When Wright was installed as pastor at TUCC on 1 March 1972, the congregation was composed of fewer than one hundred active members. When he retired in 2008 the church numbered over eight thousand. Under his leadership, TUCC experienced not only an increase in numbers, but also an increase in prestige, organizational strength, and the expansion of its programs. One of Wright's first acts as pastor was to radically transform the music of the church. Founded in 1961 by the Rev. Dr. Kenneth B. Smith, TUCC was a decidedly middle-class black church and the music of its worship services reflected that sensibility, as well as the denomination's Congregational and Puritan roots. With Wright's support and under the leadership of

a new choir director, the church embraced lively black gospel music and incorporated West African instruments and dance into its worship services. Wright also posted a "Free South Africa" sign in support of the African National Congress on the church's lawn at 532 West 95th Street and did not remove it until the end of apartheid in 1994. That year, the congregation moved into a much larger edifice at 400 West 95th Street, paying off the mortgage just ten years later.

Wright stalwartly implemented TUCC's motto, "unashamedly black, unapologetically Christian," during a time of heightened black consciousness and the spread of black liberationist thought during the 1970s. He steered the church away from its "middle-classness" to a keen focus on Afrocentrism and the concerns of the poor. Over seventy ministries he organized at the church included those centered on Africa, HIV-AIDS, domestic violence, seniors, and child care. By the 1990s TUCC was one of the most prestigious and socially active African American congregations in Chicago, counting among its membership and frequent visitors BARACK OBAMA, hip-hop artist Common, and OPRAH WINFREY.

In 1993 *Ebony* magazine proclaimed Wright one of the fifteen greatest black preachers in the United States. Seven honorary doctorates accompany his four earned degrees, including those from Valparaiso University, Chicago Theological Seminary, Bethune Cookman College, and Colgate University. He sat on numerous boards and advisory councils, lectured extensively, and held several guest and adjunct professorships. Among his many publications are four books, *What Makes You So Strong: Sermons of Joy and Strength from Jeremiah A. Wright, Jr.* (1994); *Adam! Where Are You?: Why Most Black Men Don't Go to Church* (1994); *Good News!: Sermons of Hope for Today's Families* (1995); and *What Happens When We Pray: A Daily Devotional.* In 2008 Wright received the Carver Medal from Simpson College in Iowa in recognition for his leadership in the field of religion and his humanitarian efforts.

Wright gained international attention in March 2008 when ABC News excerpted a few of his sermons in a story by Brian Ross and Rehab El-Buri. Spreading quickly over the Internet and other media outlets, especially the avowedly conservative FOX News, the sermon excerpts were considered racially divisive and unpatriotic by many viewers and generated a firestorm of controversy. They also created significant problems for the presidential campaign of TUCC member and junior Senator from Illinois BARACK OBAMA. Senator Obama sought to end the controversy with a speech he delivered in Philadelphia, entitled "A More Perfect Union," where he distanced himself from Wright's statements but not from Wright himself. In June 2008, however, he resigned his membership at TUCC after Wright rose to his own defense in a series of public appearances, seemingly affirming statements made in the sermon excerpts and suggesting that the media scrutiny on him was an attack on the black church. Wright was granted emeritus status when he retired after thirty-six years as senior pastor and TUCC continued under the leadership of its new pastor, Rev. Otis Moss, III.

FURTHER READING

Obama, Barack. *Dreams from My Father: A Story of Race and Inheritance* (2004).

Speller, Julia. *Walkin' the Talk: Keepin' the Faith in Afrocentric Congregations* (2005).

Walker, Clarence, and Gregory Smithers. *The Preacher and the Politician: Jeremiah Wright, Barack Obama and Race in America* (2009).

WALLACE D. BEST

Wright, Jonathan Jasper (11 Feb. 1840–18 Feb. 1885), politician and jurist, was born in Luzerne County, Pennsylvania. Little is known of his parents except that his father was a farmer and that the family moved to Susquehanna County, Pennsylvania, during Wright's childhood. Wright attended Lancasterian University in Ithaca, New York, and later studied law at the offices of Bently, Fith, and Bently in Montrose, Pennsylvania. He also taught school and read law in the office of Judge O. Collins of Wilkes-Barre, Pennsylvania. Wright attended the 1864 national black convention in Syracuse, New York, that opposed slavery, supported universal manhood suffrage, and endorsed equality before the law.

At the end of the Civil War in April 1865, the American Missionary Association sent Wright to Beaufort, South Carolina, where he taught adult freedmen and soldiers of the 128th U.S. Colored Troops. In November 1865 he served as a delegate to the Colored Peoples' Convention in Charleston. Disappointed that the state's recent all-white, all-male constitutional convention relegated the black population to second-class status through a series of measures known as the "Black Code," the forty-five delegates to the Charleston convention supported

the enfranchisement of black men and the abolition of the Black Code, appealing for "even handed justice." Seven years later, in a speech assessing black political progress, Wright denounced the code as an attempt to keep blacks virtually enslaved by depriving "the colored people of all and every opportunity of being elevated an iota above their former condition. They were left totally at the mercy of the white man."

In 1866 Wright returned to Pennsylvania, where he became the first black admitted to the state bar. A few months later he was back in Beaufort as a legal adviser for the Freedmen's Bureau, representing the interests of former slaves and offering legal advice to the bureau's commanding officer in South Carolina, General Robert K. Scott. Though some bureau agents were accused of cooperating closely with white planters and ignoring the needs of the freedmen, Wright insisted that he would not do the bidding of white men. "Had I been contented to settle down, and been what the masses of white persons desired me to be (a boot-blacker, a barber, or a hotel waiter) I would have been heard of less."

When Congress authorized the reorganization of the southern states and adopted universal manhood suffrage in the 1867 Reconstruction Acts, Wright promptly joined in organizing the Republican Party and speaking on its behalf. At a rally in July 1867, he urged the party to nominate a black man for U.S. vice president in 1868. He resigned from the Freedmen's Bureau in 1868 and was elected to represent Beaufort at the state constitutional convention.

Wright played a prominent part in the convention, serving as one of two black vice presidents (of five total vice presidents) and as a member of the Judiciary Committee. He persuaded the convention to support the legislative election of judges to fixed terms rather than to permit gubernatorial appointment of judges for life. Wright was also deeply concerned about education. Like most of the convention's delegates (black and white), he showed little interest in integrated public schools, claiming that he did "not believe the colored children will want to go to the white schools, or vice versa."

Wright was involved in a major controversy when he supported the adoption of a one-dollar poll tax, the proceeds of which would be devoted to education. Wright and FRANCIS L. CARDOZO believed the tax was necessary to finance the establishment of public schools, while other black delegates led by ROBERT BROWN ELLIOTT feared the failure to pay the tax would disenfranchise large numbers of black voters. The tax was not included in the constitution.

In 1868 Wright, Elliott, and WILLIAM J. WHIPPER were the first three black men admitted to the South Carolina bar. Shortly thereafter Wright was elected to the South Carolina Senate, representing Beaufort County. In 1869, while traveling through Virginia, Wright was removed from a first-class, all-white coach on the Richmond and Danville Railroad. He subsequently won a $1,200 lawsuit against the railroad.

On 1 February 1870 the general assembly elected Wright to the state supreme court to fill the unexpired term of Solomon L. Hoge, who had been elected to Congress. The following December, Wright was elected to a full six-year term. Wright's elevation to the court was part of a larger effort by South Carolina black leaders to secure the election of more black men to major political offices. In 1870 black men were elected lieutenant governor, treasurer, speaker of the house, and to three seats in Congress.

Wright's seven-year tenure on the three-member court was largely uneventful. Only his most biased critics considered him less than competent and effective. Wright participated in 425 cases; he wrote 87 opinions and dissented on just one occasion. Wright's judicial career ended in controversy in 1877 during the prolonged dispute involving the results of the 1876 gubernatorial election, when Democratic candidate Wade Hampton and Republican incumbent Daniel Chamberlain each claimed victory. In a supreme court case testing Hampton's authority as governor, Wright and Associate Justice A. J. Willard upheld a pardon issued by Hampton. (Chief Justice Franklin Moses Sr. was ill.) Two days later Wright attempted to reverse his decision as well as the order releasing the prisoner.

The revocation of the order was not accepted, and rumors circulated that black Republicans bribed Wright or had gotten him drunk to compel him to change his position. Counter rumors contended that the black Republican legislator THOMAS E. MILLER was offered a bribe by Democrats to testify that Wright was drunk. Other reports claimed that Wright was threatened by one party or the other. A month later Hampton's claim to executive authority was supported by Republican president Rutherford B. Hayes, and the Republican Party lost political control of South Carolina. Though a special legislative committee under Democratic control recommended the impeachment of Wright

for misconduct for allegedly accepting a bribe to uphold Hampton's pardon, no formal charges were presented. Wright resigned from the court on 6 August 1877.

Wright resumed his career as a lawyer. He supported Hampton's reelection in 1878, and in 1879 he moved to Charleston and opened a law practice on Queen Street. In 1881 the Board of Trustees of Claflin University in Orangeburg, South Carolina, authorized Wright to teach law courses for the university. He offered the courses in Charleston on behalf of Claflin until his death. He died of tuberculosis in Charleston.

Wright was one of the vanguard of black men who rose to political power in the 1860s and 1870s and is noteworthy as the only black state supreme court justice in the nineteenth century. Moderate in his political views and restrained in his legal decisions, he nevertheless persistently sought expanded political influence for African Americans while defending the rights they so recently had gained. His life and career illustrate both the possibilities and the limitations that black men encountered in the post–Civil War era.

FURTHER READING

Holt, Thomas. *Black over White: Negro Political Leadership in South Carolina during Reconstruction* (1977).

Oldenfield, J. R. "A High and Honorable Calling: Black Lawyers in South Carolina, 1868–1915." *Journal of American Studies* 23 (1989).

Rogers, George C., Jr. *Generations of Lawyers: A History of the South Carolina Bar* (1992).

Tindall, George B. *South Carolina Negroes, 1877–1900* (1952).

Williamson, Joel. *After Slavery: The Negro in South Carolina during Reconstruction, 1861–1877* (1965).

Woody, Robert H. "Jonathan Jasper Wright, Associate Justice of the Supreme Court of South Carolina, 1870–1877," *Journal of Negro History* 18 (Apr. 1933).

Obituary: (Charleston) *News and Courier*, 20 Feb. 1885.

This entry is taken from the *American National Biography* and is published here with the permission of the American Council of Learned Societies.

WILLIAM C. HINE

Wright, Louis Tompkins (22 July 1891–8 Oct. 1952), surgeon, hospital administrator, and civil rights leader, was born in La Grange, Georgia, the son of Ceah Ketcham Wright, a physician and clergyman, and Lula Tompkins. After his father's death in 1895, his mother married William Fletcher Penn, a physician who was the first African American to graduate from Yale University Medical School. Raised and educated in Atlanta, Wright received his elementary, secondary, and college education at Clark University in Atlanta, graduating in 1911 as valedictorian of his class. His stepfather was one of the guiding influences that led to his choice of medicine as a career.

Wright graduated from Harvard Medical School, cum laude and fourth in his class, in 1915. While in medical school he exhibited his willingness to take a strong stand against racial injustice when he successfully opposed a hospital policy that would have barred him (but not his white classmates) from the practicum in delivering babies (obstetrics) at Boston-Lying-In Hospital. Despite an early record of publications, because of restrictions based on race, Wright completed an internship during 1915–1916 at Freedmen's Hospital, the teaching hospital at the Howard University School of Medicine in Washington, D.C., one of only three black hospitals with approved internship programs at that time.

While he was an intern at Freedmen's, Wright rejected a claim in the medical literature that the Schick test for diptheria could not be used on African Americans because of their heavy skin pigmentation. A study he conducted proved the validity of the usefulness of this test on dark-skinned people and was the basis of his second published paper, "The Schick Test, with Especial Reference to the Negro" (*Journal of Infectious Diseases* 21 [1917]: 265–268). Wright returned to Atlanta in July 1916 to practice medicine. In Atlanta he launched his civil rights career as a founding member of the Atlanta branch of the NAACP, serving as its first treasurer (1916–1917).

With the onset of World War I, Wright applied for a military commission and became a first lieutenant in the U.S. Army Medical Corps. A month before going overseas in June 1918, he married Corrine M. Cooke in New York City. They had two daughters, both of whom became physicians: Jane Cooke Wright and Barbara Penn Wright.

While Wright was in France, his unit was gassed with phosgene, causing him permanent lung damage. Because his injury (for which he received a Purple Heart) imposed physical limitations, he served out the rest of the war in charge of the surgical wards at three field hospitals. As a medical officer he introduced the intradermal method for smallpox vaccination ("Intradermal Vaccination against Smallpox," *Journal of the American Medical Association* 71 [1918]: 654–657), which was officially adopted by the U.S. Army.

In 1919, when Wright settled in Harlem to start a general medical practice, Harlem Hospital, a municipal facility with a 90 percent black patient population, had no African American doctors or nurses on staff. With an assignment effective 1 January 1920 as a clinical assistant (the lowest rank) in the Out-Patient Department, he became the first African American to be appointed to the staff of a New York City hospital. His steadfast and successful efforts during the 1920s working with hospital administrators and with city officials led gradually to appointments for other African Americans as interns and attending physicians. His push for greater opportunities for African American professionals at Harlem Hospital culminated in a reorganization mandated in 1930 by William Schroeder, commissioner of the Department of Hospitals for the City of New York. The result was the first genuine effort to racially integrate the entire medical staff of a major U.S. hospital. By then Wright had risen to the position of visiting surgeon, and in October 1934 he became the second African American to be admitted to the American College of Surgeons (established in 1913). In 1938 he was appointed to a one-year term as the hospital's director of surgery. In 1929 he had achieved yet another breakthrough, as the first African American to be appointed as a police surgeon through the city's competitive civil service examination. He retained the position until his death.

In 1935 Wright was elected chairman of the national board of directors of the NAACP, a position he held until 1952. As a civil rights leader he opposed the establishment of hospitals exclusively for black people, and in the 1940s he argued for national health care insurance; he also challenged discriminatory policies and practices of the powerful American Medical Association. In a published open letter (dated 28 Jan. 1931) in response to an offer from the Julius Rosenwald Fund to build a hospital for blacks in New York City, Wright wrote: "A segregated hospital makes the white person feel superior and the black person feel inferior. It sets the black person apart from all other citizens as being a different kind of citizen and a different kind of medical student and physician, which you know and we know is not the case. What the Negro physician needs is equal opportunity for training and practice—no more, no less."

Treating common injuries in the surgical wards of Harlem Hospital led Wright to develop, in 1936, a device for handling fractured and dislocated neck vertebrae. In addition to this neck brace, he also designed a special metal plate to treat certain fractures of the femur. He became an expert on bone injuries and in 1937 was asked to write the chapter on head injuries for Charles Scudder's monumental textbook *The Treatment of Fractures* (1938), this being the first contribution by an African American to a major authoritative medical text.

Wright became ill with tuberculosis in 1939 and for nearly three years was confined to Biggs Memorial Hospital in Ithaca, New York. In 1939, while hospitalized, he was elected a diplomate of the American Board of Surgery. The year before, *Life* magazine had recognized him as the "most eminent Negro doctor" in the United States. In 1940 he was awarded the NAACP's prestigious Spingarn Medal for his achievements and contributions to American medicine.

In 1942, after returning to Harlem Hospital, Wright was appointed director of surgery, a position he held until his death. In 1945 he established a certified four-year residency program in surgery, a first for a black hospital. In 1948 he led a team of resident doctors in the first clinical trials of the antibiotic aureomycin with human beings. This pioneering testing at Harlem Hospital and subsequently at other hospitals paved the way for the approval of this drug and eventually other antibiotics by the U.S. Food and Drug Administration. In 1948 he established and became director of the Harlem Hospital Cancer Research Foundation, funded by the U.S. Public Health Service. Perhaps his crowning achievement was his election, that year, as president of the hospital's medical board.

Over the course of his long career at Harlem Hospital, Wright welded together into a harmonious whole the various white and black groups within the hospital. He recognized and confronted directly the problems faced by other ethnic professionals, particularly Jewish and Italian American physicians, so that shortly before his death, at the dedication of the hospital's Louis T. Wright Library, he said, "Harlem Hospital represents to my mind the finest example of democracy at work in the field of medicine."

Wright died in New York City. His presence at Harlem Hospital and on the national civil rights scene, and his voice and actions in public and private health forums and debates, had significant consequences for American medicine in three areas: it led to a rapport between black and white doctors that generated scientific and clinical research yielding important contributions in several areas of medicine; it dispensed with myths regarding black physicians that excluded them from any hospital staff on grounds other than those related to individual competence and character; and it led to the admittance of qualified physicians who were African American into local and national medical and scientific societies.

FURTHER READING

Wright published eighty-nine scientific articles in leading medical journals: thirty-five on antibiotics, fourteen in the field of cancer, six on bone trauma, and others on various surgical procedures on the colon and the repair of gunshot wounds.

Cobb, William Montague. "Louis Tompkins Wright, 1891–1952," *Journal of the National Medical Association* 45 (Mar. 1953): 130–148.

de L'Maynard, Aubre. *Surgeons to the Poor: The Harlem Hospital Story* (1978).

Obituary: *New York Times*, 9 Oct. 1952.

This entry is taken from the *American National Biography* and is published here with the permission of the American Council of Learned Societies.

ROBERT C. HAYDEN

Wright, Mary Herring (29 Dec. 1924–), author, was born in Iron Mine, North Carolina, to Ben and Helena Herring, farmers who raised crops of tobacco and strawberries to take to market. Mary and her five siblings shared the labor of the farm and household, which often included schoolteachers for Iron Mine's two-room schoolhouse who boarded with her family. Mary attended the racially segregated school, which encompassed grades one through seven; an education in grades eight through eleven was available in another town only if a student found someone in town with whom to live, since the segregated school bus to town was for whites only.

Herring's world changed when she was about eight years old as she began losing her hearing; she became completely deaf by age ten. The condition was nerve deafness but the cause was unknown. She learned to communicate through lipreading and note writing but became socially isolated; at school she was shunned or pitied. She continued to speak, however, and throughout her life she retained both the memory of the sounds she once knew and her love for music.

In 1935 her family sent her to the North Carolina School for the Blind and Deaf in Raleigh. A state school with African American teachers, it could accommodate about three hundred black children. Mary learned sign language there and her ability to speak was reinforced as she was instructed to continue speaking. In addition to academic subjects, she learned handicrafts such as knitting, crocheting, embroidery, and rug weaving. She learned to cook and sew both at school and at home. She found the resources to cope with deafness through the development of her abilities, school friends with whom she could communicate, her faith, and her family with whom she lived each summer.

Traversing a variety of milieus that influenced her education, Herring learned to adjust to home life and the hearing world as well as to school life and the world of the disabled. On train trips home for the summer, she sat in a railway car designated for deaf and blind students only, which resulted in both black and white students' riding in the same car. This occurred during the mid-1930s when public places, such as the beach her family utilized for recreation, were segregated. At home, she finger spelled to communicate with family members. In the summer of 1939, as a young woman interested in popular tunes, she accompanied family members to nightspots in town, learning the words from hit song magazines, and the beat from jukeboxes and records played at home. She also learned to dance in spite of her deafness.

While attending the Raleigh school, she discovered the library, which had been avoided by others because it was used for detention purposes. Motivated by her love of reading, Herring requested and obtained permission to use it. Seeing typewriters for the blind students in the library, she began teaching herself to type.

Having retained her speaking ability, Herring was able to talk to the blind students. She made friends with blind girls and understood them when they learned to sign or finger spell by feeling her hand form each letter of the alphabet. While the blind students used their sense of touch to read Braille, she learned how to read and write in Braille from them by using her sight.

Herring's introduction to politics occurred at the school when the blind girls perceived injustices by teachers and alerted the deaf students through Herring to unite with them in protest. She became chief spy for the deaf girls and used her eyes to report what she saw while the blind girls used their ears to report all they heard. After they went to a program in town at the school for white blind children and were given a tour of their campus, the students were depressed and angry about the better facilities at the school for whites. Eventually changes were made to improve their own school. Mary's own idea of progress was to have typewriting lessons given to deaf girls, an idea put into effect when she approached a teacher about it.

Her autobiography provides insights into the world of the deaf. Her ability to speak was an asset in situations where she acted as interpreter for the deaf to hearing people. Her speaking ability was also a basis for her ability to write sentences; she saw that deaf students who used only sign language to communicate were not able to write so that hearing people could understand what was written, because one or two signs can communicate a whole sentence.

Herring wanted to become a nurse, but saw her deafness as a barrier. She worked as a volunteer in the school infirmary, rolling bandages, copying health reports into a ledger, and feeding patients. The school physician was Dr. Delany, a man whose sisters BESSIE and SADIE DELANY later became famous authors when they were elderly women.

Herring graduated from high school at the North Carolina School for the Blind and Deaf in 1941, and she returned to the school that autumn as a teacher. She taught home economics and classroom work under the guidance of an experienced teacher. To students who had been born deaf, she taught the meaning of sound and of talking. As a teacher she continued to lead in signing the spirituals and other songs in the school's chapel services as she had done during her years as a student at the school. Churches in town and other places invited African Americans from the school to sign for their programs.

After a year of teaching, Herring moved to Washington, D.C. In 1943, during World War II, she became a clerk for the U.S. Department of the Navy, working on reports for ships in the Muster Roll Department. As everyone in the office was able to hear and none signed or finger spelled, she was able to communicate with them through speech reading (lipreading) and note writing. In spite of her disability, she felt content with both the opportunity to become financially self-supporting and to have a good place to live. During her term of work there, signs were posted announcing that all facilities such as restrooms and cafes were to be used by all government employees regardless of race, color, or creed. In the mid-1940s she resigned in order to return to her roots in North Carolina.

Back in Iron Mine, she taught the beginners' class in Sunday school. Later when her own children were in school, the school personnel requested her to use her skills as a seamstress to make costumes for school plays. She also taught a fourth-grade class to knit, crochet, and sew.

In North Carolina she met James Wright. They were married in 1950 and remained married until his death in 1982. They had four daughters, whom she raised to value an education, in the same way that her family had raised her.

Mary Herring Wright was awarded an honorary bachelor of arts degree from Gallaudet University in May 2004. She was the author of two books. The first, *Sounds Like Home, Growing Up Black and Deaf in the South*, was published in 1999; the second, *Far from Home, Memories of World War II and Afterward*, was published in 2005.

ROSE PELONE SISSON

Wright, Richard (4 Sept. 1908–28 Nov. 1960), author, was born Richard Nathaniel Wright in a log cabin in the backwoods of Adams County, Mississippi. He was the eldest of the two sons of Nathaniel Wright, an illiterate sharecropper, and Ella Wilson, a semiliterate schoolteacher. Since the boll weevil had ravaged the local cotton industry, the family moved to Memphis, Tennessee, and shortly afterward, Nathaniel Wright abandoned them.

Ella Wright eked out a living by working as a servant in white households, but after a severe stroke in 1918, she was never able to work again. She and the boys went to live with her parents, Richard and Margaret Wilson, in Jackson, Mississippi. Wright's autobiographical narrative *Black Boy* (1945) gives a vivid picture of those difficult years in his grandparents' house. There were constant arguments and violent beatings. The family resources were stretched to the limits, and his grandmother, the family matriarch, bitterly resented Richard's independent spirit. She was a devout Seventh-day Adventist who believed that all books other than the Scriptures were "Devil's Work," and pressured Wright to be "saved" by the church. Wright remained an atheist all his life.

After a year at the Negro Seventh-day Adventist School in Jackson, Wright attended the Jim Hill Primary School and, in eighth grade, the Smith Robertson Elementary School. For the first time, he came into contact with the striving black middle class, whose models were people like W. E. B. DuBois and BOOKER T. WASHINGTON. He blossomed and soon proved an outstanding student. In 1925 Wright was the school valedictorian. That same year, he had a short story published in the *Southern Register*, a local African American weekly.

A black high school opened in Jackson for the first time that year, but Wright could not buy books or clothes from the money he earned from odd jobs after school. In November 1925 he left behind the hostile atmosphere in his grandmother's house and took the train to Memphis to seek full-time work.

His job opportunities were severely curtailed by the color of his skin. The best he could find was work as a messenger in an optical company. One day, in the local newspaper, he came across the name H. L. Mencken. It would prove a turning point. As a black man, Wright was not able to borrow books from the public library, but he persuaded an Irish coworker to lend him his card, and he went to the library, pretending to be picking up books for this white man. He took out two books by Mencken. Wright was excited to discover that the iconoclastic Baltimore journalist and literary critic used words like a weapon. He realized he wanted nothing more than to do the same. With Mencken's *A Book of Prefaces* as his guide, Wright began to read voraciously. He was painfully aware that his formal education extended only to the eighth grade, and that famous writers, as well as their subject matter, were invariably white.

Wright left the segregated South in November 1927. For the next ten years he lived in Chicago. He was one of 12 million black people who made that journey from the rural South to the industrial North during the Great Migration of 1916–1928, and he would describe it as the most traumatic journey of his entire life. His narrative *Twelve Million Black Voices* (1941), accompanied by WPA photographs, movingly conveys the two different worlds.

Wright soon landed a job as an unskilled laborer, sorting mail on the night shift at the Chicago Post Office—the best-paying job in town for a black man. Wright brought his mother, brother, and aunt to live with him in Chicago. During the Depression, however, Wright took whatever work he could find, while also pursuing his reading and writing with extraordinary determination.

In the fall of 1933 a white friend from the post office told him about the John Reed Club, a national organization of "proletarian artists and writers" founded by the Communist Party. Wright went along and met other aspiring artists and writers— mostly sons of Jewish immigrants. Stimulated by this environment, he began to write poems, several of which were published in Communist magazines. His poem "I Have Seen Black Hands" was printed in the national weekly *The New Masses* in June 1934.

Richard Wright in New York City, 27 March 1945. (AP Images.)

Early in 1934 Wright was pressured to join the Communist Party. Since it consciously fought racism and was one of the few places in the United States where blacks and whites mixed on an equal footing, Wright decided to do so, but from the beginning there were conflicts. He disliked being told what to do, and in his spare time, his writing was far more important to him than party work. Nevertheless, the party provided crucial support to Wright, both as an artist and as a bulwark against racism in America. He did not leave it until 1944, when he became an outspoken anti-Communist. He was disgusted that the Communist Party put civil rights issues on hold during World War II, at a time when blacks were expected to fight in segregated armed forces, and as he explained in his famous essay, "I Tried To Be a Communist," published in the *Atlantic Monthly* in August and September 1944, while the party claimed to be democratic, it actually took its orders from Moscow.

The Works Progress Administration (WPA) was established by President Franklin Roosevelt in May 1935, with the Federal Writers Project as one of its offshoots. Wright, who by now had published two short stories and thirteen poems, was signed on to the Illinois Writers Project as a supervisor. He could hardly believe his luck. This was a thirty-hour-a-week job, and the U.S. government was paying him to write. In his spare time Wright wrote a volume of short stories, *Uncle Tom's Children* (1938), and a novel, *Lawd Today!* (1963).

Wright was influenced by Marxism and the Chicago School of Sociology, which related neurotic behavior and crime to environment, and both were important influences on the South Side group of black writers that Wright organized in 1936. Other members who became well-known writers were FRANK MARSHALL DAVIS, MARGARET WALKER, and THEODORE (TED) WARD.

In May 1937 Wright moved to New York City. He became a friend and mentor to RALPH ELLISON, encouraged the young JAMES BALDWIN, and championed CHESTER HIMES and GWENDOLYN BROOKS. Wright was briefly the Harlem correspondent for the Communist Party newspaper *The Daily Worker*, before he was transferred to the New York Writers Project. In February 1938 his writing career took off when he won a national competition of WPA writers for his collection of short stories *Uncle Tom's Children*, which portrayed the barbarism of black life and lynching in the Jim Crow South. Harper and Brothers published the book, which won Wright national recognition. In 1939 a Guggenheim Fellowship allowed Wright to work full-time on his novel *Native Son* (1940). With its negative depiction of black ghetto life and its hint of interracial sex, the novel was controversial at the time and would remain so for decades to come. Promoted by the Book-of-the-Month Club, though the judges insisted on deleting nearly all allusions to interracial sexual attraction, the book sold a quarter of a million copies. Wright became the first best-selling African American writer. In 1941 the play *Native Son*, written by Wright and Paul Green and directed by Orson Welles, opened on Broadway to rave reviews. In 1945 Wright's autobiographical narrative *Black Boy*, again promoted by the Book-of-the-Month Club, sold an incredible half million copies. The original manuscript, entitled *American Hunger*, referring to the spiritual hunger of oppressed American blacks, portrayed Wright's formative years up to the beginning of the war, focusing on his experience of racism in both the deep South and in the North. The Book-of-the-Month Club insisted that he cut the second half, with its depiction of racism in the North and Wright's experiences in the Communist Party. Similarly, the judges disliked the unpatriotic title, and finally Wright changed it to *Black Boy*. The original manuscript was finally published posthumously in 1977 under its original title.

After a brief marriage to Dhimah Meidman in 1939, Wright married Ellen Poplowitz in March 1941, and their daughter Julia was born in 1942. His marriage to a white woman and the taunts that followed them when they walked together around New York and when Ellen went out with Julia reinforced Wright's desire to leave the country. He desperately wanted to expand his horizons and see the world. Encouraged by Gertrude Stein, who lived in Paris and whose work he greatly admired, Wright and his family left for Paris in May 1946. Their second daughter, Rachel, was born in Paris on 17 January 1949.

Wright was thirty-eight and in his prime when he left for Europe, but that ship voyage across the Atlantic marked a dramatic downturn in his career.

For the next fourteen years he continued to write prolifically, both fiction and nonfiction. In Europe his work was celebrated by the famous existentialists Jean-Paul Sartre and Simone de Beauvoir. He was interviewed frequently and his work was widely translated. He was regarded as an important American writer and public intellectual. But in the United States he was largely ignored. Even today, few Americans have heard of the titles he wrote after he left the United States—*The Outsider* (1953), *Savage Holiday* (1954), *Black Power* (1954), *The Color Curtain* (1956), *Pagan Spain* (1957), *White Man, Listen!* (1957), *The Long Dream* (1958), *Eight Men* (1961), and *Haiku: This Other World* (1998). Wright's exile writing had the same power, the same emotional persuasiveness. His nonfiction—a mixture of travel essay, memoir, biographical sketch, and political commentary—was in many ways ahead of its time. But in the highly conservative atmosphere of the McCarthyist 1950s, hard-hitting critiques of American racism and Western imperialism—and protest literature, in general—were no longer in vogue.

Wright's world opened up considerably after he left the United States. In 1949–1950 he spent almost a year in Argentina, where he played Bigger Thomas in the movie *Native Son*. (The film, made in an adverse political climate, with the forty-year-old Wright badly miscast as an eighteen-year old, was a financial flop.) In 1953 he visited the Gold Coast, a trip he chronicled in *Black Power*. In 1955 he attended the Bandung Conference in Indonesia, an experience he recalled in *The Color Curtain*. He spent time exploring life in Franco's Spain for the book *Pagan Spain* (1957), and he gave lectures that were collected in *White Man, Listen!* (1957).

American critics often refer to Wright's last fourteen years as his "exile" years. The term is hardly appropriate, however, since Wright's entire body of work prior to his departure for France was a passionate portrayal of what it was like to live as an exile in his native land. The prevalent view, even today, is that living abroad was bad for his writing, that it cut him off from the reality of contemporary America, from his roots, and from the anger that fueled his writing. Others claim that Wright did not lose his power in the 1950s. What changed were the historical circumstances in which he was writing.

Wright died in Paris at the age of fifty-two. His death certificate gives a heart attack as the cause, but the circumstances of his premature death have always aroused suspicion, especially as it is known that the U.S. State Department watched him closely, throughout the 1950s. As someone who ceaselessly criticized American racism from his prominent vantage point as a black intellectual in Europe, Wright was something of a threat to the 1950s propaganda war.

Richard Wright was the first African American writer to enter mainstream American literature. A watershed figure in African American literature, he pushed back the horizons for black writers, expanding their possible subject matter. At the beginning of the twenty-first century, Wright's writing continued to provoke passionate responses, from deep admiration to vehement hostility. He is an *uncomfortable* writer. He challenges, he tells painful truths, he is a disturber of the peace. He was never interested in pleasing readers. Wright wanted his words to be weapons.

FURTHER READING

Fabre, Michel. *The Unfinished Quest of Richard Wright* (1973).
Kinnamon, Keneth, and Michel Fabre, eds. *Conversations with Richard Wright* (1993).
Rowley, Hazel. *Richard Wright: The Life and Times* (2001).
Walker, Margaret. *Richard Wright: Daemonic Genius* (1988).
Webb, Constance. *Richard Wright: A Biography* (1968).
Obituary: *New York Times*, 30 Nov. 1960.

HAZEL ROWLEY

Wright, Richard Robert, Sr. (16 May 1855–2 July 1947), educator and banker, was born in Whitfield County, Georgia, the son of Robert Waddell and Harriet (maiden name unknown), both slaves. His father, of mixed African and Cherokee descent, was the coachman on a plantation where his mother was a house servant. When Richard was two years old, his father escaped to free territory. Richard and his mother were taken by their slave owner to Cuthbert, Georgia, where she married Alexander Wright and had two children. After emancipation Harriet Wright moved with her three children to Atlanta to take advantage of the recent opening of a Freedman's Bureau School for Negroes. While Harriet supported the family by running a boarding house, Richard entered Storrs School, which was run by the American Missionary Association. In 1866 General Oliver Otis Howard, then current commissioner of the Freedmen's Bureau, visited the Sunday school at the Storrs Church and asked the students what message he should tell the children

of the North about them. The young Wright stood up and said, "Tell them we are rising." This incident inspired the poem "Howard at Atlanta" by the great abolitionist John Greenleaf Whittier. Wright attended Atlanta University where he received a B.A. and was valedictorian of the university's first graduating class in 1876. Wright married Lydia E. Howard in 1869, and they had nine children.

After graduation from Atlanta University, Wright became the principal of a primary school in Cuthbert. In Cuthbert he helped organize local farmers into cooperatives and coordinated the state's first county fair for blacks. In 1878 he organized the Georgia State Teachers' Association (for black educators), served as its first president, and began publishing the association's *Weekly Journal of Progress*, later called the *Weekly Sentinel*. Wright represented Georgia at the 1879 National Conference of Colored Men of the United States, held in Nashville, Tennessee, which sought primarily to assist in the plight of African Americans.

In 1880 Wright was asked to set up and direct Ware High School in Augusta, Georgia, which became the state's first public high school for blacks. His political activities definitely aided his career in education. Wright was an alternate delegate in 1880 to the Republican National Convention in Chicago, a participant at the conference of the Afro-American League in Minneapolis (1881), a member of the State Republican Central Committee (1882), a special agent for the U.S. Department of the Interior Development in Alabama (1885), and a delegate for Georgia to the Republican National Convention through 1896. In return for his political influence with the black voters, Wright was appointed by President William McKinley to the position of paymaster in the army with the rank of major during the Spanish-American War.

In October 1891 the Georgia legislature established the Georgia State Industrial College for Colored Youth in Savannah. Wright, an obvious candidate to lead the school because of his long experience in teaching and administration, remained president for thirty years, until his retirement in 1921. One of the members of his faculty was MONROE NATHAN WORK, who later wrote the well-known *Bibliography of the Negro in Africa and America*.

Wright's tenure as president was troubled by the control of an all-white board of trustees for the college that objected to higher education for blacks. Especially controversial were Wright's efforts to include classical education in the curriculum. Early in his presidency he organized the Negro Civic Improvement League in Savannah. This political organization proved to be very unpopular with the college trustees, and, under much pressure from them, Wright withdrew from the organization and politics in general. He decided to follow the emphasis placed by many black scholars and leaders of the day, such as BOOKER T. WASHINGTON, on programs of self-help and cooperative efforts with whites. It was during this time that Wright wrote *A Brief Historical Sketch of Negro Education in Georgia* (1894), which addressed his inability to obtain sufficient support for an adequate curriculum at the college.

In 1921 Wright retired as president of the Georgia State Industrial College for Colored Youth and began a new career as a banker and elder statesman. Along with a son, Richard R. Wright Jr., and a daughter, Lillian W. Clayton, Wright founded in Philadelphia, Pennsylvania, in 1921 the Citizens and Southern Bank and Trust Company. Wright's reputation as an honest and well-qualified man provided the kind of stability needed to survive such economic crises as the 1929 stock market crash and the Great Depression of the 1930s. The fact that Wright managed to maintain banking operations during the Depression can be credited to both the diversity of his investment portfolio and the conservative policy of his bank.

In 1945 he attended the conference in California that organized the United Nations. A banquet was held at the conference in recognition of his long career, which included the presidency of the National Association of Presidents of A&M Colleges (1906–1919) and the presidency of the National Association of Teachers of Colored Schools (1908–1912). He helped to establish the National Freedom Day Association, supported a 1940 commemorative stamp for Booker T. Washington, and gathered information for the Georgia Archives about African Americans who fought in the First World War. In 1946, a year before his death, Wright accepted the Muriel Dobbin's Pioneers of Industry Award from the business community of Philadelphia. He died in Philadelphia.

FURTHER READING

Wright's papers are held by his family, the majority with Emanuel C. Wright of Philadelphia and others with Wright's daughter Harriet B. S. Hines of Glenarden, Maryland.

Bond, Horace Mann. *The Black American Scholars: A Study of Their Beginnings* (1972).

Hall, Clyde W., ed. *One Hundred Years of Educating at Savannah State College, 1890–1990* (1990).

Haynes, Elizabeth Ross. *The Black Boy of Atlanta* (1952).

Logan, Rayford W. *The Betrayal of the Negro* (1965).

Meier, August. *Negro Thought in America, 1888–1915* (1963).

Obituary: *New York Times*, 3 July 1947.

This entry is taken from the *American National Biography* and is published here with the permission of the American Council of Learned Societies.

ROBERT C. MORRIS

Wright, Stan (11 Aug. 1921–6 Nov. 1998), track coach, teacher, and administrator, was born Stanley Van Dorne Wright in Englewood, New Jersey, the son of Spencer Wright, a sanitation worker and truck driver, and Mildred (Prime) Wright, a seamstress and cook. Growing up in a northern city proved no shield from racism. In junior high and high school, Wright had little option but to follow a curriculum for black students that de-emphasized academics. His parents, however, taught him to value education.

Unfortunately, America's involvement in World War II interrupted his schooling. Soon after Pearl Harbor, Wright joined the Army Air Corps. However, he failed to complete pilot training, and his responsibilities at an airbase in Kansas consisted primarily of office tasks. While in the Air Corps, in late 1944, he married Hazel Mathes and they would have four children. In 1945 Wright was reassigned to an airbase in Massachusetts. He completed his military duty in early 1947. Wright enrolled in Springfield College in Massachusetts and graduated in 1949 with a bachelor's degree in Health and Physical Education. The following year he obtained a master's degree from Columbia University Teachers College.

Upon graduation, Wright discovered that his job prospects were limited. He wanted to teach and coach, but no college offered him a position. Frustrated, Wright accepted the directorship of a YMCA in Detroit. In 1951 he was hired as a physical education instructor and head track coach at Texas Southern University, a historically black university in Houston and a member of the National Association of Intercollegiate Athletics (NAIA). An exceptional recruiter, Wright transformed Texas Southern's lackluster track program into a national powerhouse. Dubbed the "Flying Tigers," his squads captured multiple Southwestern Athletic Conference championships and won the NAIA national title in 1961 and 1962. Also in 1962 Texas Southern became the first historically black university to compete in the Texas Relays. Wright's team routed the competition, finishing first in five events and setting five meet records for the college category. No other team had ever triumphed as much in one year at the Texas Relays. For their efforts, the Flying Tigers were selected the most outstanding squad. Wright's 1963 and 1967 Texas Southern teams earned the same honor. Wright also received numerous accolades. *Track and Field News* named him national coach of the year for 1961, as did the NAIA for 1966. In 1967 Wright, unable to get along with a newly hired athletic director, left Texas Southern to become the coach at Western Illinois University, a predominantly white university in rural Illinois. That same year he helped coach the successful American team at the Pan-Am Games in Canada. In 1969 he took over the head coaching position at Sacramento State University in California, remaining its coach until 1975, when he assumed the position of athletic director. In 1979 he was hired as the athletic director at Fairleigh Dickinson University in New Jersey. Six years later he retired from Fairleigh Dickinson.

During his lifetime, Wright carved a path for African Americans in track and field. The impressive achievements of his Texas Southern teams helped persuade track coaches at predominantly white universities in the South to recruit African American athletes, thereby helping to break the accepted practice below the Mason-Dixon Line that kept black athletes off white intercollegiate sports rosters. Wright also shared his talents with foreign teams. Through a State Department program, he served as coach of the Singapore squad at the 1962 Asian Games and, in 1964, of the Malaysian Olympic team. The American track and field establishment noticed Wright's abilities too. He was picked in 1966 to coach an American team for a meet against Poland and for another against the Soviet Union—the first time an African American had been chosen to oversee a U.S. track squad. However, the meets never took place. Polish and Soviet officials pulled their squads in response to the increased military operations of the United States in Vietnam. Nevertheless, an alternate competition featuring Wright's American team versus a collection of British Commonwealth track standouts was held at the Los Angeles Coliseum. Wright's team performed superbly. The 4 x 400-meter relay squad, which included Lee Evans and Tommie Smith, posted a new world mark of 2:59.6

seconds. Wright was an assistant coach on the 1968 U.S. Olympic track team, arguably the best track squad in Olympic history. The Olympians under his direction not only garnered six gold medals but also established five world records. Jim Hines, one of Wright's sprinters at Texas Southern, set a new world record for the 100-meters in a speedy 9.95 seconds. In 1969 Wright became the first African American to head the track and field committee of the Amateur Athletic Union (AAU)—a post he held until 1973. Because of Wright's experience and credentials, many expected him to be named head coach of the 1972 U.S. Olympic track team in Munich. But he finished a close second in the voting and ended up serving again as an Olympic assistant.

For much of his career, Wright battled the injustices of racism. In 1961, for example, he pulled his Texas Southern squad out of a meet in Houston when he learned that spectators would be seated in segregated areas of the stadium. Yet some African Americans—particularly those associated with the Olympic Project for Human Rights (OPHR), an organization founded by the black sports activist HARRY EDWARDS that pushed for an African American boycott of the 1968 Mexico City Olympics—called Wright a racial accommodationist. In large part the label stemmed from his perceived obedience to the white-controlled track establishment and from his open opposition to the suggested Olympic boycott. Yet Wright sympathized with two of the OPHR's more outspoken proponents. When the U.S. Olympic Committee (USOC) ejected two sprinters, TOMMIE SMITH and John Carlos, for staging a Black Power protest on the medal dais at the Mexico City Olympic Games, Wright disagreed with the move. He believed that the USOC and the International Olympic Committee (IOC), which had pressured the American committee into barring the two sprinters, had acted unjustly and had neglected Smith and Carlos's rights as Olympic participants. On another occasion Wright could have been named the first African American to coach a U.S. Olympic track team had it not been for an error he committed as an assistant during the 1972 Olympic Games in Munich. Eddie Hart and Rey Robinson, two of America's fastest sprinters, never appeared for their qualifying heats because Wright, who had been following an old schedule, had given them the incorrect times for the start of their races. Wright never evaded culpability for the mistake, even though some American and Olympic track officials, who knew of the revised schedule, had not informed him of the changes. At the Montreal Olympic Games four years later, the legendary Leroy Walker became the first African American to coach a U.S. Olympic track squad.

In his later years, Wright stayed active on the national track scene, heading the Budget and Finance Committee of the Athletic Congress, then becoming its treasurer. He also acted as an adviser for USA Track and Field (USATF). A member of the NAIA, Texas Southern University, USATF, and U.S. Track Coaches Association Halls of Fame, Wright helped dismantle racial barriers in track and field and create opportunities for African Americans in the sport. He succumbed to renal failure in Houston in 1998.

FURTHER READING

Dorr, Dave, "Classic Blunder and Shower of Gold Medals for US," *Sporting News* (16 Sept. 1972).

Hendershott, John, "Mexico City Boycott Reverb: How Black Coach Stan Wright Reacted," *Track & Field News* (1 March 1972).

Maule, Tex, "Record-Breaking Day in Austin," *Sports Illustrated* (16 Apr. 1962).

Who's Who among African Americans, 19th ed. (2006).

Wright, George. *Stan Wright: Track Coach; Forty Years in the "Good Old Boy Network"* (2005).

Obituaries: *New York Times*, 8 Nov. 1998; *Sacramento Bee*, 8 Nov. 1998; *Sacramento Observer*, 18 Nov. 1998.

CHRIS ELZEY

Wright, Theodore Sedgwick (1797–25 Mar. 1847), black Presbyterian minister and reformer, was born in New Jersey and brought up in Schenectady, New York, the son of R. P. G. Wright, an early opponent of the American Colonization Society's program of returning American blacks to Africa. His mother's name is unknown. He was named after a distinguished Massachusetts jurist, Theodore Sedgwick, whose defense of a slave woman against her master's claim of ownership had effectively abolished slavery in that state.

Wright received a good education in spite of rejection by a number of colleges to which he applied. After several years at New York's African Free School, he was admitted into Princeton Theological Seminary in New Jersey in 1825 at the age of twenty-eight. Well treated there by both fellow students and faculty, he graduated in 1828, thus becoming the first African American to complete a theological seminary program. That same year

Wright was chosen to be pastor of New York City's First Colored Presbyterian Church, which had been founded some years earlier by the journalist SAMUEL CORNISH. Wright devoted the remaining two decades of his life to building this church into a large (more than four hundred members) and socially concerned black congregation.

Angered by racism and discrimination, Wright became a social activist on many fronts. He and Cornish were charter members of the largely white American Anti-Slavery Society (AASS), founded in 1833. They served for several years with white radicals Arthur and Lewis Tappan on the society's executive committee. Both of them withdrew from the Presbytery of New York because of its opposition to censuring southern Presbyterian slave owners and joined the abolition-inclined Third Presbytery. When the New York Vigilance Committee was founded in 1835 to combat the kidnapping of free blacks off the streets of Manhattan for slavery, and to help fugitive slaves, Wright became its first chairman. In 1839, when the American Anti-Slavery Society's founder and chief staff member William Lloyd Garrison denounced political activity as a means of reform, Wright withdrew from the AASS. He had become a strong supporter of the most extensive African American political effort to date: the New York State campaign to recover full voting rights for black males by securing signatures on petitions to the state legislature and by lobbying individual legislators.

Wright's blend of spiritual fervor, clarity of thought, anger over racial discrimination, and political activism helped to influence young black pastors such as CHARLES RAY, HENRY HIGHLAND GARNET, and AMOS BEMAN, who later became leaders of the drives for reenfranchisement in New York State and Connecticut. Wright's speeches to gatherings of mostly white abolitionists, denouncing slavery, the American Colonization Society, and prejudice against free blacks, commanded their rapt attention.

Bitter personal experience lay behind Wright's denunciation of prejudice. During an alumni gathering at Princeton, he had been publicly humiliated by being called "nigger" and kicked several times by a Princeton alumnus. Several years later, in excoriating discriminatory treatment of black passengers on shipboard, Wright cited three cases of black people whose deaths had resulted from the exposure forced on them when, refused cabins, they had had to stay on deck through a cold and stormy night. One of those casualties had been his young wife, whom he probably married in 1828 and who had died in 1829, a few months after such exposure on a boat from Brunswick, New Jersey, to New York City and again on her passage up the Hudson to Schenectady. Wright had suffered in less dramatic ways too, by being made to feel like a pariah at presbytery meetings when white clergy entered the pew where he was sitting at prayer, saw that he was black, and hastily withdrew to another pew.

For Wright the exclusion of blacks from equal education was, next to slavery, American society's greatest crime against his race. "They keep us down," he agonized in 1836, "drive us out of their schools, mob and break down our schools and then point at us in scorn as an inferior race of men. 'Can't learn anything.' Why don't they let us try?" Wright was a central figure in the founding of the Phoenix Society, a many-faceted educational enterprise for blacks in New York City. Begun in 1833, the society aimed to provide basic schooling for children and assistance to young men toward apprenticeships and long-term employment as "mechanics." That same year Wright, Cornish, and the black Episcopal priest PETER WILLIAMS JR. opened a private high school for black men; they established one for women three years later. But by 1838 both schools had to close for lack of funds.

In May 1837 Wright married Adeline T. Turpin of New Rochelle, New York. Wright died in New York City. His death at age fifty was said to have been hastened by overwork and by undue exposure to the elements in covering a huge parish on foot—blacks risked humiliation and physical injury if they tried to board the "horse cars." Thousands attended his funeral or joined in an extended funeral march through the streets of lower Manhattan. William Lloyd Garrison, setting aside earlier bitter disagreement with Wright over political action, published a lengthy and generally laudatory obituary in his weekly, the *Liberator*.

FURTHER READING

Gross, Bella. "Life and Times of Theodore S. Wright, 1797–1847," *Negro History Bulletin* 3 (1939–1940).

Swift, David E. *Black Prophets of Justice: Activist Clergy before the Civil War* (1989).

Woodson, Carter, ed. *Negro Orators and Orations* (1925).

This entry is taken from the *American National Biography* and is published here with the permission of the American Council of Learned Societies.

DAVID E. SWIFT

Wright, Wild Bill (6 June 1914–1997), Negro League baseball player, was born Burnis Wright in Milan, Tennessee, a town in the western part of the state between Memphis and Clarksville. The names and occupations of his parents are unknown. He began pitching at age five, and though he had a passion for pitching, his lack of control led to the nickname "Wild Bill." He started playing with the Milan Buffaloes, a local all-black team, in 1931.

In 1932 Wright had a tryout with the Nashville Elite Giants, a team in the Negro Southern League, but he hurt his arm and was converted to an outfielder. A right-handed thrower with a strong if not always accurate arm, he played all outfield positions. Wright stood six feet four inches, weighed 220 pounds, and was one of the fastest players in the Negro Leagues, using his speed to cover considerable ground on defense. He was reportedly able to circle the bases in 13.2 seconds. A switch-hitter with power who generally batted cleanup, Wright was a better hitter from the left side of the plate and had notable success with the drag bunt.

Growing up in the South, Wright experienced the limited opportunities and daily indignities forced upon African Americans living in a racially segregated society. American baseball mirrored the rapid expansion of legal and de facto segregation that occurred in America more generally in the 1880s and 1890s. The color line in baseball was drawn in 1884 when MOSES FLEETWOOD WALKER became the last African American to don a major league uniform until JACKIE ROBINSON joined the Brooklyn Dodgers in 1947.

Racial segregation made it more difficult for black players to earn a livelihood than their white counterparts. Most games were played on the road and were scheduled on short notice against local semiprofessional black or white teams. It was not unusual for players to play two games in a day against different teams and in different locations. The baseball fields were rudimentary and usually without locker rooms. Since black ballplayers were not allowed to stay in white-owned hotels, they typically found a black-owned boardinghouse, stayed with a black family, or slept outside. Meals were often taken out through the back doors of restaurants because blacks were not allowed to sit in white eateries. It was not unusual for teams to fold during the season. Profits were slim to none, so payrolls were kept to a minimum with small rosters, which meant that injured men often played and pitchers were expected to field a position when not on the mound. Low salaries necessitated black ballplayers either to play in winter leagues in Latin America or California or to hold off-season jobs.

The final indignity heaped upon black baseball players was scant record of their games, which denied them recognition by their contemporaries and succeeding generations. Press coverage was limited because of both the racism of white-owned newspapers and the games' haphazard schedule. Baseball is celebrated mainly through statistics, and the dearth of newspaper coverage meant that many games, even when they were mentioned in the press, did not include box scores. The careers of black ball-players during the era of segregation lack the historical record of their white counterparts, so trying to analyze a specific player's career is difficult.

From 1932 through 1939 Wright played for the Elite Giants, a franchise that relocated from Nashville to Columbus to Washington, D.C., and finally to Baltimore. In 1939 he won the Negro National League batting title with a .402 average, and the Elite Giants won the championship series against the perennial powerhouse, the Homestead Grays. A higher salary lured Wright to the Santa Rosa team in the Mexican League in 1940, where he batted .360—fifth best in the league—and tied for the league lead in doubles. In 1941 he played for Mexico City, stole twenty-nine bases, and led the league with a .390 batting average, finishing ahead of JOSH GIBSON and RAY DANDRIDGE, both of whom were later inducted into the National Baseball Hall of Fame.

Wright's military draft status brought him back to play for the Baltimore Elite Giants in 1942, but he enjoyed a career season upon his return to Mexico City in 1943, winning the triple crown. He hit .366 to surpass Dandridge for the batting title, and he tied Dandridge with seventy runs batted in. He also hit seventeen home runs, one more than future Hall of Famer ROY CAMPANELLA. Wright's twenty-one stolen bases fell one short of the league lead. In 1945, his last year in the Negro Leagues, Wright hit .382. His average batting average, in eleven seasons in the Negro Leagues, was .336.

Wright returned to the Mexican League in 1946, preferring the relative lack of racial discrimination south of the border. The Mexican League season also required considerably less travel than the Negro Leagues, and travel in Mexico was in the relative comfort of trains rather than in the buses used by Negro League teams. Lazaro Salazar convinced Wright to join the Nuevo Laredo team in 1951. Wright batted .365 and helped his team win the championship.

Wright retired after that season, with a .335 batting average during his ten seasons in the Mexican League. He coached for three additional seasons and then opened Bill Wright's Dugout, a popular restaurant in Aguascalientes, Mexico. In 1958 Wright returned to the United States to appear as a surprise guest on the weekly television show *This Is Your Life*. The show's featured celebrity was Campanella, who had recently been paralyzed in an automobile accident. Prior to his Hall of Fame career with the Brooklyn Dodgers, Campanella had roomed with Wright. This was Wright's last visit to America until he attended a sports card show in Chicago as a member of the Negro League Baseball Players Association. Wright died in Mexico.

In the United States Wright did not achieve the official recognition of peers like Josh Gibson and Ray Dandridge, who—although they never played in the white major leagues—were admitted to the National Baseball Hall of Fame. Unlike Campanella, Wright was too old to play in the racially integrated major leagues. The baseball historian and statistician Bill James has ranked Wild Bill Wright as the fourth best right fielder ever to play in the Negro Leagues. During his lifetime Wright received the recognition and respect of baseball fans and fellow players in the Negro and Mexican leagues. He was inducted into the Mexican Baseball Hall of Fame in 1972.

FURTHER READING

Cisneros, Pedro Treto. *The Mexican League: Comprehensive Player Statistics, 1937–2001* (2002).

Holway, John B. *Black Diamonds: Life in the Negro Leagues from the Men Who Lived It* (1989).

James, Bill. *The New Bill James Historical Baseball Abstract* (2001).

McNeil, William F. *Baseball's Other All-Stars: The Greatest Players from the Negro Leagues, the Japanese Leagues, the Mexican League, and the Pre-1960 Winter Leagues in Cuba, Puerto Rico, and the Dominican Republic* (2000).

Rogosin, Donn. *Invisible Men: Life in Baseball's Negro Leagues* (1995).

PAUL A. FRISCH

Wrighten, John (10 July 1921–15 Oct. 1996), attorney, symbolic legal figure, pastor, was born John Howard Wrighten to Rosa Wrighten on 10 July 1921 in Edisto Island, South Carolina. While Wrighten grew up living "fairly well" with both parents along with his siblings, little is known of his father (Baker, p. 64). According to the 1930 federal manuscript census, Wrighten's father was not listed, and his mother was listed as a widow. Wrighten attended Central Elementary School between 1929 and 1934. He was encouraged to pursue secondary education past the seventh grade when public support for African American education ended. Many African Americans in the lowcountry area moved to Charleston to enroll at the all-black Burke Industrial School. Wrighten, however, managed to save money for tuition and attend Avery Normal Institute in Charleston. Organized in 1865, Avery Normal Institute was the first African American accredited school in Charleston. Initially serving the prominent African Americans in Charleston, Avery became a public institution in 1947 and would subsequently close in 1954 upon the ruling of *Brown v. Board of Education*.

Due to financial reasons, Wrighten dropped out of Avery. As he worked to support his family, he married Dorothy Lillian Richardson (they would be married for the next fifty-six years) and was able to reenroll in Avery in 1941 as a junior. However, with U.S. entry into World War II on the horizon, Wrighten was drafted into the U.S. Army. Entering the service on 22 August 1942, Wrighten trained with the Army-Air Force, training at Fort Jackson (South Carolina), Fort Benning (Georgia), and Greenville (South Carolina) Army-Air Force Base. He served with the 92nd Aviation Squadron out of Tampa, Florida. He received an honorable medical discharge in 1943. After his discharge, Wrighten returned to Avery and graduated in the spring of 1943. Taking advantage of the GI Bill, Wrighten enrolled at South Carolina State College (State College), the state's land grant college for African Americans, in 1943. He majored in sociology and was considered "a superb student" (Baker, p. 75). Wrighten was heavily influenced by his professors to openly critique and challenge the racial status quo in South Carolina. He became an active member of the NAACP youth chapter of Orangeburg and wrote editorials that challenged racial segregation in the student newspaper, *The Collegian*. This experience influenced Wrighten to pursue law.

In the summer of 1946 (the summer before his senior year), Wrighten, along with Daniel George Sampson, applied to the all-white University of South Carolina Law School. Both were denied admission solely on race. By 1946 South Carolina had one law school that only admitted white applicants. African Americans who sought graduate/professional school education were funded through a special scholarship, a railway ticket and tuition scholarship, by the State of South Carolina to pursue graduate/professional education outside of the state. This was popular a trend in other southern states. However, no funds in the state of South Carolina were earmarked for legal education. In 1947 with the support of the South Carolina NAACP state president James Hinton and the legal advice of Thurgood Marshall, Wrighten filed a lawsuit which was heard by Judge John J. Waites Waring of the U.S. District Court of South Carolina. In July 1947 Judge Waring ruled in favor of the plaintiff. Waring stipulated that the University of South Carolina had to desegregate its law school or the state of South Carolina had to create a separate but equal law school for African Americans. If there was no action, Waring further ruled that the state of South Carolina could not provide any legal education (for either whites or African Americans). The state of South Carolina chose to maintain segregation and opened a law school on the campus of South Carolina State College. Thurgood Marshall advised Wrighten not to attend the newly created law school because there were previous court decisions—*Missouri ex rel. Gaines v. Canada* (1938)—that had set a legal precedence to desegregate the University of South Carolina School of Law. Wrighten, who was teaching back at his alma mater Avery Institute, chose to attend the law school at State College because he was financially strapped and eager to pursue a law degree.

Two weeks following the ruling, State College hired BENNER C. TURNER, a 1930 Harvard Law School graduate and current law professor at the all-black North Carolina Central College of Law in Durham, to serve as the dean of the law school. Turner would serve as the dean of the law school for the next three years before being elected as the fourth president of State College in 1950. State College hired several African American attorneys to serve as law professors and created a permanent home on the campus, Moss Hall, which "contained six classrooms, two seminar rooms, two reading rooms a moot courtroom, a library, stacks for 50,000 volumes and office space for faculty and the dean" (Burke and Hine, p. 35). Although the law school shut its doors at the close of the 1965–66 academic year, when the University of South Carolina desegregated its law school, the law school served as a catalyst for personal and social change. It enabled many of its graduates, who otherwise would have not had the opportunity to do so, to pursue law. Many of those graduates were instrumental in helping to dismantle segregation in

South Carolina. Along with Wrighten, who graduated in 1950, the most notable graduates include Ernest A. Finey (class of 1954), who would later serve as the first African American Chief Justice of the South Carolina Supreme Court, and Matthew Perry (class of 1951), who would serve as the first African American federal court judge in the state of South Carolina.

When Wrighten graduated in June of 1952, he faced another legal roadblock. In the wake of the *Waring* ruling in 1947, the South Carolina state legislature, in fear of an influx of African American lawyers, repealed the traditional "double ceremony" in which new law school graduates received their diplomas and were sworn in as members of the court simultaneously. The state legislature passed a bill that introduced a policy that required new law school graduates in South Carolina to successfully pass the bar exam in order to practice law in the state of South Carolina. The state legislator who proposed this bill stated its purpose was to "bar Negroes and undesirable whites" (Baker, p. 84). In fact, between 1953 and 1973, 15 percent of African American law candidates passed the bar exam, in comparison to 90 percent of their white counterparts. Wrighten ultimately passed the bar exam in November of 1953, but it was a long and frustrating process, requiring four attempts.

Wrighten returned to Charleston and began practicing law in early 1954. Like many African American attorneys during the era of segregation and the civil rights movement, he served in capacities that addressed African American educational equality and access. Wrighten served as the legal advisor to the Charleston branch of the NAACP. He personally drafted the petition, submitted to the local school board, to desegregate the Charleston school district, as well as filed a lawsuit to end segregation at the local beaches. Moreover, Wrighten along with other attorneys was influential in helping two thousand African American Charlestonians register to vote in 1957. It also must be noted that Wrighten represented many protesters, often students who participated in sit-ins in the effort to desegregate lunch counters as well as other public facilities.

In 1976 Wrighten's law career came to an abrupt halt. Accused of "failure to account for and misappropriating funds belong to clients," Wrighten was disbarred (*Wrighten v. United States of America*, 1977). Despite appeals, the ruling was upheld. Upon being disbarred, Wrighten moved to Connecticut on the invitation of one of his children and would live there, serving as a church pastor, until his death in 1996.

In spite of his legal career downfall, Wrighten's legacy as being part of the first wave of African Americans who openly challenged racial segregation at the graduate- and professional-school level should be acknowledged. In comparison to Lloyd Gaines, HEMAN SWEATT, and ADA SIPUEL, Wrighten's legal challenge to desegregate the University of South Carolina is obscure. And yet, as noted by Wrighten's law school classmate and later law partner Russell Brown, "When it comes to Black attorneys, he was considered to be the granddaddy of us all ("John H. Wrighten, Civil Rights Leader and Legal Figure, Succumbs." *Jet Magazine* 28 Oct. 1996).

FURTHER READING

Baker, R. S. *Paradoxes of Desegregation: African American Struggles for Educational Equity in Charleston, South Carolina, 1926–1972* (2006).

Burke, William L., and Hine, William C. "The South Carolina State College Law School: Its Roots, Creation, and Legacy." In *Matthew J. Perry: The Man, His Times, and His Legacy*, edited by W. Lewis Burke and Belinda F. Gergel, 17–61 (2004).

John H. Wrighten, William C. Hine Oral History Interview, 6 June 1989.

John Howard Wrighten v. United States of America, 550 F.2d 90 (U.S. Court of Appeals, Fourth Circuit, 1977).

Obituary: "John H. Wrighten, Civil Rights Leader and Legal Figure, Succumbs." *Jet Magazine*, 28 Oct. 1996.

TRAVIS D. BOYCE AND
WINSOME CHUNNU

Wyatt, Addie (8 March 1924–28 March 2012), labor organizer, civil rights and feminist activist, and minister, was born Addie Cameron in Brookhaven, Mississippi, to Maggie Cameron and Ambrose Cameron. She was the second of their eight children. In 1930, at the age of six, Wyatt moved with her family to Chicago, Illinois. She would go on to graduate from DuSable High School with honors, and while a student at DuSable she met Claude Wyatt, whom she married shortly after her graduation. Within five years of their marriage the couple became parents of not only their own two children but Wyatt's six younger siblings as well. They were compelled to shoulder this responsibility after the unexpected death of Wyatt's mother.

With eight children to look after, Wyatt had to work full-time outside of the home in order to help

Addie Wyatt holding a framed photo of her friend, the Rev. Martin Luther King Jr., at her Chicago home on Thursday, 13 January 2005. (AP Images.)

support her family. Her first job was at Armour & Company, packing meat into cans. She was not at the meatpacking plant long before she filed her first grievance. Black women at the company were routinely assigned the dirtiest and least desirable positions. Often they were forced to work on the "stew line," cleaning waste or worms from the intestines of animals and packing the finished product into cans. Wyatt was no exception to this general rule and she worked for months on the stew line.

Eventually, Wyatt was assigned a less arduous task that she liked far more, placing tops on the cans. Her time in this position, however, did not last long as she was quickly forced to return to the stew line when a white woman was hired. Angered by her demotion, Wyatt appealed to the union stewardess, a black woman, for help. Wyatt admitted that she was unsure whether two black women would have any influence on the company officials. Despite their reservations, both women walked into the foreman's office and demanded that Wyatt be allowed to return to her previous job assignment. To Wyatt's surprise, the voices of two

black women union members were heard, and she returned to her preferred assignment. From that moment forward, she appreciated the importance of having the support of a union, rather than being a lone voice trying to force change.

Ultimately, Wyatt was laid off from the Armour & Co. in the midst of company downsizing. In 1947 she was hired at the Illinois Meat (Packing) Company in Chicago where she worked for seven years, peeling potatoes and slicing bacon. Wyatt was inspired to become more active in the union after attending a local union meeting where she witnessed a racially diverse group of workers discussing the "problems of decent wages and working conditions," alongside "the struggles of black people, Hispanic people, and women" (*Labor's Heritage*, 27). She described this meeting as helping to cement her belief that collective organizing offered an effective way for all workers to challenge the problems faced by oppressed people both inside and outside the workplace.

Despite seeing a diverse union membership and winning her first grievance because of union support, Wyatt never considered becoming a union leader until she attended the United Packing House

Workers of America (UPWA) "Anti-Discrimination and Women's Conference." At this conference, she observed women in prominent leadership positions. Emboldened by this experience, Wyatt returned to her local union with other women from the conference and searched for a woman to run for the local union vice presidency. When no one volunteered, Wyatt's coworkers convinced her that there was no need to look any further; she was the perfect candidate. Wyatt was elected as vice president and after only a few months she succeeded to the presidency of Local 56 of the United Packing House Workers of America. This appointment made Wyatt the first woman and first African American to be elected into this leadership position at the majority white male union.

Over the next thirty years Wyatt held various leadership positions within the union. For example, in 1954 Wyatt was an international representative of the UPWA, and after the merger in 1968 of the UPWA with the Amalgamated Meat Cutter and Butcher Workmen of North America she became an international vice president and the director of the Civil Rights and Women's Affairs Department. Wyatt held this position until her retirement in 1984.

Wyatt worked throughout her career to connect union politics to both civil rights and feminist organizing. A key figure in the civil rights struggle in Chicago, Wyatt in 1956 became the labor liaison to Reverend MARTIN LUTHER KING JR. and was a founder of Operation Breadbasket, a program that provided spiritual guidance and practical assistance to communities in need. Additionally, she was a founder and board member of Rainbow PUSH Coalition, the organization that grew out of Operation Breadbasket, under the direction of Reverend JESSE JACKSON. During the 1980s this multicultural international initiative worked for social justice, challenging human rights abuses in the United States and abroad. As a union leader, Wyatt worked steadily to challenge the discrimination women experienced. She was particularly interested in such issues as job security, equal pay for comparable work, and improving pregnancy leave. She recalled in an interview that "we were winning equal rights for women before the women's movement of the 1960s and 1970s really took off" (personal interview with subject, 1 June 2005). In 1963 John F. Kennedy and Eleanor Roosevelt appointed her to the President's Commission on the Status of Women, where she worked on the Protective Legislation committee and helped prepare *The Presidential Report on American Women*, published in 1963. Wyatt later became one of the founding members of national women's organizations such as the National Organization for Women (NOW) in 1966 and the Coalition of Labor Union Women (CLUW) in 1974. Both groups benefited greatly from Wyatt's extensive knowledge and her experience with working on issues and with groups that stressed challenging multiple forms of oppression.

An ordained minister since 1960, Wyatt described the black church as offering a site where she could work with both men and women to push for political and social change. Beginning in the late 1960s she and her husband helped build and copastor the Vernon Park Church of God and the Wyatt Community and Family Life Center in Chicago, Illinois. A significant aspect of their work involved community organizing in low-income communities in the Chicago area.

Like her contemporaries FLO KENNEDY, SHIRLEY CHISHOLM, and PAULI MURRAY, Addie Wyatt's political work demonstrated that twentieth-century black feminists rarely worked within one social movement or organization. Like other black feminists she could best be described as a radical humanist with a commitment to not only liberating black women, but liberating humanity and reconstructing social relations more broadly.

In March 2012, Addie Wyatt died in Chicago. She was 88.

FURTHER READING

Cobble, Dorothy Sue. *The Other Women's Movement: Workplace Justice and Social Rights in Modern America* (2004).

Wyatt, Addie, Rick Halperin, and Roger Horowitz. "'An Injury to One is an Injury to All' Addie Wyatt Remembers the Packinghouse Workers Union." *Labor's Heritage* 12:1 (2003).

Obituary: *Chicago Tribune*, 1 April 2012.

SHERIE RANDOLPH

Wynn, Albert R. (10 Sept. 1951–), United States congressman, was born Albert R. Wynn in Philadelphia, Pennsylvania, the son of Albert Wynn, a farmer, and Rose Russell Wynn, a schoolteacher. After his father secured a position with the U.S. Department of Agriculture, he and his family moved to the greater Washington, D.C., area, where he attended public schools. Wynn then attended the University of Pittsburgh, where he studied political science. He graduated with a B.S. degree in 1973. In his early twenties, Wynn had already displayed a keen interest in politics. Following his time in Pittsburgh,

Wynn attended Howard University and studied public administration. He did not graduate; however, he subsequently enrolled in law school at the Georgetown University Law Center. Wynn received his J.D. degree in 1977 and pursued a career in government and law. Wynn has been married twice; his first marriage to Jessie Wynn ended in a divorce. He later married the art teacher Gaines Clores. He has two daughters, Meredith and Gabrielle.

Following his interest in public life after law school, Wynn served as director of the consumer protection commission in Prince George's County. By 1982 Wynn had opened his own law firm. Wynn, in 1982, also ran successfully for a seat in the Maryland House of Delegates. He served two terms, from 1983 to 1987. In 1986, ambitious and seeking bigger challenges, Wynn ran for the Maryland state senate. Continuing his string of successful campaigns, he won and served until 1993. Albert Wynn was an up-and-comer in Prince George's County political circles. It was a fortuitous place for a young, African American politico to be. Like many states following the 1990 congressional redistricting, Maryland created a minority-majority district that bordered the District of Columbia. Since the early 1970s Prince George's County had been notable for its increasingly up-scale, highly educated African American community. Further, since most residents of the county worked in Washington, many had relocated to the district to escape the grind of living in an increasingly dangerous city, as did other, more recent African American transplants of the county. Determined to take on a larger political role, Wynn jumped into the race for the 4th Congressional District, defeated a crowded field with 28 percent of the vote, and easily won the general election. On 3 January 1993, Albert Wynn was sworn in as a United States representative.

Reflecting the district that he was serving, Wynn served on the Financial Services committees, Foreign Affairs, and Post Office and Civil Service committees. Wynn proved to be a reliably moderate or left-of-center Democrat, attentive to the values of the middle- and upper-middle-class residents of the 4th Congressional District. This was demonstrated by his service on the Commerce committee, firm support for federal workers (many of whom lived in the district), and strong efforts to win government contracts for infrastructure projects in his home district. In Congress, Wynn also was a prominent member of the Congressional Black Caucus. As a result of his hard work, Congressman Wynn has been twice a recipient of the Small Business

Administration Administrator's Leadership Award. However, his tenure in Congress has not been without controversy.

In his reelection campaign in 2000, Wynn's former wife, Jessie, worked for his Republican opponent. She claimed that he had wronged her, and, by extension, all black women, by leaving her for a white woman. Still, most voters were unmoved by these claims, and Wynn won reelection in the heavily Democratic district with 87 percent of the vote. By 2006, however, Wynn ran into more serious electoral difficulty as he faced the most serious political challenge of his career from the Maryland community activist DONNA EDWARDS. Wynn's moderate positions, including support for the Iraq War, the Bankruptcy Reform Act of 2005 (all of which Edwards opposed), and other policies considered closely aligned with the Republican George W. Bush administration, Wynn became increasingly vulnerable. Even the *Washington Post* endorsed the more liberal Edwards over Wynn. He barely won the Democratic nomination by three percentage points before winning the general election with more than 80 percent of the vote. Further complicating Wynn's political situation was the congressional redistricting after the 2000 elections. Effectively, the Maryland legislature shaved off several precincts that were heavily Democratic from Wynn's district, thereby adding to the political diversity of the 4th Congressional District.

In 2008 Donna Edwards returned for a second run at the Wynn seat. This time Edwards defeated Wynn with 60 percent of the vote. Congressman Wynn left Congress on 31 May 2008. He subsequently worked as a lawyer for the tobacco industry, energy companies, and the Teamsters union.

FURTHER READING

"Divorce Scandal Erupts in Maryland Rep. Albert Wynn's Reelection Campaign." *Jet*, 18 Sept. 2000.

Helderman, Rosalind S. "Edwards Overpowers Wynn; 8-Term Congressman Concedes after Heated Race; Gilchrest in Tough Fight." *Washington Post*, 13 Feb. 2008.

U.S. Congress, House, Committee on House Administration of the U.S. House of Representatives. *Black Americans in Congress, 1870–2007* (2008).

DARYL A. CARTER

Wysinger, Edmond (1816–1891), slave, California pioneer, and miner, was born on a South Carolina plantation to a Cherokee Indian father and a slave mother whose names are not now known. In 1849, when he was thirty-two years old, he accompanied his master to the California gold mines, where he was permitted to work in the mines to buy his freedom. After obtaining his freedom, Wysinger settled in Grass Valley, California. In 1853 he married Pernesa Wilson and moved to Visalia, California, in the San Joaquin Valley. They had six boys and two girls, and Wysinger was determined that his children would have access to an education. He became a leading advocate for school desegregation in California.

Visalia had no school for African American children, although an 1869 state law required any town with ten or more black children to provide a school for them or to allow them to attend a school for whites, if the parents of the white children did not object. As a rule, white parents opposed the presence of African American children in white schools, thus most black children went without an education. Wysinger refused to accept the laws that effectively prevented his children from receiving an education and appeared before the Tulare County school board to request that it establish a school for his children. After a struggle Wysinger triumphed, and the county opened a school for black students.

During the Civil War Visalia stood with "El Monte" as a stronghold of the Confederacy in the West. The open display of support for the Confederacy in Visalia can be explained by the fact that many of its inhabitants came from the South. By the end of the Civil War, Visalia had segregated schools, and this was supported by California law, specifically California Political Code sections 1669, 1670, and 1671. Section 1669 read, "The Education of children of African descent and Indian children must be provided for in separate schools." Arthur Wysinger, Edmond Wysinger's son, had attended the school for African American children in the outskirts of Visalia. When it came time to attend secondary school on 1 October 1888, Edmond Wysinger placed his son in the only secondary school in Visalia, located on Locust Street. According to the principal S. A. Crookshank's own testimony, he stopped the Wysingers, informed them that because Arthur was black he could not enroll in his school, and immediately sent them to the school for black children.

On 4 October 1888 Wysinger hired two lawyers, Oregon Sanders and W. A. Gray, to file a lawsuit against Crookshank in the Superior Court of Tulare County, California. When the case was argued before the superior court, the defense anticipated the arguments of *Plessy v. Ferguson* (1896), advancing the concept of separate but equal, which supported the idea that as long as facilities for African Americans were equal, segregation was an acceptable practice. Crookshank endeavored to demonstrate that the facilities for African Americans were equal to those for whites in the physical aspects as well as in the quality of the teachers. He also emphasized that he was obeying the decision made by Visalia's school board to keep the children separated. Wysinger stated that his son had finished elementary school and was ready to proceed with further education, and his lawyers asserted that the law had been amended and now called for all children to be admitted without regard to race. In spite of this the superior court denied Arthur Wysinger the right to attend the "for whites only high school," arguing that the Visalia school board's decision was better for both races.

The Superior Court of Tulare County's decision did not discourage Wysinger. He and his lawyers filed for a retrial since California did not have a court of appeals until 1904. When the retrial was denied, they petitioned the Supreme Court of California. In the supreme court Crookshank reiterated his arguments about the equality of the school for whites and the school for blacks. He also stated that he did not allow Arthur Wysinger in his school because he was "colored." He stated: "I told him to take his boy to Mr. McAdams, who taught the colored school. I refused to admit his boy to the public school on Locust Street because he was colored, and because this public school was established by the board of education, who has instructed me to send the colored children to that school." The court asserted that California law regarding segregation for reasons of race had been amended on 7 April 1880. Sections 1669, 1670, and 1671 of the Political Code were repealed. The amended law read, "Every school, unless otherwise provided by law, must be open for the admission of *all* children" (emphasis added). The supreme court stated that a school board's decisions or rules do not supersede the law. Quoting the law as it stood in 1890, Judge C. Foote stated, "The board of education has the power to make, establish, and enforce all necessary and proper rules and regulations *not contrary to law*." Since the law had been amended, the court ruled that the school board of Visalia had no right to deny Arthur Wysinger admission to the secondary school of Visalia and ordered him admitted.

At the age of seventy-two Wysinger bravely challenged the pro-Confederate town of Visalia and the racial custom and prejudice of the law. His refusal to accept Visalia's school board decision allowed his son to continue his schooling and graduate from secondary school. The Supreme Court of California's decision in *Wysinger v. Crookshank* opened the doors of California schools to other African Americans. Wysinger died in Visalia in 1891, a year after the court's decision.

FURTHER READING

Beasley, Delilah. *Negro Trail Blazers of California* (1919).

Lapp, Rudolph M. *Afro-Americans in California*, 2d ed. (1987).

Wysinger, Myra, ed. "An African American Trail Blazer of California, Edmond Edward Wysinger, 1816–1891," *California Black History*, accessible online at http://www.homestead.com/wysinger/courtcase.html.

ALICIA J. RIVERA

X, Louis. *See* Farrakhan, Louis Abdul.

X, Malcolm. *See* Malcolm X.

Xuma, Madie Hall (1894–10 Sept. 1982), educator, organizer, and activist, was born Madie Beatrice Hall in Winston-Salem, North Carolina, the first girl among the four children of H. H. Hall, the first black doctor in the city and founder of the first black city hospital, and Ginny (Cowen) Hall, a real estate entrepreneur in Salisbury and Asheville, North Carolina. Ginny Hall had a profound influence on Madie's view of the power women could hold in society.

Madie Hall attended Shaw University and earned a B.S. degree from Teachers' College in Winston-Salem and an M.A. from Columbia University Teachers College in 1937. Her work in education and social welfare elevated her to a position of prominence in Winston-Salem, where both her father and her brother worked as physicians. Despite her privileged life, she worked to improve the lives of the poor in the United States.

Hall met Alfred Bitini Xuma, a widower, when he visited the United States during a speaking tour in 1937–1938. Xuma, a medical doctor born and educated in South Africa, was eager for professional and political advancement and had arrived in New York in 1913 to earn a medical degree. He opened a surgical practice in Sophiatown, South Africa, in 1931, married Priscilla Mason, and lost his wife in childbirth three years later. Hall and Xuma met at Columbia University when Hall was taking master's classes and Xuma was taking advanced classes

in medicine. Hall went to Atlanta University to study social work but agreed to marry Xuma after several years of correspondence. They married in 1940; Madie went to live in South Africa with her husband and his two children from his previous marriage.

Alfred Xuma served as president of the African National Congress (ANC) from 1940 through 1949. The ANC, established in 1912, underwent alternating periods of strength and waning popularity. Xuma brokered an agreement between the conservative politicians and the young, more radical factions, and Madie Xuma played an important role in the organization by helping the politically underrepresented women and children. She viewed women as the foundation of the family, and through assisting women and families, she felt changes could be made in the country and its political structures with little violence. As an American, she expected women to take an active role and criticized men who kept their wives and daughters away from political activities. The women's movement in South Africa eventually took a more prominent part, stressing nonviolent action and protesting the use of exclusionary laws. Prior to this time, men had always taken the more active role in protesting government actions.

Madie Xuma accepted the appointment as the first president of the Women's League of the African National Congress (ANCWL) in 1943 and also served as president of the National Council of African Women in an effort to combine the two organizations into a united front. The women's movement of South Africa began to be formally organized after World War I, and Xuma, like her husband, believed that improvement of the social conditions in the country must rely on slow and gradual change. There were two camps in the women's movement at that time: one saw the "modern woman" in a negative light, and the other saw women who worked outside the home, wore fashionable dress and makeup, and joined in political movements in a positive light. Xuma played an important role in organizing South African women and a critical part in integrating the women's branch of the ANC with the men's branch of the organization. Women were granted full membership in the organization during her husband's presidency.

Madie Xuma also played a key leadership role in promoting jazz music and vaudeville acts as catalysts for political change. She encouraged the members of the ANC in their efforts to integrate a strong African voice into South African music and traveling dramatic performances. The younger members of the ANCWL advocated music and drama to promote a message of equality, and Xuma wrote, produced, and directed a show that promoted the goals of the women's branch of the ANC. Xuma's leadership of the ANCWL, which lasted until 1948, helped shape the organization's goals around the need to interest African women in the struggle for freedom and equality. She encouraged women to organize to solve their own social problems and to work to spread the mission of the ANC. Ironically, her ideals of the role of women would have aligned better with the ANCWL's goals in the 1980s and 1990s. With the election of the more militant Ida Mtwana in 1948, Xuma left the presidency.

The Zenzele Clubs were a special project for Xuma. The clubs were apolitical organizations led by mission-educated African women who brought information about child rearing, health care, and food preparation to rural African women. Xuma viewed progress in these areas as a step toward the general betterment of women in South Africa. Eventually the Zenzele Clubs became affiliated with the South African Young Women's Association, and Xuma was elected president of its national council in 1955. Xuma's efforts were instrumental in expanding the number of locations and allowing black women to enroll at YMCA facilities. By the 1950s the women's protest began to be incorporated into the general movement against apartheid. Even though she no longer held a major leadership position, Xuma continued to work for political advancement. She was a major mover, along with Maggie Resha and Kate Mxakatho, in organizing protests against laws requiring travel passes for blacks.

Her husband died in Johannesburg in 1962, and Xuma returned to Winston-Salem the next year. She was viewed as a living symbol of women's activism. Xuma made a world speaking tour in 1966 and continued to work with the YWCA organization before her death. The Xuma home in Sophiatown, a suburb of Johannesburg, became a museum in 2007 with exhibits chronicling the couple's work in South Africa. Xuma is remembered as a pioneer of the African women's movement.

FURTHER READING

Berger, Iris. "An African American 'Mother of the Nation': Madie Hall Xuma in South Africa, 1940–1963," *Journal of Southern African Studies* 27 (Sept. 2001).

Gerhart, Gail M., and Thomas G. Karis, eds. *From Protest to Challenge: A Documentary History of African Politics in South Africa: 1882–1990*, vol. 4, *Political Profiles, 1882–1964* (1977).

Schadeberg, Jurgen, comp. and ed. *The Fifties People of South Africa* (1987).

PAMELA LEE GRAY

Yancey, Mama (1 Jan. 1896–4 May 1986), blues singer, was born Estella Harris in Cairo, Illinois. Her parents' names are unknown. She moved to Chicago at six months of age and was raised there. Her interest in music developed early; as a child she frequently sang in the local church choir and as a youth learned to play guitar, perhaps from her mother who was a singing guitarist. Her mother died when Estella was thirteen, after which she was raised by her father. In 1917 (some sources cite 1919) she married Jimmy Yancey, a boy she had grown up with in Chicago. They probably had at least one child, but details are unavailable. At the time, Jimmy was a singer and dancer, but according to an interview with Mama Yancy by Bob Rusch, he became interested in blues piano in 1919, after which he began traveling around playing for house "rent" parties, at which the occupants charged guests a fee to help them pay their rent. Jimmy subsequently developed a unique blues piano style that contained certain basic principles of the boogie style and is said to have influenced a host of pianists, including MEADE LUX LEWIS and ALBERT AMMONS.

Mama Yancey's father discouraged his daughter from singing on stage, and in the beginning, she and her young husband tried settling down to a steady home life. As she later said, "I had a very strict father and my father is the one that held me back. See, he never wanted me to go on the stage no kind of way, shape, or fashion. Then after he died I was thirty-two, then I just had my own way after he died" (Rusch, 3). Jimmy worked steadily for thirty-three years as a Chicago White Sox groundskeeper.

However, in addition to rent parties he also frequently played at other local private parties and various music clubs. Mama Yancey sometimes joined her husband, performing for gatherings at their home or at parties on Chicago's South Side, but she sang primarily only for her husband. Influences on her life included Lottie Grady (a friend of her father's), MEMPHIS MINNIE, and BESSIE SMITH. Singing on stage taught Yancey that it was no place for a married woman because "when you're on the road, you're here tonight, you may be having an engagement in London, England, tomorrow. Look at the hopping around that you gotta do, and you're changing beds from night to night."

Yancey's musical development was different from other "classic" blues singers of her generation. She did not sing in theaters, cabarets, or vaudeville and tent shows. In fact she rarely broke out of the boundaries of her own home; therefore, she was not forced to maintain the large musical repertoire characteristic of other working blues singers. Instead she chose to sing a small number of songs over and over again—songs that were important primarily to her. Since she rarely sought employment as a singer, her talent became an outlet for self-expression. She actually deplored the commercialization of blues music, stating that "blues is what comes from your heart."

To Yancey, her marriage, her occasional work as a Democratic precinct captain, which began in 1945 and continued through the 1960s, and her friends and family came first. Her home became a gathering spot for students from around the Chicago area. Yancey boasted that her house was the place to be on Saturday nights, adding that it was "crowded like a dance parlor and people had to wedge in with a shoehorn."

Her first documented performance was with her husband, four songs recorded by Phil Featheringill for the Session label in December 1943. In 1945 she sang with Richard Jones at the Art Institute in Chicago, and with Jimmy Yancey and KID ORY, among others, at Carnegie Hall in New York City. In 1948 she sang with her husband at Chicago's Orchestra Hall and, from 1948 to 1950, occasionally sang with him on his weekend gigs at Chicago's Bee Hive Club. Mama and Jimmy recorded again, this time in 1951, for Atlantic Records. "When we cut that session," Mama later recalled, "all the time [Jimmy] was playing I was bathing his face in cold water with a washcloth. Jimmy was diabetic. It wasn't two weeks after that session that he went into a coma and passed away."

During the next twenty-five years Yancey returned to her more private life, interspersed with a few performances and recordings. In 1952 she recorded with Don Ewell for the Windin' Ball label, Chicago; worked Sugar Hill Club, San Francisco, 1961; recorded with LITTLE BROTHER MONTGOMERY, Riverside label, Chicago, 1961; worked Chicago's Limelight and Red Lion clubs in 1962 and the Touch of Olde Club in 1964; recorded with Art Hodes, Verve-Folkways label, Chicago, 1965; and appeared with Hodes on *Jazz Alley*, PBS-TV in 1969.

When Yancey turned eighty in 1976, she returned to performing in earnest. During the next eight years she appeared with the pianist Erwin Helfer at numerous events, including the University of Chicago folk festival. Together they released the recording *Maybe I'll Cry* in 1983. She also performed during those years with EARL HINES at Northwestern University in 1977, and sang with the German pianist Axel Zwingenberger in 1982–1983, although their recordings were not released until 1988.

Yancey's recorded repertoire includes approximately twenty-four songs, several of which she wrote the lyrics for, including "Mama Yancey's Blues," "Death Letter Blues," "Maybe I'll Cry," and "Four O'clock Blues." In live performances she is known to have sung another dozen songs that she improvised onstage. Of the twenty-four recorded songs, eight were recorded more than once, and seven constituted her central repertoire. Her favorite songs, "Make Me a Pallet on Your Floor" and "How Long Blues," were both recorded six

times and were sung at nearly every one of her performances that can be documented. She died in Chicago.

Since she mostly stayed away from the commercial jazz scene, Yancey was able to develop her own style according to her own needs and desires. Her music, therefore, contains personal insights often missing from the repertory of other blues singers. She sang with urgency in a "dry, salty voice, full of feeling, and full of the blues" (Stewart-Baxter, 3). Rudi Blesh, author of *Shining Trumpets* (1946), considers Yancey to be the greatest blues singer.

Mama Yancey sang with unusual wisdom. As she explained it, "The world is like a piano, and everybody's playing their own song."

FURTHER READING
Bowers, Jane. "The Meanings of the Blues of Estella 'Mama' Yancey," *American Music* 11 (Spring 1993).
Bruyninckx, Walter. *Sixty Years of Recorded Jazz, 1917–1977* (1980).
"Mama Yancey and the Revival Blues Tradition." *Black Music Research Journal* 12 (Fall 1992).
Mandel, Howard. "No Blues Now for Mama Yancey," *Chicago Tribune*, 20 Jan. 1977.
Rusch, Bob. "Mama Yancey: Interview," *Cadence* 4 (Fall 1978).
Stewart-Baxter, Derrick. "Mama and Jimmy Yancey," *Jazz Journal* 8 (Oct. 1954).
This entry is taken from the *American National Biography* and is published here with the permission of the American Council of Learned Societies.

NANETTE DE JONG

Yarbrough, Manny (5 Sept. 1964–), sumo wrestler, judo and mixed martial arts competitor, and football player, was born Emmanuel Yarbrough in Rahway, New Jersey, and holds the *Guinness* record as the largest living athlete in the world. Affectionately known as "Tiny," a nickname he earned at Morgan State University because of his large size, he stood six feet seven inches and, at one point, tipped the scale at well over eight hundred pounds. In sixth grade Manny was already five feet eleven inches and 260 pounds. Coaches and school administrators wanted him to play football, but at age eleven he was not ready for the intensity of the game and refused to play. However, by the time he entered high school, his confidence had grown and so, too, had his body; in ninth grade Manny was six feet four inches and weighed 320 pounds. As a high school senior starting tackle, he played football and helped his team advance to the state finals. Yarbrough discovered wrestling in college. At four hundred pounds, he was one of the heaviest competitors in college wrestling history. He was a three-time All-American wrestler (in 1983, 1985, and 1986) at Morgan State University, where he also played football and was an All-American offensive tackle.

The NCAA implemented a weight restriction that rendered Yarbrough ineligible for competition, effectively ending Yarbrough's college wrestling career. He left school the following year. Yarbrough considered wrestling professionally, but was not comfortable with the theatrics of the popular World Wrestling Federation (WWF). Putting his dream of becoming a professional athlete on hold, Yarbrough began driving a delivery van and worked as a nightclub bouncer. Then a friend introduced Yarbrough to Yoshisada "Yone" Yonezuka, the sensei (teacher) at Cranford, New Jersey's Judo and Karate Center. Yone was in search of exceptionally large men with wrestling experience to compete on the Olympic judo team. At more than four hundred pounds, Yarbrough was the right fit. He placed third in the 1989 nationals, but a knee injury ended any hopes of further judo competition. Once again, Yone would provide an opportunity for Yarbrough. In 1992 the new International Sumo Federation was seeking wrestlers. Yone, who was an amateur sumotori in high school in Japan, suggested Yarbrough. After arriving in Japan and undergoing three days of intensive training, Yarbrough was competing in the first Sumo World Championships. He reached the finals, although he did not win.

He continued to compete in other wrestling-related events: Ultimate Fighting Championship III, Pride I, and Pride III, in Tokyo, Japan. Despite newfound celebrity, and being a seven-time member of the U.S. national team, Yarbrough battled for three years before becoming the 1995 amateur world sumo champion in the open weight division. In a 2003 Doghouseboxing.com interview Yarbrough spoke about winning the 1995 championship: "It felt great because I realized this is something we're not well-versed in. ... I actually beat a Japanese guy in the finals. ... It felt like a weight lifted because I was so close before."

He became a sensation. In 2001, at more than seven hundred pounds, Yarbrough won his only North American Championship. He is known as "International Sumo's Greatest Ambassador." Outside of Japan, when the conversation is about sumo, Yarbrough's name is usually the first one mentioned. Outside of Japan, Hawaii is perhaps

sumo's best known home. Most wrestlers who hail from the islands are Polynesian, but on the mainland Yarbrough is the face of sumo. Many of the current and upcoming sumotori are either African American or Latino, mainly because of Yarbrough's efforts.

Yarbrough has appeared on many television programs, such as the *Tonight Show with Jay Leno*, *Late Night with David Letterman*, *Regis and Kathie Lee*, *Roseanne*, *Jon Stewart*, the *Jimmy Kimmel Show*, *Conan O'Brien*, and HBO's *Oz*. Yarbrough made countless personal appearances abroad as well. "We had an awesome reception in Poland." Nearly six thousand people turned out for a demonstration in a town hall. "Sumo is really catching on there." Yarbrough claimed to have been culturally enriched by many people he has met through his travels.

Yarbrough began to spend much of his time trying to lose the weight that made him a celebrity, hoping to qualify for the 2008 Summer Olympics as a wrestler. Yarbrough lost 180 pounds on his quest to reach a three-hundred-pound wrestling weight. Through a campaign called "GET TINY," he began sharing his story with young people across the country in an effort to reduce childhood obesity. With help from Health Platinum Products, Body Mechanics, and a lot of prayer, Yarbrough once said, "nothing is unobtainable."

FURTHER READING
Callahan, Derek. Interview with Emmanuel Yarbrough. Doghouseboxing.com. http:www.doghouseboxing. com (2003).
Yang, Jeff. "Size Matters," *Village Voice* (Dec. 1998).

JAHAAN MARTIN

Yarrow, Mamout (c. 1730–1824), slave, was born in West Africa, possibly in Futa Jallon (later Senegal-Gambia). The exact year of his birth is unknown, and little is known of his early life in Africa. While his name is often given as Yarrow Mamout, Yarrow is his surname, the spelling of which has appeared over time as Yarrah, Yorro, and Yoro. Yarrow's appearance in two portraits painted in his old age has led modern scholars to suggest that he may have been a member of the Fulani/Fulbe people. A Muslim, Yarrow fell victim to intra-African religious conflicts when he was captured as a young man and sold into slavery in North America.

According to the painter and naturalist Charles Willson Peale's diary account of meeting Mamout Yarrow, the captain of the ship on which Yarrow endured the Middle Passage was Captain Dow. Though no Captain Dow has been located in surviving shipping records, a slaver captain called Robert How made seven transatlantic trips between 1755 and 1767. Yarrow estimated his age at the time of his enslavement to be thirty-five years, while his enslavers reckoned him to be fourteen. Two factors explain the discrepancy in these figures. Slave marketers typically gave rough age estimates, particularly because younger slaves would be more attractive to traders, and as a Muslim, Yarrow would probably have used the Islamic lunar calendar to calculate the years of his life. Working within the range of ages given for Mamout Yarrow and the framework of the dates of Captain How's slave runs, it is reasonable to suggest that he was born in the mid-1730s.

As is often the case with African American slaves, any written details of Yarrow's life history can only be traced through the biographies and legal papers of his owners. In America Yarrow was purchased by Samuel Beall of Montgomery County, Maryland. When Beall died in 1778, possession of Yarrow transferred to his son, Brooke Beall, a merchant and importer. Brooke Beall and his household moved from rural Montgomery County to Georgetown, D.C., in 1783, to a house at Lot 73 on Water Street. Yarrow Mamout worked as an enslaved manual laborer for the Beall family and apparently began a family of his own. His son Aquilla (possibly named for Aquila Beall, a brother of Brooke) was born in 1789. Aquilla's mother's identity and whether she and Mamout were married are not known.

Brooke Beall hired out Yarrow to work as a day laborer, and of course Yarrow also labored for his owner, making the bricks for Beall's planned new mansion on Congress Street. Beall promised Yarrow that he would manumit the now rather old man after work on the new Georgetown estate was completed, but before construction could begin, Beall passed away. The 1796 inventory of Beall's estate lists "Negro Yarrow" as a sixty-year-old man, with a value of seven pounds sterling.

Brooke Beall's son and executor, Upton Beall, signed an order of manumission that established Yarrow's freedom on 22 August 1796. The manumission was recorded in Montgomery County, Maryland, where Upton Beall was also clerk of court. Margaret Beall, widow of Brooke, is sometimes credited for this manumission as an act of good faith meant to fulfill her late husband's pledge, but the actual order states, "At the request of Yorro

the following manumission is recorded … that I Upton Beall of Montgomery County and State of Maryland do manumit and set free negro Yorro" (Montgomery County LRC No. 385 [1796]).

Mamout Yarrow remained in Georgetown. He continued to do day labor and at night made baskets and nets to sell for additional income. By the early 1790s Yarrow owned stock shares in the second chartered bank in the new nation, the Columbia Bank, whose stockholders included George Washington. He may have been aided in this investment endeavor by the Bealls, to whom he still belonged at that point. After his manumission, having saved money for retirement, Yarrow by 1800 was able to purchase a home at 3300 Dent Place. In the next few years he searched for further profitable investments for his money. His first investment of $100 was lost when the man to whom he had entrusted the money died suddenly. Subsequently he invested $100 with a young merchant, who went bankrupt. A third investment of $200 in the Columbia Bank proved more profitable.

By the 1810s Yarrow had achieved some local celebrity. White residents of Georgetown knew him by sight on the streets, and he was well regarded. He appeared in an 1816 survey and inventory of Georgetown as one of the neighborhood's most well-known and distinctive characters, a free black man, proclaiming his Islamic faith in public and gently teasing and joking with white Georgetowners. Yarrow remained in good physical shape by swimming regularly into his eighties when contemporary accounts described him as still "active, cheerful, and good-natured" (Warden, 49).

In 1819 the artist Charles Willson Peale was in Washington to paint a portrait of President James Monroe when his interest was piqued by rumors of a man who was 134 years old; the artist wished to learn how he had achieved such advanced age. Peale became determined to meet the old man, interview him, and paint his portrait, and he soon arranged through mutual acquaintances to meet Mamout Yarrow. Yarrow sat for Peale on 30 and 31 January 1819. Peale recorded in his diary that his subject's advanced age might be attributed both to his general good nature and his temperate habits. In particular, Peale noted, Yarrow did not eat pork or drink alcohol, both of which his faith prohibited. Yarrow's likeness was hung in Peale's Museum in Philadelphia, Pennsylvania, along with the portraits of Revolutionary War heroes who were Peale's stock in trade until the museum closed and its contents were sold in 1854. Later this portrait would be housed in the collections of the Historical Society of Pennsylvania.

While Yarrow was indeed an old man by the time he met Peale, it is highly unlikely that he was actually more than 130 years old. Legal papers plausibly put Yarrow's age at the time of Brooke Beall's death in 1796 at 60, making him an octogenarian by the time he met Peale, who was likewise nearly 80. A few years later James Simpson, the drawing and painting instructor at Georgetown College, painted another portrait of the esteemed old man that would later be displayed in the Peabody Room at the Georgetown Public Library. In Simpson's less skilled portrait Yarrow looks noticeably older and more wizened. Whether Simpson painted the portrait from life or copied Peale is unknown.

Yarrow was financially comfortable in his old age. His investments earned enough of a return that he could even afford to lend money. On 23 March 1821 Yarrow loaned nearly $200 to William Hayman, a loan that was never repaid. Having achieved freedom and financial solvency in the land where he had been enslaved, Mamout Yarrow died in Georgetown. Nineteen years after Yarrow's death a free black woman named Nancy Hillman appeared before the Chancery Court of the District of Columbia. Hillman identified herself as Yarrow's niece and filed claim for the proceeds of an auction of the late William Hayman's property. The court ruled in her favor, and she was awarded $451 for principal and interest on the old loan.

Mamout Yarrow was a remarkable man for many reasons. He arrived in America as a slave, convinced his owner to manumit him, and in his old age attained a fair measure of material wealth and fame. He did reach an advanced age, although not perhaps as fantastically advanced as some of his contemporaries believed, and he continued in good health into his dotage. Although he was not as famous as some of his fellow Columbia Bank stockholders, Yarrow was a well-known and well-liked public figure in Georgetown. Perhaps most strikingly he continued to openly proclaim his Islamic faith in an environment not generally conducive to such expressions. Among his many achievements Mamout Yarrow is an important example of the survival of Islamic faith despite the experience of the Middle Passage and American slavery.

FURTHER READING

Gomez, Michael. "Muslims in Early America," *Journal of Southern History* 60:4 (1994).

Johnson, James H. "Yarrow Mamout," *The Montgomery County Story* (May 2004).

Miller, Lillian, ed. *The Selected Papers of Charles Willson Peale and His Family*, vol. 3 (1991).

Warden, David. *Chorographical and Statistical Description of the District of Columbia* (1816).

ELIZABETH KUEBLER-WOLF

Yates, James (1906–7 Nov. 1993), activist and volunteer in the Abraham Lincoln Brigade in the Spanish civil war, was born in Quitman, Mississippi, the middle child of sharecroppers Ida and George Washington Yates. In the year Yates was born the State of Mississippi did not register the birth of African Americans, so the exact date of his birth is unknown. When James was about six years old, in 1912, his parents and some other families pooled their money to hire a private teacher. Because of the cost most of the families could not pay the teacher; as a result, Yates's schooling was sporadic. Determined that their son would receive an education, George and Ida Yates sent him walking ten miles one way to a one-room schoolhouse that operated only five months of the year. Jim Crow laws permeated the South, and from an early age Yates witnessed racism and intimidation against African Americans. It was after witnessing the rage of the Ku Klux Klan directed at his family that Yates began to dream about living in the North and having greater freedom.

At age thirteen he quit school, frustrated by the lack of opportunities. He took menial labor jobs where he witnessed more inequality against African Americans. In his memoir *Mississippi to Madrid* (1989) he recalled working at a brickyard where white workers were paid three dollars a week in cash, while black workers were paid three dollars a week in vouchers for the company store. In 1923 at age seventeen, Yates left Mississippi and eventually settled in Chicago, Illinois, where he found work in the Chicago stockyards. He was hired in 1927 as busboy in the dining car for the Pennsylvania Railroad, hoping to work his way up to a waiter's position. That same year, he married Bessie (her maiden name is now unknown), a girl from his hometown in Mississippi who had also migrated to Chicago. Their daughter Louise was born in 1928 and son Richard in 1930.

As the Great Depression gripped the United States, Yates was laid off from the railroad. He often spent time listening to socialists speak in a soap-box forum called the Bug Club in Washington Park near the University of Chicago. It was here that he first learned of socialist causes and witnessed demonstrations for relief from the Depression. In 1932 Yates was rehired as a relief waiter for the Pennsylvania Railroad. The following year, President Franklin Delano Roosevelt's National Industrial Recovery Act (later declared unconstitutional) temporarily gave workers the right to organize unions without interference from their employers. With the federal government behind him, Yates began organizing black waiters into the Dining Car Waiters Union to fight discrimination and low wages. As a result, Yates was labeled an agitator and he found it difficult to obtain long-term assignments with the railroad.

Frustrated by the lack of job opportunities in Chicago in 1935, Yates migrated to New York City to find work. As in Chicago, socialists gathered to speak of their causes in Union Square Park. It was there that Yates learned of fascism in Europe and he realized the similarities between fascism and racism, which led to his decision to fight for the Republican cause in the Spanish civil war. In 1937 Yates made his way to Spain, answering a call for volunteers to help the democratically elected Spanish Republican government fight against the fascism of the dictator Francisco Franco. During the conflict the U.S. State Department was enforcing an embargo barring Americans from traveling to Spain. Yates, along with other volunteers, had to take a circuitous route through France and make a treacherous mountain crossing in the Pyrenees. As a volunteer in the Abraham Lincoln Brigade, an organization of Americans formed to fight fascist forces in the Spanish civil war, he served as an ambulance and ammunition driver and was wounded twice.

In 1939, because of his injuries, Yates left Spain and the Abraham Lincoln Brigade and settled in New York City. When the United States entered World War II in 1941, Yates enlisted in the U.S. Army and remained stateside in a medic unit at Bushnell Army Hospital in Utah. After an infection hospitalized him, Yates was honorably discharged. Serving in the army qualified him for college tuition paid under the GI Bill, and he earned a degree in electronics at the RCA Institute in New York City. Yates found it difficult to find a job in the 1950s McCarthy era owing to his involvement with the Abraham Lincoln Brigade and his leftist political leanings. Unable to find work, Yates opened his own television repair shop in New York's Greenwich Village and continued to be involved in the civil rights movement and the struggle for equality. He served from 1964 to 1968 as president of the Greenwich Village–Chelsea chapter of the NAACP.

In 1986 Yates returned to Spain with other veterans of the Abraham Lincoln Brigade, who were honored in Madrid for their service. Yates published his memoir, *Mississippi to Madrid: Memoir of a Black American in the Abraham Lincoln Brigade,* in 1989. James Yates died at age eighty-seven in New York City.

FURTHER READING
The archives of the Abraham Lincoln Brigade are housed at New York University's Tamiment Library.
Yates, James. *Mississippi to Madrid: Memoir of a Black American in the Abraham Lincoln Brigade* (1989).
Obituary: *New York Times,* 11 Nov. 1993.

WENDY PFLUG

Yates, Josephine Silone (15 Nov. 1859–3 Sept. 1912), clubwoman, educator, and civic leader, was born in Mattituck, Suffolk County, New York, the daughter of Alexander Silone and Parthemia Reeve. She attended schools in New York until she was eleven, at which time she went to live with an uncle in Philadelphia, Pennsylvania. There she enrolled in the Institute for Colored Youth. Later Josephine moved to Newport, Rhode Island, and attended Rogers High School. The only African American student in her class, she graduated as valedictorian in 1877. She earned a teaching certificate enabling her to teach in public schools in Newport, the first African American to do so in that city. Yates then attended and graduated from the Rhode Island State Normal School in Providence in 1879, also the only African American graduate that year. She later received an M.A. from National University in Illinois.

In 1879 Yates began her teaching career at Lincoln Institute (later Lincoln University) in Jefferson City, Missouri. Employed as the chairperson of the Department of Natural Science, Yates held the distinction of being the first woman elected to a professorship at the school. For the next ten years she devoted her life to teaching and educating the students at Lincoln Institute. In 1889 she left the school to marry William Ward Yates, the principal of the Wendell Phillips School in Kansas City, Missouri. The couple had two children. Not without an opportunity to influence public education, Josephine Yates, while in Kansas City, conducted a private school for domestics and others who had not had the opportunity to attend school previously.

In addition to her experience and devotion to the field of education, Yates also became involved in the activities of numerous women's clubs. She assisted in organizing the Kansas City League and served as its first president in 1893. On the national level, Yates served as vice president of the National Association of Colored Women from 1897 to 1899, as treasurer from 1899 to 1900, and as president from 1900 to 1904. During her tenure as president, Yates used her leadership to incorporate the National Association of Colored Women, as well as to affiliate the organization with the National Council of Women. Following her term as the national president, Yates also served as state president of the Missouri Association of Colored Women from 1907 to 1911.

During this time, however, Yates had not lost her desire to teach, and in 1902 the Lincoln Institute's new president, Benjamin Franklin Allen, had convinced her to return to the school. In her new position, Yates served as the chairperson of the departments of English and history. In 1908, when she attempted to resign from the institution for a second time, the school's Board of Regents refused her resignation and convinced her to stay. At that time Yates's duties at Lincoln Institute increased, and in addition to teaching, she also began to advise students. Along with her roles as both teacher and adviser, Yates also continued to work with numerous women's clubs and traveled the country giving lectures. She gained considerable reputation as a speaker, especially in locations such as Chicago, Kansas, and New York. During her public appearances she discussed the benefits of the work accomplished by the National Association of Colored Women and the importance of that organization to African American women. She called the group a "non-sectarian body organized for the definite and avowed purpose of race elevation."

After her husband died in 1910, Yates left Lincoln Institute to take over the care of her family and home in Kansas City. For the next two years she worked for the Kansas City Board of Education, teaching young people until her death.

In addition to her success as an educator, Yates also earned fame as a writer, contributing many articles to magazines and newspapers during her career. She served as editor of the *Negro Educational Review* in 1904 and wrote articles for inclusion in the *Boston Herald*, the *Transcript*, the *Los Angeles Herald*, and the *Pacific*. Under the pseudonym "R. K. Potter," Yates also wrote "The Isles of Peace," as well as other poems and works. In *Twentieth Century Negro Literature*, Yates wrote concerning the status of African Americans in society. She addressed her concerns to advancements made in the nineteenth century and how those advancements, or lack thereof, affected African Americans in the twentieth century. Of particular interest were achievements in education, morality, and wealth, as well as any opportunities available to black individuals. In discussing the advancements made, Yates wrote, "The measure of the success of a race is the depths from which it has come...we conclude that educationally, morally, financially, the Negro has accomplished by means of the opportunities at his command about all that could be expected of him or any other race under similar conditions." However, Yates also spoke of the success of women in society, of which she said, "The women of a race forms, perhaps, the surest index of its real advancement." Emphasizing the importance of teaching, she concluded that "future success ... is ours, if we hew to the line in teaching our sons and daughters to love virtue and that a good name is rather to be chosen than great riches."

FURTHER READING

Yates's papers are at the Ethnic Studies Center, Inman E. Page Library, Lincoln University.

Carter-Brooks, Elizabeth. "Josephine Silone Yates, Second President of the N.A.C.W.," in *Lifting as They Climb*, ed. Elizabeth L. Davis (1933).

Dannett, Sylvia G. L., and the Negro Heritage Library. *Profiles of Negro Womanhood*, vol. 1 (1964–1966).

Kerlin, Robert T. *The Voice of the Negro* (1920, 1968).

This entry is taken from the *American National Biography* and is published here with the permission of the American Council of Learned Societies.

STEPHANIE A. CARPENTER

Yates, William Henry (27 Apr. 1816–6 Sept. 1868), activist, was born to a free father, a Baptist minister named Beverly Yates, and an enslaved mother, whose name is not now known, in the Alexandria, Virginia–Washington, D.C., area. Owned by Eliza Black, Yates was hired out as a child. It may have been this early work outside his owner's home that spurred his desire for liberty. While he was still in his early teens, Black began to allow Yates to hire himself as a porter at the prestigious Fuller's Hotel in Washington, D.C. (across from the U.S. Treasury Department). He married his first wife (whose name is also now unknown) in 1835. He eventually purchased his freedom—some sources suggest with money made from additional work as a janitor for the U. S. Supreme Court—and was manumitted on 15 May 1841.

Although most sources agree that he worked as a hack driver and purchased his wife and two children out of slavery, sources vary as to when and why he left Washington, D.C. He had been active in the black community, founding the first black literary and debating society, a temperance society, and a military band. Some sources suggest that he was driven from the nation's capital because of rumors of Underground Railroad involvement. Regardless, when his wife died in 1849, he moved to New York for a brief period about which nothing is known.

He went west in 1851 on the ship, *Golden Gate*, and settled in San Francisco. He served as a steward on the luxury steamers *Chrysopolis* and *Eclipse*, bought real estate, and quickly rose to prominence within the black community. Elected the chair of the state's first Colored Convention in 1855, he was active in the fight for equal education, the right of blacks to testify in court, and civil rights in general. He helped establish the Executive Committee that planned several later conventions, as well as the Franchise League and the San Francisco *Mirror of the Times*. He was also an active Mason. As such, he worked with figures ranging from community activists such as WILLIAM H. HALL and JEREMIAH BURKE SANDERSON to journalists like PETER ANDERSON and PHILIP A. BELL.

By 1860 he had accumulated over $1,500 in real estate and lived in a home on Pacific Street with his second wife Mary Jane, their daughter Francis (Fanny), and three daughters from his first marriage. He remained a key figure among blacks in California, and often spoke at various conventions and Masonic functions. Late in his life, he wrote fairly regularly for the San Francisco black press—sometimes under his own name and sometimes under the pen name "Amego." The 16 October 1868 San Francisco *Elevator* remembered "his versatility as an orator, poet, essayist and general writer." The eulogy continued, "He [was] determined to be FREE. He was what slaveholders call a bad boy."

He apparently considered returning to his birthplace to retire—and even purchased a house in Washington, D.C.—but he died while visiting Alexandria. He was so prominent within California's black community that the *Elevator* ran obituaries and remembrances for almost a full month after his death; the *Elevator* also published a poem written for his daughter Fanny by columnist

"Semper Fidelis" (JENNIE CARTER). In addition to bequests to his large family, his will included a provision to donate $50 to each of San Francisco's black churches. His wife decided to stay in San Francisco, and her holdings were valued at almost $20,000 in 1870.

An important pioneer in black California, Yates was rightly remembered by his contemporaries as a Renaissance man.

FURTHER READING
Lapp, Rudolph. *Blacks in Gold Rush California* (1977).
Primus, Marc. *Monographs of Blacks in the West* (1976).
Obituary: San Francisco *Elevator*, 16 Oct. 1868.

ERIC GARDNER

Yerby, Frank (5 Sept. 1916–29 Nov. 1991), writer, was born Frank Garvin Yerby in Augusta, Georgia, the son of Rufus Garvin Yerby, a postal worker, and Wilhelmina Smythe. As a child, he was shy and bookish, and by the time he was a teenager he was writing verse, some of which he published locally. He became interested in pursuing writing as a career after his sister, a student at Fisk University in Nashville, Tennessee, showed some of his poems to JAMES WELDON JOHNSON, who was a teacher there, and Johnson commented favorably on them. Yerby attended segregated schools in Augusta, and after graduation from high school he enrolled at Paine College, a black institution in that city, and contributed poems and short stories to college publications and small magazines.

After receiving his undergraduate degree in 1937, Yerby did graduate work in English at Fisk, earning a master's degree a year later. He then moved to Chicago, where he did further graduate work at the University of Chicago while working for the Federal Writers' Project, a Depression-era program sponsored by the U.S. government. As part of the Writers' Project, a nationwide enterprise that extensively documented various aspects of American life, Yerby worked in the so-called Ethnics Unit and was assigned to write about a Muslim religious sect living in the city. He later described the experience, which included training in how to do detailed research, as the best preparation possible for an aspiring writer.

Yerby moved to Tallahassee, Florida, in 1939 to teach English at Florida A&M College, another all-black institution, and after a year there went on to teach at the all-black Southern University, in Scotlandville, Louisiana. It was at this time, in 1941, that he married Flora Williams, with whom he had four children. He moved north to Detroit in the summer of 1942 to work in a defense plant in Dearborn for several years, then moved east to spend another year working at an aircraft factory in Long Island, New York. During this period Yerby wrote short stories about racial tensions in contemporary America and submitted them to magazines, but most of them were rejected. He did score one success with "Health Card," which appeared in *Harper's* in May 1944. An account of a black couple mistreated by military police, it received an O. Henry Memorial Prize Award and was reprinted that year in the annual O. Henry collection of outstanding short stories.

Pleased to have recognition at last, Yerby nevertheless realized that little money would be made from short stories—he now had a family to support—and he shifted his focus to writing a popular novel that he hoped would become a best seller. The result was *The Foxes of Harrow*, a historical potboiler filled with melodrama, set in the antebellum South, and featuring the stock characters, predictable incidents, and steamy sex of the genre that came to be known as "costume fiction." Although black people appeared in the book, albeit it as slaves, and were sympathetically depicted, the story focused on the rise to riches and power of a white protagonist—an unusual subject for a black novelist at that time. Critical opinion seemed to divide along racial lines. White critics writing in mainstream publications, while treating the novel respectfully and looking for political significance, found themselves struggling to find something to praise and usually focused on the authenticity of "period detail." Black critics, on the other hand, seemed somewhat defensive on Yerby's behalf; determined to take the book seriously—perhaps more so than the author had intended—they saw it as a breakthrough for the black novelist in America.

In one way it was: *The Foxes of Harrow* was no literary masterpiece, but it became a runaway best seller. Within a year more than a million copies had been sold, excerpts from the book had been reprinted in both black and white periodicals, and Twentieth Century Fox had bought the film rights; a movie version starring Rex Harrison and Maureen O'Hara was released in 1947. The book was reprinted many times and over the next forty years sold an estimated 10 to 12 million copies. Yerby's astonishing success encouraged him to stay with a winning formula, and he never looked back. Thenceforth he turned out historical novels in a similar vein at the rate of nearly one a year, writing a total of thirty-three books that were translated into more than a dozen languages. Nearly all of them were best sellers.

Most of Yerby's novels after *Harrow* were also set in the nineteenth-century South and featured the standard melodramatic panoply of the costume novel. They included *A Woman Called Fancy* (1951), *An Odor of Sanctity* (1965), *The Dahomean* (1971), and *A Darkness at Ingraham's Crest* (1979). But occasionally Yerby moved his locales: *Goat Song* (1967) is set in ancient Greece; *Judas, My Brother* (1969) in the early Christian era; and *Western* (1982) is subtitled *A Saga of the Great Plains*. Yerby defended these and several other works as "serious novels" rather than costume fiction, but most critics did not agree, concluding that his books indulged in two-dimensional characters and historical stereotypes. The public, seemingly oblivious to the conflict, kept on buying his books—close to 60 million copies by 2007. Though Yerby was obliquely accused of betraying his early promise by not writing novels of social protest, especially as the civil rights movement captured national attention during the 1950s and 1960s, he defended his work as popular entertainment, putting himself in the company of other best-selling novelists such as Thackeray and Dickens and declaring his refusal to write what he called "sociological tracts."

By this time Yerby had become an expatriate, having settled in Spain in 1952. There he continued to write best-selling fiction. Having divorced his first wife, he married his secretary and translator, Blanca Calle-Perez, in 1956. His last novel, *McKenzie's Hundred*, was published in 1985. Yerby died of heart failure in a hospital in Madrid.

FURTHER READING
Bone, Robert A. *The Negro Novel in America* (1965).
Current Biography Yearbook (1946).
Fuller, H. W. "Famous Writer Faces a Challenge," *Ebony*, June 1966.
Obituary: *New York Times*, 8 Jan. 1992.
This entry is taken from the *American National Biography* and is published here with the permission of the American Council of Learned Societies.

ANN T. KEENE

Yerby, William James (22 Sept. 1867–3 July 1950), physician and career diplomat, was born in Oldtown, Philips County, Arkansas, one of six children of Robert Milton and Clementina Yerby. As a youth, Yerby moved to Memphis, Tennessee, with his widowed mother and his one surviving brother. There he attended public schools and the city's Le Moyne Normal and Commercial Institute (now Le Moyne-Owen College) before entering Nashville's Baptist-affiliated Roger Williams University, where he received his bachelor's degree.

Yerby worked for six years in the publishing and printing business, before beginning medical studies in 1895 at Meharry Medical Department (now Meharry Medical College) of Central Tennessee College in Nashville. After receiving an M.D. degree from Meharry in 1898, Yerby immediately established his medical practice in Memphis, where he also became active in the Republican Party.

On 30 June 1897, Yerby was married to Cecilia Carolyn Kennedy, a Henderson, Kentucky, schoolteacher and a fellow graduate of Roger Williams University. The couple had two daughters: Edwina (Church) and Clementine (Tyler, Doram). The family, including Yerby's mother, maintained their residence in Memphis for many years, where Cecilia Yerby first taught at the Howe Institute in Memphis and later served as a school library supervisor during her husband's consular service abroad. She studied privately for several years at the Ecole Pigier, in Paris, France, and later took private lessons in French history (Mather, p. 294).

In 1906 Yerby was among a number of African Americans recommended to President Theodore Roosevelt for appointment to federal office by Republican leaders in Tennessee. Roosevelt selected Yerby as the U.S. consul to the British colony of Sierra Leone in West Africa, succeeding the McKinley appointee Dr. JOHN T. WILLIAMS in that post. Yerby was commissioned as a U.S. consul on 28 June 1906, and remained in the consular service for more than a quarter of a century, spending nineteen years in Africa. He eventually became one of the first black career officers in the service of the Department of State.

Yerby served as U.S. consul in Freetown until at least 1912. Although his pending transfer to Istanbul, Turkey, was duly reported in *The Crisis* (February 1913), that transfer never occurred. Mrs. Yerby returned to Memphis to live and work in 1913, and by 1915, Yerby went instead to Dakar, in the French colony of Senegal, West Africa. In Dakar, he served as U.S. consul for more than a decade, until 1925. From there he provided periodic updates on African commercial and economic issues, including the palm and kernel oil industry, the subject of a 1915 report from Dakar published by the U.S. Department of Commerce.

In 1915 Dr. Yerby was promoted to a Class 7 consul by the State Department, and in 1920 he was elevated to Class 6. By that year, he was one of just five black U.S. diplomatic and consular officers left at the State Department, and one of only a handful of Republican-era appointees to be retained by the Democratic president Woodrow Wilson, who appointed few new black diplomats. Indeed, the Wilson administration witnessed a decline in opportunities for blacks within the federal government more generally.

Yerby visited Washington occasionally, making reports to his superiors at the Department of State, as noted in the *American Consular Bulletin* (April 1921) after Yerby's 1920 home leave in Chicago. In 1924 Yerby and his colleagues WILLIAM H. HUNT and James G. Carter became the first three African Americans in the consular ranks to be commissioned as Foreign Service Officers under the Rogers Act, congressional legislation that reformed and combined the consular and diplomatic services.

When Yerby's tour in Dakar ended in May 1925, he was briefly reassigned to the U.S. consulate at La Rochelle, France, before being transferred in late 1926 to Oporto, Portugal. He served for four years in Oporto, before his transfer as U.S. Consul to Nantes, France, in 1930.

At the end of his tour in Nantes, Dr. Yerby returned to work at the State Department in Washington, D.C., sailing home from Le Havre, France, aboard the *President Harding* with his family in late June 1932. Soon thereafter, he retired from the consular service. He and his wife then returned to Chicago, where both his daughters now lived and where the family remained until his death.

A devout Baptist, Yerby was also a member of the South Center Community Council in Chicago, and a member of the city's Citizens Civic and Economic Welfare Council. Described as being "for 30 years a career diplomat at the State Department" (*New York Times*, 4 July 1950), Yerby died at his Chicago home at age eighty-two.

FURTHER READING
Mather, Frank L. *Who's Who of the Colored Race* (1915).
Who Was Who in America, 1943–1950 (1950).
Obituary: *New York Times*, 4 July 1950.

BENJAMIN R. JUSTESEN

Yergan, Max (19 July 1892–11 Apr. 1975), YMCA secretary, missionary, theologian, and anti-Communist ideologue, was born in Raleigh, North Carolina, the son of Elizabeth Yeargan, a literate seamstress.

Nothing is now known about his father. The family name has appeared variously as "Yeargin," "Yeargan," "Yergin," "Yergan," and even "Yergen." The spelling "Yergan" was apparently adopted during his early adulthood, while there is evidence that his mother employed "Yeargan" until at least the second decade of the twentieth century.

Raised by his mother and maternal grandfather Frederick Yergan, Max Yergan grew up in a household in which Christian values held sway. This was evident in his attendance at the St. Ambrose Episcopal Parish School and Shaw Institute (now Shaw University). Frederick Yergan served as both deacon and trustee of the Baptist church from which Shaw grew; years later Max recalled his zeal in seeing his grandson become a missionary to "our people in Africa" as a "priceless memory."

Active in Shaw's YMCA since 1911, his sophomore year, by the time of his grandfather's death in 1912 Yergan had announced a change in career plans from law to "some form of Christian service" (Anthony, 15). The "Colored Work" department of the YMCA afforded him a bully pulpit for doing so. Upon graduation in 1914 he sought further training to help him perform the managerial duties associated with YMCA endeavors and therefore enrolled in a secretarial course at the YMCA's Springfield College. By 1916, following the outbreak of World War I in Europe and galvanized by a persuasive appeal from Edward Clark (Ned) Carter, director of YMCA War Work in the East, Yergan answered a "call" to assist British-led troops in Bangalore, India. Six months later, he transferred to the East African front, a fateful request for which his grandfather may posthumously be credited.

Yergan's Indian and East African experiences exposed him to a wider world than he had known in Raleigh, North Carolina. Moreover, these experiences occurred in times and under circumstances that left lasting impressions upon him for the remainder of his life. At the outset of his overseas experiences, Yergan's worldview had been shaped chiefly by the faith of his family and immediate social milieu—broadly Protestant, as shown in his schooling. YMCA education exposed him to the Social Gospel strain of ecumenical thought that proved significant in late-nineteenth- and early-twentieth-century North American Protestantism. The high level of mobility afforded by the YMCA conference network brought him into direct contact with clerical and lay authors, educators, missionaries, and philanthropists of various nationalities, in the United States, Britain, and the broader reaches of the British Empire. In this sense, his World War I service made him more cosmopolitan. It also made him color-conscious in a new way, not merely as an American of African descent, but as one who moved within worlds of color that were made vastly more complicated by imperialism and colonialism.

In letters home from Asia and Africa, Yergan revealed traces of this new consciousness. As a high-profile African American role model in a sea of "nonwhite" colonial subjects, he forged bonds of commonality with people of color in India, Kenya, and mainland Tanzania, impressing imperial hosts and their colonial charges.

Although his reputation among the British officers to whom he reported was sufficient to earn him nomination as first permanent YMCA secretary of Kenya, this aim was blocked in 1919 by colonial governor Sir Edward Northey, reportedly on the grounds that he did not think it "advisable" to admit more blacks into East Africa "of a different calibre from those already there" (Anthony, 41). What happened next, however, was the beginning a surprising turn of events.

Soon after his rejection in Kenya, Yergan received word of an offer for him to consider coming to South Africa to assist recruitment of African youth and students into what was a racially and ethnically segregated YMCA movement. Not only was this YMCA chapter vastly underrepresented in terms of black participation, the organization reflected the society's cultural cleavages between Anglophone and Afrikaans-speaking whites. Indeed, despite the movement's British origins, the majority of South Africa's YMCA members were Boers (a word that means "farmers" in Dutch, it refers to white South Africans of Dutch descent).

The complexity of the South African situation immediately became apparent to Yergan, as one of his correspondents pointed out that he should expect minimal informal contact with whites or unfettered access to vehicles of conveyance or public accommodations, unless he could pass as mixed-race rather than black. He was nonetheless assured that black and mixed-race South Africans would welcome him.

Suffering delays for reasons very similar to those that stymied his appointment in Kenya, Yergan was initially prevented from entry into South Africa by the South African government, which was very suspicious about the intentions of "American Negroes" relative to the African majority. W. E. B. DuBois and Gold Coast nationalist J. E. K. Aggrey—who had officiated at Yergan's 16 June 1920 marriage to fellow Shaw graduate Susie Wiseman—came to his support by lobbying on his behalf, vouching for him and causing the government to reverse its position later in 1921.

Arriving with his spouse and infant son, Frederick, in January 1922, Yergan spent fifteen years in South Africa; the majority of these years on the campus of Fort Hare "Native" College (now University) in Alice in the old Ciskei district of the Eastern Cape. During most of that time, Susie Yergan was a homemaker, but she was also an informal missionary in her own right, founding a "ladies' auxiliary" sometime in the 1920s. Meanwhile, Yergan was organizing and monitoring branches of the Student Christian Association throughout South Africa, using Fort Hare as his base. He also participated in regular chapel rotations and became an ecumenical interlocutor.

Yergan's time in South Africa became noteworthy in several ways. It set the tone for a lifelong connection to the African continent in general and to South Africa in particular. By the 1930s, however, prolonged exposure to racism in both its legal and customary guises, coupled with the growing radicalism characteristic of the Depression era both locally and globally, began to transform him into a political radical. This was indicated in his writings home and in a body of remarkable articles printed in South African periodicals as well as organs affiliated with the Student Christian Association, World Student Christian Federation, and other constituencies connected to the international YMCA. By the mid-1930s he had reinvented himself as a revolutionary socialist for whom YMCA work was passé.

Returning to the United States in 1936, Yergan cut a new profile as a "race leader" in the new National Negro Congress, which he joined at its inception that year. The next year he and PAUL ROBESON cofounded an organization called the International Committee (later Council) on African Affairs and he began teaching black history at the City College of New York. By 1940 he had risen to the post of president of the National Negro Congress, succeeding A. PHILIP RANDOLPH in a controversial election that RALPH BUNCHE apparently considered a "coup" led by Communist forces within the group. From 1937 to 1947, Yergan was seen as a stalwart member of American left-wing politics and an advocate of Communist principles. Then his career trajectory changed again.

With the death of Franklin D. Roosevelt, the end of World War II, and the rise of cold war hysteria, the former New Deal progressive coalition lost its cohesion; Yergan and many others began drifting between left-wing and right-wing political ideas. For many and varied reasons Yergan expressed a loss of confidence in Communism as a potential solution to the problems capitalism posed at a time when most on the left were being subjected to surveillance and intimidation by the intelligence community. From 1947 onward, he at first retreated from activism, and then he gradually reemerged as an anti-Communist ideologue. He testified at hearings against Communist influence in black organizations in both the United States and Africa and traveled to several African nations including South Africa at the height of the Defiance Campaign in 1952 to denounce Communist influence within the mass democratic movement. For the remainder of his life, some two-and-a-half decades, he positioned himself as an apologist for apartheid and minority rule in South Africa and its allies such as Belgium and Portugal; and by 1965 he was a supporter of Rhodesia as it declared a Unilateral Declaration of Independence to forestall the advent of African majority rule.

Thus, after having been in the vanguard of the democratic opposition to fascism in the 1930s, a leader in the struggle against lynching and Jim Crow laws in the 1940s, by the 1950s and 1960s he became identified with forces of racial reaction worldwide, including many that were racist and reactionary, such as the breakaway Rhodesian Unilateral Declaration of Independence (UDI) of 1965, the pro-apartheid Nationalist Party that ruled South Africa from 1948 to 1990, the Belgian industrialists who opposed the rule of the first Prime Minister of an independent People's Republic of the Congo, and the Portuguese government that opposed reforms in their colonies of Guinea-Bissau, Angola, and Mozambique. He died of natural causes in 1975 in Ossining, New York.

FURTHER READING

Anthony, David H., III. *Max Yergan: Race Man, Internationalist, Cold Warrior* (2006).

Duberman, Martin Bauml. *Paul Robeson, A Biography* (1988).

Edgar Robert R., ed., *An African American in South Africa: The Travel Notes of Ralph J. Bunche, 28 September 1937–1 January 1938* (1992).

Gish, Stephen. *Alfred Bitini Xuma: African, American, South African* (2000).

Lewis, David L. *W. E. B. DuBois: The Fight for Equality and the American Century, 1919–1963* (2001).

DAVID H. ANTHONY III

York (c. 1772–before 1832), explorer, slave, and the first African American to cross the North American continent from coast to coast north of Mexico, is believed to have been born in Caroline County, Virginia, the son of an enslaved African American also named York (later called Old York), owned by John Clark, a member of the Virginia gentry and father of the famous George Rogers Clark and William Clark. York's mother is unidentified; it is likely that she, too, was a Clark family slave. A slave named Rose is sometimes listed as York's mother, but sources best identify her as his stepmother. York is believed to have been assigned while a child to William Clark as his servant and companion. Since such relationships were generally between children of about the same age, with the slave sometimes a few years younger, York may have been about two or three years Clark's junior. As the boys grew older, their roles would have become more sharply defined as master and slave. York would have learned everything necessary to serve properly as the body servant of a young Virginia gentleman. He was essentially following in his father's footsteps, since Old York was John Clark's body servant and a trusted slave. York would not have received any formal schooling and was most likely illiterate.

In March 1785 the John Clark family settled in Jefferson County, Kentucky, near Louisville. Once in Kentucky, York would have learned many of the same frontier skills as William Clark did. York probably accompanied Clark during the latter's service as a lieutenant in the U.S. Army from 1792 to 1796. A letter of 1 June 1795 by Clark mentioning that his "boy" had arrived at Fort Greenville, Ohio, might be the earliest known reference to York (Holmberg, 273, 274n). The first certain record of York is his listing in the July 1799 will of John Clark. By that will York officially became the property of William Clark.

In 1803 Clark accepted Meriwether Lewis's invitation to join him as coleader of the famous Lewis and Clark expedition (1803–1806) to the Pacific Ocean, and he took his slave with him. Thus, York was one of the earliest members of the Corps of Discovery and part of the important foundation formed in 1803 at the Falls of the Ohio, at Louisville. York was not an official member of the corps; he was carried on the rolls as Clark's servant and received no pay or land grant for his service. Nonetheless, he was an important member of the expedition, and Clark would have had little hesitation in taking him. Clark had traveled widely as a soldier and a civilian, and York almost certainly traveled with him on some, if not most, of his trips. Thus, York was an experienced traveler by land and water and possessed many of the same abilities the captains required of expedition recruits.

It was a bonus to have York present as a servant to make camp life easier for the captains. And York would have had a definite presence. Expedition-related documents provide a basic physical description of him as a large man (apparently both in height and weight), very strong, agile for his size, and very black. A personality also emerges. York was loyal, caring, and determined, and he had a sense of humor. The expedition journals also give us a basic understanding of York's experience on the journey. The dangers and hardships of the expedition had a leveling effect on the men of the corps. While York never would have completely escaped his slave status, his participation in the daily experiences and work of the corps resulted in his acceptance as one of the group at a level he never would have enjoyed before the expedition. Additional evidence of this is York's inclusion in the November 1805 vote of expedition members regarding the location of their winter quarters. The very fact that York's opinion was sought and recorded with the others' votes reflects his acceptance and status.

An additional benefit for the corps, and a revelation to York, was realized when the explorers encountered American Indians who had never before seen a black man. Those native people almost always greeted York with awe and respect. In their cultures his uniqueness gave him great spiritual power. They also admired his enormous size, strength, and agility. The Arikara Indians named him "Big Medicine." York was consequently used to help advance the expedition. For his part, this was a new and enlightening experience. In only a couple of years he had gone from a societal and racial inferior to a position of relative equality in a primarily white group and even to being viewed by many Indians as superior to his white companions.

On 23 September 1806 the explorers arrived in St. Louis on their return from the Pacific Ocean. The men were discharged and other business taken care of before traveling eastward. On 5 November 1806 Lewis, Clark, York, and others arrived in Louisville, where York was reunited with his wife. (Only one other returning member of the expedition was married.) The names of York's wife and her owner are unknown. When York was married is not known either, though it was before October 1803, when the nucleus of the corps pushed off from the Louisville area. Nor is it known whether they had any children. There are oral traditions among some of the Indian tribes the corps visited that York left behind descendants, and Clark also made a reference in 1832 to stories he had heard that York left descendants among the Indians of the Missouri River.

Over the next year and a half Clark traveled between Louisville, St. Louis, and Virginia. York almost certainly went with him as his servant. In June 1808 Clark and his bride, Julia Hancock, moved to St. Louis to establish their permanent residence, bringing with them a number of their slaves, including York. The situation now changed for York. The years of periodic travel had meant separation from his wife, but York also knew he would be returning. Now his visits to her would be periodic and probably short. York went so far as to ask to be hired out or sold to someone in Louisville. Clark refused to grant this request and told him to forget about his wife. York persisted until Clark relented and allowed him to go for a visit, though he was angry enough to threaten to sell York or hire him out to a severe master if he tried to "run off" or failed to "perform his duty as a slave" (Holmberg, 160). A month later Clark noted that because of York's "notion about freedom and his immense services," he doubted York would ever be of service to him again (Holmberg, 183).

By spring 1809 York had returned to St. Louis, but only briefly. His attitude was no better, in Clark's opinion, and punishment failed to improve it. Clark therefore determined to keep York in Louisville. But rather than sell him, Clark hired him out for at least the next six years. In November 1815 York was still a slave, working as the wagon driver in a freight-hauling business that Clark and a nephew started in Louisville. From then until 1832 York disappears from known records.

In 1832 Clark reported to Washington Irving that he had freed York and set him up in a freight-hauling business between Nashville, Tennessee, and Richmond (Kentucky, it is believed), that York had proved a poor businessman, that he had regretted getting his freedom, and that while trying to return to Clark in St. Louis, he had died of cholera in Tennessee. A happier, but unsubstantiated, ending has York returning to the West, where he lived in the Rocky Mountains as a chief among the Crow Indians, but despite some possible slaveholder rationalization, there is no reason to doubt the main points of Clark's statement. The possibility that York traveled deeper into slave territory upon being freed is indeed unusual. It may be that York's wife's owner had moved to Nashville and that York followed her there after being manumitted.

An assessment of his participation in the Lewis and Clark expedition shows that York made definite contributions to its success. His experience undoubtedly altered his perspective on race and his place in society. Even though doing so alienated him from Clark and brought him further hardship and unhappiness, he spoke up for the rights and freedom he believed he had earned by his years of loyal service and his role in the expedition. It is ironic that the very thing that made him a slave and inferior in white society—the color of his skin—marked him as someone to be respected and admired among many of the Indian tribes encountered on one of the most famous journeys in U.S. history.

FURTHER READING

Betts, Robert B. *In Search of York: The Slave Who Went to the Pacific with Lewis and Clark*, revised with a new epilogue by James J. Holmberg (2000).

Holmberg, James J., ed. *Dear Brother: Letters of William Clark to Jonathan Clark* (2002).

JAMES J. HOLMBERG

Young, Al (31 May 1939–), writer and musician, was born Albert James Young in Ocean Springs, Mississippi, the son of Albert James, a musician and autoworker, and Mary Campbell. Life in the rural South, on the Gulf of Mexico not far from New Orleans, shaped his early interest in storytelling, music, and lives within and beyond familiar landscapes. By the time the family settled in Detroit in 1946, spirituals, blues, the "hollers" in Mississippi fields, birdcalls, and the tinkle of spoons against glasses had already imprinted their magic on Young's boyhood imagination. Often he would sit before the coal heater in his house, watching the flames, under the spell of the Ravens Quartet, the Mills Brothers, and Johnny Mercer, his imagination transporting him.

From 1957 to 1961 Young attended the University of Michigan, where he entertained thoughts of becoming a writer, a Spanish teacher, and a lawyer, but dropped out in his senior year, restless and eager to experience the world for himself. He worked in the Ann Arbor and Detroit areas as a disc jockey, warehouseman, medical photographer, typist, janitor, clerk, lab aide, and film narrator, and began publishing poems, stories, and articles. Although he did not thrive as a musician until he moved to California in 1961, the 1950s marked the beginning of his career as a blues singer and guitarist. In 1963 he married Arlin June Belch, a freelance artist, with whom he had a son, Michael James.

After completing his B.A. in Spanish at the University of California, Berkeley, in 1969 Young revisited his earlier resolution never to enter the world of academia or to teach creative writing. Still, he needed to work, and so over the next decades he accepted long-term and visiting positions at the University of California (at Berkeley, Santa Cruz, and Davis), Rice University, Stanford University, the University of Michigan, the University of Washington, the University of Arkansas, San Jose State University, and Appalachian State University. He traveled throughout the United States and abroad—to what was then the country of Yugoslavia, Israel, Bangladesh, India, Italy, Kuwait, Bahrain, and the Czech Republic—giving readings and lectures, conducting workshops, and sharing his talents and knowledge with unrelenting generosity and passion. Anchored in African American traditions while continuously attuned to the local and global realities of his time, Young's writing thrived and matured over the years into a polyphonic, cross-cultural, and multi-genre body of work.

Young's first book of poems, *Dancing* (1969), was followed by *The Song Turning Back into Itself* (1971), *Geography of the Near Past* (1976), *The Blues Don't Change: New and Selected Poems* (1982) (all four collected in *Heaven: Collected Poems, 1956–90* [1992]), and *The Sound of Dreams Remembered: Poems 1990–2000* (2001). His belief in the "sheer physicality of poetry and music" and his view of poetry as "sonic medium" shine through in the soulful or deliberately jarring, invariably fresh, and inventive rhythms of his poetic opus (Dick, 27). As Young declared in an interview, working in received forms sharpened his ear for "melody and pulse," allowing him better control of open form (Dick, 28). Yet since "[p]oetry from the beginning always belonged to the people, to everybody everywhere," his paramount task was to preserve its oral richness, to make it vibrate, as Walt Whitman had, with the "blab of the pave" (Young in Gonzales, Part 1, 3). Aural, visual, and oral pleasures intersect and enhance each other in the poems' inventive rhythms, lifting the words off the page.

Just as places and people from all corners of the world are often grafted onto Young's poetic canvas through the universal language of jazz and blues, his memories, too, enter the autobiographical genre through musical portals. His four "musical memoirs" (as Young called them) sing personal and communal histories back into existence through affective or associative, rather than chronological, accounts of encounters with blues, jazz, and grassroots artists. Music imposes order on memory and assists the latter into exacting meaning.

Like many other African American writers, including his hero LANGSTON HUGHES, Young was sometimes criticized for his disengaged stance toward "black anger" and for his work's lack of overt militancy. A declared challenger of all coteries and theories, especially those courting essentialism and the marketing of racial struggle, Young parodied this and similar charges in poems such as "A Dance for Militant Dilettantes" and "Your Basic Black Poet," and through the persona of O. O. Gabugah, an alter-ego invention drawing on Tarzan movies, the South African trumpeter Hugh Masekela's *Americanization of Ooga Booga*, and Langston Hughes's Jess B. Semple.

Like his multi-tiered characters, whose ineluctable complexity both encumbers and ennobles their searches, Al Young resists easy categorization. His creative output extended to editorial work for various journals and anthologies, film scripts for SIDNEY POITIER, BILL COSBY, and RICHARD PRYOR, the 1994 video documentary *Color: A Sampling of African American Writers*, and regular contributions of liner notes to the Verve Jazz Masters series. A recipient of Wallace Stegner, Guggenheim, Fulbright, and National Endowment for the Arts fellowships, the PEN-Library of Congress Award for Short Fiction, the PEN-USA Award for Non-Fiction, two American Book Awards, a Pushcart Prize, and two New York Times Notable Book of the Year citations, Al Young was offered the key to the city of Detroit in 1982—a symbolic gesture of reciprocation for the doors he opened onto the human soul.

FURTHER READING

Dick, Bruce Allen. "A Conversation with Al Young," *Cold Mountain* 32.1 (Fall 2003).

Gonzales, Ray. "An Interview with Poet, Essayist, Novelist & Memoirist Al Young: Part I," *Bloomsbury Review* 21.5 (2001).

Gonzales, Ray. "Part II," *Bloomsbury Review* 21.6 (2001).

Lee, Don. "About Al Young," *Ploughshares* 19.1 (Spring 1993).

MIHAELA MOSCALIUC

Young, Andre. *See* Dr. Dre.

Young, Andrew Jackson, Jr. (12 Mar. 1932–   ), civil rights leader, United Nations ambassador, U.S. congressman, and mayor, was born in New Orleans, Louisiana, the son of Andrew Jackson Young, a dentist, and Daisy Fuller, a teacher. Young received a B.S. degree in Biology from Howard University in 1951 and a Bachelor of Divinity degree from Hartford Theological Seminary in Connecticut in 1955. In the same year he was ordained as a minister in the United Church of Christ. As a pastor, he was sent to such places as Marion, Alabama, and Thomasville and Beachton, Georgia. During this time the civil rights movement was reaching its height under the leadership of MARTIN LUTHER KING JR. and others who followed the nonviolent resistance tactics of Mohandas Gandhi, the pacifist who had led Indian opposition to British colonial rule. By the time of the Montgomery, Alabama, bus boycott in 1955, Young and several of his parishioners had decided to join the movement. Young himself was actively engaged in voter registration drives.

In 1957 Young returned north to serve as associate director of the Department of Youth Work of the National Council of Churches in New York City. The United Church of Christ then solicited him in 1961 to lead a voter registration drive, focusing on southern blacks who were unaware of their voting rights. Around this time he became involved with King's organization, the Southern Christian Leadership Conference (SCLC). By 1962 Young had become an administrative assistant to King, and in 1964 he was appointed SCLC's executive officer. Although Young originally opposed King's decision to support a strike by sanitation workers in Memphis, Tennessee, he finally joined and was there at the Lorraine Motel when King was assassinated on 4 April 1968.

King's death signaled the end of one phase of the civil rights movement, but Young soon became active in the movement's new focus on electoral politics. In 1970 Young entered the race for the Democratic nomination in Georgia's Fifth Congressional District, whose boundaries encompassed much of the southern part of metropolitan Atlanta and contained 40 percent of the area's African American population. Young's opponents were two white candidates and an African American, Lonnie King, an NAACP activist and a former leader of the Atlanta sit-in movement. Although Young was victorious in the Democratic primary, he lost the general election to the Republican challenger, Fletcher

Andrew Jackson Young, then U.S. Ambassador to the United Nations, 6 June 1977. (Library of Congress.)

Thompson. Inclement weather on election day and a failure to energize some black voters contributed to Young's defeat.

Following that loss, Young became the chairman of Atlanta's Community Relations Commission (CRC) and fought for a better public transit system and against Atlanta's growing drug trafficking and drug use problems. These actions increased his visibility and popularity across the Fifth District, and in 1972 he again sought a seat in the House. After running a more aggressive campaign, particularly in African American communities, Young received approximately 52 percent of the vote in the general election. By accomplishing this feat, even in a district that was 62 percent white, Young became the first black congressman elected from Georgia since the end of Reconstruction. Indeed, that year Young and BARBARA JORDAN were the first African Americans elected to Congress from any southern state since North Carolina's GEORGE WHITE in 1898. Young was reelected, by comfortable margins, in 1974 and 1976. During the presidential campaign of 1976, he became a strong supporter of the Democratic candidate, Jimmy Carter, a former Georgia governor.

In 1977, after Carter was elected president, he appointed Young as U.S. ambassador to the United Nations. As ambassador, Young championed African issues and visited the African continent several times. He also vehemently attacked the South African system of racial apartheid. But, after only two-and-one-half years in office, Young resigned his ambassadorial post in August 1979. This came shortly after a meeting with Zehdi Lahib Terzi, the UN observer for the Palestinian Liberation Organization (PLO). The PLO, at this time, was considered an international terrorist group by the United States government. By meeting with a PLO representative, Young violated state department rules prohibiting official contact with the Palestinian organization. Following his resignation, Young told the *Atlanta Journal* that efforts for peace in the Middle East were at a crucial and perhaps pivotal juncture, and that he had met with the PLO because a chance for peace had to be pursued.

After resigning as UN ambassador, Young returned to Atlanta and founded a consulting firm called Law International, Inc. (later GoodWorks International). The company promoted trade, especially with African nations. Seemingly satisfied with his new and financially lucrative career in business, Young, in 1981, became a reluctant candidate for mayor of Atlanta, after being urged to do so by CORETTA SCOTT KING, outgoing mayor MAYNARD JACKSON, and others. During his campaign Young made a special effort to reach out to white businessmen, many of whom had been alienated by the affirmative action policies of the administration of Jackson, Atlanta's first black mayor. Young received 55 percent of the total vote in the election of 1981 and was reelected by a larger margin in 1985. His administrations were marked by renewed economic growth, including a revitalization of the Underground Atlanta tourist attraction, increased convention trade in the city, and a decrease in overall crime. It also was credited with a major triumph when Atlanta won the right to host the Democratic National Convention in 1988. By 1984 white business leaders were already telling publications like *Ebony* magazine that the city's reputation had improved in the boardrooms of corporate America. The Young administration, however, drew broad criticisms for its historic preservation and neighborhood revitalization policies. The city's Urban Design Commission and neighborhood activists consistently protested proposals to demolish historic buildings and housing in favor of new commercial buildings and highways—and during and after the 1988 Democratic National Convention, the administration was chastised for its rough handling of anti-abortion demonstrators.

Young's mayoral term ended in 1989, but his political aspirations remained strong. The next year he made an unsuccessful run for governor of Georgia against the state's popular lieutenant governor, Zell Miller. Remaining active in business and civic affairs, Young then led a bid by the city of Atlanta to host the 1996 summer Olympic Games. Atlanta's success in winning the bid to host the Centennial Games was largely attributed to Young's popularity and influence among African and other Third World members of the International Olympic Committee (IOC). During the pre-Olympic and Olympic period in Atlanta (a span of more than four years), Young served as cochairman of the Atlanta Organizing Committee.

After the Olympics left Atlanta, Young returned full time to his international consulting firm and continued to serve on several corporate boards, including Delta Airlines, as well as the boards of several academic and humanitarian institutions. In 1999 he returned, in a sense, to his career origins when he was elected president of the National Council of Churches. In February 2006 Young drew criticism for taking on a position as chairman of the national steering committee of Working Families for Wal-Mart. Further controversy arose when Young, in attempting to defend Wal-Mart's benefit to America's poor, suggested that Jewish, Korean, and Arab shopowners in urban areas had exploited African Americans in the past. He resigned shortly afterward and apologized for his comments.

Young was married to JEAN CHILDS YOUNG (a civil rights and civic activist) for forty years, until her death in 1994. The couple had three children. Young married Carolyn McClain in 1995.

Unlike many of his contemporaries in the southern civil rights movement, Andrew Young's most enduring contributions came after the great legal and political battles of the 1960s had been won. Serving as a congressman, a United Nations ambassador, and a mayor of a large American city, he affected international, national, and local policies for more than twenty-five years. In each of his roles, but particularly as UN ambassador, he was a principal liaison between the United States and the Third World.

FURTHER READING

Young, Andrew. *An Easy Burden: The Civil Rights Movement and the Transformation of America* (1996).

Young, Andrew. *A Way Out of No Way: The Spiritual Memoirs of Andrew Young* (1994).

DeRoche, Andrew J. *Andrew Young: Civil Rights Ambassador* (2003).

Gardner, Carl. *Andrew Young, A Biography* (1978).

Garrow, David J. *Bearing the Cross: Martin Luther King, Jr., and the Southern Christian Leadership Conference, 1955–1968* (1986).

Hornsby, Alton, Jr. *A Short History of Black Atlanta* (2003).

ALTON HORNSBY JR.

Young, Buddy (5 Jan. 1926–5 Sept. 1983), football player and sports executive, was born Claude H. Young in Chicago, Illinois. His parents' names and occupations are unknown. He attended Wendell Phillips High School, where he was an outstanding athlete in both track and football. Young's success as a football player was remarkable because of his size; he was five feet five and weighed 165 pounds. Young entered the University of Illinois in 1944. Although he knew the sting of racial discrimination, Young believed that his small stature was an equal handicap—at least on the football field. Recalling his initial football season at Illinois, Young remarked, "I could never stop proving myself. I had to work harder, play better, block better than the big guys. ... At my first practice they acted like I was some kind of sideshow, like I was supposed to go out with the band at halftime."

As a freshman at Illinois, Young became one of the most exciting wartime players. Playing halfback against Iowa in his first collegiate game, he ran 64 yards for a touchdown on the first play from scrimmage. On his second carry, Young sprinted 30 yards for another score. During that season he had touchdown runs of 93, 92, 74, 64, and 63 yards. Young averaged 8.9 yards a carry and scored thirteen touchdowns, equaling the Big Ten Conference record set by Red Grange in 1924. Illinois coach Ray Eliot called Young "the best running back I have ever seen." After his first year of college football, Young was named to a number of All-America teams. In addition to his prowess on the gridiron, he was an outstanding sprinter. In 1944 he won the national collegiate championships in the 100- and 200-yard dashes and was the Amateur Athletic Union's 100-meter champion; he tied world records for the 45- and 60-yard dashes.

In January 1945 Young was drafted into the navy. After first reporting to the Great Lakes Naval Training Station, he was transferred to the naval base at Fleet City, California, where he played for the Fleet City Bluejackets football team, one of the best squads on the West Coast. The Bluejackets were made up of many college All-Americans and National Football League (NFL) players. In one of his greatest games, Young led Fleet City to a 45-28 victory over the El Toro, California, marines in the West Coast service championship game in 1945. Before 65,000 fans in Los Angeles, Young exploded for kickoff return runs of 94 and 88 yards for touchdowns and added another on a 30-yard run from scrimmage. El Toro coach Dick Hanley, who formerly coached at Northwestern, called Young "the greatest college back I've ever seen."

Despite rumors that he would turn professional after his service obligation was fulfilled, Young returned to the University of Illinois in the fall of 1946. He helped lead the Fighting Illini to their first Big Ten championship since 1928. In the Rose Bowl game on 1 January 1947, Illinois defeated the highly regarded UCLA team by a score of 45-14. Young rushed for 103 yards in twenty carries and scored two touchdowns in the game. The following summer Young was named the most valuable player in the College All-Star game, defeating the Chicago Bears 16-0 before more than 105,000 fans in Chicago. In 1946 Young married his high school sweetheart Geraldine (maiden name unknown); they had three children.

In 1947 the New York Yankees of the All-America Football Conference (AAFC) signed Young to a multiyear contract amid great fanfare. The previous year the AAFC had reintegrated big-time professional football, which had not included black players since 1933. In one of the early tests of fan reaction to professional football's integration, Young led the Yankees against the Cleveland Browns, which included African American stars Bill Willis and MARION MOTLEY. More than 70,000 fans, including 25,000 African Americans, turned out at Yankee Stadium on 24 November 1947 to watch the 28-28 tie. A number of commentators speculated that the game ensured that professional football owners would continue with the experiment in integration. During 1947 Young helped lead the Yankees to the AAFC Eastern Division title, but the New Yorkers lost the championship game to the Cleveland Browns, 14-3.

In addition to his tenure with the AAFC New York Yankees (1947–1949), after the league's demise Young played in the NFL for the New York Yanks (1950–1951), the Dallas Texans (1952), and the Baltimore Colts (1953–1955). He was best known for his sensational run-backs of kickoffs and punts, and he was rated as the best in this category during the 1950s. During his professional career, Young rushed for 2,727 yards and seventeen touchdowns. He also caught 179 passes for 2,711 yards and twenty-one touchdowns. He averaged 27.7 yards per kickoff return. After his retirement as a player in 1955, Young became an assistant general manager of a radio station and worked as a public relations official for the Baltimore Colts. In 1964 Young became a special assistant to NFL commissioner Pete Rozelle, a position that made him the first African American executive hired by a major sports league. In 1968 he was elected as a member of the College Football Hall of Fame. Young died in an automobile accident in Texas while on NFL business.

FURTHER READING

McCallum, John, and Charles H. Pearson. *College Football USA, 1869–1971* (1971).

Neft, David S., and Richard M. Cohen. *The Sports Encyclopedia: Pro Football, the Early Years, 1892–1959* (1987).

Smith, Thomas G. "Outside the Pale: The Exclusion of Blacks from the National Football League, 1934–1946." *Journal of Sport History* 15 (Winter 1988).

Treat, Roger L. *The Encyclopedia of Football* (1979).

Obituary: *New York Times*, 6 Sept. 1983.

This entry is taken from the *American National Biography* and is published here with the permission of the American Council of Learned Societies.

JOHN M. CARROLL

Young, Charles (12 Mar. 1864–8 Jan. 1922), army officer, was born in Mayslick, Kentucky, the son of Gabriel Young and Armintie Bruen, former slaves. When he was nine years old, the family moved north to Ripley, Ohio. Young graduated from Wilberforce University in Ohio and then embarked on a career as a public school teacher. Inspired by Ohio native John H. Alexander, the second African American to graduate from West Point, Young sought and won his state's nomination to the military academy in 1884. He graduated from West Point in 1889,

despite an atmosphere of racial prejudice and the hostility of his fellow cadets.

On leaving West Point, Young was assigned as second lieutenant with the Tenth Cavalry. He was transferred to the Ninth Cavalry in 1889. In 1894 he was assigned to Wilberforce University as a professor of military science and tactics—one of a very small number of assignments available to black officers. While at Wilberforce, Young taught French, German, and mathematics and helped to run the university's drama group. His record at Wilberforce so impressed the president of nearby all-white Antioch College that Young was asked to teach a course in military training there. Young remained intellectually active throughout his career and displayed artistic talent in a number of areas. In addition to a collection of poetry and a monograph entitled *Military Morale of Nations and Races* (1912), Young wrote a play about the leader of the Haitian slave revolt, Toussaint Louverture. As a musician, he wrote numerous compositions and played the piano, harp, ukelele, and cornet. While in the Philippines he would add a proficiency in Spanish to the two languages he had learned in college, German and French.

Young's primary calling, however, was in the military, and he devoted the bulk of his energy to climbing the ranks of the officer corps. Following the death of John H. Alexander in 1894, Young became the highest-ranking black officer in the U.S. Army. He would own this distinction and the racial burden that accompanied it until his death. By the time the Spanish-American War broke out in 1898, he had been promoted to first lieutenant. As the only black commissioned officer in the army, he was assigned to command and oversee the training of the Ninth Ohio Battalion, a black volunteer unit. While Young's regular regiment, the Ninth Cavalry, saw action in Cuba, the Ninth Ohio Battalion never left the United States. In 1901 Young was promoted to captain, and for the following year he saw service with the Ninth Cavalry in quelling the Philippine Insurrection. Young questioned the pervading view in the army that black troops could succeed only under the command of white officers, when he wrote in 1912 that the experience of the Spanish-American War and the Philippine Insurrection demonstrated clearly the ability of black officers to command their own men.

Young's race, however, continued to undermine his military assignments. Between 1904 and 1907 he served in Haiti as U.S. military attaché, a post for which the *Army and Navy Journal* believed black officers were best suited because they could deal better with the local population than could their white counterparts. Also in 1904 he married Ada Mills of Xenia, Ohio; they would have two children. While in Haiti Young surveyed the military preparedness and the terrain of the island nation. According to the U.S. ambassador to Haiti, Young took great personal risk in his endeavors, traveling deep into previously uncharted territory. By the time he left the country, Young had completed a map of Haiti and written a monograph entitled *Handbook of Creole as Spoken in Haiti*. His work would later prove invaluable to the U.S. Marines during their occupation of the Caribbean republic. In 1912 Young was promoted to the rank of major, and in the same year he was once again assigned as a military attaché, this time to the African Republic of Liberia. Young's assignment, as part of the 1912 loan agreement between the administration of President William Howard Taft and the Liberian government, was to oversee the training and reorganization of the country's defense forces, the Liberian Frontier Force. Although he saw himself as an adviser, leaving the day-to-day command to three African American officers he appointed to assist him, Young was occasionally called on to command troops. In one incident, he led a force deep into the Liberian interior to rescue a fellow American, Captain Arthur A. Browne. Browne and an attachment of Liberian troops were trapped by a group of native Africans, who were rebelling against the Americo-Liberian government, the descendants of freed American slaves who had founded the country and who monopolized power by excluding the African population from any form of political participation. Young's expedition succeeded in rescuing Browne, and during his tour of duty the Liberian Frontier Force succeeded in quelling numerous native rebellions. Young believed that Liberia was "a heritage" for all black people; it is ironic that his successful performance of duty there helped to perpetuate an oligarchy that for many years to come would remain ethnically exclusive.

Upon his return to the United States in 1915, Young was awarded the NAACP's Spingarn Medal in recognition of his work in Africa. In 1916 he reunited with the Tenth Cavalry to take part in General John Joseph Pershing's Punitive Expedition to Mexico, where he distinguished himself by leading the rescue of a unit of the Thirteenth Cavalry at Parral. During his tour of duty in Mexico he was promoted to lieutenant colonel. Racism, however, was to bring a premature end to Young's career in the regular army. Fearing that the United States's entry in World War I in 1917 would result in Young's being given command of the Tenth Cavalry, the white officers in the regiment protested the prospect of serving under a black officer. Their protests were taken up by a number of U.S. senators, causing the War Department to force Young into early retirement, ostensibly for medical reasons. Young sought to demonstrate his health by riding his horse from his home in Ohio to Washington, D.C., but to no avail. He was retired in 1917 with the rank of colonel, the highest rank ever achieved by an African American officer. Although Young was recalled to train troops in the last days of the war, the actions of the War Department in 1917 cost him the prospect of promotion to brigadier general. Young returned to Liberia as U.S. military attaché in 1919, and while visiting Lagos, Nigeria, he contracted Bright's disease and died. His body was returned to the United States, and he was buried with full military honors at Arlington National Cemetery.

FURTHER READING

Chew, Abraham. *A Biography of Colonel Charles Young* (1923).

Fletcher, Marvin. *The Black Soldier and Officer in the United States Army, 1891–1917* (1972).

Kilroy, David P. *For Race and Country: The Life and Career of Colonel Charles Young* (2003).

Nalty, Bernard C. *Strength for the Fight: A History of Black Americans in the Military* (1986).

This entry is taken from the *American National Biography* and is published here with the permission of the American Council of Learned Societies.

DAVID P. KILROY

Young, Coleman (24 May 1918–29 Nov. 1997), mayor, was born in Tuscaloosa, Alabama, the son of William Coleman Young, a barber and a tailor, and Ida Reese Jones Young. After his family moved to Detroit in 1923, Young grew up in the Black Bottom section of town, where his father ran a dry-cleaning and tailoring operation and also worked as a night watchman at the post office. Although Young enjoyed his early years in the then ethnically diverse neighborhood, his family did not altogether escape discrimination. A gifted student, he was rejected by a Catholic high school because of his race, and after graduating from public Eastern High, he lost out on college financial aid for the same reason. Young became an electrical apprentice at Ford Motor

Coleman A. Young, November 1985. (AP Images.)

Company, only to see a white man with lower test scores get the job. He then worked on Ford's assembly line but was fired for fighting a thug from Harry Bennett's Service Department who had identified Young as a union member.

After his dismissal from Ford, Young went to work for the National Negro Congress, a civil rights organization that focused on labor issues. While with the NNC, he worked at the post office and continued the fight to unionize Ford. When Henry Ford accepted a union contract, Young turned his attention to other issues such as open housing. Fired from his job in the post office for union activity, he was drafted into the army in February 1942. Young initially served in the infantry with the Ninety-second Buffalo Division before transferring to the U.S. Army Air Forces, where he underwent pilot training with the famed Tuskegee airmen. Washed out of the pilot program—an action Young blamed on FBI interference based on his years of unionizing and associating with so-called radicals—he spent the rest of the war fighting for equal accommodations for African American servicemen on a number of military bases.

Discharged from the air forces as a second lieutenant in December 1945, Young returned to Detroit, regained his position at the post office, and resumed his union-organizing activities. In January 1947 he married Marion McClellan; the couple had no children before divorcing in 1954. Shortly thereafter he married Nadine Drake; that childless marriage also ended in divorce a few years later. As a member of the United Public Workers, he soon ran afoul of Walter Reuther, whose conservative

brand of anticommunist leadership within the United Auto Workers extended to the Congress of Industrial Organizations (CIO). Although Young had been elected to an executive post with the Wayne County, Michigan, chapter of the CIO, he lost his position in 1948 on account of Reuther's political machinations. Following a disastrous run for the state senate as a candidate of Henry Wallace's Progressive Party that same year, Young drifted through a series of jobs before becoming the executive secretary of the newly formed National Negro Labor Council, which achieved some successes nationwide in increasing the range and number of job opportunities for African Americans. Targeted by the federal government as a subversive group, however, the organization folded under pressure in the spring of 1956. After a few more years of drifting between jobs, Young lost a bid for Detroit's Common Council in 1960. Encouraged by the election results, he successfully gained a seat at Michigan's Constitutional Convention. Following the convention Young spent several successful years as an insurance salesman for the Municipal Credit Union League before reentering politics for good in 1964, when he gained election to the Michigan State Senate. Young remained until 1973 in the senate, where he supported open housing and school busing legislation and eventually became Democratic floor leader. In 1973 he ran for mayor of Detroit and, with substantial union support, narrowly won a racially charged contest against former police commissioner John F. Nichols. After the election Young pledged to work together with business and labor to help turn around the badly troubled city, which was then reeling from high unemployment, rampant crime, white flight, the effects of the gasoline embargo, and the loss of its industrial base. Young presided over the 1977 opening of Renaissance Center, a downtown office-retail complex designed to revitalize the city's riverfront, and was also instrumental in building new manufacturing plants for Chrysler and General Motors. Faced with the city's possible bankruptcy, he persuaded voters to approve an income tax increase and gained wage and benefit concessions from municipal workers. Having run on a campaign of reforming the Detroit police department (long viewed as a source of oppression among African American residents), he increased the number of blacks and minorities on the force and also disbanded STRESS (Stop the Robberies, Enjoy Safe Streets), a special police decoy unit that was the focus of many complaints of brutality.

Reelected four times, Young enjoyed a particularly good relationship with President Jimmy Carter. Among the first to endorse Carter's presidential campaign in 1976, Young served as vice chairman of the Democratic National Committee between 1977 and 1981, and from 1981 until 1983 headed the United States Conference of Mayors. He fared less well under Carter's Republican successors, however, and also had to deal with long-running feuds with the local press as well as nearby suburban governments. Despite his long-held emphasis on racial cooperation, the blunt-spoken Young—who for years had a sign on his desk that read "Head Motherfker in Charge"—never gained the trust of many white voters, who deplored his confrontational style and his frequent overseas vacations. In addition to being the subject of federal criminal investigations, none of which resulted in any charges, Young was the target of a paternity suit by former city employee Annivory Calvert, with whom he had a son.

In declining health, Young chose not to run for reelection in 1993. He died in a Detroit hospital. Despite having to face a host of problems with resources that were limited at best, Young proved himself game in his efforts to preserve and revitalize one of America's major metropolitan centers.

FURTHER READING

Young's papers are divided between the Walter Reuther Library at Wayne State University and the African American Museum in Detroit.

Young, Coleman, with Lonnie Wheeler. *Hard Stuff: The Autobiography of Coleman Young* (1994).

Rich, Wilbur C. *Coleman Young and Detroit Politics: From Social Activist to Power Broker* (1989).

Obituaries: *Detroit Free Press*, 5 Dec. 1997; *New York Times*, 30 Nov. 1997.

This entry is taken from the *American National Biography* and is published here with the permission of the American Council of Learned Societies.

EDWARD L. LACH JR.

Young, James Hunter (26 Oct. 1858–11 Apr. 1921), editor, federal official, Republican activist, and state legislator, was born in Henderson, North Carolina, the son of a slave woman of whom nothing is known but that she was owned by Capt. D. E. Young, a wealthy farmer. His father, who was never named publicly, was described as a prominent white resident of Henderson who financed his son's education. Although little is known of his early life before 1865, James Young attended the common schools of Henderson after the war, and in 1874 he entered the private Shaw University in Raleigh, North Carolina.

In early 1877 Young left Shaw to accept a position as messenger in the office of Col. J. J. Young, the U.S. collector of internal revenue for the Raleigh district, and thus began a lengthy, intermittent career in federal service. In 1881 he married his first wife, Bettie Ellison (1862), a daughter of Raleigh political associate STEWART ELLISON. The couple would have two daughters, Maude and Martha.

A committed Republican, Young rose to become chief clerk and cashier for the collector's office, a position he held until his removal from office in July 1885, during the first administration of President Grover Cleveland. But in 1886 he was appointed chief clerk and deputy register in the Wake County office of the register of deeds.

In 1889, after Republican President Benjamin Harrison's inauguration, Young became a special collector of U.S. customs in Wilmington, an appointment engineered by his close friend, Rep. HENRY P. CHEATHAM (R-N.C.), another Henderson native. In 1890 Young was nominated for collector of customs for the city, one of the state's most lucrative federal patronage jobs, and was selected for reappointment by Harrison in 1891. Although never confirmed by the U. S. Senate, Young served in the position until 1893.

Young's nomination sparked a vigorous battle among Democrats, who blocked his confirmation and targeted him, increasingly, as symbolic of the alleged "Negro domination" within the state's Republican Party. After losing the special collector's position during the second Cleveland administration in 1893, Young purchased the Raleigh *Gazette*, a flourishing weekly newspaper operated by JOHN H. WILLIAMSON, which Young published until the late 1890s. It was the state's largest and most influential black publication.

For the first time, Young now pursued an active political career, serving as an at-large delegate to the Republican National Convention in 1892 and running in 1894 as a Republican for the North Carolina House of Representatives from Wake County. After winning a narrow victory for one of three county seats, he was appointed to a number of influential House committees—judiciary, finance, and special election law among them—by the new "fusion" leadership of Republicans and Populists, an alliance that Young, an indefatigable

Republican negotiator with the leaders of the new Populist Party, had helped orchestrate.

His strongest interests lay in the areas of education, penal reform, and state-run schools for the disabled. Young then defeated Democratic opponent Needham B. Broughton to win reelection in 1896. An increasingly influential figure within state Republican ranks, Young helped broker the 1896 congressional nomination of attorney GEORGE HENRY WHITE of Tarboro in the so-called Black Second district, a gerrymandered congressional district composed primarily of the predominantly black eastern counties. In so doing, he helped defeat White's brother-in-law and major rival (and Young's erstwhile ally), former-two-term congressman Henry P. Cheatham. Young also allied himself with white leaders, especially the enigmatic Daniel L. Russell, the successful Republican nominee for governor.

So long as fusionists remained in power, Young had little to fear politically from disgruntled Democrats such as newspaper publisher Josephus Daniels, whose News and Observer openly attacked Young. The men had feuded since Young's purchase of the Gazette from Williamson, who was a friend of Daniels, and Daniels clearly loathed both Young and his new Republican allies: Russell, White, and U.S. Senator Jeter C. Pritchard. A member of the new governor's inner circle of advisors, Young soon emerged as the highest-ranking African American in state government, following appointments in 1897 by Russell as chief fertilizer inspector and as a member of the board governing institutions for the deaf, dumb, and blind. Despite the state's small number of black legislators and officeholders, Young's energetic public image tended to reinforce unfounded charges, by white supremacists, of "Negro domination" in the state government.

After war broke out with Spain, Russell selected Young as the colonel of a state regiment of African American volunteers being raised for use in the Cuban invasion. The Third North Carolina Regiment traveled to Florida but never left the United States during the brief Spanish-American War, but Young's otherwise capable legacy was distorted by the Democratic press as an outrage, stoking public resentment during the tempestuous 1898 campaign. Democrats swept the state legislature in a fraud-marred landslide, effectively destroying the fusion movement.

In 1899 the Democratic-controlled North Carolina legislature voted to remove Young's name permanently from the cornerstone of the newly built state school for the deaf, dumb, and blind. It was the first action in a political war to obliterate memories of the so-called Negro domination. The general assembly also oversaw an action that led to passage in 1900 of a constitutional amendment disenfranchising most African American voters through strict new literacy requirements. For more than half a century after 1900, no African American served as state legislator or congressman, and few wielded any political power outside specific racial circles. Even Young's popular Gazette ceased publication by 1900, the victim of Young's declining political fortunes and dwindling advertising revenue.

Although it is not known when Young's first wife died, he remarried around 1900 Mrs. Mary A. Christmas, a widow with one daughter, Pearl.

Despite his political setbacks Young persevered, securing a final federal appointment from the sympathetic administration of President William McKinley in 1899 as deputy collector of revenue for the Raleigh district. Despite heavy Democratic opposition, Young held that position for the next 14 years, reappointed successively by Presidents Theodore Roosevelt and William Howard Taft, until the first Woodrow Wilson administration. After Young's tenure as deputy federal revenue collector ended in 1913, he devoted himself to business interests, including insurance, real estate, an undertaking firm, and a pharmaceutical company. A devout Baptist, he served as church clerk and Sunday school superintendent for Raleigh's black First Baptist Church and as president of his state Sunday school convention. He was an active Mason and member of the Odd Fellows, Knights of Pythias, and the Household of Ruth. A lifelong proponent of racial moderation and patriotic cooperation, he was criticized by some for seeking moderation on both sides during periods of racial tension.

While the death of his second wife (or dissolution of the marriage by divorce) is unrecorded, Young married his third wife, Lula Evans, in 1913. He also continued to serve his country unofficially by advising federal selective service officials during World War I. Young died of natural causes at his home in Raleigh, and the funeral was held at First Baptist Church. An overflow crowd, consisting of both black and white mourners, attended his 1921 funeral.

FURTHER READING
Anderson, Eric. Race and Politics in North Carolina, 1872–1901: The Black Second (1981).

Kenzer, Robert C. *Enterprising Southerners: Black Economic Success in North Carolina, 1865–1915* (1997).

Obituary: Raleigh *News and Observer*, 14 April 1921.

BENJAMIN R. JUSTESEN

Young, Jean Childs (1 July 1933–16 Sept. 1994), advocate for civil rights, education, and women's and children's welfare, was born Jean Childs in Marion, Alabama, the youngest of five children of Norman Childs, proprietor of a bakery, grocery, soda fountain, and candy store, and Idella Childs, a fifth-grade teacher. Jean Childs was born into a family of educated property owners who, as longtime residents of Marion, demonstrated a long-standing commitment to seeking justice for Marion's black community. Growing up in segregated Perry County, Childs attended Marion's Lincoln School, an early American Missionary Association school opened in the Reconstruction era. After graduating from high school, she enrolled in Manchester College, an institution affiliated with the Church of the Brethren, located in North Manchester, Indiana.

In 1952, while visiting home from college, she met the Reverend ANDREW YOUNG, who would become the first African American elected to Congress from the South since 1901, a U.S. ambassador to the United Nations, and mayor of Atlanta, Georgia. When she and Young met, he was serving as pastor of a church in Marion. In the summer of 1953 Childs was awarded a six-week fellowship from the Church of the Brethren to travel to Europe and work in an Austrian refugee camp. Andrew Young borrowed money from his parents to travel along, and while Childs worked with children in a camp in Linz, he helped build a community center in Reid.

In 1954 Childs graduated from Manchester College and married Young on 7 June of that year. The union would produce four children—Lisa, Paula, Andrea, and Andrew III—and marked the formalized beginning of Jean's partnered civil rights advocacy with Andrew. Together they moved to southwestern Georgia, where he received his first pastorate at Bethany Congregational Church in Thomasville and Evergreen Congregational Church a few miles away in Beachton. Jean Young assisted her husband in his role as co-chair of the Thomasville voter registration drive organized around the 1956 presidential race between Adlai Stevenson and Dwight Eisenhower.

In 1957 the Youngs moved to Queens, New York, when he was called to serve as a minister in the youth division with the National Council of Churches. She taught in Hartford, Connecticut, and earned a master's degree from Queens College in Flushing, New York, in 1961. Her master's thesis replicated the Swiss psychologist Jean Piaget's child developmental stages experiments. Using her own children as subjects, she demonstrated that her children showed no developmental deficits, indeed exceeding Piaget's timetable. Her findings suggested that disadvantage was more accurately explained as the result of a disadvantaged environment than as the result of innate characteristics—a controversial conclusion given a climate in which social scientific research labeled black children as disadvantaged because they were innately inferior.

Also in 1961, inspired by a NBC television program called "The Nashville Sit-in Story," which described the activities of several leaders of the student arm of the civil rights movement, the Youngs decided to return to the South. By November 1961 they were in Atlanta pursuing their commitment to civil rights, with Andrew Young working closely with MARTIN LUTHER KING JR.'s newly founded Southern Christian Leadership Conference (SCLC). Jean Young helped develop educational materials in citizen education for the SCLC. Together the couple helped register black voters and participated in the 1961 boycott of downtown lunch counters in Atlanta, the 1963 March on Washington for Jobs and Freedom, the 1964 St. Augustine marches, the Selma march which led to the passage of the Voting Rights Act of 1965, and the 1968 Poor People's Campaign in Washington, D.C.

Young continued her commitment to education in several ways. Upon the Youngs' return to Atlanta, the family joined the First Congregational Church and she became a Sunday school teacher. She also served as a classroom teacher, coordinator of elementary and preschool programs for the Atlanta Public School System, and as a leader in the Teacher Corps. Young was a member of the team that helped develop Atlanta Junior College (renamed Atlanta Metropolitan College), serving as an instructor, its first public relations officer, and later, a member of its board of advisers.

In 1978, shortly after Andrew Young's 1977 appointment as U.S. ambassador to the United Nations by President Jimmy Carter, Jean Young was appointed by Carter to chair the National Commission on the International Year of the

Child, 1979, a United Nations program intended to challenge governments and private organizations to focus attention on how well they were meeting the needs of children. The United Nations did not declare a unified action plan, schedule an international conference, or appropriate a large budget. Despite these limitations, under Young's leadership a network of commissions and task forces charged with the mission of developing their own projects for children was established in forty-eight states and four U.S. territories. She also fostered dialogue among nongovernmental organizations. Among those she brought to the table were state coordinators of International Year of the Child committees, representatives from America's African American, Latino, Asian American, and Native American communities, and a national youth advisory panel. The emergence of a national agenda for change in critical areas of children's lives led to new coalitions, projects, funding sources, supporters of children's welfare, and legislation that lived on well beyond their 1979 origins.

When her husband was mayor of Atlanta in the 1980s, she established the Atlanta Task Force on Education and sponsored the Mayor's Scholars Program and the Dream Jamboree, a college and career fair that brought together Atlanta high school seniors and college and trade school recruiters. She was co-founder of the Atlanta-Fulton Commission on Children and Youth, which was charged with the task of youth development by teaching youth how to organize community activities and projects, such as public hearings for Atlanta children and youth, in response to issues affecting their lives.

In July 1991 she was diagnosed with cancer, which led to her death in 1994 at Crawford Long Hospital of Emory University in Atlanta. A public funeral was held at the Atlanta Civic Center. The legacy of Jean Childs Young lives on through her personal and professional contributions to children's welfare, nationally and globally.

FURTHER READING

DeRoche, Andrew J. *Andrew Young: Civil Rights Ambassador* (2003).

Young, Andrea. *Life Lessons My Mother Taught Me* (2000).

Young, Andrew. *An Easy Burden: The Civil Rights Movement and the Transformation of America* (1996).

Obituary: *Atlanta Journal-Constitution*, 17 Sept. 1994.

TRACY R. RONE

Young, Kevin (8 Nov. 1970–), poet, editor, and teacher, was born in Lincoln, Nebraska, to Azzie Young, a chemist and healthcare administrator, and Paul Young, an ophthalmologist. The family moved frequently during his childhood, living in the Boston area, Chicago, Illinois, and Syracuse, New York, before settling in Topeka, Kansas, where Young graduated from high school in 1988. After graduating from Harvard University with an AB in English and American Literature, in 1992 Young received a Stegner Fellowship in poetry at Stanford University. He went on to study at Brown University, where he studied with MICHAEL HARPER. He was the recipient of two fellowships from the MacDowell Colony in 1993 and 1995.

His debut collection of poems, *Most Way Home*, was selected for the National Poetry Series by LUCILLE CLIFTON and published in 1995; it received the John C. Zacharis First Book Award from *Ploughshares* in 1996. That year, Young also received his MFA from Brown. In 2000 Young was editor of the collection *Giant Steps: The New Generation of African American Writers.*

Young describes his second collection of poems, 2001's *To Repel Ghosts*, as a "double album"—in which the sections are divided into discs and sides, like records—inspired by the work of the late artist JEAN-MICHEL BASQUIAT. The *Village Voice* named Young one of their "Writers on the Verge" that year, and he explained the inspiration for the collection. "I saw his work [Basquiat's] in San Francisco, and it haunted me," he told the *Village Voice*'s David Mills. "I had to respond." Of the mammoth 340-page collection, Mills writes: "Young's voice melds LANGSTON HUGHES's lyrical empiricism with John Berryman's humor. His words inhabit the cityscapes Basquiat and his subjects brought to life—from CHARLIE PARKER and Andy Warhol to pugilists JACK JOHNSON and MUHAMMAD ALI" (Mills, 104). The collection was a finalist for the James Laughlin Prize from the Academy of American Poets.

Young's third collection, 2003's *Jelly Roll: A Blues*, shies away from the formal restraints of some blues music (that is, the complicated pattern of repeating choruses) and aims instead to capture the coy mix of pleasure and pain, and joy and despair that embodies the blues. In "Ragtime," for instance, the speaker tells his lover that he loves her "like warm / bread & cold / cuts, butter / sammiches," and later, in "Riff," he laments:

I am all itch,
total, since you done

been gone—zero
sum, empty set—
counting. Calculated.

Young's emotions ranged from sensual to silly to serious in these mostly short-lined, compact poems. In the brief (two-line) "Early Blues," the speaker somewhat humorously complains "Once, I ordered a pair of shoes / But they never came," while "Anthem" begins "God, you are gorgeous— / and gone—" With titles like "Jive," "Bluegrass," "Rhapsody," and "Country (& Western)," the poems themselves transcend readers' expectations of what blues poems can do. *Jelly Roll* was a finalist for both the National Book Award for poetry and the Los Angeles Times Book Award in 2003, and received the Patterson Poetry Prize in 2004. Around this time, Young was editor of the poetry collections *Everyman's Library Blues Poems* (2003) and *John Berryman: Selected Poems* (2004). In 2005 Young was named Atticus Haygood Professor of Creative Writing and English and curator of the Raymond Danowski Poetry Library at Emory University in Atlanta. In May 2005 he married Kate Tuttle, an academic editor, and in 2006 they had a son, Paul McCullough Young. In September 2005 Knopf published a shortened edition of Young's second book, calling it *To Repel Ghosts: The Remix.*

Perhaps one of Young's most notable traits as an author was his willingness to experiment with different forms, not only in individual poems but also in full-length books. He did not merely compile his poems into a book. Instead, he composed a "double album" (in the case of *To Repel Ghosts*), a "blues" (in the case of *Jelly Roll*), and, in *Black Maria*, a "serial noir drama."

Black Maria took its title from the nickname for a police wagon or a hearse. Divided into five "reels," each with its own introductory voiceover, the collection followed the misadventures of singer Delilah Redbone and detective A.K.A. Jones in the fictional noir-tinged Shadowtown. Young structured each reel dramatically to pique readers' curiosity about the characters, making them want to read more. In true cliffhanger form, for instance, the first reel, "Honeymoon Rain," ends with the poem "The Suspects." The poem describes a scene filled with seedy characters: the "boozy, / overdressed dame," the "one-armed pickpocket / with a nose // for the horses," the "Newshound nosing round / the place." "Here comes the bribe," the speaker quips halfway through the poem. Later, the sinister scene is described more clearly:

The once-over
The okie-doke
The moon a thumb-
print pressed
in the black police book
kept by the night
Put your hands
where I can see em

The poem ends with the image of Death as a "well- / dressed doorman, // his pockets stuffed with cash." *Black Maria* traced Delilah Redbone's struggles against the Boss and A.K.A. Jones's struggles to make good on his debts. The couple sneaks around, gets caught, gets separated, and reunites, all in the tight, deliberate lines that characterized Young's style. "The Hideout" opens with Jones admitting he "Woke up dead // tired," and in "Stills" he describes his first encounter with Delilah as "He say, she say / foreplay, amscray." The book ends like an old movie, with poems titled "Farewell," "The End," and "Credits," with Delilah Redbone and A.K.A. Jones walking into the sunset—separately, of course.

In 2006 Young was the editor of the poetry collection *Jazz Poems*, and in 2007 the Providence Black Repertory Theater staged *Black Maria* as a play. Also in 2007 Young's fifth collection of poems, *For the Confederate Dead*, was published by Knopf. In addition to his poetry collections, his work appeared in *Callaloo*, the *Kenyon Review*, the *New Yorker*, the *Paris Review*, *Poetry*, and other magazines and literary journals. He was also the recipient of a Guggenheim Foundation Fellowship in 2003 and received a fellowship from the National Endowment for the Arts in 2005. He was a former assistant professor at the University of Georgia and Ruth Lilly Professor of Poetry at Indiana University.

FURTHER READING

Mills, David. "Writers on the Verge," in the *Village Voice* (2001).

Rowell, Charles H. "An Interview with Kevin Young," in *Callaloo* (1998).

Whitehead, Colson. "A Short Distance to the Blues: A Conversation with Kevin Young," *Poets & Writers* (2003).

MAGGIE GERRITY

Young, Lester (27 Aug. 1909–15 Mar. 1959), jazz musician, was born in Woodville, Mississippi, the son of Willis Handy Young, a musician, and Lizetta (maiden name unknown). "Prez," or "the

President," as BILLIE HOLIDAY dubbed him in the 1930s, spent his early childhood in Algiers, Louisiana, across the river from New Orleans. When his parents divorced in 1919, he moved to Minneapolis with his father, who headed a family band that played in carnivals and vaudeville shows. Young played drums in the band, but he changed to the alto saxophone at age thirteen. Unwilling to tour the South and suffer the racist humiliations that accompanied such trips, he left the band in 1927. He played briefly with WALTER PAGE's Blue Devils and Art Bronson's Bostonians, where he switched to the tenor saxophone. In 1931 he settled again in Minneapolis and then toured with the Blue Devils in 1932. When they disbanded, he moved to Kansas City, traveling and playing with a variety of groups, including KING OLIVER's band. He also was married for the first time in 1931, to a white Jewish girl named Bess Cooper. They had one child, but shortly after giving birth, his wife underwent surgery and bled to death. Young was grief-stricken. His constant traveling forced him to place his infant daughter with foster parents, but he always maintained close contact with her.

Early in 1934 Young joined the COUNT BASIE band for several months, but he left in March to join FLETCHER HENDERSON's band. One night he had come to hear Henderson's tenor player, COLEMAN HAWKINS, but Hawkins failed to appear, and Young ended up replacing him for the evening. Henderson was impressed enough to hire Young as a replacement when Hawkins later left the band, but the job lasted only a few months. Young's style and tone were so different from Hawkins's that band members complained, and Henderson's wife spent hours playing the band's records for Young in an effort to teach him how to play like Hawkins. By 1936 Young was back with Basie.

He made his first recordings with a Basie-led group in November of that year, immediately producing several classic solos in tunes like "Lady Be Good," "Shoe Shine Boy," "Boogie Woogie," and "Evenin'." He had already created a fully developed style. Influenced by Jimmy Dorsey and especially by Frankie Trumbauer on C-melody saxophone and by Bix Beiderbecke, he had a light tone, almost without vibrato, a breathtaking sense of melodic beauty, rhythmically relaxed phrasing, and a linear approach to improvising that contrasted sharply with the more harmonic, chordal approach of Hawkins. He played in a ceaselessly variegated, sometimes flurrying, unexpectedly accented legato style that could be said to mark the beginning of modern jazz, and his solos unfolded in a daring, freshly logical, and strikingly balanced flow of ideas. Like all great jazz playing, his solos told a story, and there is a sense of inevitability and "rightness" in them that commands total attention.

Young also left a personal imprint on the jazz world. Musicians loved him, and he epitomized the sense of "hip" that characterized many black communities of the South and Southwest at that time. He specialized in giving other musicians nicknames (he named Billie Holiday "Lady Day"), and he invented a myriad cryptic expressions that dotted his language; he had "big eyes," for instance, for things he liked, or "no eyes" for those he did not. He loved to play practical jokes, such as ringing a bell onstage when a band member made a mistake. But Young also was introverted, a shy man whose sensitivity and concern for the underdog endeared him to his colleagues and left him vulnerable to the pain and humiliation of the racist society he lived in. He spoke frequently of his anger at this racism, and he sought release in alcohol and marijuana, although he avoided hard drugs. Music was his real life, offering him the total escape he desired. Equally therapeutic was his close, platonic friendship with Holiday, whom he recorded with frequently during the late 1930s. His soft, tender accompaniments on tunes like "All of Me" reveal a profoundly empathetic artistic partnership.

Young stayed with the Basie band through the 1930s, touring and making several hundred recordings and live broadcasts. He also played clarinet occasionally during these years; even Benny Goodman expressed admiration for Young's skill on the instrument. The death of his friend and fellow saxophonist Herschel Evans in early 1939, however, affected him deeply, and business and artistic differences led him to leave Basie in 1940 to form a small band of his own. He later co-led a group with his brother Lee Young, a drummer, playing lengthy engagements in New York City and Los Angeles. He also freelanced widely until rejoining Basie by December 1943, and he recorded a series of widely influential sessions for Keynote Records in late 1943 and early 1944. He now began to attract wider public notice, winning the *Down Beat* poll for tenor saxophone in 1944. Beginning in 1942 his playing underwent the first of two major stylistic changes, as his sound became broader and heavier and his style more overtly emotional.

In September 1944 Young was drafted. Army discipline was antithetical to his personality, and he quickly alienated his superiors with his indifference. They confiscated his saxophone and refused to allow him to play in the jazz band at Fort McClellan, Alabama, where he was stationed. After being hospitalized for a minor injury, Young became addicted to painkillers. When a white officer discovered a picture of Young's second wife, Mary (who was white and whom he had married in 1937), he also found pain medication that Young had obtained illegally. The army subsequently court-martialed Young, gave him a dishonorable discharge, and sentenced him to a year in the detention barracks at Fort Gordon, Georgia. The entire experience left him emotionally scarred.

After his discharge, Young made a series of recordings for the Los Angeles–based Aladdin company, producing classic performances on such tunes as "These Foolish Things." Starting in 1946 he toured almost annually with Norman Granz's well-paying Jazz at the Philharmonic. He appeared often with groups of his own and as a guest with Basie's band, and his popularity rose dramatically. His domestic life became more settled. He was married for a third time, to another woman named Mary, in 1946; the two moved into a house in Queens, New York, and had two children. But Young also continued to drink and smoke heavily, and by now he was suffering from malnutrition, alcoholism, and cirrhosis of the liver. Although he kept his musical commitments, he grew suspicious, uncommunicative, and increasingly uncomfortable around whites. As he noted in a Paris interview shortly before he died, "They want everybody who's a Negro to be an Uncle Tom, or Uncle Remus, or Uncle Sam, and I can't make it."

Some critics claim that Young's later recordings, particularly those made after 1950, were vastly inferior to those he made during the late 1930s. But while his style changed, it was not necessarily inferior. He continued to explore new musical conceptions; he preferred to work with younger musicians, and by the late 1940s his groups were playing in a more modern, bop-influenced style. His tone also became fuller and rounder, partly as a result of his use of a new mouthpiece and his temporary adoption of plastic reeds. Although his tone weakened after 1950, he often played with his old self-assurance. This was particularly true when he was surrounded by musicians of a similar aesthetic. The pianist JOHN LEWIS often played with Young in 1951 and 1952, and Lewis's light, linear style allowed Young to return to his light tone and float airily over the accompaniment. He found a similarly sympathetic partner in 1952 recordings with OSCAR PETERSON, and in two wonderful 1956 quartet sessions with TEDDY WILSON on piano. His live sessions with a trio at Olivia's Patio Lounge in Washington, D.C., contain some of his best later work. But after 1953 Young's recordings were less consistent. He suffered from painful toothaches and sporadic epileptic attacks, and he was hospitalized several times for alcohol-related problems. He moved out of his home and into the Alvin Hotel, across the street from Birdland, where he often played in his later years. His last great moment came on the December 1957 television show *The Sound of Jazz* in a poignant reunion with Lady Day. Young was so ill that the show's producers considered canceling his appearance, and they decided to allow him only a brief solo. When his time came, he rose and played an exquisite forty-five-note chorus on Holiday's classic "Fine and Mellow." The two never saw each other again.

Young seemed to recover a bit during the final year of his life, reducing his drinking and gaining weight, and in January 1959 he opened an engagement at the Blue Note Club in Paris. But he stopped eating and began to drink heavily again. Ill and in great pain, he returned to New York on 13 March and died of heart failure two days later in his hotel room.

Lester Young once said that originality should be the goal of both life and art. He remains the most original, influential figure in the history of jazz between LOUIS ARMSTRONG and CHARLIE PARKER. He spawned dozens of imitators and complained that he could not go anywhere without hearing himself. His diatonic style pointed the way toward the bop era and even to the modal jazz of the 1950s and 1960s. His playing reflected his inner self. A kind, gentle man, he sought the same qualities in his music: "It's got to be sweetness, you dig?" And more than anything else, his playing reflected the essence of great jazz: "The blues? Great Big Eyes! … Everybody has to play the blues and everybody has them too."

FURTHER READING

Büchmann-Møller, Frank. *You Just Fight for Your Life: The Story of Lester Young* (1990).

McDonough, John. *Lester Young* (1980).

Porter, Lewis. *Lester Young* (1985).

Porter, Lewis, ed. *A Lester Young Reader* (1991).

Schuller, Gunther. *The Swing Era: The Development of Jazz, 1930–1945* (1989).

This entry is taken from the *American National Biography* and is published here with the permission of the American Council of Learned Societies.

RONALD P. DUFOUR

Young, Nathan Benjamin (15 Sept. 1862–19 July 1933), educational leader of the early twentieth century, was born in Newborn, Alabama, a rural town near the bustling coastal city of Mobile, to a slave mother, Susan Smith. Nathan's mother was born in 1842 on a slave plantation in Chatham, Virginia, where her owner died around her fourteenth birthday. Upon his death, Smith was given the choice of being sold to a local owner who was known for his abusive nature or being sold to a slave trader, who would potentially sell her away from her family. After some convincing from her mother, Susan decided that her best option was to be sold to the slave trader, who eventually marched her and a number of other slaves to Alabama.

Once in Alabama, the slave trader sold Susan to a Newborn cotton planter, who in turn sold her to the plantation's overseer in 1862, the same year of Nathan's birth. At the summation of the war, Susan traveled with Nathan to Tuscaloosa, where she met and eventually married a local black man by the name of Frank Young. It was Frank who served as Nathan's father figure, not only by bequeathing young Nathan with his surname, but also by helping Susan to mold him into one of the most respected black educational leaders of his day.

Newly freed and married, Susan desired for Nathan to receive an education, an ambition that her son made a reality in short order. First, he was enrolled in several rural schools for black youth in the Alabama countryside. Once Nathan grasped the three Rs, he went on to receive his first formal schooling at Alabama's Talladega College. It was during his time at Talladega that Nathan gained his first classical-type education in the college's normal school. Shortly after earning his high school diploma, Nathan accepted a position as principal of a secondary school in Jackson, Mississippi. After only two years as a high school administrator, Nathan quickly understood the need for advanced studies. This led the educator to Oberlin College in Ohio, where he received one of the finest liberal arts educations available in the United States for whites and blacks. At Oberlin he embraced the philosophy that a liberal arts education for the African American community was equally as important as vocational studies. Nathan earned a bachelor's degree in 1888 and a master's degree in 1891. Thereafter, he returned to work in his native state, this time as principal of a black elementary school in Birmingham.

During his second stint in Alabama, Nathan's focus quickly shifted from education to his personal life. Particularly, the educator strove to establish a family. The first step in Nathan's family development was laid in 1891 when he married the former Emma Mae Garette of Selma. To their union eventually came Nathan's first two children, Nathan B. Young Jr. and Gareth Young. Shortly after his family unit was in place, a great career opportunity was presented to Nathan. BOOKER T. WASHINGTON, one of the most influential black educators of the late nineteenth and early twentieth centuries, extended him an offer to teach history and English at the Tuskegee Institute. At first, Nathan enjoyed great success in his new position, leading Washington to promote him as head of the Academic Department and as teacher of pedagogy. Nathan labored in this capacity from 1893 to 1897.

However, Young's belief that liberal arts education should carry equal weight as vocational instruction led him into direct confrontation with Washington. In a clear rebuke to Young's approach to leading the Academic Department at the Tuskegee Institute, Washington lambasted his understudy. "You do not respect authority," Washington asserted, "and this defect is fatal in an institution where the will and policy of the Principal are expected to be carried out even in the remotest corner of the school in the actions of teachers and students through the head of a department." While it appears that the two men parted on a sour note, Young later recalled that his time working for the Wizard of Tuskegee was a privilege and inspirational although "it became necessary occasionally to disagree with his educational views and methods." Although the two men separated in 1897, historical evidence reveals that Washington was largely responsible for Nathan's selection in 1901 as the second president of the Florida State Normal and Industrial School for Negroes (FSNIS), the precursor to Florida A&M University.

Prior to that selection, however, Nathan accepted a teaching position at the Georgia Industrial School and College (GISC) in Savannah in 1897, which was under the direction of RICHARD R. WRIGHT SR. At GISC, Nathan served as a professor of economics and moral philosophy. While in this position Young once again found himself dissatisfied and at odds with his supervisors because members of the board of trustees wanted to emphasize industrial education. The presidency of the FSNIS came open after the state of Florida ousted Thomas DeSalle Tucker, the institution's first principal, for not adhering to Booker T. Washington's idea of black higher education. While searching for someone to replace the liberal arts–minded Tucker, William N. Sheats, the superintendent for public instruction in the state of Florida, forwarded Washington correspondence in search of a candidate he felt would fit the Tuskegee principal's mold. Ironically, Washington gave Nathan Young a strong recommendation to lead Florida's only publically funded historically black college in the midst of the Jim Crow era.

Under Young's leadership, FSNIS underwent enormous change, with the first being its name. To secure more federal funds from the Morrill Fund, which guaranteed monies to land grant institutions, Young changed the name of the school to Florida Agricultural and Mechanical College for Negroes (FAMC). Along with the name change, the addition of academic programs satisfied the Morrill Fund committee, and the college received an additional $5,994.79 from the land grant by 1902. Two years later, Nathan's wife Emma died of fever, leaving the college administrator single with two children. The bereaved president only remained single for one year. He married the former Margaret Buckley in 1905. Their union produced three children, William, Frank, and Julia Young.

For the next twenty years, Nathan served as the president of FAMC in the midst of a political climate where white state legislators required that his institution's focus remain limited to industrial education. Nevertheless, during those years he was able to disguise his liberal arts agenda by publically placing more emphasis on his vocational programs. Nonetheless, by 1921 Cary Augustus Hardee, Florida's newly elected governor, initiated a political attack on Young for his pro–liberal arts agenda at FAMC. This attack ended on 3 June 1923 when Young announced that he was leaving the college immediately to assume the presidency of Lincoln University in Jefferson City, Missouri. Nathan reflected on his time in Florida and the manner of his treatment by the southern white politicians as follows: "This is the way the South treats Negroes who are men once its gets them in power. There are few colored state schools left in the South whose presidents dare to call their souls their own."

Once at Lincoln, Nathan found that the battle against liberal arts education was not confined to the Deep South, and he was removed from his position as president of the Missouri HBCU in 1927. Nevertheless, in 1929 with the election of a new governor that had a more progressive agenda for black education, Young was reseated as the president of Lincoln. His second stint at the university was also short-lived, and Nathan was ousted for the last time in 1931. Notwithstanding the circumstances surrounding his departure from Florida, Young remained attached to the state. In fact, at the age of seventy, he moved back to the Sunshine State to close out his life. Under his daughter's care, he died in Tampa on 19 July 1933. Nathan Benjamin Young is remembered for his continuous fight to make a space for liberal arts education alongside vocational instruction in black higher education.

FURTHER READING

Ellis, Reginald. "Nathan B. Young: Florida A&M College's Second President and His Relationships with White Public Officials." In *Go Sound the Trumpet! Selections in Florida's African American History*, ed. David H. Jackson and Canter Brown (2005).

Holland, Antonio F. *Nathan B. Young and the Struggle over Black Higher Education* (2006).

REGINALD K. ELLIS

Young, Plummer Bernard (27 July 1884–9 Oct. 1962), newspaper editor and publisher and civic leader, was born in Littleton, North Carolina, the son of Sallie Adams and former slave Winfield Scott Young, a businessman, newspaper editor, and officeholder. Young founded his own monthly paper, the *Argus*, in 1904. He attended St. Augustine's College in Raleigh, North Carolina, at the same time that he taught printing and produced the school's publications. In 1906 he married Eleanor Louise White, the adopted daughter of the college's president, and went to work as foreman at his father's printing shop. The next year, after the birth of the first of their two children, the couple moved to Norfolk, Virginia's second largest city. There Young began work as plant foreman for the *Lodge Journal and Guide*, a weekly newspaper published by the Supreme Lodge Knights of Gideon, an African American fraternal order of which his father was a member.

Young spent the rest of his life in the newspaper business in Norfolk. By 1909 he had become editor, and in 1910 he bought the paper from the Gideons and changed its name to the *Norfolk Journal and*

Guide. Over the years Young built up the paper until it had the largest circulation of any African American weekly published in the South. From a four-page paper with a circulation of about 1,000 at the time he took it over, he transformed it into an eight-page paper with a circulation of 4,000 by 1920 and a sixteen-page paper with a circulation of 28,000 by 1935. In the 1940s circulation topped 60,000. Young incorporated the business in 1913 and became president. His wife was treasurer, his brother Henry Cheatham Young was plant manager and then secretary, and his father was circulation manager. Young was publisher of the *Journal and Guide* for fifty-two years, from 1910 until his death, though he turned over most of the responsibility to his sons in 1946.

Young allied himself with BOOKER T. WASHINGTON in his early years in Norfolk and continued to take an accommodationist approach to civil rights after Washington's death in 1915. "Build up, don't tear down," he exhorted. But as times changed, so did his approach to civil rights. In 1917 he organized a local chapter of the National Association for the Advancement of Colored People (NAACP). Young came to politics as a committed Republican, a position he maintained into the 1920s. Then he exemplified the switch among African Americans to the Democratic Party. The Republican Party in Virginia adopted a "lily-white" hue, and in 1921 a group of black Virginians responded by running a "lily-black" slate for state office. The group offered Young the nomination for the lieutenant governorship, but Young had misgivings about the strategy, and he was also miffed that the gubernatorial nomination had gone to his rival, JOHN MITCHELL, editor of the *Richmond Planet*, so he declined, though he and the others later joined forces. Young served as a delegate to the 1924 Republican National Convention in Cleveland, but the party's near exclusion of black delegates from the 1928 convention in Kansas City led him to support Democrat Alfred E. Smith's candidacy that year. He supported Franklin D. Roosevelt in 1932, embraced the New Deal, and attended Roosevelt's second inaugural in 1936. Young served from 1943 to 1944 on the Fair Employment Practices Committee, which President Roosevelt had established in 1941 in response to A. PHILIP RANDOLPH's planned march on Washington.

Young entered into the civic life of his adopted city and state, as he promoted his newspaper as a voice for black Norfolk and the South. He and his wife joined the Grace Protestant Episcopal Church as soon as they arrived in Norfolk; he was elected to the vestry in 1910 and later served for many years on the board of trustees. At one time or another he served as vice president of the statewide Negro Organization Society, led the Negro Forward Movement as it pushed for improvements in Norfolk, presided over the board of the Norfolk Community Hospital, and chaired the advisory committee to the Norfolk Redevelopment and Housing Authority. Young served on the Howard University board of trustees for twenty-one years, from 1934 to 1955, and chaired it for six years, from 1943 to 1949. He was also a board member at Hampton Institute and at St. Paul's College.

Young used the *Journal and Guide* to campaign against many of the ills that beset black Virginians. Between the revival of the Ku Klux Klan in 1915 and passage in 1928 of a state antilynching law, he campaigned against lynching. He publicized a criminal proceeding in Norfolk in 1931 that led not only to the black defendant's being acquitted on the charge of rape but also to the imprisonment of his white accuser for perjury. From the 1920s into the 1940s he pushed for better housing, and he campaigned to pave dirt roads in black neighborhoods. He editorialized against the white Democratic primary in Virginia, until a court decision invalidated it in 1929 (*West v. Bliley et al.*), and against the poll tax as an impediment to black voting. Concerned about scant employment opportunities for black citizens, by December 1916 Young was developing an approach that later emerged as the "double-duty dollar" or "buy where you work," a precursor to the "don't shop where you can't work" movement that swept many American cities in the 1930s. In 1941, though troubled by A. Philip Randolph's March on Washington Movement, Young campaigned to open defense jobs in the Norfolk area to black workers. Meanwhile, Young's home was a perennial meeting place for discussing strategy and ideology when JAMES WELDON JOHNSON, WALTER WHITE, ROY WILKINS, and other NAACP leaders visited Norfolk, as well as when the National Urban League's WHITNEY YOUNG did. Correspondents for his paper included NANNIE HELEN BURROUGHS, GORDON BLAINE HANCOCK, and CARTER G. WOODSON.

Young hesitated to attack segregation directly, but he strived to secure greater equality within the framework of "separate but equal." On 21 June 1913 he editorialized about segregated streetcar transportation, "We do not object to separate cars, but we want equal accommodations." He was a founding member of the Southern Commission on Interracial Cooperation in 1919 and its successor organization, the Southern Regional Council, in 1944. In the 1930s he campaigned for such public facilities as parks, bathing beaches, and a new elementary school for black residents of Norfolk. During World War II he pushed successfully for the appointment of black police officers in Norfolk. He involved himself in the establishment of a black community college in Norfolk in 1935 (later Norfolk State University) and chaired its advisory board. In the 1930s and 1940s he publicized the inferior physical facilities and teachers' salaries that characterized black public schools, and he fostered the breakthrough court case (MELVIN OVENUS) ALSTON *v. Board of Education of the City of Norfolk*, which in 1940 secured the principle of salary equalization.

"Mr. P.B.," as he was called, edited a newspaper about which it was often said, "See what the *Guide* says about it." Tall and fair-skinned in appearance, grave and unemotional in demeanor, proud yet cautious in character, pragmatic yet prodding in politics, Young achieved prosperity, respect, and influence. He received numerous honors, and the National Newspaper Publishers Association named him Distinguished Editor of the Year in 1960. Eleanor Young died in 1946, and Young married Josephine Tucker Moseley in 1950. After he died in Norfolk, his sons carried on the family business.

FURTHER READING

Suggs, Henry Lewis. *P. B. Young, Newspaperman: Race, Politics, and Journalism in the New South, 1910–62* (1988).

Obituaries: *Richmond Times-Dispatch*, 10 Oct. 1962; *Washington Post*, 11 Oct. 1962; *New York Times*, 12 Oct. 1962; *Norfolk Journal and Guide*, 13 Oct. 1962.

This entry is taken from the *American National Biography* and is published here with the permission of the American Council of Learned Societies.

PETER WALLENSTEIN

Young, Purvis (4 Feb. 1943–24 April 2010), a self-taught artist who rose from the slums to prominence as a muralist, was born in the historically black Liberty City section of Miami. His Bahamian mother encouraged him to draw spontaneously as a child. Unfortunately, he did not stick with drawing and, at eighteen, received a four-year sentence in Raiford State Prison in Florida for armed robbery. While behind bars, Young discovered a love for the arts. He started to draw again. Reading a book on Chicago mural artists shortly after his release prompted Young to realize that he could paint rather than stand on a street corner all day. He quickly began drawing and collaging books, taping up sketches and paintings on his walls, and covering scraps of wood, bottles, and carpet rolls with washes of color and exuberant figuration.

Young is a product of the popular mural movement that emerged in the late 1960s in black, Chicano, Latino, and other ethnic neighborhoods. He saw that ordinary people could paint the stories of their own communities and give them mythic importance. His first public project, consisting of hundreds of pictures painted with house paint on plywood that he affixed to boarded-up buildings along a subsection of Miami's historically black Overtown, appeared in the early 1970s. The name of the stretch of road, Goodbread Alley, referred to a bakery that had been destroyed, along with many other businesses and homes, by unrealized urban development plans and a highway through the heart of the neighborhood. The paintings reflected Young's emotions. He has spent most of his life in Overtown and uses art to channel both his fury and his compassion.

Young is a sophisticated painter who cites Rembrandt, El Greco, and van Gogh as his favorite artists because they paint their feelings. In 1979 he received a fellowship from the National Endowment for the Arts because of the high quality of his art. Yet Young has a very complex relationship with anything that smacks of commercialism and control by white people, or to use his term, "blue eyes." As he paints, Young prefers to listen to public broadcasting, particularly television shows on Africa and American Indians, as well as jazz and classical music stations because, in his view, the news and history as told by white people omit the black viewpoint. A very prolific artist, he paints people who are not happy and who are reaching (often literally) for a better life. His paintings present a perspective that is rooted in an African American view of things. Young also prefers to work with found materials on the grounds that you do not have to pay anyone for them. In short, he is a very race-conscious and fiercely independent artist who believes that a white-dominated establishment is determined to control black culture.

As a fairly inarticulate and awkward man, the contrast between Young's talent and his social status has been the controlling factor in his reception as an artist. Critics charge that his work has remained essentially unchanged because he has not developed the critical sense needed for self-editing. This lack of artistic evolution has been noted by John Ollman, director of the Fleisher/Ollman Gallery in Philadelphia, which represents a significant body of Young's work. Ollman observes that Young's paintings are less cluttered than in the past, chiefly because collectors purchase them before Young can add too much. The artist is not evolving possibly because he is an outsider and, as such, is somewhat isolated. Young identifies himself as an aborigine of the ghetto and claims that his instincts are keyed into this environment, thereby embracing his outsider status.

Shortly after the Goodbread Alley exhibit, Barbara Young (no relation), head of the art section of the Dade County Public Library, observed Young poring over the art books and drawing his own pictures. She gave him the opportunity to paint a mural on the outside walls of the Overtown Branch Library (now destroyed). In the 1980s, Young received a commission from the Dade County Art in Public Places Trust to install a work in the Northside Metrorail Station. He has had more than two dozen solo exhibitions in France, Canada, and the United States. His work hangs in the Corcoran Gallery of Art in Washington, D.C.; the Houston Museum of Fine Art; the New Orleans Museum of Art; and many other major institutions.

In 2010, Young died in Miami of cardiac arrest and pulmonary edema. He was 67.

FURTHER READING
Blazier, Wendy, ed. *Purvis Young: Paintings from the Street* (2006).
Wertkin, Gerard, et al. *Self-Taught Artists of the 20th Century: An American Anthology* (1998).
Obituary: *New York Times,* 24 Apr. 2010. http://www. nytimes.com/2010/04/24/arts/24young.html.

CARYN E. NEUMANN

Young, Roger Arliner (1899–9 Nov. 1964), zoologist, was born in Clifton Forge, Virginia, to parents whose names have not been recorded. When she was a child, Young's family moved to Burgettstown, Pennsylvania. In 1916, when she was seventeen, Young entered Howard University in Washington, D.C., to study music. In what would prove to be a recurrent pattern in Young's life, she studied hard and long but struggled to achieve high or even passing grades. In 1921, however, she took her first

science course, with the head of Howard's zoology department ERNEST EVERETT JUST, who encouraged her to pursue a career in science after her graduation in 1923.

Young remained at Howard, where she was appointed assistant professor of zoology and began working as a research assistant for Just, while also studying on a part-time basis in the summer for a master's degree at the University of Chicago. In spite of her hectic schedule her grades improved dramatically, and on 12 September 1924 Young became the first African American woman scientist to publish in her field of zoology, when her article, "On the Excretory Apparatus in the Paramecium," appeared in *Science*, one of the most important journals in the sciences. Young's study of the paramecium, an aquatic single-celled microorganism, preceded by two months the publication of similar findings by Dmitry Nasonov, the world-renowned Russian cell physiologist. Largely on the strength of her *Science* article, which was referenced in many academic journals, Young was invited in 1926 to join Sigma Xi, the national honor society of the biological sciences. Shortly afterward the University of Chicago awarded Young a master's degree in zoology.

In the summer of 1927, while still at Howard, Young began work with her mentor Just at the Marine Biological Laboratory at Woods Hole, Massachusetts. There she studied a range of marine organisms and began to focus on a study of the effects of ultraviolet light on marine eggs, including *Arbacia, Chaetopterus, Nereis,* and *Platynereis*. She also worked closely with Just on a study of the role of electrolytes in hydration and dehydration. Meanwhile the highly regarded Just introduced Young and her work to a number of notable zoologists, including Professor L. L. Woodruff of Yale University and Professor C. M. Child of the University of Chicago. Woods Hole also presented Young with a vibrant community of talented and ambitious young zoologists, and she apparently fit in well there, in social affairs as well as in the laboratory. Even though most of her colleagues had enjoyed more extensive training in the sciences than she had, Young had greater experience of life in the classroom. The only black woman at Woods Hole, she was also one of only a handful of African Americans pursuing doctoral studies in the natural sciences at that time.

In January 1930, however, Young's promising career was delayed by failure in her doctoral exams. Perhaps because of severe eyestrain, a consequence of her experiments using ultraviolet light, as well as anxiety, she proved unable to answer her examiner's questions, even on topics she had previously shown expertise in at Howard, Woods Hole, and as a master's student at Chicago. Rejected by the Chicago doctoral program, Young suffered a severe mental collapse. Establishing a pattern that would recur in later life Young ran away from the academic world, perhaps to look after her mother, who was suffering from a long illness, and whom she had struggled to support on her meager stipend. "I seem to have lost my grip all round," she later wrote a friend (Manning, *Black Apollo*, 218). Young attributed her failure to the fact that her duties at Howard and Woods Hole had left her little time to study. She also appears to have blamed Just—with whom she may have had an affair—for his frequent foreign travel, which left her as the primary zoology lecturer at Howard and as sole department administrator. These duties, Young believed, had required her to give up a prized doctoral fellowship.

Young later returned to Howard to teach and perform administrative duties, but her relationship with Just was increasingly strained. The reasons were partly professional—Just believed that Young's failures reflected badly on himself, since he had so actively championed her—but mostly personal. Just, who was married, reportedly began an affair with a white woman he had met while serving as a visiting lecturer in Europe in 1930. Young intercepted mail from this woman to Just, and confronted him with it. She also revealed the contents of the letter to members of the Howard administration, which did little to enhance either Just's reputation or her own. Just, for his part, accused Young of incompetence, carelessness, frequent absences, and poor teaching methods, and he dismissed her in 1936.

Though it was intended to be the end of her academic career, Just's sacking of Young may instead have revitalized it. She transferred to the University of Pennsylvania and produced four scientific papers between 1935 and 1938, working with Professor L. V. Heilbrunn, whom she had met at Woods Hole. When Penn awarded Young the Ph.D. degree in 1940, she became the first black woman to receive a doctorate in zoology. Her dissertation examined "The Indirect Effect of Roentgen Rays on Certain Marine Eggs" of simple marine organisms. Upon receiving her doctorate, Young moved to North Carolina in 1940 to teach zoology, first at the North Carolina College for Negroes in Durham and then as head of the biology department at Shaw University in Raleigh, North Carolina. Young was also prominent in civil rights activities in the state during World War II. Energetically and successfully she campaigned to increase NAACP membership in North Carolina. Young's financial and mental health problems continued, however, and her relationships with fellow faculty members at Shaw were cool. She returned to the North Carolina College for Negroes in 1947 but only taught there for a year.

Between 1947 and 1962 Young held temporary teaching appointments at Paul Quinn College in Dallas, Texas, and Jackson State University in Mississippi, and also as a kindergarten teacher in Waco, Texas. Increasingly she suffered from depression, particularly after the death of her mother in 1953. While in Mississippi in the late 1950s she received treatment at the Mississippi State Mental Asylum. Discharged from that institution in December 1962, Young secured an appointment as a visiting lecturer at Southern University in Baton Rouge, Louisiana. Young died penniless in New Orleans. She had never married. Although Dr. Young's work as a zoologist in the 1920s and 1930s was largely ignored at the time of her death, she was posthumously recognized for her pioneering efforts as a black woman in the academic sciences.

FURTHER READING

Manning, Kenneth. *Black Apollo of Science: The Life of Ernest Everett Just* (1983).
Manning, Kenneth. "Roger Arliner Young: Scientist," *Sage: A Scholarly Journal on Black Women* 6:2 (Fall 1989).

STEVEN J. NIVEN

Young, Rosa Jinsey (14 May 1890–30 June 1971), Lutheran educator and founder of schools for African Americans, was born in Rosebud, Wilcox County, Alabama, the fourth of ten children of the Reverend Grant Young, an itinerant minister in the African Methodist Episcopal Church, and his wife Nancy, whose maiden name is unknown. The poverty so common in rural Alabama at the time defined Rosa's early life, as she and her siblings picked cotton to supplement their father's meager income. Determined that their children would have opportunities to break the cycle of poverty, Young's parents provided for their children's education. Rosa outperformed her siblings, gaining the title of "family teacher." After finishing public school, Rosa attended Payne University in Selma, Alabama, where she distinguished herself by becoming the valedictorian of her class. She titled her valedictory, delivered on 1 June 1909, "Serve the People." In it she encapsulated what became her life's work. Education, she said, "has opened a fountain of knowledge for the colored youth of my race. Good service is an unfailing guide to success. ... There is nothing more reputable to a race or nation than Christian service. So let us not hesitate, but grasp every opportunity that will enable us to do some good for others" (Young, 41–42).

Young immediately began creating her own opportunities. By 1912 she had established a small private school that initially totaled seven pupils but soon grew to 215 students. It expanded so quickly that it outstripped its resources and jeopardized its future. Appeals to a number of church agencies resulted in no immediate help. In a move that changed Young's life, she wrote to Booker T. Washington of Tuskegee Institute, who suggested she approach the Evangelical Lutheran Synodical Conference, specifically its largest member, the Lutheran Church–Missouri Synod (LCMS), for help. On 27 October 1915 Young wrote to the Reverend C. F. Drewes, asking if "your conference will take our school under your auspices" and noting that "both white and colored folk are interested in this school" (Young, 104). While the LCMS was still a largely German-speaking church body, it had been interested in parochial school work from its inception in 1847. The synod sent the Reverend Nils J. Bakke (1853–1921) to meet with Young. By this time the sixty-year-old Bakke, an immigrant who spoke German and English in addition to his native Norwegian, had been involved in mission work in the South, including among African Americans, for more than thirty years. Bakke immediately impressed Young, and though she had been baptized in the African Methodist Episcopal Church, she soon became a Lutheran. Bakke's arrival in Alabama provided Young with an advocate and a partner (he and his successors taught the formal religion classes that led to confirmation in the Lutheran Church), which allowed the school to expand and thrive.

Young was remarkably active over the course of her fifty-year ministry to her church and community. She started at least thirteen schools in congregations and missions, including twelve Alabama sites: Christ, Rosebud; St. Paul, Oak Hill; Our Savior, Possum Bend; St. Andrew, Vredenburgh; St. James, Buena Vista; Mt. Olive, Tinela; Mt. Carmel, Midway; Zion, Tait's Place; Bethany, Nyland; St. Phillip, Catherine; Gethsemane, Hamburg; and Grace, Ingomore. Several of the congregations and schools continued to operate in the early twenty-first century.

Young, however, is best remembered for her role in helping establish the Alabama Lutheran Academy and Junior College in Selma, Alabama, now Concordia College, Selma. The academy was founded as a specifically African American institution whose mission was to train pastors and teachers for the Lutheran Church. Classes began in 1922, and the campus was dedicated in 1925. In 1983 the school received full accreditation as a junior college from the Commission on Colleges of the Southern Association of Colleges and Schools and in 1994 was accredited as a baccalaureate degree–granting institution.

Young's impact on the LCMS was substantial. At its 2004 convention the LCMS recognized "the pioneer work of Dr. Rosa Jinsey Young" and its importance for the mission of the synod, particularly among African Americans (LCMS Proceedings, 2004, Res. 2-06, 125). In 1961 the faculty of Concordia Theological Seminary in Springfield, Illinois, awarded her an honorary doctorate. Noting her "dedicated, unselfish and intelligent service to the Lutheran church," the seminary also recognized that she was "probably the first woman to be awarded an honorary degree by a Lutheran Seminary" (PR Release, CTS, 1961).

Such recognition from a conservative church body at a time when the question of integration increasingly came to the forefront of American society is striking. Young's schools had been largely segregated (apart from the white clergy that taught in them), specifically established for African Americans. She seems to have been guarded on the question, reportedly believing in integration, but thinking that neither whites nor blacks were fully prepared for it. Social and political tools would not solve the integration problem, Young believed; it was God's working through human hearts that would accomplish these goals.

That work summed up Young's life, the story she told in her autobiography, *Light in the Dark Belt* (1929). That perspective is captured in a letter to E. A. Wescott, president of the Selma Academy (6 Oct. 1942): "I have given my life for this work. I began this work when I was quite young in the morning of my life and have given all my life to its cause. ... Yes, God is still working in his own way with regards to this mission. We are on the high seas. We do not see nor know where we shall land. All I am doing is looking to God. Trusting in God. I will not be surprised at nothing that happens nows [sic]." Rosa Young died at age eighty-one.

FURTHER READING

Young's personal correspondence and the records of her life are at the Concordia Historical Institute, Department of Archives and History of the Lutheran Church–Missouri Synod, St. Louis, Mo.

Young, Rosa. *Light in the Dark Belt: The Story of Rosa Young as Told by Herself* (1929).

Dickinson, Richard C. *Roses and Thorns: The Centennial Edition of Black Lutheran Mission and Ministry in The Lutheran Church–Missouri Synod* (1977).

Gude, George J. "The Home Mission Work of the Evangelical Lutheran Synodical Conference: A Description and Evaluation," ThD thesis, Concordia Seminary, St. Louis, Mo. (1991).

Johnson, Jeff G. *Black Christians: The Untold Lutheran Story* (1991).

King, Robert H., ed. *African-Americans and the Local Church* (1996).

Lueking, F. Dean. *Mission in the Making* (1964).

LAWRENCE R. RAST JR.

Young, Trummy (12 Jan. 1912–10 Sept. 1984), jazz trombonist, was born James Osborne Young in Savannah, Georgia. His father was a railroad worker and his mother was a schoolteacher and seamstress (both names unknown). His uncle was a trombonist who played with JAMES REESE EUROPE's ragtime band. After moving to Richmond, Virginia, following his father's death in 1918, Young began playing trumpet and then trombone in the school band and took lessons from John Nick, a brass teacher from the Jenkins Orphanage Band. Young left school before graduation and moved to Washington, D.C., where he took a job as an elevator operator and began to play music professionally, first with Frank Betters and then with Booker Coleman's Hot Chocolates. Young also played with the Hardy Brothers Orchestra and Elmer Calloway before joining the band of drummer Tommy Myles, who gave Young his nickname "Trummy" (likely a reference to the trombone, the only instrument he played after turning professional). In early 1933, while in Washington for an engagement, the pianist EARL HINES heard the Myles group and was so impressed with its sound that he hired Myles's arranger and tenor saxophonist JIMMY MUNDY for his own band. Once established, Mundy suggested that Hines also hire Young, who joined the band in October at their regular stand in Chicago. Young remained with Hines through August 1937, although he also worked summers in the small groups of ALBERT AMMONS and ROY ELDRIDGE.

Trummy Young, jazz trombonist, with Jimmie Lunceford (left), early 1940s. (© William P. Gottlieb; www.jazzphotos.com.)

After leaving Hines, he toured briefly with the Midwest band of Jimmy Raschel before joining the JIMMIE LUNCEFORD orchestra in September. While with Lunceford he achieved his first widespread exposure on records, both as a high note specialist on trombone and as a singer of rhythm novelties. Young left Lunceford in March 1943 and spent the balance of the year with Charlie Barnet's racially mixed orchestra. In November 1943 Young briefly led his own group, but in early 1944 he began working as a sideman again for TINY GRIMES, Roy Eldridge, and CLAUDE HOPKINS, as well as playing in the CBS staff orchestra of Paul Baron and occasionally appearing as a guest star on Mildred Bailey's radio show. Beginning in the summer of 1944 he worked for eight months in Boyd Raeburn's progressive jazz orchestra, and in February 1945 he joined Benny Goodman's band.

Young remained with Goodman until August, when he left to form his own sextet with the young modernists Leo Parker, John Malachi, and Tommy Potter. In the fall of 1945 Young worked with the Tiny Grimes Sextet in New York City, where they accompanied BILLIE HOLIDAY and played their own sets opposite the ART TATUM trio. He then spent most of 1946 and the early part of 1947 touring with

Jazz at the Philharmonic, after which he rejoined Claude Hopkins in mid-1947. In October he went to Hawaii with Cee Pee Johnson, a Los Angeles drummer whose band also included GERALD WILSON, DEXTER GORDON, and Red Callender.

When the Johnson job ended, Young decided to stay in Honolulu, where he married his second wife (name unknown) and worked locally with the Art Norkus Trio and his own groups. While on tour with his All Stars, LOUIS ARMSTRONG heard Young play in Honolulu and asked him to replace his current trombonist, who was himself a temporary substitute for Jack Teagarden. Young accepted and in September 1952 joined the All Stars, a position he maintained until New Year's Day 1964, when he returned to Hawaii to resume his family life and local work. In September 1971 he appeared at a weekend-long all-star jazz party at the Broadmoor Hotel in Colorado Springs and worked with Hines at Disneyland. After a serious illness in 1975 Young continued to tour Europe, record, and lead his own groups in Hawaii. He died in San Jose, California.

Rejecting the older style of tailgate trombone, Young initially was impressed by the smooth tone and fluent, Armstrong-like improvisations of Jimmy Harrison and BENNY MORTON, but by the late 1930s he had adopted Armstrong himself as his primary model. He concentrated on developing a powerful upper register on trombone, and it was this technique, along with his softly intoned, highly rhythmic singing style, that made him such a valuable member of the Lunceford band. Of the records he made with Hines between October 1933 and February 1937, "Copenhagen," "Cavernism," "Disappointed in Love," and "Japanese Sandman" offer the best examples of his Morton-tinged style. However, he came into more prominence on the Lunceford records of November 1937 through June 1942. Here, his technically liberated, increasingly vocalized delivery surfaces on "Annie Laurie," "Margie," "'Tain't What You Do," "The Lonesome Road," "Blue Blazes," "Easter Parade," "Think of Me," "Dinah," "Battle Axe," and "Hi Spook," with several of these as well as others also featuring his singing. Young's only other recordings during the 1930s were with Mundy in March 1937 and TEDDY WILSON in November 1938.

It was only after he left Lunceford that Young began to participate more regularly in small-band record sessions. In February 1944 he emerged for the first time as a major jazz stylist on "Blue Moon" and "Thru' for the Night" from a COZY COLE septet date featuring Hines and COLEMAN HAWKINS. On these titles his tone and phrasing suggest the growing influence of DICKY WELLS and VIC DICKENSON, especially in their use of unconventional timbres. Demonstrating his acceptance by younger, more modern jazzmen, in January 1945 he played on a Clyde Hart session with DIZZY GILLESPIE, CHARLIE PARKER, and DON BYAS, teamed once again with Byas on Gillespie's first leader date, and in February, along with Gillespie and ERROLL GARNER, recorded with Georgie Auld's modern big band.

Between February and August 1945 Young recorded only with Benny Goodman, but starting in 1946 he took part in sessions led by Benny Carter, BUCK CLAYTON, Grimes, ILLINOIS JACQUET, Lunceford, and Billy Kyle. Understandably, Young received more consistent exposure than ever before while he was a featured member of Armstrong's All Stars, but in deference to the more traditional style of the band, he also simplified his phrasing, broadened his tone, and deepened his range, as can be heard on the hundreds of studio and concert recordings and telecasts he made with Armstrong between October 1952 and December 1963. During this period, however, he also participated in a March 1954 Buck Clayton jam session date, a June 1957 Lunceford tribute album directed by Billy May, and an April 1958 All Stars session led by Armstrong-styled trumpeter Teddy Buckner. From 1953 on, Young had also recorded with various European bands while on tour with the All Stars, but his last American sessions were with his own bands in Hawaii in the mid-1970s and a final tribute album to Armstrong with Peanuts Hucko and Billy Butterfield in October 1983. Young also recorded several times as the leader of his own small groups between February 1944 and December 1955. During his years with Lunceford and as a freelancer on modern swing records in the mid-1940s, Young influenced an entire generation of younger trombonists, including Bill Harris, J. J. JOHNSON, Kai Winding, and Al Grey.

FURTHER READING

Bruyninckx, Walter. *Traditional Jazz Discography, 1897–1988* (6 vols.).

Dance, Stanley. *The World of Earl Hines* (1977).

McCarthy, Albert. *Big Band Jazz* (1974).

Morgenstern, Dan. *Jazz People* (1976).

Rust, Brian. *Jazz Records, 1897–1942* (1982).

This entry is taken from the *American National Biography* and is published here with the permission of the American Council of Learned Societies.

JACK SOHMER

Young, Whitney Moore, Jr. (31 July 1921–11 Mar. 1971), social worker and civil rights activist, was born in Lincoln Ridge, Kentucky, the son of Whitney Moore Young Sr., president of Lincoln Institute, a private African American college, and Laura Ray, a schoolteacher. Raised within the community of the private academy and its biracial faculty, Whitney Young Jr. and his two sisters were sheltered from harsh confrontations with racial discrimination in their early lives, but they attended segregated public elementary schools for African American children and completed high school at Lincoln Institute. In 1937 Young, planning to become a doctor, entered Kentucky State Industrial College at Frankfort, where he received a B.S. in 1941. After graduation he became an assistant principal and athletic coach at Julius Rosenwald High School in Madison, Kentucky.

After joining the U.S. Army in 1942, Young studied engineering at the Massachusetts Institute of Technology (MIT). In 1944 he married Margaret Buckner, a teacher whom he had met while they were both students at Kentucky State; they had two children. Sent to Europe later in 1944, Young rose from private to first sergeant in the all-black 369th Anti-Aircraft Artillery Group. His experience in a segregated army on the eve of President Harry Truman's desegregation order drew Young to the challenges of racial diplomacy. In 1946, after his discharge from the army, he entered graduate study in social work at the University of Minnesota. His field placement in graduate school was with the Minneapolis chapter of the National Urban League, which sought increased employment opportunities for African American workers. In 1948 Young completed his master's degree in Social Work and became industrial relations secretary of the St. Paul, Minnesota, chapter of the Urban League. In 1950 he became the director of the Urban League chapter in Omaha, Nebraska. He increased both the Omaha chapter's membership and its operating budget. He became skilled at working with the city's business and political leaders to increase employment opportunities for African Americans. In Omaha he also taught in the University of Nebraska's School of Social Work.

In 1954 Young became dean of the School of Social Work at Atlanta University. As an administrator, he doubled the school's budget, raised faculty salaries, and insisted on professional development. In these early years after the Supreme Court's decision in *Brown v. Board of Education of Topeka, Kansas*, Young played a significant advisory role within the leadership of Atlanta's African American community. He was active in the Greater Atlanta Council on Human Relations and a member of the executive committee of the Atlanta branch of the NAACP. He also helped to organize Atlanta's Committee for Cooperative Action, a group of business and professional people who sought to coordinate the social and political action of varied black interest groups and organized patrols in African American communities threatened by white violence. He took a leave of absence from his position at Atlanta University in the 1960–1961 academic year to be a visiting Rockefeller Foundation scholar at Harvard University.

In January 1961 the National Urban League announced Whitney Young's appointment to succeed Lester B. Granger as its executive director. Beginning his new work in fall 1961, Young came to the leadership of the Urban League just after the first wave of sit-in demonstrations and freedom rides had drawn national attention to new forms of civil rights activism in the South. Among the major organizations identified with the civil rights movement, the Urban League was the most conservative and the least inclined to favor public demonstrations for social change. Young was resolved to move it into a firmer alliance with the other major civil rights organizations without threatening the confidence of the Urban League's powerful inside contacts. In 1963 he led it into joining the March on Washington and the Council for United Civil Rights Leadership, a consortium initiated by Kennedy administration officials and white philanthropists to facilitate fund-raising and joint planning. In his ten years as executive director of the Urban League, Young increased the number of its local chapters from sixty to ninety-eight, its staff from 500 to 1,200, and its funding by corporations, foundations, and federal grants. After the assassination of President John Kennedy, Young developed even stronger ties with President Lyndon Johnson's administration. Perhaps Young's most important influence lay in his call for a "Domestic Marshall Plan," outlined in his book *To Be Equal* (1964), which influenced President Johnson's War on Poverty programs.

By the mid-1960s, however, the civil rights coalition had begun to fray. In June 1966 Young and ROY WILKINS of the NAACP refused to sign a manifesto drafted by other civil rights leaders or to join them

Whitney Moore Young Jr. (center) meets with President John F. Kennedy and Henry Steeger (right) at the White House in 1962. (Library of Congress.)

when they continued the march of JAMES MEREDITH from Memphis, Tennessee, to Jackson, Mississippi. Young continued to shun the black power rhetoric popular with new leaders of the Congress of Racial Equality and the Student Nonviolent Coordinating Committee. Simultaneously, in consideration of the vital alliance with the Johnson administration, he was publicly critical of MARTIN LUTHER KING JR.'s condemnation of the U.S. pursuit of the war in Vietnam. At the administration's request, he twice visited South Vietnam to review American forces and observe elections there. Before Young left office in 1969, Lyndon Johnson awarded him the Medal of Freedom, the nation's highest civilian citation.

After Richard Nixon's inauguration in 1969, however, Young modified his earlier positions, condemning the war in Vietnam and responding to the black power movement and urban violence by concentrating Urban League resources on young people in the urban black underclass. He continued

to have significant influence, serving on the boards of the Federal Reserve Bank of New York, MIT, and the Rockefeller Foundation and as president of the National Conference on Social Welfare (1967) and of the National Association of Social Workers (1969–1971). Subsequently, Young's successors as executive director of the Urban League, ARTHUR FLETCHER, VERNON JORDAN, and John Jacob, maintained his legacy of commitment to the goals of the civil rights movement by sustained engagement with centers of American economic and political power.

In March 1971, while Young was at a conference on relations between Africa and the United States in Lagos, Nigeria, he suffered either a brain hemorrhage or a heart attack and drowned while swimming in the Atlantic Ocean. Former attorney general Ramsey Clark and others who were swimming with him pulled Young's body from the water, but their efforts to revive him were to no avail.

FURTHER READING

The Whitney M. Young Jr. Papers are in the Rare Book and Manuscript Library of Columbia University; the National Urban League Papers are at the Library of Congress.

Moore, Jesse Thomas, Jr. *A Search for Equality: The National Urban League, 1910–1961* (1981).

Parris, Guichard, and Lester Brooks. *Blacks in the City: A History of the National Urban League* (1971).

Weiss, Nancy J. *Whitney M. Young Jr. and the Struggle for Civil Rights* (1990).

Obituary: *New York Times*, 12 Mar. 1971.

This entry is taken from the *American National Biography* and is published here with the permission of the American Council of Learned Societies.

RALPH E. LUKER

Younge, Samuel Leamon (17 Nov. 1944–3 Jan. 1966), U.S. Navy veteran, Tuskegee student, SNCC worker, and civil rights martyr, was born in Tuskegee, Alabama, son of Renee and Samuel Younge Sr. His mother was an elementary school teacher, and his father was an occupational therapist, head of the department of Physical Medicine and Rehabilitation at Veterans' Hospital (Tuskegee) and later attached to the U.S. Forest Service. Younge's life was marked by a series of uncompromising role models within and beyond his family. In the town of Tuskegee itself, he grew up in a black middle-class enclave that valued both education and self-respect. Yet even among this relatively privileged enclave that existed for Tuskegee's educated African American elite, Samuel L. Younge Jr.'s childhood was far more individualistic than most. Credit for this belonged to his mother, Renee, who, although conscious of the negative power of racist stereotypes in limiting the horizons of talented black youth, courageously encouraged him to express himself, even if this self-expression was unconventional. He was educated at Cornwall Academy in Great Barrington, Massachusetts, from September 1957 through January 1960, but graduated from Tuskegee Institute High School in May 1962.

Color complicated his life immeasurably; for, like his mother, Sammy Jr. was extremely light-skinned, to the extent that both child and parent were at times mistaken for white. Younge and his mother would often play along with people who so mistook them, occasionally exploiting Jim Crow "whites only" policies and using other tactics to expose the frequently absurd contradictions of the racist system. Throughout his youth, he continued to treat the "race problem" with characteristic humor.

After high school, a stint in the U.S. Navy from 1962 to 1964 exposed him to further discrimination. The most egregious example of naval discrimination occurred through medical neglect. In September 1963, serving on the USS *Independence*, Younge had complained frequently about having a severe backache and was ignored until he collapsed and was rushed into emergency surgery at a Portsmouth, Virginia, hospital where he was found to be suffering kidney failure. In the ensuing months, he lost one kidney and suffered extensive malfunctions in the other, and he eventually received a medical discharge.

Still uncertain about the direction his life should take, Younge enrolled in Tuskegee University early in January 1965, six months following his exit from the navy. The period during which this transition occurred was one of profound transformation for Alabama, the South, and the entire nation. During the months when Sammy Younge Jr. served in the armed forces, the Student Nonviolent Coordinating Committee (SNCC) had stepped up its militant confrontations with the system of segregation, most notably in Mississippi, whose 1964 Freedom Summer voter education and registration project had accelerated the process of social change. Within a year, SNCC and the Southern Christian Leadership Conference (SCLC) had set their sights upon an Alabama initiative that would address some of the same issues. This movement was in full swing by the time Younge entered Tuskegee. Two months later, in March 1965, he emerged from relative obscurity to a prominent place in Alabama's freedom movement.

On 10 March 1965 Tuskegee Institute students presented a petition to Alabama governor George Wallace protesting his state's treatment of African Americans. Three days earlier police, under the direction of Selma's sheriff Jim Clark, had attacked and routed demonstrators intending to march across the Edmund Pettus Bridge en route from Selma to Montgomery in a confrontation later recalled as "Bloody Sunday." Since the autumn of 1964 SNCC had deployed what it designated as "campus travelers" to Tuskegee in connection with its nascent Alabama Project. Locally SNCC was aided by a campus organization called the Tuskegee Institute Advancement League (TIAL). TIAL supported a massive demonstration aimed at Montgomery in response to a statewide call by

Dr. MARTIN LUTHER KING JR. Sammy Younge Jr. took over fund-raising for the campaign.

From 10 to 16 March 1965 hundreds of Tuskegee Institute students mounted demonstrations in Montgomery in coalition with SNCC and in communication with allies on the Tuskegee campus. Despite his fragile health, Younge was committed to the Montgomery action and spent time on the barricades with other students during the weeklong siege. Protesters were met with fierce police action, from arrests to intimidation.

Younge, worried about by his health, was intensely committed, yet also extremely cautious. He had changed from a well-dressed, distinguished man on campus with a car to a dedicated SNCC worker who severed all ties to his formerly comfortable middle-class life. During this time he joined the efforts of FANNIE LOU HAMER, a militant sharecropper who was one of the founders of the Mississippi Freedom Democratic Party. He also initiated voter registration drives in several rural localities. In this way he became a skilled organizer.

Younge and fellow TIAL activists worked to desegregate public accommodations in Tuskegee. They boycotted and picketed an A&P store that only had one black employee. Younge's activism brought him unwanted attention from school and civil authorities. He was involved in attempts to desegregate swimming pools, churches, and stores—supporting boycotts where necessary. Younge at times allowed emotion to overrule reason and gained a reputation for impulsiveness as a result.

In late 1965 Younge's behavior became increasingly erratic, and he departed from SNCC and flirted with various other radical strategies to alter the status quo in Alabama, many of these actions showing his increasing isolation, alienation, frustration, and desperation at the slow pace of change. On 3 January 1966 Younge played a leading role in a voter registration effort at the Macon County Courthouse, attending on one of the two days per month when blacks were permitted to register. Later, at the end of a long day spent facing off against the authorities and registering scores of black voters, Younge spent time with friends until he left them at around 11 P.M. After midnight Younge's mother received a call that he had been found dead, after being shot by a sixty-nine-year-old white man named Marvin Segrest. Segrest was never convicted of the murder.

Sammy Younge Jr.'s murder galvanized large numbers of youth in and around Tuskegee, including those with Tuskegee roots who were then studying at other historically black colleges such as Fisk University in Nashville, Tennessee. It inspired others to drop out to devote themselves full time to the movement. It reached antiracist white allies such as the Southern Student Organizing Committee (SSOC). Younge's death also marked the deepening of fissures within and beyond SNCC on the subjects of organizing strategy, goals, and the larger purposes of the freedom struggle. It was used by some SNCC members to tie responsibility for domestic racism to those responsible for the beginnings of the Vietnam War in Southeast Asia. On 6 January 1966, three days following the murder of Sammy Younge Jr., SNCC issued this statement:

"The murder of Samuel Younge in Tuskegee, Alabama, is no different than the murder of peasants in Vietnam, for both Younge and the Vietnamese sought—and are seeking—to secure rights guaranteed them by law. In each case, the United States bears a great part of the responsibility for these deaths. Samuel Younge was murdered because U.S. law is not being enforced. Vietnamese are murdered because the United States is pursuing an aggressive policy in violation of international law. The United States is no respecter of persons or law when such persons or laws run counter to its needs and desires" (Forman, 223).

FURTHER READING

Carson, Clayborne. *In Struggle! SNCC and the Black Awakening of the 1960s* (1981).

Forman, James. *Sammy Younge, Jr: The First Black Student to Die in the Black Liberation Movement* (1986).

Norrell, Robert J. *Reaping the Whirlwind: The Civil Rights Movement in Tuskegee* (1998).

DAVID H. ANTHONY III

Zampty, John Charles (12 July 1889–28 Apr. 1980), founder of the Detroit division of the Universal Negro Improvement Association (UNIA), was born in Belmont, Port-of-Spain, Trinidad, in the British West Indies. His mother, Matilda Cadett, was from a French-speaking family of bakers. Little is known about his father. Charles, as he was known, attended a Catholic primary school in Trinidad and a local public high school, and enrolled at St. Mary's College, a Catholic secondary institution on the island.

Zampty's early career exemplifies the experience of thousands of migrant workers in the colonial Caribbean. For a brief period in 1909 he secured employment as a mechanic with the Trinidad Oil Company. He left the company to work for the Trinidad Sanitary Inspection Corporation, which sent him to Lagos, Nigeria. He asked the company to send him back to Trinidad when he discovered his wages were significantly less than those specified in the labor contract he had signed. Returning home in 1912, his ship docked in Colón, Panama, where he obtained employment with the Isthmus Canal Commission.

Zampty soon discovered a pay differential between black and white workers on the Panama Canal during his employment for the commission. His discovery marked an awareness of the economic realities of racial discrimination that led to his increasing political consciousness. He then helped found the Colón Federal Labor Union, which sought redress of canal workers' grievances and mirrored the efforts of similar groups throughout Central America and the Caribbean. While employed with the commission, Zampty attempted to obtain a civil service position with the British West Indies Regiment. Although white civil servants received their positions without appearing before a board of determination, British officials told Zampty that to obtain the position he would have to travel to Bermuda to appear before such a board. Rejecting the blatantly discriminatory hiring practice of the British government, he instead traveled to Chile and Brazil, where he found work constructing a railroad in the South American interior. While on this assignment, he contracted malaria. He then returned to Panama.

When Zampty returned to Colón, he met MARCUS GARVEY, who had come from Jamaica to address the newly organized labor union. Garvey found a kindred spirit in Zampty, and the two shared the belief that the lack of black-owned enterprises stood as the central problem of blacks throughout the African diaspora. Zampty's political activities resulted in his dismissal from the Canal Commission. He married a woman in 1914 while living in Panama. Although her name is not known, the couple had a daughter, Florence. He married at least two more times after his later arrival in Detroit. He married his second wife, Bessie, a nurse, in the early 1930s. In 1957 he married Irmah Cooke, a teacher, who became his business partner.

During World War I, Zampty sent an application to the Ford Motor Company seeking a managerial position. Impressed with his credentials, the company encouraged him to come to the United States. Leaving Panama in 1918, he went to New York, where he had relatives. Garvey had come to New

York in 1916 and established the first Universal Negro Improvement Association (UNIA) division in the United States. Zampty joined the fledgling organization when he arrived in the city two years later. He left New York for Detroit, Michigan, in 1919 to begin the job Ford had offered him. When he appeared at the personnel office, however, Zampty was informed that the company did not hire blacks for managerial positions, although the company conceded that he was clearly qualified for the position. He accepted a position as a carpenter at Ford but for much less money than he expected and less than whites employed in the same capacity received. It was not what he had anticipated, but he needed a job; he would retire from the company in 1957.

Garvey came to Detroit in 1919 to sell stock in the UNIA steamship company, the Black Star Line, and Zampty subsequently played an instrumental role in founding Division 407 of the organization in 1920. Detroit, along with other cities of the industrialized northern states, witnessed a massive increase in its black population between 1910 and 1920. UNIA appealed to thousands of black migrants who left the Jim Crow South only to find a subtler but still virulent form of discrimination in the North. The organization helped assuage the worst aspects of migration for the masses of black southerners attempting to adjust to their new environment. Caribbean immigrants such as Zampty held a disproportionate majority of the leadership positions within UNIA in Detroit and in other cities where the organization had a large following. Many of the members of Division 407 were employed at Ford, and their relatively high wages made it one of the most prosperous chapters throughout the Americas, Africa, and the Caribbean. With over 4,000 members, the Detroit division became one of the largest in UNIA during the 1920s. Other branches formed in the city and caused internal rivalries, but Division 407 remained the most organized, best funded, and most visible for over eight decades.

Zampty assisted in the purchase of a building, Liberty Hall, on Detroit's east side, where the organization's meetings were held. He helped organize various economic enterprises under the auspices of the division, including laundries, restaurants, and benevolent societies. By 1922 Zampty had accompanied Garvey across the United States, acting as auditor for the association. In spite of Garvey's conviction for mail fraud in 1925 and deportation to Jamaica in 1927, Zampty remained active for sixty years in Division 407 as auditor. Later he was auditor general for the international body. In the early twenty-first century the division remained one of the active chapters of UNIA.

Zampty put into practice the organization's credo of economic self-determination and pride in African heritage by becoming an importer of African art, which he sold from the store he opened in 1957, when he retired from Ford. Many generations of Detroiters became familiar with the tenets of Garveyism by visiting Zampty's store. At his memorial service, local and national Pan-African groups gathered to honor him with a service accorded royalty in West Africa.

FURTHER READING

Martin, Tony. *The Pan-African Connection: From Slavery to Garvey and Beyond* (1983).

Smith-Irvin, Jeannette. *Footsoldiers of the Universal Negro Improvement Association* (1989).

Stein, Judith. *The World of Marcus Garvey: Race and Class in Modern Society* (1986).

Thomas, Richard W. *Life for Us Is What We Make It: Building Black Community in Detroit, 1915–1945* (1992).

KATHRYN L. BEARD

Zanders, Roosevelt Smith (13 July 1910–20 May 1995), laborer, entrepreneur, and celebrity procurer was born in Valdosta, Georgia, the son of Reverend Arthur Zanders and Ethel Smith Zanders. His family relocated to Youngstown, Ohio, where he attended public school. In 1930, Zanders was employed as a lockerroom attendant at the Mahoning Valley Country Club. He roomed with Pink and Irene Ward, who also worked at the club as a steward and cook, respectively. In 1943, Zanders was working as a construction engineer on the Alcan Highway in Alaska when he developed the concept of offering combined limousine and concierge services. This idea was inspired by his difficulty in obtaining simple things that were not readily available.

Zanders moved to New York in 1935. More than a chauffeur, Zanders ran a highly regarded concierge service that catered to local and visiting celebrities in New York City. He started Zanders Auto Rental Service in 1946 in Harlem when he borrowed $3,000 to buy his first Cadillac. He soon increased his fleet to 16 Cadillacs and one custom-made Rolls-Royce that he drove himself. Two years after starting his business, and ever with an eye to good publicity, he provided NAT KING COLE and his new bride Maria Ellington (MARIA COLE) free limousine service for their wedding in

1948. He later became well known in the celebrity arena when Gertrude Lawrence, the British actress, became his client. A maid for Lawrence's attorney was a neighbor of Zanders, and it was through this connection that he was hired. Lawrence introduced him to the Duke and Duchess of Windsor as well as other clients.

According to a 1959 article by the journalist Gay Talese, Zander charged his clients $150 for an entire day of his services. This included not only chauffeur-driven Cadillacs but also personal services such as arranging hotel and restaurant reservations, babysitters, dry cleaning, and banking, as well as obtaining theater tickets for his clients. Zanders was very successful and earned an annual salary of nearly $90,000 in 1960—a figure that was more than twenty times the American average and forty times the median salary of African American males. His services were used by diplomats, dignitaries, presidents, businessmen, actors, and actresses. His client list included Ethel Merman, Margot Fonteyn, Winston Churchill, Eleanor Roosevelt, Harry S. Truman, John F. Kennedy, Richard M. Nixon, William Holden, Red Skeleton, Clark Gable, Lana Turner, Danny Kaye, Eddie Fisher, Nat King Cole, and Aristotle Onassis.

Some of his most famous requests included:

- Sending 100 pounds of shrimp to John Wayne while he was in Paris
- Delivering a special kind of shrimp to a yacht in Monte Carlo
- Delivering $200,000 in cash to an apartment in the United Nations plaza for Aristotle Onassis in May 1968
- Sending two tiger cubs to the president of Panama
- Renting an entire hotel floor, hiring a maid and a butler, and buying all the food for a Christmas visit by the Gerber (baby food) family
- Arranging for a log cabin from the Black Forest in Germany to be relocated to South America for use as a hunting lodge (When the client's workers could not read the assembly instructions, he had them translated into Spanish.)
- Securing theater tickets for the Sadler's Wells Ballet for impresario Sol Hurok when he discovered Hurok had not reserved enough tickets for his own guests.

In 1961, Zanders traveled on a seven-week, thirteen-nation "goodwill tour," during which he stopped in Ghana and was welcomed by president Kwame Nkrumah. The following year he was hired for a special luncheon in Hyde Park for one hundred top world figures during the wake for Eleanor Roosevelt. He could not find a glass when President Kennedy asked for a refreshment, so Zanders hurried to the home next door to secure stemware before he was even missed.

Understanding the power of marketing, Zanders was featured in an October 1963 New York Life Insurance ad in *Ebony* magazine with the caption "Like my custom Rolls-Royce, my New York Life insurance is a wonderful investment." He also befriended several stars, including John Wayne, who invited Zanders to visit him on location in Durango, Mexico, where he was filming *The Sons of Katie Elder* (1965). In 1976, he was interviewed by Lee Israel for a biography about American journalist Dorothy Kilgallen, who was one of Zanders's former clients. He revealed that he had driven her from New York to Washington, DC, during a blizzard so she could report on the inauguration of President Kennedy. Immediately after the inauguration he drove her to a New York hospital. When asked if her condition was alcohol-related, he replied, with customary respect for his clients' reputations, "I don't say 'drunk.' One of the things that brought it about was having one or two drinks and not eating. Her system ran down that way."

According to Zanders's daughter Roxanne, he wrote an autobiography that was stolen from his home in Harlem before it could be sent to a publisher. He retired in 1985 and sold Zanders Auto Rental Service. Roosevelt Smith Zanders died on 20 May 1995 at the Jewish Home and Hospital in Manhattan.

FURTHER READING

Hamilton, Esther. "Zanders, Once Locker Room Boy Here, Is Now Chauffeur for the Stars," *Youngstown Vindicator*, 1 May 1960.
Talese, Gay. "A Chauffeur with a Chauffeur Rode a Boyish Dream to Fortune," *New York Times*, 17 Apr. 1959.
Obituary: *New York Times*, 26 May 1995.

KENYATTA D. BERRY

Zeno, Joseph François. *See* Lewis, George (Joseph François Zeno).

Zollar, Jawole (21 Dec. 1950–), choreographer, founder, and artistic director of the Urban Bush Women dance company, was born Willa Jo Zollar in Kansas City, Missouri, the third of the six children of Alfred Jr. and Dorothy Delores Zollar, about whom little is known. Nor is it known when she changed her name from "Willa Jo" to "Jawole," an African word meaning "she enters the house." It is known that she began studying dance at an early age when her mother, who had studied dance and jazz singing, took Zollar and one of her sisters to the local Conservatory of Music to take classes with a Russian ballet teacher who was apparently willing to take black students during that era. Unhappy in the almost completely segregated class, Zollar switched to a community school run by Joseph Stevenson, a former ballroom dancer who had also studied with KATHERINE DUNHAM. Stevenson gave Zollar a thorough grounding both in traditional black jazz dance and in Afro-Cuban forms; she also received extensive performance experience. As young as six years of age, Zollar appeared professionally onstage in "kiddie shows" with her sister.

Zollar's creative vision and movement vocabulary were not only developed in school or on stage. Another important component of her dance education was the social dancing that surrounded her in the streets and, when she was older, in the clubs. Zollar made up dances and sang doo-wop while hanging out with her friends on the stoops; she later incorporated these memories into some of her best-known pieces, including "Lipstick: A Doo-Wop Drama" (1990). Additionally, her time as a majorette and on the drill team introduced her to other movement options, such as marching formations, which she integrated into various signature pieces for her company, Urban Bush Women, such as "I Don't Know, But I Been Told, If You Keep Dancin' You'll Never Grow Old" (1989).

After a brief, unsatisfactory stint in college, Zollar dropped out, and then returned in 1970 to the University of Missouri, Kansas City, to major in dance; she earned her degree in 1975. She worked with the choreographer Milton Myers in his company Black Exodus and later took over the directorship of the group. Myers's work, which Zollar described as militant, filled with African dance, and accompanied by poems, influenced her own later choreography.

The early 1970s was a time of political, social, and cultural turmoil, all of which made an impact on Zollar. After graduating from the University of Missouri, Zollar went to Florida State University a year later to study for her MFA, which she received in 1979. At Florida State University, she became involved with the Black Players Guild, a group dedicated to staging theater and dance pieces, and created highly activist and feminist choreography. Zollar also saw groundbreaking antiwar pieces like Daniel Nagrin's "Peloponnesian War"; and found inspiration in the aesthetic of such contemporary choreographers as Eleo Pomare, Murray Louis, and Alwin Nikolais, who worked with dancers whose bodies broke the balletic ideal and who looked at both the dramatic and theatrical aspects of dance in fresh ways. Though her distance from the New York City dance center meant that she had little opportunity to view much of the emerging postmodern choreography—which used non-technical, "ordinary," and task-related movement rather than more theatrical dance vocabularies like ballet or Martha Graham's—she did get to see some and it helped liberate and justify her aesthetic choices. Although Zollar's dances for Urban Bush Women seemed to have little in common with these definitively nonnarrative works, she found a point of contact with them, noting that their reliance on the "pedestrian … validated my possibility of using the vernacular" (Sommer, 53). Zollar felt free to transform, and put on the concert stage, the everyday social dances, games, and movement styles she had seen in her childhood.

In 1977 she became the Nancy Smith Fichter Professor of Dance at Florida State. In 1980 she went to New York to study with Dianne McIntyre, a choreographer noted for her work on stage and screen. Four years later Zollar founded Urban Bush Women. The ensemble, in Zollar's words, "seeks to bring the untold and under-told histories and stories of disenfranchised people to light through dance. We do this from a woman-centered perspective, as members of the African Diaspora Community." Her dance aesthetic embraced a wide variety of movement techniques that included traditional jazz, African vernacular, and modern dance as well as dramatic gesture. Her musical choices had an equally diverse range, from the traditional (African American southern chants) and popular (blues, hip-hop) to contemporary commissioned scores. Her performances generally integrate speech and song. In order to create such dynamic dance-theater pieces, she collaborated closely with other artists, including Laurie Carlos, who wrote the text for several of her dances, and musicians.

Almost all of Zollar's works involved a rich and potent mixture of the political and personal placed in highly nuanced historical context. "We can't just go out there and make shapes onstage," she told a newspaper reporter (*Boston Globe*, 26 Feb. 1988). The link of past and present, of painful memory and present-day political redemption and recovery, is a recurrent theme in her work. "Shelter" (1988) examined homelessness, while "Womb Wars" (1992) took on the issue of abortion, making it clear that reproductive rights were but one battle in women's—particularly black women's—ongoing struggle to control their own bodies. Other dances, like "Batty Moves" (1998) and "Hair Stories" (2002), examined the often-fraught issues of black women's beauty. The first, with its hip-hop music and hip emphatic movements, playfully celebrated the buttocks and not having to "tuck it in," while the second focused on "good" and "bad" hair and their meanings in the black community. The full-evening work "Bones of Ash" (1995), based on writing by the novelist Jewelle Gomez, told a vampire story but altered the tradition significantly. Here the vampire embodied living memory, particularly of slavery.

Zollar has received numerous honors for her choreography, including an honorary doctorate from Columbia College in 2002, the American Dance Festival Doris Duke Award in 1997, a Capezio Award for outstanding achievement in dance (1994), as well as two Bessie Awards: one in 1992 for *River Songs*, a collective work, and another for "Walking with Pearl" (2006), a piece she created in honor of the groundbreaking choreographer, dancer, and anthropologist PEARL PRIMUS. Zollar appeared in the PBS series *Free to Dance* about African American dance history, and her piece "Praise House" (1991), directed by JULIE DASH, aired on PBS as well.

FURTHER READING

"Interview with Jawole Willa Jo Zollar," conducted by Sally Sommer for the Oral History Project, Dance Division (2 Mar. 2002), is in the New York Public Library.

Albright, Ann Cooper. *Choreographing Difference: The Body and Identity in Contemporary Dance* (1997).

Chatterjea, Ananya. *Butting Out: Reading Resistive Choreographies through Works by Jawole Willa Jo Zollar and Chandralekha* (2004).

Gottschild, Brenda Dixon. *The Black Dancing Body: A Geography from Coon to Cool* (2003).

Urban Bush Women Dance Company. http://www.urbanbushwomen.org.

KAREN BACKSTEIN

Zuber, Paul Burgess (20 Dec. 1926–6 Mar. 1987), lawyer and professor, was born in Williamsport, Pennsylvania, the son of Paul A. Zuber, a postal worker, and Jennie Baer. He attended school in Williamsport through third grade. In 1934 his family moved to Harlem, New York, and he enrolled in the all-black P.S. 157. After graduating from Thomas Jefferson High School in Brooklyn, Zuber entered Brown University, where he played football, basketball, and track. He was drafted into the U.S. Army Quartermasters Corps during World War II and was stationed at Camp Lee, Virginia. Upon his discharge he returned to Brown, graduating in 1947 with an AB in Premedical Studies. He was reactivated for the Korean War and served as chief of psychological testing at Murphy Army Hospital in Massachusetts. In 1953 he married Barbara Johnson, an artist. They had two children.

Zuber worked for the New York City Health Department while attending night classes at Brooklyn Law School. He earned his JD in 1956. The day after being admitted to the bar, he filed his first lawsuit against the New York City Board of Education. He represented Mae Mallory, who sought to enroll her daughter in a racially mixed junior high school instead of the all-black school to which she had been assigned.

In 1958 Zuber defended boycotting African American parents who sought to force the board to transfer their children to better-staffed integrated schools. Four defendants were found guilty in Domestic Relations Court for keeping their children out of school. Two weeks later, however, a different judge, Justine Wise Polier, dismissed charges against two other defendants, ruling that children attending Harlem schools received "inferior educational opportunities in those schools by reason of racial discrimination" (*In the Matter of Charlene Skipworth and Another*, Domestic Relations Court of the City of New York, December 15, 1958). Although Polier lacked authority to order the board to remedy these conditions, her ruling was hailed as a victory over de facto segregation.

In 1960 Zuber sued the New Rochelle Board of Education on behalf of African American parents who wanted to enroll their children in a predominantly white elementary school. At their trial he demonstrated that the concentration of black students in Lincoln School was the result of deliberate actions. Judge Irving R. Kaufman concluded that the board operated a segregated school system. He wrote, "It is of no moment whether the segregation is labeled by the defendant as 'de jure' or 'de facto,' as long as the Board, by its conduct, is responsible for its maintenance" (*Taylor v. New Rochelle Board of Education*). Kaufman ordered the board to prepare a desegregation plan. His ruling was upheld by the court of appeals and affirmed by the Supreme Court. *Taylor v. New Rochelle Board of Education* was the first case to successfully apply *Brown v. Board of*

Education to a northern school district. Zuber maintained that northern racism was more difficult to identify and root out than the southern variety. He observed: "Down home our bigots come in white sheets. Up here they come in Brooks Brothers suits and ties" (*New York Times*, Man in the News profile, 26 Feb. 1962).

In August 1961 Zuber represented African American parents protesting overcrowding and double sessions in Chicago public schools. Superintendent Benjamin Willis maintained that Chicago schools were not segregated, but when black parents were unable to enroll their children in underutilized white schools, Zuber filed suit in federal court in *Webb v. Board of Education*. The plaintiffs' suit initially was dismissed by Judge Julius Hoffman. One year later, however, the case was reinstated. On 29 August 1963 the parties announced a settlement that required an independent panel to develop a desegregation plan. Zuber also was counsel in school desegregation cases in Newark and Englewood, New Jersey, and Malverne, Hempstead, and Mount Vernon, New York.

Zuber also entered politics, running unsuccessfully for the New York State Senate in 1958. In 1962 he challenged Congressman ADAM CLAYTON POWELL JR. but later withdrew. Zuber entered the New Hampshire Republican presidential primary in 1963, using his candidacy to focus attention on civil rights issues.

Zuber's career reached a low point in 1969. His problems began when he accused the New York City patrolman Gerald Vassilatos of planting marijuana on one of his clients. The officer sued for defamation of character. When Zuber failed to appear in court, Justice Harold Baer awarded the officer $450. Zuber refused to pay and on 30 December 1968 was arrested and jailed for six days. His troubles increased in September 1969, when he was charged with professional misconduct. The court cited four instances that "showed complete lack of responsibility of his obligations as an attorney" and found that "he was guilty of conduct tending to bring the profession into disrepute" (*New York Times* 10 Sept. 1969) and he was suspended from the bar for two years.

Zuber's legal practice had never flourished, so he seized an opportunity to enter teaching. He became an associate professor of law and urban studies at Rensselaer Polytechnic Institute (RPI) in Troy, New York. Two years later he was appointed director of the Center for Urban Environmental Studies, a position he held until his death. In 1979 he became

a full professor, the first African American to attain this rank at RPI. He died of a heart attack in his home near the RPI campus.

Zuber was a lifelong activist, working tirelessly to improve community conditions. He was moderator of a weekly television program, columnist for a community newspaper, and host of a local radio program. He served on numerous boards in his adopted city of Troy, including the mayor's task forces on fair housing and community development. He wrote the city's fair housing law and affirmative action plan. Associates and opponents alike described Zuber as independent and outspoken. These were his greatest strengths and principal weaknesses. He was never reluctant to speak his mind, exposing bias and incompetence wherever he found it. He frequently described himself as "a bull in a china closet." Zuber was a solo practitioner whose difficulty in forming alliances limited his effectiveness. Nevertheless, his pioneering litigation against northern school segregation established important legal precedents.

FURTHER READING

Back, Adina. "Exposing the 'Whole Segregation Myth': The Harlem Nine and New York City's School Desegregation Battles," in *Freedom North: Black Freedom Struggles outside the South, 1940–1980*, eds. Jeanne F. Theoharis and Komozi Woodard (2003).

"Integration Vendetta in a Northern Town," *Life*, 5 May 1966.

Obituary: *New York Times*, 10 Mar. 1987.

PAUL T. MURRAY

Zydeco, Buckwheat (14 Nov. 1947–), zydeco musician, was born Stanley Joseph Dural Jr., the fourth of thirteen children near Lafayette, Louisiana, where his parents owned a farm. As a child, he took odd jobs—besides helping his parents on the farm or when they took outside jobs picking cotton in the nearby fields to make ends meet. His hair resembled that of the character Buckwheat in the popular *Little Rascals* film shorts series, thereby earning him his enduring nickname. His was also a musical upbringing: Zydeco learned to play piano and organ as a very young boy and was performing in paying gigs in the local jukes by the time he was ten.

Lafayette at the time was a center of the Creole music scene, and it was there that Zydeco began to develop his style. His father wanted him to play Creole accordion—as he himself did—but Zydeco preferred R&B, much to his father's dismay. The zydeco style—with its quick tempo and folksy,

Buckwheat Zydeco performs at the 2006 New Orleans Jazz & Heritage Festival. (AP Images.)

old-fashioned instrumentation—was far from Zydeco's mind. He insisted that he would be an R&B or funk performer. In 1971 Zydeco formed the band Buckwheat & the Hitchhikers, a local favorite that played gigs for five years and had a modest hit in "It's Hard To Get." In 1977, shortly after the Hitchhikers' breakup, Zydeco's father introduced him to the zydeco great CLIFTON CHENIER. Chenier asked Zydeco to perform backup for his band, and the young man agreed. He later reported that the experience opened his eyes to the power of zydeco music and forever changed the path of his musical career. He played keyboard at first, but soon took up the accordion, and within a year was ready to start his own band.

The change in musical styles was as rapid as it was successful. At the time, the zydeco style was undergoing something of a popular revival, not just in Louisiana but throughout much of the country. Zydeco took advantage of the fad. In 1979

he recorded *One for the Road* for Blues Unlimited and then had a short stay at another small label before coming to the attention of Rounder, one of the leading record labels for folk and Americana. Soon after, Zydeco and his group recorded *Turning Point* (1983). The album was nominated for a Grammy. The year 1985 saw *Waitin' for My Ya Ya* and another Grammy nod. In 1986 he signed with Island Records, becoming the first zydeco artist to be recruited by such a big-name studio. Their first effort together was 1987's *On a Night Like This*. The album won yet another Grammy nomination. That same year, Zydeco's music was featured on the soundtrack to the popular movie thriller *The Big Easy*.

Bigger things followed. In 1988 he toured with Eric Clapton. He went on to tour or appear with a number of major recording stars: Robert Plant, Paul Simon, and MAVIS STAPLES. He continued to tour and record, appearing on the major festival circuit, including at the Newport Folk and Montreaux Jazz festivals. In 1998 he formed Tomorrow Recordings, at least in part to give himself a more stable home in a buy-out and takeover-churned recording industry. His first recording for Tomorrow was 1999's celebratory *Buckwheat Zydeco Story: A 20 Year Party.* Among his more recent recordings is *Down Home Live* (2001), *Jackpot!* (2005), and *Lay Your Burden Down* (2009). In 2006 Island released a major retrospective, *The Best of Buckwheat Zydeco: Millennium Collection.* Zydeco also performed on an album to benefit survivors of Hurricane Katrina, *Our New Orleans: A Benefit Album for the Gulf Coast.*

FURTHER READING

Gould, Philip. *Cajun Music and Zydeco* (1992).
Lichtenstein, Grace. *Musical Gumbo* (1993).

JASON PHILIP MILLER

Directory of Contributors

Louis M. Abbey
Dummett, Clifton O., Sr.
Melina Abdullah
Burke, Yvonne Brathwaite
Lee, Barbara
Waters, Maxine
Donna M. Abruzzese
Clark, Mamie Phipps
Logan, Arthur Courtney
Lloyd Ackert
Thomas, Vivien Theodore
Martha Ackmann
Jemison, Mae
Johnson, Mamie Peanut
Morgan, Connie
Stone, Toni
Michael Adams
Brown, Charles
Brown, Clarence "Gatemouth"
Freeman, Al, Jr.
Lanier, Willie
Moore, Lenny
Parker, Jim
Perry, Joe
Rampersad, Arnold
Watts, André
Williamson, Fred
Tiffany Adams
Dance, Daryl Cumber
Ulrich Adelt
Campbell, Luther
Gaynor, Gloria
Jones, Booker T.
Thomas, Rufus
Watson, Johnny "Guitar"
Kellie N. Adesina
Alexander, Joyce London
Vanessa Agard-Jones
Grosvenor, Verta Mae Smart
Wilbert H. Ahern
Adams, John Quincy (1848–1922)
Anthony Aiello
Prince
Thomas Aiello
Burley, Dan

Jane Ailes
Redman, John
Angela Aisevbonaye
Canty, Marietta
Evan J. Albright
Lewis, William Henry
Otis D. Alexander
Ward, Calvin Edouard
Philip Alexander
Branson, Herman Russell
Starla Alexander-Evilsizor
Bradford, Mark
Omar H. Ali
Fulani, Lenora Branch
Lytle, Lutie A.
Pattillo, Walter Alexander
Y. Jamal Ali
Kemp-Rotan, Renee
Yasmine Ali
Brown, Addie
Paul Alkebulan
Hampton, Carl B.
Richard B. Allen
Celestin, Papa
William A. Allison
Smith, Lydia Hamilton
Eugenie P. Almeida
Fox, Lillian Thomas
Garland, Hazel B.
Richard Alperin
Cheswell, Wentworth
Cheryl A. Alston
Guyton, Tyree
Monika R. Alston
Brown, Corrine
Davis, Lelia Foley
Clayton, Eva McPherson
Donald Altschiller
Blakely, Allison
Amalia K. Amaki
Artis, William Ellisworth
Bailey, Herman Kofi
Battey, Cornelius Marion (C. M.)
Bedou, Arthur
Burnett, Calvin Waller

Goreleigh, Rex
Hutson, Bill
Knight, Gwendolyn
Painter, Nell Irvin
Polk, Prentice Herman (P. H.)
Wallace, William Onikwa
Whitten, Jack
Williams, Carla

The *American National Biography* Editors
Dolphy, Eric

Christopher J. Anderson
Stewart, John

Eric Anderson
O'Hara, James Edward
White, George Henry

Virginia Anderson
Bullins, Ed

Edward E. Andrews
Quamino, Duchess
Quamino, John

Stephen W. Angell
Early, Jordan Winston
Singleton, Benjamin
Turner, Henry McNeal

David H. Anthony, III
Abu Bakr Al-Siddiq
Dean, Harry Foster
Hunter, Charles Norfleet
Moon, Henry Lee
Russell, George Allen
Teamoh, George
Webster, Milton Price
Yergan, Max
Younge, Samuel Leamon

Michael A. Antonucci
Dixon, "Big" Willie James
Forrest, Leon
Gibson, Althea
Payton, Walter
Southern, Eileen

R. Iset Anuakan
Morrow, Willie Lee
Taborn, Earl "Mickey"
Tyson, Cicely
Uncle Jack

Krystal Appiah
Brooks, Hallie Beachem
Flood, Elizabeth Thorn Scott
Washington, Mary Parks

Lauren Araiza
Pratt, Geronimo

Madalyn Ard
Coles, Solomon Melvin

Adria N. Armbrister
Hale, Mamie Odessa

Donald S. Armentrout
Jones, Absalom

Felix L. Armfield
Jones, Eugene Kinckle

Susan Armitage
Flowers, Ruth Cave

Monifa Love Asante
Edwards, Mel
Hunt, Richard

Lillian Ashcraft-Eason
Michaux, Lightfoot Solomon

Dora Jean Ashe
Spencer, Anne

Jacqueline Asher
Ligon, Glenn

Thabiti Asukile
Rogers, Joel Augustus

Deborah F. Atwater
Kelly, Sharon Pratt

Louis E. Auld
Cox, Ida

Allan D. Austin
Abd Al-Rahman, Ibrahima
Bilali
Delany, Martin Robison
Jallo, Job ben Solomon
Kebe, Lamine
Said, Umar ibn
Salih Bilali

Samuel Autman
Roundtree, Richard

Richard L. Aynes
Jackson, Leo Albert

Natasha Baafi
Dash, Julie

George Baca
Taylor, Council

Karen Backstein
Adams, Carolyn
Benjamin, Fred
Destine, Jean-Leon
Zollar, Jawole

Reid Badger
Europe, James Reese

Sara Bagby
Jernigan (or Jernagin), William H.
Price, Hugh Bernard

Julius H. Bailey
Steward, Rebecca Gould

Chasity Bailey-Fakhoury
Moody, Charles David

David R. Bains
McGuire, George Alexander

Barbara Bair
Hawkins, William Ashbie
Ridley, Florida Ruffin

Therese Duzinkiewicz Baker
Collins, Janet

William J. Baker
Owens, Jesse

Lewis V. Baldwin
Spencer, Peter

James Fargo Balliett
Heath, Jimmy
Hite, Mattie
Monroe, Vernon Earl "The Pearl"
Washington, Grover, Jr.
Webb, Wellington Edward

William E. Bankston
Ammi, Ben
Homer, LeRoy
Shakur, Assata
Smith, Will

Charles Pete Banner-Haley
McGruder, Aaron
Rhodes, Eugene Washington
Vann, Robert L.

Arthur Banton
Fisher, Gail
Tyus, Wyomia

Edward E. Baptist
Thomas, Irma

Lang Baradell
McGirt, James Ephraim

André Barbera
Walker, T-Bone
Washington, Dinah

Roland Barksdale-Hall
Beard, Andrew Jackson

Kenneth C. Barnes
Bouey, Harrison N.

Rhae Lynn Barnes
Deslandes (Deslondes), Charles
Lopes, Lisa (Left Eye)
Smallwood, Thomas

Sharon L. Barnes
Gilbert, Mercedes

Simone Monique Barnes
Briggs, Martha Bailey

Regina N. Barnett
Grandmaster Melle Mel (Melvin Glover)
Jam Master Jay

McDaniels, Darryl
Reverend Run

Bruce Barnhart
Blythe, Arthur

John Herschel Barnhill
Factor, Pompey
Mulzac, Hugh Nathaniel

Alwyn Barr
Bellinger, Charles

Kevin Barrett
Thompson, Joseph Pascal

Frederica Harrison Barrow
Washington, Forrester Blanchard

Leland Conley Barrows
Wright, Elizabeth Evelyn

William David Barry
Bowens, Beverly Elizabeth Dodge

Mathew J. Bartkowiak
Lee, Arthur

Juluette Bartlett-Pack
Bambaataa Aasim, Afrika
Connerly, Ward
Heard, Marian Nobelene Langston

Carolyn Terry Bashaw
Smith, Lucy Harth

Ellen Baskin
Wattleton, Alyce Faye

Jack Bass
Sellers, Cleveland L., Jr.

Angela Bates
Garland, Samuel
Hickman, Daniel
Switzer, Veryl Allen
Vanduvall, Ernestine Caroline

Erin Royston Battat
Adams, Elizabeth Laura
James, Anna Louise

Alexander Battles
Foxx, Redd

Lillian Baulding
Wheatstraw, William Bunch "Peetie"

Dale Baum
Hearne, Azeline

Roland M. Baumann
Patterson, Mary Jane

Betty Winston Bayé
Wickham, DeWayne

Bijan C. Bayne
Wood, William Vernell

Annemarie Bean
Sissle, Noble

Jonathan J. Bean
Fuller, S. B.
Wallace, Charles

Kathryn L. Beard
Craigen, Joseph A.
Daniel, Everard Washington
DeBaptiste, John
Richards, Fannie Moore
Zampty, John Charles

E. Beardsley
Bousfield, Midian Othello
Evans, Matilda Arabella
McClennan, Alonzo Clifton
Murray, Peter Marshall

Michael J. Beary
Demby, Edward T.

William K. Beatty
Dailey, Ulysses Grant
Williams, Daniel Hale

M. Kelly Beauchamp
Blackman, Pompey
Butler, Nace
Charlton, Samuel
Freeman, Jordan

Camille Beazer
Thompson, Priscilla Jane

Chris Bebenek
Belafonte, Harry
Jones, James Earl

H. Kenneth Bechtel
Bouchet, Edward Alexander

Sheila Beck
Caesar, Adolph

Thea Gallo Becker
Brown, Emma V.
Hope, Lugenia Burns
Hunton, Addie Waites

Geraldine Rhoades Beckford
Anderson, Caroline Virginia Still Wiley
Brown, Lucy Manetta Hughes
Burton, Thomas
Grier, Eliza Anna

Joseph W. Becton
Fry, Windsor

Silvio A. Bedini
Banneker, Benjamin

Jayne R. Beilke
Davis, Allison
Davis, John Aubrey
Minkins, Shadrach
Player, Willa Beatrice
Tate, Merze

David T. Beito
Howard, T. R. M.

Linda Royster Beito
Howard, T. R. M.

Gregory S. Bell
Bell, Travers, Jr.
Graves, Earl
Johnson, John (1918–2005)
O'Neal, Stanley
Parsons, Richard Dean
Raines, Franklin Delano
Sutton, Percy

Susan E. Bell
Logan, Myra Adele

Richard J. Bell
Couvent, Marie Bernard
Jea, John
Romain

Donnie D. Bellamy
Hunt, Henry Alexander, Jr.

Lois Bellamy
Baker, Ruth Baytop
Berksteiner, Constance
Boatner, Edward Hammond
Jones, R. Wellington
Pritchard, Robert Stalling, II

Elvatrice Parker Belsches
Edwards, Tommy
Ferguson, David Arthur
Jones, Robert Emmett, Sr.
Jones, Sarah Garland Boyd
Kenney, John Andrew, Sr.
Randolph, Virginia Estelle
Stubbs, Frederick Douglass
Turner, John Patrick

Christopher Benfey
Rillieux, Norbert

Jody Benjamin
Ben Jochannan, Yosef Alfredo Antonio
Bogle, Donald E.
Troupe, Quincy Thomas, Jr.

Jeff Berg
Boyer, Frances
Williams, Clara Belle

Christopher Berkeley
Carter, Stephen L.

Edward A. Berlin
Chauvin, Louis
Harney, Ben R.

Wendi Berman
Bagneris, Vernel Martin
Neville Brothers

Nataly Bernard
Canty, Marietta
Alice Bernstein
Abbott, Israel Braddock
Curry, George Edward
DeLaine, Joseph Armstrong
Perry, Matthew James, Jr.
Slyde, Jimmy
Watson, James Lopez
David Bernstein
Charleston, Oscar McKinley
White, Solomon
Mark Berresford
Sweatman, Wilbur Coleman
Kenyatta D. Berry
Baltimore, Jeremiah Daniel
July, Johanna
Lanier, Robert White
Levy, James Richelieu
Zanders, Roosevelt Smith
Mary Frances Berry
House, Callie Delphia
Michael Berthold
Dubois, Silvia
Eugene H. Berwanger
Hardin, William Jefferson
Curwen Best
Queen Latifah
Wallace D. Best
Wright, Jeremiah A., Jr.
James Bethea
Hubbard, Philip Gamaliel
Adele Beverly
Scales, Jesse
Michael Bieze
Adams, John Henry, Jr.
Adam Biggs
Brooks, Walter Henderson
Roger Biles
Dinkins, David N.
Deborah Bingham Van Broekhoven
Fayerweather, Sarah Ann Harris
Fleming, Louise "Lulu" Cecelia
Washington, James Melvin
Jeffrey L. Birk
Singleton, Alvin
Dedra McDonald Birzer
Esteban
Angela Black
Bowen, Ruth Jean
Sampson, Edith Spurlock
Sklarek, Norma Merrick
Thomas, Franklin Augustine

Cheryl Black
Cooke, Marvel Jackson
Harvey, Georgette Mickey
Mitchell, Abbie
Thomas, Edna Lewis
Samuel W. Black
Black, John Lincoln
Cole, Allen Eugene
Dorsey, James Arthur
R. J. M. Blackett
Chester, Thomas Morris
Day, William Howard
Pamela Blackmon
Alcorn, George Edward, Jr.
Guy, Edna
Renfroe, Earl Wiley
Frederick H. Blake
Stokes, Louis (Lou)
Allison Blakely
Hunt, William Henry
Waller, John Louis
Charles Blancq
Baquet, Achille
Baquet, George
Bolden, Buddy
Cheatham, Doc
Higginbotham, J. C.
Sterling Lecater Bland, Jr.
Mars, James
Parker, William (1822?–?)
De Anne Blanton
Williams, Cathay
Ellesia A. Blaque
Dumas, Henry
Jeff Bloodworth
Hawkins, Augustus Freeman
Lawson, James
Owens, Major Robert Odell
John Bloom
Bonds, Barry Lamar
Haggler, Joseph, Jr.
Maxwell Bloomfield
Jones, Scipio Africanus
Kenneth J. Blume
Clark, Alexander G.
Heard, William Henry Harrison
Powell, William Frank
Thompson, John E. W.
Edith L. Blumhofer
Osborne, William T.
Kristina D. Bobo
Mebane, Mary Elizabeth
Thomas, Piri

Mary Anne Boelcskevy
Alston, Charles Henry
Bowman, Laura
Brown, Ada
Edmonds, S. Randolph
Fauset, Arthur Huff
Harleston, Edwin Augustus
Walrond, Eric
Wilson, Frank H.

Charles Boewe
Williams, Kenny J.

Richard J. Boles
Levington, William

John K. Bollard
Stagolee

Todd Bolton
Dihigo, Martin
Taylor, C. I.

Bruce D. Bomberger
Ruth, William Chester

Gregory Travis Bond
Bullock, Matthew Washington
Cable, Theodore
Flippin, George Albert
Follis, Charles W.
Jackson, William Tecumseh Sherman
Marshall, Bobby
Marshall, Napoleon Bonaparte
Poage, George Coleman
Shippen, John
Sifford, Charlie
Weir, Reginald S.

Melinda Bond Shreve
Dandridge, Vivian
Miller, Loren
Teer, Barbara Ann

F. N. Boney
Brown, John

Alice Bonner
Maynard, Robert Clyve

Barbara Bonous-Smit
Blake, "Blind" Arthur
Bowman, Euday Louis
Brown, Buster
Bumbry, Grace
Hobson Pilot, Ann
Hyman, Phyllis
Jarreau, Alwyn Lopez (Al)
Redman, Joshua
Stone, Fred
Vodery, William Henry Bennett ("Will")

Teresa A. Booker
Anderson, Charles W., Jr.

Holland, William H.
Wright, Binkley T.

Joseph A. Boromé
Purvis, Robert

David Borsvold
Davis, Willie
DeJohnette, Jack
Duke, Bill
Edwards, Gaston Alonzo
Futch, Eddie
Hailstork, Adolphus
Holmes, Larry
Peters, Brock
Quarles, Norma
Sanders, Barry David
Shaw, Bernard
Short, Bobby
Thomas, Isiah Lord, III

Thomas N. Boschert
Church, Robert Reed, Jr.

Joseph Boskin
Cambridge, Godfrey

Nan Bostick
Guy, Harry P.

Greer C. Bosworth
Bellamy, Sherry
Talbert, Naomi

Henry Warner Bowden
Gregg, John Andrew
Grimké, Francis James
Tanner, Benjamin Tucker

J. D. Bowers
Poindexter, James Preston
Somerville, John Alexander

Ryan Reid Bowers
Paige, Rod

Linda Bowles-Adarkwa
Vroman, Mary Elizabeth
Wall, Fannie Franklin

Rob Bowman
Brown, James
Hayes, Isaac

Travis Boyce
Finney, Ernest A.
Gaines, Lloyd L.
Turner, Benner C.
Whittaker, Miller F.
Wrighten, John

Robin Brabham
Gantt, Harvey
Watt, Mel

William H. Brackney
Tindley, Charles Albert

Fuhr, Grant Scott
O'Ree, Willie

Andrea A. Burns
Arnold, Juanita Delores Burnett

William E. Burns
Da Costa, Mathieu
Ferguson, Katy
Sash, Moses

Denise Burrell-Stinson
Everett, Percival

Todd Steven Burroughs
Rideau, Wilbert

Zisca Isabel Burton
Phillips, Carl
Woods, Mattiebelle

Charles Butler
Griffin, Archie

Johnnella E. Butler
Whitfield, James Monroe

Melvin L. Butler
Brewster, William Herbert
Crouch, Andrae

Storm Butler
Percy, Leonard

Marilyn Demarest Button
Cuthbert, Marion Vera
Rogers, Elymas Payson

Kevin Byrne
Dudley, Sherman Houston
Kersands, Billy

Arphelia K. Cabell
Tyner, McCoy

Christopher Caines
Lee, Canada

H. Zahra Caldwell
Holstein, Casper
Johnson, Ellsworth "Bumpy"

Laura M. Calkins
Brown, Arthur McKimmon
Chiles, James Alexander
Fitzbutler, William Henry
Francis, John Richard
Graham, Mary Henrietta
Howell, Abner Leonard
Jones, Sophia Bethena
Roberts, Grace
Rollins, Ida Gray Nelson
Watson, Samuel Codes
Williams, Emily Augustine Harper

Cynthia A. Callahan
Butler, Octavia E.
Petry, Ann

Agnes Kane Callum
Brashear, Carl Maxie
Cain, Lawrence

Michelle Madsen Camacho
Waddles, Mother

Leslie E. Campbell
Campbell, Bebe Moore

Penelope Campbell
Russwurm, John Brown

Joyce A. A. Camper
Egypt, Ophelia Settle

Patricia E. Canson
Chisholm, Shirley

David Alvin Canton
Alexander, Raymond Pace
Bruce, John Edward

Gregg Cantrell
Rayner, John Baptis

Dominic J. Capeci
Dancy, John Campbell, Jr.
Grigsby, Snow Flake
Hill, Charles Andrew
McClendon, James Julius

Christopher Capozzola
Roberts, Needham

Joy Gleason Carew
Atkins, Jasper Alston
Smith, Homer
Tynes, George W.

Brycchan Carey
Equiano, Olaudah

Charles W. Carey Jr.
Cox, Elbert Frank
Davis, Benjamin Jefferson (1870–1945)
Dunbar, Paul Laurence
Ferguson, Angella Dorothea
Flora, William
Julian, Percy Lavon
Kornegay, Wade M.
Langford, George Malcolm
Lewis, Julian Herman
Owens, Joan Murrell
Rouse, Carl Albert
Walls, Josiah Thomas
Washington, Warren Morton

Patrick W. Carey
Tolton, Augustus

Richard Carlin
Handy, W. C.
Hayden, Scott
Jones, Thad
Marshall, Arthur

Terry, Sonny
Turpin, Tom
Rodney P. Carlisle
Lynch, John Roy
Iris Carlton-LaNey
Haynes, Elizabeth Ross
Stephanie A. Carpenter
Yates, Josephine Silone
Glenda R. Carpio
Colescott, Robert
Smith, Bessie
Amy E. Carreiro
Parish, Robert L.
Vincent Carretta
Gronniosaw, James Albert Ukawsaw
Bruce R. Carrick
Bigard, Barney
John M. Carroll
Jackson, Peter
Lipscomb, Eugene Alan "Big Daddy"
McDonald, Henry
Pollard, Fritz
Slater, Duke
Tunnell, Emlen
Young, Buddy
Clayborne Carson
Abernathy, Ralph
King, Martin Luther, Jr.
Malcolm X
Daryl A. Carter
Booker, Cory A.
Cummings, Elijah E.
Diggs, Charles Coles, Jr.
Ellison, Keith M.
Jackson, Lisa P.
Kirk, Ronald "Ron"
Meek, Kendrick B.
Nutter, Michael A.
Steele, Michael
Wynn, Albert R.
Linda M. Carter
Andrews, Raymond
Bristol, Johnny
Brown, Cora
Burton, Annie Louise
Campbell, Israel S.
Day, John, Jr.
Driskell, David
Fakir, Abdul "Duke"
Fuqua, Harvey
Gordy, Berry, Sr.

Guy, Rosa Cuthbert
Holland, Brian
Holland, Edward "Eddie"
Isley, Ernest "Ernie"
Johnson, Isaac
Knight, Gladys
Mason, Isaac
Smyth, John H.
Talley, André Leon
Vandross, Luther
Whitfield, Norman Jesse
Marva Griffin Carter
Cumbo, Marion
Fletcher, Tom
Jessye, Eva Alberta
Love, Josephine Harreld
Steven R. Carter
Hansberry, Lorraine Vivian
Tomeiko Ashford Carter
Gayle, Addison, Jr.
Adrienne Carthon
Shinhoster, Earl
Charles F. Casey-Leninger
Berry, Theodore M.
Floris Barnett Cash
Matthews, Victoria Earle
Derek Charles Catsam
Shuttlesworth, Fred Lee
Frank Cha
Burrill, Mary P.
Bruce Guy Chabot
Wilson, J. Finley
Faye A. Chadwell
Carter, Eunice Hunton
Mou Chakraborty
Sandifer, Jawn Ardin
Malca Chall
Albrier, Frances Mary
Chris Chan
Blockson, Charles L.
Nat Charles
Hendricks, Barbara
Marcia Chatelain
Little Rock Nine, The
Linda Chavers
Bassett, Angela
Tucker, C. DeLores
Wallace McClain Cheatham
Arroyo, Martina
Davy, Gloria
Frierson, Andrew Bennie
Lee, Everet Astor
Lee, Sylvia Olden

McGinty, Doris Evans
Moore, Dorothy Rudd
Shirley, George Irving
Warfield, William Caesar
Williams, Camilla Ella

Aimee Lee Cheek
Copeland, John Anthony, Jr.
Langston, John Mercer

William Cheek
Copeland, John Anthony, Jr.
Langston, John Mercer

Alexander J. Chenault
Barthelemy, Sidney J.
Boyce, Mildred L.
Evans, Melvin Herbert
Hall, Amos T.
Johnson, Mildred Louise
Jones, Levi
Nagin, C. Ray

Margaret Cheney
Mercer, Mabel

Boyd Childress
Bethea, Elvin
Bol, Manute
Dawkins, Darryl
Gilchrist, Carlton Chester "Cookie"
Moses, William Henry

Arthur Ben Chitty
Green, Ely
Russell, James Solomon

Laura M. Chmielewski
Montjoy, Zilpah

James Chrismer
Baker, Harriet Ann

Anna Christian
Crosse, Rupert
Williams, Frances E.

Samuel Christian
Dandridge, Dorothy

Winsome Chunnu
Childs, Francine C.
Finney, Ernest A.
Gaines, Lloyd L.
Whittaker, Miller F.

Patrick Chura
Early, Gerald
Steele, Shelby

Barbara L. Ciccarelli
Fort, Syvilla
Patterson, William L.

Mark Clague
Adams, Alton Augustus, Sr.

Benjamin, Bennie
Hinderas, Natalie

Randall Clark
Capers, Virginia
Everett, Francine
McNeil, Claudia

Thomas Clarkin
Bunche, Ralph
Dubuclet, Antoine

Stanley Bennett Clay
Harris, E. Lynn
Hines, Gregory

Kathleen N. Cleaver
Newton, Huey P.

Patrick Cliff
Jones, James Francis

Suzanne Cloud
Ballard, Butch
Bridgewater, Cecil
Bridgewater, Dee Dee
Bryant, Ray
Dockery, Sam
Green, Eddie
Simms, Evelyn

Shirley M. Carr Clowney
Harvey, Bessie

William J. Cobb
Pickens, William
Randolph, A. Philip

Rachel Cody
DeFrantz, Faburn
Garrett, Bill

Harvey Cohen
Williams, Clarence

Thomas Burnell Colbert
Jones, Laurence Clifton
McCabe, Edwin Prescott

Johnnetta B. Cole
Simmons, Ruth J.

Stefanie Cole
Luper, Clara

Florence M. Coleman
Barrow, Peter
Burch, Charles Eaton

Paulette Coleman
Cole-Talbert, Florence O.
Epps, Anna Cherrie
Thompson, Robert Louis (Bob)
Tolliver, William

James Lincoln Collier
Ellington, Duke

Camille A. Collins
Africa, John
Bennett, Estelle
Collins, Sam "Crying"
Edwards, Bernard
Smith, Mabel Louise "Big Maybelle"
Stanton, Alysa

Lisa Gail Collins
Lawrence, Jacob Armstead

Sharon M. Collins
Lowry, James H.

Thomas W. Collins
Leonard, Buck
Moore, Archie

Michelle D. Commander
Fields, Mamie Elizabeth Garvin

Tonia M. Compton
Beasley, Mathilda Taylor
Peake, Mary S.

Kirsten Condry
Clash, Kevin

Paula Conlon
Eckstine, Billy

Eugene H. Conner
Lattimore, John Aaron Cicero

Susan C. Cook
Wooding, Sam

Nicole A. Cooke
Delaney, Sarah Peterson
Jones, Clara Stanton

Princess Mhoon Cooper
Cummings, Blondell
Waters, Sylvia

Dennis Michael Corcoran
Green, Percy, II

Mary F. Corey
Coker, Daniel

Caleb A. Corkery
Newsome, Mary Effie Lee
Ray, Henrietta Cordelia

Íde Corley
Duse, Mohammed Ali

Nathan M. Corzine
Cooper, Andy "Lefty"
Grant, Frank
Horton, William R., Jr.

Caryn Cossé Bell
Dumas, Francois Ernest
Lanusse, Armand
Savary, Charles Joseph

Richard Hauer Costa
Gordone, Charles

Angelo Costanzo
Hammon, Briton

P. J. Cotroneo
Jackson, Milt

Debbie Maudlin Cottrell
Branch, Mary Elizabeth

Robert P. Crease
Rector, Eddie
Tucker, Snake Hips

Jeff Crocombe
Prout, Mary Ann
Weir, Samuel

J. Vern Cromartie
Lewis, Joan Tarika

Adelaide M. Cromwell
Cromwell, Otelia

Ginny Crosthwait
Allen-Noble, Rosie
Williams, Stanley "Tookie"

Lou-Ann Crouther
Dickens, Dorothy Lee

Samantha Crowell
Richardson, Judy

Donnamaria Culbreth
Cobb, James Adlai
Poole, Cecil F.

Prudence D. Cumberbatch
Mfume, Kweisi
Murphy, Carl

Rosalind Cummings-Yeates
Reid, Vernon
Walker, Albertina
White, Barry

Isabel Shipley Cunningham
Jefferson, Roland M.

Mark D. Cunningham
Chappelle, Dave
Hughes, Albert and Allen

Valerie Cunningham
Whipple, Dinah

Cynthia Current
Lane, Lunsford

Blanche Radford Curry
Edmonds, Helen
Weems, Renita J.

Ginette Curry
Chase-Riboud, Barbara
Senna, Danzy

Jennifer Curry
Gladwell, Malcolm
Gordon, Bruce S.

Kimberly Curtis
Chandler, Dana C., Jr.
Donaldson, Jeff
Greene, Lorenzo Johnston

Colleen Cyr
Jeffrey, George S.
Linda Dahl
Donegan, Dorothy
Maceo Crenshaw Dailey
Moton, Robert Russa
Napier, James Carroll
Daniel A. Dalrymple
Barkley, Charles
Bettis, Jerome
Blount, Mel
Greene, Joe
Stallworth, John
Karen C. Dalton
Baker, Josephine
Lisa Daniels
Powell, Michael Anthony (Mike)
Robin M. Dasher-Alston
Ross Barnett, Marguerite
Antje Daub
Alexander, Clifford Leopold, Jr.
Gourdin, Edward Orval
Lee, Joseph E.
Brian J. Daugherity
Green, Calvin Coolidge
Hill, Oliver White
Leo J. Daugherty
Stewart, Bennett McVey
Marlene L. Daut
Beaty, Powhatan
Brown, Wilson
Estabrook, Prince
Hamlet, James
Elizabeth K. Davenport
Jackson McCabe, Jewell
LaFontant, Jewel Stradford
Rolark, Wilhelmina Jackson
Keay Davidson
Osborne, Estelle Massey Riddle
Peck, David Jones
Althea T. Davis
Franklin, Martha Minerva
Pinn, Petra Fitzalieu
Amanda J. Davis
Naylor, Gloria
Smith, Barbara (1946–)
Barbara Toomer Davis
Brown, Joan Myers
Faison, George
LeTang, Henry
Cyprian Davis
Dorsey, John Henry
Healy, Eliza
Rudd, Daniel

Hugh Davis
Gordon, Emmanuel Taylor
Horne, Frank
John Davis
Blind Boone
Blind Tom
Gottschalk, Louis Moreau
LaRose M. Davis
Whitman, Albery Allson
Lisa Kay Davis
Bingham, Howard
Luckett V. Davis
Armstrong, Henry
Dixon, George
Flowers, Tiger
Langford, Samuel
Lewis, John Henry
Walcott, Joe
Robert "Bob" Davis
McCain, Franklin
Robert Scott Davis
Dabney, Austin
Ryan J. Davis
Franks, Gary
Wayne Dawkins
Jackson, Fay M.
Tanita Jasmine Dawson
Fabio, Sarah Webster
Aaron L. Day
Butler, Mary Dell
Jared N. Day
Payton, Philip A., Jr.
David de Clue
Anderson, Michael
Pandit, Korla
Warwick, Dionne
Mary De Jong
Smith, Amanda Berry
Nanette De Jong
Yancey, Mama
Dominique-René de Lerma
Bledsoe, Jules
Moore, Undine
Perry, Julia
Simmons, Calvin Eugene
Christopher C. De Santis
Tolson, Melvin Beaunorus
David M. Dean
Holly, James Theodore
Pamala S. Deane
Edwards, James
Gilpin, Charles Sidney
Gines, Bernadine Alberta Coles
Randolph, Amanda

Simms, Hilda
Washington, Mary Helen
LaNesha NeGale DeBardelaben
Alexander, Virginia Margaret
Burroughs, Margaret Taylor Goss
Freeman, Frankie Muse
Lindsay, Inabel Burns
Morton, Lena Beatrice
Thomas F. DeFrantz
Borde, Percival
Williams, Bert and George Walker
Crystal A. deGregory
Gloster, Hugh Morris
Lawson, James Raymond
William Dejong-Lambert
Checker, Chubby
Domino, Fats
Theodore C. DeLaney
Chavis, John
Brenda K. Delany
Gentry, Herbert
Jeannine DeLombard
Ball, Charles
Dianne Dentice
Conner, Jeffie Obrea Allen
Dupree, Anna Johnson
Adebe DeRango-Adem
Christian, Barbara
Isaac, Ephraim
Spillers, Hortense J.
Mary Krane Derr
Amini, Johari
Anderson, Hallie L.
Bessent, Hattie
Blake, Margaret Jane
Bowman, Thea
Brown, Linda Carol
Byrd, Bobby
Carter, Nell
Chatmon, Sam
Collins, Cardiss Robertson
Davis, Danny K.
Duster, Alfreda Barnett
Guillory, Ida Lewis
Gwaltney, John Langston
Harrison, Faye Venetia
Hernandez, Aileen
Hill, Anita Faye
Jackson, Mattie J.
Jones, Edith Mae Irby
Jones, Stephanie Tubbs
Loguen Fraser, Sarah Marinda
Martin, Sallie

Mr. Imagination
Nash, Helen Elizabeth
Patton, Georgia E. L.
Petioni, Charles Augustin
Petioni, Muriel Marjorie
Reynolds, Melvin Jay
Roberts, Shearley Oliver
Rodgers, Carolyn M.
Starr, Edwin
Steele, Carrie
Stubbs, Levi
Suggs, Eliza G.
Sylvester
Temple, Ruth Janetta
Turpin, Waters Edwards
Ward, Aida
Wheeler, Emma Rochelle
Woods, Geraldine Pittman
Sylvia M. DeSantis
Che-cho-ter
Figgs, Carrie Law Morgan
Gleason, Eliza Veleria Atkins
Taylor, Mildred D.
Barbara A. Desmarais
Heuston, Francis
Stakeman, Randolph
James I. Deutsch
Strode, Woody
John Patrick Deveney
Randolph, Paschal Beverly
Christopher Devine
Battey, Earl
Gibson, Bob
Jackson, Reggie
Walker, Weldy
Watson, Bob "The Bull"
Paul Devlin
Dean, Lillian Harris "Pig Foot Mary"
Edwards, Jodie "Butterbeans"
Hampton, Slide
Huff, Leon
Johnson, George W.
Lew, Barzillai (or Barsillai)
McAdoo, Robert (Bob) Allen, Jr.
Peete, Calvin
Rawls, Lou
Reed, Eric
Snow, Valaida
Stone, Sly
Caroline DeVoe
Crawford, Anthony P.
Kerry Dexter
Bibb, Leon

Firouzeh Dianat
  Pierce, Ponchitta
Ed Diaz
  Cayton, Horace Roscoe, Sr.
  Cayton, Revels Hiram
  Cayton, Susie Sumner Revels
Simon Dickel
  Hemphill, Essex
Bill Dickens
  Wharton, Clifton R., Jr
Dennis C. Dickerson
  Cannon, George Dows
  Cannon, George Epps
Robert M. Dixon
  Massey, Walter Eugene
Makeba G. Dixon-Hill
  Moorhead, Scipio
  Smith, Marvin and Morgan Smith
Marty Dobrow
  Abdul-Jabbar, Kareem
  Griffith-Joyner, Florence
Jualynne E. Dodson
  Lee, Jarena
Jacob Doerfler
  Quy, Libbeus
Elvita Dominique
  Davis Trussell, Elizabeth Bishop
Daniel Donaghy
  Harris, Franco
  Komunyakaa, Yusef
  O'Neal, Shaquille Rashaun
  Thompson, John Robert, Jr.
  Walker, George Theophilus
  Wideman, John Edgar
  Williams, Sherley Anne
Bobby Donaldson
  Floyd, Silas Xavier
  Walker, Charles Thomas
  White, William Jefferson
Jamal Donaldson Briggs
  Browne, Robert Span
  Herman, Alexis Margaret
Joe Dorinson
  Doby, Larry
  Irvin, Monte
Davison M. Douglas
  Robinson, Jackie
George H. Douglas
  Anderson, Eddie Rochester
Seth Dowland
  Hooks, Benjamin Lawson

Lynn Downey
  Pleasant, Mary Ellen
Jennifer Drake
  Cortez, Jayne
  Dent, Tom
  Evans, Mari E.
  Harper, Michael Steven
  Joans, Ted
  Kaufman, Bob
Noah D. Drezner
  Hayre, Ruth Wright
Anne K. Driscoll
  Bacon-Bercey, June
  Bentley, Gladys
  Bohannon, Horace
  Green, Jonathan
  Hall, Charles "Buster"
  Hawkins, Jalacy J. "Screamin' Jay"
  Lucas, C. Payne
  Perry, Carrie Saxon
Alice Drum
  Cary, Lorene
  Crouch, Stanley
Cheryl Dudley
  Brown, Homer S.
  Jones, E. Edward, Sr.
  Jones, Edward P., Sr.
Ronald P. Dufour
  Abrams, Muhal Richard
  Allen, Geri Antoinette
  Berry, Chu
  Braxton, Anthony (Delano)
  Byas, Don
  Chambers, Paul
  Christian, Charlie
  Coleman, Bill
  Davis, Anthony Curtis
  Hawkins, Coleman
  Henderson, Fletcher
  Hill, Andrew
  Hodges, Johnny
  Jackson, Mahalia
  Johnson, Bunk
  Lateef, Yusef
  Redman, Don
  Roach, Max
  Rollins, Sonny
  Shepp, Archie Vernon
  Shorter, Wayne
  Silver, Horace

Taylor, Cecil Percival
Williams, Mary Lou
Williams, Tony
Wilson, Teddy
Young, Lester

Peter J. Duignan
Roye, Edward James

Bethany K. Dumas
Baugh, John
Butler, Melvin Arthur
Rickford, John R.
Smitherman, Geneva
Turner, Lorenzo Dow

Eve E. Dunbar
Kennedy, Adrienne

Russell Duncan
Campbell, Tunis Gulic

Christine Dureau
Guillén, Nicolás

Diana Kristine Durham
Franklin, Charles Sumner
Jenkins, Norman A.
Sebastian, Simon Powell

Peg Duthie
Cullen, Frederick Ashbury
Love, Rose Leary
Rush, Gertrude Elzora Durden

Ervin Dyer
Kelly, Leontine Turpeau Current
Lincoln, C. Eric
McNairy, Francine

De Witt S. Dykes
Dykes, De Witt Sanford, Sr.

Gerald Early
Ali, Muhammad
Flood, Curt
Foster, Rube

Mary Frances Early
Johnson, Hall
Martin, Roberta

Alice Knox Eaton
Brown, William Wells
Chuck D (Carlton Douglas Ridenhour)
Cobb, Charles E., Jr.
Coffee
Davis, Thulani
Dunbar-Nelson, Alice
Harris, Louise "Mamma"
Hopkins, Pauline Elizabeth
Jacobs, Phebe Ann
Prince, Mary
Sanchez, Sonia

Shange, Ntozake
Turner, Darwin T.

Margaret E. Edds
Wilder, Douglas

Ramona Hoage Edelin
Lewis, William Charles, II
Phinazee, Alethia Annette Lewis Hoage

Joanne H. Edey-Rhodes
Battle, Effie Dean Threat
Battle, Wallace Aaron, Sr.

Justin D. Edwards
Kincaid, Jamaica

Pamela C. Edwards
Bath, Patricia
Boone, Sarah
Goode, Sarah E.
Johnson, Katherine G.
Joyner, Marjorie Stewart

Thomas O. Edwards
Carson, Ben

Yvonne Jackson Edwards
Mease, Quentin Ronald "Quent"

Marta J. Effinger-Crichlow
Jones, Madame Sissieretta Joyner

Douglas R. Egerton
Gabriel
Turner, Nat

Walter Ehrlich
Scott, Dred

Lois J. Einhorn
McCray, Carrie Anderson Allen

Harry Elam
O'Neal, Frederick Douglass
Parks, Suzan Lori

Michele Elam
Walker, Kara

Sean Elias
Toussaint, Allen
Washboard Sam

William G. Elliott
Blake, Eubie

Nadia Ellis
Patterson, Orlando

Chris Elzey
Matthews, Vince
Wright, Stan

Caroline Emmons
Hurley, Ruby

David J. Endres
Healy, Sherwood
Rivers, Clarence Rufus Joseph
Uncles, Charles Randolph

Saul Engelbourg
Lewis, Reginald Francis
Kent J. Engelhardt
Parker, Charlie
Bertis English
Berry, Lawrence S.
Green, Jim
Turner, William V.
Kristal L. Enter
Cunningham, Edgar V., Sr.
Hawkins, Virgil Darnell
Hollowell, Donald Lee
Kennard, Clyde
Martin, Lazarus "Lesra"
Ward, Horace Taliaferro
Lia B. Epperson
Alexander, Sadie Tanner Mossell
Edward M. Epstein
Simpson, Lorna
Kitty Kelly Epstein
Hodges, Sylvester
Paul A. Erickson
Cobb, William Montague
John Ernest
Hughes, Louis
Karenga, Maulana
Keona K. Ervin
Calloway, DeVerne Lee
Stephen Eschenbach
Brown, Earl
Pride, Curtis
Thompson, Henry Curtis (Hank)
Onita Estes-Hicks
Anderson, Regina
Nance, Ethel Ray
David Evans
Johnson, Blind Willie
Stephanie Y. Evans
Evans, William Leonard, Jr.
Lyle, Ethel Octavia Hedgeman
Bruce J. Evensen
Mills, Harry
Michael Ezra
Norton, Kenneth (Ken) Howard
Patterson, Floyd
Sayers, Gale
Terrell, Ernie
Duncan F. Faherty
Hammon, Jupiter
David M. Fahey
Artrell, William Middleton
Browne, William Washington

Ina J. Fandrich
Massiah, Louis Joseph
Montana, Allison Marcel "Tootie"
Caroline M. Fannin
Bullard, Eugène
Julian, Hubert F.
Lawrence, Robert Henry, Jr.
Andrew M. Fearnley
George, Zelma Watson
Wayne Federman
Thompson, David
Alex Feerst
McCall, Nathan
Smith, William Gardner
Steve Feffer
Dozier, Lamont Herbert
R. J. Fehrenbach
Easton, William Edgar
Lynne B. Feldman
Gaston, A. G.
Nail, John E.
Pettiford, William Reuben
Kenneth R. Fenster
Peeples, Nat
Leslie T. Fenwick
Futrell, Mary Hatwood
Gerard Fergerson
Johnson, Peter August
Moira Ferguson
Kincaid, Jamaica
SallyAnn H. Ferguson
West, Dorothy
Wanda F. Fernandopulle
Allen, Richard (1830–1909)
Jeri Chase Ferris
Mason, Biddy Bridget
Marcie Cohen Ferris
Council, Mildred "Mama Dip"
Allyson N. Field
Wayans, Keenen Ivory
Robert Fikes
Anderson, Jervis
Arrington, Richard, Jr.
Bristow, Lonnie Robert
Coons, Orlando
Cose, Ellis Jonathan
Ferguson, Lloyd Noel
Gilliam, Earl B.
Kimbrough, Jack
Lee Smith, Hughie
Morrison, Harry Lee
Murphy, Isaac
Organ, Claude H., Jr.

Linda J. Frazier
Shankle, James and Winne Brush
Yvonne Davis Frear
Craft, Juanita Jewel Shanks
Flanagan, Minnie
John C. Fredriksen
Flipper, Henry Ossian
Jacob Andrew Freedman
Allensworth, Allen
Bond, Scott
Latta, Morgan London
Leonard, Sugar Ray
Morgan, Joe
Sanders, Deion Luwynn
Taylor, Lawrence
Wilkens, Lenny
Williams, Isaac D.
Williams, Sally Isaac (Aunt Sally)
Greg Freeman
Shines, Johnny
Simmons, Philip
Williams, J. Mayo "Ink"
Lisa D. Freiman
Delaney, Beauford
Saar, Betye
John French
Blakeley, Adeline
Manson, Jacob
Manson, Roberta
Ruth C. Friedberg
Price, Florence B.
Nathaniel Friedman
Alexander, Arthur
Blackwell, Ed
Burke, Solomon
Cherry, Don
Haynes, Roy
Sledge, Percy
Turner, Ike
Womack, Bobby
Paul A. Frisch
Ferrell, Frank J.
Griffey, Ken, Jr.
Smith, Wendell
Torriente, Cristobal
Wells, Willie
Wright, Wild Bill
Jan Marie Fritz
Gomillion, Charles Goode
Gary L. Frost
Temple, Lewis
Woods, Granville T.
Jennifer Reed Fry
Coleman, Maude B.

Dickerson, Addie Whiteman
Griffin, Mary (Mazie) Campbell Mossell
Stephen M. Fry
Valentine, Kid Thomas
Linda K. Fuller
Beavers, Louise
Timothy E. Fulop
Perry, Rufus Lewis
Brett Gadsden
Belton, Ethel Lee
Bulah, Sarah
Mitchell, Littleton Purnell
Redding, Louis Lorenzo
C. Dale Gadsden
Mitchell, Arthur
Larvester Gaither
Guyot, Lawrence
Obadele, Imari
Washington, Craig
Robert L. Gale
Gardiner, Leon
Lee, Ulysses Grant
Julie Gallagher
Hedgeman, Anna Arnold
Jackson, Ada B.
Richardson, Maude B.
Speaks, Sara Pelham
Mar Gallego
Lee, Andrea
Louis B. Gallien
Middleton Hairston, Jeanne
Perkins, John M.
Francesca Gamber
Boykin, Keith
Nabrit, James Madison, Jr.
Vanessa Northington Gamble
Jefferson, Mildred Fay
Hope Hazard Gamboa
Foster, Autherine Lucy
Larry Gara
Still, William
David F. Garcia
Rodríguez, Arsenio
Eric Gardner
Brown, Josephine
Bruce, Josephine Beall Willson
Burton, Walter Moses
Carter, Dennis Drummond
Carter, Jennie
Cassey, Peter
Corbin, Joseph Carter
Detter, Thomas
Dickson, Moses
Douglass, Grace Bustill

Drumgoold, Kate
Dunlap, Mollie Ernestine
Duplex, Edward P.
Fletcher, Barney
Fordham, Mary Weston
Forte, Ormond Adolphus
Gilliard, James E. M.
Greenfield, Elizabeth Taylor
Hall, William Henry
Hubbard, James H.
Johnson, Amelia Etta Hall
Johnson, Harvey
Jones, Friday
Jones, Sarah Emily Gibson
McKoy, Millie and Christine McKoy
Moore, John Jamison
Mossell, Gertrude Bustill
Newby, William H.
Offley, Greensbury Washington
Parker, Allen
Paul, Susan
Perry, Fredericka Douglass Sprague
Pyles, Charlotta Gordon
Ray, Henrietta Green Regulus
Rock, John Stewart
Ruby, George Thompson
Russel, Chloe
Scott, Harriet Robinson
Selika (Marie Smith Williams)
Sims, Thomas
Sprague, Rosetta Douglass
Townsend, Jonas Holland
Vashon, Susan Paul Smith
Ward, T. M. D.
Webb, Frank J.
Webb, Mary
Williams, James
Yates, William Henry

S. L. Gardner
Armstead, Robert "Bob"

Jim Garrett
Coffey, Cornelius Robinson

Shennette Garrett
Calloway, Blanche Dorothea Jones
Cole, Robert A.
Herndon, Norris B.
Hilyer, Amanda Victoria Gray
Scott, R. C.
Stewart, Sallie W.
Wilson, Sunnie

John Garst
Baker, Frankie
Delia

Duncan, Harry
John Hardy
John Henry
Speed, Ella

John Bryan Gartrell
Bluford, Guion (Guy) Stewart, Jr.
Greer, Hal
McNair, Ronald Erwin

Wendi Berman Gary
French, Robert "Bob"

Marybeth Gasman
Johnson, Charles Spurgeon

David Barry Gaspar
Walcott, Derek

Billie Gastic
Beam, Joseph Fairchild

Willard B. Gatewood
Cook, John Francis
Cook, John Francis, Jr.
Mitchell, John, Jr.

Chris Gavaler
Long, Sylvester

Mary Lisa Gavenas
Williams, Dudley Eugene

James Gavin
Jackson, Michael
Jones, Quincy
Vaughan, Sarah

Jason Geary
Wilson, Olly

Marilyn L. Geary
Davis, Belva
Gaston, Felecia Gail

Elshaday Gebreyes
Jones, Bill T.

Stephen M. Gennaro
Gwynn, Tony
Henderson, Rickey

Andy Gensler
Johnson, Francis
Wonder, Stevie

Nadine George-Graves
Whitman, Alice, Alberta, Essie, and Mabel

David A. Gerber
Clark, Peter Humphries

Mary Reginald Gerdes
Lange, Mary Elizabeth

Larry R. Gerlach
Ashford, Emmett Littleton
Fowler, Bud
Howard, Elston
Robeson, Paul
Walker, Moses Fleetwood

Maggie Gerrity
Glave, Thomas
Young, Kevin

Jerry Gershenhorn
Austin, Louis Ernest
Elder, Alfonso
Pearson, Conrad Odell
Thorpe, Earlie Endris

David A. Gerstner
Riggs, Marlon

Louis S. Gerteis
Montgomery, Benjamin Thornton

Anthony Gerzina
Prince, Abijah
Terry, Lucy

Paula J. Giddings
Wells Barnett, Ida Bell

Steven P. Gietschier
Washington, Kenny

Justin David Gifford
Beck, Robert "Iceberg Slim"
Cooper, Clarence, Jr.
Heard, Nathan Cliff
Jefferson, Roland Spratlin

Laura Jane Gifford
Washington, Valores J. (Val)

Daniel R. Gilbert
Davis, Ernie

Jenifer W. Gilbert
McKissick, Floyd Bixler
Ottley, Roi

Freda Scott Giles
Bubbles, John
McKay, Claude

Glenda E. Gill
Waters, Ethel

Teresa Gilliams
Holman, Steve

Brian Gilmore
Bell, Derrick Albert, Jr.
Lynn, Conrad J.

Glenda E. Gilmore
Smalls, Robert

Jennifer Glaser
Johnson, Mat

Zipporah G. Glass
Boyd, Richard Henry

Stephen D. Glazier
Arnett, Benjamin William
Brown, John Mifflin

Charles A. Gliozzo
Jones, John

Geoffrey Gneuhs
Plummer, Henry Vinton

Richlyn Faye Goddard
Forsythe, Albert E.
Hyers, Anna Madah
Hyers, Emma Louise
Still, James

Jacqueline Goggin
Taylor, Alrutheus Ambush
Woodson, Carter Godwin

Marv Goldberg
Ricks, James Thomas "Jimmy"
Til, Sonny

Nancy Goldstein
Ormes, Jackie

Vincent F. A. Golphin
Brandon, Brumsic, Jr.
Marino, Eugene Antonio
Perry, Harold Robert

Angela M. Gooden
Lynch, Damon, III

Frank H. Goodyear
Gordon

Lewis R. Gordon
West, Cornel

Maxine Gordon
Higgins, Billy
Scott, Shirley

Stephanie Gordon
Reeves, Bass

William B. Gould, IV
Gould, William B.

Leslie Gourse
Brown, Cleo
Liston, Melba
McFerrin, Bobby
Peterson, Oscar
Sanders, Pharoah

Dennis Gouws
Dill, Augustus Granville
Jackman, Harold

Kevin Grace
Steward, Emanuel

Nathan L. Grant
Bush-Banks, Olivia Ward

Will Gravely
Brown, Morris

Christine Rauchfuss Gray
Richardson, Willis

Michael Gray
Carr, Leroy

Pamela Lee Gray
Aaron, Jesse
Bradley, Edward
Browne, Roscoe Lee
Campbell, Elmer Simms

Chenier, Clifton
Daylie, Holmes "Daddy-O"
De Lavallade, Carmen
Dédé, Edmond
Ellington, Mercedes
Farrow, William McKnight
Goines, Donald Joseph
Hall, Arsenio
Havens, Richie
Holder, Geoffrey
Johnson, Earvin "Magic," Jr.
Lomax, Louis Emanuel
Lymon, Frankie
McCovey, Willie
Moore, Kevin (Keb' Mo')
Pickett, Wilson, Jr.
Seals, Frank Son
Sims, Howard "Sandman"
Solomons, Gus, Jr.
Townsend, Robert
Weston, Maudelle Bass
Xuma, Madie Hall

Tarice Sims Gray

Johnson, Marjorie Witt

Valerie A. Gray

Arter, Jared
Kelley, William

Lloyd J. Graybar

Ford, Len

Adam W. Green

Alou, Felipe
Arrieta, Saturnino Orestes Armas Miñoso ("Minnie Miñoso")
Ballance, Frank Winston, Jr.
Bishop, Sanford Dixon, Jr.
Blackwell, John Kenneth (Ken)
Campbell, William Craig "Bill"
Carew, Rod
Carter, Anson
Cepeda, Orlando
Clarke, Yvette Diane
Clay, William Lacy (Bill), Sr.
Collins, George Washington
Dawes, Kwame Senu Neville
Dawson, Andre Nolan
Dickerson, Eric Demetric
Garrison, Zina Lynna
Gaston, Clarence Edwin "Cito"
Golden, Lily
Haskins, James S.
Hinton, Chuck
Jenkins, Ferguson "Fergie" Arthur, Jr.
Lott, Ronald Mandel "Ronnie"
Marichal, Juan

Murray, Eddie
Pérez, Tony
Puckett, Kirby
Raines, Timothy, Sr.
Reliford, Joe Louis
Rudd, Wayland
Smith, Ozzie
Strawberry, Darryl Eugene
Virgil, Osvaldo José
Walker, Herschel Junior
Williams, Billy Leo
Winfield, Dave

Frank L. Green

Bush, George Washington

Jeffrey Green

Johnson, Thomas Lewis
Loudin, Frederick Jeremiah

Patricia E. Green

Thurman, Sue Bailey

Stanton W. Green

Mays, Willie

Robert M. Greenberg

Hayden, Robert Earl

Bob Greene

Johnson, James Alloyd
Lowry, "Tiger" Ted
Nichols, Barbara Ware
Ruby, Reuben

Christina Greene

Atwater, Ann

Janice L. Greene

Baker, Henry Edwin
Clarke, Milton

Sally Greene

Roberts, Meshack "Shack" R.

Cynthia Greenlee-Donnell

Evans, Minnie Jones
Giddens, Rhiannon

Sheila T. Gregory

Banks, William Venoid

Farah Jasmine Griffin

Holiday, Billie
Marshall, Paule

David R. Griffiths

Robinson, John C.

Elizabeth Gritter

Smith, Maxine Atkins

Dalton Gross

Braithwaite, William Stanley Beaumont

Kahlil Gross

Merriweather, "Big Maceo"
Washington, Sarah Spencer

Mary Jean Gross

Braithwaite, William Stanley Beaumont

James R. Grossman
Jackson, Robert R.

Kathryn Grover
Jackson, William
Jacobs, John S.
Johnson, Nathan

John Gruber
Ganaway, King Daniel

Dolph Grundman
Barksdale, Don
Baylor, Elgin Gay
Haynes, Marques Oreole
Jones, K. C.
Lloyd, Earl Francis
Robertson, Oscar Palmer
Unseld, Westley Sissel

Pamela Grundy
Washington, Ora

Richard Grupenhoff
Tucker, Lorenzo

Gerard Gryski
Taylor, Anna Diggs

Thomas Edward Guastello
Bowe, Riddick

Betty Kaplan Gubert
Brown, Willa
Farmer, James
Schomburg, Arthur Alfonso

Lawrence Gushee
Oliver, King

LaVerne Gyant
Davis, Henrietta Vinton

Chuck Haddix
McShann, Jay
Williams, Claude Fiddler

Matthew A. Hafar
Estes, Simon Lamont
Pratt, Awadagin

Monica Hairston
Bogan, Lucille (Bessie Jackson)
Rupaul

Douglas Hales
Cuney, Norris Wright

Eric Allen Hall
Edwards, Harry

Stephen Gilroy Hall
Cromwell, John Wesley

Carl V. Hallberg
Dart, Isom

Brian Hallstoos
Bradford, Alex

Campbell, Delois Barrett
Jones, Willa Saunders
Williams, Marion

John E. Hallwas
Goodwin, Ruby Berkley

Donna L. Halper
Cooper, Jack Leroy
Coppin, Levi Jenkins
Funnye, Capers C., Jr.
Gibson, Joseph Deighton (Jack)
Gordon, Eugene F.
Higgins, Bertha Grant DeLard
Hill, "Rabbi" David
Jackson, J. J.

Edward C. Halperin
Donnell, Clyde Henry
Moore, Aaron McDuffie

Tiffany T. Hamelin
Hutton, Bobby
Moore, Amzie

Daniel W. Hamilton
Randolph, Benjamin Franklin

Lawrence E. Hamilton
Laine, Henry Allen

Debi Hamlin
Holland, Annie Welthy Daughtry
Hyman, John Adams

Françoise N. Hamlin
Henry, Aaron E.
Pigee, Vera Mae

Mary Jessica Hammes
Holmes, Hamilton

Theresa A. Hammond
Blayton, Jesse Bee
Cromwell, John W., Jr.
Gines, Bernadine Alberta Coles
Harris, John Benjamin
Harris, Ruth Coles
Mitchell, Bert Norman
Ross, Frank K.
Washington, Mary Thelma
Wilson, Milton James

Monte Hampton
Evans, Henry

Fiona J. L. Handley
Coincoin, Marie-Thérèse
Doclas, Nicholas
Metoyer, Augustin
Metoyer, Louis
Pacalé, Yves

Antoinette Handy
Anderson, Marian
Austin, Lovie

Dixon, Dean
Durham, Eddie
Freeman, Harry Lawrence
Pierce, De De and Billie Pierce
Scott, Hazel Dorothy
Spivey, Victoria

Rebecca L. Hankins
Cartwright, Marguerite D.
Harvey, Clarie Collins

John Hanners
Grier, Rosey
Johnson, John Henry

Mary Anne Hansen
Carr, Sister Wynona

Moya B. Hansen
Bush, William Owen
Denny, John
Morrison, George

Mathias Hanses
Crogman, William Henry
Hooks, Mathew "Bones"
Lane, Wiley
Moore, Louis (or Lewis) Baxter
Snowden, Frank Martin, Jr.
Williams, Daniel Barclay

Renée R. Hanson
Hathaway, Isaac Scott

Verity J. Harding
Brooks, Lucy Goode
Hare, Nathan
Jones, James Monroe "Gunsmith"

Peggy J. Hardman
Holloway, Josephine Amanda Groves

Claude Hargrove
Hawkins, Edler Garnett

Jon M. Harkness
Fuller, Solomon Carter

Richard Harmond
Delany, Bessie and Sadie Delany

Donna Waller Harper
Allen, Debbie

Jorjet Harper
Harper, Minnie Buckingham

Judith E. Harper
Douglass, Anna Murray
Early, Sarah Woodson
Logan, Adella Hunt

Jamie Walker Harris
Johns, Moses

Janelle Harris
Carson, Robert
Malone, Vivian Juanita

Jessica Christina Harris
Schmoke, Kurt

Joseph E. Harris
Hansberry, William Leo

Leonard Harris
Locke, Alain Leroy

Matthew L. Harris
Broteer (Venture Smith)

Nolen Harris
Carter, Betty

Robert L. Harris
Barnett, Claude Albert
Douglas, H. Ford
Holland, Jerome Heartwell (Brud)
Wesley, Charles Harris

Stephen L. Harris
Butler, William
Fillmore, Charles W.
Johnson, Herman A.

William C. Harris
Bruce, Blanche Kelso
Washington, Harry

John Harris-Behling
Benson, Al
Bowie, Lester
Harris, Eddie
Jamal, Ahmad
St. Cyr, Johnny (John Alexander)

Daphne Duval Harrison
Hunter, Alberta
Sullivan, Maxine
Wilson, Edith Goodall

Christopher Harter
Randall, Dudley
Thomas, Lorenzo

Jim Haskins
Bricktop

Tim Haslett
Jafa, Arthur

James V. Hatch
Anderson, Garland

Cynthia Hawkins
Billops, Camille
Morgan, Norma
Overstreet, Joe

Fred J. Hay
Cannon, Gus
Dranes, Arizona
Memphis Minnie
Wilkins, Joe Willie

Samuel A. Hay
Davis, Ossie
Dee, Ruby

Robert C. Hayden
Chinn, May Edward
Crosthwait, David Nelson, Jr.

DeGrasse, John Van Surly
Freeman, Robert Tanner
Hinton, William Augustus
Mossell, Nathan Francis
Steward, Susan Maria Smith McKinney
Wright, Louis Tompkins
Camille Hazeur
Cousins, Laura Cheatham
Jennifer Lynn Headley
O'Grady, Lorraine
Sligh, Clarissa
Willis, Deborah
Leslie Heaphy
Allen, Newt
Jessup, Gentry
Marcelle, Oliver
Jenny Heil
Hodges, Augustus M.
Michael F. Hembree
Powell, William Peter
Alexa Benson Henderson
Herndon, Alonzo Franklin
Perry, Heman Edward
Edwin B. Henderson
Henderson, Edwin B. and Mary Ellen Henderson
Nikki Graves Henderson
Henderson, Edwin B. and Mary Ellen Henderson
Gerald S. Henig
Simmons, Ellamae
Taylor, Susan (Susie) Baker King
Tillman, William
Mary T. Henry
Adams, John Hurst
Tanu T. Henry
Davis, Benjamin O., Jr.
Oliver Herbel
Morgan, Raphael
Elizabeth A. Herbin
Campbell, T. M.
David F. Herr
DeBaptiste, George
Wallace Hettle
Gooding, James Henry
Leslie Heywood
Coachman, Alice
Stokes, Louise
Jared Winston Hickman
Tilmon, Levin
Carmon Weaver Hicks
Morton-Finney, John
Kyra E. Hicks
Benberry, Cuesta Ray
Cummings, Michael
Hacker, Benjamin Thurman

Mazloomi, Carolyn
Ricks, Martha Ann
Roberts, Jane Rose Waring
F. Michael Higginbotham
Edwards, Harry Thomas
Constance Valis Hill
Baby Laurence
Bates, Peg Leg
Bradley, Buddy
Coles, Honi
Green, Chuck
Lane, William Henry
Robinson, Bill
DaMaris B. Hill
Baker, Augusta Braxton
Golden, Marita
Nzinga Hill
Nelson, Rachel West
Ruth Edmonds Hill
Harrison, Samuel
Adriel A. Hilton
Simmons, Howard L.
Wheelan, Belle S.
Darlene Clark Hine
Bethune, Mary McLeod
Obama, Michelle
Parks, Rosa
Thoms, Adah Belle Samuels
William C. Hine
Cain, Richard Harvey
Miller, Thomas Ezekiel
Rainey, Joseph Hayne
Ransier, Alonzo Jacob
Wright, Jonathan Jasper
Peter Hinks
Walker, David
Kaavonia Hinton
Bennett, Lerone, Jr.
Elzy, Ruby Pearl
Emanuel, James
Polite, Carlene Hatcher
Scott-Heron, Gil
Robert Hinton
Delany, Hubert T.
James S. Hirsch
Carter, Rubin "Hurricane"
Burgsbee L. Hobbs
Romney, Lionel
Willie Hobbs
Love, Edward
Poussaint, Alvin
Brian P. Hochman
Henderson, Joe
Mackey, Nathaniel

Natalie Hodge Cook
Manns Israel, Adrienne

Graham Russell Hodges
Cooke, Sam
Cornish, Samuel Eli
Hopkins, Lightnin'
Reason, Charles Lewis
Ruggles, David
Saunders, Prince
Williams, Peter, Jr.

Michael H. Hoffheimer
White, Josh

G. Robert Hohler
Hampton, Henry

Antonio F. Holland
Page, Inman Edward

William H. Holland
Laine, Henry Allen

Lawana Holland-Moore
Holley, Susie Catherine
Honeywood, Varnette
Moutoussamy-Ashe, Jeanne

Donna Tyler Hollie
Cummings, Ida Rebecca
Dean, Jennie
Fernandis, Sarah Collins
Flake, Green
Holloman, John Lawrence Sullivan, Jr.
Johnson, Kathryn Magnolia
Lewis, Edna Regina
Locks, John W.
Patterson, Frederick Douglass
Scarborough, William Sanders
Williams, William Taylor Burwell

Peter C. Holloran
Jones, Sam (1933–)
Trotter, Geraldine Louise Pindell

Camara Dia Holloway
Allen, James Latimer

James J. Holmberg
York

Arthur Matthew Holst
Brown, Willie (1934–)
Goode, W. Wilson
Nix, Robert
Street, John Franklin

Elvin Holt
Brewer, John Mason

Thomas C. Holt
Du Bois, W. E. B.

John B. Holway
Dandridge, Ray
Hill, Pete
Poles, Spottswood

Redding, Dick
Stearnes, Turkey

Maureen Honey
Earley, Charity Adams

Jari Christopher Honora
Landry, Pierre Caliste

Olive Hoogenboom
Greener, Richard Theodore

Briallen Hopper
Baldwin, Maria Louise
Tillman, Katherine Davis Chapman

Michelle D. Hord
Hord, Noel Edward

Adam R. Hornbuckle
Drew, Howard Porter
Johnson, Cornelius Cooper
Tolan, Eddie

Gerald Horne
Davis, Benjamin Jefferson (1903–1964)

Alton Hornsby
Young, Andrew Jackson, Jr.

Laurel Horton
Snoddy, Dilsey

Sara E. Hosey
Austin, Doris Jean

SaFiya D. Hoskins
Allison, Luther
Berry Newman, Constance
Blanchard, Terence
Bland, Bobby "Blue"
Bradley, Wallace "Gator"
Brown, Chuck
Buchanan, Beverly
Canady, Herman George
Collins, Kathleen
Davis, Artur
Dixon, Sheila
Edwards, Donna
Faggs, Mae
Fenty, Adrian
Fort, Jeff
Franklin, Shirley
French, George Tony, Jr.
Guillaume, Robert
Harpo, Slim
Hawkins, Tramaine
Hemsley, Sherman
Jackson Lee, Sheila
Madhubuti, Haki R.
Majette, Denise
Milton, Little
O'Neal, Ron
Price, Lloyd

Pugh, Charles
Rakim
Rashad, Phylicia Ayers-Allen
Roberts, Leon Cedric
Robinson, David
Rucker, Darius
Ruffin, David
Sloan, Albert J. H., II
Stone, Jesse
Walker, Jimmie
Watson, Diane
Wright, Jeffrey

Ann Hostetler
Mosley, Walter
Mullen, Harryette
Trethewey, Natasha
Watkins, Mel

Søren Henry Hough
Seymour, Lloyd Garrison

Benjamin Houston
Bevel, James

Julian Houston
Atkins, Thomas Irving
Jones, Edward Paul

George Hovis
Kenan, Randall

Courtney A. Howard
Bozeman, Sylvia Trimble

Damond L. Howard
Twiggs, Leo

John R. Howard
Berry, Mary Frances
Bolin, Jane Matilda
Carter, Robert Lee
Cochran, Johnnie
Gray, Fred D.
Stout, Juanita Kidd
Sweatt, Heman Marion

Sharon Howard
Hutson, Jean Blackwell

Sheena C. Howard
Drexler, Clyde A.
Payne, Donald Milford

Kenneth Wayne Howell
Adams, George

Ron Howell
Baker, Bertram L.
Sharpton, Al

Nina Davis Howland
Wharton, Clifton Reginald
Watson, Barbara Mae

Kenneth J. Hreha
Cockrel, Kenneth V.

Hua Hsu
Dr. Dre
Ice Cube
Jay-Z

Michael E. Hucles
Tarrant, Caesar

Mark Andrew Huddle
Roper, Moses
Thompson, John

Mary E. Huddleston
Johnson, Cernoria McGowan

Diane Hudson
Parris, Pedro Tovookan
Pope.L, William

Joan B. Huffman
Killens, John Oliver

Brandi Hughes
Delaney, Emma B.

Charles L. Hughes
Ballard, Florence
Barrier, Eric
Bell, Al
Blackwell, Otis
Butler, Jerry
Clinton, George
Hunter, Ivory Joe
Isley, Ronald
Jackson, Al, Jr.
LL Cool J
Melvin, Harold
Porter, David
Prater, David
Robinson, William "Smokey"
Staples, Roebuck "Pops"
Tex, Joe

Yvonne L. Hughes
Kearse, Amalya Lyle
Seaton, Willie Mae

Jean McMahon Humez
Jackson, Rebecca Cox

Karen Jean Hunt
McKane, Alice Woodby
Remond, Sarah Parker
Stone, Chuck

Steve Huntley
Gibson, Truman Kella, Jr.

Elliott S. Hurwitt
Brooks, Shelton
Brymn, Tim
Cato, Minto
Collette, Buddy
Cooke, Charles "Doc"
Dabney, Ford

Grainger, Porter
Kildare, Dan
Mack, Cecil
Morgan, Frank
Spiller, Isabele Taliaferro
Spiller, William
Thompson, Ulysses "Slow Kid"
Tyers, William H.

Aida Ahmed Hussen
Cuney-Hare, Maud

Genevieve Hyacinthe
Weems, Carrie Mae

Raymond Pierre Hylton
Boone, Clinton Caldwell, Sr.
Ellison, John Malcus
Fauntroy, Walter Edward
Gravely, Samuel Lee, Jr.
Holloman, John Lawrence Sullivan, Jr.
Roberts, Joseph Jenkins
Scott, Robert Cortez "Bobby"
Walker, Wyatt Tee

Lena Hyun
Blackburn, Robert Hamilton

Tim Ianna
Moore, Johnny "Dizzy"

Michaeljulius Idani
Ford, Harold Eugene, Jr.
Ford, Harold Eugene, Sr.
Johnson, Eddie Bernice
Keyes, Alan
McCall, Herman Carl, Jr.
Meeks, Gregory
Rush, Bobby L.
Towns, Edolphus
West, Togo, Jr.

Elizabeth L. Ihle
Garnet, Sarah Smith Tompkins

Thomas M. Inge
Herriman, George Joseph

John N. Ingham
Banks, Charles
Binga, Jesse
Cohen, Walter L.
Merrick, John
Pace, Harry Herbert
Wormley, James

E. Renée Ingram
Bruce, Roscoe Conkling, Sr.
Hargrave, Frank Settle

Germaine Ingram
Robinson, LaVaughn

Lolita K. Buckner Inniss
Coker, Marie Jones Austin Dickerson

J. James Iovannone
Gumby, Levi Sandy Alexander
Johnson, Helene V.

Russell W. Irvine
Freeman, Martin Henry

Rochell Isaac
Clark, Charles Henry

J. Susan Isaacs
Johnson, Joshua
Pippin, Horace

Adrienne Israel
Robinson, Lizzie

Susan B. Iwanisziw
Bowser, David Bustill
Burgaw, Israel
Dexter, James Oronoko

Barbara Garvey Jackson
Bonds, Margaret Jeannette Allison

Benjamin A. Jackson
Cobb, Jewell Plummer
Gordon, Edmund Wyatt

Cassandra Jackson
Harper, Frances Ellen Watkins

David H. Jackson, Jr.
Height, Dorothy
Howard, Perry Wilbon
Settle, Josiah Thomas
Stringer, Thomas W.

Debra Jackson
Cooper, Ada Augusta Newton
Hamilton, Robert
Hamilton, Thomas
Newton, Alexander Herritage

Eric R. Jackson
Dabney, Wendell Phillips
Frazier, E. Franklin
Pendergrass, Teddy
Pinchback, P. B. S.

Gregory S. Jackson
Bibb, Henry Walton
Clarke, Lewis G.

J. D. Jackson
Billingsley, Orzell, Jr.
Jackson, Emory Overton

John P. Jackson
Cayton, Horace Roscoe

Mark Allan Jackson
Handcox, John

Miles M. Jackson
Allen, Anthony
Maples, William Lineas

Timothy L. Jackson
Jackson, Jay
Milai, A. Sam

Jolie A. Jackson-Willett
Edelin, Ramona Hoage
Hunt, Ida Alexander Gibbs
Sloan, Edith Barksdale
Wilson, Butler

Sylvia M. Jacobs
Boone, Eva Roberta (or Mae) Coles
Gordon, Nora Antonia
Gorham, Sarah Everett
Howard, Clara Ann
Jones, Nancy
Thomas, Cora Ann Pair

Daniel Christopher Jacobson
Broadnax, Wesley Jerome

Steven B. Jacobson
Ashford, Evelyn
Hawkins, Connie
Joyner Kersee, Jackie
Watts, J. C.

William A. Jacobson
Ashford, Evelyn

Alfreda S. James
Forten, Margaretta
Purvis, Harriet Davy Forten
Purvis, Sarah Louisa Forten

Donald James
Adderley, Nat
Wilson, Gerald

Michael James
Wilkerson, Doxey

Portia P. James
McCoy, Elijah

Robert Janis
Archibald, Nathaniel
Brown, Lawrence, Jr.
Green, Darrell
Griffith, Emile
Houston, Kenneth Ray
Kid Gavilan
Mitchell, Bobby

Kenneth Robert Janken
Logan, Rayford Whittingham
White, Walter Francis

Wilnise Jasmin
Mitchell Bateman, Mildred

Régine Michelle Jean-Charles
Poitier, Sidney

Paul Jefferson
Reid, Ira De Augustine

Robert F. Jefferson
Coggs, Pauline Redmond
McGee, Henry Wadsworth

Randal Maurice Jelks
Mays, Benjamin E.

Glen Pierce Jenkins
Lambright, Middleton H.

McKay Jenkins
Ashe, Arthur

James Phillip Jeter
Murphy, John Henry, Sr.

John V. Jezierski
Goodridge, Glenalvin J.

David Joens
Thomas, John W. E.
White, Jesse Clark, Jr.

Clifton H. Johnson
Beman, Amos Gerry
Cullen, Countée
Lafon, Thomy

Eric D. Johnson
Hemphill, Jessie Mae

Joan Marie Johnson
Butler, Susie Dart

Judith R. Johnson
Harris, Patricia Roberts

Kristine Johnson
Wilkinson, Marion Birnie

Michael P. Johnson
Ellison, William

Patrice D. Johnson
James, Sharpe
Lewis, Ida Elizabeth

Robert Johnson, Jr.
Hawkins, Walter Lincoln
Knox, William Jacob
McAfee, Walter Samuel
Mitchell, Charles Lewis
Taylor, George Edwin

Sharon D. Johnson
Carroll, Vinnette
Grier, Pam
Haizlip, Shirlee Taylor
Hull, Gloria Thompson (Akasha)
McNair, Barbara

Tekla Ali Johnson
Shanks, Lela Knox
We Langa, Wopashitwe Mondo Eyen
Wilson, Alyce McCarroll

Twinette L. Johnson
Francis, Norman C.

Whittington B. Johnson
Marshall, Andrew Cox

Adrienne Lash Jones
Bowles, Eva Del Vakia
Garvin, Charles Herbert

Andrew W. Kahrl
  Burnside, R. L.
  Jefferson, Lewis
Sara Kakazu
  Delaney, Lucy Ann Berry
  McCline, John
  Slew, Jenny
Vickey Kalambakal
  Hill, Stephen Spencer
  Pico, Andrés
James Kalyn
  Lewis, George (Joseph François Zeno)
Sylvie Kandé
  Piper, Adrian Margaret Smith
  Till Mobley, Mamie
Nancy Kang
  Bass, George Houston
  Marvin X
Ayesha Kanji
  Amos, Wally
  Fitzhugh, Howard Naylor
  Fudge, Ann Marie
  Simmons, Russell
Richard L. Kaplan
  Baquet, Dean P.
Terri A. Karis
  powell, john a.
Amber Karlins
  Whipper, Leigh
Mark Katz
  GrandWizzard Theodore
Casey Kayser
  Blakely, Nora Brooks
  Joseph, Allison
Janis F. Kearney
  O'Leary, Hazel R.
Ann T. Keene
  Dorman, Isaiah
  Hayes, Roland
  Jordan, Barbara
  Yerby, Frank
Allison Kellar
  Barnett, Etta Moten
  Blanks, Birleanna
  Sessions, Lucy Stanton Day
Andrew James Kellett
  Fulson, Lowell
  Moon, Harold Warren
Baron Kelly
  Brown, Anne
  Kelly, Paula
Sandra Kelman
  Gaddy, Bea

Edward A. Kemmick
  Bivins, Horace Wayman
Randall Kennedy
  Obama, Barack
Gary Kerley
  Page, Clarence
  Sowell, Thomas
Barry Kernfeld
  Ammons, Albert C.
  Ammons, Gene
  Anderson, Cat
  Anderson, Ivie
  Ashby, Irving C.
  Barbarin, Paul
  Bernhardt, Clyde
  Bostic, Earl
  Bradford, Perry
  Brown, Lawrence
  Buckner, Milt
  Carney, Harry Howell
  Catlett, Big Sid
  Clark, Sonny
  Clarke, Kenny
  Clayton, Buck
  Criss, Sonny
  Davis, Eddie "Lockjaw"
  Dickerson, Carroll
  Dutrey, Honore
  Ervin, Booker
  Forrest, Jimmy
  Garland, Red
  Gonzales, Babs
  Green, Grant
  Grimes, Tiny
  Hall, Adelaide
  Hall, Al
  Hall, Edmond
  Hardwick, Toby
  Harris, Little Benny
  Heard, J. C.
  Hegamin, Lucille
  Henderson, Horace W.
  Hill, Chippie
  Hines, Earl "Fatha"
  Hite, Les
  Hope, Elmo
  Hopkins, Claude
  Humes, Helen
  Jefferson, Eddie
  Johnson, James P.
  Johnson, Pete
  Jones, Jo
  Jones, Sam (1924–1981)

Keppard, Freddie
Kersey, Kenny
Kirby, John
Kirk, Andy
Lee, George E.
Lee, Julia
Leonard, Harlan "Mike"
Lewis, Meade Anderson "Lux"
Lindsay, John
Lunceford, Jimmie
Lyons, James Leroy (Jimmy)
Machito
Marable, Fate
McGhee, Howard B. "Maggie"
McRae, Carmen
Miles, Lizzie
Millinder, Lucky
Mitchell, George
Montgomery, Little Brother
Montgomery, Wes
Morgan, Sam
Nanton, Joe
Newborn, Phineas
Oliver, Sy
Ory, Kid
Page, Hot Lips
Paul, Emmanuel
Perez, Manuel
Peyton, Dave
Picou, Alphonse
Piron, Armand John
Razaf, Andy
Richmond, Dannie
Roberts, Luckey
Robinson, Jim
Rouse, Charlie
Shavers, Charlie
Shaw, Woody
Simeon, Omer
Smith, Clara
Smith, Mamie
Smith, Pine Top
Smith, Stuff
Smith, Trixie
Smith, Willie "the Lion"
Stewart, Slam
Stitt, Sonny
Sun Ra
Taylor, Eva
Thomas, Joe
Timmons, Bobby
Tio, Lorenzo, Jr.
Trent, Alphonso

Turrentine, Stanley William
Vick, Harold
Waits, Freddie
Ware, Wilbur
Watkins, Julius
Webb, Chick
Whetsol, Artie
Wilson, Shadow
Woodyard, Sam

Tammy L. Kernodle
Smith, Willie Mae Ford

Melissa A. Kerr
Wilson, John Woodrow

M'Lissa Kesterman
Hunster, Richard L.

Joseph D. Ketner
Duncanson, Robert S.

Connor Killian
Pearson, William Gaston

David Killingray
Hercules, Felix
LoBagola, Bata Kindai Amgoza Ibn

Judith Kilpatrick
Branton, Wiley Austin

David P. Kilroy
Young, Charles

Howard Kimeldorf
Fletcher, Benjamin Harrison

Leigh Kimmel
Burris, Roland

Joy G. Kinard
Mason, Vivian Carter
Price, Joseph Charles

Larry Sean Kinder
Florence, Virginia Proctor Powell
Matheus, John Frederick
Sanford, Isabel

Jason King
Cosby, Bill
Parks, Gordon, Jr.
Washington, Denzel

Patricia Miller King
Cass, Melnea

Anne Kingery
Scott, Joyce J.

Elise K. Kirk
Norman, Jessye
Price, Leontyne

Hasaan A. Kirkland
Barnes, Ernie

Amy Helene Kirschke
Douglas, Aaron

Harvey Klehr

Perry, Pettis

Stacy Klein

Knight, Etheridge

Christine Knauer

Reynolds, Grant

John T. Kneebone

Burrell, William Patrick

Michael F. Knight

Dorsey, Decatur

Fleetwood, Christian Abraham

Greaves, Clinton

Stance, Emanuel

Walley, Augustus

Glenn Allen Knoblock

Africanus, Scipio

Anderson, Aaron

Anderson, Bruce

Anderson, Webster

Ashley, Eugene, Jr.

Atkins, Daniel

Austin, Oscar Palmer

Barnes, William Henry

Bell, Dennis

Blake, Robert

Bolden, Melvin R.

Boyne, Thomas

Briscoe, Neliska Ann "Baby"

Brock, Lou

Bronson, James H.

Brown, Benjamin

Brown, James

Brown, Robert

Brown, William H.

Bryant, Richard Renard

Bryant, William Maud

Bundy, William F.

Carlisle, Cato

Carter, Edward, Jr.

Cato, Willmer Reed

Charlton, Cornelius H.

Collins, Hannibal

Combs, Osie V., Jr.

Crafus, Richard

Cromwell, Oliver (1752–1853)

Dailey, London

Daly, James A.

David, Charles Walter, Jr.

Davis, John (d. 1812)

Davis, John (d. 1903)

Dees, Clement

DeYampert, Warren Traveous

Dickinson, Castor

Dowden, Leonard E.

Etheridge, Louis Cullen, Jr.

Ezra

Fortune, Vilot

Fort-Whiteman, Lovett

Gardner, James Daniel

Girandy, Alphonse

Gilchrist, Samuel

Grooms, Bruce E.

Hall, Jude

Haney, Cecil D.

Hardy, Isaac

Harmon, Leonard Roy

Harris, James H.

Hawkins, Thomas R.

Hazard, Newport

Hector, Edward (Ned)

Hilton, Alfred B.

Holland, Milton Murray

Holloway, Tommie Lee

Huff, Edgar R.

Huiswoud, Otto Eduard Gerardus Majella

Isom, Roger G.

James, Miles

James, Willy F., Jr.

Jenkins, Edmund

Jenkins, Robert H., Jr.

Joe

Joel, Lawrence

Johnson, Dwight Hal

Johnson, Gilbert

Johnson, Henry

Johnson, John (d. 1912)

Johnson, John (b. 1839)

Johnson, Mess

Johnson, Ralph H.

Johnson, William

Kelly, Alexander

Kimmons, Carl Eugene

Langhorn, Garfield McConnell

Lawson, John

Lee, Fitz

Lee, William

Leonard, Matthew

Long, Donald Russell

Mays, Isaiah

McBryar, William

Mifflin, James

Miles, John "Mule"

Miller, Robert

Noil, Joseph

Olive, Milton Lee, III
Payne, Adam
Payne, Isaac
Peagler, Robert J.
Pease, Joachim
Penn, Robert
Peterson, Joseph P.
Pinckney, William
Pinn, Robert
Pitts, Riley Leroy
Porter, Marion Anthony
Ratcliff, Edward
Rivers, Ruben
Roberts, George R.
Rogers, Charles Calvin
Runnels, Peleg
Sampson
Sanders, Frank Cook
Sargent, Ruppert Leon
Sasser, Clarence Eugene
Sermon, Isaac
Shaw, Thomas
Sims, Clifford Chester
Smith, Andrew Jackson
Smith, John
Sneed, Floyd
Staines, Ona Maria Judge
Starlins, Mark
Stedman, Cato
Stowers, Freddie
Swann, Alonzo Alexander, Jr.
Sweeney, Robert Augustus
Thomas, Charles Leroy
Thomas, Jack
Thompkins, William H.
Thompson, William H.
Tiffany, Cyrus
Tye, Colonel
Tzomes, C. A. "Pete"
Vaird, Lauretha
Veale, Charles
Walls, Jesse
Warren, John Earl
Warrior, John, Aka John Ward
Watson, Anthony J.
Watson, George
Webb, Rothchild Roscoe
Williams, Anthony
Williams, Jesse
Williams, Melvin, Jr.
Williams, Melvin, Sr.
Williams, Moses
Wilson, William Othello

Woods, Brent
Woodson, Waverly B., Jr.
Jane Knowles
Hundley, Mary Gibson
Carole E. Knowlton
Jones, John W.
Betty K. Koed
Moseley Braun, Carol
Greta Koehler
Gates, William "Pop"
Khazan, Jibreel
Morial, Marc
Richmond, David
Tate, Claudia
David Koenigstein
Glover, Danny
Rita Kohn
Blackburn, Alpha
Blackburn, Walter Scott
Amy Sparks Kolker
Clifton, Lucille
Hamilton, Virginia Esther
Smith, Lucy Wilmot
Tyson, Neil deGrasse
Edward Komara
Patton, Charley
Waters, Muddy
Heather Miyano Kopelson
Force, Nathaniel and Daniel Force
Constance Koppelman
Greene, Belle da Costa
Chaitali Korgaonkar
Primus, Holdridge
Theodore Kornweibel
Owen, Chandler
Karen Kossie-Chernyshev
Horace, Lillian B.
Beth Kraig
Jones, Grace
McKinney, Cynthia
Isaac Kramnick
Lawrence, Margaret Morgan
David Krasner
Cole, Bob
Cook, Will Marion
Gary R. Kremer
Turner, James Milton
Michael L. Krenn
Brown, Joe
Charles, Ezzard Mack
Dudley, Edward Richard
Foreman, George
Foster, Robert Wayne "Bob"

Frazier, Joe
Gans, Panama Joe
Hagler, Marvin
Hearns, Thomas
Ihetu, Richard "Dick Tiger"
Jack, Beau
Kid Norfolk
Richmond, Bill
Spinks, Michael
Todman, Terence
Wallace, Coley
Wills, Harry

Mikael D. Kriz
Bailey, Walter T.

Ondra Krouse Dismukes
Babb, Valerie Melissa
Sapphire

Elizabeth Kuebler-Wolf
Dave The Potter
Lafayette, James Armistead
Stewart, Charley
Yarrow, Mamout

Michelle Kuhl
Burdett, Samuel
Johnson, W. Bishop
Nance, Lee

Bruce Kuklick
Fontaine, William Thomas

Kenneth L. Kusmer
Green, John Patterson
Malvin, John
Smith, Harry Clay

Constance Ky
Jackson, Allen F.

Jennifer Ky
Primus, Nelson A.

Modupe Labode
Ford, Justina Laurena Carter

Edward L. Lach
Brown, Charlotte Eugenia Hawkins
Burrell, Berkeley Graham
Higginbotham, A. Leon, Jr.
Sinkler, William H., Jr.
Stokes, Carl
Young, Coleman

Lisa C. Lakes
Ross, Fran
Taulbert, Clifton

Alan K. Lamm
Asher, Jeremiah
Prioleau, George Washington

Jane G. Landers
Biassou, Jorge (Georges)

Garrido, Juan
Menéndez, Francisco
Witten, Juan Bautista "Big Prince"

Jennifer Lang
Roberts, Kay George

Michael Lang
Ware, David S.

Gaynol Langs
Rudolph, Wilma

Meron Langsner
Dove, Ulysses
Henderson, Stephen McKinley

Rudolph M. Lapp
Lee, Archy

Cheryl Janifer LaRoche
Quinn, William Paul

Jennifer Larson
Menard, John Willis
Ruffin, George Lewis

Kate Clifford Larson
Green, Sam

Michael E. Latham
Lewis, W. Arthur

Yvonne Latty
McPhatter, Thomas Hayswood

Maria Lauret
Walker, Alice Malsenior

David Todd Lawrence
Neal, Larry

Ellen Nickenzie Lawson
Stanley, Sara G.

Cheryl Laz
Hale, Clara McBride

Arlene Lazarowitz
Carter, William Beverly, Jr.

Daniel J. Leab
Still, William Grant

Jeffrey B. Leak
Grooms, Anthony

Leora Maltz Leca
Amos, Emma Veoria
Stout, Renée
Wilson, Fred

Zachary J. Lechner
Bartholomew, Dave
Johnson, Johnnie
Summer, Donna

Candace L. LeClaire
Dial, Thornton, Sr.

Julia Sun-Joo Lee
Cooper, Thomas
Davis, Noah
Grandy, Moses

Green, Jacob D.
Randolph, Peter
Voorhis, Robert

Carson Grath. Leftwich
Johnson, Pauline Byrd Taylor

Steven Leikin
Dennis, Lawrence

Theresa Leininger-Miller
Ball, James Presley
Barthe, Richmond
Bell, Mary A. (1873–1941)
Bennett, Gwendolyn
Hayden, Palmer
Johnson, Sargent Claude
Lion, Jules
Prophet, Elizabeth
Reason, Patrick Henry
Smith, Albert Alexander

Thomas M. Leonard
Durham, John Stephens

Dália Leonardo
Brashear, Donald
Byard, Gloria
Hardy, David
Iginla, Jarome
Watts, Frederick

Richard J. Leskosky
Baskett, James F.
Rucker, Benjamin H. "Black Herman"

Larry Lester
Day, Leon
De Moss, Elwood
Foster, William Hendrick
Johnson, Grant
Mackey, Biz
Pickett, Bill
Smith, Hilton
Suttles, George Mule
Walcott, Jersey Joe

Benjamin Letzler
Ferguson, Clarence Clyde, Jr.
Glass, Dick

Kevin M. Levin
Paul, Robert Austin

Deborah I. Levine
Elders, M. Joycelyn

Donny Levit
Miller, Bebe
St. Clair, Stephanie ("Queenie")
White, Slappy

Frank R. Levstik
Jenkins, David

Parker, John P.
Vashon, George Boyer

Alan Levy
Burleigh, Henry Thacker
Dett, R. Nathaniel

Devra Hall Levy
Henderson, Luther
Levy, John

Eugene Levy
Johnson, James Weldon

Peter B. Levy
Richardson, Gloria St. Clair Hayes

Sholomo B. Levy
Ali, Noble Drew
Angelou, Maya
Baraka, Amiri
Brimmer, Andrew Felton
Brown, Claude
Butts, Calvin Otis, III
Cleveland, James Edward
Cox, Oliver Cromwell
Cruse, Harold W.
Davis, Sammy, Jr.
Dellums, Ronald
Farrakhan, Louis Abdul
Father Divine
Flake, Floyd Harold
Ford, Arnold Josiah
Fortune, T. Thomas
Franklin, C. L.
Franklin, John Hope
Garvey, Amy Euphemia Jacques
Gomez, Joseph
Gordy, Berry, Jr.
Green, Al
Hampton, Lionel Leo
Henry, Thomas W.
Henson, Matthew Alexander
Himes, Chester Bomar
Hood, James Walker
Hope, John
Johnson, William H.
Jordan, Vernon
Keeble, Marshall
King, B. B.
King, Don
Levy, Levi Ben
Lorde, Audre
Matthew, Wentworth Arthur
McBride, James
Proctor, Samuel DeWitt
Reverend Ike

Snowden, John Baptist
Toomer, Jean
Twilight, Alexander Lucius
Ward, Clara
Wilson, August
Woods, Tiger
Catherine E. Lewis
Osbey, Brenda Marie
George Lewis
Hawkins, Ted
Heron, Giles
Kathleen McCree Lewis
McCree, Wade Hampton, Jr.
Meharry H. Lewis
Lewis, Felix Early
Tate, Mary Lena Lewis
Tracey M. Lewis-Giggetts
Wells, Henrietta Bell
Rita Liberti
Glover, Ruth
Miller, Cheryl
William Lichtenwanger
Bland, James Allen
William E. Lightfoot
Baker, Etta
Shultz, Arnold
Dawn Lille
Blunden, Jeraldyne
Theodore Lin
Brown, Kate
Richard C. Lindberg
Du Sable, Jean Baptiste Pointe
Beverley Rowe Lindburg
Howard, Milton
Fred Lindsey
Conyers, John F., Jr.
Aaron M. Lisec
Dunn, Oscar James
Devorah Lissek
Johnson, William
Leon F. Litwack
Huggins, Nathan Irvin
Lili Cockerille Livingston
Ailey, Alvin
Brynley A. Lloyd-Bollard
Hudson, Hosea
Mamie E. Locke
Bell, James Madison
Gaines, Irene McCoy
Hamer, Fannie Lou
Martin, John Sella
Plessy, Homer Adolph
Turner, Jack

Whipper, William
Williams, Fannie Barrier
Jeff Loeb
Willmott, Kevin
Kathryn Lofton
Brazier, Arthur
Chavis, Benjamin Franklin, Jr.
Sadye L. Logan
Newman, Isaiah DeQuincey
Azhia Long
Kennedy, Yvonne
Hugh K. Long
Washington, Ford Lee "Buck"
Thomas Long
Creed, Cortlandt Van Rensselaer
Minor, Jane
Sam Lorber
Frankie, Crocker
Kip Lornell
Campbell, Lucie E.
Cotton, Elizabeth
Dorsey, Thomas Andrew
Wells, Junior
Wilson, Orlandus
Rainer E. Lotz
Davis, Belle
Douglas, Louis
Fields, Arabella
Garland, William (Will)
Hampton, Pete
Hill, Lethia
Hyers, May C.
Johnson, Charles Edward "Chas"
Spyglass, Elmer
Walker, Ruth "Rudy" and Frederick "Fredy"
Weeks, Seth
Spencie Love
Drew, Charles Richard
Paul E. Lovejoy
Baquaqua, Mahommah Gardo
Alec Lowman
Welch, Eileen Watts
David Lucander
Lofton, James
Bernita D. Lucas
Pickett, Tidye
John A. Lucas
Hubbard, William DeHart
M. Lois Lucas
Drewry, Elizabeth Simpson
Meadows, Lucile Smallwood
Ralph E. Luker
Barber, Jesse Max

Blackwell, Randolph Talmadge
Bowen, John Wesley Edward
DeBerry, William Nelson
Haley, Alex
Hurston, Zora Neale
Johns, Vernon Napoleon
King, Martin Luther, Sr.
Proctor, Henry Hugh
Ransom, Reverdy Cassius
Steward, Theophilus Gould
Walden, Austin Thomas
Walters, Alexander
Young, Whitney Moore, Jr.

John S. Lupold
King, Horace

Christine Lutz
Hunton, Alphaeus
Hunton, William

Henry Lyman
MacAlpine, Arthur

Theresa C. Lynch
Eve, Arthur O., Sr.
Rollins, Howard E., Jr.
Washington, Jerome

Hugh C. MacDougall
Swails, Stephen A.

Morris J. MacGregor
Miller, Dorie

Vince J. Mack
Custis, Lemuel Rodney

Rei Magosaki
Birtha, Becky

Jeffery Othele Mahan
Baker, Vernon Joseph
Fox, John

Michael Maiwald
Fisher, Rudolph
Thurman, Wallace

Rachel Malcolm-Woods
Bullock, Dick

Kimberly L. Malinowski
Bailey, John B.
Brown, Richard Lonsdale
Dodd, Joseph Eldridge
Reece, Cortez Donald

Devona A. Mallory
Marrant, John

Jerry Malloy
Lloyd, John Henry "Pop"
Rogan, Bullet

Lawrence H. Mamiya
Muhammad, Elijah

Kimberley Mangun
Cannady, Beatrice Morrow

Kenneth R. Manning
Hawthorne, Edward William
Hill, Henry Aaron
Just, Ernest Everett
Matzeliger, Jan Ernst
McKinney, Roscoe Lewis
Poindexter, Hildrus Augustus
Turner, Charles Henry
Wilkerson, Vernon Alexander

Martin J. Manning
Parks, Lillian Rogers

Lou Manzo
Johnson, George Chappie
Martinez, Pedro
Seay, Richard (Dick)
Wilson, Ernest Judson

David Marc
Childress, Alvin
Wilson, Flip

Maha Marouan
Bradley, David

Barry Marshall
Baker, LaVern
Hopkins, Linda

Jennifer L. Freeman Marshall
Diggs, Ellen Irene

John F. Marszalek
Whittaker, Johnson Chesnut

Charles H. Martin
Herndon, Angelo

Frank Martin
Delaney, Joseph
Fax, Elton
Rose, Arthur

Heather Martin
Bryant, Hazel Joan

Jahaan Martin
Yarbrough, Manny

Kameelah L. Martin
Ansa, Tina McElroy
Nunez, Elizabeth

Ruth E. Martin
Colvin, Claudette
Crockett, George William, Jr.

Sandy Dwayne Martin
Agyeman, Jaramogi Abebe
Brawley, Edward McKnight
De Baptiste, Richard
Hosier, "Black Harry"
Morris, Elias Camp

Hutto, J. B.
James, Elmore
James, Skip
Lenoir, J. B.
Lipscomb, Mance
Magic Sam
McDowell, Mississippi Fred
McTell, Blind Willie
Memphis Slim
Nighthawk, Robert
Professor Longhair
Sykes, Roosevelt
Tampa Red
Taylor, Eddie
Taylor, Hound Dog
White, Bukka
Williams, Big Joe
Williamson, Sonny Boy (1899?–1965)
Williamson, Sonny Boy (1914–1948)

Clyde O. McDaniel
Clement, Rufus Early

Karen Cotton McDaniel
Kidd, Mae Taylor Street
Powers, Georgia Davis
Smith, Mary Levi

W. Caleb McDaniel
Beman, Jehiel C.
Grimes, Leonard A.

Pellom McDaniels, III
Allen, Marcus
Bell, Bobby Lee
Buchanan, Junious "Buck"
Shell, Art, Jr.
Upshaw, Eugene Thurman, Jr.
White, Reginald Howard (Reggie)

John McDermott
Rice, Condoleezza

Trevy A. McDonald
Fulwood, Sam
Jarrett, Vernon D.

Erik S. McDuffie
Moore, Queen Mother
Thompson Patterson, Louise

Nicole McFarlane
Owens, Carl

Robyn McGee
Calvin, Floyd

Sharon Renee McGee
Flack, Roberta
Riperton, Minnie

Doris Evans McGinty
Childers, Lulu Vere
Marshall, Harriet Gibbs

Nadine McIlwain-Massey
Page, Cedric Alan

Christine G. McKay
Harrington, Oliver W.

Adam McKible
Williams, Edward Christopher

Casey McKittrick
Carr, Sister Wynona

Diane Savage McLaughlin
Savage, John Anthony

Timothy J. McMillan
Caldwell, Wilson
Candy
Pomp
Singleton, William Henry
Vanderpool, Jacob

Linda O. McMurry
Carver, George Washington
Work, Monroe Nathan

Connie L. McNeely
Marrett, Cora Bagley
Nixon, Lawrence Aaron

Genna Rae McNeil
Houston, Charles Hamilton

Jim McWilliams
Johnson, Charles Richard

Susan J. McWilliams
Dixon, Julian Carey
Hamilton, Grace Towns
Payton, Carolyn Robertson
Welcome, Verda Freeman

Carl E. Meacham
Mitchell, Matt

Eddie S. Meadows
Allen, Red
Dameron, Tad
Jordan, Louis
Mitchell, Blue
Strayhorn, Billy
Tatum, Art

Krystofer A. Meadows
Thompson, Mildred Jean

Connie Meale
Roudanez, Louis Charles

Frank Mehring
Massaquoi, Hans J.

Dick Meister
Dellums, C. L.

Joseph S. Mella
Adams, Ron

Danielle D. Melvin
Melvin, Chasity
Peck, Carolyn

Charles Messinger
McGhee, Brownie
David Michel
Blackwell, Lucien Edward
Boyd, Henry Allen
Carey, Archibald James, Jr.
Cherry, Frank S.
Evers, Charles
Fisher, Miles Mark
Harsh, Vivian Gordon
Haywood, G. T.
Jemison, T. J.
Jones, Charles Price
Karim, Benjamin Goodman
Kilgore, Thomas, Jr.
Lightner, Gwendolyn
Mallory, Arenia Cornelia
McKenzie, Vashti Murphy
Morton, Paul Sylvester
Mossell, Mary Ella
Patterson, Gilbert Earl
Patterson, James Oglethorpe
Rivers, Eugene F.
Robinson, Ida Bell
Smith, Lucy
Stallings, George Augustus, Jr.
Vedrine, Soliny
Ward, Gertrude Mae
White, Charles
White, Charley C.
Ronald E. Mickens
Bharucha-Reid, Albert Turner
Imes, Elmer Samuel
Moore, Willie Hobbs
Wilkins, J. Ernest, Jr.
Richard T. Middleton IV
Espy, Michael Alphonso
Thompson, Bennie Gordon
La'Tonya Rease Miles
Harris-Stewart, Lusia "Lucy"
Otesa Middleton Miles
Farmer, Sharon
Chandra M. Miller
Bayne, Thomas
Nash, Charles Edmund
Jake C. Miller
Moore, Harry Tyson
James A. Miller
Fuller, Hoyt William
Jason Philip Miller
Baker, Anita
Ball, William
Ballard, Hank

Barney, Lem
Benson, George
Betsch, MaVynee
Blue, Vida
Brady, Xernona Clayton
Briscoe, Marlin
Brooks, Avery
Brown, Willie (1940–)
Burns, Ursula M.
Butterfield, G. K.
Capehart, Harry Jheopart
Cleaver, Emanuel
Coleman, Anita Scott
Coleman, Gary
Cowans, Adger W.
Cundieff, Rusty
Dismukes, William "Dizzy"
Dungy, Tony
Elder, Larry
Elliott, Missy
Erving, Julius
Grier, Mike
Gunn, Moses
Hastings, Alcee Lamar
Herbert, Bob
Ice-T
Innis, Roy
James, Rick
Jones, Robert Elijah
Khanga, Yelena
King, Slater
KRS-One
LaSalle, Denise
Lemon, Meadowlark
Loving, Alvin D., Jr.
Mackey, John
Mathis, Johnny
Mayfield, Percy
McDonald, William Madison
McNair, Steve
McWhorter, John
Mitchell, Juanita Jackson
Mooney, Paul
Morris, Garrett
Mr. T
Myers, Walter Dean
Parker, Junior
Prosser, Inez Beverly
Ribbs, Willy T.
Rice, Jerry
Rice, Norm
Savage, Augustus "Gus"
Shipp, E. R.

Sidat-Singh, Wilmeth
Singletary, Mike
Smith, Lovie Lee
Spinks, Leon
Tomlin, Mike
Vereen, Ben
Walker, Hazel Mountain
Ward, Vera
Williams, Wayne
Wilson, Nancy Sue
Winn, Mississippi
Witherspoon, Jimmy
Zydeco, Buckwheat
Jim Miller
Ali, Rashied
Hart, Billy
Heath, Tootie
Kristie Miller
De Priest, Oscar Stanton
Michael C. Miller
Brown, Roosevelt "Rosey"
Elder, Robert Lee
Hayes, Bob
Hoskins, Dave
Joiner, Charlie
Lane, Dick "Night Train"
McKegney, Tony
Renfro, Mel
Rhodes, Ted
Selmon, Lee Roy
Smith, Emmitt, Jr.
Warfield, Paul
Williams, Doug
Wills, Maury
R. Baxter Miller
Dykes, Eva Beatrice
Sam Miller
Henry, Ernie
Nathaniel Millett
Pritchard, "Gullah" Jack
Frederick V. Mills
Allen, Richard (1760–1831)
Bragg, George Freeman, Jr.
Margot Minardi
Hall, Primus
Spear, Chloe
Robert Mirandon
Nance, Ray
Pullen, Don
Singleton, Zutty
Carl Mirra
Cone, James Hal
Woodbey, George Washington

Elizabeth Mitchell
Bishop, Stephen
John Hanson Mitchell
Gilbert, Robert Alexander
Koritha Mitchell
Livingston, Myrtle Smith
Richard M. Mizelle
Blackwell, David
Satcher, David
Michael Mizell-Nelson
Barker, Danny
Christian, Marcus Bruce
Thomas A. Mogan
Chaney, John
Staley, Dawn
Stokes, Maurice
Carl Moneyhon
Bush, John Edward
Gaines, Matthew
Philip M. Montesano
Bell, Philip Alexander
Shirley C. Moody
Brown, Lloyd Louis
Cosby, Camille
Christopher Paul Moore
Browne, Robert Tecumtha
Rodrigues, Jan (Juan)
Diana Moore
Sands, Diana
James Ross Moore
Eldridge, Roy
Gaillard, Slim
Garner, Erroll
Mills, Florence
Williams, Joe
Janet E. Moorman
Brooks, Elizabeth Carter
Chinwe Morah
Tatum, Jack "Assassin"
Lois Baldwin Moreland
Ray, Charlotte E.
Douglas Morgan
Crowdy, William Saunders
Marcyliena Morgan
Shakur, Tupac Amaru
Marilyn Morgan
Johns, Barbara
Woods, Sylvia
Sharon Leslie Morgan
Lawless, Theodore Kenneth
Sengstacke, Robert Abbott
William A. Morgan
Blanton, John W.

Beverly Morgan-Welch
Patrick, Deval

Edward T. Morman
Cornely, Paul Bertau
Edelin, Kenneth Carlton
Maynard, Aubre de Lambert

Robert C. Morris
Wright, Richard Robert, Sr.

Vanessa J. Morris
Tate, Thelma Horn

Dewey Franklin Mosby
Tanner, Henry Ossawa

Mihaela Moscaliuc
Young, Al

Shelia Patrice Moses
Gregory, Dick

Wilson J. Moses
Crummell, Alexander

Juanita Patience Moss
Johnson, William Henry
Patience, C. Edgar
Patience, Crowder
Rolac, John

Byron Motley
Bankhead, Sam
Barnhill, David
Brown, Larry
Crutchfield, John William
Davis, Piper
Hughes, Samuel Thomas
Kimbro, Henry Allen
Pearson, Lennie

Lisa Mott
Brown, Sue M. Wilson

Jacqueline-Bethel Mougoué
Pelham, Robert A., Jr.

Amber Moulton-Wiseman
Briggs, Cyril Valentine
Gray, William Herbert, III
Morton, Theophilus B.
Stewart Lai, Carlotta

J. Todd Moye
Carter, Mae Bertha
Dryden, Charles Walter
Gooden, Dwight Eugene
Lewis, Furry
McGee, Charles Edward
O'Neil, Buck
Spencer, Chauncey Edward

Linda Everett Moyé
Bowden, Artemisia

William F. Mugleston
Fuller, Thomas
Garvey, Marcus
Love, Nat
Washington, Booker T.

Precious Rasheeda Muhammad
Muhammad, Clara

Lisa Muir
Danticat, Edwidge

Peter Muir
Blythe, Jimmy
Davenport, Charles Edward "Cow Cow"
Scott, James Sylvester

Kevin Mulroy
Horse, John

Gayle Murchison
Caesar, Shirley Ann
Harris, Wynonie (Mr. Blues)
Hill, Arzell "Z. Z."
Hughes, Revella
Jacquet, Illinois
Jenkins, Edmund Thornton
Jones, Bessie
Rushen, Patrice Louise
Taylor, Koko
Work, John Wesley, III
Work, John Wesley, Jr.

Laura Murphy
Aaron
Black, Leonard
Bruner, Peter
Clement, Samuel Spottford
Ferebee, London R.
Ferrill, London
Gaines, Wesley John
Garlick, Charles
Garner, Margaret
Green, William
Lewis, Joseph Vance
Mapps, Grace A.
Smith, James Lindsay

Michael J. Murphy
Baker, General

Paul T. Murray
Block, Samuel
Corbitt, Ted
Peacock, Wazir
Steele, C. K.
Zuber, Paul Burgess

Peter C. Murray
Brawley, James P.
Golden, Charles Franklin

Barbara A. Seals Nevergold
Seals, Willie Brown
Gerald G. Newborg
Thompson, Era Bell
Dalyce Newby
Abbott, Anderson Ruffin
Augusta, Alexander Thomas
Carney, William Harvey
Davis, Frances Elliott
Purvis, Charles Burleigh
Shadd, Furman Jeremiah
Pamela Newkirk
Rowan, Carl Thomas
Marti K. Newland
Hogan, Moses
McLin, Lena
Euthena M. Newman
Gaines, Clarence Edward
Kurt Newman
Grimes, Henry
Mark Newman
Brooks, Owen
Dahmer, Vernon Ferdinand
Richard Newman
Allen, Sarah and Flora Allen
Brown, Henry "Box"
Grace, Charles Emmanuel
Haynes, Lemuel
Healy, Patrick Francis
Moorland, Jesse Edward
M. Cookie E. Newsom
Badger, Roderick
Scot Ngozi-Brown
Fagen, David
Mildred T. Nichols
Nichols, Charles H.
Timothy Nicholson
Chappell, Edward Carter, Jr.
Luke Nichter
Johnson, John Howard
Leland, Frank C.
Martin, John B.
Taylor, Benjamin H.
Steven J. Niven
Aarons, Charlie
Adams, Henry
Adams, Dock
Albright, George Washington
Alexander, Kelly Miller
Allain, Théophile T.
Anderson, Osborne Perry
Antoine, Caesar Carpetier
Baker, Lena

Bates, Daisy
Bell, Mary A. (1852–?)
Berry, Halle
Bethea, Rainey
Bond, John Robert
Bradley, Thomas
Brown, Ruth
Caldwell, Charles
Calloway, Cab
Cardozo, Thomas W.
Carter, James
Carter, Uless
Celia (d. 1848)
Celia (d. 1855)
Chamberlain, Wilt
Chaney, James Earl
Charles, Robert
Clark, Kenneth Bancroft
Clash, Kevin
Collins, Addie Mae
Cook, Fields
Cook, George F. T.
Cox, Minnie
Cox, Wayne Wellington
Cromwell, Oliver (fl. 1875–1889)
Davis, Alexander K.
Davis, Madison
Deveaux, John H.
Doctor Jack
Durham, Tempie Herndon
Ellington, Arthur
Fauset, Crystal Bird
Fields, Alonzo
Finch, William
Gaetjens, Joe
Galloway, Abraham Hankins
Garlic, Delia T.
Garvey, Amy Ashwood
Gillam, Cora T.
Gillam, Isaac T.
Graweere, John
Gray, Ralph
Gray, Simon
Hancock, Gordon Blaine
Higginbotham, Evelyn Brooks
Hose, Sam
Hunt, Gilbert
Hyman, Flora "Flo"
Jackson, Jimmy Lee
Jemmy
Jennings, Darius T.
Johnson, Jack
Jones, Bill T.

Jones, Edward Smyth
Key, Elizabeth
Laveaux, Marie
Lee, William Mack
Lewis, Channing
Liston, Sonny
Logan, Onnie Lee
Louis, Joe
Lucas, Bohlen
Martin, Louis E.
McCray, John Henry
McCrorey, Mary Jackson
McDaniel, Hattie
McDonald, Gabrielle Kirk
McKaine, Osceola
McNair, Denise
Meredith, James Howard
Mitchell, Arthur Wergs
Mollison, Irvin C.
Mollison, Willis E.
Montgomery, William Thornton
Moses, Robert P.
Murray, Albert
Nash, William Beverly
Noll, Malinda
Obama, Barack
Onesimus
Otabenga
Parker, Mack Charles
Parker, Noah B.
Pettey, Sarah Dudley
Pollard, Auburey
Poston, Ted
Powell, Colin
Pride, Charley
Rainey, Ma
Rice, Condoleezza
Rice, Spotswood
Rivers, Prince
Robertson, Carole
Rustin, Bayard Taylor
Schuyler, George Samuel
Scottsboro Boys
Sheppard, William Henry
Shorey, William T.
Simkins, Modjeska
Simkins, Paris
Simpson, O. J.
Smith, Margaret Charles
Smith, Owen L. W.
Spaulding, Asa Timothy
Spaulding, Charles Clinton
Thomas, Clarence
Thompson, Holland

Thompson, Jacob
Walker, Edwin G.
Wesley, Cynthia
Wheeler, John Hervey
Whipper, Ionia Rollin
Whipper, William J.
Williams, Robert Franklin
Wright, Cleo
Young, Roger Arliner

M. Margarita Nodarse
Hernández, Rafael
Sherri J. Norris
Abron, Lilia Ann
Harvard, Beverly
Terri L. Norris
Brooks, Carolyn Branch
Hughes, Cathy
Ana Nunes
Perry, Phyllis Alesia
Erich Nunn
Payne, Rufus "Tee Tot"
Thomas, William
Yusuf Nuruddin
Kilson, Martin Luther, Jr.
Patricia Williamson Nwosu
Lee, Mollie Huston
Justin Nystrom
Trévigne, Paul
Ann O'Bryan
Stephens, Charlotte Andrews
Rafael Ocasio
Burgos, Juliade
Stephen J. Ochs
Cailloux, André
Susan E. O'Donovan
Joiner, Philip
Floyd Ogburn
Bowles, Charles
Crum, William Demos
Green, Elisha Winfield
James, Thomas
Richardson, Archie Gibbs
Thorne, Jack
Walker, William
Waller, Odell
W. Farrell O'Gorman
Cotter, Joseph Seamon, Sr.
Terence J. O'Grady
Hendrix, Jimi
Marian M. Ohman
Smith, N. Clark
Jonette O'Kelley Miller
McKinney, Nina Mae
Woodard, Beulah Ecton

Sykes, Roosevelt
Tampa Red
Taylor, Eddie
Taylor, Hound Dog
White, Bukka
Williams, Big Joe
Williamson, Sonny Boy (1899?–1965)
Williamson, Sonny Boy (1914–1948)
Rudy Pearson
Hill, Edwin Shelton
Unthank, DeNorval
Jane H. Pease
Steward, Austin
William H. Pease
Steward, Austin
Diane Pecknold
Simpson, Valerie
Nadine D. Pederson
Séjour, Victor
Nan Peete
Harris, Barbara
Lara Pellegrinelli
Fitzgerald, Ella
Horn, Shirley
Lincoln, Abbey
Wilson, Cassandra
A. J. Peluso, Jr.
Selby, Joe
Aisha Peña
Dinwiddie Quartet
Sabrina Pendergrass
Steele, Claude
James L. Penick
Railroad Bill
Lisa M. Penn
Devine, Annie Belle Robinson
Lisa K. Perdigao
Gaines, Ernest J.
Jackson, Angela
Malin Pereira
Alexander, Elizabeth
Govan, Sandra
Harris, Trudier
Moss, Thylias
Burton W. Peretti
Basie, Count
Foster, Pops
Claranne Perkins
Collins, Marva Delores
de Passe, Suzanne Celeste
Gaines, Patrice Jean
Simpson, Carole

Smith, Barbara (1949–)
Stringer, C. Vivian
Linda M. Perkins
Coppin, Fanny Jackson
Jonna Perrillo
Mason, E. Harold
Jeffrey B. Perry
Harrison, Hubert Henry
Marilyn Elizabeth Perry
Parsons, Lucy
White, Eartha Mary Magdalene
Dahlia Patrice Perryman
Baxter, Freddie
Eric W. Petenbrink
Hall, Harry Haywood
Barbara Bennett Peterson
Stockton, Betsey
Bernard L. Peterson
Bailey, Pearl
Muse, Clarence E.
M. A. Peterson
Fletcher, Arthur Allen
Miriam J. Petty
Fetchit, Stepin
Preer, Evelyn
Welch, Elisabeth
Denyce Porter Peyton
Washington, Fanny Smith
Sarah K. Pfatteicher
Crumpler, Rebecca Davis Lee
Wendy Pflug
Brown, Elaine
Yates, James
Christopher Phelps
Abu-Jamal, Mumia
Boggs, James
James, C. L. R.
Lester, Julius
McKinney, Ernest Rice
Moore, Cecil Bassett
J. Alfred Phelps
James, Daniel, Jr.
Otis Westbrook Pickett
Jenkins, Esau
Kerry Pimblott
Hayes, Charles A.
Sherrow O. Pinder
Anderson, William T.
W. Brian Piper
Vivian, Cordy Tindell (C. T.)
Michael W. Pipkin
Thompson, Emeline

Merline Pitre
Leland, Mickey
White, Lulu Belle

Martha Pitts
Bibb, Joseph Dandridge
Sims, Naomi

Reginald H. Pitts
Goldsby, Crawford (Cherokee Bill)
Lewis, Robert Benjamin

Bailey Thomas Player
Griffey, Ken, Sr.
Jenkins, Clarence (Fats)
Strong, Ted

Betty E. Plummer
Durham, James

Fritz G. Polite
Robinson, Eddie

Paulette K. Polley-Edmunds
Thomas Graham, Pamela

Carol Polsgrove
Forman, James
Padmore, George

Millery Polyné
Plinton, James O., Jr.
Williams, Lavinia

David L. Porter
Metcalfe, Ralph Harold

Deborah Post
Keith, Damon Jerome

Sarah Powers
Piper, Rose

Robert A. Pratt
James, Etta
Loving, Mildred Delores Jeter

Stephen Preskill
Moten, Lucy Ellen

Delaina A. Price
McCarty, Oseola

H. H. Price
Foy(e), William Ellis
Greene, Bob
Talbot, Gerald "Jerry" Edgarton

Kimala Price
Avery, Byllye
Kennedy, Flo
Ross, Loretta

Marseille M. Pride
Parks, Henry Green, Jr.

Wendell E. Pritchett
Weaver, Robert Clifton

Luca Prono
Battle, Kathleen

Davis, Frank Marshall
Delany, Samuel R.

Bernadette Pruitt
Grovey, R. R.
Houston, Joshua
Washington, Margaret Murray

Sharon Pruitt
Amaki, Amalia

Robert Pruter
Mayfield, Curtis

Linda Przybyszewski
Harlan, Robert

Sarah J. Purcell
Hull, Agrippa
Ranger, Joseph

William W. Quivers
Quivers, William Wyatt, Sr.

Christopher M. Rabb
Freeman, Amos Noë

Howard N. Rabinowitz
Elliott, Robert Brown

Albert J. Raboteau
Thurman, Howard W.

Allana Radecki
Briggs, Bunny

Arnold Rampersad
Ellison, Ralph Waldo

Adah Ward Randolph
Ferguson, Thomas Jefferson

Sherie Randolph
Wyatt, Addie

Lawrence R. Rast, Jr.
Young, Rosa Jinsey

Jamal Ratchford
McGuire-Duvall, Edith
Temple, Edward S.

Susan J. Rayl
Cooper, Tarzan
Douglas, Robert L.

Maria Elena Raymond
Brown, Clara (Aunt Clara)
Ford, Barney Launcelot
McClain, Leanita

Ann Rayson
Baldwin, James
Larsen, Nella

Marina Reasoner
Glover, Nathaniel, Jr.

Shana L. Redmond
Brown, Lawrence Benjamin
King, Rodney Glenn

Notorious B. I. G.
Rock, Chris

Dwandalyn R. Reece
McQueen, Butterfly

Teresa L. Reed
Batson, Flora
LaBelle, Patti

Vonzele David Reed
Combs, Sean
Grandmaster Flash (Joseph Saddler)

De Anna J. Reese
Houston, Drusilla Dunjee

Linda W. Reese
McLaurin, George W.

Debra A. Reid
Hunter, Mary Evelyn Virginia
Smith, Robert Lloyd
Thorburn, W. Garth

Mark A. Reid
Lee, Spike

Patricia Reid-Merritt
Barrow, Willie Taplin

Joseph P. Reidy
Bradley, Aaron Alpeora

Rachel B. Reinhard
Clark, Robert

Robert Repino
Childs, Faith
Clemons, Michael "Pinball"

Susan M. Reverby
Laurie, Eunice Verdell Rivers
Pollard, Charlie Wesley
Shaw, Herman

Angelita D. Reyes
Gregory, Louis George
Rhinelander, Alice Jones

Althea E. Rhodes
Bonner, Marita Odette

Darren Rhym
Robinson, Max Cleveland

Nicole S. Ribianszky
Butcher, Elizabeth
Johnson, Amy
Johnson, Ann Battles
Leiper, Fanny
Price, Nelly

Connie Park Rice
Clifford, John Robert
Cook, Coralie Franklin
Davis, John Warren
Payne, Christopher Harrison
Starks, Samuel W.

Frank O. Richards
Sinkler, William H., Jr.

Janine Richardson
Smith, Nolle R., Sr.

Joe M. Richardson
Gibbs, Jonathan C.

Susan Richardson-Sanabria
Bey, James Hawthorne

James W. Riddlesperger, Jr.
Brown, Jesse

David Riehle
James, Charles Edmund

Steven A. Riess
Gans, Joe

Brenton E. Riffel
Booker, James Carroll, III
Estes, Sleepy John
Rachell, James "Yank"
Turner, Big Joe

James A. Riley
Bell, Cool Papa
Gibson, Josh
Johnson, Judy
Williams, Smokey Joe

Marinelle Ringer
Beals, Melba Pattillo

Susan Knoke Rishworth
Morton Jones, Verina Harris

Michael J. Ristich
Boutelle, Frazier Augustus
Burch, J. Henri
Cromwell, Robert I.

Donald A. Ritchie
Dunnigan, Alice Allison
Lautier, Louis Robert
Moss, Annie Lee
Payne, Ethel Lois

Alicia J. Rivera
Wysinger, Edmond

Pamela S. Rivers
Motley, Marion "Tank"

Lisa E. Rivo
Beckwourth, Jim
Brown, Grafton Tyler
Brown, Hallie Quinn
Catlett, Elizabeth
Cole, Johnnetta
Cole, Rebecca
Davis, Benjamin O., Sr.
Day, Thomas
Dove, Rita Frances
Dunham, Katherine Mary
Fields, Mary
Fuller, Meta Warrick
Gilliam, Sam
Hackley, Emma Azalia

Jackson, Shirley Ann
Jones, Lois Mailou
Jordan, June
Kelly, Patrick
Kitt, Eartha Mae
Lewis, Edmonia
Micheaux, Oscar
Morgan, Garrett Augustus
Mungin, Lawrence
Parks, Gordon, Sr.
Powers, Harriet
Puryear, Martin
Richards, Michael
Ringgold, Faith
Rose, Edward
Savage, Augusta
Simone, Nina
Sul Te Wan, Madame
Thomas, Alma
Van Peebles, Melvin
VanDerZee, James Augustus Joseph
Walker, Maggie Lena
Wells, James Lesesne
Wilson, Ellis
Wilson, Harriet E.
Winfrey, Oprah
Wolfe, George C.
Woodruff, Hale Aspacio

Hildred Roach
Joplin, Scott
Andree Layton Roaf
Edwards, Ballard Trent
Gloria Grant Roberson
Buccau, Quamino
Heth, Joice
Brian R. Roberts
Downing, Henry Francis
Kevin D. Roberts
Adams, John Quincy (1845–?)
Gilbert, John Wesley
Rita Roberts
Moore, Frederick Randolph
Edward J. Robinson
Cassius, Samuel Robert
Taylor, Preston
Gerard Robinson
Brown, Roscoe Conkling, Jr.
Leonard, Walter J.
Washington, Walter E.
J. Bradford Robinson
Hartley, Henry Alexander Saturnin
Nancy T. Robinson
Branch, Wallace

Gumbel, Bryant
Hart, William H. H.
Hendon, Ernest
Marsh, Vivian Osborne
Moore, Melba
Shaw, Patricia Walker
Van Engle, Dorothy
Gail Robinson-Oturu
Duncan, Robert Todd
Ian Rocksborough-Smith
O'Dell, Jack
Katharine Rodier
Nelson, Marilyn
Edward W. Rodman
Burgess, John
Dennis, Walter Decoster
Juan Carlos Rodriguez
Cruz, Celia
Michael Rodriguez
Plumpp, Sterling
William W. Rogers
Turner, Benjamin Sterling
Jarod H. Roll
Whitfield, Owen
Tracy R. Rone
Young, Jean Childs
Michele Valerie Ronnick
Gilbert, John Wesley
Hartley, Henry Alexander Saturnin
Lightfoot, George Morton
Noliwe Rooks
Malone, Annie Turnbo
Douglas Fleming Roosa
Darby, Dorothy
Jones, Willie "Suicide"
Santop, Louis
Smith, Ida Van
Vails, Nelson
Tom Rose
Thompson, Willie
Adam Rosen
Carroll, Hattie
Charles Rosenberg
Abner, David, Sr.
Allen, Mary Rice Hayes
Antoine, Felix C.
Ballard, John
Beckham, Albert Sidney
Bedford, Robert Edward
Blue, Thomas Fountain
Bolivar, William Carl
Bowling, Frank
Brodhead, John Henry

Dawson, William Levi (1886–1970)
Gaye, Marvin
Gryce, Gigi
Hamid, Sufi Abdul
Majors, Monroe Alpheus
Morgan, Clement Garnett
Morton, Benny
Pozo, Chano
Redding, Otis
Washington, Harold

Elizabeth A. Russey
Dawson, William Levi (1899–1990)
Houston, Ulysses L.

Anna Russo
Scott, Alberta Virginia

Nichole T. Rustin
Mingus, Charles, Jr.

Howard Rye
Curtis, King
Tharpe, Rosetta

Kelly Boyer Sagert
May, Lee

John Saillant
Paul, Nathaniel
Preston, William Everett "Billy"
Sanderson, Jeremiah Burke
Swan, Frederic W.
Teage, Hilary
Walker, Quok
Withers, William (Bill)

Frank A. Salamone
Drake, St. Clair, Jr.
Gibbs, James Lowell
Willis, William Shedrick, Jr.

Dorothy Salem
Fleming, Lethia C.

James M. Salem
Ace, Johnny
Robey, Don D.
Thornton, Willie Mae

Mark J. Sammons
Whipple, Prince

Brenna Sanchez
Abdul, Raoul
Burks, Mary Fair
White, John H.

Crystal Renée Sanders
Adams, Victoria Jackson Gray
Bowser, Rosa
Tatum, Beverly

Joshunda Sanders
Africa, Ramona
Anderson, Ada C.

Anderson, Violette Neatley
Banks, Tyra
Collins, Newton Isaac, Sr.
Dash, Leon Decosta, Jr.
DeCarava, Roy
Jones, Amanda
Madgett, Naomi Long
McNatt, Rosemary Bray
McPherson, James Alan
Mills, David
Mitchell, Elvis
Nelson, Jill
White, Armond
Wilkerson, Isabel

Justin Sanders
Sanders, Hayes Edward "Big Ed"

Sophie Sanders
Biggers, John

Martha A. Sandweiss
King, Ada

David Sanjek
Diddley, Bo
McNeely, Cecil James (Big Jay)
Milburn, Amos
Phillips, Esther
Spann, Otis

Xiomara Santamarina
Eldridge, Elleanor
Freeman, Elizabeth

Carol Baker Sapora
Day, Caroline Stewart Bond

Monica R. Saunders
Lewis, Oliver

Richard Saunders
Estes, James F., Sr.
Herenton, Willie Wilbert
Looby, Z. Alexander

Janet Marie Savage
Savage, Howard Thornton

Steven P. Savage
Simms, Willie

Todd L. Savitt
Lynk, Miles Vandahurst

Miriam Sawyer
Bragg, Janet

Elizabeth D. Schafer
Branche, George Clayton
Cesar
Dibble, Eugene Heriot, Jr.
Dorsette, Cornelius Nathaniel
Garrett, Leroy
Hinson, Eugene Theodore
Marchbanks, Vance Hunter, Jr.

Moten, Pierce Sherman
Tildon, Toussaint Tourgee
Don Schanche
Brooks, Tyrone
Randall, William P. "Daddy Bill"
Thurmond, Michael
Jeffry D. Schantz
Fortune, Amos
Richard Schechner
Smith, Anna Deavere
N. Elizabeth Schlatter
Basquiat, Jean-Michel
Leonard Schlup
Cheatham, Henry Plummer
Christopher W. Schmidt
Robinson, Frank
Stovey, George Washington
Michael Schmidt
Hancock, Herbie
Little, Booker, Jr.
Christine Schneider
Artemus, John C.
Thomas, Jesse O.
Ingrid Schorr
Chanticleer, Raven
Hampton, James
David Schroeder
Boyd, Gerald M.
Fuller, Howard
Stewart, Thomas McCants
Elizabeth R. Schroeder
Jones, Richard "Dick Jones" Lee
Malini Johar Schueller
Dorr, David F.
Gunther Schuller
Blanton, Jimmy
Lois Massengale Schultz
Summers, Jane Roberta
Roger A. Schuppert
Brawley, Benjamin
Ruffin, Josephine St. Pierre
Kelsey Schurer
Glover, Nathaniel, Jr.
Roxanne Y. Schwab
Avery, Margaret
Coleman, Lucretia Newman
Falana, Lola
Jeffers, Lance
Jones, Etta
Roker, Roxie
Uggams, Leslie
Weeks, James

Philip J. Schwarz
Newby, Dangerfield
Loren Schweninger
Bayley, Solomon
Burris, Samuel D.
Coleman, Warren Clay
Gibbs, Mifflin Wistar
Haralson, Jeremiah
Johnson, Andrew N.
McKinlay, Whitefield
Meachum, John Berry
O'Kelly, Berry
Rapier, James Thomas
Stanly, John Carruthers
Karla Sclater
Ray, Emma J. Smith
Billy Scott
Barnes, William Harry
Hill, Mary Elliott
Smith, Relliford Stillmon
Donald Scott
Allen, Ethel D.
Brown, Wesley A.
Catto, Octavius Valentine
Gloucester, John
Staples, Brent
Laine A. Scott
Grimké, Angelina Weld
Olivia A. Scriven
Falconer, Etta Zuber
Granville, Evelyn Boyd
Guy-Sheftall, Beverly
Hammonds, Evelynn Maxine
Haynes, Martha Euphemia Lofton
Manley, Audrey Forbes
Mayes, Vivienne Lucille Malone
McBay, Shirley Mathis
Eileen Scully
Sands, Sarah
Nicole Sealey
Appiah, Kwame Anthony
hooks, bell
Smith, Patricia
Wade-Gayles, Gloria
Michael N. Searles
Nigger Add
Wallace, Daniel Webster
William Seraile
Billy
Laura Isabel Serna
Fishburne, Laurence
Murphy, Eddie

Joel M. Sipress
Ward, William

Kimberly A. Sisson
Clifford, Carrie Williams

Rose Pelone Sisson
Cameron, James Herbert
Carson, Julia May Porter
Knox, George Levi
Wilson, Mary
Wright, Mary Herring

Lyde Cullen Sizer
Bowser, Mary Elizabeth

Rebecca L. Skidmore
Jones, Gayl

Beverly Lanier Skinner
Davis, Arthur Paul

Genevieve Skinner
Burleigh, Angus Augustus

Nico Slate
Sykes, Rozzell

Kevin Sliman
Lacy, Rubin

Gerard Sloan
Banks, Willie
Murphy, Calvin

Genevieve Slomski
Clark, Ed

Patricia Carter Sluby
Jackson, Giles Beecher
Johnson, Lonnie G.

Jessica Smedley
McMillan, Terry

Robert Smieja
Primus, Holdridge

Andrew Smith
Shakur, Sanyika (Kody Scott)
Tyson, Michael Gerard

Carlton Elliott Smith
Smith, Eddie Lee, Jr.

Cherise Smith
Sleet, Moneta, Jr.

David Lionel Smith
Northup, Solomon

Eric Ledell Smith
Brown, E. C. (Edward Cooper)
Evanti, Lillian Evans
Gibson, John Trusty

Erin A. Smith
Fauset, Jessie Redmon

Gary Scott Smith
Powell, Adam Clayton, Sr.

Gera Smith
Radcliffe, Alec
Radcliffe, Ted "Double Duty"

Jessie Carney Smith
Johnson, Halle Tanner Dillon

John David Smith
Councill, William Hooper
Thomas, William Hannibal

John Howard Smith
Fraunces, Samuel
Jeremiah, Thomas
Johnson, Anthony
McPherson, Christopher
Populus, Vincent

Johnie D. Smith
Allen, Macon Bolling

Larissa M. Smith
Robinson, Spottswood William, III

Maureen M. Smith
Smith, Tommie
Whitaker, Mark
Williams, Serena and Venus Williams

Robert C. Smith
Jackson, Jesse L., Sr.
Lewis, John
Rangel, Charles

Shanna L. Smith
Majozo, Estella Conwill

Susan L. Smith
Ferebee, Dorothy Boulding

Valerie Smith
Morrison, Toni

Dorsía Smith Silva
Lutcher, Nellie
Christian-Christensen, Donna M.
Dyson, Michael Eric
Herron, Carolivia

David F. Smydra, Jr.
Brown, Jim
Horne, Lena
Jordan, Michael
McLendon, Johnny
Pryor, Richard
Reed, Ishmael
Ross, Diana
Russell, Bill
Scott, Wendell

Terri L. Snyder
Webb, Jane

Richard Sobel
Banks, Ernie
Beamon, Bob
Carew, Jan

Chenault, Kenneth Irvine
Dumas, Charles "Charley" Everett
Ellis, Larry
Guinier, Lani
Jackson, Jesse Louis, Jr.
Thomas, John Curtis

Jack Sohmer
Archey, Jimmy
Armstrong, Lil
Bailey, Buster
Braud, Wellman
Carey, Mutt
De Paris, Sidney
De Paris, Wilbur
Dickenson, Vic
Dodds, Johnny
Johnson, Bill
Johnson, Budd
Miley, Bubber
Newton, Frankie
Nicholas, Albert
Procope, Russell
Robinson, Prince
Russell, Luis Carl
Sedric, Gene
Smith, Jabbo
Smith, Joe
Stewart, Rex
Wells, Dicky
Williams, Cootie
Young, Trummy

Gabriel Solis
Monk, Thelonious

David W. Southern
Turner, Thomas Wyatt

Albert B. Southwick
Taylor, Major

Wayne Sparkman
Bottoms, Lawrence Wendell

DeCarlous Spearman
Doyle, Henry Eman
Woods, Lois Lee Prestage

Linda Spencer
Austin, H. Elsie
Bowen, Uvelia Atkins
Brown, Solomon G.
Chesnutt, Helen Maria
Mix, Sarah Ann Freeman
Simpson, Georgiana Rose
Tarry, Ellen
Walcott, Bess Bolden
Williams, Ella V. Chase

David E. Spies
Ayler, Albert
Holley, Major
Kelly, Wynton
Mobley, Hank
Morgan, Lee
Moten, Bennie
Nichols, Herbie
Pettiford, Oscar
Quebec, Ike

Yolanda L. Watson Spiva
Lewis, Shirley A. R.
Morley Ball, Joyce A.
Simon, Marguerite Francis
Sizemore, Barbara Ann
Sudarkasa, Niara

Jocelyn Spragg
Amos, Harold

Kimberly Springer
Cooper, Anna Julia Haywood
Evers-Williams, Myrlie

Kathryn L. Staley
Garrison, Memphis Tennessee
Potter, Eliza

Lucia C. Stanton
Hemings, Sally
Jefferson, Isaac

Cynthia Staples
Harrison, Juanita

Richard D. Starnes
Fuller, Thomas Oscar

John Stauffer
Smith, James McCune

Liz Stephens
Ikard, Bose

Randall J. Stephens
Fuller, William Edward, Sr.
Lowery, Irving E.

Tom Stephens
Doram, Dennis

Robert Stepto
Brown, Sterling Allen

J. Deborah Johnson Sterrett
Dwight, Ed
McClendon, Dorothy V.
Washington, James W., Jr.

Alva Moore Stevenson
Lu Valle, James Ellis
Píco, Pío

Elizabeth P. Stewart
Frisby, Herbert

Milton Stewart
Brown, Clifford

Paul Stillwell
Arbor, Jesse Walter
Barnes, Samuel Edward
Cooper, George Clinton
Lee, John Wesley, Jr.
Martin, Graham Edward
Reagan, John Walter
Reason, Joseph Paul
Sublett, Frank Ellis, Jr.
White, William Sylvester, Jr.

Robert L. Stone
Eason, Willie Claude

Jared T. Story
Withers, Ernest C.

Glenn Stout
Newcombe, Donald
Whiteside, Larry

Michelle M. Strazer
Butler, Selena Sloan

Joe Street
Kendricks, Eddie
Knuckles, Frankie
May, Derrick
Rodgers, Nile, Jr.
Sherrod, Charles

Rodger Streitmatter
Trotter, William Monroe

Steve Strimer
Dorsey, Basil
Jones, Rev. Thomas H.

Melissa Nicole Stuckey
Franklin, Buck Colbert
Haynes, Thomas
Leftwich, John C.
Turner, David J.

Sterling Stuckey
Cook, Vivian E. J.
Faulkner, William John
Stuckey, Elma

Rick Suchow
Jamerson, James

James D. Sullivan
Brooks, Gwendolyn

Patricia Sullivan
Bond, Julian

Terrie Sultan
Marshall, Kerry James

Allison M. Sutton
Jones, Virginia Lacy

Karen E. Sutton
Doner, Sam
Freedom, British
Jackson, Dinnah

Nickens, Armistead Stokalas, Jr.
Nickens, James
Poor, Salem
Washington-Williams, Essie Mae

Jay Sweet
Lewis, John Aaron

Ray Swick
Simmons, Robert W., Sr.

David E. Swift
Ray, Charles Bennett
Wright, Theodore Sedgwick

Bruce Sylvester
McPhatter, Clyde

Marcia G. Synnott
Burroughs, Nannie

Klara Szmánko
Greenlee, Sam

John Szwed
Davis, Miles

Morgan Taggart-Hampton
Logan, Myra Adele

Suzi Takahashi
Archer (Adams), Osceola Macarthy

S. Sherrie Tartt
Hilliard, David
Huggins, Ericka

Cornelia Akins Taylor
Byrd, Flossie Marian

Deborah Lois Taylor
Canady, Alexa I.
Kilpatrick, Carolyn Cheeks
West, Miguel S.

James Lance Taylor
Shabazz, Hajj Bahiyah "Betty"

Theodore Taylor
Brown, Jesse Leroy

Yuval Taylor
Grimes, William

Leonard Ray Teel
Polite, Carlene Hatcher
Scott, William Alexander, II

Jerome Teelucksingh
Greene, Maurice
Holyfield, Evander

Emily A. Teitsworth
Ladd, Florence

Harmony A. Teitsworth
DePreist, James

Matthew Teorey
Major, Clarence

Rosalyn Terborg-Penn
Quarles, Benjamin Arthur

Carol Parker Terhune
Gardner, Eliza Ann
McCray, Mary F.

Rose C. Thevenin
Blocker, Sarah
Collier, Nathan White
Gray, William Herbert, Jr.
Porter, Gilbert Lawrence

Herman E. Thomas
Pennington, James William Charles

Jennifer R. Thomas
Penn, Irvine Garland

Kenneth F. Thomas
Calloway, Ernest

Melanie R. Thomas
Clayton, Mayme
Coleman, L. Zenobia
Lattimore, Benjamin
Marshall, Albert P.
Thomas, Sally

Rhondda Robinson Thomas
Johnson, Lucy Bagby
Shadd, Abraham Doras

Roger K. Thomas
Sumner, Francis Cecil

Sheila Gregory Thomas
Gregory, James Monroe
Gregory, Thomas Montgomery
Hancock, Hugh Berry

Elaine E. Thompson
Pierce, Billy

George A. Thompson, Jr.
Brown, William Alexander
Hewlett, James

Julius E. Thompson
Greene, Percy

Kathleen Thompson
Bass, Charlotta

Katrina D. Thompson
Herc, DJ Kool
Lewis, Roscoe E.
Snoop Dogg

Lisa K. Thompson
Kern Foxworth, Marilyn

Pamela Felder Thompson
Ogbu, John Uzo

Patricia J. Thompson
Brown, George S.
Holmes, Isabella Snowden
Mars, John N.
Snowden, Isaac Humphrey
Snowden, Samuel

William Thomson
Rushing, Jimmy
Snowden, Elmer

J. Mills Thornton
Nixon, Edgar Daniel
Robinson, Jo Ann

Sarah C. Thuesen
Shepard, James Edward

Timothy N. Thurber
Brooke, Edward
Wilkins, Roy

Donald F. Tibbs
Jones, Nathaniel Raphael

Frank Tirro
Adderley, Cannonball
Armstrong, Louis
Gordon, Dexter Keith

Danica Tisdale
Lane, Isaac

W. S. Tkweme
Brown, H. Rap

Diane Todd Bucci
George, Nelson
Giddings, Paula J.
Jones, Grace Morris Allen

Margaret E. M. Tolbert
Brown, Jeannette Elizabeth

Susan D. Toliver
Premice, Josephine
Spencer, Margaret Beale

Barbara B. Tomblin
Johnson-Brown, Hazel

Charlie T. Tomlinson
Brown, Willie (1962–)
Cooper, John Walcott
Potter, Richard
Sandfield, Richard
Tyler, Willie
Williams, Aaron

Beth Tompkins Bates
Lampkin, Daisy

Brian Tong
Brown, Kate

Edgar Allan Toppin
Haynes, George Edmund
Jackson, Luther Porter
Scott, Emmett Jay

Simon Topping
Rivers, Francis Ellis

William P. Toth
Bennett, Hal

Steven C. Tracy
Hooker, John Lee

Hughes, Langston
Jacobs, Little Walter
Jefferson, Blind Lemon
Johnson, Lonnie
Johnson, Robert

Sarah L. Trembanis
Malarcher, David Julius "Gentleman Dave"
Trouppe, Quincy Thomas

Zoe Trodd
Crafts, Hannah
Green, Shields
Leary, Lewis Sheridan
Washington, Madison

C. James Trotman
Anderson, Matthew

Joe W. Trotter
Davis, Richard L.

Carole Watterson Troxler
Outlaw, Wyatt

Debra Thomas Truhart
Weaver, Anna Bolden
Weaver, William B.

Stephen Truhon
Guthrie, Robert Val
Jenkins, David Martin
Long, Howard Hale
Thompson, Charles Henry

David M. Tucker
Church, Robert Reed

Vernitta Brothers Tucker
Du Bois, Shirley Lola Graham

Anne M. Turner
Thierry, Camille

Brian Turner
Askin, Luther B.

John G. Turner
Fearing, Maria
Jakes, T. D.
Sheppard, Lucy Gantt

T. Natasha Turner
Westbrook, Peter

Mark Tushnet
Marshall, Thurgood
Waddy, Joseph C.

Kate Tuttle
Wamba, Philippe Enoc

William M. Tuttle, Jr.
Williams, Eugene

Akinyele K. Umoja
Carter, Alprentice "Bunchy"

Wayne J. Urban
Bond, Horace Mann

Constance Porter Uzelac
Coleman, Bessie

Porter, James Amos
Wesley, Dorothy Burnett Porter

J. E. Vacha
Hall, Juanita

Vanita Vactor
Cleage, Pearl

Peter Valenti
Aaron, Hank

Katrien Van der Aa
Moore, Johnny "Dizzy"

Karen Van Outryve
Washington, Mildred

Randall K. Van Schepen
Harris, Lyle Ashton

Betti Carol VanEpps-Taylor
Aaron, Jesse
Abbott, Cleveland Leigh
Blair, Norval
Blakey, Theodore Robert
Campbell, Sarah (Aunt Sally)
Marchbanks, Lucretia

Andre D. Vann
Alexander-Ralston, Elreta
Blue, Daniel T., Jr.
Brice, Carol Lovette
Browne, Marjorie Lee
Browne, Rose Butler
Chambers, Julius LeVonne
Cole, Maria Hawkins
Cole, Natalie
Frye, Henry E.
Kennedy, William Jesse, Jr.

Debra A. Varnado
Crouch, Hubert Branch, Sr.
Martin, Archie Alexander "A. A." and Nancy Candler
    Martin
Massie, Samuel Proctor, Jr.

Jennifer Vaughn
America, Richard F.
Loury, Glenn C.
Williams, Walter E.

Cynthia Haveson Veloric
Hendricks, Barkley
Saunders, Raymond

Cassandra Veney
Prosser, Nancy
Robinson, James Herman
Robinson, Randall

Sudhir Alladi Venkatesh
Wilson, William Julius

Leandi Venter
Odrick, Alfred

Arthur C. Verge
Russell, Clayton

Elizabeth Zoe Vicary
Henson, Josiah
Johnson, Edward Austin
Leidesdorff, William Alexander
Payne, Daniel Alexander
Melissa Vickery-Bareford
Aldridge, Ira
Hill, Abram
McClendon, Rose
Stephen Vincent
Roberts, Carl Glennis
Paul Von Blum
Beasley, Phoebe
Lewis, Samella
Outterbridge, John
Pajaud, William
Albert von Frank
Burns, Anthony
Stefan Vranka
Johnson, J. J.
Mary A. Waalkes
Boynton Robinson, Amelia
Williams, Hosea
Carl A. Wade
Spence, Eulalie
Wilkinson, Henry B.
Margaret Wade-Lewis
Applegate, Joseph R.
Bailey, Beryl Isadore Loftman
Morgan, Raleigh, Jr.
Spears, Arthur K.
Venise Wagner
Allensworth, Josephine Leavell
Keith Wailoo
Blackwell, David
Satcher, David
Billie E. Walker
Rollins, Charlemae Hill
Paul Walker
Kelley, Edmond
Mountain, Joseph
William S. Walker
Bowers, Thomas J.
Brandon K. Wallace
DeRamus, Lawrence DePriest, Sr.
MacDavid, Mary Foster
Peter Wallenstein
Alston, Melvin Ovenus
Delany, Bessie and Sadie Delany
Hastie, William Henry
Murray, Pauli
Newsome, Joseph Thomas
Poe, L. Marian
Powell, Adam Clayton, Jr.

Ransom, Leon Andrew
Young, Plummer Bernard
Kelli Cardenas Walsh
Putney, Martha
Waddy, Harriet West
Julie Walters
Louveste, Mary
Ronald Walters
Brown, Ron
Elise Virginia Ward
Ward, Theodore (Ted)
Harry M. Ward
Attucks, Crispus
Tom J. Ward
Frederick, Rivers
Eaton, Hubert A.
Carolyn Warfield
Slaughter, Moses
Warfield, George William
Clare J. Washington
Brown, Jill
Roberts, Lillian Davis
Dorothy A. Washington
Brown, Fredi Sears
Clack, Doris Hargrett
Edward T. Washington
Hill, Errol
Roberta Washington
Greene, Beverly Lorraine
Tandy, Vertner Woodson
Salim Washington
Bechet, Sidney
Coleman, Ornette
Clifford Edward Watkins
Lowery, P. G.
Denton L. Watson
Jackson, Lillie Mae Carroll
Mitchell, Clarence Maurice, Jr.
Jack Borden Watson
Arnold, Hendrick
Nigel Watson
Hill, Barney
Tiffany K. Wayne
Beckham, Ruth Winifred Howard
Darden, Christine Voncile Mann
Bethany Waywell Jay
Jai, Anna Madgigine
A. M. Weaver
Bullock, Barbara
Bret A. Weber
Bussey, Charles
Morial, Ernest Nathan "Dutch"
Watson, Lauren

Eleanor F. Wedge
Bearden, Romare
Melinda E. Weekes
Hawkins, Edwin
George P. Weick
Attaway, William Alexander
Parker, Toni Trent
Donovan S. Weight
Flipper, Joseph Simeon
Free Frank (Frank McWorter)
Hinard, Eufrosina
Teri B. Weil
Adams-Ender, Clara
McElroy, Colleen J.
Daniel Wein
Sweet, Ossian H.
Norman Weinstein
Coleman, Steve
Hood, Walter
Robert E. Weir
Harris, E. Victor
Zach Weir
Whitehead, Colson
Eric Weisbard
Little Richard
Judith Weisenfeld
Haynes, Daniel
Ellen Weiss
Taylor, Robert Robinson
Kimberly Welch
Blyden, Edward Wilmot
Redding, J. Saunders
Judith Wellman
Morel, Junius C.
Christopher Wells
Atkins, Charles "Cholly"
Brown, Ernest "Brownie"
McFerrin, Robert, Sr.
Donna M. Wells
Davis, Griffith Jerome
Freeman, Daniel
Hernandez, Nestor, Jr.
McNeill, Robert H.
Scurlock, George Hardison
Sorrell, Maurice B.
Dennis Wepman
Carmichael, Stokely
Cinque
Walker, Margaret
Paul Wermager
Ball, Alice Augusta
Johnston, Albert

C. S'thembile West
Beatty, Talley
Primus, Pearl
Nicholas Westbrook
Bush, John
Taylor, Prince
Rachel Westley
Harrison, Paul Carter
Martha L. Wharton
Elaw, Zilpha
Foote, Julia A. J.
Plato, Ann
Prince, Nancy
Stewart, Maria W.
David Wheat
Mongoula, Nicolas
Sara Graves Wheeler
Johnson, Mordecai Wyatt
Barbara A. White
Boston, Absalom
Cooper, Arthur
Crawford, James
Ross, Eunice
Melanye White Dixon
Cuyjet, Marion Helene Durham
Jamison, Judith
K. Wise Whitehead
Lyons, Maritcha R.
Rollin, Frances (Frank)
Washington, Olivia Davidson
Thomas N. Whitehead
Hunter, Clementine
Keith Whitescarver
Reed, Willis, Jr.
Harvey Amani Whitfield
Peters, Thomas
Preston, Richard
Salem, Peter
Stephen J. Whitfield
Till, Emmett Louis
Alexis Whitham
Singleton, John
Whitaker, Forest
Flint Whitlock
Green, Marlon D.
Eunice Angelica Whitmal
Duncan, Thelma Myrtle
Watson, Ella
David O. Whitten
Durnford, Andrew
Kevin Alan Whittington
Rolle, Esther
Slater, Jackie Ray

Cook, Joyce Mitchell
Jones, Gilbert Haven

Jamane Yeager
Easley, Annie J.

Shirley J. Yee
Cary, Mary Ann Shadd

Eric S. Yellin
Trotter, James Monroe
Waldron, J. Milton

Jean Fagan Yellin
Jacobs, Harriet

Jeffrey R. Yost
Gourdine, Meredith C.
Hall, Lloyd Augustus
Henry, Warren Elliott

Barbara Kraley Youel
Michaux, Lewis H.

Cynthia A. Young
Burnett, Charles
Jones, Claudia

Karen Beasley Young
Joyner, Tom
Smiley, Tavis

Mary L. Young
Holtzclaw, William Henry
Smith, Charles Spencer

William H. Young
Dodds, Baby
Page, Walter

Natalie Zacek
Evers, Medgar

Ann Zeidman-Karpinski
Robeson, Eslanda Cardozo Goode
Spikes, Dolores Margaret Richard

Benjamin T. Zeigler
Clyburn, James Enos

John H. Zimmerman
Adams, Alton Augustus, Sr.

Kristal Brent Zook
Beasley, Delilah Leontium
Brandon, Barbara
Coston, Julia Ringwood
Milburn, Rodney "Hot Rod"
Stewart, Ella Nora Phillips
Taylor, Susan Lillian

Nathan Zook
Alexander, Avery C.
Fattah, Chaka

Jacob Zumoff
Cleaver, Eldridge
Domingo, Wilfred Adolphus
Moore, Richard Benjamin
Seale, Bobby

African American Prizewinners, Medalists, and Members of Congress

Spingarn Medal Winners

The Spingarn Medal is awarded annually by the NAACP for outstanding achievement by a black American.

1915	Ernest E. Just	1954	Theodore K. Lawless
1916	Major Charles A. Young	1955	Carl J. Murphy
1917	Harry T. Burleigh	1956	Jack R. Robinson
1918	William S. B. Braithwaite	1957	Martin Luther King, Jr.
1919	Archibald H. Grimké	1958	Daisy Bates and the Little Rock Nine
1920	W. E. B. Du Bois	1959	Edward Duke Ellington
1921	Charles S. Gilpin	1960	J. Langston Hughes
1922	Mary B. Talbert	1961	Kenneth B. Clark
1923	George Washington Carver	1962	Robert C. Weaver
1924	Roland T. Hayes	1963	Medgar W. Evers
1925	James Weldon Johnson	1964	Roy O. Wilkins
1926	Carter G. Woodson	1965	M. Leontyne Price
1927	Anthony Overton	1966	John Harold Johnson
1928	Charles W. Chesnutt	1967	Edward W. Brooke, III
1929	Mordecai W. Johnson	1968	Sammy Davis, Jr.
1930	Henry A. Hunt	1969	Clarence M. Mitchell, Jr.
1931	Richard B. Harrison	1970	Jacob Lawrence
1932	Robert Russa Moton	1971	Leon H. Sullivan
1933	Max Yergan	1972	Gordon Parks, Sr.
1934	William T. B. Williams	1973	Wilson C. Riles
1935	Mary McLeod Bethune	1974	Damon J. Keith
1936	John Hope	1975	Hank Aaron
1937	Walter F. White	1976	Alvin Ailey, Jr.
1938	*No award given*	1977	Alexander P. Haley
1939	Marian Anderson	1978	Andrew J. Young, Jr.
1940	Louis T. Wright	1979	Rosa L. Parks
1941	Richard N. Wright	1980	Rayford W. Logan
1942	A. Philip Randolph	1981	Coleman A. Young
1943	William H. Hastie	1982	Benjamin E. Mays
1944	Charles R. Drew	1983	Lena Horne
1945	Paul B. Robeson	1984	Thomas Bradley
1946	Thurgood Marshall	1985	William H. Cosby, Jr.
1947	Percy L. Julian	1986	Benjamin L. Hooks
1948	Channing Heggie Tobias	1987	Percy E. Sutton
1949	Ralph J. Bunche	1988	Frederick Douglass Patterson
1950	Charles H. Houston	1989	Jesse L. Jackson
1951	Mabel K. Staupers	1990	L. Douglas Wilder
1952	Harry T. Moore	1991	Colin L. Powell
1953	Paul R. Williams	1992	Barbara C. Jordan

1993	Dorothy I. Height	2003	Constance Baker Motley
1994	Maya Angelou	2004	Robert L. Carter
1995	John Hope Franklin	2005	Oliver W. Hill
1996	A. Leon Higginbotham, Jr.	2006	Benjamin S. Carson, Sr.
1997	Carl T. Rowan	2007	John Conyers, Jr.
1998	Myrlie Evers-Williams	2008	Ruby Dee
1999	Earl G. Graves, Sr.	2009	Julian Bond
2000	Oprah Winfrey	2010	Cicely Tyson
2001	Vernon E. Jordan, Jr.	2011	Frankie Muse Freeman
2002	John Lewis		

Nobel Prize Winners

1950	Ralph Bunche (Peace)	1993	Toni Morrison (Literature)
1964	Martin Luther King, Jr. (Peace)	2009	Barack Obama (Peace)
1992	Derek Walcott (Literature)		

Pulitzer Prize Winners

1950	Gwendolyn Brooks	Poetry
1969	Moneta Sleet, Jr.	Journalism (Photography)
1970	Charles Gordone	Drama
1973	*Washington Post* (team member Roger Wilkins)	Journalism (Public Service)
1974	*Newsday* (team member Les Payne)	Journalism (Public Service)
1975	Matthew Lewis	Journalism (Photography)
	Ovie Carter	Journalism
1976	Scott Joplin	Music (posthumous)
1977	Acel Moore	Journalism
	Alex Haley	for *Roots*
1978	James Alan McPherson	Fiction
1982	Charles Fuller	Drama
	John H. White	Journalism
1983	Alice Walker	Fiction
1984	Kenneth Cooper and Norman Lockman	Journalism
1985	Dennis Bell and Ozier Muhammad	Journalism
1986	Michel duCille (as part of team)	Journalism (Photography)
1987	August Wilson	Drama
	Rita Dove	Poetry
1988	Dean Baquet (as part of team)	Journalism
	Michel duCille	Journalism (Photography)
	Toni Morrison	Fiction
1989	Clarence Page	Journalism
1990	August Wilson	Drama
1991	Harold Jackson (as part of team)	Journalism
1994	David Levering Lewis	Biography
	Isabel Wilkerson	Journalism

	William Raspberry	Journalism
	Yusef Komunyakaa	Poetry
1995	Leon Dash (as part of team)	Journalism
	Margo Jefferson	Journalism
	Virgin Islands Daily News (for the work of Melvin Claxton)	Journalism (Public Service)
1996	E. R. Shipp	Journalism
	George Walker	Music
1997	Wynton Marsalis	Music
1998	Clarence Williams	Journalism (Photography)
1999	Angelo B. Henderson	Journalism
	Duke Ellington	Music (posthumous)
2001	Gerald Boyd	Journalism
	David Levering Lewis	Biography
2002	Suzan-Lori Parks	Drama
2003	Colbert I. King	Journalism
2004	Leonard Pitts	Journalism
	Edward P. Jones	Fiction
2005	Dele Olojede	Journalism
2006	Trymaine Lee	Journalism
	Robin Givhan	Journalism
2007	Irwin Thompson (shared)	Journalism
	Quinton Smith	Journalism
	Cynthia Tucker	Journalism
2009	Annette Gordon Reed	History
	Eugene Robinson	Journalism
	Lynn Nottage	Drama
	Damon Winter	Journalism (Photography)

Recipients of the Presidential Medal of Freedom

1963	Marian Anderson	1985	Count Basie
	Ralph Bunche		Jerome H. Holland
1964	Lena F. Edwards	1988	Pearl Bailey
	Leontyne Price	1991	Colin Powell
	A. Philip Randolph		Leon Sullivan
1969	Duke Ellington	1992	Ella Fitzgerald
	Ralph Ellison		Leon H. Sullivan
	Roy Wilkins	1993	Arthur Ashe
	Whitney M. Young, Jr.		Thurgood Marshall
1976	Jesse Owens		Colin Powell
1977	Martin Luther King, Jr.	1994	Dorothy Height
1980	Clarence M. Mitchell		Barbara Jordan
1981	Eubie Blake	1995	William T. Coleman, Jr.
	Andrew Young		John Hope Franklin
1983	James Edward Cheek		A. Leon Higginbotham
	Mabel Mercer	1996	John H. Johnson
1984	Jackie Robinson		Rosa Parks

1998	James L. Farmer	2004	Edward Brooke
1999	Oliver W. Hill	2008	Benjamin Carson
2000	Marian Wright Edelman	2009	Joseph Lowery
	Jesse Jackson		Sidney Poitier
	Gardner C. Taylor	2011	Maya Angelou
2002	Hank Aaron		John Lewis
	Bill Cosby		Bill Russell
	Roberto Clemente		

Recipients of the Congressional Gold Medal

1973	Roberto Clemente		Joseph A. DeLaine
1977	Marian Anderson		Harry Briggs
1982	Joe Louis		Eliza Briggs
1984	Roy Wilkins		Levi Pearson
1988	Jesse Owens	2004	Martin Luther King, Jr.
1991	Colin Powell		Coretta Scott King
1998	The Little Rock Nine	2006	Tuskegee Airman
1999	Rosa Parks	2008	Edward William Brooke, III
2003	Jackie Robinson		
	Dorothy Height		

Recipients of the National Medal of Arts

1985	Ralph W. Ellison, Sr.	1996	Lionel Hampton
1986	Marian Anderson	1997	Betty Carter
1987	Ella Fitzgerald, Romare Bearden	1998	Fats Domino
1988	Gordon Parks, Sr.	2000	Maya Angelou, Benny Carter
1989	Katherine Dunham	2001	Judith Jamison
1990	Jacob Lawrence, B. B. King	2002	Smokey Robinson
1991	Honi Coles, Pearl Primus	2003	Buddy Guy
1992	James Earl Jones, Billy Taylor	2006	Roy R. DeCarava
1993	Cabell "Cab" Calloway, Ray Charles	2008	Henry "Hank" Jones
1994	Celia Cruz, Harry Belafonte	2009	Jessye Norman
1995	Ossie Davis and Ruby Dee, Gwendolyn Brooks, Arthur A. Mitchell	2010	Quincy Jones, Sonny Rollins

Recipients of the National Humanities Medal

1990	Henry Hampton	2001	Eileen Jackson Southern
1993	John Hope Franklin	2002	Thomas Sowell
1994	Dorothy Porter Wesley	2003	Frank M. Snowden
1995	Bernice Johnson Reagon	2009	Annette Gordon Reed, David Levering Lewis
1996	Rita Dove	2010	Arnold Rampersad
1998	Henry Louis Gates, Jr.		
1999	August Wilson		
2000	David C. Driskell, Ernest J. Gaines, Quincy Jones, Toni Morrison		

African American Members of Congress

Name	Years of Service	State	Party
SENATORS			
Revels, Hiram Rhoades	1870–1871	Mississippi	Republican
Bruce, Blanche Kelso	1875–1881	Mississippi	Republican
Brooke, Edward W.	1967–1979	Massachusetts	Republican
Moseley Braun, Carol	1993–1999	Illinois	Democrat
Obama, Barack	2005–2008	Illinois	Democrat
Burris, Roland	2009–2010	Illinois	Democrat
REPRESENTATIVES AND DELEGATES			
Menard, John Willis	1868	Louisiana	Republican
Long, Jefferson F.	1870–1871	Georgia	Republican
Rainey, Joseph H.	1870–1879	South Carolina	Republican
DeLarge, Robert C.	1871–1873	South Carolina	Republican
Turner, Benjamin S.	1871–1873	Alabama	Republican
Walls, Josiah T.	1871–1873, 1873–1876	Florida	Republican
Elliott, Robert B.	1871–1874	South Carolina	Republican
Rapier, James T.	1873–1875	Alabama	Republican
Ransier, Alonzo J.	1873–1875	South Carolina	Republican
Cain, Richard H.	1873–1875, 1877–1879	South Carolina	Republican
Lynch, John R.	1873–1877, 1882–1883	Mississippi	Republican
Haralson, Jeremiah	1875–1877	Alabama	Republican
Hyman, John Adams	1875–1877	North Carolina	Republican
Nash, Charles E.	1875–1877	Louisiana	Republican
Smalls, Robert	1875–1879, 1882–1883, 1884–1887	South Carolina	Republican
O'Hara, James E.	1883–1887	North Carolina	Republican
Cheatham, Henry P.	1889–1893	North Carolina	Republican
Langston, John Mercer	1890–1891	Virginia	Republican
Miller, Thomas E.	1890–1891	South Carolina	Republican
Murray, George W.	1893–1895, 1896–1897	South Carolina	Republican
White, George Henry	1897–1901	North Carolina	Republican
DePriest, Oscar Stanton	1929–1935	Illinois	Republican
Mitchell, Arthur W.	1935–1943	Illinois	Democrat

Name	Years of Service	State	Party
Dawson, William L.	1943–1970	Illinois	Democrat
Powell, Adam Clayton, Jr.	1945–1967, 1967–1971	New York	Democrat
Diggs, Charles	1955–1980	Michigan	Democrat
Nix, Robert N. C., Sr.	1958–1979	Pennsylvania	Democrat
Hawkins, Augustus F.	1963–1991	California	Democrat
Conyers, John	1965–present	Michigan	Democrat
Chisholm, Shirley	1969–1983	New York	Democrat
Stokes, Louis	1969–1999	Ohio	Democrat
Clay, William	1969–2001	Missouri	Democrat
Collins, George W.	1970–1972	Illinois	Democrat
Metcalfe, Ralph	1971–1978	Illinois	Democrat
Mitchell, Parren	1971–1987	Maryland	Democrat
Fauntroy, Walter E.	1971–1991	District of Columbia	Democrat
Dellums, Ron	1971–1998	California	Democrat
Rangel, Charles B.	1971–present	New York	Democrat
Young, Andrew	1973–1977	Georgia	Democrat
Burke, Yvonne Brathwaite	1973–1979	California	Democrat
Jordan, Barbara	1973–1979	Texas	Democrat
Collins, Cardiss	1973–1997	Illinois	Democrat
Ford, Harold, Sr.	1975–1997	Tennessee	Democrat
Stewart, Bennett M.	1979–1981	Illinois	Democrat
Evans, Melvin H.	1979–1981	Virgin Islands	Republican
Leland, Mickey	1979–1989	Texas	Democrat
Gray, William H., III	1979–1991	Pennsylvania	Democrat
Dixon, Julian C.	1979–2000	California	Democrat
Crockett, George W., Jr.	1980–1991	Michigan	Democrat
Washington, Harold	1981–1983	Illinois	Democrat
Dymally, Mervyn	1981–1993	California	Democrat
Savage, Gus	1981–1993	Illinois	Democrat
Hall, Katie	1982–1985	Indiana	Democrat
Hayes, Charles	1983–1993	Illinois	Democrat
Wheat, Alan	1983–1995	Missouri	Democrat
Owens, Major	1983–2007	New York	Democrat
Towns, Edolphus	1983–present	New York	Democrat
Waldon, Alton R., Jr.	1986–1987	New York	Democrat
Espy, Michael Alphonso	1987–1993	Mississippi	Democrat
Mfume, Kweisi	1987–1996	Maryland	Democrat
Flake, Floyd H.	1987–1998	New York	Democrat
Lewis, John R.	1987–present	Georgia	Democrat
Washington, Craig Anthony	1989–1995	Texas	Democrat
Payne, Donald M.	1989–present	New Jersey	Democrat
Blackwell, Lucien E.	1991–1995	Pennsylvania	Democrat
Franks, Gary	1991–1997	Connecticut	Republican
Collins, Barbara-Rose	1991–1997	Michigan	Democrat
Jefferson, William J.	1991–2009	Louisiana	Democrat
Waters, Maxine	1991–present	California	Democrat
Norton, Eleanor Holmes	1991–present	District of Columbia	Democrat

Name	Years of Service	State	Party
Clayton, Eva M.	1992–2003	North Carolina	Democrat
Reynolds, Melvin J.	1993–1995	Illinois	Democrat
Tucker, Walter	1993–1995	California	Democrat
Fields, Cleo	1993–1997	Louisiana	Democrat
Hilliard, Earl F.	1993–2003	Alabama	Democrat
Meek, Carrie P.	1993–2003	Florida	Democrat
McKinney, Cynthia	1993–2003, 2005–2007	Georgia	Democrat
Wynn, Albert	1993–2008	Maryland	Democrat
Bishop, Sanford	1993–present	Georgia	Democrat
Brown, Corrine	1993–present	Florida	Democrat
Clyburn, James E.	1993–present	South Carolina	Democrat
Hastings, Alcee	1993–present	Florida	Democrat
Johnson, Eddie Bernice	1993–present	Texas	Democrat
Rush, Bobby	1993–present	Illinois	Democrat
Scott, Robert C.	1993–present	Virginia	Democrat
Watt, Mel	1993–present	North Carolina	Democrat
Thompson, Bennie	1993–present	Mississippi	Democrat
Frazer, Victor O.	1995–1997	Virgin Islands	Independent
Watts, J. C.	1995–2003	Oklahoma	Republican
Fattah, Chaka	1995–present	Pennsylvania	Democrat
Jackson-Lee, Sheila	1995–present	Texas	Democrat
Jackson, Jesse, Jr.	1995–present	Illinois	Democrat
Millender-McDonald, Juanita	1996–2007	California	Democrat
Cummings, Elijah	1996–present	Maryland	Democrat
Carson, Julia	1997–2007	Indiana	Democrat
Ford, Harold, Jr.	1997–2007	Tennessee	Democrat
Kilpatrick, Carolyn Cheeks	1997–2011	Michigan	Democrat
Davis, Danny K.	1997–present	Illinois	Democrat
Christian-Christensen, Donna	1997–present	Virgin Islands	Democrat
Meeks, Gregory W.	1998–present	New York	Democrat
Lee, Barbara	1998–present	California	Democrat
Jones, Stephanie Tubbs	1999–present	Ohio	Democrat
Watson, Diane	2001–2011	California	Democrat
Clay, William Lacy, Jr.	2001–present	Missouri	Democrat
Ballance, Frank	2003–2004	North Carolina	Democrat
Majette, Denise	2003–2005	Georgia	Democrat
Davis, Artur	2003–2011	Alabama	Democrat
Meek, Kendrick	2003–2011	Florida	Democrat
Scott, David	2003–present	Georgia	Democrat
Butterfield, G. K.	2004–present	North Carolina	Democrat
Cleaver, Emanuel	2005–present	Missouri	Democrat
Green, Alexander N. "Al"	2005–present	Texas	Democrat
Moore, Gwen	2005–present	Wisconsin	Democrat
Clarke, Yvette D.	2007–present	New York	Democrat
Ellison, Keith	2007–present	Minnesota	Democrat
Johnson, Hank	2007–present	Georgia	Democrat
Richardson, Laura	2007–present	California	Democrat

Name	Years of Service	State	Party
Carson, André	2008–present	Indiana	Democrat
Edwards, Donna	2008–present	Maryland	Democrat
Fudge, Marcia	2008–present	Ohio	Democrat
Bass, Karen	2011–present	California	Democrat
Clarke, Hansen	2011–present	Michigan	Democrat
Richmond, Cedric	2011–present	Louisiana	Democrat
Scott, Tim	2011–present	South Carolina	Republican
Sewell, Terri	2011–present	Alabama	Democrat
West, Allen	2011–present	Florida	Republican
Wilson, Frederica	2011–present	Florida	Democrat

African American Recipients of the Medal of Honor

(Arranged chronologically by war)

Name	Rank	Service	War	State	Awarded
Anderson, Aaron (aka Sanderson, Aaron)	Landsman	Navy	Civil War	NC	1865
Anderson, Bruce	PVT	Army	Civil War	NY	1914*
Barnes, William H.	PVT	Army	Civil War	MD	1865
Beaty, Powhatan	1SG	Army	Civil War	OH	1865
Blake, Robert	Contraband	Navy	Civil War	VA	1864
Bronson, James H.	1SG	Army	Civil War	OH	1865
Brown, William H.	Landsman	Navy	Civil War	MD	1864
Brown, Wilson	Boy	Navy	Civil War	MS	1864
Carney, William H.	SGT	Army	Civil War	MA	1900*
Dorsey, Decatur	SGT	Army	Civil War	MD	1865
Fleetwood, Christian A.	SGT	Army	Civil War	MD	1865
Gardiner, James	PVT	Army	Civil War	VA	1865
Harris, James H.	SGT	Army	Civil War	MD	1874*
Hawkins, Thomas	SGM	Army	Civil War	PA	1870*
Hilton, Alfred B.	SGM	Army	Civil War	MD	1865
Holland, Milton M.	SGT	Army	Civil War	OH	1865
Kelly, Alexander	1SG	Army	Civil War	PA	1865
James, Miles	CPL	Army	Civil War	VA	1865
Lawson, John	Landsman	Navy	Civil War	PA	1864
Mifflin, James	Cook	Navy	Civil War	VA	1864
Pease, Joachim	Seaman	Navy	Civil War	NY	1864
Pinn, Robert	1SG	Army	Civil War	OH	1865
Ratcliff, Edward	1SG	Army	Civil War	VA	1865
Smith, Andrew Jackson	Color SGT	Army	Civil War	IL	2001*
Veal, Charles	PVT	Army	Civil War	VA	1865
Boyne, Thomas	SGT	Army	Indian Campaign	MD	1882
Brown, Benjamin	SGT	Army	Indian Campaign	VA	1890
Denny, John	SGT	Army	Indian Campaign	NY	1894

Name	Rank	Service	War	State	Awarded
Factor, Pompey	PVT	Army	Indian Campaign	AK	1875
Greaves, Clinton	CPL	Army	Indian Campaign	MD	1879
Johnson, Henry	SGT	Army	Indian Campaign	VA	1890
Jordan, George	SGT	Army	Indian Campaign	TN	1890
McBryar, William	SGT	Army	Indian Campaign	NY	1890
Mays, Isaiah	CPL	Army	Indian Campaign	OH	1890
Paine, Adam	PVT	Army	Indian Campaign	TX	1875
Payne, Isaac	PVT	Army	Indian Campaign	AK	1875
Shaw, Thomas	SGT	Army	Indian Campaign	KY	1890
Stance, Emanuel	SGT	Army	Indian Campaign	LA	1870
Walley, Augustus	PVT	Army	Indian Campaign	MD	1890
Ward, John	SGT	Army	Indian Campaign	TX	1875
Williams, Moses	1SG	Army	Indian Campaign	LA	1896
Wilson, William O.	CPL	Army	Indian Campaign	MN	1891
Woods, Brent	SGT	Army	Indian Campaign	KY	1894
Atkins, Daniel	Cook	1c Navy	Interim 1871–1898	VA	1898
Davis, John	Seaman	Navy	Interim 1871–1898	NJ	1884
Johnson, John	Seaman	Navy	Interim 1871–1898	PA	1872
Johnson, William	Cooper	Navy	Interim 1871–1898	NY	1884
Noil, Joseph B.	Seaman	Navy	Interim 1871–1898	NY	1872
Smith, John	Seaman	Navy	Interim 1871–1898	NY	1884
Sweeney, Robert A.	Seaman	Navy	Interim 1871–1898	NJ	1881
Sweeney, Robert A.	Seaman	Navy	Interim 1871–1898	NJ	1883**
Baker, Edward L.	SGM	Army	Spanish American	WY	1902
Bell, Dennis	PVT	Army	Spanish American	DC	1899
Penn, Robert	Fireman	1c Navy	Spanish American	VA	1898
Thompkins, William H.	PVT	Army	Spanish American	NJ	1899
Wanton, George H.	PVT	Army	Spanish American	NJ	1899
Girandy, Alphonse	Seaman	Navy	Interim 1901–1911	PA	1902
Stowers, Freddie	CPL	Army	WWI	SC	1991*
Baker, Vernon	1LT	Army	WWII	WY	1997*
Carter, Edward	SSG	Army	WWII	CA	1997*
Fox, John R.	1LT	Army	WWII	OH	1997*
James, Willy F.	PFC	Army	WWII	MO	1997*
Rivers, Ruben	SSG	Army	WWII	OK	1997*
Thomas, Charles	MAJ	Army	WWII	MI	1997*
Watson, George	PVT	Army	WWII	AL	1997*
Charlton, Cornelius	SGT	Army	Korea	WV	1952
Thompson, William	PFC	Army	Korea	NY	1951
Anderson, James C.	PFC	USMC	Vietnam	CA	1967
Anderson, Webster	SFC	Army	Vietnam	SC	1967
Ashley, Eugene, Jr.	SGT	Army	Vietnam	NY	1968
Austin, Oscar P.	PFC	USMC	Vietnam	AZ	1969
Bryant, William Maud	SFC	Army	Vietnam	MI	1969
Davis, Rodney M.	SGT	USMC	Vietnam	GA	1967
Jenkins, Robert H., Jr.	PFC	USMC	Vietnam	FL	1969
Joel, Lawrence	Spec/6	Army	Vietnam	NY	1967

Name	Rank	Service	War	State	Awarded
Johnson, Dwight Hal	Spec/5	Army	Vietnam	MI	1968
Johnson, Ralph H.	PFC	USMC	Vietnam	CA	1968
Langhorn, Garfield M.	PFC	Army	Vietnam	NY	1969
Leonard, Matthew	SGT	Army	Vietnam	AL	1967
Long, Donald Russell	SGT	Army	Vietnam	KY	1968
Olive, Milton L.	PFC	Army	Vietnam	IL	1966
Pitts, Leroy Riley	CPT	Army	Vietnam	KS	1967
Rogers, Charles Calvin	Brig. Gen.	Army	Vietnam	WV	1968
Sargent, Ruppert Leon	1LT	Army	Vietnam	VA	1967
Sasser, Clarence E.	Spec/5	Army	Vietnam	TX	1968
Sims, Clifford Chester	SGT	Army	Vietnam	FL	1968
Warren, John E., Jr.	1LT	Army	Vietnam	NY	1967

*Medal of Honor awarded after a review by the Department of the Army.

**This is the second Medal of Honor awarded to Robert A. Sweeney.

Index by Subject Area and Realm of Renown

Dance

Mason, Lena Doolin
Mayfield, Percy
McCray, Carrie Anderson Allen
McElroy, Colleen J.
McGirt, James Ephraim
McKay, Claude
McMillan, Terry
Menard, John Willis
Miller, May
Moorhead, Scipio
Moss, Thylias
Mullen, Harryette
Neal, Larry
Nelson, Marilyn
Newsome, Mary Effie Lee
Osbey, Brenda Marie
Phillips, Carl
Plato, Ann
Plumpp, Sterling
Popel, Esther
Purvis, Sarah Louisa Forten
Randall, Dudley
Ray, Henrietta Cordelia
Razaf, Andy
Reason, Charles Lewis
Reed, Ishmael
Rodgers, Carolyn M.
Rogers, Elymas Payson
Sanchez, Sonia
Sapphire
Scott-Heron, Gil
Shakur, Assata
Shakur, Tupac Amaru
Shange, Ntozake
Smith, Patricia
Southerland, Ellease
Spencer, Anne
Stuckey, Elma
Suggs, Eliza G.
Talbert, Naomi
Terry, Lucy
Thierry, Camille
Thomas, Joyce Carol
Thomas, Lorenzo
Thomas, Piri
Thompson, Clara Ann
Thompson, Eloise Bibb
Thompson, Priscilla Jane
Tillman, Katherine Davis Chapman
Tolson, Melvin Beaunorus
Trethewey, Natasha
Troupe, Quincy Thomas, Jr.
Turner, Darwin T.

Vashon, George Boyer
Vroman, Mary Elizabeth
Wade-Gayles, Gloria
Walcott, Derek
Walker, Alice Malsenior
Walker, Margaret
Ward, T. M. D.
Washington, Jerome
Washington, Mary Helen
We Langa, Wopashitwe Mondo Eyen
Webb, Frank J.
Wheatley, Phillis
Whitfield, James Monroe
Whitman, Albery Allson
Wilkinson, Henry B.
Williams, Edward Christopher
Williams, Robert Franklin
Williams, Sherley Anne
Wilson, August
Wright, Charles S.
Wright, Richard
Yates, Josephine A.
Young, Al
Young, Charles
Young, Kevin

Publishing
Adams, Ron
Allen, Elise Ford
Atkins, Jasper Alston
Bennett, Lerone, Jr.
Calloway, DeVerne Lee
Calvin, Floyd (Joseph)
Cannady, Beatrice Morrow
Carter, Elmer Anderson
Carter, William Beverly, Jr.
Cayton, Horace Roscoe, Sr.
Cayton, Susie Sumner Revels
Chase, William Calvin
Childs, Faith
Clarke, Charles Henry
Cleage, Pearl (Michelle)
Clifford, Carrie Williams
Clifford, John Robert
Cooper, Edward Elder
Cooper, Thomas
Cose, Ellis Jonathan
Coston, Julia Ringwood
Cromwell, John Wesley
Cromwell, Robert I.
Crowdy, William Saunders
DeBerry, William Nelson
Dill, Augustus Granville
Evans, William Leonard, Jr.

Music

Simmons, Russell
Simms, Hilda
Simpson, O. J.
Simpson, Valerie
Sims, Howard "Sandman"
Singleton, Zutty
Slyde, Jimmy
Smiley, Tavis
Smith, Anna Deavere
Smith, George Walker
Smith, Lucy
Smith, Marvin and Morgan Smith
Smith, N. Clark
Smith, Ozzie
Smith, Stuff
Smith, Will
Snoop Dogg
Solomons, Gus, Jr.
Steele, Shelby
Steward, Emanuel
Stewart, Maria W.
Stewart, Slam
Still, William Grant
Stokes, Carl
Stone, Chuck
Stone, Sly
Strode, Woody
Sublett, Frank Ellis, Jr.
Sullivan, Maxine
Sutton, Percy
Takeall, Arthur Oliver
Thomas, Rufus
Townsend, Robert
Uggams, Leslie
Vails, Nelson
Van Peebles, Melvin
Verrett, Shirley
Walker, Jimmie
Wallace, William "Onikwa"
Ward, Theodore (Ted)
Warfield, Paul
Warwick, Dionne
Washington, Mary Helen
Waters, Ethel
Wayans, Keenen Ivory
Wilder, Douglas
Wilkens, Lenny
Wilkins, Joe Willie
Williams, Aaron
Williams, Lavinia
Williams, Robert Franklin
Williams, Serena and Venus Williams
Williams, Walter E.

Williamson, Fred
Williamson, Sonny Boy (1899?–1965)
Wills, Maury
Wilson, Flip
Wilson, Frank
Wilson, Mary
Winfield, Paul
Winfrey, Oprah
Withers, Ernest C.
Wright, Wild Bill
Zuber, Paul Burgess

Religion and Spirituality

Baptist

Abernathy, Ralph
Alexander, Avery
Allensworth, Allen
Allensworth, Josephine Leavell
Arter, Jared
Asher, Jeremiah
Banks, William Venoid
Barrow, Peter
Black, Leonard
Booker, Joseph Albert
Boone, Clinton Caldwell, Sr.
Boone, Eva Roberta (or Mae) Coles
Boothe, Charles Octavius
Bouey, Harrison N.
Bowles, Charles
Boyd, Richard Henry
Brawley, Edward McKnight
Brewster, William Herbert
Brooks, Walter Henderson
Bryan, Andrew
Butts, Calvin Otis, III
Cain, Lawrence
Campbell, Lucie E.
Carter, Uless
Cary, Lott
Clarke, Charles Henry
Cleveland, James Edward
Cook, Fields
Corrothers, James David
Crawford, James
Davis, Gary D.
Davis, Noah
Day, John, Jr.
De Baptiste, Richard
DeBerry, William Nelson
Dennis, Lawrence
Edwards, Ballard Trent
Ellison, John Malcus, Sr.
Faulkner, William John
Fauntroy, Walter Edward

Sports

Amateur Sports and the Olympics

Index by Birthplace

Africa. *See also individual African countries.*

Black River
Bailey, Beryl Isadore Loftman
Chatham
Anderson, Jervis
Frome
Patterson, Orlando
Kingston
Bennett, Louise
Davis, John
Domingo, Wilfred Adolphus
Garvey, Amy Euphemia Jacques
Herc, DJ Kool
Kildare, Dan
Moore, Johnny "Dizzy"
Somerville, John Alexander
Kingstown
Heron, Giles
Negril
Rogers, Joel Augustus
Port Antonio
Garvey, Amy Ashwood
Russwurm, John Brown
St. Ann's Bay
Garvey, Marcus

Kansas

Arkansas City
Davis, Frank Marshall
Atchison
Hilyer, Amanda Victoria Gray
Baldwin City
Porter, Gilbert Lawrence
Coffeyville
Jessye, Eva Alberta
Eureka
Gregg, John Andrew
Fort Scott
Wilkerson, Vernon Alexander
Hiawatha
McLendon, Johnny
Junction City
Stout, Renée
Willmott, Kevin
Kansas City
Brown, Ada
Dwight, Ed
Greene, Maurice
Rivers, Francis Ellis
Spears, Arthur K.
Lawrence
Brown, Lawrence
Williams, Bert and George Walker

Leavenworth
Asberry, Nettie J.
Smith, N. Clark
Nicodemus
Van Duvall, Ernestine Caroline
Parsons
Clayton, Buck
Topeka
Brooks, Gwendolyn
Brown, Linda Carol
Cable, Theodore
De Moss, Elwood
DeFrantz, Faburn
Douglas, Aaron
Hamlin, Albert Comstock
Lowery, P. G.
Wichita
Anderson, Garland
Bacon-Bercey, June
Hollowell, Donald Lee
McDaniel, Hattie
Sanders, Barry David
Sayers, Gale
Thomas, Andre J.
Woodard, Lynette

Kentucky

Ballard, John
Bishop, Stephen
Burdett, Samuel
Campbell, Sarah (Aunt Sally)
Gloucester, John
McCray, Mary F.
Randolph, Benjamin Franklin
Shankle, James
Spaulding, James Morrow
Bardstown
Cotter, Joseph Seamon, Sr.
Rudd, Daniel
Walters, Alexander
Boone County
Garner, Margaret
Bourbon County
Baltimore, Priscilla
Green, Elisha Winfield
Bowling Green
Grainger, Porter
Hampton, Pete
Hogan, Ernest
Brandenburg
Steward, William Henry
Burgin
Black, John Lincoln